THE OXFORD HANDB

GW00357958

POLITICAL
COMMUNICATION

THE OXFORD HANDBOOK OF

POLITICAL

COMMUNICATION

Edited by

KATE KENSKI

and

KATHLEEN HALL JAMIESON

OXFORD
UNIVERSITY PRESS

OXFORD
UNIVERSITY PRESS

Oxford University Press is a department of the University of Oxford. It furthers
the University's objective of excellence in research, scholarship, and education
by publishing worldwide. Oxford is a registered trade mark of Oxford University
Press in the UK and certain other countries.

Published in the United States of America by Oxford University Press
198 Madison Avenue, New York, NY 10016, United States of America.

CIP data is on file at the Library of Congress
ISBN 978–0–19–979347–1 (hardcover); 978–0–19–009045–6 (paperback)

CONTENTS

MEDIA AND POLITICAL COMMUNICATION

Political Systems, Institutions, and Media

Construction and Effects

Political Communication and Cognition

INTERPERSONAL AND SMALL GROUP POLITICAL COMMUNICATION

THE ALTERED POLITICAL
COMMUNICATION LANDSCAPE

CONCLUSION

Contributors

Sean Aday, George Washington University

Michael Barthel, Pew Research Center

W. Lance Bennett, University of Washington

William L. Benoit, Ohio University

David S. Birdsell, Baruch College (CUNY)

Jay G. Blumler, University of Maryland

Daniel M. Butler, Washington University in St. Louis

Joseph N. Cappella, University of Pennsylvania

Allison Carnegie, Columbia University

Dan Cassino, Fairleigh Dickinson University

Jihyang Choi, Indiana University

Kevin Coe, University of Utah

Stephen Coleman, University of Leeds

Ann N. Crigler, University of Southern California

Claes H. de Vreese, University of Amsterdam

Michael X. Delli Carpini, University of Pennsylvania

Nina Eliasoph, University of Southern California

William P. Eveland Jr., The Ohio State University

Timothy W. Fallis, Hawai'i Pacific University

Lauren Feldman, Rutgers University

Andrew J. Flanagin, University of California, Santa Barbara

Laura Lazarus Frankel, Duke University

Oscar H. Gandy Jr., University of Pennsylvania

R. Kelly Garrett, The Ohio State University

John Gastil, Pennsylvania State University

Jason Gilmore, Utah State University

Saar Golde, Revolution Analytics

Doris A. Graber, University of Illinois at Chicago

Donald P. Green, Columbia University

James T. Hamilton, Stanford University

Bruce W. Hardy, Temple University

Roderick P. Hart, University of Texas at Austin

Andrew F. Hayes, The Ohio State University

Parker R. Hevron, Texas Woman's University

Robert Huckfeldt, University of California, Davis

Shanto Iyengar, Stanford University

Lawrence R. Jacobs, University of Minnesota

Patrick E. Jamieson, University of Pennsylvania

Kathleen Hall Jamieson, University of Pennsylvania

Sharon E. Jarvis, University of Texas at Austin

Philip R. Johnson, Syracuse University

Elihu Katz, University of Pennsylvania

Kate Kenski, University of Arizona

Katherine R. Knobloch, Colorado State University

R. Lance Holbert, Temple University

Rebecca LaVally, California State University, Sacramento

Nam-jin Lee, College of Charleston

Milton Lodge, Stony Brook University

Eeva Luhtakallio, University of Tampere, Finland

Jörg Matthes, University of Vienna

Nicole Maurantonio, University of Richmond

Robert W. McChesney, University of Illinois at Urbana-Champaign

Maxwell McCombs, University of Texas at Austin

Jack McLeod, University of Wisconsin

Miriam J. Metzger, University of California, Santa Barbara

Joel Middleton, University of California, Berkeley

Darwin W. Miller III, RAND Corporation

Patricia Moy, University of Washington

Norman H. Nie, Stanford University and the University of Chicago

Lilach Nir, Hebrew University of Jerusalem

Diana Owen, Georgetown University

Thomas E. Patterson, Harvard University

Victor Pickard, University of Pennsylvania

Vincent Price, University of Pennsylvania

Markus Prior, Princeton University

Jaime R. Riccio, CUNY LaGuardia Community College

S. Robert Lichter, George Mason University

Daniel Romer, Annenberg Public Policy Center, University of Pennsylvania

Dietram A. Scheufele, University of Wisconsin

Michael Schudson, Columbia University

Dhavan V. Shah, University of Wisconsin

Pamela J. Shoemaker, Syracuse University

Brian G. Southwell, RTI International and University of North Carolina at Chapel Hill

John Street, University of East Anglia

Jennifer Stromer-Galley, Syracuse University

Natalie Jomini Stroud, University of Texas at Austin

D. Sunshine Hillygus, Duke University

Charles Taber, Stony Brook University

Michael Tesler, University of California, Irvine

Kjerstin Thorson, Michigan State University

Yariv Tsfati, University of Haifa

Nicholas Valentino, University of Michigan

Sebastián Valenzuela, Catholic University of Chile

Allyson Volinsky, University of Pennsylvania

L. Matthew Vandenbroek, NeighborWorks America

David H. Weaver, Indiana University

Ilana Weitz, University of Pennsylvania

Chris Wells, University of Wisconsin

Carol Winkler, Georgia State University

Kenneth M. Winneg, University of Pennsylvania

Dannagal G. Young, University of Delaware

John Zaller, University of California, Los Angeles

Jingwen Zhang, University of California, Davis

THE OXFORD HANDBOOK OF

POLITICAL COMMUNICATION

INTRODUCTION

....

CHAPTER 1

POLITICAL COMMUNICATION

Then, Now, and Beyond

....

KATHLEEN HALL JAMIESON AND KATE KENSKI

As a discipline, communication was shaped by real-world concerns such as those "over the effects of World War I and Nazi propaganda" (Schramm, 1983, 7) and by hopes, fears, and forecasts about the effects of new media—film and radio. This meant, of course, that the findings of early researchers such as Berelson and Lazarsfeld "were peculiar to the political conditions and media systems of the 1940s and that many of their generalizations don't hold up today" (Rogers and Chaffee, 1983, 22). As we hurtle into an increasingly individualized and fragmented media landscape filled with campaigns operating in a post–*Citizens United* world, what we know about political communication and how we know it is changing yet again and, in the process, raising questions about the applicability of the findings generated in the all-but-bygone mass-media era.

Just as media structures have changed, so, too, have the resources available to study them. Among the innovations that have invigorated research in political communication are computers able to digest and manipulate large data sets; new ways of making sense of data such as meta-analyses; the availability of readily searchable news, advertising archives, and presidential speech archives; computerized means of content analysis; access to ad buy data; and the availability of Internet panels and rolling cross-sectional designs. Our primary focus, however, is not on our methods of knowing, but rather on the answers they generate. (For a valuable treatment of the methods employed in political communication research, we recommend turning to the essays in Bucy and Holbert's *Sourcebook for Political Communication Research* [2011].)

Transformations in media structure, content, and delivery matter to scholars and voters alike, because, as Chaffee argued, "the structure of communication shapes the structure of politics, both because so much of political activity consists of communication and because constraints on communication limit the exercise of power" (2001, 237–238). Believing that this is, as a result, an opportune time to reprise political communication's past and forecast its future, as editors of the *Oxford Handbook of Political Communication,* we commissioned the essays by political communication scholars found in this volume.

To anchor it with a working notion of what we mean by political communication, we begin by exploring three sets of definitions: those inherited from earlier periods and work; the self-definitions offered by the political communication divisions of the major communication and political science associations; and those that emerged from an Annenberg Public Policy Center conference attended by those who contributed to this handbook. We then turn to noting some of the institutional forces that contributed to the emergence and sustenance of the burgeoning hybrid field of political communication. We close with a cursory overview of this handbook and a caution that many of its essays could easily have been placed in any of a number of the sections into which we somewhat arbitrarily have divided this volume.

DEFINING POLITICAL COMMUNICATION

A quick look at defining statements made more than two-thirds of a century ago by Harold Lasswell—one of the founders appropriated by both political science and communication—reveals how much the study of each has changed since he probed propaganda techniques, language, and the content analytic means of unpacking both in the thirties and forties. Whereas in the study of politics his concern was "who gets what, when, how" (Lasswell, 1936), in communication it was "who/says what/ in which channel/to whom/ with what effect" (Lasswell, 1948). Welding this classic distributional definition of politics and a unidirectional, linear model of communication together might lead one to define political communication as the study of who gets what, when, (and) how by saying what, in which channel, to whom, with what effect.

Not so today. Instead, in *A New Handbook of Political Science*, politics is cast as "the *constrained use of social power*" (Goodin and Klingemann, 1996, 7).[1] Similarly, in communication scholarship the transmission model has been supplanted by or supplemented with one that "conceptualizes communication as a constitutive process that produces and reproduces shared meaning"(cf. Craig, 1999, 125 crediting Carey, 1989; Pearce, 1989).

Because communication is the noun grounding the definition and field of political communication, it is unsurprising that there is more of "symbolic exchange" and less, indeed nothing at all, about "shared power" in the first sentences of the self-descriptions memorialized on the web pages of the political communication divisions of the American Political Science Association (APSA), the International Communication Association (ICA), and the National Communication Association (NCA):

- The creation, shaping, dissemination, processing and effects of information within the political system—both domestic and international—whether by governments, other institutions, groups or individuals (American Political Science Association).

- The interplay of communication and politics, including the transactions that occur among citizens, between citizens and their governments, and among officials within governments (International Communication Association).
- The communicative activity of citizens, individual political figures, public and governmental institutions, the media, political campaigns, advocacy groups and social movements (National Communication Association).

Nonetheless each description reveals ancestral assumptions about what matters, with the ICA and NCA divisions embracing the word "citizens," and the one housed in the APSA featuring "the political system." Although in practice all three divisions are methodologically pluralistic, and their memberships overlap substantially, it is the one whose scholars admit to practicing rhetorical criticism that champions "a variety of methodologies" (NCA), and the one whose discipline pioneered the National Election Studies (ANES) that includes "effects." And the NCA division reveals its parent's more message-centric focus by situating as the subject of its sentence "The communication activity of citizens, individual political figures . . ."

Drawing on these traditions, those whose work is included in this handbook defined political communication as "making sense of symbolic exchanges about the shared exercise of power" and "the presentation and interpretation of information, messages or signals with potential consequences for the exercise of shared power."

CREATION OF A HYBRID FIELD

As we have implied, hybrid fields are conceived when scholars learn that others are contributing insightful answers to shared questions and decide to engage rather than disregard these potential colleagues. In the case of political communication, shared interests converged on such questions as, "Under what circumstances, if at all, and, if so, how, are voters, leaders, and the political system affected by media?" "How, if at all, and, if so, for whom or what does presidential rhetoric matter?" "How do exchanges among individuals and groups affect what they know and how they know and act about politics?" Additionally, a nascent field will expire unless a number of conditions are met. The impulse to engage must be fostered by individuals with standing in both disciplines who bring their colleagues to the table. There must be common spaces in which interested scholars can engage each other's ideas thoughtfully. And resources must be available to fund needed research. Political communication would not have institutionalized as a hybrid field had there not been places to converse, common publishing venues, and, at opportune moments, funding.

Places to converse: Chapter 2's narrative of origins chronicles the impact of boundary-defying intellectual omnivores. By publishing in a related discipline's major journals, engaging the ideas of its leading lights, and coauthoring cross-disciplinary work, those interested in political communication purchased legitimacy for its research questions and modes of inquiry. Early points of cross-disciplinary intersection in political communication included not only Kraus's *Great Debates* (1962), which brought together work by scholars in sociology, rhetoric and public address, mass communication, and political science, but also more targeted forays by a scholar in one discipline into a journal hosted by another. Examples of this include political scientist Tom Patterson's essay on "Television News and Political Advertising" in *Communication Research* in 1974, political scientist Lance Bennett's "The Ritualistic and Pragmatic Bases of Political Campaign Discourse," in the *Quarterly Journal of Speech* three years later, and mass communication scholars Weaver, McCombs, and Spellman's (1975) "Watergate and the Media: A Case Study of Agenda-Setting" in *American Politics Quarterly* in 1975. Among the first cross-disciplinary book-length manuscripts was Weaver, Graber, McCombs, and Eyal's *Media Agenda-Setting in a Presidential Election* (1981). Boundary-breaking field-building occurred as well when Steven Chaffee "played a significant role" in the "development and eventual inclusion of a large media use battery in the quadrennial NES election surveys . . ." (Iyengar, 2001, 226) and political scientist John Zaller instigated the 1994 meeting of communication scholars and political scientists at the Annenberg School at Penn that examined ways to assess communication effects and forged the relationships that led to the creation of the National Annenberg Election Survey.

Common publishing venues: Before the advent of *Political Communication*, two influential journals—*Public Opinion Quarterly* and *Journal of Communication*—set scholars on a road toward institutionalization of the political communication field by welcoming high-quality work on the subject without regard to disciplinary origin. The former was home to Klapper's "What We Know About the Effects of Mass Communication: The Brink of Hope" (1957); Eulau and Schneider's "Dimensions of Political Involvement" in 1956; Katz's "The Two-Step Flow of Communication: An Up-to-Date Report on an Hypothesis" in 1957; Converse's "Information Flow and the Stability of Partisan Attitudes" in 1962; McLeod, Ward, and Tancill's "Alienation and Uses of the Mass Media" in 1965; McCombs and Shaw's "The Agenda-Setting Function of Mass Media" in 1972; Chaffee and Choe's "Time of Decision and Media Use During the Ford-Carter-Campaign" in 1980; and Behr and Iyengar's "Television News, Real World Cues, and Changes in the Public" in 1985.

In the decades before *Political Communication* became an APSA-ICA journal, *The Journal of Communication* was a second hospitable venue for those working at the intersections of politics and communication. As a result, Elisabeth Noelle-Neuman, director of communication, University of Mainz, published "The Spiral of Silence: A Theory of Public Opinion" there in 1974. The journal's 1983 "Ferment in the Field" issue featured work by Noelle-Neuman as well as that of mass communication scholars Wilbur Schramm and Jay Blumler, sociologists Elihu Katz, Kurt Lang, and Gladys Lang, and polymath Ithiel de Sola Pool, among others.

Funding: Because the laws of supply and demand affect the world of research as surely as they do markets, the availability of resources shaped the questions political communication scholars addressed, the answers they discovered, and, as a result, the contours of political communication's parent disciplines as well as of the field itself. The focus of communication research on the individual and on the social psychology of short-term persuasion was, for example, an "outgrowth … of media- and advertiser-sponsored research, Rockefeller Foundation intervention, and the federal government's war-time propaganda mobilization" (Pooley and Katz, 2008). Indeed, some argue that "the mainstream effects tradition was crucially shaped, in the mid-1930s, by the Rockefeller Foundation's interest, first, in educational broadcasting and, after 1939, in anti-Nazi propaganda" (Pooley, 2008, 48).

If the presence of a willing donor matters, so, too, does the absence of one. Had the Ford Foundation not responded to pressure from "Congressional McCarthyites in 1952 and, notably, 1954's Reece Commission" (Morrison, 2008) by backing out of its "major commitment to fund a series of television studies at Lazarsfeld's Bureau … a whole body of television research might have found its ways onto sociologists' bookshelves to complement Lazarsfeld's pioneering radio research" (Pooley and Katz, 2008, 773). Where a decision by the Ford Foundation closed off an opportunity in 1955, decisions by the Carnegie and Rockefeller Foundations opened ones in 1952 and 1956. The political science classic *The American Voter* was made possible by support from the Carnegie Corporation of New York in 1952 and the Rockefeller Foundation in 1956 (Campbell, et al., 1960, viii).

Money mattered in more recent times as well. Patterson and McClure's (1976) *The Unseeing Eye* was supported by a grant from the National Science Foundation (7). Iyengar's *Is Anyone Responsible? How Television Frames Political Issues* (1991) was underwritten by grants from the Political Science Program of the National Science Foundation and the John and Mary R. Markle Foundation. The fieldwork in Cappella and Jamieson's *Spiral of Cynicism: The Press and the Public Good* (1997) was made possible by the Markle and Robert Wood Johnson Foundations. Funding from the National Science Foundation ensured the survival of the NES, and the largesse of the Annenberg Foundation underwrote the rolling cross-sectional and panel studies of the NAES.

How this Volume will Address "Then, Now, and Beyond"

We have asked the authors in this handbook to reflect upon their areas of expertise and address four questions: What is the importance of your area of study? What are the major findings to date, including areas of scholarly disagreement, on the topic? What is your perspective on the topic? And, What are unanswered questions for future research to address?

Their answers reveal that, like political economy and political psychology, political communication is a hybrid with complex ancestry, permeable boundaries, and interests that overlap with those of related fields, such as political sociology, public opinion, rhetoric, neuroscience, and the new hybrid on the quad, media psychology. What Blumler and Gurevitch observed of mass communication in 1987 is also true of its off-spring, political communication, which is "a notoriously eclectic enterprise, drawing on and borrowing from a wide range of social science and humanistic disciplines" (17). Accordingly, it is unsurprising that many of our authors claim visiting rights, if not primary residence, in another of those fields. Indeed, like the founders, they appropriate from sociology, psychology, political science, and communication. Most of those who identify with political communication are intellectual omnivores whose work in such areas as agenda setting, priming, framing, and inoculation is indebted to the work of individuals and groups unlikely to describe themselves as political communication theorists.

To assess the "then, now, and beyond" of this eclectic, interdisciplinary field, we have invited chapters from scholars with homes or pedigrees in economics (e.g., James Hamilton), psychology (e.g., Milton Lodge and Charles Taber), and sociology (e.g., Nina Eliasoph and Michael Schudson), as well as a majority who consider their home base to be political science, mass communication, or the rhetoric tradition within departments of speech communication, communication arts, or communication studies. Though most are housed in US institutions, we draw as well from work conducted at the University of Amsterdam (Claes de Vreese), the University of East Anglia (John Street), the University of Haifa (Yariv Tsfati), the University of Helsinki (Eeva Luhktakallio), Hebrew University of Jerusalem (Lilach Nir), University of Leeds (Stephen Coleman), and the University of Zurich (Jorg Matthes). In addition, we include two peripatetic scholars occasionally based in the United States who have created significant research both inside and outside its boundaries (Elihu Katz and Jay Blumler).

To identify the nucleus that enables us to gather the work of this wide array of scholars under the label "political communication," we start by asking, What do mainstream scholars in political science and communication mean by each, and how do those who identify as political communication scholars define what they do (Chapters 2–7)? We proceed to offer our take on the origins of the field of political communication—a story involving strands of research in sociology, psychology, and political science that found their way into and were, in the process, poked and prodded by those focused on politics and communication in areas identified as mass communication, radio TV-film, and various divisions within speech departments, including one known as rhetoric and public address. In the process, we identify work that foreshadows that of the scholars in this handbook.

Consistent with the notions of political communication as "making sense of symbolic exchanges about the shared exercise of power" and "the presentation and interpretation of information, messages or signals with potential consequences for the exercise of shared power," this volume includes essays clustered under the titles Political Discourse: History, Genres, and the Construction of Meaning (Chapters 8–16), Media and Political Communication focusing on Political Systems, Institutions, and Media (Chapters 17–24), Construction and Effects (Chapters 25–35), Political Communication and Cognition (Chapters 36–46), and Interpersonal and Small Group Political Communication

(Chapters 47–53). Because, as we noted a moment ago, changes in media and media systems alter the nature, function, and effects of political communication, we include as well a cluster of essays on The Altered Political Communication Landscape (see Chapters 54–61). Given the interdisciplinary nature and complexity of political communication research, we acknowledge that this scheme for organizing the volume contains some unavoidable choices of categorizing chapters that could be placed in one or more other sections.

Since "Then and Now" is one of our themes, it is important to remember that much of the work in our handbook is consistent with the focus of Steven Chafee's 1975 edited volume (*Political Communication: Issues and Strategies for Research*) on "behavior and cognition rather than on attitudes, the need for experimentation with different methods of measurement, an understanding of a campaign as unfolding in distinct phases over time, a homogenization of mass media and interpersonal communication as sources of information and influence, and the need for comparative cross-national scholarship" (Chafee, 2001, 239). Those foci foreshadow this handbook's sections on Political Communication and Cognition, Construction and Effects, and Interpersonal and Small Group Communication, as well as its chapter on comparative political communication research (chapter by Claes de Vreese), anticipate the experimentation with different methods that in subsequent decades produced sophisticated field experiments (chapters by Tesler and Zaller and Green, Carnie, and Middleton) and laboratory experiments (chapter by Cassino, Lodge, and Taber), refined use of the rolling cross-sectional method, and innovative ways of tracking citizen deliberation (chapter by Cappella, Zhang, and Price).

Less likely to be foreseen by those writing in 1975 was a field of political communication encompassing scholarship on elites' use of polls (chapter by Jacobs), media systems (chapter by McChesney and Pickard), niche communication (chapter by Frankel and Hillygus), narrowcasting (chapter by Metzger), the social media (chapters by Winneg et al., Owen, and Stromer-Galley), the politics of entertainment media (chapters by Delli Carpini and Young), and scholarship theorizing about the effects produced by implicit attitudes (chapter by Cassino, Lodge, and Taber) and moderated by affect (chapter by Crigler and Hevron). If the sophistication and scope of political communication research continues apace, we expect our successors forty and fifty years hence to be as bemused by our work as we are by the notion that, in 1960, the state-of-the-art move in research on the Kennedy-Nixon debates consisted of interviewing 200 respondents whose names had been drawn from the Indianapolis city telephone directory (Kraus and Smith, 1962, 290).

NOTE

1. Lurking in the meaning of "social," of course, is symbol-using between and among individuals and groups for, as Dewey notes, society exists "*by* transmission, *by* communication, but it may fairly be said to exist *in* transmission, *in* communication" (Dewey, 1921, 184). In Dewey's view, "Democracy is primarily a mode of associated living, of conjoint communicated experience" (Dewey, 1915, 87).

REFERENCES

Behr, R., and Iyengar, S. 1985. Television news, real world cues, and changes in the public agenda. *Public Opinion Quarterly* 49: 38–57.

Bennett, L. 1977. The ritualistic and pragmatic bases of political campaign discourse. *Quarterly Journal of Speech* 63: 219–238.

Blumler, J., and Gurevitch, M. 1987. The personal and the public: Observations on agendas in mass communication research. In Michael Gurevitch and Mark R. Levy (Eds.), *Mass Communication Review Yearbook Volume 6* (pp. 16–21). Newbury Park, CA: Sage.

Bucy, E., and Holbert, R. L. (Eds.). 2011. *Sourcebook for political communication research: Methods, measures, and analytical techniques.* New York: Routledge.

Campbell, A., Converse, P., Miller, W., and Stokes, D. 1960. *The American voter.* Chicago: University of Chicago Press.

Cappella, J., and Jamieson, K. H. 1997. *Spiral of cynicism: The press and the public good.* New York: Oxford University Press.

Chaffee, S. (Ed.). 1975. *Political communication: Issues and strategies for research.* Beverly Hills: Sage.

Chaffee, S. 2001. Studying the new communication of politics. *Political Communication* 18: 237–244.

Chaffee, S. and Choe, S. 1980. Time of decision and media use during the Ford-Carter campaign. *Public Opinion Quarterly* 44: 53–69.

Converse, P. 1962. Information flow and the stability of partisan attitudes. *Public Opinion Quarterly* 26: 578–599.

Craig, R. 1999. Communication theory as a field. *Communication Theory* 9: 119–161.

Eulau, H., and Schneider, P. 1956. Dimensions of political involvement. *Public Opinion Quarterly* 20: 128–142.

Goodin, R., and Klingemann, H. (Eds.). 1996. *A new handbook of political science.* New York: Oxford University Press.

Iyengar, S. 1991. *Is anyone responsible? How television frames political issues.* Chicago: University of Chicago Press.

Iyengar, S. 2001. The method is the message: The current state of political communication research. *Political Communication* 18(2): 225–229.

Katz, E. 1957. The two-step flow of communication: An up-to-date report on a hypothesis. *Public Opinion Quarterly* 21: 61–78.

Klapper, J. 1957. What we know about the effects of mass communication: The brink of hope. *Public Opinion Quarterly* 21(4): 453–474.

Kraus, S. (Ed.) 1962. *The great debates: Background, perspective, effects.* Bloomington: Indiana University Press.

Kraus, S., and Smith, R. 1962. Issues and images. In Sidney Kraus (Ed.), *The great debates: Background, perspective, effects* (pp. 289–312). Bloomington: Indiana University Press.

Lasswell, H. 1936. *Politics: Who gets what, when, how?* New York: Whittlesey House.

Lasswell, H. 1948. *Power and personality.* New York: W.W. Norton.

McCombs, M., and Shaw, D. 1972. The agenda-setting function of mass media. *Public Opinion Quarterly* 36(2): 176–187.

McLeod, J., Ward, S., and Tancill, K. 1965. Alienation and uses of the mass media. *Public Opinion Quarterly* 29: 584–594.

Morrison, D. 2008. Opportunity structures and the creation of knowledge: Paul Lazarsfeld and the politics of research. In D. Park and J. Pooley (Eds.), *The history of media and communication research: Contested memories* (pp. 179–204). New York: Peter Lang.

Noelle-Neumann, E. 1974. The spiral of silence: A theory of public opinion. *Journal of Communication* 24(2): 43–51.

Noelle-Neumann, E. 1983. The effect of media on media effects research. *Journal of Communication* 33(3): 157–165.

Patterson, T. 1974. Television news and political advertising. *Communication Research* 1: 3–31.

Patterson, T., and McClure, R. 1976. *Unseeing eye: The myth of television power in national elections.* New York: G.P. Putnam's Sons.

Pearce, B. 1989. *Communication and the human condition.* Carbondale: Southern Illinois University Press.

Pooley, J., and Katz, E. 2008. Further notes on why American sociology abandoned mass communication research. *Journal of Communication* 58(4): 767–786.

Rogers, E., and Chaffee, S. 1983. Communication as an academic discipline: A dialogue. *Journal of Communication* 33(3): 18–30.

Schramm, W. 1983. The unique perspective of communication: A retrospective view. *Journal of Communication* 33(3): 6–17.

Weaver, D., McCombs, M., and Spellman, C. 1975. Watergate and the media: A case study of agenda-setting. *American Politics Quarterly* 3: 458–472.

Weaver, D., Graber, D., McCombs, M., and Eyal, C. 1981. *Media agenda setting in a presidential election: Issues, images and interest.* Westport, CT: Greenwood.

CONTEXTS FOR VIEWING THE FIELD OF POLITICAL COMMUNICATION

CHAPTER 2

CREATING THE HYBRID FIELD OF POLITICAL COMMUNICATION
A Five-Decade-Long Evolution of the Concept of Effects

KATHLEEN HALL JAMIESON

INTRODUCTION

IN 1993, Bill Clinton was sworn in as the forty-second president of the United States, the World Wide Web came online for public use, *Political Communication* published its inaugural issue under the auspices of divisions of the American Political Science Association and the International Communication Association, and three essays signaled an emerging view in political science that under certain circumstances, communication's role in producing the outcome in presidential elections might be worth studying after all. Explaining why presidential election polls are so variable when votes are so predictable, Gelman and King (1993) argued that "the news media have an important effect on the outcome of presidential elections—not through misleading advertisements, sound bites, or spin doctors, but rather by conveying candidates' positions on important issues" (409). Reexamining the minimal effects model, Finkel (1993) contended that presidential campaigns do not ordinarily affect presidential election outcomes because the communicative efforts of the competent professionals on one side cancel out those on the other, and in a one-two punch at conventional wisdom, Bartels (1993, 268) attributed "the pervasive pattern" of past "negative [media effects] findings and non-findings in part to limitations of research design and in part to carelessness regarding measurement," and specified "a model of opinion formation that can help to 'pinpoint the exact contribution which mass media make to the individual's cognitions, feelings, and actions . . . .'"

My goal in this chapter is sketching some of the byways that led to the emergence of a cross-disciplinary cadre of scholars whose representatives in this volume detail the insights and unanswered questions native to the hybrid field of political communication. Since many of the chapters begin their story in the 1990s, in its efforts to identify work that shaped the kinds of questions asked by political communication researchers, this retrospective will concentrate on the decades before then. Concentrating on the period between the 1940s and 1993, I will telegraph the influence of the disciplines of sociology, political science, psychology and communication on the emerging field, outline the factors that created the convergence needed to ground it, and in the process reveal why the three articles cited a moment ago foreshadow political communication research indebted to both the political science and communication disciplines.

How Did We Get Here?

My chronicle is in some ways similar and in others different from that offered in 1987 by Elihu Katz who is both a contributor and heir to the tradition of research created in the late 1930s and early 1940s by polymath Paul Lazarsfeld and his Columbia colleagues at the Bureau of Applied Social Research (see Katz and Lazarsfeld's *Personal Influence: The Part Played by People in the Flow of Mass Communications* [1955]). With Lazarsfeld, Katz centered interpersonal and group communication at the heart of political influence (1955), sidelining a focus on mass media along the way.

In the fiftieth anniversary issue of *Public Opinion Quarterly* (1987), Katz recalled that after Klapper (1960) codified the conclusion that mass communication produced only limited effects, sociology "abandoned" communication research (1987, S26). What saved the otherwise orphaned research area was being "institutionalized in schools, colleges, and departments of communications, building on mergers of traditions of rhetoric and speech, journalism and publizistik, critical traditions in film and literature and socio-psychologically oriented media research" (S40). Later, in the 1980s, some political scientists and sociologists gave communication research a second look. "There is a flocking back to the field of communication research by humanists, film theorists, political scientists who had gone off in their different directions 30 years ago," recalled Katz in 1987, "even the sociologists are coming back" (S40).

In a moment, I will suggest that political communication did not emerge as a field until the notion that mass media don't much matter had been dispatched. Making the case that media effects are worthy of study even if they do not often affect presidential election outcomes were sociologists, political scientists, psychologists and communication scholars from speech, radio-TV-film, and mass communication departments whose interest in the nascent field persisted after sociology, in Katz's narrative, abandoned it. Taken together, their research not only challenged the received wisdom expressed in the narrowly focused minimal effects model but, as this handbook attests, also drew into the political communication tent the study of political discourse, its history, underlying regularities, genres, and capacities to construct meaning; the roles of interpersonal, group, and mass communication in and about politics; the ways in which political media and messages interact with, affect and are affected by feelings, cognition, and behaviors; and the relationships among media systems and political systems, content, and behavior. Across the decades of interest here, those toiling in this emerging field expanded their scope of inquiry beyond the earlier studies' focus on the short-term influence of communication on opinions, attitudes and actions. In the process, they embraced methods capable of detecting the impact of a wider range of communicative behavior and created the cross-disciplinary collaborations required to establish political communication as a hybrid field existing at the intersection of political science and communication.

Origins of the Minimal Effects Model

As humans we tend to exaggerate the significance of our own new work by, in Kurt and Gladys Lang's words, manufacturing "false dichotomies that [make] the break with the past appear sharper than it actually was" (Lang and Lang, 1993). Both the presumption of powerful media and the view "of media power as severely limited, a view often characterized as the 'minimal effects model'" are "parodies that functioned as straw men in a non-existing controversy that distracted . . . scholars from investigating issues that deserve our full attention" (Lang and Lang, 1993, 93). This distraction occurred because the dichotomous "minimal vs. massive effects" frame foreclosed the possibility that, if broadly defined, media effects usually fall someplace in between, and, at the same time, suppressed such important questions as "effects on whom and on what?" Additionally the digestive notion of minimal effects obscured the fact that such phenomena as learning, cultivation of worldview, creating a spiral of silence, agenda setting, and reinforcement of predispositions are important outcomes in their own right.

Where the presumption of powerful media effects—cast in the poorly conceived metaphors of the "magic bullet" and "hypodermic needle"—fueled mass communication research in the 1930s and 1940s, the minimal effects model threatened to mothball that embryonic research area with such relics as the elocution machine even as it contributed to our understanding of factors such as selective perception and partisan predispositions that blunt the "direct" effects of mass media. Although scholars in three well-established disciplines—sociology, political science, and psychology—legitimized the minimal effects model, in succeeding years, others bearing the same disciplinary crests joined those in communication departments to reconsider the evidence supporting it and, in the process, recast it.

Minimal Effects in the Columbia Tradition

With Roosevelt and Wilke on the ballot in 1940, the Columbia team led by Lazarsfeld focused its attention on voters in Erie Country, Ohio. Eight years later the Columbia scholars turned their lens on voters in Elmira, New York, who were trying to decide between Truman and Dewey. In each campaign, flyers, newspapers, and radio were the media of the day. If a voter wanted to see an actual candidate in action, she had to travel to an event or watch the newsreels played after the cartoons and before the main feature in movie theatres.

From their inception in Erie in 1940 (Lazarfeld, Berelson, and Gaudet, 1944), the classic Columbia multiwave panel studies (cf. Lazarsfeld et al., 1944; Berelson, Lazarsfeld, and McPhee, 1954; Katz and Lazarsfeld, 1955) seemed to confirm that the impact of mass communication was both minimal and largely indirect, a notion capsulated in two-step flow. Although the campaign stimulated interest and information seeking (1944, 76–79), these sociologists found (1944, 102–104) that it reinforced existing predispositions more often than it changed them. For half of those who were tracked throughout the election cycle, political communication did not initiate "new decisions" but instead "had the effect of reinforcing the original vote decision" (1944, 87). Of course with 8 percent of those studied in Erie leaving "the Democratic fold" (Lazarsfeld et al., 1944, 102), one could as well have interpreted that study to say that communication could affect the outcome of a close election.

Their bottom line: When media influence occurs, it is likely to be indirect. Specifically, "ideas often flow *from* radio and print *to* opinion leaders and *from* them to the less active sections of the population" (Lazarsfeld et al., 1944, 151). In short, word-of- mouth from trusted individuals (i.e., opinion leaders) was more likely to change the views of late deciders than was mass communication. Where the media reinforced existing predispositions, the trustworthy personal communication of "opinion leaders" could change at least some votes. So influential was two-step flow that one scholar reported in 1968 that "few formulations in the behavioral sciences have had more impact" (Arndt, 1968). However, by the mid-1980s, its basic insight had been challenged. In 1987, Katz, whose work with Lazarsfeld (1955) had canonized the concept, observed that "the hypothesis is still about and still controversial" (1987, S26).

Rather than sounding a death knell for US mass communication research about elections, two-step flow could have invited scrutiny of the relationship among interpersonal, group, and mass communication, a line of inquiry hospitable to German public opinion scholar Noelle-Neumann's (1974) spiral of silence theory, which was introduced to English-speaking scholars in an essay titled "Return to the Concept of Powerful Mass Media" (1973) that credited the 1940 Erie County study with bringing "into view the interaction between the opinions of an individual member of society and the distribution of opinions in the environment" (92). Writing in the *Journal of Communication* (1974, 1983), she argued that silencing spirals occur when media and the mutterings of others prompt those holding what they perceive as minority views to fall silent rather than championing them. But in the main, successive studies of two-step flow focused on topics other than politics.

Still, lingering in the Columbia data are many of the phenomena that interest political communication scholars today. The Elmira study, for example, correlated media use both with higher turnout (Berelson et al., 1954, 248) and an increase in accurate reports of candidate issue positions (248). Priming effects lurked there as well (273), with the media's focus on issues favorable to the Democratic nominee affecting both the salience of those matters and the preferences of some voters near the end of the campaign. Presuppositions of Downs' *An Economic Theory of Democracy* (1957, 222, 229, 243, 298–299) that would figure in later understandings of the ways in which cognitive shortcuts operate when individuals process political content (see Popkin, 1991) are rooted in the Columbia studies as well.

Minimal Effects in the Michigan Tradition in Political Science

Like the 1940 and 1948 contests, the general election campaigns of 1952 and 1956 did not really start until the candidates were officially nominated at their respective conventions. Only on Labor Day, did the national efforts begin in earnest. However, by the 1950s, what was meant by mass communication was changing. Political party conventions were now being televised. Moreover, in 1952, both Ike and Adlai insinuated television ads into the media mix.

The interests underlying the Columbia and Michigan studies differed dramatically. "The early Columbia studies focused on demographics such as religion and rural/urban residence, although they also considered the media and the interpersonal influence exerted within families and friendships," notes Katz. "In contrast the more psychologically minded Michigan studies focused on party identity, attitudes, and issue positions as more proximate predictors of the vote" (Katz and Warshel, 2001, 2). Where the community-based Columbia studies were vulnerable to the charge that the settings were idiosyncratic and the voters atypical, the Michigan ones constituted panels designed to represent the nation as a whole. Sacrificed in this methodological shift was the ready ability to examine the influence of interpersonal networks and local media content, including targeted advertising. Had media content been comparable across the country, and the Michigan researchers asked the questions needed to capture advertising's influence, the shift to a national model would not have mattered. But in both 1952 and 1956 paid advertising was reaching some markets and not others, and in 1960, the Kennedy campaign sought to mobilize the Catholic vote in part by reairing an edited version of JFK's speech to the Houston ministers in predominantly Catholic markets (see Jamieson, 1984).

Neither the earlier Columbia studies nor the Michigan Survey Research Center (SRC) ones of the 1952 and 1956 presidential elections (Campbell et al., 1960) denied that campaign communication affects some voters. Rather the Michigan political scientists surmised that the primary influence on voting decisions was party identification (1960, 121). As a result, from 1948 through 1972, their instruments asked single questions about exposure to radio, TV, newspapers, and magazines and treated the answers "as instances of political participation" (Chaffee and Hochheimer, 1985, 284). Unsurprisingly then, *The American Voter* (1960, 92) devotes a single paragraph to the use of mass media. This relegation of "media-related activity to the status of a minor mode of political participation" meant that "the Michigan studies through the 1960s inadvertently ensured perpetuation of the limited-effects model of mass communication. No new data relevant to the question of media effects would be gathered, so no new interpretations could be reached" (Chaffee and Hochheimer, 1985, 284). The same can be said of Nie, Verba, and Petrocik's *The Changing American Voter* (1979), which, as Patterson notes (1980, vii), makes "almost no mention of the mass media or their impact."

In the 1950s and 1960s, conventional wisdom in political science (Campbell, 1954; Campbell et al., 1960; Converse, 1962) held that voting decisions were largely in place by the end of the party conventions and hence before "the campaign" began (1960) and were driven primarily by partisan loyalties. Past performance of the incumbent party was thought to trump communication as well. "Campaigning does change votes and it does bestir people to vote. Yet other influences doubtless outweigh the campaign in the determination of the vote. As voters mark their ballots they may have in their minds impressions of the last TV political spectacular of the campaign," noted V.O. Key and Cummings in 1966, "but, more important, they have in their minds recollections of their experiences of the last four years" (9). Also diverting attention from the roles communication might be playing was the ability of forecasters to predict the winner from variables such as economic conditions and presidential approval (Fair, 1978; Rosenstone, 1983).

Whether, and, if so, how political party conventions and other forms of campaign communication affect party identification, and what role, if any, forms of personal and mass communication play in a person's identification as a Democrat or Republican, were not of interest in these studies. But if one honors the assumptions of the Michigan model, as party identification levels drop, as they did from the early 1950s to the late 1980s (Wattenberg, 1990), the influence of other factors such as candidate-centered politics (Wattenberg, 1991) would presumably rise. Moreover nothing in the model denies the possibility that media play a role in political socialization (cf. Chaffee, Ward, and Tipton, 1970) or set the criteria on which candidates are assessed.

Although they did not call it a communication effect, as early as the 1920s political scientists had confirmed that, as Key would later put it, campaigns can "bestir people to vote." Field experiments conducted in local elections demonstrated, for example, that letters (Gosnell, 1927, 85) and leaflets (Hartmann, 1936–1937, 86) produced upticks in turnout. Personal contact affected turnout as well (Eldersveld and Dodge, 1954; Eldersveld, 1956; Wolfinger, 1963). SRC evidence entered the picture when Kramer (1970) drew on four election's worth of it (1952–1964) to estimate that "door–to–door canvassing during a presidential campaign" increased turnout but had "little effect on voter preferences for national or local offices" (572). In later years, scholars using more sophisticated methods would confirm the existence of campaign-driven turnout effects (cf. Popkin, 1991, 227; Rosenstone and Hansen, 1993).

An early sign that election scholars in political science might find common ground with their colleagues in other departments interested in communication occurred in 1976 when, in *The Changing American Voter*, Nie, Verba, and Petrocik (1976) isolated a campaign-driven learning effect arguing that "[a] simple but important theme runs through much of this book: the public responds to the political stimuli offered it. The political behavior of the electorate is not determined solely by psychological and sociological forces, but also by the issues of the day and by the way in which candidates present those issues" (319). In evidence that the streams flowing toward a political communication field were not yet in active conversation, they fail to note the learning effects found by Katz and Feldman (1962), Trenaman and McQuail (1961), Blumler and McQuail (1969), or McClure and Patterson (1974).

The Minimal Effects Tradition in Psychology

Political communication's focus on psychological theories and processing models and its increasing embrace of controlled experiments have roots in the investigations into persuasion and attitude change pioneered by Yale psychologist Carol Hovland and his colleagues.[1] So, too, do concepts that anchored the minimal effects model. In *Experiments on Mass Communication* (1949), for example, Hovland's team isolated the role of attitude anchoring in blunting communication effects. Specifically, "film communications had a significant effect on opinions related to straight-forward interpretations of policies and events, but had little or no effect on more deeply entrenched attitudes and motivations" (Hovland, 1959, 16, commenting on Hovland et al., 1949). A similar notion appeared a decade later when the Michigan studies of voting (Campbell et al., 1960, 269–270) were able to predict a vote from "the partisan direction and intensity of his [the voter's] attitude toward six discernible elements of the world of politics. . . ." "To say whether any given person will vote Republican or Democratic," they conclude, "we need to know where he falls on those dimensions of partisan feeling, that is, whether his attitude toward each political object is pro-Republican or pro-Democratic and with what strength."

Of course it is possible that communication could work its wiles on those whose attitudes were less firmly set. Moreover, the Hovland studies confirmed that films and hence presumably political campaigns can affect learning, a finding that should be more pronounced when a massed audience is exposed to sustained communication as it is in debates (cf. Katz and Feldman, 1962; Chaffee, 1978). Still, in a 1986 review article, Hovland's co-author William McGuire (1986) dismissed as myth the notion that "television and other mass media have sizeable impacts on the public's thoughts, feelings, and actions" and reported that "most empirical studies indicate small to negligible effects" (1986, 174).

DOCUMENTING THE IMPORTANCE OF COMMUNICATION AND MASS COMMUNICATION

In my telling, after some leading lights in sociology abandoned mass communication research, others from that discipline as well as those in political science, communication (i.e., mass communication, speech and radio-TV-film) documented effects lurking in the minimal effects studies, uncovered them in the television age as well and in the process intellectually grounded the hybrid field of political communication, while also ensuring that it would be open to a wide range of methods and inquiry. The prime pro-tagonists in my narrative are Katz, Lang and Lang, Edelman, and Graber, with support-ing roles played by others.

Sociology: Katz

With works ranging from his dissertation-based *Personal Influence* (Katz and Lazarsfeld, 1955) to *Media Events,* with Daniel Dayan (1992), Elihu Katz's scholarship demonstrated the value of systematically studying communication through a variety of methods. In the decades after sociology's exit, he co-authored a synthesis of findings from studies of the Kennedy-Nixon debates (Katz and Feldman 1962), reopened the question of selectivity in exposure to mass media (1968), argued that political parties were better served by polit-ical campaigns than were voters (1971), examined the ways in which media function in wartime (Peled and Katz, 1974), explored whether authentic cultures can survive new media (1977), and with Liebes documented cross-cultural differences in viewers inter-pretations of the soap opera "Dallas"(1990). Along the way he co-authored a book on diffusion (Coleman, Katz, and Menzel, 1966), with Jay Blumler and Michael Gurevitch, incorporated uses of mass communication through a gratifications approach into the communication research agenda (Blumler and Katz, 1974; Katz, Blumler, and Gurevitch, 1974), and in 1988 forecast an argument that he and Dayan would body in *Media Events* (1992), namely: "Effects, of course, need not be limited to . . . cognitive effects. . . . Indeed, a badly neglected effect in research on mass communication is that the media may tell us how to *feel* And they may situate us in certain *roles*—family members, consumers, stu-dents, farmers, or citizens. . . . If television can make hundreds of millions of people feel something, that's a powerful effect—and one that's very neglected in our research. An example is the integrative effect of mass communication—the way in which the mass media can sometimes make the society feel as one" (Katz, 1988, 367).

Consistent with my assumption that this story's protagonists reveal the state of the art at given points in time, in 1968 Katz noted a shift in the assumption underlying mass communication research. "Whereas the media had been thought capable of impressing their message on the defenseless masses," he noted, "it now appears as if the audience has quite a lot of power of its own. Indeed, the fashion in research nowadays is not to ask 'what the media do *to* people' but 'what people do *with* the media,' or at least to be sure to ask the second question before the first" (1968, 788). Performing the same func-tion two decades later, Katz observed that the two-step flow of communication had been "[a]mended in a dozen ways to prefer influence over information, talk between equals over opinion leaders, multiple steps over two steps, etc." (1987, S26).

Sociology: Lang and Lang

The notion that media construct or co-create meaning was inherent in Kurt and Gladys Lang's 1953 conclusion that television viewers experienced both the MacArthur Day parade and their relationship with the general differently than did observers on the parade route (Lang and Lang, 1953, 1968). This germinal essay earned them a place in the canon of communication research (Katz and Dayan, 2003), foreshadowed Dayan and Katz's *Media Events* (1992), and established that television constructs our view of those political events that we have not directly experienced. Embrace of this view opens the possibility that variables in the forecasting models such as the well-being of the economy, its past performance, the popularity of the incumbent, and perhaps even party identification (Johnston, Hagen, and Jamieson, 2004; Kenski, 2004; Winneg and Jamieson, 2005, 2010) are themselves influenced by or their effects activated by campaign communication and media coverage through such phenomena as agenda setting, framing, and priming.

Educated in the Chicago School of Sociology by symbolic interactionist Herbert Blumer, who had authored two of the twelve Payne studies of the filmic effects on children, and Tamotsu (Tom) Shibutani, best known in communication circles for *Improvised News: A Sociological Study of Rumor* (1966), the Langs not only retained an interest in political communication through the 1960s, 1970s, and 1980s, but like Katz, published their results in venues that would nurture the emerging political communication field including Kraus's *Great Debates* (1962), the *Journal of Communication* (Lang and Lang, 1993), and *Public Opinion Quarterly* (Lang and Lang, 1978).

Like Katz, this pair of sociologists employed the qualitative or quantitative method best suited to the question they were probing and explored both the flow of influence and the ways in which audiences, messages, and contexts contribute to the construction of meaning. Between 1960 and 1981, Gladys and Kurt Lang analyzed the effects of the Kennedy-Nixon (in Kraus 1962) and Ford Carter debates (1978), television and politics (1968a), the implications of broadcasting returns before the polls close (1968b), and the battle for public opinion over Watergate (1981). Because their 1968 book *Television and Politics* "pays attention to what the *communicators* said, what the *audience heard*, and how they were *affected*," Ithiel de sola Pool hoped that it would set a trend. "Many studies report only one or two links in the chain from what was said to its consequences," he argued. "There are numerous studies of attitude change in an audience that do not try to identify the way in which the particular content of messages caused the change (most of the best voting studies would be examples)" (1969, 287).

Political Science: Edelman, Graber, and the Constructionist Tradition

Considered a founder of both the fields of political psychology and mass communication, Lasswell was an "original and productive political scientist" (Almond, 1996, 249) who considered making sense of the meaning of events (1948) one of the key functions of mass communication. His focus on the use of symbols in the exercise of power links him to the constructionist tradition in political science, rhetoric and public address, and sociology now found in the field of political communication (cf. *Propaganda Technique in the World War* [1927], *The Comparative Study of Symbols* [1952], written with Daniel

Lerner and Ithiel de Sola Pool,[2] *The Language of Politics* [Lasswell et al., 1965], *Political Communication: The Public Language of Political Elites in India and the United States* [Arora and Lasswell, 1969],[3] and the three-volume *Propaganda and Communication in World History* [1980]).[4]

Like Lasswell, University of Wisconsin political scientist Murray Edelman explored the ways in which uses of political symbols enable people to displace "their inner tensions and needs onto public objects" (see Hershey 1993, 122; and Edelman's "Symbols and Political Quiescence" [1960], *The Symbolic Uses of Politics* [1964], *Politics as Symbolic Action* [1971], and *Political Language: Words that Succeed and Policies that Fail* [1977]). In Edelman's view, campaigns matter not so much because they elect, but because they create a political spectacle that makes it difficult for citizens to realize that their interests are not being well served by those who govern. Specifically, "not only does systematic research suggest that the most cherished forms of popular participation in government are largely symbolic, but also that many of the public programs universally taught and believed to benefit a mass public in fact benefit relatively small groups" (Edelman, 1964, 4). Like literary theorist Kenneth Burke (1950), Edelman conceived his object of inquiry as the "interplay in politics among acts, actors, settings, language, and masses" (1964, 21).

There is a discernible difference between the questions framed and methods employed by positivist social science and those arising from Edelman's constructionist epistemology. For the latter, as Bennett notes (1993), "traditional scientific claims about properties of public opinion are not hypotheses that describe some independently existing world but are political statements that are actively part of the political construction of opinion itself" (109).

Like Katz and Lang and Lang, political scientist Doris Graber focused both on the construction of meaning and on its effects. In *Verbal Behavior and Politics* (1976), she draws on Edelman to contend, "People no longer need to see and experience to believe. They need merely to hear, or to hear and see a little and then project from the little they see, in order to create a new 'reality' which furnishes symbolic gratifications for needs for which material gratifications would otherwise be expected" (65). Consistent with Lang and Lang and Edelman, that book's chapter on mass media emphasizes "the type of verbal environment which is created by the mass media and which is likely to influence politically significant reality perceptions which, in turn, may influence actual politics" (140). In a similar vein, *Processing the News: How People Tame the Information Tide* (1984) uncovered what people make of televised content by exploring "thinking patterns though intensive interviews of small panels of registered voters" (viii) and linking them "to each person's social and cultural contexts" (viii). Among the first US political scientists to co-author with those formally identified with mass communication departments, Graber contributed to a book that helped ground agenda setting—one of the more important theories in political communication (Weaver et al.'s *Media Agenda Setting in a Presidential Election* [1981]).

A focus on construction of meaning emerged as well in the rhetoric and public address tradition in speech communication departments when scholars there shifted from a focus on assessing the fidelity of individual speeches to an Aristotelian ideal to the study of rhetoric as symbolic action (Sillars, 1964; Campbell, 1982) and in the process entertained the notion that rhetoric is constitutive (cf. McGee, "The 'Ideograph': A Link between Rhetoric and Ideology" [1980]; Charland's "Constitutive Rhetoric: The case of the Peuple Quebecois" [1987] and Jamieson's [1992] *Dirty Politics: Deception: Distraction and Democracy* which is dedicated to Edelman). This new direction broadened the scope of inquiry to include the rhetoric of social movements (cf. Scott and Brockriede's *The Rhetoric of Black Power* [1969]) and underlying rhetorical regularities in discourse that construct meaning (cf. Rosenfield's "A Case Study in Speech Criticism: The Truman–Nixon Analog" [1968]; Ivie's "Images of Savagery in American Justifications for War" [1980]; Denton's *The Symbolic Dimensions of the American Presidency* [1982]; Hart's *Political Pulpit* [1977], *Verbal Style and the Presidency* [1984]; and *The Sound of Leadership* [1987]). Driving this change were the writings of Kenneth Burke, whose work was introduced into the Speech tradition by the co-editor of *History and Criticism of Public Address*, Marie Hochmuth [Nichols] in 1952, as well as Black's *Rhetorical Criticism: A Study in Method* (1965), and Perelman and Olbrechts-Tyteca's *The New Rhetoric* (1969).

Other important early constructionist political communication works by scholars in political science, communication, and sociology include Altheide's *Creating Reality: How TV News Distorts Events* (1974); Nimmo's *Popular Images of Politics* (1974) and his coauthored *Mediated Political Realities* (1990)[5]; Elder and Cobb's *The Political Uses of Symbols* (1983); Hinkley's *The Symbolic Presidency: How Presidents Portray Themselves* (1990); and Bennett's *News: The Politics of Illusion* (1988).

Among these, Neuman, Crigler, and Just's *Common Knowledge: News and the Construction of Political Meaning* (1992) stands out for displacing the notion of a one-way flow of communicative influence with a multi-methodological constructionist "research perspective which focuses on the subtle interaction between what the mass media convey and how people come to understand the world beyond their immediate life space" (xv). Drawing on survey data, content analysis, interviews, and experiments, Neuman and his colleagues demonstrated that by actively reinterpreting and integrating mass media images into their existing beliefs and knowledge, audiences "construct" candidates and political knowledge into composites that may differ voter to voter.

RESPECT FOR OR HOSTILITY TOWARD ALTERNATIVE WAYS OF KNOWING?

At this point in my narrative, we have some scholars focused on the flow of influence using quantitative methods, others concentrating on explicating the making of meaning, usually but not exclusively, employing qualitative ones, and still others doing both.

Importantly those whose inquiry is centered on understanding the making of meaning and its implications are not expressing disdain for the work of their colleagues using quantitative social scientific methods to track influence. Indeed in 1979 Kurt Lang argued that "there is no *inherent* incompatibility between the 'positivism' of administrative communication research and the critical approach associated with the Frankfurt School" (1979, 83) and concluded, "In the interest of gaining valid and meaningful knowledge—which is not the monopoly of any single tradition or school—we are all critical, with or without a capital 'C'" (95). Nor are those whose sleuthing methods include panels, surveys, and experiments belittling the work of Edelman and his epistemic kin.

By contrast, in the 60s and 70s, some in part of the communication discipline were engaged in a contretemps involving hallway asides such as "If you can't quantify it, it's not worth knowing" or "Anything you can quantify is trivial." While such skirmishes can serve as entertainment in a mature discipline, they are suicidal in a fledging one. Rapprochement occurred, and disciplinary self-interest prevailed when each granted that the other employed a valuable, different but complementary and legitimate way of knowing, a resolution signaled by the publication of *The Handbook of Rhetorical and Communication Theory* (Arnold and Bowers, 1984), co-edited by a leading social scientist and rhetorical critic. Interestingly, a decade later speech communication departments did not splinter into warring factions when constructionists argued that the "variables" that preoccupy the positivist tradition are socially or rhetorically constructed and the privileged intellectual status claimed for the methods of science and social science simply a particularly appealing body of symbols whose use obscures the powerful role that definition and framing play in constructing knowledge and knowledge paradigms (cf. Nelson, McCloskey, and Megill, 1986; Simons, 1989, 1990). Nonetheless, some who had weathered that earlier storm, experienced déjà vu when political scientist George Edwards advanced the notion that public address scholars cannot warrant conclusions about the power of a speech from textual analysis in the absence of public opinion data (Edwards, 1996, 208).

However, had the constructionists in my narrative such as Edelman canonized sociologist Todd Gitlin's 1978 assault on the Columbia and Yale traditions of inquiry, the hybrid field of political communication as we know it probably would not have emerged. "Whether in Lazarsfeld's surveys or the laboratory experiments of Carl Hovland and associates," wrote Gitlin, "the purpose was to generate *predictive* theories of audience response, which are necessarily—intentionally or not—consonant with an administrative point of view, with which centrally located administrators who possess adequate information can make decisions that affect their entire domain with a good idea of the consequences of their choices" (211). "In this historical situation," he argued, "to take a constancy of attitude for granted amounts to a choice, and a fundamental one, to ignore the question of the sources of the very opinions which remain constant throughout shifting circumstances. Limiting their investigation thus, Katz and Lazarsfeld could not possibly explore the institutional power of mass media: the degree of their power to shape public agendas, to mobilize networks of support for the policies of state and party, to condition public support for these institutional arrangements themselves. Nor could they even crack open the questions of the sources of these powers" (1978, 215–216).

In 1987 Elihu Katz responded with a reframing that addressed "three challenges to the paradigm of limited effects" which Katz called "institutional, critical [i.e. Gitlin], and technological" and "their three alternative theories of powerful effects—information, ideology [i.e. Gitlin], and organization . . . " (1987, S39) by casting them as complementary parts of "a continuing search for an adequate conceptualization of effect" (S39). Especially important is his claim that the "*empirical* research" resulting from these three "is certainly convergent with work stemming from the Bureau paradigm" (S40), which, in a fashion similar to Lang (1979), Katz argued had been wronged by narrow constructions of what and how it studied communication. Note that in a Big E-tented "search for an adequate conceptualization of effects," there is space for the constructionists, including Edelman and within that tradition for those such as Gitlin who embrace critical theoretical assumptions, and also space for such key players in the hybrid field of political communication as Iyengar and Kinder who, in Gitlin's construction of the world would be cast as "generat[ing] predictive theories through use of controlled experiments."

The hybrid field of political communication is built from Lang and Katz's encompassing view that values both positivist and constructionist communication research. Among other things this means that scholars who identify with the political communication field recognize the complementarity of Gitlin's argument in *The Whole World Is Watching: Mass Media in the Making & Unmaking of the New Left* (1980) that "media frames" are "largely unspoken and unacknowledged" ways in which journalists organize the world (7) and Iyengar's in *Is Anyone Responsible? How Television Frames Political Issues* (1991) that "exposure to episodic news makes viewers less likely to hold public officials accountable for the existence of some problem and also less likely to hold them responsible for alleviating it" (2–3). What Iyengar's work demonstrates is that use of surveys and experiments to generate predictive theories does not sideline questions about institutionalized media power. "By discouraging viewers from attributing responsibility for national issues to political actors," argues the scholar who would become *Political Communication*'s fourth editor, "television decreases the public's control over their elected representatives" (3). Indeed, I would suggest that Iyengar confirmed with other methodological means the 1985 conclusion of Bennett and Edelman that different meanings are constructed when we attribute "any social problem to official policies, the machinations of those who benefit from it, or the pathology of those who suffer from it. . . . In choosing any such ultimate cause we are also depicting a setting, an appropriate course of action, and sets of virtuous and evil characters . . . " (159–160).

The ability of the constructionists and positivists to co-habit a space such as *Political Communication* is made possible by the fact that unlike some in the constructionist tradition, Edelman granted the "central importance" of actual "situations and conditions" even as he explicated the meanings that human minds constructed and were led to construct (1971, 85). Meanwhile, even when working within or drawing from the positivist heritage, Katz, Lang and Lang, and Graber found value in educing nonobvious insight about constructed meaning from their and their audiences' interpretation of texts.

By devoting a 1993 issue of *Political Communication* to a symposium on Edelman's work and installing Graber as the founding editor of *Political Communication* in 1993, political communication scholars signaled their hybrid field's openness to a range of methodologies and viewpoints. Fittingly, Graber, Katz and the Langs were the first three winners of the APSA political communication division's lifetime achievement award, an honor named for Murray Edelman.

Locating Communication Effects, Broadly Construed, and Specifying the Constraints Within Which They Operate

Because of his role in creating the classic Columbia studies (cf. Lazarsfeld et al., 1944; Berelson et al., 1954), when Bernard Berelson mourned the fact that those who had stimulated the mass communication tradition had abandoned it and opined that communication research was "withering away" (1959, 3), those holding stock in mass communication research futures took note. In response, Wilbur Schramm, the founder of the first Ph.D. program in mass communication (at the University of Iowa) and the first communication research institute (at the University of Illinois), observed that the corpse "seemed extraordinarily lively" (1983, 6 reporting on 1959, 6–9). Nodding in agreement were those sharing custody of the body in schools and departments originally founded to teach public speaking, group discussion, journalism, and the production of radio, TV, and film. The reason? As a result of the mass exodus of talent to which Berelson's emigration contributed, mass communication research had lost "its place as a major concern within the conventionally recognized academic disciplines, such as sociology and political science. . . ." but survived in "departments of journalism and other vocationally oriented faculties [that had] moved in to fill the vacuum" (Lang and Lang, 1993, 130). Taken together these departments and schools educated the researchers now identifying themselves with the communication discipline in the political communication field and contributed to the common culture required to sustain a new joint cross-disciplinary enterprise. They did so by joining some in sociology and political science to challenge the minimal effects model and in the process broaden the notion of effects in the way Katz had imagined.

Among those leading the charge in Great Britain were Blumler and McQuail (1968, 1970) and in US communication departments, Swanson (1972, 1978) in speech communication, Kraus (1973) and Kraus and Davis (1976) in radio-TV-film, and Chaffee (1975) and McCombs and Shaw (1972) and Gerbner (1959) in mass communication. Each defined the state of play of political communication research in the 1970s. Each contributed significant work advancing the field. After reviewing over 800 studies Kraus and Davis spoke for communication scholars when they concluded in *The Effects of Mass Communication on Political Behavior* (1976) that "what we know is not what we thought we knew and what we thought we knew is more persistent in the literature than what we know" (283).

In a demonstration of the power of rhetorical constructions of reality, Joseph Klapper's (1960) *The Effects of Mass Communication* is remembered for inscribing on marble the conventional wisdom that media tend to produce "minimal effects." Forgotten is his caution that "under conditions and in situations other than those described in this volume, the media of mass communication may well have effects which are quite different and possibly more dramatic or extensive than those which have here been documented" (1960, 252). Identifying those conditions and situations became a raison d'etre of the emerging communication discipline. In a quest driven by an instinct for disciplinary self-preservation, these researchers featured underplayed facets of the Columbia studies and excavated unnoticed media effects from Columbia data while arguing that the Michigan scholars were sauntering past communication effects because they weren't looking for them. They also adopted methods able to capture effects that had proven elusive and broadened the concept of influence in ways that translated previous nonfindings into significant ones and centered new topics on the research agenda. In the process, some research confirmed and some confounded Columbia results. So for example, where the 1948 Elmira study (Berelson et al., 1954) had found a relationship between media exposure and both interest in the campaign and higher turnout, Blumler and McLeod's (1974) panel study in the 1970 British general election suggested a link between TV use and reduced turnout among better educated and informed potential voters. In the United States in the 1980s, however, exposure to news in print media was linked positively with turnout (McLeod and McDonald, 1985).

Challenging the Minimal Effects Model in the Columbia Studies

Attacking the minimal effects inference drawn from the Columbia studies, Becker, McCombs, and McLeod (in Chaffee, 1975) located mass media effects in the Columbia data (28–33), noting, for example, that in the Erie study, "Among persons with Republican predispositions *and* predominantly Republican media exposure, only 15% voted for the Democratic candidate; but the Democratic vote among Republicans with predominantly Democratic exposure is 47%" (29). A decade later, Chaffee and Hochheimer dismissed most of the generalizations from the Elmira study as time bound at best, disproved at worst (278). "Had not the focus been exclusively on the vote," they argued, "and specifically on within-campaign changes in voting intentions, and had not each case been weighted equally and relative frequencies been taken as the indicator of theoretical importance, a very different interpretation of the role of mass media could have been derived from the findings of the 1940 study—and of every election study since" (279). Where the Columbia studies counterposed interpersonal influence and that of the mass media, later work that explored the influence of one on the other found not only that attention to media and public affairs stimulated interpersonal discussion

(McLeod, Bybee, and Durall, 1979) but interpersonal canvassing increased attention to campaign news as well (Popkin, 1991).

Meanwhile, in a challenge to the concept of two-step flow, Deutschmann and Danielson (1960) demonstrated that major news stories diffused directly to individuals through radio and television and not, as Katz and Lazarsfeld had surmised (see Katz and Lazarsfeld, 1955, 82) through personal channels. After a decade of this sort of work, the theory of two-step flow had been "weakened by increasingly deviant findings" (Lin, 1971, 33) or in Katz's construction "amended."

Those in departments devoted to studying communication were not the only ones throwing caution flags at the minimal effects model. In 1959, for example, Lang and Lang reminded readers that the information transmitted by opinion leaders came from the media to start with and also posited that by influencing the political climate or the images of the parties and candidates, mass media may sway votes. In 1978, Gitlin weighed in with the claim that the two-step flow theory "does not hold up in its own terms." Specifically, "Respondents were being asked to name as influentials those individuals who they thought were most tuned in to the mass media." Katz and Lazarsfeld were taking for granted the power of mass media to define news; and they were therefore discovering not "the part played by people in the flow of mass communications," but the nature of the *channels* of that flow (1978, 218).

In the process of reexamining the Columbia model, mass communication scholars recast findings of media's impotence as confirmation of significance. "Theoretical refinements," noted Comstock (1983), "such as 'two-step flow' . . . the notion that the media often reinforce predispositions or present behavior . . . and the cataloguing of conditions under which the media are ineffective . . . had appeared only as confirmations of media ineffectiveness; today, they are more likely to appear as conditions qualifying media effects or as effects in themselves . . . " (44).

To this evolving conversation, Katz added that critics erred "in assuming that the 'dominant' paradigm is standing still while only theirs are moving ahead" (1987, S40). Not so, he argued. Instead "the somewhat distorted paradigm of limited effects" and "the twin emphases on selectivity and interpersonal influence. . . . in turn, led to the revival of gratifications research and to work on the diffusion of innovation which, in their next incarnation, have become occupied, respectively, with 'decoding' and 'networks.' These recurrent themes—that of *meaning* (selectivity, gratifications, uses, text, reading, decoding) and of *flow* (networks, information, influence, technology)—appear to be the major dimensions underlying the field" (S39). By integrating psychological processes into "meaning," one could easily parse the essays in the handbook into those two themes as Katz defines them.

Challenges to Hovland and McGuire's Minimal Effects Conclusion in Psychology

Recall that McGuire dismissed the notion that "television and other mass media have sizeable impacts on the public's thoughts, feelings, and actions," a conclusion that did not rule out the possibility of modest but nonetheless important effects. While political scientists were tracking factors that directly affected voting behavior and psychologists were pursuing evidence of attitude and behavior change, mass communication scholars were asking whether, and, if so, how, media affected cognition, specifically the pictures in our heads (Lippmann, 1922). Their answer: through agenda setting and cultivation, some types and genres of media do in fact produce statistically significant albeit modest effects on our "thoughts" with larger effects occurring in some populations, for example those with a high need for cognition or little direct experience with the issue or image being trafficked by media. Unsurprisingly, a study of major communication journals covering 1956–2000 found that agenda setting and cultivation were two of the top three most heavily cited communication theories (Bryant and Miron, 2004, 673). The third, uses and gratifications, is bodied in the work of Blumler and McQuail that I will address in a moment.

Captured in Bernard Cohen's (1963) memorable axiom, the press "may not be successful much of the time in telling people what to think, but it is stunningly successful in telling its readers what to think about" (13), the theory of agenda setting played a central role in the emergence of the field of political communication by demonstrating the relationship between the most often covered issues in media and what the audience considers important. After correlating undecided Chapel Hill, North Carolinians' perceptions of which issues were important in 1968 with those featured in the media, McCombs and Shaw (1972) posited that media set the agenda by telling susceptible voters what to think about. Since candidates offer competing issue agendas, this phenomenon had the potential to advantage one aspirant over another. By the early 1990s, agenda-setting scholarship had refined Cohen's formulation by showing that "that the media not only tell us what to think about, but also how to think about it, and, consequently, what to think" (McCombs and Shaw, 1993, 65).[6] Agenda setting also elicited an early cross-disciplinary exchange when Erbring, Goldenberg, and Miller (1980) broke from what they saw as McCombs and Shaw's "reliance on a 'mirror-image' model of media effects" to introduce an " 'audience-effects' model which treats issue-specific audience sensitivities as modulators, and news coverage as a trigger stimulus, of media impact on issue salience, issue by issue" (Erbring et al., 1980, 16).

Developed by Annenberg School scholars George Gerbner and Larry Gross, cultivation presupposed that over time, heavy viewers of prime time television would adopt television's distorted view of reality. Their research confirmed that at least some heavy viewers of violence-saturated, prime-time programming were indeed more likely to believe that the world is a meaner and scarier place than it actually is. At its core, the theory contended that television "is an agency of the established order and as such serves primarily to extend and maintain rather than to alter, threaten, or weaken conventional conceptions, beliefs and behaviors" (Gerbner and Gross, 1976, 175; for a contrary view see Hirsch, 1980, 1981; for meta-analyses see Morgan and Shanahan, 1997, 2010). Of particular interest here is the derivative explanation that over-time high exposure to crime-saturated local news elicited the public belief that crime remained a significant national problem even after clear drops in the crime rate occurred (Romer, Jamieson, and Aday, 2003, 88). Gerbner and Gross's focus on the effects of exposure to prime-time television both challenged the minimal effects assumption and presaged later work on the political effects of non-news media.

Where McCombs and Shaw and Gerbner and Gross relied on content analysis and survey data, the next major assault on the minimal effects model would come from controlled experiments. In political communication's ledger sheet, the Yale tradition deserves credit for integrating that method into political communication research. Just as Hovland (1959) urged Lazarsfeld (15) to replace the panel method with the controlled experiment so as to better capture the complexity of communication and justify causal inferences, so, too, his colleagues and co-authors, William McGuire and Robert Abelson (see Hovland, McGuire, Abelson, and Brehm's *Attitude Organization and Change: An Analysis of Consistency Among Attitude Component* [1966]), offered encouragement when Iyengar and Kinder were "not yet fully persuaded that the political effects of television could be studied usefully by experimental means" (vii).[7] In an instance of historical symmetry, the work reported in *News That Matters* was begun at Yale.

Ignoring Patterson's later work (1980), Iyengar and Kinder—two of the political scientists Katz espied flocking to communication research in the 1980s—used the power of the experimental method to argue that "Patterson and McClure's [1976] conclusion—that 'network newscasts are neither very educational nor very powerful'—is quite thoroughly mistaken" (1). In the process of making that case, in *News That Matters,* they (1987) centered a mechanism capable of producing media effects in the political communication scholar's repertoire by showing that "by priming certain aspects of national life while ignoring others, television news sets the terms by which political judgments are rendered and political choices made" (4).

The behavioral impulse in the speech field was fed by insights drawn from Hovland, Janis, and Kelley's 1953 *Communication and Persuasion*, among other works,[8] and championed by psychologists such as Charles Woolbert at the University of Illinois, who served as president of the speech field's professional association in 1920, and Franklin Knower at Ohio State (see Delia, 1987, 43). The laboratory experiments of speech scholars explored the impact of classical rhetorical elements such as ethos—later called source credibility—(cf. Haiman, 1949) and argument (cf. Knower 1936) and studied the effects of medium on messages and audiences response to them (cf. Ewbank's exploration of radio techniques, 1932), a line of work that prefigured findings of medium-related learning differences (cf, Neuman, Crigler, and Just, 1992). I cite these essays in particular because each earned recognition in Hovland's 1954 "Effect of Mass Media of Communication."

McGuire's work influenced not only Iyengar and Kinder's (1987, 73) but also that of the cross-disciplinary team of Pfau and Kenski (1990) and that of political scientist John Zaller (1992) who reported that McGuire's "masterly synthesis of research on attitude change has provided the starting point for all my work in this area" (xi). Originally conceptualized by psychologists Lumsdaine and Janis (1953) as part of propaganda studies and refined by psychologist McGuire (McGuire and Papageorgis, 1961; McGuire, 1961), inoculation was the subject of communication scholar Michael Pfau and political scientist Henry Kenski's *Attack Politics: Strategy and Defense* which built on work by

Pfau (Pfau and Burgoon, 1988; Pfau et al., 1990) to show that employing an inoculative strategy could create resistance to both character and issue attacks (Pfau and Kenski, 1990).[9]

Drawing on both Converse (1962) and McGuire (1968), Zaller's (1992) Receive Accept Sample (RAS) model explained the circumstances and mechanisms involved in determining who would be influenced by media. In the RAS, attitude change is most likely among individuals in the middle of the distribution of motivation whose exposure is high enough to encounter new information but whose disposition to counterargue is sufficiently low to permit attitudinal impact. Although it appeared after 1993, I include as well Zaller's argument that evidence of minimal ultimate effects does not preclude massive media influence (1996, 17) because it explicitly responds to McGuire's minimal effects synthesis. In "The Myth of Massive Media Impact Revisited: New Support for a Discredited Idea" Zaller argued that "models that assume that more exposure leads in additive fashion to more media influence are of little use in disentangling the effects of crosscutting communication" (20). Instead, he showed that because "members of the public who are heavily exposed to one message tend to be heavily exposed to its opposites as well" each message "has its effects, but the effects tend to be mutually canceling in ways that produce the illusion of modest impact" (20).

By situating political communication within the cognitive revolution (see Beniger and Gusek, 1995), these bodies of scholarship broadened its concept of effects to include sustaining the status quo as well as such outcomes as learning, agenda setting, cultivation, and creating spirals of silence. At the same time, they tied such message structures as inoculation and framing to audience response and specified the circumstances and individual characteristics most susceptible to communicative influence. In the process, the idea that audiences are uniform and passive gave way to one in which individuals counter-argue (Pfau and Kenski, 1990), agenda-setting effects are likely when issues are unobtrusive (cf. Weaver et al., 1981) but unlikely when they are not, and the cultivation power of media is minimized when television's images contradict lived experience and magnified when one is consistent with the other (Morgan, 1983).

The importance of the robust finding that campaigns can increase political knowledge was on display at a 1999 seminar convening by Katz to guide the Annenberg Public Policy Center's National Annenberg Election Survey. There McGuire argued that the "knowledge (information) variable should be a high priority for inclusion in future election studies because it has a good track record for entering into a variety of confirmed hypotheses as an effect in its own right, as well as a theorized mediator or interaction variable that helps explain hypothesized relations" (2001, 49).

Challenging the Political Science Minimal Effects Model

Where Deutschmann and Danielson questioned the Columbia tradition's notion of two-step flow, and McCombs and Shaw and Gerbner and Gross showed that media affect the pictures in our heads, election studies by Blumler and McQuail and their colleagues in Britain and one by Mendelsohn and O'Keefe in the United States recast the study of effects by replacing the transmission model of influence with a transactional one. Because they are often excluded from histories of the field, let me note that pioneering studies of British elections include Trenaman and McQuail's *Television and the Political Image* (1961), Blumler and McQuail's analysis of the 1964 general election *Television in Politics: Its Uses and Influences* (1968), Blumler and McQuail's (1970) *The Audience for Election Television*, and Blumler and McLeod's (1974) *Communication and Voter Turnout in Britain*. Consistent with earlier work, Trenaman and McQuail (1961) correlated increased television exposure with heightened levels of information about proposed policies. Unlike the study by Trenaman and McQuail, Blumler and McQuail's study of the 1964 parliamentary election isolated the effects of television on attitudes.

Designed "to explore the paradox of high exposure to campaign communication coupled with low propensity to change," the Blumler and McQuail study (1969), focused "on the perception of the campaign by voters and on their motivations for viewing political television. A guiding idea was that the influence of campaign communication might turn not so much on its volume but on how and why it is received by its intended or unintended audience" (Blumler and McQuail, 2001, 226).

This uses and gratifications approach assaulted the minimal effects model with "new measures of political communication effects that do not involve a reversion to outdated mass persuasion models of media influence" (Blumler and McLeod, 1974, 309). Responding to the "modest role that the Columbia findings attributed to the media," they proposed instead "a more interactional approach to the reception of mediated information by different kinds of citizen-voters" (Katz and Warshel, 2001, 2). In conclusions consistent with those that Zaller would reach decades later, they (for an explanation, see Blumler and McQuail, 2001, 230) concluded that "a number of effects go in quite different directions and are obscured if one only looks at net changes." They also determined: "The less habitually politically inclined were 'brought into line' in informational and even attitude terms with trends affecting the majority" (230).

Following Blumler and McQuail's lead were US mass communication scholars Mendelsohn and O'Keefe (1976) whose 1972 election study *The People Choose a President: Influences on Voter Decision* showed that "simplistic models of vote prediction based upon demographic and/or political indicators alone" tell an incomplete story. "It is," they concluded," the interactions between those and more subtle variables, such as image and issue perception, that seem to lead to more important differences in electoral decision-making" (123). Like Patterson and McClure's *The Unseeing Eye*, also published in 1976, Mendelsohn and O'Keefe's book was based on detailed work conducted in a single community. But where Mendelsohn and O'Keefe found important media effects in their 1972 data, political scientists Patterson and McClure did not. In the process, they did however isolate a learning effect from ads. Specifically, "presidential ads were ineffective at manipulating voters but better at increasing their understanding of candidate issue positions . . . " However, "among the voters they studied, network news was neither very powerful nor every educational" (1976, 22–23, 90).

Shortly thereafter a second study by Patterson concluded that although newspapers were "the superior transmitter of information" (1980, 146), television news had power of its own. In particular "when only the voters' impressions about the candidates' personalities and leadership capacities are considered, television's impact is more apparent" (143) and not "insignificant" (146). "It appears," noted Patterson, "that continued exposure to a candidate, whether on television or the newspaper, encourages the voter to make judgments about a candidate's character" (146). Importantly "[e]arly impressions, many of which have no obvious political significance, affect later ones, and provide resistance to partisan leanings" (152).

By replacing the community-based panel designs and cross-sectional model dominating US elections research with the kind of rolling cross-sectional method briefly tried out by ANES in 1984, Richard Johnston and a team of Canadian political scientists were able to confirm that "rhetoric" produced election effects in its own right. Campaign rhetoric, they concluded, not only persuades people in campaigns but also "possibly" plays "its biggest role—by directing voters towards a specific agenda and considerations surrounding that agenda" (Johnston et al., 1992, 249). Because Johnston incorporated the rolling cross-sectional method into the inaugural 100,000 interview, year 2000 run of the National Annenberg Election Study, the two political scientists and one communication researcher who superintended the project (Johnston, Hagen, and Jamieson, 2004) were able to explain why the forecasters' predictions of a decisive 2000 Gore win against George W. Bush were off base. Specifically, and here our story comes full circle—analysis of the 2000 NAES rolling cross-sectional data confirmed that Gelman and King (1993) were prescient when they surmised that communication plays a key role in activating the effects of fundamental factors in voters (i.e., Gore violated an assumption of the political science forecasters by failing to prime the economy), Finkel (1993) was correct in anticipating communication effects when the efforts of the two sides are out of balance (i.e., Bush won the battleground by outspending Gore on ads in the final weeks), and Bartels (1993) was on target in arguing that with a good research design and measurements, one should be able to isolate media effects (i.e., early in the general election, Republican ads primed negative trait perceptions about Gore; in the week before the election, a Republican ad advantage in the battleground protected Bush from attacks on his Social Security plans made by Gore in unrebutted appearances in network news).[10]

Because a number of its findings echo those in the Columbia data, the Johnston, Hagen, and Jamieson study (2004) brings us full circle in a second sense as well. There are after all important parallels between their explanation of the 2000 outcome and those advanced by the Columbia scholars. "Political campaigns are important," noted Lazarsfeld and his colleagues (1944, 74) in *The People's Choice*, "primarily because they *activate* latent predispositions." Communication mattered in both elections. Where in that earlier one, Democratic campaign communication activated latent dispositions, in 2000 the relative Democratic silence on the economic successes of the Clinton-Gore years undercut the potency of a fundamental factor that should have propelled the vice president to victory in the electoral college as well as the popular vote.

CONCLUSION

This chapter has tracked the byways that led to the emergence of a cross-disciplinary cadre of scholars identified with the hybrid field of political communication. Concentrating on the period between the mid 1940s and mid 1990s, it has telegraphed the influence of the disciplines of sociology, political science, psychology, and communication on the emerging field; recounted how scholars such as Elihu Katz, Kurt and Gladys Lang, Murray Edelman, and Doris Graber seeded the intellectual ground from which the field would grow; catalogued the emergence of a concept of effects that includes such phenomena as learning, the construction of political meaning, and agenda setting; and featured a study that isolated the role of communication in activating the variables from which forecasting models predict presidential election outcomes.

The chapters in this handbook reveal the questions currently vexing scholars identified with political communication, the answers they have uncovered and the extent to which they have been able to replace the "minimal effects" model with compelling alternatives that yield nonobvious insight about symbolic exchanges about the shared exercise of power.

NOTES

1. Books by Hovland and his Yale colleagues included *Communication and Persuasion* (1953), *The Order of Presentation in Persuasion* (1957), *Personality and Persuasibility* (1959), *Attitude Organization and Change* (1960) and *Social Judgment: Assimilation and Contrast Effects in Communication and Attitude Change* (1961).
2. Unsurprisingly, the Ithiel de Sola Pool lecture presented every third year at the APSA Annual Meeting is the one tradition at APSA outside the political communication division that has featured those identified with the political communication division (i.e., Lance Bennett [1988], Kathleen Hall Jamieson [2001] and Manuel Castells [2004]) among the invited lecturers.
3. Another tributary of Lasswell's flowed from his books *Psychopathology and Politics* (1930) and *Power and Personality* (1948) to the theorizing of James David Barber whose typology reported in the *Presidential Character: Predicting Performance in the White House* (1972) led him to predict accurately in 1969 at a meeting of the American Political Science Association, "The danger is that Nixon will commit himself irrevocably to some disastrous course of action" (Fox, 2004). Barber's psycho-biographies of presidents fitted them into one of four categories based on childhood background and cues embedded in the interstices of their discourse.
4. But where the concerns about the power of Nazi propaganda that drove the Lasswell tradition assumed that its effects were massive, the later work by the sociologists found them

to be small. One explanation is the difference in rigor and method. Another is the difference in the object of inquiry. Where those focused on propaganda studied single, long-lived streams of intense communication in media (film and radio) that drew large audiences united by a common threat, all conditions conducive to media influence, the Columbia studies focused on elections which by their nature included multiple, conflicting flows of information and potential influence that were likely to evoke selective perception.

5. Nimmo is important as well for co-editing the first *Handbook of Political Communication* (Nimmo and Sanders, 1981).

6. In *News That Matters*, Iyengar and Kinder dismiss McCombs and Shaw's empirical case for agenda setting without offering justificatory evidence. "Although research on agenda—setting has proliferated over the last decade" they write, "so far, unfortunately, the results add up to little" (3).

7. A Ph.D. in social psychology, Kinder had earlier co-authored with Abelson (Kinder et al., 1980; Abelson et al., 1982).

8. Among them Pearce includes George Miller's *Language and Communication*; Shannon and Weaver's *The Mathematical Theory of Communication*; Ruesch and Bateson's *Communication: The Social Matrix of Psychiatry*; Cherry's *On Human Communication*; and, somewhat later, Watzlawick, Beavin, and Jackson's *Pragmatics of Human Communication* (Pearce, 1985, 270).

9. Lin and Pfau (2007) rely on Pfau, Tuding, Koerner, et al.'s model involving threat, counter-argument, refutational preemption, and involvement to address the question "Can inoculation work against the spiral of silence?" (155).

10. Communication's effects were not limited to activating variables in the traditional political science model. After integrating a comprehensive data set of radio-TV and cable buys into the rolling cross-sectional NAES 2008 survey data, Kenski, Hardy, and Jamieson (2010) concluded that "the fundamentals—specifically, an unpopular incumbent, a faltering economy, and a party-identification advantage for the Democrats—had impressive predictive power in 2008" explaining three-fourths of the variance in vote disposition. "But with almost 15% of the variance in the satchels, messages shifted vote intention as well, & the effects of the advertised messages were in part a function of Obama's capacity to significantly outspend McCain on advertising" (301–2). In particular, "[a] 100 GRP advantage for Obama in local TV advertising increases by 1.5% the probability that a person with a baseline probability of 50% will say that if the election were held of the day on the interview she would cast an Obama vote, cable produces a 4.1% impact, and radio, a 5.5% one" (274). Whether these are effects at all and, if so, whether they are minimal or not so, is a function of how one frames the finding.

REFERENCES

Abelson, R., Kinder, D., Peters, M., and Fiske, S. 1982. Affective and semantic components in political person perception. *Journal of Personality and Social Psychology* 42: 619–630.

Almond, G. 1996. Political science: The history of the discipline. In Robert Goodin and Hans-Dieter Klingemann (Eds.), *A new handbook of political science* (pp. 50–96). Oxford: Oxford University Press.

Altheide, D. 1974. *Creating reality: How TV news distorts events*. Beverley Hills: Sage.

Arndt, J. 1968. A test of the two-step flow in diffusion of a new product. *Journalism Quarterly* 45: 457–465.

Arnold, C., and Bowers, J. W. 1984. *Handbook of rhetorical and communication theory.* Boston: Allyn and Bacon.

Arora, S. K., and Lasswell, H. D. 1969. *Political communication: The public language of political elites in India and the United States.* New York: Holt, Rinehart and Winston.

Barber, J. 1972. *The presidential character: Predicting performance in the White House.* Englewood Cliffs: Prentice-Hall.

Bartels, L. 1993. Messages received: The political impact of media exposure. *The American Political Science Review 87:* 267–285.

Becker, L., McCombs, M., and McLeod, J. M. 1975. The development of political cognitions. In S. Chaffee (Ed.), *Political communication: Issues and strategies for research,* (pp. 21–63). Beverly Hills: Sage.

Beniger, J. R., and Gusek, J. A. 1995. The cognitive revolution in public opinion and communication research. In T. L. Glasser and C. T. Salmon (Eds.), *Public opinion and the communication of consent* (pp. 217–248). New York: Guilford.

Bennett, L., and M. Edelman, M. 1985. Toward a new political narrative. *Journal of Communication 35:* 156–171.

Bennett, L. 1988. *News: The politics of illusion.* New York: Longman.

Bennett, L. 1993. Constructing publics and their opinions, *Political Communication,* 101–118.

Berelson, B., Lazarsfeld, P., and McPhee, W. 1954. *Voting: A study of opinion formation in a presidential campaign.* Chicago: University of Chicago Press.

Berelson, B. 1959. The state of communication research. *Public Opinion Quarterly 23:* 1–6.

Black, E. 1965. *Rhetorical criticism: A study in method.* Madison: University of Wisconsin Press.

Blumler, J., and McQuail, D. 2001. Political communication scholarship. In E. Katz and Y. Warshel (Eds.), *Election studies: What's their use?* (pp. 219–246). Boulder: Westview.

Blumler, J., and McQuail, D. 1968. *Television in politics: Its uses and influence.* London: Faber and Faber.

Blumler, J., and McQuail, D. 1969. *Television in politics: Its uses and influence.* Chicago: University of Chicago Press.

Blumler, J., and McQuail, D. 1970. The audience of election television. In J. Tunstall (Ed.), *Media sociology: A reader,* (pp. 452–478). London: Constable.

Blumler, J., and McQuail, D. 2001. Political communication scholarship: The uses of election research. In E. Katz and Y. Warshel (Eds.), *Election Studies. What's Their Use,* (pp. 219–245). Boulder: Westview.

Blumler, J., and Katz, E. 1974. *The uses of mass communications: Current perspectives on gratifications research. Sage annual review of communication research,* Volume 3. Beverly Hills: Sage.

Blumler, J., and McLeod, J. 1974. Communication and voter turnout in Britain. In Timothy Leggatt (Ed.), *Sociological theory and survey research: International change and social policy in Great Britain,* (pp. 265–312). Beverly Hills: Sage.

Bryant, J., and Miron, D. 2004. Theory and research in mass communication. *Journal of Communication 54:* 662–704.

Burke, K. 1950. *A rhetoric of motives.* New York: Prentice Hall.

Campbell, A. 1954. *The voter decides.* Evanston: Row, Peterson.

Campbell, A., Converse, P., Miller, W., and Stokes, D. 1960. *The American voter.* Chicago: University of Chicago Press.

Campbell, K. K. 1982. *The rhetorical act.* Belmont: Wadsworth.

Chaffee, S., Ed. 1972. *Political communication: Issues and strategies for research.* Beverly Hills: Sage.

Chaffee, S. 1978. Presidential debates—Are they helpful to voters? *Communication Monographs* 45: 330–346.

Chaffee, S., and Hochheimer, J. 1985. The beginnings of political communication research in the United States: Origins of the "limited effects" model. In E. M. Rogers and F. Balle (Eds.), *The media revolution in America and Western Europe,* (pp. 267–296). Norwood: Ablex.

Chaffee, S., Ward, S., and Tipton, L. 1970. Mass communication and political socialization. *Journalism Quarterly 47:* 647–659.

Charland, M. 1987. Constitutive rhetoric: The case of the Peuple Quebecois. *Quarterly Journal of Speech 73:* 133–150.

Coleman, J., Katz, E., and Menzel, H. 1966. *Medical innovation: A diffusion study.* New York: Bobbs-Merrill.

Cohen, B. 1963. *The press and foreign policy.* Princeton: Princeton University Press.

Comstock, G. 1983. The legacy of the past. *Journal of Communication, 33,* 42–50.

Converse, P. 1962. Information flow and the stability of partisan attitudes. *Public Opinion Quarterly 26:* 578–599.

Dayan, D., and Katz, E. 1992. *Media events: The live broadcasting of history.* Cambridge, MA: Harvard University Press.

de Sola Pool, I. 1969. Review of the book *Television and Politics* by Kurt Lang; Gladys Lang. *Public Opinion Quarterly 33:* 287–289.

Delia, J. 1987. Communication research: A history. In C. Berger and S. Chaffee (Eds.), *Handbook of communication science,* (pp. 20–98). Newbury Park, CA: Sage.

Denton, R. 1982. *The symbolic dimensions of the American presidency: Description and analysis.* Long Grove: Waveland Press.

Deutschmann, P., and Danielson, W. 1960. Diffusion of knowledge of the major news story. *Journalism Quarterly 37:* 345–355.

Downs, A. 1957. *An economic theory of democracy.* New York: Harper and Row.

Edelman, M. 1960. Symbols and political quiescence. *American Political Science Review 54:* 695–704.

Edelman, M. 1964. *The symbolic uses of politics.* Urbana: University of Illinois Press.

Edelman, M. 1971. *Politics as symbolic action: Mass arousal and quiescence.* New York: Academic Press.

Edelman, M. 1977. *Political language: Words that succeed and policies that fail.* New York: Academic Press.

Edwards, G. 1996. Presidential rhetoric: What difference does it make? In, M. J. Medhurt (Eds.), *Beyond the rhetorical presidency,* (pp. 199–217). College Station: Texas A&M Press.

Elder, C., and Cobb, R. 1983. *The political uses of symbols.* New York: Longman.

Erbring, L., Goldenberg, E., and Miller, A. 1980. Front-page news and real-world cues: A new look at agenda setting by the media. *American Journal of Political Science 24:* 16–49.

Ewbank, H. 1932. Exploratory studies in radio techniques. In, J. MacLatchy (Ed.), *Education on the air, yearbook of the Institute for Education Radio, Volume 3,* (pp. 231–245). Columbus: Ohio State University Press.

Fair, R. 1978. The effect of economic events on votes for president. *The Review of Economics and Statistics 60:* 159–173.

Finkel, S. E. 1993. Reexamining the "minimal effects" model in recent presidential campaigns. *Journal of Politics 55:* 1–21.

Fox, M. 2004. James D. Barber, expert on presidents, dies at 74. *New York Times*, September 15. Retrieved from http://www.nytimes.com.

Gelman, A., and King, G. 1993. Why are American presidential election campaign polls so variable when votes are so predictable? *British Journal of Political Science* 23: 409–451.

Gerbner, G., and Gross, L. 1976. Living with television: The violence profile. *Journal of Communication* 26: 172–194.

Gitlin, T. 1978. Media sociology: The dominant paradigm. *Theory and Society* 6: 205–253.

Gitlin, T. 1980. *The whole world is watching: Mass media in the making & unmaking of the new left*. Berkeley: University of California Press.

Gosnell, H. 1927. *Getting-out-the-vote: An experiment in the stimulation of voting*. Chicago: University of Chicago Press.

Graber, D. 1976. *Verbal behavior and politics*. Urbana: University of Illinois Press.

Graber, D. 1984. *Processing the news: How people tame the information tide*. New York: Longman.

Haiman, F. S. 1949. An experimental study of the effects of ethos in public speaking. *Speech Monographs* 16: 190–202.

Hart, R. 1977. *The political pulpit*. West Lafayette: Purdue University Press.

Hart, R. 1984. *Verbal style and the presidency: A computer-based analysis*. Orlando: Academic Press.

Hart, R. 1987. *The sound of leadership: Presidential communication in the modern age*. Chicago: University of Chicago Press.

Hershey, M. R. 1993. Election research as spectacle: The Edelman vision and the empirical study of elections. *Political Communication* 10: 121–139.

Hinkley, B. 1990. *The symbolic presidency: How presidents portray themselves*. New York: Routledge.

Hirsch, P. (1980). The "scary world" of the nonviewer and other anomalies: A reanalysis of Gerbner et al.'s findings on cultivation analysis, part I. *Communication Research* 7: 403–456.

Hirsch, P. 1981. On not learning from one's own mistakes: A reanalysis of Gerbner et al.'s findings on cultivation analysis, part II. *Communication Research* 8: 3–37.

Hochmuth, M. 1952. Kenneth Burke and the "new rhetoric". *Quarterly Journal of Speech* 38: 133–144.

Hovland, C. 1954. The effects of the mass media of communication. In G. Lindzey *Handbook of social psychology*, (pp. 1062–1103). Cambridge: Addison-Wesley.

Hovland, C., Ed. 1957. *The order of presentation in persuasion*. New Haven: Yale University Press.

Hovland, C. 1959. Reconciling conflicting results derived from experimental and survey studies of attitude change. *American Psychologist* 14: 8–17.

Hovland, C., and Janis, I. Eds. 1959. *Personality and persuasibility*. New Haven: Yale University Press.

Hovland, C., Janis, I., and Kelley, H. 1953. *Communication and persuasion: Psychological studies of opinion change*. New Haven: Yale University Press.

Hovland, C., Lumsdaine, A., and Sheffield, F. D. 1949. *Experiments on mass communication*. Princeton: Princeton University Press.

Hovland, C., and Rosenberg, M. Eds. 1960. *Attitude organization and change: An analysis of consistency among attitude components*. New Haven: Yale University Press.

Hovland, C., McGuire, W., Abelson, R., and Brehm, J. W. 1966. *Attitude organization and change: An analysis of consistency among attitude component. Yale Studies in Attitudes and Communication, Volume 3*. In Milton Rosenberg (Ed). New Haven: Yale University Press.

Ivie, R. 1980. Images of savagery in American justifications for war. *Communication Monographs 47*: 279–294.

Iyengar, S. 1991. *Is anyone responsible? How television frames political issues*. Chicago: University of Chicago Press.

Iyengar, S., and Kinder, D. 1987. *News that matters: Television and American opinion*. Chicago: University of Chicago Press.

Jamieson, K. H. 1984. *Packaging the presidency: A history and criticism of presidential campaign advertising*. New York: Oxford University Press.

Jamieson, K. H. 1992. *Dirty politics: Deception, distraction and democracy*. New York: Oxford University Press.

Johnston, R., Blais, A., Brady, H., and Crête, J. 1992. *Letting the people decide: Dynamics of a Canadian election*. Montreal: McGill Queen's University Press.

Johnston, R., Hagen, M., and Jamieson, K. H. 2004. *The 2000 presidential election and the foundations of party politics*. Cambridge: Cambridge University Press.

Katz, E., and Feldman, J. J. 1962. The debates in the light of research: A survey of surveys. In S. Kraus (Ed.), *The great debates: Background, perspective, effects*, (pp. 173–223). Bloomington: Indiana University Press.

Katz, E. 1968. On reopening the question of selectivity in exposure to mass communications. In R. Abelson (Ed.), *Theories of cognitive consistency: A sourcebook*, (pp. 788–796). Chicago: Rand McNally.

Katz, E. 1971. Platforms & windows: Broadcasting's role in election campaigns. *Journalism & Mass Communication Quarterly 48*: 304–314.

Katz, E. 1977. Can authentic cultures survive new media? *Journal of Communication 27*: 113–121.

Katz, E. 1987. Communications research since Lazarsfeld. *Public Opinion Quarterly 51*: S25–S45.

Katz, E. 1988. On conceptualizing media effects: Another look. In S. Oskamp (Ed.), *Television as a social issue, Applied Social Psychology Annual*, (pp. 361–374). Newberry Park, CA: Sage.

Katz, E., Blumler, J., and Gurevitch, M. 1974. Utilization of mass communication by the individual. In J. Blumler and E. Katz (Eds.), *The uses of mass communications: Current perspectives on gratifications. Sage Annual Reviews of Communication Research Volume 3*, (pp. 19–32). Beverly Hills: Sage.

Katz, E., and Dayan, D. 2003. The audience is a crowd, the crowd is a public: Latter day thoughts on Lang and Lang's MacArthur Day in Chicago. In E. Katz, J. D. Peters, T. Liebes and A. Orloff (Eds.), *Canonic texts in media research*, (pp. 121–136). Cambridge: Polity Press.

Katz, E., and Liebes, T. 1990. Interacting with Dallas cross cultural readings of American TV. *Canadian Journal of Communication 15*: 45–66.

Katz, E., and Lazarsfeld, P. 2006/1955. *Personal influence: The part played by people in the flow of mass communication*, 2nd edition. New Brunswick: Transaction.

Katz, E., and Warshel, Y. 2001. Introduction. In E. Katz and Y. Warshel (Eds.) *Election studies: What's their use?* (pp. 1–14). Boulder: Westview.

Kenski, K. 2004. The rolling cross-section design. In D. Romer, K. Kenski, P. Waldman, C. Adasiewicz, and K. H. Jamieson (Eds.), *Capturing campaign dynamics: The National Annenberg Election Survey* (pp. 56–65). New York: Oxford University Press.

Kenski, K., Hardy, B., and Jamieson, K. H. 2010. *The Obama victory: How media, money and message shaped the 2008 election*. New York: Oxford University Press.

Key, V. O., and Cummings, M. C. 1966. *The responsible electorate: Rationality in presidential voting, 1936–1960.* Cambridge, MA: Harvard University Press.

Kinder, D., Peters, M., Abelson, R., and Fiske, S. 1980. Presidential prototypes. *Political Behavior 2:* 4315–337.

Klapper, J. 1960. *The effects of mass communication.* Glencoe: Free Press.

Knower, F. H. 1936. Experimental studies of changes in attitude II. A study of the effect of printed argument on changes in attitude. *Journal of Abnormal and Social Psychology 30:* 522–532.

Kraus, S., Ed. 1962. *The great debates: Background, perspective, effects.* Bloomington: Indiana University Press.

Kraus, S. 1973. Mass communication and political socialization: A re-assessment of two decades of research. *Quarterly Journal of Speech 59:* 390–400.

Kraus, S., and Davis, D. 1976. *The effects of mass communication on political behavior.* University Park: Pennsylvania State University Press.

Kramer, G. H. 1970. The effects of precinct-level canvassing on voter behavior. *Public Opinion Quarterly 34:* 560–572.

Lang, K., and Lang, G. E. 1953. The unique perspective of television and its effects: A pilot study. *American Sociological Review 18:* 3–12.

Lang, K., and Lang, G. E. 1959. The mass media and voting. In E. J. Burdick and A. J. Brodbeck (Eds.), *American voting behavior,* (pp. 217–235). Glencoe, IL: Free Press.

Lang, K., and Lang, G. E. 1968a. *Politics and television.* Chicago: Quadrangle Books.

Lang, K., and Lang, G. E. 1968b. *Voting and nonvoting: Implications of broadcasting returns before polls are closed.* Waltham: Blaisdell.

Lang, G. E., and Lang, K. 1978. Immediate and delayed responses to a Carter-Ford debate: Assessing public opinion. *Public Opinion Quarterly 42:* 322–341.

Lang, G. E., and Lang, K. 1981. Watergate: An exploration of the agenda-building process. In G. Cleveland Wilhoit and Harold de Bock (Eds.), *Mass Communication Review Yearbook 2,* (pp. 447–468). Beverly Hills: Sage.

Lang, K., and Lang, G. E. 1993. Perspectives on communication. *Journal of Communication 43:* 92–99.

Lasswell, H. 1927. *Propaganda technique in the World War.* New York: Peter Smith.

Lasswell, H. 1930. *Psychopathology and politics.* Chicago: University of Chicago Press.

Lasswell, H. 1948. *Power and personality.* New York: W.W. Norton.

Lasswell, H., Lerner, D., and de Sola Pool, I. 1952. *The comparative study of symbols.* Stanford: Stanford University Press.

Lasswell, H., Lerner, D., and Speier, H. 1979–1980. *Propaganda and communication in world history: Volume 1—The symbolic instrument in early times; Volume 2—Emergence of public opinion in the West; Volume 3—A pluralizing world in formation.* Honolulu: University Press of Hawaii.

Lasswell, H., Leites, N., Fadner, R., Goldsen, J., Grey, A., Janis, I., Kaplan, A., Mintz, A., De Sola Pool, I., Yakobson, S., and Kaplan, D. 1965. *The language of politics: Studies in quantitative semantics.* Cambridge: MIT Press.

Lazarsfeld, P., Berelson, B., and Gaudet, H. 1944. *The people's choice: How the voter makes up his mind in a presidential campaign.* New York: Duell, Sloan and Pearce.

Lin, W., and Pfau, M. 2007. Can inoculation work against the spiral of silence? A study of public opinion on the future of Taiwan. *International Journal of Public Opinion Research 19:* 155–172.

Lin, N. 1971. Information flow, influence flow and the decision-making process. *Journalism Quarterly 48*: 33–61.

Lippmann, W. 1922. *Public opinion*. New York: Harcourt.

Lumsdaine, A., and Janis, I. 1953. Resistance to counterpropaganda produced by one-sided and two-sided propaganda presentations. *Public Opinion Quarterly 17*: 311–318.

McClure, R. D., and Patterson, T. E. 1974. Television news and political advertising the impact of exposure on voter beliefs. *Communication Research 1*: 3–31.

McCombs, M., and Shaw, D. 1993. The evolution of agenda-setting research: Twenty-five years in the marketplace of ideas. *Journal of Communication 43*: 58–67.

McCombs, M., and Shaw, D. 1972. The agenda-setting function of mass media. *Public Opinion Quarterly 36*: 176–187.

McGee, M. C. 1980. The ideograph link between rhetoric and ideology: A link between rhetoric and ideology. *Quarterly Journal of Speech 66*: 1–16.

McGuire, W. 1961. Resistance to persuasion conferred by active and passive prior refutation of the same and alternative counterarguments. *Journal of Abnormal and Social Psychology 63*: 326–332.

McGuire, W., and Papageorgis, D. 1961. The relative efficacy of various types of prior belief-defense in producing immunity against persuasion. *Journal of Abnormal and Social Psychology 62*: 327–337.

McGuire, W. 1968. The nature of attitudes and attitude change. In Gardner Lindzey and Elliot Aronson (Eds.), *Handbook of social psychology, 2nd Edition, Volume 3*, (pp. 136–314). Reading: Addison Wesley.

McGuire, W. J. 1986. The myth of massive media impact: Savagings and salvagings. In George A. Comstock (Ed.), *Public communication and behavior, Volume 1*, (pp. 173–257). Orlando: Academic Press.

McLeod, J. M., C. R. Bybee, and Durall, J. A. 1979. Equivalence of informed political participation: The 1976 presidential debates as a source of influence. *Communication Research 6*: 463–487.

McLeod, J. M., and McDonald, D. G. 1985. Beyond simple exposure media orientations and their impact on political processes. *Communication Research 12*: 3–33.

Mendelsohn, H., and O'Keefe, G. J. 1976. *The people choose a president: Influences on voter decision making*. New York: Praeger.

Morgan, M. 1983. Symbolic victimization and real world fear. *Human Communication Research 9*: 146–157.

Morgan, M., and Shanahan, J. 1997. Two decades of cultivation research: An appraisal and meta-analysis. In B. R. Burleson (Ed.), *Communication Yearbook 20*, (pp. 1–45). Newbury Park, CA: Sage.

Morgan, M., and Shanahan, J. 2010. The state of cultivation. *Journal of Broadcasting & Electronic Media 54*: 337–355.

Nelson, J., McCloskey, D., and Megill, A. 1986. *The rhetoric of the human sciences*. Madison: University of Wisconsin Press.

Neuman, W. R., Crigler, A., and Just, M. 1992. *Common knowledge: News and the construction of political meaning*. Chicago: University of Chicago Press.

Nie, N. H., Verba, S., and Petrocik, J. R. 1979. *The changing American voter*. Cambridge: Harvard University Press.

Nimmo, D. 1974. *Popular images of politics: A taxonomy*. Englewood Cliffs: Prentice Hall.

Nimmo, D., and Sanders, K. Eds. 1981. *Handbook of political communication*. Beverly Hills: Sage.

Nimmo, D. D., and Combs, J. E. 1990. *Mediated political realities, 2nd Edition*. New York: Longman.

Noelle-Neumann, E. 1973. Return to the concept of powerful mass media. *Studies in Broadcasting* 9: 67–112.

Noelle-Neumann, E. 1974. The spiral of silence: A theory of public opinion. *Journal of Communication* 24: 43–51.

Noelle-Neumann, E. 1983. The effect of media on media effects research. *Journal of Communication* 33: 157–165.

Patterson, T., and McClure, R. D. 1976. *Unseeing eye: The myth of television power in national elections*. New York: G.P. Putnam's Sons.

Patterson, T. E. 1980. *The mass media election: How Americans choose their president*. New York: Praeger.

Pearce, W. B. 1985. scientific research methods in communication studies and their implications for theory and research. In Thomas Benson (Eds.), *Speech Communication in the 20th century*, (pp. 255–281). Carbondale: Southern Illinois University Press.

Peled, T., and Katz, E. 1974. Media functions in wartime: The Israel home front in October 1973. In Jay Blumler and Elihu Katz (Eds.), *The uses of mass communications: Current perspectives on gratifications research, Sage Annual Reviews of Communication Research, Volume 3*, (pp. 49–69). Beverly Hills: Sage.

Perelman, C., and Olbrechts-Tyteca, L. 1969. *The new rhetoric: A treatise on argumentation*, translated by J. Wilkinson and P. Weaver. Notre Dame: University of Notre Dame Press.

Pfau, M., and Burgoon, M. 1988. Inoculation in political campaign communication. *Human Communication Research* 15: 91–111.

Pfau, M., and Kenski, H. 1990. *Attack politics: Strategy and defense*. New York: Praeger.

Pfau, M., Kenski, H., Nitz, M., and Sorenson, J. 1990. Efficacy of inoculation strategies in promoting resistance to political attack messages: Application to direct mail. *Communication Monographs*, 57, 25–43.

Popkin, S. 1991. *The reasoning voter: Communication and persuasion in presidential campaigns*. Chicago: University of Chicago Press.

Romer, D., Jamieson, K. H., and Aday, S. 2003. Television news and the cultivation of fear of crime. *Journal of Communication* 53: 88–104.

Rosenfield, L. A. 1968. Case study in speech criticism: The Nixon-Truman analog. *Speech Monographs* 35: 435–450.

Rosenstone, S. J. 1983. *Forecasting presidential elections*. New Haven: Yale University Press.

Rosenstone, S., and Hansen, J. M. 1993. *Mobilization, participation and democracy in America*. New York: MacMillan.

Schramm, W. 1983. The unique perspective of communication: A retrospective view. *Journal of Communication* 33: 6–17.

Schramm, W. 1959. Comments on The state of communication research. *Public Opinion Quarterly* 23: 6–9.

Scott, R., and Brockriede, W. 1969. *The rhetoric of black power*. New York: Harper and Row.

Sherif, M., and Hovland, C. 1961. *Social judgment: Assimilation and contrast effects in communication and attitude change*. New Haven: Yale University Press.

Shibutani, T. 1966. *Improvised news: A sociological study of rumor*. Indianapolis: Bobbs-Merrill.

Sillars, M. 1964. Rhetoric as act. *Quarterly Journal of Speech* 50: 277–284.

Simons, H., Ed. 1990. *The rhetorical turn: Invention and persuasion in the conduct of inquiry.* Chicago: University of Chicago Press.

Simons, H., Ed. 1989. *Rhetoric in the human sciences.* London: Sage.

Swanson, D. L. 1972. The new politics meets the old rhetoric: New directions in campaign communication research. *Quarterly Journal of Speech 58:* 31–40.

Swanson, D. L. 1978. Political communication: A revisionist view emerges. *Quarterly Journal of Speech 64:* 211–222.

Trenaman, J., and McQuail, D. 1961. *Television and the political image: A study of the impact of television on the 1959 general election.* London: Methuen and Co, Ltd.

Wattenberg, M. P. 1990. *The decline of American political parties, 1952–1988.* Cambridge, MA: Harvard University Press.

Wattenberg, M. P. 1991. *The rise of candidate-centered politics.* Cambridge, MA: Harvard University Press.

Weaver, D., Graber, D., McCombs, M., and Eyal, C. 1981. *Media agenda setting in a presidential election: Issues, images and interest.* Westport: Greenwood.

Winneg, K., and Jamieson, K. H. 2005. Elections: Party identification in the 2004 election. *Presidential Studies Quarterly 35:* 576–589.

Winneg, K., and Jamieson, K. H. 2010. Party identification in the 2008 presidential election. *Presidential Studies Quarterly 40:* 247–263.

Zaller, J. 1992. *The nature and origins of mass opinion.* New York: Cambridge University Press.

Zaller, J. 1996. The myth of massive media effects revived: Empirical support for a discredited idea. In Mutz, D. Sniderman, P., and Brody, R. (Eds.), *Political persuasion and attitude change.* Ann Arbor: University of Michigan Press.

CHAPTER 3

....

THE SHAPE OF POLITICAL COMMUNICATION

....

JAY G. BLUMLER

DOES political communication have a shape? Does it matter? If so, how might we characterize it? The whole, it is sometimes said, is greater than its parts. Could this proposition be true of political communication, and if so, how and why? As other chapters in this volume show, lines of empirical political communication research are often specifically focused, aiming to generate cumulative knowledge from closely and carefully studied "parts." This leaves open, however, questions about what they might add up to overall. Five reasons explain why these questions should also be explored.

One reason is the complexity of the political communication process, which is organized "within a Chinese-boxes-like set of levels" (Blumler, McLeod, and Rosengren, 1992, 14), linking a political, economic, and cultural environment; political advocates of all kinds; journalistic and other mediators of all kinds; the messages and other content that they produce; and bodies of heterogeneous and varyingly involved citizens. We need to be able to travel across these levels (as well as to home in on particular ones) with concepts that can help us to understand how these relationships work, how they feed on each other, how they evolve with regard to each other, and in what ways their interrelations may matter. As Blumler, McLeod, and Rosengren (1992, 10) put it, we need to bear in mind "the ever-continuing interplay between macro and micro. . . in the realm of communication."

The second reason is that if only dealt with in isolation, some of the organizations and actors involved in political communication could at times be incompletely understood, perhaps misunderstood. Key communicators can only rarely put across messages entirely as they would like without the involvement of others or their mediation by others or by taking advance account of the possible reactions of intended recipients. Mutual expectations, even mutual dependencies, consequently underlie much of the political communication process. This is particularly true of the sometimes collaborative, sometimes conflictual, sometimes even incestuous relationship of politicians and journalists—forming, according to David Swanson's (1997) metaphor, a virtual "political-media complex."

Third, it has been evident from time to time that broadly environmental changes can affect a range of phenomena, rippling down through the political communication system, as it were. Examples that come to mind are the onset of increased electoral volatility in Western democracies from the 1970s onward; the commercialization of formerly public service broadcasting systems in Western Europe; the switch from limited-channel television services to an ecology of media and communication abundance; and the current declining viability of network television news and the mainstream printed press. All these developments have affected political communication behaviors and responses.

Fourth, to assess political communication in a normative spirit, criticisms of specific bodies of content (e.g., of negative news for generating "media malaise") or of particular message makers (e.g., deceitful politicians or sensationalizing reporters) can have only a limited value. That is because "system-based features of political communication give characteristic shape to a society's public sphere, favouring certain sources and styles of political discourse over others and enabling or impeding a democratic engagement of leaders with citizens" (Blumler and Gurevitch, 1995, 203). In other words, what troubles us on the visible surface of political communications may often have deeper roots.

Fifth, with the increasing internationalization of political communication scholarship comes a need for single-country studies to be supplemented by, sometimes enlarged into, cross-national, comparative research. Among other things, such research is "an essential antidote to naïve universalism, or the tendency to implicitly presume that political communication research findings from one society (normally one's own!) are applicable everywhere" (Gurevitch and Blumler, 1990a, 308). Well-designed comparative research will therefore be based on a sense of how different systems may be different or similar as "wholes," that is, try to take account of differing "macro-social, system-level characteristics and influences on significant political communication phenomena" (Gurevitch and Blumler, 1990a, 306).

In short, whether the whole is always greater than the parts in political communication may be debatable, but it is undoubtedly essential to a fuller understanding of those parts as well as to the provision of insights into the process overall.

How, then, might the political communication process be grasped in the round? Harold Lasswell (1948) once depicted political communication as a matter of who says what, in which channel, to whom, and with what effect. That characterization, however, (a) is unduly linear, (b) ignores the shaping significance of communicator interrelationships, and (c) fails to mention a host of surrounding societal and organizational influences. In thinking about all this, it is important to bear in mind that political communication arrangements may be exposed to forces of both stability and change. Even in fast-moving news situations, political communicators often adopt and follow essentially similar routines over and over, making it easier for them to cope as well as to anticipate how other individuals significant for them will behave or react, given their involvement in equally entrenched routines. But neither are political communication systems frozen in cement. A major source of their unsettlement can be change in the technologies by which political messages are produced and disseminated. This may offer politicians new opportunities for projecting their messages and may reconfigure relations among key communicators and receivers. Other changes in the political communication process include changes in news media markets and competition patterns, changes in voters' orientations to the major political parties, and changes in political culture (such as attitudes of political skepticism or trust).

An attempt to generate a more holistic perspective on these matters arose in the 1970s and centered on the concept of a "political communication system" (as in Blumler and Gurevitch, 1977; Gurevitch and Blumler, 1977). (A current treatment of this notion may be found in Pfetsch and Esser, 2013.) Its emergence reflected two features of the period.

First, it represented something of a reaction against the predominant disciplinary influence of social psychology on the mass communication research field at the time, with many US scholars in particular having focused on individual-level phenomena, such as those of media effects—whether limited or powerful, attitudinal or cognitive, likely to reinforce or to change prior views, direct or indirect, and so forth (Klapper, 1960; Becker, McCombs, and McLeod, 1975). In contrast, originators of the concept of a political communication system aimed to introduce perspectives from political science and sociology into the field, for example, analyzing relationships of media institutions to political and other societal institutions (Gurevitch and Blumler, 1977).

Second, these scholars had witnessed and were responding to a major technological source of change: the comprehensively transforming impact of television on democratic politics from the 1960s onward. This change had enlarged and restructured the political audience (Blumler, 1970); transmitted visual images alongside verbal ones; stood for norms of fairness, impartiality, and neutrality rather than staunch partisanship; and directly entered the home, feeding political conversations inside and beyond it. But eventually the most important feature of this transformation was probably the positioning of television news as a pivot of the political communication process, one that voters (particularly less politically minded ones) derived much of their information and impressions of politics from (increasingly so as their party allegiances weakened) and that parties and politicians were keen, even desperate, to get their messages into. Indeed, with few national channels for politicians to address and for viewers to use—only three in the United States and two in Britain at first, later three—television must have seemed a veritable system-cementing medium. And as anyone familiar with television in both the United States and Britain at the time could readily see, their political broadcasting arrangements, one run on commercial, the other on public service, lines, did differ considerably—and precisely *as* systems.

But what does the notion of a political communication system involve? More generally, it draws attention to two features that lay perspectives, even practitioner perspectives, have rarely taken into account. One is that no single source of influence or practice is usually responsible for what political communication at a given time or place is like; rather, it typically stems from a composite of interacting influences. The other is that change in one part of a political communication system will usually trigger responses or changes in other parts—a matter of continual action and reaction. Such is the nature of a system (McLeod and Blumler, 1987).

And how is a political communication system constituted? Structurally, it comprises two sets of institutions, political and media organizations, which are involved in the course of message preparation in much horizontal interaction with each other, while on a vertical axis they are separately and jointly engaged in processing and disseminating ideas to and from the mass citizenry. The bulk of message production arises from the interface of political and media organizations, whose personnel continually "read" and take account of each other, and although these prime communicators may also be influenced by certain images they hold of audience members' interests and predilections and by opinions that they believe are widespread in the electorate at large, the audience consists predominantly of receivers (not makers) of communications, whose information and perceptions are more often products of what has come their way than reflective of ideas they have independently formed to pass on to others. And as indicated previously, the patterns and outcomes of these triangular relationships will be shaped in turn by prevailing communication technologies and will be embedded within surrounding political systems, media systems, and political cultures—all of which may change over time and differ across societal space (Blumler and Gurevitch, 1995).

What does this conceptualization offer to political communication scholarship? It has been applied in analysis and research in four main ways:

1) To conduct detailed explorations of the roles, perceptions, and strategies involved in media-politics interactions. On the media side, a key distinction between "sacerdotal" and "pragmatic" orientations to the reporting of political institutions, events, and messages has emerged, the former regarding such material as inherently deserving of news coverage due to its civic importance, the latter insisting that news values alone should determine the extent and manner of its coverage (Blumler, 1969). On the political side, depiction of a highly considered, elaborate, and power-oriented approach to daily news publicity has emerged. Termed "strategic communications" by Bennett and Manheim (2001) and the "modern publicity process" by Blumler (1990), this approach centers on a "competitive struggle to influence and control public perceptions of key issues and events through the major mass media" (1990, 103). More recently, Mazzoleni and Schulz (1999) have coined the notion of "mediatization" to convey how political actors are increasingly impelled to tailor their publicity efforts and messages to media logics, media requirements, and media perspectives on reality, with specifiable consequences for public communication and ultimately for the workings of democracy. Since then, other scholars have taken this idea further, dividing up the mediatization process into four distinct phases (each more media-oriented) and postulating how societies with different political and media systems might be positioned at different way stations along this mediatization route (Stromback, 2008).

2) To conduct longitudinal analyses of political communication arrangements and practices over time. This has centered especially on the increasing professionalization of political advocacy for news management purposes (as detailed internationally in Swanson and Mancini, 1996), on the one hand, and on a journalistic fight

back to keep ownership of the political message and defend professional auton- omy, on the other (as portrayed in Blumler and Gurevitch, 1995 and in Zaller's "Theory of Media Politics," 2001) Also considered in this line of analysis are the kinds of materials that these approaches tend to produce, such as increased neg- ativity and an increased reporting of politics as a tactical game rather than as a forum of policy debate (Jamieson, 1992; Patterson, 1993), as well as how they might affect public perceptions of politics, politicians, and political communication itself, including increased cynicism and an overall impoverishment of communi- cation for citizenship (Blumler and Gurevitch, 1995).

3) To design comparative, cross-national analyses of political communication sys- tems (see also de Vreese in this volume). Barely out of infancy in the mid-1970s (Blumler and Gurevitch, 1975), this approach eventually matured into "some- thing of a growth stock" (Swanson, 1992). Not all cross-national research stems from a macro-social point of departure, however, which is what concerns us here. Systemically oriented comparative research would identify in advance cer- tain ways in which macro-social features may be similar and/or different in two or more societies; postulate how such features might be reflected in similarities and differences at other levels of political communication (e.g., media contents or audience awareness, knowledge, and perceptions); carry out empirical research to verify, disconfirm, or modify such expectations; and then revisit the hypothesized macro-level influences in light of the results. Studies that have adopted something like this approach have multiplied in recent years, have usually yielded illuminat- ing results, and have created promising platforms for further research in turn. They include an analysis of influences on national levels of turnout in European parliamentary elections (Blumler, 1983); the framing of European Community news in different member countries' media reports (de Vreese, 2003); the forma- tion of election campaign agendas in the United Kingdom and the United States (Semetko et al., 1991); journalists' political roles in five countries (Patterson and Donsbach, 2006); innovations in election campaigning across eleven democra- cies (Swanson and Mancini 1996); news coverage of immigration issues in France and the United States (Benson, 2010); the portrayal of politicians as "spin doctors" in Germany, the United Kingdom, and the United States (Esser, Reinemann, and Fan, 2001); tests of Bennett's (1990) "indexing hypothesis" about the relationship of political reporting to the structure of inter-elite debate in the news systems of the United States, Italy, France, and Pakistan (Archetti, 2010); the personalization of mediated political output in twenty democracies (Downey and Stanyer, 2010); and the role of news management in British and Dutch politics (Brown, 2011). The conceptual armory of comparative communication analysis has also been sub- stantially advanced by Hallin and Mancini (2004), who have comprehensively described and differentiated three models of political communication systems extant in the nations of North America and Western Europe, as well as specify- ing four dimensions of political and media structure on which these are based. They have latterly sought to extend this framework to a number of less mature

democracies in Eastern Europe, South America, Africa, and Asia as well (Hallin and Mancini, 2012).

4) To consider normative issues. This is a particularly complicated subject, since scholars—and others of course—differ over the values that political communication should serve (Christians et al., 2009). So far as the present author is concerned, political communication should help citizens understand the main choices their society faces at a given time; engender confidence that what they are being told and shown about them can be trusted (or tested for its trustworthiness); and encourage them to play some part in, rather than merely kibitz over, what is going on. From this point of view, the concept of a political communication system can be normatively sobering. It can highlight disparities between civic ideals and political realities—between what communication-for-democracy should be like and what political communicators actually produce. For example, in "Political Communication Systems and Democratic Values," Gurevitch and Blumler (1990b) identified four different system-based constraints on the ability of the news media to serve democratic goals well. Indeed, after looking at political communication through systemic glasses, some scholars concluded that "our civic arteries" are "hardening," diagnosed a "crisis of communication for citizenship" (Blumler and Gurevitch, 1995), and maintained that in Britain at least (and perhaps elsewhere) political communication was in "freefall" (Blumler and Coleman, 2010). A systems outlook on political communication can thus heighten normative concern. Yet it also suggests that the main problems and deficiencies of political communication are deep-seated and are not due merely to the failings of certain blameworthy actors, but often stem from the constraints and pressures of an overall system. Of course this perspective makes the task of recommending feasible reform difficult. Reform-minded scholars have tried to overcome this problem in various ways: by addressing political communication practitioners through reviews and reports, sometimes commissioned by media organizations themselves or think tanks (e.g., Blumler, Gurevitch, and Ives, 1977; Downie and Schudson, 2009); by suggesting ways of building on the more constructive possibilities of already introduced political communication innovations (cf. chapter 15 of Blumler and Gurevitch, 1995; Coleman, 2011); by systematically exposing erroneous claims in political advertisements (Jamieson and Jackson, 2007); and latterly by examining and elaborating upon the democratic potential of the Internet (Coleman and Blumler, 2009). But none of this is straightforward or easy!

Although the concept of a political communication system has attracted little criticism in the literature, certain of its limitations should be mentioned. One is the normative impasse that may arise from it, as described above. Another is the confinement of most of its comparative research locales so far to North America and Western Europe, although a few scholars have recently endeavored to redress this geographical imbalance, including Hallin and Mancini (2012), Curran and Park (2000), Voltmer (2006), and Waisbord (2010). Third, authors in the political economy school of communication research (see McChesney in this volume) might well feel that the analysts of political communication systems have not taken sufficient account of the impact of economic power and other market-based factors on media performance in the civic sphere.

But much has changed (again, technologically driven) since the concept of a political communication system was promulgated, elaborated in analyses, and drawn on to frame empirical research. Two fundamental trends have jointly transformed the conditions in which political communicators, producers, and receivers alike operate. One has been the onset, accelerating since the late 1980s, of communication abundance, greatly increasing the numbers and genres of outlets in which political materials may appear and which people may choose to patronize. The other has been the extensive dissemination and utilization of Internet facilities, heightening the salience of the communication roles of what used to be known as "audience members" and increasing the flows of communication (both direct and interactive) to and from political and media elites and among themselves.

The resulting political communication process is undoubtedly more complex than its network-television-dominated predecessor was, more riddled with cross-currents, and facing many of its actors with greater choice and uncertainty. Can it still be understood holistically? It is important to try to do so, especially for comparative, cross-national, and longitudinal political communication research to continue to prosper. But can the notion of a political communication system itself still effectively serve such holistic needs? Or should it be modified? Or are fresh conceptualizations required at this level? At this stage it is difficult to say. Perhaps the best we can do at present is keep an eye on certain developments that could eventually be significant beyond themselves for the nature of political communication overall. These include the following:

1) Communication abundance presumably intensifies the competition among most, if not all, message makers (politicians, journalists, bloggers, etc.) to gain and hold the attention of their intended auditors. What strategies are consequently pursued, how do they differ among different communicators, and with what consequences for political communication contents?

2) The professionalization of political advocacy will presumably continue apace, but may change in important ways. In addition to targeting mainstream news media, politicians must now address all sorts of electors differently through all sorts of channels with a medley of objectives in mind, and often more interactively than before. Are their publicity machines differently organized, staffed, and resourced as a result? Might the mediatization process itself become less all-consuming or be modified in some other way? How may politicians juggle their concern to stay in communication and policy control against the need to heed the upward-gathering views of ordinary people from below?

3) In its heyday, limited-channel television was a predominantly centripetal medium, offering little choice of agendas, policy frames, and accredited witnesses. Consequently, some of the most influential theories of political communication effects presupposed consonance rather than diversity in the media's coverage of

public affairs—as with the agenda-setting function of the mass media, the spiral of silence, cultivation effects, and neo-Marxists' perceptions of the media as ideological sources of support for the status quo. But with the explosion of communication channels, the creation of online journalistic enterprises, and the advent of blogging, has the tendency to consonance appreciably slackened, and if so, in what channels? Is it still dominant in mainstream journalism if less evident in other outlets—or do they sometimes interact in this respect?

4) Until recently, a commonsensical notion of citizenship tended to prevail. In essence, this maintained that democratic citizens should be able to exercise informed choices and hold their political leaders to account for their decisions at periodic intervals. (A more participatory view of citizenship was also in play, but was rarely voiced by practitioners.) This notion underpinned a great deal of research, showing what voters learned (or did not learn) from campaigns, for example, what media they derived most information from, how they differed from each other in this respect (as in Tichenor, Donohue, and Olien's [1970] "knowledge gap" hypothesis). De Beus, however, has noted "the lack of a fixed technical term" for democracy "in postmodern Western societies" nowadays (2011, 19). It seems that the advance of the Internet has germinated an array of different notions of citizenship (some analytical, some normative), such as Dutton's (2009) depiction of the Internet as a fifth estate; Manin's (1997) concept of "audience democracy"; Blumler's (2011, 11) concerns about a "hit and run democracy"; and a swelling army of advocates of "deliberative democracy" (see Stromer-Galley "Political Discussion and Deliberation Online" in this volume). The staying power and evolution of this last concept will demand (and garner) much attention in the future. It brings to the fore the idea of a citizen who can enter into serious discussion of political questions with others—rationally, fairly, and openly—aiming to arrive at a better and more inclusive understanding of what is at stake. A "growth stock," undoubtedly this has become something of a movement, with its own dedicated literature, lines of empirical research, websites, and activist programs. It is important to follow the progress of this movement, including whether and how far it can eventually penetrate the precincts of political and communication power.

In the face of all this, political communication scholars are striving to further holistic understandings along two different avenues. Some are still producing analytically and empirically creative and insightful studies of political communication systems in something like their original sense—such as Aeron Davis's (2013) mapping of the intricacies of political-media inter-elite relationships in Britain, and Pfetsch, Meyerhoffer, and Moring's (2014) comparisons of the numerous cultural orientations that underpin politician-journalist relationships in nine European countries. Others, however, have adopted different points of conceptual departure, which they regard as more in line with current and foreseeable conditions. Arnold Chadwick (2013), for example, has advanced the notion of a hybridized news system, the messages of which emerge and evolve through both offline and online communication channels, blending the contributions of elite and nonelite communicators. For their part, Esser and Stromback (2014) have situated earlier ideas about the mediatization of politics within a more fully developed theoretical framework, which they maintain should help us to understand the very "transformation of Western democracies."

It may be argued, however, that these perspectives can and should be incorporated into a more encompassing notion of a political communication system, albeit one that involves much interactive reciprocity and reflexivity among prime forces and actors and that is exposed to significant currents of change (such as mediatization). After all, "hybridity" was built into the first formulations of such a system, in which political communications typically stemmed from a composite of interacting influences (see above). And some of the latest versions of mediatization theory stipulate "that the agenda interactions between politics and media are essentially bidirectional" (Van Aelst et al., 2014) and actually recommend the adoption of "a systems approach" to the analysis of political mediatization (Marcinkowski and Steiner, 2014).

REFERENCES

Archetti, C. 2010. *Explaining news: National policies and journalistic cultures in global context.* Basingstoke, Hampshire, UK: Palgrave Macmillan.

Becker, L. B., McCombs, M. E., and McLeod, J. M. 1975. The development of political cognitions. In S. H. Chaffee (Ed.), *Political communication: Issues and strategies for research* (pp. 21–63). Beverly Hills and London: Sage Publications.

Bennett, W. L. 1990. Toward a theory of press-state relations in the United States. *Journal of Communication* 40(2): 103–125.

Bennett, W. L., and Manheim, J. B. 2001. The big spin: Strategic communication and the transformation of pluralist democracy. In W. L. Bennett and R. M. Entman (Eds.), *Mediated Politics: Communication in the future of democracy* (pp. 279–286). Cambridge, UK: Cambridge University Press.

Benson, R. 2010. What makes for a critical press? A case study of French and U.S. immigration news coverage. *International Journal of Press/Politics* 15(1): 3–24.

Blumler, J. G. 1969. Producers' attitudes towards television coverage of an election campaign: A case study. *Sociological Review Monograph* 13: 85–115.

Blumler, J. G. 1970. The political effects of television. In J. Halloran (Ed.), *The Effects of Television* (pp. 69-104). London: Panther Books.

Blumler, J. G., and Gurevitch, M. 1977. Linkages between the mass media and politics: A model for the analysis of political communication systems. In J. Curran, M. Gurevitch, and J. Woollcott (Eds.), *Mass communication and society* (pp. 270–290). London: Edward Arnold.

Blumler, J. G. (Ed.) 1983. *Communicating to voters: Television and the first European parliamentary elections.* London: Sage Publications.

Blumler, J. G. 1990., Elections, the media and the modern publicity process. In M. Ferguson (Ed.), *Public communication: The new imperatives* (pp. 101–113). London, New Delhi de Vreese and Newbury Park: Sage Publications.

Blumler, J. G., and Gurevitch, M. 1995. *The crisis of public communication.* London and New York: Routledge.

Blumler, J. G., and Coleman, S. 2010. Political communication in freefall: The British case—and others? *International Journal of Press/Politics* 15(2): 139–154.

Blumler, J. G., and Gurevitch, M. 1975. Toward a comparative framework for political communication research. In S. H. Chaffee (Ed.), *Political communication: Issues and strategies for research* (pp. 165–193). Beverly Hills and London: Sage Publications.

Blumler, J. G., Gurevitch, M., and Ives, J. 1977. *The challenge of election broadcasting.* Leeds UK.: Leeds University Press.

Blumler, J. G., McLeod, J. M., and Rosengren, K. E. 1992. *Comparatively speaking: Communication and culture across space and time.* Newbury Park, London, and New Delhi: Sage Publications.

Brown, R. 2011. Mediatization and news management in comparative institutional perspective. In K. Brants and K. Voltmer (Eds.), *Political communication in postmodern democracy: Challenging the primacy of politics* (pp. 59–74). Basingstoke, Hampshire, UK: Palgrave Macmillan.

Chadwick, A. 2013. *Hybrid media system: Politics and power.* Oxford, UK: Oxford University Press.

Coleman, S. (Ed.). 2011. *Leaders in the living room: The prime ministerial debates of 2010; evidence, evaluation and some recommendations.* Oxford, UK: Reuters Institute for the Study of Journalism.

Coleman, S., and Blumler, J. G. 2009. *The Internet and democratic citizenship: Theory, practice and policy.* Cambridge UK, and New York: Cambridge University Press.

Christians, C., Glasser, T., McQuail, D., Nordenstreng, K., and White, R. 2009. *Normative theories of the media: Journalism in democratic societies.* Champaign: University of Illinois Press.

Curran, J., and Park, M. J. 2000. *De-Westernizing media studies.* New York: Routledge.

Davis, A. 2013. *Promotional cultures.* Cambridge, UK: Polity Press.

de Vreese, C. H. 2003. *Framing Europe: Television news and European integration.* Amsterdam: Aksant.

Downey, J., and Stanyer, J. 2010. Comparative media analysis: Why some fuzzy thinking might help. *European Journal of Communication* 25(4): 332–347.

Downie, L., Jr., and Schudson, M. 2009. The reconstruction of American journalism. *Columbia Journalism Review.* http://www.cjr.org/reconstruction/the_reconstruction_of_american.php

Dutton, W. H. 2009. The fifth estate emerging through the network of networks. *Prometheus* 27(1): 1–15.

Esser, F., Reinemann, C., and Fan, D. 2001. Spin doctors in the United States, Great Britain and Germany: Metacommunication about media manipulation. *International Journal of Press/Politics* 6(1): 16–45.

Esser, F., and Stromback, J. (Eds.). 2014. *Mediatization of politics: Understanding the transformation of Western democracies.* Houndsmills, Basingstoke, Berkshire, UK: Palgrave Macmillan.

Gurevitch, M., and Blumler, J. G. 1977. Mass media and political institutions: The systems approach. In G. Gerbner (Ed.), *Mass media policies in changing cultures* (pp. 251–268). New York, London, Sydney, Toronto: John Wiley & Sons.

Gurevitch, M., and Blumler, J. G. 1990a. Comparative research: The extending frontier. In D. L. Swanson and D. Nimmo (Eds.), *New directions in political communication: A resource book* (pp. 269–289). Newbury Park, London, and New Delhi: Sage Publications.

Gurevitch, M., and Blumler, J. G. 1990b. Political communication systems and democratic values. In J. Lichtenberg (Ed.), *Democracy and the mass media* (pp. 305–325). Cambridge, UK: Cambridge University Press.

Hallin, D. C., and Mancini, P. 2004. *Comparing media systems: Three models of media and politics.* Cambridge UK: Cambridge University Press.

Hallin, D. C., and Mancini, P. (Eds.). 2012. *Comparing media systems beyond the Western world.* Cambridge UK: Cambridge University Press.

Jamieson, K. H. 1992. *Dirty politics: Deception, distraction and democracy.* New York and Oxford, UK: Oxford University Press.

Jamieson, K. H., and Jackson, B. 2007. *Un-spun: Finding facts in a world of disinformation.* New York: Random House.

Klapper, J. T. 1960. *The effects of mass communication.* Glencoe, IL: Free Press.

Lasswell, H. D. 1948. The structure and function of communication in society. In L. Bryson, *The Communication of Ideas.* New York: Institute for Religious and Social Studies.

Manin, B. 1997. *The principles of representative government.* Cambridge, UK: Cambridge University Press.

Marcinkowski, F., and Steiner, A. (2014). Mediatization and political autonomy: A systems approach. In F. Esser and J. Strömbäck (Eds.), *Mediatization of politics: Understanding the transformation of western democracies* (pp. 74–89). Basingstoke, UK: Palgrave Macmillan.

Mazzoleni, G., and Schulz, W. 1999. "Mediatization" of politics: A challenge for democracy? *Political Communication* 16(3): 247–261.

McLeod, J. M., and Blumler, J. G. 1987. The macrosocial level of communication science. In C. R. Berger and S. H. Chaffee (Eds.), *Handbook of communication science* (pp. 271–322). Newbury Park, Beverly Hills, London, and New Delhi: Sage Publications.

Patterson, T. E. 1993. *Out of order.* New York: Alfred A. Knopf.

Patterson, T. E., and Donsbach, W. 2006. Psychology of news decisions: Journalists as partisan actors. *Political Communication* 13(4): 455–468.

Pfetsch, B., and Esser, F. 2013. Comparing political communication. In F. Esser and T. Hanitzsch (Eds.), *Handbook of comparative communication research.* New York: Routledge.

Pfetsch, B., Meyerhoffer, E., and Moring, T. 2014. National or professional? Types of political communication culture across Europe. In B. Pfetsch (Ed.), *Political communication cultures in Europe: Attitudes of political actors and journalists in nine countries* (pp. 76–102). Houndsmills, Basingstoke, Berkshire, UK: Palgrave Macmillan.

Semetko, H. A., Blumler, J. G., Gurevitch, M., and Weaver, D. H. 1991. *The formation of campaign agendas: A comparative analysis of party and media roles in recent American and British elections.* Hillsdale, NJ, Hove, and London: Lawrence Erlbaum.

Stromback, J. 2008. Four phases of mediatization: An analysis of the mediatization of politics. *International Journal of Press/Politics* 13(3): 228–246.

Swanson, D. L. 1992. Managing theoretical diversity in cross-national studies of political communication. In J. G. Blumler, J. M. McLeod, and K. R. Rosengren (Eds.), *Comparatively speaking: Communication and culture across space and time* (pp. 19–34). Newbury Park, London, and New Delhi: Sage Publications.

Swanson, D. L. 1997. The political-media complex at 50: Putting the 1996 presidential campaign in context. *American Behavioral Scientist* 40(8): 1264–1282.

Swanson, D. L., and Mancini, P. (Eds.). 1996. *Politics, media and modern democracy: An international study of innovations in electoral campaigning.* Westport, CT, and London: Praeger.

Tichenor, I. J., Donohue, G. A., and Olien, C. N. 1970. Mass media flow and differential growth in knowledge. *Public Opinion Quarterly* 34(2): 259–270.

Van Aelst, P., Thesen, G., Walgrave, S., and Vliegenhardt, R. 2014. Mediatization and political agenda-setting: Changing issue priorities? In F. Esser and J. Stromback (Eds.), *Mediatization of politics: Understanding the transformation of western democracies* (pp. 200–220). Houndsmills, Basingstoke, Berkshire, UK: Palgrave Macmillan.

Voltmer, K. (Ed.). 2006. *Mass media and political communication in new democracies.* New York: Routledge.

Waisbord, S. 2010. The pragmatic politics of media reform: Media movements and coalition building in Latin America. *Global Media and Communication* 6(2): 133–153.

Zaller, J. 2001. The rule of product substitution in presidential campaign news. In E. Katz (Ed.), *Election studies: What's their use?* (pp. 247–269). Boulder, CO, and Oxford, UK: Westview Press.

CHAPTER 4

....

A TYPOLOGY OF MEDIA EFFECTS

....

SHANTO IYENGAR

THE role of media presentations in shaping the beliefs, attitudes, and behavior of the audience is a paradigmatic question that defines the field of political communication. In this chapter, I describe the evolution of media effects research from the early preoccupation with attitude change through the development of the agenda-setting, priming, and framing paradigms (which occurred in response to findings of minimal attitude change) to the current revival of persuasion research.

In the propaganda or persuasion model, the definitional criterion of "effects" is some change in political attitudes or preferences, and the causal variable is typically the slant or direction of a given media message. Thus, news reports favoring one candidate over another are expected to increase the vote share of the candidate accorded more favorable media treatment. In the context of political campaigns, the early research demonstrated that media-based campaigns reinforced rather than shifted prevailing preferences. These findings disappointed scholars of political communication. But rather than abandon the idea of influential mass communication, they substituted changes in beliefs about the state of the political world for changes in attitudes as the standard for assessing media effects. In this new approach, the causal variable was not the direction or slant of messages, but rather, the sheer quantity of programming devoted to particular subjects. Based on the returns from numerous studies, news organizations came to be judged as powerful agenda setters.

After surveying and classifying definitions of media effects, I briefly consider how fundamental transformations in the media environment brought about by information technology may work to reshape scholarly understandings of the relationship between news sources and audiences. The availability of multiple sources makes it possible for consumers to be more selective in their exposure to news programs. Selective exposure means that people with limited interest in politics may bypass the news entirely, while the more attentive may tailor their exposure to suit their political preferences. Both of these trends imply a weakening of persuasion effects.

A Chronology and Typology
of Effects Research

Persuasion

The origins of media effects research can be traced to the 1920s, following the large-scale diffusion of radio. Dramatic events in Europe associated with the rise of Nazism and fascism suggested that mass publics could easily be swayed by demagoguery. Alarmed by this possibility, officials in the US Defense Department commissioned a series of studies to understand the dynamics of propaganda campaigns.

The DOD research was carried out by psychologists at Yale University under the leadership of Hovland (Hovland et al., 1953; Hovland et al., 1949). The team designed a series of experiments to identify the conditions under which people underwent persuasion. Their research program, which remains a foundation of the media effects literature, was guided by an analytic framework known as "message learning theory." Message learning theory can be summarized by the simple rhetorical question—who says what to whom? The likelihood and extent of persuasion is contingent on evaluations of information sources, the content of incoming messages, and attributes of the receiver.

Assessments of source credibility—favorable or unfavorable—were assumed to condition receivers' willingness to accept messages. The key attributes of sources that enhanced their credibility included expertise and objectivity, that is, the perception that the source intended to inform rather than persuade. Message factors represent the "rational" pathway to attitude change in the sense that messages are more effective when they present strong arguments and high-quality evidence.

The most important insight from the message-learning paradigm, however, concerns attributes of the receiver that influence her susceptibility to persuasion. The search for receiver-related explanations led to the identification of two very different pathways to persuasion. As developed by William McGuire, the distinction between exposure to a message and acceptance of the message became critical to understanding the outcome of persuasion campaigns. Consider the case of political interest. People with little interest in politics cannot be persuaded by the news because news programs rarely reach them; these individuals are low on the exposure dimension. If political messages did reach them, they would be persuaded because they are unable to resist, that is, they are high on the acceptance dimension. Persuasion requires both exposure and acceptance. The more-interested pass the exposure test, but fail to accept; interest makes them both motivated to disagree and capable of rebutting messages with which they might disagree. The less-interested, on the other hand, are highly acceptant, but fail the exposure test. Thus, in the final analysis, both groups are equally *unaffected* by the media (for illustrations of the exposure-acceptance axiom, see McGuire, 1968; Zaller, 1992).

The findings from the Hovland lab gradually diffused to the study of election campaigns (see Lazarsfeld, Berelson, and Gaudet, 1948). A series of studies revealed no net change in vote choice over the course of the campaign. Instead, in keeping with the insights of message learning theory, attentive and inattentive voters were both generally unaffected by the campaign. People who entered the campaign with a party preference only became all the more convinced of their preferences over the course of the campaign (Klapper, 1960).

The repeated inability of survey researchers to find evidence of persuasion in campaigns gradually led them to abandon the persuasion paradigm in favor of a more "limited influence" model of media effects. In this new approach, the media were thought to act as gatekeepers—selecting issues for presentation—rather than as a platform for advocates or marketers.

Agenda Setting and Priming

The argument that the media could not directly sway public opinion but could direct the public to pay attention to particular issues or events came to be known as media agenda setting. To borrow Walter Lippmann's famous metaphor, the media act as a "searchlight," (Lippmann, 1922, 364) directing attention to issues deemed important by journalists; the more media coverage accorded an issue, the greater the level of public concern for that issue.

The earliest formulation of the agenda-setting hypothesis was provided by Cohen (1963); the media, he said, "may not be successful most of the time in telling people what to think, but it is stunningly successful in telling its readers what to think *about*" (13). The hypothesis was tested and replicated in hundreds of research studies during the 1970s and 1980s (for a review, see Dearing and Rogers, 1996). The classic study by McCombs and Shaw (1972) surveyed a random sample of Chapel Hill (NC) voters and asked them to identify the key campaign issues. Simultaneously, they monitored the print media available to residents of the Chapel Hill area to track the level of news coverage given to different issues. They found almost a one-to-one correlation between the rankings of issues based on amount of newspaper coverage and the number of survey respondents citing the issue as important.

Because of well-known limitations of the correlational approach, agenda-setting researchers later turned to experimentation. In a series of experiments administered in the early 1980s, Iyengar and Kinder manipulated the level of television news coverage accorded particular issues (see Iyengar and Kinder, 1987). In virtually every case, they found that concern for the "target" issue was elevated following exposure to their experimental treatments.

A further genre of agenda-setting research tracks changes in news coverage and public concern over time, thus establishing whether it is the media that lead public concern or vice versa (see MacKuen, 1981; Baumgartner et al., 2008). In one such study, the first to test explicitly for "feedback" from the level of public concern to news coverage, the authors found no traces of shifts in the amount of news devoted to the economy attributable to changes in public concern for economic issues (Behr and Iyengar, 1985). The authors thus effectively dismissed the possibility that the news media pandered to the concerns of the audience.

The agenda-setting effects of news coverage also extend to political elites. When public opinion seizes upon an issue, elected officials recognize that they need to pay attention to it. Legislators interested in regulating the tobacco industry, for instance, are more likely to succeed in enacting higher taxes on cigarettes when the public believes the public health consequences of smoking are a serious problem (see Baumgartner and Jones, 1993 for evidence of media influence on the elite agenda). Thus, media coverage moves not only public opinion but also serves to motivate elected officials.

As scholars began to refine the idea of media agenda setting, they gradually discovered that the state of the political agenda could contribute, at least indirectly, to attitude change by altering the criteria on which people evaluated public officials. This phenomenon came to be known as priming (see Iyengar et al., 1982). A simple extension of agenda setting, priming describes a process by which individuals assign weights to particular issues when they make summary political evaluations, such as voting choices. In general, voters give weight to opinions on particular policy issues in proportion to the perceived salience of these issues: the more salient the issue, the greater the impact of opinions about that issue on any given appraisal or evaluation (for reviews of priming research, see Druckman, 2004; Lenz, 2010).

The dynamic nature of priming effects makes them especially important during campaigns. Consider the case of the 2008 American election. Two months before the election, following the collapse of the banking sector of the US economy, American voters were subjected to a non-stop flow of news reports about the declining stock market, company bankruptcies, and the impending prospects of a severe depression (for evidence on the volume of news coverage, see Holbrook, 2009). Given the choice between Obama and McCain, the sudden elevation of the economy as the most important campaign issue provided a significant boost to the former. In the US, Republicans are generally seen as the party that favors business interests; in the context of the 2008 economic crisis, voters were disinclined to support a candidate who would favor the very interests that were seen as responsible for the crisis (for evidence of the shift in public opinion following the onset of the crisis, see Erickson, 2009).

Media priming effects have been documented in a series of experiments and surveys, with respect to evaluations of presidents (Iyengar and Kinder, 1987; Iyengar and Simon, 1993), legislators (Kimball, 2005), and lesser officials (Iyengar, Lowenstein, and Masket, 2001), as well as with respect to a variety of attitudes ranging from voting preferences (Druckman, 2004), to assessments of incumbents' performance in office and ratings of candidates' personal attributes (Druckman and Holmes, 2004; Druckman, 2004; Mendelberg, 1997), to racial and gender identities (Schaffner, 2005; Givens and Monohan, 2005). In recent years, the study of priming has been extended to arenas other than the United States, including a series of elections in Israel (Sheafer and Weimann, 2005), Germany (Schoen, 2004) and Denmark (de Vreese, 2004).

If, by making a particular issue more salient, campaigns also make voters more sensitive to their opinions on that issue when they cast their vote, that would seem quite

similar to persuasion. Because the criteria on which they assess a candidate's performance have changed, voters arrive at different choices. Thus, ironically, the abandon-
ment of the persuasion paradigm in favor of agenda setting led researchers to evidence
that media campaigns could persuade. In the aftermath of repeated failures to document widespread persuasion during campaigns, the media were assigned a more
limited, agenda-setting role. As agenda-setting research proliferated, scholars realized that perhaps agenda setting could eventually produce effects that were similar to
persuasion.

Framing Effects

The concept of framing, the subject of a different chapter, will receive limited treatment here. Conceptually, framing resembles persuasion, but rather than focusing on
messages that might persuade, the causal factor is presentation. To frame is to present
information in a particular manner. In the classic studies by Tversky and Kahneman,
framing outcomes as financial gains or losses (Tversky and Kahneman, 1981) powerfully
influenced subjects' choices between these outcomes.

In the political arena, the two principal "presenters" are the news media and public
officials. Scholars have identified media frames—presentations associated with particular news sources or genres of journalism—as well as topical frames associated with subject matter emphases in news coverage or elite rhetoric.

As developed by Druckman (2001, 2001a), definitions of the framing concept can be
arranged along a continuum ranging from presentations that differ only minimally in
substantive content ("equivalence" framing) to presentations accompanied by numerous content differences ("emphasis" framing). The great majority of framing studies
produced by political science and mass communications scholars embody the emphasis-oriented, less precise definition of framing.

A final basis for cataloguing the framing literature corresponds to the distinction
between one-sided and two-sided messages in persuasion research. Scholars have
recently begun to incorporate more elaborate framing designs in which study participants are exposed simultaneously to not just one, but a pair of competing emphases on
contentious issues. When exposed to two-sided framing, the competing frames tend to
"cancel out" and individuals tend to fall back on general predispositions as opinion cues
(see, for instance, Sniderman and Theriault, 2004; Chong and Druckman, 2007, 2008).

As this description of the media effects literature suggests, the field has gradually
turned full circle over the past forty years. Initially researchers were preoccupied with
questions of persuasion, but lost interest in the face of evidence suggesting that media
campaigns persuaded few people to cross party lines. Agenda setting became the paradigm of choice and agenda-setting researchers discovered that changes in the public
agenda prompted changes in political attitudes. In the case of the framing concept, as
researchers gravitated to an emphasis-oriented definition of frames, framing effects
have morphed into persuasion effects.

CHANGES IN THE MEDIA
ENVIRONMENT: IMPLICATIONS
FOR MEDIA EFFECTS

Fifty years ago, television dominated the media landscape. On a daily basis, close to one-half the adult population watched one of the three network evening newscasts. Moreover, it made little difference which network Americans watched because their offerings were so homogeneous that the same content reached virtually everyone. In the era of old media, therefore, exposure to the same set of news reports was near universal; the news represented an "information commons."

Both the development of cable television in the 1980s and the explosion of media outlets on the Internet more recently have contributed to a more fragmented audience. Obviously, the rapid diffusion of new media has made available a wider range of media choices, providing much greater variability in the content of available information. Thus, on the one hand, the attentive citizen can—with minimal effort—access news-papers, radio, and television stations the world over. On the other hand, the typical citizen—who is relatively uninterested in politics—can consume vast amounts of media but avoid news programming altogether.

The availability of increased programming choices is likely to have at least two impor-tant consequences for media effects research. First, the less politically engaged strata of the population may now have close to zero exposure to news. Second, the more attentive may decide to follow news outlets whose programming they find more agreeable. Both possibilities suggest a possible return to the era of minimal consequences, as least in the case of persuasion.

The Demise of the Inadvertent Audience

During the heyday of American network news, the combined audience for the three evening newscasts exceeded sixty million viewers. A significant component of the audi-ence was uninterested in politics; it watched the news mainly to await the entertainment program that followed. Exposure to political information was driven not by political motivation, but rather by loyalty to a particular sitcom or other entertainment program (Robinson, 1976; Prior, 2007). These "inadvertent" viewers may have been watching tel-evision rather than television news. Precise estimates are not available, but the inadvert-ent audience is likely to have accounted for a significant share of the total audience for network news.

Because the news audience of the 1970s included politically unmotivated viewers, exposure to television news had a leveling effect on the distribution of information. Inattentive viewers exposed to the news were given an opportunity to "catch up" with their more attentive counterparts. But once the major networks' hold on the national audience was loosened, first by the advent of cable, then by the profusion of local news programming, and eventually by the Internet, unmotivated exposure to news was no longer a given. Between 1968 and 2010, the total audience for network news fell by more than thirty million viewers (see Iyengar, 2011). The decline in news consumption occurred disproportionately among the less politically engaged segments of the audience, thus making exposure to information more tied to motivational factors. Paradoxically, just as technology has made possible a flow of information hitherto unimaginable, the size of the total audience for news has shrunk substantially.

To reiterate, the increased availability of media channels and sources makes it possible for people who care little about political debates to substitute entertainment for news programming. As a result, this group is likely to encounter very little information about political issues and events. Their reduced exposure to news programming and to a low level of political information implies that on those infrequent occasions when they do happen to encounter political messages, they will be easily persuaded.

Selective Exposure among Information Seekers

The extinction of the inadvertent audience is symptomatic of one form of selective exposure—avoidance of political messages among the politically uninvolved. But the increasing abundance of news sources also makes it necessary for the politically attentive to exercise more active control over their exposure to information. In particular, enhanced media choices make it possible for consumers to avoid exposure to information they expect will be discrepant or disagreeable and to seek out information that they expect to be congruent with their preexisting attitudes (for a more detailed discussion of selective exposure research, see the chapter in this volume by Stroud).

The new, more diversified information environment makes it not only more feasible for consumers to seek out news they might find agreeable but also provides a strong economic incentive for news organizations to cater to their viewers' political preferences (Mullainathan and Schleifer, 2005). The emergence of Fox News as the leading cable news provider is testimony to the viability of this "niche news" paradigm. Between 2000 and 2004, while Fox News increased the size of its regular audience by some 50 percent, the other cable providers showed no growth (Pew Center, 2004b).

CONCLUSION

The repeated findings of significant media effects in the second half of the twentieth century contributed to an image of strong media. One of the factors contributing to the ability of media to set the public agenda, prime, frame, and persuade public opinion was the dominance of the broadcast media. Exposure to television news during the 1970s and 1980s was extraordinarily high. Both the disappearance of the politically inattentive from the news audience and the tendency of partisans to select sources that reflect their worldview result in a fundamentally altered news audience. Instead of a vast heterogeneous audience, today, there are fragmented audiences, each consisting of like-minded individuals. News stories reach only the more attentive, who also hold strong opinions on political issues. This subset of the population, not surprisingly, is the most difficult to sway. In the world of niche media, the prospects for large-scale, media-induced changes in public opinion are slight. As media audiences become increasingly self-selected, it becomes less likely that media messages will do anything other than reinforce prior predispositions. Most media users will rarely find themselves in the path of attitude-discrepant information.

The increasing level of selective exposure thus presages a new era of minimal consequences, at least insofar as persuasive effects are concerned. But other forms of media influence, such as agenda setting or priming may continue to be important. Put differently, selective exposure is likely to erode the influence of the slant or tone of news messages (vis-à-vis elected officials or policy positions) but may not similarly undermine media effects that are based on the sheer volume of news.

The increased stratification of the news audience based on level of political involvement conveys a different set of implications. The fact that significant numbers of Americans avoid news programming altogether means that this segment of the electorate knows little about the course of current issues or events. On those infrequent instances when they can be reached by political messages, therefore, they are easily persuadable. When political events reach the stage of national crises and news about these events achieves a decibel level that is sufficiently high or loud so that even those preoccupied with entertainment are exposed to information, the impact of the news on these individuals' attitudes will be immediate and dramatic. In the case of the events preceding the US invasion of Iraq, for instance, many Americans came to believe the Bush administration's claims about the rationale for the invasion since that was the only account provided by news organizations (see Bennett, Lawrence, and Livingston, 2007). The inattentive audience, in short, is a manipulable audience.

To sum up, the changing shape of the media universe has made it increasingly unlikely that the views of the attentive public will be subject to any media influence. But as increasing numbers of citizens fall outside the reach of the news, they become more vulnerable to the persuasive appeals of political elites.

REFERENCES

Baumgartner, F. R., De Boef, S. L., and Boydstun, A. E. 2008. *The decline of the death penalty and the discovery of innocence.* New York: Cambridge University Press.

Baumgartner, F. R., and Jones, B. D. 1993. *Agendas and instability in American politics.* Chicago: University of Chicago Press.

Behr, R. L., and Iyengar, S. 1985. Television news, real-world cues, and changes in the public agenda. *Public Opinion Quarterly* 49: 38–57.

Bennett, W. L., Lawrence, R. G., and Livingston, S. 2007. *When the press fails*. Chicago: University of Chicago Press.

Cohen, B. E. 1963. *The press and foreign policy*. Princeton, NJ: Princeton University Press.

Chong, D., and Druckman, J. N. 2007. Framing public opinion in competitive democracies. *American Political Science Review 101*: 637–655.

Chong, D., and Druckman, J. N. 2008. Dynamic public opinion: Framing effects over time. Unpublished manuscript, Department of Political Science, Northwestern University.

Dearing, J. W., and Rogers, E. 1996. *Agenda-setting*. Thousand Oaks, CA: Sage Publications.

De Vreese, C. H. 2004. Primed by the euro: The impact of a referendum campaign on public opinion and evaluations of government and political leaders. *Scandinavian Political Studies 27*: 45–64.

Druckman, J. N. 2001. On the limits of framing effects. *Journal of Politics 63*: 1041–1066.

Druckman, J. N. 2004. Priming the vote: Campaign effects in a U.S. Senate election. *Political Psychology 25*: 577–594.

Druckman, J. N., and Holmes, J. W. 2004. Does presidential rhetoric matter? Priming and presidential approval. *Presidential Studies Quarterly, 34*(4): 755–778.

Erickson, R. S. 2009. The American voter and the economy in 2008. *Political Science and Politics 42*: 467–472.

Givens, S. M. B., and Monahan, J. L. 2005. Priming mammies, jezebels, and other controlling images: An examination of the influence of mediated stereotypes on perceptions of an African American woman. *Media Psychology 7*: 87–106.

Holbrook, T. M. 2009. Economic considerations and the 2008 presidential election. *Political Science and Politics 42*: 479–484.

Hovland, C. I., Janis, I. L., and Kelley, H. H. 1953. *Communications and persuasion: Psychological studies in opinion change*. New Haven, CT: Yale University Press.

Hovland, C. I., Lumsdaine, A. A., and Sheffield, F. D. 1949. A baseline for measurement of percentage change. In C. I. Hovland, A. A. Lumsdaine, and F. D. Sheffield (Eds.), *Experiments on mass communication* (pp. 284–289). Princeton, NJ: Princeton University Press.

Iyengar, S. 2011. *Media politics: A citizen's guide*. New York: W. W. Norton.

Iyengar, S., and Kinder, D. R. 1987. *News that matters: Television and American opinion*. Chicago: University of Chicago Press.

Iyengar, S., Kinder, D. R., and Peters, M. D. 1982. Experimental demonstrations of the "not-so-minimal" consequences of television news programs. *American Political Science Review 76*: 848–858.

Iyengar, S., Lowenstein, D. L., and Masket, S. 2001. The stealth campaign: Experimental studies of slate mail in California. *Journal of Law and Politics 17*: 295–332.

Iyengar, S., and Simon, A. F. 1993. News coverage of the Gulf War and public opinion: A study of agenda-setting, priming, and framing. *Communication Research 20*: 365–383.

Kimball, D. C. 2005. Priming partisan evaluations of Congress. *Legislative Studies Quarterly 30*: 63–84.

Klapper, J. T. 1960. *The effects of mass communications*. New York: Free Press.

Lazarsfeld, P. F., Berelson, B. R., and Gaudet, H. 1948. *The people's choice*. New York: Columbia University Press.

Lippmann, W. 1922. *Public opinion*. New York: Harcourt, Brace.

MacKuen, M. B. 1981. *More than news: Media power in public affairs*. Beverly Hills, CA: Sage Publications.

McCombs, M. E., and Shaw, D. L. 1972. The agenda setting function of mass media. *Public Opinion Quarterly 36*: 176–187.

McGuire, W. J. 1968. Personality and susceptibility to social influence. In E. F. Borgatta and W. F. Lambert (Eds.), *Handbook of personality theory and research* (pp. 1130-1187). Chicago: Rand-McNally.

Mendelberg, T. 1997. Executing Hortons: Racial crime in the 1988 presidential campaign. *Public Opinion Quarterly 61*: 134–157.

Mullainathan, S., and Shleifer, A. 2005. The market for news. *American Economic Review 95*: 1031–1053.

Pew Research Center for the People and the Press. 2004a. Cable and internet loom large in fragmented political news universe. http://people-press.org/reports/display.php3?ReportID=200

Pew Research Center for the People and the Press. (2004b). News audiences increasingly politicized: Online news audience larger, more diverse. http://people-press.org/reports/display.php3?ReportID=215

Prior, M. 2007. *Post-broadcast democracy*. New York: Cambridge University Press.

Robinson, M. J. 1976. Public affairs television and growth of political malaise: The case of the "selling of the Pentagon." *American Political Science Review 70*: 409–432.

Schaffner, B. F. 2005. Priming gender: Campaigning on women's issues in US Senate elections. *American Journal of Political Science 49*: 803–817.

Sheafer, T., and Weimann, G. 2005. Agenda building, agenda setting, priming, individual voting intentions, and the aggregate results: An analysis of four Israeli elections. *Journal of Communication 55*: 347–365.

Sniderman, P. M., and Theriault, S. M. 2004. The structure of political argument and the logic of issue framing. In W. E. Saris and P. M. Sniderman (Eds.), *Studies in public opinion* (pp. 133-165). Princeton, NJ: Princeton University Press.

Tversky, A., and Kahneman, D. 1981. The framing of decisions and the psychology of choice. *Science 211*: 453–458.

Zaller, J. 1992. *The nature and origins of mass opinion*. New York: Cambridge University Press.

CHAPTER 5

....

THE POWER OF POLITICAL COMMUNICATION

....

MICHAEL TESLER AND JOHN ZALLER

FOR most of the past generation, Klapper's (1960) claim that the effects of mass communication are minimal has been the worthy foil of review essays. At this point, however, the evidence is overwhelming: Media effects are "far from minimal," as Iyengar and Simon wrote in 2000, and "quite impressive," as Kinder put it in a 2003 review.

The general question raised by Klapper nonetheless remains vital: Exactly how much power do the mass media possess to shape public opinion? More specifically:

- How politically consequential are the effects of mass communication? Media-induced changes in mass attitudes that neither affect the political system nor perhaps matter very much to the individuals expressing the opinions should not be taken as evidence of media power.
- How durable are the effects of mass communication? Several studies that investigate this question find duration to be low. How powerful can communication be if its effects are fleeting?
- To what extent is the impact of mass communication due to more or less *factual reports* about conditions in the world, to *political cues* that originate with politicians and other interest groups, or to *information dug out by journalists*?
- If mass communication can influence opinion, can it also run roughshod over it? What, if any, are the boundaries of media influence?

None of these questions has a clear answer in extant research and some have scarcely been raised. Happily, however, research in the past decade has provided better building blocks for answering them than ever before. Our aim in this paper is to capitalize on this new research to answer these questions and construct an assessment of the power of mass communication.

A Turn Toward Field Studies

A notable feature of media research has been ongoing dialogue between laboratory experiments and field studies (e.g., Ansolabehere and Iyengar, 1995; Kinder, 2003). But laboratory studies, with crisp results on such topics as source effects, priming, and framing, have led the communication studies agenda. A big reason is that laboratory experiments can readily establish causality, which field studies often cannot.

The leading role of laboratory experiments in the study of communication may, however, be ending. Very large rolling cross-section and panel surveys are now done with relative ease, and researchers have become adept at leveraging temporal variation in these and older data sets into causally valid arguments. The result is a flurry of field studies able to make strong claims to both internal and external validity. Our review centers on this body of work.

The Size of Communication Effects

By happy coincidence, three well-designed field studies have made estimates of what can be seen as the same parameter: The effect of slanted news coverage on voting in national elections. In this section, we review the three estimates and consider their implications for the general question of media power.

In the first study, Gerber, Karlan, and Bergan (2009) conducted a baseline survey to identify northern Virginia residents who did not subscribe to either the liberal-leaning *Washington Post* or the more conservative *Washington Times*; these individuals were then randomly assigned to receive a free subscription to one of the two papers or to a control condition. The major finding of the post-treatment survey was that voters receiving the *Post* were about 11 percentage points more likely than controls to vote Democratic in the Virginia gubernatorial election.

In the second of these studies, Ladd and Lenz (2009) turned up a sterling research opportunity in an older data set: a multiyear panel survey that bracketed the decision by publishers of the *Sun* and of three other British newspapers to change their usual endorsements in the 1997 general election. Using several estimation techniques, the investigators showed that the newspaper switches caused a shift of about 11 percentage points among all readers of the affected papers and 20 points among habitual readers.[1] These pro-Labour votes, as was further shown, constituted about 14 percent of Tony Blair's overall margin of victory (405).

The third study, by Della Vigna and Kaplan (2007), leverages the largely idiosyncratic diffusion of cable systems carrying Fox News at the time of the 2000 presidential election into an estimate of Fox's political effect, which they estimated to be a 0.55 percentage point vote gain for George W. Bush in Fox markets (1211). For individuals who actually watched Fox News, however, the effect was bigger: About 12 percentage points.[2]

These three studies are, to our knowledge, the first to estimate the effect of news slant on voting in national elections. What we learn from them is that the effect is big enough to be politically consequential—big enough, that is, to have swayed the very close US presidential election of 2000 and quite possibly others. But let's look more closely. Exactly how big are the effects of slanted news?

This question turns out to be quite tricky. Consider the Fox News effect. Fox was the first conservative TV news source in the markets it entered. As such, it may have attracted voters ripe for conversion, and a 12 percent rate of conversion among favorably disposed viewers does not seem very great. But big or small, the effect is hard to view in general terms: It says that people who chose to see news with a certain slant changed their politics toward the slant; but what does that say about the effect of slanted news on other people who do not choose such news?

To be clear: We do not doubt that Fox News had a true causal effect on voting preferences. But we cannot tell whether we should be impressed by the size of the effect or what the estimate tells us about the effect of slanted news more generally.

The setup for the Ladd and Lenz newspaper study seems closer to what scholars have in mind when thinking about the effect of slanted news: A set of four UK papers traditionally covered politics from one partisan point of view and then suddenly changed sides. Readers did not choose the newspaper because of its new slant and may actually have preferred the old one. Hence there is no element of choice in the causal impact.

Yet to interpret the effect in this study—an 11 percent shift toward Labour among persons subscribing to one of the four papers before the change of endorsement—one must keep in mind the characteristics of the newspapers, their audiences, and the politician they endorsed. The papers were national newspapers in the British journalistic tradition, which means that they supported their endorsee not only in editorials but also in aggressively partisan news coverage. The newspaper subscribers tended to be downscale and accustomed to partisan news reporting. And the endorsed candidate was the moderate Tony Blair. One must ask whether *USA Today* could do what these newspapers did and have the same effect. Probably not. We have, then, a clear, valid finding but also a circumscribed one.

The adjectives *clear, valid,* and *circumscribed* apply similarly to the causal effect demonstrated in the Virginia newspaper study. Recall that this study gave free subscriptions of the *Washington Post* or *Washington Times* to persons not already subscribing to one of these papers. However, only 34 percent of those given free subscriptions to the *Post* said afterward that they read the paper, and only 13 percent claimed to have read the *Times.* Some actually refused their free subscriptions. The authors duly reported newspaper effects for all respondents selected to receive the newspapers, whether they said they had read them or not. In the language of experimental analysis, they report the "intent to treat" effect. They did not estimate the "treatment on treated" effect, which is the effect on the people who actually looked at the newspapers.

Yet for purposes of gauging the power of mass communication, researchers must care more about the latter effect. To see why, consider another kind of experimental study—a study of the effect of door-to-door canvassing to increase voter turnout. The purpose of such work is to learn how to reach and mobilize people who are not voting. Such studies need a statistic that includes information about both reaching and converting the treated. The intent-to-treat statistic does exactly that. Yet studies of the power of mass communication are not usually concerned about effects on people outside the media system. They care, rather, about the people who regularly and voluntarily receive media "treatment." The intent-to-treat statistic says little about such people.

The treatment-on-treated effect, if validly estimated, would tell us the effect of newspapers on people who normally shun them. Researchers might, for some purposes, want to know exactly this. However, researchers could not use the treatment-on-treated statistic as a basis for inference about people already in the media system—unless, of course, they were willing to assume that effects would be the same for those who read a newspaper on their own and those who read it only when someone gave it to them free. There are strong reasons, however, to believe that populations differing in their attentiveness to news would not be equally susceptible to media influence (Zaller, 1992, 1996; Sears and Kosterman, 1994; Deli Carpini and Keeter, 1996; Kinder, 2003).

We thus conclude that the field's most compelling causal estimates are inappropriate for developing a general estimate of the effect of media bias. They are individually interesting but tell us little about the most common situations of potential media bias in the United States.

Political scientist Tim Groseclose, however, takes another view. In *Left Turn: How Liberal Media Distort the American Mind* (2011), he uses the effect sizes from the Fox News and Virginia studies for exactly the purpose for which we have just said they are unsuitable: the construction of a general estimate of the effect of news on public opinion. His work provides an excellent example of what media scholars should, in our view, make more of an effort to do but cannot yet do with extant findings.[3]

In previous work, Groseclose and Mylo (2005) develop a method of assigning ideological locations to individual news media outlets. In his recent book, Groseclose applies the method to all media groups—national TV news, local TV news, newspapers, and radio—and constructs a measure, weighted by audience share, of the American news media's ideological location. He calculates that the media's overall score is 60 on a 100-point scale, where high values are more liberal and the average American is at 50.

To estimate the effect of the media's liberal slant, Groseclose notes that the entry of Fox News to the national mix reduced average media liberalism by about one point (to about 59) and moved the aggregate Republican vote share (per Della Vigna and Kaplan) about half a percent to the right. With some rescaling and a simple model, Groseclose leverages these results into an estimate that the "natural" ideological location of the average American—that is, the public's location absent the influence of the liberal media—is 31 on his 100-point scale. This score compares with 38 for Fox News and 18 for the average Republican member of Congress.

Moving the American public from 31 to 50 on a 100-point ideology scale indicates substantial media power, but is the estimate valid? Beside the general reason already given, we see two specific reasons for doubt. One is that neither partisan voting, trends in party attachment, nor the positions of the two major political parties have been drifting to the left in recent decades, as would be expected if the liberal media had so much power. The other is that when Groseclose applied his method to the effect size reported in the Virginia newspaper study, he obtained an estimate that was more than three times greater than its theoretical maximum, a problem he acknowledged.

Despite our reservations about Groseclose's point estimates, we see his general approach to media effects as bold and well conceived: Measure the overall slant of the news and estimate the effect of small changes in that slant on overall voter opinion. With more appropriate measurements of key inputs, it may bear fruit. In the meantime, limitations on the available quantitative evidence impel us to a qualitative approach to gauging the power of mass communication.

THE POLITICAL CONSEQUENCES
OF POLITICAL COMMUNICATION

In another field experiment, Gerber, Green, Gimpel, and Shaw (2011) managed to persuade an actual candidate in a Texas gubernatorial primary to experimentally vary his advertising over a one-month period and twenty media markets. This study disclosed that ad buys of 1,000 gross ratings points (GRPs) per week moved opinion about 5 percentage points toward the sponsoring candidate. Meanwhile, a study of the 2000 presidential election found that the effect of a 3,500-GRP advantage in the final week of the campaign gained George Bush about 0.75 percentage points of vote share (Hill, Lo, Vavreck, and Zaller, 2011). Thus, GRP for GRP, ads seemed to matter much more in the gubernatorial contest.

One cannot, of course, take this difference at face value: Because preferences in the final week of a presidential campaign are likely to be firmer than preferences at the beginning of a gubernatorial primary, ads must get more credit for moving the former than the latter. An analyst could adjust for this problem by imposing a control for attitude strength or importance. The result would be a general estimate of the unit effect of advertising GRPs on vote preference, ceteris paribus. Such an estimate would have interest for psychologists, who focus on individual-level effects. Ultimately, however, our aim is to estimate effects at the level of the political system. From that perspective, what strikes us most strongly about the two ad effects is how little one mattered and how much the other did. The Texas candidate allowed academics to randomly assign his advertising precisely because he knew it didn't much matter. By contrast, a handful of ads at the very end of a long presidential campaign was just enough to move Florida into Bush's Electoral College tally and thereby change the outcome of the presidential election, as first documented by Johnston, Hagen, and Jamieson (2004). Notably, Bush's campaign advisers understood that final-week ads could have this effect and conserved cash for this purpose.

Communication that affects important political outcomes are obviously powerful, and especially so if political agents can deploy it at will for this purpose. This is true whether it meets a psychological criterion of changing strong attitudes or only weak ones and whether many or few people are swayed.

In the remainder of this essay, we use this system-level criterion to gauge the power of communication. We cannot always determine with certainty when communication has affected political outcomes, but we can do so often enough to make the criterion useful.

The Duration of Communication Effects

The Texas field experiment was designed not only to provide a causal test of the impact of advertising but also to test the duration of its effects. The design was random assignment of advertising that turned on and off in media markets at different times. Results disclosed that only traces of ad effects survived for as long as one week. The on-and-off feature of the design, along with the certainty that ads were not being run more often where consultants felt they were more needed, make a compelling demonstration that, whatever is true about the size of persuasive impacts, the rate of their decay can be massive.

The tendency toward rapid decay of experimentally induced persuasion has been well known for many decades.[4] Yet few studies have been designed to detect it and most that do give it short shrift (although see Chong and Druckman, 2010). Reviewing three such studies, Kuklinski, Gaines, and Quirk (2007, 6) comment that authors typically reported "the lack of enduring effects as an aside. Suppose, instead, that they had included the words 'transitory effects' in their original titles?"

Scholars interested in the power of mass communication should not regard decay as any sort of artifact; they should see it, rather, as feature of the persuasion process.

Communication effects that decay rapidly are not necessarily less powerful for that reason. They may create different winners and losers. For example, Hill and colleagues (2011) observe that the rapid decay of advertising effects can work to level the playing field in elections, as it prevents the better-financed candidate from building an ever more insurmountable lead over the campaign. The general point here—communication closer to the point of decision matters more—has wide relevance, as we show below.

What Part of the Message Matters?

If communication studies of the past fifty years have taught us anything, it is that communication has many different facets that may independently affect impact. Prominent among them are the frame, source, strength, and primacy or recency of messages. Field research cannot capture most of these factors. Extant field studies do, however, permit some distinctions: They can distinguish party versus journalist or sponsored communication and can also roughly distinguish the effects of the raw ingredients of news from the packaged news product. We argue that these distinctions, as applied in field studies, generate useful insights into the power of communication.

Consider first the effects of the 9/11 attacks on public opinion. Since most Americans learned of the attacks in the mass media, it is natural to attribute the effect to the mass communication that carried it, including any slant given to it by journalists. Yet when foreign enemies attack a nation, citizens are likely to become alarmed about it regardless of how journalists frame the news. So how much did the journalistic frame matter? Two recent studies have plausibly argued that, at least for the case of 9/11, the attack itself was more important to the public's response than how the news played it or politicians responded (Atlhaus and Coe, 2011; Kam and Ramos, 2008; see, however, Bennett, Livingston, and Lawrence, 2007).

Laboratory studies could, in principle, address this question by testing the effect of competing news frames or cues. But we wonder whether competing experimental scripts could adequately capture the news that Americans experienced in real time—"*my country has been attacked!*"—and, if not, whether the tests of competing frames of the news would be fair. We wonder as well whether any frame strong enough to affect opinion in a laboratory study could realistically have been deployed in the event itself, when even entertainers were constrained to tread carefully.[5] Thus, the findings of the two field studies may yield results not available from a laboratory study.

Presidential elections are a particularly fruitful domain in which to explore the effects of message content. We begin our analysis with the following rough calculation: In the last three weeks of the 2000 election, the average resident of a battleground state viewed forty campaign ads—or roughly 20 minutes of party-controlled communications—per day (Hill et al., 2011). We are aware of no comparable estimate for how many minutes of televised news content about the presidential election the average citizen absorbed in the final weeks of the campaign but estimate that it was less than 20 minutes.[6] Some TV news is given over to reports of candidate activity and hence is partly controlled by partisan sources, but the larger fraction is devoted to horserace, hoopla, and other matter not intended to sway votes (Patterson, 1993; Project for Excellence in Journalism, 2008). Our conclusion, therefore, is that parties control the larger part of the televised communication openly aimed at influencing the outcomes of US presidential elections. The Fox News study demonstrates, however, that journalistic slant does have a real effect.

Raw news ingredients also matter in presidential elections, foremost among them the performance of the national economy in the few months prior to the election. The correlation between percent change in real disposable income and vote share of the incumbent party is above 75 percent, which indicates that more than half the variation in vote swing in US elections is explained by this one raw news ingredient. Other raw news ingredients—such as war, scandal, terms in office, and personal qualities of the candidates—no doubt explain an additional fraction of vote outcomes.

How do these effects compare? If the Della Vigna and Kaplan estimate is correct, the bias of the mainstream news is a regular advantage for the Democrats. And if Groseclose and Milyo (2004) are right, that Fox is the lone major TV outpost of conservatism in a sea of liberal voices, the overall pro-Democratic effect could be more than the Della Vigna and Kaplan estimate of half a percent. We'll guestimate 2 percent. Bartels (2008), meanwhile, has estimated that the Republican Party typically outspends the Democrats by nearly $2 per vote and that this adds an average of 2 percentage points to its vote share.[7] These two effects may thus be about equally big—and also big enough to sway even a not-so-close election. So by our criterion of size, each effect is big. Meanwhile, variation in the performance of the economy causes swings in the presidential vote that are typically about 4 percent from one election to the next.[8]

We have, then, three effects—from liberal TV news, the normal Republican edge in advertising, and the performance of the economy. Although none of the estimated effects is anything like razor-sharp, they are sharp enough that we can roughly compare them. This level of precision in the estimate of three different effects is all but unattainable in laboratory studies. And knowing magnitudes, we can gauge political importance. We can estimate, in particular, that the liberal TV and Republican money advantage may roughly cancel each other out, leaving the probably larger effect of the economy decisive.

Another area in which firm evidence exists on the relative influence of news sources is popular support for war. For several decades, scholars have highlighted different influences. One group emphasized the cues of party and government leaders as transmitted by professional journalists (e.g., Bennett, 1990; Cohen, 1963; Zaller, 1992), while another focused on foreign casualties (Burk, 1999; Feaver and Gelpi, 2004; Gartner and Segura, 1998; Mueller, 1973). In studies of American wars from World War II through the war in Iraq, Berinsky (2009) pitted the two causal claims against one another. Focusing on changes in party cues and casualties across time in these wars, he found that that public opinion responded much more to cues than to casualties. In a time-series analysis of public support for the Iraq War, Baum and Groeling (2010) report support for a novel theory arguing that in the early stages of war, "partisan rhetoric" has much more impact on opinion that do war casualties, but that if war continues, casualties may have moderately more important than party rhetoric. Overall, however, party cues tend to matter more than events on the ground in Americans' support for war.

Party-sponsored communication thus seems to dominate the raw ingredients of news. Other studies, however, show that the story is more complicated. Local casualties have very large impacts on local opinion; death for death, their impact is 100 times greater on local opinion than national opinion. Presumably this reflects the personalized coverage of local war heroes by local media. But rather than cumulate over time toward greater impact, the local effects instead decay rapidly. According to one study, effects of local casualties survive only about two weeks (Hayes and Myers, 2009); according to another, impacts fall to a fraction of their original size after about two months (Althaus, Bramlett, and Gimpel, 2011). The reason, then, that party cues dominate casualties in influence on national opinion may be that the former are continually present in the national debate, whereas, with few exceptions, the latter are brief events in local media.

Hence, decay accentuates the importance of one kind of communication and limits that of another.

Despite limits in the available evidence, we wish to examine two additional cases: public opinion about national health insurance and global warming. In 1993 and 2009, Democratic presidents, buttressed by favorable public opinion polls, attempted to persuade Democrat-controlled congresses to enact national health insurance. In the first case Democrats failed completely, and in the second they settled for half a loaf. Those two episodes can be sketched as profiles in the power of different kinds of communication.

For years prior to the presidential initiatives, the health issue was framed in terms of the unmet needs of the uninsured and resulting stress on the healthcare system. The frames came from health professionals and interest groups and were featured in the news reports of professional journalists. Once consideration of legislation began, a new source became important: the partisan rhetoric of Democratic and Republican leaders and their allied groups (Jacobs and Shapiro, 2000). The newly prominent frames included such ideas as fairness, government doctors, the Constitution and the Tenth Amendment, Hillarycare and Obamacare, "death panels," and greedy private insurance companies. The effect of the party-sponsored frames was rapid and readily visible in published polls: a drop in support for national health insurance among Republicans and Independents, leading to an overall decline in public support and a deeper polarization of Democrats/liberals versus Republicans/conservatives.[9] In these conditions, wary Democratic legislators from swing districts pulled back—and still often lost their seats for being on what had initially seemed to be the popular side. In the heat of legislative decision-making, party-sponsored communication thus seemed more important than other kinds, transforming a proinsurance majority into opposing partisan camps. That parties were (in our rough account) less active in setting the agenda for legislation did not prevent them from coming in at the end and shaping the outcome.

The media's reporting on party-sponsored communications also appears to dominate scientific information in mass opinions about global warming. Tesler (2013) finds that conservatives doubt the existence of global warming in large part because of Republican rhetoric. The finding is based on the following: (1) news reception is perhaps the strongest predictor of conservatives' climate change skepticism; (2) the United States, where political elites are far more divided over the causes of global warming than any other country, is the only nation where news reception significantly predicts conservatives' doubts about climate change; (3) news-attentive conservatives were actually more likely to believe scientists' warnings about global warming in the 1990s, before, as content analysis showed, the media began to cover climate change as a partisan issue; (4) an experiment showing that Americans in general and conservatives in particular would be less skeptical about human-made warming if more Republicans in Congress endorsed the idea.

Where in the past Congress and the president worked behind mostly closed doors to shape legislation, national policymaking now occurs in the media spotlight and the court of public opinion (Kernell, 2007). The extended debates over healthcare proposals and global warming are thus representative of a large class of important cases. From our rough examination, the role of communication in these two areas appears similar to the case of war policy: Party cues trump the raw ingredients of news, including even scientific facts, in shaping public opinion and determining outcomes. Journalistic frames may set the stage of legislation, but they don't close the deal. Obviously these assessments are more than a little rough, but we think they are sufficiently plausible to be worth stating.

Which leads to a final question: Few would worry if it were shown that the raw ingredients of news have more effect on public opinion than the slants that party or journalists give them. But party-sponsored communication, as it has emerged in our analysis, is a strong, elite-controlled, and potentially worrisome force. How strong? Can it override even the strong feelings and basic perceptions of the citizens who receive it?

Changing Sides or Changing Minds?

When parties and their leading politicians adopt new positions or focus attention on older ones, voters may respond by either changing their minds to the salient party position or changing sides to the other party. Which do they do? If the former, it highlights the power of party-sponsored communication to shape citizen opinion. If the latter, it suggests that citizens can stand up to at least some mass communication.

Two political scientists, Thomas Carsey and Geoffrey Layman, framed their 2006 study of party position taking on abortion in these admirably clear terms. Their answer was mixed, but mixed in a revealing way. Citizens for whom the issue was salient tended to maintain their views on abortion and to switch to the party closer to those views. Voters who cared less about the issue but followed politics closely enough to be aware of party position taking tended to follow the lead of their traditional party by adjusting their views on abortion. Although Carsey and Layman do not emphasize it, many citizens seem to have taken the option of ignoring the new party position. This pattern is consistent with the view that party-sponsored communication, though often influential, does not override strongly held opinion.

Three recent studies utilize panel data to examine some twenty additional cases in which parties offered voters a choice of changing sides or changing minds. These studies—having other fish to fry—do not focus explicitly on this frame but do report evidence bearing directly on it, as follows.

Lenz (2009, 2012) demonstrates how a variety of prominent campaign issues—such as public works in 1976, defense spending in 1980, and Social Security privatization in 2000—typically led voters to change their minds about policies in order to become consistent with the positions of the candidates they had already decided to support.

Lenz (2012) also shows, however, that for another class of issues—what he calls performance issues—citizens respond differently. Most importantly, citizens who have decided that the economy is strong or weak do not change their views on this as campaigns focus attention on it; rather, they switch to the party indicated by their prior performance evaluation.

Tesler (2012) further clarifies the conditions under which voters are likely to change sides or change minds. He notes that in most of the cases where Lenz finds voters changing their minds involve policy issues on which, as studies since Converse (1964) have argued, citizens often have weak or nonexistent views. But Tesler finds that campaign appeals to more deeply rooted predispositions—notably attitudes about Catholics in the 1960 elections, homophobia in the 2004 presidential election, and religiosity in the elections of the 1980s and 1990s—cause voters to change partisan preferences rather than change values or predispositions. He also notes evidence from a long-term panel study showing that voters changed sides rather than minds when race became a salient party issue in the 1960s (Sears and Funk, 1999; for additional cases see also Kinder and Kam, 2009; Tesler and Sears, 2010; Hillygus and Jackman, 2003).

These studies are consistent with the view that party-sponsored communication can shape political attitudes, but they also show that it does not run roughshod over all voter attitudes.

THE POWER OF POLITICAL COMMUNICATION

We began our essay with four questions about the power of political communication. Based mainly on results of field studies, we now supply our answers. To the question of whether political communication can affect political outcomes, our answer is strongly positive. From a variety of sources, it is clear that long-term journalistic slant, party-sponsored advertising, and raw news ingredients have effects that are large enough to swing the outcome of national elections. Some of these effects may tend to cancel out, but the raw effects are nonetheless clear.

As to the duration of communication effects, evidence is limited, but all of it points to the fairly short duration (or rapid decay) of most persuasion effects. But short duration does not imply lack of political importance if the persuasive communication continues over a long period of time (as in the case of news slant) or targets political decision-making (as in party-sponsored communication on policy questions). On the other hand, short-term or one-shot communication that targets general attitudes independent of any relevant political decision—as may typify many nonpartisan news reports—may have little political consequence.

The third question is whether some kinds of communication are more persuasive than others. Our tentative answer is that some raw ingredients of news—the performance of the economy, perhaps the 9/11 terrorist attack—may have more power to shape opinion than either long-term journalistic slant or party-sponsored communication. It is nonetheless clear, however, that long-term journalistic slant (e.g., Fox News) and party-sponsored communication (e.g., on healthcare reform) can have effects that are big enough to sway political outcomes.

An important question is what happens when party-sponsored communication clashes with journalist-sponsored communication. From limited evidence—our sketch of healthcare and global warming communications—we suspect that partisan communication is the more powerful. It was widely believed that journalists' investigation of Watergate led to President Richard Nixon's resignation from office, but journalists made little dent in President Clinton's popularity during the Lewinsky scandal. It should be remembered that the national economy was much better during the Lewinsky matter than during Watergate, and that Democratic members of the House Judiciary Committee were more supportive of Clinton in 1998 and 1999 than their Republican counterparts were of Nixon in 1974. This constitutes evidence that, in a conflict between party- and journalist-sponsored messages, the fraction of the public that sides with journalists seems to be rather insignificant.[10]

Our fourth question is whether political communication can override strong personal beliefs. There is evidence that it cannot.

In sum, political communication cannot easily override strong personal beliefs and does not usually produce enduring effects. Of the three kinds of communication we identified—factual reports, partisan cues, and journalist-initiated news—the first two are the more powerful and can sometimes influence political outcomes. The power of the third is uncertain. Surely it is important, but it is not clear how.

The state of existing evidence does not permit us to offer these conclusions with any confidence, but we think they are the right conclusions to be investigating in our post-Klapper world and urge researchers to focus their energies accordingly.

NOTES

1. This is the average of the multivariate estimates in Table 2, 400.
2. This is the average of the four estimates reported on p. 1222.
3. Conflict of interest declaration: Groseclose teaches at UCLA, where Zaller is on the faculty; until recently, Tesler was a graduate student there. Neither read his book until it was in press.
4. See, for example, a 1978 review essay by Cook and Fey, "The Persistence of Experimentally Induced Persuasion."
5. E.g., "Terrorist Attacks Spark Cowardly Debate," ABC News. September 26, 2001. Available at: http://abcnews.go.com/Politics/story?id=121312&page=1#.UZbozpXCHZY
6. Survey data indicate that Americans watch about 30 minutes of TV news a day (Pew Research Center, 2010). Separately, the Project for Excellence in Journalism reports that coverage of the 2008 election accounted for 52 percent of the total news hole in the final three weeks of the campaign (see http://www.journalism.org/news_index/101).
7. Bartels estimated effect is 3.5 percent of vote margin, which translates into about 2 percentage points of share.
8. The variance of incumbent share of the two-party vote from 1948 to 2012 is about 30, about half of which is, as noted, explained by changes in real disposable income. The typical vote swing explained by the economy is then about 4 percentage points ($15^.5 \sim 4$)
9. A CBS News Poll from February 2007, for instance, disclosed that 67 percent of Independents and 41 percent of Republicans thought the federal government should

guarantee health insurance for all Americans. After the intense debate over healthcare reform legislation in the summer of 2009, however, according to a CBS poll in September 2009, only 42 percent of Independents and 23 percent of Republicans supported such a guarantee. See also Henderson and Hillygus (2011) for declining public support in panel data.

10. In our accounting, any persuasion effects from MSNBC or Fox would be due to partisanship rather than journalism.

References

Althaus, S. L., and Coe, K. 2011. Priming patriots: Social identity processes and the dynamics of public support for war. *Public Opinion Quarterly* 75(1): 65–88.

Ansolabehere, S., and Iyengar, S. 1995. *Going negative: How political advertisements shrink and polarize the electorate*. New York: Free Press.

Bartels, L. M. 2008. *Unequal democracy: The political economy of the new gilded age*. New York: Russell Sage Foundation.

Baum, M. A., and Groeling, T. J. 2010. *War stories*. Princeton, NJ: Princeton University Press.

Bennett, W. L. 1990. Toward a theory of press-state relations. *Journal of Communication* 40: 103–127.

Bennett, W. L., R. Lawrence, and Livingston, S. 2007. *When the press fails: Political power and the news media from Iraq to Katrina*. Chicago: University of Chicago Press.

Berinsky, A. J. 2009. *In time of war: Understanding American public opinion from World War II to Iraq*. Chicago: University of Chicago Press.

Berinsky, A. J., and Kinder, D. R. 2006. Making sense of issues through media frames: Understanding the Kosovo crisis. *Journal of Politics* 68(3): 640–656.

Burk, J. 1999. Public support for peacekeeping in Lebanon and Somalia: Assessing the casualties hypothesis. *Political Science Quarterly* 114(1): 53–78.

Carsey, T. M., and Layman, G. C. 2006. Changing sides or changing minds? Party identification and policy positions in the American electorate. *American Journal of Political Science* 50: 464–477.

Chong, D., and Druckman, J. N. 2007. Framing theory. *Annual Review of Political Science* 10: 103–126.

Chong, D., and Druckman, J. N. 2010. Dynamic public opinion: Communication effects over time. *American Political Science Review* 104(4): 663–680.

Cohen, B. 1963. *The press and foreign policy*. Princeton, NJ: Princeton University Press.

Converse, P. E. 1964. The nature of belief systems in mass publics. In D. E. Apter (Ed.), *Ideology and discontent* (pp. 206–261). New York: Free Press.

Cook, T. D., and Flay, B. R. 1978. The persistence of experimentally induced attitude change. *Advances in Experimental Social Psychology* 11: 1–57.

DellaVigna, S., and Kaplan, E. 2007. The fox effect: Media bias and voting. *Quarterly Journal of Economics* 122: 1187–1234.

Delli Carpini, M. X., and Keeter, S. 1996. *What Americans know about politics and why it matters*. New Haven, CT: Yale University Press.

Feaver, P. D., and Gelpi, C. 2004. *Choosing your battles: American civil-military relations and the use of force*. Princeton, NJ: Princeton University Press.

Gaines, B. J., J. H. Kuklinski, and Quirk, P. J. 2007. The logic of the survey experiment reexamined. *Political Analysis* 15: 1–20.

Gartner, S. S. 2008. The multiple effects of casualties on public support for war: An experimental approach. *American Political Science Review* 102 (1): 95–106.

Gartner, S. S., and Segura, G. M. 1998. War, casualties and public opinion. *The Journal of Conflict Resolution* 42(3): 278–300.

Gerber, A. S., J. G. Gimpel, D. P. Green, and Shaw, D. R. 2011. How large and long-lasting are the persuasive effects of televised campaign ads? Results from a randomized experiment. *American Political Science Review* 105: 135–150.

Gerber, A., D. Karlan, and Bergan, D. 2009. Does the media matter? A field experiment measuring the effect of newspapers on voting behavior and political opinions. *American Economic Journal: Applied Economics* 1: 35–52.

Groseclose, T. 2011. *Left turn: How liberal media bias distorts the American mind.* New York: St. Martin's Press.

Groseclose, T., and Milyo, J. 2005. A measure of media bias. *Quarterly Journal of Economics* 120: 1191–1237.

Hayes, A. F., and Myers, T. A. 2009. Testing the "proximate casualties hypothesis": Local troop loss, attention to news, and support for military intervention. *Mass Communication and Society* 12(4): 379–402.

Henderson, M., and Hillygus, D. S. 2011. The dynamics of health care opinion, 2008-2010: Partisanship, self-interest, and racial resentment. *Journal of Health Politics, Policy and Law* 36(6): 945–960.

Hill, S. J., J. Lo, L. Vavreck, and Zaller, J. 2011. The duration of advertising effects in political campaigns. Unpublished manuscript. University of California, Los Angeles, Department of Political Science.

Hillygus, D. S., and Jackman, S. 2003. Voter decision making in election 2000: Campaign effects, partisan activation, and the Clinton legacy. *American Journal of Political Science* 47: 583–596.

Iyengar, S., and Simon, A. 2000. New perspectives and evidence on political communication and campaign effects. *Annual Review of Psychology* 51: 149–169.

Jacobs, L. R., and Shapiro, R. Y. 2000. *Politicians don't pander: Political manipulation and the loss of democratic responsiveness.* Chicago: University of Chicago Press.

Johnston, R., M. G. Hagen, and Jamieson, K. H. 2004. *The 2000 presidential election and the foundations of party politics.* New York: Cambridge University Press.

Kam, C. D., and Ramos, J. M. 2008. Joining and leaving the rally: Understanding the surge and decline in presidential approval following 9/11. *Public Opinion Quarterly* 72(4): 619–650.

Kernell, S. 2007. *Going public: New strategies of presidential leadership,* 4th ed. Washington, DC: CQ Press.

Kinder, D. R. 2003. Communication and politics in the age of information. In D. O. Sears, L. Huddy, and R. Jervis (Eds.), *Oxford handbook of political psychology* (pp. 357–393). Oxford, UK: Oxford University Press.

Kinder, D. R., and Kam, C. D. 2009. *Us against them: Ethnocentric foundations of American opinion.* Chicago: University of Chicago Press.

Klapper, J. T. 1960. *The effects of mass communication.* New York: Free Press.

Ladd, J. McDonald, and Lenz, G. S. 2009. Exploiting a rare communication shift to document the persuasive power of the news media. *American Journal of Political Science* 53: 394–410.

Lenz, G. S. 2009. Learning and opinion change, not priming: Reconsidering the priming hypothesis. *American Journal of Political Science* 53: 821–837.

Lenz, G. S. 2012. Follow the leader? How voters respond to politicians' policies and performance. Chicago: University of Chicago Press.

Mueller, J. E. 1973. *War, presidents and public opinion.* New York: Wiley.

Patterson. T. 1993. *Out of order.* New York: Vintage Books.

Pew Research Center. September 12, 2010. Americans spending more time following the
news. Washington, DC: Author. Available at: http://www.people-press.org/2010/09/12/
americans-spending-more-time-following-the-news/

Pew Research Center's Project for Excellence in Journalism. October-November, 2008.
Campaign coverage index: 2008 weekly analyses. Available at: http://www.journalism.org/
news_index/101

Sears, D. O., and Freedman, J. L. 1967. Selective exposure to information: A critical review.
Public Opinion Quarterly 31: 194–213.

Sears, D. O., and Funk, C. L. 1999. Evidence of the long-term persistence of adults' political predispositions. *Journal of Politics 61:* 1–28.

Sears, D. O., and Kosterman, R. 1994. Mass media and political persuasion. In S. Shavitt and
T. C. Brock (Eds.), *Persuasion: Psychological insights and perspectives* (pp. 251–278).
Needham Heights, MA: Allyn & Bacon.

Tesler, M. 2012. Priming predispositions and changing policy positions: An account of when
priming and opinion change occur. Unpublished manuscript. Providence, RI: Brown
University.

Tesler, M. 2013. When science and ideology collide: Explaining public doubts about global
warming and evolution. Unpublished manuscript. Providence, RI: Brown University.

Tesler, M., and Sears, D. O. 2010. *Obama's race: The 2008 election and the dream of a post-racial
America.* Chicago: University of Chicago Press.

Zaller, J. R. 1992. *The nature and origins of mass opinion.* New York: Cambridge University Press.

Zaller, J. R. 1996. The myth of massive media impact revisited. In D. C. Mutz, P. M. Sniderman,
and R. A. Brody (Eds.), *Political persuasion and attitude change* (pp. 17–78). Ann Arbor:
University of Michigan Press.

CHAPTER 6

....

NOWHERE TO GO

Some Dilemmas of Deliberative Democracy

....

ELIHU KATZ

THE last few decades have seen the revival of the once-classic ideal of Deliberative Democracy. My interest in social networks of influence has placed me on the sidelines—sometimes in and sometimes out—of this old/new trend. Therefore, the present attempt to identify theory and research in this area cannot claim to be comprehensive. Mostly, I will report on a small selection from the findings of others, but will also draw on work conducted jointly with Joohan Kim and Robert Wyatt some years ago, in which we examined the links among exposure to the news, political conversation, quality of opinion, and political action, following in the footsteps of Gabriel Tarde (1901).

A range of definitions surrounds the concept. However, there seems to be general agreement (e.g., Delli Carpini and Cook, 2004; Jacobs et al., 2009; Pan, 2006; Chambers, 2003) that Deliberative Democracy—at least in its "bottom-up" version—refers to (1) open-minded citizens, who are (2) interested in public affairs, (3) attentive to the several sides of most issues, (4) have access to spaces for deliberation, (5) engage in agonistic conversation with each other, (6) on an equal and mutually respectful basis, (7) form considered opinions after weighing the competing arguments and their rationales, (8) prioritize the common good, and (9)[1] act to advance their opinions in public.

Who can resist the attractiveness of this model of government "of, by, and for the people?" It evokes the image of concerned and even-tempered citizens informally gathered on tree-shaded lawns—as well as at pubs, cafes, and salons—to discuss and debate issues on the political agenda. It is easy to understand why aspiring (and established) students of political communication continue to observe this phenomenon—and to earn a PhD, and perhaps a suntan, in the process.

And yet, Deliberative Democracy seems to attract opposition at every turn—normatively ("is this the system we really want?"), theoretically ("do its parts fit together?"), and empirically ("does it work?").

The most basic objection emerges at the normative level, exemplified in the "debate" (Schudson 2008) between Walter Lippman and John Dewey. Lippman felt that the mass public was incapable of coping with the vast and complex issues of modernity, while Dewey had faith in the grass roots, that is, in the interaction of press, conversation, public opinion, and widespread political action. Dewey's argument for deliberation echoes Tocqueville's observations of the participatory character of early American democracy, as well as that of his compatriot, Tarde, writing about France. Lippman had little use for deliberation, preferring to have experts on call to advise the leadership. The nostalgia for mass participation in the "public sphere" has resurfaced more recently in the writings of Jurgen Habermas (1989) and in the lament of Robert Putnam (2000) over the waning of sociability in the United States. Michael Schudson (1997) sides with Lippman, arguing that true deliberation is not a parlor game but an intensive confrontation between ideological rivals that requires rules of order and an umpire, such as exists in parliaments but not, typically, in parlors. Schudson believes that we should keep close watch on our representatives and express our support or discontent in the ballot box.

And what would be wrong, ask some normative critics, if deliberations were based not on the meeting of disembodied minds but on the interaction of whole persons with existing identities—such as class, gender, ethnicity, disability—and particular interests? The idea of multiple types of public was raised in criticism of Habermas by Nancy Fraser (1992). And is consensus-aiming deliberation really better than bargaining and compromise? Peters (1995) takes us even further in his appraisal of objections to classic liberal doctrine, citing those who question whether the valorizing of argumentation may not be dysfunctional for a political system. A (rightist) critique, says Peters, would sound like this: "The liberal public is nihilistic; its moral indecisiveness, its perpetual postponement of the most difficult questions, and its creation of a self and a public which are so preoccupied with arguments that neither self nor public are able to act" (1995, 659).

There are many objections at the theoretical level as well, some of which border also on the normative and the empirical. Most salient of these is the objection that Deliberative Democracy, by focusing so exclusively on opinion formation in small-group interactions, ignores the larger political system of which these groups are a part. Thus, political parties have all but disappeared, in favor, perhaps, of some ideal of the "independent voter." By "bracketing" the identity and interests of those who participate in the public sphere, Habermas posits that rationality rules, and that the best idea—not the best man, or the most popular party—wins. Participants are asked to check their identities at the door! And what is the role of the media in Deliberative Democracy? For canonic Habermas (1989)—but later amended (Habermas, 2006; Dahlgren, 2005; Benson, 2015)—present-day media, and audio-visual "representation" in general (Peters, 1993), were thought to undermine rationality.[2] And whatever happened to parliament? These are key elements in a democratic system, and even the most rational and creative deliberations cannot exist without a theory of how they are interrelated. Many theorists seem to lose sight of this larger context in which deliberation is embedded. Coleman and Blumler (2011) go so far as to suggest the irony that the very ideal of "deep listening" by government and "rich deliberation" by the public may be incompatible with a system of contemporary winner/loser politics.

In this connection, it is worth noting that the "situation of contact" (Freidson, 1953) in which the media are consumed is changing before our eyes. The new media networks are not only connecting activists, they are bringing them into the streets! In an earlier day, political activity, often raucous, was conducted in public (Brewin, 2003; Schudson, 1997). Then, broadcasting moved politics off the streets and into the home (Katz, 2009). Now, it seems that the social media are moving politics "outside" again. But mass mobilization, no more than intimate political talk, typically has nowhere "to go." Perhaps talk can undermine a system, but it can't build a new one.

Even if we pay attention to Deliberative Democracy as a separate unit—even if we permit its decontextualization for purposes of close consideration—we would need to theorize the process of aggregating opinion. In other words, we would expect theory to answer the question of how to bundle the opinions that percolate in these myriad groups.

Through what means do they become packaged as Public Opinion? Are opinion polls the end-product of mass deliberation? Is talkback? Is data-mining? Do the media perform this task? What about voting? How are these supposed to provide direction to public affairs? And, again, to whom are these opinions delivered? How (and when) do they enter legislative deliberations or governmental decision-making?

Those are external problems, so to speak, about the institutional context in which Deliberative Democracy presumably belongs. But there are also internal problems of a theoretical nature, those that ask whether the constituent elements of the Deliberative Democracy model actually fit well together. One such objection—a major one—asks whether it is at all possible to achieve equality and mutual understanding in political deliberation when participants come from different backgrounds, and thus possess different linguistic and conceptual abilities. Kohn (2000), for one, insists that this is the case, and furthermore, that such disparities invite the kinds of manipulation and domination that the Deliberative Democracy model is meant to overcome (see also Peters, 1995). And where do the rules regulating conversation come from?, asks Kohn. If they are not imposed by an umpire, do they come from the larger (shared) culture (and are thus known in advance by deliberants), or are they, in the unlikely case, generated in the process of deliberation itself?

It is at the empirical level, however, where most questions and objections arise. If such deliberative interactions actually take place, how do they work in practice? Here, one would want to know—referring back to the elements in the definition—(1) the extent of citizen interest in politics, (2) the extent of political talk, (3) whether everyday conversation includes political talk, (4) the extent to which talk goes on among persons with opposing opinions, (5) whether people change their minds in such deliberations, (6) how often consensus is reached, and (7) what political action follows when persons agree/disagree with each other? These are questions that have some answers.[3]

1. On the question of political interest, the Lazarsfeld, Berelson, and Gaudet (1944) studies of the forties and fifties set the stage, and the answers may still apply. When people are asked how interested they are in public affairs, there is a high

affirmative response (Hampton et al., 2009), then as well as today. When people are asked about their interest in election campaigns, the answers vary by election and by proximity to the polling date. The important point for our purposes, however, is the strong relationship between partisanship and interest. This is hardly a surprise until one is struck by the further fact that it is voters with low interest who are more likely to hear (or overhear) both sides of a political debate, more likely to talk with somebody whose opinion is different, more likely to change intention during an election campaign, and more likely to decide late for whom to vote. In other words, the less-interested voter behaved more like the ideal citizen of the deliberative model. Indeed, as Berelson et al. (1954) note more explicitly, the classic "independent voter" of high interest but low partisanship is a deviant case. We have long known that most voters—certainly the more interested ones—know their vote intention before the campaign begins, and do not change during the campaign. This is the received wisdom—but things may be different now, even if political interest continues high.

2. The extent of political talk is also high. Jacobs et al. (2009) report that over two-thirds of Americans engaged in talk about some political issue at least several times per month "in the past year," and Ingelhart (in Mutz, 2006) finds that Americans score ahead of citizens of Britain, Singapore, Canada, and most of South America (but behind Israel, Poland, Sweden, Greece, and the Netherlands) in extent of political talk. The Pew study by Hampton et al. (2011) suggests that the average American has 2.16 confidants "with whom they discuss important matters," more than in earlier years, partly due to the Internet. The more politically interested are also more likely to participate in talk about public affairs, and vice versa (Pan et al., 2006). Such talk goes on among intimates—family, friends, and acquaintances—and in the workplace (Kim et al., 1999). In these data, of both national and international subjects, Mutz (2006) discerns a correlation between amount of talk and the extent to which the discussion partners share the same opinion. Thus, the United States stands out as a nation with much political talk, of which a very high percentage is "homophilous," as the Columbia group early discovered. Citing Noelle-Neumann (1984), Wyatt et al. (2000) also find that feeling "free to talk" (in general, and in particular loci) and feeling that one shares the majoritarian opinion, further encourage participation in political talk. Deliberation accounts for an increase in various forms of civic and electoral participation (even after controlling for demographics), report Jacobs et al. (2009).

3. If so, what is the basis of the persistent concern that people, typically, "avoid politics," as Nina Eliasoph (1997) concludes from her ethnographic studies of informal social groups in an American city? Even groups engaged in avowedly civic projects, she finds, manage not to discuss political issues at the ideological level. The answer, almost surely, is that people who work together wish to avoid disagreement. Noelle-Neumann (1984) suggests that this is particularly true of those who feel embarrassed, and fall into silence, when they discover that their opinions differ from those of the (perceived) majority (as in Asch, 1956). Mutz believes,

too, that, in a pluralist society, people avoid taking sides because it might alienate them from certain others (Mutz, 2008). "Heterophilous" talk, she finds, is more likely to go on among less intimate associates, among people connected by what Granovetter (1973) calls "weak ties."

4. Even if political interest and political talk are more prevalent than one might have imagined, we need to know more about the extent of political disagreement in these deliberations. On one hand, it seems that most talk goes on among those who agree with each other, interpolated in daily conversation about other things— as in the home (Wyatt, 2000) or in the workplace (Mutz and Mondak, 2006) And if earlier theory still holds true, "disagreement," while relatively infrequent, may be located, ironically, among the less interested. Shamir and Shamir (2000) also find that education is negatively related to willingness to talk politics with a stranger. But this may be changing. According to Hampton's study for Pew (2011), users of social networks are no less likely than non-users to limit their relationships to like-minded others (as was feared). And Pan et al. (2006) report high levels of disagreement in talk during an election campaign. Indeed, Jacobs et al. (2009) find that almost half of Americans (47%) tried to persuade somebody to change their minds about one or another public issue during the last year!

5. So far, so good. If the extent of political interest, talk, and disagreement in informal deliberation is currently far more extensive than Berelson, Noelle-Neumann, and Eliasoph had led us to expect, the present-day climate for Deliberative Democracy seems considerably improved. However, one important hurdle still needs to be negotiated, namely, the relationship between "hearing the other side" and political action. In her brilliant book by the same name, Diana Mutz (2006) has revived one of the most interesting hypotheses of the Columbia voting studies, namely, that "cross-pressure"—that is, exposure to influence from more than one side of a partisan debate—has a "paralyzing" effect; voting decisions are made later in the campaign and turnout is negatively affected (Lazarsfeld et al., 1944). Nir (2011) reports a similar finding. At a minimum, cross-pressure creates an ambivalence about how to act, or whether to act. But even when it works to enlighten—to clarify and crystallize the arguments, to become aware of the rationale for opposing viewpoints, to increase tolerance (Mutz, 122)—cross-pressure may cause people to keep their opinions to themselves. Noelle-Neumann would agree. Mutz concludes that political participation is not a product of agonistic deliberation, but of single-mindedness. It is also worth noting that Mutz's research involves actual cross-pressures between discussion pairs, far outdistancing Lazarsfeld's early effort to infer cross-pressures from respondents' reports of the occupations and religions of their associates.[4]

6. Empirical research seems stuck at this point. The evidence supports the prevalence of persuasion attempts, but one encounters little evidence of being persuaded. On the other hand, there is evidence of hardening effects, sometimes called polarizing effects, as a result of deliberation. Delli Carpini et al. (2004) cite such effects, as does Wojcieszak (2011) in her finding that strong prior opinions on

issues of same-sex marriage or abortion became even stronger after deliberation—especially when the extremists are aware that there is disagreement in the group. Latter-day Habermas (2006) willingly concurs. At this point we are forced to conclude that there is still room for argument over the consequences of arguing, the agonistic element in the definition of Deliberative Democracy.

DISCUSSION

This review, however cursory, suggests that the empirical study of Deliberative Democracy has been reduced, essentially, to the study of interpersonal communication about public affairs. While this focus on the extent and dynamics of political talk in small groups is surely worthy, it falls far short of constituting a system of governance. On the most rudimentary level, it pays little attention to the role of the media, to the problems of how public opinion aggregates, and how it is transmitted to policymakers. Even more glaring is the absence of attention to the several institutional branches of government—legislative, judicial, and executive. If Deliberative Democracy is meant to be reconciled—rather than competitive—with a model of representative democracy, somebody should say so, more often. Rhetorically, at least, it is typically proposed as a project in itself. Instead, it deserves study as part of a system in which deliberation has an important part at various stages of policymaking and relates to the system's no-less-important other parts.[5] This disconnect of one component from interlocking others echoes the classic concerns of Lazarsfeld and Merton (1948) and Hallin and Mancini (1984) about whether exposure to the news "goes" anywhere, for example, whether it serves as an input into the political system. More recently, this question is being raised in a different guise and in a global context by Boltanski 1999), Chouliaraki (2006), and Frosh and Pinchevski (2009), who have focused on the ethical obligations of witnessing devastation on television. Studies of media reception, like studies of the deliberative process, are pieces that have to fit into a larger puzzle. That is one of the major conclusions of this cursory review.

As for the study of the internal elements of deliberation, much of the empirical research seems to add up. Political talk—albeit interspersed with daily talk at home and elsewhere—seems surprisingly frequent; interest in public affairs is high, and may be even higher when issues such as health and education are included; talk often leads to civic engagement, such as taking an active role in an election campaign. Talk goes on, mostly, among people with similar backgrounds and similar outlooks; thus, consensus is more likely to precede discussion rather than to follow from it. Social media may mobilize such networks for political action. And, the news may echo this activity. This is a mini-system that hangs together. Political cultures differ, of course, and it is worth noting that we are not here dealing with authoritarian regimes, or with societies in revolt. Each of these offer different views on the power of political talk.

Talk in democracies does not do much, apparently, to change opinions or attitudes toward policies. While discussants report rather frequent influence-attempts, there is only little evidence of resultant change. Social media, so called, may, however, be facilitating movements for change. But, on the whole, argument is rare—and is as likely to reinforce prior positions, or to create ambivalence and even withdrawal. A "willingness to argue" is also associated with non-mainstream action ("complaining" rather than "campaigning," as Wyatt et al. [2000] have dubbed them). It is true, apparently, that "hearing the other side" is not something that activates citizens—although much work is still needed on this point. What is clear, however, is that engaging with others helps to clarify one's own opinions and promotes greater understanding of others' opinions (Cappella et al., 2002), thus enhancing the quality of opinion.

AUTHOR NOTE

Thanks to Kathleen Hall Jamieson for encouragement, and to John Durham Peters, Magdalena Wojcieszak, Robert Wyatt, Lilach Nir, Jefferson Pooley, and Christopher Ali for comments and criticism.

NOTES

1. Deliberative Democracy may also refer to transparent policymaking procedures initiated by governments that share their decisions with citizens, along with the rationale for doing so. Lilach Nir points out, correctly, that the present article refers, rather, to political talk, mostly of an informal kind, initiated by citizens, as idealized in current American political theory. For the case of Britain, see Coleman and Blumler (2011).
2. This revisionist paper of Habermas seeks to resituate deliberation in the context of the other institutions of representative democracy, including the media of mass communication, thus addressing the central issue raised in the present article. I thank John Peters for calling this to my attention, even though fair disclosure requires me to admit that I was in the audience when Habermas presented this thesis to the International Communications Association in Dresden in 2006. The present article would have been considerably improved if its author had paid closer attention.
3. In the absence of field studies, Tali Mendelberg (2002) reviews a large number of laboratory studies of small-group interaction, rightly arguing that this genre of experimental social psychology essentially simulates the kinds of real-life deliberations that theorists postulate. She attempts to infer likely outcomes (consensus, polarization, etc.) as a function of variations in group structure (homogeneous vs. mixed education, politically independent vs. party membership, etc.), and types of issues discussed (national budget deficit, intergroup relations, etc.).
4. Jefferson Pooley points out how closely these findings about homophilous talk fit the classical concerns of social psychology with "selective exposure" and "cognitive dissonance."
5. Habermas (2006) is rather more optimistic (1) about the changes in opinion that may result from deliberation, citing Fishkin (1995), for example, and (2) about the success of several attempts by policymakers to incorporate the results of such deliberation—citing

an example from Berlin reported by Van den Daele and Neidhardt (1996). Coleman and Blumler (2011) are much more pessimistic. In what may be a new turn in the institution-alization of Deliberative Democracy, the mass protests in Tel Aviv in 2011 against the neo-Liberal policies of government deserve study for (1) the role of the social media in making different sectors aware of a common interest, that is, in overcoming "pluralistic ignorance," (2) the role of the new media in facilitating consensual (i.e., homophilous) deliberation among the like-minded, (3) the combined role of these media and of such deliberation in mobilizing a mass demonstration in the city streets, partly inspired by the so-called Arab Spring, (4) the cautious admission by government of the legitimacy of this opposition, its right to organize and to be heard, and (5) the founding of a mechanism for deliberation between protesters and establishment, offering the prospect of genuine response, both ide-ological and practical.

References

Asch, S. 1956. Studies in independence and submission to group pressure. *Psychological Monographs* 70(4l6).

Benson, R. 2015. Public spheres, fields, networks: Western concepts for a de-Westernizing world?. In C. C. Lee (Ed.), *Internationalizing international communication* (pp. 258–280). Ann Arbor: University of Michigan Press.

Berelson, B., Lazarsfeld, P. F., and McPhee, W. N. 1954. *Voting*. Chicago: University of Chicago Press.

Boltanski, L. 1999. *Distant suffering: Morality, media and politics*. Cambridge: Cambridge University Press.

Brewin, M. W. 2003. *Celebrating democracy: The mass mediated ritual of Election Day*. New York: Peter Lang.

Cappella. J., Price, V., and Nir, L. 2002. Argument repertoire as a reliable and valid measure of opinion quality. *Political Communication* 75: 287–316.

Chambers, S. 2003. Deliberative democratic theory. *Annual Review of Political Science* 6: 307–326.

Chouliaraki, L. 2006. *The spectatorship of suffering*. London: Sage.

Coleman, S., and Blumler, J. G. 2011. The wisdom of which crowd? On the pathology of a listen-ing government. *Political Quarterly* 82(3): 355–364.

Dahlgren, P. 2005. The public sphere: Linking the media and civic cultures. In E. W. Rothenbuhler and M. Coman (Eds.), *Media anthropology* (pp. 318–327). Thousand Oaks, CA: Sage.

Delli Carpini, M. X., and Cook, F. L. 2004. Public deliberation, discursive participation, and citizen engagement: A review of the empirical literature. *Annual Review of Political Science* 7: 315–344.

Eliasoph, N. 1997. "Close to home": The work of avoiding politics. *Theory and Society* 20(5): 605–664.

Fishkin, J. 1995. *The voice of the people: Public opinion and democracy*. New Haven: Yale University Press.

Fraser, N. 1992. Rethinking the public sphere: A contribution to the critique of actually existing democracy. In C. Calhoun (Ed.), *Habermas and the public sphere* (pp. 109–142). Cambridge, MA: MIT Press.

Freidson, E. 1953. The relation of the social situation of contact to the media in mass communication. *Public Opinion Quarterly* 17: 230–238.

Frosh, P., and Pinchevski, A. 2009. *Media witnessing: Testimony in the age of mass communication.* London: Palgrave/Macmillan.

Granovetter, M. 1973. The strength of weak ties. *American Journal of Sociology* 78: 1360–1380.

Habermas, J. 1989. *The structural transformation of the public sphere.* Cambridge, MA: MIT Press.

Habermas, J. 2006. Political communication in media society: Does democracy still enjoy an epistemic dimension? The impact of normative theory on empirical research. *Communication Theory* 16: 411–426.

Hallin, D., and Mancini, P. 1984. Speaking of the president: Political structure in American and Italian news. *Theory and Society* 13: 829–850.

Hampton, K., Goulet, L., Eun Ja Her, Rainie, L. 2009. Social isolation and new technology: How the internet and mobile phone impact Americans' social networks. Washington, D.C. Pew Internet and American Life Project.

Hampton, K., Goulet, L. S., Rainie, L., and Purcell, K. 2011. Social networking sites and our lives. Pew Research Center. 16 June 2011.

Jacobs, L. R., Cook, F. L., and Delli Carpini, M. X. 2009. *Talking together: Public deliberation and political deliberation in America.* Chicago: University of Chicago Press

Katz, E. 2009. Introduction. In E. Katz and P. Scannell (Eds.), The end of television? Its impact on the world so far. *Annals of the American Academy of Political and Social Science* 625: 6–18.

Kim, J., Wyatt, R. O., and Katz, E. 1999. News, talk, opinion, participation: The part played by conversation in deliberative democracy. *Political Communication* 16(4): 361–386.

Kohn, M. 2000. Language, power and persuasion: Toward a critique of deliberative democracy. *Constellations* 7(3): 408–429.

Lazarsfeld, P. F., Berelson, B., and Gaudet, H. 1944. *The people's choice.* New York: Duell, Sloan and Pearce.

Lazarsfeld, P. F., and Merton, R. K. 1948. Mass communication, popular taste and organized social action." In L. Bryson (Ed.), *The communication of ideas* (pp. 95–118). New York: Harper.

Mendelberg, T. 2002. The deliberative citizen: Theory and evidence. In M. X. Delli Carpini et al., (Eds.), *Political decision making: Deliberation and participation* (pp. 151–193). Chicago: JAI Press.

Mutz, D. 2006. *Hearing the other side: Deliberative vs. participatory democracy.* Cambridge: Cambridge University Press.

Mutz, D., and Mondak, J. J. 2006. The workplace as a context for cross-cutting political discourse. *Journal of Politics* 68(1): 140–155.

Mutz, D. 2008. Is deliberative democracy a falsifiable theory? *Annual Review of Political Science* 11: 521–538.

Nir, L. 2011. Disagreement and opposition in social networks: Does opposition discourage turnout? *Political Studies* 59: 674–692.

Noelle-Neumann, E. 1984. *The spiral of silence: Public opinion—our social skins.* Chicago: University of Chicago Press.

Pan, Z. 2006. Mobilizing public talk in a presidential campaign. *Communication Research* 33: 315–345.

Peters, J. D. 1993. Distrust of representation: Habermas on the public sphere. *Media, Culture and Society* 15(4): 541–571.

Peters, J. D. 1995. Publicity and pain: Self-abstraction in Adam Smith's Theory of Moral Sentiments. *Public Culture* 7: 657–684.

Putnam, R. 2000. *Bowling alone: The collapse and revival of American community.* New York: Simon and Schuster.

Schudson, M. 1997. Why conversation is not the soul of democracy. *Critical Studies in Mass Communication* 14: 297–300.

Schudson, M. 2008. The "Lippman-Dewey Debate" and the invention of Walter Lippman as an anti-democrat. 1986–1996. *International Journal of Communication* 2: 1–20.

Shamir, J., and Shamir, M. 2000. *The anatomy of public opinion.* Ann Arbor: University of Michigan Press.

Tarde, G. 1901. "La Conversation," in L'opinion et la foule, Paris: Alcan.Translated in Katz, E., Ali, C. and Kim, J. (2014) *Echoes of Gabriel Tarde: What we know better or different 100 years later.* Los Angeles: The Annenberg Press.

Van den Daele, W., and Neidhardt, F. 1996. Government by discussion: On attempts to do politics with the help of argument. In Van den Daele and Neidhardt (Eds.), *Kommunikation und Einscheidung* (German) (pp. 9–50). Berlin: WZB Yearbook, Rainer Bohn Verlag.

Wojcieszak, M. 2011. Deliberation and attitude polarization: What happens when people with extreme views encounter disagreement. *Journal of Communication* 61: 596-617.

Wyatt, R. O., Kim, J., and Katz, E. 2000. Bridging the spheres: Political and personal conversation in public and private spaces. *Journal of Communication* 50: 71–92.

CHAPTER 7

HOW TO THINK NORMATIVELY ABOUT NEWS AND DEMOCRACY

MICHAEL SCHUDSON

THE premise of this chapter is that democracy is the best, or the least bad, form of government, and that the news media have a significant role in helping to make democracy work. Specifying that role is difficult. In the large literature on the media and democracy, there is little clarity about what democracy is or what the various forms of democracy are, and there is no more clarity about just what work journalism does on democracy's behalf, which tasks matter most, or what combinations of them serve democracy best.

In this chapter I offer a list of what seem to me the major democratic functions of the press and make suggestions about what understanding of democracy is implicit in the American news media. In my view, American journalists misread democracy's greatest strengths and almost completely miss the boat in grasping major changes in the character of democratic government in the United States since 1945 that call for rethinking journalism's democratic role.

FUNCTIONS OF THE NEWS MEDIA IN DEMOCRACY

How do the media serve, and how could the media better serve democracy? This is a familiar topic, but it has usually been addressed in superficial ways, in self-congratulatory sermons at journalism's ceremonial occasions or in high-minded pronouncements that skirt the most difficult and complex issues. In the widely used textbook on journalism, *The Elements of Journalism*, a work that takes these matters very seriously, journalists Bill Kovach and Tom Rosenstiel ask, "How does the free press actually work as a bulwark of liberty? Does it work at all?" and they begin their reply, "Journalists don't usually consider these questions explicitly. It may seem slightly ridiculous to ask: what is the theory of democracy that drives your TV news operation or your newspaper?" (Kovach and Rosenstiel, 2007, 21). Whatever that theory may be, it is almost surely out of date, because the structure and operation of the American state has greatly changed since 1945 and even since 1965; US government has moved from a representative democracy to what might be termed a postlegislative democracy, characterized by a greatly expanded administrative state, coupled with a new network of accountability in which government is held responsible not only by voters at the next election but also by agencies of civil society that monitor the performance of government, society, and the economy on a daily, ongoing basis. These agencies include the news media, think tanks, universities, opinion polling, and partisan and nonpartisan NGOs. They include also, as I shall indicate, newly institutionalized accountability practices inside government itself. The result is a political system quite distant from what eighteenth-century republicans envisioned or what textbooks still outline, but there has been no corresponding adjustment of conventional understandings of the role the news media do play or should play.

Most of the key philosophical works that lay out a case for democracy or republican or representative government do not mention journalism. This is not surprising—there was no journalism in ancient Greece. Nor were the fledgling news journals in England, the Netherlands, and France in the 1600s and 1700s, or in the American colonies, of great consequence. Occasionally pamphleteers sometimes played a political role, and by the middle of the eighteenth century in France so did criticism of the king circulated in songs, doggerel, and an underground, vulgar literature, all of which had a corrosive effect on the authority of the king (Darnton, 2000). Even toward the end of the eighteenth century, when the thinkers at the American founding argued for republicanism in the pages of weekly newspapers, they paid only cursory attention to the role of the press. The Federalist papers barely mention the press and, as important as the First Amendment has become, it began as more of a prohibition on federal power (as opposed to the power of state governments) rather than as a ringing affirmation of the necessity of the press for democracy.

Journalism exists and has long existed without democracy—think of Chile under Pinochet or Spain under Franco or India during Indira Gandhi's "Emergency" in the mid-1970s when, as one critic put it, "journalists were told to bend but chose to crawl" (Jeffrey, 2010, 190). Journalism existed in the Soviet Union yesterday, and it exists in China today, sometimes even daring to criticize the government—but without bringing China appreciably closer to democratic political institutions.

Journalism exists without democracy, but it is much harder to imagine democracy without journalism—at least, it is difficult to imagine democracy without protections for the freedom to speak and write, including to speak and write about and against the government. But it is not hard to picture a democracy in which people comment freely about government but have little access to government information and little interest in reporting—rather than commenting on—governmental activities. The identification of journalism with reporting is a development of the nineteenth century, not before. Even late in the nineteenth century, many Europeans thought of "reporting" as an American or Anglo-American brand of journalism, and they were resistant to its diffusion to the Continent (Chalaby, 1996).

Today people tend to place reporting as the leading function of journalism and its most important contribution to democracy. I do not disagree with this, but I observe, in the untidy list that follows, that standard daily informational reporting is just one of seven things that the press does or could do for democracy. There is no canonical list of the contributions of news to democracy. While this list is long enough to be ungainly, and surely incomplete even so, it has the virtue of linking lofty goals to particular journalistic forms and genres, and it does not assume that one or another of the multiple things journalism does is the single most vital contribution that the press makes to democracy:[1]

1. Information: the news media can provide fair and sufficient information so citizens can make sound political choices. Informational journalism often focuses on breaking news—anticipated and unanticipated events and actions that have taken place in the very recent past, usually the past twenty-four hours.

2. Investigation: the news media can investigate concentrated sources of power, particularly governmental power. Investigation often requires planning, teamwork, and the allocation of scarce journalistic resources and may absorb weeks or months of work to yield published reports.

3. Analysis: the news media can provide intelligible frameworks of interpretation to help citizens comprehend a complex world. Analysis is sometimes contributed by columnists, editorial writers, or bloggers, but it also appears when reporters who regularly cover a beat step back to offer a broader overview or more context than normally appears in their daily news coverage. The informational, investigative, and analytical functions of the media, insofar as they focus particularly on government, can be collectively identified as "watchdog journalism" or "accountability journalism."

     Also within the range of analysis is the capacity of the media to make "pretty good sense of very large and complex events quickly" (Lemann, 2011). Columbia Journalism School dean Nicholas Lemann praises here as democratically useful something that media analysts often disparage but that many people rely on, what Lemann calls "an important middle level of understanding." It is neither "just the facts" nor is it in-depth investigation or analysis, but it is a rough first stab at making meaning, usually built more on conventional wisdom and common sense than on anything more searching or soulful, and for all that of real value.

4. Social empathy: journalism can tell people about others in their society and their world so that they can come to appreciate the viewpoints and lives of other people, especially those less advantaged than themselves. As the philosopher Joseph Raz has argued, it is important in a pluralistic democratic society for the media to portray and thereby implicitly legitimate various styles of life in society, giving them "the stamp of public acceptability" (1994, 140). Social empathy reporting

often comes in the form of "soft" or feature reporting. It may be related to breaking news but typically is a follow-up to a breaking news story. It may be done in a day or it may require more substantial research and appear as a long story or a series of several stories.

5. Public forum: journalism can provide a forum for dialogue among citizens and serve as a common carrier of the perspectives of various groups and interests in society. In the nineteenth century and well into the twentieth, the American news media were collectively a public forum more than they were individually. Newspapers became individually more a forum for a variety of opinions in the 1970s with the decline of competitive urban dailies and the rise of "op-ed" pages that typically offer a range of political perspectives, including views at variance with the opinions of the newspaper's own editorials.

6. Mobilization: the news media can advocate for particular party or political programs and perspectives and mobilize people to act on their behalf. For the nineteenth-century American newspaper, this was understood to be their primary function; newspapers were closely identified with political parties. With a growing independence of newspapers from parties in the twentieth century and the growing professionalization of journalism as a field at the same time, mobilization began to be seen as a failing rather than a purpose. It is only with the emergence of explicitly partisan cable television political coverage and partisan online news outlets that mobilizing has begun—unevenly—to regain some legitimacy. Still, when a news outlet puts mobilization or advocacy first, it may undermine the integrity of the informational and investigative functions.

7. Democratic education: news can be educative about democracy itself. This is not the widespread paternalist model of journalism as a school in which cultural elites exercise a tutorial leadership of the masses. It is, instead, a journalistic allegiance to the values of democratic governance themselves. The first six functions listed above are not inconsistent with a relatively populist view of democracy, one in which the audience addressed is invariably the general public and the assumption held is that democracy means broad citizen participation whenever practically feasible. But the media abdicate their democratic educational function when they give the impression that democracy means simply majority rule or realizing some mystical will of the people. There is no "will of the people" that endures beyond the moment of its expression (say, in an election) apart from the methods of "realizing" it and the constitution and institutions through which it gains its sustaining legitimacy. The media should contribute to a view of democracy as a system of checks and balances operating within a system of free and fair elections with protections for civil liberties, human rights, and the rule of law, regardless of what a particular moment, popular mood, or apparent meaning of an election might appear to dictate. In other words, journalism should seek to educate its audiences in a sophisticated concept of democracy that locates it not in popular expression but in a system of elections, laws, and rights in which popular expression holds an honored, but not unconstrained, place.

Journalism in the Context of Changing Democratic Structures

Does American journalism have an implicit political theory? I think it does. To discover it, one could examine newspaper editorials on or just before election day, analyze public addresses of journalism's leaders, or develop other empirical measures. What I suspect such investigation would find is an implicit endorsement of representative democracy in which citizens make up their minds about a wide range of specific policies and then vote for, contribute to the campaigns of, and otherwise support candidates and representatives who advocate the policies those citizens favor. There is little or no attention in this view to the ways that representation itself might improve upon direct democracy and produce better outcomes than an aggregation of individual preferences can. What journalists support, if I am reading between the lines correctly, is representative democracy as a kind of attenuated direct democracy. They understand representative democracy as the pragmatic compromise that a large, populous society must make to retain a taste of the preferable town-meeting, face-to-face, and fully participatory democracy—so the closer elections are to policy referenda, the better. In this, they do not take seriously the arguments—from James Madison in Federalist No. 10 to political philosopher George Kateb (1992)—that representative democracy has moral, not just practical, benefits that direct democracies real and imagined cannot match.

Philosophically journalism has yet to actually accept representative democracy as anything more than a decidedly second-best system to people gathering in town meetings or other assemblies to govern themselves. Given that we are, by the practicalities of living in a populous society, saddled with this second-best system of representation, journalism tries to make the best of it by keeping citizens well informed on the issues before legislators. This view is, in my judgment, an unnecessarily lukewarm endorsement of representative democracy. It is also insensitive to changes—one might arguably say improvements—in how US democracy has actually come to function in the past half century.

Today, for various reasons, the election of representatives and the operation of legislatures is a smaller element in the actual governance of the nation than it used to be, and one might even say we have entered into an era of postrepresentative democracy. This is true in at least three respects. First, citizens' access to governance comes not only from electing representatives but also from influencing them through a variety of civil society organizations that monitor legislative behavior. Second, citizens' access to governance comes also through litigation, and this avenue to participation through the courts rather than the legislature has expanded greatly from the civil rights movement on. Third, the executive has become so vast since 1945 that a kind of veiled system of government accountability has emerged of which the general public is largely unaware—I have in mind the expansion of varieties of governmental self-monitoring and self-surveillance, which I will discuss shortly.

Are we in or moving into a postlegislative phase of democracy? French political theorist Bernard Manin offers one useful periodization that makes such a claim. He describes a move from eighteenth-century "parliamentary democracy," in which voters were supposed to select a "person of trust" to represent them, a local "notable" who would then vote his own conscience based on his understanding of the public good, to nineteenth-century "party democracy," in which representatives were members of parties expected to maintain a large degree of loyalty to the priorities of their party platforms. Then, largely in the post-1945 era, party democracies gave way to "audience democracy," in which candidates were again freed from party rule and able to respond more individually and idiosyncratically to public opinion and an increasingly wide array of interest groups, experts, and others (Manin, 1997).

Australian political theorist and media scholar John Keane offers a related view, with more extensive discussion of the post-1945 era. In his periodization, democracy has shifted from the "assembly democracy" model of ancient Greek city-states to the "representative democracy" model that emerged in the eighteenth century and which, in its different variants, has to this day been identified with modern democracy. But for Keane, as for Manin, social changes since 1945 have altered the conditions of popular government sufficiently to force upon us a new label for today's democratic forms. For Keane, two features stand out in shaping democracy today. First, there is what he calls "communicative abundance." If assembly democracy is linked to the spoken word and representative democracy to print culture, today's democracy—what Keane calls "monitory democracy"—emerges with the rise of multimedia societies (Keane, 2009, 737). The multiple forms of news media give new force to the print-era aspirations of journalism to serve as a "watchdog" on government. But journalism is by no means the only significant monitor of governmental activity. As Keane observes, today we have not only a rapidly proliferating array of civil society organizations that scrutinize government, but even organizations (he mentions the Democratic Audit Network and the Global Accountability Project) in the business of second-order assessment, monitoring the quality and effectiveness of the power-scrutinizing work of other civil society organizations. "In the era of monitory democracy, the constant public scrutiny of power by hosts of differently sized monitory bodies with footprints large and small makes it the most energetic, most dynamic form of democracy ever" (Keane, 2009, 743). How the media should work with these alternative institutions of accountability when the press cannot serve as the sole watchdog on leviathan government is something that media theory has not attended to at all.

Keane's "monitory democracy" may sound like a recipe for governmental paralysis. Indeed, in the concluding chapter of Keane's ambitious work, he reprints a drawing of Lemuel Gulliver tied to stakes in the ground by a flock of Lilliputians. But this is not, for Keane, a dystopian image. In fact, he makes the case that today democracy should be understood not as the "rule by the people" but as rule by "nobody." Probably the key quotation in his book is from C. S. Lewis, who wrote that he was a democrat "because I believe in the Fall of Man. I think most people are democrats for the opposite reason. A great deal of democratic enthusiasm descends from the ideas of people . . . who believed in a democracy because they thought mankind so wise and good that every-one deserved a share in the government. The danger of defending democracy on those grounds is that they're not true." Lewis was a champion of democracy, he avowed, not because human beings can govern themselves but because "mankind is so fallen that no man can be trusted with unchecked power over his fellows" (Keane, 2009, 865). The moral value of democracy is that it is provisional and revisable, not that it always reflects or expresses the will of the people, if such a thing as the "will of the people" could even be practically designated.[2]

Keane articulated his views on the role of the media in democracy in another work nearly two decades earlier. In *The Media and Democracy*, he emphasizes that democracy is not simply a participatory form of government or a government in which the majority rules. It "comprises procedures for arriving at collective decisions in a way which secures the fullest possible and qualitatively best participation of interested parties. At a minimum ... democratic procedures include equal and universal adult suffrage; majority rule and guarantees of minority rights, which ensure that collective decisions are approved by a substantial number of those entitled to make them; the rule of law; and constitutional guarantees of freedom of assembly and expression and other liberties, which help ensure that the people expected to decide or to elect those who decide can choose among real alternatives" (Keane, 1991, 168–169). Keane insists that Enlightenment hopes that free expression would be the agency for "absolute knowledge and the spread of a rational democratic consensus" are simply "obsolete" and that a new justification for a close connection of a free press and democracy is still to be crafted (Keane, 1991, 175). What democracy provides is not "good decisions," in his view, but the opportunity for citizens "to judge (and to reconsider their judgments about) the quality of those decisions" (Keane, 1991, 190). Reconsideration, revision, second thoughts—for Keane, the virtue of democracy is the humility of its operation, and the place of a free press in democracy is that it, too, is revisable and at its best, honors revisability, not to mention a multiplicity of voices and a forum for contestation of facts, interpretations, policies, goals, and values.

Both Keane and Manin point to remarkable changes in our governing systems that deserve attention when we think about the role of media in democracy. Our conceptual grasp of what the media do and should do is lagging about half a century behind substantial and enduring changes in how American and other democracies work. Keane takes note of developments in Australia in recent decades of operations within government itself that create quasi-independent oversight agencies, and there have been similar changes in US government. These include the increased authority of the Government Accountability Office (once the General Accounting Office) and the Congressional Budget Office; the creation of inspectors general for all of the major federal agencies (by the Inspectors General Act of 1978); and the complicated, sometimes vexing, but nonetheless powerful Freedom of Information Act (passed in 1966 and strengthened in 1974), which became a model for similar efforts around the world to make it possible for individuals to request government-held information and to sue for its release if government authorities deny it. For the news media to operate as watchdogs on government, they must work in relationship to and work with these self-surveilling bodies, including also the reports filed with the Federal Elections Commission (1971, 1974) and the issuing of environmental impact statements authorized by the National Environmental Policy Act (1969) and other legislatively ordained disclosures of public information (Schudson, 2010). Efforts to make government activity more transparent to the general public have grown rapidly with the Internet and the relative ease of making vast quantities of government data available online. Increasingly, this information is not only available but searchable—even if it has required the efforts of private citizens, news organizations, nongovernmental organizations, and universities to do the work to make government data actually useable.

Constructing a Democracy-Relevant Journalism

Suppose that the news media can serve the multiple democratic functions I have listed. What factors support the press in these efforts? What are the social, cultural, political, legal, economic, technological, and institutional features that are most likely to help establish and nurture the kind of media most likely to serve democracy well?

First and foremost, the press should be free. If journalists fear for their lives or livelihood when they publish truthful accounts of government activity, news will not serve democracy. The problem with the concept of press freedom is that there is a difference between the absence of constraints—which is what is usually meant—and the presence of relevant informational substance, investigative vigor and critical stance, professional norms and values, and a diversity of viewpoints, not to mention adequate public access to information. All of these are key elements of what we mean by (but do not reliably measure or measure at all with respect to) a free press.

That said, we can distinguish between "freedom of the press" as a condition of possibility—is the press legally and politically sufficiently free to cover politics and society usefully, responsibly, compassionately, and critically?—and "freedom of the press" as a realized condition: *does* the sufficiently free press in fact cover the news usefully, responsibly, compassionately, and critically?

The basic level of press freedom is dependent on political and legal institutions of a society designed to foster an independent media and the commitment of the national political culture to free expression. Without this, the press cannot serve democracy. With it, effective news organizations become possible—but are not guaranteed. What factors encourage a high quality of democratically relevant discourse to actually emerge?

This question is not as easy to answer as it may at first seem to be. Some people—particularly American journalists—would insist that effective news coverage can only come from organizations completely insulated from government subsidy and government control. And yet this is not universally so. Some news organizations widely respected for the quality of their news coverage are publicly funded—in the wider world, the most distinguished case is the BBC. Not only are there state-supported broadcasters that have established a strong reputation for independent news gathering (including the Public Broadcasting Service and National Public Radio in the United States), but in some notably successful democracies with widely admired news organizations, there is even direct government subsidy of daily newspapers—this subsidy represents a relatively small portion of the papers' total funding, but it has survived in operation for several decades in all of the Scandinavian countries and several other European democracies as well.

Some critics, from another angle, point to what has been called "market censorship" rather than state censorship and argue that there are grave dangers in any advertising-based and corporate-controlled news media. The weakness of public service broadcasting in the United States compared with many of the democracies of Western Europe is held up as evidence that US media are in constant danger of being little more than propaganda mouthpieces for capitalism, even if it may be "responsible" capitalism or capitalism with a human face. Put in terms of day-to-day news decisions, the fear is that bottom-line judgments will invariably trump news judgment, and news coverage that focuses on what is important will give way to news decisions that highlight what is interesting to consumers and likely to sell.

While this line of critique makes conceptual sense, and it is easy to list instances in which commercial considerations have blocked pure journalistic instincts, it is important to recognize that "pure" journalistic instincts are never, in fact, pure. In many ways, commercial considerations have been a considerable boon for the role of media in serving democracy. Consider media historian Marcel Broersma's study of the last century of Dutch newspapers. He observes that for the first half of the twentieth century, Dutch newspapers were organized "vertically"—in unrelieved columns of type, the second article beginning, separated only by a short line or dash, immediately after the article before it. Nowhere were adjustments made for the "news value" of the story. Journalism was understood as an educational service, and readers were expected to do some work to get through a newspaper. In contrast, what the Dutch saw as the "Anglo-American" system or the "American system" used a system of page layout and design to highlight "the news value of the items." And then Broersma writes, in telling language, "After 1945 Dutch journalism increasingly adopted the Anglo-American conventions, which meant that the emphasis shifted to news value. Journalists were no longer expected merely to record happenings but to extract the news from an event" (Broersma, 2007, 187).

If journalism is not "extracting the news from an event," what is it? If clarifying for readers what is more and what is less worthy of their notice is not part of the job of journalists and especially of editors, what are they doing? And yet Dutch journalists before 1945 took themselves to be and were treated as journalists. Likewise, eighteenth- and early nineteenth-century American newspapers were visually very much like the 1900–1945 Dutch newspapers Broersma describes. The "American" system was made in this country but was not born on the Fourth of July, 1776. It emerged as part of an increasingly commercial system—but a commercial system that at the same time gave rise to

greater authority for "news judgment" and greater deference to the independent authority of the journalists themselves.

All of this is to say that commercialism, although it can be the enemy of professionalism, has historically also been its ally and its enabling condition. This is not to suggest that there is clarity about what norms and values of professionalism should be most
prized. European news media tend to favor coherent and consistent philosophical or
political perspectives in journalism as a very high value, American news media tend
to favor "objectivity," although it is clear that in the past two generations, leading US
news organizations have increasingly and insistently blended this with offering context
and analysis. The difficulty in assessing "professionalism," then, at least as it might be
gleaned from news texts themselves, would be in judging what professional values journalists should be upholding in their daily work.

One might also look for the *absence* of norms and values that work *against* good
journalism. I have in mind the views common in journalism in times past—and still
today in local journalism and community journalism and perhaps not there alone—
that controversy should be avoided. This was part of the early mandate of the BBC, for
instance, in the 1920s. And even in the early days of television news, there were formal
provisions to prevent the BBC from covering topics that could be expected to come
before the parliament in the next two weeks. The "fourteen-day rule" was designed
(until its demise in 1956–1957) to keep the center of public discussion located in the
parliament and not on television. Swedish public broadcasting all through the 1950s
likewise adhered to a highly deferential attitude to government officials and ventured
essentially nothing critical or controversial. These were not accidents of omission
but explicit and self-conscious efforts to adhere to certain standards of appropriate
decorum. In the American case, sociologist Steven Clayman and his colleagues have
shown with a very careful sociolinguistic analysis of a large sample of presidential
news conference transcripts that the questions journalists asked at White House press
conferences in the 1950s were rarely aggressive, and they rarely sought to hold presidents accountable for their words or actions before 1968 (Clayman et al., 2007, 2010).
The level of critical questioning leapt upward in the 1968–1972 period, and although it
has varied up and down since then, at no point has it returned to the lower levels that
consistently prevailed before 1968.

Besides legal and political guarantees of freedom and appropriate journalistic professionalism (difficult as the latter is to define, and plural and fuzzy as acceptable professional standards are likely to be), one might also look for conditions that sponsor the
availability of multiple perspectives on contemporary affairs.

The difficult problem here is whether one wants to assess diversity within a given publication or across publications or news outlets available to people of a given city or community, what has been termed "internal pluralism" and "external pluralism" (Hallin and
Mancini, 2004, 29). In talking about diversity within a publication, one thinks immediately of letters to the editor and op-ed columns. But one would want to know, even more,
how many different sources are quoted in news stories—and how diverse those sources
are in relation to the story at hand. There are academic studies of the uses of sources,

but not very many (Hallin, Manoff, and Weddle, 1993; Steele, 1995). The ones I know assess relatively small samples of media, but they are then able to be nuanced (and interesting) in assessing the strengths and weaknesses of the sourcing patterns they find. It would be a safe bet that the reason there are relatively few studies is that they are hard to do! They cannot be done well from the text of the news outlet alone but require background knowledge or additional research to identify just who are the sources the media rely on. More familiar and more common are studies, often undertaken by advocacy media criticism groups, of the political affiliation or gender of guests on television news shows. Such studies are easier to do, and they can be done much more comprehensively because the news shows one might want to study are few and guests typically appear one at a time.

Finally, a condition of the adequacy of the media for democracy would surely have to be that journalists have access to relevant government information and relevant information from or about other institutions that exercise power in society. Moreover, the general public needs to have adequate access to the news media. Does a large percentage of the population (approaching 100 percent of adults) have relatively convenient and relatively inexpensive access to the Internet, television and radio news, and newspapers and magazines? Ideally, people would have such access in their homes and also in public facilities (like schools and libraries). Access would be simple, widespread, unsupervised, and unrestrained by surveillance or public fear of surveillance. Does a large percentage of the population (approaching 100 percent of adults) have sufficient education, literacy, and background political knowledge to make sense of news?

When we can give serious attention to all of these questions, we will be able to say we have a normative understanding of the role of the news media in democracies. We should not assume that news institutions are the same or should be the same across different democracies, or across all news organizations within a single democracy, nor that the institutions central to one democracy must be central to another (apart from regular elections, competition among two or more parties, the constitutional protection of minority rights, the rule of law, and constitutional guarantees for freedom of speech, press, and association—and the specific forms of even these essential features may differ substantially from one country to the next). Nor should we assume that one of the seven (or more) functions the news media serve in democracies is paramount, but rather that each makes an important contribution of its own. And we will certainly not assume, in this era of a rapidly changing informational environment, that there is or ever was a One True Journalism from which all democratic blessings flow.

NOTES

1. This list is a revised and condensed version of what was originally published as "Six or Seven Things News Can Do for Democracy" in Schudson (2008, 11–26).
2. Kateb (1992, 36–56) is a brilliant account of what makes representative democracy a moral improvement over "assembly democracy" or participatory democracy.

REFERENCES

Broersma, M. 2007. Visual strategies: Dutch newspaper design between text and image 1900–2000. In M. Broersma (Ed.), *Form and style in journalism* (pp. 177–207). Leuven, Netherlands: Peeters.

Chalaby, J. 1996. Journalism as an Anglo-American invention. *European Journal of Communication* 11: 303–326.

Clayman, S., Heritage, J., Elliott, M., and McDonald, L. 2007. When does the watchdog bark? Conditions of aggressive questioning in presidential news conferences. *American Sociological Review* 72: 23–41.

Clayman, S., Elliott, M., Heritage, J., and Becket, M. 2010. A watershed in White House journalism: Explaining the post-1968 rise of aggressive presidential news. *Political Communication* 27: 229–247.

Darnton, R. 2000. An early information society: News and the media in eighteenth-century Paris. *American Historical Review* 105: 1–35.

Hallin, D., Manoff, R., and Weddle, J. K. 1993. Sourcing patterns of national security reporters. *Journalism Quarterly* 70: 753–766.

Hallin, D. C., and Mancini, P. 2004. *Comparing media systems*. Cambridge, UK: Cambridge University Press.

Jeffrey, R. 2010. *India's newspaper revolution*. 3rd ed. New Delhi: Oxford University Press.

Kateb, G. 1992. The moral distinctiveness of representative democracy. In G. Kateb, *The Inner Ocean*, 36–56. Ithaca, NY: Cornell University Press.

Keane, J. 1991. *The media and democracy*. Cambridge, UK: Polity Press.

Keane, J. 2009. *The life and death of democracy*. London: Simon & Schuster.

Kovach, W., and Rosentiel, T. 2007. *The elements of journalism*. New York: Three Rivers Press.

Lemann, N. 2011. Personal communication.

Manin, B. 1997. *The principles of representative government*. Cambridge, UK: Cambridge University Press.

Raz, J. 1994. *Ethics in the public domain*. Oxford: Clarendon Press.

Schudson, M. 2008. *Why democracies need an unlovable press*. Oxford: Polity Press.

Schudson, M. 2010. Political observatories, databases and news in the emerging ecology of public information. *Daedalus* 139: 100–109.

Steele, J. 1995. Experts and the operational bias of television news: The case of the Persian Gulf War. *Journalism and Mass Communication Quarterly* 72: 799–812.

POLITICAL DISCOURSE: HISTORY, GENRES, AND THE CONSTRUCTION OF MEANING

....

CHAPTER 8

NOT A FOURTH ESTATE BUT A SECOND LEGISLATURE

....

RODERICK P. HART AND REBECCA LAVALLY

INTRODUCTION

EVERYONE has an opinion about political news, and for good reason: (1) it is political and (2) it is news. Because it is political, it trades in power—who has it and who does not— and that reminds us that life is unfair. Because the news is news—because it features an ever-changing tableau—it reminds us that problems persist and that the future is vexingly uncertain. So political news can include the salacious and is sometimes reviled even when consumed voraciously. Political news fills up our days—during the morning commute, at the office water cooler, via iPhone and Facebook news feeds. Even those who detest political news cannot get enough of it.

Oddly, though, not enough is known about political news. What, for example, makes some people Fox news addicts? How do those who refrain from reading a newspaper learn what is going on? Can citizens really trust the news or is it partisan to the core? Are reportorial norms changing with the advent of the new media? We know that better-informed citizens vote regularly and become more involved in civic activities, but what is it about the news that drives them to the voting booth or the soup kitchen? The news is all around us—always and inevitably—and yet it remains a stranger to us.

THE PURPOSE OF THIS ESSAY

This essay highlights some of the scholarly literature on political news, focusing specifically on its linguistic qualities. To be sure, the popularity of television news and web-based videos quickly reminds us that language is only part of the news story. But language remains central to journalism because even dramatic pictures can overwhelm us with their ambivalence and multivalence. So we must inspect language to find the story behind the news story—why it was told in a particular way and why consumers reacted as they did. To address these questions, we here examine the linguistic scaffold upon which the news is erected.

PRIOR RESEARCH

Some years ago, Hart (2000) identified four functions served by news coverage of political events, each of which was associated with specific linguistic markers. To wit: (1) *the disciplinary function*—compared with other rhetorical entities, news is reliably negative, in part because it is heavily infused with polling stories, a normative choice that inevitably features disagreements among the American people rather than their common aspirations; (2) *the energizing function*—the press builds a suggestive and involving narrative that features constant motion among political actors, a set of devices that builds heightened psychic involvement but that may, paradoxically, decrease actual citizen engagement; (3) *the exploratory function*—the news is heavily interpretive—it tells us what events mean—and that makes it seem exhaustive, a quality that distinguishes it from the very careful things that politicians themselves say; (4) *the objectivity function*—popular protestations to the contrary, research has consistently failed to find systematic political biases in news coverage; indeed, the first author's research shows an actual *increase* in "detachment" or objectivity over the years. In short, the news becomes the news by following a predictable rhetorical course.

RECENT RESEARCH

Research published between 2000 and 2010 on political news has been particularly provocative, in part because of the tumultuous events of that decade: In the United States, these included the disputed presidential election of 2000, the war on terror, domestic issues such as abortion and immigration, economic dislocation, and the convergence of old and new media enterprises. Global events have reflected profound turmoil as well, even as social media set the pace of coverage. A news climate under renegotiation, we argue, invites a new metaphor for news—political journalism as a Second Legislature. That is, after examining scholarly studies in the area, we conclude that journalism is not really a Fourth Estate that takes note of occurrences but a far more transactional entity, one that proposes and disposes, proclaims and denounces, and bargains and bargains and bargains. Where can we find evidence for such a claim? In the news text itself. Journalists pick the terms of debate—the words that will be used, advantaging those in power or sometimes those seeking it. If all politics is local, so essentially is *news* of politics, fashioned by reporters in constituents' vernacular. Although a legislature barters among powerful interests, it must heed disaffection at the grassroots. News, like legislation, reveals where the influence lies. Specifically, we find six ways in which journalism acts as a quintessentially political entity and as a Second Legislature.

By Being a Vessel of Accommodation

Journalists actively negotiate how to discuss political torture and international threats. Jones and Sheets (2009) report that US news accounts often characterized the infamous treatment of prisoners by American troops at Abu Ghraib as abuse or mistreatment, while German, Italian, and Spanish journalists called it torture. In between, although a bit closer to the American characterization, were those of the Australian, British, and Canadian press. In the aftermath of the 2001 terrorist attacks on the World Trade Center in New York City and the Pentagon, for example, American broadcasters and print reporters—as well as newspaper editorials—echoed President George W. Bush's oft-repeated themes of *September 11* and *external threats*. Yet these outlets paid far less attention to Bush's oft-voiced associations between *evil* and Iraq's *Saddam Hussein* (John, Domke, Coe, and Graham, 2007). Two contrasting explanations for the media's apparent aversion to the term *evil*, both of which are grounded in notions of a bargaining press, have been offered by Sue Lockett John and her colleagues (2007). On one hand, they say, journalists may have considered the word to be excessively inflammatory. On the other, there may have been a strong presumption that calling Saddam evil was not particularly newsworthy in and of itself.

In other words, there is some evidence that the press tries to balance popular constructions of current events with the preferred understandings of the regime in power. In another study related to the Bush administration's war on terror, Erjavec (2009) reports that Slavic news media moved from portraying Islamics positively as an *us* group in 1995 to emphasizing revocations of Islamic citizenship in a global antiterror campaign against *them* in 2007. Sometimes this sort of shift involves appropriation of a given administration's preferred locutions. For example, in explaining his decision to bomb Yugoslavia in 1999, President Bill Clinton compared the slaughter then occurring in Kosovo to the Holocaust of World War II. Clinton's analogy was repeated on more than 200 US broadcasts and in more than 300 articles published in the top 50 US newspapers during the week of the American bombings (Bates, 2009). This kind of political echoing may be a natural out-of-consciousness response by reporters to changing linguistic fashion. But even if that is the case, such forms of imitation carry parapolitical resonance as well.

Along these same lines, a study comparing terminology for the human embryo during congressional deliberations on banning late-term abortions in *New York Times* coverage found that use of the word *baby* by members of the US House of Representatives "significantly predicts [its] usage in news content" (Simon and Jerit, 2007, 261). These linguistic choices matter, Simon and Jerit assert, because surveys suggest that exclusive use of *baby* or *fetus* in news articles can significantly influence public support for or against such a ban. These are mere words, perhaps, but they connect to mere attitudes which, in many cases, can be linked to mere policies.

At times, the news can even reflect a kind of "public diplomacy," a function normally relegated to governmental entities. Cheng's (2002) analysis of news accounts from CNN.com and ChinaOnline.com revealed that successful talks to resolve a spy-plane crisis between the United States and China in 2001 evolved through stages linked to the appearance of the face-saving word *if*. Naturally, members of the press—staunch defenders of objectivity that they are—would scoff at the notion that they had unknowingly become adjuncts to the government in power. But words are empirical things and word traces are discoverable. To imagine that reporters are, to some extent, unwitting agents of a political system in which they have been raised hardly seems strange, especially when examined from a distance.

By Prioritizing Nativist Agendas

Although journalists often see themselves as doyens of the cosmopolitan, they frequently become localist in orientation. Studies find, for example, that the news text often contains within it subtle and not-so-subtle signals of nationalism. Linguistic modifiers describing a Danish newspaper's 2005 publication of controversial cartoon images of the Prophet Mohammed, for example, grew increasingly negative as the news source moved from Western-generated reports to Arabian news outlets (Hakam, 2009). Too, Murata (2007) found a markedly different lexicon in newspaper stories about whaling published in Great Britain, a former whaling nation now critical of the practice, and those published in Japan, which continues to welcome the whaling industry. The British press quoted British officials denouncing Japanese seafaring practices and seldom published contrasting views, Murata reports. Word choice and syntax in the British coverage excoriated Japanese agents for carrying out dreadful acts against these giants of the sea, animals inevitably described as passive victims of a heartless and unthinking commercial enterprise. Conversely, Japanese articles on whaling were "characterized by brevity and a factual tone with little loaded or provocative lexis." Supportive background information made these latter stories "sound relatively objective," Murata reports (2007, 755), implying that politics rarely stops at the water's edge.

The politics of news coverage can also take on characteristics of a super-, even tribal, politics. Consider, for example, the issues of gender and ethnicity. Feature articles about women entrepreneurs in India, for example, used adjectival phrases—*nimble fingers, aesthetic touch, tall frame, fine-boned face,* and *flowing tresses*—to stress a kind of feminized entrepreneurship (Iyer, 2009, 248). In Germany, Johnson and Suhr (2003) discovered that terms described in the conservative German newspaper *Die Welt* as "politically correct" or "politically incorrect" clearly mirrored the nation's postwar struggle to define its national identity. In another study comparing how Scottish newspapers and a selection of UK and English newspapers covered Scottish parliamentary elections, Higgins

(2004) found more locational references in the Scottish papers, perhaps reflecting that nation's more ambiguous national status and even a village-centric imaginary.

Such location-based attitudes and assumptions become especially apparent during times of strife. So, for example, a computerized analysis of word groupings in US and UK newspapers revealed dissimilar patterns in the coverage of terrorism. While US papers focused on specific events, British journalists took a more global stance, portraying terrorism "as a complex condition" (Papacharissi and de Fatima Oliveira, 2008, 64). Within the United States, too, newspapers reflected differences grounded in locale. The *New York Times* placed emphasis on those who participated in the unfolding terrorist drama—the flesh-and-blood people who were its perpetrators and its victims. In the nation's capital, in contrast, the *Washington Post*'s coverage stressed different words— *combatant, enemy, Islamic, radical, policy, Geneva Convention*—thereby providing a policy orientation to events that the *New York Times* had made social and psychological.

By Reproducing Regnant Power Dynamics

If read with sufficient subtlety, the news text often tells us who is influential and who is not, which views hold sway and which have gone by the boards. Xinhua News Agency, the official press service of the People's Republic of China, shifted how it used the word *boss* between 1978 and 1989, an adaptation paralleling China's governmental and cultural change from a politically oriented, prereform Marxism to a postreform, proeconomic posture (Pan, 2009). It is also the case that the news frequently superimposes dominant frames on subgroups whose self-understandings may be quite different. In northern Scandinavia, we are told, indigenous Arctic peoples prefer to be called *Sami* and yet are described in Finnish newspapers as *Lapps, natives, a group of Northern people, nomads,* or *tribesmen*. These terms, Pietikäinen (2003) observes, reflect the Sami's organizational challenges and imply an inadequate political cohesion. So, for example, articles in *Helsingin Sanomat*, a leading Finnish newspaper, discursively placed the Sami and Finnish at opposite poles by representing Sami rights as an *unsettled issue*, something *struggled for* and *struggled over*. Meanwhile, "the state, various ministries, boards or committees were frequently represented as *doing, changing* and *challenging* these rights" (Pietikäinen, 604, italics in original).

Paul Baker (2010), in analyzing Islam-related articles published before and after 9/11 in a dozen British newspapers, found that tabloids—which unerringly focused on British interests—employed an emotionally laden vocabulary centered on religious extremism in referring to Muslims. In contrast, broadsheets, newspapers having a more international outlook, used less passionate language and took a more restrained political stance. Ironically, though, because the broadsheets placed Muslims in a wider geopolitical context, Muslim-related wars and violence were featured more prominently, thereby creating a Hobbesian choice for Muslims—to be seen as mindless religious zealots or as war-mongering opportunists.

Reporters, consciously or unconsciously, sometimes characterize groups in debilitating ways. An analysis of *Los Angeles Times* stories during a 1994 California debate over denying public services to illegal immigrants, for example, found immigrants described as *quarry being hunted* by federal agents or *lured* by employers who *hungered* for low-wage workers (Santa Ana, 1999, 200–201). In New Zealand, a study of newspaper articles on political conflicts involving indigenous Polynesian people found that journalists sometimes described groups challenging dominant positions as *radical*, thereby giving a political inflection to processes that might otherwise have been described in didactic or academic terms (Phelan and Shearer, 2009). The authors report that New Zealand's mainstream newspapers were also inclined to make *activist* a left-leaning assignation even though the term is relatively open ended in its original construction.

All of this is not to say that the press is inevitably establishmentarian or colonialist, even though its readers (not to mention its advertisers and government overseers) may be both. One often finds progressive overtones in reportage. Headlines in three major Taiwanese newspapers, for instance, have increasingly mingled the words of different languages and dialects across a span of two decades, thereby showcasing a fresh political dynamic. English, Japanese, and Cantonese, reports Kuo (2009), were often mixed with the predominant Mandarin to reflect "an emerging new Taiwan identity, which can be characterized by multilingualism, multiculturalism, and multiple identities" (239).

By Emphasizing Traditionalist Values

Stereotypically, the press is seen as a goad to the current political order, an entity that comforts the afflicted and afflicts the comfortable. Scholarly research, however, finds a more complicated pattern. Institutional priorities are often emphasized (Ferree, Gamson, Gerhards, and Rucht, 2002) and governmental viewpoints sanitized (John, Domke, Coe, and Graham, 2007). In analyzing pro and con abortion discourse in elite American and German newspapers across a span of twenty-four years, Ferree (2002) and her colleagues found that inflammatory language was attributed to just 5 percent or fewer of German and US speakers, thereby "normalizing" centrist attitudes. "Hot button" words likely to outrage opponents such as *murder, persecution,* or *barbarity* were often eschewed, as were extreme expressions of incivility. Especially in the elite press, traditional behavioral patterns were reinforced (outright or subtly), suggesting "a norm that journalists feel an obligation to uphold" (239). When reporters did quote obstreperous personalities, they typically compensated by also including "legislative or government speakers" who decried "the use of such inflammatory language" (244).

At other times, the press resists "progressivist" tendencies entirely, turning to long-accepted norms to describe novel political personalities and relationships. American journalists during the 2008 Democratic presidential primaries seldom labeled Obama, son of a black African father and a white American mother, as *biracial* or *multiracial*, a finding determined by computer-assisted analysis of words and phrases in major US publications (Squires and Jackson, 2010, 380). Variations on the word *racial* were printed more frequently than *racism* or *racist*, possibly because the latter words suggested that *structural* problems related to race still existed in the United States. Referenced least often in these publications were phrases like *racial discrimination* and *racial profiling*, further suppressing "discussion and/or acknowledgment of the material, social, and political impacts of racism" in American political reporting (Squires and Jackson, 2010, 383).

On still other occasions, the news can appear downright protectionist when the civil order seems threatened. Neighborhood protests in Great Britain targeted homes of convicted and suspected pedophiles in 2000 after the *News of the World* published names and addresses of sex offenders in a controversial campaign to expose the whereabouts of released sex criminals. Coverage of the protests by more than three-dozen British newspapers contained over fifty references to *mob* and more than twenty to *mob rule* (Drury, 2002). Rarely was the more neutral term *crowd* used to describe the gatherings, aimed at forcing pedophiles, in particular, to move elsewhere. Drury argues that these semantic choices stand as evidence of the press's silent repudiation of disorder and unlawfulness and, further, its persistent attempt to uphold traditional British sensibilities. Sometimes, says Drury (48), metaphors of *fire* were also used in describing popular protest movements, a device implying that they were "easily liable to turn to indiscriminate destruction."

By Emphasizing Proletarian Attitudes

Can the press be both master and slave, both patrician and plebian? After all, if it is a protolegislative body, it must constantly be ready to address multiple constituencies, to tilt in one direction today, in another tomorrow. So, for example, the news is often earnestly populist in tone, deploying everyday metaphors to make things clear and compelling. Jennifer Jerit (2006) studied the differential use of fifty-three words associated with Social Security debates in the United States. Specifically, she compared how often and in what context they were used by elected officials compared to print and broadcast coverage. Three words—*save, reform,* and *fix*—were used in nearly 70 percent of the officeholders' rhetoric. In contrast, Jerit's media sample contained less sober phraseology in an attempt to extend the "reach" of the debate to the common person. Jerit (2006, 22) found the press using dramatic words such as *run out of money, bankrupt, shortfall,* and *repair*—which were more likely to expose the grassroots implications of a looming crisis.

Researchers have found several other ways in which the press includes "pedestrian" codes in its reportage. For example, British, German, and US television news programs dramatize election coverage with metaphors of *war, sports,* and *contestation,* subtle ways of showing how politics is relevant to everyday life. Too, Scheithauer (2007) found that broadcasters frequently compared elections to a *journey*, a universally shared experience of transition and change. Jameson and Entman (2004) discovered that the press often uses *game* metaphors to describe politics, sometimes stressing that certain budget items were *on* or *off* the table. By stressing the adversarial nature of politics, observe Jameson and Entman, reporters not only amp up political interest in their audiences but also acclimate voters to the win-loss nature of political life (as opposed, say, to its accommodating possibilities).

Geoffrey Baym (2010), in his book *From Cronkite to Colbert: The Evolution of Broadcast News*, argues that broadcast journalism's central metaphor shifted from one of a *searchlight* illuminating politics' dark recesses (during the Watergate era) to one of a *floodlight* dousing all political actors (during the Monica Lewinsky scandal). These shifting metaphors of light, says Baym, point up transitions from the earnest, dispassionate press of the old network era to today's multichanneled, highly personal media promising complete transparency of all things political.

The proletarian aspects of news coverage are also revealed when hard news and soft news are compared, with factual reportage dominating the former and mythic invocations the latter. An examination of 180 articles (including editorials and letters) in the *Chicago Tribune* concerning a 2007 debate over declaring English the official US language revealed narratives of assimilation in soft news and opinion pieces that were absent from hard-news accounts. Phrases such as *my grandparents, my ancestors,* and *previous generations* relayed seemingly irrefutable myths of assimilation, thereby inscribing both the emancipatory and inclusionary possibilities of US citizenship (Tardy, 2009, 280).

By Being Presentistic in Orientation

An enlightened legislature takes the long view of issues, consulting the past to better understand the present. Equally often, however, public officials are expedient to the core. Reading a newspaper can also be a study in provisional biases and transitory understandings of the political order. A content analysis of US newspapers from 1981 through 2003, for example, reveals that the meaning of *Judeo-Christian* has changed dramatically from earlier in the twentieth century (Hartmann, Zhang, and Wischstadt, 2005). At one time, the term evoked "fairly liberal connotations of expanding social boundaries to include minority groups and affirm church-state separation" (223). More conservative social and political stances are now being implied, the researchers report, with *Judeo-Christian* being "deployed in the context of culture-wars–type debates about morality and cultural preservation" (223).

Such research suggests that news coverage may no longer provide the kind of cultural anchor it offered in times past. For instance, popular calls for stricter immigration and asylum controls are now more likely to be questioned by Britain's broadsheets than by its tabloids, Baker and his colleagues (2008) have determined. They find that broadsheets used the phrase *pose as* in positive contexts about refugees, asylum seekers, immigrants, and migrants almost twelve times more often than did the tabloids, which took "a predominantly negative stance." In another British study, a computer-assisted analysis found that the term *politically incorrect* and related terms were used during the 1990s to characterize gaps between the promises of the Left and actual life on the street. Conservative factions, on the other hand, were not subjected to similarly dismissive labels (Johnson, Culpeper, and Suhr, 2003). In other words, news coverage can sometimes become a compass—objectively telling us which way to go—and sometimes a weathervane—subjectively telling us which way the wind is blowing.

A sample of major American newspapers between 1991 and 2004 showed that politicians were labeled *conservative* more often than *liberal*, according to Eisinger, Veenstra, and Koehn (2007). They suggest, however, that these appellations were more a function of political pragmatics than journalistic bias. The authors point to an influx of congressional conservatives in 1994, which brought forth an attendant "political pejorativization of the word *liberal*" (Eisinger et al., 2007, 17). Negative associations with the term *liberal* may have inhibited Democrats from identifying themselves as such even as Republicans were proudly calling themselves *conservatives*. In other words, reporters not only *reflect* changing cultural mores but, by reflecting them, sometimes also *reinscribe* them. Over time, perhaps, these constantly updated labels may balance leftist and rightist leanings, but that brings small comfort to at least two constituencies: (1) news consumers who expect more from journalism than sheer presentism, and (2) political interest groups who are linguistically out of favor at a given point in time. In a perfect world, then, the news should be *new* without glorifying the *transient*. Understanding that distinction is what makes great journalism great journalism.

Conclusion

Political journalists, then, legislate the news. Serving not as a Fourth Estate of dispassionate onlookers but as a Second Legislature of engaged debaters, they negotiate, vacillate, accommodate. Reporters construct political events by weighing popular notions against officially preferred interpretations, by favoring local attitudes and assumptions over the distant. Their dominant story frames may isolate or overpower the same subgroups dismissed by legislators. Journalists stand guard against disorder, giving sway to institutional priorities and even sanitizing government views. Yet, like any functional legislating body, the press is not the same all of the time. Journalism can be a cultural bellwether, capable of farsightedness and inclusion. Although it might lean one way today, it may change direction tomorrow given its populist bent on connecting with everyday people. Its currency is not votes but metaphors, liberally applied to foster relevance and nurture myth. Like a legislature, the political press may resist change or facilitate it.

Perhaps it seems heretical to describe the news in such crude political terms. Viewing journalism as an institution devoted to cutting the best possible deal—of hewing this way, then that—can seem dismissive of the men and women in the press who struggle each day, sometimes at considerable personal risk, to enlighten the body politic. But those same traits—the daily struggle, accepting risks, advancing the commonweal—also apply to those who make our laws and suffer opprobrium as a result. To conceive of the press as a Second Legislature cannot possibly be an affront unless one also assumes that politics itself is eternally corrupt. We make no such assumption here. In describing reporters as legislators, we bestow upon them one of the highest compliments a democracy can pay to its various sectors and citizens.

References

Baker, P. 2010. Representations of Islam in British broadsheet and tabloid newspapers 1999–2005. *Journal of Language and Politics* 9(2): 310–338. doi: 10.1075/jlp.9.2.07bak

Baker, P., Gabrielatos, C., KhosraviNik, M., Krzyżanowski, M., McEnery, T., and Wodak, R. 2008. A useful methodological synergy? Combining critical discourse analysis and corpus linguistics to examine discourses of refugees and asylum seekers in the U.K. press. *Discourse & Society*, 19(3): 273–306. doi: 10.1177/0957926508088962

Bates, B. R. 2009. Circulation of the World War II/Holocaust analogy in the 1999 Kosovo intervention: Articulating a vocabulary for international conflict. *Journal of Language and Politics* 8(1): 28–51. doi: 10.1075/jlp.8.1.03bat

Baym, G. 2010. *From Cronkite to Colbert: The evolution of broadcast news.* Boulder, CO: Paradigm.

Cheng, M. 2002. The standoff—What is unsaid? A pragmatic analysis of the conditional marker "if." *Discourse & Society* 13(3): 309–317. doi: 10.1177/0957926502013003050

Drury, J. 2002. "When the mobs are looking for witches to burn, nobody's safe": Talking about the reactionary crowd. *Discourse & Society* 13(1): 41–73. doi: 10.1177/0957926502013001003

Eisinger, R. M., Veenstra, L. R., and Koehn, J. P. 2007. What media bias? Conservative and liberal labeling in major U.S. newspapers. *Harvard International Journal of Press/Politics* 12(1): 17–36. DOI: 10.1177/1081180X06297460

Erjavec, K. 2009. The "Bosnian war on terrorism." *Journal of Language and Politics* 8(1): 5–27. doi: 10.1075/jlp.8.1.02erj

Ferree, M. M., Gamson, W.A., Gerhards, J., and Rucht, D. 2002. *Shaping abortion discourse: Democracy and the public sphere in Germany and the United States.* Cambridge, UK: Cambridge University Press.

Hakam, J. 2009. The "cartoons controversy": A critical discourse analysis of English-language Arab newspaper discourse. *Discourse & Society* 20(1): 33–57. doi: 10.1177/0957926508097094

Hart, R.P. 2000. *Campaign talk: Why elections are good for us.* Princeton, NJ: Princeton University Press.

Hartmann, D., Zhang, X., Wischstadt, W. 2005. One multicultural nation under God? Changing uses and meanings of the term "Judeo-Christian" in the American media. *Journal of Media and Religion* 4(4): 207–234.

Higgins, M. 2004. Putting the nation in the news: The role of location formulation in a selection of Scottish newspapers. *Discourse & Society* 15(5): 633–648. doi: 10.1177/0957926504045035

Iyer, R. 2009. Entrepreneurial identities and the problematic of subjectivity in media-mediated discourses. *Discourse & Society* 20(2): 241–263. doi: 10.1177/0957926508099004

Jameson, J. K., and Entman, R. M. 2004. The role of journalism in democratic conflict management: Narrating the New York budget crisis after 9/11. *Harvard International Journal of Press/Politics* 9(2): 38–59. doi: 10.1177/1081180X03262443

Jerit, J. 2006. Reform, rescue, or run out of money? Problem definition in the Social Security reform debate. *Harvard International Journal of Press/Politics* 11(1): 9–28. doi: 10.1177/1081180X05283781

John, S. L., Domke, D., Coe, K., and Graham, E. S. 2007. Going public, crisis after crisis: The Bush administration and the press from September 11 to Saddam. *Rhetoric & Public Affairs* 10(2): 195–220.

Johnson, S., Culpeper, J., and Suhr, S. 2003. From "politically correct councillors" to "Blairite nonsense": Discourses of "political correctness" in three British newspapers. *Discourse & Society* 14(1): 29–47. doi: 10.1177/0957926503014001928

Johnson, S. and Suhr, S. 2003. From "political correctness" to "politische Korrektheit": Discourses of "PC" in the German newspaper, *Die Welt. Discourse & Society* 14(1): 49–68. doi: 10.1177/0957926503014001929

Jones, T. M., and Sheets, P. 2009. Torture in the eye of the beholder: Social identity, news coverage, and Abu Ghraib. *Political Communication* 26: 278–295. doi: 10.1080/10584600903053460

Kuo, S. 2009. Multilingualism, multiculturalism, and multiple identities: Analyzing linguistic hybridization in Taiwanese newspaper headlines. *Journal of Asian Pacific Communication* 19(2): 239–258. doi: 10.1075/japc.19.2.05kuo

Murata, K. 2007. Pro- and anti-whaling discourses in British and Japanese newspaper reports in comparison: A cross-cultural perspective. *Discourse & Society* 18(6): 741–764. doi: 10.1177/0957926507082194

Pan, J. 2009. Mediating ideology and cultural realities: The changing meaning of "boss" in China's Xinhua News, 1978–1989. *Journalism Studies* 10(6): 805–820. doi: 10.1080/14616700902975038

Papacharissi, Z., and de Fatima Oliveira, M. 2008. News frames terrorism: A comparative analysis of frames employed in terrorism coverage in U.S. and U.K. newspapers. *Harvard International Journal of Press/Politics* 13(1): 52–74. doi: 10.1177/1940161207312676

Phelan, S., and Shearer, F. 2009. The "radical," the "activist" and the hegemonic newspaper articulation of the Aotearoa New Zealand foreshore and seabed conflict. *Journalism Studies*, 10(2): 220–237. doi: 10.1080/14616700802374183

Pietikäinen, S. 2003. Indigenous identity in print: Representations of the Sami in news discourse. *Discourse & Society* 14(5): 581–609. doi: 10.1177/09579265030145003

Santa Ana, O. 1999. "Like an animal I was treated": Anti-immigrant metaphor in US public discourse. *Discourse & Society* 10(2): 191–224. doi: 10.1177/0957926599010002004

Scheithauer, R. 2007. Metaphors in election night television coverage in Britain, the United States and Germany. In A. Fetzer and G. E. Lauerbach (Eds.), *Political discourse in the media: Cross-cultural perspectives* (pp. 75–106). Amsterdam and Philadelphia: John Benjamins.

Squires, C. R., and Jackson, S. J. 2010. Reducing race: News themes in the 2008 primaries. *Harvard International Journal of Press/Politics* 15(4): 375–400. doi: 10.1177/1940161210372962

Simon, A. F., and Jerit, J. 2007. Toward a theory relating political discourse, media, and public opinion. *Journal of Communication* 57: 254–271. doi: 10.1111/j.1460-2466.2007.00342.x

Tardy, C. M. 2009. "Press 1 for English": Textual and ideological networks in a newspaper debate on US language policy. *Discourse & Society* 20(2): 265–286. doi: 10.1177/0957926508099006

CHAPTER 9

....

PRESIDENTIAL ADDRESS

....

KEVIN COE

IMPORTANCE OF THE AREA

....

MOST observers, if forced to choose, would identify the president of the United States as the single most important political figure in the country, perhaps the world. As such, presidential actions of any kind—from the advisers presidents select, to the policies they support, to the events they attend, to the words they speak—have substantial meaning and importance. Among these actions, speaking to the public is particularly significant because it is a central function—some would argue *the* central function—of the modern presidency. Presidents are expected to address the public regularly to mark momentous occasions, advocate for their preferred legislation, and respond to tragedies or crises. The speeches are not only attempts to persuade but also opportunities to construct a broad American identity that can highlight the common goals and shared interests of a diverse populace (Beasley, 2004; Stuckey, 2004). As Rossiter noted decades ago, the president is the only politician elected by the entire citizenry and thus assumes the role of voice of the people: "The president is the American people's one authentic trumpet, and he has no higher duty than to give a clear and certain sound" (1960, 34).

Scholars interested in presidential address study presidents' performance of this crucial role. Work in this area typically focuses on *how* (the content of the message), *why* (the production of the message), and/or with *what effect* (the consequences of the message) presidents address the public. Traditionally, research focused almost exclusively on oratory, but now includes all manner of presidential communication aimed at the public, including forms that are spoken, written, or visual, as well as those that are formal or informal. Scholars of communication—particularly those trained in the rhetorical tradition—and political scientists have produced the bulk of this scholarship, though historians and others have also made considerable contributions (for a history of research in this area, see Medhurst, 2008).

Scholars who analyze presidential address often do so because they believe it has substantial consequences for those who encounter it—presidential rhetoric *matters*, the argument goes. Leaving aside for a moment the question of whether presidential address has observable effects on the media or the public (a question taken up in the second section), it is clear that presidential address does indeed matter. Campbell (2005) has observed that rhetors are key "points of articulation," "inventors" who give voice to a variety of competing forces at work in a single moment of rhetorical action. Accordingly, presidents' public communications are an amalgam of various perspectives and influences (e.g., they reflect concerns about public sentiment, decisions about media suitability, and the closed-door negotiations of various members of the executive). Close examination of these communications can provide insight into the confluence of these forces during a particular historical moment. In a world that is increasingly constructed via public communication—a vast array of mediated discourse in particular—it is as important as ever to understand how presidents use language to navigate and shape the political environment.

Major Findings

Countless studies have examined presidential address, with a particularly substantial body of work focusing on twentieth- and twenty-first-century presidents (for extended reviews at three different points in history, see Aune and Medhurst, 2008; Stuckey and Antczak, 1998; Windt, 1984). The irony is that this extensive area of research lends itself to few generalizations because much of the research in this area, though certainly not all of it, is based on case studies of key speeches, presidents, or eras. As the National Task Force on the Theory and Practice of the Rhetorical Presidency observed, "Case studies of rhetorical practice comprise a substantial amount, if not a majority, of the research. . . . [O]ur attention as a field remains centrally on the case" (2008, 345). By design, then, much of the scholarship on presidential address seeks to illuminate what makes a given speech, president, or era *different* from other speeches, presidents, or eras. It comes as no surprise that there is considerable variation in the patterns these studies uncover.

If there is an overarching framework that pulls research in this area together, it is the "rhetorical presidency." Initially conceptualized by Ceaser, Thurow, Tulis, and Bessette (1981), then developed and popularized by Tulis (1987), the rhetorical presidency argument holds that the presidency of the twentieth century—especially since the Woodrow Wilson administration—has differed from the presidency of past centuries. Central among the differences is in that century speaking directly to the public, and making policy appeals in these speeches, became a primary and valued form of leadership in a way it had not previously been. The role of the president thus became less about being head of state and more about being a constant campaigner for public attention and support. This, in turn, changed the institution of the presidency itself. Numerous other major works have identified similar patterns in presidential address, drawing out different nuances but all indicating the increasing importance of public communications to the modern presidency (e.g., Hart, 1987; Hinckley, 1990). Kernell (2007), for instance, identified a pattern in which modern presidents "go public" to gain support for their policies. By appealing directly to the American people, presidents hope to use popular support to encourage other political leaders to fall in line behind presidential policy.

Several scholars have critiqued the idea of the "rhetorical presidency," but rarely do they dispute Tulis's characterization of the modern presidency as a rhetorical one. Rather, they argue that popular leadership through public address has *always* been crucial to the presidency—an "essential constitutional role" of the office (Nichols, 1994; see also Dorsey, 2002; Ellis, 1998). One result of the introduction of this paradigm is that, especially in the decade immediately following its introduction, scholarship on presidential address has been somewhat divided between focusing on the functions of the presidency as an institution (rhetorical presidency) and focusing on the capacity of an individual president to identify the available means of persuasion in a given speaking situation (presidential rhetoric) (Medhurst, 1996; Stuckey and Antczak, 1998).

Among the three components of research on presidential address considered here—how, why, and with what effect presidents communicate with the public—the "how" of presidential rhetoric (i.e., the particulars of its content) has received the most attention from scholars. Generalizing about the specific content of presidential addresses is difficult, as noted, but rhetorical "genres" provide valuable assistance in this respect. A genre is a category of presidential address that has shared contextual features; speeches within a genre thus tend to exhibit similar rhetorical themes. In understanding the genres of presidential address, Campbell and Jamieson's *Deeds Done in Words* (originally published in 1990, then updated and re-titled in 2008) is a singular accomplishment. Undertaking an extensive rhetorical analysis of presidential speech throughout US history, Campbell and Jamieson identify the key genres of presidential address: inaugural addresses; special inaugural addresses (i.e., those of ascendant vice presidents); national eulogies; pardoning rhetoric; state of the union addresses; veto messages; signing statements; presidential war rhetoric; presidential rhetoric of self-defense; the rhetoric of impeachment; and farewell addresses.[1] Each of these genres has characteristics that set it apart from the others, and different presidents speaking in the same genre usually sound themes that are similar, albeit not uniform. Thus genres provide a kind of predictive power, specifying which themes presidents are likely to use in specific speaking circumstances.

Despite the constraints of genre, presidential address often varies across individual presidents and changes over time owing to the different exigencies each president faces. Indeed, even *within* a particular genre, change over time is not uncommon (e.g., Sigelman, 1996). Various studies have identified longitudinal changes in the content of presidential addresses. Some shifts that are especially well documented include increases in the frequency with which presidents address the public (e.g., Hart, 1987); in rhetoric that positions the president symbolically as one with the American people (e.g., Hinckley, 1990; Teten, 2003); and, at least in the last several decades, in moral, religious, and nation-focused rhetoric (e.g., Domke and Coe, 2008; Shogan, 2006). These changes have been accompanied by a decline in intellectualism and an increasingly abstract and conversational tone (e.g., Lim, 2002, 2008).

Intricately tied to the question of how presidents address the public is the question of why they do so; that is, what factors determine the particular rhetorical choices that a president makes when addressing the public? One answer to this question is genre, where the constraints of the office restrict presidents' rhetorical options—and, in turn, presidents' rhetorical choices shape the very institution of the presidency (Campbell and Jamieson, 2008). Numerous other factors are at work as well, many of them unique to the particular historical moment that a president occupies. Among the broader factors that consistently influence presidential speechmaking are changes in the media environment, particularly the growth of television as presidents' primary means of reaching the public (e.g., Jamieson, 1988; Stuckey, 1991); changes in the electorate, such as the political mobilization of previously disengaged groups (e.g., Domke and Coe, 2008); partisan differences among presidents, with some themes used more commonly by one party than the other (e.g., Coe, 2007; Jarvis, 2005); and the various individual characteristics of each president, such as their worldviews, personalities, and leadership styles (e.g., Greenstein, 2004; Winter, 2002). One other important source of presidential rhetoric is the team of speechwriters that generates much of the content for modern presidents' public communications. Although these ghosts undoubtedly do influence presidential rhetoric (e.g., Ritter and Medhurst, 2003; Lim, 2008), it is important to keep in mind that, as Medhurst puts it, presidents are far more than "marionettes who merely mouth the words that others write for them" (2003, 8).

The final element of research on presidential address—one of considerable recent interest to the scholarly community—is the question of effects. Does presidential address matter and, if so, in what ways? Because this is an area of considerable scholarly debate, it is useful to group effects into two general categories: effects on the press and effects on the public. There is greater scholarly consensus that presidents generate the former than the latter. Presidential address is thought to have a considerable, if inconsistent, impact on news coverage. This happens primarily via an agenda-setting process in which a president selects areas of emphasis (e.g., particular policies to pursue), journalists take notice, and the president becomes a key source of quoted material in news stories about that topic (e.g., McDevitt, 1986; Smith and Norris, 1974). Presidents are not unfettered in their ability to drive the agenda and often end up following the lead of news media rather than leading the charge. Nevertheless, US heads of state are a regular focus of news content and, given the right circumstances, can exercise considerable control over the rhetorical themes that show up in news content (e.g., Domke, 2004; Entman, 2004; but see Coe, 2011).

On the question of whether presidential address affects the public, scholars are somewhat divided. To an extent this divide maps onto the disciplinary distinctions present in political communication research: political scientists have been more skeptical of presidents' capacity to influence the public via rhetoric, whereas communication scholars—especially rhetoricians—have largely taken for granted that presidents have such ability. Stuckey and Antczak note that this divide has a long history: political scientists have predominately been interested in communication as "instrumental" (i.e., does it affect surveyed public opinion), but many communication scholars take seriously the "constitutive" aspects of rhetoric, which suggest that "political reality is partly or wholly created from and sustained in rhetoric" (1998, 406).

Substantial fodder for this debate was provided by the publication of Edwards' (2003) *On Deaf Ears: The Limits of the Bully Pulpit*. This work, as the title suggests, argues that presidents are limited in their ability to use rhetoric to directly sway public opinion. The primary critique of this work was that it conceived of effects too narrowly—primarily as significant movement in public attitudes as measured by survey data. Several scholars, including Hart (2008) and Zarefsky (2004), offered rebuttals focusing on the possibility that there are much broader and less easily measured effects of presidential address, such as its ability to define the terms of political debate, shift the public's attention, and alter what is thought to be "common sense" in the political environment. At the same time, culling the extant scholarship does reveal examples of research demonstrating a measurable (by social scientific standards) impact of presidential communication on the public. For example, Druckman and Holmes (2004) demonstrate that presidential rhetoric can prime the public and, in doing so, influence the level of approval it grants the president.[2]

CURRENT ISSUES

The question of effects is central among the current issues in the study of presidential address. The debate that emerged out of the publication of Edwards' work appears to have had a beneficial effect on the field. Those scholars who are convinced that presidential rhetoric matters have been encouraged to think harder about exactly *how*, while also cautioned to avoid the direct causal claims that they sometimes employed carelessly in the past (Zarefsky, 2004). Meanwhile, several recent books—many of which rely on longitudinal data and employ sophisticated empirical techniques—have dug more deeply into exactly when and how presidential address influences the public (e.g., Canes-Wrone, 2006; Rottinghaus, 2010; Wood, 2007). The growing consensus appears to be something of a middle ground. Presidents are sometimes able to find key moments when favorable conditions allow specific messaging strategies to influence the public in very important ways. Nevertheless, they are often quite constrained in what they are able to accomplish. Edwards (2009) himself, in a more recent book, appears to support this view.

A second current issue in the study of presidential address deals with a transformation that is taking place in the nature of the "texts" that scholars work with to study presidential discourse. This issue has two components. In part, the study of presidential address is burgeoning because of the development in the past decade of several online repositories that house nearly every public presidential communication that scholars might hope to analyze (e.g., The American Presidency Project at www.americanpresidency.org and American Rhetoric at www.americanrhetoric.com). Such wide availability of texts—and of new means with which to analyze them (see the fourth section)—has encouraged some scholars to focus their attention on broader patterns across many different speeches and, in some cases, many different presidents (e.g., Domke and Coe, 2008; Lim, 2008). At the same time, what constitutes a presidential address is changing. Rhetoricians have long understood that a "text" has many more components than just the specific words that a president says in a particular moment. With a host of new ways for presidential messages to circulate—via forwarded emails, social networking sites, and an ever more diverse mediascape—these texts, and likely the interpretations of them among different audiences, are changing rapidly. Scholars are still very much wrestling with what this will mean for the study of presidential address.

Finally, scholars of presidential address are coming to grips with the reality that the traditional form of speech with which they have long concerned themselves—the major presidential speech—may cease to be the most familiar and studied form of presidential communication. Looking at the body of scholarship in this area over the past half century, it is clear that the substantial majority of that work focuses on what might be thought of as major presidential addresses (see Coe and Neumann, 2011). These are carefully crafted spoken messages in which the president, without interruption, addresses a large audience (primarily via television since the mid-twentieth century) and receives substantial notice from journalists and the public. Inaugural addresses, state of the union addresses, and a host of other key presidential speeches fit this category. But as the media environment becomes more fragmented, presidents are seeking nontraditional means of reaching audiences. During Barack Obama's first term, for example, the president visited *The Tonight Show with Jay Leno, The Oprah Winfrey Show*, and gave an interview to political commentator Bill O'Reilly during the 2011 Super Bowl pregame show. At the same time, the changing media environment is providing presidents with increased opportunities for "narrowcasting" (Jacobs, 2005) and "going local" (Cohen, 2010). The traditional model of addressing as large an audience as possible is giving way to sophisticated targeting of specific audiences (especially ideologically homogenous groups who are predisposed to react favorably to the message). These changes have potentially profound implications for the production, content, and effects of presidential address, and future researchers will be tasked with making sense of these.

EMPIRICAL APPROACHES

Scholars have employed various methods to understand the different aspects of presidential address, from its content, to the factors that influence the production of that content, to its likely effects. Specific patterns in content, the focus of the largest proportion of the research in this area, have usually been uncovered via one of two approaches. The less common employs quantitative content analysis, identifying key themes and tallying their frequency (e.g., Lim, 2002; Teten, 2003). This approach has the advantages of being able to work with a substantial number of speeches and to specify presidential emphasis quite precisely. Increasingly, scholars are relying on computer programs to undertake such analyses. Though this approach has a long history in the study of presidential address (e.g., Hart, 1984), the growing sophistication of the programs, and the wide availability of presidential texts, has made this approach more feasible and more popular.

The more common approach to understanding the content of presidential address is to engage in a close reading. Rhetorical analysis, discourse analysis, and textual analysis—methods that different scholars understand somewhat differently, but all of which employ qualitative interpretation of a text to make sense of its meaning and import—are all typical approaches, though rhetorical analysis/criticism is far and away the most widely used. Work in this tradition often focuses in great detail on a single speech, single president, or single historical era (e.g., Houck, 2002; Kraig, 2004; Winkler, 2006; Zarefsky, 1986), drawing insights not just from the text but also from the context to interpret the rhetorical choices the speaker made, argue for the suitability of (or problems with) these choices, and explore the possible outcomes these choices might invite. Much of this work thus also directly considers the production of content, examining the decisions that led a certain speech to sound the way it did. Archival research to explore drafts, internal memos, and other documents that shed light on the behind-the-scenes decision-making process is invaluable in this regard. A useful but less common approach to understanding production is to interview speechwriters directly (e.g., Lim 2008).

As for the effects of presidential address, the rhetorical approach does consider effects via the interpretation of a given rhetorical moment. As Zarefsky explains:

> [C]hoices—about such matters as argument selection, framing, phrasing, evidence, organization, and style, as well as about staging, choreography, and other aspects of the presidential performance—are embodied in the text that the rhetor composes and the context in which it is delivered. An audience, also influenced by context, perceives this text, interprets it, participates thereby in determining what it means, and is affected by it. (2004, 609)

In contrast, research that takes a quantitative empirical approach to the study of effects typically conceives of presidential communication as an independent variable and some quantifiable component of media discourse or public perceptions as a dependent variable, employing the typical battery of social scientific methods and statistics to capture effects (e.g., Canes-Wrone, 2006; Rottinghaus, 2010; Wood, 2007). Increasingly this work is able to analyze large bodies of text via sophisticated statistical models, which should ultimately improve scholars' confidence in the evidence brought to bear on the crucial question of what effects presidential address has on the media and the public.

Unanswered Questions

As an area of research interested largely in the particular—in the nuances of a given speech, president, rhetorical genre, or historical era—the study of presidential address will never have a shortage of questions for scholars to tackle. Each new president invariably brings along some previously unasked questions, as well as new answers to the questions that have always drawn researchers' attention: What is the substance of this president's rhetoric? How did the president come to employ these themes as opposed to others? What will be the consequences of this president's rhetorical decisions? Adding to these broad queries, I suggest three more specific issues to which scholars of public address might productively turn their attention in the coming years.

The first has to do with the technological revolution that has swept the United States over the past few decades. Reviewing research on the rhetorical presidency more than a decade ago, Stuckey and Antczak observed: "Whatever the consequences computer technologies may have for democracy, scholars. . . need to develop theories and methods for testing those theories if we are going to understand the rhetorical presidency in an increasingly electronic age" (1998, 425). This is perhaps even truer today than it was then. Many of the key new questions facing scholars of presidential address pertain directly to the role of presidential communications in the new media environment. For example, how will web-based messages and an Internet-based press transform presidential address? Will presidential messaging become almost entirely focused on particular subsets of the populace and, if it does, what will this say about the capacity for presidential address to serve as a primary vehicle for national and cultural identity formation (e.g., Ryfe, 2005; Stuckey, 2004)? How should scholars understand and study messages and audiences in an era when a major presidential speech might draw a smaller audience than a popular reality television program? As scholars explore these questions, they should not assume that technology will change everything; but they should be prepared to assess those changes that do occur, some of which will no doubt have considerable impact.

The second issue has to do with the visual aspects of presidential address. In surveying the field of political communication, Graber (2005) bemoaned the lack of attention to audiovisual material. The same concern might be raised about research on presidential address in particular. This is an area of study that has been, throughout its history, centrally concerned with the spoken word. There is nothing wrong with that—unless that tradition discourages scholars from dealing with the reality that, in the twenty-first century, visuals are too integral to presidential communication to be ignored. Visual rhetoric is a growing area of research that has produced some excellent treatments of visuals vis-à-vis the presidency (e.g., Finnegan, 2005). But much more needs to be done to incorporate the study of visuals centrally into research on presidential address. How, for example, do the words and visuals that presidents present to an audience work together to produce effects? And how might we understand the meaning of presidential addresses more fully if we conceive of them primarily as a text that is both heard and seen? As web-based communications become the norm and audiences increasingly interact directly with video clips of presidential communication, such questions will need answers.

Finally, scholars of presidential address need to think harder about what role theory should play in their research. As an area of study, presidential address has comparatively little engagement with any core set of theories, and does even less in terms of building its own from the findings of its voluminous body of research. Numerous theories of the presidential leadership exist (e.g., Greenstein, 2004; Skowronek, 2011). However, with only a few exceptions (e.g., Cohen, 2010; Rottinghaus, 2010), they do not deal centrally with presidential rhetoric. Those that do tend to focus on the question of effects as opposed to the equally important questions of content and production. The result is that research on presidential address is subject to the charge of being "merely" descriptive.

Being richly descriptive need not be a sign of weakness in an area of research, but a more direct, substantial, and focused engagement with theory would benefit our understandings of presidential address. Consider just the issue of content. Outside of what genres can tell us, there is little extant research that could produce meaningful predictions about the content of presidential address. A theory, or set of theories, that could do so would benefit the field. A clear parallel exists in the content of campaign communication: William Benoit's functional theory of political campaign discourse (see "Functional Theory of Political Campaign Communication" essay) helps predict how presidential candidates will communicate. Similar approaches might be used to understand better the communication of those who attain the office as well. Clearly, theory building need not be the sole focus of scholars who study presidential address, but making it more central than it is at present would be a positive development. Addressing these questions, and generating many others, will ensure that the study of presidential address will retain the intellectual vitality and importance it has had throughout its long history.

NOTES

1. Other works have identified additional genres, many of which are about rhetoric beyond just the presidency and subsume some of the genres identified by Campbell and Jamieson. For example, epideictic/ceremonial rhetoric would encompass, at a minimum, inaugurals, special inaugurals, and farewell addresses. For a broader perspective on how genres function in rhetoric, see Miller (1984).

2. There is also ample empirical evidence that messages matter in presidential campaigns (e.g., Kenski, Hardy, and Jamieson, 2010; Shaw, 1999).

REFERENCES

Aune, J. A., and Medhurst, M. J., Eds. 2008. *The prospect of presidential rhetoric.* College Station: Texas A&M University Press.

Beasley, V. B. 2004. *You, the people: American national identity in presidential rhetoric.* College Station: Texas A&M University Press.

Campbell, K. K. 2005. Agency: Promiscuous and protean. *Communication and Critical/Cultural Studies* 2: 1–19.

Campbell, K. K., and Jamieson, K. H. 2008. *Presidents creating the presidency: Deeds done in words.* Chicago: University of Chicago Press.

Canes-Wrone, B. 2006. *Who leads whom? Presidents, policy, and the public.* Chicago: University of Chicago Press.

Ceaser, J. W., Thurow, G. E., Tulis, J., and Bessette, J. M. 1981. The rise of the rhetorical presidency. *Presidential Studies Quarterly* 11: 158–171.

Coe, K. 2007. The language of freedom in the American presidency, 1933–2006. *Presidential Studies Quarterly* 37: 375–398.

Coe, K. 2011. George W. Bush, television news, and rationales for the Iraq War. *Journal of Broadcasting and Electronic Media* 55: 307–324.

Coe, K., and Neumann, R. 2011. The major addresses of modern presidents: Parameters of a data set. *Presidential Studies Quarterly* 41: 727–751.

Cohen, J. E. 2010. *Going local: Presidential leadership in the post-broadcast age.* New York: Cambridge University Press.

Domke, D. 2004. *God willing?: Political fundamentalism in the White House, the "war on terror," and the echoing press.* London: Pluto Press.

Domke, D., and Coe, K. 2008. *The God strategy: How religion became a political weapon in America.* New York: Oxford University Press.

Dorsey, L. G., Ed. 2002. *The presidency and rhetorical leadership.* College Station: Texas A&M University Press.

Druckman, J. N., and Holmes, J. W. 2004. Does presidential rhetoric matter? Priming and presidential approval. *Presidential Studies Quarterly* 34: 755–778.

Edwards, G. C., III. 2003. *On deaf ears: The limits of the bully pulpit.* New Haven, CT: Yale University Press.

Edwards, G. C., III. 2009. *The strategic president: Persuasion and opportunity in presidential leadership.* Princeton, NJ: Princeton University Press.

Ellis, R. J., Ed. 1998. *Speaking to the people: The rhetorical presidency in historical perspective.* Amherst: University of Massachusetts Press.

Entman, R. M. 2004. *Projections of power: Framing the news, public opinion, and U.S. foreign policy.* Chicago: University of Chicago Press.

Finnegan, C. A. 2005. Recognizing Lincoln: Image vernaculars in nineteenth-century visual culture. *Rhetoric and Public Affairs* 8: 31–58.

Graber, D. A., with Smith, J. M. 2005. Political communication faces the 21st century. *Journal of Communication* 55: 479–507.

Greenstein, F. I. 2004. *The presidential difference: Leadership style from FDR to George W. Bush* (2nd ed.). Princeton, NJ: Princeton University Press.

Hart, R. P. 1984. *Verbal style and the presidency: A computer-based analysis.* Orlando, FL: Academic Press.

Hart, R. P. 1987. *The sound of leadership: Presidential communication in the modern age.* Chicago: University of Chicago Press.

Hart, R. P. 2008. Thinking harder about presidential discourse: The question of efficacy. In J. A. Aune and M. J. Medhurst (Eds.), *The prospect of presidential rhetoric* (pp. 238–248). College Station: Texas A&M University Press.

Hinckley, B. 1990. *The symbolic presidency: How presidents portray themselves.* New York: Routledge.

Houck, D. W. 2002. *FDR and fear itself: The first inaugural address.* College Station: Texas A&M University Press.

Jacobs, L. R. 2005. Communicating from the White House: Presidential narrowcasting and the national interest. In J. D. Aberbach and M. A. Peterson (Eds.), *Institutions of American democracy: The executive branch* (pp. 174–217). New York: Oxford University Press.

Jamieson, K. H. 1988. *Eloquence in an electronic age: The transformation of political speechmaking.* New York: Oxford University Press.

Jarvis, S. E. 2005. *The talk of the party: Political labels, symbolic capital, and American life.* Lanham, MD: Rowman & Littlefield.

Kenski, K., B. W. Hardy, and K. H. Jamieson. 2010. *The Obama victory: How media, money, and message shaped the 2008 election.* New York: Oxford University Press.

Kernell, S. 2007. *Going public: New strategies of presidential leadership* (4th ed.). Washington, DC: CQ Press.

Kraig, R. A. 2004. *Woodrow Wilson and the lost world of the oratorical statesman.* College Station: Texas A&M University Press.

Lim, E. T. 2002. Five trends in presidential rhetoric: An analysis of rhetoric from George Washington to Bill Clinton. *Presidential Studies Quarterly* 32: 328–366.

Lim, E. T. 2008. *The anti-intellectual presidency: The decline of presidential rhetoric from George Washington to George W. Bush.* New York: Oxford University Press.

McDevitt, M. 1986. Ideological language and the press: Coverage of Inaugural, State of the Union addresses. *Mass Communication Review* 13: 18–24.

Medhurst, M. J., Ed. 1996. *Beyond the rhetorical presidency.* College Station: Texas A&M University Press.

Medhurst, M. J., Ed. 2003. Presidential speechwriting: Ten myths that plague modern scholarship. In K. Ritter and M. J. Medhurst (Eds.), *Presidential speechwriting: From the New Deal to the Reagan Revolution and beyond.* (pp. 3–19). College Station: Texas A&M University Press.

Medhurst, M. J., Ed. 2008. From retrospect to prospect: The study of presidential rhetoric, 1915–2005. In J. A. Aune and M. J. Medhurst (Eds.), *The prospect of presidential rhetoric* (pp. 3–27). College Station: Texas A&M University Press.

Miller, C. R. 1984. Genre as social action. *Quarterly Journal of Speech* 70: 151–167.

National Task Force on the Theory and Practice of the Rhetorical Presidency. 2008. Report of the National Task Force on the Theory and Practice of the Rhetorical Presidency. In In J. A. Aune and M. J. Medhurst (Eds.), *The prospect of presidential rhetoric* (pp. 340–354). College Station: Texas A&M University Press.

Nichols, D. K. 1994. *The myth of the modern presidency.* University Park: Pennsylvania State University Press.

Ritter, K., and Medhurst, M. J., Eds. 2003. *Presidential speechwriting: From the New Deal to the Reagan Revolution and beyond.* College Station: Texas A&M University Press.

Rossiter, C. 1960. *The American presidency* (2nd ed.). New York: Harcourt, Brace.

Rottinghaus, B. 2010. *The provisional pulpit: Modern presidential leadership of public opinion.* College Station: Texas A&M University Press.

Ryfe, D. M. 2005. *Presidents in culture: The meaning of presidential communication.* New York: Peter Lang.

Shaw, D. R. 1999. The effect of TV ads and candidate appearances on statewide presidential votes, 1988–96. *American Political Science Review* 93: 345–361.

Shogan, C. J. 2006. *The moral rhetoric of American presidents*. College Station: Texas A&M University Press.

Sigelman, L. 1996. Presidential inaugurals: The modernization of a genre. *Political Communication* 13: 81–92.

Skowronek, S. 2011. *Presidential leadership in political time: Reprise and reappraisal* (2nd ed.). Lawrence: University Press of Kansas.

Smith, H. E., Jr., and Norris, L. 1974. *Newsmakers: The press and the presidents*. Reading, MA: Addison-Wesley.

Stuckey, M. E. 1991. *The president as interpreter-in-chief*. Chatham, NJ: Chatham House.

Stuckey, M. E. 2004. *Defining Americans: The presidency and national identity*. Lawrence: University Press of Kansas.

Stuckey, M. E., and Antczak, F. J. 1998. The rhetorical presidency: Deepening vision, widening exchange. *Communication Yearbook* 21: 405–441.

Teten, R. L. 2003. Evolution of the modern rhetorical presidency: Presidential presentation and development of the State of the Union address. *Presidential Studies Quarterly* 33: 333–346.

Tulis, J. K. 1987. *The rhetorical presidency*. Princeton, NJ: Princeton University Press.

Windt, T. O., Jr. 1984. Presidential rhetoric: Definition of a field of study. *Central States Speech Journal* 35: 24–34.

Winkler, C. K. 2006. *In the name of terrorism: Presidents on political violence in the post-World War II era*. Albany: State University of New York.

Winter, D. G. 2002. Motivation and political leadership. In L. O. Valenty and O. Feldman (Eds.), *Political leadership for the new century: Personality and behavior among American leaders* (pp. 25–47). Westport, CT: Praeger.

Wood, B. D. 2007. *The politics of economic leadership: The causes and consequences of presidential rhetoric*. Princeton, NJ: Princeton University Press.

Zarefsky, D. 1986. *President Johnson's war on poverty: Rhetoric and history*. Tuscaloosa: University of Alabama Press.

Zarefsky, D. 2004. Presidential rhetoric and the power of definition. *Presidential Studies Quarterly* 34: 607–619.

CHAPTER 10

···

POLITICAL MESSAGES
AND PARTISANSHIP

···

SHARON E. JARVIS

POLITICAL parties play many important roles in democratic life. These groups organize to gain elected office, control governing processes, mobilize majorities, structure dissent and opposition, recruit future political leaders, socialize voters, and serve as a connection between campaigns and governance. Parties can vary with regard to ideological commitments, elite- and mass-based memberships, and electoral viability. Unless they are forbidden by law, parties have emerged in most systems as the natural evolution of like-minded interests organizing for political influence. Indeed, comparative scholars contend that parties are fixtures of all advanced democracies and can be regarded as a definitive component of a democratic state (Aldrich, 1995; Linz and Stepan, 1996; Schlesinger, 1985; Sorauf and Beck, 1988).

Even though many systems are passionately ambivalent about the conflict fostered by political parties, few are truly nonpartisan. Consider how they developed in the United States. Conspicuously absent in our foundational documents—and warned against in President George Washington's Farewell Address—parties nonetheless formed quickly here. As Aldrich (1995) observes, they emerged naturally around the *fundamental problem* of the desirable size and scope of the burgeoning federal government. Orren (1982, 4) contends that their development is "a remarkable innovation" as "political parties had to battle the personal prejudices of the Founding Fathers" and take hold in a system featuring a "deeper anti-organizational spirit" than other democracies. Nevertheless, parties formed, in Orren's mind, for one simple reason: they were indispensable. As he (1982, 5) writes,

> In no other democracy has there been a greater need for an integrating mechanism like a political party. This need is rooted in two particular characteristics of American politics. First, America retains an archaic, eighteenth century form of government in which power is fragmented within and among many institutions which share authority. The vast number of veto points in this system makes action difficult and

inaction easy. Parties serve as a method for aggregating popular choices, tying these conflicts over courses of action to a broader program, and thus making compromise rather than veto the general form of resolution. Second, the demand for widespread popular participation emerged earlier and has proceeded further in the United States than elsewhere. The American public has achieved a greater voice in political affairs through the steady extension of the franchise, increases in the number of public officials subject to popular approval at the polls, and the involvement of citizens in the selection of party nominees. Political parties are needed to harness the participation of a powerful citizenry and fashion a coherent message out of the din of voices.

Important work in political science explains the indispensability of parties. Indeed, some scholars have advanced seminal research on the parties' *campaign functions*—detailing how they organize elections, collect and spend money, and provide cognitive and psychological shortcuts for voters (Aldrich, 1995; Downs, 1957; Schlesinger, 1985). Others have addressed the parties' *governing functions*—describing how they facilitate legislatures, aggregate interests, create space for bargaining, and reconcile group conflict (Aldrich, 1995; Eldersveld, 1982; Polsby, 1983). Still others have applauded the parties' *stabilizing functions*—acknowledging how strong party systems institutionalize popular control of government and underscoring how parties are hallmarks of all developed democracies (Chambers and Burnham, 1975; Linz and Stepan, 1996; Schmitter and Karl, 1996). Additionally, scholars have taken *historical approaches* in studying critical elections, realignment and dealignment (Burnham, 1965, 1970), and *alternative approaches* in examining third-party candidates and movements (Rosenstone, Behr, and Lazarus, 1984).

Scholars have even engaged in a debate surrounding the *vitality* of parties in the United States (coined both as the *decline of parties* thesis and the *deathwatch*; see Cotter, Gibson, Bibby, and Huckshorn, 1984). Work published between the late 1960s and 1980s has pointed to patterns of party-reform, split-ticket voting, and television viewing as threats to party well-being (Broder, 1972; Wattenberg, 1986, 1992). And research published from the late 1990s to the present contends that "many measures scholars have used as evidence of mass party decline now point to party resurgence" (Hetherington, 2001, 619; Bartels, 2000).

In contrast to the depth of this long-lived tradition of work, scholars have only begun to investigate the parties' *rhetorical functions*—namely, inquiring into the meaning and influence of partisan labels (Hofstadter, 1969; Jarvis, 2005; Sanders, 1988) and the strategy and impact of partisan styles (Benoit, 2004; Petrocik, 1996; Weaver, 1953). For party organizations and their nominees, partisan messages can reveal priorities, highlight objectives, imply political strategies, and offer images of their desired brands (Jarvis, 2005). For the citizenry, partisan messages can serve as a primary means of becoming familiar with and developing opinions about political matters.

This chapter discusses the importance of attending to partisan messages, examines the major findings on the uses and effects of party labels and partisan styles in the United States, addresses unanswered questions in this area, and shows how the talk surrounding parties in the United States, to date at least, underscores their indispensable roles in the polity.

THE IMPORTANCE OF ATTENDING
TO PARTISAN MESSAGES

At least four assumptions justify attending to party labels and party styles. To begin, public communication practices are the primary way modern citizens become involved in public affairs. As Edelman (1964, 1977) put it, people are more likely to experience the language about political events rather than the events themselves. This statement is particularly relevant to political parties, for American voters are more likely to be subjected to the discourse of partisanship than to actual partisan events (e.g., attending party meetings or rallies, studying roll-call votes, or examining campaign donations). How entities are depicted in discourse is influential, Edelman (1971) continues, for political events are often understood through the language used to describe them, and people's understandings of political institutions rest on their beliefs or perceptions of them, whether or not those cognitions are accurate. Thus attending to how party labels and partisan styles have appeared in political discourse should reveal, to paraphrase Burke (1968), how Americans have used such terms and have been used by them as well.

Second, political elites have been credited with managing the meanings of party labels and patterns of partisan communications (Benoit, 2004; Hart, 2000; Jarvis, 2005). Attending to their word choices is important, for as Converse (1964) and Zaller (1992) have observed, elite voices help to guide understandings of politics and are critical to the development of public opinion. Moreover, as Edelman (1964, 1977) has elaborated, elite depictions of politics structure the expectations people have not only of politicians, parties, and government but also the very nature of political power. Often, Edelman contends, the word choices and rhetorical styles of political elites lead to an accepting relationship of mass publics to authority and help to perpetuate the power these very elites hold over the citizenry.

Third, party labels and partisan styles function as powerful shortcuts in modern life and have been shown to have important psychological effects on citizens. Key works contend that party cues provide shortcuts (Downs, 1957) that shape political attitudes and evaluations (Campbell, Converse, Miller, and Stokes, 1960) and help individuals to predict issue positions (Conover and Feldman, 1981) and to vote (Rahn, 1993). While the power of cues is not absolute—indeed studies question when, exactly, party labels aid decision-making (Coan, Merolla, Stephenson, and Zechmeister, 2008; Lupia and McCubbins, 1998)—these words are generally regarded to be accessible and relevant to political decision-making (Huckfeldt, Levine, Morgan, and Sprague, 1999).

Fourth, the meanings of political terms can shift with time, becoming broader or narrower or changing entirely. Consider research on the labels *Democratic, Republican, liberal,* and *conservative.* Baumer and Gold (1995) detail how, during the Ronald Reagan presidency, "as the economic decline of the 1970s gave way to the apparent prosperity of the 1980s, the Democrats lost what had been an advantage of the promotion of economic prosperity" (35). Accordingly, the label *Democratic* became associated with an inability to manage government and the economy. During those same years, Baumer and Gold also found that the label *Republican* was increasingly viewed as strong on defense, a champion of low taxes, and committed to traditional and conservative values. Conover and Feldman (1981) show a similar type of shift for the terms *liberal* and *conservative.* They describe how the nature of the political environment in the 1960s and 1970s made the word *liberal* more visible and then more salient to citizens, such that it had a stronger impact on decision-making than did the term *conservative.* In the authors' minds, the prominence of the "New Left" and the social issues it championed tended to dominate political discourse in the United States and thus put the *liberal* label more prominently in the minds of many. Writing in the 1980s, however, they note that the emergence of the "New Right" and the concomitant ascendancy of the *conservative* label might mean that this term will have "a stronger impact on self-identification in the coming years" (630). Additionally, Menefree—in a charming study published in the 1930s— reveals how labels change over time. In that work, he reports that *liberalism* was regarded as a positive term by 83 percent of his sample and that it was the most popular of the eight stereotyped words in his study (other words being *conservatism, fascism, patriotism, pacifism, radicalism, socialism,* and *communism*). Menefree (1936) comments that these types of words "are being used constantly as an important means of social control" and elaborates how such practices may indicate that these political elites understand that stereotyped words (like *radicalism, socialism,* and *communism*) "are powerful weapons against persons and policies with whom they do not agree"(621).

Studies on the effects of party labels show that these terms can exert a powerful influence on individuals as they make sense of politics. And the research on party styles indicates how elites often attempt to connect with audiences by emphasizing partisan cues, stereotypes, and values.

PARTY LABELS

Party labels provide simple, direct, and consequential information in shaping individual's perceptions and are considered by many to be the chief cue influencing how people make decisions about candidates and issues (Baumer and Gold, 1995; Herrera, 1996–1997; Schaffner and Streb, 2002). Findings from survey and experimental research suggest that labels help people make sense of their political environments in the following ways.

Labels Are Broadly Understood

A set of projects has detailed how labels are understood by citizens of high and low political sophistication as well as high and low levels of participation. Herrera's (1996–1997) examination of the meanings of the labels *liberal* and *conservative*, for instance, found that even though political elites were more likely to correctly depict the meanings of these terms, most citizens could identify those meanings. That the meanings are shared, writes Herrera, points to a quite remarkable linkage between the mass public and the political elite with regard to political terminology. In his words, "prior studies may have over emphasized constraint and sophistication as criteria for political engagement by the mass citizenry. In sum, perhaps little is needed to obtain a rudimentary understanding of the language of politics. . . . The building blocks for a politically informed electorate may already be in place" (635). Similarly, Snyder and Ting (2002) have observed that citizens are far more knowledgeable about party labels and their ideological implications than they are of particular candidates. These researchers contend that voters are far better at discussing the differences between the major party labels than they are at discussing the differences between the liberals and conservatives within the parties.

Labels Increase the Likelihood That Citizens Will Make Decisions

Findings from decision-making research have shown that individuals are more likely to rely on heuristics when there is a high need for cognitive efficiency (Mondak, 1993). A related finding for party labels has been advanced by Schaffner and Streb (2002): A voter is more likely to choose a candidate when a partisan term is provided. As they explain, party labels help "voters not only to participate but also to participate intelligently in our political system. Without the party label, voters become less likely to vote and less able to link their own party affiliations to their vote choices" (579). Even though Schaffner and Streb found that highly educated respondents had an easier time selecting candidates to support in the absence of partisan information, the role of the party label helped all citizens make decisions with confidence and efficiency. Several projects confirm that individuals with fewer political resources are the most likely to employ cognitive shortcuts; yet citizens of all levels of sophistication make decisions more efficiently when labels are present (Herrera, 1996–1997; Rahn, Aldrich, and Borgida, 1994; Fiske, Kinder, and Larter, 1983).

Labels Are Viewed Through Partisan Screens

Sanders (1988) found that citizens who have an ideological view of the parties are more likely to see differences between them, almost always preferring their party's label to that of the opposition. Conover and Feldman (1981) have located a similar result for ideological terms, showing that identification with a party affects how individuals interpret the labels *liberal* and *conservative*. Interestingly, these authors found that symbolic factors played a more pivotal role than issue positions in determining the evaluation of these labels. Specifically, they observed that positive attitudes toward the *liberal* label "were primarily a function of positive feelings toward the symbols of the radical and reformist left" (634). In contrast, positive evaluations of the *conservative* label were influenced by "a positive affect towards the symbol of capitalism, the status quo, social control symbols, and a conservative stance on racial issues" (635). These patterns led Conover and Feldman to conclude that "ideological labels, and consequently self-identifications, have largely symbolic, non–issue-oriented meaning to the mass public" (641).

Labels Are Regarded as Distinct

Research from a variety of scholars—including Baumer and Gold (1995), Trilling (1976), and Sanders (1988)—shows that citizens see differences between the party labels and are comfortable in identifying a distinct set of generalizations that separate the two major parties. The data reveal that individuals viewed Democrats as those willing "to rely on government intervention, whether to regulate the economy and businesses or to assist the economically disadvantaged" (Baumer and Gold, 1995, 35) and Republicans as those opposed to government intervention in the economy, as "champions of low taxes and of bringing businesslike efficiency to government," and as "supporters of entrepreneurial activity" (Baumer and Gold, 1995, 36). Individuals have also connected these understandings of the parties to favored groups; notably, voters associated Democrats with an array of interests (e.g., labor unions, welfare recipients, gays and lesbians, feminists, and minorities), whereas Republicans have been recognized as business elites and those committed to traditional conservative values. Additionally, with regard to party philosophies, "the Democrats' dominant image has been one of liberalism, humanism, equality, and support for government activity and social change. The Republican image has been more or less the opposite; it has featured conservatism, anticommunism, property rights, and opposition to government activity and social change" (Baumer and Gold, 1995, 44).

Labels, then, are influential for a score of reasons: They are accessible; they help individuals make decisions with efficiency (particularly individuals with lower levels of information); and they point to perceived differences between the two major parties in the United States. Because of their prominence and value, these labels also present themselves as desired entities for ambitious candidates, groups, organizations, and movements.

Partisan Styles

Scholars have also examined the partisan styles of political actors as well as how such styles influence audiences. In his seminal rhetorical work, Weaver (1953) contends that a primary goal of political parties is to persuade; to do so they must have a strategic style. Weaver identifies two such partisan approaches, explaining how conservatives argue from definition as they base their positions on fundamental principles and liberals argue from circumstance as they base their cases on conditions and contingencies. A member of the New Conservatives at the time that his *The Ethics of Rhetoric* was published, Weaver clearly prefers the argument from definition to the argument from circumstance. He regards the argument from definition as the most ethical type of claim as it considers ideal objectives, embraces principles, and demonstrates that a leader "has the courage to define" (Weaver, 1953, 114). In contrast, he views the argument from circumstance as the nearest of all arguments to pure expediency because it privileges the present (or the facts around a situation) and prevents individuals from seeing matters of cause and effect ("since theoretically, it stops at the level of perception of fact" [Weaver, 1953, 57]).

Psychological inquiry has documented patterns similar to Weaver's, although with less of a normative edge. Specifically, Tetlock (1983) has employed his *integrative complexity coding system* to document how Republicans are more cognitively simple than Democrats. His research shows how conservatives are more parsimonious in their arguments whereas centrists and liberals express issues in more complex and multidimensional ways (Tetlock, 1983; Tetlock, Hannum, and Micheletti, 1984). Tetlock is careful to explain that these rhetorical patterns do not suggest that Republicans are less intelligent than Democrats; instead, the recommending force of his findings underscores Weaver's observations that Republicans speak in a more direct manner than do Democrats. Subsequent analyses show that conservative rhetors are also more comfortable with and loyal to their party label, less trusting of the opposition, more aware of their enemies, and less ambivalent and guilty when making decisions than are centrists and liberals (Gershtenson, 2007; Morris, Carranza and Fox, 2008; Skitka and Tetlock, 1993).

Textual analyses of speeches further document how Democratic and Republican leaders employ distinctive partisan styles. A first set of projects embraced computerized textual analysis to spot trends over time. In an analysis of presidential campaign speeches from 1948 to 1996, Hart (2000) shows show how Democrats spoke in grounded ways (employing familiar terms), humanistic ways (using common, collective appeals), and institutional ways (talking about leaders and political parties). In contrast, Republicans emphasized themes of inspiration, liberation, and patriotism. In an examination of debates, television spots and acceptance addresses from 1948 to 2000, Benoit (2004) reveals how Democrats discuss policy, Democratic issues, and empathy more than Republicans, whereas Republicans detail character, Republican issues, sincerity, and morality more than Democrats. In a review of Democratic and Republican presidential campaign speeches, Jarvis (2004) shows how, in order to rhetorically bring the various subgroups of their coalition together, Democrats use more nouns per verb than Republicans, whereas Republicans employ a more unified, direct approach that rhetorically betrays their tendency toward a more hierarchical organizing style. All three projects acknowledge, however, that these party styles have decreased somewhat since 1948.

Other projects also find differences between the parties, particularly with regard to protecting their labels. In a study of party nomination acceptance addresses from 1948 to 2000, Jarvis (2001) uncovers how Republicans have used party labels more divisively than Democrats. In a follow-up study from those years, Jarvis and Jones (2005) expose how Republicans are more protective of their labels (*Republican* and *conservative*) than are Democrats of their labels (*Democrat* and *liberal*). And, in his longitudinal work, Benoit (1999) shows that Republicans are more likely to go on the attack than Democrats (especially on the issue of character; see Benoit, 2004).

Several works have examined how the theory of *issue ownership* influences both partisan statements and media coverage of such statements. Petrocik (1996) contends that the parties have reputations for how they have handled issues in the past and that it behooves candidates to call attention to those that their party "owns" (1) to make such concerns salient to voters and (2) to increase the likelihood that voters will regard party loyalists more fit for office than opponents of the other party. Content analyses document how victorious Democratic and Republican presidential candidates emphasize the issues owned by their own party more frequently than do losing candidates (Benoit, 2007), how the issues owned by Democrats (education, healthcare) became more commonly discussed in the 1990s (Benoit and Hansen, 2004), and how issues traditionally owned by the Democrats became particularly more common in congressional campaigns (compared with presidential contests; see Brazeal and Benoit, 2008). Studies analyzing the media coverage of issue ownership unpacks how both candidates and journalists contribute to the issues partisans own (Walgrave and De Swert, 2007) and how candidates receive more favorable coverage when they focus on issues their party owns (with Democrats benefiting particularly for focusing on social welfare topics; see Hayes, 2008).

Talk of the Party

Inspired by Sander's (1988) call for deeper analysis of the meanings of party labels across time and circumstance, I conducted an extensive analysis of how four elite voices (presidential candidates, elite journalists, members of the US House of Representatives, and political scholars) discussed six party labels (*Democrat, Republican, Independent, liberal, conservative,* and *party*) over a fifty-six-year time period (1948–2004). The goals were to uncover how these actors treated parties in two key contexts (presidential campaigns and moments of governance) over a half-century featuring periods of considerable party allegiance (1948 to early 1960s), party decline (late 1960s to 1980s), and party resurgence (1990s to 2004). The project tracked over 3,000 party labels on ten theoretically derived content analytic categories and yielded the following insights.

Even though Americans have been passionately ambivalent about parties, the talk surrounding these groups has been remarkably accommodating. When all labels and speakers were examined en mass, it was striking to see how labels were used continuously (despite shifting levels of party allegiance in the electorate) and deferentially (despite periods of questioning their power in elections and governance). When the labels were examined in light of political time, the data revealed that political elites were particularly protective of party labels between 1961 and 1979, rarely casting these terms as weak, unproductive, or harmful during this period of cultural tensions and political reforms. Attending to individual actors, the meanings of these labels shifted somewhat depending on who was using them. Legislators deployed labels to sharpen partisanship and mobilize teamwork; journalists used labels to identify the two major teams battling for political influence; presidential candidates used labels to identify with audiences; and scholars celebrated and inflated the meanings of parties (oddly enough, even while questioning their political capital). The data also showed how journalists relied on these labels the most, regularly crediting partisans with the task of organizing campaigns and facilitating legislatures, critiquing candidates who departed from party platforms, and preserving expectations of how Democrats and Republicans should act. And, when the labels were examined individually, it appeared that elites largely protected the terms *Democrat, Republican,* and *party;* praised the term *independent;* vilified (and failed to stand up for) the term *liberal:* and largely ignored the term *conservative* (save George W. Bush's attention to this term in 2000 and 2004).

Ultimately, the project advanced two key conclusions: First, Republican candidates and legislators exercised considerable discipline between 1948 and 2004 in debasing the term *liberal,* in placing the *Republican* brand name closer to citizens, and in forestalling critique of the term *conservative;* second, American elites have a strong tradition of talking about parties and have used party terms in ways that contribute to parties' political potency in the United States, even when the conversation has sometimes turned sour. This broader argument advances what may seem to be an obvious point: the major parties enjoy political capital because voices in the United States discuss parties in light of their impact on the system. As long as elites continue to bow symbolically to political parties—thereby giving them the limelight time and time again—it stands to reason that they will not be far from power in the polity. Intriguingly, even conversations about the *deathwatch* of parties revealed how parties are depicted in terms of influence and inevitability. This broad analysis contends, then, that as long as political elites discuss the strength of the party system (for good or ill), the parties will never be far from governing the political imaginary.

UNANSWERED QUESTIONS

Traditionally, the lion's share of research has focused on what parties *are* and what they *do* (Finer, 1980). Less work has examined the talk surrounding partisanship, possibly because of a number of methodological challenges: Specifically, this work can be descriptive and therefore nonfalsifiable; this research can generate more research questions than hypotheses and is therefore difficult to test; this research can capture broad meanings and therefore cannot be neatly generalized to the individual. And yet, as this chapter details, party labels and party styles merit close attention because they are widely understood, help individuals make decisions, serve as partisan screens, and are regarded as distinct. What these labels mean to individuals and how they are managed by elites begs surveillance.

Three sets of questions invite additional inquiry. First, how will (the reemergence and rise of) partisan outlets influence how elites and journalists deploy party labels and partisan styles? Will partisan outlets make favored party cues more salient, familiar, and trustworthy to audience members (Coan, Merolla, Stephenson, and Zechmeister, 2008; Petrocik, 1996)? Will the voices on these outlets continue to perpetuate party reputations (Hayes, 2008), or will these voices inflate the meanings of preferred party labels and demean the meanings of other party labels (Jarvis, 2005)? Research shows that candidates who are more partisan than their opponents typically lose (Benoit, 2004; Hart, 2000; Jarvis, 2001). Will conservative outlets invite more extreme conservative communications from their guests? Will liberal outlets invite more liberal communications from their guests? How will such rhetoric be received by other voices in the media and the voting public (both within and beyond these partisan outlets)?

Second, how will a period of "rude democracy" (Herbst, 2010) influence how party labels and styles are deployed and interpreted? While the notion of incivility in the United States is not new, the amount of messaging in the media environment continues to grow. Marketing estimates suggest that individuals were faced with roughly 200 brand impressions a day in the 1950s. By the early 2000s, that number had likely risen to 5,000 a day (with individuals noticing roughly 300 and recalling roughly 130; see Jarvis, 2005). Strategic communicators know that short attack messages are effective means of breaking through this overcommunicated environment. What might the contemporary emphasis on brevity and negativity mean for party labels and party styles (Herbst, 2010)? To date, Republicans have been more likely to go on the attack, have been savvier with keeping their messages brief, and have been more focused in protecting their labels and in demoting those of the opposition than have Democrats (Benoit, 1999; Jarvis, 2005). Will these trends continue? Will Democrats develop a strategy of their own to break through the clutter? What might it look like? And, how might such developments influence the meaning(s) of party labels and public support for them?

Third, how will innovations in communication technologies (and the increased ability of citizens to voice their concerns and comment on elite discourses such as news content and political websites) influence how citizens use party labels and styles? Will citizen use of these cues continue to follow elite practice (Converse, 1964; Zaller, 1992)? Will some groups of citizens be more disciplined in their label use than others (Jarvis, 2005)? Will citizens help to expand or contract the meanings of labels? And will elites (either journalists, political figures, or both) change their communications in response to such patterns? Tracking non-elite uses of such cues can provides some insight into the relevance, familiarity, favorability, and trust individuals place in party labels.

Conclusion

The last thing a political party will give up is its vocabulary, argued Tocqueville, for crowds will forget the ideas of politics far sooner than they will forget the words they have learned. Political parties play a pivotal role in democratic states, and the linguistic symbols surrounding them play a pivotal role too. This chapter has reviewed how individuals are more likely to be subject to the language of partisanship than actual party events, how party labels and party styles are largely controlled by elites, how these labels and styles change over time, and how they serve as powerful shortcuts in democratic life. This chapter also has revealed how the talk surrounding partisanship underscores the power of these groups in the polity. An intriguing element of the scholarship on partisan messages is that despite Americans' frustration with the parties and despite the efforts of elite actors (particularly Republicans) to use their own labels strategically, discussions of partisanship do little to challenge the indispensable nature of these groups or their inevitable place in the United States (Orren, 1982). At least not the most visible partisan communicators—and at least not yet.

References

Aldrich, J. H. 1995. *Why parties? The origin and transformation of political parties in America.* Chicago: University of Chicago Press.

Bartels, L. M. 2000. Partisanship and voting behavior, 1952–1996. *American Journal of Political Science* 44: 35–50.

Baumer, D. C., and Gold, H. J. 1995. Party images and the American electorate. *American Politics Quarterly* 23: 33–61.

Benoit, W. L. 1999. Acclaiming, attacking, and defending in presidential nominating acceptance addresses, 1960–1996. *Quarterly Journal of Speech* 85: 247–267.

Benoit, W. L. 2004. Political party affiliation and presidential campaign discourse. *Communication Quarterly* 52: 81–97.

Benoit, W. L. 2007. Own party issue ownership in presidential television spots. *Communication Reports 20*: 42–50.

Benoit, W. L., and Hansen, G. J. 2004. Issue ownership in primary and general presidential debates. *Argumentation & Advocacy 40*: 143–154.

Brazeal, L. M., and Benoit, W. L. 2008. Issue ownership in congressional campaign television spots. *Communication Quarterly 56*: 17–28.

Broder, D. S. 1972. *The party's over: The failure of politics in America*. New York: Harper & Row.

Burke, K. *Language as symbolic action: Essays on life, literature and method*. Berkeley: University of California, 1968.

Burnham, W. D. 1965. The changing shape of the American political universe. *American Political Science Review 59*: 7–28.

Burnham, W. D. 1970. *Critical elections and the mainsprings of American politics*. New York: Norton.

Campbell, A., P. E. Converse, W. E. Miller, and Stokes, D. E. 1960. *The American voter*. New York: Wiley.

Chambers, W., and Burnham, W. D. 1975. *The American party systems: Stages of political development*. New York: Oxford University Press.

Coan, T. G., J. L. Merolla, L. B. Stephenson, and Zechmeister, E. J. 2008. It's not easy being green: Minor party labels as heuristic aids. *Political Psychology 29*: 389–405.

Converse, P. E. 1964. The nature of belief systems in mass publics. In D. E. Apter (Ed.), *Ideology and discontent* (pp. 206–261). New York: Free Press.

Conover, P. J., and Feldman, S. 1981. The origins and meaning of liberal/conservative self-identifications. *American Journal of Political Science 25*: 617–645.

Cotter, C., J. L. Gibson, J. F. Bibby, and Huckshorn, R. J. 1984. *Party organizations in American politics*. New York: Praeger.

Downs, A. 1957. *An economic theory of democracy*. New York: Harper & Row.

Edelman, M. 1964. *The symbolic uses of politics*. Urbana: University of Illinois Press.

Edelman, M. 1971. *Politics as symbolic action: Mass arousal and quiescence*. New York: Academic Press.

Edelman, M. 1977. *Political language: Words that succeed and policies that fail*. New York: Academic Press.

Eldersveld, M. J. 1982. *Political parties in American society*. New York: Basic Books.

Finer, S. E. 1980. *The changing British party system, 1945–1979*. Washington DC: American Enterprise Institute.

Fiske, S. T., D. R. Kinder, and Larter, W. M. 1983. The novice and the expert: Knowledge-based strategies in political cognition. *Journal of Experimental Social Psychology 19*: 381–400.

Gershtenson, J. 2007. Primaries, parties, and candidate positioning in US Senate elections. *Journal of Elections, Public Opinion & Parties 17*: 165–179.

Hart, R. P. 2000. *Campaign talk: Why elections are good for us*. Princeton, NJ: Princeton University Press.

Hart, R. P., S. E. Jarvis, W. P. Jennings, and Smith-Howell, D. 2005. *Political keywords: Using language that uses us*. New York: Oxford University Press.

Hayes, D. 2008. Party reputations, journalistic expectations: How issue ownership influences election news. *Political Communication 25*: 377–400.

Herbst, S. 2010. *Rude democracy: Civility and incivility in American politics*. Philadelphia: Temple University Press.

Herrera, R. 1996–1997. Understanding the language of politics: A study of elites and masses. *Political Science Quarterly 111*: 619–637.

Hetherington, M. J. 2001. Resurgent mass partisanship: The role of elite polarization. *American Political Science Review 95*: 619–631.

Hofstadter, R. 1969. *The idea of a party system: The rise of legitimate opposition in the United States, 1780–1840*. Berkeley: University of California Press.

Huckfeldt, R., J. Levine, W. Morgan, and Sprague, J. 1999. Accessibility and the political utility of partisan and ideological orientations. *American Journal of Political Science 43*: 888–911.

Jarvis, S. E. 2001. Campaigning alone: Partisan versus personal language in the presidential nominating acceptance addresses, 1948–2000. *American Behavioral Scientist 44*: 2152–2171.

Jarvis, S. E. 2004. Partisan patterns in presidential campaign speeches, 1948–2000. *Communication Quarterly 52*: 403–419.

Jarvis, S. E. 2005. *The talk of the party: Political labels, symbolic capital & American life*. Lanham, MD: Rowman & Littlefield.

Jarvis, S. E., and Jones, E. B. 2005. Party labels in presidential acceptance addresses:1948–2000. In L. C. Han and D. J. Heith (Eds.), *In the public domain: Presidents and the challenge of public leadership* (pp. 29–48). Albany, NY: SUNY Press.

Linz, J. J., and Stepan, A. 1996. *Problems of democratic transition and consolidation: southern Europe, South America and post-communist Europe*. Baltimore, MD: Johns Hopkins University Press.

Lupia, A., and McCubbins, M. D. 1998. *The democratic dilemma: Can citizens learn what they need to know?* Cambridge, UK: Cambridge University Press, 1998.

Menefree, S. 1936. The effect of stereotyped words on political judgments. *American Sociological Review 1*: 614–621.

Mondak, J. J. 1993. Public opinion and heuristic processing of source cues. *Political Behavior 15*: 167–192.

Morris, M. W., E. Carranza, and Fox, C. R. 2008. Mistaken identity: Activating conservative political identities induces "conservative" financial decisions. *Psychological Science 19*: 1154–1160.

Orren, G. R. 1982. The changing styles of American party politics. In J. L. Fleishman (Ed.), *The future of American political parties: The challenge of governance* (pp. 4–41). Englewood Cliffs, NJ: Prentice Hall.

Petrocik, J. R. 1996. Issue ownership in presidential elections, with a 1980 case study. *American Journal of Political Science 40*: 825–850.

Polsby, N. W. 1983. *Consequences of party reform*. Oxford, UK: Oxford University Press.

Rahn, W. M. 1993. The role of partisan stereotypes in information processing about political candidates. *American Journal of Political Science 37*: 472–496.

Rahn, W. M., J. H. Aldrich, and Borgida, E. 1994. Individual and contextual variations in political candidate appraisal. *American Political Science Review 88*: 193–199.

Rosenstone, S. J., R. Behr, and Lazarus, E. H. 1984. *Third parties in America: Citizen response to major party failure*. Princeton, NJ: Princeton University Press.

Sanders, A. 1942. The meaning of party images. *Political Research Quarterly 41*: 583–599.

Schattschneider, E. E. *Party government*. New York: Holt, Rinehart and Winston.

Schaffner, B. F., and Streb, M. J. 2002. The partisan heuristic in low information elections. *Public Opinion Quarterly 66*: 559–581.

Schlesinger, J. A. 1985. The new American political party. *American Political Science Review 79*: 1152–1169.

Schmitter, P. C. and Karl, T. L. 1996. What democracy is . . . and is not. In L. Diamond and M. F. Plattner (Eds.), *The global resurgence of democracy*, 2nd ed. (pp. 49–62). Baltimore, MD: Johns Hopkins University Press.

Skitka, L. J., and Tetlock, P. E. 1993. Providing public assistance: Cognitive and motivational processes underlying liberal and conservative policy preferences. *Journal of Personality & Social Psychology 65*: 1205–1223.

Snyder, J. M., and Ting, M. M. 2002. An informational rationale for political parties. *American Journal of Political Science 46*: 90–110.

Sorauf, F. J., and Beck, P. A. 1988. *Party politics in America*, 6th ed. Glenview, IL: Scott, Foresman.

Tetlock, P. E. 1983. Cognitive style and political ideology. *Journal of Personality and Social Psychology 45*: 118–126.

Tetlock, P. E., K. A. Hannum, and Micheletti, P. M. 1984. Stability and change in the complexity of senatorial debate: Testing the cognitive versus rhetorical style hypothesis. *Journal of Personality and Social Psychology 46*: 979–990.

Trilling, R. J. 1976. *Party image and electoral behavior*. New York: Wiley.

Walgrave, S., and De Swert, K. 2007. Where does issue ownership come from? From the party or from the media? Issue party identifications in Belgium, 1991–2005. *Harvard International Journal of Press/Politics 12*: 37–67.

Wattenberg, M. P. 1992. *The rise of candidate-centered politics: Presidential elections of the 1980s*. Cambridge, MA: Harvard University Press.

Wattenberg, M. P. 1986. *The decline of American political parties, 1952–1988*. Cambridge, MA: Harvard University Press.

Weaver, R. M. 1953. *The ethics of rhetoric*. Chicago: Regnery.

Zaller, J. 1992. *The nature and origins of mass opinion*. Cambridge: Cambridge University Press.

CHAPTER 11

POLITICAL ADVERTISING

TIMOTHY W. FALLIS

IN the more than two centuries since the country's first contested election, the technology of political advertising has changed, but the attack and advocacy strategies have remained much the same. Attack content vilifies; advocacy venerates. Marshaling minimal if any evidence, the makers of political propaganda identify their candidate with esteemed individuals and popular sentiments, all the while denigrating their rivals. In short, from the Republic's earliest days, sloganeering, not substance, has been the stuff of politics in the United States (see Jamieson, 1984).

Within the field of political communication, the study of political advertising has attempted to relate its content to posited effects. Most of this inquiry has been conducted using one (or some combination) of three methods: survey, experiment, and content analysis. As a result, a picture of what political advertising does and why and how it does it has emerged. This chapter synthesizes findings by outlining what we know about the content of political ads and suggesting that differences in spending on political advertising can affect vote choice, advertising's effects on vote choice are mediated by very specific factors, and that, under some circumstances, political advertising can affect electoral outcome.

THE CONTENT OF POLITICAL ADS

Scholars affix varying labels to the content of political ads. Where Geer divides the ad world into appeals that raise "doubts about the opposition (i.e., negative) or [state] why the candidate is worthy of your vote (i.e., positive)" without a "middle category" (Geer, 2006), Jamieson, Waldman and Sherr (2000) parse the terrain into attack, contrast, and advocacy, whereas Freedman, Wood, and Lawton (1999) segment attack into "personal" and "issue" appeals. The Jamieson, Waldman, and Sherr (2010) content analysis finds that conflating contrast with negative overstates the amount of deceptive advertising; as a result, they argue, we falsely criticize candidates when their discourse is actually informative and accountable. Geer's content analysis, which treats as "negative" ads that Jamieson et al. would call "contrast," finds that negative advertising often offers strong, substantive information that is useful to voters. The difference between the Jamieson et al. and Geer results is largely a result of varying definition and data sets: Jamieson et al. included 5-minute ads and excluded ads that never aired.

William Benoit's alternative typology categorizes ads as acclaiming (emphasizing good reasons voters should lend their support), attacking (focusing on the opponent's faults as reasons why he or she should be shunned by voters), or defending (countering the accusations leveled by the candidate's opponent) (Benoit, Blaney, and Pier, 1998). Results from this content-analytic approach to ads of the 1980 through 1996 presidential campaigns show Democrats more likely to acclaim than to attack and Republicans tending to do the opposite. Incumbents are also more likely to take advantage of their record and acclaim rather than attack, while, without a record to reference, challengers are more likely to attack than to acclaim; for all four groups, ads that defend are rare (Benoit, 2001; Benoit, Blaney, and Pier, 1998). A content analysis of 584 spots featured in the year 2000 presidential, gubernatorial, congressional, and local elections found that 67 percent acclaimed, 32 percent attacked, and only 1 percent defended the sponsor against attack (Airne and Benoit, 2005). Fearful of alienating potential supporters, candidates do not usually include obvious cues about party affiliation in political advertisements (Vavreck, 2001).

Using a definition closer to Geer's, another study that parsed political advertising into positive or negative ads (the latter defined as those "intended to make the opposing candidate look bad by attacking personal characteristic, political issues, or affiliated party") found that negative and positive spots tend to emphasize different issues. Positive ones are more often informal in style, use a more cognitive (i.e., "ads [that] directed viewers to think, reason, and consider") vocabulary, highlight social issues and achievement, and seek to contrast the present with a potentially brighter future. Negative and even mixed-format ads tend to focus on financial issues, evoke a more sensory than cognitive reception, and laud the past while expressing anger about the present (Gunsch, Brownlow, Haynes, and Mabe, 2000).

Some argue that constructive attack ads are valuable and may encourage voters to exercise their franchise, whereas ads that merely disparage candidates or their issues or engage in what are perceived to be inaccurate or unfair assertions are perceived as unhelpful (Jamieson, 2000) and may lead voters to feel that their ballot is a useless gesture and therefore to stay home (Kahn and Kenney, 1999; Gronbeck, 1992).

An "attack" advertisement is not necessarily "negative" or "dirty," and some argue (see Jamieson, Waldman, and Sherr, 2000) that conflating the terms, as many studies on political advertising do, obscures the important distinctions between legitimate and illegitimate attack. Further, it is important to note that in the presidential general election campaigns from 1952 to 1996, deception was no less likely in advocacy and self-promotional ads than it was in attack ads (Jamieson, Waldman, and Sherr, 2000).

Richardson (2001) also argues that because studies that examine negative advertising are conceptualizing it poorly, they ask the wrong questions: "In short, negativity has been defined in ways that are too broad ... insufficiently holistic, too pejorative, and ultimately irrelevant in a constitutional framework grounded on free speech and retrospective accountability."

POLITICAL ADVERTISING EFFECTS

Like political communication in general, political ads are more likely to reinforce existing beliefs than to change attitudes (Ansolabehere and Iyengar, 1995). However they can affect individual voting decisions (Valentino, Hutchings, and Williams, 2004) as well as vote share (Althaus, Nardulli, and Shaw, 2002), and in close contests may prove decisive (Shaw, 2006; Johnston, Hagen, and Jamieson, 2004).

Differences in Spending

Although the effect is not inevitable, spending more than an opponent tends to carry electoral advantages. Bartels, for example, finds that in five instances the Republican presidential candidates' "popular vote margin was at least four points larger than it would have been, and in two cases—1968 and 2000—Republican candidates won close elections that they very probably would have lost had they been unable to outspend incumbent Democratic vice presidents" (2008, 122–3). Although they disagree about the size of the effect, scholars have also found that spending more on ads than an opponent translates into vote choice (Shaw, 1999; Huber and Arceneaux, 2007; Johnston, Hagen, and Jamieson, 2004).

Increased spending on political advertising increases awareness of a candidate, which in the case of disparities in spending may change the outcome of an election though an increased likelihood of voting for that candidate (see for example Goldstein and Freedman, 2000). Johnston, Hagen, and Jamieson (2004) demonstrate voters' responsiveness to differences in the level and content of political advertising in the 2000 presidential election and attribute Bush's win in the electoral college in part to the fact that the "ad signal became decisively unbalanced" in the battleground in the final weeks of the campaign (13). Combining data from the Annenberg National Election Survey with a reconstruction of the 2008 presidential campaign, Kenski, Hardy, and Jamieson (2010) showed that by outspending McCain on ads, the Democrats affected pro-Obama vote intentions. In addition, the fact that the Obama campaign had enough money to pay for all of his advertising (rather than having to partly rely on the Democratic Party or other advocacy groups) allowed it to control and focus its message for maximum effect (Franz and Ridout, 2010).

Duration of Effect

The suasive effect of political advertising is of limited duration. A 2006 field experiment—involving the randomized placement of $2 million of real advertising for Rick Perry's Texas gubernatorial re-election campaign coupled with extensive daily tracking interviews—showed that TV advertising had a strong vote-shift effect within one week of audience exposure, a smaller/equivocal effect in the second week, and no effect at all by the third week (Gerber, Gimpel, Green, and Shaw, 2011). Similarly using National Annenberg Election Survey data from 2000, Hill et al. (2008; see also Hill et al., 2013) showed that the effect of any specific ad on vote preference disappeared within a week with long-term effects evident only in "the most politically aware voters." This finding suggests that a priming model, wherein the message temporarily weights the considerations that inform a voter's response to a vote choice—rather than an online processing model, where new information affects an opinion even after the instigating information is forgotten—may account for the voter learning effects of political advertising.

The reliance on self-reports of intention to vote is a problematic aspect of research looking into the relationship between political advertising and actual ballot choices. A variety of methodologies, including surveys, focus groups, content analyses, and lab experiments, have been used in this research. However, all ask voters their intention to vote. As Vavreck (2007) points out, this is a problem for a number of reasons, among them are voters not carrying through with their stated intention, and a range of factors that may inspire respondents to respond dishonestly. This same concern casts doubt on whether we know whether political advertising is successful at accomplishing its primary goal, namely winning votes for its sponsors (Goldstein and Ridout, 2004).

Effects on Turnout

Scholars differ on whether negative political advertising affects voter turnout, viewers' political efficacy, and viewer cynicism about government. Those finding suppression of turnout include Ansolabehere, Iyengar, Simon, and Valentino (1994), whose experimental study correlated exposure to negative ads with a weakened sense of political efficacy. They argued that such exposure creates more cynicism in government and weakens the intention to vote. Their subsequent work concluded that negative advertising suppresses turnout by driving away independents and pushing others toward party extremes (Ansolabehere and Iyengar, 1995), and also confirmed that political consultants know this and deploy negative ads for this purpose (see also Diamond and Bates, 1984). An even larger study suggested that negative advertising results in voter suppression (Ansolabehere, Iyengar, and Simon, 1999).

Other studies have arrived at a different conclusion. Although viewers report that they do not like negative political advertisements generally and dislike them more than they do positive ads (in truth, they don't like ads at all except to the extent that they subsidize television programming [Mittal 1994]), some research has shown that attack spots do not decrease voter turnout. Meirick and Nisbett (2011) show that while negative ads lower viewer intention to vote for the candidate the ad supports, overall voting is not reduced. Other studies show that while negative advertising is not without effect, it does not reduce the likelihood of voting (Wattenberg and Brians, 1999; Finkel and Geer, 1998; Goldstein, 1997; Clinton and Lapinski, 2004; Krasno and Green, 2008; Garramone, Atkin, Pinkleton, and Cole, 1990; Franz, Freedman, Goldstein, and Ridout, 2008).

Indeed some argue that negative ads may increase voter turnout. Phillips, Urbany, and Reynolds (2007) agree that although viewers dislike negative ads, they increase one's likelihood of voting for one's preferred candidate; Freedman and Goldstein (1999) also found that negative advertising increases voter turnout (also see Wattenberg and Brians, 1999; Goldstein and Freedman, 2002). The seemingly contradictory research on the effects of negative ads on turnout may be explained by the varying definitions involved in the competing studies- or may be a function of the timing of exposure to attack. So for example, Krupnikov finds that "it is not negativity in general that has an effect on turnout—but negativity under two specific conditions: 1) negativity after a selection and 2) negativity about an individual's selected candidate" (Krupnikov, 2011, 805). A meta-analysis by Allen and Burrell (2002) offered cautious support for the conclusions that "negative information produces a larger effect on opinion formation when compared to positive information, whether for a position . . . or a candidate. . . ." Two large meta-analyses report that although attack is more memorable and does tend to stimulate more knowledge, negative advertising is no more effective at yielding votes for the sponsoring party than are positive ads. Both studies found that negative advertising has no particularly deleterious effect on political systems and does not suppress turnout (Lau, Sigelman, Heldman, and Babbitt, 1999; Lau, Sigelman, and Rovner, 2007).

Effects on Voter Cynicism

The relationship between negative advertising and cynicism is also unclear. Tedesco (2002) found that, in a 2000 Senate campaign, exposure to political attack ads expressing negative emotions predicted overall voter cynicism; those ads that intentionally elicit fear (of the opposing candidate or his party, the economy, the world) breed such cynicism especially. Other research has found that "negative" ads (defined as "a one-sided attack designed to draw attention to the target's weaknesses such as character flaws, voting record, public misstatements, broken promises, and the like") are indeed less useful for decision making and tend to create disgust with politics but do not affect cynicism, efficacy, or apathy (Pinkleton, Um, and Austin, 2002). Others have found that "negative" advertising does not lower trust in government (Jackson, Mondak, and Huckfeldt, 2009; Martinez and Delegal, 1990); however, viewers who already harbor lower levels of such trust do tend to be more affected by negative ads.

Voter Learning

Because political ads contain a substantial amount of issue information (Kaid and Johnston, 1991), it is unsurprising that exposure to them increases voter knowledge about candidate issue positions (Patterson and McClure, 1976; Just, Crigler, and Wallach, 1990) and prompts issue-based assessments of candidates (Ansolabehere and Iyengar, 1995; Brians and Wattenberg, 1996). Political ads can also spread inaccurate information (Kenski, Hardy, and Jamieson, 2010, 281–283).

Emotional Appeals

A 1990 survey (Perloff and Kinsey, 1992) of political consultants found that they believe that emotional appeals characterize the most effective political ads. Although cognition and emotion are not readily separable, the effects of political advertising are magnified when it generates an emotional response such as enthusiasm, fear, or anger. Emotion focuses attention on certain aspects of the advertisement and may affect the way the information presented in the ad is processed by the viewer (Lang, 1991). A 1990 experiment by Kaid, Leland, and Whitney found that ads run by George Bush in the 1988 election helped that candidate, while the ads of his opponent Michael Dukakis largely did not; the difference was attributed to an emotional response generated by the Bush ads that the Dukakis pieces failed to elicit (Kaid, Leland, and Whitney, 1992). The emotional appeals in ads are able under some circumstances to affect participation and vote choice (Brader, 2005).

Contrastive Ads

A survey conducted by Jamieson (2000) found that the American electorate considers contrast ads (those wherein a candidate makes claims both favorable to his or her own candidacy and critical of his or her opponent) more responsible and useful for making voting decisions than they do attack ads, and much less of a turn-off to the political process. Comparative political advertising elicits more viewer involvement with the message, and hence more processing activity; an experimental study (Muehling, Stoltman, and Grossbart, 1990) found that viewers also considered comparative ads more relevant, paid more attention to them, and were better able to elaborate on and recall them than other types of ads (see also Putrevu and Lord, 1994). Comparative ads also produce less criticism of the ad source (backlash), prompt more support arguments, and are viewed more favorably than attack ads (Meirick, 2002). In a content analysis of presidential general election ads from 1952 through 1996, Jamieson, Waldman, and Sherr (2000) found that comparative advertising is the one most likely to contain the information needed to make informed voting decisions.

Trait Effects

Although it is impossible to completely disentangle assessments of a candidate's character or traits from assessment of his or her stands on issues, scholars have drawn general distinctions among the types of ads dominated by one form of claim rather than the other. Trait assessments provide voters with an easily accessible heuristic allowing them to elicit predictions about the future behavior of a candidate if she or he is elected (Hardy, forthcoming). Ad-driven trait assessments can affect vote intention (Johnston, Hagen, and Jamieson, 2004).

Issue vs. Character

Experimental data from 1989 show that political advertisements that focus on policy or governance issues rather than the personal qualities of candidates tend to create a more positive attitude toward the ad itself, the sponsor of the ad, and the issue highlighted; they also increase the likelihood of voting (Thorson, Christ, and Caywood, 1991). One survey found that negative issue ads (which decry the foolishness of a position rather than advocate an alternative) broadcast on radio are judged to be fair, while negative character (sometimes called "image") ads are considered unfair (Shapiro and Rieger, 1992). In a 2000 experiment, critical news stories produced lower opinions of candidates when those stories focused on character advertising, but elicited no change when the subject was issue advertising (Leshner, 2001). Another experiment found, in the 2008 presidential election, that young people reported greater feelings of political efficacy when exposed to issue-based rather than character-driven advertising (Kaid, Fernandes, and Painter, 2011), although Shyles's content analysis (1984) concluded that character content in 1980 presidential campaign ads aided voting decisions. Combining content analysis with experimental data, Schenck-Hamlin et al. found that viewers were more likely to be cynical regarding the government and more likely to hold politicians accountable in response to ads centered on candidate character than those focused on issues (Schenck-Hamlin, Proctor, and Rumsey, 2000); however, another experiment suggested that issue-based attack ads can also lead to cynicism and lower perceptions of self-efficacy (Dardis, Shen, and Edwards, 2008; see also Groenendyk and Valentino, 2002).

Agenda Setting

In so far as political advertising has an agenda-setting effect, it can frame issues and candidates in a way that suggests what viewers should think about (McCombs and Shaw, 1972); by heightening the salience of specific attributes, it can also produce a second-order agenda-setting effect that shapes how viewers think about issues and candidates.

Separate studies found this to be the case in both American elections (Golan, Kiousis, and McDaniel, 2007) and those in Spain (McCombs, Llamas, Lopez-Escobar, and Rey, 1997).

Issue Convergence and Ownership

The various issues on which opposing candidates focus over the course of a campaign tend to increasingly converge as the overall amount of money spent on the campaigns increases. Kaplan, Park, and Ridout (2006) found that candidates are rarely able to "own" particular issues to a significant degree; the need to cover a variety of issues, and the expense of doing so via political advertising may explain why the issues on which a candidate focuses in his or her own advertising are frequently not the same as those on which his or her party will concentrate.

Candidates are able to enhance their chance of winning an election with advertising that highlights issues they own. Using experimental data, Ansolabehere, Iyengar, Simon, and Valentino (1994) showed that candidates who choose to focus on issues they own are able to create more resonance for their campaigns than those who concentrate on issues only because they are featured prominently in news. Although one study has found that Democratic and challenger advertising tends to be more aligned with public priorities than the ads of Republicans or incumbents, it did not find any such difference between election winners and losers (Hansen and Benoit, 2002).

AUDIENCE VARIABLES IN EFFECTS OF POLITICAL ADVERTISEMENTS

Negativity Bias

Humans have a negativity bias, weighing negative experiences more heavily than positive ones, holding the valence of the two constant (Rozin and Royzman, 2001). Negative information carries more weight than positive information, as well (Kellermann, 1989). In general, attack is processed more quickly and recalled more readily than advocacy. The effectiveness of negative political advertising can be explained by expectancy theory (i.e., messages violate norms and expectations of language use and so are memorable for being out of the norm) (Pfau, Parrott, and Lindquist, 1992). Lau, Sigelman, and Rovner (2007) also show that negative advertising is more memorable than advocacy advertising and stimulates more knowledge. Some experimental data show that negative political ads cause viewers to reflexively turn away in avoidance, exhibit and report greater physiological arousal than when exposed to more moderate ads, and better recognize the information presented (Bradley, Angelini, and Lee, 2007).

Confirmation Bias

Consistent with confirmation bias, voters scrutinize advertised claims with which they disagree more critically than those that support their existing dispositions. A 1996 Budesheim, Houston, and DePaola experiment involving negative advertising showed that "although participants were sensitive to message content from both in-group [defined as those with whom they identify, are similar to them, or who belong to the same social group] and out-group sources, less stringent criteria were used when evaluating out-group political messages than when evaluating in-group political messages." In addition, the particular content of the negative message and the strength of the justification for claiming it also affect viewers' evaluations of the ad (Budesheim, Houston, and DePaola, 1996). A study employing survey and advertising data from the 2000 presidential campaign and two 1998 gubernatorial campaigns showed that while voters' distaste for negative advertising may affect their judgment of the campaign itself, it does not necessarily affect their judgment of the information offered by the ad, as viewers tend to separate those judgments (Sides, Lipsitz, and Grossmann, 2010).

Issue and Campaign Awareness

The level of a voter's issue and campaign awareness prior to viewing an ad will moderate its persuasive effect. The least aware are more susceptible to persuasion not only because they only pick up on the simplest part(s) of the message and do not devote analytical energy to make sense of more subtle information cues, but also because they have little context against which to compare/evaluate the presented information.

The amount of information that viewers glean from political advertising is mediated by how informed they were to begin with and by the degree to which they follow other media. Those who are least informed about candidates and issues before exposure to political advertising learn the most from these ads, because the issues highlighted in them become more salient (Atkin and Heald, 1976). Political advertising's effect on voting intention is also stronger for those who are least informed initially, regardless of the strength of their party affiliation or whether they are politically independent (Franz and Ridout, 2007; Surlin and Gordon, 1977). In addition, one study found that viewers who tend to pay more attention to television newscasts are more strongly affected by political advertising, although newspaper reading reduces the impact of negative advertising that is seen on TV (Faber, Tims, and Schmitt, 1993). Because political ads tend to be clustered around local newscasts and the likelihood that their inaccuracies will be corrected there is slight, local news viewing has been associated with increased belief in repeatedly aired distortions featured in political ads aired in adjoining space (Jamieson and Gottfried, 2010). Viewers are more likely to recall political advertising by candidates they support, though in one study one-third of viewers couldn't recall anything whatsoever about political ads they may have seen; recall is more related to attitude than television exposure or demographics (Faber and Storey, 1984).

Need for Cognition

Since the most aware have a higher level of information demand or "need for cognition" (Cacioppo, Petty, Feinstein, and Jarvis, 1996), they will learn the most from ads; but with a larger body of knowledge, they will be little swayed by each new input (Patterson and McClure, 1976; Valentino, Hutchings, and Williams, 2004). Those with a high awareness of politics are more likely to understand and retain information but less likely to change their minds as a result (Delli Carpini and Keeter, 1996). Since the most aware have already made up their minds, messages consistent with an opinion reinforce it while contrary messages are resisted (Kaid and Tedesco, 1999). The RAS (receive, accept, sample) model predicts that the most aware will learn the most from ads but will change their minds the least, while the least aware will learn the least but change their minds the most (Zaller, 1992).

Political Efficacy and Party Identification

Whether a viewer will find the assertions offered in political advertisements believable depends on his or her political involvement, sense of personal political efficacy, and party affiliation. Voters who are more involved in following the political process may be less likely to believe ads than are those who are less so. Viewers who perceive they have some influence on the political process (political efficacy) and are more satisfied with government are more likely to accept ads at face value, and the content of any particular ad is more likely to be believed if it is offered by the viewer's own party rather than by the opposition (O'Cass, 2005). The fact that campaign rhetoric within a party tends to be consistent, regardless of other campaign restraints, helps make one's party a trustworthy source of information (Spiliotes and Vavreck, 2002). Those with lower levels of trust in government and politicians are more affected by negative ads than those with higher levels of trust (Martinez and Delegal, 1990).

Attack ads can be effective against the target if there is no response; however, a strong response may turn viewer emotions back against the ad sponsor (Sonner, 1998). Consistent with research that indicates public disapproval of negative ads generally, Roddy and Garramone (1988) found that viewers prefer that responses to attack be positive; nevertheless, a counterattack is more effective in discrediting the original attacker. Messages in attack advertising that are backed by a credible source can be effective in damaging the electability of an attacked candidate, but if the allegation is denied by another credible source, the effect of the attack can be nullified; if that denial is accompanied by a counterattack, the attacked candidate may come off better than before the exchange began (Calantone and Warshaw, 1985). Pfau and Kenski (1990) agree that candidates must defend against negative messages but find that inoculation strategies against anticipated attacks are more effective than ad hoc responses.

Negative advertising can have a third-person effect. Viewers deny that negative advertising about someone they support will affect them but do posit a probable effect on others; by contrast, they report that negative advertising about someone they do not support affects them but hypothesize that it would probably not affect others (Cheng and Riffe, 2008; Cohen and Davis, 1991; Shen, Dardis, and Edwards, 2011). When viewers become convinced that they must get to the polls and counteract the ballots of their gullible neighbors, the third-person effect can lead to increased voting (Golan, Banning, and Lundy, 2008).

Under some conditions, negative political advertising can damage the sponsoring candidate more than the intended target. Scholars have found that viewers find negative advertising distasteful and tend to attach that distaste to the candidate or party sponsoring (or intended to benefit from) the ad (Garramone, 1984; Hill, 1989; Jasperson and Fan, 2002; Kahn and Geer, 1994; Pinkleton, 1998); they especially don't care for ads that use inflammatory language, attack a candidate's personal life, or are misleading (Jamieson, 2000). This effect can be muted by party allegiance (Bowen, 1994; Robideaux, 2004) and party loyalty (Sorescu and Gelb, 2000), the perceived credibility of the information source cited in the attack (Calantone and Warshaw, 1985), and whether the ad includes insult or is more substantive (Roese and Sande, 1993). The chance of a backlash from negative advertising can be significantly reduced by using a contrastive approach rather than outright attack (Pinkleton, 1997).

Unanswered Questions

Experimental research on the impact of political ads has had difficulty mimicking the actual campaign environment in which multiple channels carry complementary advertising content and in which competing ads contain responses, re-framings and counterattacks. The rolling cross sectional surveys that have identified ad effects (Johnston, Hagen, and Jamieson, 2004; Kenski, Hardy, and Jamieson, 2010) have had the benefit of across time analysis of the competing message environment, but despite their inclusion of television buys in 2000 and television, cable and radio in 2008 failed to track Internet advertising content in either and had no way of confirming actual exposure to messages aired in the survey respondent's media market. The rise of micro-targeted messaging through mobile devices increases the difficulty of tracking the actual content to which subgroups of persuasible voters are exposed.

Summary

Although its effects are mediated by party affiliation, political knowledge, political involvement, and media exposure, political advertising can affect voting. In addition to persuading viewers to vote for a specific candidate or issue, political ads can also have agenda-setting and third-person effects that can indirectly affect voter intention. Because political advertising is a potent tool for influencing voter choice, differences in the amount of money alternative campaigns have available to pay for such ads can affect outcome. Although viewers don't report that they like negative or attack advertising, it can nevertheless be effective in shaping voting decisions; however, this effect may be the opposite of what the ad sponsor intended. Negative ads do seem to affect cynicism regarding government and can reduce voter turnout under specific conditions, but they do not significantly affect overall voter turnout. Political advertisements need to elicit both emotional and cognitive responses in order to move votes. Print and broadcast news abet the power of political ads by legitimizing the format and giving the ads free airplay.

Despite the criticism that political advertising receives for manipulating voters, it does underscore the existence of choices in a system of government and assert that they are consequential.

References

Airne, D., and Benoit, W. L. 2005. Political television advertising in campaign 2000. *Communication Quarterly* 53(4): 473–492.

Allen, M., and Burrell, N. The negativity effect in political advertising. In J. P. Dillard and M. Pfau (Eds.), *The persuasion handbook: Developments in theory and practice* (pp. 83–96). Thousand Oaks: Sage, 2002.

Althaus, S. L., Nardulli, P. F., and Shaw, D. R. 2002. Candidate appearances in presidential elections, 1972–2000. *Political Communication* 19(1): 49–72.

Ansolabehere, S., Iyengar, S., Simon, A., and Valentino, N. 1994. Does attack advertising demobilize the electorate? *American Political Science Review* 88(4): 829–838.

Ansolabehere, S. and Iyengar, S. 1995. *Going negative: How political advertisements shrink and polarize the electorate*. New York: Free Press.

Ansolabehere, S., Iyengar, S., and Simon, A. 1999. Replicating experiments using aggregate and survey data: The case of negative advertising and turnout. *American Political Science Review* 93(4): 901–909.

Atkin, C., and Heald, G. 1976. Effects of political advertising. *Public Opinion Quarterly* 40(2): 216–228.

Bartels, L. M. 2008. *Unequal democracy: The political economy of the new gilded age*. New York: Russell Sage.

Benoit, W. L., Blaney, J. R., and Pier, P. M. 1998. *Campaign '96: A functional analysis of acclaiming, attacking, and defending*. Westport, CT: Praeger.

Benoit, W. L. 2001. The functional approach to presidential television spots: Acclaiming, attacking, defending 1952–2000. *Communication Studies* 52(2): 109–126.

Bowen, L. 1994. Time of voting decision and use of political advertising: The Slade Gorton-Brock Adams senatorial campaign. *Journalism and Mass Communication Quarterly* 71(3): 665–675.

Bradley, S. D., Angelini, J. R. and Lee, S. 2007. Psychophysiological and memory effects of negative political ads: Aversive, arousing, and well remembered. *Journal of Advertising* 36(4): 115–127.

Brader, T. 2005. Striking a responsive chord: How political ads motivate and persuade voters by appealing to emotions. *American Journal of Political Science* 49(2): 388–405.

Brians, C. L., and Wattenberg, M. P. 1996. Campaign issue knowledge and salience: Comparing reception from TV commercials, TV news, and newspapers. *American Journal of Political Science* 40: 172–193.

Budesheim, T. L., Houston, D. A., and DePaola, S. J. 1996. Persuasiveness of in-group and out-group political messages: The case of negative political campaigning. *Journal of Personality and Social Psychology* 70(3): 523–534.

Cacioppo, J. T., Petty, R. E., Feinstein, J. A., and Jarvis, W. B. G. 1996. Dispositional differences in cognitive motivation: The life and times of individuals varying in need for cognition. *Psychological Bulletin* 119: 197–253.

Calantone, R. J., and Warshaw, P. R. 1985. Negating the effects of fear appeals in election campaigns. *Journal of Applied Psychology* 70: 627–633.

Cheng, H., and Riffe, D. 2008. Attention, perception, and perceived effects: Negative political advertising in a battleground state of the 2004 presidential election. *Mass Communication and Society* 11(2): 177–196.

Cho, J. 2011. The geography of political communication: Effects of regional variations in campaign advertising on citizen communication. *Human Communication Research* 37(3): 434–462.

Clinton, J. D., and Lapinski, J. S. 2004. "Targeted" advertising and voter turnout: An experimental study of the 2000 presidential election. *Journal of Politics* 66(1): 69–96.

Cohen, J., and Davis, R. G. 1991. Third-person effects and the differential impact in negative political advertising. *Journalism and Mass Communication Quarterly* 68(4): 680–688.

Dardis, F. E., Shen, F., and Edwards, H. H. 2008. Effects of negative political advertising on individuals' cynicism and self-efficacy: The impact of ad type and message exposures. *Mass Communication and Society* 11(1): 24–42.

Delli Carpini, M. X., and Keeter, S. 1996. *What Americans know about politics and why it matters.* New Haven, CT: Yale University Press.

Diamond, E., and Bates, S. 1984. *The spot: The rise of political advertising on television.* Cambridge. MA: MIT Press.

Drew, D., and Weaver, D. 1998. Voter learning in the 1996 presidential election: Did the media matter? *Journalism and Mass Communication Quarterly* 75(2): 292–301.

Faber, R. J., and Storey, M. C. 1984. Recall of information from political advertising. *Journal of Advertising* 13(3): 39–44.

Faber, R. J., Tims, A. R., and Schmitt, K. G. 1993. Negative political advertising and voting intent: The role of involvement and alternative information sources. *Journal of Advertising* 22(4): 67–76.

Finkel, S. E., and Geer, J. G. 1998. A spot check: Casting doubt on the demobilizing effect of attack advertising. *American Journal of Political Science* 42(2): 573–595.

Franz, M. M., and Ridout, T. N. 2007. Does political advertising persuade? *Political Behavior* 29(4): 465–491.

Franz, M. M., and Ridout, T. N. 2010. Political advertising and persuasion in the 2004 and 2008 presidential elections. *American Politics Research* 38(2): 303–329.

Franz, M. M., Freedman, P., Goldstein, K., and Ridout, T. N. 2008. Understanding the effect of political advertising on voter turnout: A response to Krasno and Green. *The Journal of Politics* 70: 262–268.

Freedman, P., and Goldstein, K. 1999. Measuring media exposure and the effects of negative campaign ads. *American Journal of Political Science* 43(4): 1189–1208.

Freedman, P., Wood, W., and Lawton, D. 1999. Do's and don'ts of negative ads: What voters say. *Campaigns and Elections* 20(9): 20–25.

Garramone, G. M. 1984. Voter responses to negative political ads. *Journalism and Mass Communication Quarterly* 61(2): 250–259.

Garramone, G. M., Atkin, C. K., Pinkleton, B. E., and Cole, R. T. 1990. Effects of negative political advertising on the political process. *Journal of Broadcasting and Electronic Media* 34(2):
299–311.

Geer, J. G. 2006. *In defense of negativity: Attack ads in presidential campaigns.* Chicago:
University of Chicago Press.

Gerber, A. S., Gimpel, J. G., Green, D. P., and Shaw, D. R. 2011. How large and long-lasting are
the persuasive effects of televised campaign ads? Results from a randomized field experiment. *American Political Science Review* 105(1): 135–150.

Golan, G. J., Kiousis, S. K., and McDaniel, M. L. 2007. Second-level agenda setting and political advertising: Investigating the transfer of issue and attribute saliency during the 2004 US
presidential election. *Journalism Studies* 8(3): 432–443.

Golan, G. J., Banning, S. A., and Lundy, L. 2008. Likelihood to vote, candidate choice, and the
third-person effect: Behavior implications of political advertising in the 2004 presidential
election. *American Behavioral Scientist* 52(2): 278–290.

Goldstein, K. August 1997. Political advertising and political persuasion in the 1996 presidential campaign. Paper delivered at the annual meeting of the American Political Science
Association, Washington DC.

Goldstein, K., and Freedman, P. 2000. New evidence for new arguments: Money and advertising in the 1996 Senate elections. *The Journal of Politics* 62(4): 1087–1108.

Goldstein, K., and Freedman, P. 2002. Campaign advertising and voter turnout: New evidence
for a stimulation effect. *The Journal of Politics* 64(3): 721–740.

Goldstein, K., and Ridout, T. N. 2004. Measuring the effects of televised political advertising in
the United States. *Annual Review of Political Science* 7: 205–226.

Groenendyk, E. Q., and Valentino, N. A. 2002. Of dark clouds and silver linings: Effects of
exposure to issue versus candidate advertising on persuasion, information retention and
issue salience. *Communication Research* 29(3): 295–319.

Gronbeck, B. E. 1992. Negative narratives in 1988 presidential campaign ads. *Quarterly Journal
of Speech* 78(3): 333–346.

Gunsch, M. A., Brownlow, S., Haynes, S. E., and Mabe, Z. 2000. Differential linguistic content
of various forms of political advertising. *Journal of Broadcasting and Electronic Media* 44(1):
27–42.

Hansen, G. J., and Benoit, W. L. 2002. Presidential television advertising and public policy priorities, 1952–2000. *Communication Studies* 53(3): 284–296.

Hardy, B. W. forthcoming. Candidate traits and political choice, in K. Kenski and K. H.
Jamieson (Eds.), *The Oxford handbook of political communication.* New York: Oxford
University Press.

Hill, R. P. 1989. An exploration of voter responses to political advertisements. *Journal of
Advertising* 184: 14–22.

Hill, S. J., Lo, J., Vavreck, L., and Zaller, J. 2008. The duration of advertising effects in political
campaigns. Paper presented at the Midwest Political Science Association.

Hill, S. J., Lo, J., Vavreck, L., and Zaller, J. 2013. How quickly we forget: the duration of persuasion effects from mass communication. *Political Communication* 30: 521–547.

Huber, G. A., and Arceneaux, K. 2007. Identifying the persuasive effects of presidential advertising. *American Journal of Political Science* 51(4): 957–977.

Jackson, R. A., Mondak, J. J., and Huckfeldt, R. 2009. Examining the possible corrosive impact
of negative advertising on citizens' attitudes toward politics. *Political Research Quarterly*
62(1): 55–69.

Jamieson, K. H. 2000. *Everything you need to know about politics and why you're wrong.* New York: Basic Books.

Jamieson, K. H., and Gottfried, J. A. 2010. Are there lessons for the future of news from the 2008 presidential campaign? *Daedalus 139*(2): 18–25.

Jamieson, K. H., Waldman, P., and Sherr, S. 2000. Eliminate the negative? Defining and refining categories of analysis for political advertisements. In J. A. Thurber, C. Nelson, and D. Dulio (Eds.), *Crowded airwaves* (pp. 44–64). Washington DC: Brookings.

Jasperson, A. E., and Fan, D. P. 2002. An aggregate examination of the backlash effect in political advertising: The case of the 1996 U.S. Senate race in Minnesota. *Journal of Advertising 31*(1): 1–12.

Johnson, T. J., Braima, M. A. M., and Sothirajah, J. 2000. Measure for measure: The relationship between different broadcast types, formats, measures, and political behaviors and cognitions. *Journal of Broadcasting and Electronic Media 44*(1): 43–61.

Johnston, A., and Kaid, L. L. 2002. Image ads and issue ads in U.S. presidential advertising: Using videostyle to explore stylistic differences in televised political ads from 1952 to 2000. *Journal of Communication 52*(2): 281–300.

Johnston, R., Hagen, M. G., and Jamieson, K. H. 2004. *The 2000 presidential election and the foundations of party politics.* New York: Cambridge University Press.

Just, M., Crigler, A., and Wallach, L. 1990. Thirty seconds or thirty minutes: What viewers learn from spot advertisements and candidate debates. *Journal of Communication 40*(3): 120–133.

Kahn, K. F., and Geer, J. G. 1994. Creating impressions: An experimental investigation of political advertising on television. *Political Behavior 16*(1): 93–116.

Kahn, K. F., and Kenney, P. J. 1999. Do negative campaigns mobilize or suppress turnout? Clarifying the relationship between negativity and participation. *American Political Science Review 93*(4): 877–889.

Kaid, L. L., and Johnston, A. 1991. Negative versus positive television advertising in the U.S. presidential campaigns, 1960–1988. *Journal of Communication 41*(3): 53–64.

Kaid, L. L., Leland, C. M., and Whitney, S. 1992. The impact of televised political ads: Evoking viewer responses in the 1988 presidential campaign. *Southern Communication Journal 57*: 285–295.

Kaid, L. L., and Tedesco, J. C. 1999. Tracking voter reactions to television advertising. In L. L. Kaid and D. G. Bystrom (Eds.), *The electronic election: Perspectives on the 1996 campaign communication* (pp. 233–246). Mahwah, NJ: Erlbaum.

Kaid, L. L., Fernandes, J., and Painter, D. 2011. Effects of political advertising in the 2008 presidential campaign. *American Behavioral Scientist 55*(4): 437–456.

Kaplan, N., Park, D. K., and Ridout, T. N. 2006. Dialogue in American political campaigns? An examination of issue convergence in candidate television advertising. *American Journal of Political Science 50*(3): 724–736.

Kellermann, K. 1989. The negativity effect in interaction: It's all in your point of view. *Human Communication Research 16*(2): 147–183.

Kenski, K., Hardy, B., and Jamieson, K. H. 2010. *The Obama victory: How media, money and message shaped the 2008 election.* New York: Oxford University Press.

Krasno, J. S., and Green, D. P. 2008. Do televised presidential ads increase voter turnout? Evidence from a natural experiment. *The Journal of Politics 7*: 245–261.

Krupnikov, Y. 2011. When does negativity demobilize: tracing the conditional effect of negative campaigning on voter turnout? *American Journal of Political Science 55*: 797–813.

Lang, A. 1991. Emotion, formal features, and memory for televised political advertisements. In F. Biocca (Ed.), *Television and political advertising: Vol. 1. Psychological processes* (pp. 221–243). Hillsdale, NJ: Lawrence Erlbaum.

Lau, R. R., Sigelman, L., Heldman, C., and Babbitt, P. 1999. The effects of negative political advertisements: A meta-analytic assessment. *American Political Science Review* 93(4): 851–875.

Lau, R. R., Sigelman, L., and Rovner, I. B. 2007. The effects of negative political campaigns: A meta-analytic reassessment. *The Journal of Politics* 69(4): 1176–1209.

Leshner, G. 2001. Critiquing the image: Testing image adwatches as journalistic reform. *Communication Research* 28(2): 181–208.

Martinez, M. D., and Delegal, T. 1990. The irrelevance of negative campaigns to political trust: Experimental and survey results. *Political Communication* 7(1): 25–40.

McCombs, M. E., and Shaw, D. L. 1972. The agenda-setting function of mass media. *Public Opinion Quarterly* 36(2): 176–187.

McCombs, M. E., Llamas, J. P., Lopez-Escobar, E., and Rey, F. 1997. Candidate images in Spanish elections: Second-level agenda-setting effects. *Journalism and Mass Communication Quarterly* 74(4): 703–717.

Meirick, P. 2002. Cognitive responses to negative and comparative political advertising. *Journal of Advertising* 31(1): 49–62.

Meirick, P. C., and Nisbett, G. S. 2011. I approve this message: Effects of sponsorship, ad tone, and reactance in 2008 presidential advertising. *Mass Communication and Society* 14(5): 666–689.

Mittal, B. 1994. Public assessment of TV advertising: Faint praise and harsh criticism. *Journal of Advertising Research* 34: 35–53.

Muehling, D. D., Stoltman, J. J., and Grossbart, S. 1990. The impact of comparative advertising on levels of message involvement. *Journal of Advertising* 19(4): 41–50.

O'Cass, A. 2005. Political campaign advertising: Believe it or not. *Journal of Nonprofit and Public Sector Marketing* 14(1): 205–246.

Patterson, T. E., and McClure, R. D. 1976. *The unseeing eye: The myth of television power in national politics.* New York: Putnam.

Petrevu, S., and Lord, K. R. 1994. Comparative and noncomparative advertising: Attitudinal effects under cognitive and affective involvement conditions. *Journal of Advertising* 23: 77–90.

Perloff, R. M., and Kinsey, D. 1992. Political advertising as seen by consultants and journalists. *Journal of Advertising Research* 32(3): 53–60.

Pfau, M., and Kenski, H. C. 1990. *Attack politics: Strategy and defense.* New York: Praeger.

Pfau, M., Parrott, R., and Lindquist, B. 1992. An expectancy theory of the effectiveness of political attack television spots: A case study. *Journal of Applied Communication Research* 20(3): 235–253.

Phillips, J. M., Urbany, J. E., and Reynolds, T. J. 2007. Does confirmation trump valence? Confirmation and the effects of negative and positive political advertising. *Advances in Consumer Research* 34: 208.

Pinkleton, B. E. 1997. The effects of negative comparative political advertising on candidate evaluations and advertising evaluations: An exploration. *Journal of Advertising* 26, 19–29.

Pinkleton, B. E. 1998. Effects of print comparative political advertising on political decision-making and participation. *Journal of Communication* 48(4): 24–36.

Pinkleton, B. E., Um, N.-H., and Austin, E. W. 2002. An exploration of the effects of negative political advertising on political decision making. *Political Advertising* 31(1): 13–25.

Richardson, G. W., Jr. 2001. Looking for meaning in all the wrong places: Why negative advertising is a suspect category. *Journal of Communication* 51(4): 775–800.

Robideaux, D. R. 2004. A longitudinal examination of negative political advertising and advertisement attitudes: A North American example. *Journal of Marketing Communication* 10(3): 213–224.

Roddy, B. L., and Garramone, G. M. 1988. Appeals and strategies of negative political advertising. *Journal of Broadcasting and Electronic Media* 32: 415–427.

Roese, N. J., and Sande, G. N. 1993. Backlash effects in attack politics. *Journal of Applied Social Psychology* 23(8): 632–653.

Rozin, P., and Royzman, E. B. 2001. Negativity bias, negativity dominance, and contagion. *Personality and Social Psychology Review* 5(4): 296–320.

Schenck-Hamlin, W. J., Procter, D. E., and Rumsey, D. J. 2000. The influence of negative advertising frames on political cynicism and politician accountability. *Human Communication Research* 26(1): 53–74.

Shapiro, M. A., and Rieger, R. H. 1992. Comparing positive and negative political advertising on radio. *Journalism Quarterly* 69(1): 135–145.

Shaw, D. R. 1999. The effect of TV ads and candidate appearances on statewide presidential votes, 1988–96. *American Political Science Review* 93(2): 345–361.

Shaw, D. R. 2006. *The race to 270: The electoral college and the campaign strategies of 2000 and 2004*. Chicago: University of Chicago Press.

Shen, F., Dardis, F. E., and Edwards, H. H. 2011. Advertising exposure and message type: Exploring the perceived effects of soft-money television political ads. *Journal of Political Marketing* 10(3): 215–229.

Shyles, L. 1984. The relationships of images, issues and presentational methods in televised spot advertisements for 1980's American presidential primaries. *Journal of Broadcasting* 28(4): 405–421.

Sides, J., Lipsitz, V., and Grossmann, M. 2010. Do voters perceive negative campaigns as informative campaigns? *American Politics Research* 38(3): 502–530.

Spiliotes, C. J., and Vavreck, L. 2002. Campaign advertising: Partisan convergence or divergence? *The Journal of Politics* 64(1): 249–261.

Sonner, B. S. 1998. The effectiveness of negative political advertising: A case study. *Journal of Advertising Research* 38(6): 37–42.

Sorescu, A. B., and Gelb, B. D. 2000. Negative comparative advertising: Evidence favoring fine-tuning. *Journal of Advertising* 29(4): 25–40.

Surlin, S. H., and Gordon, T. F. 1977. How values affect attitudes toward direct reference political advertising. *Journalism Quarterly* 54(1): 89–98.

Tedesco, J. C. 2002. Televised political advertising effects: Evaluating responses during the 2000 Robb-Allen senatorial election. *Journal of Advertising* 31(1): 37–48.

Thorson, E., Christ, W. G., and Caywood, C. 1991. Effects of issue-image strategies, attack and support appeals, music, and visual content in political commercials. *Journal of Broadcasting and Electronic Media* 35: 465–486.

Valentino, N. A., Hutchings, V. L., and Williams, D. 2004. The impact of political advertising on knowledge, Internet information seeking, and candidate preference. *Journal of Communications* 54(2): 337–354.

Vavreck, L. 2001. The reasoning voter meets the strategic candidate: Signals and specificity in campaign advertising, 1998. *American Politics Research* 29(5): 507–529.

Vavreck, L. 2007. The exaggerated effects of advertising on turnout: The dangers of self-reports. *Quarterly Journal of Political Science* 2: 325–343.

Wattenberg, M. P., and Brians, C. L. 1999. Negative campaign advertising: Demobilizer or mobilizer? *American Political Science Review* 93(4): 891–899.

Zaller, J. R. 1992. *The nature and origins of mass opinion*. New York: Cambridge University Press.

CHAPTER 12

....

POLITICAL CAMPAIGN
DEBATES

....

DAVID S. BIRDSELL

IN US presidential elections, candidate debates are marquee events, drawing the largest audiences of the campaign: 63.2 million for the second 2008 Obama-McCain debate, nearly 70 million for the Biden-Palin exchange,[1] and 67.2 million the first of the 2012 debates between Romney and Obama. These events dominated the news coverage for days leading up to and immediately following each one. While presidential candidates could at one time treat the decision to debate as a strategic choice—there were no debates in 1964, 1968, or 1972—debates have, since 1984, been obligatory performances accompanied by briefings and rehearsals focused on highlighting candidate strengths, opponents' weaknesses, and avoiding the kind of gaffe that can torpedo message strategies and sink campaigns. Scholars have responded accordingly, devoting a great deal of attention to these contests since the first presidential debate in 1960. The vast majority of this scholarship has focused on presidential debates per se—and on general election presidential debates at that—rather than the much larger and more diverse array of campaign debates across the spectrum of American politics. This chapter therefore focuses on presidential debate scholarship, including, where possible, what we know about the wider range of campaign debates overall.

These limitations of scope notwithstanding, over the United States' five decades of experience with presidential debates, debate research has focused with some consistency on several core questions. Scholars have asked how, if at all, debates affect viewer learning and voting, whether and how format affects debaters' performance, and the way viewers (or listeners) understand debates; they have assessed the role of the participants themselves in debates and the nature of the claims they advance during them; they have examined media coverage of debates and the media's apparent influence on learning and voter preference. A central question throughout is the impact of debates overall: Do they matter, for whom, and how? Scholarship on these questions is divided; the most recent studies have tended to support the notion that debates affect both learning and voter preference although not usually electoral outcome. This chapter is organized around the questions asked most consistently by debate scholars, noting under each category divergent points of view and remaining research questions.

WHETHER TO DEBATE AND UNDER WHAT AUSPICES?

Debates have become obligatory at the presidential level, but this was far from clear until the 1990s. There were no debates in 1964, 1968, and 1972; the 1980 schedule was uniquely thin; and the League of Women Voters, which had sponsored the debates from 1976 to 1984, gave up that role for the 1988 cycle. As a result, well into the 1990s, scholarly and professional attention was devoted in part to the question of whether there would be presidential debates, and if so, employing what format(s) under what sponsorship.

The first volume published on presidential debates, *The Great Debates: Kennedy Nixon, 1960* (Kraus, 1962), consisted of articles dealing with the genesis of the Kennedy-Nixon debates, their formats and audience effects. Joel Swerdlow (1987) also looked at sponsorship issues and particularly at the transition from the League of Women Voters to the Commission on Presidential Debates, which was established in 1987 "to ensure that debates, as a permanent part of every general election, provide the best possible information to viewers and listeners." Minow and Lemay (2008) brought to bear Minow's decades of experience as a debate negotiator both from the campaign perspective (Kennedy in 1960) and as an adviser to both the League of Women Voters and the Commission.

As presidential debates have become more nearly certain, fewer scholarly analyses have attended to their likelihood. There has, on the other hand, been increasing attention to the Commission's conditions for considering whom to include in debates, to third party access overall (e.g., Open Debates, n.d.; Newton, Sloan, and Angulo, 1999; Farah, 2004) and continuing interest in format among scholars. Negotiations over number, sequencing, invitations, and format will remain a matter of scholarly interest unless campaign regulations were to require debates of a particular format on a particular schedule with clear rules for including and excluding participants.

FORMAT

Format refers primarily to the flow of events in a debate and secondarily to the physical arrangement of the stage, together with the placement of the television cameras transmitting images of the event. A third set of considerations is editorial: which camera feed to put onscreen, whether to split the screen for reaction shots or other image pairings, whether to allow voice-over commentary, and so on. Since the first general election debates in 1960, campaign operatives have negotiated over format issues in all three categories (Minow and Lemay, 2008; Schroeder, 2008; Swerdlow, 1987), seeking advantage for their respective candidates where possible, but even more concentrating on ensuring (perceived) equity, control, and predictability. Scholars have tried to test many of these assumptions and to measure the impact of the results on audiences.

Some formats have elicited controversy. Press panels—the only debate format employed at the presidential level through 1988—were criticized in the 1970s and 1980s for fragmented attention to issues, sensationalism, and other infirmities (Bitzer and Rueter, 1980; Jamieson and Birdsell, 1988; Swerdlow, 1987). The press panel in its original form disappeared after the 1988 cycle, replaced by what has been a stable mix from 1992 to 2008 of two single-moderator debates with the presidential candidates standing at podiums, one audience/town hall debate with the candidates seated but permitted to get up and walk toward questioners or the opponent (as a wandering John McCain demonstrated during the town hall debate in 2008; see coverage of comedians' attention to that behavior in the *Huffington Post*, 2008), and a vice presidential debate, also superintended by a single moderator. The stability of these formats precludes evaluating the differential impact of format decisions in any given race; the status quo can be compared only to the press panels of 1988 and before.

Several studies have found that camera angle and other variables, such as split-screen shots (see Mutz and Holbrook, 2003; Mutz and Reeves, 2005), influence audience perception of debates. In a study in which students were shown a Bush-Kerry debate from the 2004 cycle in both split- and single-screen formats, Scheufele, Kim, and Brossard (2007) found that students who entered the experiment favoring Bush became more extreme in their positive and negative impressions of Bush and Kerry under the split-screen condition, while Kerry supporters showed little change based on format. Kepplinger and Donsbach (1987) found that camera angles could make a difference in audience perceptions of a candidate among those favorably disposed toward a candidate, those ill-disposed toward a candidate, and previously neutral observers. An unpublished study of the visual dimensions of debate by Westcott-Baker (2008) found that camera placement—one of the prime determinants of camera angle—in at least one 2000 presidential debate made Democratic Party nominee Al Gore appear less central to the conversation than his opponent, George W. Bush. As Scheufele and his colleagues note, "this area of debate research is surprisingly understudied, especially given the controversy surrounding" the closed process between the candidates and the Commission on Presidential Debates leading up to format and coverage decisions (16-17).

Stage arrangement per se received more attention in the era of the press panel than it has since the status quo mixture of single-moderator and town hall debates (Bitzer and Rueter, 1980; Jamieson and Birdsell, 1988). The press panel debates and contemporary primary debates have been compared with game show formats and other forms of entertainment television based primarily on the visual dimensions of debates (Schroeder, 2001).

Participants

The identity and ineffaceable personal characteristics of the participants (distinct from performance variables, which are discussed below) may affect participants' conduct as well as the press coverage and audience response to debates. Since—with the exception of Barack Obama, Geraldine Ferraro, Sarah Palin, and Hillary Clinton—general election debaters in the United States have been white men, the range of variables to test has been limited and information on differences by race or gender derived primarily from down-ballot races (e.g., Atkeson and Krebs, 2008, who did research on mayoral debates) and from races outside the United States (e.g., Gidengil and Everitt, 2003, who did research on Canadian leaders' debates).

Gender

Several studies have examined gender as a factor in the amount and character of campaign coverage. In their analysis of debate coverage in the Canadian Leaders' debates in 1993, 1997, and 2000, Gidengil and Everitt (2003) found that female candidates were more likely to be portrayed in conflictual postures than their male counterparts, holding constant the verbal and gestural content that their coding scheme associated with aggressive behavior.

At least one study finds no gender-based differences in candidates' behavior. Banwart and McKinney (2005), in a study of mixed-gender Senate and gubernatorial debates (i.e., one or more male candidates and one or more female candidates), found that basic argumentative strategies, use of language, and issue selection did not vary significantly by gender.

Such analyses have yet to appear in the scholarly literature on presidential debates. In the United States, three women have participated in general election debates, at the vice presidential level: Democrat Geraldine Ferraro in 1984 and Republican Sarah Palin in 2008 and in 2016 Hillary Clinton. These cases do not offer a platform on which to pivot an analysis of gender variables. Representative Ferraro was the first woman nominated to a major party ticket, and Governor Palin and Secretary Clinton were anomalous choices on several dimensions that could confound any analysis of gender. Indeed, there has been limited academic attention to vice presidential debates overall, providing no baseline performance for male candidates (Dole-Mondale, Quayle-Bentsen, Quayle-Gore-Stockdale, Gore-Kemp, Lieberman-Cheney, and Edwards-Cheney) against which to compare the treatment of women candidates. To date, this is inviting but underexplored and inconclusive territory.

Voice

Research suggests that vocal qualities evinced by participants in general election debates mirror the candidates' respective "social dominance" and correlate strongly with electoral outcomes. Gregory and Gallagher (2002) examined the fundamental frequency of phonation (represented as F_0) in nineteen general election presidential debates through the year 2000. They explain:

> The F_0 is a critical component of human vocalization. When the voice is filtered electronically, however, allowing only the F_0 to pass, the resulting sound is perceived as a low-pitched and segmented hum absent of any clearly discernible verbal content. When experimental subjects' vocal frequencies beneath F_0 are filtered from the normal conversational signal . . ., the perceived quality of interaction, as measured by outside judges hearing an unfiltered version of the experimental subjects' conversational exchange, is diminished significantly (Gregory et al., 2000; Gregory et al., 1997). Thus it is evident from previous studies that the low-frequency band beneath F_0 is crucial for communicating critical social information. (298)

This information related to perceived social status, with lower-status individuals accommodating their vocalizations to those of the higher-status persons involved in the conversation. Gregory and Gallagher find that this phenomenon applies in presidential debates and correlates in every one of the nineteen cases examined with the ultimate electoral outcome.

This tantalizing study finds a strong correlation between a physical, nonverbal characteristic of voice and electoral outcome independent of any other factors. Gregory and Gallagher did not, however, test audience perceptions of social dominance, relying only the outcomes of the elections as a marker of the success of a socially dominant performance as measured by F_0, which have, of course, been explained by any number of other factors as well. In that sense they leave unresolved the question of F_0 influence on responses to debates.

DEBATES AFFECT LEARNING, PERCEIVED VIABILITY, AND SUPPORT

A meta-analysis of the extant literature concluded that viewing debates increases one's ability to distinguish candidates' positions on issues (Benoit, Hansen, and Verser, 2003). However until recently most studies had found that debates, while providing opportunities to learn about candidates' positions, did very little to influence perceptions of viability or voters' allegiances (Holbrook, 1994; Lanoue and Schrott, 1991; Sears and Chaffee, 1979; Zhu, et al., 1994). In the years since, the availability of different data sources and different methodologies has allowed scholars to identify influences that either went undetected in earlier studies or had been washed out in the totality of campaign and other factors (cf. Johnston, Hagen, and Jamieson, 2004; Kenski. Hardy, and Jamieson, 2010). So, for example, using the National Annenberg Election Survey (NAES) data, Johnston et al. (2004) found a shift in the impact of Social Security on voter intention after the first and third presidential debate of 2000 (168), and Kenski et al. (2010) found that exposure to the final debate of 2008 improved McCain's prospects.

Decomposing the Audience

Improved methods have made it possible for scholars to characterize debate viewers (and the electorate as a whole) in terms of their levels of political awareness, their prior voting records, the candidate and/or issue preferences they express before watching a debate, and other factors that might influence an individual's response to a debate (or any other campaign message). Noting limitations in data available in prior cycles, Hillygus and Jackman (2003) summarized the inherent weakness of univocal analyses of campaign effects in an article on the 2000 campaign.

> Much of this research relies on data that measures presidential campaigns as mono-lithic, time-invariant events that have the same average effect for all people during all points of the campaign (Wlezien and Erikson 2001). Clearly, the campaign is not so simplistic. Presidential campaigns consist of a series of events, activities, and efforts, and the candidates may do better or worse on each of these efforts. Intuitively, we might expect, for instance, that the effect of a Bush ad in Virginia might be different from the effect of a Gore rally in California. More fundamentally, we expect that an individual's reactions to campaign events may be influenced by that individual's prior beliefs and preferences. (584)

Writing in that same year, Waldman and Jamieson (2003) showed that voters' issue awareness and misperceptions of issue positions produced different results for different candidates, with position misattributions benefiting George W. Bush and hurting Al Gore in the 2000 campaign.

Thomas Holbrook, an early skeptic on the influence of debates on voter knowledge and choice (Holbrook, 1994), wrote in 1999 that debates and other campaign messages did show modest influence on learning and voter preference (67) and elaborated the impact on debate viewers with different levels of issue knowledge. He found that more engaged voters are the ones more likely to learn from political debates (84). He found further that the sequence of exposure and the lack of information on a given candidate make a difference as well: voters learn most about the candidates with whom they are least familiar and more from the first debate in any series than from subsequent debates. This comports with research finding the greatest debate-specific impact from primary debates and with Freedman, Franz, and Goldstein's (2004) "differential effects" hypothesis, which posits that different message forms produce different results in different viewers/voters.

New Sources of Data

As Hillygus and Jackman noted in 2003, the new century ushered in data sets that had been available on a limited basis or not at all prior to 2000. These tools afford scholars unprecedented insight into voters' reactions to campaign events.

Hillygus and Jackman use data from Knowledge Networks (KN), a "probability-based panel designed to be statistically representative of the U.S. population" (Knowledge Networks, http://www.knowledgenetworks.com/ganp/index.html). The inherent qualities of the panel design—accessible through KN on a routine basis for price points far below what would have been possible a decade earlier—make it possible to identify attitude changes at the individual level over time, which cannot be achieved with cross-sectional surveys. Using data from KN, scholars can uncover individuals' attitude changes following specific events or messages, such as a debate or a series of political advertisement, revealing movement in voter preference during a campaign that may or may not result in a given Election Day choice.

KN is not the only innovation in data collection that bears on the analysis of presidential debates. In 2000, 2004, and 2008, the Annenberg Public Policy Center at the University of Pennsylvania conducted the rolling cross-sectional National Annenberg Election Survey (NAES), which collected data on political attitudes in the 2000, 2004, and 2008 presidential election cycles. The NAES "has a particular emphasis on the effects of media exposure through campaign commercials and news from radio, television and newspapers" and "measures the effects of other kinds of political communication, from conversations at home and on the job to various efforts by campaigns to influence potential voters" (http://www.annenbergpublicpolicycenter.org/ProjectDetails. aspx?myId=1). In 2008, this study reached more than 57,000 respondents by phone prior to Election Day, another 95,000 online, and 3,737 for a postelection panel. The size and frequency of the survey, together with its emphasis on campaign messaging, allows for much more detailed analysis of voter/viewer responses to campaign events than is possible through previously available surveys, including the American National Election Studies.

Taken together, the data gleaned through KN and the NAES permit more sensitive analyses of what voters/viewers have seen or heard, how preevent attitudes relate to the likely impact of an event on postevent attitudes, and reveal opinion formation to be, for at least some voters, a more volatile process than previously supposed, with exposure to debates, advertisements, and other campaign messages moving attitudes toward a given candidate or party up or down with each successive event. Scholars using KN and/or the NAES have discovered message impacts, including impact for debates (Hillygus et al., 2003; Johnston, Hagen, and Jamieson, 2003; Kenski, Hardy, and Jamieson, 2010).

DEBATES ARE STRUCTURALLY PREDICTABLE BUT THE EFFECT OF PERFORMANCE ON PERCEPTION REMAINS ELUSIVE

Performance variables take place against a backdrop of remarkable consistency with respect to basic message patterns. Relying on their functional theory of campaign communication (e.g., Benoit, 2007; Benoit and Brazeal, 2002; Benoit and Hansen, 2004;

Benoit and Harthcock, 1999), William Benoit and colleagues have documented that basic messaging strategies are remarkably consistent across debates in all of the cycles and at all of the levels that they have examined, with a consistent balance of acclaims (positive statements about a candidate's character, record, or programs), attacks (negative comments about an opponent's character, record, or programs), and rebuttals or defenses (responses to an opponent's attacks). They show that acclaims are the most common statements in debates, followed by attacks and rebuttals/defenses, in that order. They also document that policy topics feature more prominently in debate than discussions of character. Incumbents, with a record to defend and arguing for reelection at least partly based on prior performance, are more positive and less likely to talk about character than are their challengers. While the primary focus of Benoit and colleagues has been on presidential debates during general elections, they have also covered primary debates, down-ballot debates, and debates in other nations (Benoit et al., 2002; Benoit, Brazeal, and Airne, 2007; Benoit and Klyukovski, 2006; Benoit and Sheafer, 2006; Benoit, Wen, and Yu, 2007). In short, with very few exceptions that can be explained by unique electoral circumstances (e.g., Choi and Benoit, 2009), statements made by debaters are positive and issue-focused, with predictable strategic differences between incumbents and challengers.

It is then all the more puzzling—given the gross content consistencies across levels of debate, cultural circumstances, differences in political organization, and formats—that researchers have been unable to provide a clear, empirically driven set of criteria that predict a good or poor performance. As Hillygus and Jackson (2003) note, the "research cannot distinguish what specifically about each campaign event was influential" (594); the same point can be made with respect to debate scholarship overall.

Performance is at one level the most obvious and available element of a debate—every pundit on television freely opines on candidates' fluency, organization, concision, emotional appropriateness, physically grace, empathy, command, and so forth—and the most difficult to characterize with precision. Expectations play an important role, as one candidate's lackluster performance may count as another's breakthrough. An otherwise dominant debate performance may be perceived as mean and alienating. There is no universal standard to distinguish a "commanding" debater from an "aggressive" one.

In addition to the inherent instability of these assessments is the variable of media coverage. A "gaffe" identified as such by the press and repeated on news programs for days if not weeks after a debate can become a millstone even if viewers who watched only the debate and not the coverage saw no gaffe at all. Sears and Chafee (1979) found that Gerald Ford's assertion that "there is no Soviet domination of Eastern Europe" became widely perceived as a gaffe among television viewers who watched coverage of the debate; it was not a salient feature for those polled immediately after watching the debate itself. Jamieson and Waldman (2003) found that perceptions of Al Gore's veracity were negatively influenced by those who watched coverage but not the debate itself; opinions of his veracity were relatively stable among those who watched the actual debate, irrespective of how much coverage they subsequently saw. *Saturday Night Live* and *The Daily Show* may have as much to do with the lasting impression of a debate performance as either network news or the debaters themselves. Candidates must attend not only to how their performances scan within the context of the debate per se but also within snippets on YouTube and the highlight "reels" of pundits across the spectrum of digital media.

Answering questions about the effects of debate performance will require collecting data over a period of time and in several settings (i.e., during a debate and during follow-on coverage of that debate in a variety of media). Such assessments will require capturing not only the language that candidates use but also their physical performance, nonverbal cues, opponents' responses, press reactions, and responses in entertainment venues, such as comedy sketches. They will also have to account for candidates' performance in venues outside of debate, their advertising strategies, and, increasingly, on campaign media created on their behalf by third-party organizations such as Super-PACs. And they must account for change over time. Comedian Darrell Hammond's imitation of Al Gore intoning "lock-box" in response to every question posed in the skit effectively required that Gore find a new phrase or risk association with a witheringly funny—and undermining—characterization every time he referred to that key campaign theme. Gore did not shift away from "lock-box," and public perception of him firmed up—though surely not for that reason alone—along the lines of the stiff, out-of-touch policy wonk who contrasted poorly with Bush's "approachable" candidacy.

MOST DEBATE HAPPENS OUTSIDE OF PRESIDENTIAL GENERAL ELECTION CAMPAIGNS AND WE KNOW TOO LITTLE ABOUT IT

Observers (e.g., Benoit, Brazeal, and Airne, 2007a; McKinney and Carlin, 2004) have pointed to the paucity of attention to nonpresidential debates. As Benoit and colleagues (2007) note after reviewing a handful of studies addressing debates outside of presidential general election campaigns, "these studies are a useful beginning, but the sample of debates, candidates and years is still very small" (77). This is particularly concerning in light of the fact that most campaign debates occur in other contexts.

Scholars have paid little attention to the increasing number of presidential primary debates and their growing ubiquity at the subpresidential level as well. Consider that in 2000 there were twenty-two primary debates overall, thirteen among Republican and 9 among Democratic candidates (http://www.gwu.edu/~action/primdeb/primdebm.html). Eight years later there were at least twenty-five Democratic debates and twenty-one debates among GOP candidates in a contest with no incumbent. The 2012 cycle featured twenty-seven among the GOP contestants (Election Central, 2012). As primary seasons have lengthened, primary debates have burgeoned in turn, with the first primary debate of the 2012 campaign taking place a full 18 months before Election Day (Fox News and South Carolina Republican Party, May 5, 2011; in 2000, both Republicans and Democrats waited until October 1999 to begin the debate season, a mere 13 months ahead of the general election). This lack of attention is particularly concerning given that evidence does exist that primary debates can be influential in shaping voter opinion (Yawn et al., 1998).

In 2000, there were thirty-four contested Senate races, 59 percent of which featured campaign debates. By 2010, with thirty-eight contested races (John Thune was reelected in South Dakota but did not have an opponent in the general election), only six failed to hold a debate, making debates part of 84 percent of the contested Senate elections that year. Of the thirty states that held debates (New York had two Senate races that year), 81 percent held at least two.

Debates are even more common in gubernatorial races. All eleven gubernatorial races in 2000 included general election face-offs. While the percentage shrank somewhat in 2010, the number soared. Of thirty-seven governors' races, only Nebraska's failed to produce a single debate. Among the remaining thirty-six states, Texas's incumbent Governor, Rick Perry was the only major party candidate not to participate in a debate. Of those thirty-six races, thirty involved at least two debates. Minnesota alone held a pace-setting twenty-six.

There are many hundreds of other debates in down-ballot contests at all levels of government. In some localities, debates are required as a condition for receipt of public funds (Malbin and Brusoe, 2010). In one such jurisdiction, New York City, All fifty-one City Council seats feature debates during a general election, as do all five borough president races and the three citywide offices. Even Michael Bloomberg, who opted out of the public finance system and paid for all three of his mayoral campaigns himself, felt compelled to engage during each cycle in the minimum of one official Campaign Finance Board debate mandated for recipients of public money (but not self-funders) under New York election law (the Campaign Finance Act).

In sum, general election presidential debates constitute a tiny fraction of political debating overall. But as we have seen, the scholarly literature on political debates focuses almost exclusively on this fraction, begging the question of whether other venues for political debating should be understood in the same way as the general election presidential matchups. There is good reason to believe that the "rules" may differ quite substantially in presidential primary and down-ballot races. The primaries often feature large numbers of candidates, particularly in the early portion of the season when the field has yet to sort itself into a contest among a handful of top contenders. With eight or more contenders on stage and perhaps months between a given debate and an actual election (or caucus), candidates' performance needs differ substantially from those of their general election counterparts. Coverage is far less extensive than for general election debates; viewers are more partisan (these are, after all, party primary debates); and audiences are smaller overall. While general election debates employed only press-panel formats through 1988, beginning to introduce audience questions and other format variables in 1992, presidential primary debates have used a wide range of formats, in part in response to the need to accommodate many more debaters in often cluttered primary fields. Primary debate formats have included audience questions, questions received via email, questions embedded in videos, and remote-site questioning of candidates. Statewide and local races feature a similarly wide range of formats and performance variables; they sometimes include press panelists from non-English-language newspapers and television outlets, such as Univision or Telemundo. Down-ballot debates have also employed a range of formatting and staging strategies that are unlikely soon to find their way into general election contests at the presidential level.

How do these other campaign debates differ from presidential ones? Do they affect viewers' understanding of debates overall and of presidential matchups in particular? Do cartoonish events such as New York's gubernatorial debate in 2010 (with seven candidates, including Anti-Prohibition Party nominee and former madam Kristin Davis; Jimmy McMillan, the glove-wearing, elaborately coiffed, mildly profane candidate of the Rent Is Too Damn High Party; colorful candidates nonetheless upstaged by the GOP's Carl Paladino, who left his seat to go to the restroom during closing remarks) discredit debates overall and make it less likely that they will be examined for substance rather than theater? The short answer is that we do not know. However with the proliferation of debates below the presidential level, it would be imprudent to assume that these debates are the same as the tiny fraction at the top of the political ladder or that their variety of formats, coverage, participants, and practices does not influence the reputation and reception of debates overall.

CONCLUSION

Debate scholarship has attended consistently, for more than four decades, to the auspices under which debates are constituted; the formats negotiated by sponsors and candidates; behavioral, attitudinal, and coverage variables that may or may not flow from aspects of candidates' identities; the verbal and visual content of debates; and debate's influence on issue knowledge and candidate support across a wide range of audiences. Available evidence strongly suggests that debate answers consist of a predictable mixture of strategic choices, pay closer attention to policy than to character, and work through advocacy or acclaims rather than attack. Debates influence audiences, but they influence different audiences in different ways; prior beliefs matter, as do preexisting levels of issue knowledge, and perceptions of particular candidates.

A systematic understanding of performance and performance variables remains beyond the scope of debate scholarship, as do debates that take place below the presidential level. While there have been careful studies of debates in countries outside the United States, some of them finding patterns similar to those observed in the United States, these constitute a tiny fraction of the debate literature. A comprehensive, cross-cultural account of the roles and functions of debates has yet to appear.

NOTE

1. http://latimesblogs.latimes.com/showtracker/2008/10/final-obamamcca.html

REFERENCES

Atkeson, L. R., and Krebs, T. B. 2008. Press coverage of mayoral candidates: The role of gender in news reporting and campaign issue speech. *Political Research Quarterly* 61: 239–252.

Banwart, M. C., and McKinney, M. S. 2005. A gendered influence in campaign debates? Analysis of mixed-gender United States Senate and gubernatorial debates. *Communication Studies* 56: 353–373.

Banwart, M. C., Bystrom, D. G., and Robertson, T. 2003. From the primary to the general: A comparative analysis of candidate media coverage in mixed-gender 2000 races for governor and U.S. Senate. *American Behavioral Scientist* 46: 658–676.

Benoit, W. 2007. *Communication in political campaigns.* New York: Peter Lang.

Benoit, W. L., and Brazeal, L. M. 2002. A functional analysis of the 1988 Bush-Dukakis presidential debates. *Argumentation and Advocacy* 38: 219–233.

Benoit, W. L., Brazeal, L. M., and Airne, D. 2007. A functional analysis of televised U.S. Senate and gubernatorial campaign debates. *Argumentation and Advocacy* 44: 75–89.

Benoit, W. L., and Hansen, G. J. 2004. Issue ownership in primary and general presidential debates. *Argumentation and Advocacy* 40: 143–154.

Benoit, W. L., Hansen, G. J., and Verser, R. M. 2003. A meta-analysis of the effects of viewing US presidential debates. *Communication Monographs* 70: 335–350.

Benoit, W. L., and Harthcock, A. 1999. Functions of the great debates: Acclaims, attacks, and defense in the 1960 presidential debates. *Communication Monographs* 66: 341–357.

Benoit, W. L., and Klyukovski, A. A. 2006. A functional analysis of the 2004 Ukrainian debates. *Argumentation* 20: 209–225.

Benoit, W. L., Pier, P. M., Brazeal, L. M., McHale, J. P., Klyukovski, A., and Airne, D. 2002. *The primary decision: A functional analysis of debates in presidential primaries.* Westport, CT: Praeger.

Benoit, W. L., and Sheafer, T. 2006. Functional theory and televised discourse: Televised debates in Israel and the United States. *Journalism and Mass Communication Quarterly* 83: 281–297.

Benoit, W. L., Wei-Chun Wen, and Tzu-hsiang Yu. 2007. A functional analysis of 2004 Taiwanese political debates. *Asian Journal of Communication* 17: 24–39.

Bitzer, L., and Rueter, T. 1980. *Carter versus Ford: The counterfeit debates of 1976.* Madison: University of Wisconsin Press.

Campaign Finance Act. 2007. Available at: http://www.nyccfb.info/act-program/CFACT.htm?sm=press_ap2 (Retrieved August 4, 2011.)

Choi, Y. S., and Benoit, W. L. 2009. A functional analysis of French and South Korean debates. *Speaker and Gavel* 46: 59–78.

Commission on Presidential Debates. 2012. Candidate selection criteria. Available at: http://www.debates.org/index.php?page=candidate-selection-process

Democractic Debates. 2008. Available at: http://en.wikipedia.org/wiki/Democratic_Party_(United_States)_presidential_debates,_2008

Election Central. 2012. Available at: http://www.2012presidentialelectionnews.com/2012-debate-schedule/2011-2012-primary-debate-schedule/

Farah, G. 2004. *No debate: How the Republican and Democratic Parties secretly control the presidential debates.* New York: Seven Stories Press.

Freedman, P., Franz, M., and Goldstein, K. 2004. Campaign advertising and democratic citizenship. *American Journal of Political Science* 48(4): 723–741.

Fridkin, K. L., Kenney, P. J., Gershon, S. A., Shafer, K., and Woodall, G. S. August 2007. Capturing the power of a campaign event: The 2004 presidential debate in Tempe. *The Journal of Politics* 69(3): 770–785. Available at: http://www.jstor.org/stable/4622579

Gidengil, E., and Everitt, J. 2003. Conventional coverage/unconventional politicians: Gender and media coverage of Canadian leaders' debates, 1993, 1997, 2000. *Canadian Journal of Political Science* 36(3): 559–578.

Gregory, S. W., Jr., and Gallagher, T. J. September 2002. Spectral analysis of candidates' nonverbal vocal communication: Predicting U.S. presidential election outcomes. *Social Psychology Quarterly* 65(3): 298–308.

Gregory, S. W., Jr., Green, B. E., Carrothers, R. M., Dagan, K. A., and Webster, S. 2000. Verifying the primacy of voice fundamental frequency in social status accommodation. *Language and Communication* 21: 37–60.

Gregory, S. W., Jr., Dagan, K., and Webster, S. 1997. Evaluating the relation of vocal accommodation in conversation partners' fundamental frequencies to perceptions of communication quality. *Journal of Nonverbal Behavior* 21: 37–60.

Hillygus, D. S., and Jackman, S. 2003. Voter decision making in election 2000: Campaign effects, partisan activation, and the Clinton legacy. *American Journal of Political Science* 47(4): 583–596.

Holbrook, T. M. 1994. The behavioral consequences of vice-presidential debates: Does the undercard have any punch? *American Politics Quarterly* 22: 469–482.

Huffington Post. November 10, 2008. The McCain wander. Available at: http://www.huffingtonpost.com/2008/10/10/the-mccain-wander_n_133775.html

Jamieson, K. H., and Birdsell, D. S. 1988. *Presidential debates: The challenge of creating an informed electorate.* New York: Oxford University Press.

Jamieson, K. H. and Waldman, P. 2003. *The press effect: Politicians, journalists, and the stories that shape the political world.* New York: Oxford University Press.

Johnston, R., Hagen, M. G., and Hall Jamieson, K. 2004. *The 2000 election and the foundations of party politics.* New York: Cambridge University Press.

Kenski, K., Hardy, B. W., and Jamieson, K. H. 2010. *The Obama victory: How media, money, and message shaped the 2008 election.* New York: Oxford University Press.

Kenski, K., and Jamieson, K. H. 2006. Issue knowledge and perceptions of agreement in the 2004 presidential general election. *Presidential Studies Quarterly* 36(2): 243–259.

Kepplinger, H. M., and Donsbach, W. 1987. The influence of camera perspective on the perception of a politician by supporters, opponents and neutral viewers. In D. L. Paletz (Ed.), *Political communication research: Approaches, studies, assessments* (pp. 62–72). Norwood, NJ: Ablex.

Kraus, S. (Ed.). 1962. *The great debates: Kennedy vs. Nixon, 1960.* Bloomington: Indiana University Press.

Lanoue, D., and Schrott, P. 1991. *The joint press conference.* New York: Greenwood.

Malbin, M., and Brusoe, P. W. December 2010. Small donors, big democracy: New York City's matching funds as a model for the nation and states. Available at: http://www.cfinst.org/pdf/state/NYC-as-a-Model_Malbin-Brusoe_RIG_Dec2010.pdf (Retrieved August 4, 2011).

McKinney, M. S., and Carlin, D. B. 2004. Political campaign debates. In L. L. Kaid (Ed.), *Handbook of political communication research* (pp. 203–234). Mahwah, NJ: Lawrence Erlbaum.

Mutz, D. C., and Holbrook, R. A. April 2003. Televised political conflict: Nemesis or necessity? Paper presented at the annual convention of the Midwest Political Science Association, Chicago.

Mutz, D. C., and Reeves, B. 2005. The new videomalaise: Effects of televised incivility on political trust. *American Political Science Review* 99(1): 1–15.

Minow, N. N., and Craig L. LeMay. 2008. *Inside the presidential debates: Their improbable past and promising future*. Chicago: University of Chicago Press.

Minow, Newton N., Sloan, C. M., and Angulo, C. T. 1999. *Opening salvos: Who should participate in presidential debates*. New York: Century Foundation.

Open Debates. Available at: http://www.opendebates.org/theissue/

Republican Debates. 2008. Available at: http://en.wikipedia.org/wiki/Republican_Party_(United_States)_presidential_debates,_2008

Scheufele, D. A., Kim, E., and Brossard, D. February 2007. My friend's enemy: How split-screen debate coverage influences evaluation of presidential debates. *Communication Research* 34(1): 3–24. Available at: http://crx.sagepub.com/content/34/1/3.full.pdf+html (Retrieved February 11, 2012).

Schroeder, A. 2008. *Presidential debates: Fifty years of high-risk TV*. New York: Columbia University Press.

Sears, D., and Chaffee, S. 1979. Uses and effects of the 1976 debates: An overview of empirical studies. In S. Kraus (Ed.), *The great debates: Carter vs. Ford, 1976* (pp. 223–261). Bloomington: Indiana University Press.

Swerdlow, Joel (Ed.). 1987. *Presidential debates: 1988 and beyond*. Washington, DC: Congressional Quarterly Press.

Waldman, P., and Jamieson, K. H. 2003. Rhetorical convergence and issue knowledge in the 2000 presidential election. *Presidential Studies Quarterly* 33(1): 145–163.

Westcott-Baker, A. November 2008. Gore de-fanged: Camera angles, construction of space and Gore's marginalization in the second 2000 presidential debate. Paper presented at the 94th Annual National Communication Association Convention, San Diego, CA; also presented in April 2007 at Media Fields, University of California Santa Barbara.

Wlezien, C., and Erikson, R. S. 2002. The timeline of presidential election campaigns. *The Journal of Politics* 64(04): 969–993.

Yawn, M., Ellsworth, K., Beatty, B., and Kahn, K. F. 1998. How a presidential primary debate changed attitudes of audience members. *Political Behavior* 20(2): 155–181.

Zhu, Jian-Hua, Milavsky, J. R., and Biswas, R. 1994. Do televised debates affect image perception more than issue knowledge? A study of the first 1992 presidential debate. *Human Communication Research* 20: 302–333.

CHAPTER 13

NICHE COMMUNICATION IN POLITICAL CAMPAIGNS

LAURA LAZARUS FRANKEL
AND D. SUNSHINE HILLYGUS

INTRODUCTION

MOST of what we know about campaign communication has come from the study of television advertising. This is hardly surprising because this is where candidates have spent the bulk of their campaign money for at least the last half a century. But dramatic changes in communication technology and the information environment in recent years have changed not only our daily lives, but also campaign communications. With each new election cycle, candidates seem to add to the expanding list of communication technologies used—smartphones, Facebook, blogs, and the like—to get their message to intended recipients.

In this essay, we review the limited, but growing, research that examines candidates' use of niche campaign communications, conceptualized here as any communication medium candidates employ to directly and narrowly target a particular audience. There is a tendency to think of the use of new technologies as a supplemental communication tool for conducting politics as usual—altering the style or mode of communication but not the basic structure of political interaction (Margolis and Resnick, 2000).[1] We suggest, however, that new communication technologies have changed not only how candidates communicate with the public, but also whom they contact and what they are willing to say. Whereas candidates once focused on broad mass appeals to voters, campaign strategies now involve the tailoring of messages to specific voters and households (Hillygus and Shields, 2008), with implications for the nature and influence of campaign discourse. In other words, niche communications have actually changed some fundamental aspects of candidate strategy and campaign dynamics.

BACKGROUND

Today's media and informational environment is characterized by its diversity, fragmentation, and complexity. With the introduction of cable television, websites, blogs, social media, and the like, the public no longer relies on just broadcast news and newspapers for information. These new technologies have changed how the public communicates, gathers information, and interacts with political campaigns (Mossberger et al., 2008). In this essay, we consider the implications of this new environment for candidate communications.

The evolution in candidate communications has been driven by opportunity and necessity—the combination of a basic desire to improve the efficiency and effectiveness of those messages and new resources with which to do so. Candidates now face a higher "cost-per-impression" to reach a voter with a broadcast message. The expansion of media choice (on television, cable, and the Internet) and the widespread use of technologies such as remote controls and TIVO make it is easier than ever for the public to avoid political advertising (Prior, 2007). As new media technologies and alternative forms of access to voter information have provided candidates with the ability to target subgroups of voters, the declining efficiency of broadcast communication has incentivized campaigns to make increasing use of this new technology.

The emergence of microtargeted communications rests on the combination of new communication technologies and the increased availability of information about individual voters. The political parties have built enormous databases that contain information about every registered voter in the United States. Statewide, electronic voter registration files—mandated by the 2002 Help America Vote Act—are the cornerstone of these databases. These files typically include a person's name, home address, turnout history, party registration, phone number, and other information, and are available to parties and candidates (and, in most states, anyone else who wants it). Consumer, census, political, and polling data are then merged to these files to better predict who is going to turn out, what their beliefs and attitudes are, and, ultimately, how they are going to vote. These predictions then drive candidate messaging (Hersh, 2011).

STATE OF THE FIELD

Unfortunately, the body of research on niche communications is theoretically and empirically underdeveloped. The frantic pace at which new technologies are being introduced means that scholarship about the nature and influence of niche communications is never current. Politicians seem to continually play catch-up to the technologies used by teenagers, and scholars continually play catch-up to the politicians. Not only is there minimal research on many of the newer communication technologies, the research that does exist is largely descriptive—simply documenting the use of a new technology in the political realm. There is a sense that the impact of research in this area is also limited; given the length of publication cycles, the hottest new technology may well be replaced by the next best thing before research is in print.[2] Moreover, much of recent knowledge about the effectiveness of new communications is coming not from published academic studies but from the campaigns themselves as more and more have started embedding research experiments into their communication campaigns (Issenberg, 2012).

The fragmentation that characterizes the information environment today is also apparent in the existing scholarship. Scholarship on niche communications is scattered across the academic fields of communications and political science, and across different subfields. At most, this work is organized by mode of contact or research methodology, which we will argue has a limiting effect on the theoretical development of the field. Before offering our view of the most fruitful directions for future research, we first provide a brief overview of the existing research covering each of the various communication modes that might be deemed a niche medium.

Face-to-Face Canvassing

When we think about niche communications, it typically invokes images of Facebook and Twitter in twenty-first-century campaigns. But the most personal form of electoral messaging, face-to-face interaction, was the first niche communication and dates to the earliest political campaigns (Wielhouwer, 2003). Even as campaigns focused primarily on broadcast communications beginning in the mid-twentieth century, they continued some "on the ground" efforts to mobilize core supporters. In the past decade or so, campaigns have increased their ground efforts. In the 2004 US presidential elections, the two major-party presidential campaigns knocked on over 17 million doors (Bergan et al., 2005).

Considerable research has demonstrated that face-to-face canvassing succeeds at increasing turnout (e.g., Gerber and Green, 2000; Green et al., 2003). Compared to other modes of contact, it is thought that the personal nature of the communication makes it especially effective (Dale and Strauss, 2009; Gerber and Green, 2000; Green and Gerber, 2004). Much of the research on the effectiveness of personal canvassing has focused on the question of turnout, largely reflecting its historical use for getting partisans to the polls. But with information about *every* registered voter, campaigns now attempt to persuade as well as mobilize. Recently scholars have begun to evaluate the persuasive effects of door-to-door canvassing and found it can increase candidate support (Arceneaux, 2007).

There remains very little research, however, about the candidate strategy behind face-to-face communication—who is most or least likely to be targeted, when they are contacted, or the content of the messaging. Using the American National Election Study (ANES), Panagopoulos and Wielhouwer (2008) show previous voters and those living in battleground states are especially likely to report contact. Unfortunately, the ANES contact question fails to account for the changing nature of campaign communication, as it does not distinguish between contact via face-to-face contact, email, phone, or the like.[3] If candidates target different groups for email communication than for face-to-face contact, for instance, we are especially limited in our ability to understand candidate strategy using this measure. In evaluating the nature and influence of face-to-face contact, researchers should account for the characteristics of the canvasser and the recipient (e.g., matched race, familiarity, etc.), as well as the content of the message—including not only if it is a mobilization or persuasion message, but also the issue content, tone, and complexity. In many respects, the literature needs to better heed Lasswell's maxim, "who says what to whom in which channel" in examining the effects of face-to-face campaign communication

Telephone/Text

Along with personal canvassing, Get Out the Vote (GOTV) efforts using telephone calls have been standard practice in political campaigns for many decades. In the 2004 US presidential election, the two major-party presidential campaigns were estimated to have completed 50.7 million phone calls (Bergan et al., 2005). As with the research on face-to-fact contact, analyses of this type of campaign communication have typically focused on its effectiveness for mobilizing voters. Research has generally found that campaign calls are less effective than is face-to-face contact, which is often attributed to the fact that phone calls are less personal than canvassing and fail to increase feelings of social connectedness (Gerber and Green, 2000; Green and Gerber, 2004).

There is, however, perhaps no starker example of the diversifying nature of campaign communication than the telephone. We simply cannot generalize about the nature or effectiveness of telephone communication given its diversity today; telephone communication can be by landline, cell phone, text message, email via smartphone, personal contact vs. robocall. We are just starting to see work that distinguishes types of telephone communication. For instance, research finds that phonebank efforts for GOTV can produce a mobilizing effect (McNulty, 2005; Nickerson, 2006; Nickerson et al., 2006; Ramirez, 2005; Wong, 2005), but nonconversational communication, such as robocalls, often has little effect (Garcia Bedolla and Michelson, 2009; Green and Gerber, 2004; Michelson et al., 2007). A recent field experiment conducted by Shaw et al. (2012) attempted to determine whether source credibility impacts the effectiveness of robocalls on vote turnout. Their experiment produced weak but statistically significant effects suggesting that, if done well, robocalls can be an effective campaign tool. Yet despite the framework of social connectedness that may lead us to expect the contrary, emerging work finds that GOTV reminders via text message produce results (Dale and Strauss, 2009; Malhotra et al., 2011). To explain this contradiction, Dale and Strauss (2009) propose a "Noticeable Reminder Theory" which posits that a noticeable and salient reminder can be effective despite the impersonal medium, if a recipient is already intending to vote. As Manjoo (2008) notes, unlike other directed but automated messages "text messages show up on a device that you carry with you all day long—and because you probably get only a handful of them each day, you're likely to read each one."

The strength of this new work lies in its consideration of the characteristics of the communication, rather than just the mode. But there remain many unanswered questions and many other factors (mobility, complexity of message, etc.) that might shape campaign strategy and effectiveness. Here again, for instance, little is known about the effectiveness of these messages for persuasion. We might expect that texting registered voters is effective simply because all that is needed is a reminder, whereas persuasion would seem much more difficult in 160 characters.

Direct Mail and Email

Political direct mail dates back to at least 1914 when Woodrow Wilson mailed 300,000 campaign communications (Pfau et al., 1990), but it has seen a reemergence in the last couple of decades (Monson, 2004). Between 2000 and 2004, spending on direct mail more than doubled from $242 million to an estimated $564 million (Lieberman, 2004).[4] Its appeal is that, compared to television advertising, it is less expensive, allows more detail, and is more easily targetable.[5]

Reflecting its potential for microtargeting, Hillygus and Shields (2008) demonstrate that direct mail discusses a greater variety of policy issues and is more likely to discuss divisive issues than is television advertising. They find that Bush and Kerry mentioned more than seventy-five different policy issues in their direct mail communications in the 2004 presidential campaign. In addition, while fewer than 1 percent of television ads mentioned the wedge issues of abortion, gay marriage, and stem cell research, nearly 10 percent of direct mail mentioned them.

With regard to the effects of direct mail for turnout and persuasion, the results of a series of field experiments reveal mixed results. Some research demonstrates that direct mail is ineffective for increasing turnout and persuading voters (Cardy, 2005; Gerber and Green, 2000, 2003). However, other studies find both turnout effects (Green and Gerber, 2008) and small persuasive effects (Gerber, 2004). Results from a more recent field experiment in a Kansas attorney general race indicate that direct mail had a substantial persuasive effect—a 10 percentage point increase in the amount of mail sent to a precinct increased vote share by approximately 3 percentage points (Gerber et al., 2011). The authors of the latter study attribute the differences in findings across studies to the low level of information voters had about this down-the-ballot race.

In our daily lives, snail mail has been replaced by email communication, so it seems natural to question if the same will happen with campaign communication. Certainly, campaigns are utilizing email to communicate with the electorate. In 2008, the Obama campaign sent a total a total of 1 billion emails, comprised of 7,000 distinct messages, over the course of the campaign (Vargas, 2008). Email is a notable campaign asset because of its low-cost, flexibility, mass reach, and ease of construction (Shea, 2009; Williams and Trammell, 2005). Additionally, it is not restricted in volume by the cost constraints of other mediums (Shea, 2009). Campaigns are able to email a large volume of messages with little overhead or lead time.

Yet, email has a number of characteristics that might lead us to expect that it is not a direct substitute for traditional direct mail. To begin, because of the volume of emails most individuals already receive, the existence of spam filters, and the tendency of individuals to delete emails without reading them, there is reason to believe that sending an email does not equate with a recipient reading it (Looney, 2004). Moreover, even if the email is read, recent survey analysis casts doubt on its effectiveness in shaping voter attitudes when compared to television and radio advertisements (Overby and Barth, 2009). Results from field experiments in the context of voter registration drives show that emailed outreach produces no increase in the level of voter registration and, in some cases, actually depresses registration and turnout (Bennion and Nickerson, 2010; Nickerson, 2007).

More importantly, however, candidates do not have similar access to email addresses as they do mailing addresses, which are readily available in voter registration files.[6] There is no public directory of email addresses, and while some email addresses may be available through various lists and databases, there seems to be a consensus among practitioners that political spam is risky, such that "most mainstream political organizations should find that the dangers of relying on others' email lists outweigh the benefits" (Krueger, 2006, 763). As a consequence, candidates typically rely on individuals to sign-up to receive emails through their websites. Of course, those most likely to do so tend to be already supportive and politically engaged, potentially limiting the usefulness of email for persuading swing voters.

As a consequence, email lists are most widely used for fundraising and mobilization efforts and, indeed, their use in this regard is growing. The 2008 Obama email list contained some 13 million email addresses generated primarily from traffic to their campaign's websites. Due to email's increasing use and relative newness there is much more research to be done. For instance, is there a difference in effectiveness between a truly personal email and an individualized email blast? Is there a way for unsolicited political email to be effective for persuasion? While political spam remains rare, which candidates are using it and to what effect?

Internet/Websites

It can be difficult to study the role of the Internet in political campaigns because nearly *everything* can be done on the Internet–fundraising, virtual "town hall" meetings, voter registration, debates, and the like. It is sometimes hard to believe that it has been only 15 years since the first presidential election in which the candidates maintained websites (Klotz, 2004; Howard, 2006). In a very short period of time, candidate websites have become the norm. In 1998, only 35 percent of Democratic and Republican congressional candidates created websites (Kamarck, 1999), but by 2006 this number more than doubled to over 80 percent (Gulati and Williams, 2007).

Candidate website content has been the subject of considerable research. Gulati and Williams (2007) find that website content is typically designed for fundraising, engaging supporters, organizing volunteers, and disseminating candidate information. Foot and Schneider (2006) similarly break campaigns' online content into four strategic motivations: informing, involving, connecting, and mobilizing.[7] Xenos and Foot (2005) conclude that websites have increased the overall amount of information campaigns provide about policy issues. In coding congressional websites from 2002 to 2006, Druckman et al. (2009) find systematic differences between incumbent and challenger sites. Incumbents tend to rest on their laurels, emphasizing experience and what they've accomplished. In contrast, challengers, especially in competitive races, are more likely to take risks such as going negative and using Web 2.0 technologies, incorporating explicitly interactive components, like a blog, or linking to other more interactive sites like YouTube. These choices are likely based on assumptions about how websites affect voters, something that is quite difficult to evaluate.

A Pew Study of the 2008 election found that the majority of Internet users (74%) went online to participate in, or to get news and information about the campaign. However, a survey cannot cleanly distinguish voter utilization of *candidate* websites from other online information sources. Moreover, given the extent of linking across websites—through advertising pop-ups, and the like—it can often be difficult for users themselves to know what sites they are accessing. Estimating the impact of a candidate website is further complicated by the general recognition that visitors to candidate websites are more likely to be supporters than detractors or swing voters (Bimber and Davis, 2003). As Klotz (2004) puts it, there is a "low incidence of accidental exposure" (640).

And while the knowledge that those who access candidate sites do so through selective exposure may lead us to assume that the information provided is targeted to those already disposed toward the candidate, the wide accessibility of websites means that content must be broadly constructed to avoid alienating less supportive voters. So while we know little about the distinct effects of candidate websites, their similarities to broadcast media may help us understand the strategic choices campaigns make when building them.[8] Reflecting this concern for broad appeal, while many candidates are using tools from the blogosphere (Lawson-Borders and Kirk, 2005), some research concludes that campaigns are creating a façade of interaction, for example, using a blog format for carefully-screened, press-release-type content (Baker and Stromer-Galley, 2006).

Of course, as the Internet now contains nearly *everything*, candidate websites do not exist in a vacuum. As the interconnectivity of different types of media and the technological capabilities of online tools increase, it is becoming difficult to separate direct campaign communication on the web from a mediated message. To this end, we cannot hope to extensively cover the types of Internet communication with which candidates are concerned but, rather, are restricting this essay to direct communications from the candidates. However, given the preponderance of information on candidate websites and their role as a link to other online tools—social media, blogs, YouTube, etc.—it seems increasingly important to understand the flow of information. How, for example, does a particular YouTube video become a sensation? What role can a campaign play in controlling this flow, and how does it try?

Nowhere is the fuzzy divide between direct and indirect Internet communication more clearly reflected than in forms of social media. On sites such as Facebook and Myspace candidates only have direct control over a sliver of the messages communicated by the medium.

Social Media

Social media, like Facebook and Twitter, are the hottest new technology. As of December 2013, Facebook has 1.23 billion active users, and as of January 2014, Twitter has upwards of 645 million users. (Facebook, 2013; http://www.statisticbrain.com/twitter-statistics/). Not surprisingly, then, campaigns are increasingly trying to use these new technologies to communicate with the electorate. In 2008, the Obama campaign had more than 3.2 million supporters on Facebook alone, and turned the Facebook Group "Students for Barack Obama" into an official part of the campaign after it proved an enormously effective organizing tool for college students (Vargas, 2008).[9] By 2012, the official Obama campaign Facebook page had nearly 28 milliom "likes" (Pew, 2012: http://www.journalism.org/2012/08/15/attention/).

Some predict that the political import of these technologies will continue to grow, as social media become more enmeshed in "mainstream" political institutions and news (Sanson, 2008). Candidates for the Republican Presidential nomination, for example, held a "Twitter debate" in July 2011 (Holt, 2011). Research from recent elections notes that the "e-momentum" that arose on social networks was subsequently communicated and amplified through more mainstream mediums, like network news (Hull and Morgan, 2010; Williams and Gulati, 2013).

Social media communications represent a very different form of communication from that previously discussed. First, by definition, by tapping into social networks, they create the potential to increase the spread and impact of messages. Second, social media technologies are more interactive in nature than previous modes. Whereas candidates control the content they put on their own websites, social networking sites allow users to contribute content. Because information can flow in both directions, this is a much riskier form of communication for campaigns. Third, many of these communication technologies are not monolithic in their mode like email or text messaging. For example, Facebook allows candidates to maintain a profile page, post status updates, post on "walls," send direct private messages, link themselves with other groups or individuals, target particular demographic groups with niche advertising, and host live forums that mimic town halls. When he mistakenly sent all of his followers rather than a single college co-ed what he thought was a private image of his self-described "package" and what some media outlets described as a "crotch shot," former Congressman Anthony Weiner learned the hard way that twitter has both public and private messaging capabilities.

While research on social media is just emerging, scholars and journalists have observed some patterns that distinguish its use from other communication modes. Given the risky nature of social media communications, they are most often used by challengers and candidates running in competitive races (Williams and Gulati, 2013). It is also clear that they can be used for very narrow microtargeting on a mass scale. Sanson (2008) describes how the 2008 Obama campaign microtargeted social media users based on their profiles and group memberships on various social networking sites. Moreover, the campaign was able to make the most of its resources by strategically targeting individuals who held central roles in different networks (ibid).

While it is difficult to measure the effectiveness of social media communications, work on voter interaction with these technologies hints at their potential role. In 2006, 13 percent of all Facebook users expressed support for a candidate (Williams and Gulati, 2013), and in 2008 over 5 million Facebook users clicked the "I Voted" button that the site provided (Vargas, 2008). Based on Obama's success in the 2008 campaign, especially among younger voters, there is speculation that social networking sites can serve to mobilize and engage the electorate, but research evaluating the effectiveness of social media is in its infancy. In tracking measures of candidate support in social networking media, Hull and Morgan (2010) find suggestive evidence of momentum building and bandwagon effects in the nomination stage of the 2008 campaign. A randomized experiment during the 2010 midterm election found those receiving a mobilization message through Facebook were 0.39 percent more likely to vote than those who did not receive a message (Bond et al., 2012). This study hints at the potential of social media for persuasion, though more research is clearly needed in this area.

Clearly, there is both more to learn about the strategic use of social media and many ways in which the study of it and its impact can be improved. Much of the current scholarship operationalizes social network communication too narrowly, for example, by only analyzing candidates' profile pages, walls, or status updates (Sanson, 2008). But social media communications are highly multi-faceted and interwoven, something that is increasingly true of many new communication technologies. This suggests that we should be cautious in making claims about the general effects of Facebook, Twitter, or any other social media, broadly defined.

Radio

Although radio was the first nonprint medium that allowed candidates to broadcast messages to a large number of voters (Weeks, 1964), we include it here because it is now so clearly niche communication. The fragmentation of audiences coupled with the proliferation of radio stations has facilitated its use to narrowcast messages and target specific groups. For example, in the 1988 election, Michael Dukakis used radio ad buys on predominantly black radio stations to take a position on gun control that directly contradicted the position he espoused in his broadcast television ads (Oreskes, 1988).

Despite its rich history, research on radio has been rather limited, with a couple of notable exceptions that examine the effectiveness of radio advertising. Analyzing the effects of exposure to advertising on reported likelihood to vote for a candidate during the 2008 campaign, Kensksi et al. find that radio advertising is more effective than either cable or local broadcast television advertising (2010). Field experiments have also demonstrated that radio advertisements can increase turnout (Panagopoulos and Green, 2008). We know much less about the strategic use of radio advertising by campaigns. Radio spots are numerous, prolific, and often fragmented, which, we suspect, is one of the reasons that there exists less scholarship on radio than other advertising mediums. Indeed, it is the elusive nature of radio advertising that makes it so useful for narrowcasting. Taking advantage of personal connections with a campaign, Overby and Barth (2011) offer a rare comparison of television and radio advertising in Tom Kaine's 2005 gubernatorial run. They find that radio ads were much more targeted, especially to black voters. We consider this to be a very fruitful area for future research.

DIRECTIONS FOR FUTURE RESEARCH

Although we have reviewed the existing literatures by mode of communication here, we argue that it is not the most compelling way to conceptualize research on niche communication. Technological advancements, increased access to voter data, and the interconnectivity of new communication technologies (and old) mean that different communication modes can provide a diverse variety of types of contact, all of which may have differing effects. As an example, within the "mode" of social networks, direct messaging on Facebook may produce forms of influence more similar to email than to Facebook status updates. Further, a targeted radio advertisement may feel more personal to voters than does a pre-recorded robocall, even though phone contact is typically conceptualized as a more personal mode of contact than radio broadcast.

We therefore suggest that future scholarship on campaign communication look beyond mode and, instead, focus on the context and characteristics of communication, such as who delivers the message, how, to whom, and what the content is. For example, does the medium transmit a message from one person to many (e.g., Twitter posts) or one to one (e.g., Twitter private messages)? Is the message easily shared with individuals beyond the intended recipient (e.g., email)? Is the medium mobile (e.g., cell phone)? Is it interactive, such that it expects a response from the recipient (e.g., a personal email as compared to an email blast)? Is the communication exchange anonymous (e.g., blog commentary), identifiable by some (Facebook), or fully identified and public? Undoubtedly there are other characteristics we have not mentioned, but the power of thinking in terms of communication characteristics is that it not only more accurately captures the increasingly blurry lines across modes and the diversity within mode, but also advances theory building. This approach inherently guides us toward explanations of why a communication might be effective or not. Further, it helps us build expectations not just about existing communication technologies, but also about the role of technologies that do not yet exist. As a field in a constant state of playing "catch up," this more nuanced approach may assist us in getting "ahead of the game"—i.e., building theory.

As literature on niche communications continues to develop, one of the more vexing problems will be methodological in nature. While field experiments represent a potent way to measure the effect of a communication on the public, it is far more complicated to get a clear portrait of the niche communication actually occurring in campaigns. For one, the fragmented and often elusive nature of these communications makes it more difficult to collect data on the volume and content of the messages. In contrast, television advertising is routinely collected and coded. The groups who receive television advertising are clearly designated by geographic boundaries, as these messages vary by media market. In contrast, niche communications vary from one household to the next. Moreover, there is far greater regulatory oversight, and subsequent record keeping, of television and radio advertising, than of many niche communications. The definition of electioneering communication in the 2002 Bipartisan Campaign Reform Act is limited to advertisements made by "broadcast, cable, or satellite communication." For example, broadcast advertisements have strict disclosure and disclaimer requirements to the Federal Election Commission that do not apply to direct mail, emails, or face-to-face communications.

Nonetheless, it is a worthy task to understand the strategic use of niche communications by political candidates, in no small part because of the normative implications. Some politicos and academics have called microtargeting a "welcome" development in American politics because personalized contact might increase interest and participation amongst the electorate (Dulio, 2004). Unfortunately, there exist a number of potentially negative implications.

First, niche communications threaten to exacerbate inequalities in political information and engagement. Because voter registration files are often the basis for niche communications, citizens who are not registered to vote are especially vulnerable to being ignored by political elites. Hillygus and Shields (2008) show that direct mail, telephone calls, and face-to-face visits were targeted to registered voters with an active vote history, despite existing research suggesting that campaign communications can have their largest effect on those least likely to participate (Arceneaux and Nickerson, 2009). More generally research has shown that the proliferation of sources of political information is widening disparities in knowledge and participation amongst the electorate (Prior, 2005) because it is easier than ever for those not interested in politics to ignore it entirely. These disparities parallel other systematic inequalities, such as socio-economic status, level of education, and race. As campaigns are increasingly able to contact only those who are likely supportive or persuadable voters, persistent inequalities in political participation and knowledge amongst those with low SES may be exacerbated.

Second, we must consider what the fragmentation in delivery of candidate platform and messages means for democratic theories of governance. Specifically, when campaigns highlight and voters cast ballots based on different issues, what are the implications for public discourse and for elected officials' ability to govern a unified citizenry?

For example, Bush and Kerry mentioned 75 distinct issues in their direct mail campaigns in 2004, and households rarely received mailings from different candidates about the same issue (Hillygus and Shields, 2008). At its extreme, a fragmented campaign dialogue undercuts the very notion that a collective public opinion exists, and disavows the possibility that an elected official has a legitimate mandate to pursue a specific policy agenda. Despite the reluctance of many empiricists to broach normative theory, these topics deserve further attention.

Final Thoughts

Research on niche communication in political campaigns is in its infancy. Indeed, the pace of technological innovation means that we are unlikely to ever have a firm grasp on its nature and influence. But the clearest path for development within the field is to concern ourselves not just with the adoption of the latest and greatest new technology by political campaigns, but with understanding the nature of its use. Who is being contacted? What is the content of the messages being communicated? And with what effect? To answer these questions, we must consider not just the general mode of communication, but also its characteristics. A political message sent by phone cannot just be called a phone call—it could be a text message, a robocall, a voicemail, an email, a social media interaction, or any number of other forms of communication. And each of these has a set of characteristics that could make it more or less distinctive from just a phone call. Since it seems inevitable that the lines between communication modes will continue to blur, it is all the more important for research to try to understand how candidates are using various communication technologies and why various communications have a particular effect. In developing better theories of niche communications, this field moves from a specialized body of work to fundamentally building on our understanding of candidate strategy and campaign dynamics.

Notes

1. M. Margolis and D. Resnick 2000. *Politics as usual: The "Cyberspace revolution."* Thousand Oaks, CA: Sage.
2. Indeed, this chapter was first drafted in 2010, predating a number of communication innovations in the 2012 campaign. As just one example, Obama participated in a popular Reddit AMA ("Ask Me Anything").
3. Question Wording: "As you know, the political parties try to talk to as many people as they can to get them to vote for their candidate. Did anyone from one of the POLITICAL PARTIES call you up or come around and talk to you about the campaign this year?"
4. Lieberman, D. (2004, August 18). Cable, satellite, Net grab chunk of election ad bucks, *USA Today*, p. B1.
5. The 2002 Bipartisan Campaign Reform Act indirectly encouraged ground war efforts because it focused campaign finance regulations almost exclusively on broadcast

communications (Kang, 2005). Indeed, the definition of electioneering communication is limited to advertisements made by "broadcast, cable, or satellite communication." Broadcast advertisements also require immediate reporting to the Federal Election Commission, while there are no equivalent requirements for direct mail, emails, or face-to-face communications.

6. Some states have email as an optional field, but most indications are that it is not often used.

7. This is similar to Bimber and Davis (2003) break of website functions into (1) opinion reinforcement, (2) activism, (3) donating, and (4) voter registration and mobilization.

8. This may be changing as some research suggests that new technologies may actually enable campaigns to tailor displayed website content to the data file associated with a visitor's IP address, undermining the assumption that websites can only be used for "mass" messaging (Howard, 2003).

9. This is contrast to the 190,000 Howard Dean supporters connected through Meetup.com, the first social media, in 2004 (Trippi, 2004).

REFERENCES

Arceneaux, K. 2007. I'm asking for your support: The effects of personally delivered campaign messages on voting decisions and opinion formation. *Quarterly Journal of Political Science*, 2(1), 43–65.

Arceneaux, K., and D. Nickerson. 2009. Who is mobilized to vote? A re-analysis of 11 field experiments. *American Journal of Political Science*, 53, 1–16.

Bennion, E., and D. W. Nickerson. 2010. The cost of convenience: An experiment showing email outreach decreases voter registration. *Political Research Quarterly*. Retrieved from http://prq.sagepub.com/content/early/2010/09/23/1065912910382304

Bergan, D. E., A. S. Gerber, D. P. Green., and C. Panagopoulos. 2005. Grassroots mobilization and voter turnout in 2004. *The Public Opinion Quarterly*, 69(5), 760–777.

Bimber, B., and R. Davis. 2003. *Campaigning online: The Internet in U.S. elections*. New York, NY: Oxford University Press.

Bond, R. M., C. J. Fariss, J. J. Jones, A. D. Kramer, C. Marlow, J. E. Settle, and J. H. Fowler. 2012. "A 61-million-person experiment in social influence and political mobilization." *Nature* 489, no. 7415: 295–298.

Cardy, E. A. 2005. An experimental field study of the GOTV and persuasion effects of partisan direct mail and phone calls. *Annals of the American Academy of Political and Social Science*, 601, 28–40.

Carlson, N. 2011. Chart of the day: How many users does twitter really have? *Business Insider*. Retrieved from http://www.businessinsider.com/chart-of-the-day-how-many-users-does-twitter-really-have-2011-3#ixzz1IH31klUW

Dale, A., and A. Strauss. 2009. Don't forget to vote: Text message reminders as a mobilization tool. *American Journal of Political Science*, 54(4), 787–804.

Druckman, J. N., M. Kifer., and M. Parkin. 2009. Campaign communications in U.S. congressional elections. *American Political Science Review*, 103(3), 343–366.

Dulio, D. A. 2004. *For better or worse? How political consultants are changing elections in the United States*. Albany, NY: SUNY Press.

Facebook. 2013. Statistics. Facebook.com. Retrieved from http://newsroom.fb.com/Key-Facts

Foot, Kirsten A., and Steven M. Schneider. 2006. *Web campaigning*. Cambridge, MA: MIT press.

Garcia Bedolla, L., and M. R. Michelson. 2009. What do voters need to know? Testing the role of cognitive information in Asian-American voter mobilization. *American Politics Research*, 37(2), 254–274.

Gerber, A. S. 2004. Does campaign spending work? Field experiments provide evidence and suggest new theory. *American Behavioral Scientist*, 47(5), 541–574.

Gerber, A. S., D. P. Kessler, and M. Meredith. 2011. The persuasive effects of direct mail: A regression discontinuity based approach. *Journal of Politics*, 73, 140–155.

Gerber, A. S., and D. P. Green. 2000. The effects of canvassing, telephone calls and direct mail on voter turnout: A field experiment. *American Political Science Review*, 3, 653–663.

Gerber, A. S., and D. P. Green. 2003. Partisan mail and voter turnout: Results from randomized field experiments. *Electoral Studies*, 22, 63–579.

Green, D. P., and A. S. Gerber. 2004. *Get out the vote: How to increase voter turnout.* Washington, D.C.: Brookings Institution Press.

Green, D. P., and A. S. Gerber. 2008. *Get out the vote: How to increase voter turnout: Second Edition.* Washington, D.C.: Brookings Institution Press.

Green, D. P., A. S. Gerber., and D. W. Nickerson. 2003. Getting out the vote in local elections: Results from six door-to-door canvassing experiments. *Journal of Politics*, 65, 1083–1096.

Gulati, G. J., and C. B. Williams. 2007. Closing the gap, raising the bar: Candidate web site communication in the 2006 campaigns for Congress. *Social Science Computer Review*, 25(4), 443–465.

Hersh, E. 2011. At the mercy of data: Campaigns' reliance on available information in mobilizing supporters. Working Paper. Retrieved from http://www.eitanhersh.com/uploads/7/9/7/5/7975685/atthemercyofdata.pdf

Hillygus, D. S., and T. Shields. 2008. *The persuadable voter.* Princeton, NJ: Princeton University Press.

Holt, K. 2011. Republican presidential candidates to face off in Twitter debate. Scribbal.com. Retrieved from www.scribbal.com/2011/06/republican-presidential-candidates-to-face-off-in-twitter-debate/

Howard, P. N. 2003. Digitizing the social contract: Producing American political culture in the age of new media. *Communication Review*, 6, 213–245.

Howard, P. N. 2006. *New media campaigns and the managed citizen.* New York: Cambridge University Press.

Hull, C. C., and B. Morgan. 2010. Friending Obama: How netroots technology is altering presidential nomination dynamics. Paper presented at the annual meeting of the Northeastern Political Science Association, Boston, MA.

Issenberg, Sasha. 2012. *The victory lab: The secret science of winning campaigns.* Random House LLC.

Kamarck, E. C. 1999. Campaigning on the Internet in the elections of 1998. In *Democracy.com: Governance in a networked world,* ed. E. C. Kamarck and J. S. Nye, Jr. Hollis, NH: Hollis.

Kang, M. 2005. From to narrowcasting: The emerging challenge for campaign finance law. *George Washington Law Review,* 73(5/6), 1070.

Klotz, R. J. 2004. *The politics of Internet communication.* Oxford: Rowman and Littlefield.

Krueger, B. S. 2006. A comparison of conventional and Internet political mobilization. *American Politics Research,* 34(6), 759–776.

Lawson-Borders, G., and R. Kirk. 2005. Blogs in campaign communication. *American Behavioral Scientist,* 49(4), 548–559.

Lieberman, D. 2004. Cable, satellite, Net grab chunk of election ad bucks. *USA Today*, 18 August, B1.

Looney, S. 2004. Civic participation and the Internet: Indicators from the 2004 presidential campaigns. *LBJ Journal of Public Affairs*, 16, 49–61.

Malhotra, N., T. Rogers, and A. A. Valenzuela. 2011. Text messages as mobilization tools: The conditional effect of habitual voting and election salience. *American Politics Research*, 39(4), 664–681.

Manjoo, F. 2008. Texts you can believe in. Slate.com. Retrieved from http://www.slate.com/id/2203146

Margolis, M., and D. Resnick. 2000. *Politics as usual: The cyberspace revolution*. Thousand Oaks, CA: Sage.

McNulty, J. E. 2005. Phone-based GOTV—What's on the line? Field experiments with varied partisan components, 2002–2003. *Annals of the American Academy of Political and Social Science*, 601, 41–65.

Michelson, M. R., L. G. Bedolla., and D. P. Green. 2007. *New experiments in minority voter mobilization: A report from the California Votes Initiative*. San Francisco, CA: The James Irvine Foundation.

Monson, J. Q. 2004. Get on television versus get on the van: GOTV and the ground war in 2002, in D. B. Magleby and J. Q. Monson, ed. *The last hurrah? Soft money and issue advocacy in the 2002 congressional elections*. Washington, D.C.: Brookings Institution Press.

Mossberger, K., C. Tolbert, and R. McNeal. 2008. *Digital citizenship: The Internet, society and participation*. Cambridge, MA: MIT Press.

Nickerson, D. 2006. Volunteer phone calls can increase turnout. *American Politics Research*, 34(3), 271–292.

Nickerson, D. W. 2007. Does email boost turnout? *Quarterly Journal of Political Science*, 2(4), 369–379.

Nickerson, D. W., R. K. Friedrichs., and D. C. King. 2006. Partisan mobilization campaigns in the field: Results from a statewide mobilization campaign in Michigan. *Political Research Quarterly*, 59(March), 85–97.

Oreskes, M. 1988. Thrust of TV campaign ads can vary with the territory. *The New York Times*, 1 November.

Overby, L. M., and J. Barth. 2009. The media, the medium, and malaise: Assessing the effects of campaign media exposure with panel data. *Mass Communication and Society*, 12(3), 271–290.

Overby, L. M., and J. Barth. 2011. Broadcasting vs. narrowcasting: Television ads, radio ads, and niche marketing in an American political campaign. *European Political Science Association (Dublin)*.

Panagopoulos, C., and D. P. Green. 2008. Field experiments testing the impact of radio advertisements on electoral competition. *American Journal of Political Science*, 52, 156–168.

Panagopoulos, C., and P. Wielhouwer. 2008. Polls and elections: The ground war 2000–2004: Strategic targeting in grassroots campaigns. *Presidential Studies Quarterly*, 38(2), 347–362.

Pfau, M., H. C. Kenski, M. Nitz., and J. Sorenson. 1990. Efficacy of inoculation strategies in promoting resistance to political attack messages: Application to direct mail. *Communication Monographs*, 57(1), 25–43.

Prior, M. 2005. News vs. entertainment: How increasing media choice widens gaps in political knowledge and turnout. *American Journal of Political Science*, 49(July), 577–592.

Prior, M. 2007. *Post-broadcast democracy: How media choice increases inequality in political involvement and polarizes elections.* New York: Cambridge University Press.

Ramirez, R. 2005. Giving voice to Latino voters: A field experiment on the effectiveness of a national nonpartisan mobilization effort. *Annals of the American Academy of Political and Social Science, 601*(September), 66–84.

Sanson, A. 2008. Facebook and youth mobilization in the 2008 presidential election. *Gnovis, 8*(3), 162–174.

Shea, D. M. 2009. Young voters, the Obama net-roots campaign, and the future of local party organizations. Retrieved from https://www.uakron.edu/pages/bliss/docs/SheaSOPpaperfor the2009conference.pdf

Stromer-Galley, J., and A. B. Baker. 2006. Joy and sorrow of interactivity on the campaign trail: Blogs in the primary campaign of Howard Dean. In *The Internet election: Perspectives on the web in campaign 2004*, ed. A. P. Williams and J. C. Tedesco. Lanham, MD: Rowman and Littlefield.

Trippi, J. 2004. *The revolution will not be televised.* New York: Regan Books.

Vargas, J. A. 2008. Obama raised half a billion online. *The Washington Post.* Retrieved from http://voices.washingtonpost.com/44/2008/11/obama-raised-half-a-billion-on.html

Weeks, L. E. 1964. The radio election of 1924. *Journal of Broadcasting, 8*, 223–243.

Wielhouwer, P. W. 2003. In search of Lincoln's perfect list: Targeting in grassroots campaigns. *American Politics Research, 3*(6), 632–669.

Williams, A. P., and K. D. Trammell. 2005. Candidate campaign email messages in the presidential election 2004. *American Behavioral Scientist, 49*(4), 560–574.

Williams, C., and Gulati, J. 2013. Social networks in political campaigns: Facebook and the congressional elections of 2006 and 2008. *New Media & Society, 15*(1): 52–71.

Wong, J. 2005. Mobilizing Asian American voters: A field experiment. *Annals of the American Academy of Political and Social Science, 601*, 102–114.

Xenos, M. A., and K. A. Foot. 2005. Politics as usual, or politics unusual: Position-taking and dialogue on campaign web sites in the 2002 U.S. elections. *Journal of Communication, 55*, 169–185.

......

CHAPTER 14

THE FUNCTIONAL THEORY OF POLITICAL CAMPAIGN COMMUNICATION

......

WILLIAM L. BENOIT

POLITICAL election campaigns are ubiquitous—and no more so than in the United States. Candidates run for a myriad of elective offices including mayor, city council, congress (state and federal), senate (state and federal), governor, president, and in some jurisdictions, judgeships. In elections in other countries, US style campaigning seems to be spreading. Presidential debates have been held in many countries, including Australia, Canada, France, Germany, Iran, Israel, Italy, Northern Ireland, Poland, Scotland, South Korea, Spain, Taiwan, Ukraine, the United Kingdom, and Wales. The use of television spots is limited in some countries, but others allow use of this message form during elections.

IMPORTANCE OF ELECTION CAMPAIGNS

......

Of course, some citizens do not exercise their right to vote, but those who do have a say in the direction of their city, county, congressional district, state, or country. For example, regardless of which candidate one preferred in 2000, there is no doubt Texas Governor George W. Bush and Vice President Al Gore would each have reacted differently to the tragedy of 9/11. Although some citizens do not actively seek out information on the campaign (and one important purpose of television spots is to reach such people), they do learn about the candidates and their issue positions during the course of campaigns. Meta-analysis has confirmed that political campaign messages (debates and TV spots) are capable of having significant effects on those who consume these messages (Benoit, Hansen, and Verser, 2003; Benoit, Leshner, and Chattopadhyay, 2007). Accordingly, political election campaigns are vital to the democratic form of government and unquestionably merit scholarly attention. This chapter explicates the functional theory of political campaign discourse, one approach to understanding election campaigns.

THE FUNCTIONAL THEORY
OF POLITICAL CAMPAIGNS

Functional theory views utterances in an election campaign as *functional*, or means to an end. It begins with several assumptions about the nature of political campaigns. First, voting is a comparative act. To win office, candidates only need to appear—and it is important to keep in mind the fact that political campaigns are about perceptions—preferable to their opponents.

Second, political candidates must contrast themselves with their opponents. Those aspiring to lead do not need to disagree with their competitors on every salient issue. Who would oppose creating jobs or keeping one's country safe? But voters cannot prefer one candidate to another if each is an exact copy of the other. Candidates must differ from opponents on at least some points of comparison if they are to have a chance to appear preferable to opponents. Communication enters elections at this stage.

The third assumption of functional theory is that voters learn candidate distinctions through political messages disseminated by a variety of sources, including supporters, the news media, supporters of opposing candidates, and special interest groups. Candidates use messages in a variety of media to inform voters (directly and indirectly, as other sources pass along some of the ideas from their campaign messages) about themselves and their policies and to identify points of distinction with opponents. Figure 14.1 illustrates how information flows from candidates and media to voters.

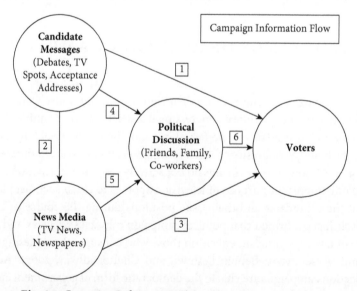

FIGURE 14.1. Election Campaign Information Flow.

This diagram reflects the fact that multiple sources are active in an election campaign as well as the fact that multiple ways exist for information to reach voters. Path 1 represents messages from candidates that reach a voter directly (e.g., from watching a TV spot). The second path includes messages that move from candidates to the news media. Path 3 reflects messages from the media to a voter (which can include information generated by the media and/or obtained from candidates). Path 4 represents information from a candidate that reaches one voter and then is passed along, via political discussion, to another voter (path 6). Path 5 includes information from the media that reaches one voter directly and then other voters by political discussion (path 6 again).

Fourth, candidates establish preferability through acclaiming, attacking, and defending. Acclaims address a candidate's strengths or advantages. Attacks expose an opponent's weaknesses or disadvantages. Defenses respond to, or refute, attacks against a candidate. Together, these three functions work as an informal form of cost-benefit analysis. Conceptualizing vote choice as a variant of cost-benefit analysis does not mean that functional theory assumes that voters quantify benefits (acclaims) or costs (attacks and defenses) or engage in mathematical calculations to make vote choices. Acclaims, if persuasive, have a tendency to increase perceived benefits. Attacks, if accepted by the audience, are prone to increase apparent costs of an opponent. When embraced by voters, defenses tend to reduce a candidate's perceived costs. Of course, the attitudes and existing knowledge of audience members and how they perceive messages from and about candidates are very important. A candidate who advocates healthcare legislation through acclaims (or who attacks an opponent's healthcare proposal) may simultaneously attract and repel different groups of voters.

Campaign discourse occurs on both policy and character. A candidate's resources for acclaiming, attacking, and defending are *who he or she is* (character) and *what he or she has done or will do* in office (policy). Voters develop perceptions of candidates' character and policy, and, as noted earlier, are exposed to information from many sources that influence perceptions of the candidates and their policy positions. But policy and character are the two topics on which candidates acclaim, attack, and defend to foster the impression that they are more worthy of election than the others seeking the office. To succeed, a candidate must win a majority (or a plurality) of the votes cast in an election (or a majority in the Electoral College for US presidential elections). Given that the electorate is divided on multiple contested issues (e.g., some preferring federal financing of healthcare, others opposing it), it is likely that many voters prefer one candidate on some issues and an opponent on others. But to be elected, political candidates need not win the support of everyone potentially in the electorate but need only to secure sufficient votes from those who actually bother to ballot. Table 14.1 offers hypothetical illustrations of acclaims, attacks, and defenses on policy and character.

Functional theory also distinguishes among three forms of policy (past deeds, which facilitate retrospective voting; future plans [means]; and general goals [ends]; the latter two forms facilitate prospective voting). It also distinguishes three forms of character (personal qualities, leadership ability, and ideals [values, principles]).

Table 14.1 Acclaims, Attacks, and Defenses on Policy and Character

	Policy	Character
Acclaim	"I will reduce inflation."	"I will always be honest with you."
Attack	"Job creation fell during my opponent's administration."	"My opponent cannot be trusted."
Defend	"My opponent is wrong to say I raised taxes."	"It is simply false to say I don't care about people."

Functional theory (Benoit, 2007; see also Benoit 2014a, 2014b; Benoit, Blaney, and Pier, 1998; Benoit, McHale, Hansen, Pier, and McGuire, 2003; Benoit, Stein, McHale, Chattopadhyay, Verser, and Price, 2007) advances several hypotheses about political campaign messages, including these:

H1. Political candidates will use acclaims more frequently than attacks, and attacks more often than defenses.

H2. Debates will have more defenses than other media.

H3. Policy comments will be more frequent than character comments in political campaign discourse.

H4. General goals and ideals will be used more often to acclaim than to attack.

H5. Messages from candidates will use more acclaims and fewer attacks than messages from other sources (e.g., political parties, independent groups).

H6. Incumbents acclaim and defend more, and attack less, than challengers.

H7. Incumbents will be more likely than challengers to use past deeds to acclaim; challengers use past deeds to attack more than do incumbents.

H8. Acclaims are more common, and attacks less so, in primary than in general campaign messages.

H9. A focus on character is more common, and concentration on policy less so, in primary than in general campaign messages.

H10. Attacks in the primary will be more likely to target candidates who are members of the attacker's own party than candidates of the other party.

H11. Attacks in primaries will be more likely to target the front runner than other candidates.

H12. The front runner attacks candidates from the opposing party more than other candidates.

H13. Campaign winners discuss policy more, and character less, than do losers.

H14. Campaign winners attack more on policy, and less on character, than losers.

H15. News coverage will overrepresent attacks and defenses and underrepresent acclaims.

H16. News coverage will focus on the horse race (e.g., who is ahead in the polls or who is campaigning where today).

H17. News coverage will overrepresent character and underrepresent policy.

Research driven by functional theory has investigated US presidential campaign messages for a variety of media and offices, including presidential TV spots (Benoit, 1999); presidential debates (e.g., Benoit and Hartcock, 1999; Benoit and Brazeal, 2002); vice presidential debates (Benoit and Airne, 2005); announcement speeches (Benoit, Henson, Whalen, and Pier, 2008); nominating convention acceptance addresses (Benoit, Wells, Pier, and Blaney, 1999); and direct mail brochures (Benoit and Stein, 2005). The theory has also been applied to US gubernatorial and Senate debates (Benoit, Brazeal, and Airne, 2007); US gubernatorial, Senate, and House TV spots (Brazeal and Benoit, 2006; Benoit and Airne, 2009). Non-US TV spots (e.g., Wen, Benoit, and Yu, 2004) and debates (e.g., Benoit and Klyukovski, 2006) have also been studied. Functional theory has been extended to understand news coverage of political campaigns. Predictions include (1) horse race coverage will be more common than policy or character, (2) news coverage of campaigns will report attacks more frequently than candidates use attacks in their messages, and (3) news coverage of elections will discuss character more, and policy less, than candidate messages. Benoit, Stein, and Hansen (2005) content analyzed *New York Times'* coverage of US presidential campaigns, 1952–2000. Benoit, Hemmer, and Stein (2010) applied functional theory to *New York Times'* coverage of presidential primary campaigns.

Over multiple years (1948–2012), studies of offices (president, vice president, governor, senator, congressman, mayor, prime minister, chancellor); media (e.g., TV spots, debates, speeches, websites, newspapers); and countries (e.g., Australia, Canada, Israel, South Korea, Taiwan, the United Kingdom) support functional theory (see Benoit 2007). Only rarely, for example in the 2004 Ukraine debates (Benoit and Klyukovski, 2006), does a candidate attack more than he or she acclaims. However, that campaign was negative for two reasons: accusations of vote fraud meant the first vote was declared invalid and a second election was held; one of the candidates accused his opponent of having poisoned him.

One consistent exception to the general preference for acclaims over attacks occurs in non-candidate messages (Benoit, 2007). Functional theory concerns what might be best understood as reasons rather than causes. For example, candidates have a reason to avoid excessive reliance on attacks: Many voters say they dislike mudslinging. This does not mean candidates must acclaim more than they attack, just that there is a reason to do so—and most candidates do in fact acclaim more than they attack (and use defense the least). For example, we have data from 114 announcement speeches; six used more attacks than acclaims. In those exceptions the two functions occurred at similar frequencies (e.g., John Kerry in 2004 used forty-eight acclaims and forty-nine attacks). So, exceptions occur but this prediction is almost always confirmed in election messages from political candidates.

However, spots sponsored by political parties and interest groups tend to attack more than candidate-sponsored ads. The assumption most likely at work is that an attack from a candidate is more likely to backfire (upset voters who dislike mudslinging) than an attack from a surrogate source. Another exception—from another type of surrogate source—occurs when nominating convention keynote speeches typically have more attacks (and fewer acclaims) than the candidates' nomination acceptance addresses.

Defenses were never more common than acclaims or attacks in these data. Functional theory (Benoit, 2007) argues that candidates have three reasons to use few defenses. Most attacks occur on a candidate's weaknesses, so responding to those attacks likely takes the candidate off-message. Second, defending could make the candidate appear reactive rather than proactive. Finally, in order to defend against an attack the candidate must identify the criticism being refuted; doing so could remind or inform voters of a potential weakness. However, defenses are consistently more frequent in debates than in other media. Functional theory argues that one of the reasons to minimize attack—reminding or informing the audience of a potential weakness—does not apply in debates, given that the candidate is probably responding to an attack just made by an opponent.

Research on US presidential and non-presidential campaign messages, as well as that on election debates held in other countries, has established that political candidates tend to discuss policy more often than character (Benoit, 2007; TV spots in some countries are exceptions: Kaid and Holtz-Bacha, 1995). Rather than being a mirror held up to reflect the candidates' messages, news coverage of campaigns addresses character more, and policy less, than candidate messages; news coverage reports attacks more frequently than candidates use them; and the most common topic of newspaper coverage is the horse race (see Benoit, Stein, and Hansen, 2005; Benoit, Hemmer, and Stein, 2010).

Research (Benoit, 2007) consistently reports that general goals and ideals are used more often as the basis for acclaims than attacks. It is easier to advocate more jobs (a goal) or equality (an ideal) than to attack either idea.

As noted earlier, the nature of the source of a political campaign message influences functions: Candidates tend to use more acclaims and fewer attacks than other sources. Nomination acceptance addresses tend to be more positive than keynote speeches. In presidential TV spots candidates are prone to be more positive than narrators or other speakers (Benoit, 1999). TV spots sponsored by the political parties and interest groups tend to attack more, and acclaim less, than ads sponsored by candidates (Benoit, 2007).

Incumbent party candidates are typically more positive (use more acclaims and fewer attacks) than challenger party candidates (Benoit, 2007). This is in large part a function of how the candidates use past deeds or record in office in their campaign messages. Incumbents have a record of performance in the office sought; with an occasional exception (none for US presidential campaigns in recent history) challengers do not. Arguably, the best evidence of how a candidate will perform in an office is how that candidate has performed in that office. Accordingly, both incumbents and challengers talk about the incumbent's record more than the challenger's record. Of course, when incumbents discuss their own record they acclaim; when challengers discuss incumbents' records they attack.

Primary and general election campaign messages have significant differences (Benoit, 2007). Attacks are more common in the general campaign than the primary. When seeking their party's nomination, candidates tend to use fewer attacks than after they become the nominee. First, more policy differences (opportunities to attack) exist between members of different parties (general election) than between members of the same party (primary election). Second, a candidate hoping to become the nominee may wish to moderate attacks on opponents in the primary in order to obtain their support in the general election—and the support of party members who preferred the winner's opponents. In the primary campaign, most attacks target other candidates from the source's own political party and there is a direct relationship between a candidate's position in the poll and the number of attacks targeting that candidate in primary debates; the front runner is more likely than other candidates to attack opposing party candidates (Benoit, Pier, Brazeal, McHale, Klyukovksi, and Airne, 2002).

Research has also established that policy is discussed more frequently in the general election than in the primary campaign (Benoit, 2007). Many candidates in the primary phase are relatively unknown (think Dennis Kucinich or Hermann Cain) and they usually begin by introducing themselves. As noted earlier, more policy differences exist between members of different parties (general election) than among members of the same party (primary). This means there are more opportunities to discuss policy in the general election. Finally, some primary candidates continue to develop policy positions as the campaign unfolds; in other words, especially at the beginning of the primary season some candidates have fewer policy positions to discuss.

Election winners tend to discuss policy more, and character less, than losers ("winner" refers to candidates who win their party's nomination or the general election; it has nothing to with which candidate is believed to have "won" a debate or whether a candidate won a caucus or primary; Benoit, 2003). Functional Theory argues that most voters consider policy to be a more important determinant of their presidential vote than character (public opinion polls support this explanation). Furthermore, when they attack, election winners are more likely to criticize their opponents' policy than their opponents' character (Benoit, 2004); some evidence suggests that voters consider attacks on character more offensive than attacks on policy (Johnson-Cartee and Copeland, 1989).

News coverage of election campaigns features more attacks and fewer acclaims than the candidates employ in their campaign messages. As noted earlier, news coverage of campaigns focuses on the horse race. When it does focus on policy and character, news stories about elections privilege character over policy (Benoit, Stein, and Hansen, 2005).

NEED FOR MORE RESEARCH

Although the effects of attack in political advertising have been extensively studied (see Fallis, this handbook), there has been little systematic research assessing the effects of attacks, acclaims, and defenses on audiences for other campaign genres, such as speeches and debates (see, e.g., Reinemann and Maurer, 2005). Typologies of traits found in political messages include Benoit and McHale's (2004) typology of personal qualities (e.g., honesty, determination, empathy), the trait batteries of Kinder (1986) and Miller et al. (1986), and the catalogue of traits in ads compiled by Geer (2006). The effect of character appeals also merits further study (see Hardy, this handbook). Indications that people may react more favorably to attacks on policy than on character (Johnson-Cartee and Copeland, 1989) justify research investigating functions and topics jointly—as well as research on functions and topics in other campaign media. Further analysis of candidates' use of personal qualities in campaign messages should be pursued in future research. It would be interesting to combine functional theory with the elaboration likelihood model (ELM) (Petty and Cacioppo, 1986) or the theory of planned behavior (TPB) (Fishbein and Ajzen, 2009) to do audience effects research. Two key elements of the ELM are arguments and credibility, which correspond roughly to policy and character. The ELM concerns how messages—which could be such campaign messages as TV spots or debates—are processed by audience members. The TPB has potential because its approach to integrating information and functional theory argues that candidate messages supply information to voters in the form of acclaims, attacks, and defenses. Recall the discussion of the three functions as an informal variant of cost-benefit analysis, where voters must integrate the information provided by acclaims, attacks, and defenses. Furthermore, sufficient data has been accumulated to permit longitudinal analysis of US presidential campaigns, which could be very productive.

Unanswered Questions

Functional theory focuses on selected aspects of political campaign messages (functions and topics). It does not, for example, investigate other message features such as argument structures or metaphors (although one study has investigated the use of evidence in TV spots—evidence is more likely to be deployed in support of attacks than acclaims or defenses; Henson and Benoit, 2010). Other variables related to message production (besides, e.g., incumbency status, campaign phase, or political party affiliation), such as competitiveness of race, merit attention. Some research has investigated the functions and topics of non-presidential campaign messages (e.g., Airne and Benoit, 2005; Benoit, Brazeal, and Airne, 2007; Benoit, Henson, and Maltos, 2007) but more could be done here. Similarly, studies have begun to apply functional theory to non-US campaign messages (e.g., Benoit and Henson, 2007; Benoit and Klyukovski, 2006; Benoit and Sheafer, 2006; Benoit, Wen, and Yu, 2007; Lee and Benoit, 2004; Wen, Benoit, and Yu, 2004), but further work in this area would be helpful. Political content in social media (e.g., Facebook, Twitter) is also a fertile ground for research using functional theory.

References

Airne, D., and Benoit, W. L. 2005. Political television advertising in campaign 2000. *Communication Quarterly* 53: 473–492.

Benoit, W. L. 1999. *Seeing spots: A functional analysis of presidential television advertisements from 1952–1996.* New York: Praeger.

Benoit, W. L. 2003. Topic of presidential campaign discourse and election outcome. *Western Journal of Communication* 67: 97–112.

Benoit, W. L. 2004. Election outcome and topic of political campaign attack. *Southern Communication Journal* 69: 348–355.

Benoit, W. L. 2007. *Communication in political campaigns*. New York: Peter Lang.

Benoit, W. L. 2014a. *A functional analysis of presidential television advertisements* (2nd ed.). Lanham, MD: Lexington Books.

Benoit, W. L. 2014b. *Political election debates: Informing voters about policy and character*. Lanham, MD: Lexington Books.

Benoit, W. L., and Airne, D. 2005. A functional analysis of American vice presidential debates. *Argumentation and Advocacy* 41: 225–236.

Benoit, W. L., and Airne, D. 2009. A functional analysis of non-presidential TV spots in campaign 2004. *Human Communication* 12: 91–117.

Benoit, W. L., and Benoit-Bryan, J. M. (2013). Debates come to the UK: A functional analysis of the 2010 British prime minister election debates. *Communication Quarterly* 61: 463–478.

Benoit, W. L., Blaney, J. R., and Pier, P. M. 1998. *Campaign '96: A functional analysis of acclaiming, attacking, and defending*. New York: Praeger.

Benoit, W. L., Blaney, J. R., and Pier, P. M. 2000. Acclaiming, attacking, and defending: A functional analysis of nominating convention keynote speeches, 1960–1996. *Political Communication* 17: 61–84.

Benoit, W. L., and Brazeal, L. M. 2002. A functional analysis of the 1988 Bush-Dukakis presidential debates. *Argumentation and Advocacy* 38: 219–233.

Benoit, W. L., Brazeal, L. M., and Airne, D. 2007. A functional analysis of televised U.S. Senate and gubernatorial campaign debates. *Argumentation and Advocacy* 44: 75–89.

Benoit, W. L., Hansen, G. J., and Verser, R. M. 2003. A meta-analysis of the effects of viewing U.S. presidential debates. *Communication Monographs* 70: 335–350.

Benoit, W. L., and Harthcock, A. 1999. Functions of the Great Debates: Acclaims, attacks, and defense in the 1960 presidential debates. *Communication Monographs* 66: 341–357.

Benoit, W. L., Hemmer, K., and Stein, K. 2010. *New York Times'* coverage of American presidential primary campaigns, 1952–2004. *Human Communication* 13: 259–280.

Benoit, W. L., and Henson, J. R. 2007. A functional analysis of the 2006 Canadian and 2007 Australian election debates. *Argumentation & Advocacy* 44: 36–48.

Benoit, W. L., Henson, J., Davis, C., Glantz, M., Phillips, A., and Rill, L. 2013. Stumping on the Internet: 2008 presidential primary candidate campaign webpages. *Human Communication* 16: 1-12.

Benoit, W. L., Henson, J. R., and Maltos, S. 2007. A functional analysis of mayoral debates. *Contemporary Argumentation and Debate* 28: 20–37.

Benoit, W. L., Henson, J. R., Whalen, S., and Pier, P. M. 2008. "I am a candidate for president": A functional analysis of presidential announcement speeches. *Speaker & Gavel* 45: 3–18.

Benoit, W. L., and Klyukovski, A. A. 2006. A functional analysis of 2004 Ukrainian presidential debates. *Argumentation* 20: 209–225.

Benoit, W. L., Leshner, G. M., and Chattopadhyay, S. 2007. A meta-analysis of political advertising. *Human Communication* 10: 507–522.

Benoit, W. L., and McHale, 2004. Presidential candidates' personal qualities: Computer content analysis. In K. Hacker (Ed.), *Presidential candidate images: Issues of theory and measurement* (pp. 49–63). Lanham, MD: Rowman & Littlefield.

Benoit, W. L., McHale, J. P, Hansen, G. J., Pier, P. M., and McGuire, J. P. 2003. *Campaign 2000: A functional analysis of presidential campaign discourse*. Lanham, MD: Rowman & Littlefield.

Benoit, W. L., Pier, P. M., Brazeal, L. M., McHale, J. P., Klyukovksi, A., and Airne, D. 2002. *The primary decision: A functional analysis of debates in presidential primaries*. Westport, CT: Praeger.

Benoit, W. L., and Sheafer, T. 2006. Functional theory and political discourse: Televised debates in Israel and the United States. *Journalism & Mass Communication Quarterly* 83: 281–297.

Benoit, W. L., and Stein, K. A. 2005. A functional analysis of presidential direct mail advertising. *Communication Studies* 56: 203–225.

Benoit, W. L., Stein, K. A., and Hansen, G. J. 2005. *New York Times*' coverage of presidential campaigns, 1952–2000. *Journalism & Mass Communication Quarterly* 82: 356–376.

Benoit, W. L., Stein, K. A., McHale, J. P., Chattopadhyay, S., Verser, R., Price, S. 2007. *Bush versus Kerry: A functional analysis of campaign 2004*. New York: Peter Lang.

Benoit, W. L., Wells, W. T., Pier, P. M., and Blaney, J. R. 1999. Acclaiming, attacking, and defending in presidential nomination convention acceptance addresses, 1960–1996. *Quarterly Journal of Speech* 85: 247–267.

Benoit, W. L., Wen, W-C., and Yu, T. 2007. A functional analysis of 2004 Taiwanese political debates. *Asian Journal of Communication* 17: 24–39.

Brazeal, L. M., and Benoit, W. L. 2006. On the spot: A functional analysis of congressional television spots, 1980–2004. *Communication Studies* 57: 401–420.

Fishbein, M., and Ajzen, I. 2009. *Predicting and changing behavior: The reasoned action approach*. New York: Psychology Press.

Geer, J. G. 2006. *In defense of negativity: Attack ads in presidential campaigns*. Chicago: University of Chicago Press.

Henson, J. R., and Benoit, W. L. 2010. Because I said so: A functional theory analysis of evidence in political TV spots. *Speaker & Gavel* 47: 1–15.

Johnson-Cartee, K. S., and Copeland, G. 1989. Southern voters' reactions to negative political ads in the 1986 election. *Journalism Quarterly* 66: 888–893, 986.

Kaid, L. L., and Holtz-Bacha, C. 1995. Political advertising across cultures. In L. L. Kaid and C. Holtz-Bacha (Eds.), *Political advertising in western democracies* (pp. 206–227). Thousand Oaks, CA: Sage.

Kinder, D. R. 1986. Presidential character revisited. In R. R. Lau and D. O. Sears (Eds.), *Political cognition: The 19th Annual Carnegie Symposium on cognition* (pp. 233-255). Hillsdale, NJ: Lawrence Erlbaum.

Lee, C., and Benoit, W. L. 2004. A functional analysis of presidential television spots: A comparison of Korean and American ads. *Communication Quarterly* 52: 68–79.

Miller, A. H., Wattenberg, M. P., and Malanchuk, O. 1986. Schematic assessment of presidential candidates. *American Political Science Review* 80: 521–540.

Petty, R. E., and Cacioppo, J. T. 1986. *Attitudes and persuasion: Central and peripheral routes to attitude change*. New York: Springer-Verlag.

Reinemann, C., and Maurer, M. 2005. Unifying or polarizing short-term effects and post-debate consequences of different rhetorical strategies in televised debates. *Journal of Communication* 55: 775–794.

Wen, W-C., Benoit, W. L., and Yu, T-H. 2004. A functional analysis of the 2000 Taiwanese and US presidential spots. *Asian Journal of Communication* 14: 140–155.

CHAPTER 15

....

THE POLITICAL USES
AND ABUSES OF CIVILITY
AND INCIVILITY

....

KATHLEEN HALL JAMIESON, ALLYSON VOLINSKY,
ILANA WEITZ, AND KATE KENSKI

CIVILITY is a social norm and a standard "of behavior. . . based on widely shared beliefs [about] how individual group members ought to behave in a given situation" (Fehr and Fischbacher, 2004, 185). Put differently, "A *norm of civility* defines the kinds of behavior that persons can rightfully expect from others" (Sinopoli, 1995, 613). Like other injunctive norms, civility "specif[ies] what people approve and disapprove within the culture and motivate[s] action by promising social sanctions for normative or counternormative conduct" (Reno et al., 1993, 104).

After exploring the challenges involved in defining incivility, this chapter addresses the evolution of the concept, notes the dispute over trend lines, précises work on its psychological effects, outlines some functions served by civility and incivility, and flags questions worthy of additional attention.

THE CHALLENGES OF DEFINITION

....

Scholars agree that providing a settled definition of civility is all but impossible because, as Benson notes, the "communicative, rhetorical practices" of civility and incivility "are always situational and contestable" (2011, 22). Put differently, "[c]ivility in discourse is a matter of socially secured agreements to conform to the local culture. . . . What is normal in public discussion in some places is rude in others; and what is considered a normal way of showing respect in some venues seems mannered and arid in others" (Ferree et al., 2002, 313–314). For that reason, among others, Sapiro observes, "It would take an advanced degree in alchemy, not political science, to draw a tidy but reasonably comprehensive definition out of the literature to which one must turn to learn about civility as it is understood today" (quoted in Herbst, 2010, 12).

What most definitions do share is the notion that civility connotes a discourse that does not silence or derogate alternative views but instead evinces respect. Often the object of respect is one's interlocutor or fellows. So for Carter, civility involves "an attitude of respect, even love, for our fellow citizens" (1998, xii); for Shils, "respect for the dignity and the desire for dignity of other persons" (1997, 338); for Hayek, a "method of collaboration" (1976, 3); and for Sobieraj and Berry, "political argumentation characterized by speakers who present themselves as reasonable and courteous, treating even those with whom they disagree as though they and their ideas are worthy of respect" (2011, 20). For Coe, Kenski, and Rains, incivility refers to "features of discussion that convey an unnecessarily disrespectful tone toward the discussion forum, its participants, or its topics" (2014, 660); for Andersson and Pearson, "low-intensity deviant behavior with ambiguous intent to harm the target, in violation of workplace norms of mutual respect" (1999, 457). However, for other scholars the object of respect or disrespect is broader. For example, Papacharissi (2004, 267) argues: "Civility is positive collective face; that is, deference to the social and democratic identity of an individual. Incivility can be defined as negative collective face; that is, disrespect for the collective traditions of democracy." As scholars have shifted to a constructionist perceptive, civility has been less likely to be defined in terms of use of specific words or practice and more likely to be cast as a mode of interaction and a perception. "Everyday incivility can be thought of as commonplace actions and interactions that are perceived to be rude or inconsiderate," write Phillips and Smith (2003, 85).

Much contemporary theorizing about civility is tied to presuppositions about the nature of deliberation and to discussions of the appropriate forms that disagreement on moral matters should take in a political system such as ours. Political philosophers derive their sense of the role of civility in the public sphere from their concept of deliberation and the public good. For example, Rawls's duty of civility not only entails a moral duty to explain how an advocated policy "can be supported by the political values of public reason," but also "involves a willingness to listen to others and a fairmindedness in deciding when accommodations to their views should reasonably be made" (1996, 217).

From earlier times to more recent ones, rudeness and civility have been cast as antonyms. Accordingly, Chaucer notes of the carpenter in *The Miller's Tale* (n.d., 119): "He knew nat Catoun [a Latin handbook on appropriate behavior], for his wit was rude," and in *The American Commonwealth* Lord Bryce observes, "Yet neither are they rude for to get on in American politics one must be civil and pleasant" (1921, Part 1, 148).

The Evolution of the Concept
of Incivility

Although lexically kin to the Roman's *civis* (citizen) and *civitas* (citizenship) (Simpson, 1960, 109), the word civility (*civilitas*) did not become fashionable (Gillingham, 2002, 281) until publication of Erasmus's sixteenth-century *De Civilitate Morum Puerilium* (Knox, 1995; Carter, 1998, 14). That work's ancestors include the twelfth-century *Liber Urbani* of Daniel of Beccles and the much older, third-century "commonplace secular morality" of the *Distichs of Cato* (Gillingham, 2002, 267). Widely circulated in the Middle Ages, the *Distichs of Cato* was published in the colonies by Benjamin Franklin.

In early modern England and Western Europe, "the terms 'civil' and 'civility' gradually displac[ed] 'courteous' and 'courtesy' as the fashionable terms denoting approved conduct" (Gillingham, 2002, 267), a transformation documented by Elias (2000), Becker (1988), and Bryson (1998), among others. In the process, "during the sixteenth century the term 'civility' began to take on some of the connotations of 'civilization' as the opposition between the 'civil' and the 'barbaric' implicit in classical writings was allegedly developed in response to the challenge presented by the discovery of the 'savage inhabitants of the New World, and then applied in a contrast between English civility and Irish barbarity" (Gillingham, 2002, 269).

Incivility Trends

Depending on how one defines the term, measures the phenomenon, and brackets the period of study, civility in general either is (Carter, 1998, xi) or is not on a downward slope (see Altschuler and Blumin, 2000). Similarly, comity in Congress either is (Uslaner, 1996) or is not on a downward path (Nickels, 1995; Jamieson and Falk, 2000). An alternative view is that congressional civility rises and falls with the changes driven by the interaction of individuals and events. The patterns revealed by a charting of both the requests to take down words in the House and of requests that led to a ruling indicates that 1946 and 1995 were high points of incivility and that "those who believe that incivility has been on an upward course since the Vietnam war are, by this measure, mistaken" (Jamieson and Falk, 2000, 108).

There is nonetheless general agreement that, whether or not twenty-four-hour-a-day cable talk, talk radio, and the Web have increased the amount of uncivil discourse, "the uncivil tendencies in American culture are more apparent and abundant thanks to pervasive media" (Herbst, 2010, 26). After examining ten weeks of data from political blogs, talk radio, and cable news analysis programs, Sobieraj and

Berry found that outrage, a specific kind of incivility that involves trying to provoke a visceral response from an audience, "punctuates speech and writing across formats" (2011, 26), and "89.6% of cases included in the sample contained at least one outrage incident." Coe, Kenski, and Rains found that in the online discussions they analyzed from a newspaper website, "more than one out of every five comments were uncivil, and 55.5% of the article discussions contained at least some incivility" (2014, 673).

Incivility's Psychological Effects

There is general agreement that uncivil discourse is emotionally arousing (Mutz, 2007). Moreover, being the target of uncivil remarks (including insults and rude behavior in public) can elicit strong responses (cf. Vasquez et al., 2013); reduce effective cognitive processing, productivity, and creativity (Porath and Erez, 2007, 2009; Rafaeli et al., 2012, 931); and elicit reciprocal aggression (Andersson and Pearson, 1999).

The effects of viewing uncivil behavior are less settled. In a study focused on exchanges on a talk show, Mutz and Reeves concluded that "political trust is adversely affected by levels of incivility" in televised political exchanges arguing that "the format of much political television effectively promotes viewer interest, but at the expense of political trust" (2005, 1). Anderson and colleagues found that "uncivil blog comments can polarize... along the lines of religiosity and issue support" (2014, 274) in their study on risk perceptions of emerging technologies. By contrast, Brooks and Geer find: "While uncivil messages in general—and uncivil trait-based messages in particular—are usually seen by the public as being less fair, less informative, and less important than both their civil negative and positive counterparts, they are no more likely to lead to detrimental effects among the public. In fact, incivility appears to have some modest positive consequences for the political engagement of the electorate" (2007, 1).

Other research has shown that when a news article was embedded in an uncivil blog post, the article's perceived credibility increased (Thorson, Vraga, and Ekdale, 2010). Borah (2013) found that incivility increased perceptions of credibility of a news article, but it also decreased political trust and efficacy. In a study of online comments, Coe, Kenski, and Rains (2014) found that uncivil commenters were slightly more likely to include statistics as evidence; uncivil comments were also more likely to receive more reactions from readers in the form of thumbs-down ratings. Depending on one's point of view, negative reactions to online posts could be considered harmful, but for others, the mere fact that people are responding at all could be considered beneficial to public discourse as a sign of increased participation.

THE FUNCTIONS OF INCIVILITY
AND CIVILITY

Because civility and incivility are "strategic assets used by those pursuing specific interests, whether humanitarian efforts or far less admirable ones" (Herbst, 2010, 124), we parse the remainder of this chapter into sections on the various functions served by civility and incivility. In the process of so doing, we outline the differentiating, mobilizing, expressive, and silencing functions of incivility; the social and deliberative functions of civility; and the ways in which calls for civility can be used to disempower.

The Functions of Incivility

Incivility's Differentiating and Mobilizing Functions

Insults and invective are a powerful means of differentiating an in-group from an out-group, an opponent from an ally. Since members of a group tend to exaggerate their differences with out-groups (Robbins and Krueger, 2005)—believing out-group members to be rather homogeneous and in-group members less so (Linville and Fischer, 1993), holding members of out-groups to be less human than those in the in-group (Leyens et al., 2003), and perceiving out-group attitudes to be more extreme than they actually are (Gawronski, Bodenhausen, and Banse, 2005; Jamieson and Cappella, 2008)—the fact that forms of attack such as ad hominem are employed against out-group members should be unsurprising.

Precisely because it evokes a strong emotional response, incivility is also a strategic tool in the arsenal of individuals seeking dramatic social or political change. Those carrying the flag for strategic incivility argue, as Schudson does, that "democracy may require withdrawal from civility itself. . . . We call the people who initiate such departures from civility [as social movements, strikes, demonstrations] driven, ambitious, unreasonable, self-serving, rude, hot-headed, self-absorbed—the likes of Newt Gingrich and Martin Luther King and William Lloyd Garrison" (1997, 308).

As the record of agitators such as Garrison confirms, invective can serve as an assertion of identity and power by those who are being marginalized by a majority community (Murray, 1983). It can also act as an expression of outrage against evils such as genocide or slavery, which exist on a scale and of a kind that rupture the assumptions of the social order (see Aminzade and McAdam, 2002; Gould, 2009).

"[O]ffering up an 'enemy'. . . as the source of the problem" is a way of harnessing anger, an "emotion political organizers need to capture and channel" (Ost 2004, 229). As a result, invective has been a primary weapon of those arguing that an opponent is a heretic, a miscreant, or worse; unsurprisingly, such assaults elicit the kind of reciprocation in kind revealed by the psychological studies cited earlier. So, for example, Martin Luther attacked the "'brainless and illiterate beast in papist form,'" Thomas More called Luther both "an apostate and a pimp" (Furey, 2005, 469), and Thomas Cooper (1792) used invective against invective in his *Reply to Mr. Burke's Invective Against Mr. Cooper, and Mr. Watt*.[1]

Incivility as a Means of Marginalizing the Powerless

Just as incivility can be a tool of insurrection, it can also be marshaled against those seeking power by those in control. Some argue that online flaming "is an expression of cyberspace machismo which is often practiced more often against women and women's online groups as a kind of sexual harassment" (Vrooman, 2002, 53), a finding consistent with evidence from 2008 attacks on the Web posts by women objecting to sexist portrayals of the candidacy and person of Democratic presidential aspirant Hillary Clinton (Jamieson and Dunn, 2008).

Incivility's Expressive Function

Whether incivility is to be lauded or lamented is answered differently by different theorists and variously in different times, places, and circumstances. Accordingly, in ancient Rome, what was appropriate in one venue was frowned upon in another. In that tradition, *vituperatio*, the speech of reproach, was as much a part of the curriculum as the speech of praise (*laus*) and as such treated in Cicero's *De Inventione* (2:28–31, 177–178) and in the *Ad Herrennium* (3:10–15). To disparage or blame, the rhetor attacked the target for lacking the positive attributes that are the focus of a speech of praise, for example achievements, desirable characteristics such as speed or health, and virtues. By Craig's count there were "seventeen conventional *loci* of invective established in Greek and Roman practice by Cicero's time" (2004, 4–5): embarrassing family origin; being unworthy of one's family; physical appearance; eccentricity of dress; gluttony and drunkenness, possibly leading to acts of *crudelitas* and *libido*; hypocrisy for appearing virtuous; avarice, possibly linked with prodigality; taking bribes; pretentiousness; sexual misconduct; hostility to family; cowardice in war; squandering of one's patrimony/financial embarrassment; aspiring to *regnum* or tyranny; cruelty to citizens and allies; plunder of private and public property; and oratorical ineptitude.

Exemplifying what many would define as invective, in his widely praised attack on Piso, Cicero called his adversary a monster, a butcher, a scoundrel, and a gelded pig (Arena, 2007, 152). What was rhetorically appropriate when condemning an enemy was less so when addressing friends. So, for example, in *De Officiis* (Book 1, 49–51), "What one can observe in human society as a whole is fundamental. The bond of that society is reason and speech; they reconcile men to each other and join them in a sort of natural community by teaching, by learning, by communicating, by discussing, by judging."

The Function of Civility in Deliberation

If the public sphere is to be inclusive, productive, and deliberative, it requires norms of interpersonal exchange. Unsurprisingly then, in his *Manual of Parliamentary Practice*,

Thomas Jefferson observed, "It is very material that order, decency, and regularity be preserved in a dignified public body" (1868, 14). Adopted on April 7, 1789, the House of Representatives' rules of decorum specified, among other things, that a member "shall confine himself to the question under debate, avoiding personality" (Jefferson, 1868, 38). In short, a member should not arraign or impugn the motive of another member.

Spaces predicated on cooperative engagement commonly adopt similar rules. For example, *Wikipedia* proclaims: "Civility is part of Wikipedia's code of conduct and one of Wikipedia's five pillars. The civility policy is a standard of conduct that sets out how Wikipedia editors should interact. Stated simply, editors should always treat each other with consideration and respect. . . . Someone may *very well* be an idiot. But *telling them so* is neither going to increase their intelligence nor improve your ability to communicate with them" (Civility, n.d.).

Codes such as Jefferson's and *Wikipedia's* are consistent with political theorists' notion, expressed by Gutmann and Thompson, that mutual respect "lies at the core of reciprocity and deliberation in a democracy" (1996, 79; see also Darwall, 1977). Democracies cannot, in Lynch's (2011) phrase, be "spaces of reasons" unless we are able "to find common currency with those with whom we must discuss practical matters." Because "civility . . . is really the very glue that keeps an organized society from flying apart" (Burger, 1975),"it makes practical sense to embrace civility as a norm . . . in the rhetorical exchanges that occur between those in an ongoing relationship, and . . . those who have come together as a community to address problems" (Jamieson, 2000, 4–5). For some, this means that deliberative civility focuses not on "what is communicated, whether these be reasons, arguments, propositions, or whatever. . ., [but rather on] *how* I address you and *how* I interpret and respond to your claims and arguments" (Bohman and Richardson, 2009, 272), with the "point of civility" being "to engage the other as possessing practical intelligence, and so as capable of revising goals in the light of new understandings of one's circumstances and of reaching new understandings of one's circumstances in the light of newly accepted goals" (271).

The Negative Functions of Calls for Civility

Silencing or Subjugating a Marginalized Group

Just as incivility itself can be used to silence a minority view, condemnations of the "incivility" of those holding such views can function as a silencing mechanism or means of harassing a feared or subordinated group. The notion that calls for civility can be a means of social control (Strachan and Wolf, 2012, 47) is a long-lived one. In *On Liberty*, John Stuart Mill opined:

> With regard to what is commonly meant by intemperate discussion, namely invective, sarcasm, personality, and the like, the denunciation of these weapons would deserve more sympathy if it were ever proposed to interdict them equally to both sides; but it is only desired to restrain the employment of them against the prevailing opinion: against the unprevailing they may not only be used without general

disapproval, but will be likely to obtain for him who uses them the praise of honest zeal and righteous indignation. Yet whatever mischief arises from their use is greatest when they are employed against the comparatively defenceless. (1910, 150)

Mill's observation is consistent with Lendler's claim that "inevitably, an appeal for enforced 'civility' becomes an argument for a specific side in a conflict" (2004, 424) and with concerns that condemnations of incivility can act "against a fully democratic order and in support of special interests, institutions of privilege, and structures of domination" (Kasson, 1990, 3), by functioning "discursively to restrict content and participation though the limits they place on acceptable style" (Ferree et al., 2002, 313–314). For this reason, DeMott argues that the "'new incivility' needs to be recognized, in short, for what it is: a flat-out, justified rejection of the leader-class claims to respect, a demand that leader-class types start looking hard at themselves" (1996, 14). "The civility movement," argues Kennedy (1998) "is deeply at odds with what an invigorated liberalism requires: intellectual clarity; an insistence upon grappling with the substance of controversies; and a willingness to fight loudly, openly, militantly, even rudely for policies and values that will increase freedom, equality, and happiness in America and around the world."

UNANSWERED QUESTIONS AND AREAS REQUIRING FUTURE RESEARCH

Synthesizing scholarly work on the effects of incivility is complicated by the fact that operationalizations of the term differ widely. In Mutz and Reeves's experiments (2005, 5) the "uncivil" conditions included statements such as "You're really missing the point here, Neil" and "What Bob is *completely* overlooking is"; "The candidates also raised their voices and never apologized for interrupting one another, nonverbal cues such as rolling of the eyes and rueful shaking of the head from side to side were also used to suggest lack of respect." By contrast, Brooks and Geer include explicit direct ad hominem attacks (e.g., "my unprincipled opponent," "my cowardly opponent," "my gutless opponent") on an opponent in the ads used in their experiments. Note, however, that consistent with our earlier point, the two projects do share the notion that incivility shows lack of respect for the views of another.

Those attempting to assess changes in civility across time within an institution or across media face other challenges. Reliably tracking behavior within the House of Representatives, for example, is complicated by the fact that before the 104th Congress changed the procedure, members were able to clean up their floor remarks before they were memorialized in the *Congressional Record* (Jamieson and Falk, 2000, 105). Moreover, those trying to determine whether the level of civility on cable talk shows differs from one time to another must deal with the facts that the networks differ in the number of shows whose transcripts they release, some programs are repeated multiple times with slight alterations from airing to airing, and many programs are short lived. For example, four of the nine hosts whose shows Sobieraj and Berry (2011, 24–25) examined over a ten-week period in 2009 no longer have a home on the studied network.

We close with the problem raised at the beginning of this chapter. The meaning attached to the concept of civility differs from one period to another and from one theorist to the next. One way to determine what the culture means by incivility at a given point in time is to ask what sorts of behaviors are awarded that label by dissimilar individuals commenting on the same body of discourse. Following that lead, Weitz, Volinsky, Jamieson (Jamieson, 2012), and a team of coders at the Annenberg Public Policy Center found agreement among hosts on Fox, MSNBC, and CNN that the following classes of acts were uncivil:

- analogizing an opponent to Hitler or the Nazis
- extreme characterizations of opponents (e.g., as "barbarians" or a "mob")
- use of the language of violence (including Governor Perry's mock threat to get "ugly" with Fed chair Ben Bernanke if he were to go to Texas after pursuing loose monetary policy and Teamster leader Jimmy Hoffa's call to "take these sons of bitches out")
- extreme characterizations of legislation (including the notion that senior citizens would die under the opposing side's health plan)
- allegations that the president of an opposing party had lied (Rep. Wilson's "You lie" and statements by Democrats on the floor of the House alleging that President George W. Bush had done the same)
- dismissive or demeaning references to the president (i.e., calling President George W. Bush a "loser" and President Obama "kind of a dick")
- dismissive or demeaning references to others (e.g., labeling a female lobbyist a "K street whore" and a female senator a "hooker")

The study also explained why conservatives and progressive viewers enclaved within Fox or MSNBC programming might be disposed to consider incivility a problem plaguing only those on the other side of the aisle. Whereas Obama-Hitler analogies were more likely to be decried on MSNBC and CNN, Nazi analogies applied to Republican governor Walker were more often criticized on Fox. Whereas a FOX viewer was more likely to learn that Democrat Alan Grayson had labeled an advisor to Federal Reserve chairman Bernanke a "K Street whore," the viewer tuned to MSNBC was more likely to hear that conservative Glenn Beck had characterized Democratic senator Mary Landrieu as a hooker. The differences between FOX and MSNBC were significant and could be predicted by knowing the ideology of the transgressor.

NOTE

1. For the definitive treatment of invective in ancient Rome, see Koster (1980). For a sophisticated treatment of Cicero's use of invective, see Craig (2004, 187–213).

REFERENCES

Altschuler, G., and Blumin, S. 2000. *Rude republic: Americans and their politics in the nineteenth century*. Princeton, NJ: Princeton University Press.

Aminzade, R., and McAdam, D. 2002. Emotions and contentious politics. *Mobilization: An International Quarterly* 7(2): 107–109.

Anderson, A. A., Brossard, D., Scheufele, D. A., Xenos, M. A., and Ladwig, P. 2014. The "nasty effect:" Online incivility and risk perceptions of emerging technologies. *Journal of Computer-Mediated Communication* 19: 373–387.

Andersson, L., and Pearson, C. 1999. Tit for tat? The spiraling effect of incivility in the workplace. *Academy of Management Review* 24(3): 452–471.

Arena, V. 2007. Roman oratorical invective. In W. Dominik and J. Hall (Eds.), *A Companion to Roman Rhetoric* (pp. 149–160). Oxford, UK: Blackwell.

Becker, M. 1988. *Civility and society in Western Europe, 1300–1600*. Bloomington: Indiana University Press.

Benson, T. 2011. The rhetoric of civility: Power, authenticity, and democracy. *Journal of Contemporary Rhetoric* 1(1): 22–30.

Bohman, J., and Richardson, H. S. 2009. Liberalism, deliberative democracy, and "reasons that all can accept." *The Journal of Political Philosophy* 17(3): 253–274.

Borah, P. 2013. Interactions of news frames and incivility in the political blogosphere: Examining perceptual outcomes. *Political Communication* 30: 456–473.

Brooks, D., and Geer, J. 2007. Beyond negativity: The effects of incivility on the electorate. *American Journal of Political Science* 51(1): 1–16.

Bryce, J. 1921. *The American commonwealth*. Vol. 1. New York: Macmillan.

Bryson, A. 1998. *From courtesy to civility: Changing codes of conduct in early modern England*. Oxford, UK: Oxford University Press.

Burger, W. 1975. The necessity for civility. *Litigation* 1(1): 8–10, 62–63.

Carter, S. 1998. *Civility: Manners, morals, and the etiquette of democracy*. New York: Basic Books.

Chaucer, G. n.d. *The Canterbury tales*. Librarius Online Publication. Retrieved October 21, 2014 from http://www.librarius.com/canttran/mttrfs.htm.

Civility. n.d. In *Wikipedia*. Retrieved February 19, 2014, from http://en.wikipedia.org/wiki/Wikipedia:Civility.

Coe, K., Kenski, K., and Rains, S. A. 2014. Online and uncivil? Patterns and determinants of incivility in newspaper website comments. *Journal of Communication* 64: 658–679.

Cooper, T. 1792. *A reply to Mr. Burke's invective against Mr. Cooper, and Mr. Watt: In the House of Commons on the 30th of April, 1792*. Vol. 10, No. 6. London: J. Johnson, . . . , and M. Falkner and Co.

Craig, C. 2004. Audience expectations, invective, and proof. In J. Powell and J. Paterson (Eds.), *Cicero the Advocate* (pp. 187–214). Oxford, UK: Oxford University Press. doi:10.1093/acprof:oso/9780198152804.003.0008.

Darwall, S. 1977. Two kinds of respect. *Ethics* 88(1): 36–49.

DeMott, B. 1996. Seduced by civility: Political manners and the crisis of democratic values. *Nation* 263(19): 11–19.

Elias, N. 2000. *The civilizing process: Sociogenetic and psychogenetic investigation*. Oxford, UK: Blackwell.

Fehr, E., and Fischbacher, U. 2004. Social norms and human cooperation. *Trends in Cognitive Sciences* 8(4): 185–190.

Ferree, M., Gamson, W., Gerhards, J., and Rucht, D. 2002. Four models of the public sphere in modern democracies. *Theory and Society* 31(3): 289–324.

Furey, C. 2005. Invective and discernment in Martin Luther, D. Erasmus, and Thomas More. *Harvard Theological Review* 98(4): 469–488.

Gawronski, B., Bodenhausen, G., and Banse, R. 2005. We are, therefore they aren't: Ingroup construal as a standard of comparison for outgroup judgments. *Journal of Experimental Social Psychology* 41(5): 515–526.

Gillingham, J. 2002. From civilitas to civility: Codes of manners in medieval and early modern England. *Transactions of the Royal Historical Society (Sixth Series)* 12: 267–289.

Gould, D. 2009. *Moving politics: Emotion and ACT UP's fight against AIDS*. Chicago: University of Chicago Press.

Gutmann, A., and Thompson, D. 1996. *Democracy and disagreement*. Cambridge, MA: Harvard University Press.

Hayek, F. 1976. *Law, legislation and liberty. Vol. 2, The mirage of social justice*. Chicago: University of Chicago Press.

Herbst, S. 2010. *Rude democracy: Civility and incivility in American politics*. Philadelphia: Temple University Press.

Jamieson, K. H. 2000. *Incivility and its discontents: Lessons learned from studying civility in the US House of Representatives*. Boston: Allyn and Bacon.

Jamieson, K. H. 2012. Cable news networks increase amount and public accessibility of incivility. March 27. Retrieved from http://www.flackcheck.org/press/press-release-incivility-in-public-discourse/.

Jamieson, K. H., and Cappella, J. 2008. *Echo chamber: Rush Limbaugh and the conservative media establishment*. New York: Oxford University Press.

Jamieson, K. H., and Dunn, J. 2008 The "B" word in traditional news and on the web. *Nieman Reports* (Summer). Retrieved from http://www.nieman.harvard.edu/reports/article/100020/The-B-Word-in-Traditional-News-and-on-the-Web.aspx.

Jamieson, K. H., and Falk, E. 2000. Continuity and change in civility in the House. In J. Bond and R. Fleisher (Eds.), *Polarized politics: Congress and the president in a partisan Era* (pp. 96–108). Washington, DC: Congressional Quarterly Press.

Jefferson, T. 1868. *A manual of parliamentary practice: For the use of the Senate of the United States*. New York: Clark & Maynard Publishers.

Kasson, J. F. 1990. *Rudeness and civility: Manners in nineteenth-century urban America*. New York: Hill and Wang.

Kennedy, R. 1998. The case against civility. *American Prospect* 9(41): 84–89.

Knox, D. 1995. Erasmus' "De Civilitate" and the religious origins of civility in Protestant Europe. *Archiv für Reformationsgeschichte* 86: 7–55.

Koster, S. 1980. *Die invektive in der griechischen und römischen Literatur*. Mesienheim am Glan, DE: Hain.

Lendler, M. 2004. Equally proper at all times and at all times necessary: Civility, bad tendency, and the sedition act. *Journal of the Early Republic* 24(3): 419–444.

Leyens, J., Cortes, B., Demoulin, S., Dovidio, J., Fiske, S., Gaunt, R., Paladino, M., Rodriguez-Perez, A., Rodriguez-Torres, R., and Vaes, J. 2003. Emotional prejudice, essentialism, and nationalism: The 2002 Tajfel lecture. *European Journal of Social Psychology* 33(6): 703–717.

Linville, P., and Fischer, G. 1993. Exemplar and abstraction models of perceived group variability and stereotypicality. *Social Cognition* 11(1): 92–125.

Lynch, M. 2011. Reasons for reason. *New York Times*, October 2. Retrieved from http://opinion-ator.blogs.nytimes.com/2011/10/02/reasons-for-reason/?_php=true&_type=blogs&_r=0.

Mill, J. 1910. *Utilitarianism, liberty, & representative government*. New York: E.P. Dutton.

Murray, Stephen O. 1983. Ritual and personal insults in stigmatized subcultures. Gay—Black—Jew. *Maledicta 7*: 189–211.

Mutz, D. 2007. Effects of "in your face" television discourse on perceptions of a legitimate opposition. *American Political Science Review 101*(4): 621–635.

Mutz, D., and Reeves, B. 2005. The new videomalaise: Effects of televised incivility on political trust. *American Political Science Review 99*(1): 1–15.

Nickels, I. 1995. *Decorum in the House*. Washington, DC: Congressional Research Service.

Ost, D. 2004. Politics as the mobilization of anger. *European Journal of Social Theory 7*(2): 229–244.

Papacharissi, Z. 2004. Democracy online: Civility, politeness, and the democratic potential of online political discussion groups. *New Media and Society 6*(2): 259–283.

Phillips, T., and Smith, P. 2003. Everyday incivility: Towards a benchmark. *Sociological Review 51*(1): 85–108.

Porath, C., and Erez, A. 2007. Does rudeness really matter? The effects of rudeness on task performance and helpfulness. *Academy of Management Journal 50*(5): 1181–1197.

Porath, C., and Erez, A. 2009. Overlooked but not untouched: How rudeness reduces onlookers' performance on routine and creative tasks. *Organizational Behavior and Human Decision Processes 109*(1): 29–44.

Rafaeli, A., Erez, A., Ravid, S., Derfler-Rozin, R., Treister, D., and Scheyer, R. 2012. When customers exhibit verbal aggression, employees pay cognitive costs. *Journal of Applied Psychology 97*(5): 931–950.

Rawls, J. 1996. *Political liberalism: The John Dewey essays in philosophy*. New York: Columbia University Press.

Reno, R., Cialdini, R., and Kallgren, C. 1993. The transsituational influence of social norms. *Journal of Personality and Social Psychology 64*(1): 104–112.

Robbins, J., and Krueger, J. 2005. Social projection to ingroups and outgroups: A review and meta-analysis. *Personality and Social Psychology Review 9*(1): 32–47.

Schudson, M. 1997. Why conversation is not the soul of democracy. *Critical Studies in Media Communication 14*(4): 297–309.

Shils, E. 1997. Civility and civil society: Good manners between persons and concern for the common good in public affairs. In S. Grosby (Ed.), *The virtue of civility: Selected essays on liberalism, tradition and civil society* (pp. 63–102). Indianapolis, IN: Liberty Fund.

Simpson, D. 1960. *Cassell's new Latin dictionary. Latin-English, English-Latin*. New York: Funk and Wagnalls.

Sinopoli, R. 1995. Thick-skinned liberalism: Redefining civility. *American Political Science Review 89*(3): 612–620.

Sobieraj, S., and Berry, J. 2011. From incivility to outrage: Political discourse in blogs, talk radio, and cable news. *Political Communication 28*(1): 19–41.

Strachan, J., and Wolf, M. 2012. Calls for civility: An invitation to deliberate or a means of political control? In D. M. Shea and M. P. Fiorina (Eds.), *Can we talk? The rise of rude, nasty, stubborn politics* (pp. 41–52). New York: Pearson.

Thorson, K., Vraga, E., and Ekdale, B. 2010. Credibility in context: How uncivil online commentary affects news credibility. *Mass Communication and Society 13*: 289–313.

Uslaner, E. 1996. *The decline of comity in Congress.* Ann Arbor: University of Michigan Press.

Vasquez, E., Pedersen, W., Bushman, B., Kelley, N., Demeestere, P., and Miller, N. 2013. Lashing out after stewing over public insults: The effects of public provocation, provocation intensity, and rumination on triggered displaced aggression. *Aggressive Behavior* 39(1): 13–29.

Vrooman, S. 2002. The art of invective performing identity in cyberspace. *New Media & Society* 4(1): 51–70.

CHAPTER 16

....

THE POLITICS OF MEMORY

....

NICOLE MAURANTONIO

As Thelen (1989) states, "Remembering, we tend to think, is a process by which peo-ple search some kind of storage system in their minds—a filing cabinet or computer 'memory,' perhaps—to see whether they can retrieve some objective record of a fact or experience they had learned or observed at some earlier point" (1119). Memories consti-tute the metaphorical "files" retrieved in this process. In remembering, we are called to engage with the past, with history. Yet, remembering signals more than an act of cogni-tive recall. As Schwartz (1982) argues, "To remember is to place a part of the past in the service of conceptions and needs of the present" (374). Thus consideration of memory requires less attention to issues of "accuracy" or "authenticity" than it does to the values, beliefs, and norms shaping cultures at a particular historical juncture. Whether memo-ries present a past that can be deemed objectively "true" is beside the point. As Sturken (1997) writes, "What memories tell us, more than anything, is the stakes held by indi-viduals and institutions in attributing meaning to the past" (9). Memory is a dynamic entity, crafted and recrafted in dialogue with the political, social, and cultural impera-tives of the present.

Out of this acknowledgement of memory's malleability, some have focused on the "politics of memory" as a means of sharpening the bounds of the interdisciplinary enterprise of memory studies. Summarized by Confino (1997) as "a subjective experi-ence of a social group that essentially sustains a relationship of power," the politics of memory engages the questions of "who wants whom to remember what, and why" (1393). In focusing on the politics of memory, we move from the individual and more psychologically oriented frameworks for studying memory and toward a more socially oriented understanding that considers memory as part of a broader network of rela-tionships. Such an approach is especially well suited to communication studies, given the field's particular emphasis upon issues of identity formation, power, and politics. However, in moving toward considerations of memory as a social phenomenon, mem-ory studies open themselves up to the questions raised by the need to engage a shifting cultural, political, and technological landscape.

This chapter revisits some of the scholarly pleas for a more conceptually precise rendering of memory and considers the various sites of memory study that have emerged within the field of communication. Specifically, this chapter reviews sites of memory and commemoration, ranging from places such as museums, monuments, and memorials, to textual forms, including journalism and consumer culture. Within each context, I review the ways in which these sites have interpreted and reinterpreted traumatic pasts bearing great consequence for national identity, from the World War II and Vietnam Veterans Memorials in Washington, DC, to the Take Back the Memorial website created by the families of the victims of the terrorist attacks of September 11, 2001. I focus on places and texts engaging traumatic pasts as particularly illustrative sites of memory, or what Nora (1989) refers to as *lieux de mémoire*. In the wake of trauma, as Berkowitz (2010) notes, "meanings and values in society become confounded and ambiguous" (644), as the public searches for ways to make sense of what has occurred and return to normalcy. Memory sites thus assume a particular cultural role in helping collectives manage and work through trauma. In this process, as Sturken (1997) argues, "Questions of who is sanctioned to speak of particular memories are often raised, and issues of difference and exclusion from the 'imagined community' of the nation come to the fore" (13). This chapter points to the ways in which "imagined communities," as theorized by Anderson (1983/2006), have been configured and ultimately reconfigured through memory. It then concludes with a discussion of the challenges set forth by new media for scholars engaging in studies of the politics of memory and identifies areas worthy of future research.

DEFINING MEMORY

Memory is, as Davis and Starn (1989) argue, "polymorphic" and thereby interpreted variously, depending on the context within which it is used (2). As such, memory studies can be envisioned as stretching along a "spectrum of experience," as Thelen (1989) notes, "from the personal, individual, and private to the collective, cultural, and public" (1117). Consequently it is important to parse these "modifiers" (e.g., individual, social, collective, and public)—a term I borrow from Blair, Dickinson, and Ott (2010)—to stress not so much memory's distinctive forms but the conceptual implications of embracing them (6). Although some have spilt considerable ink differentiating these concepts as kinds of memory (Casey, 2004), here I suggest that their differences are significant but mostly heuristic in nature. As a result, this chapter focuses on collective memory as the central concept around which memory studies orbit when approached by scholars within the field of communication. I work from the assumption articulated by Olick (1999) when he noted that "we need to inquire into the value added by the term [collective memory], to specify what phenomena the term sensitizes us to as well as what kind of a sensitivity this is" (333–334).

Since the publication of Maurice Halbwachs's influential work (1952/1992) theorizing memory as a fundamentally social phenomenon, scholarly attention has focused largely upon the formulation, interpretation, and dissemination of collective/social memory. For Halbwachs (a follower of Emile Durkheim), individual acts of recollection are dependent upon the social frameworks within which one is situated (e.g., class, family, and religion). Scholars such as Schudson (1995) have argued, echoing Halbwachs, that "there is no such thing as individual memory" (346), claiming that memory resides within institutions and what Schudson refers to as "dedicated memory forms." These forms—including books, statues, and souvenirs—are deliberately imbued with meanings that serve specific ends and fulfill particular rhetorical functions (346–347). Such material forms of memory evidence but one basic premise, as Zelizer (1995) argues, for collective remembering. In addition to being material, Zelizer states, memory is unpredictable, usable, both universal and particular, as well as processual (218–234). Understanding collective memory in this way—as a dynamic entity subject to reinterpretation in time and space—invites inquiry into the ways in which meaning is made—how it functions and is ultimately "contested, subverted and supplanted by other memories" (Phillips 2004, 2). If conceptualized in this way, memory is a communicative process that occurs in terrain that is simultaneously contested and negotiated. Memory is political.

DISCIPLINARY POLITICS OF MEMORY

The coexistence of varied approaches to the study of memory has compelled scholars to contend with questions of disciplinary ownership and authority. Who wields the power to analyze how the past is remembered? Which disciplinary tool kit is best suited to the study of memory? Such questions necessarily identify historians as the scholars with the most at stake in memory's rise as an academic enterprise. If memory is in fact contingent and multiple, how does one explain memory's relationship to history—the discipline that trades in narratives of the past?

Just as Halbwachs considered collective memory a fundamentally social phenomenon, he envisioned memory as under attack by the discipline of history. This perspective, echoed years later by French historian Pierre Nora (1989), suggests that memory and history exist in a state of fundamental opposition. For example, Nora writes,

> Memory is a perpetually actual phenomenon, a bond tying us to the eternal present; history is a representation of the past. Memory, insofar as it is affective and magical, only accommodates those facts that suit it; it nourishes recollections that may be out of focus or telescopic, global or detached, particular or symbolic. . . . History, because it is an intellectual and secular production, calls for analysis and criticism. (8–9)

This divide—between the dynamic and the static, between the lived experience and the presentation of it—elicited initial skepticism of memory studies among historians. Memory was firmly grounded in the present; history in the past. If memory ensures that the grand narratives offered by the historian are inherently flawed and incomplete, what of history's future?

Since Halbwachs's and later Nora's expressed concerns regarding the opposition of history and memory, historians have taken a decidedly less antagonistic approach to memory studies. Some historians have argued that a more productive approach is to emphasize the interdependence of memory and history. Rather than envisioning history and memory as inherently antithetical, Davis and Starn (1989) write, "If anything, it is the tension or outright conflict between history and memory that seem necessary and productive. The explosive pertinence of a remembered detail may challenge repressive or merely complacent systems of prescriptive memory or history; memory, like the body, may speak a language that reasoned inquiry will not hear" (5). Historians, however, were not always so willing to see memory's potential to enhance historical practice.

I feature this tension between memory and history not simply because it has informed memory studies broadly but also because it emphasizes the analytic potential of communication studies scholarship. In discussing what they term "public memory"—a form of collective memory that is highly visible and accessible within the public sphere—Blair, Dickinson, and Ott (2010) argue that rhetoric, concerned with the "meaningfulness" of texts—including not simply speeches but performance, visual imagery, commodities, and other forms of popular culture—is particularly well suited to the type of work at the center of collective memory studies. As such, communication moves beyond some of the more functionalist explanations of memory's place within culture (e.g., Blair, Dickinson, and Ott's review of critiques of Hobsbawm and Ranger's [1983] "invention of tradition" model) to consider the ways in which texts are imbued with meaning. Romano and Raiford (2006) summarize as follows: "Representations of the past can be mobilized to serve partisan purposes. They can be commercialized for the sake of tourism; they can shape a nation's sense of identity, build hegemony, or serve to shore up the political interests of the state; and they can certainly influence the ways in which people understand their world" (cited in Hume 2010, 181). However, as Schwartz (1991) and Schudson (1992) remind us, these modes of remembering are not without limits. Communication studies' particular emphasis upon identity formation, power, and politics suggests that this inherently interdisciplinary field is well equipped to bring its array of tools and interests to bear on questions of the collective and to mediate between history and memory.

METHODOLOGICAL AND THEORETICAL POLITICS OF MEMORY

The disciplinary politics surrounding memory's academic study raise a central methodological question in memory studies: Whose memory do we study and how? Although there is no "correct way to 'do' memory," as Confino (1997) contends, the different entry

points into memory studies within the field of communication broadly suggest the multiple ways in which rhetorical analyses, discourse analyses, and textual analyses may
be brought to bear on different memory sites. The following categories, though hardly
exhaustive, constitute the dominant sites for memory study in communication scholarship: place, journalism, consumer culture, and new media. Through these sites of struggle, we gain insight into the stakes involved in the politics of memory as well as their
implications for the present.

In considering the construction of the World War II Memorial on the Washington
Mall and several popular texts representing the Second World War—such as the film
Saving Private Ryan, Tom Brokaw's book *The Greatest Generation,* and the Women in
Military Service for America Memorial—Biesecker (2002) argues that "these extraordinarily well-received reconstructions of the past function rhetorically as civics lessons
for a generation beset by fractious disagreements about the viability of U.S. culture and
identity" (394). Rather than teach about the past, Biesecker (2002) argues, such texts
become primers on how to become "good" citizens, serving as modes of establishing
social consensus. This need to unite collectives—to build community—rests at the core
of each of the four memory sites discussed here. As such, these sites transcend the events
they commemorate, offering collectives the opportunity to reaffirm identities in the face
of national crises. However, the processes by which these sites have come to be are often
highly contested, bringing the "politics of memory" to the fore and in turn opening up
areas for future research.

"Memory places," according to Blair, Dickinson, and Ott (2010), "may function as the
secular oracles for the current moment of a civic culture, offering instructions in public identity and purpose not only through proclamation, parable, or proverb, but even
more importantly by modes of interaction and contact in the place" (27). The significance of sites such as museums, monuments, and memorials rests in their rhetorical
power to act upon bodies and cultivate narratives that provide anchors for collective
identity. Memorials, Ehrenhaus (1988) argues, "speak" to communities. Inscriptions at
the Lincoln Memorial in Washington, DC, he suggests, "focus and direct our appreciation of that greatness, and instruct us in the manner in which we *ought* to interpret our
encounter with the memorial" (47). In so doing, "memory places" guide communities
toward particular interpretations of the past, often limiting the possibility for alternate
readings. However, as studies have shown, efforts to create consensus through place
have hardly been seamless, generating controversies surrounding commemorative form
and narrative as well as questions regarding "appropriate" uses of the past.

Nowhere are these issues engaged as dramatically as in sites grappling with traumas
such as war. Building upon Biesecker's (2002) claim regarding the ideological function
of World War II within American political culture, Balthrop, Blair, and Michel (2010)
offer a reading of the World War II memorial on the Washington Mall deemed "culturally illegible" by critics. Cited for its "surfeit of symbolism" (Balthrop, Blair, and Michel,
2010, 174), the World War II memorial was criticized for its inappropriate and confusing
symbolism as well as its lack of emotional resonance with visitors. However, when read
against the memorial's dedication events, Balthrop, Blair, and Michel (2010) argue, the

World War II Memorial can be made legible as a tool advancing a US imperialist agenda. Serving to bolster support for the US invasion of Iraq, the World War II Memorial, argue Balthrop, Blair, and Michel (2010), broke with the event being commemorated to speak to more presentist aims, leading them to question whether the past was indeed "hijacked."

The issue of the hijacking of history was similarly considered by Linenthal and Engelhardt (1996) in their volume analyzing the controversy surrounding the National Air and Space Museum's attempt to create an exhibit including the *Enola Gay*, the plane from which the atomic bomb was dropped on Japan, ending World War II. As Engelhardt and Linenthal (1996) argue, the *Enola Gay* controversy offers a case in which historians "found their work debated or attacked, misused and abused, and themselves accused of aiding and abetting the post-Vietnam War fragmentation of an American consensus" (5). An exemplar of the "history wars," the *Enola Gay* controversy illuminates the ways in which collectives have sought to strategically "forget" or exclude elements of the past that complicate and challenge preexisting narratives of the "good war." The eventual cancellation of the exhibit signaled the political stakes involved in crafting a narrative that might retell the war's end.

Monuments, memorials, and museums relating to civil rights have similarly been identified as rhetorically powerful sites where arguments of consensus and reconciliation largely overshadow conflict and struggle (DeLaure, 2011; Gallagher, 1999). Gallagher (1999) argues Birmingham, Alabama's Civil Rights Institute advances a discourse of progress that allows for an interpretation of the past that privileges hope. In such cases, the desire to establish a consensus interpretation of the past translates into a form of cultural amnesia (Gallagher, 1999), whereby elements of the past are finessed so as to minimize conflict. Dickinson, Ott, and Aoki (2006) argue that a similar phenomenon is at work at the Plains Indian Museum in Cody, Wyoming, where narratives of Euro-American colonization and the decimation of the native population are positioned so as to instill a "rhetoric of reverence" that simultaneously serves to advance both a degree of respect for the Native Americans and cultural distance from the native "Other."

Although most of the aforementioned case studies have focused on the ways in which the past has been seized to bolster national unity in the present, studies of the Vietnam Veterans Memorial in Washington, DC, have pointed instead to the ambiguities surrounding the war's memorialization, begging the question "How is commemoration without consensus, or without pride, possible?" (Wagner-Pacifici and Schwartz, 1991, 379). Unlike World War II, the Vietnam War itself was a site of fierce contest on the home front. The Vietnam War's commemoration was no less contentious. Wagner-Pacifici and Schwartz (1991) argue that the Memorial designed by Maya Lin, "informed by ambivalence about both the cause and its participants," was moved "in the direction of the muted and unobtrusive" (392). In contrast to the World War II memorial, so laden with symbolism as to render the structure inchoate according to critics (Balthrop, Blair, and Michel, 2010), the Vietnam Veterans Memorial is so controversial because it lacked the markers of traditional war memorials. Instead of offering a clear message, the memorial,

Ehrenhaus (1988) claims, "places both the burden and the freedom upon us to discover what these past events mean, whether these deaths do have meaning, what virtue is to be found in sacrifice, and what our own relationship should be to our political institutions" (55). The Vietnam Veterans Memorial reflects, according the Blair, Jeppeson, and Pucci (1991), the "'both-and' of postmodern architectural practice." They argue, the Memorial "does not suggest one reading or the other, but embraces even contradictory interpretations. The Memorial both comforts and refuses comfort. It both provides closure and denies it. It does not offer a unitary message but multiple and conflicting ones" (281).

Collectively, these exemplars of "memory places" have largely emphasized "official" memory, or memory sanctioned by individuals/institutions wielding power and on the dominant discourses that emanate from them. However, studies have also emerged that consider not simply "vernacular" or "popular" memory as official memory's relatively powerless opposite, which emanates from the ground up, but also the tension generated between such types of memory. Rather than being distinct and fundamentally opposing entities, as some have charged (e.g., most notably Bodnar, *Remaking America*, 1992), one can envision official and vernacular memories as coming into direct conflict and producing, in some cases, a more robust understanding of the past. Armada's (1998) study of the National Civil Rights Museum in Memphis, Tennessee, and the countermemorial forged by former Lorraine Motel resident and civil rights protester Jacqueline Smith suggest that the consumption of memory is made more productive by Smith's presence, whether one agrees with her critiques or not. When Smith was removed from her home at the Lorraine Motel by police in the 1988, leading her to create a makeshift countermemorial across the street, she called visitors to the eventual museum to consider the use of the space and the legacy of Dr. Martin Luther King, Jr., who was assassinated at the site in 1968.

Studies of place, focusing largely on the meanings imbued by those with power, will necessarily leave out the experiences of those who were not privy to the decision-making process. Doing so, argues Confino (1997), reduces memory to its very political core and consequently "underplay[s] the social" (1394). As a result, "we miss a whole world of human activities that cannot be immediately recognized (and categorized) as political, although they are decisive to the way people construct and contest images of the past. We can think of the family, voluntary association, and workplace but should also include practices such as tourism and consumerism" (Confino, 1997, 1395). The two sites on which I focus next, journalism and consumer culture, answer this call specifically.

Despite eliciting relatively little scholarly attention as a site of memory, journalism functions, as Zelizer (2008) argues, in often unrecognized ways as a source of collective memory and medium of memory's dissemination. The cliché that "journalists write the first draft of history" suggests a significant role for journalists in collective memory formation, as Edy (1999) notes. This role extends beyond written text to news images, which as Zelizer (1998) has argued, "need to be considered as markers of both truth-value and symbolism" (10). However, comparatively few inquiries into the memory work performed by journalism reveal how little traction journalism has gained as an area of memory inquiry within the academy. Recent work has sought to fill this void (e.g., Berkowitz and Gutsche, Jr., 2012; Carlson, 2006, 2010; Carlson and Berkowitz, 2012; Hoerl, 2009; Maurantonio, 2008; Robinson, 2006, 2009; Serazio, 2010; Zelizer and Tenenboim-Weinblatt, 2014); yet, as Zelizer (2008) argues, there is still considerable work to be done.

Studies have shown the ways in which journalists function as public historians through commemorative practices that occur on special occasions, such as anniversaries (Kitch, 2002a, 2006) as well as news media's work in "creat[ing] and convey[ing] a feeling of (temporary) national consensus" (Kitch 2003, 213), particularly in the wake of disasters such as the events of September 11, 2001, and the 1995 Oklahoma City bombing. In the face of crisis, journalists are called to make sense of events for their audiences. They must tell stories (Bird and Dardenne, 1997), rendering the often inexplicable accessible. One strategy for doing so is to rely on collective memory, thereby transforming the unknown into the familiar, as the cases of the 2003 Columbia space shuttle destruction (Edy and Daradanova, 2006) and the 2007 Virginia Tech shooting (Berkowitz, 2010) demonstrate.

In addition to conveying information to audiences, journalists also, as Berkowitz (2010) notes, "bring people together for catharsis through the stories they tell" (644). Journalists do this through the construction and maintenance of myth, which, as Lule (2005) argues, "is an essential social narrative, a rich and enduring aspect of human existence" (102). Myths help legitimate collectives, providing them with modes of interpretation. As Kitch (2002b) argues in her analysis of coverage of the death and funeral of John F. Kennedy Jr., mythical narratives "offer a promise of hope and healing, a message meant not just to console, but also to restore the social and political status quo" (305). The implications of these narrative decisions, however, are not all unproblematic. As Serazio (2010) argues in his analysis of sports journalism in the wake of Hurricane Katrina, triumphalist narratives of recovery pervaded journalistic discourse, providing an escape from the traumatic memories of Katrina and the harsh realities of a city where recovery is far from over.

Journalists' stories, however, not only facilitate audience understandings of traumatic events. They simultaneously bolster the interpretive authority of the institution (Zelizer, 1992). As a form of "imagined community," Carlson (2006) argues, journalism can be seen "as a symbolic collective connected by common normative ideas and a shared history that positions it within the larger cultural framework" (108). As an "interpretive community" (Zelizer, 1993), journalists rely on shared understandings of the past to maintain the cohesiveness of the institution.

Just as journalism provides one site of scholarly inquiry and an outlet through which individuals and collectives alike engage in the politics of memory, in considering the politics of grief and trauma, Sturken (2007) considers an alternate entry point: consumer culture. The linkage between consumption and politics did not emerge in the twenty-first century, as Dickinson (2005) reminds us. However, in analyzing the ways in which acts of consumption depoliticize trauma and grief, Sturken (2007) argues that an existing "culture of comfort" that takes refuge in kitsch commemorative objects such as teddy bears and snow globes allows consumers to distance themselves from broader political contexts. Examining objects that proliferated in the wake of traumas such as the Oklahoma City bombing and the attacks of September 11, 2001, Sturken (2007) argues that "an American public can acquiesce to its government's aggressive political and military policies, such as the war in Iraq, when that public is constantly reassured by the comfort offered by the consumption of patriotic objects, comfort commodities, and security consumerism" (6). In so doing, Americans are situated, according to Sturken (2007), as "tourists of history."

The emergence of new digital media technologies that have made archiving and accessing of memory possible has raised a series of new questions for scholars working within each of these subfields. As Savoie (2010) notes, "new media's democratizing role in memory work makes the translations and tradeoffs included in the production of collective memory increasingly visible" (3). Specifically, digital technologies such as blogs, memorial sites, and online archives change the ways in which we memorialize. After analyzing the September 11 digital archive, Haskins (2007) argues that "digital memory, more than any other form of mediation, collapses the assumed distinction between modern 'archival' memory and traditional 'lived' memory by combining the function of storage and ordering on the one hand, and of presence and interactivity on the other" (401). While presenting opportunities for individuals to engage with pasts they may not have experienced, new media give individuals access to sources that were previously unavailable. With these possibilities come consequences.

The vaunted democratization attributed to the Internet has raised theoretical questions both about new media's democratic function as well as new media's role as a space to contest the authority to interpret memory. Although contests surrounding interpretive authority did not emerge with the development of the Internet (see, for instance, Heyse, 2010), the Internet has provided a new arena within which such contests can unfold. As Donofrio (2010) argues in her analysis of the Take Back the Memorial (TBM) website, the families of the victims of the September 11, 2001, attacks eschewed "politics," locating themselves in opposition to the left-leaning academics, commercial interests, and politicians who might have seized the 9/11 memorial to capitalize on the suffering of others. In so doing, the families staked claim to interpretive authority by virtue of their suffering. Yet, as Donofrio (2010) notes, TBM's declared opposition to what they deemed "political" meant that the organization would "privilege a narrative of American innocence and dismiss entreaties to engage in larger a conversation about the US's role in international politics" (163). In advancing this argument, Donofrio builds upon Sturken's (2007) claims surrounding the use of consumer goods to distance individuals from the political stakes involved in memory.

In exploring these four sites where the politics of memory are considered centrally within the field of communication, we see both the possibilities as well as potential challenges for scholarly inquiry. Some have criticized studies examining the politics of memory for overemphasizing sites of memory and correspondingly paying little attention to issues of reception, or how audiences make sense of these sites (Confino, 1997). This latter concern, however, is one communication studies is well equipped to address, given the field's interests in the ways audiences make meaning from different texts. Reception remains, however, an area open for future research.

FUTURE RESEARCH IN POLITICS OF MEMORY

The disciplinary, methodological, and theoretical stakes involved in memory studies are high. In exploring the politics of memory, we examine not only what is being remembered but how and why. In so doing, we necessarily beg the questions of identity and collectivity that strike at the core of human experience. Communication scholars confronting issues of memory must consider further how various voices are privileged and marginalized in memory's construction, the ways in which memory is shaped and appropriated by individuals and collectives, and the ways in which memory's very existence is being challenged by new media. These future directions require greater attentiveness to two central issues: forgetting and reception.

Memory is not simply about what we remember or opt to recall, as the case may be. Just as remembering is contingent, so too is forgetting, as Connerton (2008) reminds us. Although Connerton (2008) claims that "forgetting" is commonly associated with a failure of memory, forgetting, like remembering, is differentiable. Just as there are modes of remembering, there are modes of forgetting. Forgetting can be directed by the state, can emanate from what may be seen as pure interests, can emerge from lack of information, or can be a form of "planned obsolescence." The categories do not end there (Connerton, 2008). Acknowledging the dialectic between remembering and forgetting invites further interrogation of this relationship. As Vivian (2010) argues, remembering and forgetting are part and parcel of larger processes by which "we construct, amend, and even revise altogether our public perceptions of the past, including our collective interpretations of its lessons, in response to the culture and politics of the day" (10). Rather than opposing forces, they are intimately connected. Within this framework, not all forgetting may be necessarily bad, as Vivian (2010) suggests.

Closer attention to forgetting as a subject of scholarly inquiry opens possibilities to address laments that studies of the "politics of memory" overemphasize "visible places and familiar names, where memory construction is explicit and its meaning palpably manipulated" (Confino, 1997, 1395). Consequently Confino (1997) calls scholars to search for memory "where it is implied rather than said, blurred rather than clear, in the realm of collective mentality" (1395). Such a call might seem easier said than done—seek out the subtlety, complement the visible. Perhaps now more than ever, with the enhanced ability to record, archive, and preserve, we stand at a moment of great potential. We may not only catalogue history as it unfolds but also give voice to those whose pasts may have been, even if only temporarily, forgotten. Reception studies offer a productive entry point to address these issues, leading to more nuanced understandings of the ways in which individuals and collectives negotiate memory as it is contested.

The value of such studies, however, rests not merely in added dimensionality. Surely it is important to grapple with the complexity of the past and the individuals who inhabited it. With greater access to traces of the past via new media, we have a greater capacity to explore how memory is used, moving beyond the sites where memory is commemorated to how it is enacted and performed. While much scholarship has considered the rhetoric of the monument, memorial, or museum exhibit, less attention has been paid to how visitors to these places respond to them. Similarly, journalism studies have tended to emphasize particular news items rather than how audiences make meaning from them. In adopting more audience-centered approaches to the study of the politics of memory, we may develop a more complete understanding of the "imagined communities" at stake and deeper insight into the collectives that form the fabric of the nation.

REFERENCES

Anderson, B. 1983/2006. *Imagined communities: Reflections on the origin and spread of nationalism.* London: Verso.

Armada, B. J. 1998. Memorial Agon: An interpretive tour of the National Civil Rights Museum. *Southern Communication Journal,* 63(3): 235–243.

Balthrop, V. W., Blair, C., and Michel, N. 2010. The presence of the present: Hijacking "the good war"? *Western Journal of Communication,* 74(2): 170–207.

Blair, C., Jeppeson, M. S., and Pucci, E. Jr. 1991. Public memorializing in postmodernity: The Vietnam Veterans Memorial as prototype. *Quarterly Journal of Speech,* 77(3): 263-288.

Berkowitz, D. 2010. The ironic hero of Virginia Tech: Healing trauma through mythical narrative and collective memory. *Journalism,* 11(6): 643–659.

Berkowitz, D. and Gutsche, , R. E. Jr. 2012. Drawing lines in the journalistic sand: Jon Stewart, Edward R. Murrow, and memory of news gone by. *Journalism & Mass Communication Quarterly,* 89(4): 643-656.

Biesecker, B. A. 2002. Remembering World War II: The rhetoric and politics of national commemoration at the turn of the 21st century. *Quarterly Journal of Speech,* 88(4): 393–409.

Bird, S. E., and Dardenne, R. W. (1997). Myth, chronicle and story: Exploring the narrative qualities of news. In D. Berkowitz (Ed.), *Social meanings of news.* Thousand Oaks, CA: Sage.

Blair, C., Dickinson, G., and Ott, B. L. (Eds.). 2010. Introduction: Rhetoric/memory/place. In *Places of public memory: The rhetoric of museums and memorials* (pp. 1–54). Tuscaloosa: University of Alabama Press.

Bodnar, J. 1992. *Remaking America: Public memory, commemoration, and patriotism in the twentieth century.* Princeton, NJ: Princeton University Press.

Carlson, M. 2006. War journalism and the "KIA journalist": The cases of David Bloom and Michael Kelly. *Critical Studies in Media Communication,* 23(2): 91–111.

Carlson, M. 2010. Embodying deep throat: Mark Felt and the collective memory of Watergate. *Critical Studies in Media Communication,* 27(3): 235–250.

Carlson, M., and Berkowitz, D. A. 2012. Twilight of the television idols: Collective memory, network news and the death of Walter Cronkite. *Memory Studies,* 5(4): 410-424.

Casey, E. S. 2004. Public memory in place and time. In K. R. Phillips (Ed.), *Framing public memory* (pp. 17–44). Tuscaloosa: University of Alabama Press.

Confino, A. 1997. Collective memory and cultural history: Problems of method. *The American Historical Review*, 102(5): 1386–1403.

Connerton, P. 2008. Seven types of forgetting. *Memory Studies*, 1(1): 59–71.

Davis, N. Z., and Starn, R. 1989. Introduction (special issue: memory and counter-memory). *Representations*, 26: 1–6.

DeLaure, M. B. 2011. Remembering the sit-ins: Performing public memory at Greensboro's International Civil Rights Center and Museum. *Liminalities: A Journal of Performance Studies*, 7(2): 1–28.

Dickinson, G. 2005. Selling democracy: Consumer culture and citizenship in the wake of September 11. *Southern Communication Journal*, 70(4): 271–284.

Dickinson, G., Blair, C. and Ott, B. L., (Eds.), 2010. *Places of public memory: The rhetoric of museums and memorials*. Tuscaloosa: University of Alabama Press.

Dickinson, G., Ott, B., and Aoki, E. 2006. Spaces of remembering and forgetting: The reverent Eye/I at the Plains Indian Museum. *Communication and Critical/Cultural Studies*, 3(1): 27–47.

Donofrio, T. A. 2010. Ground Zero and place-making authority: The conservative metaphors in 9/11 families' "take back the memorial" rhetoric. *Western Journal of Communication*, 74(2): 150–169.

Edy, J. A. 1999. Journalistic uses of collective memory. *Journal of Communication*, 49(2): 71–85.

Edy, J. A., and Daradanova, M. 2006. Reporting through the lens of the past: From Challenger to Columbia. *Journalism*, 7(2): 131–151.

Ehrenhaus, P. 1988. Silence and symbolic expression. *Communication Monographs*, 55(1): 41–57.

Engelhardt, T., and Linenthal, E. T. 1996. Introduction: History under siege. In *History wars: The Enola Gay and other battles for the American past* (pp. 1–7). New York: Holt.

Gallagher, V. J. 1999. Memory and reconciliation in the Birmingham Civil Rights Institute. *Rhetoric & Public Affairs*, 2(2): 303–320.

Halbwachs, M. 1952/1992. *On collective memory*, Edited, translated, and with introduction by L. A. Coser. Chicago: University of Chicago Press.

Haskins, E. 2007. Between archive and participation: Public memory in a digital age. *Rhetoric Society Quarterly*, 37(4): 401–422.

Heyse, A. 2010. Women's rhetorical authority and collective memory: The United Daughters of the Confederacy remember the South. *Women & Language*, 33(2): 31–53.

Hobsbawm, E. J., and Ranger, T. (Eds.). 1983. *The invention of tradition*. Cambridge, UK: Cambridge University Press.

Hoerl, K. 2009. Commemorating the Kent State tragedy through victims' trauma in television news coverage, 1990–2000. *The Communication Review*, 12(2): 107–131.

Hume, J. 2010. Memory matters: The evolution of scholarship in collective memory and mass communication. *Review of Communication*, 10(3): 181–196.

Kitch, C. 2002a. Anniversary journalism, collective memory, and the cultural authority to tell the story of the American past. *Journal of Popular Culture*, 36(1): 44–67.

Kitch, C. 2002b. "A death in the American family": Myth, memory, and national values in the media mourning of John F. Kennedy Jr. *Journalism & Mass Communication Quarterly*, 79(2): 294–309.

Kitch, C. 2003. "Mourning in America": Ritual, redemption, and recovery in news narrative after September 11. *Journalism Studies*, 4(2): 213–224.

Kitch, C. 2006. "Useful memory" in Times Inc. magazines. *Journalism Studies*, 7(1): 94–110.

Linenthal, E. T., and Engelhardt, T. (Eds.). 1996. *History wars: The Enola Gay and other battles for the American Past*. New York: Holt.

Lule, J. 2005. News as myth: Daily news and eternal stories. In E. W. Rothenbuhler and M. Coman (Eds.), *Media anthropology* (pp. 101–110). Thousand Oaks, CA: Sage.

Maurantonio, N. 2008. Justice for Daniel Faulkner? History, memory, and police identity. *Journal of Communication Inquiry*, 32(1): 43–59.

Nora, P. 1989. Between memory and history: *Les Lieux de Mémoire*. *Representations*, 26(1): 7–24.

Olick, J. K. 1999. Collective memory: The two cultures. *Sociological Theory*, 17(3): 333–348.

Phillips, K. R. (Ed.). 2004. Introduction. In *Framing public memory* (pp. 1–14). Tuscaloosa: University of Alabama Press.

Robinson, S. 2006. Vietnam and Iraq: Memory versus history during the 2004 presidential campaign coverage. *Journalism Studies*, 7(5): 729–744.

Robinson, S. 2009. "If you had been with us": Mainstream press and citizen journalists jockey for authority over the collective memory of Hurricane Katrina. *New Media & Society*, 11(5): 795–814.

Romano, R. C., and Raiford, L. (Eds.). 2006. *The civil rights movement in American memory*. Athens: University of Georgia Press.

Savoie, H. 2010. Memory work in the digital age: Exploring the boundary between universal and particular memory online. *Global Media Journal*, 9(16): 1–22.

Schudson, M. 1992. *Watergate in American memory: How we remember, forget, and reconstruct the past*. New York: Basic Books.

Schudson, M. 1995. Dynamics of distortion in collective memory. In D. L. Schacter (Ed.), *Memory distortion: How minds, brains, and societies reconstruct the past* (pp. 346–364). Cambridge, MA: Harvard University Press.

Schwartz, B. 1982. The social context of commemoration: A study in collective memory. *Social Forces*, 61(2): 374–402.

Schwartz, B. 1991. Iconography and collective memory: Lincoln's image in the American mind. *The Sociological Quarterly*, 32(3): 301–319.

Serazio, M. 2010. When the sportswriters go marching in: Sports journalism, collective trauma, and memory metaphors. *Critical Studies in Media Communication*, 27(2): 155–173.

Sturken, M. 1997. *Tangled memories: The Vietnam War, the AIDS epidemic, and the politics of remembering*. Berkeley: University of California Press.

Sturken, M. 2007. *Tourists of history: Memory, kitsch, and consumerism from Oklahoma City to Ground Zero*. Durham, NC: Duke University Press.

Thelen, D. 1989. Memory and American history. *The Journal of American History*, 75(4): 1117–1129.

Vivian, B. 2010. *Public forgetting: The rhetoric and politics of beginning again*. University Park, PA: Penn State University Press.

Wagner-Pacifici, R., and Schwartz, B. 1991. The Vietnam veterans memorial: Commemorating a difficult past. *American Journal of Sociology*, 97(2): 376–420.

Zelizer, B. 1992. *Covering the body: The Kennedy assassination, the media, and the shaping of collective memory*. Chicago: University of Chicago Press.

Zelizer, B. 1993. Journalists as interpretive communities. *Critical studies in mass communication*, 10(3): 219–237.

Zelizer, B. 1995. Reading the past against the grain: The shape of memory studies. *Critical Studies in Mass Communication*, 12(2): 214–239.

Zelizer, B. 1998. *Remembering to forget: Holocaust memory through the camera's eye.* Chicago: University of Chicago Press.

Zelizer, B. 2008. Why memory's work on journalism does not reflect journalism's work on memory. *Memory Studies,* 1(1): 79–87.

Zelizer, B., and Tenenboim-Weinblatt, K. (Eds.). 2014. *Journalism and Memory.* Palgrave Macmillan.

MEDIA AND POLITICAL COMMUNICATION

Political Systems, Institutions, and Media

CHAPTER 17

FREEDOM OF THE PRESS

Theories and Realities

DORIS A. GRABER

THE CONCEPT OF FREEDOM OF THE PRESS

THE idea that government control of news media content should be minimal and that freedom of the press should be guaranteed by the state's most fundamental laws has become popular in countries throughout the world. Most modern constitutions explicitly promise their citizens the right to freely express and publicize their political views. In the United States, a democratic country, the Bill of Rights of the US Constitution, for example, prohibits the national legislature from passing any law abridging the freedom of speech or the freedom of the press. But freedom of the press is also legally protected even in states where authoritarian forms of government prevail. In Russia, which has traditionally had authoritarian governments, Article 29 of the Constitution nonetheless explicitly guarantees freedom of speech and thought, unhindered public access to information, and freedom of the media from government pressure to control news coverage. Censorship is expressly forbidden. Those are the constitutional provisions; whether governments obey them is a matter of debate.

The fact that hands-off relationships between governments and the news media are routinely mentioned in constitutions shows that people everywhere realize that the power to control political news carries the power to destroy popular sovereignty. News media transmit political information that potentially reaches everyone within a state's borders and even beyond. These messages can, and often do, shape the views and actions of message recipients. In modern times battles over control of mass-mediated information flows have been relentless and pervasive. There are many contenders, but governments have always been among the fiercest because they want political information streams to reflect and buttress their political goals and to weaken or smother information that might benefit their opponents. They need the media to circulate government propaganda, counter or squelch unfavorable stories, and demonize their opposition.

Theories and Assumptions

The broad agreement that news media should be protected from government censorship rests on theories about the nature of human beings and their inherent rights. The underlying assumption is that all normal human beings are rational and have inalienable rights of self-determination, including choosing and monitoring their governments. Ordinary people presumably can understand the problems that their communities face and are able to judge the merits of policies designed to deal with these problems.

The idea that average people are smart enough to understand their political world was revolutionary in the seventeenth and eighteenth centuries, when it spread through much of Europe. It was grounded in Enlightenment theories about the rationality of all normal human beings. These theories were developed and espoused by political philosophers such as John Locke (1632–1704), the Baron de Montesquieu (1689–1755), and Jean-Jacques Rousseau (1712–1788). The political importance of free expression was widely discussed and debated by intellectuals, government leaders, and ordinary citizens. Most saw great benefits in free speech and the ability to circulate it widely through news media. There was broad agreement that truth will emerge only from battles of clashing ideas in which these ideas about shared problems are freely and rationally discussed.

If people have an inherent right to determine the nature of their governments, they need ample and diversified information about conditions at home and abroad to perform citizenship tasks adequately. For instance, they must know enough about current political issues to cast intelligent votes and to express sound opinions about public policies and government performance. They also must know how to render required citizen services properly, like paying taxes or serving in the military.

It followed from this assumption that news media are an essential element of public life because they provide the facts on which productive discussions are based. They also publicize the public dialogue and its ultimate outcomes. A press that is free to present a wide array of contradictory claims and opinions, including views that challenge government authority and legitimacy, is therefore a prerequisite for sound government. It safeguards people's presumably inalienable rights to express their ideas and to share them as widely as possible with others.

Rational assessments of human behavior also convinced Enlightenment philosophers that all humans are fallible and prone to engage in socially damaging behaviors. Political leaders in particular are apt to abuse their substantial official powers because they have many opportunities to do so. To forestall or detect abuse and end and punish it requires a vigilant public. The public needs the news media as its eyes and ears. A free press, beyond the control of government and acting on behalf of citizens, can monitor the activities of government officials so that they can be held accountable. Accordingly, a constitutional requirement that speech and press must be free from government control keeps government actions transparent and forestalls abuses and tyranny.

Balancing Conflicting Rights

The Enlightenment philosophers were fully aware that news media were not necessarily the ideal servants of the public that theorists postulated. Published views could be wrong, incomplete, intentionally deceptive, one-sided, and harmful to public interests. Thomas Jefferson, a founding father of the United States and a two-term president, complained about the "putrid" state of newspapers and "the malignity, the vulgarity, and mendacious spirit of those who write for them" (Levy, 1963, 67). Nonetheless, like other framers of the US Constitution and later political leaders, he was willing to accept a free press, marred by misbehaviors, in preference to a better-behaved press, hemmed in by government controls. He argued that "our liberty depends on the freedom of the press, and that cannot be limited without being lost" (Levy, 1963, 67).

Like all human rights, the right of free expression through an uncensored press is limited by other individual or collective rights. State security needs or concerns about governmental stability are likely to trump the right to enjoy the unhampered exchange of political messages. Most constitutions explicitly forbid treasonable communications and directly or indirectly prioritize security needs over countervailing rights. The Constitution of Iran, for example, guarantees freedom of the press for all people, including ethnic minorities, but it also lists broad exceptions. The press is free except for situations that the authorities consider "detrimental to the fundamental principles of Islam or the rights of the public." The country's criminal code mandates prison terms and even the death penalty for "propaganda" against the state or "insults" to religion. The scope of these exceptions is left undefined. The government can interpret them broadly or narrowly, as suits its political needs.

The locations of the boundary lines between exercising press freedom and protecting the safety and security of the population vary widely. In many states, high-level courts define the specific circumstances when freedom of expression must yield to security concerns. Usually, courts in liberal democracies give much greater weight to freedom of expression than courts in states with authoritarian forms of government. But there is no clear dividing line between liberal democracies and dictatorships when one assesses them on a scale that ranges from complete press independence to the reality of total control over all mass-mediated communication.

Societal Constraints

When governments put few restrictions on the press, it does not mean that there are no limits on what it can publish or must ignore. The most potent limits on press freedom flow from the norms that the press adopts. These norms vary depending on the types of governments and their theories about the role of the news media in their society. One well-known book, *Four Theories of the Press* (Siebert, Peterson, and Schramm, 1956), claims that news media operate to support the existence and goals of either strict or liberal regimes. When operating in authoritarian or totalitarian modes, the news media's chief goal is to protect the survival of the state and its government. They sing its praises, hail its laws, expose its enemies, and limit critical comments to a minimum. Alternatively, when news media subscribe to "libertarian" or "social responsibility" theories, the public's welfare rather than the government's survival becomes the prime concern. In the libertarian mode news media take their cues from what their audiences want and need. News stories will be a mixture of entertainment and information that may contain mild or sharp criticism of government. Social responsibility journalism demands that journalists keep important social goals in mind when they select and interpret news stories. They do not merely ask what their audiences want to know; they also ask what they need to know as responsible citizens. A responsible press is, in many respects, a restrained press, though its reins are much looser than is the case in author-itarian and totalitarian regimes. Being socially responsible is made easier for journal-ists when laws specify topics that should not be publicized because they may create social harm.

Many governments pass laws that outlaw the type of news that is deemed socially harmful. For example, democratic countries, like France or Germany or the United States, ban publication of stories likely to engender racial and religious hatred, justify-ing war crimes, promoting child pornography, or endangering the lives of military and law-enforcement personnel. Authoritarian states have similar rules, which they enforce more diligently. Their prohibitions are usually far more extensive, with much harsher penalties for violations. In China, for instance, "throughout 2010, some 60,000 websites containing 'harmful materials' were forcibly shut down, and an estimated 350 million articles, photographs, and videos were deleted" (Reuters, 2010). Even in a country as large and populous as China, these are huge numbers.

The unwritten rules of ethics and professional behavior that journalists obey are another constraint on the content of news stories. These norms reflect each country's political culture and dominant political philosophies. Professional associations, such as India's Press Council, often reinforce these norms. The Council is an independent body, but its members include politicians, along with journalists and publishers. The Council investigates complaints about misconduct or irresponsible reporting by print media. Broadcast journalism has self-imposed controls as well. The Indian News Broadcasters Association checks the social appropriateness of news, with special attention to cover-age of stories about crime, violence, and national security. As is true of most informal controls, violations of the norms are all too common, with few serious adverse conse-quences for offending journalists.

Self-censorship induced by fear about harsh penalties for publishing sensitive stories is another, highly significant curb on journalists' reporting. Journalists are likely to keep silent if they anticipate that telling particular stories will expose them to public censure, prison terms, the death penalty, or physical assault or murder. Consequently, many important stories about alternative policies or about misdeeds by government officials or abuses by powerful individuals remain hidden. The evidence shows that journalists and their organizations who tell unwelcome stories about corrupt politics, organized crime, or drug cartel wars are at substantial risk. That very real danger has led to an increase in self-censorship, especially in countries where governments do little to bring thugs and assassins to justice.

The Reality of Modern Press Freedom

What does press freedom really mean in countries around the world in the twenty-first century? It has turned out to be an elusively elastic concept. A small number of studies have examined the reality of press freedom in individual countries, like Iran, India, or Brazil (Semati, 2008; Rajapal, 2009; Matos, 2008). But studies covering press freedom in a broader array of states or even the entire world are rare. Even more unusual are studies, such as those done by Freedom House, that update the information annually, based on well-defined criteria. Freedom House is a US-based nonprofit, nonpartisan research organization that has measured freedom of the press in all of the world's states annually since 1980. Its teams of experts gather and evaluate information systematically in each of the world's 196 states.

Freedom House Classifications

Freedom House classifies states as free, partially free, or not free. The data collected in 2010 show that 35 percent of the world's states allow press freedom, another 33 percent have a "partly free" press, and 32 percent lack press freedom, even when their constitutions promise it explicitly (Freedom House, 2010). In terms of the world's population in 2010, that meant that only 15 percent of the world's people, just one in six, lived under conditions in which the news media were free from strict governmental and nongovernmental restraints imposed on the content of print and broadcast messages. Approximately 44 percent of the people in the modern world lived in states where the press was only partly free, and 40 percent lived in states where many of the essentials of press freedom were lacking. Although there are annual fluctuations in these numbers, the overall pattern of an almost equal tripartite division appears to be stable.

The analysis of press freedom that follows is based on careful scrutiny of the full Freedom House reports for 2009 and 2010, which were two relatively ordinary years with no unusual incidents of violence or catastrophic economic upheavals. The data reveal the countless ways in which governments can and do impair press freedom for print news, over-the-air broadcasts, and Internet news suppliers. Some critics have questioned the completeness, accuracy, and fairness of the Freedom House data in general or for specific states.[1] Challenges are most common when the ratings are negative. China, for example, calls its "not free" rating "ridiculous" and "not worth commenting on. . . . The Chinese media enjoy sufficient freedom in reporting. Meanwhile, like in any other countries of rule of law, the Chinese media should conduct their work within the scope of the Constitution and law"[2] (Yu, 2007). Irrespective of the disputes about the scores that Freedom House assigns to specific states and of the weaknesses that inevitably plague huge research projects, there is broad agreement among scholars and pundits that Freedom House reports present a solid overview of the status of press freedom in today's world.[3]

Freedom House divides the indicators by which it judges press freedom into three categories: legal, political, and economic. Circumstances uniquely characteristic of each of these areas can support or curtail the independence of the press. Governments tend to have most direct control over the legal realm; less control over the political realm, where they may have to cope with powerful opponents; and generally least control over the economic environment. The power of news media institutions to resist government efforts to control the news also hinges on legal, political, and economic conditions that prevail in each of these types of environments.

Legal Environments

Major features of the legal environment that affect press freedoms include laws and regulations that deliberately or incidentally influence media content and governments' inclination to use them sparingly or incessantly. Freedom House experts assess the positive, negative, or neutral impact that legal and constitutional guarantees may have on press freedoms of expression in each of the world's states. For example, on the positive side, some countries, such as the United States, have "freedom of information" laws that allow journalists to compel government agencies to release information that these agencies would prefer to hide. Like the proverbial sword of Damocles, the power to compel exposure deters abuses as well as punishing them.

Also on the positive side, in the past governments in many states enjoyed a monopoly over news broadcasting or were the dominant news provider. Most, but by no means all, have now relinquished that power by allowing competition from privately controlled enterprises. In England, for example, the British Broadcasting Company (BBC), which represents official government views and dominated the field for a long time, has been joined by multiple privately controlled broadcast stations. Nonetheless, government influence often continues even when there are many competitors in the broadcast field. For example, in France many print and broadcast outlets are owned by companies that have close contacts with the country's leading politicians. In Italy, which has many private media companies, media mogul Silvio Berlusconi controlled nearly all of them even when he was prime minister.

In many states the courts have acted as a counterweight to encroachments on press freedom by the government's executive and legislative branches by invalidating many severe restrictions. For example, Brazil's Supreme Federal Tribunal overturned a law that imposed harsh criminal penalties on journalists who had criticized government actions. The law had been adopted in 1967 when the country was under military rule.

Courts have also served as protectors of press freedom when journalists were sued for libel for telling stories and naming names about government incompetence, corruption, and cover-ups or when they were held responsible for offending content presented by visitors to their websites. On the negative side, many courts are highly politicized or even corrupt. They dismiss cases in which breaches of press freedom are charged and are overly zealous in punishing journalists accused of dispensing dangerous information.

Turning to laws that impede press freedom, the penal codes of many states and laws designed to protect the state against domestic and foreign terrorism severely curb free expression, either explicitly or by threatening harsh penalties for violations. Venezuela, for example, imposes harsh penalties for vaguely defined transgressions like offending or denigrating the authorities or spreading hatred. Penalties for criticizing or insulting the country's political leaders are common. Even the very liberal Dutch courts fined the Associated Press in 2009 for publishing photographs of the royal family on vacation. Many states, like Israel and China, require publishers and journalists to register. Such laws can be easily manipulated to admit only admirers of the current government and exclude potential critics.

Political Environments

Evaluation of each state's political environment involves assessing the degree of political control over the selection and framing of news content. Freedom House researchers check how much editorial independence state-owned and privately owned media enjoy and to what extent they are throttled by censorship laws. They also look for evidence of self-censorship. In the process, they check whether local and foreign reporters can cover the news freely without harassment and intimidation by governments or other powerful groups within society. Common methods of intimidation include detention of journalists for unspecified reasons and long prison sentences if they are convicted for publishing stories that allegedly endanger the nation's security. As mentioned, incidents of physical violence against journalists are commonplace, making journalism an increasingly hazardous occupation for journalists committed to open reporting. In states such as Mexico or Colombia, drug cartels regularly assault or murder journalists who report about drug-related crimes. In politically unstable regions of Pakistan, four journalists were allegedly murdered in a single year.

Ease of access to information and to the people and organizations that supply it is another important indicator of the openness of the political environment to press surveillance. Freedom House researchers assess the diversity of news available within each country and its vibrancy. Their reports give demerits to countries like Iran for suspending or shutting down hundreds of publications that criticized the government or reported about topics like a faltering economy, ethnic tensions, or nuclear policies. Offending journalists and bloggers were imprisoned, contrary to constitutional guarantees of press freedom.

Economic Environments

Assessments of the economic environment for the media include examining the structure of media ownership to determine who owns and therefore influences them and how concentrated or dispersed ownership is. Other important factors in the economic environment are the costs of establishing and operating news media and the selective granting or withholding of advertising or subsidies. Steep costs regularly bar small opposition groups and poor citizens from making their voices heard. Corruption and bribery can also have a strong impact on what gets published and what is omitted. More generally, Freedom House analysts weigh how economic circumstances affect the status of a state's news media.

Comparing Environments

Which of these three environments—legal, political, or economic—generates the greatest problems for press freedom? A comparison of a balanced sample of fifteen randomly selected free, partly free, and not free states provides answers. Australia, Canada, Chile, the United Kingdom, and the United States represented the "free" category. The sample of "partly free" countries included Brazil, India, Mexico, South Africa, and Turkey. The "not free" category was represented by China, Libya, Russia, Saudi Arabia, and Venezuela. All of these countries were quite typical of their categories, so the total scores listed for each are well within the limits of the Freedom House scoring system. In fact, the scores are close to the group medians of 20, 45, and 80, respectively, indicating that the sample data depicted in Table 17.1 are, indeed, representative of the universe.

The symmetry of the data across the various levels of freedom is striking. Irrespective of the level of press freedom, Table 17.1 shows that restraints imposed by the political environment received the highest scores, confirming that they are the strongest barriers to the exercise of press freedom. Although the numbers are partly an artifact of the scoring system that assigns penalty points according to the seriousness of the infraction, with some political offenses rating at the top, real-world events bear them out. Freedom House reports about individual states confirm that the greatest threats to press freedom do indeed occur in the political realm. That is both good and bad news. It is good because most political constraints can be eliminated fairly readily and quickly; it is bad because that is unlikely to happen. Power struggles are endemic to politics, and contenders know that control over the news media can determine the outcome.

In comparison to political factors, economic ones were unexpectedly minor impediments to press freedom. In fact, contrary to prevailing views that economic issues shape the course of politics, they were the least important element in the total count of restraints. It is also interesting that the numbers in the legal, political, and economic columns increase in roughly symmetrical patterns. As one moves from one freedom level

Table 17.1 Comparative Legal, Political, and Economic Scores*

Country Categories	Legal Factors 30%	Political Factors 40%	Economic Factors 30%	Weighted Factor Average	Total Country Score
Free	6.2	9.2	6.2	7.4	22.2
Partly Free	14.0	18.8	11.0	15.0	45.0
Not Free	27.0	32.6	23.8	28.2	84.6
Averages	15.7	20.2	13.6	16.5	50.6

* Freedom House scores range from 0 to 30 points for constraints due to legal or economic factors and from 0 to 40 points for constraints due to political factors. The "Free" category ends at a total of 30 points; the "Partly Free" category ends at a total of 60 points; the "Not Free" category runs from 61 to 100 points.

to the next, the numbers double, suggesting that the differences between the various levels are substantial.

WHAT DOES THE FUTURE HOLD?

What is the key explanation for the sharp variations in the extent of press freedom in free, partly free, and nonfree states? All of these states hail the importance of press freedom and claim that their policies respect it. When pushed to explain obvious restraints, the universal official justification is that these rules are needed to protect the laws of the land and national security. As discussed at the start of this chapter, most constitutions explicitly acknowledge that important security needs may trump press freedoms. The crucial question is at what point security becomes paramount.

The ratings and justifications reported by Freedom House suggest that the answer to that question depends on the values that various governments place on the freedom of the press compared to other goals. When either state survival or government survival is at stake, governments based on authoritarian or totalitarian philosophies weigh order and stability far more heavily than liberty. Governments grounded in social responsibility or libertarian theories weigh press freedom and security needs more evenly. However, the scales dip more readily toward security needs when state survival, rather than the survival of an incumbent government, is at stake. In fact, according to libertarian and social responsibility theories, it may be the special privilege or even duty of the press to expose the faults of governments and encourage their overthrow if that serves the public's interests.

While values are important, the realities of political life carry the greatest weight. All states will suspend press freedoms when they are at war or feel threatened by war or terrorism. Most citizens and external observers will condone curtailments under such circumstances. What about other circumstances? This chapter shows that restraints on press freedom are common during times of peace as well. Keeping the press in line with the government's goals is fully compatible with principles of authoritarianism, but democratically oriented states also do it and justify it, especially when their governments are under stress. Israel, for example, has seesawed between free and partly-free status depending on the state of tension in its relationships with neighboring countries. At times of higher stress, it has tightened travel restrictions for reporters and has tried to influence the thrust of news coverage. When dangers pass, restraints may be lifted, and political leaders often apologize for muzzling the press. The prevalence and severity of restrictions on press freedom depend, in all types of government, largely on the risk tolerance of political leaders and on the population's willingness to tolerate curbs on press freedom without protesting forcefully.

In sum, the strongest reason for violating press freedoms is the vulnerability of most modern governments to attacks on their leadership and on their major policies. Democratic and authoritarian governments alike fear that they may succumb to opposition forces. Most lack strong and vibrant popular support for the government and the media. The chances are remote that governments will feel strong and secure in the foreseeable future and that attacks on news media will therefore diminish. Violations of press freedoms may even become more constricting, because advancing technologies make the tools for repression ever more sophisticated.

Who will win in this power struggle over control of the information that reaches the public? In the past, governments have always been the winners because their legal status gives them a distinct advantage. But that could change, considering that the tools for foiling repression are also becoming more prevalent and potent.

QUESTIONS FOR FUTURE RESEARCH

President Theodore Roosevelt cautioned Americans to "keep your eyes on the stars and your feet on the ground." In tune with that advice, researchers should continue to explore the theories and assumptions that support the free press ideal and the practices that violate it. If the ideals are violated consistently, are they flawed?

Questioning the Concepts

Most important, is a press that is free from government control essential for allowing all citizens to publicize their political views? Where the press is partly free, or lacks freedom, have news flows differed in major ways from their counterparts in free-press countries? Is it true that an unrestrained flow of conflicting opinions produces truth, or does it obscure truth and often generate confusion? In sum, do unelected news media really need and deserve to be beyond the control of popularly elected governments?

Press Performance

Have journalists delivered the important political goods that press freedom theories promise? Have they been wise in choosing their information sources, topics, and frames? Have irresponsible free media done more harm than good in the past? Has press freedom hurt unstable countries where critical stories may make governing impossible? Does the universal suspension of press freedoms in wartime mean that it is a peacetime luxury for stable, economically secure states?

These are huge and troubling questions. Well-researched answers may discover new guiding stars to better the interplay between governments and news media.

Notes

1. For a general discussion of the limitations of comparative international data analysis, see Munck and Verkuilen (2002). For an overview of cross-national data sets, see Munck (2003).
2. Jiang Yu, a spokesperson for the Chinese Foreign Ministry, posted this statement on the website of the Chinese embassy in London on May 11, 2007.
3. For a comprehensive, comparative analysis of the validity of the Freedom House data, see Burgess (2010).

References

Burgess, J. 2010. Evaluating the evaluators: Media freedom indexes and what they measure. National Endowment for Democracy. Retrieved from http://cima.ned.org/docs/CIMA-Evaluating_the_Evaluators_Report.pdf.

Freedom House. 2010. Freedom of the press 2010: Broad setbacks to global media freedom. Retrieved from http://www.freedomhouse.org/template.cfm?page=251&year=2010.

Levy, L. W. 1963. *Jefferson and civil liberties: The darker side*. Cambridge, MA: Harvard University Press.

Matos, C. 2008. *Journalism and political democracy in Brazil*. Lanham, MD: Rowman & Littlefield Publishers.

Munck, G. L. 2003. Measures of democracy, governance and rule of law: An overview of cross-national data sets. Retrieved from http://siteresources.worldbank.org/INTMOVOUTPOV/Resources/2104215-1148063363276/071503_Munck.pdf.

Munck, G. L., and Verkuilen, J. 2002. Conceptualizing and measuring democracy: Evaluating alternative indices. *Comparative Political Studies* 35(1): 5–34.

Rajapal, A. (Ed.). 2009. *The Indian public sphere.* New Delhi: Oxford University Press.

Reuters. 2010. China shuts over 60,000 porn websites this year. December 30. Retrieved from http://www.reuters.com/article/idUSTOE6BT01T20101230.

Semati, M. (Ed.). 2008. *Media, culture and society in Iran.* New York: Routledge.

Siebert, F. S., Peterson, T., and Schramm, W. 1956. *Four theories of the press: The authoritarian, libertarian, social responsibility, and Soviet communist concepts of what the press should be and do.* Urbana, University of Illinois Press.

Yu, J. 2007. Foreign Ministry spokesperson Jiang Yu's remarks on the report of the US human rights group Freedom House. May 11. Retrieved from http://www.chinese-embassy.org.uk/eng/fyrth/t322250.htm.

CHAPTER 18

....

PRESS–GOVERNMENT RELATIONS IN A CHANGING MEDIA ENVIRONMENT

....

W. LANCE BENNETT

JUST when it seemed that the persistent media controversy about the authenticity of President Obama's birth in the United States had finally died down, the real estate developer and reality TV impresario Donald Trump announced on a morning television program that he might run for president and that he was skeptical about the already extensive evidence offered about Obama's birthplace (ABC News, 2011). The ensuing media attention led Trump to more media appearances, fueled by his continuing challenges to the president's birth status. As a result, a dubious story was back in the news despite having been refuted repeatedly over several years through the production of documents by the president, various public officials, and FactCheck.org, all demonstrating the authenticity of his birth in Hawaii. For example, FactCheck (2008) issued this assessment amid the rumors of the 2008 presidential campaign: "FactCheck.org staffers have now seen, touched, examined and photographed the original birth certificate. We conclude that it meets all of the requirements from the State Department for proving U.S. citizenship. Claims that the document lacks a raised seal or a signature are false. We have posted high-resolution photographs of the document as 'supporting documents' to this article. Our conclusion: Obama was born in the U.S.A. just as he has always said."

A growing dilemma for the press is how to hold the news gates against the swarms of suspect political claims that fly in the face of authoritative evidence. Such factually dubious narratives have appeared as news on a variety of issues, foreign and domestic, including challenges to scientific evidence about climate change, frightening claims about how the healthcare reforms of 2010 would threaten people who already had health insurance, and assertions that the use of torture by the Bush administration helped President Obama get Osama bin Laden.

Why did the mainstream press report such known distortions, particularly from sources such as Trump, who would seem to have little standing to challenge more authoritative views? Candy Crowley, a prominent CNN reporter and anchor—who joined the legions in interviewing Trump—said this: "There comes a point where you can't ignore something. . . . The question was, 'Is he driving the conversation?' And he was" (Rutenberg, 2011). The larger question of course is just what is "the conversation," and who is moderating it, if not the press?

All of this raises interesting questions about relations between the press and official-dom, and in particular, about whether the gatekeeping process has changed, and if so, how. It seems clear that with the rise of the Internet, the proliferation of cable chan-nels, and the business crisis facing most news organizations in the United States (and many other democracies as well), the capacity to report critically has become vastly diminished (McChesney and Nichols, 2010). This diminished journalistic product may contribute to the erosion of audience numbers and pubic confidence in the quality of journalism itself (Patterson, 2000; Cook, 2005). Indeed, some observers are pronounc-ing the mass media news regime over, although there are not yet enough discernible trends to know what sort of information regime will replace it (Prior, 2007; Bennett and Iyengar, 2008; Williams and Delli Carpini, 2012).

In sorting out these complex currents that characterize the embattled legacy press system, this chapter reviews how the classic model of press-state relations has adapted to such factors as diminished journalism capacity, the proliferation of dubiously sourced information flowing across more densely interconnected communication networks, and audiences that exercise greater choice about what to believe. Among the related issues explored in the remainder of this chapter are the following:

- Where, and with what consequences, does indexing—the journalistic filtering of news sources and content through perceived government power balances—continue to hold sway? This discussion examines the continuing role of the leg-acy media in constructing the symbolic political record. Perhaps the main irony surrounding the loss of public respect and audience ratings is that the legacy news media have become an insider game, serving as a sort of surrogate public against which elites play out their frame contests.
- Is there countervailing evidence for a decline of gatekeeping and a rise of narrative-driven news in which the telling of entertaining and dramatic stories becomes the filtering mechanism for sources and facts? Perhaps the decline of journalism resources and the desperate quest for paying customers makes it more difficult to resist the dramatic, if dubious, stories that circulate online and in ever more fanci-ful talk radio and television programs. If so, how do indexing and narrative- driven news intersect?
- What are the consequences of a changing news system for public engagement and democratic legitimacy? This discussion explores the implications of the increasing *democratization of truth* as the news system loses the capacity to assess evidence, reject groundless narratives, and anchor public debates in reasonable standards.

THE LEGACY PRESS AND
THE INDEXING PROCESS

Among the more established perspectives on press politics is the idea that the press operates as a de facto branch of government. This approach has developed into a theoretical formulation termed a *new institutionalism*, following parallel schools of thought in sociology and political science (Cook, 2006; Sparrow, 2006; Ryfe, 2006). At the core of the theoretical puzzle in new institutionalist thinking is how such a large system of highly competitive organizations produces such remarkably similar content at the end of the day (Cook, 2005). One answer is that the core dynamic of the institutional organization of news involves filtering stories according to power balances in political institutions being covered (Bennett, 1990; Bennett, Lawrence, and Livingston, 2007). This indexing process gives the media-as-institution its remarkable homogeneity in terms of what stories matter, what sources are used to frame those stories, and what narrative lines emerge as stories develop.

During the era of the high modern press in the United States and elsewhere, news organizations have tended to rely overwhelmingly on official, authoritative sources to frame news stories (government officials, heads of business and interest organizations, and other public figures). In different press systems decisions about balance and inclusion of content tend to be based on a combination of the political stance of the press organization and weighing sources according to their role in party or government and their capacity to affect policy outcomes, which entails somewhat more complex indexing rules that vary from system to system. Beyond these core considerations, press systems also differ depending on the importance of party-affiliated news outlets, the development and independence of public service media, and norms about the role of journalism in society (Blumler and Kavanagh, 1999; Hallin and Mancini, 2004). In the US press system, the prevailing norms have been independence (or press freedom) and impartiality (or neutrality), resulting in claims about objectivity in an earlier era, or more recently, fairness and balance. While these foundations of press politics are beginning to change, they continue to produce a remarkable level of uniformity in mainstream media reporting—so much that, as noted above, scholars have described the US news media as an institution. In this highly institutionalized system, much of the political reality in news reporting is filtered through implicit journalistic calculations about power within official circles, rather than, say, through reference to other possible credible sources offering evidence about the issues being reported that is independent of the standpoints of officialdom.

The role of indexing has introduced a variety of anomalies or paradoxes into the US press system. When democratic institutions are performing well, the press system works well. However, reporting often proves limited or incomplete when government is operating less transparently, or the range of policy debate is restricted due to the influence of money or other political calculations—even when credible evidence challenging official claims may exist outside of official circles. As a result, in cases where democracy most needs an independent press to serve as a watchdog against poorly performing public institutions, journalism often fails to deliver independent critical reporting. Thus, Bush administration claims about weapons of mass destruction and links between Iraq and al Qaeda were largely unchallenged in the run-up to the Iraq War because the Democratic Party proved reluctant to take a party position challenging a then popular president, depriving the press of another side of the (official) story. The continuing challenges to administration claims by UN weapons inspectors, among others, were not acceptable under indexing logic as sources that could sustain a counter frame in a contest with Bush administration spin. The statements of UN weapons inspectors from the International Atomic Energy Agency (IAEA) were noted for the record, but not reported often enough to constitute a credible frame challenge to Bush administration claims. The failure to grant such knowledgeable challengers a balanced amount of coverage was not due to lack of external source credibility: the IAEA and its director, Mohamed ElBaradei, were awarded the Nobel Prize in 2005, in part for their efforts to verify Bush administration claims about WMDs in Iraq.

Despite admissions of poor performance from leading news organizations about their failure to investigate other sides of the Bush administration Iraq story, the strength of the indexing norm continued to trump journalistic independence as the war went on. The next critical episode of the Iraq story involved the tortured news coverage of the interrogation of prisoners in US detention facilities at Abu Ghraib and elsewhere. Again, despite independent reports of programmatic violations of Geneva Conventions by observers such as the Red Cross, and accounts in the foreign press of rendition and torture, the US press did not raise torture to a competing news frame until Senator John McCain eventually challenged the president on the issue (Bennett, Lawrence, and Livingston, 2007).

In this model of press politics, the news gates may be under continuous siege, but when one scratches the surface of the resulting stories, one often finds that officials and other authoritative sources provide the cuing that reporters need to consider them "driving the conversation." Donald Trump was, after all, thinking about a presidential run, and had shown in the polls as a contender, even if only briefly. And, as shown in the next section, the challenges to established climate science that "balanced" the news on that issue for over a decade were cued by powerful members of the Bush administration and by members of Congress who could influence the outcomes of climate legislation.

To some observers, however, the appearance of such high-profile stories seems at odds with the impression that news organizations are somehow vulnerable to sensational stories that are too good to fact check. How else could so many grandiose stories get into the news? Perhaps the journalistic allure of a good drama, scandal, or people-pleasing narrative is simply too good to resist. There is little doubt that the news feeds on sensation, but this does not settle the question of whether stories that may be too good to be true get through the news gates independently on those grounds alone, or whether they are escorted through with cueing by sources who meet indexing criteria. Indeed, when acceptable sources spin scandals against opponents or offer convenient denials about the scientific evidence for climate change, the news may have a win-win situation: a "talker" story that also passes the indexing test. This is essentially what the CNN reporter acknowledged earlier about the Trump challenge to Obama's birth. Indeed, Murray Edelman (1988) long ago noted that there were few better sources of political spectacle than public officials themselves. As a result, we need to sort out how many of the seemingly fanciful narratives cycling in the news may have officials promoting them. If insider spin still rules, it seems important to reconcile this view with the alternative current of thinking that finds news discourses to be more cultural constructions in which journalists have more agency as storytellers.

IS NARRATIVE-DRIVEN NEWS ON THE RISE?

Stories such as the Obama birth controversy or the denial of the consensus account of climate scientists about the scale and significance of human-created global warming (just to cite two very different cases) may give the appearance that the gatekeeping process has become more porous, or that narrative-driven news is on the rise, perhaps even displacing indexing. Indeed, there is evidence that journalists have stepped more into the center of news stories than in earlier periods. Hallin (1992a) found that TV sound bites (air time given to sources to speak) shrank dramatically, from an average of 43 seconds in 1968 to under 10 seconds by 1988. The incredible shrinking sound bite continued to shrink, to 7.3 seconds by the 2000 presidential campaign (Center for Media and Public Affairs, 2000). This trend complements Patterson's (2000) finding that there was an increase in airtime given to journalists who talked over sources and interpreted their statements for viewers. In addition, the 24/7 news cycle calls for more commentary and updating of stories even when there is little new to add. These and other factors suggest that journalists may have a growing capacity to stir stories, provoke reactions, and turn rumors into leading questions, all of which may contribute to greater license to create narratives themselves. This narrative license may be particularly evident in so-called event-driven situations, in which big events that shock the nation place journalists at a news scene before official framing strategies point to clear plot developments. Events such as floods, hurricanes, terrorist attacks, or school shootings can set somewhat independent narratives in motion (Lawrence, 2000a; Bennett and Lawrence, 1995).

This collection of factors pointing toward greater journalistic intervention in story development appears to support a second broad perspective in the literature on press politics: an account that portrays the press as a cultural storyteller—narrating the national collective identity (Gans, 1979; Barnhurst and Nerone, 2001). This viewpoint is implicit in much of the agenda-setting literature, which has never been satisfactorily reconciled with indexing, although there have been steps toward such a theoretical synthesis. (Walgrave, van Aelst, and Bennett, 2011).

What may make more sense than setting up an "either/or" contrast here is to hypothesize that some combination of indexing and narrative license may drive big stories, with the edge going to narrative license for those grand events that invite celebration or reiteration of hallowed American themes (e.g., the triumph of freedom in the fall of the Berlin Wall, or heroism under adversity during 9/11). By contrast, more mundane, day-to-day political reporting requires considerably less literary imagination and a good deal more routine indexing work to figure out the sources who are most likely to influence the outcome of the story.

Even in big event-driven stories, the process of fashioning narratives around frames is not likely to be driven entirely by journalistic narratives or by indexing, alone. For example, Lawrence and Birkland (2004) studied news framing of a major high school shooting incident in Columbine, Colorado. They found an important overlap between policy debates in Congress and news frames of gun control (suggesting the role of indexing), but they also found that the second most prominent news frame was about whether violence in popular culture triggered such incidents, which was more a cultural narrative than a politically indexed story. This suggests that even event-driven news may reflect a mix of culturally familiar press narratives and politically indexed ones (Lawrence, 2010). For example, the proverbial political game frame, which seems to be largely a press narrative, often crops up in coverage of policy fights, even as key players in the contest strive to get their preferred frames into coverage via indexing (Lawrence, 2000b).

This suggests that the press may not have been entirely culpable of pure sensationalism in granting substantial coverage to Tea Party activists who revived charges that President Obama was not actually a native citizen and invented claims that he was simultaneously a communist and a fascist. While some of these charges may have originated with pseudo-journalists (such as Rush Limbaugh and Glen Beck), they also cycled through the mainstream legacy media as part of their coverage of Tea Party activities. The high volume of rather positive coverage given to the often rude and disruptive Tea Party differed from the often negative and dismissive coverage typically given to similarly disruptive protest movements. This curious departure from coverage patterns suggests that indexing was operating at some level to get the Obama attack narratives into the news.

After it was revealed (not surprisingly) that most Americans who doubted Obama's native birth got their supporting evidence from the media, the staff of the *Washington Post* "44" blog decided to find out where the media got their information. The answer turned out to involve a high degree of cueing from prominent Republican politicians, primarily members of Congress or political candidates. Indeed, the *Post* found no fewer than twenty-two instances of prominent Republicans casting doubt on Obama's status as a real American and even as a Christian. Counted among these sources were vice presidential candidate Sarah Palin, the director of new media for the Republican National Committee, and some prominent members of both the Senate and House. The members of Congress included sponsors of legislation requiring presidential candidates to prove their birthplaces and endorsers of independent lawsuits seeking greater disclosures of records from Obama (*Washington Post*, 2010).

A similar story emerges about how so much climate science denial entered mainstream reporting on global warming. For example, Boykoff and Boykoff (2004) examined coverage of climate change and global warming in the national prestige press between 1988 and 2002 and found that nearly 53 percent of the articles contained challenges to scientific consensus about human causes of warming. This pattern continued through the Bush administration in the 2000s and was routinely cued by a combination of administration officials and Republican members of Congress, who followed the spin moves outlined in a coordinated strategic communication campaign developed by Republican communication consultant Frank Luntz. One result was that public concern for global warming as a policy priority declined, paralleling the declining numbers who believed that there were human causes of global warming. The very existence of global warming began to be questioned in opinion polls, as the percentage believing that it was even happening dropped from 71 to 57 percent between 2008 and 2010 (Bennett, 2011, 115–118).

Venerable *New York Times* climate reporter Andrew Revkin described a debate between journalists and climate scientists at an annual meeting of the American Association for the Advancement of Science. His reaction to scientists thinking that their knowledge should somehow be preeminent on the subject was to claim that they simply represented one belief system among others and were thus guilty of propounding an "ism" that he called *scientism*: "Scientism tends to suppose a one-size-fits-all notion of truth telling. But in the public sphere, people don't think that way. They bring to the table a variety of truth standards: moral judgment, common-sense judgment, a variety of metaphysical perspectives, and ideological frameworks. The scientists who communicate about climate change may regard these standards as wrong-headed or at best irrelevant, but scientists don't get to decide this in a democratic debate" (Revkin, 2011).

In this revealing statement, Revkin appears to provide insight into how even the best journalists approach their reporting by simply distilling competing social truths into news stories. Yet how journalists know valid truths from preposterous ones that they deem beyond the journalistic pale is not explained by Revkin, or by most other reporters. Since one might easily regard the denial of climate science as preposterous, Revkin's gloss on journalism avoids explaining how he can recognize it as a credible "truth standard" that qualifies as news. The way in which competing truths—in this case, denials of science as a valid basis for public policy—most often get into the news is that they are promoted by authoritative sources such as prominent politicians and experts affiliated with think tanks funded by carbon energy interests (Bennett, 2011). If these are the "truth" mechanisms at work, then there is a hollow ring to Revkin's claim about the legitimacy of many of the competing truths in the public media sphere. On the contrary, the process at work behind the journalistic parlor trick of simply "knowing" which truths are valid involves the indexing norm, which means that the truth standard is power. If a calculus of power determines truth, the press has become the handmaiden of power. There would seem little that would hasten the demise of democracy faster than this. To relegate science in this scenario to just another "ism" seems woefully naïve about the corruptions of power on both truth and democracy, not to mention the naïveté of a press that fails to understand its handmaid's role in the process.

The overarching point here is that it does not make sense to juxtapose indexing and narrative news theories, but to better understand how they combine and inter-act. Equally important is to sift through the seemingly naïve stances of journalists, like Revkin, who often claim to be passively transmitting received social truths with little concern for the ways in which those truths are manufactured or spun. The next section explores how these elements of press passivity (in the midst of changing audience habits and multiplying information sources) may affect the future of news and ultimately the health of democracy. When the origins of many influential news accounts fall little short of propaganda, the result is to invite popular self-selection of convenient truths. The outcome is a disorienting democratization of truth in the contemporary media system.

A Passive Press and the Democratization of Truth

The modern press system has always been procedurally vulnerable to reporting incomplete versions of stories or failing to report challenges from outside of officialdom. At the dawn of the modern press system in the United States, Walter Lippmann (1922) warned that the public seldom received the unvarnished truth about political events. At the same time, Lippmann seemed to think that as long as high-minded motives accounted for the official stories, the uneasy interests of democracy, business, and global power could be balanced. Thus, the old indexing system relied on an important measure of faith on the part of journalists that officials operated in good faith with the public interest. At the same time, greater commitments to investigative reporting during the "high modern" era of the US press (1950s–1980s)—along with government and industry commitments to public responsibility norms—may have introduced greater probity into the calculations of both press and politicians (Hallin, 1992b). Nonetheless, serious breakdowns in information quality have occurred when news sources abuse good faith assumptions, sometimes with the too-easy compliance of a willing press (Entman, 2003; Bennett, Lawrence, and Livingston, 2007).

Given these conflicting forces at work, press performance was uneven during the high modern era, as government secrecy and corruption hid many questionable activities from the public. However, the willingness of concerned officials to leak information to reporters, combined with the willingness of editors and publishers to report those leaks, led to remarkable moments of accountability journalism, such as reporting on failures of Vietnam War policies in the late 1960s and the abuses of power in the Watergate scandal of the 1970s.

As both the old political order and the media system on which it depended began to crumble toward the end of the twentieth century, a number of factors seemed to encourage the advancement of win-at-any-cost communication practices. One inducement for partisan bending of claims about reality is the flood of money into politics, resulting in large numbers of politicians beholden to corporate interests and dependent on the flow of that money to win ever more expensive election contests. Even Barack Obama, who ran on a promise to clean up special interest politics, supported weak regulatory responses and no legal prosecutions among heads of the big financial firms who brought about the economic collapse of the new century (Bernard Madoff's infamous Ponzi scheme notwithstanding, as it was not related to the causes of the larger investment bank collapse). Despite rounds of record Wall Street bonuses following the collapse and the general failure to use government bailout money to meaningfully increase normal bank lending or significantly adjust shaky mortgages, the most serious action Obama took against the financial titans was to call them "fat cats." Although this might seem a mild rebuke given the magnitude of the offenses, it resulted in general anger and haughty dismay from members of the banking community. Their reaction to even such a mild rhetorical sanction created a situation in which the president was forced to curry favor among this powerful interest sector by inviting many of them to a private dinner at an exclusive New York restaurant, and he personally called key players who did not attend. Despite the peace overture, many were reportedly still offended at the indignity of being called "fat cats" and at the prospect of any regulatory restrictions on their highly lucrative, if dangerous, investment practices. As a result, some of Obama's key Wall Street supporters from 2008 did not support his 2012 campaign (Confessore, 2011). One can only imagine the reaction from the financial titans had the Obama Justice Department prosecuted anyone from the big banks who might appear to have committed fraud in the trading practices that triggered the collapse.

Large shares of the flood of political money go into ever more sophisticated communication operations. In the process, questions of reason and truth in public discourse seem to have become largely academic concerns. Compounding this palpable decline in information quality at its political source are the proliferating information channels that feed into the tendency for audience self-selection biases. When audiences increasingly seek reinforcement for prior beliefs, the result is an unfortunate feedback loop that signals to political information producers that there is diminished popular concern about grounding information in evidence or reason. As policy advocates recognize the utility of simply inventing facts and arguments to suit their preferred outcomes, misinformation becomes more prevalent. The misinformation cycle is completed as leaders (and implicitly the press) invite the people, in effect, to choose what they want to believe. This is a vicious cycle that diminishes the capacity for reasoned debate and independent (journalistic) assessment of competing truth claims. This journalistic lacuna reveals the conceit of the earlier statements by Revkin and Crowley about the seemingly natural occurrence of self-evident truths in the public sphere.

Herein lies the danger of a press system that operates as an institution that so closely filters information through the claims of government officials and powerful interests: when those operating inside the system begin to play loose with facts, and when the audiences increasingly can choose what they want to hear, the barbarians have effectively begun to operate inside the gates. The result is that truth becomes democratized and less subject to authoritative monitoring and gatekeeping (Bennett, 2005). For journalists like Revkin to claim that only legitimate claims somehow float into the news, and that they have equal standing as truth claims, is either an act of supreme naïveté or regrettable cynicism.

Looking beyond the press, the democratization of truth can be understood more broadly in the context of a larger set of changes occurring in institutions of late modern democracies. The postindustrial democracies have experienced important changes in social and political organization, media and communication systems, and political participation that all affect how political information is produced, consumed, and shared (Bennett, 1998). Changes such as the decline of group memberships and the growing individuation of social identity have impacted the institutional authority systems of societies as people drift away from institutional memberships and allegiances and even become hostile to many institutions. Under such conditions, institutional authorities hold less sway and at the same time may become more desperate to reach and persuade publics, leading to greater reliance on spin and strategic communication. When information systems invite people to pick convenient realities, the result may be a loss of public cohesion and the capacity to generate what philosophers have termed political will. With the decline of these public sphere qualities, so goes the capacity to have reasoned, transparent, and somewhat conclusive policy debates.

All of these broader social changes feed back into the decline of legitimacy and confidence in key democratic institutions such as press, Congress, and the president, which, not coincidentally, comprise the core triad of US national news. It is not unreasonable to suppose that the growing levels of public disdain may drive the press, even if inadvertently, into greater isolation and implicit cooperation with its political sources. Indeed, such symbiotic news production makes for easy parody, as revealed in the frequent episodes of *The Daily Show* that jump from one newscast to another, showing dozens of journalists saying the same thing about the same spin. One result of this strange mutuality of interest between news organizations and their sources is the increasing loss of audience confidence and attention. In the end, the news looks like an insider game, largely because it has, in fact, become one. In the process, journalists become surrogate publics for politicians, who look to the news for indicators of how well their spin is working (Herbst, 1998).

As this insider syndrome develops, journalists conduct a back and forth game of setting different sides against each other and getting official reactions. Since the updates and developments need to be interpreted, journalists also become sources for each other, fashioning narratives around the official frames. This process involves both indexing and narrativity.

For their part, publics are not entirely innocent victims in this communication system. As alternating inattention and self-selection of agreeable content become more dominant public information norms, the dwindling partisan audiences offer political leaders and journalists few rewards for efforts to sort out complex events amid cries of bias from politicians who are losing the spin contests. The much discussed cynical tone of the press may reflect an understanding that this process renders facts highly malleable, while audiences and politicians offer few rewards for sorting them out. Thus, an implicit acceptance of the plasticity of reality may settle in with journalists.

CONCLUSION

Amid the many changes involving audience fragmentation, the proliferation of information channels and new technologies, and the shifting economic foundations of the news business, some key aspects of conventional press-state relations formed during the high modern era of the last century remain largely the same. For example, in the United States, most mainstream news organizations continue to *index* news frames to perceived power balances among key political actors. Yet various changes surrounding this traditional core of press politics may complicate this process in many cases. For example, the proliferation of radio and cable pundits and online information flows may challenge the gatekeeping capacity of the legacy press by introducing something of a prisoner's dilemma game, in which mainstream news organizations that resist reporting thinly sourced information circulating in these channels may discover that competitors will run with it. This may relax indexing requirements so that relatively less official cueing is needed to carry a story. If this is the case, the news-making power of individual sources (e.g., Donald Trump or the members of Congress who contributed to "birther" stories about President Obama) may be increased if they are willing to promote audacious claims. Thus, it becomes difficult to avoid reporting the growing number of stories that are hyperbolic, sensational, distracting, or simply wrong. Indeed, avoiding such stories may mean that audiences will get them through other channels, making legacy news organizations irrelevant. The problem is that reporting such stories lends them credibility, while diminishing the hold of journalism on information quality. Herein lies the nexus between journalists as storytellers and as practitioners of a remarkably uniform system of indexing truth to power.

The often ludicrous news stories that can be attributed to more porous news flows across different media gradients (e.g., from Internet gossip sites to mass media) may explain why there is increasing experimentation with new public information forms that are emerging outside of conventional news formats entirely. For example, a large volume of credible information is being produced directly by technology-equipped citizens, partisan commentators, and bloggers, as evidenced in reporting on the uprisings in the Middle East in recent years. Other forms of hybrid news are being produced through WikiLeaks and its successors.

Changing information habits of citizens may lead them to prefer such content instead of news. Audiences may mix and confound conventional news with partisan commentary, political comedy, or information obtained from direct searches of databases and other online sources. At the same time, as noted earlier, increasing numbers of citizens are avoiding news altogether. Thus, while the shell of the high modern news system remains intact, it is under siege from a combination of forces. Aspects of these trends have been developing for some time, but the contrast between the old rules of engagement amid declining public confidence seems to have reached a chronic state with the journalism crisis in the early 2000s and the high degree of political polarization in Washington.

Despite these currents of change, the news remains important to the governance process, as evidenced by politicians and their consultants, who continue to spin it in order to promote their policies and themselves. Indeed, the legacy media still offer the main public stage for making claims, and those claims may still shape public opinion. In this system, power continues to be the compass that guides the course of information. The result is that, even if political claims may be absurd, they can end up driving the conversation when they are issued by powerful politicians or by aspirants with electoral credibility. As power is left unchallenged by the press, it corrupts the very system on which it ultimately depends for legitimacy. The ultimate irony of this system is that the legacy press clings to the very norm that inhibits fundamental changes in how it might gather, interpret, and package political information more convincingly.

Even modest experimentation with other norms might produce salutary effects, such as raising levels of public confidence, restoring young audiences, and perhaps encouraging politicians to exercise greater restraint in bending realities to serve their interests. Yet the most innovative information formats seem to be coming from outside of journalism, ranging from WikiLeaks, to Twitter streams from the scenes of events, to citizen videos circulating virally on YouTube. Even as the journalism crisis reaches dire proportions, the core institutions of journalism seem strangely unable to reinvent themselves, preferring to look back to a romantic era of accountability journalism that still serves as an underlying model for many reform efforts.

References

ABC News. 2011. One-on-one. Trump's tough talk: Going too far on birther issue? April 19) Retrieved on May 20, 2011, from http://abcnews.go.com/GMA/video/trump-obama-healthcare-abortion-1340665.

Barnhurst, K. G., and Nerone, J. 2001. *The form of news: A history*. New York: Guilford Press.

Bennett, W. L. 1990. Toward a theory of press-state relations in the U.S. *Journal of Communication* 40(2): 103–125.

Bennett, W. L. 1996. An introduction to journalism norms and representations of politics. *Political Communication* 13(4): 373–384.

Bennett, W. L. 1998. The uncivic culture: Communication, identity, and the rise of lifestyle politics. *P.S.: Political Science and Politics* 31(4): 41–61.

Bennett, W. L. 2005. News as reality TV: Election coverage and the democratization of truth. *Critical Studies in Media Communication* 22: 171–177.

Bennett, W. L. 2011. *News: The politics of illusion*. 9th ed. New York: Longman/Pearson.

Bennett, W. L., and Iyengar, S. 2008. A new era of minimal effects? The changing foundations of political communication. *Journal of Communication* 58(4): 707–731.

Bennett, W. L., and Lawrence, R. G. 1995. News icons and the mainstreaming of social change. *Journal of Communication* 45(3): 20–39.

Bennett, W. L., Lawrence, R. G., and Livingston, S. 2007. *When the press fails: Political power and the news media from Iraq to Katrina.* Chicago: University of Chicago Press.

Blumler, J. G., and Kavanagh, D. 1999. The third age of political communication: Influences and features. *Political Communication* 16: 209–230.

Boykoff, M. T., and Boykoff, J. M. 2004. Balance ad bias: Global warming and the US prestige press. *Global Environmental Change* 14: 125–136.

Center for Media and Public Affairs. 2000. The incredible shrinking sound bite. September 28. Retrieved on June 13, 2011, from http://www.google.com/cse?cx=012326687056111711 469%3Axkzmk-k_fla&ie=UTF-8&q=sound+bite+2000&sa.x=0&sa.y=0&siteurl=www. cmpa.com%2Fstudies.htm.

Confessore, N. 2011. Obama seeks to win back Wall Street cash. *New York Times*, June 13. Retrieved June 13, 2011, from http://www.nytimes.com/2011/06/13/us/politics/13donor. html?hp=&pagewanted=all.

Cook, T. E. 2005. *Governing with the news: The news media as a political institution.* 2nd ed. Chicago: University of Chicago Press.

Cook, T. E. 2006. The news media as a political institution: Looking backward and looking forward. *Political Communication* 23: 159–172.

Edelman, M. 1988. *Constructing the political spectacle.* Chicago: University of Chicago Press.

Entman, R. M. 2003. Cascading activation: Contesting the White House's frame after 9/11. *Political Communication* 20(4): 415–432.

FactCheck.org. 2008. Born in the USA: The truth about Obama's birth certificate. August 21. Retrieved May 20, 2011, from http://factcheck.org/2008/08/born-in-the-usa/.

Gans, Herbert. 1979. *Deciding what's news: A study of CBS Evening News, NBC Nightly News, Newsweek, and Time.* New York: Pantheon.

Hallin, D. C. 1992a. Sound bite news: Television coverage of elections, 1968–1988. *Journal of Communication* 42(2): 5–24.

Hallin, D. C. 1992b. The passing of the "high modernism" of American journalism. *Journal of Communication* 42(3): 14–25.

Hallin, D. C., and Mancini, P. 2004. *Comparing media systems: Three models of media and politics.* New York: Cambridge University Press.

Herbst, S. 1998. *Reading public opinion: How political actors view the democratic process.* Chicago: University of Chicago Press.

Jamieson, K. H., and Cappella, J. N. 2009. *Echo chamber: Rush Limbaugh and the conservative media establishment.* New York: Oxford University Press.

Lawrence, R. G. 2000a. *The politics of force: Media and the construction of police brutality.* Berkeley: University of California Press.

Lawrence, R. G. 2000b. Game-framing the issues: Tracking the strategy frame in public policy news. *Political Communication* 17(2): 93–114.

Lawrence, R. G. 2010. Researching political news framing: Established ground rules and new horizons. In P. D'Angelo and J. A. Kuypers (Eds.), *Doing News Framing Analysis: Empirical and Theoretical Perspectives* (pp. 265–285). New York: Routledge.

Lawrence, R. G., and Birkland, T. A. 2004. Guns, Hollywood, and school safety: Defining the school-shooting problem across public arenas. *Social Science Quarterly* 85(5): 1193–1207.

Lippmann, W. 1922. *Public opinion.* New York: Free Press.

McChesney, R. W., and Nichols, J. 2010. *The death and life of American journalism: The media revolution that will begin the world again.* Philadelphia: Nation Books.

Patterson, T. E. 2000. Doing well and doing good: How soft news and critical journalism are shrinking the news audience and weakening democracy—And what news outlets can do about it. Joan Shorenstein Center on the Press, Politics, and Public Policy, Kennedy School of Government, Harvard University.

Prior, M. 2007. *Post-broadcast democracy: How media choice increases inequality in political involvement and polarizes elections.* New York: Cambridge University Press.

Revkin, A. C. 2011. Do fights over climate communication reflect the end of "scientism"? *New York Times*, February 23. Retrieved June 6, 2011, from http://dotearth.blogs.nytimes.com/2011/02/23/do-fights-over-climate-communication-reflect-the-end-of-scientism/.

Rutenberg, J. 2011. Trump bows out, but spotlight barely dims. *New York Times*, May 16. Retrieved May 20, 2011, http://www.nytimes.com/2011/05/17/us/17trump.html?_r=3&hp=&pagewanted=all.

Ryfe, D. M. 2006. The nature of news rules. *Political Communication* 23: 203–214.

Sparrow, B. H. 2006. A research agenda for an institution media. *Political Communication* 23: 145–157.

Walgrave, S., van Aelst, P., and Bennett, W. L. 2011. Beyond agenda-setting. Towards a broader theory of agenda interactions between individual political actors and the mass media. Unpublished manuscript.

Washington Post. 2010. 44: Lawmakers and the "birther"/Muslim myths (blog). August 30. Retrieved June 6, 2011, from http://voices.washingtonpost.com/44/2010/08/lawmakers-who-push-the-birther.html.

Williams, B. A., and Delli Carpini, M. X. 2012. *After broadcast news: Media regimes, democracy, and the new information environment.* New York: Cambridge University Press.

CHAPTER 19

NEWS MEDIA AS POLITICAL INSTITUTIONS

ROBERT W. MCCHESNEY AND VICTOR PICKARD

INTRODUCTION

THE study of news media as political institutions refers to the policies, laws, and subsidies that create and shape the organizational structures and practices that form the basis of the news media.[1] Such research treats news media institutions as political actors, makes certain assumptions about journalism's importance within a democratic society, and emphasizes the role of various structures in shaping journalism. Specifically, it focuses on the nature of public policies and subsidies that determine news media institutions, as well as the policymaking process—that is, the politics behind the policies—that bring about these arrangements. Understood this way, such research is a subfield of political communication. Unfortunately it has had, overall, a marginal presence in American mass communication research over the past few generations, generally relegated to areas such as "media law" or "broadcasting policy."

THE GREAT DISCONNECT

There has been an ironic and long-standing tension concerning the study of news media as political institutions. Historically, government policies and subsidies have been understood as being of central importance when examining news media systems in other countries, especially communist or developing ones. What governments did or did not do in these states was of paramount importance. In the United States, however, the conventional wisdom often assumed that the marketplace could be trusted to provide the news media system necessary for self-government. As long as the state did not

intervene in media markets, went the argument, the private sector would provide a sufficient quantity and quality of journalism.

If one granted these assumptions, there was important work for communication
scholars to do to understand and improve the quality of the news and to assess how
different interest groups affected the news, and how audiences received the news and
with what effect. But the nature of the news media system itself was treated like a foreor-
dained permanence, and a benevolent one at that. Even the "critical" work of past generations that has emphasized the importance of corporate ownership and commercialism
to journalism's development—generally as an antidemocratic force—has tended to take
commercial news media as a given, and effectively an unalterable one. Because the commercial system was assumed to be natural and inevitable, there was not much interest in
studying it as if its structure were an open question. The research questions in media law
and broadcasting policy therefore tended to deal with smaller issues, not the big picture,
assuring a relatively marginal status for more structural questions.

With the crisis of journalism unfolding in the United States in recent years, the study
of news media as political institutions is attracting more attention. A long-standing
assumption has been that the news media form the Fourth Estate, that absolutely necessary branch of the political system that makes self-government and the rule of law
possible. The founders of the American republic understood this imperative, and it is
a cornerstone of virtually all democratic theory. Our laws and the US Supreme Court
have routinely acknowledged the special and crucial role of news media in the political
system. News media are core political institutions in any type of governing system and
carry an enormous burden in self-governing societies.

Justice Potter Stewart put it best four decades ago: "The Free Press guarantee is, in
effect, a *structural* part of the Constitution" (1974–1975; emphasis in original). "The primary purpose of the constitutional guarantee of a free press was," he added, "to create a
fourth institution outside the Government as an additional check on the three official
branches." Stewart concluded: "Perhaps our liberties might survive without an independent established press. But the Founders doubted it, and, in the year 1974, I think
we can all be thankful for their doubts" (9–11). In this sense the study of news media as
political institutions is arguably as important as any area in communication; it should be
at the center of the field. And the possible dissolution of our primary news media should
concern all communication scholars.

The major reason for the gradual collapse of journalism has been the economic crisis
of news media institutions, which have been in sharp decline for the past decade. The
commercial interests that dominate news media industries increasingly are finding traditional journalism a less profitable undertaking. The Internet does not appear to be filling the void. *Why* this situation has occurred is where much research is directed, as we
discuss below. First, however, it is important to provide more detail on the crisis of news
media as political institutions.

A study that encapsulated the crisis was a report by the Pew Center for the People and
the Press that examined in exhaustive detail the "media ecology" of the city of Baltimore
for one week in 2009 (Pew Research Center, Project for Excellence in Journalism,

2010).[2] The objective was to determine how, in this changing media moment, "original" news stories were being generated, and by whom. The study tracked old media and new, including newspapers, radio, television, websites, blogs, and even Twitter "tweets" from the police department. The researchers' first conclusion was an unsettling one: despite the seeming proliferation of media, "much of the 'news' people receive contains no original reporting. Fully eight out of ten stories studied simply repeated or repackaged previously published information." In looking at where the "original" reporting came from, the study found that more than 95 percent of original news stories were still generated by old media, particularly the *Baltimore Sun* newspaper. In other words, a great many of the much-heralded online sites—even some that proudly labeled themselves as "news" operations—simply disseminated what was being produced by traditional old media. But here is an even more startling fact: the *Sun's* production of original news stories was itself down more than 30 percent from ten years before and down 73 percent from twenty years before.

Baltimore is not a unique case. The 30 percent decline is precisely the same figure that the Pew Project for Excellence in Journalism settled on in its assessment of the loss of reporting and editing capacity at American newspapers since 2000.[3] For an example of what this means tangibly, consider the following pattern. The revelation of the spectacular corruption over the past decade that brought down Jack Abramoff, Tom DeLay, and Randall "Duke" Cunningham, among others, was instigated to a significant extent by reporters who subsequently were "downsized" and/or whose positions no longer exist. The United States is losing its most experienced and engaged investigative reporters (see, e.g., Walton, 2010). This pattern is great news for the next generation of Abramoffs, DeLays, and Cunninghams, as transgressions by corrupt public officials will be increasingly less likely to be reported, and when the reporting stops so too in all likelihood will the prosecutions. The implications for our governing system are self-evident and grounds for deep concern.

Unfortunately, the precipitous drop in original reporting was not the most alarming part of Pew's Baltimore study. Of the "original" stories identified by Pew, whether generated by old media or new, only 14 percent were developed by journalists defining an issue and pursuing it. A staggering 86 percent of the stories originated with official sources and press releases, suggesting that dominant news narratives are being pushed increasingly by those with power.

These trends continue to worsen as public relations (PR) replaces journalism. Official sources and PR have long played a major role in shaping the news, and the best reporters always struggled so that such prepackaged stories would not be taken at face value. But the previous ratio of stories generated by PR and official sources versus stories created by journalists used to be less stark. As the Pew study concludes: "The official version of events is becoming more important. We found official press releases often appear word for word in first accounts of events, though often not noted as such."

As journalism declines, there will still be plenty of "news," but it will be increasingly unfiltered PR. The hallmark of great PR is that it is not recognized by the public as manipulation of the facts; it is surreptitious. In 1960 there was less than one PR agent for every working journalist, a ratio of 0.75/1. By 1990 the ratio was just over 2/1. In 2011 the ratio was *four* PR people for every working journalist. At the current rate of change, the ratio may well be 6/1 within a few years (McChesney and Nichols, 2010, app. 3). There are far fewer reporters to interrogate the spin and the press releases, so the likelihood that this public relations material gets presented as legitimate "news" has become much greater.

In summary, the Fourth Estate is in an existential crisis because an increasing number of the commercial institutions that produce journalism are no longer solvent. It is necessary to understand the crisis and to see what can be done to create and sustain credible news media institutions. This project, therefore, is a defining issue for communication scholars, because much of what interests the field is rendered irrelevant if the foundation for credible self-government and freedom collapses.

MAJOR FINDINGS OF EXISTING RESEARCH

Two sets of historical and economic research projects provide necessary context for the study of news media as political institutions. First is the significant body of work that has examined the role of the postal service and federal printing subsidies in founding and supporting the free press system of the first several generations in American history. McChesney and Nichols draw from this tradition in *The Death and Life of American Journalism*, as do scholars such as John (1995), Kielbowicz (1989), Cook (1998 and 2005), Martin (2001), Baldasty (1992), and Smith (1977), among others. For example, if the US government subsidized journalism today at the same level of GDP that it did in the 1840s, the government would have to spend in the neighborhood of $30–35 billion annually (McChesney and Nichols, 2010). Federal press subsidies—for example, postal subsidies and paid government notices—have diminished in real terms to only a small fraction of their nineteenth-century levels, though they still exist.

More broadly, in 2004 McChesney and Starr each published major works explaining the crucial role of government policies and subsidies in creating the American news media throughout history. Starr relied on secondary sources but nonetheless did a masterful job of marshaling the evidence and chronicling how the US government has "created" the media with a series of policies and subsidies since the beginning of the republic. In these historical accounts, there was no natural "free market" default option. Lloyd makes a compatible argument about the centrality of government policies to the formation of the communication system in *Prologue to a Farce: Democracy and Communication in America* (2007). It is safe to say that the "immaculate conception" notion of the American news media system—that it was birthed by Adam Smith's free market—once accepted without comment, is no longer regarded as credible by most scholars in the area, whatever their political leanings. At the same time, this history is largely unknown outside of a small circle of scholars and has only recently begun to be appreciated by the broader realm of communication researchers and policymakers.

Second, an emerging body of work has concentrated on the history and nature of public policy debates over how best to structure media systems. Some of that material is covered in the work mentioned above, but there is another body of detailed archival research of core communication policy debates, primarily over the past century. McChesney's *Telecommunications, Mass Media and Democracy: The Battle for the Control of U.S. Broadcasting, 1928–1935* (1993) was among the first major works in this area. Others of note include Lawson's study of the 1912 Newspaper Act (1993), Stole's monograph on the debates over advertising regulation (2006), Scott's research on journalism in the 1930s (2009), Schiller's research on telecommunication policy fights (2007), Fones-Wolf's book on postwar labor struggles around broadcast reform (2006), and Pickard's work on core media policy debates and reform efforts in the 1940s (2010a, 2010b, 2011a, 2014).

Two general conclusions can be reached. First, significant debates surrounded the genesis of many of our major communication media, and a credible case can be made that our media could have been developed in a significantly different manner. The second conclusion is that powerful commercial interests have dominated policy debates, with the support of the commercial news media, and the general public has usually been excluded as an effective participant. However, the research also demonstrates that at key moments a significant number of Americans did organize to get involved in core communication policy debates—even as political and economic elites tried to ignore or suppress them—and sometimes were able to influence the outcomes. This history is only beginning to get widespread recognition.

Although there has been impressive progress in the areas described above, a great deal of research remains to be done, particularly around historical critical junctures when media could have been developed along different trajectories. This history is important for correcting the record and for legitimating alternative models. It is also of particular importance to citizens who wish to engage in the policymaking process but are not affiliated with commercial interests.

The remaining core research questions address four related areas. First, what factors specifically explain the decline of commercial journalism? Existing research emphasizes a number of factors, including commercial pressures that degraded the quality of journalism, concentrated media ownership, and in particular, the role of the Internet in undermining the commercial news business model. There is considerable debate and no consensus on these issues. To the extent one can generalize, those more inclined to be critical tend to put somewhat greater emphasis on issues of commercial ownership and control as undermining journalism, whereas those who think commercial journalism was of acceptable quality tend to emphasize the Internet as an exogenous factor that came in to disrupt an otherwise relatively ideal system.

Second, how effective will the Internet be in solving the journalism problem? For most American scholars and journalists, this is the preferred solution, as it would allow for an independent commercial news media (King, 2010). At present there is considerable activity and research along these lines, but there is no evidence that the Internet will call forth a news media sector with anything remotely close to the per capita resources of the dying media system. Accordingly, research should assess what government policies might support the possibility of commercial journalism in the digital realm. There is also the concurrent question of whether Internet-based journalism may become even more dependent on pleasing advertisers, as its need to attract commercial support is dire, the competition intense, and the amount of available funds well short of what is needed.

One of the most optimistic claims about the Internet was that through the blogosphere it empowered everyday people—sometimes referred to as "citizen journalists"—to go online, launch new websites, and have the same caliber of Internet access to the world's attention as the mightiest media conglomerate. Some argue that these trends will combine with online commercial media to solve the journalism problem in the digital world. If nothing else, it will allow for a much more competitive and diverse news media marketplace. However, the evidence to support that claim is at present thin.

Although there are an all but infinite number of websites, human beings are only capable of meaningfully visiting a small number of them on a regular basis. The Google search mechanism strongly encourages implicit censorship, in that sites that do not end up on the first or second page of a search effectively do not exist for most Internet users. As Michael Wolff (2010) put it in *Wired*: "[T]he top 10 Websites accounted for 31 percent of US pageviews in 2001, 40 percent in 2006, and about 75 percent in 2010." "Big sucks the traffic out of small," Wolff quotes Russian Internet investor Yuri Milner. "In theory you can have a few very successful individuals controlling hundreds of millions of people. You can become big fast." And once you get big, you stay big.[4]

Hindman's incisive book *The Myth of Digital Democracy* (2009) provides research on journalism, news media, and political websites that is striking in this regard. What has emerged is a "power law" distribution in which a small number of political or news media websites get the vast majority of traffic (51–54). These are dominated by the traditional giants with name recognition and resources. There is a "long tail" of numerous websites that get little or no traffic, and few people have any idea that they exist. There is also no "middle class" of robust, moderately sized websites; that aspect of the news media system has been wiped out online. All of this leads Hindman to conclude that the online news media are *more* concentrated than the old media world. This is true, too, of the vaunted blogosphere, which has effectively ossified. Its traffic is highly concentrated in a handful of sites, operated by people with elite pedigrees (Foster and McChesney, 2011, 19–20).[5]

Third, how can government policies promote independent and competitive news media? Our previous work, as well as work by the late C. Edwin Baker, Mark Cooper, and Bruce Ackerman, among others, has generated a number of proposals for public policy approaches to the journalism crisis, ranging from a variety of public subsidies to adjusting existing tax laws to allow for more non- and low-profit journalistic models.[6] As the journalism crisis deepens and the Internet does not appear to be solving the problem, more scholarly attention is turning to this line of inquiry. Much of this research no doubt will involve comprehensive examinations of what is currently being done online and what can be learned from recent experiments.

Fourth, the experience of other advanced democratic nations, in Europe and north-east Asia in particular, now becomes highly relevant to American scholars. They are all huge press subsidizers compared to the United States. If America subsidized public media at the same per capita rate as nations with similar political economies, such as Canada, Australia, and New Zealand, US public broadcasters would have a government subsidy in the $7–10 billion range. If America supported public media at the same per capita rate as nations such as France ($51.56), Japan ($54.03), or the United Kingdom ($90.70), US public broadcasters would have a government subsidy in the $15–27 billion range. If America subsidized public media at the same per capita rate as Denmark ($130.52), Germany ($131.27), or Norway ($133.57), US public broadcasters would have a government subsidy in the neighborhood of $39–40 billion (Benson and Powers, 2011, 61).

This assessment does not even factor in the extensive newspaper subsidies that several democracies employ. If the US federal government subsidized newspapers at the same per capita rate as Norway, it would make a direct outlay of approximately $3 billion annually. Sweden spends slightly less per capita and has extended the subsidies to digital newspapers. France is the champion at newspaper subsidies. If a federal government subsidy provided the portion of the overall revenues of the US newspaper industry that France does for its publishers, it would have conservatively spent $6 billion in 2008 (Benson and Powers, 2011, 49–53, 34).[7]

Instead, as noted, the total US subsidy for public broadcasting sits at a paltry $1.1 billion. American scholars have paid too little attention to the experiences of other democratic nations with press subsidies. This oversight must end, as these kinds of comparative analyses could provide some of the most important lessons for what options are available to address the journalism crisis.

ADDRESSING MARKET FAILURE

In our view the evidence points in one direction: if we in the United States are serious about reversing course and dramatically expanding and improving journalism, the only way this can happen is with massive public subsidies. The market is not supporting the journalism required by a democratic society, and there is little reason to assume that it will anytime in the near future. Therefore, a significant expansion of the nonprofit news media sector is necessary. First and foremost, it is imperative to discontinue the practice of regarding journalism as a "business" and evaluating it by business criteria (Levy and Kleis, 2010).[8] Instead, it is necessary to embrace the public-good nature of journalism. That is our approach here (Pickard et al., 2009; McChesney and Nichols, 2010; Pickard, 2014).

To clarify what we mean by the "public-good" nature of journalism, journalism is something society requires but that the market cannot produce in sufficient quality or quantity. Readers or final news consumers have never provided sufficient funds to subsidize the popular journalism system self-government requires. For the first century of American history the public-good nature of journalism was understood implicitly and was addressed by massive postal and printing subsidies. For the past century the public-good nature of journalism has been masked by the infusion of advertising to provide the vast majority of revenues supporting the news. But advertising has no specific attachment to journalism and is disinvesting in traditional news media as better alternatives present themselves in the digital media world, especially as news media appear less commercially attractive. In turn, financially strapped news organizations are disinvesting in news production and focusing more on less costly and more sensationalistic media, such as commentary-driven fare.

Understanding "journalism as a public good" also helps explain one of the more persistent questions posed within the context of the journalism crisis. The question generally begins, "If people wanted good journalism, isn't it logical to expect the commercial news media to give it to them?" On the surface this seems like such a solid premise that it is generally posed as a rhetorical question. However, public-good theory convincingly explains that no matter how strong the consumer demand, it will never be sufficient to provide the resources for a popular democratic journalism. Even when Americans have been most engaged with news and politics, there was not sufficient demand to subsidize a popular news media.

But public-good theory is important in another way: it also highlights the market's inability to accurately gauge popular support for the news. The market cannot express all of our values; we cannot individually "purchase" everything we value. A preponderance of Americans, including younger Americans notorious for their lack of interest in newspapers and conventional news media, stand to gain from having credible reporting on corporate and government affairs, even if they do not necessarily plan to read or view the news reports thereby produced. In many cases, less attentive citizens still want to know that the work is being done and that people in power are being held accountable and issues are being covered, and they are willing to use their tax dollars to pay for journalism even if they themselves prefer to watch a reality TV show or listen to their iPods. To cite one recent example of general attitudes toward subsidizing public media, a CNN poll (2011) found that a majority of those interviewed dramatically overestimated how much of the US budget goes toward funding public broadcasting—nearly a whopping $178 billion instead of the actual $430 million per year—and yet a majority of those polled believed that such overinflated expenditures should be maintained or even increased.[9]

Nonetheless, the notion of government support for the press strikes many as downright un-American, a dangerous measure that would more likely beckon a dystopian future than enhance journalism, freedom, and self-government. This is a common refrain; it has become so deeply ingrained in American political consciousness—across the political spectrum—that it requires no evidence to be asserted categorically and end all further debate. Yet when it is actually examined, the evidence points in a different direction. According to Britain's *The Economist* (2010), which every year produces a highly acclaimed "Democracy Index," the top four most democratic nations on the list—Norway, Iceland, Denmark, and Sweden—are among the top six or seven per capita press subsidizers in the world. The United States ranks seventeenth, and all six-teen nations in front of the United States have larger, generally much larger, subsidies for journalism.[10]

Then there is the research conducted by Freedom House, an American organization created in the 1940s to sponsor freedom and oppose totalitarianism of the left and right, with special emphasis on the left. Every year it, too, ranks all the nations of the world on the basis of how free and effective their press systems are. Its detailed and sophis-ticated research is particularly concerned with any government meddling whatsoever with private news media. Typically the list is dominated by the democratic nations with the largest per capita journalism subsidies in the world. For example, four of the first five nations listed by Freedom House in 2010 are the same nations that topped *The Economist*'s "Democracy Index," and all rank among the top seven per capita press sub-sidizers in the world.[11] That should be no surprise, as one would expect the nations with the freest and best press systems to rank as the most democratic nations. What has been missing from the narrative is that *the nations with the freest press systems are also the nations that make the greatest public investment in journalism* and therefore provide the basis for being strong democracies. Furthermore, recent research on the European press concludes that as journalism subsidies increased, the overall reporting in those nations did not kowtow to but in fact grew *more* adversarial toward the government in power (Benson, 2011).

Our point is not that the United States should adopt foreign models willy-nilly. It is simply that journalism subsidies are compatible with a democratic society, a flourish-ing, uncensored, private news media, and an adversarial journalism. The record is clear that the problem of creating a viable free press system in a democratic and free society is solvable. There may not be perfect solutions, but there are good and workable solutions.

UNANSWERED QUESTIONS AND FUTURE DIRECTIONS

There is a crucial role for communication scholars in addressing these problems, as research questions abound. At the very least, more data are needed to address the sus-tainability of news media institutions during the current structural transformations. More historical and international work is also needed to underscore the contingency and vulnerabilities of our current system, as well as to recover alternatives from the past and to highlight best practices from abroad (Pickard, 2011b). At present, misconceptions about the operations of other democracies and about historical models in the United States stand in the way of intellectual clarity regarding the public policy approach that the journalism crisis requires. The good news is that the expertise that political commu-nication scholars of news institutions can bring to bear on these problems is needed now more than ever.

Notes

1. This approach overlaps with, but is distinct from, the rich area of institutionalist research, sometimes referred to as "political institutionalism" or "new institutionalism." For a discussion of the latter, see, for example, Benson (2006).
2. All quotations and statistics are from Pew Research Center, Project for Excellence in Journalism (2010).
3. Pew Research Center, Project for Excellence in Journalism (2010).
4. Wolff (2010).
5. This discussion of Hindman relies on Foster and McChesney (2011).
6. Many of these proposals are found in McChesney and Pickard (2011). See also Pickard, Stearns, and Aaron (2009).
7. Benson and Powers (2011, 49–53, 34). The French government provides roughly 13 percent of the revenues of the French newspaper industry. The total revenue of the US newspaper industry in 2008 was approximately $48 billion. See the data of the Newspaper Association of America at http://www.naa.org/TrendsandNumbers.aspx. Our estimate does not include the emergency three-year $950 million subsidy the French government made to address the crisis facing French newspapers. On a per capita basis that would be like the US government making a three-year, $5 billion additional subsidy.
8. See, e.g., Levy and Nielsen (2010).
9. Retrieved on June 26, 2014, from http://i2.cdn.turner.com/cnn/2011/images/03/31/rel4m.pdf. The poll is based on interviews with 1,023 adult Americans conducted by telephone by Opinion Research Corporation on March 11–13, 2011. The margin of sampling error for results based on the total sample is plus or minus three percentage points.
10. *Economist* (2010).
11. Freedom House (2010).

References

Baldasty, G. 1992. *The commercialization of news in the nineteenth century.* Madison: University of Wisconsin Press.

Benson, R. 2011. Public funding and journalistic independence: What does the research tell us? In Robert W. McChesney and Victor Pickard (Eds.), *Will the Last Reporter Please Turn Out the Lights* (pp. 314–319). New York: New Press.

Benson, R. 2006. News media as a "journalist field": What Bourdieu adds to new institutionalism, and vice versa. *Political Communication* 23: 197–202.

Benson, R., and Powers, M. 2011. *Public media around the world: International models for funding and protecting independent journalism.* Washington, DC: Free Press.

Cable News Network. 2011. CNN opinion research poll, April 1. Retrieved from http://i2.cdn.turner.com/cnn/2011/images/03/31/rel4m.pdf.

Cook, T. E. 1998. *Governing with the news: The news media as a political institution.* Chicago: University of Chicago Press.

Cook, T. E. 2005. Public policy toward the press: What government does for the news media. In G. Overholser and K. H. Jamieson (Eds.), *The Press* (pp. 248–262). Oxford and New York: Oxford University Press.

Economist. 2010. Democracy index 2010: Democracy in retreat. Retrieved from http://graph-ics.eiu.com/PDF/Democracy_Index_2010_web.pdf.

Fones-Wolf, E. 2006. *Waves of opposition: Labor and the struggle for democratic radio.* Urbana: University of Illinois Press.

Foster, J. B., and McChesney, R. W. 2011. The Internet's unholy marriage to capitalism. *Monthly Review* (March): 19–20.

Freedom House. 2010. Freedom of the press 2010. Retrieved from http://www.freedomhouse.org/uploads/pfs/371.pdf.

Hindman, M. 2009. *The myth of digital democracy.* Princeton, NJ: Princeton University Press.

John, R. 1995. *Spreading the news: The American postal system from Franklin to Morse.* Cambridge, MA: Harvard University Press.

Kielbowicz, R. B. 1989. *News in the mail: The press, post office, and public information, 1700–1860s.* Westport, CT: Greenwood Press.

King, E. 2010. *Free for all: The Internet's transformation of journalism.* Evanston, IL: Northwestern University Press.

Lawson, L. 1993. *Truth in publishing: Federal regulation of the press's business practices, 1880–1920.* Carbondale: Southern Illinois University Press.

Levy, D. A. L., and Nielsen, R. K. (Eds.). 2010. *The changing business of journalism and its implications for democracy.* Oxford, UK: Reuters Institute for the Study of Journalism.

Lloyd, M. 2007. *Prologue to a farce: Democracy and communication in America.* Urbana: University of Illinois Press.

Martin, R. W. T. 2001. *The free and open press: The founding of American press liberty, 1640–1800.* New York: New York University Press.

McChesney, R. W. 1993. *Telecommunications, mass media, and democracy: The battle for the control of U.S. broadcasting, 1928–1935.* New York: Oxford University Press.

McChesney, R. W. 2004. *The problem of the media: U.S. communication politics in the 21st century.* New York: Monthly Review Press.

McChesney, R. W., and Nichols, J. 2010. *The death and life of American journalism: The media revolution that will begin the world again.* New York: Nation Books.

McChesney, R. W., and Pickard, V. (Eds.). 2011. *Will the last reporter please turn out the lights: The collapse of journalism and what can be done to fix it.* New York: The New Press.

Pew Research Center, Project for Excellence in Journalism. 2010, January 11. The study of the news ecosystem of one American city. Retrieved from http://www.journalism.org/analysis_report/how_news_happens.

Pickard, V. 2010a. Reopening the postwar settlement for U.S. media: The origins and implications of the social contract between media, the state, and the polity. *Communication, Culture & Critique* 3(2): 170–189.

Pickard, V. 2010b. "Whether the giants should be slain or persuaded to be good": Revisiting the Hutchins Commission and the role of media in a democratic society. *Critical Studies in Media Communication* 27(4): 391–411.

Pickard, V. 2011a. The battle over the FCC Blue Book: Determining the role of broadcast media in a democratic society, 1945–1949. *Media, Culture & Society* 33(2): 171–191.

Pickard, V. 2011b. Can government support the press? Historicizing and internationalizing a policy approach to the journalism crisis. *The Communication Review* 14 (2): 73—95.

Pickard, V. (2014). *America's battle for media democracy: The triumph of corporate libertarianism and the future of media reform.* New York: Cambridge University Press.

Pickard, V., Stearns, J., and Aaron, C. 2009. *Saving the news: Toward a national journalism strategy*. Washington, DC: Free Press.

Schiller, D. 2007. The hidden history of U.S. public service telecommunications, 1919–1956. *INFO* 9(2/3): 17–28.

Scott, B. 2009. Labor's New Deal for journalism: The newspaper guild in the 1930s. PhD diss., University of Illinois.

Smith, C. H. 1977. *The press, politics, and patronage*. Athens: University of Georgia Press.

Starr, P. 2004. *The creation of the media: Political origins of modern communications*. New York: Basic Books.

Stewart, P. 1974–1975. Or of the press. *Yale Law Report* 21(2): 9–11.

Stole, I. L. 2006. *Advertising on trial: Consumer activism and corporate public relations in the 1930s*. Urbana: University of Illinois Press.

Walton, M. 2010. Investigative shortfall. *American Journalism Review* (September). Retrieved from http://www.ajr.org/article.asp?id=4904.

Wolff, M. 2010. The web is dead; long live the Internet: Who's to blame: them. *Wired* 18(September): 122–127, 166.

CHAPTER 20

MEASURING SPILLOVERS IN MARKETS FOR LOCAL PUBLIC AFFAIRS COVERAGE

JAMES T. HAMILTON

INFORMATION about public affairs has value in part because it may change the decisions that readers and viewers make as voters. Doing a cost-benefit analysis that would tell us whether the optimal (i.e., efficient) amount of information is provided by the news media about public affairs is difficult. In part this is because it is hard to trace out the chain of causation that links voters to changes in policy; in part it is because we need models of political communication and representation to understand the different ways people might economize on information in the political decision-making process and not need to be fully informed to cast the correct ballots (from their perspective); and in part because it is difficult to monetize the benefits and costs of policies.

Yet theories of economics and politics do suggest places we might look for gaps in coverage of local and state public affairs and suggest evidence we might look for (Downs, 1957; Hamilton, 2004). Coverage of public affairs is not highly demanded by voters, even though it can have a large impact on the operation of government. At least four problems generate a low expressed demand for news about government: information in general is a public good; news about government feeds into the creation of other public goods, such as holding officials accountable; the low probability of an individual's political action having an impact means that information costs will often outweigh its benefits; and the positive spillovers that we generate for others by casting an informed vote don't often factor into our decisions to become informed. In the language of economics, problems of public goods and positive externalities mean that many people won't seek out news about the city council. This means local media outlets cannot monetize many of the effects their coverage has on government, which leads them to underinvest in public affairs stories.

What types of issue coverage involve positive spillovers and are thus likely to be underprovided? Education, environment, health, and accountability are frequently mentioned in popular (and some academic) accounts of what is missing. Another way to think about the coverage "gap" is that for a given audience demand, stories about public affairs will be less likely to be written if they are more costly. Types of stories that involve high costs include investigative pieces that require lots of time, lots of document and records work, and potential false starts; stories in which government officials actively resist the disclosure of records and information, thereby raising the cost of writing; and stories that involve knowledge best gained through beat reporting, since understanding some policy areas involves spending time observing a set of institutions and issues. These cost considerations suggest that less than ideal amounts of local coverage will be produced when the stories are costly because of the nature of the investigation, resistance from government (e.g., accountability or corruption stories), or the need to spend sustained time on the story to understand what is going on.

Gaps can also arise because of the mismatch between media markets and the geographic boundaries of political jurisdictions. Consider a metro paper that covers a region with many small towns and a central city. The fixed costs of covering a city council may mean that it does not pay for the paper to cover all city councils in the region. The audience's interest in city councils may only extend to the area they happen to live in, which means that the metro paper may not find much reader curiosity about city councils' actions except for those affecting a large number of people in the region. Overall, we would expect less than "ideal" amounts of local public affairs coverage when stories involve positive spillovers, high fixed costs, or a mismatch between market and political boundaries.

This chapter reviews how far academic evidence on media effects in local markets can take us in determining the spillovers that arise from local public affairs coverage. When an individual reads a news story, she may gain utility simply from following the narrative or learning new facts. If a news story influences a reader's decisions about turning out to vote, supporting an incumbent, or selecting a particular party's candidates, these decisions may have spillovers on other people in the community. If politicians anticipate these spillover effects when making their own choices, or if they learn new facts that cause them to change their public actions, then this is another way that the media can affect local politics. In this chapter "local" politicians are defined as municipal, congressional, or state officials, and I explore the evidence on how media coverage generates spillovers that influence the election and actions of local politicians.

EVIDENCE OF MEDIA SPILLOVERS
IN LOCAL MEDIA MARKETS

One of the hardest things to demonstrate statistically in media research is the impact of news coverage on the operation of government. The problem for a researcher is that the quality and quantity of news coverage is endogenous. This means if we see a relationship between high levels of local accountability coverage and good outcomes in society, we cannot simply make a causal claim. It could be the case that if people in a community are highly educated and very interested in politics, they will both monitor what their officials are doing/be politically active AND subscribe to the newspaper in large numbers. It would pay for an editor to push coverage of civic affairs because of reader interest in this community. But it could be the underlying civic activity and interests of the voters, rather than the coverage targeted toward them, that was driving the low levels of corruption in the city.

The challenge for researchers is to isolate a separate impact from news coverage, an impact that is unlikely to be confounded by the endogeneity of news. Researchers have tried to go beyond correlation and examine causation in local media effects using five different types of analyses. Studies have explored how media content changes political opinions and actions by examining (1) the imperfect overlap between media markets and political boundaries, (2) the introduction of new communication technologies (e.g, radio, broadcast TV, cable) and new outlets (e.g., Fox News, Spanish local news broadcast, local delivery of the *New York Times*), (3) the interruption or closure of local newspapers, (4) the delivery of new bundles of facts or stories in a community, and (5) lab experiments using news content. Each of these approaches has established that local media content does generate spillovers by affecting political decisions by voters and policymakers.

Overlap between Media and Political Markets

Snyder and Stromberg (2010) offer the most complete analysis to date of how media content affects local political accountability. They start with the observation that different factors drive the economic boundaries of media markets and the politically derived boundaries of congressional districts. They treat the match or congruence between a newspaper market and congressional district as exogenous and define congruence based on the fraction of a newspaper's readership residing in a particular district. They find that the greater the congruence between the newspaper's market and the district, the more likely the paper is to write about the representative. This variation in news coverage, which arises not out of variation in interest in politics or taste for news but simply because of the variation in borders, allows them to explore how news coverage affects actions by voters and politicians.

Snyder and Stromberg find that a greater congruence between a newspaper's market and the congressional district results in many more articles about the local member of Congress. This translates into voters in more congruent areas being more able to identify their representative and place the member on an ideological scale. The representatives respond to this scrutiny. In more congruent areas, the representatives are more likely to work for constituents by testifying at committees and are less likely to vote a party line. The media scrutiny also translates into policy actions, with the result that federal spending per capita is higher in areas with greater congruence between media markets and electoral boundaries. Summarizing these results, Snyder and Stromberg note (2010, 402):

> Quantitatively, the effects of news coverage on voter information, politicians' actions, and policy are large. We estimate that increasing Congruence by one standard deviation induces around 50 additional newspaper articles about the House representatives per congress, it increases voters' ability to correctly name the candidates in the House race by 10% and their willingness to describe and rate the representative by 6-8%, it increases the representatives' witness appearances by 10%, and it reduces the gap between Republican and Democratic ideological differences in voting by 5%. Finally, it increases federal spending per capita by 3%. Effects on voter participation and the incumbency advantage are significant but not large.

Introduction of Media Technologies, Publications, and Programs

The introductions of radio and then television technologies offer opportunities to study the link between media information and political outcomes. Strömberg (2004) found that governors were more likely to allocate New Deal relief expenditures to counties with more radios and higher voter turnout, that the spread of radio increased voter turnout, and that the impact of radio on government spending was particularly strong in competitive elections and in rural areas (which were less likely to have newspapers already providing political information). To explore potential omitted variable bias, in some specifications he uses ground conductivity (a measure of the ability of AM radio waves to travel through the ground) and the degree that a county is covered by woodland, two factors that affect the quality of AM radio reception, as instrumental variables to estimate radio penetration. Overall, he concludes (2004, 215):

> Governors allocated more relief funds to areas where a larger share of the population had radios. The effects are not only statistically significant, but also economically important. The estimates of this study imply that for every percentage increase in the share of households with radios in a certain county, the Governor would increase per capita relief spending by 0.6%. A one-standard-deviation increase in the share of households with radios would increase spending by 9%, and a change from the lowest to the mean share of households with radios in the sample increases spending by 60%.

Counties in the United States vary in when television was introduced, variations in timing that arose in part because of World War II and in part because of a licensing freeze by the Federal Communications Commission from 1948 to 1953. Gentzkow (2006, 931) uses this variation to explore the impact of television on voter turnout, finding that

[t]he estimated effect is significantly negative, accounting for between a quarter and a half of the total decline in turnout since the 1950s. I argue that substitution away from other media with more political coverage provides a plausible mechanism linking television to voting. As evidence for this, I show that the entry of television in a market coincided with sharp drops in consumption of newspapers and radio, and in political knowledge as measured by election surveys. I also show that both the information and turnout effects were largest in off-year congressional elections, which receive extensive coverage in newspapers but little or no coverage on television.

Gentzkow, Shapiro, and Sinkinson (2009) explore the impact of newspapers by studying the effects of entry and exit of daily newspapers on political outcomes for the period 1869–2004. They note that newspaper entry and exit cause "large, discrete changes in newspaper readership" and that their "basic strategy is to look at changes in political outcomes in counties that experience an entry or exit relative to other counties in the same state and year that do not" (2009, 3). They also find that

> newspapers have a robust positive effect on political participation. In the years 1869-1928, one additional newspaper increases presidential turnout by 0.3 percentage points. This effect is similar for congressional and presidential elections, and is robust to a range of alternative specifications. Turning to the role of competition, we find that the effect of the first entrant to a market on turnout is 1.0 percentage point, while the effect of later entrants is significantly smaller. The competition results are consistent with the hypothesis that all turnout effects are proportional to the effect on the share of eligible voters reading at least one newspaper, and imply that reading a newspaper increases the probability of voting by 4 percentage points. The effect of newspapers on presidential turnout diminishes after the introduction of radio and television, while the effect on congressional turnout remains similar up to recent years. (3)

The introduction of particular types of political information offers another way to see media's impact on local politics. Studying how the expansion of local television news programming in Spanish affected Hispanic turnout, Oberholzer-Gee and Waldfogel (2009) find that about a quarter of a local market's Hispanics turn from English to Spanish local news when the programming becomes available. They estimate that nearly 20 percent of these switchers start voting, which yields an overall increase of about 5 percentage points in Hispanic voter turnout. DellaVigna and Kaplan (2007) take advantage of the natural experiment generated by the introduction in local markets at different times of another type of differentiated news product, the Fox News channel. They find that areas with Fox News had a higher Republican vote share for president in the 2000 elections and trace this in part to non-Republican viewers choosing to vote for the Republican party. They find that Fox News increased the vote share for Republican Senate candidates by 0.7 percentage point. Given that most Senate races were rarely mentioned on Fox News, they note that this impact on local elections is evidence that Fox News exposure caused a shift in general ideology rather than a reaction linked to a specific candidate. Both the Spanish local news and Fox News studies take steps to show that their results capture the effect of exposure to new types of news programming and are not simply correlations generated by selection of particular markets to receive the news programming.

George and Walfogel (2006) chart how the introduction of another national news source, the *New York Times*, affected local information markets. Using the rollout of the home delivery option of the *Times* across more than 100 cities in the late 1990s, they find that the availability of the *Times* reduced circulation of the local newspaper among more highly educated readers, the target demographic of the *Times*. Local newspapers responded by increasing their focus on local news and decreasing emphasis on topics more heavily covered by the *Times*, such as national and international news. George and Walfogel (2008) find that after the introduction of the *Times*, voting among highly educated readers targeted by the *Times* expansion went down in congressional elections. These results are consistent with highly educated readers being drawn away from the local newspapers to reading the *Times* and the resulting drop in exposure to local news generating lower turnout in local elections.

Prior (2007) shows how the expansion of cable television allowed people less interested in political news to opt for entertainment programming, which changed the mix of voters in congressional elections. He concludes (2007, 244):

> Greater media choice reduced turnout rates among entertainment fans. They are more moderate or politically indifferent than the rest of the electorate. Their abstention makes the voting public more partisan. This compositional change is complemented by partisan news junkies becoming even more reliable in going to the polls and casting ideologically motivated votes. . . . Cable television and the Internet set in motion a re-sorting of the electorate that polarized elections without necessarily making anyone more partisan.

After showing how cable TV allowed those with a strong preference for entertainment to avoid news programming and that this reduced exposure decreased their turnout, he concludes that the "timing of [the] cable effect thus strengthens the case for greater media choice as an important cause of polarization in Congress."

Closure of Media Outlets

Sometimes the impact of a local newspaper on community life becomes more apparent when it is gone. In 1977 the *Cincinnati Enquirer* and *Cincinnati Post* formed a joint operating agreement that merged their business operations, a 30-year agreement the papers set to expire on December 31, 2007. On that date, the *Cincinnati Post* published its last edition, as the E.W. Scripps Co. shut the paper down and left the market to the Gannett-owned *Enquirer*. Schulhofer-Wohl and Garrido (2009) argue that since this shutdown is unlikely to be related to short-run local economic or political factors, the closure can be used to examine what happens to local politics when a news source is removed. They pursue a difference-in-differences strategy by comparing electoral outcomes before and after the *Post*'s closure in a set of Kentucky suburbs, which were covered in varying degrees by the *Post*.

For forty-eight municipalities in Kentucky counties in the core circulation area of the *Post*, they gathered data on the two newspapers' local coverage for 2003 through 2008 and data on school board, city council, and county commission races from 2004 through 2008. While noting that they are looking at short-run effects in a small sample, they find that (2009, 1) "the *Post*'s closing made municipal politics in the Kentucky suburbs less competitive among several dimensions: Fewer people voted in elections for city council, city commission and school board; fewer candidates sought those seats; the remaining candidates spent less money on their campaigns; and, for councils and commissions, incumbents' chances of retaining office improved. These changes happened even though the *Enquirer* increased its coverage of the *Post*'s former strongholds." Although indicating that some of their results are statistically imprecise and sensitive to modeling decisions, they conclude overall that (2009, 26) "if voter turnout, a broad choice of candidates and accountability for incumbents are important to democracy, we side with those who lament newspapers' decline."

When an 8-month newspaper strike in 1992 left Pittsburgh, Pennsylvania, without a major local newspaper, Mondak (1995) used this as a quasi-experiment to test the impact of local newspapers on political knowledge. He surveyed residents of Pittsburgh, left without a newspaper because of the strike, and Cleveland, where the *Plain Dealer* continued to be published. After giving survey respondents seventeen questions about national and international affairs, he concluded that the results between the two cities did not differ in a meaningful way. This is not necessarily surprising, since Pittsburgh residents still had access to media outlets such as local television news and network news broadcasts, which covered these topics. Mondak concluded that in the 1992 time period (1995, 520), "local newspapers apparently do not uniquely augment information acquisition, in national and international affairs." When he asked about self-reported knowledge about elections, he also found (1995, 524) that "voters without access to a major local newspaper perceived themselves to be at least as well informed about the 1992 presidential and senate elections as voters who did have access to a local newspaper." But Mondak found that people in Pittsburgh were less likely to report they were knowledgeable about House races, leading him to conclude (1995, 524): "Pittsburgh voters were not able to find fully satisfactory alternatives to the striking newspapers for news about the local U.S. House races."

Field Experiments and New Information Bundles

Field experiments using randomized control groups, often used in medical studies and increasingly used in development economics research, offer another way to study media effects in local markets for political information. Gerber, Karlan, and Bergan (2009) studied the impact of local newspapers by literally dropping newspapers on the door-steps of nonsubscribers. From a sample of households in Prince William County in Virginia in 2005, the researchers randomly assigned some nonsubscribing households to get a free subscription to the *Washington Post*, some to get the *Washington Times*, and some to get neither. They compared the opinions and actions of those who received the papers with the control group, based on surveys conducted before and after the sub-scriptions started and on voting records. Though one might assume that differences in content across the two papers might give rise to differences in learning, Gerber, Karlan, and Bergan (2009, 37) found

> no effect of receiving either paper on knowledge of political events, opinions of those events, or on voter turnout in the 2005 gubernatorial election. However, receiv-ing either paper led to more support for the Democratic candidate, suggesting that media slant mattered less in this case than exposure to media. There was also some evidence of increased voter turnout in the 2006 election among those receiving either paper.

The magnitudes of these effects are large. The researchers don't know how much the newspapers dropped on the doorstep were read, but those in the treatment group who received the free bundle of stories in fall 2005 did change their reported preferences in the Virginia gubernatorial race. Relative to those who did not get the free subscrip-tion to the *Washington Post* (often seen as leaning left) or the *Washington Times* (often seen as leaning right), for those who got a free newspaper there was an increase of about 7 percentage points in the likelihood of voting for the Democratic gubernatorial candi-date (a conservative-leaning Democrat who won the election). Though the papers did not appear to affect turnout rates in the 2005 election, state voting records indicate that turnout in the treatment group was about 3 percentage points greater in the 2006 mid-term elections (though this effect was "of only borderline statistical significance").

These field experiments show that spillovers from local newspapers are real. When political information, in the form of local newspaper articles, is (randomly) provided, turnout and the selection of candidates can change. Both of these changes have spill-overs on society that go beyond the impact on the readers whose choices are changed by the media. The nature of the media as an experience good, defined as one in which consumption may be required to understand quality and product dimensions, also finds confirmation in the experiment. Three months after the free subscriptions had ended, the *Washington Post* told the researcher that 17 percent of those in the treatment group had bought their own subscriptions after the experience of reading the paper for free.

Investigative reporting series that uncover and bring to light previously hidden or unknown information offer a different type of field experiment opportunity. In *The Journalism of Outrage* (1991), Protess and coauthors explored through six case studies the reactions generated by investigative reports. Since they were alerted by journalists ahead of the publication or airing of stories, the researchers were able to do public opin-ion surveys before and after the reports circulated and contrast changes in knowledge and opinions among those exposed to the media reports and those who were not. In some cases, they were able to interview policymakers before and after the reports were released. Four of the six cases involved investigations by local media: a series on rape by the Chicago *Sun-Times*; the "Beating Justice" series by the NBC television affiliate in Chicago, on police officers repeatedly charged with brutality; the same station's exposé about how the University of Chicago dealt with hazardous and radioactive waste; and the *Philadelphia Inquirer*'s series, later widely distributed by the news wire joint venture between Knight Ridder and Tribune Company, on dialysis programs funded by the federal government.

Protess and colleagues trace out three types of policymaking changes that can result from the release of these investigative reports (1991, 240):

> Deliberative results occur when policy makers hold formal discussions of policy problems and their solutions, such as legislative hearings or executive commissions. Individualistic outcomes occur when policy makers apply sanctions against particular persons or entities, including prosecutions, firings, and demotions. Finally, substantive results include regulatory, legislative, and/or administrative changes.

The *Inquirer* report "Dialysis: The Profit Machine" resulted in all three types of change. The deliberative effects included the introduction of federal and state legislation about dialysis. Individualistic changes included stricter enforcement of state codes at dialysis centers. Substantive changes in the regulatory regime included the hiring of additional inspectors.

The ways that these investigative reports generated change varied widely. In some cases journalists interacting with policymakers as they did the investigation caused the government officials to consider changes even before the reports were released. In other cases public opinions changed and an issue moved up the agenda. In one case, the investigative report injected an issue into a local political campaign. As the authors note, the pathways of influence can be very different (Protess et al. 1991, 204):

> Once published, some investigative stories have profound policy consequences without regard for public opinion. Other stories arouse the public without changing policy-making agendas. Still others mobilize interest groups, which then exert pressure on policymakers.

The contribution of these case studies is to show how a shock to the local political system, in the form of new information generated by the media, can sometimes generate spillovers. As Protess and colleagues summarized these effects (1991, 241):

> The rape reports made legislative changes an immediate priority and engendered community hearings that were not previously planned. The police brutality broadcasts mobilized political actors and produced swift and fundamental revisions of regulations regarding police misconduct. The dialysis series fueled state and federal

debate over the regulation of clinics and, in particular, the reuse of dialyzers. In each case, agenda building resulted in substantive reforms.

Evidence from the Lab

Lab experiments offer researchers the opportunity to expose participants to different media content on a randomized basis and observe short-term changes in opinions and actions. While political advertising and national news content have been the subject of significant lab research, investigations of the impact of local news content are less frequent. Gilliam and Iyengar (2000) used the lab to explore a staple of local television news broadcasts, crime coverage. They note that local broadcasters frequently cover crime using a standard script, which involves description of violence and portrayal of a suspect. To test how viewers are affected by crime stories, they had participants in a lab watch a news broadcast in which the crime content was varied by the researchers. The experiment was designed so that (2000, 563)

> [f]our levels of the manipulation were established. First, some participants watched a story in which the alleged perpetrator of a murder was an African-American male. Second, other subjects were given the same news report, but this time featuring a white male as the murder suspect. A third set of participants watched the news report edited to exclude information concerning the identity of the perpetrator. Finally, a control group saw no crime.

The researchers used digital technology to alter the appearance of the suspect's skin color in a news story. This meant that (2000, 563) "the perpetrator featured in the 'white' and 'black' versions of the story was equivalent in all respects but race." By looking at how survey responses in the lab varied with the type of crime story presented, Gilliam and Iyengar (2000, 560) found that "exposure to the racial element of the crime script increases support for punitive approaches to crime and heightens negative attitudes about African-Americans among white, but not black, viewers." With crime content a key factor in how stations differentiate themselves within a market (Hamilton, 1998), these results from the lab show how the images generated in local TV news can affect viewers' opinions about public policies such as capital punishment and mandatory sentencing.

FUTURE RESEARCH AND POLICY QUESTIONS

Research to date clearly shows that local media outlets can generate spillovers in society. Some of these might be positive impacts that arise from increases in voter turnout, changes in candidate selection, or alterations in policies implemented. Some could be negative spillovers, if the allure of cable entertainment or the depth of the *New York Times* causes some people to skip local media and stop voting in local elections. The challenge for media scholars will be to continue to explore how the rapidly changing local information environment results in changes in policies and politicians.

Between 2006 and 2009, one out of every four jobs in daily newspaper newsrooms was eliminated (Project for Excellence in Journalism, 2011). One avenue for future research will be exploring how the reduction in the number of print journalists has affected accountability coverage at the local and state levels. The decline in information outlets supported by advertising and subscription, however, may also be accompanied by increases in information motivated by nonprofit, partisan, or expressive goals (Hamilton, 2011). Research questions about public affairs information created by these incentives are numerous: How does the coverage provided by an increasing number of nonprofit local public affairs outlets help fill holes left by shrinking commercial media? Can partisan information provision, through expenditures by independent groups, candidates, and political parties, provide information that helps substitute for what local commercial media once provided? Do social media lower the costs of holding local and state officials accountable?

Policymakers care about political information and political action for intrinsic reasons (e.g., knowledge is a distinct good; voting is a good in and of itself) and for instrumental reasons (e.g., media consumption translates into political actions, which have value as they are translated into policy outcomes). In the chain of causation linking media content and policy outcomes, future research on the existence of spillovers will help policymakers understand more about the impact of media policy on real-world outcomes. There are many policy-relevant questions remaining: How could we assess the claim that the public interest defines the public interest, versus claims about the failures of local media to provide sufficient information to hold officials accountable? How far are we from measuring the magnitude of the market failures associated with inadequate provision of local public affairs information, if these failures exist? If media outlets do help educate voters and increase participation in civic affairs, should the Internal Revenue Service add media providing public affairs coverage to the set of institutions treated as qualifying for nonprofit status because they are "educational"? Future research on local media content, political accountability, and policymaking outcomes will contribute to both scholarly and policy debates about the magnitude and meaning of the spillovers generated in media markets.

REFERENCES

DellaVigna, S., and Kaplan, E. 2007. The Fox News effect: Media bias and voting. *Quarterly Journal of Economics* 122(3, August): 1187–1234.

Downs, A. 1957. *An economic theory of democracy*. New York: Harper Books.

Gentzkow, M. 2006. Television and voter turnout. *Quarterly Journal of Economics* 121(3, August): 931–974.

Gentzkow, M., Shapiro, J. M., and Sinkinson, M. 2009. The effect of newspaper entry and exit on electoral politics. National Bureau of Economic Research Working Paper No. 15544.

George, L. M., and Waldfoegel, J. 2006. The *New York Times* and the market for local newspapers. *American Economic Review* 96(1): 435–447.

George, L. M., and Waldfoegel, J. 2008. National media and local political participation: The case of the *New York Times*. In R. Islam (Ed.), *Information and public choice: From media markets to policy making* (ch. 3). Washington, DC: World Bank.

Gerber, A. S., Karlan, D., and Bergan, D. 2009. Does the media matter? A field experiment measuring the effect of newspapers on voting behavior and political opinions. *American Economic Journal* 1(2): 35–52.

Gilliam, F. D., Jr., and Iyengar, S. 2000. Prime suspects: The influence of local television news on the viewing public. *American Journal of Political Science* 44(3): 560–573.

Hamilton, J. T. 1998. *Channeling violence: The economic market for violent television programming*. Princeton, NJ: Princeton University Press.

Hamilton, J. T. 2004. *All the news that's fit to sell: How the market transforms information into news*. Princeton, NJ: Princeton University Press.

Hamilton, J. T. 2011. What's the incentive to save journalism? In R. W. McChesney and V. Pickard (Eds.), *Will the Last reporter please turn out the lights: The collapse of journalism and what can be done to fix it* (ch. 26). New York: New Press.

Mondak, J. J. 1995. Newspapers and political awareness. *American Journal of Political Science* 39(2): 513–527.

Oberholzer-Gee, F., and Waldfogel, J. 2009. Media markets and localism: Does local news en Español boost Hispanic voter turnout? *American Economic Review* 99(5): 2120–2128.

Project for Excellence in Journalism. 2011. The state of the news media: An annual report on American journalism. Pew Research Center. Retrieved from http://stateofthemedia.org/.

Prior, M. 2007. *Post-broadcast democracy: How media choice increases inequality in political involvement and polarizes elections*. New York: Cambridge University Press.

Protess, D. L., Cook, F. L., Doppelt, J. C., Ettema, J. S., Gordon, M. T., Leff, D. R., and Miller, P. 1991. *The journalism of outrage: Investigative reporting and agenda building in America*. New York: The Guilford Press.

Schulhofer-Wohl, S., and Garrido, M. 2009. Do newspapers matter? Evidence from the closure of the *Cincinnati Post*. NBER Working Paper No. 14817.

Snyder, J. M., and Stromberg, D. 2010. Press coverage and political accountability. *Journal of Political Economy* 118(2): 355–408.

Strömberg, D. 2004. Radio's impact on public spending. *Quarterly Journal of Economics* 119(1, February): 189–221.

CHAPTER 21

....

COMPARATIVE POLITICAL COMMUNICATION RESEARCH

....

CLAES H. DE VREESE

INTRODUCTION

....

COMPARATIVE political communication research is en vogue. Finding only a few cross-national political communication studies almost forty years ago, Blumler and Gurevitch (1975) surmised that the field was in its infancy. Two decades later, they concluded that this area of work remained "patchy," but nonetheless saw signs of adolescence. A few years ago Norris concluded that despite an increase in both the number of studies with a comparative focus and advances in comparative theorizing, comparative political communication scholars still need " sharper, cleaner and more precise concepts" (2009, 340). In the meantime, several large-scale comparative projects have yielded important new insights and in the process signaled that the political communication subfield has attained early adulthood.

Why should political communication researchers care about cross-national comparisons? First of all, they deliver an important, sobering antidote to the assumption that anything we find based on a single case study at one point in time generalizes, with few or no limitations, across space and time. As Esser and Pfetsch aptly note, "every observation is without significance if it is not compared with other observations" (2004, 5). Indeed, comparative research not only helps us become more aware and knowledgeable about other contexts; it also helps us to understand our own context and its particularities. Comparative research has the "capacity to render the invisible visible" (Blumler and Gurevitch, 1995, 76). Indeed, Graber sees comparative political communication research as one of the future highlights of the field and notes that given the variation in the contents of political communication, it is "important and instructive to study it from different cultural perspectives" (2005, 502). In the words of Sartori (1996, 245): "He who knows only one country knows none."

In communication science, political communication is one of the more international and comparatively oriented subfields. However, compared to such fields as political science and sociology, comparative political communication research is deficient. As de Vreese and Vliegenthart note (2011), comparative political scientists have developed specific journals (e.g., *Comparative Political Studies*), been involved in the development of large-scale data collection efforts (such as the European election study), created a tradition of utilizing large-scale social sciences data sets (such as the Eurobarometer, the European Social Survey, and the World Value Survey; see Kittilson [2007] for an overview), and collected key indicators about political systems and economic developments.

In political science, following the tradition of Lijphart (1977) and Przeworski and Teune (1970), comparative politics is defined as a combination of a *substantive focus* (e.g., on countries' political systems) and as a *method* of identifying and explaining similarities and differences between different countries while using underlying common concepts. Drawing on this definition, in this chapter I outline a typology of comparative political communication research (CPCR), review key findings in CPCR, and pose a number of questions worthy of future research.

Types of Comparative Political Communication Research

Comparative political communication research can mean many things. It may imply a comparison *across time*, such as Dan Hallin's (1992) work on how politicians' sound bites have shrunk in US news, Tom Patterson's (1993) demonstration of the increase in the use of the game frame in US newspapers between the 1960s and 1990s, and Schulz and Zeh's (2005) longitudinal analysis of German news coverage of elections; *across media*, such as Semetko and Valkenburg's (2000) analysis of news framing in television news and newspapers; or *across units* (e.g., countries and media markets), such as Köcher's (1986) comparison of German and British journalists, Ridout and colleagues' (2004) analysis of political advertising in different US media markets, and Norris's (2000) analysis of how news in Europe reports about the European Union (EU). The choice of a comparative research strategy should be driven by the research question. Different analytical strategies can be chosen to answer different research questions. In the process, different types of CPCR can be distinguished (see the typology by Vliegenthart 2012 and de Vreese and Vliegenthart 2011).

One type of comparison is mostly *descriptive* in nature. Studies in this tradition ask to what extent a phenomenon occurs. An example is Blumler and Gurevitch's (2001) studies of news in the United States and Britain, in which the journalistic approach in both places is analyzed and described. In a similar vein, Trenz (2004) showed how news in different countries differs in the extent to which, for example, it makes reference to other European countries. De Vreese, Peter, and Semetko (2001) offered an internationally comparative analysis of news framing and showed how news in different countries applied news frames differentially. While descriptive in nature, such studies are often explorative and bent on explanation, in that they investigate whether differences in media coverage between, for example, countries can be attributed to such factors as the positions of political actors and journalistic values and norms. Typically, as pointed out by Vliegenthart (2012), though the differences in, for example, news coverage between countries in such studies may be in line with expectations derived *theoretically* from different political and journalistic practices, these relationships cannot be tested formally, in a *statistical* sense. Researchers encounter the problem of too few cases and too many variables. There may be multiple factors that account for differences between the countries, even when a mostly similar system design (assuming that the countries are very similar in many of their structural characteristics) (Przeworski and Teune, 1970) is adopted.

A second type of study is *explanatory* in nature. Studies in this tradition rely on characteristics of units to explain differences in some kind of output variable that is usually measured within each unit. So, for example, Peter, Lauf, and Semetko (2004) showed how the European parliamentary elections were covered in television news in 1999 and, using multivariate analyses, established that there is more coverage of the European elections on public broadcasting channels and in countries where citizens are dissatisfied with their national governments. Schuck and colleagues (2013) investigated the factors that *explain* the variation in campaign coverage of the 2009 European parliamentary elections, using a cross-national media content analysis conducted in all twenty-seven EU member states. Their findings revealed that time, country, and media characteristics all explained the way media frame elections. Conflict framing especially was contingent on the medium, the electoral system, and public aversion against the EU. In such explanatory work, there is sometimes sufficient leverage in the data to conduct multivariate analyses, but a considerable number of cases are required.

A third type of study looks at the same relationships among variables in different contexts. In his typology, Vliegenthart (2012) identifies such work by its focus on the *comparison of relation* types of research questions. An example is provided by Holtz-Bacha and Norris (2001). In their study on the effects of public television preferences on political knowledge, they demonstrate that this relation holds for ten of the fourteen European countries included in the analysis. As their study shows, to answer this type of research question, multiple analyses must be done—for each unit separately. De Vreese (2005) showed that the level of strategic news framing in two countries (Denmark and the Netherlands) varied and that the effect of exposure to news in each country was different, contingent upon the degree of strategy news framing. Van Dalen, Albæk, and de Vreese (2011) analyzed the level of political cynicism among journalists in the United Kingdom, Denmark, Germany, and Spain. They found that in Denmark and Germany more experienced political journalists are significantly less cynical. Four separate regression models revealed that when journalists perceive politicians to be driven by media salacity, their level of political cynicism is higher.

A fourth type of CPCR focuses on *explaining variation in relations across units*. Studies of CPCR employing this type of question are relatively scarce. Shehata and Strömback (2010), for example, showed that the effects of political interest and education on newspaper reading are contingent upon the degree of newspaper concentration in a country. High newspaper circulation decreases gaps in newspaper reading between those with high and low levels of education and political interest. This conclusion was drawn from cross-nationally collected data at the system level and at the individual level, as well as the interaction terms between the different levels.

This type of study conceptually nests citizens in larger systems. It offers explanations at both the individual and system levels and takes their interaction into consideration, typically using multilevel modeling. Using this approach, US scholars have found that the effect of individual exposure to political advertising is contingent upon characteristics of the media market (Goldstein and Freedman, 2002). In related research, Schuck, Vliegenthart, and de Vreese (2014), using panel survey data and media content analyses in twenty-one EU countries, found that exposure to conflict-driven news positively affected turnout in the 2009 European parliamentary election, especially in countries in which the media depiction of the EU is mostly positive. This implies that in those instances when the news showcases conflict and disagreement between political elites, it offers citizens a choice that mobilizes them to turn out to vote.

AREAS OF CPCR

In addition to different *types* of CPCR, several key *areas* of research can be identified. In this chapter my focus is on comparative research on (1) media and political systems, (2) political and election news, (3) political communication in the EU, and (4) political journalists.

Media and Political Systems

Knowledge about the media and political systems in which political communication is created and consumed is of key interest to both European and US comparativists. In the early 1980s the Euromedia research group set out to "collect and exchange information and to develop and apply frameworks that help to describe and analyse developments in media structure and policy in the European region" (EMRG). Since then, this network of European scholars has produced a series of books and overview volumes with systematic information about media systems, media governance, distribution, availability, and consumption of media products. In the main, this body of work has concentrated on providing overviews and country descriptions.

In 2004 Hallin and Mancini published *Comparing Media Systems: Three Models of Media and Politics*. Focusing on historical developments and structural relationships between media and politics, they classify the media systems in Western democracies as democratic corporatist, liberal, and polarized pluralist. Although the typology, as well as Hallin and Mancini's selection of underlying dimensions, has been criticized (see, e.g., Norris, 2009), the book, like Esser and Pfetsch's (2004) and Esser and Hanitsch's (2012) edited volumes on comparative research, quickly became a must-read in CPCR. All three works have stimulated empirical studies and new thinking about comparisons.

Hallin and Mancini (2004) in particular provoked an increase in the number of studies testing how media structures influence the content produced by journalists (e.g., Strömbäck and Dimitrova, 2006; Strömbäck and Luengo, 2008; see also Engesser and Franzetti, 2011). Hallin and Mancini's approach both sparked discussion beyond Western Europe about the applicability of their model and prompted work on other dimensions distinguishing media systems in other parts of the world (e.g., Dobek-Ostrowska et al., 2010; see also Voltmer 2006, 2011). One of the more important foci of comparative system research in Western democracies has been the role of public broadcasting and its positive relation to the availability of political information (see Esser et al., 2012, for a comparative, over time, cross-national analysis of the availability of political information in Europe; see also Aalberg, van Aelst, and Curran, 2010).

Political and Election News

One of the more studied topics in CPCR is news. Pioneering work focused on both how television viewers across the globe (including in the United States, India, Mexico, Italy, Denmark, Israel, and Belarus) respond to the increasing availability of information from news programs and on how news viewing is incorporated into everyday life (Bruhn Jensen, 2000). So, for example, Shoemaker and Cohen's (2006) *News Around the World* examines how local notions of newsworthiness make a crucial difference in what stories are reported throughout the world. Drawing on examples from Australia, Chile, China, Germany, India, Israel, Russia, South Africa, and the United States, their book shows how and why news stories are reported (or not reported) across the globe. Similarly, a new ongoing study led by Cohen looks at the production and contents of foreign news in more than a dozen countries.

Particular attention is given in CPCR to the study of election campaigns and election news. Among the key reasons given by Blumler and McQuail (2001) for the intermingling of election and political communication research is that election campaigns lend themselves to cross-national and comparative political communication research. The *Handbook of Election News Coverage Around the World* (Strömbäck and Kaid, 2008) offers an excellent overview of election campaign communication in different countries and in the process issues an important caution to those eager to generalize the conclusion in the US-based literature that substantive news coverage has been largely driven out by procedurally focused strategic news coverage. Specifically, in several countries substantive coverage dominates, and there is considerable cross-national variation in the focus on strategy and the reliance on horse race news (see Kaid and Strömbäck, 2008, 424).

News has also been treated as an independent variable in CPCR that concentrates on citizens' political knowledge and learning from the media. One common conclusion is that news exposure is—ceteris paribus—conducive to learning and political participation and that public service news and newspapers play a particularly positive role in this process. In a cross-national study relying on panel studies and media content analysis, de Vreese and Boomgaarden (2006) found that exposure to news outlets with high levels of political content (such as public television news and broadsheet newspapers) not only contributes more than commercial news and tabloid papers to knowledge gains, but also increases the propensity to vote. In similar work, Curran and colleagues (2009) found that public service television devotes more attention to public affairs and international news and fosters greater knowledge in these areas. Combining a content analysis of broadcast news with a national survey measuring public awareness of various events, issues, and individuals in the news, Iyengar and colleagues (2010) found that properties of national media systems influence both the supply of news and citizens' awareness of events in the news. This body of scholarship warrants an important conclusion: specifically, since public-service-oriented media systems deliver hard news more frequently than market-based systems, the opportunity costs of exposure to hard news are significantly lower for citizens living under public service regimes. Lowered costs allow less-interested citizens to acquire political knowledge.

Political Communication in the EU

In the context of European integration, a body of CPCR, pioneered by Blumler (1983), has asked how the EU is covered in the news media in Europe and beyond (see de Vreese et al., 2006, and Maier and Maier 2008 for overviews). By making it possible to study the occurrence of a single election (for the European Parliament) that takes place across national boundaries at the same time, the EU provides a unique laboratory for CPCR. This "laboratory" for testing social science theories today counts no less than twenty-seven member states (de Vreese and Boomgaarden, 2011).

A stellar example of comparative descriptive research is Trenz's analysis of broadsheet newspapers in 2000 in Germany, France, Britain, Italy, and Spain. Trenz (2004) found evidence of a "transnational resonance of political communications," implying that in relation to specific actors and institutions, cross-references are present. Similarly, de Vreese and colleagues' (2006) work on the news coverage of the 1999 and 2004 European parliamentary elections identified an increasing salience of the elections in the news and an increasing Europeanization over time as well as significant differences among the European countries.

In a time-series analysis including seven countries, Vliegenthart and colleagues (2008) examined how variation in information contexts, in particular the framing of the EU, affects public support for the EU. This study is an example of how media content analyses can be integrated with survey data, at the *aggregate* level, to understand changes in public opinion in a cross-nationally comparative perspective.

Finally, Boomgaarden and colleagues (2013) looked at the interaction among different levels of *explanations* for cross-national and over-time variation in the news media coverage of EU affairs. Drawing on large-scale media content analyses of newspapers and television news in EU-15 (1999), EU-25 (2004), and EU-27 (2009) in relation to European Parliament elections, their study found that national parties that were intensely divided about the EU led heightened news visibility.

Political Journalists

A fourth area in which CPCR has flourished is journalism studies and politics. Work in this area has been inspired by general journalist surveys (such as in *The American Journalist* [Weaver and Wilhoit, 2006] and the *Global Journalist* [Weaver and Wilnat, 2012]), as well as comparative journalist surveys such as the Worlds of Journalism project (http://worldsofjournalism.org/), directed by Thomas Hanitzsch (see Hanitzsch et al., 2011).

Focusing cross-nationally on political journalists, pioneers Blumler and Gurevitch's (1991, 2004) comparison of US and UK television journalists introduced the distinction between a pragmatic and sacerdotal journalistic approach to politics (see also Semetko et al., 1991). Building on this early tradition of inquiry, Donsbach and Patterson's (1996) survey of political journalists in five countries (United States, United Kingdom, Germany, Italy, and Sweden) concluded that journalists in Western democracies define themselves primarily as news professionals who are committed to a form of journalism marked by its objectivity and neutrality. Importantly, the journalists in some countries acknowledged partisanship as part of daily news coverage. In a similar vein, van Dalen and van Aelst (2012) found that although the role conceptions of journalists in eight countries were highly similar, their source relationships were highly variable and dependent on the degree of journalistic political autonomy.

Looking at mutual relations between journalists and politicians and their "power struggle," Van Aelst and Walgrave's (2011), comparative survey of members of parliament in four small parliamentary democracies—Belgium, the Netherlands, Sweden, and Denmark—showed that MPs consider the mass media to be one of the key political agenda setters directly competing with the prime minister and the powerful political parties. Van Aelst, Shehata, and van Dalen's (2010) unique survey of members of parliament (MPs) in five democratic corporatist countries (Belgium, the Netherlands, Sweden, Norway, and Denmark) showed that parliamentary experience and institutional position increase the frequency of contacts that MPs have with journalists.

Building on a comparative project on political journalism from the University of Southern Denmark, van Dalen, Albæk, and de Vreese (2011) investigated the claim that journalists spread a cynical view of politics since their relation with politicians is characterized by mistrust and hyper-adversarialism. Their survey of over four hundred political reporters from the United Kingdom, Denmark, Germany, and Spain found that Spanish journalists have the most cynical view of politicians, which can partly be explained by feelings of political pressure. In this study, journalists were considered cynical if they had a negative view of the role of spin doctors and believed that politicians used the media as a podium to be in the spotlight (see also Albæk et al., 2014).

First results are also emerging from a large-scale, comparative project on political communication culture in Western Europe directed by Pfetsch. The study's objective is analyzing the attitudes, norms, and values that drive the relationship between political elites and the media. By so doing it hopes to detect the underlying patterns of political communication behaviors in eleven Western democracies. Eventually, the aim of the study is to systematically map the types of political communication cultures in Europe and detect similarities and differences across countries (for first results see Maurer 2011).

Several studies have also focused specifically on EU journalists (as well as EU officials and correspondents). Statham (2008) provides a general picture of how journalism has responded to the transformation of politics resulting from advancing European integration. This work also asks whether, based on journalists' assessments, this has involved a transformation of the practices and norms of journalism (see also Baisnée 2004; Lecheler and Hinrichsen 2010). In another study of European journalistic practice, de Vreese (2003) identified a number of cross-national differences in the approach and coverage of reporters in three European countries. While the visibility of the campaign was low to modest in all countries, the news organizations differed substantially in their contribution to the agenda formation process. British news reflected the politicians' agenda to a greater extent than Dutch news, where the elections were largely neglected, while Danish news organizations played a proactive role in setting their own news agenda. Wessler and colleagues (2008) looked at public opinion, country size, and power, and—in this context most importantly—the number of correspondents in Brussels and the editorial missions, to explain differences in the coverage of European affairs. Finally, Martins, Lecheler, and de Vreese (2011) showed that journalists from several countries are strongly negative about the press work of each EU institution.

Conclusion

This chapter is an introduction to and synthesis of CPCR. In service of this objective, it provides a typology of different *types* of CPCR, ranging from descriptive to explanatory studies, and outlines the key *areas* in which CPCR is most vibrant, including media systems research, news and elections research, EU political communication, and political journalism.

The contributions of CPCR are many and various. Comparative research has shown how a media system defines the context in which journalists operate and citizens receive information. It also has revealed that news across the world varies and that in strong public broadcasting systems the availability of political information is greater, the degree of substantive political news coverage higher, and citizen knowledge greater. Comparative political communication research has also demonstrated that EU news is more readily available when political elite contestation is high, and that political journalists in many Western democracies perceive their roles in similar ways, but also experience different autonomy and vary in their perception of politicians and political power. Comparative research has not only rendered the invisible visible, but also has taught us more about the conditions under which specific patterns hold up and when they do not.

One area of research that this chapter has not addressed is the role of the Internet in CPCR. Recent studies have looked at the role of online communication in relation to elections (Kluver et al., 2007; Ward, 2008). Many studies so far offer descriptive comparative accounts of the availability, contents, and uses of political communication online, but systematic comparative and explanatory analyses are rare. An exception is Groshek (2009), whose data from 152 countries revealed that, at the aggregate level, increased Internet diffusion was a predictor of more democratic regimes.

Where should CPCR go next? Several challenges and unanswered questions are apparent. It is flourishing, and cross-national comparisons are especially popular. The field has developed from its initial niche position to become an important mainstream subfield. However, several authors point to the need to push the field and the research further. A number of challenges are at the top in the field's quest for adulthood:

Geographical bias. Most published studies in political communication pertain to the United States, with findings from these studies rarely compared to other locations. In essence this creates a "single-country bias" in much of our extant knowledge. Most comparative studies focus on Western democracies or, even more narrowly, Western Europe. Only recently has research generated knowledge about, for example, Eastern Europe and democracies in transition (e.g., Voltmer, 2011). Testing and, importantly, rethinking our concepts and assumptions in other parts of the world is necessary if we are to assess the often assumed universal nature of our theories.

Understanding levels and time. CPCR is often, implicitly or explicitly, faced with questions and theories that involve different levels and time. For example, citizens exposed to different political messages in different media are typically nested within specific states, media systems, or language areas, and new information is consumed in the context of an existing individual and situational media environment. This calls for appropriate thinking about the interdependency of levels and time of many observations.

Improving designs, data collection, and analyses to improve theory. CPCR needs to take itself seriously and strive to add more to our knowledge base than descriptive accounts. This necessitates thinking more about designs that are appropriate to answer dynamic and complex questions, collaborative and concerted research efforts, the criteria for case selection, and appropriate tests and statistical analyses. The latter can include small *n* approaches (e.g., fuzzy set analyses) as well as large *n* ones (e.g., multilevel modeling). Only when these criteria are met can we improve our theorizing (Blumler and Gurevitch, 2004). New opportunities emerge quickly in the realm of "big data," though accessibility, usefulness, and quality are not always evident.

Not in the ghetto. CPCR faces the challenge of having to improve and advance as a subdiscipline without ending up in the "intellectual ghetto." It is imperative to create outlets in which CPCR can flourish and theoretical and empirical exchanges can take place (akin to comparative political studies). However, it is even more important that CPCR not be written off as an entirely independent subdiscipline, void of relevance for general (political) communication research. It is important to include CPCR in mainstream journals to increase the dialogue between findings based on single cases and findings from CPCR that can draw inferences about time and/or place.

Infrastructure. As noted by Norris (2009), cross-national media content analyses are needed "to accompany the growing range of cross-national social surveys that now include measures of media use." Too much CPCR hinges on the flash drives, servers, and drop boxes of individual scholars. To take the field forward, we need data sharing and documentation in publicly accessible data repositories, with data sets, documentation, and codebooks with standardized measures, much along the lines of survey data repositories.

REFERENCES

Aalberg, T., van Aelst, P., and Curran, J. 2010. Media systems and the political information environment: A cross-national comparison. *International Journal of Press/Politics* 15(3): 255–271.

Albæk, E., van Dalen, A., Jebril, N, and de Vreese, C. H. 2014. *Political journalism in comparative perspective.* Cambridge, UK: Cambridge University Press.

Baisnée, O. 2004. The politics of the Commission as an information source. In A. Smith (Ed.), *Politics and the European Commission: Actors, interdependence, legitimacy* (pp. 134–155). London: Routledge.

Blumler, J. G. (Ed.). 1983. *Communicating to voters: Television in the first European parliamentary elections.* London: Sage.

Blumler, J. G., and Gurevitch, M. 1975. *Towards a comparative framework for political communication research.* Beverly Hills, CA: Sage.

Blumler, J. G., and Gurevitch, M. 1995. *The crisis of public communication.* London: Sage.

Blumler, J. G., and Gurevitch, M. 2001. Americanization reconsidered: UK-US campaign communication comparisons across time. In L. Bennett and R. Entman (Eds.), *Mediated Politics* (pp. 380–405). Cambridge, UK: Cambridge University Press.

Blumler, J. G., and Gurevitch, M. 2004. State of the art of comparative political communication research. Poised for maturity? In F. Esser and B. Pfetsch (Eds.), *Comparing Political Communication* (pp. 325–344). Cambridge, UK: Cambridge University Press.

Blumler, J. G., and McQuail, D. 2001. Political communication scholarship: The uses of election research. In E. Katz and Y. Warshel (Eds.), *Election Studies: What's Their Use* (pp. 219–246). Boulder, CO: Westview.

Boomgaarden, H. G., de Vreese, C. H., et al. 2013. Across time and space: Explaining variation in news coverage of the European Union. *European Journal of Political Research* 52(5): 608–629.

Bruhn Jensen, K. 2000. *News of the world.* London: Routledge.

Curran, J., Iyengar, S., Lund, A. B., and Salovaara-Moring, I. 2009. Media system, public knowledge and democracy: A comparative study. *European Journal of Communication* 24: 5–26.

De Vreese, C. H. 2003. Television reporting of second-order elections. *Journalism Studies* 4(2): 183–198.

De Vreese, C. H. 2005. The spiral of cynicism reconsidered: The mobilizing function of news. *European Journal of Communication* 20(3): 283–301.

De Vreese, C. H., Banducci, S. A., Semetko, H. A., and Boomgaarden, H. G. 2006. The news coverage of the 2004 European parliamentary campaign in 25 countries. *European Union Politics* 7(4): 477–504.

De Vreese, C. H., and Boomgaarden. H. G. 2006. News, political knowledge and participation: The differential effects of news media exposure on political knowledge and participation. *Acta Politica* 41: 317–341.

De Vreese, C. H., and Boomgaarden, H. G. 2012. Explaining variation in the news: News coverage of European parliamentary elections as an example of comparative communication research. in F. Esser and T. Hanitzsch (Eds.), *Handbook of comparative communication* (pp. 327–340). New York: Routledge.

De Vreese, C. H., Peter, J., and Semetko, H. A. 2001. Framing politics at the launch of the euro: A cross-national comparative study of frames in the news. *Political Communication* 18(2): 107–122.

De Vreese, C. H., and Vliegenthart, R. 2011. Europe: A laboratory for comparative communication research. In I. Voltmer (Ed.), *Handbook of global media research* (pp. 470–484). Chichester: WileyBlackwell.

Dobek-Ostrowska, B., et al. 2010. *Comparative media systems: European and global perspectives.* Budapest: Central European University Press.

Donsbach, W., and Patterson, T. E. 1996. News decisions: Journalists as partisan actors. *Political Communication* 13: 455–458.

Engesser, S., and Franzetti, A. 2011. Media systems and political systems: dimensions of comparison. *International Communication Gazette* 17(4): 273–301.

Esser, F., de Vreese, C., Strömbäck, J. van Aelst, P., Aalberg, T., Stanyer, J., Lengauer, G., Berganza, R., Legnante, G., Papathanassopoulos, S., Salgado, S., Sheafer, T., and Reinemann, C. 2012. Political information opportunities in Europe: A longitudinal and comparative study of 13 television systems. *International Journal of Press/Politics* 17(3): 247–274.

Esser, F., and Hanitzsch, T. 2012. *Handbook of comparative communication research.* London: Routledge.

Esser, F., and Pfetsch, B. 2004. *Comparing political communication: Theories, cases, and challenges.* Cambridge, UK: Cambridge University Press.

Goldstein, K., and Freedman, P. 2002. Campaign advertising and voter turnout: New evidence for a stimulation effect. *Journal of Politics* 64(3): 721–740.

Graber, D. A. 2005. Political communication faces the 21st century. *Journal of Communication* 55(3): 479–507.

Groshek, J. 2009. The democratic effects of the Internet, 1994–2003: A cross-national inquiry of 152 countries. *International Communication Gazette* 71(3): 115–136.

Hallin, D. C. 1992. Sound bite news: Television coverage of elections, 1968–1988. *Journal of Communication* 42: 5–24.

Hallin, D. C., and Mancini, P. 2004. *Comparing media systems: Three models of media and politics.* Cambridge, UK: Cambridge University Press.

Hanitzsch, T., et al. 2011. Mapping journalism cultures across nations: A comparative study of 18 countries. *Journalism Studies* 12(3): 273-293.

Holtz-Bacha, C., and Norris, P. 2001. "To entertain, inform, and educate": Still the role of public television. *Political Communication* 18: 123-140.

Iyengar, S., Curran, J., Lund, A. B., Salovaara-Moring, I., Hahn, K. S., and Coen, S. 2010. Cross-national versus individual-level differences in political information: A media systems perspective. *Journal of Elections, Public Opinion & Parties* 20: 291-309.

Kaid, L. L., and Strömbäck, J. 2008. Election news coverage around the world: A comparative perspective. In J. Strömbäck and L. L. Kaid (Eds.), *The handbook of election news coverage around the world* (pp. 412-431). New York: Routledge.

Kittilson, M. C. 1997. Research sources in comparative political behavior. In R. Dalton and H-D. Klingemann (Eds.), *The oxford handbook of political behavior* (pp. 865-895). Oxford, UK: Oxford University Press.

Köcher, R. 1986. Bloodhounds or missionaries: Role definitions of German and British journalists. *European Journal of Communication* 1: 43-64.

Kluver, R., Jankowski, N., Foot, K., and Schneider, S. (Eds.). 2007. *The Internet and national elections: A comparative study of web campaigning.* Milton Park, UK: Routledge.

Lecheler, S., and Hinrichsen, M. 2010. Role conceptions of Brussels correspondents from new member states. *Javnost—The Public* 17: 73-86.

Lijphart, A. 1977. *Democracy in plural societies: A comparative exploration.* New Haven, CT: Yale University Press.

Maier, M., and Maier, J. 2008. News coverage of EU Parliamentary elections. In J. Strömbäck and L. L. Kaid (Eds.), *The handbook of election news coverage around the world* (pp. 403-425). New York: Routledge.

Martins, A., Lecheler, S., and de Vreese, C. H. 2011. Information flow and communication deficit: Perceptions of Brussels-based correspondents and EU officials. *Journal of European Integration* 34(4): 305-322.

Maurer, P. 2011. Explaining perceived media influence in politics: An analysis of the interplay of context and attitudes in four European democracies. *Publizistik* 56: 27-50.

Norris, P. 2000. *A virtuous circle: Political communications in postindustrial societies.* New York: Cambridge University Press.

Norris, P. 2009. Comparative political communications: Frameworks or Babelian confusion? *Government and Opposition* 44: 321-340.

Patterson, T. E. 1993. *Out of order?* New York: Alfred Knopf.

Peter, J., Lauf, E., and Semetko, H. A. 2004. Television coverage of the 1999 European parliamentary elections. *Political Communication* 21(4): 415-433.

Przeworski, A., and Teune, H. 1970. *The logic of comparative social inquiry.* New York: Wiley-Interscience.

Ridout, T. N., Shah, D. V., Goldstein, K. M., and Franz, M. M. 2004. Evaluating measures of campaign advertising exposure on political learning. *Political Behavior* 26(3): 201-225.

Sartori, G. 1996. Comparing and miscomparing. *Journal of Theoretical Politics* 3: 243-257.

Schuck, A. R. T., Vliegenthart, R., Boomgaarden, H., Elenbaas, M., Azrout, R., van Spanje, J., and de Vreese, C. H. 2013. Explaining campaign news coverage: How medium, time and context explain variation in the media framing of the 2009 EP elections. *Journal of Political Marketing* 12(1), 8-28.

Schuck, A. R. T., Vliegenthart, R., and de Vreese, C. H. 2014. Who is afraid of conflict? *British Journal of Political Science.* http://dx.doi.org/10.1017/S0007123413000525

Schulz, W., and Zeh, R. 2005. The changing election coverage of German television: A content analysis 1990–2002. *Communications* 30(4): 385–407.

Semetko, H. A., and Valkenburg, P. M. 2000. Framing European politic: A content analysis of press and television news. *Journal of Communication* 50: 93–109.

Semetko, H. A., et al. 1991. *The formation of campaign agendas: A comparative analysis of party and media agendas in American and British elections.* Hillsdale, NJ: Lawrence Erlbaum.

Shehata, A., and Strömbäck, J. 2010. A matter of context: A comparative study of media environments and news consumption gaps in Europe. *Political Communication* 28(1): 110–134.

Shoemaker, P., and Cohen, A. 2006. *News around the world: Content, practitioners, and the public.* New York: Routledge.

Statham, P. 2008. Making Europe news: How journalists view their role and media performance. *Journalism: Theory, Practice & Criticism* 9(4): 398–422.

Strömbäck, J., and Dimitrova, D. V. 2006. Political and media systems matter: A comparison of election news coverage in Sweden and the United States. *Harvard International Journal of Press/Politics* 11(4): 131–147.

Strömbäck, J., and Luengo, O. G. 2008. Polarized pluralist and democratic corporatist models: A comparison of election news coverage in Spain and Sweden. *International Communication Gazette* 70(6): 547–562.

Strömbäck, J., and Kaid, L. L. (Eds.). 2008. *The handbook of election news coverage around the world.* New York: Routledge.

Trenz, H.-J. 2004. Media coverage on European governance: Exploring the European public sphere in national quality newspapers. *European Journal of Communication* 19(3): 291–319.

Van Aelst, P., Shehata, A., and Van Dalen, A. 2010. Members of Parliament, equal competitors for media attention? An analysis of personal contacts between MPs and political journalists in five European countries. *Political Communication* 27(3): 310–325.

Van Aelst, P., and Walgrave, S. 2011. Minimal or massive? The political agenda setting power of the mass media according to different methods. *International Journal of Press Politics* 16(3): 295–313.

Van Dalen, A., and Van Aelst, P. 2012. Political journalists: Covering politics in the democratic corporatist media system. In D. Weaver and L. Wilnat (Eds.), *The global journalist in the 21st century* (pp. 511–525) London: Routledge.

Van Dalen, Albæk, E., and de Vreese, C. H. 2011. Suspicious minds: Explaining political cynicism amount political journalists in Europe. *European Journal of Communication* 26: 147–162.

Vliegenthart, R. 2012. Advanced strategies for data analysis: Opportunities and challenges of comparative data. In F. Esser, and T. Hanitzsch (Eds.), *Handbook of comparative communication research* (pp. 486–500). New York: Routledge.

Vliegenthart, R., Schuck, A., Boomgaarden, H. G., and de Vreese, C. H. 2008. News coverage and support for European integration 1990–2006. *International Journal of Public Opinion Research* 20(4): 415–439.

Voltmer, K. (Ed.). 2006. *Mass media and political communication in new democracies.* London: Routledge.

Voltmer, K. 2011. *The media in transitional democracies.* Cambridge, UK: Polity.

Ward, S. 2008. *Making a difference: A comparative view of the role of the Internet in election politics.* Lanham, MD: Rowman & Littlefield.

Weaver, D. H., and Wilhoit, C. 2006. *The American journalist in the 1990s*. Mahwah, NJ: Lawrence Erlbaum.

Weaver, D. H., and Wilnat, L. (Eds.). 2012. *The global journalist in the 21st century*. New York: Routledge.

Wessler, H., Peters, B., Brüggemann, M., Kleinen-von Königlow, K., and Sifft, S. 2008. *Transnationalization of public spheres*. Basingstoke, UK: Palgrave Macmillan.

CHAPTER 22

....

MEDIA RESPONSIVENESS IN TIMES OF CRISIS

....

CAROL WINKLER

CRISES occur when situations perceived to be outside the realm of the normal warrant consequential decision-making. Political, economic, social, environmental, and natural events can all qualify as crises. Here my focus is on studies of terrorism, war, natural disasters, transportation accidents, and environmental catastrophes, with particular attention on how the American media respond to such events occurring at home and abroad. Consistent with Stephen Cottle's view that crises are "conducted in and through news media as well as being communicated by it" (2009, 110), this chapter briefly describes the parameters of the media's influence and then concludes with an analysis of the sources, messages, and audiences related to the media's coverage of crisis events.

THE ROLE OF THE MEDIA

....

When faced with national events labeled as crises, the public focuses its attention on the media. In recent years most individuals have selected television as their primary medium of choice to learn about crises (Grusin and Utt, 2005, 10); now, the majority of Americans utilize digital formats to access their news (Pew Research Center, 2014, 6). Receiving limited or no information about crisis situations otherwise, members of the public frequently rely on the media to determine the events that will enter the public sphere and achieve issue salience (Soroka, 2003, 43). By choosing what catastrophic events to include, emphasize, or ignore within their scope of coverage, members of the news media play an influential role in defining crises. Media outlets both present the cause of the crises and identify a range of appropriate solutions. They identify the organization(s) responsible for addressing the crises and provide the public with criteria for assessing the effectiveness of the response. Typically, the nation's leadership reacts to the media's crisis coverage by tracking the mediated depictions of public sentiment associated with both the nature of the crisis and alternative response options. In certain contexts, leaders react by foreclosing or narrowing the range of acceptable responses (Robinson, 2002, 121–126).

MEDIA SOURCES IN TIMES OF CRISIS

While members of the media are making decisions about how to report crisis events, they maintain a symbiotic relationship with other entities that also seek to influence the substance and style of crisis coverage. Key factors include the government, the military, perceived enemies, corporations, and the public. Each vies to sway media reporting in accordance with its own interests. At times, framing goals of the competing groups converge; at others, one source dominates the media reporting (Entman, 2004, 1-22). While scholars generally agree that multiple sources shape how the press presents the news, they differ on both the extent to which and the conditions under which any group is capable of exerting substantial influence on crisis reporting.

In general, media outlets rely heavily on government officials as sources during times of crisis. With both unique access to and control over information, officials become central figures in the media's crisis coverage. While serving as sources, government spokespersons can appeal to wide audiences in an effort to advocate their own agendas and legitimize their agencies (Bennett, Lawrence, and Livingston, 2007, 1–6). When government officials disagree, the news media include their alternative views in their coverage. (For a review of studies on the indexing hypothesis, see Bennett and Cook, 1996, 371–481). The National Task Force on the Presidential Rhetoric in Times of Crisis provides a useful overview of how the nation's leadership deploys message strategies during crisis situations (Bostdorff et al., 2008, 361–368).

While some crises are natural occurrences, others are man-made. American governmental officials, having institutional authority over both classified information and response agencies, are key actors in the social construction of the nation's "threats." Various academic fields have offered explanations for the motivations behind leaders' desire to help shape media depictions of enemies. From the perspective of political science, Edelman (1988) explains that national leaders often construct enemies through nonempirically verifiable assumptions related to evil, warped, immoral, or pathological characters. Officials do so to coalesce allies, win political support for leaders, garner material advantages for those who construct them, mask true threats, and reinforce existing power relations (66–89). From the view of social psychology, Rousseau (2006) dismisses standard premises of both realism and liberalism by presenting the nation's threats as grounded in society's perceptions of "self" and "other," both concepts built on individuals' prior beliefs and values that remain open to manipulation or priming by both leaders and the media (210–212). From literary theory, Burke (1966) insists that humans, consumed by guilt caused by our capacities as symbol-using animals, seek order, invent the negative, and obtain "catharsis by scapegoating" (18). Taken together, the varied disciplinary perspectives offer persuasive explanations for why threat construction will remain an ongoing, important topic for political communication scholars.

When government officials attempt to influence depictions of crisis events, they typically do so through fairly predictable, identifiable public frameworks. In natural and man-made environmental disasters, for example, officials rely on the image restoration strategies of apology, excuses, and accounts (Benoit, 1995, 1–5). Two other event types—war and terrorism—have garnered particularly focused attention by scholars interested in how sources attempt to influence the media in times of crisis.

As US leaders justify the need to go to war, they typically employ rhetorical resources proven over time to persuade domestic audiences. For example, presidents have historically repeated three lines of argument or *topoi* that distinguish the United States from its enemies: force vs. freedom, irrational vs. rational, and aggression vs. defense (Ivie, 1980, 283–292). Official sources typically employ generic rhetorical appeals to address audience expectations during such periods by indicating that their decision to go to war was a product of thoughtful deliberation, by deploying narratives that function as the basis of argumentative claims, by exhorting the public to unify and commit to the mission, by warranting the use of commander-in-chief powers, and by increasing their use of strategic misrepresentation (Campbell and Jamieson, 2008, 221–252). Having framed American foreign policy for more than four decades, the strategic, metaphorical, and ideological perspectives prominent during the Cold War identified by Medhurst and colleagues are frequently utilized by the nation's leaders in their efforts to justify war (1990, 203–207). Not restricted to conventional attacks on US citizens or their property, official discourse on war also has applicability to other types of crises. As David Zarefsky in *President Johnson's War on Poverty: Rhetoric and History* reveals, the leader's use of the war metaphor as an approach for socially constructing crises helps garner support during the inception phase of policy campaigns. It can also, however, lead to the public's perception of failure of specific social policies and liberalism more broadly conceived when government officials cannot deliver on the expectations created by the war metaphor (1986, 1–275).

US leaders exercise wide latitude for enemy selection and response framing to justify counterterrorism policies, given the lack of an international, or even a national, consensus on the definition of the term "terrorism." Contemporary government officials adopt enemy labeling strategies that emphasize certain actors, acts of violence, regions, targets, and goals to advance their own foreign policy objectives, while deemphasizing others less productive or even counterproductive to their interests. They utilize modified Cold War or crime narratives based on presidential political party and employ ideographs to maintain a unified community of supporters while warranting wide response powers to the commander-in-chief (Winkler, 2006, 189–212; see also Aday in this volume). Examining governmental rhetoric about the post-9/11 war on terrorism, Zulaika reveals a self-fulfilling counterterrorism narrative that combines linear temporality with future and past references to turn allies into arch-terrorists. The narrative also characterizes nonresponse as defenselessness, promotes responses that foster more terrorism, and relies on a frame of political moralism that rationalizes immoral practices to achieve victory (2009, 207–213). Focusing on the visual rather than the verbal, Mitchell traces government involvement in the initial construction and subsequent cloning of iconic images used by the media during the war on terror to reawaken "figures of sovereignty and abjection in Christian, Jewish and Muslim traditions" (2011, xv).

Closely aligned with official sources but worthy of consideration on its own, the nation's military functions as a second key source that influences the media in times of crisis. Historically, the media and the military have negotiated an ongoing tension among operational security concerns, the need for sustained public support for the military's mission, and the public's right to know. As Brandenburg chronicles, the view of the military leaders during the 1991 Persian Gulf War shifted from a preference for press censorship (based on their perception that the media were responsible for turning support against the Vietnam War) to a recognition of the potential value of the media in achieving their own defense objectives (2005, 227–229). To strengthen its position via the media during crisis, the military began embedding reporters in field operations during the 2003 Iraq War. These journalists produced stories that were more positive about the military, more emotional about the troops, less graphic, and more episodic than those of their nonembedded counterparts (Fuchs, 2005, 199–201). Recent critical perspectives, such as the one offered by Entman, Livingston, and Kim decry the gaps between public statements of military officials and actual conditions on the ground (2009, 686–708). They also condemn the increasingly close relationship between the military and the media establishment. Der Derian, for example, describes the existence and growth of the military-industrial-media-entertainment complex and denounces its outcome as promoting "a vision of bloodless, humanitarian, hygienic wars" (2001, xv). Stahl concludes that while the media coverage during the 1991 Persian Gulf War produced spectacles that rendered citizens passive, the period since 9/11 has "featured certain institutional, political, technological, and culture shifts that began to describe the 'virtual citizen-soldier,' a subject invited to step into a fantasy of first-person, interactive war" (2010, 140). While the growing influence of the military in crisis coverage is virtually undisputed, the implications of that power remain relatively unexplored.

Those constructed as the nation's "enemies" represent a third source of influence on crisis media coverage. Particularly noteworthy in this category are those cast as "terrorists" who depend on the media to amplify their acts of violence, raise morale in their own ranks, and undercut their opposition's morale. Analyzing speeches, written texts, online media, and websites of Islamist extremists in particular, Halverson, Goodall, and Corman identify twelve recurrent master narratives used to frame these groups' messages (2011, 27–178). Examining groups and individuals labeled "terrorists" more broadly, Schmid and de Graaf were early adopters of the view that terrorism as a whole "can best be understood as a violent communication strategy" that attempts to change the broader public or enemy rather than the immediate victims (1982, 15). They explain how terrorists use the media to provide information, reduce inhibitions against violence, and motivate participation in the terrorists' causes (142). Notably, many terrorist groups' reliance on the live, immediate, and visual coverage of television to convey their messages expands their influence due to the media's attraction to events based on those same characteristics (Hoskins and O'Loughlin, 2007, 188–189).

Several content analyses of the coverage of terrorism attempt to discern which variables attract and sustain the attention of media outlets. Drawing a distinction between terrorists who are traditionally motivated and those who are media motivated, Weimann and Winn examine the "theatre of terrorism" by analyzing US network news coverage and nine global newspapers to document the impact of attack location, victims' identity, perpetrator's identity, types of media events, professional journalistic practices, media outlet, and terrorists' motivations on frequency of coverage (1994, 1–280). Similarly, Nacos's (2002) systematic examinations of media stories related to terrorism conclude that press coverage focuses on acts of political violence, underreports nonviolent anti- or counterterrorist measures, and ignores the reasons motivating terrorist attacks. Since 9/11, the media have reported more contextual stories. Media stories also employ infotainment formats, provide unlimited access to government officials, and fixate on terrorist leaders, granting them celebrity status and focusing disproportionate attention to their causes and threats of future violence (Nacos, 2002, 194).

However, recent decisions by US networks to censor terrorists' messages have resulted in a shift by such groups to Arab satellite networks and online websites to convey their messages. Weimann, noting a "proliferation of radical Islamic websites" (2006, 7), catalogs examples of terrorists' communication practices and instrumental uses of the Internet, discusses the Internet as a potential weapon of terrorists, and identifies solutions and their potential costs (49–242). To date, crisis scholars have not systematically examined the ways in which terrorists' message strategies may have changed or what their impact has been on potential recruits, funders, or the public.

Corporations are a fourth source that shapes crisis coverage. The most influential are those that acquire, consolidate, and directly control the news media. Simmons's work reveals that the five corporations that now control traditional US media outlets also dominate the most popular Internet websites. Reviewing the growing body of research about the outcomes of media concentration, she finds that consolidation leads to less local reporting, more critical reporting of local institutions, and more repackaged news stories (2010, 106, 110–112). The influence of the corporate elite on crisis reporting, however, extends beyond those entities that directly control media industry holdings. Pettigrew and Reber find that businesses vulnerable to claims of responsibility for crisis situations deploy spokespersons who appear frequently in crisis coverage (2010, 421). Englehardt, Sallot, and Springston provide a taxonomy of message strategies capable of restoring a corporation's reputation. Although the relative effectiveness of these approaches is context dependent, the strategies include mortification, ingratiation, nonexistence, distancing, shifting blame, and suffering (2004, 128–133). Klein critiques the role of corporate actors as "disaster capitalists," a label she employs to mark the use of the shock and chaos associated with catastrophes to drive otherwise controversial social and economic policy changes that benefit large, multinational corporations (2007, 175–176).

The public is the fifth and final source discussed here that influences the media during times of crisis. While victim groups can draw media attention for short periods of time, a more sustained public influence on crisis coverage stems from conspiracy theorists, who link fragments of information regarding crisis events in nonfalsifiable ways to supposedly divine the secret workings of powerful actors. Although early examinations, such as Hofstadter's "The Paranoid Style in American Politics" view conspiracy theorists as pathological (1964, 77–86), more recent scholarship, such as Fenster's *Conspiracy Theories: Secrets and Power in American Culture*, argues that they function as popular protesters by providing a voice to those who feel they lack either recognition or representation in the public realm due to the sublimation of civil society to the neoliberal state (1999, xiv–xv). Goodnight and Poulakos theorize the persuasive strategies of conspiracy theorists in a study that shows how such actors invert conventional rhetorical appeals by debunking the norms of evidentiary standards, source credibility, and expressed feelings (1981, 229–316). Public blogs and other methods of online communication provide first-person accounts of crisis events, distribute information regarding damage assessment and community relief/rescue efforts, assess responder effectiveness, and provide emotional support to those victimized. The reach and influence of these efforts remain largely open to debate, but the mainstream media's focus on the blogosphere suggests that such groups are positioned to gain influence.

MESSAGE STRATEGIES IN TIMES OF CRISIS

How the news media choose to craft their coverage is another key focus of crisis scholars. Although studies of online venues are on the rise, most of the published work analyzes newspaper and television coverage in an effort to identify the defining characteristics, recurrent patterns, and emergent trends in crisis reporting. While much of the scholarship concludes that the style and substance of media reporting utilize predictable frameworks that generalize across variable crisis contexts, other studies maintain that the media's message strategies are context specific.

To make the case that crisis reporting relies on a generally consistent, predictable framework, scholars have identified a limited set of media practices that characterize the core of the media's coverage of crisis events. In particular, crisis stories tend to be episodic, with a focus on "specific events or particular cases," rather than thematic, which "places political issues and events in some more general context" (Iyengar, 1991, 2, 26–45). They also tend to emphasize spectacles or "media events" written through the scripts of contests (i.e., "rule-governed battles of champions"), conquests (i.e., those that redress conflict, restore order, or institute change), or coronations (i.e., ceremonial celebrations of the hero) (Dayan and Katz, 1992, 25–27). At the same time, they routinely feature personal narratives of trauma and tragedy that create identification between those individuals directly affected by the crisis and those who experience it indirectly through media consumption. In the process, negative stereotypes that render minorities and the poor as savages, criminals, or worse tend to pervade crisis media coverage, with such groups frequently blamed for their own suffering (cf. Dyson in *Come Hell or*

High Water: Hurricane Katrina and the Color of Disaster [2006, 144–145]). Media message strategies reinforce a "politics of fear" through repetition of stories about crime and war, media logics that both are ideological and reflect entertainment formats, and event frames that generally stoke the need for more social control (Altheide, 2006, 210–217).

Crisis reporting, however, is far from monolithic, with the media's message foci changing even throughout the course of a single crisis event. Initially, media outlets disseminate available, fragmented information that upon more careful examination may or may not turn out to be accurate. Further, they speculate about the causes of the crisis and the likely response options. Over the duration of the crisis, the media tend to produce a more coherent narrative that corrects earlier inaccuracies and explains events within a broader context (Graber 2010, 115–118). Mistaken early media accounts reporting that Arab Muslims were responsible for the 2005 bombing of the Alfred P. Murrah Federal Building in Oklahoma City illustrate the point. Subsequent reports on Timothy McVeigh's interpretation of the federal intervention at the Waco compound helped explain who was responsible, the motivation behind the attack, and the broader context of domestic right-wing extremism.

Message strategies employed in crisis reporting also differ according to the media channel presenting the crisis coverage. So, for example, in their pioneering work *Nightly Horrors: Crisis Coverage by Television Network News*, Nimmo and Combs (1985) conclude that the three major networks presented distinct rhetorical visions in their crisis coverage of the 1978 Jonestown murder/suicides, the 1979 Three Mile Island nuclear plant meltdown, the 1979 crash of American Airlines Flight 191, the 1980 eruption of Mount St. Helen's, the 1979–1981 Iranian Hostage Crisis, and the 1982 Tylenol poisonings. Specifically, they found that ABC relied on a more subversive, sensationalist approach; CBS on a more factual style heavily dependent on expert opinion; and NBC on a more pluralistic, feature-oriented style (1985, 195–198). Recent comparative studies have examined the differing message strategies of cable newscasts, with a particular focus on CNN and the Fox News Channel. They also compare the crisis message strategies of online vs. more conventional media outlets, US media vs. regional and other global competitors, and economically challenged media outlets vs. those that are profitable.

Crisis messaging strategies also vary according to the crisis situation being reported. An and Gower (2009) demonstrate the approach by identifying five recurrent media frames. They conclude that the news media emphasized an attribution of responsibility frame in instances in which the actors had control and intentionality, but utilized a morality frame when the crisis was preventable. When organizational responsibility was present, however, the news media deployed an economic effects frame (107–112).

Recently, scholars of political communication have augmented the field's primary focus on text-based examinations of messages in crisis coverage with ones that examine the visual images contained in such stories. Zelizer's (2010) examination of US journalistic practice introduces the "about-to-die trope" employed repeatedly in crisis coverage of events such as wars, acts of terrorism, suicides, transportation accidents, and environmental disasters. She maintains that images of impending death, including ones in which death is presumed, possible, or certain, introduce the subjunctive voice ("as if" instead of "as is") in ways that stimulate viewers' imagination, emotion, and contingency (1–27). Zelizer's study provides key insights into how particular images in the news media's crisis coverage retain or expand their currency in the process of recirculation.

AUDIENCE EFFECTS IN TIMES OF CRISIS

Scholars agree that media coverage during times of crisis is influential because it satisfies a need in the audience. Various publics seek information, reassurance, and protection when events fall outside the realm of the ordinary. Whether explicitly stated or implicitly assumed, less agreement exists on the factors that generate these audience needs.

The relationship between the audience's need for information and crisis media coverage is a recurrent topic of crisis scholarship. Studies document the public's acceptance of factual inaccuracies initially disseminated by the nation's leadership and reinforced through the media's portrayals of crisis events (Bennett, Lawrence, and Livingston, 2007, 131–164). Researchers have also explored how media framing during crisis periods leads to distorted audience perspectives. Jenkins (2003), for example, documents how interactions among interest groups, the government, and the media have led to both the news media and the broader popular culture misrepresenting terrorism in many ways. These include underestimating the threat from domestic terrorism; producing sympathy for Israeli, rather than Arab, victims; and drawing attention away from many of the more potent, dangerous groups (143–157).

Crisis scholars also examine linkages between news coverage and the audience's need for reassurance. Hoskins and O'Loughlin (2007) acknowledge that the news media's repetition of crisis stories offers the comfort of the known during such chaotic events. Moreover, they note that the media's adherence to professional standards of sanitized terrorism and war coverage minimizes public alarm (188–189). Other studies are more critical of the media's role. For instance, Meek maintains that the media's repeated emphasis on the need for empathy and human solidarity renders the audience a shocked, passive body particularly vulnerable to manipulation (2010, 195). In a similar vein, Cloud stresses that the therapeutic frame treats audience members as clients, not citizens, and silences those who disagree with the government's view, such as antiwar protesters, by marginalizing them into mere victims of personal traumas (1998, 159).

Associations between the public's need for protection and media crisis coverage also attract the attention of the scholarly community. Altheide (2006) was among the first to theorize the ways in which the media heighten public fear during times of crisis. He conceptualizes a "politics of fear" that allows decision-makers to capitalize on the public's assumptions about danger in order to justify social controls. At the same time, he insists that the politics of fear not only operates during times of crises but also "gradually inform[s] policy and everyday-life behavior, even if there are occasional bouts of resistance." However, in Altheide's view, this strategy needs to be carefully calibrated. "The longer fear is promoted," he notes," the less effective it is. . . . It cannot endure indefinitely; for it to be effective, there must be respites but not a predictable rhythm." He cautions, however, that decision-makers can circumvent the public's tolerance level by simply removing fear from the public arena for certain periods of time (2006, 208–209).

The community of crisis scholars varies considerably in what it considers the central factors that produce audiences' needs. Some treat the crisis situation itself as the primary motivator behind the public's need to understand the nature, extent, causes, and solutions of such events, with the media positioned as the entity best able to collect and convey relevant information quickly (e.g., Grusin and Utt, 2005, 10). Others argue that the predilections of particular target audiences prompt the media's behavior during crises. For them, the media are simply providing what their target audiences want, as illustrated in Iskandar's conclusion that during the Iraq War, Fox News Channel (FNC) tapped into "a large market for opinionated news with a patriotic twist" and that "FNC's successful formula is one that most US networks have emulated to capitalize on audience preferences" (2005, 162). Finally, many crisis scholars maintain that the reporting community itself is responsible for creating the public's needs. So, for example, Robinson's *The CNN Effect* suggests that US leaders have historically reacted to how they perceive the public would respond to empathy-framed reporting about international crises (2002, 128). (For an alternative view see Aday in this volume.) Similarly, Moeller identifies the media, with their heavy saturation of disaster coverage, as a key contributor to public boredom about global crisis events (1998, 10–11).

FUTURE IMPLICATIONS FOR STUDIES OF CRISIS MEDIA COVERAGE

The rapidly changing media environment will continue to transform crisis media coverage. Increased globalization and dramatic advances in telecommunication technology dictate that media sources, messages, and audiences are far from static. Due to their mutual dependence and interactivity, changes in any one have implications for the others.

During times of crisis, media sources will continue both to work together and to compete to advance their own interests. While the symbiotic relationships among government officials, the public, and the media have dominated previous crisis scholarship, comparatively less attention has focused on the military, including the sharp rise in privatized, spin-off companies regularly contracting with it and other government agencies. Those cast as the nation's "enemies" also deserve renewed attention, given the sharp rise in terrorist websites documented by Salem, Reid, and Chen (2008, 605–626). Because relevant multinational corporations, including regional media competitors, have their own interests and seek influence over crisis media coverage, they too warrant further study. While el-Nawawy and Iskandar's (2003) research on Al-Jazeera is a good first step, the network's recent channel acquisitions and its rapidly changing political landscape invite a rethinking of past work.

The standard features of media messages during times of crisis also warrant reconsideration. The introduction of affordable and readily available Web 2.0 applications has transformed speeches, news coverage, and other popular culture artifacts into source material for re-edited, recontextualized messages that reach online audiences. While Iyengar (1991) has documented that crisis news coverage in certain contexts is episodic in its first instantiation, that same coverage may now be included as part of one or more broader thematic treatments by other voices both during or in the aftermath of the crisis. Terrorists, for example, embed news clips from traditional media outlets in the video messages they distribute through YouTube, their websites, and regional media outlets. Similarly, Dayan and Katz's (1992) media events can be recast as the subject of parody in ways that promote competing social constructions of rules, standards for success, and hero veneration.

Future studies should also examine differences in crisis message strategies in relation to new media formats. Just as the audience standards for eloquence changed when the leaders spoke through television rather than through radio or, before that, directly to their audiences (Jamieson, 1988, 67–89), new media may change the ways in which leaders deploy rhetoric as they create or address crises. The impact of merging media platforms on the development of message strategies has received too little scholarly attention. The victims' narratives and media spectacles, to name but a few, may also function differently across unique media platforms.

Further, audience studies during times of crisis warrant additional scrutiny. Altheide's politics of fear, as well as Meek's and Cloud's discussion of therapeutic frames, each conclude that media framing renders the public vulnerable to social control and manipulation. Winkler's (2006, 83–95) study of terrorism discourse, however, reveals that the nation's leaders have a more nuanced approach for gauging public acceptance of policy change during times of crisis, including the probable time frame they have to exercise policy latitude before experiencing public criticism, the parameters of change the public is willing to accept, and the underlying causes of the public's sense of powerlessness that are available as resources for the officials' use. Future studies of media frames in times of crisis should address these and other factors that contribute to the constraints and opportunities for social change.

Audience studies should also attend more carefully to population subgroups during trying times. Iskandar's (2005) study of the differing niche audiences attracted to the Fox News Channel and CNN is an approach that bears repeating in other contexts that also have subgroups functioning as important audiences of their own. Understanding the informational needs of the audience by income level, for example, might have helped prevent the high death toll during Katrina.

Unanswered Questions

To conclude, scholars of media responsiveness during times of crisis should maintain their focus on media sources, messages, and audiences. Research on sources should continue to examine the full range of actors attempting to frame the crisis message, what interests they have within and related to the crisis environment, what strategies they use in pursuit of their goals, and what environmental factors affect their relative influence. Research on messages should examine trends in the media's framing and how recirculation alters the original framing, with particular attention to visual stills, moving image clips, and verbal messages in emerging media environments. Finally, audience studies of the media messaging during crises should more critically examine the impact of domestic media strategies on niche and global audiences, with a special focus on the precise means used to legitimize and counter social controls.

References

Altheide, D. L. 2006. *Terrorism and the politics of fear.* Lanham, MD: Alta Mira.

An, S., and Gower, K. K. 2009). How do the news media frame crises? A content analysis of crisis news coverage. *Public Relations Review, 35*(2): 107-112.

Bennett, W. L., Lawrence, R. G., and Livingston, S. 2007. *When the press fails: political power and the news media from Iraq to Katrina.* Chicago: University of Chicago Press.

Benoit, W. L. 1995. *Accounts, excuses, and apologies: A theory of image restoration strategies.* Albany: State University of New York Press.

Bostdorff, D. M., Carcasson, M., Farrell, J. M., Ivie, R. L., Kiewe, A., and Smith, K. B. 2008. Report of the National Task Force on Presidential Rhetoric in Times of Crisis. In J. A. Aune and M. J. Medhurst (Eds.), *The prospect of presidential rhetoric* (pp. 355–378). College Station: Texas A&M Press.

Brandenburg, H. 2005. Journalists embedded in culture: War stories as political strategy. In L. Artz and Y. R. Kamilipour (Eds.), *Bring 'em on: Media and politics in the Iraq war* (pp. 225-238). Lanham, MD: Rowman and Littlefield.

Burke, K. 1966. *Language as symbolic action: Essays on life, literature, and method.* Berkeley: University of California Press.

Campbell, K. K., and Jamieson, K. H. 2008. *Presidents creating the presidency: Deeds done in words.* Chicago: University of Chicago Press.

Cloud, D. L. 1998. *Control and consolation in American culture and politics: Rhetoric of therapy.* London: Sage.

Cottle, S. 2009. *Global crisis reporting: Journalism in the global age.* New York: Open University Press.

Dayan, D., and Katz, E. 1992. *Media events: The live broadcasting of history.* Cambridge, MA: Harvard University Press.

Der Derian, J. 2001. *Virtuous war: Mapping the military-industrial-media-entertainment network.* Boulder, CO: Westview.

Dyson, M. E. 2006. *Come hell or high water: Hurricane Katrina and the color of disaster.* Cambridge, MA: Basic Civitas.

Edelman, M. 1988. *Constructing the political spectacle*. Chicago: University of Chicago Press.

El-Nawawy, M., and Iskandar, A. 2003. *Al-Jazeera: The story of the network that is rattling governments and redefining modern journalism*. Cambridge, MA: Westview Press.

Englehardt, K. J., Sallot, L. M., and Springston, J. K. (2004). Compassion without blame: Testing the accident decision flow chart with the crash of ValuJet Flight 592. *Journal of Public Relations Research*, 16(2): 127–156.

Entman, R. M. 2004. *Projections of power: Framing news, public opinion, and U.S. foreign policy*. Chicago: University of Chicago Press.

Entman, R. M., Livingston, S., and Kim, J. 2009. Doomed to repeat: Iraq news 2002–2007. *American Behavioral Scientist*, 52(5): 680–708.

Fenster, M. 1999. Conspiracy theories: Secrecy and power in American culture. Minneapolis: University of Minnesota Press.

Fuchs, C. 2005. The mass media, politics, and warfare. In L. Artz and Y. R. Kamalipour (Eds.), *Bring 'em on: Media and politics in the Iraq war* (pp. 189–207). New York: Rowman & Littlefield.

Goodnight, G. T., and Poulakos, J. 1981. Conspiracy rhetoric: From pragmatism to fantasy in public discourse. *The Western Journal of Speech Communication*, 45, 299–316.

Graber, D. A. 2010. *Mass media and American politics*. 8th ed. Washington, DC: Congressional Quarterly Press.

Grusin, E. K., and Utt, S. H. (Eds.). 2005. *Media in an American risis: Studies of September 11, 2001*. Lanham, MD: University Press of America.

Halverson, S. R., Goodall, H. L., Jr., and Corman, S. R. 2011. *Master narratives of Islamist extremism*. New York: Palgrame Macmillan.

Hofstadter, R. 1964. *Anti-intellectualism in American life*. New York: Alfred A. Knopf and Random House.

Hoskins, A. and O'Loughlin B. 2007. *Television and terror: Conflicting times and the crisis of news discourse*. New York: Palgrave MacMillan.

Iskandar, A. 2005. "The great American bubble": Fox News Channel, the "mirage" of objectivity, and the isolation of American public opinion. In L. Artz and Y. R. Kamalipour (Eds.), *Bring 'em on: Media and politics in the Iraq war* (pp. 155–174). Lanham: Rowman & Littlefield.

Ivie, R. L. 1980. Images of savagery in American justifications for war. *Communication Monographs* 47: 279–291.

Iyengar, S. 1991. *Is anyone responsible?* Chicago: University of Chicago Press.

Jamieson, K. H. 1988. *Eloquence in an electronic age: The transformation of political speechmaking*. New York: Oxford University Press.

Jenkins, P. 2003. *Images of terror: What we can and can't know about terrorism*. New York: Walter de Gruyter.

Klein, N. 2007. The shock doctrine: The rise of disaster capitalism. New York: Macmillan.

Medhurst, M. J., Ivie, R. L., Wander, P., and Scott, R. L. 1990. *Cold War rhetoric: Strategy, metaphor, and ideology*. New York: Greenwood.

Meek, A. 2010. *Trauma and media: Theories, histories & images*. New York: Routledge.

Mitchell, W. J. T. 2011. *Cloning terror: The war of images, 911 to the present*. Chicago: University of Chicago Press.

Nacos, B. L. 2002. *Mass mediated terrorism: The central role of the media in terrorirsism and counterterrorism*. Lanham, MD: Rowman & Littlefield.

Nimmo, D., and Combs, J. E. 1985. *Nightly horrors: Crisis coverage in teleivsion network news*. Knoxville: University of Tennessee Press.

Pettigrew, J. E., and Reber, B. H. 2010. The new dynamic in corporate media relations: How Fortune 500 companies are using virtual press rooms to engage the press. *Journal of Public Relations Research*, 22(4): 404–428.

Pew Research Center. 2014, March. State of the news media 2014: Key indicators in media and news. Retrieved from http://www.journalism.org/files/2014/03/Key-Indicators-in-Media-and-News-2014.pdf

Robinson, P. 2002. *The CNN effect: The myth of news, foreign policy, and intervention.* New York: Routledge.

Rousseau, D. L. 2006. *Identifying threats and threatening identifies: The social construction of realism and liberalism.* Stanford, CA: Stanford University Press.

Salem, A., Reid, E., Chen, H. 2008. Multimedia content coding and analysis: Unraveling the content of jihadi extremist groups. *Studies in Conflict and Terrorism* 31(7): 605–626.

Schmid, A. P., and de Graaf, J. 1982. *Violence as communication: Insurgent terrorism and the Western news media.* London: Sage.

Soroka, S. N. 2003. Media, public opinion, and foreign policy. *Harvard International Journal of Press/Politics* 8: 27–48.

Stahl, R. 2010. *Militainment, Inc.: War, media, and popular culture.* New York: Routledge.

Weimann, G. 2006. *Terror on the Internet: The new arena, the new challenges.* Washington, DC: United States Institute of Peace6.

Weimann, G., and Winn, C. 1994. *The theatre of terror: Mass media and international terrorism.* New York: Longman.

Winkler, C. 2006. *In the name of terrorism: Presidents on political violence in the post-World War II era.* Albany: State University of New York Press.

Zarefsky, D. 1986. *President Johnson's War on Poverty: Rhetoric and history.* Tuscaloosa: University of Alabama.

Zelizer, B. 2010. *About to die: How news images move the public.* New York: Oxford Press.

Zulaika, J. 2009. *Terrorism: The self-fulfilling prophecy.* Chicago: University of Chicago Press.

CHAPTER 23

....

THE US MEDIA, FOREIGN POLICY, AND PUBLIC SUPPORT FOR WAR

....

SEAN ADAY

POLITICAL communication scholars have long been interested in the role of the news media in shaping and reporting on the foreign policy of the United States and how that coverage (or lack of it) influences domestic public opinion and policymakers' priorities and decisions. That said, the amount of scholarly attention to this area has increased markedly in the last twenty-five years, and—undoubtedly owing to the United States waging two wars (and a "global war on terror") in the aftermath of the 9/11 terrorist attacks—the area has seen an even greater quantity and quality of theoretical, empirical, and qualitative contributions over the last ten years. Still, in many ways, it would be fair to say that political communication scholars' understanding of media, foreign policy, and war is still in its relative infancy, certainly as compared with other areas such as American politics, domestic public opinion, social movements, and media influence generally. Yet as the area has grown, it has become clear that what scholars have learned about media coverage, source-journalist dynamics, and media influence sometimes but not always maps from the domestic to foreign policy domains.

With this in mind, this chapter focuses on the relationship between news media and US foreign policy, with a particular emphasis on war—a subset of the latter—since that has been a concern of a disproportionate amount of scholarship in the area. Although interest in this topic goes back arguably to the roots of mass communication research, this chapter focuses on the explosion of research of the last quarter century. In particular, it emphasizes current theoretical and empirical approaches with an eye toward delineating what former Defense Secretary Donald Rumsfeld memorably called the "known unknowns."

GENERAL THEORIES OF US NEWS MEDIA AND FOREIGN POLICY

Over the years, mass communication researchers have consistently found that mainstream media tend to reinforce dominant sociocultural norms and values, confer status upon that which is covered (and thus relegate to "nonevents" that which is not), and make decisions about coverage that are heavily routinized and source-driven (Fishman, 1980; Gans, 1979; Gitlin, 1980; Katz and Lazarsfeld, 1955; Klapper, 1960; Lazarsfeld and Merton, 1948; Sigal, 1973). These conclusions are, if anything, even more true when it comes to media and foreign affairs, and especially when it comes to war coverage. In addition, severe budget cutbacks in US news divisions since the early 1980s have led to a drastic reduction in the amount of international news available to American audiences via the mainstream media (Auletta, 2001; Fenton, 2005; Pew, 2011). In sum, even more than domestic policy coverage, foreign policy tends to be (1) ethnocentric (e.g., employing racial stereotypes of enemies [Dower, 1987]), (2) elite-driven, (3) uncritical (especially in the run-up to and early stages of war), and (4) episodic (usually covering other countries when senior White House officials travel to or otherwise prioritize them). In arguing for a central role for media in the study of foreign policy and public opinion, Baum and Potter (2008) echo others in suggesting that perhaps the press, for a variety of market-based and other institutional reasons, isn't particularly well-suited to performing the critical task of informing citizens about international affairs. Put another way, in the foreign policy domain the press is far less likely to adequately fulfill its Fourth Estate function than it is in the domestic policy arena.

Perhaps the most important foundational political communication theory in contemporary research on media coverage of foreign policy is Bennett's indexing hypothesis, which posits that media coverage of foreign affairs, especially foreign policy crises (e.g., war), tends to be "indexed" to the range of elite opinion and priorities (Bennett, 1990, 1994; Bennett et al., 2007). Bennett focuses particularly on the executive and legislative branches. For him, those in the White House and Senate are the most important actors because of their constitutionally derived authority in foreign policy as well as the former's command of "the bully pulpit" and expansion of power in the foreign affairs arena in the post-WWII "Imperial Presidency" era (Entman and Page, 1994; Schlesinger, 1973). Indexing draws especially on the consistent finding (see especially Sigal [1973] and Hallin [1986]) that journalism is source-driven, with media tending to ape the frames and agendas of elites (especially elected officials). Bennett argues that elites are often either in consensus about foreign policy objectives and options (especially in wartime) or in enough agreement that the range of debate, regardless of how apparently contentious it sometimes may seem, is actually relatively constricted. Alternative approaches—especially those that favor diplomacy, are offered by antiwar protesters or challenge prevailing cultural and policy norms (e.g., Cold War assumptions in the postwar era, or counterterrorism after 9/11)—are given short shrift in policy debates and media coverage (Entman et al., 2009; Entman and Page, 1994; Gitlin, 1980; Wolfsfeld, 2004). The indexing hypothesis does, however, argue that if a foreign policy crisis stays on the policy, public, and media agendas for a prolonged period, a combination of emerging elite dissensus and journalistic norms incentivizing novel story lines (Gans, 1979) will open a window for these alternative approaches to be aired in the press.

While accepting the basic premises of the indexing hypothesis, Entman (2003, 2004, 2006) has offered an expanded "cascade network activation model" to explain media coverage of foreign affairs; this model synthesizes a wide variety of literature across multiple domains, most notably indexing, hegemony, and social cognition. Consistent with its waterfall metaphor, Entman's model envisions an elite-driven chain of influence, with the White House as the prime mover, its frames and agendas "cascading" down and setting the terms of debate for a secondary level that includes Congress and other official elites, before flowing to a third level that includes the media, and, finally, a fourth in which public opinion is shaped by the messages filtered through the first three stages of the process.

Entman's model builds on the indexing hypothesis in several ways. First, it more explicitly describes the frame contestation that occurs at various levels of the cascade and ultimately shapes the message environment to which the public is exposed through media coverage. Second, it proposes "feedback loops," at each stage of the cascade, in which this frame contestation is altered or otherwise accounted for (e.g., through rebuttal) by actors in earlier stages. So, for example, congressional debate in 2009 on the closing of the detention center at Guantanamo Bay forced the Obama White House to modify its position repeatedly. Similarly, public opinion shapes media coverage and elite discourse, primarily owing to the surveillance function served by opinion polling. Finally, Entman's model doesn't assume that all messages are created equal. Rather, he argues that the effectiveness of messages and frames, especially those from the White House that start a cascade, will depend on, among other things, the communication skills of elites and institutions (e.g., the White House) and their cultural resonance with audiences. The latter point is particularly significant: Entman is drawing on the persuasion and hegemony literature simultaneously to argue that, for example, presidents will be most effective at dominating the framing environment if their messages are consistent with the values and priorities of the public and less so the more they deviate (or can be framed as deviating from) those values.

Others have proposed models of media-elite interaction in foreign affairs that also draw on, while modifying, the indexing hypothesis. Wolfsfeld's (2004) politics-media-politics (PMP) principle, for example, proposes that the political process—debate, consensus, dissensus, etc.—shapes media coverage, which itself then alters the political discourse. The PMP principle posits active media that engage with the political process rather than serving as passive receptacles for elite frames. Wolfsfeld et al. have contrasted the PMP principle with cascading activation by arguing that the former is more dynamic.

Finally, Baum and Groeling (2010) propose a "strategic bias" theory of media-elite-public interaction in which the well-established press bias toward conflict leads the news media to present a distorted image of the foreign policy debate, focusing exces-sively on elite disagreement (what they refer to as "opinion indexing") and negative news. This, they argue, leads audiences to filter news about foreign affairs primarily through the prism of partisan predispositions, led by elite cues. Here they are drawing from and adding to a long literature in political science and political communication from multiple domains, emphasizing the importance of partisan predispositions and elite messaging in helping citizens to process complex policy information heuristically (e.g., Berinsky, 2007; Brody, 1991; Zaller, 1992). Their argument, however, goes a step further by positing an "elasticity of reality" dynamic in which presidents' ability to con-trol the framing environment in wartime ebbs over time as events and partisan divi-sions materialize. This parallels an argument made by Aday (2008) that presidents have "framing windows" during the course of a military intervention that are "bigger" (i.e., their frames influence a wider range of the public) and can overwhelm partisan predis-positions during the establishing phase and early stages of a crisis (e.g., the large number of Democrats who supported President Bush after 9/11) but shrink as events and elite dissensus—transmitted through the media—combine with partisanship to play a bigger role in shaping public opinion.

WAR COVERAGE

Perhaps the best-developed area of interest for political communication scholars who study media and foreign affairs has to do with the coverage of war, arguably the most important aspect of foreign policy. The literature in this area has been primarily con-cerned with two phenomena: (1) casualty coverage and (2) public opinion rallies. Both topics can be said to have their roots in *War, Presidents, and Public Opinion* (1973), the seminal book by John Mueller, that uses data primarily from the Vietnam and Korean wars to argue that publics will rally behind presidents who go to war, but that these ral-lies will eventually fade and support for intervention dissipate as home-country casual-ties mount over time—something known as the casualty aversion hypothesis. In some elite quarters, this has been combined with a view that the United States lost the Vietnam War not only because casualties mounted but also because television turned the conflict into a "living room war" that exacerbated the public's casualty sensitivity by making the war's human costs more vivid.

Hallin (1986) has written what remains the most important and thorough debunking of some of these assumptions while also providing a guide to trends in US war cover-age across conflicts. In his influential book *The Uncensored War*, Hallin uses extensive content analyses of media coverage of Vietnam to demonstrate that the press adopted a largely *uncritical* view of the war—which typically parroted official US military and policymaker frames, assumptions, and agendas—until prominent members of Congress began questioning the war's progress in 1967 and the Tet Offensive in early

1968. Furthermore, despite the image of a living room war, casualty images were few and far between until after Tet.

Hallin's corrective about Vietnam War coverage illuminates the nature of US war coverage and what accounts for changes in that coverage. First—as historians, political communication scholars, and others have shown across virtually all US wars— media coverage follows a familiar pattern that is invariably uncritical of official claims and arguments (especially those emanating from the White House) in the run up to and early stages of war (see for instance, Campbell [2000] and Nasaw [2000] regarding the Spanish-American War; Fussell [1989] and Pyle [1979] regarding WWII; Bennett [1990] on Nicaragua; Dickson [1995] about the invasion of Panama; Hallin [1991], Kellner [1992], Mermin [1999], and Newhagen [1994], regarding the Persian Gulf War; and Aday et al. [2005], Katovsky and Carlson [2003], and others regarding the wars in Iraq and Afghanistan). Second, and relatedly, coverage of casualties generally and of American casualties (especially those killed in action) specifically is scant to nonexistent until well into a war (if then) and certainly has never been presented in the kind of vivid and consistent manner presumed by the "living room war" metaphor (Aday, 2005). Third, contrary to the conventional wisdom in some circles that presumes media to be biased against war, in order for coverage to turn negative, certain preconditions must be met, the most important being (1) elite dissensus and (2) demonstrably and enduringly negative events on the ground. The former is consistent with findings discussed earlier regarding elite-driven news, while the latter show that reality itself may eventually influence press coverage. Still, even then, coverage may be more positive than facts on the ground would warrant (Aday, 2010a; Zaller and Chiu, 1996).

In the Vietnam case, for instance, congressional angst about the progress of the war began gaining momentum in the year before Tet (notably with prominent senators such as William Fulbright). This elite cueing is an important precursor to tonal changes in press coverage (Baum and Groeling, 2010; Bennett, 1990; Hallin, 1986). Similarly, Aday, Cluverius and Livingston (2005) have shown that elite cues about victory in Iraq, combined with a general tendency toward patriotic press coverage and cultural-historic signifiers (e.g., the fall of the Berlin Wall and statues of Lenin), led US media not only to breathlessly cover the fall of Saddam Hussein's statue in Firdos Square on April 9, 2003, as if it represented the triumphant end of the Iraq War but also American television networks to drastically reduce their coverage of the war in the week following the statue's fall.

A related finding among scholars of media and war is that political leaders often use culturally resonant historical metaphors to advocate military intervention, with a bias toward references evoking the "good war"—World War II. These analogies then receive prominent airing in the press (Aday and Kim, 2008; Dorman and Livingston, 1994). Prominent among them are comparisons analogizing the enemy leader to Adolf Hitler and his government to that of the Nazis; also comparing opponents of intervention to Neville Chamberlain and/or accusing such opponents of "appeasement" (Jervis, 1976;

Khong, 1992; Petraeus, 1987). Given the well-established finding that media coverage echoes elite framing, particularly in *support* of intervention when urged by the White House, it is not surprising that these metaphors also tend to dominate press coverage in the establishing phase and early stages of a war (Dorman and Livingston, 1994). Aday and Kim (2008), for example, found these frames to be prevalent in coverage of the Iraq War and, in experiments, more persuasive than Vietnam counterframes.

MEDIA-MILITARY RELATIONS

These findings point to the importance of military-media relations in understanding war coverage and the corresponding source-journalist dyad (Aukofer and Lawrence, 1995). The conventional wisdom is that up to Vietnam, the press was largely patriotic and supplicant to the military, but that it has been reflexively critical since. This is only partly true. Through Vietnam, journalists were allowed on the front lines with US forces but, especially in the twentieth century, their copy was censored by the military, ostensibly for operational security reasons but in fact for more propagandistic aims (Fussell, 1989; see also Prochnau, 2005). Most notably, images of dead US GIs were almost entirely forbidden in American media in the first two World Wars. This era of "postcensorship" was replaced beginning with the invasion of Grenada in 1983 with one of "precensorship." Following the lead of British media management in the Falklands/Malvinas War a year earlier and spurred by an institutional belief among many in the military and the Republican-controlled White House that the press had played a role in losing Vietnam (Petraeus, 1987; Wilson, 2001), reporters were kept away from the battle and left on boats to cover the invasion via press conference. Although this media management strategy raised hackles among the press and many critics, it also allowed the military to control the message environment and resulted in uncritical coverage of conflicts ranging from Grenada to Panama to the Persian Gulf War (Hallin, 1991; Sharkey, 2001).

This policy changed, however, with the wars in Afghanistan and Iraq, when the Pentagon switched to a modified version of the postcensorship model called embedding. The decision to attach journalists to specific units stemmed in large part from a belief that in the twenty-first-century global media environment, information wars were important components of an intervention's success (Katovsky and Carlson, 2003). Critics of the program accused journalists of being "in bed" with the military, and many reporters refused to be embedded, choosing instead to roam on their own (becoming "unilateral" journalists, a term these reporters loathed). Scholarly studies of embedded coverage show mixed results regarding whether the coverage was indeed more slanted than would be expected. Pfau and colleagues, for instance, found evidence of pro-American bias in embedded reportage (2004). Using different measures of tone, Aday, Livingston, and Hebert (2005) didn't find significant differences in the level of patriotic coverage but did find that unilateral reporters showed more casualty images in broadcast news.

PUBLIC OPINION ABOUT FOREIGN POLICY

Before turning to the question of the effects of exposure to media coverage of foreign affairs, it may be helpful to clarify the nature of public opinion about foreign policy generally. For a variety of reasons, studies consistently show that the American public knows even less about foreign affairs generally and foreign policy specifically than it does about domestic issues, although there is debate about whether citizens still make basically rational if not fully informed decisions about foreign policy (Delli Carpini, and Keeter, 1997; Holsti, 2004; Jentleson, 1992; Page and Shapiro, 1992). The public is particularly dependent on media coverage, elite messaging, and other informational cognitive shortcuts (especially ethnocentrism [Kinder and Kam, 2009]) to inform them about matters with which they are highly unlikely to have either personal experience or to know people who do (Althaus, 2003; Brody, 1991; Krosnick and Kinder, 1990; Sniderman et al., 1991; Zaller, 1992). Aldrich et al.'s (2006) summary of this literature concludes that there appears to be something of a scholarly consensus that people hold fairly stable foreign policy views that drive judgments (e.g., voting).

This has been shown to be particularly true in foreign policy crises (Boyle et al. 2004), when people seek out information from a variety of sources. Baum (2003) has shown that these include "soft news" venues such as entertainment shows, and that such media are relatively good at informing at least some viewers about basic facts regarding the crisis—a finding consistent with other literature showing that people learn about war from media (Pan et al., 1994). Yet any learning is going to be inevitably constrained by several factors, including the fact that crisis coverage (especially regarding war) is typically consensus-based and has not been preceded by consistent international coverage that might provide a store of available foreign policy-related information with which to contextualize and interpret media and elite messaging. As discussed above, press coverage of matters outside America's borders has become vanishingly rare since the early 1980s. This, coupled with the elite-driven nature of foreign coverage, leads to a public that is especially likely to base its foreign affairs opinions on elite cues filtered through the media.

There are three major implications of this set of patterns. First, because foreign policy beliefs are more likely to be based on heuristic information processing than perhaps some domestic policy issue positions are, social cognition research tells us that they are likely to be less stable and more susceptible to persuasion (Eagly and Chaiken, 1993). Since party heuristics are among those most commonly utilized for policy opinion formation, partisan elites are particularly likely to influence public opinion on international affairs. For instance, Berinsky (2007) and Berinsky and Druckman (2007) found that people's opinions about the Iraq War several years into it could be explained primarily by their attitudes toward President Bush. Berinsky (2009) has found similar dynamics at play in looking at public opinion during earlier wars dating back to WWII.

Second, because the range of elite foreign policy opinion is limited in general and more likely to be in consensus during international crises (Bennett, 1990; Mueller, 1973), media coverage can accentuate and contribute to public opinion rallies in support of White House policies (Althaus and Coe, 2011; Baum, 2002; Jordan and Page, 1992; Lian and Oneal, 1993; McLeod et al., 1994; Oneal and Bryan, 1995; Zaller, 1992) and make citizens especially susceptible to and dependent on elite messages filtered through the media (Ball-Rokeach and DeFleur, 1976; Hindman, 2004). One implication of this can be that during major foreign policy crises, trust in political and media institutions is heightened (Brewer et al., 2003, 2004). Gross et al. (2004), for example, found such heightened institutional trust following the 9/11 attacks to be associated with exposure to media coverage of the attacks and their aftermath (when, importantly, politicians gave many indications of elite consensus).

Finally, a depleted foreign affairs information environment makes citizens particularly susceptible to misinformation—a phenomenon that can take several forms. For instance, the otherwise reasonable assumption by citizens that politicians take the time to be informed about foreign policy, even crises, and base their votes and opinions on that information rather than partisanship or other political calculations, may not always be true, as the Iraq and Vietnam cases demonstrated. In addition, factual inaccuracies endorsed by elites and broadcast through the media are not only likely to be accepted by the public but to persist even after their debunking (Kull et al., 2003).

EFFECTS OF EXPOSURE TO WAR COVERAGE

The question of what role media play in generating or depressing public support for war has been of increasing interest to political communication and political science scholars over the past twenty years. In particular, Mueller's (1973, 1994, 2005) casualty aversion hypothesis has been fleshed out and contextualized by recent work that has challenged or modified its propositions (Baum, 2003; Gartner and Segura, 2000; Gartner et al., 2004; Morgan and Campbell, 1991; Reiter and Stam, 2002; Russett, 1990). The preponderance of work in this area, however, has found scant support for the casualty aversion hypothesis, at least as proposed by Mueller (Burk, 1999; Dauber, 2001; Eichenberg, 2005; Feaver and Gelpi, 2004; Gartner and Segura, 1998; Gelpi, Feaver, and Reifler, 2005; Jentleson, 1992; Jentleson and Britton, 1998; Klarevas, 2002). Instead, casualties are seen as being contextualized by citizens depending on other variables, such as cost-benefit analysis (Lacquement, 2004), elite consensus or dissensus (Berinsky, 2007, 2009; Berinsky and Druckman, 2007; Larson, 1996), the nature of the conflict (e.g., whether it addresses a serious threat to the United States or is more of a humanitarian intervention) (Jentleson 1992; Jentleson and Britton 1998) and whether the intervention is seen by the public as being likely to succeed and as righteous (Gelpi et al., 2005/2006, 2009; Feaver and Gelpi, 2004).

Still, while the emerging consensus among scholars is that casualties alone may not be the most important determinant of public support for military action, most empirical tests of the casualty aversion hypothesis do not posit media exposure as an important independent or intervening variable in determining public support for military interventions (Berinsky, 2007; Gelpi et al., 2009; Jentleson, 1992). Yet it seems reasonable to ask, for example, why the public sees a conflict as winnable, righteous, or in the interests of the United States (all variables that political scientists have argued affect public support for intervention). For example, the Vietnam and Iraq Wars were initially justified by political elites' arguments that they represented potentially existential national security threats and that victory was assured. Yet historical hindsight exposes these arguments to have been frames rather than facts (to be charitable).

THE "CNN EFFECT" AND OTHER EFFECTS STUDIES

Political communication, by contrast, has begun to address the relationship between media exposure and support (or nonsupport) for military intervention. One area of inquiry that has received a great deal of attention is the CNN effect hypothesis. With roots in Mueller, this hypothesis proposed that in an era of 24-hour broadcast news, some vivid images might spur support for intervention (e.g., images of a famine), while others, notably casualties (e.g., a dead American airman being dragged through the streets of Mogadishu) might make the public risk-averse. Since the hypothesis was crafted, most studies have found little evidence of direct effects on the public in line with it (Gilboa 2005; Livingston and Eachus, 1995; Robinson, 1999; although Hawkins [2011] argues that *lack* of media coverage of global conflicts has the important effect of banishing them from the global policy agenda). By contrast, however, policymakers' *perception* of the media's power to influence publics through such imagery, especially against interventions that inflict American casualties, has been shown to lead them to adopt policies that avoid or limit American risks (e.g., avoiding intervening to stop the Rwandan genocide in 1994) (Gilboa, 2005; Lacquement, 2004; Livingston, 1997, 2000; Robinson, 2002).

Other research suggests, however, that media coverage might matter in other ways, such as being an intervening variable between elite cues and public opinion (Boettcher and Cobb, 2006; Chanley, 1999). Jordan and Page (1992), for instance, found that favorable messages in television news from elite sources had a significant effect on changing public attitudes. Baker and Oneal (2001), Oneal and Bryan (1995), and Aday (2010b) all find that media coverage and the framing of war news is associated with the occurrence and magnitude of rally effects. Entman et al. (2009) argue that episodic and tactically oriented war stories that ignore more thematic and geostrategic implications of war and foreign policy create "accountability gaps" that prevent presidents and other elites from being held fully responsible when those policies fail or backfire (see also Aday et al., 2010; Entman et al., 2010).

But despite their prominence in normative discussions of media coverage of war, the specific effects of exposure to casualty images, especially vivid ones, remain largely unaddressed empirically. Recently, however, a few scholars have begun to investigate experimentally the influence of mediated casualty images on audience attitudes. Aday (2010b), for instance, found, in the middle of the Iraq War, that subjects tended to reframe graphic images of dead American soldiers through the prism of their partisan predispositions, with Republican-leaning participants more likely to feel pride in a heroic and worthy sacrifice while Democrats felt more negative emotions. The emotional responses were the opposite in groups exposed to more typical blood-free photos. In a series of experiments, Gartner (2008, 2011) found that "conventionalized" casualty images, such as flag-draped coffins (as opposed to "unconventional" images, such as battle pictures) have a greater tendency to shift a person from supporting to opposing a war, but that this effect is filtered through and sometimes mitigated by his or her partisanship. Still, there remains a great deal of work to be done to discern what effect, if any, exposure to the various media images of war has on audiences.

NEW MEDIA, WAR, AND CONFLICT

In the last decade the role of new and social media, from satellite television and blogs to Facebook and Twitter, in shaping foreign affairs, international conflicts, and public opinion has received increasing attention from policymakers and scholars. Interest in these media has accelerated as events from Iran's Green Movement in 2009 to the Arab Spring in 2011 appeared to be driven to some degree by them. As is often the case, pundits and policymakers were quick to declare powerful media effects, trumpeting "Twitter revolutions" and "Facebook diplomacy." Scholars, however, have mostly been more hesitant and nuanced even when they posit an important role for these media in social movements that challenge or even bring down despotic governments (Castells, 2000; Lynch, 2007; Shirky, 2011; Zuckerman, 2008). In part this is perhaps a legacy of the strong, though certainly controversial, history of the limited media effects tradition in mass communication studies (Klapper, 1960; but see Gitlin, 1978, for a spirited rebuttal). It also stems from the simple fact that powerful direct effects have been elusive in the growing number of studies that have investigated them.

But another important reason is that gathering and making sense of online data has proven extremely difficult (Aday et al., 2010a, 2010b). In doing so, researchers face several challenges. First, data collection is difficult because the universe of, say, tweets or blog posts is not only large and diverse but also not necessarily known. Second, even when tools are developed for gathering large amounts of data, the complex statistical procedures required to make sense of them are not easily applied. Finally, language barriers present critical difficulties for scholars who are working in an international setting.

Because of these difficulties, much of the research in this area has been descriptive, using occasionally innovative data collection, analysis, and visualization tools to, for example, map the international blogosphere (Kelly and Etling, 2008). Others have relied on more qualitative, less empirical approaches to argue either for the power of new media (Shirky, 2011) or the lack thereof (Morozov, 2011). However, some have used innovative techniques to assess the role of new and social media in international politics. One of the best examples to date is Howard's (2010) cross-cultural study of the relationship between information and communication technologies (ICTs) and political systems in the Islamic world. That work concludes not only that ICT diffusion is associated with the transformation of dictatorships to more democratic regimes but also that digital diffusion is a necessary and sufficient precondition for such political change.

Indeed, an emerging finding in the literature in this area is that the power of some social media and other online tools resides in their ability to organize collective action (Bimber, 2003; Bimber et al., 2005; Castells, 2009). Still, an important insight that should be drawn from past political communication research on traditional media is that it is important to parse the effects of various kinds of media (e.g., newspapers versus television) rather than treating "media" as a uniform variable. Similarly, scholars are increasingly recognizing the importance of differentiating the effects of Twitter from those of Facebook and satellite television; they are also recognizing that very often media organizations such as, for example, Al Jazeera, use multiple platforms that may have unique effects on events themselves and public opinion about them.

Finally, new media and other technological innovations are leading scholars to rethink old paradigms in political communication regarding media and foreign affairs. In particular, the press-state dynamic described earlier—in which the foreign policy press is largely dependent on and reflective of political elites in a nation-state system—is being challenged. Global media and satellite-based technologies (e.g., in the area of mapping), for instance, have empowered transnational advocacy networks (TANs) and other networked communities to gain access to publics and media (and therefore an even wider public) and challenge official framing and message dominance (Aday and Livingston, 2008, 2009; Bimber, 2003; Castells, 2000, 2009; Keck and Sikkink, 1998; Livingston, 2001). Portable satellite video technology and smartphones are giving reporters—professional and amateur—the ability, in theory at least, to circumvent official media management strategies and potentially include a wider array of sources that can now be efficiently engaged via the Internet (Livingston and Asmolov, 2010). Because old news norms die hard however, foreign policy coverage often still clings to elite source-driven framing and agendas (Bennett and Livingston, 2003; Livingston and Bennett, 2003).

CONCLUSION

Although this chapter represents only an overview of the literature on media and foreign policy, its survey has identified a few robust findings and signaled some areas in which additional work is needed. Five major conclusions about media and foreign affairs are well grounded in past work: (1) the press-state power dynamic clearly favors political elites, especially the president; (2) coverage of foreign policy outside of war tends to be scarce, elite-driven, ethnocentric, and uncritical; (3) war coverage is all of those things, only more so, plus casualty-free and tactically/episodically driven rather than focusing on geostrategic or more thematic issues and implications; (4) media coverage, especially in crises, can contribute to rallies in public opinion; and (5) these trends have become exacerbated since the early 1980s as news organizations have cut their foreign news budgets and overseas bureaus drastically.

At the same time, at least five areas of research political communication scholars are still in an embryonic stage: First, the role of emotion in both the processing of foreign policy events and media coverage of them is a growing field of study mirroring the increasing interest in affective response across scholarly domains (Aday, 2010b; Huddy et al., 2003; Kinder and Kam, 2009). Emotion clearly plays a role in how people make sense of international events and news, especially in crises, but we are only beginning to understand how and why. Second, this area of inquiry has a long way to go in explaining what, if any, effects exposure to casualty images produces. Because it involves the wide variety of variables at play, this topic, which is highly relevant to policy and newsroom ethics' debates and policies, is ideally suited to a rich research agenda. Third, despite frequent punditry to the contrary, we know precious little about the effects and role of new and social media on collective action, system support, democracy building, and message reception, to name just a few dependent variables. As noted earlier, significant methodological issues need to be worked out in this area, and it will be important to parse effects by medium rather than lumping all "new media" together. Fourth, political communication needs to pay more attention to foreign policy *not* involving wars or crises. Fifth, more attention needs to be paid in coming years to how the transition to online news, both for new and traditional media organizations, influences the media-state-public dynamic. It could be, for instance, that cheaper forms of producing and distributing international news (e.g., "backpacker" journalism and cell phone video cameras), including by amateurs, will arrest the downward spiral in the amount and caliber of foreign news available to American audiences. At this point, however, it is fair to say that despite the existence of some insightful foreign policy and war reporters,[1] a strong argument can be made in favor of the notion that the press is failing to meet its Fourth Estate challenge when it comes to foreign affairs coverage.

NOTE

1. For example: Dexter Filkins, Carlotta Gall, and Howard French of the *New York Times*; Deb Amos of NPR; Laura King of the *Los Angeles Times*; Christiane Amanpour of CNN; Rajiv Chandrasekaren of the *Washington Post*, just to name a few.

References

Aday, S. 2005. The real war will never get on television: An analysis of casualty imagery in American television coverage of the Iraq war. In P. Seib (Ed.), *Media and conflict in the 21st century* (pp. 141–156). Basingstoke, UK: Palgrave.

Aday, S. 2008. On the opening and closing of framing windows: The relative power of elites and events to shape public opinion on use of force. Paper presented to the annual meeting of the International Studies Association, San Francisco, March.

Aday, S. 2009. NGOs as intelligence agencies: The empowerment of transnational advocacy networks and the media by commercial remote sensing. *Geoforum, 4:* 514–522.

Aday, S. 2010a. Chasing the bad news: An analysis of 2005 Iraq and Afghanistan war coverage on NBC and Fox News Channel. *Journal of Communication, 60*(1): 144–164.

Aday, S. 2010b. Leading the charge: Media, elite cues, and emotion in public support for war. *Journal of Communication, 60*(3): 440–465.

Aday, S., and Kim, J. 2008. Framing matters: A multi-methodological test of the use and effects of World War II and Vietnam frames by elites. Paper presented to the annual meeting of the International Studies Association, San Francisco, March.

Aday, S., Cluverius, J., and Livingston, S. 2005. As goes the statue, so goes the war: The emergence of the victory frame in television coverage of the Iraq War. *Journal of Broadcasting & Electronic Media, 3:* 314–331.

Aday, S., Entman, R. M., and Livingston, S. L. 2010. Media, power, and US foreign policy. In H. Semetko and M. Scammell (Eds.), *Sage handbook of political communication.* Thousand Oaks, CA: Sage.

Aday, S., Farrell, H., Lynch, M., and Sides, J. 2010a. Advancing New Media Research. Special Report 250. Washington, DC: United States Institute of Peace.

Aday, S., Farrell, H., Lynch, M., and Sides, J. 2010b. *Blogs and bullets: New media in contentious politics: Peaceworks 65.* Washington, DC: United States Institute of Peace.

Aday, S., and Livingston, S. 2008. Taking the state out of state-media relations theory: How transnational advocacy networks are rewriting (some) of the rules about what we think we know about news and politics. *Media, War, and Conflict, 1*(1): 99–107.

Aday S., Livingston, S., and Hebert, M. 2005. Embedding the truth: a cross-cultural analysis of objectivity and television coverage of the Iraq War. *Harvard International Journal of Press/ Politics, 10* (1): 3–21.

Aldrich, J. H., Gelpi, C., Feaver, P., Reifler, J., and Sharp K. T. 2006. Foreign policy and the electoral connection. *Annual Review of Political Science, 9:* 477–502.

Althaus, S. L. 2003. When news norms collide, follow the lead: New evidence for press independence. *Political Communication, 20:* 381–414.

Althaus, S. L., and Coe, K. 2011). Social identity processes and the dynamics of public support for war. *Public Opinion Quarterly, 75*(1): 65–88.

Aukofer, F., and Lawrence, W. P. 1995. *America's team: The odd couple.* Nashville, TN: Freedom Forum First Amendment Center.

Auletta, K. 2001. Battle stations. *The New Yorker,* December 10, pp. 60–67.

Baker, W. D., and Oneal, J. R. 2001. Patriotism or opinion leadership? The nature and origins of the "rally 'round the flag" effect. *The Journal of Conflict Resolution, 45*(5): 661–687.

Ball-Rokeach, S. J., and DeFleur, M. L. 1976. A dependency model of mass media effects. *Communication Research, 3,* 3–21.

Baum, M. A. 2002. The constituent foundations of the rally-round-the-flag phenomenon. *International Studies Quarterly*, 46: 263–298.

Baum, M. A. 2003. Infotainment wars: Public opinion and foreign policy in the new media age. Princeton, NJ: Princeton University Press.

Baum, M. A., and Groeling, T. 2010. *War stories: How strategic journalists, citizens, and politicians shape the news about war*. Princeton, NJ: Princeton University Press.

Baum, M. A. and Potter, P. B. K. 2008. Mass media, public opinion, and foreign policy: Toward a theoretical synthesis. *Annual Review of Political Science*, 11: 39–65.

Bennett, W. L. 1990. Toward a theory of press-state relations. *Journal of Communication*, 40(2): 103–125.

Bennett, W. L. 1994. The news about foreign policy. In W. L. Bennett and D. L. Paletz (Eds.), *Taken by storm: The media, public opinion, and US foreign policy in the Gulf War* (pp. 12–42). Chicago: University of Chicago Press.

Bennett, W. L., Lawrence, R., and Livingston, S. 2007. *When the press fails: Political power and the news media from Iraq to Katrina*. Chicago: University of Chicago Press.

Bennett, W. L., and Livingston, S. 2003. A semi-independent press: Government control and journalistic autonomy in the political construction of news. *Political Communication*, 20: 359–362.

Berinsky, A. 2007. Assuming the costs of war: Events, elites, and American public support for military conflict. *Journal of Politics*, 69(4): 975–997.

Berinsky, A. 2009. *In Time of war: Understanding American public opinion from World War II to Iraq*. Chicago: University of Chicago Press.

Berinsky, A., and Druckman, J. 2007. Public opinion research and support for the Iraq War. *Public Opinion Quarterly*, 71: 126–141.

Bimber, B. A. 2003. *Information and American democracy: Technology in the evolution of political power*. Cambridge, UK: Cambridge University Press.

Bimber, B., Flanagin, A. J., and Stohl, C. 2005. Reconceptualizing collective action in the contemporary media environment. *Communication Theory*, 15: 365–388.

Boettcher, W., and Cobb, M. 2006. Echoes of Vietnam? Casualty framing and public perceptions of success and failure in Iraq. *Journal of Conflict Resolution*, 1: 831–854.

Boyle, M. P., Chmiebach, M., Armstrong, G. L., McLeod, D. M., Shah, D. V., and Pan, Z. 2004. Information seeking and emotional reactions to the September 11th terrorist attacks. *Journalism and Mass Communication Quarterly*, 81(1): 155–167.

Brewer, P., Aday, S., and Gross, K. 2003. Rallies all around: The dynamics of system support. In P. Norris, M. Kern, and M. Just (Eds.), *Framing terrorism: The news media, the government and the public*. New York: Routledge.

Brewer, P. R., Gross, K., and Aday, S. 2004. International trust and public opinion about world affairs. *American Journal of Political Science*, 48(1): 93–109.

Brody, R. A. 1991. *Assessing the president: The media, elite opinion, and public support*. Palo Alto, CA: Stanford University Press.

Burk, J. 1999. Public support for peacekeeping in Lebanon and Somalia: Assessing the casualties hypothesis. *Political Science Quarterly* 114(1): 53–78.

Campbell, W. J. 2000. *Yellow journalism: The life of William Randolph Hearst*. Boston: Houghton Mifflin.

Castells, M. 2000. *The rise of the network society*. Malden, MA: Wiley-Blackwell.

Castells, M. 2009. *Communication power*. New York: Oxford University Press.

Chanley, V. A. 1999. US public views of international involvement from 1964–1993: Time series analyses of general and militant internationalism. *Journal of Conflict Resolution, 43*(1): 23–44.

Dauber, C. E. 2001. The impact of Mogadishu on US military intervention. *Armed Forces & Society, 27*(2): 205–229.

Delli Carpini, M. X., and Keeter, S. 1997. *What Americans know about politics and why it matters.* New Haven, CT: Yale University Press.

Dickson, S. H. 1995. Understanding media bias: The press and the US invasion of Panama. *Journalism Quarterly, 4*: 809–819.

Dorman, W. A., and Livingston, S. 1994. News and historical context: The establishment phase of the Persian Gulf policy debate. In W. L. Bennett and D. L. Paletz (Eds.). *Taken by storm: The media, public opinion, and US foreign policy in the Gulf War* (pp. 63–81). Chicago: University of Chicago Press.

Dower, J. W. 1987. *War without mercy: Race and power in the Pacific War.* New York: Pantheon.

Eagly, A. H., and Chaiken, S. 1993. *The psychology of attitudes.* New York: Harcourt.

Eichenberg, R. C. 2005. Victory has many friends: US public opinion and the use of military force, 1981–2005. *International Security, 30*(1): 140–177.

Entman, R. M. 2003. Cascading activation: Contesting the White House's frame after 9/11. *Political Communication, 20*: 415–423.

Entman, R. M. 2004. *Projections of power: Framing news, public opinion, and US foreign policy.* Chicago: University of Chicago Press.

Entman, R. M. 2006. Punctuating the homogeneity of institutionalized news: Abusing prisoners at Abu Ghraib versus killing civilians at Fallujah. *Political Communication, 23*: 215–224.

Entman, R. M., Livingston, S. L., and Aday, S. 2010. Condemned to repeat: The media and the accountability gap in Iraq War Policy. In S. Koch-Baumgarten and K. Voltmer (Eds.), *Public policy and the media: The interplay of mass communication and political decision making.* London: Routledge.

Entman, R. M., Livingston, S., and Kim, J. 2009. Doomed to repeat: Iraq news, 2002–2007. *American Behavioral Scientist, 52*: 689–708.

Entman, R. M., and Page, B. I. 1994. The news before the storm: the Iraq War debate and the limits to media independence. In W. L. Bennett and D. L. Paletz (Eds.), *Taken by storm.* Chicago: University of Chicago Press.

Feaver P. D., and Gelpi, C. 2004. *Choosing your battles: American civil-military relations and the use of force.* Princeton, NJ: Princeton University Press.

Fenton, T. 2005. *Bad news: The decline of reporting, the business of news, and the danger to us all.* New York: Collins.

Fishman, M. 1980. *Manufacturing the news.* Austin: University of Texas Press.

Fussell, P. 1989. *Wartime: Understanding and behavior in the Second World War.* New York: Oxford University Press.

Gans, H. 1979. *Deciding what's news.* New York: Vintage Books.

Gartner, S. S. 2004. Making the international local: The terrorist attack on the USS Cole, local casualties, and media coverage. *Political Communication, 21*(2): 139–159.

Gartner, S. S. 2008. The multiple effects of casualties on public support for war: An experimental approach. *American Political Science Review, 102*(1): 95–106.

Gartner, S. S. 2011. On behalf of a grateful nation: Conventionalized images of loss and individual opinion change in war. *International Studies Quarterly, 55.* doi: 10.1111/j.1468-2478.2011.00655.x

Gartner, S. S., and Segura, G. M. 1998. War, casualties, and public opinion. *Journal of Conflict Resolution*, 42: 278–300.

Gartner, S. S., and Segura, G. M. 2000. Race, opinion, and casualties in the Vietnam War. *The Journal of Politics*, 62(1): 115–146.

Gartner, S. S., Segura, G. M., and Barratt, B. 2004. Casualties, positions, and Senate elections in the Vietnam War. *Political Research Quarterly*, 3: 467–477.

Gelpi, C., Feaver, P., and Reifler, J. 2005/2006. Success matters: Casualty sensitivity and the war in Iraq. *International Security*, 30 (3): 7–46.

Gelpi, C., Feaver, P. D., and Reifler, J. 2009. *Paying the human costs of war: American public opinion and causalities in military conflicts.* Princeton, NJ: Princeton University Press.

Gilboa, E. 2005. Global television news and foreign policy: Debating the CNN effect. *International Studies Perspectives*, 3: 325–341.

Gitlin, T. 1978. Media sociology: The dominant paradigm. *Theory and Society*, 6: 205–253.

Gitlin, T. 1980. *The whole world is watching.* Los Angeles: University of California Press.

Gross, K., Aday, S., and Brewer, P. 2004. A panel study of media effects on political and social trust after September 11th. *Harvard International Journal of Press/Politics*, 9(4): 49–74.

Hallin, D. 1986. *The "uncensored" war.* New York: Oxford University Press.

Hallin, D. 1991. Images of the Vietnam and the Persian Gulf Wars in US television. In L. Rabinovitz and S. Jeffords (Eds.), *Seeing through the media: The Persian Gulf War* (pp. 45–58). New Brunswick, NJ: Rutgers University Press.

Hawkins, V. 2011. Media selectivity and the other side of the CNN Effect: The consequences of not paying attention to conflict. *Media, War & Conflict*, 4(1): 55–69.

Hindman, D. B. 2004. Media system dependency and public support for the press and president. *Mass Communication and Society* 7: 29–42.

Holsti, O. R. 2004. *Public opinion and American foreign policy.* Ann Arbor: University of Michigan Press.

Howard, P. 2010. *The digital origins of dictatorship and democracy: Information technology and political Islam.* New York: Oxford University Press.

Huddy, L., Feldman, S., Lahav, G., and Taber, C. 2003. Fear and terrorism: Psychological reactions to 9/11. In P. Norris, M. Kern, and M. Just (Eds.), *Framing terrorism: The media, government, and the public* (pp. 255–278). New York: Routledge.

Jentleson, B. W. 1992. The pretty prudent public: Post-Vietnam American opinion on the use of military force. *International Studies Quarterly*, 36: 49–74.

Jentleson, B. W., and Britton, R. L. 1998. Still pretty prudent: Post-Cold War American public opinion on the use of military force. *Journal of Conflict Resolution*, 42(4): 395–417.

Jervis, R. 1976. *Perception and misperception in international politics.* Princeton, NJ: Princeton University Press.

Jordan, D. L., and Page, B. I. 1992. Shaping foreign policy opinions: The role of TV news. *Journal of Conflict Resolution*, 36(2): 227–241.

Katovsky, B., and Carlson, T. 2003. *Embedded: The media at war in Iraq.* Guilford, CT: Lyons Press.

Katz, E., and Lazarsfeld, P. F. 1955. *Personal influence: The part played by people in the flow of mass communication.* Glencoe, IL: Free Press.

Keck, M., and Sikkink, K. 1998. *Activists beyond borders: Advocacy networks in international politics.* Ithaca and London: Cornell University Press.

Kellner, D. 1992. *The Persian Gulf TV War.* Boulder, CO: Westview Press.

Kelly, J., and Etling, B. 2008. Mapping Iran's online public: Politics and culture in the Persian blogosphere. Research Publication, Internet and Democracy Case Study Series, April. Cambridge, MA: Berkman Center.

Khong, Y. F. 1992. *Analogies at war.* Princeton, NJ: Princeton University Press.

Kinder, D. R., and Kam, C. D. 2009. *Us against them: Ethnocentric foundations of American Opinion.* Chicago: University of Chicago Press.

Klapper, J. T. 1960. *The effects of mass communication.* Glencoe, IL: Free Press.

Klarevas, L. 2002. The "essential domino" of military operations: American public opinion and the use of force. *International Studies Perspectives, 3*: 417–437.

Krosnick, J. A., and Kinder, D. R. 1990. Altering the foundations of support for the president through priming. *American Political Science Review, 84*: 497–512.

Kull, S., Ramsey, C., and Lewis, E. 2003. Misperceptions, the media, and the Iraq War. *Political Science Quarterly, 118*: 569–598.

Lacquement, R. A. 2004. The casualty-aversion myth. *Naval War College Review, 57*(1): 38–57.

Larson, E. 1996. *Casualties and consensus: The historical role of casualties in domestic support for US military operations.* Santa Monica, CA: Rand.

Lazarsfeld, P., and Merton, R. 1948. Mass communication, popular taste, and organized social action. In W. Schramm (Ed.), *Mass communication* (pp. 492–503). Urbana: University of Illinois Press.

Lian, B., and Oneal, J. R. 1993. Presidents, the use of military force, and public opinion. *Journal of Conflict Resolution, 37*(2): 277–300.

Livingston, S. 1997. *Clarifying the CNN effect: An examination of media effects according to type of military intervention.* Cambridge, MA: Joan Shorenstein Center on the Press Politics and Public Policy, John F. Kennedy School of Government, Harvard University.

Livingston, S. 2000. Media coverage of the war: An empirical assessment. In A. Schabnel (Ed.), *Kosovo and the challenge of humanitarian intervention: Selective indignation, collective action, and individual citizenship* (pp. 360–384). New York: United Nations University Press.

Livingston, S. 2001. Remote sensing technology and the news media. In J. Baker, K. O'Connell, and R. Williamson (Eds.), *Commercial observation satellites: At the leading edge of global transparency,* (pp. 485–502). Santa Monica, CA: Rand Corporation and the American Society for Photogrammetry and Remote Sensing.

Livingston, S., and Asmolov, G. 2010. Networks and the future of foreign affairs reporting. *Journalism & Mass Communication Quarterly, 11*(5): 745–760.

Livingston, S., and Bennett, W. L. 2003. Gatekeeping, indexing, and live-event news: Is technology altering the construction of news? *Political Communication, 20*: 363–380.

Livingston, S., and Eachus, T. 1995. Humanitarian crises and US foreign policy: Somalia and the CNN effect reconsidered. *Political Communication, 12*: 413–429.

Lynch, M. 2007. Blogging the new Arab public. *Arab Media & Society, 1*(spring). Available at: http://www.arabmediasociety.com/?article=10

McLeod, D. M., Eveland, W. P., and Signorielli, N. 1994. Conflict and public opinion: Rally effects of the Persian Gulf War. *Journalism Quarterly, 71*(1): 20–31.

Mermin, J. 1999. *Debating war and peace: Media coverage of US intervention in the post-Vetnam era.* Princeton, NJ: Princeton University Press.

Morgan, T. C., and Campbell, S. H. 1991. Domestic structure, decision constraints, and war— So why can't democracies fight? *Journal of Conflict Resolution, 35*(3): 187–211.

Morozov, E. 2011. *The net delusion: The dark side of Internet freedom.* New York: Public Affairs.

Mueller, J. 1973. *War, presidents, and public opinion*. New York: Wiley.

Mueller, J. 1994. *Policy and opinion in the Gulf War*. Chicago: University of Chicago Press.

Mueller, J. 2005. The Iraq syndrome. *Foreign Affairs* (November/December): 44–54.

Nasaw, D. 2000. *The chief: The life of William Randolph Hearst*. Boston: Houghton Mifflin.

Newhagen, J. E. 1994. The relationship between censorship and the emotional and critical tone of television news coverage of the Persian Gulf War. *Journalism Quarterly*, 71(1): 32–42.

Oneal, J. R., and Bryan, A. L. 1995. The rally 'round the flag effect in US foreign policy crises, 1950–1985. *Political Behavior*, 17(4): 379–401.

Page, B. I., and Shapiro, R. 1992. *The rational public: Fifty years of trends in American policy*. Chicago: University Chicago Press.

Pan, Z., Ostman, R. E., Moy, P., and Reynolds, P. 1994. News exposure and its learning effects during the Persian Gulf War. *Journalism Quarterly*, 71(1): 7–19.

Pew Research Center Project for Excellence in Journalism. 2011. *The state of the news media*. Washington, DC: Pew Research Center.

Pfau, M., Haigh, M. M., Gettle, M., Donnelly, M., Scott, G., and Warr, D. 2004. Embedding journalists in military combat units: Impact on newspaper story frames and tone. *Journalism & Mass Communication Quarterly*, 81: 74–88.

Petraeus, D. H. 1987. The American military and the lessons of Vietnam: A study of military influence and the use of force in the post-Vietnam era. A dissertation to the faculty of Princeton University in candidacy for the degree of doctor of philosophy. Princeton, NJ Princeton University.

Prochnau, W. 2005. The military and the media. In G. Overholser and K.H. Jamieson (Eds.), *The press* (pp. 310–331). New York: Oxford University Press.

Pyle, E. 1979. *Here is your war*. Manchester, MA: Ayer.

Reiter, D., and Stam, A. C. 2002. *Democracies at war*. Princeton, N.J.: Princeton University Press.

Robinson, P. 1999. The CNN effect: Can the news media drive foreign policy? *Political Communication*, (25): 301–309.

Robinson, P. 2002. *The CNN effect: The myth of news, foreign policy, and intervention*. Oxford, UK: Routledge.

Russett, B. 1990. *Controlling the sword: The democratic governance of national security*. Cambridge, MA: Harvard University Press.

Schlesinger, A. 1973. *The imperial presidency*. Boston: Houghton-Mifflin.

Sharkey, J. 2001. War, censorship and the first amendment. *Media Studies Journal*, 15(1): 20–25.

Shirky, C. 2011. The political power of social media. *Foreign Affairs*, 90(1): 28–41.

Sigal, L. 1973. *Reporters and officials: The organization and politics of newsmaking*. Lexington, MA: D. C. Heath.

Sniderman, P. M., Brody, R. A., and Tetlock, P. E. 1991. *Reasoning and choice*. Cambridge, UK: Cambridge University Press.

Wilson, G. C. 2001. Media-military relations: No worse, no better. *Media Studies Journal*, 15(1): 26–31.

Wolfsfeld, G. 2004. *Media and the path to peace*. Cambridge, UK: Cambridge University Press.

Zaller, J. R. 1992. *The nature and origins of mass opinion*. Cambridge, UK: Cambridge University Press.

Zaller, J., and Chiu, D. 1996. Government's little helper: US press coverage of foreign policy crises, 1945–1991. *Political Communication*, 12: 385–405.

Zuckerman, E. 2008. Meet the bridgebloggers. *Public Choice*, 134: 47–65.

CHAPTER 24

....

JOURNALISM AND THE PUBLIC-SERVICE MODEL

In Search of an Ideal

....

STEPHEN COLEMAN

In the regulated world of Public Service Broadcasting the customer does not exist: he or she is a passive creature—a viewer—in need of protection. In other parts of the media world—including pay television and newspapers—the customer is just that: someone whose very freedom to choose makes them [*sic*] important. And because they have power they are treated with great seriousness and respect, as people who are perfectly capable of making informed judgments about what to buy, read, and go and see. Independence is sustained by true accountability—the accountability owed to customers. People who buy the newspapers, open the application, decide to take out the television subscription—people who deliberately and willingly choose a service which they value. And people value honest, fearless, and above all independent news coverage that challenges the consensus. There is an inescapable conclusion that we must reach if we are to have a better society. The only reliable, durable, and perpetual guarantor of independence is profit.

> James Murdoch, Chief Executive of News Corporation in Europe and
> Asia, MacTaggart Lecture, Edinburgh International Television Festival,
> August, 28, 2009

Many, many wholly innocent men, women and children who, at their darkest hour, at their most vulnerable moment in their lives, with no one and nowhere to turn to, found their properly private lives, their private losses, their private sorrows treated as the public property of News International—their private, innermost feelings and their private tears bought and sold by News International for commercial gain ... This nexus—this criminal-media nexus—was claiming to be on the side of the law-abiding citizen but was in fact standing side by side with criminals against our citizens. Others have said that in its behaviour towards those without a voice of their own, News International descended from the gutter to the sewers. The tragedy is that it let the rats out of the sewers.

Former UK Prime Minister, Gordon Brown MP,
speech to the House of Commons, July 13, 2011

THESE two extracts from speeches reflect the diametrically opposing perspectives that collided in what became known in the summer of 2011 as "Murdochgate." After the most popular newspaper in Britain was caught hacking into the phones of members of the public, bribing the police, and engaging in acts of political intimidation, the claim that such journalism was serving a "public interest" imploded and the nation embarked upon a process of cultural self-reflection. Inevitably, much of this focused upon specific allegations of corruption and illegality. Beyond these egregious malpractices, broader questions remain to be answered. What does it mean for journalists to provide a public service? Is the public interest synonymous with the public appetite? And can media standards be promoted (or imposed) that enhance the chances of the public being well served and curb the more brutish and anti-social elements of public communication?

As with most complex questions, the beginning of an answer lies in history. The transition from journalism as private correspondence read aloud to commodified newssheets addressed to mass publics raised important questions about accountability. When correspondents claimed to be no more than freelance chroniclers of stories from afar, any combination of personal motivation, salacious rumor-mongering or distorted observation could be passed off as journalism. As news-bearers began to claim a quasi-professional status, the quality of the knowledge they put into circulation and their commitment to the cultivation of a civic public emerged as defining features of a journalistic ethos. Journalists began to surround their practices with virtuous-sounding epithets, such as "objectivity" and "impartiality": an attempt to insert principles of Weberian impersonality into routines that could never fully escape structural or subjective bias.

Amongst the loftiest of journalism's grand claims has been the ideal of "public service," a term suggesting the antithesis of self-serving mendacity or mean-spirited motivation. To characterize oneself as a public servant is to profess a certain kind of civic virtue: an intention to act for all rather than some. At the state level, elected politicians and the permanent bureaucrats of government are expected to serve the needs of a universal public before the narrow interests of personal advancement, class privilege, or institutional loyalty. For decades, political scientists have debated about whether the state (governments, legislatures, judiciaries, and law enforcers) can ever achieve such neutral universalism in practice (Poulantzas, 1969; Miliband, 1982; Hay, 1999). This chapter considers the claims of journalists to be providers of a public service and the conditions that allow or inhibit the realization of such a high-minded aspiration. The chapter begins by exploring the grounds upon which journalists have claimed to serve the public and concludes by offering a normative framework for public-service journalism within the contemporary media ecology.

CLAIMING TO REPRESENT
THE PUBLIC INTEREST

The two most beguiling but prevalent attempts to equate journalism with the public interest should be outlined at the outset. The first is the claim made by authoritarian rulers that, because only the state can speak for the people, government-controlled media monopolies must represent the public interest. For example, China's news media reforms, introduced in 2003, prohibit the publication of newspapers or magazines with "incorrect politics" or which "have broken the law in the last five years." The Central Propaganda Ministry compels Chinese journalists to conform to the rule of "Three Meetings, Three Nods of the Head" whereby any articles critical of the government or a Communist Party official cannot be published until the reporter, the target of the criticism, and the target's superior have met and the target of criticism and his superior have both signed a certificate agreeing that the article should be published (He Qinglian, 2006). China is the biggest, but far from the sole, example of state-monopolized media, justified on the spurious grounds that only the ruling elite can determine what its subjects need—and do not need—to know.

No less disingenuous is a second widely made claim: that the public interest can be equated with the commercial consumption of news. The argument here is that the public receives the news it needs by paying for what is useful and ignoring what is not. According to this principle, if there is a consumer demand for any service or commodity, from bogus information to photos of naked bodies, the buyers have a right to receive it and the suppliers are not morally culpable for providing it. As Rupert Murdoch (1989) so characteristically put it, "Anybody who, within the law of the land, provides a service which the public wants at a price it can afford is providing a public service." Critics of this perspective point out that the public interest and commercial success do not always coincide; that there are some commodities (heroin, for example) for which there is profitable demand, but no public interest in supplying, and other services (such as schools and libraries) for which there is a powerful public interest that cannot be met by selling them for a profit. As key democratic functions of journalism are to provide the public with pluralistic information, social assurance, and cultural stimulation, these can no more effectively be left to the whims of consumer demand than the provision of other market externalities, such as literacy, road safety, or clean air. As goods or services that generate social benefits that exceed the logic of market profitability, externalities have to demonstrate their social value in terms expressible beyond monetary calculation.

If the media are to be expected to perform in ways that serve the public interest, without being tied to the priorities of the state or market, then identifying the values comprising such an interest and the means of evaluating the extent to which particular media organizations, genres, and content reflect and reinforce them, becomes a crucial question. As McQuail (1992, 4–5) has put it,

The existence of some kind and degree of public interest in the operation of the mass media has clearly been widely accepted, and it has much to do with the rise of democracy and of a "public sphere," in which opinions are formed and expressed by citizens on the basis of common knowledge and of widely held values. There are . . . problems in moving from these ideas to the identification of criteria which are relevant to communicative "performance" by mass media in their public role. The main difficulties are first, that of specifying the intended collective beneficiary and, secondly, to specify the rules for determining the balance of benefit or harm.

Although it might seem like an abstruse definition, one might say that public-service journalism is characterized by its mode of address; by its direct and consistent appeal to people as citizens, coexisting within a democratic community, rather than as mere subjects of the state or consumers in the marketplace. As citizens, people possess forms of agency that enable them to act upon the world around them, making a difference to their social reality as well as enduring its rules and routines. Citizenship describes the myriad ways in which people negotiate their way through the world as received and the world as they would like it to be. It describes the ways in which people encounter and present themselves to others, arrive at collective identities and shared meanings, and contest seemingly incompatible differences. To address people as citizens is to reflect an awareness of both the complexity and the creativity of communicative interaction; to acknowledge the social life of information in a world dependent upon various forms of cooperation and solidarity, but blighted by inequalities, hidden motives, and group herding. Reflecting upon these obstacles to shared publicness, Sunstein (2002, 117) concludes:

> A heterogeneous society benefits from shared experiences, many of them produced by the media. These shared experiences provide a kind of social glue, facilitating efforts to solve shared problems, encouraging people to view one another as fellow citizens, and sometimes helping to ensure responsiveness to genuine problems and needs, even helping to identify them as such.

The extent to which this civic mission is paramount in the remit of a media organization might be one way of determining the degree of its commitment to the public-service ideal. When the BBC (British Broadcasting Corporation) attempted to set out its case for being considered a provider of a public service, it argued:

> Broadcasting is a civic art. It is intrinsically public in ambition and effect. We may experience it individually, but it is never a purely private transaction. To turn on a TV or radio is to enter a communal space and to be constantly aware of and influenced by that fact. This shared experience may itself represent a significant public value—the communal glue which some call *social capital*. But that is only one of many potential wider benefits. A programme may make me more likely to vote, or to look at my neighbour in a new, more positive light. It may encourage both of us to spruce up our houses and improve our neighbourhood. A programme I turn to for pure relaxation

may unexpectedly teach me something of real value. In a national emergency, the right broadcast information might save my life. (BBC, 2004, 6)

In the same vein, Gavyn Davies (1999, 129), a former chairman of the BBC, suggested that "the core case for the BBC should rest not on money and markets but on culture and citizenship." To say that public-service journalism is characterized by its civic motivation is to suggest that, when challenged by competing motives, such as boosting audience ratings, making money, adding to the sum total of sensationalism, or serving political elites, the nurturing of democratic citizenship must always take priority. Some media organizations, such as the BBC, are funded specifically with a view to adopting such priorities, which are written into its charter. Others, including a number of commercial broadcasters and newspapers operating within various kinds of regulatory regimes, might not be primarily committed to serving civic ends, but are subject to regulatory controls if their actions are proved to be blatantly uncivic or antisocial. Most governments, however committed they may be to freedom of media expression, reserve the right to regulate the press and broadcasters in the public interest, even if this only amounts to ensuring that they conform to the same laws that govern the actions of all other citizens and corporate bodies.

The second challenge raised by McQuail in the passage quoted above is much more difficult: how to determine whether the media are serving or harming the public interest. The seductive simplicity of the market model is that public service can be measured crudely in terms of profit or loss. Likewise, authoritarian states, employing a command and control approach to media regulation, are able to classify any deviation from the state's self-determined interests as a failure to serve the public. From a democratic-civic perspective, the norms according to which media performance can be judged are rarely as straightforward, for they involve an inevitable trade-off between free expression and social cohesion. Nonetheless, there have been several attempts to set out such norms, albeit unsystematically. For example, in the United States, the 1947 Commission on the Press called upon newspapers to accept "a new public responsibility" to provide "a truthful, comprehensive and intelligent account of the day's events in a context which gives the meaning." In addition, newspapers should "provide a forum for the exchange of comment on criticism" and offer a "representative picture of constituent groups in society." In 1949 the US Federal Communications Commission (FCC) ruled that radio station owners were "public trustees" and therefore had an obligation to afford public debate comprising a range of contrasting views in relation to issues of public importance. (This so-called Fairness Doctrine was rescinded in the 1980s by the Reagan administration, opening the way for a number of broadcasting channels committed to an ideologically biased agenda, of which Murdoch's Fox TV is currently the most conspicuous.) Various Royal Commissions on the Press (and, later, broadcasting) in the United Kingdom have set out public-service principles and set up various forms of regulatory bodies funded by the newspapers themselves and non-binding in their decisions, with a view to responding to cases of manifest journalistic irresponsibility. While British newspapers' commitment to the public interest has only been subjected to light-touch self-regulation, British broadcasting has been strongly regulated on the basis of a set of explicitly civic values embodied in the public-service broadcasting model. The difficulty here, as McQuail rightly suggests, is determining not only whether but also how such values are served by broadcasting output? Unlike other publicly funded institutions, such as schools or hospitals, which can produce convincing metrics to demonstrate their contribution to the public interest, public-service media are faced with three formidable challenges. Firstly, not everyone agrees about what constitutes the public interest when it comes to political and civic information. Secondly, even where there is a good deal of consensus about social values—such as the need to encourage voting, or the discussion of public issues or becoming active in a local community, it is almost impossible to demonstrate how far these are promoted by exposure to media content and how far other aspects of civic socialization, such as family and peer pressure or formal education, might be responsible for encouraging them. Thirdly, it may be that the value of public-service broadcasting can only be truly perceived in its absence; like the provision of public funding for playing fields or poetry festivals, it may be only when such goods are no longer available that their loss to the public interest can be fully appreciated.

In response to the persistent criticisms of its opponents, who, like James Murdoch in the extract at the beginning of this chapter, have asserted that public-service broadcasting constrains free competition for public attention and treats its audience as inert targets of paternalistic cultivation, the BBC has attempted to devise a more sophisticated account of its contribution to the public interest. Drawing upon Moore's (1995) book, *Creating Public Value,* and Kelly and Muers's (2002) interpretation of Moore's ideas for the UK government, a distinction is made between forms of private value that translate into market profitability and public value, which can only be determined in partnership with "citizens acting through politics, rather than consumers acting through markets" (Moore, 1995, 44). According to "public value" theorists, the social utility of media output is best measured by providing citizens (as media users) with means of expressing their preferences and determining which aspects of the BBC they are willing to pay for and which do not constitute public value. Willingness To Pay (WPT) tests have been devised with a view to ascribing value on the basis of refined civic preferences, measured through surveys and aggregations of audience feedback, rather than a pricing mechanism. The BBC has thoroughly committed itself to the public value concept, declaring that tests of public value will "drive all its decisions about the scale and scope of what the organisation does." The BBC has applied public-value tests to five key aspects of its remit:

Democratic value: the BBC supports civic life and national debate by providing trusted and impartial news and information that helps citizens make sense of the world and encourages them to engage with it.

Cultural and creative value: the BBC enriches the UK's cultural life by bringing talent and audiences together to break new ground, to celebrate our cultural heritage, to broaden the national conversation.

Educational value: by offering audiences of every age a world of formal and informal educational opportunity in every medium, the BBC helps build a society strong in knowledge and skills.

Social and community value: by enabling the UK's many communities to see what they hold in common and how they differ; the BBC seeks to build social cohesion and tolerance through greater understanding.

Global value: the BBC supports the UK's global role by being the world's most trusted provider of international news and information, and by showcasing the best of British culture to a global audience. (BBC, 2004, 8)

By asking viewers and listeners how they have responded to these categories of output, and how much it is worth to them, the BBC hopes to make a non-market case for the public worth of what it produces. But, as Lee et al. (2011) have argued, audience research methodologies focusing upon surveys and feedback aggregation are only likely to capture accounts of personal media consumption, thereby failing to reflect the kind of civic responses that one might expect to emerge from public deliberation about competing media values. For example, rather than asking audience members whether they believe that the public interest is well served by the media producing specific types of output, might it not be more fruitful to embark upon the constructivist path of inviting listeners and viewers to define—and regularly redefine—the media standards that they consider to be consistent with democratic citizenship? Given that citizenship is not a normatively fixed concept, but one that is dependent upon the very reflexivity that it makes possible, it is surely a mistake to assume that its constituent values can be assessed in separation from a political debate about what such values should be and how best to reflect them.

Useful though the notion of public value might be in terms of rhetorically positioning the non-commoditized nature of public-service journalism, the question of how to define it in terms that are consistent with norms of democratic citizenship remains open. The BBC's commitment to the principle of public service originated in a hierarchical and paternalistic age when civic values were formulated by a cultural elite and handed down to a supposedly appreciative citizenry. But much has changed since then, leading some critics to believe that the case for public-service journalism is at best in need of reconfiguration and at worst unsustainable (Tracey, 1998; Tambini and Cowling, 2004; Debrett, 2010; Moe, 2011; Schlesinger and Sorice, 2011).

PUBLIC-SERVICE BROADCASTING: AN OBSOLETE TERM?

The very term public-service broadcasting suggests semantic instability. In the early days of the BBC, the public was conceived as a culturally homogeneous entity. Its first director, John Reith, argued that a positive effect of public broadcasting would be to make "the nation as one man." The BBC's mission, he argued, was to create a "unity of the nervous system of the body politic" by becoming "the integrator for democracy." This appeal to a singular national public extended from a "standard" way of speaking (which failed to register the numerous regional dialects of the BBC's linguistically diverse audience) to an ideologically consensual notion of common sense and political wisdom. The BBC was not a creature of a controlling state, but it shared with the elite who ran the state a set of values that inflected almost every minute of its output. But, as Coleman and Ross (2010) have argued,

> Definitions of the public interest that once appeared to be clear and immutable seem in recent times to have become fragile and in need of reconceptualization. The public, as an historical actor, has come to be seen as a fractured and fragmented entity, splintered by debates about identity, belonging and responsibility. As the idea of a singular, potentially univocal public is abandoned, a pluralistic conception of the public as a patchwork of co-existing and overlapping communities has emerged. This fractured public lacks the metaphysical integrity that once gave legitimacy to notions of sovereign nationhood and moral universalism.

Whether it makes more sense to speak of a pluralistic public or of publics, of a multicultural public sphere or of public sphericules (Gitlin, 1998), the notion that there can be a singular mode of address that speaks to and serves the public as a whole is no longer—if it ever was—feasible. As Silverstone (2007) has argued,

> For generations . . . we could avoid, disguise or deny such plurality. Our everyday lives were not necessarily lived in ways that forced the issue, at least on a scale beyond the face-to-face of village or community. But now they are. The mediated globe involves lifting the veil on difference. It cannot be avoided. It is seen and heard daily.

The incompatibility of appeals to public homogeneity and genuine respect for cultural difference has become a major challenge for late modernity. The failure of the traditional public-service model to meet such a challenge suggests a need for radical rethinking about what citizen-directed modes of address might sound or feel like.

Then there is the increasingly problematic term "broadcasting." While television, and to a lesser extent radio, remain major sources of public information and journalistic analysis for citizens in most countries, the boundaries between print, broadcasting, and online communication are now so porous as to raise questions about how long such discrete categories can remain meaningful. In the August 2011 street riots in London and other parts of England, some of the best video coverage appeared on the website of the *Guardian* newspaper. Was this a newspaper doing broadcasting or a website producing video news or a new news service that could neither be classified as online nor offline? Media convergence makes it difficult to think about regulating the values of content on one platform (television) when it is being received on another (the mobile phone or personal computer). The interactivity made possible by the Internet, which has broken down rigid distinctions between content production and reception, makes the very notion of *addressing* a public seem strangely old-fashioned. Publics now not only talk back to the media (and other hitherto paternalistic institutions), but also pursue their own civic practices around and beyond the institutional centers from which broadcast messages were once transmitted. In an age of communication networks, the primacy of transmission competes with the ubiquity of circulation. We might not yet be in a post-broadcast era, but neither are we any longer in a period that can be characterized as public-service *broadcasting*.

So, whatever service journalists might claim to offer along the lines of the old public-service broadcasting model, they need to take account of the changing nature of publics and publicness and of broadcasting within an ecology of media convergence. But perhaps the term "service" is itself no less problematic. Implying a sense of providing for others what they cannot provide for themselves, journalism as a professional service reflects a division of social labor between those "in the know" and those who are dependent upon the receipt of packaged information. Recent scholars of journalism, such as Bruns (2005), Deuze (2009), and Flew (2010) have suggested that this division was a product of a period in which information was scarce and citizens deferential, that "technology has given us a communications toolkit that allows anyone to become a journalist at little cost and, in theory, with global reach" (Gillmor, 2004). In contrast, scholars such as Mosco argue that new forms of citizen-generated journalism are likely to be civically impoverishing because "those telling the stories are not journalists . . . [and] are not trained in the craft" (Mosco, 2009, 350). This is a debate about the very nature of journalism. And, however strong the arguments of either side, it should be remembered that such ontological wrestling is not unprecedented, that, from their very earliest claims to serve the public interest, journalists have frequently overstated the difference between themselves and everyday storytellers, rumormongers, and social commentators and have found themselves struggling to defend a "profession" that anyone is free to join, regardless of qualifications. At the same time, it is hard to deny that, without substantial investment of both resources and talent, the quality of journalism required to serve the public interest in complex, accountable democracies is unlikely to emerge spontaneously.

SOME NEW THOUGHTS

While the current debate surrounding the future of journalism is rather lugubrious, there are some new ideas emerging, suggesting that even if the traditional public-service model is far from robust, the relationship between journalism and the public interest is still potentially vibrant. There are more contributions to this imaginative debate than can be listed here, and space does not allow for full accounts of those that are mentioned. New ideas about public-service journalism tend to fall into three categories.

Firstly, there is a now long-standing, critical tradition commonly referred to as public or civic journalism. Mainly promoted by radical journalists, academics, and community activists, its aim has been "to situate newspapers and journalists as active participants in community life, rather than as detached spectators" (Perry, 2003). There have been several examples of public journalism in practice, mainly in the United States. The argument here is that journalists have traditionally taken on too much and too little—too much insofar as they have seen themselves as the sole gatherers, gatekeepers, and interpreters of news, rather than as partners with the communities they serve—and not enough insofar as they have attempted to stand aside from the efforts of citizens to make a difference to the communities in which they live, merely commenting upon such efforts as if they were viewing them through a telescope. Some journalists, especially those working in community media and the blogosphere, have resisted these demands of objective distancing, insisting that telling the story ought not to prevent them from being part of it. This raises a question that will continue to stimulate debate for some time to come: Is it the role of journalists to help shape the public interest that they serve or should there be a clear line between constructing and serving the public interest?

Secondly, some are now arguing that the debate about what constitutes the democratic public interest should itself be democratized. In an interesting British constitutional initiative, Neal Lawson and Andrew Simms (2011) called for

> the government to set up a People's Jury to put the British public interest first. The jury would be made up of 1,000 citizens drawn at random from the electorate and funded out of the public purse. A paid secretariat will commission research and call witnesses to make our nation's elites answerable to the public. Reporting within a year of its launch the jury will report on how the public interest relates to media ownership; the role of the financial sector in the crash; MP selections and accountability; policing; and more generally on British political and corporate life.

This responds to Lee et al.'s (2011) concerns about the non-deliberative nature of current public-value tests. It also chimes well with Coleman and Blumler's (2009) proposal for an online civic commons in which citizens would be able to discuss policy ideas and feed in their collective thoughts to institutional processes of governance from which they have hitherto been generally excluded.

A third set of proposals for public-service journalism focuses on media funding, particularly at the local level (Downie and Schudson, 2009; Barnett, 2010; Picard, 2010; Fenton, 2011; McChesney, 2011). In one of the more cogent analyses of "the dramatic contaction of the news media," Currah (2009, 143) recommends that governments offer new tax concessions to those investing in news production and expand charity law so that new forms of third-sector support for journalism might be encouraged. These and other proposals for reinvention of the business case for public-service journalism offer helpful ways of promoting forms of journalism that can sustain civic values. But they should not be seen as substitutes for the public-service model that has been so successfully applied to the BBC. Such a model certainly should be dusted off, rearticulated, and made relevant to the digital media ecology. Any retreat from its basic principles would abandon the only reliable, durable, and perpetual guarantor of independence from the likes of Murdoch's News Corporation.

REFERENCES

Barnett, S. 2010. Minding the regional news gap. *British Journalism Review* 21(1): 13–18.

BBC. 2004. *Building public value.* London: BBC.

Bruns, A. 2005. *Gatewatching: collaborative online news production.* New York: P. Lang.

Coleman, S., and Blumler, J. G. 2009. *The Internet and democratic citizenship: Theory, practice and policy.* New York: Cambridge University Press.

Coleman, S., and Ross, K. 2010. *The media and the public: "Them" and "Us" in media discourse.* Oxford: Wiley-Blackwell.

Currah, A. 2009. *What's happening to our news: An investigation into the likely impact of the digital revolution on the economics of news publishing in the UK.* Oxford: Reuters Institute for the Study of Journalism.

Davies, G. 1999. *The future funding of the BBC.* Report of the Independent Review Panel to Department of Culture, Media and Sport, London: UK.

Debrett, M. 2010. Reinventing public service television for the digital future. Bristol: Intellect.

Deuze, M. 2009. The people formerly known as the employers. *Journalism* 10: 315–318.

Downie, L., and Schudson, M. (2009). The reconstruction of American journalism. *Columbia Journalism Review, 19,* 2009.

Fenton, N. 2011. Deregulation or democracy? New media, news, neoliberalism and the public interest. *Continuum* 25(1): 63–72.

Flew, T. 2010. Democracy, participation and convergent media: Case studies in contemporary online news journalism in Australia. *Communication, Politics & Culture* 42(2): 87–109.

Gillmor, D. 2004. *We the media: Grassroots journalism by the people, for the people.* Sebastapol, CA: O'Reilly.

Gitlin, T. 1998. Public sphere or public sphericules. In T. Liebes, J. Curran, and E. Katz (Eds.), *Media, ritual and identity* (pp. 168-185). London: Routledge.

Hay, C. 1999. Marxism and the state. In A. Gamble, D. Marsh, and D. Tant (Eds.), *Marxism and social science* (pp. 152–174). Urbana: University of Illinois Press.

Kelly, G., and Muers, S. 2002. *Creating public value: An analytical framework for public service reform.* London: Strategy Unit, UK Cabinet Office.

Lee, D., Oakley, K. and Naylor, R. 2011. "The public gets what the public wants"? The uses and abuses of "public value" in contemporary British cultural policy. *International Journal of Cultural Policy* 17(3): 289–300.

McChesney, R. 2011. Rejuvenating American journalism: Some tentative policy proposals. Workshop Presentation on Journalism, Federal Trade Commission, Washington, DC, March 10, 2010. *Perspectives on Global Development and Technology* 10(1): 224–237.

McQuail, D. 1992. *Media performance: Mass communication and the public interest.* London: Sage.

Miliband, R. 1982. *Capitalist democracy in Britain.* Oxford: Oxford University Press.

Moe, H. 2011. Defining public service beyond broadcasting: The legitimacy of different approaches. *International Journal of Cultural Policy* 17(1): 52–68.

Moore, M. 1995. *Creating public value.* Bridgewater, NJ: Replica.

Mosco, V. 2009. The future of journalism. *Journalism: Theory, Practice and Criticism* 10(3): 347–349.

Murdoch, R. 1989. Freedom in broadcasting. MacTaggart Lecture, Edinburgh Television Festival.

Perry, D. 2003. *The roots of civic journalism: Darwin, Dewey, and Mead.* Lanham, Md: University Press of America.

Picard, R. 2010. *The economics and financing of media companies.* New York: Fordham University Press.

Poulantzas, N. 1969. The problem of the capitalist state. *New Left Review 58*: 67–78.

Qinglian, H. 2006. *Media control in China.* China Rights Forum.

Schlesinger, P., and Sorice, M. 2011. *The transformation of society and public service broadcasting.* Series: CMCS Working Paper (1). Centre for Media and Communication Studies.

Silverstone, R. 2007. *Media and morality: On the rise of the mediapolis.* Cambridge: Polity Press.

Sunstein, C. 2002. *Republic.com.* Princeton, NJ: Princeton University Press.

Tambini, D., and Cowling, J. (Eds.). 2004. *From public service broadcasting to public service communications.* London: Institute of Public Policy Research.

Tracey, M. 1998. *The decline and fall of public service broadcasting.* Oxford: Oxford University Press.

Construction and Effects

CHAPTER 25

THE GATEKEEPING OF POLITICAL MESSAGES

PAMELA J. SHOEMAKER, PHILIP R. JOHNSON,
AND JAIME R. RICCIO

POLITICAL gatekeeping involves the selection, shaping, timing, repetition, and transmission of information from one person or organization to another. Economic and technological constraints imposed by the media on the transmission of this information result in the audience seeing a subset of all possible information (Levinson, 2001, 127). Today's rich menu of newspapers (online and print), blogs, social media, and more raises the question: What does gatekeeping theory describe, explain, and predict? The twentieth-century answer was "mass communication," but today's scholars have to consider whether Twitter, for example, is a mass medium. Stacks and Salwen (2009, 11) define *human* communication as emerging from speech and interpersonal communication scholarly traditions. They see mass communication as focusing "on mediated messages and channels of communication." *Social media* describes those communication organizations, such as Facebook and Twitter, that perform both functions. We define *gatekeeping* as the study of both mass communication organizations and the mass communication functions of the social media. By this definition, Twitter is a mass communication organization, and gatekeeping theory may be applied to it.

Gatekeeping is among the oldest theories used by mass communication scholars. Psychologist Kurt Lewin (1947a, 1947b, 1951) devised a "theory of channels and gate keepers" (1947b, 146) in the late 1940s to explain both the movement of items through multiple in-or-out decision points and the changes made in the process.[1] Although Lewin (1951, 187) suggested that his theory could address the flow of news items, it was his research assistant at the University of Iowa, David Manning White (1950), who applied the theory to communication messages. In a 1949 study, White analyzed the decisions of a local small-city newspaper wire editor—whom White called "Mr. Gates"—about whether to accept or reject stories from three news services.[2] White's use of Lewin's central constructs—gate, gatekeeper, channel, section, and force—inspired many communication scholars and generated many studies.

As applied to the study of political messages, gatekeeping theory explains the movement of information in a social system and the forces that facilitate or constrain it. The theory helps us understand why an event is interpreted as political, why the news media cover the event, and how the event is shaped and edited before it ultimately becomes news. Information is a characteristic of an event, such as a conversation, blog post, tweet, television news program, speech, and so forth. Events frame information in ways that determine whether such information is considered important, or newsworthy, or political. Information transmitted by some events may become *messages* carried to others.

As information is moved, shaped, and transmitted, the symbols and meaning from among combinations of event witnesses, other sources, news gatherers, editors and producers, communication organizations, and audience members are transformed (see Figure 25.1). All of these interact to ultimately produce a set of messages that may or may not eventually reach the audience. A message is a compilation of information—whether visual, verbal, or numerical—that can be written (and read), created as images (and seen or felt), spoken (and heard), video recorded (and seen, heard, and/or read), digitally analyzed (and interpreted), and so forth.

Messages may be given more formal descriptors, such as speech, email, post, story or article, news or feature item, film or video, program, show, book, song, and comments or discussion concerning any of the above. When used in the context of the mass media, a message is information drafted by a journalist, public relations practitioner, or other communicator (such as an individual), who sometimes passes it along to someone else for evaluation and for making decisions.

These messages are generally transmitted by media organizations, but the definition *of media organization* has significantly changed since the late 1990s, when news began migrating to the Internet. Today any person with Internet skills can create a blog or video, post messages, tweet, and be followed by audiences large enough to have been defined as a *mass* media organization in the twentieth century.

In this chapter, our emphasis is on messages that contain bits of new information. News is a social artifact (in the form of text, moving or still images, or various interactions) created to represent an event to an audience. Most news is driven by the occurrence of events, for example, a candidate's speech or voting in an election, a government agency's news conference that releases economic information, meetings with other countries' heads of state, congressional debates and the passage of bills, the release of a decision by the Supreme Court, and war. Because a vast number of political events occur each day, many decisions must be made, not only to select specific bits of information, but also to shape and present them within a certain schedule. It is up to the journalist to decipher political messages for public consumption (Neveu, 2002).

The in/out decision point for each event is a metaphorical gate operated by a gatekeeper. Although gatekeepers are often people, gatekeeping decisions are also frequently made by computer algorithms. In either case, decision-making involves the application of a set of rules. A human gatekeeper's decisions can be guided by the rules established

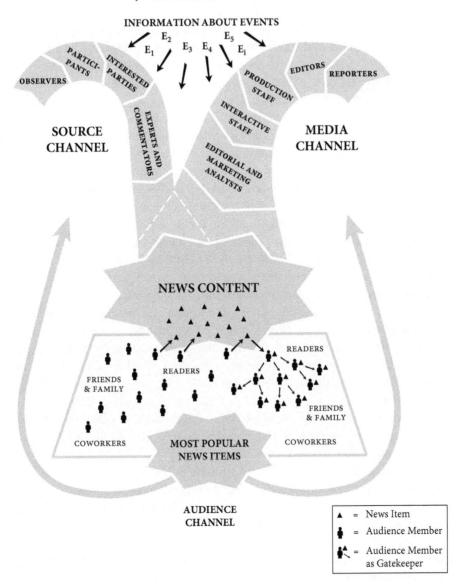

FIGURE 25.1. The three-channel gatekeeping process. Information about events flows to sources and the media and is transformed into news. Readers in the audience then transmit news about the events to others.

Based on Shoemaker, Johnson, Seo, and Wang (2010a, 2010b); Shoemaker, Seo, Johnson, and Wang (2008); Shoemaker and Vos (2009).

by journalistic values. Individual audience members increasingly customize their online information intake, based on their willingness to disclose personal information via historical search activity for a perceived advantage of getting personalized results in return (Andrade, Kaltcheva, and Weitz, 2002, 350; Norberg, Horne, and Horne, 2007, 101; Kobsa, 2007). Audience members personalize their online media by indicating a preference for or aversion to specific news topics (Sundar, 2008, 61).

Although compared to computer programs, human gatekeepers have more leeway in interpreting and applying rules, some rules are deeply ingrained. We can quit a job with disagreeable rules, but we are politically socialized from birth to think of the world in a certain way. The effectiveness of cultural rules is such that our own language, norms, cognitions, attitudes, and behaviors are seen as normal and correct; all else is the *other*. For example, US news coverage of international political events has been correlated with the normative deviance of those events (Chang and Lee, 2010; Chang and Lee, 1992).

In the case of an extremely deviant political event, such as an assassination attempt, sources of information include the people who see it happen, those drawn to the scene, medical personnel, journalists, historians, and so forth. As the event unfolds, many people become sources. Experts are consulted, and think tank experts are invited to be television commentators, often when new information is not available.

Other politicians may take the opportunity to promote messages that make themselves look good and moral—often through public relations professionals and "spin doctors." Political judgments are mediated by the news media's ability to accentuate certain issues and make them salient to audience members, who later assist in opinion formation and choice of political actors (Price and Tewksbury, 1997; Kenski, Hardy, and Jamieson, 2010). Information passes through numerous streams or channels that converge into rivers. But gatekeeping predicts that only a small amount of information is selected from the maelstrom that passes by each decision gate. As the information river becomes larger, gatekeepers become more selective.

The messages that become news are unlikely to be representative of the entire information stream; instead, rules often select the most unusual, criminal, or threatening information. Although not every decision is made consciously by a human (or the equivalent for a computer), there are few random processes involved. Information flows through *channels* that are organized into *sections*, each of which is guarded by a gate and gatekeeper. For example, news releases about candidates' stances on election issues are created by public relations workers (gate 1), who distribute them to media personnel (gate 2), who decide whether the information should be passed on to their supervisors (gate 3).[3] Editors and producers may send reporters to find more information (gate 4), which is compiled into a message about the politician (gate 5). To become news, however, the *message* (comprised of words, images, and/or interactive displays) has to pass through even more gates within media organizations, such as graphic production. The amount of work on a message does not necessarily predict its success. Many messages never become news, stopped by one of the final gatekeepers.

Politicians and their staffs spin information with their own interpretations, hoping that their points of view are able to define media coverage of an event. In gatekeeping theory, spin is a force that can help or prevent information from passing through a gate by taking positive or negative values and varying in strength. A candidate may win an election by attaching positive forces to himself or herself and negative forces to the opponent, the difference between positive and negative campaigning. Forces can be unpredictable, changing polarity after moving through a gate. For example, information may pass by a gate because a candidate's public relations staff is skilled (a propelling and strong force), only to be thrown out by journalists who look on information from public relations sources with suspicion, an inhibiting force.

IMPORTANT STUDIES

Gatekeeping theory did not originate with the study of political messages or even the study of news in general. Psychologist Kurt Lewin's "theory of channels and gate keepers" was used to explain how post–World War II food habits could be changed, with the most important gatekeeper being the family's cook (Lewin, 1947b, 146). In addition to studying the movement of food items within channels, Lewin believed that his theory could be used to study the movement of other items, including news (187).

The idea of journalist-as-gatekeeper stimulated the development of models over the next decade (e.g., see Cutlip, 1954; Gieber, 1956, 1960; Westley and MacLean, 1957; McNelly, 1959; Pool and Shulman, 1959; Stempel, 1959). Shoemaker and Vos expanded gatekeeping as a theoretical model (2009, 11; Shoemaker, 1991, 70).

With the growth of online journalism and social media, individual audience members who are focused on the dissemination of information become "users-turned-producers" (Boczkowski, 2004, 127). Bruns has suggested that the complexity of the Internet has resulted in a large number of cumulative gates, giving each less capacity to "channel the continuing flow of information into manageable portions for the audience" (Bruns, 2008, 72). Examples include collaborative news and bookmarking websites, such as Newsvine,[4] Delicious,[5] or Reddit,[6] in which individual readers explicitly (clicking a button) or implicitly (saving a link as a bookmark) vote on submitted items (Bruns, 2005, 28). Bruns argues that individuals who read these sites "support the case of those seeking information rather than that of the information providers or controllers" (Bruns 2003, 37). These sites, and other manifestations having similar most-popular lists, such as the *New York Times'* most-popular online story lists, are now part of the democratic nature of audience gatekeeping processes and news selection (Levinson, 2001, 127; Johnson and Yang, 2008, 24; Shoemaker et al., 2010a, 2010b; Shoemaker et al., 2008; Berger and Milkman, 2011).

To some, this may suggest that the Internet has killed gatekeeping. A lack of central control over decision-making suggests "gatekeeping without gates": an empowered audience that creates and shares news content without twentieth-century news gatekeeping processes (Boczkowski, 2004, 158). Levinson believes that such online sites increase the flow of viewpoints, opinions, and information that would have not made their way across gates within the usual media organization (Levinson, 2001, 128-128). Hassan (2008, 205) writes that the Internet has transformed political messages into multifaceted distortions caused by "multiple technological representations" and "sprawling and unstable" communication networks. During campaign seasons, for example, political journalists cover and critique each others' news coverage, thus spreading any bias and manipulation across media channels (Esser, Reinemann, and Fan, 2001, 39–40).

The spread of deviant information across media, across time, did not begin with online news, although certainly the Internet has expanded the speed and reach of the most ridiculous messages—*going viral* is the metaphor for the exponential rate at which information can travel online. Yet the virus metaphor describes only one-way transmission. In contrast, today's gatekeeping model includes the evolution of messages and then movement among people. Those who receive also send, and senders receive in an ever-increasing web of transmission, making the audience a powerful player in the gatekeeping process (Figure 25.1). Audiences communicate their preference for one type of information or another by emailing some messages to others, by commenting on or discussing a message online, or even by rating the message with a series of stars (Shoemaker et al., 2010a; Shoemaker et al., 2008). These direct measurements of audience preference provide key information for both media organizations and political campaign staffs.

EMPIRICAL APPROACHES

Many conventional research methodologies and statistical procedures are found in political gatekeeping research, including content analysis, survey research, experiments, and univariate (e.g., ANOVA/ANCOVA) and multivariate statistical procedures (e.g., multiple regression, structural equation modeling). The methodological focus of most gatekeeping research is on investigating media content and the players involved in creating media content (Riffe, Lacy, and Fico, 2005). Therefore, the most prominent research method in political communication scholarship is quantitative content analysis, the "systematic, objective, quantitative analysis of message characteristics" (Neuendorf, 2002, 1), to study manifest content. For example, in analyzing the citations and sources in political news stories featured in the *New York Times* between 1954 and 2004, Tan and Weaver found a relatively equal fluctuation in liberal and conservative biases, supporting the belief in a generally balanced and fair way of the media's reporting of political news (2009, 430).

Textual analysis is a qualitative approach to the study of content that focuses on latent content, in which meanings, concepts, themes, and ideas emerge as a result of interpretation of mass media messages and artifacts (McKee, 2003). In his in-depth textual analysis of four presidential speeches regarding war (two by Franklin D. Roosevelt during World War II and two from George W. Bush's addresses about the Iraq War), Oddo (2011, 312) reveals that political leaders wield a "soft power" in their ability to persuade audiences without force. This comes in large part from their privileged access to the media and close relationships sometimes formed with political journalists.

The focus group can also provide information about the actions and attitudes of journalists and the audience. Shoemaker and Cohen (2006) used data from eighty focus groups in ten countries to compare news values (a force in front of gates) of journalists, public relations practitioners, and audience members with those of their local newspapers. The groups of people had news values in common (within each city) but agreed much less with their local newspapers.

In terms of data analysis, strategies for data gathering could do a better job of testing gatekeeping-related hypotheses if scholars analyzed data using multiple levels of analysis. Although data from two levels of analysis (media routines and reporters) were collected in a study of congressional bills, information from the more macro level was aggregated down to the individual level (Shoemaker et al., 2001). If multilevel modeling had been used, the influences of the routines level would have been assessed separately from that of the individual level.

Scholars who fail to study gatekeeping within the context of multiple levels of analysis risk threats to the internal validity of their research—ignoring alternative explanations and unmistakable common causes across levels. Multilevel modeling analyses now make it possible to assess the relative importance of variables on each level. Thus, one study could assess influences on political messages from political interest groups (social institution level), the ownership patterns of media organizations (media organization level), definitions of newsworthiness (routines level), and communicators' attitudes (individual level) separately and as part of the theoretical whole. This move increases our power to interpret both the influences on political messages and their effects. For example, routine level gatekeeping forces often have a dominant influence over the individual level, particularly regarding the role of journalists (Singer, 2005; Cassidy, 2006; Shoemaker et al., 2001; Shoemaker and Reese, 2013).

FUTURE DIRECTIONS

Gatekeeping theory's scope is both a strength and a challenge and raises the question: How can scholars study political questions that involve multiple levels of analysis, the changing technology of creating and sending messages, characteristics and motivations of senders and receivers, and forces of varying strengths and polarities, all of which interact within the parts of a dynamic political field?

An important change for political communication has been the movement of many political messages to the Internet and the use of websites as gates through which money and promises of involvement flow. Candidates and advocacy groups have websites such as Facebook to communicate with their friends. Many use Twitter to give a sense of understanding to their campaigns. But who creates and disseminates these messages? Although candidates and their staffs work to give an online impression of direct access between the candidate and potential voters, this is nothing more than smoke and mirrors. For example, email messages received "directly" from candidates may appear to omit gatekeepers, when in fact they provide the same information that journalists receive from candidates: news releases and official statements or videos. The candidate's influence on message content varies. The staff's gatekeeping channel begins with multiple sources of information (including feedback from supporters and critics and the candidate's own experiences), and information is then added or subtracted by one staff member after another until the candidate is "on message."

The technology that makes the Internet possible allows communicators to hide the gatekeeping process used in creating the messages. Both constrainers and enablers exist in front of and behind gates, but not all are visible to consumers. Enablers, such as public relations and advertising staffs, try to open gates to push their candidate's messages through the channel to transmission. Constrainers work toward the opposite outcome; the staffs of opposing candidates try to manage the tone and frequency of messages about both candidates. Such positive and negative forces affect not only movement through a gate, but also the speed and the shaping of messages as they pass from one section to another in the channel. For example, if negative information about their candidate emerges, campaign strategists are unlikely to push it through a news channel gate; in fact, they may do everything they can to block it. If the information becomes public, however, it is the job of the lobbying and public relations staff to change the negative message into a neutral or even positive force for the candidate. Many a philandering husband has been repackaged by staff as a newborn family man.

An important challenge for scholars is monitoring how technology changes the content, transmission, and reception of political messages. Not every new media technology is successful (for example, videotext, eight-track music tapes). Being an "early adopter" in the study of media technology can waste research time or make the scholar an expert in an unsuccessful technology. Most gatekeeping studies have concentrated on the transmission of messages, especially news, only some of which are political. Similarly, many political messages are not part of the formal or social news media. For the gatekeeping of political messages, it is important to study not only politics as reflected in news, but also communication within organizations, small groups, and one on one. This also includes messages sent via all types of media and by people who hold all sorts of roles within the political system.

Although personal communication and the reference group have always been important aspects of political messages, the growth of social media has not only increased the volume of political messages but has also increased the importance of the individual in the political process. Gatekeeping theory offers a theoretical structure within which to study the wide diversity that is political communication.

Notes

1. Lewin (1947b, 144) was interested in how post–World War II Americans' food choices could be changed. He identified the household cook as the key gatekeeper in bringing food to the

table through two channels: buying and gardening. Each channel is divided into sections, separated by gates at either end.

2. See McQuail and Windahl (1993, 166) for a visual representation of White's (1950) model showing a single instance of a gate or "gate area" in the gatekeeping process. White's model does not take into account the possibility of multiple gates and gatekeepers in the more generally accepted systems perspective of gatekeeping. The model was expanded on by Westley and MacLean's model, depicting the organization as gatekeeper with the introduction of a mass media channel (1955, 8–9). Shoemaker (1991) later added to the model by pointing out the social system and ideological contexts in which gatekeeping decisions operate.

3. Although information may originate with politicians and their staff members, it may also come to them through preceding gates. See figure 25.1 for a model, which suggests that information can travel through multiple channels and many gates.

4. http://www.newsvine.com.

5. http://www.delicious.com.

6. http://www.reddit.com.

References

Andrade, E. B., Kaltcheva, V., and Weitz, B. 2002. Self-disclosure on the Web: The impact of privacy policy, reward, and company reputation. *Advances in Consumer Research 29*: 350–353.

Berger, J., and Milkman, K. L. 2011. What makes online content viral? *Journal of Marketing Research 49*(2): 192–205.

Boczkowski, P. J. 2004. *Digitizing the news: Innovation in online newspapers.* Cambridge: Massachusetts Institute of Technology.

Bruns, A. 2003. Gatewatching, not gatekeeping: Collaborative online news. *Media International Australia 107*: 31–44.

Bruns, A. 2005. *Gatewatching: Collaborative online news production.* New York: Peter Lang.

Bruns, A. 2008. *Blogs, Wikipedia, Second Life, and beyond: From production to produsage.* New York: Peter Lang.

Cassidy, W. P. 2006. Gatekeeping similar for online, print journalists. *Newspaper Research Journal 27*(2): 6.

Chang, K.-K., and Lee, T.-T. 2010. International news determinants in U.S. news media in the post–Cold War era. In G. J. Golan, T. J. Johnson and W. Wanta (Eds.), *International Communication in a Global Age* (pp. 71–88). New York: Routledge.

Chang, T. K., and Lee, J. W. 1992. Factors affecting gatekeepers' selection of foreign news: A national survey of newspaper editors. *Journalism Quarterly 69*(3): 554–561.

Cutlip, S. M. 1954. Content and flow of AP news—From trunk to TTS to reader. *Journalism Quarterly 31*: 434–446.

Esser, F., Reinemann, C., and Fan, D. 2001. Spin doctors in the United States, Great Britain, and Germany: Metacommunication about media manipulation. *Harvard International Journal of Press/Politics 6*(1): 16–42.

Gieber, W. 1956. Across the desk: A study of 16 telegraph editors. *Journalism Quarterly 33*: 423–432.

Gieber, W. 1960. How the "gatekeepers" view local civil liberties news. *Journalism Quarterly 37*: 199–205.

Hassan, R. 2008. *The information society, digital media and society series.* Cambridge, UK: Polity Press.

Johnson, P. R., and Yang, S. 2008, August. Popularity of news items on Digg: Toward a definition of newsworthiness for social news sites. Paper presented at the annual conference of the Association for Education in Journalism and Mass Communication. Chicago, IL.

Kenski, K., Hardy, B. W., and Jamieson, K. H. 2010. *The Obama victory: How media, money, and message shaped the 2008 election.* New York: Oxford University Press.

Kobsa, A. 2007. Privacy-enhanced personalization. *Communications of the ACM 50* (8): 24–33.

Levinson, P. 2001. *Digital McLuhan: A guide to the information millennium.* New York: Routledge.

Lewin, K. 1947a. Frontiers in group dynamics: Concept, method and reality in science; social quilibria and social change. *Human Relations 1*: 5–41.

Lewin, K. 1947b. Frontiers in group dynamics II: Channels of group life; social planning and action research. *Human Relations 1*: 143–153.

Lewin, K. 1951. *Field theory in social science: Selected theoretical papers.* New York: Harper.

McKee, A. 2003. *Textual analysis: A beginner's guide.* Thousand Oaks, CA: Sage.

McNelly, J. T. 1959. Intermediary communicators in the international flow of news. *Journalism Quarterly 36*(1): 23–26.

McQuail, D., and Windahl, S. 1993. *Communication models for the study of mass communication.* 2nd ed. New York: Longman.

Neuendorf, K. A. 2002. *The content analysis guidebook.* Thousand Oaks, CA: Sage.

Neveu, E. 2002. Four generations of political journalism. In R. Kuhn and E. Neveu (Eds.) *Political journalism: New challenges, new practices* (pp. 22–43). London: Routledge.

Norberg, P. A., Horne, D. R., and Horne, D. A. 2007. The privacy paradox: Personal information disclosure intentions versus behaviors. *Journal of Consumer Affairs 41*(1): 100–126.

Oddo, J. 2011. War legitimation discourse: Representing "us" and "them" in four U.S. presidential addresses. *Discourse and Society 22*(3): 287–314.

Pool, I. de Sola, and Shulman, I. 1959. Newsmen's fantasies, audiences, and newswriting. *Public Opinion Quarterly 23*(2): 145–158.

Price, V., and Tewksbury, D. 1997. News values and public opinion: A theoretical account of media priming and framing. In G. A. Barnett and F. J. Boster (Eds)., *Progress in the communication sciences: Advances in Persuasion* (Vol. 13, pp. 173–212). Greenwich, CT: Ablex.

Riffe, D., Lacy, S., and Fico, F. G. 2005. *Analyzing media messages: Using quantitative content analysis in research.* 2nd ed. Mahwah, NJ: Routledge.

Shoemaker, P. J. 1991. *Communication concepts, volume 3: Gatekeeping.* Newbury Park, CA: Sage.

Shoemaker, P. J., and Cohen, A. 2006. *News around the world: Content, practitioners, and the public.* New York: Routledge.

Shoemaker, P. J., Eichholz, M., Kim, E., and Wrigley, B. 2001. Individual and routine forces in gatekeeping. *Journalism and Mass Communication Quarterly 78*(2): 233–246.

Shoemaker, P. J., Johnson, P. R., Seo, H., and Wang, X. 2010a. Readers as gatekeepers of online news: Brazil, China, and the United States. *Brazilian Journalism Research 6*(1): 55–77.

Shoemaker, P. J., Johnson, P. R., Seo, H., and Wang, X. 2010b. Readers as gatekeepers of online news: Russia, China, and the United States. In E. Vartanova (Ed.), *Content, channels, and audiences in the new millennium: Interaction and interrelations* (pp. 73–103). Moscow: Faculty of Journalism, Lomonosov MSU—MediaMir.

Shoemaker, P. J., and Reese, S. D. 2013. *Mediating the message in the 21st century: A media sociology perspective.* New York: Routledge.

Shoemaker, P. J., Seo, H., Johnson, P. R., and Wang, X. 2008, October. Audience gatekeeping: A study of the *New York Times* most-emailed news items. Paper presented at the Conference on Convergence and Society: The Participatory Web (3.0). Columbia, SC: University of South Carolina.

Shoemaker, P. J., and Vos, T. P. 2009. *Gatekeeping theory*. New York: Routledge.

Singer, J. B. 2005. The political j-blogger: "Normalizing" a new media form to fit old norms and practices. *Journalism* 6(2): 173–198.

Stacks, D. W., and Salwen, M. B. (Eds.). 2009. *An integrated approach to communication theory and research*. New York: Routledge.

Stempel, G. H., III. 1959. Uniformity of wire content of six Michigan dailies. *Journalism Quarterly* 36: 45–48.

Sundar, S. S. 2008. Self as source: Agency and customization in interactive media. In E. Konijn, S. Utz, M. Tanis and S. Barnes (Eds.), *Mediated interpersonal communication* (pp. 58–74). New York: Routledge.

Tan, Y., and Weaver, D. H. 2009. Media bias, public opinion, and policy liberalism from 1956 to 2004: A second-level agenda-setting study. *Mass Communication and Society* 13: 412–434.

Westley, B. H., and MacLean, M. S., Jr. 1955. A conceptual model for communications research. *Educational Technology Research and Development* 3(1): 3–12.

Westley, B. H., and MacLean, M. S., Jr. 1957. A conceptual model for mass communications research. *Journalism Quarterly* 34: 31–38.

White, D. M. 1950. The "gate keeper": A case study in the selection of news. *Journalism Quarterly* 27: 383–390.

CHAPTER 26

....

THE MEDIA AGENDA

Who (or What) Sets It?

....

DAVID H. WEAVER AND JIHYANG CHOI

ALTHOUGH the bulk of the research on media agenda setting has focused on the relationship between news media agendas and public agendas (McCombs and Shaw, 1972; McCombs, 2004), there have been some studies of influences on news media agendas, a type of research that Dearing and Rogers (1996) have termed *media* agenda setting to distinguish it from the more common *public* agenda-setting studies that focus on influences on the public agenda. Others have called this "agenda-building" (Gilberg et al., 1980; Lang and Lang, 1981; Weaver and Elliott, 1985).

This branch of agenda-setting research includes studies of various influences on media agendas, such as news sources, other news media, the norms and traditions of journalism, unexpected events, and media audiences. It tries to unpack the original agenda-setting role of the news media assumed by many public agenda-setting studies. If the news media are often transmitting agendas set by other influential actors and institutions in society, it may not be entirely accurate to think of journalists as the original agenda setters for the public, although they still have much discretion about what to emphasize and what to ignore.

One model for thinking about the influences on news media content is an onion, the concentric layers of which represent the numerous influences on the media agenda (McCombs, 2004). This metaphor also illustrates the sequential nature of this process, with the influence of an outer layer being, in turn, affected by layers closer to the onion's core (see figure 26.1). Shoemaker and Reese (1996), in *Mediating the Message*, have proposed five layers of the onion, ranging from the prevailing societal ideology to the psychology of the individual journalist. Some of the intermediate layers representing the influence of news organizations and professional norms and media routines of journalism are the main focus of the sociology of news research studied by Breed (1955a), Tuchman (1976), and Gans (1980), among others.

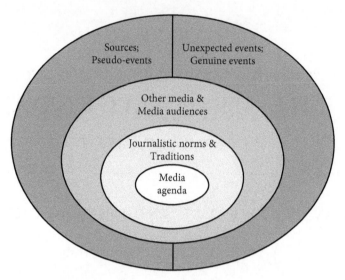

FIGURE 26.1 A metaphorical onion of media agenda setting.

In this chapter we consider five possible influences on the news media agenda: (1) *influential news sources* such as the US president, public relations activities, and political campaigns; (2) *other media* (sometimes studied under the label intermedia agenda setting); (3) the *social norms and traditions of journalism*; (4) *unexpected events* such as the earthquake and tsunami in Japan in March 2011; and (5) *media audiences*, who have more influence now than in the past because of the Internet.

NEWS SOURCES: PRESIDENTS
AND PUBLIC RELATIONS

The single most influential news source in the United States is the president. Virtually everything that a president does is considered newsworthy. One measure of the president's agenda is the legislative action proposed in his annual State of the Union address. Required by the US Constitution, for more than a hundred years this yearly report was a written document submitted to Congress. But in the late twentieth century the annual address became a major media event, broadcast live nationally by the television networks as it was delivered to a joint evening session of the House of Representatives and the Senate.

The format of this address in recent times—a listing of issues or a developed argument about a few key problems that the president wants the Congress to engage with—makes it a convenient measure of the president's priorities, or agenda. This ranking of issues can be compared with the media agenda before and after the address to get a sense of whether the president is setting the media agenda or responding to it, or both. A comparison of President Jimmy Carter's 1978 State of the Union address with the agendas of the *New York Times, Washington Post,* and three national TV networks by Gilberg, McCombs, and Nicholas (1980) found no significant impact of this address on the following month's news coverage of his eight priority issues. But there was evidence that the media coverage of these issues during the month *prior* to the address had influenced President Carter's agenda.

Another study of a very different president, Richard Nixon, by McCombs, Gilbert, and Eyal (1982), found that the agenda on fifteen issues in Richard Nixon's 1970 State of the Union address *did predict* the subsequent month's news coverage by the *New York Times, Washington Post,* and two of the three national TV networks. But there was no evidence that the *prior* news media agenda had influenced Nixon's agenda. Additional replications based on President Ronald Reagan's 1982 and 1985 State of the Union addresses by Wanta and colleagues (1989) yielded mixed evidence about the relationship between the news media agenda and the president's agenda, suggesting that the US president is sometimes able to *influence* the subsequent media agenda and sometimes *follows* earlier news media and public agendas.

In a time-series analysis of the *New York Times* and *The Public Papers of the President* from 1981 to 1996, spanning the first and second Reagan terms, the single term of the senior George Bush, and the first term of Bill Clinton, Holian (2000) found that in most instances, Republican presidents influenced the subsequent media agenda on Republican issues such as taxing and spending, government regulation, and crime and punishment. But Republican presidents Reagan and Bush tended to follow the media emphasis on the Democratic issues of Social Security, Medicare, education, and gender equality. In other words, Reagan and Bush tended to discuss these traditionally Democratic issues publicly when *others,* either the media or their political opponents, placed them on the media agenda. Democratic President Clinton, on the other hand, influenced newspaper coverage of issues related to Social Security and Medicare. Thus, there is evidence from Holian's study that the US president is more likely to influence the media agenda for issues traditionally "owned" by his political party.

Government information officers and commercial public relations practitioners are other important news sources that influence media and policy agendas. They subsidize the efforts of news organizations to cover the news by providing substantial amounts of information, frequently in the form of press or video releases (Gandy, 1982). In one of the earlier studies of this process, Sigal (1973) found that nearly half of the front-page news stories in the *New York Times* and *Washington Post* from 1949 to 1969 were based on press releases, press conferences, and other information subsidies. Considering that both newspapers are major organizations with large staffs and impressive resources, their substantial reliance on public relations sources underscores the key role that information subsidies play in the formation of all media agendas.

At the state level, Turk (1986) found that news coverage of six state government agencies in Louisiana's major daily newspapers also was based substantially on information provided by those agencies' public information officers. Slightly more than half of the information subsidies provided by these officers, mostly written news releases but sometimes personal conversations, appeared in subsequent news stories. Interviews probing the reasons for this influence of information subsidies revealed the central role of journalistic norms and routines, especially perceptions of newsworthiness.

At the local (city) level, Weaver and Elliott (1985) analyzed a year's worth of city council minutes and coverage of the council in the local newspaper. They found a strong overall correlation (+.84) between the agendas of the council and the local newspaper, suggesting that the local paper closely reflected the priorities of the city council, although for some issues the newspaper ranking of issues deviated considerably from the council ranking, especially those concerning arts and entertainment, utilities, animal protection, and awards. When asked about these discrepancies, the reporter covering the council for that year said that he consciously "boiled down" the subjects of education, animal protection, honors and awards, and historical events because they were not controversial and did not lend themselves to a good story. As with Turk's study in Louisiana, this local study reinforces the importance of journalistic norms and traditions, especially ideas about newsworthiness, in shaping the media agenda.

NEWS SOURCES: CAMPAIGNS

Political campaigns are also an important influence on media agendas, at least in countries that hold regular elections. Even though the ultimate goal is to win elections, increasingly campaigns also try to control the media agenda in hopes of influencing the public agenda (Jamieson and Campbell, 1992). Part of the media agenda is under the direct control of political campaigns. Huge amounts of money are spent on political advertising, especially on television ads, to convey candidates' agendas and images, but campaigns also exert major efforts to influence news media agendas, because these agendas are less obviously self-serving and thought to be more credible to the public than are political ads.

A comparative analysis of the 1983 British general election and the 1984 US presidential election found that politicians in Britain had considerably more influence on the news agenda than their counterparts in the United States (Semetko et al., 1991). American journalists had substantially more discretion to shape the campaign news agenda than did British journalists.

This striking difference between the influence of the US and British campaigns on the media agendas was due, in large part, to significant cultural differences in American and British journalists' orientations toward politicians and election campaigns. American election news coverage weighed election news against the newsworthiness of all other stories of the day, whereas the British journalists considered election campaigns inherently important and deserving of coverage. British journalists were also more ready to use party-initiated material, whereas US journalists were concerned that the political campaigns not be allowed to dictate the media agenda and that candidates not be given a "free publicity ride."

Another study also shows that US journalists are not likely to uncritically accept campaign agendas. This research on the 1992 US presidential election by Dalton and his colleagues (1998) found high correlations among candidate platform, media-initiated, and public agendas, but a subsequent analysis using partial correlations by McCombs (2004) showed that when the media agenda is viewed as intervening between the candidate and public agendas, the original correlation of +.78 drops to +.33, suggesting that there is still considerable discretion on the part of the media to set the public agenda in a presidential election.

A more recent comparison of the agendas of the summer 2000 national convention acceptance speeches of US presidential candidates Al Gore and George W. Bush with the agendas of the coverage of these speeches in five newspapers found an average correlation of +.48 for Bush and +.31 for Gore, suggesting that even in the reporting of major candidate speeches, the US newspaper journalists were not willing to let the candidates dictate the news agenda (Mentzer, 2001). On the other hand, the consistency of the agendas of the coverage of the acceptance addresses in the five newspapers (*USA Today, New York Times, Washington Post, Boston Globe*, and *Los Angeles Times*) was considerably higher, with an average correlation of .56 for Gore's speech and .68 for Bush's, suggesting that journalistic views of newsworthiness were an important influence on the newspaper story agendas.

At the state level in the United States, Roberts and McCombs (1994) found that in the 1990 Texas gubernatorial election, the candidates' advertising agendas exerted significant influence on the campaign agendas of the local newspaper and the local television stations even after other factors were taken into account. This analysis also found that the newspaper agenda influenced the television news agenda, rather than vice versa, and this leads to the second major influence on news media agendas, often called intermedia agenda setting.

INTERMEDIA AGENDA SETTING

Another part of the answer to the question, "Who sets the media's agenda?" can be found by looking over time at how the changes in one medium's agenda precede or follow changes in another's. This kind of interaction takes place because journalists tend to closely follow their colleagues' news stories. One of the first scholars to analyze this process was sociologist Breed (1955b), who wrote about newspaper opinion leaders and the process of standardization of newspaper content.

In the US setting, for example, there is considerable anecdotal and some empirical evidence about the agenda-setting influence of the *New York Times* on other news media (Danielian and Reese, 1989; Reese and Danielian, 1989; McCombs, Einsiedel, and

Weaver, 1991), as well as the influence of wire service news on the gatekeeping decisions of Ohio newspaper and television wire editors (Whitney and Becker, 1982).

In a book about the reporting of the 1972 US presidential election, Crouse (1973) made the phrase "pack journalism" famous when he wrote about how Johnny Apple of the *New York Times* set the agenda for the other journalists covering the Iowa caucuses: "He would sit down and write a lead, and they would go write leads. Then he'd change his lead when more results came in, and they'd all change theirs accordingly" (Crouse, 1973, 85). Although Crouse referred to this as "pack journalism," it can also be thought of as a case of intermedia agenda setting.

A more recent example of large-scale intermedia agenda setting comes from a study by Trumbo (1995) of the reporting on the issue of global warming from 1985 to 1992. He found that as the news coverage of this issue steadily accelerated toward its peak in 1989, five major newspapers—among them the *New York Times, Washington Post*, and *Wall Street Journal*—significantly influenced the agenda of the three national television networks. A major intermedia agenda-setting role also was played by science publications regularly scanned by media science writers and editors.

The major wire services, such as the Associated Press, also have an important intermedia agenda-setting influence. A study of how twenty-four Iowa daily newspapers used the AP wire found that even though each newspaper used only a small number of the available wire stories, the patterns of coverage reflected essentially the same proportion for each category of news as the total AP file (Gold and Simmons, 1965). Likewise, a reanalysis of one of the early studies of gatekeeping (White, 1950) by a wire service editor called "Mr. Gates" found a substantial correlation (+.64) between the combined agenda of the wire services he used and Mr. Gates's selections for his newspaper (McCombs and Shaw, 1976). A reanalysis of a follow-up study of Mr. Gates seventeen years later when he used only a single wire service (Snider, 1967) found a correlation of +.80 between the wire agenda and his news agenda.

An experimental study by Charles Whitney and Lee Becker (1982) also found a substantial agenda-setting influence of wire service news on experienced newspaper and television wire editors, with a correlation of +.62 between the proportions of news stories in a large wire service file and the smaller sample selected by the editors. By contrast, in the control condition, where there were an equal number of stories in each news category, there was no common pattern of selection, either in comparison with the wire service or among the editors themselves.

The interaction between newspapers and broadcast media has been another focus of interest. Generally, researchers have found that the direction of influence tends to be from newspapers to broadcast media. Using data from a 1995 election study in the Navarra region of Spain, Esteban Lopez-Escobar and his colleagues (1998) examined patterns of intermedia influence among the two local Pamplona newspapers and Telenavarra, the regional newscast produced by the national public television service. They found correlations of +.66 and +.70 between the newspapers and the subsequent television news agenda. They also found strong evidence (+.99) for the influence of newspaper advertising on television news descriptions of the candidates, in keeping with Roberts and McCombs' (1994) US finding that campaign advertising agendas can influence news coverage.

Those instances when the mainstream media's agenda is shaped by that of alternative media have also been investigated. Mathes and Pfetsch (1991, 51) studied the role of the alternative press in the agenda-building process and found that some issues spilled over from the alternative press into the established newspapers in "a multistep flow of communication within the media system." The liberal newspaper *Die Zeit* was the first established newspaper to cover a counter-issue (boycotting the 1983 German census, resisting German government plans for a new ID card), followed by other liberal daily newspapers. Shortly after the liberal papers covered the issue, the pressure to discuss it became so strong that even the conservative media were forced to report on it. As Mathes and Pfetsch put it, "Thus, the media agenda was built up in a process similar to a chain reaction. At the end of the agenda-building process, a counter-culture issue became a general, public issue" (1991, 53).

Mathes and Pfetsch also found what could be called a "second-level" agenda-setting effect: that the spillover effect from the alternative to the established media was not limited to the topic or issue of coverage because "the established media on the left of the political spectrum adopted the frame of reference for presenting the issues from the alternative media" (1991, 53), although this was not true for the conservative media. And they found this agenda-setting process also influenced the *policy* agenda, because the political elites and institutions could no longer ignore the issues that had received so much coverage in the established media.

Song (2007) similarly explored the process of second-level agenda setting from online alternative media (*Ohmynews* and *PRESSian*) to conservative mainstream media in South Korea. By tracing the reaction of online alternative media and mainstream media in setting the agenda after two Korean schoolgirls were killed by a US military vehicle in 2002, he found that the second-level agenda of alternative media—the anti-US sentiment— first moved to the progressive newspaper *Hankyoreh* and then was finally accepted by two leading conservative newspapers, *Chosun* and *Joongang*.

However, this study also revealed that the transfer of agendas from alternative to mainstream media is not a generally occurring phenomenon; for that to happen the role of a triggering external event is crucial. In the case of the death of the two schoolgirls, the not-guilty verdicts of the US military court triggered nationwide anti-US protests; consequently, even conservative media could not ignore the anti-US agenda of the alternative media.

Several studies have revealed that online media are exerting a significant intermedia agenda-setting impact on traditional media. Ku, Kaid, and Pfau (2003) investigated the direction of influence between the agendas of two presidential candidates' political websites and that of the traditional media (i.e., newspapers and television) during the 2000 US presidential election. A cross-lagged comparison revealed that the campaign issue agenda of the political websites of Bush and Gore influenced the campaign agenda of both national newspapers and television and, generally, that Bush's website had a greater intermedia agenda-setting influence on traditional media than did Gore's.

Moreover, contrary to the findings of previous studies that document the major wire services' agenda-guiding role for other media, two major online news sites in South Korea, in a reverse fashion, influenced the issue agendas of wire services, while influence in the opposite direction was not significant (Lim, 2006).

Another study suggests that the directionality of agenda setting between online media and traditional media can be reciprocal rather than mostly one-way (Lee, Lancendorfer, and Lee, 2005). This study compared the issues discussed on the Internet bulletin boards and those in newspaper coverage during the 2000 general election in South Korea. The cross-lagged comparisons indicated that, at the first level of agenda setting (issues and topics), traditional media's agenda influenced the agenda of Internet bulletin boards. But at the second level of agenda setting (attributes of issues), the Internet bulletin boards exerted an agenda-setting impact on newspapers.

These findings suggest that the intermedia agenda-setting ability of traditional media still remains powerful, even though they are losing their dominance. This is the case because often the new media are not likely to create their own agendas, but rather rely on the reporting of elite mainstream media. Findings by Roberts, Wanta, and Dzwo (2002) show that issues discussed on electronic bulletin boards (EBBs) were mainly derived from the stories that traditional news media such as newspapers and wire services produced. The *New York Times* had the strongest agenda-setting influence on issues discussed on EBBs in this study.

Studies of the intermedia agenda-setting influence of social media such as blogs and microblogs have come to similar conclusions. Network analysis is frequently adopted to explore which media are exerting more influence than others.

For example, Reese and his colleagues (2007) measured the agenda-setting effects of blogs by tracing to what extent blogs include links to professional news media and other blogs. They found that blogs tend to make links to professional news media more often (47.6 percent) than to other blogs (33.5 percent), suggesting that the blogosphere is largely dependent on issue agendas generated by professional journalists.

Likewise, a study by Meraz (2009) also assessed hyperlink usage in 2007 within the eleven newsroom political blogs of the *New York Times*, the *Washington Post*. and eighteen top US independent political blogs. This study found that more than 50 percent of the top-linked pages were those of traditional media, while 33 percent were from citizen media. Again, the *Washington Post* and the *New York Times* were the two most-linked-to sites. In the microblog setting, the pattern was similar. The most frequently "retweeted" stories on Twitter were found to be from traditional news sources such as CNN, the *New York Times*, and ESPN (Asur et al., 2011). The authors argue that "social media, far from being an alternate source of news, functions more as a filter and an amplifier for interesting news from traditional media."

As political activists start to use online media to promote their issue agendas, the impact of these media as potential agenda setters has also been assessed. However, findings show that the online media the political activists are using have only a minor influence on traditional media. Blogger activists did not succeed in affecting overall news media agendas during the "Downing Street Memo" controversy in the United Kingdom but did have a limited influence on the op-ed pages of mainstream newspapers for a short time (Schiffer, 2006). Likewise, the citizen activist–created YouTube advertisements during the 2008 US presidential election primaries did not impact the agenda of the professional activist group's official campaign ads (Ragas and Kiousis, 2010), but the issue agenda of the YouTube ads was strongly correlated with the salience of issues in coverage by partisan media (e.g., the *Nation*).

Studies also suggest that the extent of intermedia agenda setting by new media is contingent on the kinds of issues in question: some are more likely to be transferred than others. For example, a particular issue (abortion) on electronic bulletin boards (EBBs) did not exert any significant influence on traditional media, while other issues (e.g., immigration) yielded immediate and substantial correlations with the issue agendas of traditional media (Roberts, Wanta, and Dzwo, 2002). These researchers argue that controversial issues are less likely to be picked up by other media, while "unobtrusive" issues (those that do not affect most people directly) such as immigration are more likely to be.

Cornfield and colleagues (2005) also point out that the escalation of the conversation from the online environment to the mainstream media is dependent on a number of external factors, including the kinds of information discussed. Their study finds that an issue such as a political scandal is more likely to trigger a "buzz" on blogs since that kind of issue tends to lure a lot of people, including experts, into a sort of detective game.

Given that much attention has been paid to particular cases of online media functioning as strong agenda setters (e.g., bloggers' identification of flaws in CBS's reporting that during the Vietnam War George W. Bush had been given preferential access to a coveted slot in the National Guard and was derelict in discharging his duties while a Guardsman), the findings of limited intermedia agenda-setting effects of online media seem to be counterintuitive. However, some argue that the role of online media is nonetheless significant, because they may function as a channel that telegraphs the climate of public opinion to journalists (Lee, Lacendorfer, and Lee, 2005) or act as a guide for the mainstream media to the rest of the Internet (Cornfield et al., 2005).

In other words, online media sometimes have a substantial intermedia agenda-setting influence as an important source for elite media. Farrell and Drezner (2008) argue that blogs often have significant political consequences, mainly because of the high readership among journalists and other opinion leaders. While blog exposure was limited to only 7 percent of the general population in their study, more than 83 percent of journalists had used them, with 43 percent of journalists reporting use at least every week.

The outcome of this intermedia agenda setting is a *highly redundant news agenda*, at least within a single country or culture. Across countries there may be considerable variation, as Peter and de Vreese (2001) found when they compared television news programs and public surveys across five countries (Denmark, France, Germany, the Netherlands, and the United Kingdom).

Journalistic Norms and Traditions

Some of these differences are due to different cultures and norms of politics and journalism, as Pfetsch (2001) has pointed out in a comparative analysis of political communication cultures in Germany and the United States. Her study of political communicators and journalists in the United States and Germany as key actors in media agenda setting found more emphasis in the United States on the norms of objectivity, balanced content, diversity, and conflicts of interest, and less on ethically impeccable behavior, openness, and honesty.

She also found the perceived relationship between political spokespersons and journalists to be more conflictual and less harmonious in the United States than in Germany, leading to a conclusion that in the United States professional journalistic norms govern interaction between political actors and journalists, whereas in Germany political norms are more important. These different norms and interactions can result in dissimilar political agendas, as the comparative study of British and US election agendas by Semetko and her colleagues (1991) has shown.

Early studies of the media's selection of news items suggested that this process is highly subjective. Journalists tended to select or reject news items based on their own personal feelings or to reject some stories simply because there was insufficient space in a newspaper (Snider, 1967; White, 1950). However, later work has argued that the media's selection of news items not only reflects the subjective decisions of a small number of journalists, but is also a result of a series of complex interactions involving a number of factors, including social norms and traditions/routines of journalism. Shoemaker and Reese (1996) argued that various factors, including news values, journalistic norms of objectivity, and organizational structure, tend to influence individual journalist's news decisions.

It is also noteworthy that the core traditions and professional norms of journalists may be changing, as traditional media are increasingly adopting a convergence strategy with online media to attract larger audiences. Some have argued that online media tend to have different traditions and perceptions of their roles than do traditional media (Singer, 1998, 2001). For example, the online media environment tends to privilege individual viewpoints and opinions, which can challenge traditional journalistic norms of objectivity. Moreover, the Internet's unlimited news space has challenged the traditions of gatekeeping, which have also been part of the core professional norms of journalists.

However, another study by Singer (2005) revealed that the norms of objectivity and gatekeeping are so deeply ingrained among US journalists that even in the online environment of blogs, the journalists tended to "normalize" the news in order to fit their older norms and practices. Based on a content analysis of ten national and ten local blogs to which journalists affiliated with traditional media were uploading news, Singer's study revealed that among the national blogs most of the content was in the form of news digests rather than commentary. Her analysis revealed that journalist bloggers rarely included user-generated content in their blog posts, suggesting that they were trying to stick to their traditional role as gatekeepers despite the new format that provides the possibility of a more interactive and participatory environment.

UNEXPECTED EVENTS

Another group of studies has focused on how unexpected events (such as natural disasters, accidents, unanticipated violence, and dramatic terror attacks) get included on the media agenda. These unpredicted events, such as the September 2001 attack on the World Trade Towers in New York City or the March 2011 earthquake in Japan, can catapult a related issue onto the media, public, and policy agendas. As Schudson (2007, 253) puts it, "Journalists respond to events that they often have not anticipated and do not understand. . . . Events are one of the things that prevent both states and markets from taming and controlling the news." The same can be said of news agendas. Unpredicted events often lead to media agenda shifts that are not controlled by journalists, other news media, news sources, the public, policymakers, or media audiences.

Researchers have compared the effects of unexpected and pseudo-events on media's reporting, and they have, to some extent, yielded conflicting results. A study by Livingston and Bennett (2003) shows that, at least among the CNN international desk stories from 1994 to 2001, event-driven live reports that resulted from spontaneous occurrences (45 percent) outnumbered reports about the actions and pronouncement of governments (35 percent). However, it is also worth mentioning that even among the 45 percent of event-driven reports, 39 percent of the stories included interviews with official sources.

Based on content analysis of news articles and a survey of journalists in the Philippines, Tandoc and Skoric (2010) found that stories prompted by pseudo-events (60 percent) exceeded news stories based on unexpected events (40 percent). This finding stood in contrast to the self-reports from their survey of journalists, in which the majority (80 percent) answered that unexpected, spontaneous events had a better chance of getting onto the news media's agenda than did pseudo-events. The authors refer to this situation as "the pseudo-events paradox."

Moreover, it has also been argued that news media tend to have an advantage in controlling the national agenda during situations surrounding unexpected events. Lawrence (2000, 9) notes that "in institutionally driven news, political institutions set the agendas of news organizations; in contrast, as event-driven news gathers momentum, officials and institutions often respond to the news agenda rather than set it." However, it has also been noted that not every unexpected event, however dramatic and sensational it might be, influences the media agenda.

In *After Disaster*, Birkland (1997, 22) describes the kind of possible event that can influence the national agenda as one "that is sudden, relatively rare, can be reasonably defined as harmful or revealing the possibility of potentially greater future harms, inflicts harms or suggests potential harms that are or could be concentrated on a definable geographical area or community of interest, and that is known to policy makers and the public virtually simultaneously."

In another study, however, Birkland (2004) points out that only the attack on the World Trade Towers of September 11, 2001, had significant long-term effects on the agenda of the US news media, making terrorism one of the most important issues on the media's agendas, while other unexpected terror incidents, such as the first bombing of the World Trade Center, the 1995 Oklahoma City federal building bombing, and the Olympic Park bombing during the 1996 Atlanta Olympics, did not receive comparable attention from media.

Studies indicate that this is the case because media agendas do not simply result from the unexpected events themselves, but are a result of interactions among the event, the nature of the event, and the composition of the community of actors involved (Birkland, 2006). In other words, an unpredicted event's influence on the media agenda is dependent not only on the characteristics of the event itself but also on the journalists' norms and traditions. Many researchers point out that in the process of deciding whether to cover unexpected events journalists tend to rely on their normal routines (Tuchman, 1972, 1973).

Schudson (2007) describes journalists' need to respond to events that they did not expect as the "anarchy of events." As did Tuchman, he argues that journalists tend to handle this uncertainty by organizing and routinizing their process of work, as well as by assimilating the new events using available cultural resources, such as past examples of similar events.

In exploring the influence of unexpected events on media agendas, another interesting point is that one critical, dramatic real-world event can alter the media's agenda for a long period of time. This phenomenon may be referred to as the "spillover effect," in which issues related to the unexpected event are drawn onto the media's agenda. As Kepplinger and Habermeier (1995) assert, key events influence overall news criteria, and as a result, the media tend to cover stories that are relevant to those key events, even after interest in those events themselves wanes.

In line with these arguments about the spillover effect, Choi (2009) found that, due to the invasion of Iraq, related issues such as international politics and military-defense news significantly increased in the US media for a long period of time. For example, the percent of stories about international politics in the *New York Times* jumped from 17 percent in 2001 to 31 percent in 2005.

The studies mentioned above suggest that journalists do not passively report unexpected news events, but rather decide whether to cover them based on interactions between the events and their own journalistic norms and traditions.

MEDIA AUDIENCES

While agenda-setting research has mostly focused on the media's influence on public agendas, some studies have demonstrated that occasionally the influence flows in the opposite direction, from the public to the media.

Based on causality tests between media agendas (as measured by the nightly network news from 1968 to 1990) and public agendas (measured by the Gallup's Most Important Problem question), Uscinski (2009) found that for some issues, public concern tended to precede media coverage. Among nineteen issues he investigated, civil rights, the environment, energy, foreign trade, and social welfare were ones on which the public was more likely to influence the media agenda rather than the other way around. Uscinski argues that since those issues rarely are linked to obviously newsworthy external events, the media tend to carry news stories about them only when there is evident demand and concern from the public.

Scholars have frequently noted that journalists are more likely to react to spectacular and easily reportable singular events and in the process ignore issues of actual public interest due to a perceived lack of "newsworthiness" (Graber, 2010; Kosicki, 1993). However, the findings of Uscinski imply that audiences may influence the media's agenda when "obtrusive" issues (those that affect them directly, such as the environment, energy, and civil rights) are involved.

The influence of audiences on media agendas is more conspicuous in an online environment. Studies have revealed that in such a setting, readers are not guided by the agenda that the media suggest, but rather by that suggested by other audience members. This is the case because many online news sites feature "news recommendations," which show the current number of times a news story has been viewed, the most popular stories viewed within any given time span, and how readers rate a news story.

It is also true that in the highly competitive contemporary media environment, news organizations' responsiveness to the number of clicks elicited by each news story results in more news about weather, sports, crime, gossip, and entertainment than the information about political, economic, and international issues that is essential for well-informed democratic deliberation, as Boczkowski (2010) has found in his research.

Some studies have also examined how news recommendations affect the agenda of online audiences. One example is a Web-based experiment by Knobloch-Westerwick and colleagues (2005) in which three groups browsed online news that featured explicit (average rating) or implicit (times viewed) recommendations, or no recommendations. This study revealed that such recommendations influenced both the audiences' selection of news and the length of the story. In other words, this study implies that recommendation systems based on audiences' news selections function as a guiding agenda for the online media, rather than as cues of story importance, such as the display order and the headlines, that the online media typically suggest.

CONCLUSIONS

This review of media agenda-setting studies illustrates an expansion of the scope of agenda-setting research from a concern with the relationship between media and public agendas to a concern with how the media agenda is determined. Although they play a major role in shaping agendas, both of issues and attributes, journalists alone are not entirely responsible for media agendas. Future studies should focus on the conditions under which journalists' agenda-setting discretion is heightened or lessened, as well as the various influences on the formation of news media agendas discussed in this chapter.

One consistent finding from our last two national studies of US journalists (Weaver and Wilhoit, 1996; Weaver et al., 2007) is that most do not consider setting the political agenda to be a very important role for journalists as compared with investigating government claims, getting information to the public quickly, and analyzing complex problems, even though making judgments about what to emphasize in news coverage and what to downplay inevitably exerts some agenda-setting influence on the public and policymakers.

Sometimes it seems as if journalists are either not aware of the agenda-setting influence of their news media or unwilling to acknowledge it, although some prominent figures in journalism have been more forthcoming, such as the late Katharine Graham of the *Washington Post*, who was quoted as saying in 1993, "The power is to set the agenda. What we print and what we don't print matter a lot" (Freedom Forum Calendar, 1997). Likewise, David S. Broder, former longtime political journalist for the *Washington Post*, has been quoted as saying, "The premise we have to challenge as journalists is that the candidates have the exclusive rights to control the dialogue" (Randolph, 1988, 14).

Thus the evidence gathered to date on media agenda setting suggests that news agendas are constructed as a joint product between news sources and journalists, between prominent media and other media, sometimes on the basis of unexpected events and media audience preferences, and always according to the norms and traditions of journalism in different societies. As Berkowitz (1992, 81) has noted, "the creation of a news agenda is the result of a process that depends on much more than a loosely linked transferral of one group's priorities to another."

But which of these possible influences has more or less impact on this process remains uncertain, at least in relatively free and open political systems. This uncertainty only heightens interest in studying who or what influences the media agenda in different cultures and countries and during different periods of history. There surely is more to be learned in trying to determine who or what sets the media agenda and how it is done.

References

Asur, S., Huberman, B. A., Szabo, G., and Wang, C. 2011. Trends in social media: Persistence and decay. *Social Science Research Network*, February 25.http://ssrn.com/abstract=1755748.

Berkowitz, D. 1992. Who sets the media agenda? The ability of policymakers to determine news decisions. In J. D. Kennamer (Ed.), *Public opinion, the press, and public policy* (pp. 81–102). Westport, CT: Praeger.

Birkland, T. A. 1997. *After disaster: Agenda setting, public policy and focusing events*. Washington, DC: Georgetown University Press.

Birkland, T. A. 2004. "The world changed today": Agenda-setting and policy change in the wake of the September 11 terrorist attacks. *Review of Policy Research* 21: 179–200.

Birkland, T. A. 2006. *Lessons of disaster: Policy change after catastrophic events*. Washington, DC: Georgetown University Press.

Boczkowski, P. J. 2010. *News at work: Imitation in an age of information abundance.* Chicago: University of Chicago Press.

Breed, W. 1955a. Social control in the newsroom. *Social Forces 33*: 326–335.

Breed, W. 1955b. Newspaper opinion leaders and the process of standardization. *Journalism Quarterly 32*: 277–284, 328.

Choi, J. 2009. Diversity in foreign news in US newspapers before and after the invasion of Iraq. *International Communication Gazette 71*(6): 525–542.

Cornfield, M., Carson, J., Kalis, A., and Simon, E. 2005. Buzz, blogs, and beyond: The Internet and the national discourses in the fall of 2004. Pew Internet & American Life Project. Retrieved February 15, 2011, from http://www.pewinternet.org/ppt/BUZZ_ BLOGS__BEYOND_Final05-16-05 .pdf.

Crouse, T. 1973. *The boys on the bus: Riding with the campaign press corps.* New York: Ballantine Books.

Dalton, R. J., Beck, P. A., Huckfeldt, R., and Koetzle, W. 1998. A test of media-centered agenda setting: Newspaper content and public interests in a presidential election. *Political Communication 15*: 463–481.

Danielian, L., and Reese, S. 1989. A closer look at intermedia influences on agenda setting: The cocaine issue of 1986. In P. Shoemaker (Ed.), *Communication campaigns about drugs: Government, media and the public* (pp. 47–66). Hillsdale, NJ: Lawrence Erlbaum.

Dearing, J. W., and Rogers, E. M. 1996. *Agenda-setting.* Thousand Oaks, CA: Sage.

Farrell, H., and Drezner, D. W. 2008. The power and the politics of blogs. *Public Choice 134*(1–2): 15–30.

Freedom Forum Calendar. 1997. Katherine Graham, Publisher of the *Washington Post,* September 24.

Gandy, O. H. 1982. *Beyond agenda setting: Information subsidies and public policy.* Norwood, NJ: Ablex.

Gans, H. J. 1980. *Deciding what's news: A study of "CBS Evening News," "NBC Nightly News," "Newsweek" and "Time."* New York: Vintage Books.

Gilberg, S., Eyal, C., McCombs, M., and Nicholas, D. 1980. The State of the Union address and the press agenda. *Journalism Quarterly 57*: 584–588.

Gold, D., & Simmons, J. 1965. News selection patterns among Iowa dailies. *Public Opinion Quarterly 29*: 425–430.

Graber, D. 2010. *Mass media and American politics.* 8th ed. Washington, DC: CQ Press.

Holian, D. B. 2000. The press, the presidency, and the public: Agenda setting, issue ownership, and presidential approval from Reagan to Clinton. PhD diss., Department of Political Science, Indiana University-Bloomington.

Jamieson, K. H., and Campbell, K. K. 1992. *The interplay of influence: News, advertising, politics, and the mass media.* 3rd ed. Belmont, CA: Wadsworth.

Kepplinger, H. M., and Habermeier, J. 1995. The impact of key events on the presentation of reality. *European Journal of Communication 10*(3): 371–390.

Knobloch-Westerwick, S., Sharma, N., Hansen, D. L., and Alter, S. 2005. Impact of popularity indications on readers' selective exposure to online news. *Journal of Broadcasting & Electronic Media 49*(3): 296–313.

Kosicki, G. M. 1993. Problems and opportunities in agenda-setting research. *Journal of Communication 43*(2): 100–27.

Ku, G., Kaid, L. L., and Pfau, M. 2003. The impact of web site campaigning on traditional news media and public information processing. *Journalism and Mass Communication Quarterly 80*(3): 528–547.

Lang, G. E., and Lang, K. 1981. Watergate: An exploration of the agenda-building process. In G. C. Wilhoit and H. de Bock (Eds.), *Mass communication review yearbook, Volume 2* (pp. 447–468). Beverly Hills, CA: Sage.

Lawrence, R. 2000. *The politics of force: Media and the construction of police brutality.* Berkeley: University of California Press.

Lee, B., Lacendorfer, K. M., and Lee, K. J. 2005. Agenda-setting and the Internet: The intermedia influence of internet bulletin boards on newspaper coverage of the 2000 general election in South Korea. *Asian Journal of Communication* 13(1): 57–71.

Lim, J. 2006. A cross-lagged analysis of agenda setting among online news media. *Journalism and Mass Communication Quarterly* 83(2): 298–312.

Livingston, S., and Bennett, L. 2003. Gatekeeping, indexing, and live-event news: Is technology altering the construction of news? *Political Communication* 20: 363–380.

Lopez-Escobar, E., Llamas, J. P., McCombs, M., and Lennon, F.R. 1998. Two levels of agenda setting among advertising and news in the 1995 Spanish elections. *Political Communication* 15: 225–238.

Mathes, R., and Pfetsch, B. 1991. The role of the alternative press in the agenda-building process: Spill-over effects and media opinion leadership. *European Journal of Communication* 6: 33–62.

McCombs, M. 2004. *Setting the agenda: The mass media and public opinion.* Cambridge, UK: Blackwell Polity Press.

McCombs, M., Einsiedel, E., and Weaver, D. 1991. *Contemporary public opinion: Issues and the news.* Hillsdale, NJ: Lawrence Erlbaum Associates.

McCombs, M. E., Gilbert, S., and Eyal, C. H. 1982. The State of the Union address and the press agenda: A replication. Paper presented to the International Communication Association, Boston.

McCombs, M. E., and Shaw, D. L. 1976. Structuring the "unseen environment." *Journal of Communication* 26(2): 18–22.

Mentzer, T. 2001. Media agenda-building and the political process. Paper prepared for Government and Media Seminar, School of Journalism, Indiana University-Bloomington.

Meraz, S. 2009. Is there an elite hold? Traditional media to social media agenda setting influence in blog networks. *Journal of Computer-Mediated Communication* 14: 682–707.

Peter, J., and de Vreese, C. H. 2001. Another look at the public agenda: A cross-national comparative investigation of nominal and thematic public agenda diversity. Paper presented to the International Communication Association, Washington, DC.

Pfetsch, B. 2001. The normative basis of media agenda-setting: A comparative analysis of political communication culture in the United States and Germany. Paper presented to the International Communication Association, Washington, DC.

Ragas, M. W., and Kiousis, S. 2010. Intermedia agenda-settings and political activism: Moveon.org and the 2008 presidential election. *Mass Communication and Society* 13: 560–583.

Randolph, E. 1988. Now there are two "stealth" candidates. *Washington Post National Weekly Edition*, September 26–October 2, 14.

Reese, S., and Danielian, L. 1989. Intermedia influence and the drug issue: Converging on cocaine. In P. Shoemaker (Ed.), *Communication campaigns about drugs: Government, media and the public* (pp. 29–45). Hillsdale, NJ: Lawrence Erlbaum Associates.

Reese, S., Rutigliano, L., Hyun, K., and Jeong, J. 2007. Mapping the blogosphere. *Journalism* 8(3): 235–261.

Roberts, M., and McCombs, M. 1994. Agenda setting and political advertising: Origins of the news agenda. *Political Communication* 11: 249–262.

Roberts M., Wanta, W., and Dzwo, T. 2002. Agenda setting and issue salience online. *Communication Research* 29(4): 452–462.

Schiffer, A. J. 2006. Blogswarms and press norms: News coverage of the Downing Street Memo controversy. *Journalism & Mass Communication Quarterly* 83: 494–510.

Schudson, Michael. 2007. The anarchy of events and the anxiety of story telling. *Political Communication* 24(3): 253–257.

Semetko, H. A., Blumler, J. G., Gurevitch, M., and Weaver, D. H. 1991. *The formation of campaign agendas: A comparative analysis of party and media roles in recent American and British elections*. Hillsdale, NJ: Lawrence Erlbaum Associates.

Shoemaker, P. J., and Reese, S. D. 1996. *Mediating the message: Theories of influences on mass media content*. 2nd ed. White Plains, NY: Longman.

Sigal, L. V. 1973. *Reporters and officials: The organization and politics of newsmaking*. Lexington, MA: D.C. Heath & Company.

Singer, J. B. 1998. Online journalists: Foundations for research into their changing roles. *Journal of Computer-Mediated Communication* 4(1). Retrieved April 10, 2011, from http://jcmc.indiana.edu/vol4/issue1/singer.html.

Singer, J. B. 2001. The metro wide web: Changes in newspapers' gatekeeping role online. *Journalism & Mass Communication Quarterly* 78: 65–80.

Singer, J. B. 2005. The political j-blogger: "Normalizing" a new media form to fit old norms and practices. *Journalism* 6(2): 173–198.

Snider, P. B. 1967. "Mr. Gates" revisited: A 1966 version of the 1949 case study. *Journalism Quarterly* 44: 419–427.

Song, Y. 2007. Internet news media and issue development: A case study on the roles of independent online news services as agenda-builders for anti-US protests in South Korea. *New Media & Society* 9(2): 71–92.

Tandoc, E. C., and Skoric, M. M. 2010. The pseudo-events paradox: How pseudo-events flood the Philippine press and why journalists don't recognize it. *Asian Journal of Communication* 20(1): 33–50.

Trumbo, C. 1995. Longitudinal modeling of public issues: An application of the agenda-setting process to the issue of global warming. *Journalism Monographs* 152: 1–57.

Tuchman, G. 1972. Objectivity as strategic ritual: An examination of newsmen's notions of objectivity. *American Journal of Sociology* 77(4): 660–679.

Tuchman, G. 1973. Making news by doing work: Routinizing the unexpected. *The American Journal of Sociology* 79(1): 110–131.

Tuchman, G. 1976. Telling stories. *Journal of Communication* 26(4): 93–97.

Turk, J. V. 1986. Information subsidies and media content: A study of public relations influence on the news. *Journalism Monographs* 100: 1–29.

Uscinski, J. E. 2009. When does the public's issue agenda affect the media's issue agenda (and vice-versa)? Developing a framework for media-public influence. *Social Science Quarterly* 90(4): 796–815.

Wanta, W., Stephenson, M. A., Turk, J., and McCombs, M. E. 1989. How president's State of Union talk influenced news media agendas. *Journalism Quarterly* 66: 537–541.

Weaver, D. H., Beam, R. A., Brownlee, B. J., Voakes, P. S., and Wilhoit, G. C. 2007. *The American journalist in the 21st century: U.S. news people at the dawn of a new millennium*. Mahwah, NJ: Lawrence Erlbaum.

Weaver, D., and Elliott, S. 1985. Who sets the agenda for the media? A study of local agenda-building. *Journalism Quarterly* 62: 87–94.

Weaver, D. H., and Wilhoit, G. C. 1996. *The American journalist in the 1990s: U.S. news people at the end of an era.* Mahwah, NJ: Lawrence Erlbaum.

White, D. M. 1950. The "gate keeper": A case study in the selection of news. *Journalism Quarterly* 27: 383–390.

Whitney, D. C., and Becker, L. B. 1982. "Keeping the gates" for gatekeepers: The effects of wire news. *Journalism Quarterly* 59: 60–65. [Also in Protess, D. L., and McCombs, M. 1991. *Agenda Setting* (pp. 229–236). Hillsdale, NJ: Lawrence Erlbaum].

....

CHAPTER 27

GAME VERSUS SUBSTANCE IN POLITICAL NEWS

....

THOMAS E. PATTERSON

IT was one of the biggest news stories in years. A US special operations team had conducted a secret raid into Pakistan that ended in the killing of Osama bin Laden, the leader of the al Qaeda terrorist network and the mastermind of the deadly attacks on the World Trade Center and the Pentagon a decade earlier. According to the Project for Excellence in Journalism, bin Laden was the focus of 28 percent of US news stories in the week following his death (2011, 2). The major storyline was the planning and carrying out of the military raid, which accounted for a third of the bin Laden coverage.

But what was the second biggest storyline? Was it the reaction of the Arab world to the killing? Was it the operation's effect on US relations with Pakistan? Was it the effects of bin Laden's death on the fight against terrorism? "None of the above" is the answer. Second billing went to the question of the partisan impact of bin Laden's death: Would it pave the way for Barack Obama's re-election to a second term? This question accounted for a sixth of the coverage, twice the amount devoted to the national security implications of bin Laden's killing.

Political coverage is necessarily selective. Politics is complex, spanning a wide array of actors, institutions, processes, and interests. The story possibilities are endless, and journalists must find ways to narrow their selections. Almost instinctively, they find significance in the competition for power and leadership. When it comes to political coverage, substance is often subordinated to the competitive game.

THE GAME SCHEMA AS THEORETICAL PERSPECTIVE

....

The writer Paul Weaver was among the first to propose that journalists regularly frame political news as a competitive struggle between power-driven leaders:

> [As journalists see it,] politics is essentially a game played by individual politicians for personal advancement, gain or power. The game is a competitive one and the players'

principal activities are those of calculating and pursuing strategies designed to defeat competitors and to achieve their goals. . . . Of course, the game takes place against a backdrop of governmental institutions, public problems, policy debates, and the like, but these are noteworthy only insofar as they affect, or are used by, players in pursuit of the game's rewards. The game is played before an audience—the electorate— which controls most of the prizes, and players therefore constantly attempt to make a favorable impression. In consequence, there is an endemic tendency for players to exaggerate their good qualities and to minimize their bad ones, to be deceitful, to engage in hypocrisies, to manipulate appearances; though inevitable, these tendencies are bad tendencies. . . and should be exposed. They reduce the electorate's ability to make its own discriminating choices, and they may hide players' infractions of the game's rules, such as those against corruption and lying. (Weaver, 1972, 69)

Thomas Patterson used the term *game schema*[1] to describe journalists' perspective, pointing out that it dovetails with news conventions and values (1993, 60–66). He noted as well that the news by definition is what is different about today as compared with yesterday. The competitive game meets the need for novelty. It is constantly moving as politicians adjust to the tactical situation and their positions in it. The game is thus a reliable source of fresh material. By comparison, policy problems lack novelty. A sudden development may thrust a new issue into the arena or shed new light on an old one, but problems tend to be long-standing. If they came and went overnight, they would not be problems. In this sense, their day-to-day news value is comparatively small. Breaking developments catch journalists' attention. Chronic conditions do not.

The plot-like nature of political maneuvering also fits journalists' needs. Because of the requirement to attract and hold an audience, journalists prefer dramatic stories. The political game is a running drama: rising action, falling action, winners and losers. The game also embodies the conflict that journalists prize in news. Competition for power among elites "is a naturally structured, long-lasting dramatic sequence with changing scenes" (Barber, 1978, 117–118). Policy problems can also be a source of drama, but their complexity defies easy characterization. As the journalist Walter Lippmann noted, reporters prefer "the easy interest" (1965, 221).

Then, too, the news is largely a story of prominent leaders. Journalists gather where top officials are found, and most of their reports originate in what these officials do. Steele (1995) concludes that journalists have an "operational bias" that favors top leaders. News typically works from the top down, "favoring high government officials over lower government officials, government officials over unofficial groups and oppositional groups, and groups of any sort over unorganized citizens" (Schudson, 2008, 52). In this context, journalists tend naturally to see top leaders as engaged in a competition for power. Although politicians represent policy coalitions and pursue policy goals, they are also strategic actors, and this role is the most palpable. It is also a role that tempts leaders to engage in lying, cheating, and other behaviors that undermine the democratic process and that journalists in their role as watchdogs seek to identify (Delli Carpini, 2005, 31).

Finally, the news is a professional product designed for consumption by a broad audience. "The height of [Western journalists'] professional skill," says Denis McQuail, "is the exercise of a practical craft, which delivers the required institutional product, characterized by a high degree of objectivity, key marks of which are obsessive facticity and neutrality of attitude" (1994, 145). The game fits this imperative. Journalists can report the game without having to take sides. There is no overt partisanship in factual news reports on politicians' attempts to wield power. If journalists were to engage fully with partisan issues, they would risk promoting one side or the other.

In short, the game schema aligns with a number of journalists' norms and needs. It allows journalists to cover politics without having to ask constantly whether they are operating safely within the boundaries of news. Whether the game schema serves the interests of the public is a separate issue, a point discussed later in this chapter.

The Game Schema in the Context of US Presidential Elections

Presidential elections in the United States have been the focus of most research on journalists' use of the game schema. One of the earliest studies was Patterson and McClure's examination of television coverage of the 1972 US presidential general election. As reported on television, the Nixon-McGovern campaign was framed as a strategic and tactical battle waged both before crowds and behind the scenes. The three major networks—ABC, CBS, and NBC—devoted nearly four times as much airtime to the "horse race" as they did to the candidates' issue positions and nine times as much as was given to the candidates' qualifications on key personal and leadership traits (1976, 41). "The contest theme," Patterson and McClure concluded, "was carried to the campaign's very end, at the expense of the election's issues and the candidates' qualifications for office" (46).

In a 1976 election study, Patterson extended the analysis to include primary elections and the print media. Game coverage was found to be more pronounced on television and during the primary election period, but the game trumped substance at each stage of the campaign and in each medium. Patterson also analyzed candidate-controlled communication (such as their televised ads) and found it to be dominated by leadership and issue appeals, leading him to conclude that "the game emphasis [in news] primarily reflects the interests of the press" (1980, 29).

Subsequent studies, numbering in the scores, have varied in method and scope, but nearly all of them have concluded that substance is secondary to the game in presidential election reporting. In a comprehensive assessment, Farnsworth and Lichter studied news coverage of the seven presidential campaigns between 1988 and 2012. The horse race was the most heavily covered topic in each of these elections (2014, 1).

During the general election, the level of game coverage depends in part on the salience of the issues of the moment. The 2008 Obama-McCain race, for example, was waged against the backdrop of momentous issues—economic turmoil and war in the Middle East—and the Project for Excellence in Journalism found an elevated level of issue coverage: "Horse race reporting, once again, made up the majority of coverage, but less so ... than in [recent] elections" (2008, 1). When it comes to the primary election period, however, the amount of horse-race coverage is a function of the competitiveness of the race. In their analysis of the 2008 Democratic presidential primaries, Lawrence and Rose found that 89 percent of the coverage of the closely contested Obama-Clinton race was in the "horse-race/game" category, while only 7 percent was in the "issue/substantive" and "character" categories (2009, 183).

Although the level of game coverage varies from one election to the next, a long-term trend is evident. In a study of the nine presidential elections between 1960 and 1992, Patterson found that game coverage barely exceeded policy and leadership coverage in the earliest of these elections but came to dominate the coverage in the later ones (1993, 74), a change that he attributed to three developments.

One is the change in the nominating system that occurred in 1972, which resulted in an increase in the number of states using primary elections as the means of selecting their national convention delegates. The nominating campaign is when horse-race coverage is the heaviest (1993, 174–175).

A second development cited by Patterson is journalists' dependence on polls (1993, 81). In the 1960s polls were still a relatively small part of presidential election coverage, although Gallup, Harris, and other commercial pollsters were expanding their polling efforts. In the 1970s media outlets began conducting their own election polls. By 1980 polls were featured in about a fourth of election reports, often as the day's top story (Keenan, 1985, 616). Daily tracking polls soon followed, resulting in the taking of hundreds of polls during each election (Erikson and Wlezien, 1999). In the last two months alone of the 2004 election, for example, approximately 200 polls were reported by one or more of the leading US news outlets (Rosenstiel, 2005, 699).

Although journalists could use polls as a starting point for stories on leadership and issues, they seldom do so. Larson (2001) found that a mere 1 percent of poll mentions in coverage of the 2000 election referred to survey questions about the candidates' leadership qualities. Polls serve as fuel for journalists' horse-race narratives (Welch, 2002). They are used to track the candidates' positions in the race, as well as grist for strategy-centered stories. Rhee (1996) found that as poll references increase in news reports, so, too, do references to the candidates' strategies.

The third development Patterson cited is the emergence of an interpretive style of journalism (1993, 80). The older descriptive style, still dominant in the 1960s, cast the journalist in the role of reporter, which included an emphasis on the statements of candidates, often in the form of lengthy quotes or sound bites. In the 1960s, when candidates appeared in a television news story, they were usually pictured speaking. Within two decades, journalists had adopted an interpretive style, which enabled them to do most of the talking. In 1968 the average sound bite—a block of uninterrupted speech by a newsmaker on television news—was more than 40 seconds (Hallin, 1992, 10). By 1988, the average had shrunk to less than 10 seconds (Adatto, 1990, 4). In recent elections, journalists have consumed more than 70 percent of the speaking time in network election coverage, while candidates have been allotted slightly more than 10 percent (Farnsworth and Lichter, 2007, 92).

As journalists' words came to dominate coverage, their way of talking about the campaign—as a competitive game—became more prominent in election reporting. Even though candidates think strategically, their public statements are dominated by references to policy and leadership. These references receded in the news as the candidates' words were reported less often (Patterson, 1993, 81).

The interpretive style elevates the game in another way as well. To be coherent, an interpretive story requires a narrative theme. Journalists tend to construct these themes in the context of the strategic game, which has the effect of subordinating issue and leadership questions. In the lead-up to the 2008 Democratic presidential primaries, for example, Hillary Clinton went to New Hampshire to unveil her plan for helping middle-class families. Included in Clinton's speech was a proposal to extend family and sick leave. In the news, her speech was portrayed as a blatant attempt to curry favor with women voters (Lawrence and Rose, 2009, 182).

The game now pervades the news coverage of nearly every aspect of presidential campaign politics. Even the presidential debates are wrapped in a narrative about the strategic game. Pre-debate coverage is saturated with speculation on how well the candidates will perform, and post-debate coverage is dominated by assessments of how well they did perform. In 2012, even though game coverage overall was down somewhat from its usual level, it peaked during the period of the presidential debates, accounting for nearly half of election reporting. Meanwhile, foreign policy coverage fell by half during the debates, even though it was the focus of one of them (Project for Excellence in Journalism, 2012, 1). "In covering a presidential campaign," Larry Bartels concludes, "the media tell us more about who is winning and who is losing than they do about who is fit to be president" (1988, 32).

THE GAME SCHEMA IN OTHER CONTEXTS

The strategic frame is less prevalent in other reporting contexts. In the case of US congressional elections, for example, the game dominates only the coverage of national news outlets. They highlight the closely contested races, focusing on the horse race (Project for Excellence in Journalism, 2010, 2; Power and Robbins, 2014, 1). Local news outlets concentrate on congressional races within their geographical area and place relatively less emphasis on the horse race. Nevertheless, it is a theme of Senate election coverage (Kahn, 1991, 349; Druckman, 2004, 582) while also affecting the level of coverage—close Senate races get heavier coverage than lopsided ones (Kahn and Kenney, 1999). On the other hand, many House races are virtually ignored by the local media because their outcome is not in doubt. When House races get covered, the horse race is a prominent theme but not the top one, which Arnold (2004, 177) attributes to a scarcity of local analysts and opinion polls.

Regarding Congress itself, the game is an integral part of the coverage. Lichter and Amundson found that congressional news has become largely a story of power struggles and gamesmanship. Their study of the trend in television congressional coverage between 1972 and 1992 found that policy coverage dropped by nearly 20 percentage points, while coverage of competition between members and with the executive branch doubled (1994, 136). Mark Rozell examined a longer period of congressional coverage—1946–1992—and concluded that it increasingly focused on "scandal, partisan rivalry, and interbranch conflict rather than the more complex subjects such as policy, process, and institutional concerns" (1992, 110).

In part because executive power is not divided among contending parties, news coverage of the US presidency is more policy-centered (Farnsworth and Lichter, 2007, 176). Nevertheless, the game is a major component of the coverage. In a study of presidential news from 1980 to 1999, Jeffrey Cohen found that policy frames accounted for 43 percent of the coverage, while two game-related frames—conflict and ambition/power—accounted for 31 percent and 16 percent, respectively (2008, 119). He also found that use of the policy frame declined during the two decades that were studied (131).

In a study that encompassed the whole of the political process, Jamieson and Cappella (1994) tracked media coverage of the 1993–1994 US healthcare reform debate, which centered on President Bill Clinton's effort to persuade Congress to enact universal healthcare. They found that two-thirds of the print and television coverage was devoted to aspects of political process and strategy. Only a fourth of print coverage and a fifth of TV coverage focused on the issue itself. Moreover, as the debate unfolded, attention to the issue receded.

Game coverage has not been studied extensively in Europe, partly because competition for power is more constrained in European political systems. Europe's elections center on parties rather than candidates, and Europe's parliamentary systems concentrate executive and legislative power in a single leader and party. Moreover, Europe's journalists are less hamstrung than their American counterparts in how they cover partisan issues. Although European reporters aim more to inform than to persuade, partisan neutrality is not for them as strict a command (Patterson, 2007; Kleinnijenhuis and DeRidder, 1998).

As these differences would suggest, the strategic game is a comparatively smaller feature of European news coverage. It is not, however, an inconsequential feature. Studies have found that the horse-race figures prominently in election coverage in, for example, Britain (Semetko, 1991; Scammell and Semetko, 2000), Denmark (de Vreese, 2003), Germany (Kaase, 2000; Donsbach, 2001), and Sweden (Asp, 2007, Strömbäck, 2005). In Sweden, for instance, game coverage accounts for about a third of national election news, compared with more than half in the American case (Strömbäck and Dimitrova, 2006, 140).

The trend in Europe is similar to that in the United States: horse-race coverage has risen over time (Asp, 2007, 41). An increased use of opinion polls has contributed to the trend (Donsbach, 2001). Nevertheless, compared with their American counterparts, European journalists do not rely as heavily on polls (Brettschneider, 1997; Hardmeier, 1999). They also use polls more judiciously—for example, by sharply reducing the number of poll reports when covering lopsided races (Norris et al., 1999, 73).

The Effects of the Media's Game Schema

Game-centered journalism is said to deprive the public of the information it needs when choosing among candidates and policies. The game consumes news space that could be used to report on issues (Bennett, 1997, xiii). This claim has validity on its face. In a study of wire service and television coverage of the 1980 campaign, for example, Robinson and Sheehan (1983) found that about three in five election stories contained not even a single-sentence reference to policy issues. The claim also is supported by studies that have compared citizens' issue awareness across news media (Patterson, 1980, 163), countries (Holtz-Bacha and Norris, 2001, 138), and time periods (Patterson, 2002, 126).

Some scholars argue that the subordination of issues to the game also diminishes the public's interest in issues. Levy (1981) contends that by playing up the strategic game, the news media "depoliticize" issues, treating them more as tokens in the horse race than as objects to be taken seriously by the voters. Surveys show, for instance, that most Americans feel that political campaigns today seem more like theater or entertainment than something that deserves their close attention (Patterson, 2002, 56).

Game-centered journalism also warps the issue agenda. Studies indicate that the issues played up in the news differ substantially from those highlighted by candidates (Semetko et al., 1991; Vavreck, 2009, 43). Journalists prefer campaign controversies to substantive policy issues. During a long period of the 2004 presidential campaign, for example, the news media focused on personal events of three decades earlier—whether George W. Bush had fulfilled his duties as a member of the National Guard and whether John Kerry's duty in Vietnam was less than stellar. The controversy was not irrelevant, but it was not on a par with voters' worries about the economy and the Iraq war. On the other hand, the controversy served journalists' horse-race needs, serving as the basis for a running story on whether the allegations might tip the race toward one candidate or the other (Patterson, 2008, 293).

Such controversies have been a large part of election coverage since the 1970s. A short list would include the media frenzies that erupted around Carter's *Playboy* interview in 1976, Reagan's storytelling in 1980, Ferraro's tax returns in 1984, Hart's tryst with Donna Rice in 1988, Clinton's affair with Gennifer Flowers in 1992, Gore's Buddhist temple fundraising appearance in 1996, Bush's drunken-driving record in 2000, Kerry's war record in 2004, Obama's off-handed remark about "guns and religion" in 2008, and Romney's statement that "47 percent" of the voters were on the government dole and would vote for Obama "no matter what." The revelation in 2000 that Bush had been arrested a quarter century earlier for drunken driving, for example, got nearly twice the coverage on the evening newscasts in three days than did all of Bush and Gore's foreign policy statements during the entire general election (Center for Media and Public Affairs, 2000, 2).

Journalists' game schema also affects the candidate images they construct (Patterson, 1993, 116). The press is so tightly focused on the candidates and their standing in the game that it has for the most part only four stories to tell: a candidate is ahead, behind, slipping, or gaining. In each case, journalists' narratives about the candidate are fitted to the candidate's standing in the race. Whether a candidate is doing well or poorly is an obvious fact, but the reasons that the candidate is doing well or poorly are not, leaving reporters relatively free to provide explanations of their choosing. When a candidate gains strength, reporters can fix on a favorable aspect and make it the reason. When a candidate starts to slide, a negative quality can be brought forward.

So it is, for example, that candidates who are struggling in the polls are nearly always portrayed negatively in other ways as well. Journalists tend to cast them as deficient as leaders or lacking in personality or having a flawed platform. Lawrence and Rose attribute Hillary Clinton's negative coverage during the 2008 Democratic presidential nominating race in part to a game-driven narrative: "When candidates do not perform as well as predicted, that [tendency] becomes particularly harsh, as Hillary Clinton learned first-hand" (2009, 181). For his part, Barack Obama got the glowing coverage that journalists bestow on a candidate who is exceeding expectations. In the lead-up to the first contests in Iowa and New Hampshire, Obama's coverage was 50 percent more positive than Clinton's coverage (Center for Media and Public Affairs, 2007, 1).

The game-centered stories that journalists tell of the candidates are not harmless little tales. They are narratives with real consequences, because they affect for better or worse the images that voters acquire of the candidates, thereby making it easier or harder for them to obtain popular support. Studies show that journalists' narratives influence the choices of unanchored voters in fluid electoral situations such as the early phase of US presidential primaries (Patterson, 1980; Keeter and Zukin, 1983; Bartels, 1988; Kepplinger et al., 1989; Lawrence and Rose, 2009).

Studies also indicate that the media's emphasis on the strategic game stokes political cynicism (Moy and Pfau, 2000). The tendency of journalists to portray politicians as single-minded in their pursuit of power, coupled with the insinuation that they manipulate issues to advance their pursuits, is said to heighten citizens' belief that politicians are out for themselves. Michael Robinson first proposed the cynicism hypothesis in the 1970s on the basis of a study of US television network news. Noting the prevalence of strategic and conflict-based frames and the negative and anti-institutional tone of the coverage, he concluded that it served to turn viewers "against the. . . political institutions involved" (1976, 430).

Although some scholars reject this hypothesis (Norris, 2000), the bulk of the evidence supports it. Patterson found, for example, a strong correlation between the increase in game-centered coverage in the 1960–1992 period and the increase in negative political attitudes during the same period (1993, 22). In a single election study that employed a panel design, Iyengar, Norpath, and Hahn (2004) found that exposure to game-centered coverage was related to heightened cynicism about the candidates and the campaign.

In a controlled experiment, Cappella and Jamieson found that subjects exposed to strategically framed content had a heightened level of cynicism about politicians and their motives. Even exposure to other political content triggered a cynical reaction, leading Cappella and Jamieson to conclude: "A public that has accepted the belief that officials are acting in their own self-interest rather than in the interest of the common weal can be easily primed to see self-promotion in every political act" (1997, 208).

A subsequent experimental study by Valentino, Buhr, and Beckman (2001) found that strategic content lowered subjects' opinion of politics and elections. In a two-wave experimental study in the Netherlands, de Vreese (2003, 153) also found that exposure to strategic content produced a heightened level of political cynicism. In the follow-up wave a week later, the level of cynicism had regressed, leading de Vreese to conclude that its persistence requires repeated exposures to game-centered messages, which is the pattern with actual news exposure (157). In a subsequent experimental study, de Vreese and Elenbaas (2008, 265) found that game framing, as compared with issue framing, generated significantly higher levels of political cynicism.

Although the game schema has an adverse effect on the public, journalists downplay the impact. They argue that this type of reporting, whatever its weaknesses, serves a higher purpose, alerting the public to the manipulative efforts of political leaders (delli Carpini, 2005, 31). Journalists say they have a duty to look beyond politicians' words and actions to their underlying motives. In the absence of such reporting, they say, the public would fall prey to politician's ploys (Walsh, 2002). Zaller makes a related point, arguing that scholarly criticisms of news coverage are rooted in overly idealistic notions of citizenship and journalism. He argues that reporters meet their public obligation if they alert citizens at key moments to consequential developments. In this vein, a press that blows the whistle on political deception is "adequate to the informational needs of citizens in a democracy" (2003, 109).

Although scholars do not endorse game-centered reporting, they acknowledge its positive aspects. Horse-race coverage, for example, can generate interest in politics. In a study of voters' content preferences, Iyengar, Norpath, and Hahn found that "the question of who will win" is high on the list (2004, 173). However, they also found that voters have little interest in stories about candidates' strategies and tactics (173). In this context, the problem with game-based coverage is that it offers too much of what in moderation can be a good thing.

DIRECTIONS FOR FUTURE RESEARCH

Presidential elections in the United States aside, the strategic frame has not been extensively studied. There is a need for more research on its application in the reporting of governing institutions. There is also a need for more research in countries other than the United States. Studies of the use of the strategic frame elsewhere are necessary in order to better understand how its application varies with political system character-istics, news system characteristics, journalism traditions, and cultural differences, and how these factors mitigate or exaggerate its effect on news audiences.

Advances in knowledge will also require the use of common coding schemes. Researchers often have good reason to choose specialized schemes. But just as compar-ative public opinion research has benefited from the use of common sets of questions, comparative content research can benefit from the adoption of common codes. The research of Lichter and his colleagues is instructive in this respect. They have employed different coding schemes for their election, congressional, and presidential studies, blunting precise comparisons.

Research on the interaction of news frames is also needed. The game frame interacts, for example, with the conflict frame. How much of this interaction is a function of the actual situation and how much is attributable to journalists' intervention? In a study of Swedish news coverage, Westerståhl and Johansson (1986) suggested that journalists were orchestrating conflict as a means of dramatizing the competitive game. Rather than engaging in the time-intensive method of "digging" for disconfirming evidence, journal-ists used the time-efficient method of "asking" an opponent for a discrediting remark. According to Westerståhl and Johansson, "[this practice] has become a routine proce-dure among modern journalists. Instead of straight news, they prefer, on supposedly professional grounds, to support a controversy" (146–147). If the practice is widespread, traditional assumptions about journalistic objectivity and factual integrity are called into question.

Finally, there is a need for a fuller assessment of how politicians respond to journalists' use of the game schema. Is their behavior simply refracted by reporters' emphasis on the game, or have they altered their behavior to exploit it, playing "a game" within the game? Frances Lee's (2009) research on the US Senate offers a tantalizing hint to the answer. She found that the congressional parties frequently pick issues and positions with an eye to how they will play with the voters and the press rather than on the basis of legislative priorities.

CONCLUDING OBSERVATION

Harold Lasswell defined politics as the issue of "who gets what, when, and how" (1936). For citizens, the key questions are the "who" and the "what": the way in which policy costs and benefits are distributed across society. For journalists, the key question is "how": the struggle of power-driven leaders for dominance.

Although journalists sometimes claim to be in the business of guiding the public, news values are out of alignment with this goal. The media lack the incentives to present an instructive portrayal of politics on an ongoing basis. They are in the news business, and their imperative is attracting and holding an audience's attention. "Journalists are not well trained, nor are news organizations well equipped," Timothy Cook noted, "to help weigh problems, set political agendas, examine alternatives, and study implementation" (1998, 167). Journalists' needs rather than those of citizens drive the news.

NOTE

1. A schema is a person's customary way of looking at a situation and responding to it. Entering a two-way street, for example, an American driver (unlike a British driver) automatically pulls into the right lane. Like any schema, this one is constructed from past experiences. Schemas enable individuals to respond to situations without having to study them anew each time. Once ingrained, a schema takes on a life on its own, providing an almost unthinking basis on which to respond to a familiar situation.

REFERENCES

Adatto, K. 1990. Sound bite democracy: Network evening news presidential campaign coverage, 1968 and 1988. Joan Shorenstein Center on the Press, Politics, and Public Policy, Research Paper R-2, John F. Kennedy School of Government, Harvard University, Cambridge, MA.

Arnold, D. R. 2004. *Congress, the press, and political accountability*. Princeton, NJ: Princeton University Press.

Asp, K. 2007. Fairness, informativeness, and scrutiny: The role of news media in democracy. In special jubilee issue, *Nordicom Review*: 31–49.

Barber, J. D. 1978. *Race for the presidency: The media and the nominating process*. Englewood Cliffs, NJ: Prentice-Hall.

Bartels, L. M. 1988. *Presidential primaries and the dynamics of public choice*. Princeton, NJ: Princeton University Press.

Bennett, W. L. 1997 *News: The politics of illusion* (3rd ed.). New York: Longman.

Brettschneider, F. 1997. The press and polls in Germany, 1980–1994. *International Journal of Public Opinion Research* 9: 248–265.

Cappella, J., and Jamieson, K. Hall. 1997. *Spiral of cynicism*. New York: Oxford University Press.

Center for Media and Public Affairs. 2000. Campaign 2000 final. *Media Monitor XIV*(November/December): 1–6.

Center for Media and Public Affairs. 2007. Election study finds media hit Hillary hardest. December 21. Retrieved from http://www.cmpa.com/releases/07_12_21_Election_Study. pdf.

Cohen, J. E. 2008. *The presidency in the era of 24-hour news*. Princeton, NJ: Princeton University Press.

Cook, T. E. 1998. *Governing with the news*. Chicago: University of Chicago Press.

De Vreese, C. H. 2003. *Framing Europe: Television news and European integration*. Amsterdam: Aksant.

De Vreese, C. H., and Elenbaas, M. 2008. Media in the game of politics: Effects of strategic metacoverage on political cynicism. *International Journal of Press/Politics* 13(July): 285–309.

Delli Carpini, M. 2005. News from somewhere: Journalistic frames and "public journalism." In K. Callaghan and F. Schnell (Eds.), *Framing American politics* (pp. 21–53). Pittsburgh: University of Pittsburgh Press.

Donsbach, W. 2001. *Who's afraid of election polls?* Amsterdam: ESOMAR.

Druckman, J. N. 2004. Priming the vote: Campaign effects in a U.S. Senate election. *Political Psychology* 25(4): 577–594.

Farnsworth, S. J., and Lichter, S. R. 2007. *The nightly news nightmare: Network television's coverage of the U.S. presidential elections, 1988–2000* (2nd ed.). Lanham, MD: Rowman & Littlefield Publishers.

Farnsworth, S. J., and Lichter, S. R. 2014. News coverage of US presidential campaigns: Reporting on primaries and general elections, 1988–2012. APSA 2014 Annual Meeting Paper. Available at SSRN: http://ssrn.com/abstract=2454423.

Erikson, R. S., and Wlezien, C. 1999. Presidential polls as a time series. *Public Opinion Quarterly* 63: 163–177.

Hallin, D. R. 1992. Sound bite news. *Journal of Communication* 42: 5–24.

Hardmeier, S. 1999. Political poll reporting in Swiss print media. *International Journal of Public Opinion Research* 11: 257–274.

Holtz-Bacha, C., and Norris, P. 2001. To entertain, inform, and educate. *Political Communication* 18(2): 123–140.

Iyengar, S., Norpoth, H., and Hahn, K. S. 2004. Consumer demand for election news: The horserace sells. *Journal of Politics* 66: 157–175.

Jamieson, K. H., and Cappella, J. 1994. Media in the middle: Fairness and accuracy in the 1994 health care reform debate. Report of the Annenberg Public Policy Center of the University of Pennsylvania.

Kaase, M. 2000. Germany: A society and a media system in transition. In R. Gunther and A. Mughan (Eds.), *Democracy and the media: A comparative perspective* (pp. 266–302). New York: Cambridge University Press.

Kahn, K. F. 1991. Senate elections in the news: Examining campaign coverage. *Legislative Studies Quarterly* 16: 349–374.

Kahn, K. F., and Kenney, P. J. 1999. *The spectacle of U.S. Senate campaigns*. Princeton, NJ: Princeton University Press.

Keenan, K. 1985. Polls in network newscasts in 1984 presidential race. *Journalism Quarterly* 62: 616–618.

Keeter, S., and Zukin, C. 1983. *Uninformed choice: The failure of the new presidential nominating system*. New York: Praeger.

Kepplinger, H. M., Donsbach, W., Brosius, H.-B., and Staab, J. F. 1989. Media tone and public opinion: A longitudinal study of media coverage and public opinion on Chancellor Kohl. *International Journal of Public Opinion Research* 1(4): 326–342.

Kleinnijenhuis, J., and DeRidder, J. A. 1998. Issue news and electoral volatility. *European Journal of Political Research* 33: 413–437.

Larson, S. G. September 2001. Poll coverage of the 2000 presidential campaign on the network news. Paper presented at the American Political Science Association annual convention, San Francisco.

Lasswell, H. 1936. *Politics: Who gets what, when, how*. Cleveland, OH: Meridian Books.

Lawrence, R. G., and Rose, M. 2009. *Hillary Clinton's race for the White House: Gender politics and the media on the campaign trail*. Boulder, CO: Lynne Rienner.

Lee, F. E. 2009. *Beyond ideology: Parties, principles, and partisanship in the U.S. Senate*. Chicago: University of Chicago Press.

Lichter, S. R., and Amundson, D. R. 1994. Less news is worse news. in T. E. Mann and N. J. Ornstein (Eds.), *Congress, the press, and the public* (pp. 131–140). Washington, DC: American Enterprise Institute and Brookings Institution.

Lippmann, W. 1965. *Public opinion*. New York: Free Press.

McQuail, D. 1994. *Mass communication theory*. London: Sage.

Moy, P., and Pfau, M. 2000. *With malice toward all? The media and public confidence in democratic institutions*. Westport, CT: Praeger.

Norris, P. 2000. *A virtuous circle: Political communications in postindustrial societies*. New York: Cambridge University Press.

Norris, P., Curtice, J., Sanders, D., Scammell, M., and Semetko, H. A. 1999. *On message: Communicating the campaign*. London: Sage.

Patterson, T. E. 1980. *The mass media election*. New York: Praeger.

Patterson, T. E. 1993. *Out of order*. New York: Knopf.

Patterson, T. E. 2002. *The vanishing voter*. New York: Knopf.

Patterson, T. E. 2007. Political roles of the journalist. In D. Graber, D. McQuail, and P. Norris (Eds.), *The politics of news: The news of politics* (2nd ed., pp. 23–39). Washington, DC: CQ Press.

Patterson, T. E. 2008. *The American democracy* (8th ed.). New York: McGraw-Hill.

Patterson, T. E., and McClure, R. D. 1976. *The unseeing eye: The myth of television power in national elections*. New York: Putnam.

Power, L., and Robbins, D. 2014. Network news overlooks policy issues in midterm coverage. Media Matters, November 9. Retrieved from http://mediamatters.org/research/2014/11/09/network-news-overlooks-policy-issues-in-midterm/201506.

Project for Excellence in Journalism. 2008. Winning the media campaign. Pew Research Center, October 22. Retrieved from http://www.journalism.org/analysis_report/winning_media_campaign.

Project for Excellence in Journalism. 2010. 2010 midterm coverage hits a new high. Pew Research Center, October 25. Retrieved from http://www.journalism.org/index_report/pej_news_coverage_index_october_1824_2010.

Project for Excellence in Journalism. 2011. Osama Bin Laden's death continues to dominate the news. Pew Research Center, May 9. Retrieved from http://www.journalism.org/index_report/pej_news_coverage_index_may_2_8_2011.

Project for Excellence in Journalism. 2012. Winning the media campaign. Pew Research Journalism Project, November 2. Retrieved from http://www.journalism.org/2012/11/02/winning-media-campaign-2012/.

Rhee, J. W. 1996. How polls drive campaign coverage: The Gallup/CNN/USA Today tracking poll and *USA Today*'s coverage of the 1992 presidential campaign. *Political Communication* 13: 213–229.

Robinson, M. J. 1976. Public affairs television and the growth of political malaise: The case of "the selling of the Pentagon." *American Political Science Review* 70(3): 409–432.

Robinson, M. J., and Sheehan, M. A. 1983. *Over the wire and on TV*. New York: Russell Sage Foundation.

Rosenstiel, T. 2005. Political polling and the new media culture: A case of more being less. *Public Opinion Quarterly* 69(5): 698–715.

Rozell, M. J. 1994. Press coverage of Congress, 1946–92. In T. E. Mann and N. J. Ornstein (Eds.), *Congress, the press, and the public* (pp. 59–129). Washington, DC: American Enterprise Institute and Brookings Institution.

Scammell, M., and Semetko, H. A. 2000. *Media, journalism and democracy*. London: Dartmouth.

Schudson, M. 2008. *Why democracies need an unlovable press*. Boston: Polity.

Semetko, H. A. 1991. Images of Britain's changing party system: TV news and the 1983 and 1987 general election campaigns. *Political Communication and Persuasion 8*(4): 163–181.

Steele, J. 1995. Experts and the operational bias of television news: The case of the Persian Gulf War. *Journalism Quarterly 72*(4): 799–812.

Strömbäck, J. 2005. Commercialization and the media coverage of Swedish national elections in 1998 and 2002. Paper presented at the annual meeting of the American Political Science Association, Washington, DC.

Strömbäck, J., and Dimitrova, D. V. 2006. Political and media systems matter: A comparison of election news coverage in Sweden and the United States. *Harvard International Journal of Press/Politics 11*(4): 131–147.

Valentino, N. A., Buhr, T. A., and Beckmann, M. N. 2001. When the frame is the game. *Journalism and Mass Communication Quarterly 78*: 93–112.

Vavreck, L. 2009. *The message matters.* Princeton, NJ: Princeton University Press.

Walsh, K. T. 2002. *Feeding the beast: The White House versus the press.* Bloomington, IN: Xlibris Books.

Weaver, P. 1972. Is television news biased? *Public Interest 27*: 65–76.

Welch, R. L. 2002. Polls, polls, and more polls. *Harvard International Journal of Press/Politics 7*: 102–114.

Zaller, J. 2003. A new standard of news quality: Burglar alarms for the monitorial citizen. *Political Communication 20*: 109–130.

CHAPTER 28

GOING INSTITUTIONAL

The Making of Political Communications

LAWRENCE R. JACOBS

OUR everyday lives are inundated by political communications, from speeches by presidents and the dueling messages of partisans battling over legislation to campaigning by candidates for elected office. Although less strident, government programs (such as Social Security and Medicare) also churn out a steady stream of information and announcements and, of course, benefits that convey messages as well.

Although communications from election candidates, officeholders, and government programs often project an air of candor and forthrightness, they are invariably strategic, intentional, and purposive. Carefully constructed to advance agendas, they promote a campaign, sell a piece of legislation, and explain benefits and fees to constituents to simplify processing and, not incidentally, build loyalty.

Purposeful political communications are of course ancient, dating to the earliest forms of organized politics and government. However, two significant developments distinguish modern political communication, affecting its form and potency. First, political strategy has become, even over only the last few decades, enormously more sophisticated, drawing on cutting-edge survey research to track public opinion and social psychology to exploit the vulnerabilities created by the ways in which individuals process information and form evaluations. Political elites now tailor their individual words and phrasings (what I describe below as "situational framing") to the specific situations of particular campaigns and legislative debates. Even before they publicly express their "frames," they have a high degree of confidence that their messages will resonate with their intended audiences, thereby reducing uncertainty and improving the probability of influence.

The second development relates to institutional changes that have created enduring opportunities for efficacious communications. While situational framing is a common subject of study in political communications, institution-based communications and framing have received less sustained attention. This chapter addresses two elements: the substantial expansion of the White House's administrative capacity to conduct poll-driven communications and the routinized and consequential communication of established policies. Institutions-based communications have, under certain circumstances, more enduring and deeper effects than the personalistic and often time-delimited aspects of situational framing.

This chapter begins by briefly reviewing research on situational framing, proceeds to a fuller discussion of the administrative capacity for presidential communications, and then addresses the communications of institutionalized policies. It closes by considering new areas for research and the implications of institutions-based communications.

Situational Framing

Extensive research examines the effects of election campaigns, presidential speeches, and the media on audiences. "Situational" framing is a subset of this broader body of studies and focuses on the intentional efforts of political actors to target individuals within specific situations, whether an election campaign, legislative debate, or some other time-specific episode. Research by social psychologists and political psychologists, which often relies on laboratory experiments, emphasizes the importance of both the specific content of communications (i.e., their particular wording or phrasing) and audiences' established "mental organization" or "internal structures of the mind," which affect whether and how they respond to particular messages (Kinder and Sanders, 1990, 74).

The debate over healthcare reform in 2009 and 2010 illustrates situational framing. Critics (led by a largely united front of congressional Republicans) attacked the reform effort as a "Democrats-only" crusade to "jam" through a government "takeover" of health reform, one that would risk American lives by establishing "death panels." Their objective was not to create new attitudes (converting the majority of Americans who favored government assistance with health insurance into opponents), but rather to activate already existing beliefs (Jacobs and Mettler, 2011; Taber and Lodge, 2006; Lodge and Taber, 2005; Jacobs and Shapiro, 2011). Three effects resulted. First, the dueling frames prompted individuals to cue on partisan affiliations, leading about two-thirds of Democrats to favor reform while only a tenth or fifth of Republicans backed it during the legislative battle and the year or so after its passage (Kaiser Family Foundation Tracking Polls, Jan. 7-12, 2010, May 11-16, 2010, Aug. 16-22, 2010, Sept. 14-19, 2010, Nov. 3-6, 2010, and Feb. 8-13, 2011). The magnitude of the gap between the support of Democrats for health reform and the opposition of Republicans to it—which ranged between 45 and 65 percentage points—surpasses partisan differences over Social Security in the 1930s by a factor of three to more than fourfold.

Second, the dueling frames targeted and activated existing unease and suspicions about the abstract proposition of expanding "big government" (Page and Jacobs, 2009). The principal reason 82 percent of Americans gave for opposing the Affordable Care Act (ACA) in August 2010, according to polls by the Kaiser Family Foundation, was that it "gives government too big a role in the healthcare system." This supermajority expressing dread of government included even a good number of Democrats, suggesting the complexity of public opinion toward government and the potency of effectively designed frames.

Third, the concerted efforts of the reform opponents to flag the uncertainties of "massive" changes in the financing and delivery of medical care, which was obsessively covered by the media along with the broader partisan divide, fanned the public's perception of significant risk (Cappella and Jamieson, 1997; Jacobs and Shapiro, 2000, ch. 5). By the time health reform passed in March 2010 and in the months afterward, the alarming messages from reform opponents and media coverage of the conflict had tripled (to a third) the proportion of Americans who feared that the new law would make "you and your family . . . worse off" (Kaiser Family Foundation Polls).

Advocates and opponents of health reform—along with the media—generated frames that activated deep partisan attachments, suspicions of government ineptness, and unease about the risks of change, and in the process split Americans. Support and opposition among Americans ranged in the 40 to 50 percent band for several years after the summer of 2009, when the Tea Party protests at congressional town hall meetings were beamed across the country.

The extensive research on political framing and the vivid illustrations of its effects during the health reform debate, however, have generated high expectations of its impacts and insufficient attention to at least three broad conditions that affect whether and how frames impact individuals. First, individuals are not blank slates, but rather sort through frames based on existing affiliations with political parties and established public attitudes about government and specific policies, which are generally stable (Page and Shapiro, 1992). This affects their receptivity to frames depending on message and credibility of source. Individuals who affiliate with the Republican Party were predisposed, for instance, to oppose health reform when GOP leaders uniformly opposed it and stressed the Democrats' partisanship.

A second condition and an important area of new research relates to the content and environment of political communications—namely, the presence of competing frames and their persuasive strength (Druckman, 2004). Individuals are more susceptible to frames when one set dominates or monopolizes communications and the message is delivered unimpeded by a trusted source. For instance, reform advocates were justifiably frustrated when President Obama withdrew from intense public campaigning for ACA during the summer of 2009 in deference to Senate efforts to forge bipartisan legislation; as a result one-sided communications dominated by the Tea Party revolt blanketed media coverage and had the opportunity to register with many individuals, who started to express higher levels of unease about reform—an unease or outright opposition that has persisted.

It is more common, though, in electoral and policy campaigns for most frames to face countervailing political communications, which tends to diminish their impacts. The public communications of multiple and competing messages by contending sets of political elites—and by media coverage of their disputes—normally prevent any one perspective from controlling information and ensuring that individuals uniformly receive their messages. The practical effect of individuals failing to receive clear, uncontested messages is that frames within real political contexts rarely are challenged or checked.

Frames also vary in their persuasive strength, depending on the frequency of their use and the credibility of those communicating them. For instance, in the past, efforts to pass health reform (including Medicare) fought an uphill battle against the credible and frequently communicated opposition of physicians; by contrast, the 2010 health reform effort was backed by many doctors and their professional association—the American Medical Association (AMA)—which removed a convincing ally from the ranks of reform opponents (Jacobs and Skocpol, 2010; Jacobs, 1993).

The third condition relates to the personal circumstances and cognitive capacity of individuals, which of course varies considerably. Individual-level heterogeneity with regard to social and economic status, knowledge and interest in politics, and politically relevant living circumstances such as health insurance status or eligibility for Social Security may produce different reactions to identical frames. For instance, even as critics of health reform effectively activated the opposition of Republicans, the personal concerns of certain individuals—namely, their lack of health insurance coverage—led them to resist the draw of partisan affiliation and support the new law (Henderson and Hillygus, 2011). In addition, the particular experience, training, and knowledge of individuals may affect their vulnerability to frames. Training in economics and personal finance, for example, can equip individuals with the cognitive capacity to consciously inspect frames and therefore lessen susceptibility to them (Druckman, 2004).

Research on framing has revealed the impact on public opinion and citizen behavior of political communications by individual speakers within specific situations. The expansion of research methods to experimental designs has improved the precision of analysis and helped to identify the mechanisms and the psychological processes through which framing operates in discrete, time-specific episodes: election campaigns or legislative debates.

THE INSTITUTIONALIZATION OF POLITICAL COMMUNICATIONS

Political and governmental institutions are an integral but often neglected element of political communications. In certain respects, institutions augment well-studied components of political communications such as framing. The integrated administrative capacity to widely disseminate messages and track public opinion to identify words, positions, and personality traits enables frequent, widespread, and potentially influential political communications. In addition, government programs that become established—from Social Security and Medicare to veterans' benefits—convey messages that are ongoing, routine, and, under certain conditions, quite efficacious. These communications are in part the product of deliberate strategies; they also result from the routinized transactions of receiving benefits.

Institutions-enabled communications are important for several reasons. They shape the form of messages in unique ways. Their impact can be quite significant: while the effects of situational framing may be restricted to discrete and time-bound contexts in which the choices of individual speakers—such as presidents—dominate, established programs and institutions can produce changes in opinion that endure over time. The next section addresses two forms of institutions-based communications.

Administrative Capacity and Political Communications

American government and, especially, its national executive and office of the presidency, experienced two dramatic institutional developments during the twentieth century with enormous implications for political communications.

The Institutionalization of Political Communications

During the twentieth century, the presidency and the broader national executive branch developed an elaborate set of routines and offices to tailor information for public release and to distribute it widely. Creating the administrative capacity to design and disseminate political communication meant that the distribution of potent messages occurred through the organizational routines and operations of the White House rather than depending only on the personal skill of the individual holding the office. Of course individual talent mattered, but even individual presidents with limited communicative skills—such as Jimmy Carter and George W. Bush—were assured of unparalleled capacity to frame and project arguments.

The institutionalization of political communication was a sharp break from the practice of nineteenth-century politicians, who relied on political parties to mobilize supporters and on the "partisan press"—the newspapers owned and operated by the parties—for the explicit function of disseminating information that most advantaged their team in office. Beginning in the late nineteenth century and accelerating during the twentieth, presidents, executive branch departments, and other senior political leaders built new institutions and organizational routines that were geared toward controlling and centralizing information to marshal public support. These efforts included the establishment of press offices and press secretaries as well as the encouragement and then feeding of news media "beats" that were devoted to covering presidents and other specific government offices. These efforts evolved in fits and starts, from the early innovations of William McKinley (1897–1901), to the formalizing and centralizing efforts of Woodrow Wilson (1913–1921) (who restarted the personal delivery of the State of the Union address to capitalize on new publicizing opportunities), to Franklin Roosevelt's (1933–1945) expansion of public and press outreach, including the use of radio to communicate directly with Americans.

John F. Kennedy inaugurated the modern era of public communications by presidents. He identified—according to a close aide—"public communications—educating, persuading, and mobilizing . . . [public opinion]" as one of his primary responsibilities; quite a turn from his nineteenth-century predecessors, who considered public promotion undignified and inappropriate (Sorensen, 1965, 310; Tulis, 1987). The priority that Kennedy placed on mass communications propelled a series of innovations, including regular televised press conferences and a concerted effort to coordinate executive branch agencies in the feeding and managing of the press. The result was to bring Washington into the living rooms of Americans, making "normal" what had been quite extraordinary only shortly before Kennedy's election. Today we are accustomed to the Department of Defense holding regular press briefings on prime-time television as the president takes challenging questions from the press.

Kennedy's embrace of modern communications technology opened the door to the efforts of subsequent presidents to expand the White House's capacities to dominate the political information reaching Americans. The press office and press secretary in the White House and executive branch solidified their roles as the command center for focusing the attention of the press and the public on the president and on the terms sought by the administration. While the policy initiatives of George W. Bush to cut taxes and partially privatize Social Security stood in stark ideological contrast with the health reform efforts of Bill Clinton and Barack Obama, they all relied on the presidency's institutional capacities for communications and press management to centralize control over the administration's communications, develop messages that sought to favorably portray their initiatives, and saturate Americans with distinctive "messages" in the expectation that this would crowd out the messages of reform opponents.

Polling for Promotion

Public opinion polling by politicians has long been assumed to reveal an unbreakable inclination to give Americans what they want. The pejorative word, "pandering," was borrowed from the world of prostitution to demonize the presumed disposition of politicians to abandon principle to cater to voters. As popular and widespread as this assumption remains, it flies in the face of extensive and varied research. To begin with, a growing body of research on political elites finds that their decisions follow the views of higher income groups (Bartels, 2008; Gilens, 2005) and powerful economic interests in domestic and foreign policy (Milner, 1997; Rogowski, 1989; Jacobs and Page, 2005); general public opinion or the views of the less affluent or unorganized have little, if any, impact. Bartels (2008) demonstrates, for instance, that the votes of US senators are highly correlated with the preferences of higher income individuals but exhibit virtually no responsiveness to the preferences of the majority of Americans.

In a political system that rewards fidelity to the goals of party activists and campaign contributors, finely crafted political communications become more—not less—important. Political elites rely on them to signal supporters and elicit their backing while reassuring and deflecting protests from the independents and swing voters who often tilt election outcomes. Although political activists are often quite attuned to politics and nuanced communications, independents tend to be less interested in politics and more susceptible to being misled. In addition, purposeful political communications face a series of reinforcing and daunting hurdles: the stability of basic policy preferences (Page and Shapiro, 1992), the counterframes of opponents (Druckman, 2004), and the media's attraction to political conflict (Jamieson, 1992; Patterson, 1993). Winning over independents while holding the support of activists in a hostile environment has created strong incentives for presidents to develop communications that reliably and effectively resonate with electorally valuable groups.

Presidential efforts to fashion potent communications helped develop an institutionalized apparatus for routinely tracking public opinion. Beginning in earnest under Kennedy, the White House started to conduct private polls as a routine part of its operations; in the intervening years, the scope and sophistication of the White House's opinion research have grown considerably. While Kennedy's pollster (Louis Harris) supplied 15 private polling reports to the White House, the stream of regular polling took off under Lyndon Johnson (110 private surveys), Richard Nixon (173), and Ronald Reagan (204) (Jacobs and Burns, 2004). The growing number of presidential polls reflected their use as both a tool for elections and a valued instrument throughout the presidential term.

The swelling polling operations became more sophisticated over time to support three distinct forms of political communications. First, the White House used its polls to pinpoint and then cater to the intense views of politically important subgroups. Beginning under Kennedy but accelerating under Reagan, the White House routinely collected information on the economic attributes, such as income, of both voters in general and politically important subgroups in particular. The Reagan White House broadened its subgroup polling from tracking the traditional Republican base of higher income voters to the members of newer social, economic, and military conservative coalition. In addition, the administration kept close tabs on the unraveling of the New Deal coalition by tracking the ranks of independents who did not identify with either major party.

Quantitative analyses and archival records from the Reagan White House point to a consistent pattern of calibrating the president's policy statements to the views of electorally critical subgroups (Druckman and Jacobs, 2010). In particular, Reagan's policy positions systematically corresponded with the views of high-income earners who favored reducing government spending, lowering taxes, and making the Social Security program voluntary. He also responded to social conservatives (especially Baptists and Catholics) on issues such as family values and crime and to conservative Republicans on hawkish foreign policy. In this way, Reagan tailored his public communications to cater, in part, to electorally meaningful segments of his electoral coalition.

The second form of political communications informed by White House polling is message testing; this process enabled consultants to anticipate public reactions before the president spoke in order to maximize his effectiveness and minimize the risk of a backlash. For example, the White House's polling operation, which was assisted by Richard Wirthlin, conducted research in 1982 and 1983 on how to recraft the president's public communications on fiscal issues. The strategic challenge was to both mitigate the growing public unease about rising budget deficits and frustration that Reagan had not delivered on his campaign commitment to balance the budget and prevent the doubts from metastasizing into questions about the affordability of his support for more defense spending and tax cuts. Wirthlin reported back that Reagan could maintain his policy goals if he aggressively promoted a constitutional amendment to balance the budget. The White House's rationale for advocating a balanced budget amendment was not primarily on policy or political grounds (its impact and prospects were dubious), but on the strength of its popularity with Americans—it would "overcome the perception that [the President] is not fulfilling his campaign promise."[1]

The White House's message testing was also geared to avoiding unpopular and damaging positions such as on the potentially explosive issues of civil rights and modifying the Voting Rights Act. Its testing of counterframes that emphasized "rights" and "abuses" revealed "very significant political ramifications that reach far beyond the immediate issue of the Right to Vote."[2] This warning produced a more cautious and finely crafted message.

Managing and tweaking the president's personal image is the third distinctive type of political communications guided by the White House's polling operation, which tracked the public's perceptions of presidential personality traits beginning in earnest with Kennedy. Even during Kennedy's 1960 campaign, his advisors calculated that selectively accenting salient and popular issues would build a "move ahead" image for Kennedy (Jacobs and Shapiro, 1994). Their strategic objective was to win support not on issues alone but also on the basis of perceptions of Kennedy's personal traits, which broadened his appeal even among those who were uninterested in politics and policy issues.

Nixon notably expanded the scope and sophistication of the White House polling operation to include the tracking of his personal standing; this included a remarkably candid study of "The Nixon Image." While his own polling showed an antipathy to Nixon as a person, it also showed grudging respect for his ability to perform in office. Archival records and statistical analyses reveal that Nixon responded to negative evaluations of his personal competence and experience by emphasizing bold and aggressive foreign policies, signaling his personal resolve and abilities amid adversity (Druckman, Jacobs, and Ostermeier, 2004).

The establishment of enduring institutions for communications and the polling to guide them created strategic advantages for presidents and transformed their political communications. The White House's polling and communications structures provide a measure of regular, high-level capacity to design and widely disseminate messages; they do not guarantee every presidential initiative success in setting the terms of debate, but do ensure a public popularity floor even for presidents without skill. These enduring and efficacious institutions generally outstrip the often transient, uneven, and under-resourced efforts of an individual or group.

The administrative capacity and strategies of presidents and other authoritative government figures to guide and change public opinion raise fundamental questions about the nature of political representation and American democracy (Disch, 2011). These phenomena raise a troubling question: Are the concerns, preferences, and evaluations of citizens their own or a reflection of elite priorities? The institutional capacity of presidents to shape public opinion threatens democratic accountability for government performance; our heads of state now enjoy the resources to craft a personal image that appeals to voters on nonpolicy grounds, enlarging their discretion over substantively significant policy decisions.

Institutions as Communications

Institutions matter for political communications. Presidents use them instrumentally to advance their messages. But the impact of institutions on political communications goes beyond purposive situational maneuvering, as significant as that is. Institutions themselves, specifically established government programs, communicate as a normal extension of their everyday operations. A growing body of research documents the enormous effects of government programs on public attitudes and behavior.

Studying how government policies communicate and impact individuals requires a shift in the conventional portrayal of politics in which voting, mobilization by interest groups, and other forms of political participation are understood to drive policy decisions. For instance, the 2008 election of Obama and large majorities of Democrats in Congress set the parameters for health reform in 2010. This conventional approach is of course important but neglects the enduring effects of established government programs and policies in determining what changes in government programs are even considered conceivable, how interests are understood and organized, and what pressure groups form (or remain unorganized) (Schattschneider, 1960). Put another way, the 2008 elections positioned Democrats to reform healthcare, but the public's long experience with private health insurance and Medicare defined what options were considered and how stakeholders—from senior citizens to doctors—responded (Jacobs and Skocpol, 2010). Policy shifts, then, from serving as a dependent variable to acting as an independent variable that affects public opinion and political behavior.

A set of studies has identified two types of effects of policy on politics (Mettler and Soss, 2004). One reports that the design of government programs determines the degree to which their impact is tangible and visible. Social Security, for example, delivers significant and salient benefits, while its payroll tax cloaks its costs. Indeed, congressional supporters of the program sought to highlight the significant financial payoff of Social Security by mailing each eligible individual a statement akin to a bank or mutual fund report; these personal statements have improved public knowledge and confidence in the program's benefits (Cook, Jacobs, and Kim, 2010). As illustrated by AARP's formation after Social Security's passage, tangible benefits generate awareness of interests, which in turn can motivate organizations to form to serve and advance those interests.

Visibility is another critical design feature of government programs (Mettler, 2011). While Social Security's checks powerfully convey the program's benefits and help to account for its extraordinary support among supermajorities, Obama's stimulus in early 2009 buried more than a third of its investments in tax cuts that few perceived or credited to the legislation. The significance of obscure government programs is also evident in health insurance; tax credits and subsidies for employers who offer it are enormously costly and largely invisible, depressing support for explicit government insurance programs, which are seen as new "interruptions" rather than extensions of long-standing programs.

A second effect of policy on politics relates to the effects of established government programs on political attitudes and behavior. In particular, policy can impact external efficacy and the sense that government is responsive, as well as internal efficacy (namely, confidence in one's ability to take effective political action), which in turn generates political participation. Before Social Security was established, the political attitudes and behaviors of seniors were similar to other age cohorts; afterward they developed higher levels of internal and external efficacy and turned out to vote at higher levels than other age cohorts (Campbell, 2003). Moreover, as Social Security generated incentives and resources for previously disengaged citizens (seniors in particular) to increase their interest and participation in politics, politicians from both parties adjusted to compete for this new and decisive pool of votes. By contrast, programs for the poor are designed and operated to reinforce a sense of disaffection and withdrawal (Soss, 1999). Instead of seeking their votes, politicians often score points by running against welfare and other programs that serve the poor (Shapiro, Weaver, and Jacobs, 1996).

Established government programs convey a routine form of communication with political import. Although it lacks the individualized intentionality of, for instance, President Obama seeking to pass health reform, specific programs—from Social Security and Medicare to veterans' programs—can deliver persistent and credible messages through salient program benefits, which in turn exerts a lasting effect on public attitudes and political behavior.

IMPLICATIONS TO EXPLORE

Institutionally grounded communications raise several issues for further exploration. Should our study of framing at one point in time be tempered by appreciation of its possible fragility? Should the understanding of communications be broadened from individual speakers or individual media reports to take into account the effects of policy and of institutionalized communications? Under what conditions do policy effects trump situational framing? Research on policy effects underscores how the operation of established programs projects consequential messages over time that may, under certain circumstances, supersede the type of situational framing that is often a primary focus of research on political communications.

Assessing the relative impacts of situational framing and policy effects has real-world implications. Although the intense debate over the New Deal's Social Security legislation contributed to Democrats supporting it more than Republicans by ten to fifteen points during the 1930s, supermajorities of both parties back it now after decades in which beneficiaries have seen the program deliver reliable help. While discrete frames can and do influence public thinking at any one point in time, established government programs such as Social Security routinely project messages that build up and reinforce public attitudes and patterns of political engagement (Jacobs and Mettler, 2011). Looking forward, what are the implications for the split public reactions to the healthcare reform of 2010 as the new law is implemented and gradually becomes part of everyday life?

A more general issue is sorting through the volitional as compared to structural foundations of political communications. Much research and popular commentary concentrates on highly personal decisions over particular phrases and presentations in specific situations. That is important. Nonetheless, enduring institutions enable or define persistent patterns of communications. Future research on political communications would be well-served by studying the interactions of situational choices and enduring patterns of communications.

NOTES

1. Reagan Presidential Library, untitled memo, PR 15, document no. 213994.
2. Reagan Presidential Library, memo from Richard Wirthlin to Richard Richards, "Attitudes toward Voting Rights Act," June 18, 1981.

REFERENCES

Bartels, L. 2008. *Unequal democracy: The political economy of the new gilded age.* Princeton, NJ: Princeton University Press.

Campbell, A. 2003. *How policies make citizens: Senior political activism and the American welfare state.* Princeton, NJ: Princeton University Press.

Cappella, J. N., and Jamieson, K. H. 1997. *Spiral of cynicism: The press and the public good.* New York: Oxford University Press.

Cook, F. L., Jacobs, L., and Kim, D. 2010. Trusting what you know: Information, knowledge, and confidence in Social Security. *Journal of Politics 72* (April: 1–16).

Disch, L. 2011. Toward a mobilization conception of democratic representation. *American Political Science Review 105*(February): 100–114.

Druckman, J. 2004. Political preference formation: Competition, deliberation, and the (ir)relevance of framing effects. *American Political Science Review 98*(4): 671–686.

Druckman, J., and Jacobs, L. 2010. Segmented representation: The Reagan White House and disproportionate responsiveness. In C. Wlezien and P. Enns (Eds.), *Who gets represented?* (pp. 166-188). New York: Russell Sage.

Druckman, J., Jacobs, L., and Ostermeier, E. 2004. Candidate strategies to prime issues and image. *Journal of Politics 66*(November): 1205–1227.

Gilens, M. 2005. Inequality and democratic responsiveness. *Public Opinion Quarterly 69*(5): 778–796.

Henderson, M., and Hillygus, S. 2011. The dynamics of health care opinion, 2008–2010: Partisanship, self-interest, and racial resentment. *Journal of Health Politics, Policy and Law 36*: 945–960.

Jacobs, L. 1993. *The health of nations: Public opinion and the making of health policy in the U.S. and Britain.* Ithaca, NY: Cornell University Press.

Jacobs, L. R., and Burns, M. 2004. The second face of the public presidency: Presidential polling and the shift from policy to personality polling. *Presidential Studies Quarterly* 34(Fall): 536–556.

Jacobs, L., and Mettler, S. 2011. Why public opinion changes: The implications for health and health policy. *Journal of Health Policy, Politics and Law* 36(6): 917–933.

Jacobs, L. R., and Page, B. I. 2005. Who influences U.S. foreign policy? *American Political Science Review* 99(February): 107-123.

Jacobs, L. R., and Shapiro, R. Y. 1994. Issues, candidate image and priming: The use of private polls in Kennedy's 1960 presidential campaign. *American Political Science Review* 88(September): 527–540.

Jacobs, L. R., and Shapiro, R. Y. 2000. *Politicians don't pander: Political manipulation and the loss of democratic responsiveness.* Chicago: Chicago University Press.

Jacobs, L. R., and Shapiro, R. Y. 2011. Informational interdependence: Public opinion and the media in the new communications era. In R. Y. Shapiro and L. R. Jacobs (Eds.), *The Oxford handbook of American public opinion and the media* (pp. 3-21). Oxford: Oxford University Press.

Jacobs, L., and Skocpol, T. 2010. *Health care reform and American politics.* New York: Oxford University Press.

Jamieson, K. H. 1992. *Dirty politics: Deception, distraction, and democracy.* New York: Oxford University Press.

Kinder, D., and Sanders, L. 1990. Mimicking political debate with survey questions: The case of white opinion on affirmative action for blacks. *Social Cognition* 8: 73–103.

Lodge, M., and Taber, C. 2005. The utomaticity of affect for political leaders, groups, and issues: An experimental test of the hot cognition hypothesis. *Political Psychology* 26(June): 455–482.

Mettler, S. 2011. *The submerged state: How invisible government policies undermine American democracy.* Chicago: University of Chicago Press.

Mettler, S., and Soss, J. 2004. The consequences of public policy for democratic citizenship: Bridging policy studies and mass politics. *Perspectives on Politics* 2(March): 55–73.

Milner, H. 1997. *Interests, institutions, and information: Domestic politics and international relations.* Princeton, NJ: Princeton University Press.

Page, B. I., and Shapiro, R. Y. 1992. *The rational public: Fifty years of trends in American's policy preferences.* Chicago: University of Chicago Press.

Patterson, T. 1993. *Out of order.* New York: Knopf.

Rogowski, R. 1989. *Commerce and coalitions.* Princeton, NJ: Princeton University Press.

Shapiro, R. Y., Weaver, R. K., and Jacobs, L. R. 1996. Poll trends: Welfare. *Public Opinion Quarterly* 59(Winter): 606–627.

Sorensen, T. 1965. *Kennedy.* New York: Bantam Books.

Soss, J. 1999. Lessons of welfare: Policy design, political learning, and political action. *American Political Science Review* 93(June): 363–380.

Taber, C., and Lodge, M. 2006. Motivated skepticism in the evaluation of political beliefs. *American Journal of Political Science* 50(July): 755–769.

Tulis, J. 1987. *The rhetorical presidency.* Princeton, NJ: Princeton University Press.

CHAPTER 29

....

THEORIES OF MEDIA BIAS

....

S. ROBERT LICHTER

MEDIA bias is a concept the widespread use of which belies equally widespread disagreement about its meaning, measurement, and impact. Although the concept is debated by scholars and the general public alike, academic and public opinion often diverges in the meanings ascribed to the term and the conclusions drawn about its nature and prevalence. In academic circles, media bias is referenced more often as a hypothesis to explain patterns of news coverage than as a component of any fully elaborated theory of political communication. Indeed, Entman (2007, 163) recently bemoaned its status as a "curiously undertheorized staple of public discourse about the media . . . bias is yet to be defined clearly, let alone received much serious empirical attention."

Although studies have examined it in many countries, the most concentrated empirical research on the topic has taken place in the United States (Kaid and Stromback, 2008), reflecting the predominance of empirical social scientific perspectives as well as the historical development of political journalism in this country. The US commercial media system, which functions relatively free of state control and has its own professional norms, was the originator of "objective" journalism and remains its chief expositor, however objectivity is defined (Rothman, 1992; Starr, 2004). With the loosening or breakup of government control over electronic media through deregulation in recent decades, many European journalists now seek to emulate the American model, although the European conception of journalism as a literary narrative still functions as a countervailing tradition (Hallin and Mancini, 2004; Kaplan, 2009; Donsbach and Klett, 1993).

The discussion that follows deals with broad-based efforts to characterize media bias in political or ideological terms, rather than with regard to specific characteristics such as nationality, race, religion, gender, and sexual preference, or in particular political controversies such as abortion, gun control, or abortion rights. However, negativity or bad news bias is included because it is often presented as an alternative explanation for findings differently characterized as ideological or partisan bias. Where partisans may see a bias against their side, it is argued, the negative coverage may actually reflect a more general tendency to criticize all sides.

OBJECTIVITY AND BIAS

Charges of media bias draw their strength from the widespread assumption that the media should be unbiased or objective, particularly in their treatment of politics and public issues. To be sure, there are coexisting traditions, such as "watchdog" journalism, enterprise or investigative reporting, interpretive journalism, literary journalism, advocacy journalism, and most recently, civic journalism. Since the early twentieth century, however, American journalism has staked its claim to professionalism and social service primarily on the separation of facts and values in reporting (Schudson, 2001). Objectivity has become a core professional value in other countries among independent media as well, although it is interpreted somewhat differently in other national and cultural settings (Donsbach and Klett, 1993).

The development of an objectivity standard in American journalism has often been explained in terms of technological advances and changing economic incentives that occurred during the nineteenth century (Shaw, 1967; Stensaas, 1986; cf. Carey, 1989). However, Schudson (2001, 158) has argued against "economic and technological reductionism" in explaining the rise of objectivity. Instead he distinguishes between objectivity as a journalistic practice, on the one hand, and a professional norm, on the other. The adoption of objectivity as an industry standard was part of a broader societal trend toward rationalization and professionalization (Schudson, 1978, 122). Journalists thereby established their professional integrity by distinguishing themselves from the partisan manipulation of information involved in propaganda and public relations (Kaplan, 2009).

From the outset, however, there has been a stream of criticism against the adoption of objectivity as a journalistic norm. It has been described as an unattainable ideal, a subjective convention, and a mask for personal or political interests (and in that sense, itself a form of political bias) (Tuchman, 1972; Schiller, 1981; Mindich, 1998; Overholzer, 2004). Nonetheless, mainstream American journalism is still usually measured against some standard of dispassionate information-based reportage, which exhibits a concern for fairness, balance, and impartiality (Schudson, 2001).

As a result, bias is frequently conceptualized negatively, as the absence of one or more of these conditions. The term is variously used to refer to distortions of reality, favoritism or one-sidedness in presenting controversies, and closed-minded or partisan attitudes. In the process, it has been treated both as an independent variable in explaining the character of news coverage and a dependent variable to be explained by the news production process.

Scholars accounting for the sources of bias have emphasized the capitalistic system within which the media operate; the ownership and management of news organizations; organizational dynamics within those organizations; and the norms, values, and attitudes of journalists. Although studies of the nature of bias cover a wide range of material, they focus primarily on political ideology or partisanship, negativism, and various structural elements built into operational definitions of news.

Much of the literature criticizes such biases for favoring the existing power structure, hindering civic participation or democratic outcomes, and failing to provide audiences with the information they need to make rational decisions about public affairs. Television has been the leading target of such criticism, but it frequently extends to other media as well. The dramatic changes in communication introduced by digital media in recent years pose a special challenge to theories of bias, as news becomes more malleable, interactive, and audience driven.

STRUCTURAL (NONIDEOLOGICAL) BIASES

The debate over bias usually concerns the media's putative ideological or partisan tilt. However, it is often treated in a much broader context, as any deviation from an objective account of reality. This approach dismisses claims of objectivity as either irrelevant or an impediment to a real understanding of media content. Insofar as news is a specific form of discourse, any of its characteristics can be seen as bias. Such biases are often cast as structural, either to indicate that they are inherent in news or to distinguish them from political or ideological biases.

There is little agreement on the nature and derivation of structural biases. They may be traced to the effects of the economic marketplace, governmental pressures or regulation, organizational processes, and the professional norms and opinions of individuals who construct the news. For example, Cline (2009) includes the following in a lengthy list of structural biases: commercial bias, temporal bias, visual bias (for television), bad news bias, narrative bias, status quo bias, fairness bias, expediency bias, class bias, and glory bias (tendency to glorify the reporter). There is a case to be made for the existence of all these biases. As this example shows, however, listing structural biases can easily become an exercise in taxonomy, with possible overlap among categories. Moreover, the open-endedness of such exercises makes theory building problematic.

Nonetheless, researchers have found that particular structural elements can prove crucial to explaining both the content and effects of news stories. For example, Iyengar (1994) found that in experimental settings, television's tendency to frame events episodically led viewers to see individuals rather than society as responsible for social problems depicted, while thematic framing produced the opposite effect. More generally, Bennett (2004) argues that the news often creates an illusory portrait of the world, which stems from production biases such as skewed patterns of sourcing, including reliance on official sources, and with content biases toward creating dramatic, fragmented, personalized, and order-restorative depictions of reality.

CONSERVATIVE BIAS:
THE CRITICAL TRADITION

Many scholars have criticized the media for impeding social change and serving powerful interests. But the notion of a conservative media bias is most fully integrated into
the tradition of critical theory. This approach treats news as an ideological product that
shapes mass consciousness in a manner that preserves the hegemony of society's ruling
interests. A major component of this argument involves the corporate ownership and
control of the commercial news organizations that dominate the media landscape, particularly in the United States.

The most influential scholarship in this area is Bagdikian's (2004) work detailing the
ever-increasing concentration of the media industry. In Bagdikian's view, owners and
advertisers shape the news both directly and indirectly, through structural biases linked
to news production. Such biases include professional routines that define news in terms
that favor the rich and powerful, for example, through an overreliance on official sources
and beats, which marginalizes dissenting voices and activities.

The most prominent expositor of this tradition, Robert McChesney, argues that the
declining quality of contemporary journalism in the United States is ultimately rooted
in the political economy of American capitalism (McChesney, 2008). This view sees the
media as a government-sanctioned oligopoly whose misinformation serves corporate
interests, rather than providing the tools for public enlightenment and emancipation
(McChesney, 2004a). The result is the suppression or constriction of genuine debate by
the dominant media firms, which trivializes and marginalizes opposition to the status
quo (McChesney, 2004b). Professions of objectivity merely serve to divert attention
from the fact that news is an ideological expression of economic interests.

While analysts such as McChesney and Hackett (1986; Hackett and Zhao, 1998) stay
close to the neo-Marxist origins of this tradition (Jay, 1996), its most widely known
formulation is Herman and Chomsky's (1995) propaganda model. This model treats
the media as a filtering mechanism that distorts reality in a manner that serves ruling
elite interests by "manufacturing consent." The original model identified five filters—
ownership, advertising, sourcing, flak (media criticism), and anticommunism. Today
the war on terror increasingly serves as the ideological equivalent of anticommunism
(Mullen, 2009).

Critical theory treats the media primarily as agents of social control. However, some
scholars writing from a critical perspective regard journalists less as passive corporate
lapdogs and more as guard dogs who sometimes criticize the powers that be, but spring
into action to protect the system whenever a serious threat to its stability arises (Olien,
Donohue, and Tichenor, 1995).

Recent empirical studies have produced a more variegated portrait of the media's
social role as sometimes accommodating the needs of alternative and challenging groups (Demers, 2009). For example, Pollock (2007) found that local newspaper

coverage, while often tilting along an "axis of inequality," sometimes reflected the claims and interests of vulnerable and marginalized groups, rather than reinforcing inequality and elite privilege.

Notwithstanding such empirical studies, and despite its highly developed theoretical elaboration, critical theory's frequent institutional locus, reliance on case studies, fusion of analysis with prescription, and own set of journals oriented toward critical theory and cultural studies, have sometimes led it along a separate track from much of the empirical communication literature,. However, it also provides a backdrop for many other criticisms of media conservatism or status quo bias (e.g., as sexist, racist, nationalistic, etc.) that are not necessarily grounded in a formal theoretical structure (Hardt, 1992). Finally, some scholars, such as Bennett, have tried to find a middle ground between the critical tradition and a pluralist tradition that upholds the importance of objectivity as a journalistic norm (Bennett and Lawrence, 1995).

THE LIBERAL BIAS DEBATE

At the opposite end of the spectrum from the critical approach, which treats journalism as an intervening variable in the political process, are theories that portray news bias as an expression of the manifest or latent ideologies of journalists. This view is usually encountered in the context of popular media criticism from the political Right, which often takes as its starting point the political liberalism or Democratic-leaning voting patterns of major media journalists (Rusher, 1988; Goldberg, 2002; Bozell, 2004).

Attitudes vs. Content

The personal liberalism of journalists has been demonstrated by numerous surveys, which also show that liberal perspectives are most pronounced at prominent media outlets and on social and cultural issues (Lerner, Nagai, and Rothman, 1996; Kohut, 2004; Weaver et al., 2006; Noyes, 2008; Mayer, 2011). These findings hold for editors as well as reporters, although not necessarily for newspaper publishers (Media Research Center, 1998; Neuwirth, 1998).

Based partly on this evidence, Rothman (1979, 1992) posited that the national media represent the emergence of a postindustrial elite whose post-bourgeois values (Inglehart, 1971, 1977) place them at odds with traditional elites such as business and the military (cf. Bell, 1973, 1976). Lichter, Rothman, and Lichter (1990) combined survey data with content analysis to argue that journalists unconsciously project their shared, predominantly liberal, assumptions onto their coverage.

The existence of unconscious partisan biases operating in news judgments was supported by a multinational study by Patterson and Donsbach (1996). With few exceptions (Kuypers, 2002; Groseclose, 2011), however, neither the methodology nor the conclusions of this approach have been adopted by most media scholars. Few scholars have disputed the predominance of liberal attitudes among journalists, although there are exceptions here as well (Croteau, 1998). Based on a participant-observation study of network news organizations, Gans (1980) concluded that the news reflects a set of "enduring values" held by journalists, which include ethnocentrism, altruistic democracy, responsible capitalism, small-town pastoralism, individualism, moderatism, the desirability of social order, and the need for national leadership. Gans located the origin of these values in the early twentieth-century Progressive movement.

Most important, communication scholars have largely failed to find liberal bias in places where one would expect to see it, such as coverage of presidential campaigns and political institutions. For example, Niven's (2002) comparison of the tone of coverage of similar objectively measurable conditions, such as unemployment and murder rates, under Democratic and Republican administrations at different levels of government found no consistent evidence of partisan favoritism in the reports.

Similarly, in a widely cited meta-analysis, D'Alessio and Allen (2000) examined the content analysis literature evaluating presidential campaign news over several decades. They found no consistent bias toward either Democratic or Republican candidates in three areas: gatekeeping bias (selecting stories that favor one party over the other), coverage bias (the amount of coverage of each party), and statement bias (the valence or tone of coverage).

Finally, any consideration of the major media's ideological tilt must take into account the importance of two sources of overtly conservative perspectives on the news: talk radio and Fox News Channel (Alterman, 2003; DellaVigna and Kaplan, 2006; Jamieson and Cappella, 2008). Their commercial success spawned liberal counterparts such as the now defunct Air America radio network and MSNBC's shift to more liberally oriented programming (Oravec, 2005; Terwilliger, McCarthy, and Lamkin, 2011).

Increase in Partisanship

The effect of this shift toward more partisan news has been demonstrated by numerous content analyses. For example, in the 2008 general election MSNBC's coverage of Barack Obama was more positive, and Fox News's coverage was more negative, than the broadcast networks' coverage (Pew Research Center, 2008). Similarly, during the 2004 election the broadcast network coverage favored Kerry, while Fox News coverage favored Bush (Pew Research Center, 2005).

The development of avowedly partisan electronic media organs may be part of a broader tendency in recent years for news outlets to become more opinionated. For example, in a study covering a decade of newspaper coverage, Puglisi and Snyder (2011) found that Democratic-leaning newspapers (as defined by their editorial endorsements) gave more coverage to scandals involving Republican politicians than scandals involving Democratic politicians, while Republican-leaning newspapers did the opposite, with the average partisan leanings of readers held constant. Similarly, pro-Democratic newspapers systematically gave more coverage to high unemployment during Republican administrations, while pro-Republican newspapers again showed the opposite pattern (Larcinese, Puglisi, and Snyder, 2011).

Alternative Approaches

The lack of evidence of consistently liberal media bias had led to efforts to understand the widespread and growing public perception to the contrary (Media Research Center, 2011) through the lens of cognitive psychology, by applying concepts such as the hostile media phenomenon, biased attribution, and the third-person effect (Davison, 1983; Vallone, Ross, and Lepper, 1985). The central point is that people's perceptions of media bias are shaped more by their own perspectives than by actual media content (Dalton, Beck, and Huckfeldt, 1998). The public's increasing belief in liberal media bias has also been explained as the product of a rhetorical strategy of conservative political elites seeking to gain a partisan advantage by delegitimizing the media (Domke et al., 1999).

However, debate over the media's putative liberal tilt was recently rekindled by the work of Groseclose and Milyo (2005a, 2005b). Their novel methodology involved arraying media outlets along a left-to-right ideological spectrum, according to the ideological valence of activist groups and think tanks cited in news stories. Then they applied the same exercise to congressional speeches and matched the two lists. This procedure located most major media outlets to the left of the average member of Congress. Their conclusion that this finding demonstrates liberal media bias proved immediately controversial and has stimulated continuing debate (Gasper, 2011; Groseclose, 2011).

In addition, the controversy has been kept alive in recent years by an accumulating body of research done by economists, some of which appear to support the notion of a liberal bias. However, this research is sufficiently distinctive in both its theoretical orientation and its methodology to warrant separate consideration.

ECONOMIC MODELS OF BIAS

In recent years economists have played a growing role in developing new models of media bias based on supply and demand. Pioneering work by Hamilton (2004) showed that such recent changes in journalism as increased negativism and soft news, as well as an ideological tilt, could be at least partly explained as responses to changing economic incentives, many of them produced by technological advances. The fact that audiences gravitate toward news that reflects their own views (and regard news sources that challenge their views as biased) gains importance in this context, because maximum utility assumes the best match between the supply and demand sides.

Thus, a news consumer's utility from seeking out news is maximized by matching the consumer's own perspective (the demand side) with that of the news source (the supply side). As Hamilton (2004, 73) put it, "Political bias in media content is similar to product differentiation." For example, he argues that a liberal perspective on television news on issues such as crime and education may reflect the marginal utility to the networks of increasing viewership among young females, who share both an interest in these issues and a liberal perspective on them.

Hamilton's cross-disciplinary work has gained a wide audience among communications scholars. There has been less cross-pollination of other recent economic research, much of which aims at developing models that explain bias (or its absence) in terms of maximizing profitability. For example, Gentzkow and Shapiro (2008) argue that competition in the news market should lower bias, by providing consumers with feedback on inaccurate and distorted reporting (as in cities with competing newspapers). Alternatively, Mullainathan and Shleifer (2005) claim that competition is more likely to increase bias, by producing market segmentation along the lines of consumers' own biases (as it has among the cable news networks).

These studies have so far produced no overall consensus among economists on media bias. However, those that do impute bias tend to locate it to the left of center (Puglisi, 2011; cf. Sutter, 2001). For example, in a theoretical supply-side approach, Baron (2006) argued that profit-maximizing news organizations have an incentive to permit biased reporting because it is most efficient to employ journalists who define career advancement partly in terms of promoting their own worldviews. Since US journalists lean toward the left in the aggregate, so will news coverage. In an empirical demand-side approach, Gentzkow and Shapiro (2006) arrayed newspapers according to their use of politically charged phrases (such as "death tax" or "workers' rights") that matched those preferred by Democratic or Republican legislators. They found that the average newspaper's language was on the center-left, which was also close to the profit-maximizing point.

Along with the Groseclose-Milyo study, economic studies such as these have rekindled the liberal bias debate, which had seemed all but settled among communications researchers. Some of these studies rely on assumptions that may not reflect real-world conditions, and others may use imperfect measures of tone. Nonetheless, this work provides a fresh perspective that may further enrich this area of inquiry by stimulating new interdisciplinary approaches.

MEDIA NEGATIVITY

Theories of media negativism provide an alternative to those of ideological bias, while retaining a focus on journalists' personal attitudes and professional norms as causal agents. In line with the literature on cognitive distortions cited above, this concept also helps to explain the increase in public perceptions of media bias. With all else being equal, we would expect news consumers to be more likely to attribute negative media evaluations of their preferred policies and candidates to bias, while accepting negative evaluations of opposing policies and candidates as accurate reflections of reality. However, news coverage can still favor one candidate, officeholder, or policy over another, despite having an overall negative tone (Council for Excellence in Government, 2003; Farnsworth and Lichter, 2011).

In an early study, Robinson (1975, 1976) used the term "videomalaise" to describe the alienating effects of negative television news coverage of public affairs. However, media negativity first attracted sustained attention from scholars during the 1990s, as numerous studies suggested that negatively toned coverage was increasing, with detrimental effects on public discourse and civic engagement (Smoller, 1990; Patterson, 1993; Cappella and Jamieson, 1996; Just et al., 1996; Fallows, 1997). A parallel stream of research traced the increasing willingness of news organizations to focus on scandals involving the personal behavior of political actors and to adopt a prosecutorial style of coverage (Garment, 1991; Sabato, 1991; Kalb, 2001; Sabato et al., 2001).

Patterson (1993) argued that the political controversies of the 1960s and 1970s led journalists to play a more active role in politics, especially in presidential election campaigns. Instead of only reporting on candidate activities, journalists saw their new role as protecting the public from candidates' efforts to deceive them. This gave campaign coverage an increasingly negative tone. It also led journalists to become a kind of third force in American politics, criticizing both major political parties in ways that increased the influence of journalists vis-à-vis politicians. Patterson (2000) later extended this criticism to coverage of government and public affairs.

Jamieson and her colleagues argued that the problem was not only negativism but cynicism, which included the use of strategic or conflict-oriented frames (Cappella and Jamieson 1996, 1997; Jamieson and Waldman 2003). The concept of strategic frames is analogous to what Patterson (1996) termed the media's "game schema." The cynicism of strategic framing lies in its implication that politicians' rhetoric and behavior can be reduced to strategies of gaining power.

Jamieson and Cappella (1995) used experimental data to show how strategy frames produced a more cynical interpretation of politics than did issue frames. This could occur not only in campaign discourse but also in policy debates. For example, the debate over President Bill Clinton's healthcare reform plan illustrated how strategic reporting can make people cynical about public policy. Cappella and Jamieson (1997) concluded that the media were creating a "spiral of cynicism," in which cynical media portrayals of politics led audiences to view politics in a more cynical manner.

These theories of media negativism were criticized by Norris (2000a, 2000b), who argued that the effect of media exposure depends on the previous levels of trust and political engagement among audience members. Based on survey data from the United States and Western Europe, she argued that politically trusting and engaged individuals seek out more media coverage, which increases their trust and engagement. Norris termed this a "virtuous circle."

Later studies have focused on how the process is affected by differences in types of media exposure and audience characteristics, such as partisan affiliation and level of trust. The most recent research suggests that the spiral of cynicism exists most clearly for the television news audience, harking back to Robinson's early theory of videomalaise (Moy and Pfau, 2000; Valentino, Beckmann, and Buhr, 2001; Mutz and Reeves, 2005; Avery, 2009).

CONCLUSION

The debate over media bias has drawn on a wide range of theories and methods. The tradition of critical theory has produced a rich literature that portrays the news media as a conservative force in politics. To some degree, however, this conclusion is built into the theory itself. Conversely, much popular media criticism has posited that journalists' personal attitudes produce a liberal tilt in their coverage. Most scholarly studies have failed to support this conclusion, however, and the increasing public perception of liberal media bias has been linked to audience biases and strategic efforts by conservative elites. However, recent studies have rekindled this debate, while attributing biased coverage to economic incentives rather than journalists' mindsets. Finally, negativity bias provides a well-documented alternative explanation for perceptions of ideological bias in the news. However, negativity bias and ideological bias are not necessarily exclusive.

Thus, the question of whether the media have an ideological bias and, if so, in what direction it tilts is unlikely to be settled soon. In addition to competing approaches and conceptual differences, the development of theory has been slowed by the absence of agreed-upon metrics to measure bias. Much of the empirical research is based on content analyses of how individual issues or topics are covered, which do not permit generalizations about broader patterns of coverage. However, a number of approaches in recent years have sought to provide more systematic measures. These include comparisons of news coverage with measures of real-world conditions, such as economic indicators or crime rates, and attempts to link certain components of news stories, such as journalists' choice of language and citation of sources, with their counterparts in the realm of partisan politics. Other approaches that have facilitated a broader perspective include meta-analysis and computer-assisted content analysis.

Another ongoing problem for this field lies in sorting out levels of analysis, based on competing explanations from different schools of thought. The same phenomenon may be explained differently in terms of alternative explanatory frameworks. For example, negativity bias has been interpreted as a product of journalists' professional norms, an antipolitical progressive ideology, a watchdog mentality, and a conscious or unconscious response to economic incentives (cf. Schudson, 2007). Particular issues may be sorted out piecemeal, but there is currently little prospect of a fusion of theoretical approaches.

It may be that the ideologically relevant characteristics are overdetermined and cannot be broken out into separate, mutually exclusive components. Or previous research strategies may not have been sophisticated or inclusive enough. Entman (2007) takes a positive step by arguing that bias should be treated in the context of theories of media influence based on framing, priming, and agenda setting. Uses and gratifications theory, with its focus on active audience, may prove equally important in understanding the sources and dynamics of bias in the next generation of news media.

The digital revolution also poses a special challenge to theories of media bias. It is possible to overstate the impact of the Internet on the creation and distribution of news. For example, among the twenty-five most heavily trafficked news sites, twenty-two are those of legacy media or aggregators that rely heavily on traditional news organizations (Pew Research Center, 2011). Nonetheless, the study of media bias faces considerable hurdles in adapting to a media environment in which it is increasingly difficult to distinguish the journalists from the audience. News and opinion are becoming more difficult to disentangle, even as the dissemination of news becomes more interactive and user driven. Thus, a field of inquiry that is already characterized by great theoretical and methodological diversity faces new challenges in dealing with a media landscape that has a rapidly changing topography.

References

Alterman, E. 2003. *What liberal media?* New York: Basic Books.

Avery, J. 2009. Videomalaise or virtuous circle? *International Journal of Press/Politics* 14: 410–433.

Bagdikian, B. 2004. *The new media monopoly*. Boston: Beacon Press.

Baron, D. P. 2006. Persistent media bias. *Journal of Public Economics 90*: 1–36.

Bell, D. 1973. *The coming of post-industrial society*. New York: Basic Books.

Bell, D. 1976. *The cultural contradictions of capitalism*. New York: Basic Books.

Bennett, W. L. 2004. *News: The politics of illusion*. New York: Pearson/Longman.

Bennett, W. L., and Lawrence, R. G. 1995. News icons and the mainstreaming of social change. *Journal of Communication 45*: 20–39.

Bozell, B. 2004. *Weapons of mass distortion*. New York: Crown Forum.

Cappella, J. N., and Jamieson, K. H. 1996. News frames, political cynicism, and media cynicism. *Annals of the American Academy of Political and Social Science 546*: 71–84.

Cappella, J. N., and Jamieson, K. H. 1997. *Spiral of cynicism*. New York: Oxford.

Carey, J. 1989. *Communication and culture*. Boston: Unwin Hyman.

Cline, A. R. 2009. Bias. In W. Eadie (Ed.), *21st Century Communications* (pp. 479–486). Thousand Oaks, CA: Sage.

Council for Excellence in Government. 2003. *Government: In and out of the news*. Washington, DC: Council for Excellence in Government.

Croteau, D. 1998. Challenging the liberal media claim. *Extra!* (July/August): 4–9.

D'Alessio, D., and Allen, M. 2000. Media bias in presidential elections: A meta-analysis. *Journal of Communication 50*: 133–56.

Dalton, R. J., Beck, P. A., and Huckfeldt, R. 1998. Partisan cues and the media. *American Political Science Review 92*: 111–126.

Davison, P. 1983. The third-person effect in communication. *Public Opinion Quarterly 47*: 1–15.

DellaVigna, S., and Kaplan, E. 2006. The Fox News effect: Media bias and voting. *Quarterly Journal of Economics 122*: 1187–1234.

Demers, D. P. 2009. Review of "Tilted Mirrors." *Political Communication 26*: 362–364.

Domke, D., Watts, M. D., Shah, D. V., and Fan, D. P. 1999. The politics of conservative elites and the liberal media argument. *Journal of Communication* 49: 35–58.

Donsbach, W., and Klett, B. 1993. Subjective objectivity. *International Communication Gazette* 51: 53–83.

Entman, R. 2007. Framing bias: Media in the distribution of power. *Journal of Communication* 57: 163–173.

Fallows, J. 1997. *Breaking the news.* New York: Vintage Books.

Farnsworth, S., and Lichter, S. R. 2011. *The nightly news nightmare.* 3rd ed. Lanham MD: Rowman & Littlefield.

Gans, H. 1980. *Deciding what's news.* New York: Vintage Books.

Garment, S. 1991. *Scandal.* New York: Times Books.

Gasper, J. T. 2011. Shifting ideologies? Re-examining media bias. *Quarterly Journal of Political Science* 6: 85–102.

Gentzkow, M., and Shapiro, J. M. 2006. What drives media slant? NBER Working Paper No. 12707. Chicago.

Gentzkow, M., and Shapiro, J. M. 2008. Competition and truth in the market for news. *Journal of Economic Perspectives* 22: 133–154.

Goldberg, B. 2002. *Bias.* Washington DC: Regnery.

Groseclose, T. 2011. *Left turn: How media bias distorts the American mind.* New York: St. Martin's Press.

Groseclose, T., and Milyo, J. 2005a. A measure of media bias. *Quarterly Journal of Economics* 120: 1191–1237.

Groseclose, T., and Milyo, J. 2005b. A social-science perspective on media bias. *Critical Review* 17: 305–314.

Hackett, R. 1986. For a socialist perspective on the news media. *Studies in Political Economy* 19: 141–156.

Hackett, R., and Zhao, Y. 1998. *Sustaining democracy? Journalism and the politics of objectivity.* Toronto: Garamond Press.

Hallin, D. C., and Mancini, P. 2004. *Comparing media systems: Three models of media and politics.* Cambridge, UK: Cambridge University Press.

Hamilton, J. T. 2004. *All the news that's fit to sell.* Princeton, NJ: Princeton University Press.

Hardt, H. 1992. *Critical communication studies.* New York: Routledge.

Herman, E. S., and Chomsky, N. 1995. *Manufacturing consent.* New York: Vintage Books.

Inglehart, R. 1971. The silent revolution in post-industrial societies. *American Political Science Review* 65: 991–1017.

Inglehart, R. 1977. *The silent revolution.* Princeton, NJ: Princeton University Press.

Iyengar, S. 1994. *Is anyone responsible?* Chicago: University of Chicago Press.

Jamieson, K. H., and Cappella, J. N. 2008. *Echo chamber: Rush Limbaugh and the conservative media establishment.* New York: Oxford University Press.

Jamieson, K. H., and Waldman, P. 2003. *The press effect.* New York: Oxford University Press.

Jay, M. 1996. *The dialectical imagination: A history of the Frankfurt School and the Institute of Social Research, 1923–1950.* Berkeley: University of California Press.

Just, M. R., Crigler, A. N., Alger, D. E., and Cook, T. E. 1996. *Crosstalk.* Chicago: University of Chicago Press.

Kaid, L. L., and Stromback, J. (Eds.). 2008. *The handbook of election news coverage around the world.* New York: Routledge.

Kalb, M. 2001. *One scandalous story.* New York: Free Press.

Kaplan, R. 2009. The origins of objectivity in American journalism. In S. Allan (Ed.), *The Routledge companion to news and journalism studies* (pp. 25–37). New York: Routledge.

Kohut, A. 2004. How journalists see journalists in 2004. Washington, DC: Pew Research Center. Retrieved June 1, 2009, from http://people-press.org/files/legacy-pdf/214.pdf.

Kuypers, 2002. *Press bias and politics*. New York: Praeger.

Larcinese, V., Puglisi, R, and Snyder, J. M. 2011. Partisan bias in economic news. *Journal of Public Economics*. 95: 1178–1189.

Lerner, R., Nagai, A., and Rothman, S. 1996. *American elites*. New Haven, CT: Yale University Press.

Lichter, S. R., Rothman, S., and Lichter, L. S. 1990. *The media elite*. New York: Hastings House.

Mayer, W. G. 2011. The political attitudes of American journalists. Paper presented at the annual meeting of the Midwest Political Science Association, Chicago, IL.

McChesney, R. 2004a. *The problem of the media: U.S. communication politics in the 21st century*. New York: Monthly Review Press.

McChesney, R. 2004b. *Telecommunications, mass media, and democracy*. New York: Oxford University Press.

McChesney, R. 2008. *The political economy of media*. New York: Monthly Review Press.

Media Research Center. 1998. Newspaper editors voted for Clinton. Retrieved November 1, 2011, from http://www.mrc.org/mediawatch/1998/watch19980201.asp#3.

Media Research Center. 2011. How the public views the media. Retrieved June 1, 2011, from http://www.mediaresearch.org/biasbasics/biasbasics4.asp.

Mindich, David. 1998. *Just the facts: How "objectivity" came to define American journalism*. New York: New York University Press.

Moy, P., and Pfau, M. 2000. *With malice toward all?* Westport, CT: Praeger.

Mullainathan, S., and Shleifer, A. 2005. The market for news. *American Economic Review* 95: 1031–1053.

Mullen, A. 2009. The propaganda model after twenty years. *Westminster Papers in Communication and Culture* 6: 12–22.

Mutz, D., and Reeves, B. 2005. The new videomalaise. *American Political Science Review*

Neuwirth, R. 1998. Press flawed, news chiefs admit. *Editor & Publisher* 131: 10–14.

Niven, D. 2002. *Tilt? The search for media bias*. New York: Praeger.

Norris, P. 2000a. The impact of television on civic malaise. In S. J. Pharr and R. D. Putnam (Eds.), *Disaffected democracies* (pp. 231–251). Princeton, NJ: Princeton University Press.

Norris, P. 2000b. *A virtuous circle*. Cambridge, UK: Cambridge University Press.

Noyes, R. 2008. Democrats' most reliable constituents: The press. *Newsbusters*, November 2. Retrieved June 1, 2011, from http://newsbusters.org/blogs/rich-noyes/2008/11/02/democrats-most-reliable-constituents-press.

Olien, C. N., Donohue, G. A. and Tichenor, P. J. 1995. Conflict, consensus and public opinion. In T. L. Glaser and C. T. Salmon (Eds.), *Public opinion and the communication of consent* (pp. 301–322). New York: Guilford Press.

Oravec, J. A. 2005. How the left does talk. *Journal of Radio Studies* 12: 190–203.

Overholzer G. 2004. The inadequacy of objectivity as a touchstone. *Nieman Reports* 58: 4, 53.

Patterson, T. 1993. *Out of order*. New York: Vintage Books.

Patterson, T. 1996. Bad news, bad governance. *Annals of the American Academy of Political and Social Science* 546: 97–108.

Patterson, T. 2000. *Doing well and doing good*. Cambridge, MA: Harvard University Press.

Patterson, T., and Donsbach, W. 1996. News decisions: Journalists as partisan actors. *Political Communication* 13: 455–468.

Pew Research Center. 2005. The state of the news media 2005. March 15. Retrieved from http://stateofthemedia.org/2005/overview/content-analysis.

Pew Research Center. 2008. Winning the media campaign. Retrieved June 1, 2011, from http://www.journalism.org/analysis_report/winning_media_campaign.

Pew Research Center. 2011. Navigating news online. Retrieved June 1, 2011, from http://www.journalism.org/analysis_report/top_25.

Puglisi, R. 2011. Being the *New York Times*: The political behaviour of a newspaper. *B.E. Journal of Economic Analysis & Policy* 11(1). Retrieved from http://www.bepress.com/bejeap/vol11/iss1/art20.

Puglisi, R., and Snyder, J. 2011. Newspaper coverage of political scandals. *Journal of Politics*.

Robinson, M. J. 1975. American political legitimacy in an era of electronic journalism. In D. Cater and R. Adler (Eds.), *Television as a social force*. New York: Praeger.

Robinson, M. J. 1976. Public affairs television and the growth of political malaise. *American Political Science Review* 70: 409–432.

Rothman, S. 1979. The mass media in post-industrial America. In S. M. Lipset (Ed.), *The third century* (pp. 346–388). Stanford, CA: Hoover Institution Press.

Rothman, S. (Ed.) 1992. *The mass media in liberal democratic societies*. New York: Paragon House.

Rusher, W. A. 1988. *The coming battle for the media*. New York: William Morrow.

Sabato, L. 1991. *Feeding frenzy*. New York: Free Press.

Sabato, L., Stencel, M., and Lichter, S. R. 2001. *Peepshow: Media and politics in an age of scandal*. Lanham, MD: Rowman & Littlefield.

Shaw, D. L. 1967. News bias and the telegraph. *Journalism Quarterly* 44: 3–12.

Schiller, D. 1981. *Objectivity and the news*. Philadelphia: University of Pennsylvania Press.

Schudson, M. 1978. *Discovering the news*. New York: Basic Books.

Schudson, M. 2001. The objectivity norm in American journalism. *Journalism* 2: 149–170.

Schudson, M. 2007. The concept of politics in contemporary American journalism. *Political Communication* 24: 131–142.

Smoller, F. T. 1990. *The six o'clock presidency*. New York: Praeger.

Starr, P. 2004. *The creation of the media*. New York: Basic Books.

Stensaas, H. S. 1986. Development of the objectivity ethic in U.S. daily newspapers. *Journal of Mass Media Ethics* 2: 50–60.

Sutter, D. 2001. Can the media be so liberal? The economics of media bias. *Cato Journal* 20: 431–451.

Terwilliger, B., McCarthy, P. M., and Lamkin, T. 2011. Bias in hard news articles from Fox News and MSNBC. In *Proceedings of the Twenty-Fourth International Florida Artificial Intelligence Research Society Conference* (pp. 361–362). St. Petersburg, FL: Association for the Advancement of Artificial Intelligence.

Tuchman, G. 1972. Objectivity as strategic ritual. *American Journal of Sociology* 77: 660–679.

Valentino, N., Beckmann, M., and Buhr, T. 2001. A spiral of cynicism for some. *Political Communication* 18: 347–367.

Vallone, R. P., Ross. L., and Lepper, M. K. 1985. The hostile media phenomenon. *Journal of Personality and Social Psychology* 49: 577–585.

Weaver, D. H., Beam, R. A., Brownlee, B. J., Voakes, P. S., and Wilhoit, G. C. 2006. *The American journalist in the 21st century*. New York: Lawrence Erlbaum.

CHAPTER 30

....

DIGITAL MEDIA AND PERCEPTIONS OF SOURCE CREDIBILITY IN POLITICAL COMMUNICATION

....

ANDREW J. FLANAGIN AND MIRIAM J. METZGER

The Importance of Source Credibility to Political Communication

PERSUASION lies at the heart of political communication. The capacity of political communicators to persuade others is in many ways more important than—though not mutually exclusive of—their ability to formulate effective public policies, to work collaboratively with others, and to grasp the complex interplay of the diverse goals of their constituencies. It is therefore not surprising that scholars have long been concerned with the myriad factors that affect a communicator's ability to persuade audiences. An enduring and critical factor in this pursuit has been *source credibility*.

In the West, interest in understanding source credibility dates to Aristotle, for whom a central interest was persuasion in political oratory. For Aristotle, the three modes of persuasion were logos (the logic used to support a claim), pathos (emotional or motivational appeals), and ethos (the source's credibility or the speaker's/author's authority) (Kennedy, 1991). This general treatment set the foundation for the study of source credibility, and the features of logos, pathos, and ethos remain evident in modern treatments of this issue, although in revised form.

The seminal work of social psychologist Carl Hovland and his colleagues at Yale in the 1950s, for example, examined the characteristics of persuasive speakers to ascertain the factors contributing to their perceived credibility (Hovland, Janis, and Kelley, 1953; Hovland and Weiss, 1951). Their ambitious research program assessed source credibility and its influence on attitude formation, with the goal of developing a systematic theory of persuasion (Lowery and DeFleur, 1995). The Yale team suggested that source credibility is a receiver-based construct, determined by the acceptance of the speaker and of the message by the audience. Building on this notion, McCroskey (1966) and his colleagues investigated how message recipients perceived particular communicators (Perloff, 1989). This research was followed by hundreds of empirical studies that sought to determine the dimensions of source credibility from the perspective of message recipients.

Hovland and his colleagues defined source credibility in terms of the *believability* of a communicator, which is determined by the receiver's evaluation of a source's *expertise* and *trustworthiness* (Hovland, Janis, and Kelley, 1953). This basic definition persists today (see, e.g., Fogg, 2003; Gass and Seiter, 2003; Metzger et al., 2003; Sternthal, Phillips, and Dholakia, 1978), although other dimensions have been suggested, including reliability, composure, sociability, similarity to the source, goodwill, dynamism, safety, and likability (Berlo, Lemert, and Mertz, 1969; Giffin, 1967), as well as composure and sociability (Gass and Seiter, 2003; Jurma, 1981; McCroskey, 1966; Perloff, 1989; Whitehead, 1968). Although credibility is also a concern in information science, where it is conceptualized primarily as a criterion for information selection and usage, the locus of most scholarly work on source credibility has been in the fields of communication and social psychology (O'Keefe, 2002; Wilson and Sherrell, 1993; Self, 2008).

For more than half a century studies probing source credibility's influence on learning and persuasion have focused on political or policy-related topics (e.g., Hovland and Weiss, 1951; Hovland and Mandell, 1952). For example, participants in one study (Hovland and Mandell, 1952) were exposed to messages delivered by a television news commentator on the issue of changing US monetary policy. That study manipulated the source credibility of the communicator and found that less credible sources were perceived as having given a worse presentation than higher credibility speakers and were rated as less fair and honest, even though the message was held constant across conditions.

In the decades that followed, scholars concluded that source credibility is positively associated with persuasion (Albarracín and Vargas, 2010; Wilson and Sherrell, 1993), an effect moderated by factors including issue involvement, timing of source identification, and how closely the position advocated by the source matches the receiver's position and his or her own expectations (O'Keefe, 2002; see also Pornpitakpan, 2004). Some of this work looked specifically at how source credibility affects *political* persuasion, finding that greater political persuasion results from high- rather than low-credibility sources (Chebat, Filiatrault, and Perrien, 1990; see also Morton and Villegas, 2005), and that moderators such as issue involvement and the alignment between receivers' beliefs/expectations and the position advocated affect political persuasion (Iyengar and Simon, 2000; Iyengar and Valentino, 2000; Nelson and Garst, 2005). Collectively, Iyengar's research showed that source credibility can affect voters' acceptance of political campaign ads, and that voters view politicians as most credible and persuasive when they advocate issues that are consistent with their party's platform. In a similar vein, Nelson and Garst (2005) found that persuasion is greatest when voters share a political source's values and attitudes, and when the source advocates a position consistent with those values and attitudes.

An area that has received particular attention is how credibility moderates the effects of negative political campaigning. O'Cass (2002), for example, found that voters respond more favorably to high-credibility candidates who use negative campaign ads than they do to low-credibility candidates who use them. Similarly, Yoon, Pinkleton, and Ko (2005) concluded that negative advertising is more effective in capturing votes for high-credibility candidates than for low-credibility ones. At the same time, however, they found that high-involvement voters experience greater cynicism when high-credibility candidates use attack advertising. Homer and Batra (1994)'s examination of the effects of negative ads on perceptions of candidates who are targeted in the ads found that they were more effective at reducing some aspects of the attacked candidate's credibility (i.e., their trustworthiness) than others (i.e., their expertise).

Other work in this domain has focused on the role that source credibility plays in influencing public opinion. Wanta and Hu (1994) found that highly credible media sources were better able than those with lower credibility to set the public's agenda. Druckman (2001) confirmed that political sources with higher credibility are more likely to have their frames accepted by message recipients as well. And Miller and Krosnick (2000) observed greater priming effects for high- versus low-credible news sources. Together, these studies show that source credibility can magnify the effects of agenda setting, framing, and priming on public opinion.

THE RISE OF DIGITAL MEDIA AND THE EVOLUTION OF SOURCE CREDIBILITY

Recent technological changes have created a radically different information environment than the one that existed even a few decades ago. As digital network technologies have lowered the cost and complexity of producing and disseminating information, the nature of information providers has shifted. Rather than being delivered through a small number of sources, each with a substantial investment in the information production and delivery processes, information is increasingly provided by a wide range of sources, many of which can readily create and deliver information to large audiences worldwide. One consequence of this evolution in information production is an almost incomprehensibly vast number of information sources. Social software applications have extended this information and source fecundity even further, by connecting individuals directly to one another and by providing significant opportunities to share myriad types of information generated by users themselves.

While this explosion of information has created tremendous opportunities for communication and information sharing, it is also accompanied by significant challenges. In the traditional media environment there were typically a limited number of sources and high barriers for access to the public dissemination of information. In this environment of information scarcity, credible sources were often characterized by such features as formal positions indicating particular training and education or by jobs requiring specific, relevant experience. In this manner, credible sources were often recognizable by virtue of their outwardly observable and verifiable credentials, which were rooted in specific qualifications. The relative inaccessibility of these credentials ensured that the number of credible sources in most domains was small, and the difficulty in obtaining requisite skills, training, and positions perpetuated a system of elite expertise that endured over time. In this manner, source credibility has for the most part been the domain of a rather exclusive subset of individuals (e.g., doctors, experts, journalists, etc.).

Although this exclusive system of bestowing source credibility endures today in a number of domains, the evolution of networked information-sharing tools has significantly altered it in many cases. Digital media present new challenges and have in many ways magnified the burden of determining source credibility (Danielson, 2006; Fogg, 2003; Metzger et al., 2003; Rieh and Danielson, 2008). The combination of the vast quantity of and accessibility to digitally stored and transmitted information has prompted concerns about source credibility because, as Rieh and Danielson (2008) argue, this arrangement creates greater uncertainty regarding both who is responsible for information and whether it can be believed. Two important and related issues are the nature of gatekeeping in the digital media environment and the level of ambiguity surrounding both the source and context of information.

Several researchers have noted that digital media sometimes lack traditional authority indicators such as author identity and established reputation (Danielson, 2006; Fritch and Cromwell, 2002; Metzger, 2007), and yet source information is crucial to credibility because it is the primary basis upon which credibility judgments rest (Sundar, 2008). In some cases, source information is unavailable, masked, or entirely missing from a website, chat group, blog, wiki, and so forth. In other cases, it is provided, yet hard to interpret, such as when information is coproduced or repurposed from one site, channel, or application to another, or when information or news aggregators display information from multiple sources in a centralized location that may itself be perceived as the source. Indeed, Burbules (1998) has suggested that because information is presented in a similar format on websites, a psychological "leveling effect" is created that puts all information on the same level of accessibility and thus all sources on the same level of credibility.

Technological features of the Internet also can create a kind of "context deficit" for digital information (Eysenbach, 2008). The hyperlinked structure of the Web compounds this problem by making it psychologically challenging for users to follow and evaluate various sources as they move from site to site. Research by Eysenbach and Kohler (2002), for example, showed a type of digital sleeper effect such that source and message information become confused or disassociated in users' minds almost immediately after performing searches for medical information online. Various levels of source anonymity are also problematic since, under conditions of ambiguous authorship, information sources' motivations are often unclear to users, undercutting the heuristic that relies on persuasive intent to ascertain information credibility (Flanagin and Metzger, 2000, 2007).

Collectively, these factors contribute to the difficulty of evaluating news or political information in online environments. In particular, they complicate determinations of source expertise and trustworthiness, which are the core elements of source credibility. For example, as digital media allow more individuals to reach large audiences, a source's *expertise* may be difficult to determine and may derive less from his or her official credentials or organizational affiliations, and more from the number of followers, ratings, "likes," or inward links he or she has elicited. Evaluations of *trustworthiness* are complicated as well, as source identity itself is often elusive in online contexts. Moreover, the rise of narrowcasting has implications for source trustworthiness, since many news consumers today actually prefer sources that are biased toward their perspective because they see them as more credible than less congenial sources (Iyengar and Hahn, 2009; Kahan et al., 2010; Oyedeji 2010). Given this shifting media landscape and evolving news consumption preferences, we next consider what is learned from research on source credibility in newly emerging political communication contexts.

Research Findings on Source Credibility and Online Political Communication

In recent decades, scholars have produced a substantial body of research on source credibility in online contexts, some of which is directly concerned with political communication. This research falls generally into three areas: studies examining the credibility of digital versus traditional media channels as sources of news and political information; research on the credibility of political information carried by social media and Web 2.0 applications; and analyses of the credibility of other types and sources of political information online, such as research on the perceived credibility of political issue–oriented and candidate websites.

Credibility of Digital versus Traditional Channels as Sources of News and Political Information

Cross-media comparisons have sought to assess the credibility of the Internet relative to other communication channels for political or news information. Early studies by Flanagin and Metzger (2000) and Kiousis (2001) found that newspapers were rated as significantly more credible as a source of news information than other media, including the Internet/Web, magazines, radio, and television (Flanagin and Metzger, 2000; Kiousis, 2001). Schweiger (2000) found similar results in Germany, where although the

Web was viewed as a credible source of information, it was judged less credible than newspapers and television (Schweiger, 2000). Mashek (1997) found that users rated traditional media sources including newspapers and television as more fair and unbiased than their online equivalents for obtaining political information. Some research around that same period, however, found that Web-based news sources were perceived to be as credible as traditional sources (Online News Association, 2001; Kohut, 1999).

Later research produced more mixed results. Traditional news media have been found to be more credible in some cases (Mehrabi, Hassan, and Ali, 2009; Melican and Dixon, 2008), whereas in other instances online news sources were shown to be more credible (Abdulla et al., 2005). Johnson and Kaye (2010) found that among politically interested Internet users in 2004, online versions of candidate literature and cable and television news (e.g., CNN.com or cbsnews.com) were rated as more credible than their traditional counterparts, although online newspapers were rated equally credible as their print versions, and online news magazines, issue-oriented sources, and radio were rated as less so. As in their earlier studies, Johnson and Kaye (2010) also found that reliance on the Web predicts perceived credibility of a number of online sources of political information, and interestingly, that reliance on traditional media is a strong predictor of an individual's perception of the credibility of online media.

Collectively, these studies suggest that credibility perceptions of online sources may be changing with time and may depend on a variety of factors, including the extent to which people rely heavily on the Web for news and political information and the degree to which they feel that information online is consistent with their own political perspectives. For example, individuals who felt that the Internet had more information about the Iraq War that was consistent with their own attitude about the conflict rated the Internet as more credible than did those who felt the Internet offered proportionally more counterattitudinal information (Choi, Watt, and Lynch, 2006). As the Internet continues to saturate people's lives, however, differences in credibility ratings across media may recede as the distinctions among these channels disappear.

Credibility of Political Information in Social Media

Scholars have recently been investigating the special credibility problems posed both by political information carried via social media, including blogs, wikis, and news aggregators, and by political messaging between citizens using email, video sites, and online social networks.

Blogs. Given their potential for bias relative to mainstream news, and the fact that they typically are not required to adhere to professional standards of reporting, a great deal of recent work has focused on the credibility of blogs. Among their users, political blogs are rated high in believability and depth of information but low on accuracy and fairness (Johnson et al., 2008). Several studies have compared the credibility of blogs to other sources of political information, with mixed results that become coherent when considering characteristics of the evaluator. Those who rely heavily on blogs for political information judge them to be highly credible, even more so than either traditional media sources or online sources of political information such as candidate and issue websites or political chat rooms (Johnson and Kaye, 2004; Johnson et al., 2008; Johnson and Kaye, 2009; see also Banning and Sweetser, 2007). However, studies that have used either representative samples or more broad student samples find that blogs are rated lower in credibility than traditional media (Meyer, Marchionni, and Thorson, 2010; Thorson, Vraga, and Ekdale, 2010; Metzger et al., 2011). Moreover, some studies find that reliance on traditional news media negatively predicts blog credibility (except for reliance on political talk radio, which is a positive predictor; Johnson and Kaye, 2004). Political involvement, political knowledge, and information-seeking motivations (Johnson and Kaye, 2004, 2009; Johnson et al., 2008; Kaye and Johnson, 2011) also positively predict users' perceptions of blog credibility.

With regard to source credibility in the blog context, Kaid and Postelnicu (2007) found that regardless of a blogger's own source credibility (i.e., a popular actor versus a senator blogging about the privatization of Social Security), students were very trusting of information in blogs and rated the two sources as equally credible. Indeed, public perceptions of the legitimacy of blogs as information sources may be changing. For example, Messner and Disasto (2008) found that traditional news media, including the major leading newspapers, are increasingly accepting blogs as credible sources for their news stories. Carroll and Richardson (2011) suggest that blogs are changing the criteria for judging credibility, such that expertise, accuracy, and lack of bias are being supplanted by alternative criteria including interactivity, transparency, and source identification. They suggest that a new paradigm for credibility evaluation in this context is required.

Wikipedia. Although research to date has not focused on the credibility of *Wikipedia* for political information specifically, studies have shown that user-created entries in *Wikipedia* are about as accurate as well-regarded print encyclopedias such as *Encyclopaedia Britannica* (Andrews, 2007; Giles, 2005; Williams, 2008), and entries from *Wikipedia* have been evaluated as credible, particularly by area experts (Chesney, 2006). This is true despite Internet users' concerns about the credibility of the information found there (Metzger, Flanagin, and Medders, 2010; Nofrina et al., 2009), which may be driving results of studies showing that people perceive the same information to be less credible if they think it comes from *Wikipedia* than if they think it comes from *Encyclopaedia Britannica* (Flanagin and Metzger, 2011; Kubiszewski, Noordewier, and Costanza, 2011). Related to this, and to the information aggregation aspect of the wiki model, Sundar, Knobloch-Westerwick, and Hastall (2007) found that source credibility was a powerful cue affecting participants' perception of the credibility of a news story located on a news aggregator website. Well-known and highly credible news sources trumped other credibility cues, including how recently the story was uploaded and the number of related articles.

YouTube. In an experiment exposing young adults to television networks, candidate websites, YouTube's "YouChoose08'" channel, and political candidate pages on Facebook, participants rated television news and political candidate websites more trustworthy and of higher quality than social media sources, including YouTube and

Facebook (Towner and Dulio, 2011). Interestingly, however, viewers of YouTube felt greater cynicism toward the government, while those exposed to Facebook felt greater political self-efficacy. Also, those exposed to political information via the social media sources were more likely to vote.

Other research has focused on the content of YouTube videos to see how presentational differences of political issues affect perceptions of credibility. People exposed to one of three YouTube videos about healthcare that emphasized ethos (the speaker's credibility and expertise on the issue), logos (logical argument and statistical information), or pathos (humorous emotional appeal) reported that they found that the video appealing to ethos was the most credible, suggesting that "users resist being swayed by emotion or hard numbers and pay attention to message source" (English, Sweetser, and Ancu, 2011, 1). Wallsten (2011) looked at the issue of credibility and politically oriented YouTube videos from another perspective and found that political bloggers avoid posting videos that challenge their ideological positions, choosing instead to link to videos that share their views. The choices that bloggers make, he concludes, play an important role in disseminating biased political information.

Online social networks. Garrett (2011) found that political information traveling through existing social networks via email is likely to be believed more than the same information found on Web pages, suggesting the utility of relying on social networks of known others as a means of information endorsement. Studying political rumors, he found that while the Internet "accelerates and widens rumor circulation," it has no impact on recipient credulity, whereas political rumors emailed between friends or family are more likely to be believed. At the aggregate level, this can conceivably pose a threat to factual political knowledge.

Credibility of Other Types and Sources of Political Communication Online

Johnson and Kaye (2009) examined the perceived credibility of blogs, websites that provide information on political issues, electronic mailing lists/bulletin boards, and political chat rooms/instant messaging and found that blogs and political issue–oriented websites were perceived as most credible among these channels. In addition, across three election-year samples (1996, 2000, and 2004) in which they compared credibility ratings of six online sources (i.e., online counterparts of traditional newspapers, news magazines, television, radio, as well as online candidate literature and political issue–oriented websites), Johnson and Kaye (2010) found that political issue–oriented websites and online versions of traditional newspapers are consistently rated somewhat higher in credibility than the other online sources of political information, and candidate literature was deemed to be among the lowest in credibility, due in part to its potentially biased nature. Samples in both of these studies, however, were of politically interested Internet users and are thus not generalizable to the larger Internet population.

CURRENT PERSPECTIVES
ON SOURCE CREDIBILITY
AND POLITICAL COMMUNICATION ONLINE

Contemporary research on credibility examines how the online context creates both challenges and opportunities for identifying credible information, each of which can be considered in the context of how current research relates to political communication processes.

Challenges in Identifying Credible Political Information

Traditional approaches to evaluating credibility include checking the credentials of the information source, considering whether a source may be motivated to produce biased information, and verifying the currency and completeness of information (Metzger, 2007). Yet research shows that people rarely engage in such effortful information evaluation processes, instead relying on heuristic means of credibility assessment (Metzger, Flanagin, and Medders, 2010; Sundar, 2008). Metzger and colleagues, for example, found that reputation and social endorsement serve as positive credibility heuristics, whereas expectancy violations and perceived persuasive intent on the part of sources are negative credibility heuristics used by online information consumers.

Website design and navigation are important credibility heuristics (Flanagin and Metzger, 2007; Wathen and Burkell, 2002) that appear to apply to political information online as well. Chiagouris, Long, and Plank (2008), for example, found that after controlling for prior attitude toward CNN.com and MSNBC.com, ease of use and website design were most important to news consumers' perceptions of the credibility of these news websites. In spite of recent inroads, however, a good deal more research is needed to understand what heuristics consumers of online information use, and how those heuristics influence their judgments of news and political information.

Opportunities for Identifying Credible
Political Information

Digital networked technologies also offer significant opportunities to those seeking political information today. Most obviously, on even the most esoteric concerns, information consumers are currently presented with comprehensive information from a wide variety of sources. Given current Internet penetration rates, the vast majority of Americans have the capacity to access political information online, particularly among the subpopulations that are most politically concerned, aware, and active. Search engines and other information-processing tools and mechanisms (e.g., threaded online discussions, keyword identification, etc.) help to make these information repositories manageable.

Not only is political information abundant online, but features of the Web environment can also enhance individuals' capacity to accurately ascertain the credibility of information and its sources. For example, mechanisms by which people can compare their assessments of information and sources to others' evaluations can help to verify or invalidate their own opinions. Various online discussion venues (e.g., discussion groups, listservs, and bulletin boards), for instance, provide readily available opportunities for information comparison across diverse sources. Also, a host of tools designed to harness the opinions and experiences of a wide range of individuals (e.g., social information filtering tools or ratings/recommendation systems) can be applied to political information to evaluate it more reliably. Indeed, research shows that the cross-validation of sources is a prominent strategy for determining source and information credibility online (Metzger, Flanagin, and Medders, 2010). To at least some extent, the ease with which cross-validation can be achieved online provides a means of guarding against people's tendency to verify sources and their information suboptimally (Flanagin and Metzger, 2007).

UNANSWERED QUESTIONS

Open issues relevant to the production and consumption of credible online political information include (1) whether credibility may offer a theoretical explanation for selective exposure behavior that has been observed recently in online contexts; (2) the effects on political discussion and polarization when information consumers select sources based on attitude similarity; and (3) whether social media will help political information consumers navigate the sea of choices online, and, if so, the circumstances under which they are most likely to facilitate the creation and location of normatively useful political information. These issues are explored next.

Selective Exposure and Credibility

For three-quarters of a century scholars have documented the disposition of information consumers to selectively expose themselves to attitudinally consistent information sources, as opposed to seeking out a more balanced information diet that includes sources that contradict their preexisting attitudes. Though early work in this domain (Hyman and Sheatsley, 1947; Lazarsfeld, Berelson, and Gaudet, 1944) demonstrated that people tend to expose themselves selectively to attitude-consistent information, subsequent reviews were less conclusive (Sears and Freedman, 1967). In some cases, scholars concluded that evidence of selective exposure to belief-confirming sources was not particularly compelling (Kinder, 2003). For a comprehensive synthesis, see Stroud in this volume.

Recent changes to the media environment, however, have prompted reassessment of the potential for selective exposure. The ability of political information consumers to easily select from among a tremendous variety of sources suggests that citizens have greater control than ever over the number and nature of political information sources they rely on, and thus greater opportunity to selectively expose themselves to attitudinally congruent information exclusively. Research supports this view, showing strong support for selective exposure online (Iyengar and Hahn, 2009; Johnson, Bichard, and Zhang, 2009; Knobloch-Westerwick and Meng, 2009; Stroud, 2007, 2008), and an overarching tendency of people to seek out news and political information that supports their preexisting attitudes and beliefs. Moreover, selective exposure behavior is particularly pronounced under conditions of abundant information options (Fischer, Schulz-Hardt, and Frey, 2008), such as the environment of Web-based political information.

Seeking out attitudinally consistent sources, however, may come at the expense of information credibility. As people pursue attitudinally congruent information, information credibility is potentially jeopardized if they do so without attention to possible bias, the absence of which is a core component of credible information (Metzger et al., 2003). It is interesting, then, that although information consumers recognize the negative features of biased information, they still find attitude-consistent information to be more credible than counterattitudinal information (Kahan et al., 2010). In fact, not only do people tend to attribute higher levels of quality to biased but like-minded sources (Fischer et al., 2005; see also Meyer, Marchionni, and Thorson, 2010; Oyedeji 2010), but there is also evidence that they perceive attitude-consistent information as relatively *impartial* (Kahan et al., 2010). In the context of political information, the outcome is that people may be prone to ignore traditional credibility cues regarding information or source bias in their pursuit of attitudinally consistent information.

In addition, perceived credibility tends to increase as similarity between source and receiver increases (O'Keefe, 2002) and is also known to increase selection and usage of particular channels or information sources (Wheeless, 1974). Therefore, people may selectively expose themselves to attitudinally consistent information because they find information from similarly minded sources to be more credible. In this way, selective exposure provides a method whereby people are likely to obtain what they perceive as credible information, via perceived commonalities with the source. This linkage between credibility and similarity suggests a possible theoretical mechanism to explain why people selectively expose themselves to like-minded sources. In the context of political information, the net effect is that people may use attitudinally consistent information as a heuristic credibility cue when it originates from sources they perceive as similar to them, regardless of other factors, including bias.

Political Debate and Polarization

Political debate informed by a diversity of opinions forms a cornerstone of democratic engagement. As processes of selective exposure become more prominent among individuals, so too does one-sided issue knowledge, increased opinion rigidity, and group-based differences that suppress open debate. Moreover, as attitudinally congruent sources are boosted in their perceived credibility (as discussed in the previous section), the quality of political information can suffer. When people turn to attitudinally consistent political information from like-minded sources rather than to more "objective" sources of news and political information, political debate can be stifled. Indeed, current perspectives on selective exposure in digital media environments predict heightened political polarization, gridlock, and voter apathy, as well as reduced effectiveness of political campaign communications, as voters become more costly to reach due to their dispersal across vast media channels and outlets for political information.

Not only does research suggest prominent knowledge gaps among those who selectively expose themselves to attitudinally consistent information (Nir, 2011; Sweeney and Gruber, 1984; Ramsey et al., 2010), but selective exposure can also result in group polarization. Stroud (2010), for example, found evidence that repeated selective exposure to attitude-consistent information resulted in increased polarization over time, and Huckfeldt and colleagues (2004) show that attitude-confirming information in one's social network results in being more critical of out-group members with dissimilar opinions (see also Sunstein, 2001, 2009). At the societal level, this type of attitude can result in "cyberbalkanization," or social segregation that results from a number of self-interested subgroups, each of which promotes its own interests to the exclusion of other groups' views (Putnam, 2000; Sunstein, 2001). This phenomenon has raised concerns that Americans are becoming increasingly polarized along ideological lines (see Bennett and Iyengar, 2008). Overall, selective exposure means that people are less likely to experience opinion diversity, thereby potentially constraining the opportunity for informed political debate and opinion formation, as well as for compromise among opposing political groups.

The Role of Social Media and Web 2.0 Tools

When the domain of political information reaches beyond factual accounts of a politician's political platform, voting records, or views about a particular issue, it can begin to implicate citizens in new and diverse ways that are potentially enhanced by social media and Web 2.0 tools. Under conditions in which knowledge is esoteric, is diffused among many individuals, and depends on specific, situational understandings, it is often the case that the most reliable information is gleaned not from a traditional source that has been imbued with authority by virtue of position or status, but rather from a diversity of individuals lacking special training, credentials, or reputation. Indeed, not only are such circumstances common, but given the power of social media, they are increasingly sup-ported by precisely the kinds of tools required to harness the knowledge of those with the most relevant, timely, and important information. These shifts in the provision of information imply updated notions about the location and evaluation of what informa-tion and sources are most credible.

For example, the actual impact of public policy decisions is best assessed by evaluat-ing the diversity of effects they have on citizens, who are indeed the only credible sources of such information. Although public opinion polling has traditionally been used for this purpose, social media and Web 2.0 tools serve the same function, for example by provid-ing venues to share experiences, opinions, and messages using tools like social network sites, microblogging, credentialing tools, and wikis. Although such social media tools lack the representativeness of polling, their output is derived from self-engaged participation rather than solicitation, which it could be argued serves to gauge prevailing sentiment relatively accurately, particularly when aided by such diagnostic tools as trend analyses across topic, geography, and time.

Furthermore, specific instances of information sharing occurring via social media constitute both communication about political topics and instances of political com-munication itself. Grassroots sociopolitical issues that "go viral" through shared emails and other communication channels, or instances of political activism that take place in both geographic and virtual spaces, are examples of cases in which social software tools facilitate *experiential authority*, or the generation of credible political information by virtue of specific, lived experience. In such instances, rather than mass media or tradi-tional political channels, individuals are the "cognitive authorities" on political matters (Wilson, 1983) and use social media tools to aggregate and publicize their views and van-tage points. Sometimes these political acts occur with the aid of traditional mechanisms such as formal organizations that facilitate them, but increasingly they can and do arise absent the structures historically required for their formation, given the affordances of contemporary technologies (Bimber, Flanagin, and Stohl, 2012).

CONCLUSION

The rich research heritage on source credibility is in many ways fundamentally linked to processes of political communication and the provision of political information. Networked digital technologies have recently complicated the assessment of source credibility, however, by modifying the receiver's ability to determine source expertise and trustworthiness, which are the foundations upon which credibility evaluations have traditionally rested. Research has begun to address source credibility in online contexts by examining the credibility of digital versus traditional channels, the nature of polit-ical information conveyed by social media, and the dynamics of political information online. Nonetheless, important research concerns remain, including the link between credibility and selective exposure to attitudinally consistent information, the potential group polarization that might result, and the role of social media in seeking and delivering credible political information. These concerns suggest both challenges and opportunities as consumers of political information navigate the rich and varied contemporary information environment in search of the knowledge to help them become informed members of a politically engaged citizenry.

References

Abdulla, R. A., Garrison, B., Salwen, M. B., Driscoll, P. D., and Casey, D. 2005. Online news credibility. In M. B Salwen, B. Garrison, and P. D. Driscoll (Eds.), *Online news and the public* (pp. 148–163). Mahwah, NJ: Lawrence Erlbaum.

Albarracín, D., and Vargas, P. 2010. Attitudes and persuasion: From biology to social responses to persuasive intent. In S. T. Fiske, D. T. Gilbert, and G. Lindzey (Eds.), *Handbook of social psychology*, 5th ed. (vol. 1, pp. 394–427). Hoboken, NJ: John Wiley & Sons.

Andrews, S. 2007. Wikipedia uncovered. *PC & Tech Authority*. October 5. Retrieved from http://www.pcauthority.com.au/Feature/93908,wikipedia-uncovered.aspx/1.

Banning, S. A., and Sweetser, K. D. 2007. How much do they think it affects them and whom do they believe? Comparing the third-person effect and credibility of blogs and traditional media. *Communication Quarterly* 55(4): 451–466.

Bennett, W. L., and Iyengar, S. 2008. A new era of minimal effects? The changing foundations of political communication. *Journal of Communication* 58(4): 707–731. doi: 10.1111/j.1460-2466.2008.00410.x

Berlo, D. K., Lemert, J. B., and Mertz, R. J. 1969. Dimensions for evaluating the acceptability of message sources. *Public Opinion Quarterly* 33(4): 563. doi: 10.1086/267745

Bimber, B., Flanagin, A. J., and Stohl, C. 2012. *Collective action in organizations: Interaction and engagement in an era of technological change.* Cambridge, UK: Cambridge University Press.

Burbules, N. C. 1998. Rhetorics of the web: Hyperreading and critical literacy. In I. Snyder (Ed.), *Page to screen: Taking literacy into the electronic era* (pp. 102–122). London: Routledge.

Carroll, B., and Richardson, R. R. 2011. Identification, transparency, interactivity: Towards a new paradigm for credibility for single-voice blogs. *International Journal of Interactive Communication Systems and Technologies (IJICST)* 1(1): 19–35.

Chebat, Jean-Charles, Filiatrault, Pierre, and Perrien, Jean. 1990. Limits of credibility: The case of political persuasion. *Journal of Social Psychology* 130(2): 157–167. doi: 10.1080/00224545.1990.9924566

Chesney, T. 2006. An empirical examination of Wikipedia's credibility. *First Monday* 11(11): 1–13.

Chiagouris, L., Long, M., and Plank, R. 2008. The consumption of online news: The relationship of attitudes toward the site and credibility. *Journal of Internet Commerce* 7(4): 528–549. doi: 10.1080/15332860802507396

Choi, J. H., Watt, J. H., and Lynch, M. 2006. Perceptions of news credibility about the war in Iraq: Why war opponents perceived the Internet as the most credible medium. *Journal of Computer-Mediated Communication* 12(1): 209–229.

Danielson, D. R. 2006. Web credibility. In Claude Ghaoui (Ed.), *Encyclopedia of human computer interaction* (pp. 713–721). Hershey, PA: Idea Group.

Druckman, J. N. 2001. On the limits of framing effects: Who can frame? *Journal of Politics* 63(04): 1041–1066. doi: 10.1111/0022-3816.00100

English, K., Sweetser, K. D., and Ancu, M. 2011. YouTube-ification of political talk: An examination of persuasion appeals in viral video. *American Behavioral Scientist* 55(6): 733–748. doi: 10.1177/0002764211398090

Eysenbach, G. 2008. Credibility of health information and digital media: New perspectives and implications for youth. In M. J. Metzger and A. J. Flanagin (Eds.), *Digital media, youth, and credibility* (pp. 123–154). Cambridge, MA: MIT Press.

Eysenbach, G., and Kohler, C. 2002. How do consumers search for and appraise health information on the world wide web? Qualitative study using focus groups, usability tests, and in-depth interviews. *British Medical Journal* 324(7337): 573–577. doi: 10.1136/bmj.324.7337.573.

Fischer, P., Jonas, E., Frey, D., and Schulz-Hardt, S. 2005. Selective exposure to information: the impact of information limits. *European Journal of Social Psychology* 35(4): 469–492. doi: 10.1002/ejsp.264

Fischer, P., Schulz-Hardt, S., and Frey, D. 2008. Selective exposure and information quantity: How different information quantities moderate decision makers' preference for consistent and inconsistent information. *Journal of Personality and Social Psychology* 94(2): 231–244. doi: 10.1037/0022-3514.94.2.94.2.231

Flanagin, A. J., and Metzger, M. J. 2000. Perceptions of Internet information credibility. *Journalism and Mass Communication Quarterly* 77(3): 515–540.

Flanagin, A. J., and Metzger, M. J. 2007. The role of site features, user attributes, and information verification behaviors on the perceived credibility of web-based information. *New Media & Society* 9(2): 319–342. doi: 10.1177/1461444807075015

Flanagin, A. J., and Metzger, M. J. 2011. From *Encyclopædia Britannica* to *Wikipedia*: Generational differences in the perceived credibility of online encyclopedia information. *Information, Communication & Society* 14(3): 355-374. doi: 10.1080/1369118X.2010.542823

Fogg, B. J. 2003. *Persuasive technology: Using computers to change what we think and do.* San Francisco, CA: Morgan Kaufmann.

Fritch, J. W., and Cromwell, R. L. 2002. Delving deeper into evaluation: Exploring cognitive authority on the Internet. *Reference Services Review* 30(3): 242–254. doi: 10.1108/00907320210435509

Garrett, R. K. 2011. Troubling consequences of online political rumoring. *Human Communication Research* 37(2): 255–274. doi: 10.1111/j.1468-2958.2010.01401.x

Gass, R., and Seiter, J. S. 2003. *Persuasion, social influence, and compliance gaining.* 2nd ed. Boston: Allyn and Bacon.

Giffin, K. 1967. The contribution of studies of source credibility to a theory of interpersonal trust in the communication process. *Psychological Bulletin* 68(2): 104–120. doi: 10.1037/h0024833

Giles, J. 2005. Internet encyclopaedias go head to head. *Nature* 438(7070): 900–901. doi: 10.1038/438900a

Homer, P. M., and Batra, Rajeev. 1994. Attitudinal effects of character-based versus competence-based negative political communications. *Journal of Consumer Psychology* 3(2): 163–185. doi: 10.1016/S1057-7408(08)80003-4

Hovland, C. I., Janis, I. L., and Kelley, H. H. 1953. *Communication and persuasion.* New Haven, CT: Yale University Press.

Hovland, C. I., and Mandell, W. 1952. An experimental comparison of conclusion-drawing by the communicator and by the audience. *Journal of Abnormal and Social Psychology* 47(3): 581–588. doi: 10.1037/h0059833

Hovland, C. I., and Weiss, W. 1951. The influence of source credibility on communication effectiveness. *Public Opinion Quarterly* 15(4): 635. doi: 10.1086/266350

Huckfeldt, R., Mendez, J. M., and Osborn, T. 2004. Disagreement, ambivalence, and engagement: The political consequences of heterogeneous networks. *Political Psychology* 25(1): 65–95. doi: 10.1111/j.1467-9221.2004.00357.x

Hyman, H. H., and Sheatsley, P. B. 1947. Some reasons why information campaigns fail. *Public Opinion Quarterly* 11(3): 412–423.

Iyengar, S., and Hahn, K. S. 2009. Red media, blue media: Evidence of ideological selectivity in media use. *Journal of Communication* 59(1): 19–39. doi: 10.1111/j.1460-2466.2008.01402.x

Iyengar, S., and Simon, A. F. 2000. New perspectives and evidence on political communication and campaign effects. *Annual Review of Psychology* 51(1): 149–169. doi: 10.1146/annurev.psych.51.1.149

Iyengar, S., and Valentino, N. A. 2000. Who says what? Source credibility as a mediator of campaign advertising. In A. Lupia and M. D. McCubbins (Eds.), *Elements of reason: Cognition, choice, and the bounds of rationality* (pp. 108–129). New York: Cambridge University Press.

Johnson, T. J., Bichard, S. L., and Zhang, W. 2009. Communication communities or "cyberghettos"? A path analysis model examining factors that explain selective exposure to blogs. *Journal of Computer-Mediated Communication* 15(1): 60–82. doi: 10.1111/j.1083-6101.2009.01492.x

Johnson, T. J., and Kaye, B. K. 2004. Wag the blog: How reliance on traditional media and the Internet influence credibility perceptions of weblogs among blog users. *Journalism and Mass Communication Quarterly* 81: 622–642.

Johnson, T. J., and Kaye, B. K. 2009. In blog we trust? Deciphering credibility components of the Internet among politically interested Internet users. *Computers in Human Behavior* 25(1): 175–182. doi: 10.1016/j.chb.2008.08.004

Johnson, T. J., and Kaye, B. K. 2010. Still cruising and believing? An analysis of online credibility across three presidential campaigns. *American Behavioral Scientist* 54(1): 57–77. doi: 10.1177/0002764210376311

Johnson, T. J., Kaye, B. K., Bichard, S. L., and Wong, W. J. 2008. Every blog has its day: Politically-interested Internet users' perceptions of blog credibility. *Journal of Computer-Mediated Communication* 13(1): 100–122. doi: 10.1111/j.1083-6101.2007.00388.x

Jurma, W. E. 1981. Evaluations of credibility of the source of a message. *Psychological Reports* 49(3): 778-778.

Kahan, D. M., Braman, D., Cohen, G. L., Gastil, J., and Slovic, P. 2010. Who fears the HPV vaccine, who doesn't, and why? An experimental study of the mechanisms of cultural cognition. *Law and Human Behavior* 34(6): 501–516. doi: 10.1007/s10979-009-9201-0

Kaid, L. L., and Postelnicu, M. 2007. Credibility of political messages on the Internet: A comparison of blog sources. In Mark Tremayne (Ed.), *Blogging, citizenship, and the future of media* (pp. 149–164). New York: Routledge.

Kaye, B. K., and Johnson, T. J. 2011. Hot diggity blog: A cluster analysis examining motivations and other factors for why people judge different types of blogs as credible. *Mass Communication and Society* 14(2): 236–263. doi: 10.1080/15205431003687280

Kennedy, G. A. 1991. *Aristotle on rhetoric: A theory of civic discourse.* New York: Oxford University Press.

Kinder, D. R. 2003. Communication and politics in the age of information. In D. O. Sears, L. Huddy, and R. Jervis (Eds.), *Oxford handbook of political psychology*, (pp. 357–393). Oxford: Oxford University Press.

Kiousis, S. 2001. Public trust or mistrust? Perceptions of media credibility in the information age. *Mass Communication and Society* 4(4): 381–403. doi: 10.1207/S15327825MCS0404_4

Knobloch-Westerwick, S., and Meng, J. 2009. Looking the other way: Selective exposure to attitude-consistent and counterattitudinal political information. *Communication Research* 36(3): 426–448. doi: 10.1177/0093650209333030

Kohut, A. 1999. *The Internet news audience goes ordinary*. Washington, DC: Pew Research Center.

Kubiszewski, I., Noordewier, T., and Costanza, R. 2011. Perceived credibility of Internet encyclopedias. *Computers & Education* 56(3): 659–667. doi: 10.1016/j.compedu.2010.10.008

Lazarsfeld, P. F., Berelson, B., and Gaudet, H. 1944. *The people's choice: How the voter makes up his mind in a presidential election*. New York: Duell, Sloan & Pearce.

Lowery, S. A., and DeFleur, M. L. 1995. *Milestones in mass communication research: Media effects*. 3rd ed. White Plains, NY: Longman.

Mashek, J. W. 1997. *Lethargy '96: How the media covered a listless campaign*. Arlington, VA: The Freedom Forum.

McCroskey, J. C. 1966. Scales for the measurement of ethos. *Communication Monographs* 33(1): 65–72.

Mehrabi, D., Hassan, M. A., and Ali, M. S. S. 2009. News media credibility of the Internet and television. *European Journal of Social Sciences* 11(1): 136–148.

Melican, D. B., and Dixon, T. L. 2008. News on the net: Credibility, selective exposure, and racial prejudice. *Communication Research* 35(2): 151–168. doi: 10.1177/0093650207313157

Messner, M., and Distaso, M. W. 2008. The source cycle. *Journalism Studies* 9(3): 447–463. doi: 10.1080/14616700801999287

Metzger, M. J. 2007. Making sense of credibility on the Web: Models for evaluating online information and recommendations for future research. *Journal of the American Society for Information Science and Technology* 58(13): 2078–2091. doi: 10.1002/asi.20672

Metzger, M. J., Flanagin, A. J., Eyal, K., Lemus, D. R., and McCann, R. M. 2003. Bringing the concept of credibility into the 21st century: Integrating perspectives on source, message, and media credibility in the contemporary media environment. *Communication Yearbook* 27: 293–335.

Metzger, M. J., Flanagin, A. J., and Medders, R. B. 2010. Social and heuristic approaches to credibility evaluation online. *Journal of Communication* 60(3): 413–439. doi: 10.1111/j.1460-2466.2010.01488.x

Metzger, M. J., Flanagin, A. J., Pure, R. A., Medders, R. B., Markov, A. R., and Hartsell, E. H. 2011. *Adults and credibility: An empirical examination of digital media use and information credibility*.

Meyer, H. K., Marchionni, D., and Thorson, E. 2010. The journalist behind the news: Credibility of straight, collaborative, opinionated, and blogged "news." *American Behavioral Scientist* 54(2): 100–119. doi: 10.1177/0002764210376313

Miller, J. M., and Krosnick, J. A. 2000. News media impact on the ingredients of presidential evaluations: Politically knowledgeable citizens are guided by a trusted source. *American Journal of Political Science* 44(2): 301–315.

Morton, C., and Villegas, J. 2005. Political issue promotion in the age of 9–11. *Journal of Nonprofit & Public Sector Marketing* 14(1): 269–284. doi: 10.1300/J054v14n01_15

Nelson, T. E., and Garst, J. 2005. Values-based political messages and persuasion: Relationships among speaker, recipient, and evoked values. *Political Psychology* 26(4): 489–516. doi: 10.1111/j.1467-9221.2005.00428.x

Nir, L. 2011. Motivated reasoning and public opinion perception. *Public Opinion Quarterly* 75(3): 504–532. doi: 10.1093/poq/nfq076

Nofrina, H., Viswanathan, V., Poorisat, T., Detenber, B. H., and Peiqi, C. 2009. Why some wikis are more credible than others: Structural attributes of collaborative websites as credibility cues. *Observatario* 3(2). Retrieved from. http://obs.obercom.pt/index.php/obs/article/view/261

O'Cass, A. 2002. Political advertising believability and information source value during elections. *Journal of Advertising* 31(1): 63–74.

O'Keefe, D. 2002. *Persuasion: Theory & research*. 2nd ed. Thousand Oaks CA: Sage.

Online News Association. 2001. Digital journalism credibility survey. Retrieved from www.journalists.org/Programs/ResearchText.htm.

Oyedeji, T. A. 2010. The credible brand model: The effects of ideological congruency and customer-based brand equity on news credibility. *American Behavioral Scientist* 54(2): 83–99. doi: 10.1177/0002764210376312

Perloff, R. M. 1989. Ego-involvement and the third person effect of televised news coverage. *Communication Research* 16(2): 236–262. doi: 10.1177/009365089016002004

Pornpitakpan, C. 2004. The persuasiveness of source credibility: A critical review of five decades' evidence. *Journal of Applied Social Psychology* 34(2): 243–281. doi: 10.1111/j.1559-1816.2004.tb02547.x

Putnam, R. 2000. *Bowling alone: The collapse and revival of American community*. New York: Simon & Schuster.

Ramsey, C., Kull, S., Lewis, E., and Subias, S. 2010. Misinformation and the 2010 election: A study of the U.S. electorate. Program on International Policy Attitudes at the University of Maryland.

Rieh, S. Y., and Danielson, D. R. 2008. Credibility: A multidisciplinary framework. *Annual Review of Information Science and Technology* 41(1): 307–364. doi: 10.1002/aris.2007.1440410114

Schweiger, W. 2000. Media credibility—Experience or image? A survey on the credibility of the World Wide Web in Germany in comparison to other media. *European Journal of Communication* 15(1): 37–59. doi: 10.1177/0267323100015001002

Sears, D. O., and Freedman, J. L. 1967. Selective exposure to information: A critical review. *Public Opinion Quarterly* 31(2): 194. doi: 10.1086/267513

Self, C. C. 2008. Credibility. In M. B. Salwen and D. W. Stacks (Eds.), *An integrated approach to communication theory and research*, 2nd ed. (pp. 421–441). Mahwah, NJ: Erlbaum.

Sternthal, B., Phillips, L. W., and Dholakia, R. 1978. The persuasive effect of source credibility: A situational analysis. *Public Opinion Quarterly* 42(3): 285. doi: 10.1086/268454

Stroud, N. J. 2007. Media effects, selective exposure, and Fahrenheit 9/11. *Political Communication* 24(4): 415–432. doi: 10.1080/10584600701641565

Stroud, N. J. 2008. Media use and political predispositions: Revisiting the concept of selective exposure. *Political Behavior* 30(3): 341–366. doi: 10.1007/s11109-007-9050-9

Stroud, N. J. 2010. Polarization and partisan selective exposure. *Journal of Communication* 60(3): 556–576. doi: 10.1111/j.1460-2466.2010.01497.x

Sundar, S. S. 2008. The MAIN model: A heuristic approach to understanding technology effects on credibility. In M. J. Metzger and A. J. Flanagin (Eds.), *Digital media, youth, and credibility* (pp. 73–100). Cambridge, MA: MIT Press.

Sundar, S. S., Knobloch-Westerwick, S., and Hastall, M. R. 2007. News cues: Information scent and cognitive heuristics. *Journal of the American Society for Information Science and Technology* 58(3): 366–378. doi: 10.1002/asi.20511

Sunstein, C. 2001. *Republic.com 2.0.* Princeton, NJ: Princeton University Press.

Sunstein, C. 2009. *Going to extremes: How like minds unite and divide.* New York: Oxford University Press.

Sweeney, P. D., and Gruber, K. L. 1984. Selective exposure: Voter information preferences and the Watergate affair. *Journal of Personality and Social Psychology* 46(6): 1208–1221. doi: 10.1037/0022-3514.46.6.1208

Thorson, K., Vraga, E., and Ekdale, B. 2010. Credibility in context: How uncivil online commentary affects news credibility. *Mass Communication and Society* 13(3): 289–313. doi: 10.1080/15205430903225571

Towner, T., and Dulio, D 2011. The Web 2.0 election: Does the online medium matter? *Journal of Political Marketing* 10(1): 165–188. doi: 10.1080/15377857.2011.540220

Wallsten, K. 2011. Many sources, one message: Political blog links to online videos during the 2008 campaign. *Journal of Political Marketing* 10(1): 88–114. doi: 10.1080/15377857.2011.540203

Wanta, W., and Hu, Yu-Wei. 1994. The effects of credibility, reliance, and exposure on media agenda-setting: A path analysis model. *Journalism Quarterly* 71(1): 90–98.

Wathen, C. N., and Burkell, J. 2002. Believe it or not: Factors influencing credibility on the web. *Journal of the American Society for Information Science and Technology* 53(2): 134–144. doi: 10.1002/asi.10016

Wheeless, L. 1974. The effects of attitude, credibility, and homophily on selective exposure to information. *Communication Monographs* 41(4): 329–338. doi: 10.1080/03637757409375857

Whitehead, J. L. 1968. Factors of source credibility. *Quarterly Journal of Speech* 54(1): 59–63.

Williams, S. 2008. *Wikipedia* vs. *Encyclopaedia*: A question of trust? *Techradar. com: Deep Into Technology,* April 21. http://www.techradar.com/news/software/wikipedia-vs-encyclopaedia-a-question-of-trust—316163.

Wilson, E. J., and Sherrell, D. L. 1993. Source effects in communication and persuasion research: A meta-analysis of effect size. *Journal of the Academy of Marketing Science* 21(2) (March): 101–112. doi: 10.1007/BF02894421

Wilson, P. 1983. *Second-hand knowledge: An inquiry into cognitive authority.* Westport CT: Greenwood Press.

Yoon, K., B. Pinkleton, and W. Ko. 2005. Effects of negative political advertising on voting intention: An exploration of the roles of involvement and source credibility in the development of voter cynicism. *Journal of Marketing Communications* 11(2): 95–112. doi: 10.1080/1352726042000315423

CHAPTER 31

....

CANDIDATE TRAITS
AND POLITICAL CHOICE

....

BRUCE W. HARDY

INTRODUCTION

....

WHAT role do presidential candidate character traits play in vote decisions? To some, the answer is obvious as journalists and pundits frequently differentiate candidates in terms of their personal qualities. In advertisements, on the stump, and in debates, candidates routinely attack the integrity, honesty, and leadership credentials of their rivals. Casual political conversations among citizens often pivot on candidates' personalities. When pressed to explain why someone supports a candidate, personal attributes are often offered as a central reason. For example, after Republican Senator John McCain won the Florida primary on January 29, 2008, CNN.com's readers responded to a request to explain his success, and they attributed it to his character: Debbie Pike of St. Louis, Missouri, wrote, "It is very simple, actually. He comes across as an honest, trustworthy, real person." Mike Bodina of Edina, Minnesota, commented, "It's sad to say that my vote has come down to this . . . I just want to see an honest candidate. I don't necessarily agree with him on all of the issues." Geno Galindo of Santa Barbara explained, "Like myself, I think many feel character counts and McCain gets big points for character."[1] The conventional wisdom holds that candidate character influences vote decisions. Campaign strategists are among those who ardently believe this (e.g., Sosnik, Dowd, and Fournier, 2006).

Nevertheless, this conventional wisdom and the belief of those orchestrating campaigns appear to be are at odds with some empirical research that suggests that candidate character traits are important short-term forces but relatively limited in their influence on vote preference (Bartels, 2002; Miller and Shanks, 1982, 1996; Shanks and Miller, 1990, 1991). Additionally, many of the classic vote-choice and forecasting models practically ignore the role of candidate traits. In this essay, I attempt to resolve this conflict by presenting a clear conceptualization of the concept of traits, explaining how and why they may play a role in vote preference, reviewing past empirical research on the topic, and suggesting some new avenues for research on candidate character traits that may shed light on their importance in vote decisions.

CONCEPTUALIZING CANDIDATE CHARACTER TRAITS

Much of the research on this topic fails to clearly define the concept of traits—a failure that sabotages a nuanced understanding of their function and importance in vote decisions. To define candidate character traits, it is helpful to turn to a conceptualization of general personality traits offered in 1938 by Carr and Kingsbury:

> A trait is a conceptual attribute or definition of the reactive nature of an individual. The nature of the individual is defined on the basis of certain observable behavioral characteristics. Not all observable characteristics are used for this purpose. The definition is based only upon those characteristics (1) which society regards as of sufficient importance to identify and name, and (2) which are regarded as expressions or manifestations of the constitutional nature of the individual. The term "constitutional nature" refers to all of those relatively permanent and enduring organic conditions that characterize a given individual and differentiate him from his fellows, and these organic conditions may both be innate and acquired in respect to origin. (1938, 497)

These University of Chicago psychologists argued that traits are lexical categorizations of how an individual responds to his or her environment—a person's *reactive nature*. Yet, traits are much more than just descriptors. When a person reacts to his or her environment in a persistent pattern, traits are used by others to characterize the *constitutional nature* of the individual—the core of a person's character or personality. There is a sequential order in understanding a person's character. First, we view one's reaction to the environment and then name it with a trait that "society regards as of sufficient importance to identify and name" (Carr and Kingsbury, 1938, 497). After viewing this reaction repeatedly, we use this trait to characterize the person's constitutional nature (Carr and Kingsbury, 1938).

The Predictive Value of Traits

Most human transactions require trust and a level of confidence regarding how others will act. Specific behaviors are bounded to specific situations, and over time individuals manifest consistent behavioral patterns that represent their "true self" or "constitutional nature." Personality traits differ from transient mood states in that the former are relatively enduring. The identification of personality traits in others fosters interpersonal relationships because, by forecasting future behavior, trait ascription minimizes uncertainty, risk, and doubt. Relationships would be extremely difficult to manage without a means of categorizing behavior that informs expectations of future interactions. Once an individual is characterized in terms of traits, a readily accessible heuristic is available to predict his or her future behavior.

In sum:

1. Traits are attributes reflecting the reactive nature of an individual that define his or her constitutional nature.
2. The selection of important traits is a social and lexical (or communication) process.
3. Trait inferences are drawn from observed behavior.
4. Traits are useful because they provide a predictive value for future behavior.

The Predicative Value of Traits in Assessing Presidential Candidates

The predictive value of traits can be extended to voters' assessments of presidential candidates to foretell behavior in office (see Barber, 1972). Consider the 2000 contest between George W. Bush and Vice President Al Gore. This election focused mainly on domestic issues such as Social Security, Medicare, health insurance, and taxes. Nothing about the policy issues that commanded the center stage during this election would forecast how the candidates would respond to the terrorist attacks a year later. Character traits may play an important role in vote decision because of their predictive value:

1. Traits are used to capsulate trends in behavior of the presidential candidates into descriptive attributes.
2. Traits are then used in the prediction of future behavior of the candidate if elected.
3. These predictions of future behavior are then calculated into voters' decision-making processes.

LEXICAL APPROACHES TO IDENTIFYING "PROTOTYPE" PRESIDENTIAL CANDIDATE TRAITS AND HIGHER ORDER CONSTRUCTS

In past research, presidential candidate traits have been operationalized as "prototypes" consisting of only those most relevant to voters. For example, in an influential study by Kinder et al. (1980), participants responded to open-ended questions asking them to describe an "ideal" and an "anti-ideal" president. From the responses, two lists of traits, each containing sixteen items, were compiled. Respondents then selected the six most important ones from each list to construct a "profile of an ideal president" (Kinder et al., 1980, 319).[2] From these results, Kinder (1986) identified four second-order content dimensions of presidential traits that he labeled competence, leadership, integrity, and empathy. Using a confirmatory factor analysis, Funk (1996) grouped these components into two higher order factors—competence and integrity—and argued that these are universally relevant in the evaluation of presidential candidates. Work by Geer shows that most attack advertising on candidates from opposing camps focus on these two dimensions (Geer, 2006, ch. 4).

Consistent with the Kinder et al. (1980) approach, Miller, Wattenberg, and Malanchuk (1986) wrote that voters' general "schema" of a presidential candidate "will be evoked during the actual campaign period when people receive the appropriate stimuli to trigger these pre-existing cognitions" (523). This view is consistent with research that has shown that people organize their past experiences into cognitive structures known as schemas that are structured sets of expectations and rules that help make sense out of seemingly pattern-less life experiences (Fiske and Taylor, 1991). "Candidate schemas thus reduce the complexity of our impressions by enabling us to categorize and label an individual politician according to certain abstract or representative features" (Miller, Wattenberg, and Malanchuk, 1986, 524). Examining responses to open-ended questions on the American National Election Studies (ANES) from 1952 to 1984, these researchers found that perceptions of candidates were mostly focused on personality characteristics. Following Kinder and his colleagues, they constructed general categories that voters use in the evaluation of a candidate: competence, integrity, reliability, charisma, and personal.[3]

Candidate Traits as Decision-making Shortcuts

Voters rely on informational shortcuts and heuristics in making political decisions (Lodge and Stroh, 1993; Lupia and McCubbins, 1998; Popkin, 1994). Candidate traits are particularly useful heuristics because they are relatively easy to assess compared to intricate policy positions (Kinder, 1986). Candidate traits "offer an appealing shortcut for citizens to evaluate candidates on their performances without having to invest considerable time and energy into following public affairs or uncovering candidate issues" (Funk, 1996, 97). Voters use candidate traits as a relatively inexpensive way to gain information about the candidates and simplify vote decisions (Funk, 1999; Kinder et al., 1980; Miller, Wattenberg, and Melanchuk, 1986; Popkin, 1994; Rahn, Aldrich, Sullivan, and Borgida, 1990). This type of evaluation is easy, and people do it all the time. Political scientist Wendy Rahn and her colleagues (1990) suggested that voters' assessments of candidates' traits mirror their assessment of people they meet in their everyday lives.

Past Research on the Influence
of Presidential Character Traits
in Vote Decisions

Some of the more thorough tests of the influence of traits were conducted by Miller and Shanks in a series of articles and their book, *The New American Voter* (Miller and Shanks, 1982, 1996; Shanks and Miller, 1990, 1991), using data from the ANES. Focusing on the 1992 election, these researchers first examined the bivariate relationships between comparative trait evaluations and vote choice and found strong relationships. As they incrementally entered antecedent variables into their statistical model, however, the influence of traits dropped substantially, suggesting a large impact from exogenous antecedent variables—for example, party identification and policy predisposing. Yet the influence of candidate character traits never completely disappeared.

These researchers do find unique variance in vote choice explained by candidate character traits. They conclude that "these results suggest a visible—but limited—extent to which voters' choices between [Democratic candidate Bill] Clinton and [Republican incumbent President George W.] Bush may have been influenced by their comparative evaluation of Clinton and Bush concerning . . . specific personal qualities" (Miller and Shanks, 1996, 429). Referring to the series of studies by Miller and Shanks, King (2002) concluded that presidential candidate characteristics had limited influence on vote choice and no impact on determining election outcomes.

When analyzing the ANES data from 1980 to 2000, Bartels (2002) too found detectable influence of candidate traits and concluded that, for the most part, traits do have a small detectable influence on vote choice; however, this influence is not generally in play in election outcomes:

[T]he net effects of candidate trait assessments are generally quite modest in magnitude. The average effect for the six elections is 1.6 percentage points, and the *largest* effect (in 1992) is only 3.5 percentage points. By comparison, the average margin of victory in these six elections (that is the winning candidate's plurality of the two-party popular vote, including George W. Bush's small negative plurality in 2000) was about 8.7 percentage points. In three of the six elections—including the two with the largest net trait effects—the winning candidate would quite probably have won by a larger margin had personal qualities played no role in determining the election outcome. The only case in which it seems at all likely that perceptions of candidates' personal qualities had a decisive impact on the election outcome is the 2000 election, where Bush's half point advantage with respect to candidate traits was probably one of many "decisive" factors contributing to his razor-thin victory. (2002, 65)

A strong case for the effects of trait ascription can be found in the 2000 presidential election where, according to the economic forecasting models, Democratic nominee Vice President Al Gore, the candidate for the incumbent party during a good economy, should have won the election with a comfortable margin (Johnston, Hagen, and Jamieson, 2004; see the special issue of *PS: Political Science and Politics*, 2001, 34, 1). Yet, Gore did not find himself in the White House. Johnston, Hagen, and Jamieson (2004) argued that toward the end of the election Republican candidate George W. Bush outspent Gore on advertising in key "battleground" states, but Gore was more successful in getting his message across broadcast news. Therefore, Gore gained votes across the states but Bush gained more votes in the states that mattered and, thus, more electoral votes. Johnston et al. concluded:

> The typical forecast placed Gore some eight points ahead of George W. Bush. Our own data indicate that in late September Gore's margin was about where the forecasts said it should be, eight points. In most elections, this would have seemed insurmountable. Campbell's (2000) review of postwar elections suggests that Gore would lose ground but, given the late date of this eight point lead, still win decisively. What no account predicted is that a lead of eight points would disappear overnight. The inference is obvious: the election was close because the campaign made it so. (186).

The downfall of Gore, according to Johnston et al. (2004), was the direct outcome of Republican attacks on his character underscored by news coverage that emphasized what reporters saw as a tendency to exaggerate his accomplishments and misuse data. These scholars argued that the interplay between advertisements and news stories that attacked Gore's character diminished his share of the vote in the battleground and ultimately cost him the election.

THE DYNAMICS OF PRESIDENTIAL CANDIDATE TRAITS

Much of the research in this area relies on the ANES, which, unlike the National Annenberg Election Survey (NAES), does not allow for the assessment of the dynamic nature of traits. During the 2004 election, the average NAES ratings of incumbent Republican President George W. Bush and Democratic challenger Senator John Kerry on the trait "strong leader" (Figure 31.1) was rather dynamic across the general election. The divergence of the rating of the two candidates in August and September coincides with the Swift Boat Veterans for Truth (SVBT) campaign against Democratic Senator John Kerry, which attacked the Democrat's leadership credentials and trustworthiness. Similar dynamics are reported by Hardy and Jamieson (2005) in their examination of the impact of media coverage of a 2004 *Los Angeles Times* poll that reported the public thought incumbent president George W. Bush was more stubborn than his Democratic

FIGURE 31.1. Ratings of the trait "strong leader"

(0-to-10 point scale; 5-day prior moving average; from the 2004 NAES).

challenger Senator John Kerry. The findings from that study suggested that coverage of this poll magnified the perception that President Bush was indeed stubborn across time showing how trait ratings move across time. The dynamic nature of candidate character traits is further illustrated by Kenski, Hardy, and Jamieson (2010), who attributed changes in perception of candidate traits across the general election to media coverage and campaign communication.

What this suggests is that capturing the impact of candidate traits on vote choice with a cross-sectional survey design is similar to shooting at a moving target. The rolling cross-sectional design of the NAES allows for a more nuanced examination of the impact of candidate character traits on vote decision.

COMMUNICATION ENVIRONMENT, CAMPAIGN CONTEXT, AND CHARACTER TRAITS

When thinking about the impact of candidate character, researchers need to be cognizant of the communication environment, which is shaped by the campaigns,

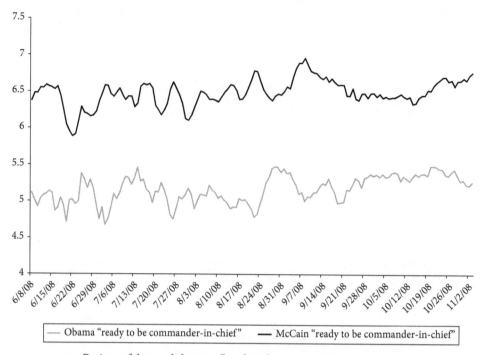

FIGURE 31.2. Ratings of the candidates on "ready to be commander-in-chief"

(0-to-10 point scale; 5-day prior moving average; from the 2008 NAES).

the news media, "real world" concerns and conditions that are central to which traits are in voters' minds, how they are used to frame the candidates, and ultimately which candidate voters support. Take the 2004 and 2008 presidential campaigns as examples. In 2004, the salience of the War on Terror and Iraq War potentially made leadership a focal trait in voters' assessment of the candidates. In contrast the worst economic meltdown since the Great Depression marked the 2008 presidential election. Even though Republican Senator John McCain was rated higher than Democratic Senator Barack Obama (see Figures 31.2 through 31.4) on perceptions of which candidate was "ready to be Commander-in-Chief," "strong leader," and "has the experience needed to be president," McCain did not find himself in the Oval Office on January 20, 2009.

To say that leadership qualities of the candidates did not matter in the 2008 presidential election would be misguided. If, instead of the economy being the most important problem, the war on Iraq was of most concern to Americans, McCain might have been elected. More Americans believed that the Republican senior senator from Arizona could better handle the Iraq War than his junior competitor from Illinois (Figure 31.5). When it came to handling the economy, Obama consistently trumped McCain (Figure 31.6). As the Iraq War receded in importance in voters' minds, McCain's military leadership credentials became less central to voting decisions. Because of the sinking economy, an unpopular incumbent, and the fact that over three-fourths of American's believed the country was on the wrong track, the 2008 election was one of "change" (see

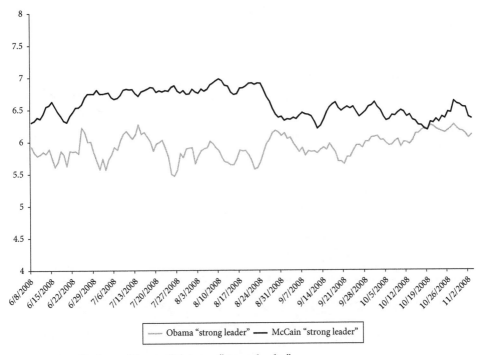

FIGURE 31.3. Ratings of the candidates on "strong leader"

(0-to-10 point scale; 5-day prior moving average; from the 2008 NAES).

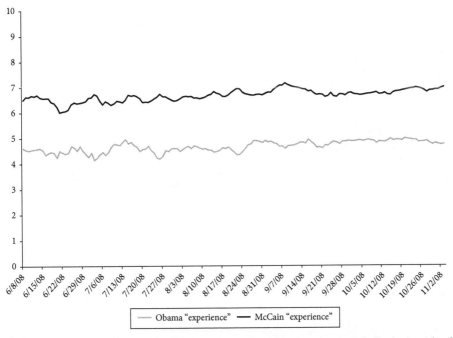

FIGURE 31.4. Ratings of the candidates on the trait "has the experience needed to be president"

(0-to-10 point scale; 5-day prior moving average; from the 2008 NAES).

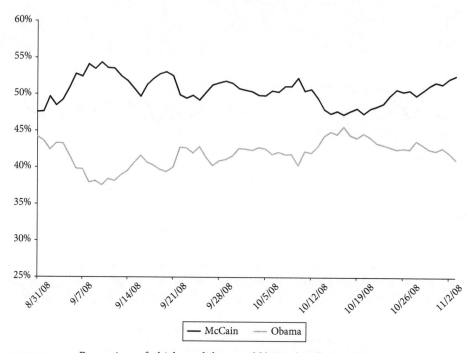

FIGURE 31.5. Perceptions of which candidate would better handle Iraq War

(0-to-10 point scale; 5-day prior moving average; from the 2008 NAES).

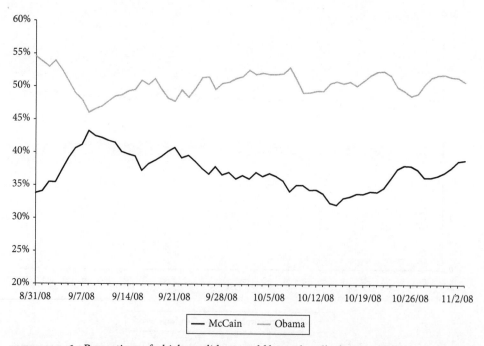

FIGURE 31.6. Perceptions of which candidate would better handle the economy

(0-to-10 point scale; 5-day prior moving average; from the 2008 NAES).

CANDIDATE TRAITS AND POLITICAL CHOICE

Kenski, Hardy, and Jamieson, 2010). Leadership was not framed by the media in terms of commander-in-chief, where McCain held the advantage, but in terms of a president's ability to inspire change. Which traits matter in vote decisions is contextual and determined by the intersection of actual conditions, campaign strategies, and media.

CONCLUSION

In an era marked by an expanding media environment, astronomical campaign spending, and candidate-centered campaigns, it seems probable that candidate traits will continue to be emphasized in future presidential races. Even though the amount of money that presidential campaigns spend rivals the national budget of some small countries, they cannot control external factors, such as the economy, war, and so forth, that heavily shape both the media's and voters' agendas. But within these boundaries, campaigns can have a significant influence on how salient issues and traits are framed and on their perceptions of which candidate possess the attributes best suited to handle the central issues.

At a minimum, researchers interested in the impact of the candidates' traits need to hold their ears to the ground to make sure that they include questions on survey instruments that reflect campaign messages. Otherwise the researcher will be left with measures that do not capture the salient traits. A promising research design would track campaign messages as they are being implemented. Such a design may find that within the boundaries of salient issues, campaign messages prove effective in shifting public opinion and corresponding votes. Only a more sophisticated research agenda with a finger on the pulse of the campaigns will be able to test such hypotheses.

The immediate challenge for political communication scholars studying presidential elections is the refining theory and explicating the contextual boundaries that foster or hinder specific communication processes that may influence trait assessments. Theories that enjoyed empirical support during the 1970s, 1980s, and 1990s, when a majority of citizens got their news from print and broadcast television, require fine-tuning as the communication environment surrounding presidential campaigns changes. The informational tide has grown into a tsunami and the number of channels in which campaigns and other motivated groups and individuals can connect to citizens will continue to increase as more mobile devices are adopted and micro-targeting advertising techniques are perfected. Each of these channels presents research opportunities on the impact of candidate character traits.

If the 2008 election is any indication, an additional and significant change in campaign dynamics that requires new theorizing and conceptualization is the growing diversity of the candidates. Are there traits that can be more easily attributed to specific ethnicities or genders? Do these traits or their salience differ when different issues are central? Such questions will be difficult to answer empirically (for example, because they require three-way interactions) but will provide a more nuanced understanding of traits, the role played by the media in how they are framed, and how these interactions affect vote preference.

Another important but undertheorized and studied phenomenon is the increasing competiveness and visibility of presidential primaries. Primaries provide a potentially fruitful setting for trait research since arguably they are more focused on character than the general election because candidates from the same party share similar issue stands and voters are unable to rely on party cues to help form opinions of the candidates.

Perhaps the greatest threat to conclusions on the impact of traits is one that all research based on cross-sectional surveys faces—the issue of causal direction. It remains possible that vote preference leads to rationalized trait evaluation; if so a respondent who prefers one candidate will rate this candidate favorably on any trait.

Providing conclusive empirical support for causal relationships between presidential candidate trait rating and vote preference would be extremely difficult. One could use an experimental design but, given the context of a presidential election and the flood of communication surrounding it, true replication could not be attained in a lab setting and, therefore, this approach would come at great expense to the validity of the findings. Alternatively, researchers could examine the impact of traits in less complex and media-saturated elections (e.g., elections within organizations, local elections, off-year elections, etc.), but generalizations from such low-information elections to high-information elections like those for US president would be tentative at best.

While the rolling cross-sectional design provides some advantages in addressing issues of causality, it is not a panacea. For example, the daily sample of the rolling cross-sectional design allows for trend analyses of cyclical patterns using statistical techniques such as Autoregressive Regressive Integrated Moving Average models. Such advanced techniques assume that causal shifts happen in longer time spans than the time in which each data point is collected. To find this type of causal relationship, a shift in vote preference would need to occur a day after, or more, a shift in a trait rating. It is quite possible that the shift in an assessment of a candidate trait and one's vote preference could occur simultaneously, or at least faster than could be detected by the survey design.

More generally, future research needs to be more sensitive to the context-dependent nature of presidential (and perhaps other) elections. The possible impact of traits can only be understood if the communication environment surrounding a presidential election is taken into account. Certain traits matter when the communication environment makes them matter. Salient issues influence both the media's selection of salient traits and their framing of them, which in turn influences vote preference.

Notes

1. http://www.cnn.com/2008/POLITICS/01/30/mccain.appeal.irpt/index.html
2. This approach in finding important candidate traits follows work in personality trait that focuses on "The Big Five" trait domains: neuroticism, extraversion, openness, agreeableness, and conscientiousness (Costa and McCrae, 1992a, 1992b). Each domain

contains "trait facets" or individual traits and the individual traits used to make up the five factors were initially selected by a lexical approach to find clusters of personality descriptors in language (De Raad, 2000). The rationale behind lexical studies of personality traits is based on the assumption that the most meaningful traits are encoded in language as single word descriptors (Carr and Kingsbury, 1938; Saucier and Goldberg, 2001).

3. The "personal" category refers to background factors such as military experience, religion, wealth, age, health, previous occupation, and so on (Miller, Wattenberg, and Malachuk, 1986, 528).

REFERENCES

Barber, J. D. 1972. *The presidential character*. Englewood Cliffs, NJ: Prentice-Hall.

Bartels, L. M. 2002. The impact of candidate traits in American presidential elections. In A. King (Ed.), *Leader's personalities and the outcome of democratic elections* (pp. 44–69). Oxford, UK: Oxford University Press.

Campbell, J. E. 2000. *The American campaign: U.S. Presidential campaigns and the national vote*. College Station: Texas A&M University Press.

Carr, H. A., and Kingsbury, F. A. 1938. The concept of traits. *Psychological Review*, 45, 497–524.

Costa, P. T., Jr., and McCrae, R. R. 1992a. *NEO PR-R professional manual*. Odessa, FL: Psychological Assessment Resources.

Costa, P. T., Jr., and McCrae, R. R. 1992b. Four ways five factors are basic. *Personality and Individual Differences*, 135, 653–665.

De Raad, B. 2000. *The big five personality factors: The psycholexical approach to personality*. Seattle, WA: Hogrefe and Huber.

Fiske, S. T., and Taylor, S. E. 1991. *Social cognition* (2nd ed.). New York: McGraw-Hill.

Funk, C. L. 1996. Understanding trait inferences in candidate images. In M. X. Delli Carpini, L. Huddy, and R. Y. Shapiro (Eds.), *Research in micropolitics: Rethinking rationality* (Vol. 5, 97–123). Greenwich, CT: JAI.

Funk, C. L. 1999. Bringing the candidate into models of candidate evaluation. *Journal of Politics*, 61, 700–720.

Geer, J. G., 2006. *In defense of negativity: Attack ads in presidential campaigns*. Chicago: Chicago University Press.

Hardy, B. W., and Jamieson, K. H. 2005. Can a poll affect the perception of candidate traits? *Public Opinion Quarterly*, 69, 725–743.

Johnston, R., Hagen, M. G., and Jamieson, K. H. 2004. *The 2000 presidential election and the foundation of party politics*. Cambridge, UK: Cambridge University Press.

Kenski, K., Hardy, B. W., and Jamieson, K. H. 2010. *The Obama victory: How media, money, and messages shaped the 2008 election*. New York: Oxford University Press.

Kinder, D. R. 1986. Presidential character revisited. In R. R. Lau, and D. O. Sears (Eds.), *Political cognition*, Hillsdale NJ: Lawrence Erlbaum.

Kinder, D. R., Peters M. D., Abelson, R. P., and Fiske. S. T. 1980. Presidential prototypes. *Political Behavior*, 2, 315–337.

King, A. 2002. Do leaders' personalities really matter? In A. King (Ed.), *Leader's personalities and the outcome of democratic elections* (pp. 1–43). Oxford: Oxford University Press.

Lodge, M., and Stroh, P. 1993. Inside the mental voting booth: An impression-driven process model of candidate evaluation. In S. Iyengar and W. McGuire (Eds.), *Explorations in political psychology* (pp. 225–263). Durham, NC: Duke University Press.

Lupia, A., and McCubbins, M. D. 1998. *The Democratic dilemma: Can citizens learn what they need to know?* Cambridge UK: Cambridge University Press;

Miller, W. E., and Shanks, J. M. 1982. Policy directions and presidential leadership: Alternative explanations of the 1980 election. *British Journal of Political Science, 12*, 299–356.

Miller, W. E., and Shanks, J. M. 1996. *The new American voter*. Cambridge MA: Harvard University Press.

Miller, A. H., Wattenberg, M. P., and Malanchuk, O., 1986. Schematic assessment of presidential candidates. *American Political Science Review, 80*, 521–540.

Popkin, S. L. 1994. *The reasoning voter: Communication and persuasion in presidential campaigns* (2nd ed.). Chicago: University of Chicago Press.

Rahn, W., Aldrich, J. H., Borgida, E., and Sullivan, J. L. 1990. A social-cognitive model of candidate appraisal. In J. Ferejohn and J. Kuklinski (Eds.), *Information and democratic processes* (pp. 136–159). Champaign: University of Illinois Press.

Saucier, G., and Goldberg, L. R. 2001. Lexical studies of indigenous personality factors: Premises, products, and prospects. *Journal of Personality, 69*, 847–878.

Shanks, J. M., and Miller, W. E. 1990. Policy direction and performance evaluation: Complimentary explanations of the Reagan elections. *British Journal of Political Science, 20*, 143–235.

Sosnik, M. J., Dowd, M. J., and Fournier, R. 2006. *Applebee's America*. New York: Simon & Schuster.

CHAPTER 32

....

POLITICAL
COMMUNICATION,
INFORMATION PROCESSING,
AND SOCIAL GROUPS

....

NICHOLAS VALENTINO
AND L. MATTHEW VANDENBROEK

THIS chapter discusses a perennially trendy notion in popular discussions of politics: the mass media powerfully alter political attitudes and behaviors by activating group identities and thus stoking group conflicts. It seems obvious that the pitting of group against group makes a story newsworthy, a political sound bite persuasive, or a policy coalition stable. In other words, many accept that Lasswell's (1935) definition of politics—who gets what, when, and how—is as true today as it was in the last century. Indeed, political scientists have long suspected that citizens think of politics mostly through the lens of group memberships and identities, not more abstract dimensions such as liberal-conservative ideology (Converse, 1964). Like most domains of human interaction (Tajfel, 1981), politics remains "group centric" (Nelson and Kinder, 1996). So what is the evidence behind claims about the media's particular role in creating, activating, and shaping group conflicts?

While it is plausible that media could indeed alter the way people perceive, think about, and act upon social group identities and conflicts, the standards of evidence for such claims must be kept high. After all, false or exaggerated fears about media influence can lead to calls for censorship and similar dangerous threats to democratic freedoms. On the other hand, if media content can systematically influence the nature, salience, and intensity of group conflicts in society, then policies, election outcomes, and the lived conditions of citizens around the world could be affected. The importance of rigorous, scientific work on these phenomena, in other words, should be obvious. Our review of the current evidence leads us to conclude that while some of Klapper's (1960) conclusions about the often-modest impact of media in the political sphere are still worth heeding, the media's role in stoking, if not creating, group tensions is also clear.

So what kinds of media messages about groups influence political outcomes, and what are the psychological mechanisms through which they operate? We review three potential domains of influence that have attracted a great deal of scholarly attention in political science, psychology, communication studies, and sociology. First, group cues could directly alter *perceptions* of group members by changing beliefs, stereotypes, or attitudes. Second, media messages could alter the *salience* of preexisting beliefs and stereotypes—a process referred to as *group priming*—so that subsequent evaluations of candidates or policies become more closely linked to these dimensions. Finally, group cues may be particularly powerful in triggering *emotions*, leading to changes in information processing and the willingness to take political risks, which subsequently affect policy preferences and actions.

Promising theories of cognition and information processing have been offered in the three areas mentioned above. Our substantive focus is heavily tilted toward race in America, in large part because this is where most of the research has occurred. There are increasingly compelling reasons, however, to pay attention to other group dimensions such as gender, religion, age, and even region. Although we discuss these whenever possible, we more often encourage further expansion of the universe of group dimensions that are ripe for scholarly attention. Along the way, we raise several unanswered questions that could lead to exciting new areas of research.

GROUP PERCEPTIONS

Since their invention, it has been tempting to imbue the electronic media of radio and television with direct, often terrifying power. To that end, early models of mass communication often employed the metaphor of a "hypodermic needle" (Scheufele and Tewksbury, 2007). These technologies, it was feared, exacerbate, if not create, horrific group conflict and violence (Kornhauser, 1959). How could Nazi propaganda vilifying and dehumanizing the Jewish people of Europe not have increased the German public's tacit if not explicit approval of genocide? One way would be if such representations were more a consequence than a cause of pervasive anti-Jewish sentiment. Most historical accounts suggest that anti-Semitism was quite rampant in Europe before, during, and after the rise of the Nazi party (Brustein, 2003). The question, then as now, is to distinguish cause and from effect in the relationship among media, culture, and society.

Indeed, the first rigorous examination of media effects suggests suggested fears of massive impact were unfounded (Klapper, 1960). Media may be influential, but they do not create group animosities out of thin air. Instead, social group attitudes and beliefs are learned early in life, usually as a result of interactions with family, and remain very stable throughout the lifespan (Allport, 1954; Katz, 1976; Porter, 1971; Proshansky, 1966). Of course this claim is less likely to hold for more abstract political groupings, such as "feminists," and the media may play a significant role in defining and stigmatizing such categories in the minds of many Americans (Huddy, 1996). Even for more familiar group dimensions, while "massive" significantly overstates the role of media effects, a number of studies have revealed important influences.

So where should we look for evidence of effects of media on mass beliefs and group attitudes? First, systematic descriptive research has continued to reveal patterns of problematic group representations in news and entertainment content. For example, content analyses document the frequent deployment of representations of minorities that reinforce, if not boost, negative stereotypes in the minds of white citizens. Blacks and Latinos are depicted as criminals more often than whites and more frequently than warranted by real-world crime statistics; at the same time these groups are less likely to be shown in occupations such as police officer and judge than their real-world incidence (Dixon and Linz, 2000a). They are also less likely to be depicted as victims in local television news than crime statistics in those communities indicate they are (Dixon and Linz, 2000b). Self-reported exposure to such news coverage is correlated with negative stereotypes about these groups (Dixon, 2008).

While these negative associations in the news are intriguing, the standard alternative explanation, endogeneity, rears its head: racially conservative individuals may self-select into the local news audience to begin with. However, experimental studies that directly manipulate the race of crime perpetrators and victims provide corroborating evidence, sometimes even demonstrating significant direct effects of such cues on negative attitudes toward blacks (Gilliam and Iyengar, 2000). Entertainment content may also propagate negative stereotypes (Entman and Rojecki, 2000), and the pairing of these representations with humor may be particularly powerful in this regard because the "joke" may relax norms against the public expression of racism and sexism (Ford and Ferguson, 2004). We encourage more work investigating the impact of entertainment programming on group attitudes, especially when these studies explore the political consequences of this content.

One hypothesis that has not yet received adequate attention highlights the potential mediating influence of real-world social interactions on exposure to negative group stereotypes in the media. Residing in diverse neighborhoods might expose people to a wider variety of social groups than would occur for those living in highly segregated, homogenous areas. Such contact, especially when positive, might provide a powerful buffer against negative media stereotypes. Crime news experiments by Gilliam, Valentino, and Beckman (2002) find evidence of this effect. White subjects who hailed from homogenous white neighborhoods reacted to stories about black criminals with significantly increased endorsement of negative stereotypes of blacks, support for punitive crime policies, and feelings of "distance" from the group. These effects, however, were entirely absent among subjects from racially integrated neighborhoods. Consistent with this is the finding that experience with elected officials from minority groups can soften the majority's negative attitudes toward the entire group (Hajnal, 2001). Stereotypes, then, can be gradually overridden as the individual gathers counter-stereotypical examples in memory. The key, however, seems to be variety; a single discrepant case generally will not suffice to change a negative stereotype (Weber and Crocker, 1983).

Historic milestones that might seem quite positive for reducing negative group sentiments may sometimes have more complicated effects. For example, the 2008 election of the nation's first black president, Barack Obama, led many to hope that the country had made a great deal of progress toward a "postracial" society. One might expect that the election would exemplify the type of significant stereotype violation demonstrated by Hajnal (2001) as capable of softening negative views of blacks in particular (Bodenhausen et al., 1995). Indeed, a nationally representative panel survey immediately before and after the election found that perceptions of racial discrimination dropped significantly (Valentino and Brader, 2011). However, the same citizens who perceived lower racial discrimination after the election also became more opposed to government policies intended to level the playing field between races. In other words, some of the imperative for affirmative action may have been lost as Obama's victory suggested great progress had already been made. This finding emerges from student samples as well (Kaiser et al., 2009). The psychological mechanism may be some form of "moral licensing" (Effron et al., 2009), whereby Obama's victory led whites to believe the country had proven itself to be racially unbiased, freeing them to express opposition to racial redistribution that they might otherwise have self-censored.

In summary, while evidence was once scant for direct effects of media representations on attitudes and beliefs about social groups, recent careful observational and experimental studies have returned modest effects. These results must not be dismissed simply because they are small. Subtle but cumulative changes in group attitudes can be politically consequential over the long haul, undermining support for policies meant to address structural inequalities that affect the opportunities and lived conditions of millions of citizens in the United States and around the world.

GROUP FRAMING AND PRIMING

Our second focus is on the activation of group attitudes via media framing and priming. Abundant evidence from psychology indicates that recent or frequent activation of ideas in memory automatically facilitates their use in subsequent judgment tasks (Banaji and Hardin, 1996; Bargh and Pietromonaco, 1982; Srull and Wyer, 1979; Taylor and Fiske, 1978). This notion is consistent with a view of memory as organized in an associative network of "schemas," or related opinion nodes (Anderson, 1983). One salient node activates other relevant nodes in memory, a process dubbed "spreading activation" (Collins and Loftus, 1975). Given the complexity of the political world, it is hardly surprising that citizens base candidate evaluations, policy opinions, and the like on considerations that are most accessible or at the "top of the head" (Iyengar and Kinder, 1987; Kinder, 2003; Taylor and Fiske, 1978). Experimental studies have shown that media messages are a particularly powerful means of altering the criteria by which citizens evaluate politics (e.g., Iyengar and Kinder, 1987). The priming of an issue domain, perhaps via exposure to a news story, boosts the correspondence between a candidate's performance on that issue and her overall evaluations. Most theoretical accounts suggest media priming is mediated by changes in the automatic accessibility of particular issue schemas triggered by the "mere attention" of the news to some issues rather than others (Kinder, 2003, 365). However, other evidence suggests a more thoughtful process: exposure alters the importance people attribute to an issue, and this importance rating mediates changes in candidate evaluations (Miller and Krosnick, 2000).

Racial priming, or more generally "group priming" (Jamieson, 1992), proposes that subtle racial cues in news coverage, political advertising, or candidate speech activates group attitudes, boosting their influence on candidate evaluation or policy opinion (Domke, 2001; Mendelberg, 2001; Valentino, 1999; Valentino, Traugott, and Hutchings, 2002). Group stereotypes seem to be activated quite automatically, and therefore operate unconsciously in a wide variety of social situations (Dovidio, Kawakami, and Gaertner, 2002; Eberhardt et al., 2004; Fazio et al., 1995). In fact, it has been suggested that such negative stereotypes are the default cognitive representations of out-groups and can therefore be suppressed only with attention and cognitive effort (Blair and Banaji, 1996; Devine, 1989).

The racialization of elite framing of social welfare policy (Gilens, 1999) and crime (Dixon and Linz 2000a; Iyengar, 1991; Peffley and Shields 1996) is well documented. This literature suggests that a wealth of subtle media cues may serve as group primes. The news media frame issues around particular group conflicts and in so doing can boost the impact of attitudes and identities linked to those groups (Kinder and Sanders, 1996; Nelson and Kinder, 1996). Media frames help audiences make sense of issues in particular ways, and group winners and losers represent a popular framing convention (Gamson and Modigliani, 1987). Elections are often framed in terms of competing group interests, and the parties develop stereotypical strengths regarding particular groups (Petrocik, 1996). When candidates violate these stereotypes—for example, when a Republican attempts to run on "women's interests"—they tend to perform poorly with voters (Iyengar et al., 1997). Specific negative stereotypes involving sexual promiscuity may lead whites to penalize black candidates for sex scandals more than white ones (Berinsky et al., 2011).

The psychological mechanism underlying framing effects can be quite automatic, linked for example to the ways humans estimate risk (Tversky and Kahneman, 1981), or to the racial and gender stereotypes people walk around with that are linked to particular policy goals (Hutchings et al., 2004; Winter, 2008). The gender gap in voting, for example, is driven not by distinct group interests of men versus women in a given election, but by differences in the degree to which men and women prioritize "compassion" issues, including racial fairness. When George W. Bush's 2000 campaign advertising suggested he would reach out to African Americans, women responded much more favorably than when he directly campaigned on "women's issues" like freedom of choice (Hutchings et al., 2004). The symbolic effort by the Republican Party during its 2000 nominating convention to present itself as racially inclusive seemed to be utterly unpersuasive to minorities but had a powerful effect on white women (Philpot, 2007). Under certain circumstances, however, more conscious and deliberative processes may drive framing effects (Druckman, 2004; Nelson, Clawson, and Oxley, 1997). In any case, it is clear that campaigns often use stigmatized groups as symbolic and rhetorical tools to cleave the electorate in ways that prove consequential on election day (Hutchings and Valentino, 2010; Jamieson, 1992).

The *subtlety* of media group cues seems to be a crucial element for racial priming (Mendelberg, 2001). A basic premise of Mendelberg's implicit-explicit (IE) model is that many whites feel ambivalent about racial matters because they are pulled in opposite directions by two powerful forces. Despite a societal shift away from explicit elite claims of biogenetic inferiority of blacks, there is persistent resentment toward blacks for their perceived refusal to adopt basic American values such as individualism and hard work, forming the basis of "symbolic racism" (Kinder and Sanders, 1996; Kinder and Sears, 1981; McConahay and Hough, 1976; Sears and Henry, 2003; Sears and Kinder, 1971). On the other hand, since the civil rights era, a strong "norm of equality" has exerted countervailing pressure on whites to reject racially biased or insensitive justifications for a given policy stand. As a result, the IE model suggests that racial attitudes will powerfully affect policy views *only* if racial cues are subtle, or "implicit." Note, however, that the mandate of cue subtlety does not seem to hold for blacks, whose in-group identity can be primed by quite explicit cues about race (White, 2007). Future work should explore variation in the power of the norm of egalitarianism among whites and other groups. If Obama's election changed perceptions of racial discrimination, perhaps it also changed the ways people think about group equality in general and how hard we should continue to work to achieve that goal.

Mendelberg (2001) operationalizes the implicit/explicit distinction dichotomously: explicit messages contain overtly racial wording such as "black" and "African American," while implicit messages cue race only with visual images of African Americans. Implicit racial messages may also employ racially coded phraseology such as "inner city," "poverty," or "welfare" (Huber and Lapinski, 2006; Valentino, 1999; Valentino et al., 2002; White, 2007). In addition to experiments, the IE model has found support in cross-sectional survey data from presidential campaigns. Jamieson (1992) and Mendelberg (2001) both report strong evidence that coded appeals in the 1988 presidential election—most notably the "Willie Horton" ad aired on behalf of George H. W. Bush's campaign—activated white voters' racial predispositions. However, whites rejected the Horton message after media accounts explicitly identified its racist undertones (Mendelberg, 2001).

Huber and Lapinski (2006) replicate tests of the IE model using an experiment performed on a large national sample. They explore whether an issue advertisement that explicitly discusses race in its appeal to end welfare primes racial attitudes more powerfully than either a message that does so implicitly (by using visual, but not verbal, race cues) or one that does not discuss race at all (a neutral message about getting out the vote). They find no support for the IE model. Instead, their results indicate that racial attitudes are quite powerful predictors of policy views regardless of whether the message is implicit or explicit. Their explanation for this null finding has to do with variation in the priming effect across levels of education; the most educated automatically bring their racial beliefs (and other predispositions) to bear on their policy views regardless of the message. The least educated can be primed, but they do not reject explicit racial messages, so their racial beliefs are triggered either way.

While plausible, Huber and Lapinski's explanation is not the only possibility, and they hint at a second one without testing it. In their discussion, the authors mention that perhaps Mendelberg's subjects "had a stronger attachment to the norm of equality than our respondents, and therefore reacted more negatively to the explicit appeal" (2006, 436). The reduced pull of egalitarianism might not simply be a function of sampling differences. Instead, it is possible that resentment has become increasingly tied to inegalitarian views in the population as a whole.[1] We have some tantalizing, if preliminary, evidence to suggest that in fact such a shift has occurred (Valentino and Vandenbroek, 2011). Explicit racial cues, as long as they cannot be seen as *racist*, are also powerful reminders about which candidates will represent which groups (Hutchings and Valentino, 2010). Furthermore, the recent rise in extreme racial discourse (e.g., *Washington Post*, 2010) calls into question whether explicitly racist speech is as powerfully rejected in post-Obama America (Pyszczynski et al., 2010).

Further investigation of the changing relationship between cherished norms such as egalitarianism, individualism, and views on race would be of significant interest and importance. In addition, expanding the study of group priming to new groups and issue domains is most welcome. By examining domains such as terrorism, globalization, and immigration, we could establish the scope of such automatic activation of group sentiments in public opinion formation.

GROUP EMOTIONS

The last area of inquiry in the intersection of group cues, information processing, and communication involves the powerful *emotions* that can sometimes be triggered by politics. Political science has recently seen a resurgent interest in emotions. While philosophers from Aristotle to the Founders warned of the threats posed by popular "passions," recent studies offer the exciting possibility of mending the divorce between emotion and reason in political attitudes and behavior. Many scholars believe emotions supply precious information about environmental stimuli and lead to cognitive and physiological changes that optimize the chances of favorable outcomes (e.g., Brader, 2006; Cosmides and Tooby, 2000; Kuklinski and Quirk 2000; Lazarus, 1991). Furthermore, once-derogated emotions such as fear and anxiety have been shown to lessen the influence of habits of mind, while stimulating political learning and attention (Brader, 2006; Marcus, Neuman, and Mackuen, 2000; Valentino et al., 2008). Such results should trigger deeper inquiry into the political role emotions play in interactions between social groups, a topic long of interest among psychologists (e.g., Mackie and Smith, 2003).

The research to date suggests three group dynamics affected by the emotions evoked in political communication: strengthening ties within social groups (closeness), intensifying competition between groups (conflict), and justifying animus against rival groups (condemnation).

Closeness—Orientation within social groups has long been seen as a central element of individuals' political attitudes and behavior (e.g., Berelson, Lazarsfeld, and McPhee, 1954; Campbell et al., 1960; Nelson and Kinder, 1996). A noteworthy example of this perspective is offered in Dawson's (1994) concept of "linked fate" driving black political activity. However, in-group emotional closeness does not appear to be chronically salient, but rather may be activated by media and candidate communications (Hutchings et al., 2006). Experimental studies suggest enthusiasm as a critical emotional trigger; messages cuing hope or pride increase the salience of group identities and predispositions (Brader, 2006; Hutchings et al., 2006; Marcus, Neuman, and Mackuen, 2000). Anger may play a similar role, helping citizens overcome the collective action problems associated with political participation (Valentino et al., 2011; Groenendyk and Banks, 2014).

Hutchings and colleagues (2006) argue that candidates are capable of generating enthusiasm among core supporters by emphasizing distinctions from their opponents on group-identity issues. During the 2000 presidential campaign, they found that blacks expressed greater enthusiasm for Al Gore after reading an experimentally manipulated news article that accentuated his differences from Bush on issues such as affirmative action. Meanwhile, Brader and Valentino (2006) show that group-based predispositions like ethnocentric prejudice against Latinos, nationalism, conservatism, and party identification predict roughly three-quarters (77 percent) of the variance in whites' enthusiasm about immigration, much more than fear (45 percent) or anger (55 percent).

Conflict—Intergroup competition appears to correspond largely with anger and anxiety, rather than enthusiasm. Uneasiness over perceived conflict has been especially linked to attitudes about immigration, independent of cognitive judgments of possible harm to the community or economy. When immigration is portrayed as primarily a "Latino" problem, whites react with strong anxiety, and this emotional mediator leads to endorsement of harsher immigration policies (Brader, Valentino, and Suhay, 2008). Material concerns, for example close competition with immigrants for jobs, can induce anxiety among whites (Brader and Valentino, 2006). However, attitudes about Latinos in particular, perhaps as a result of heightened media attention to this particular group since the early 1990s, is the primary driver of white opposition to immigration (Valentino, Brader, and Jardina, 2013; Perez, 2010). Interestingly, African Americans, who on average stand to lose more than whites from competition with low-wage immigrants and downward pressure on wages, hold significantly more favorable attitudes toward immigrants and seem to be more resistant to media messages blaming immigrants for economic problems (Brader et al., 2010). We speculate that many African Americans discount the economic threat posed by immigrants as a result of a shared minority identity linking their own lived experience to that of Latinos. Most whites do not share this strong basis for identifying with Latinos and thus are more likely to stigmatize immigrants and accept negative news frames about them, despite their relative security.

Condemnation—A most troubling normative aspect of emotional appeals is the possibility that they inspire out-group condemnation, hatred, and discrimination. We strongly suspect these effects stem from disgust and anger, both "other-condemning" emotions closely tied to moral judgments (Gutierrez and Giner-Sorolla, 2007). While these emotions are often confounded in colloquial speech and strongly correlated in self-reported affect (Bloom, 2004; Marcus, Neuman, and Mackuen, 2000; Nabi, 2002), there are clear distinctions. Disgust is uniquely tied to rejecting and avoiding impurities and violations of socio-moral taboos (e.g., Gutierrez and Giner-Sorolla, 2007; Rozin, Haidt, and McCauley, 2000). In contrast, anger is associated with aggression and is provoked by appraisals of harm, as well as blame against willful actors who transgress against the ego (Berkowitz and Harmon-Jones, 2004; Lazarus, 1991).

Of these two emotions, disgust is particularly demeaning, and potentially harmful. Evocations of biological inferiority, uncleanliness, and impurity frequently appeared in propaganda used to justify some of the darkest chapters in human history, including the Nazi Holocaust of European Jews, the American slave trade, and Jim Crow laws (Nussbaum, 2004). Experimental evidence suggests biogenetic "old-fashioned racism" is distinctly rooted in disgust, whereas modern symbolic racism is tied exclusively to anger, stemming from an appraisal blaming African Americans for willfully flouting social conventions of hard work, lawful behavior, and sexual propriety (Banks and Valentino, 2011). Meanwhile, visceral disgust at homosexuals has been shown to motivate support for legal sanctions against gays and lesbians (Inbar et al., 2009; Nussbaum, 2004; Smith et al., 2008). Negative media portrayals also appear to trigger anger and disgust toward members of Congress as a group, independent of cognitive judgments of the branch's policy outputs (Hibbing and Theiss-Morse, 1998). However, disgust does not appear to explain all derogation of out-groups. For example, Huddy and colleagues (2005) find that anxiety about perceived terrorist threats corresponds with endorsing harsh laws against Arabs.

In sum, political communications appear to powerfully influence emotional responses to groups in society. However, this research has only scratched the surface. Much remains to be learned regarding the impact of group-based emotions on political behavior. For example, it is possible that disgust toward political elites correlates with nonparticipation (Vandenbroek, 2011). In addition, little is known about the influence of affect along nonracial group dimensions (gender, partisanship, generation, and the like).

Conclusions

The role of mass media in the socialization, activation, framing, and emotional resonance of group attitudes and identities has been our focus in this chapter. While the scholarly consensus once insisted that the mass media had terrifyingly significant effects, subsequent research provided very little support for these fears. More recently, however, we have come to learn that the media can influence attitudes about groups and help to determine which identities are most salient in the opinion formation process. Thinking about the world in terms of groups and the competition among them may be universal and quite automatic, but the media can still play a fundamental role in structuring which dimensions are salient, important, and emotionally evocative. These effects are often subtle and require sophisticated measurement and rigorous experimental designs to detect. Nonetheless, we characterize as strong the evidence that media representations of groups matter for the ways citizens process information and come to decisions.

The future of the literature in this area, it seems to us, is bright with promise. In particular, we are excited about new inquiry into the linkages among the three domains of media effects reviewed here. For example, work on emotions and politics gives us an intriguing new set of tools to understand the power of group identities in structuring public opinion and policymaking. We have long debated the degree to which group attachments are a helpful shortcut for maximizing political decisions or a perceptual filter leaving them vulnerable to arguments that ultimately would undermine their own interests. The normative impact of these attachments may depend on which identities are activated and which emotions are triggered. Group identities may override careful deliberation about effective policies in the national interest primarily when the tenor of the debate is one of anger and its related appraisals, blame and control. In other words, more work on the emotional substrates of the strength and salience of group identities is sorely needed.

NOTE

1. Mendelberg (2008) criticizes Huber and Lapinski's (2006) conclusions on a number of methodological grounds. In particular, Mendelberg expresses concern about the potential for a "failure to treat" problem in the large Internet-based experiment that Huber and Lapinsky performed. The null result, in other words, could also occur if subjects in both explicit and implicit conditions failed to receive or pay attention to the advertisement. We do not take a stand on that debate, but instead replicate the basic tests and explore a distinct substantive explanation for the null result Huber and Lapinski discovered.

REFERENCES

Allport, G. W. [1954] 1988. *The nature of prejudice.* Reading, MA: Addison-Wesley.
Anderson, J. R. 1983. *The architecture of cognition.* Cambridge, MA: Harvard University Press.
Banaji, M. R., and Hardin, C. 1996. Automatic stereotyping. *Psychological Science* 7: 136–141.
Banks, A. J., and Valentino, N. A. 2011. The emotional substrates of racial attitudes. Unpublished manuscript.

Bargh, J. A., and Pietromonaco, P. 1982. Automatic information processing and social perception: The influence of trait information presented outside of conscious awareness on impression formation. *Journal of Personality and Social Psychology* 43: 437–449.

Berelson, B., Lazarsfeld, P. F., and McPhee, W. N. 1954. *Voting: A study of opinion formation in a
presidential campaign.* Chicago: University of Chicago Press.

Berinsky, A., Mendelberg, T., Hutchings, V., Shaker, L., and Valentino, N. A. 2011. Sex and
race: Are black candidates more likely to be disadvantaged by sex scandals? *Political
Behavior* 33: 179–202.

Berkowitz, L., and Harmon-Jones, H. 2004. Toward an understanding of the determinants of
anger. *Emotion* 4: 107–130.

Blair, I. V., and Banaji, M. R. 1996. Automatic and controlled processes in stereotype priming.
Journal of Personality and Social Psychology 70: 1142–1163.

Bloom, P. 2004. *Descartes' baby: How the science of child development explains what makes us
human.* New York: Basic Books.

Bodenhausen, G. V., Schwarz, N., Bless, H., and Wänke, M. 1995. Effects of atypical exemplars
on racial beliefs: Enlightened racism or generalized appraisals? *Journal of Experimental
Social Psychology* 31: 48–63.

Brader, T. 2006. *Campaigning for hearts and minds: How emotional appeals in political ads
work.* Chicago: University of Chicago Press.

Brader, T., and Valentino, N. A. 2006. Identities, interests, and emotions: Symbolic vs. material
wellsprings of fear, anger, and enthusiasm. In W. R. Neuman, G. E. Marcus, A. N. Crigler, and
M. MacKuen (Eds.), *The affect effect: Dynamics of emotion in political thinking and behavior*
(pp. 180–201). Chicago: University of Chicago Press.

Brader, T., Valentino, N. A., Ryan, T. J., and Jardina, A. E. 2010. The racial divide on immigration opinion: Why African Americans are less threatened by immigrants. Unpublished
manuscript.

Brader, T., Valentino, N. A., and Suhay, E. 2008. What triggers public opposition to immigration? Anxiety, group cues, and immigration threat. *American Journal of Political Science*
52: 959–978.

Brustein, W. I. 2003. *Roots of hate: Anti-Semitism in Europe before the Holocaust.*
New York: Cambridge University Press.

Campbell, A., Converse, P. E., Miller, W. E., and Stokes, S. E. 1960. *The American voter.* New
York: John Wiley & Sons.

Collins, A. M., and Loftus, E. F. 1975. A spreading activation theory of semantic processing.
Psychological Review 82: 407–428.

Converse, P. E. 1964. The nature of belief systems in mass publics. In D. E. Apter (Ed.), *Ideology
and discontent* (pp. 206–261). New York: Free Press.

Cosmides, L., and Tooby, J. 2000. Evolutionary psychology and the emotions. In M. Lewis and
J. M. Haviland-Jones (Eds.), *Handbook of emotions,* 2nd ed. (pp. 91–114). New York: Guilford.

Dawson, M. C. 1994. *Behind the mule: Race and class in African-American politics.* Princeton,
NJ: Princeton University Press.

Devine, P. G. 1989. Stereotypes and prejudice: Their automatic and controlled components.
Journal of Personality and Social Psychology 56: 5–18.

Dixon, T. L. 2008. Crime news and racialized beliefs: Understanding the relationship
between local news viewing and perceptions of African Americans and crime. *Journal of
Communication* 58: 106–125.

Dixon, T. L., and Linz, D. 2000a. Overrepresentation and underrepresentation of African Americans and Latinos as lawbreakers on television news. *Journal of Communication* 50(2): 131–154.

Dixon, T. L., and Linz, D. 2000b. Race and the misrepresentation of victimization on local television news. *Communication Research* 27: 547–573.

Domke, D. 2001. Racial cues and political ideology: An examination of associative priming. *Communication Research* 28(6): 728–801.

Dovidio, J. F., Kawakami, K., and Gaertner, S. L. 2002. Implicit and explicit prejudice in interracial interaction. *Journal of Personality and Social Psychology* 82: 62–68.

Druckman, J. N. 2004. Political preference formation. *American Political Science Review* 98: 671–686.

Eberhardt, J. L., Goff, P. A., Purdie, V. J., and Davies, P. G. 2004. Seeing black: Race, crime, and visual processing. *Journal of Personality and Social Psychology* 87: 876–893.

Effron, D. A., Cameron, J. S., and Monin, B. 2009. Endorsing Obama licenses favoring whites. *Journal of Experimental Social Psychology* 45: 590–593.

Entman, R. M., and Rojecki, A. 2000. *The black image in the white mind: Media and race in America*. Chicago: University of Chicago Press.

Fazio, R. H., Jackson, J. R., Dunton, B. C., and Williams, C. J. 1995. Variability in automatic activation as an unobtrusive measure of racial attitudes: A bona fide pipeline? *Journal of Personality and Social Psychology*, 69: 1013–1027.

Ford, T. E., and Ferguson, M. A. 2004. Social consequences of disparagement humor: A prejudiced norm theory. *Personality & Social Psychology Review* 8: 79–94.

Gamson, W. A., and Modigliani, A. 1987. The changing culture of affirmative action. In R. A. Braumgart (Ed.), *Research in Political Sociology*, Volume 3 (pp. 137–177). Greenwich, CT: JAI.

Gilens, M. 1999. *Why Americans hate welfare: Race, media, and the politics of antipoverty policy*. Chicago: University of Chicago Press.

Gilliam, F. D., and Iyengar, S. 2000. Prime suspects: The influence of local television news on the viewing public. *American Journal of Political Science* 44: 560–573.

Gilliam, F., Valentino, N. A., and Beckmann, M. 2002. Where you live and what you watch: Neighborhood racial context as a moderator of news exposure effects. *Political Research Quarterly* 55: 755–780.

Groenendyk, E., and Banks, A. 2014. Emotional rescue: How emotions help partisans overcome collective action problems. *Political Psychology* 35: 359–378.

Gutierrez, R., and Giner-Sorolla, R. 2007. Anger, disgust and presumption of harm as reactions to taboo-breaking behaviors. *Emotion* 7: 853–868.

Hajnal, Z. 2001. White residents, black incumbents, and a declining racial divide. *American Political Science Review* 95: 603–617.

Hibbing, J. R., and Theiss-Morse, E. 1998. The media's role in public negativity toward Congress: Distinguishing emotional reactions and cognitive evaluations. *American Journal of Political Science* 42: 475–498.

Huber, G. A., and Lapinski, J. S. 2006. The "race card" revisited: Assessing racial priming in policy contests. *American Journal of Political Science* 50(2): 421–440.

Huddy, L. 1996. Feminists and feminism in the news. In P. Norris (Ed.), *Women, the media, and politics* (pp. 183–204). New York: Oxford University Press.

Huddy, L., Feldman, S., Taber, S., and Lahav, G. 2005. Threat, anxiety, and support of antiterrorism policies. *American Journal of Political Science* 49: 593–608.

Hutchings, V. L., and Valentino, N. A. 2010. Divide and conquer: How partisan race cues polarize the electorate. In T. Philpot and I. K. White (Eds.), *Explorations in black political psychology* (pp. 157–170). New York: Palgrave Macmillan.

Hutchings, V. L., Valentino, N. A., Philpot, T., and White, I. K. 2004. The compassion strategy: Race and the gender gap in American politics. *Public Opinion Quarterly 68*: 512–541.

Hutchings, V. L., Valentino, N. A., Philpot, T. S., and White, I. K. 2006. Racial cues in campaign news: The effects of candidate issue distance on emotional responses, political attentiveness. In D. Redlawsk (Ed.), *Feeling politics* (pp. 165–186). New York: Palgrave Macmillan.

Inbar, Y., Pizarro, D. A., Knobe, J., and Bloom, P. 2009. Disgust sensitivity predicts intuitive disapproval of gays. *Emotion 9*: 435–439.

Iyengar, S. 1991. *Is anyone responsible? How television frames political issues.* Chicago: University of Chicago Press.

Iyengar, S., and Kinder, D. R. 1987. *News that matters: Television and American opinion.* Chicago: University of Chicago Press.

Iyengar, S., Valentino, N. A., Ansolabehere, S., and Simon, A. F. 1997. Running as a woman: Gender stereotyping in women's campaigns. In P. Norris (Ed.), *Women, the media, and politics* (pp. 77–98). London: Oxford University Press.

Jamieson, K. H. 1992. *Dirty politics: Deception, distraction, and democracy.* New York: Oxford University Press.

Kaiser, C. R., Drury, B. J., Spalding, K. E., Cheryan, S., and O'Brien, L. T. 2009. The ironic consequences of Obama's election: Decreased support for social justice. *Journal of Experimental Social Psychology 45*: 556–559.

Katz, P. A. 1976. The acquisition of racial attitudes in children. In P. A. Katz (Ed.), *Towards the Elimination of Racism* (pp. 125–156). New York: Pergamon Press.

Kinder, D. R. 2003. Communication and politics in the age of information. In D. O. Sears, L. Huddy, and R. L. Jervis (Eds.), *Oxford handbook of political psychology* (pp. 357–393). New York: Oxford University Press.

Kinder, D. R., and Sanders, L. 1996. *Divided by color: Racial politics and democratic ideals.* Chicago: University of Chicago Press.

Kinder, D. R., and Sears, D. O. 1981. Prejudice and politics: Symbolic racism versus racial threats to the good life. *Journal of Personality and Social Psychology 40*: 414–431.

Klapper, J. 1960. *The effects of mass communications.* New York: Free Press.

Kornhauser, W. 1959. *The politics of mass society.* Glencoe, IL: Free Press.

Kuklinski, J. H., and Quirk, P. J. 2000. Reconsidering the rational public: Cognition, heuristics, and mass opinion. In A. Lupia, M. D. McCubbins, and S. Popkin (Eds.), *Elements of reason: Cognition, choice, and the bounds of rationality* (pp. 153–182). New York: Cambridge University Press.

Lasswell, H. D. 1935. *Politics: Who gets what, when and how.* New York: McGraw-Hill.

Lazarus, R. S. 1991. *Emotion and adaptation.* New York: Oxford University Press.

Mackie, D., and Smith, S. (Eds.) 2003. *From prejudice to intergroup emotions.* New York: Psychology Press.

Marcus, G. E., Neuman, W. R., and Mackuen, M. 2000. *Affective intelligence and political judgment.* Chicago: University of Chicago Press.

McConahay, J. B., and Hough, J. 1976. Symbolic racism. *Journal of Social Issues 32*: 32–36.

Mendelberg, T. 2001. *The race card: Campaign strategy, implicit messages, and the norm of equality.* Princeton, NJ: Princeton University Press.

Mendelberg, T. 2008. Racial priming revived. *Perspectives on Politics 6*: 109–123.

Miller, J. M. and Krosnick, J. A. 2000. News media impact on the ingredients of presidential evaluations: Politically knowledgeable citizens are guided by a trusted source. *American Journal of Political Science* 44(2): 301–315.

Nabi, R. L. 2002. The theoretical versus the lay meaning of disgust: Implications for emotion research. *Cognition and Emotion* 16: 695–703.

Nelson, T., Clawson, R., and Oxley, Z. 1997. Media framing of a civil liberties conflict and its effect on tolerance. *American Political Science Review* 91: 567–583.

Nelson, T., and Kinder, D. R. 1996. Issue frames and group-centrism in American public opinion. *Journal of Politics* 58: 1055–1078.

Nussbaum, M. C. 2004. *Hiding from humanity: Disgust, shame and the law.* Princeton, NJ: Princeton University Press.

Peffley, M., Shields, T., and Williams, B. 1996. The inter-section of race and crime in television news stories: An experimental study. *Political Communication* 13: 309–327.

Pérez, Efrén O. 2010. Explicit evidence on the import of implicit attitudes: The IAT and immigration policy judgments. *Political Behavior* 32(4): 517–545.

Petrocik, J. R. 1996. Issue ownership in presidential elections, with a 1980 case study. *American Journal of Political Science* 40(3): 825–850.

Philpot, T. S. 2007. *Race, Republicans, and the return of the party of Lincoln.* Ann Arbor: University of Michigan Press.

Porter, J. D. R. 1971. *Black child, white child: The development of racial attitudes.* Cambridge, MA: Harvard University Press.

Proshansky, H. M. 1966. The development of intergroup attitudes. In L. W. Hoffman and M. L. Hoffman (Eds.), *Review of child development research*, Vol. 2 (pp. 311–371). New York: Russell Sage Foundation.

Pyszczynski, T., Henthorn, C., Motyl, M., and Gerow, K. 2010. Is Obama the Anti-Christ? Racial priming, extreme criticisms of Barack Obama, and attitudes toward the 2008 US presidential candidates. *Journal of Experimental Social Psychology* 46(5): 863–866.

Rozin, P., Haidt, J., and McCauley, C. R. 2000. Disgust. In M. Lewis and J. M. Haviland-Jones (Eds.), *Handbook of emotions*, 2nd ed. (pp. 637–653). New York: Guilford.

Scheufele, D. A., and Tewksbury, D. 2007. Framing, agenda setting, and priming: The evolution of three media effects models. *Journal of Communication* 57: 9–20.

Sears, D. O., and Henry, P. 2003. The origins of symbolic racism. *Journal of Personality and Social Psychology* 85: 259–275.

Smith, K. B., Oxley, D. R., Hibbing, M. V., Alford, J. R., and Hibbing, J. R. 2008. The ick factor: Physiological sensitivity to disgust as a predictor of political attitudes. Paper presented at the annual meeting of the Midwest Political Science Society, Chicago, IL, April.

Srull, T. K., and Wyer, R. S. 1979. The role of category accessibility in the interpretation of information about persons: Some determinants and implications. *Journal of Personality and Social Psychology* 37: 1660–1672.

Tajfel, Henri. 1981. *Human groups and social categories.* New York: Cambridge University Press.

Taylor, S. E., and Fiske, S. 1978. Salience, attention, and attribution: Top of the head phenomena. In L. Berkowitz (Ed.), *Advances in experimental social psychology* (pp. 249–288). New York: Academic Press.

Tversky, A., and Kahneman, D. 1981. The framing of decisions and the psychology of choice. *Science* 211: 453–458.

Valentino, N. A. 1999. Crime news and the priming of racial attitudes during evaluations of the president. *Public Opinion Quarterly* 63: 293–320.

Valentino, N. A., and Brader, T. 2011. The sword's other edge: Perceptions of discrimination and racial policy opinion after Obama. *Public Opinion Quarterly 75*: 201–226.

Valentino, N. A., Brader, T., Groenendyk, E., Gregorowicz, K., and Hutchings, V. L. 2011. Election night's alright for fighting: The role of emotions in political participation. *Journal of Politics 73*: 156–170.

Valentino, N. A., Brader, T., and Jardina, A. E. 2013. The antecedents of immigration opinion among U.S. whites: Media group priming versus general ethnocentrism? *Political Psychology 34*: 149–166.

Valentino, N. A., Hutchings, V. L., Banks, A. J., and Davis, A. K. 2008. Is a worried citizen a good citizen? Emotions, political information seeking, and learning via the Internet. *Political Psychology 28*: 247–273.

Valentino, N. A., Hutchings, V. L., and White, I. K. 2002. Cues that matter: How political ads prime racial attitudes during campaigns. *American Political Science Review 96*: 75–90.

Valentino, N. A., Traugott, M., and Hutchings, V. L. 2002. Group cues and ideological constraint: A replication of political advertising effects studies in the lab and in the field. *Political Communication 19*: 29–48.

Valentino, N. A. and Vandenbroek, L. M. 2011. Obama and the end of racial priming. Paper presented at the annual meeting of the International Society of Political Psychology, Istanbul, Turkey, July.

Vandenbroek, L. M. 2011. Disentangling aversion: Experimentally testing the impact of disgust and anger on political participation. Paper presented at the annual meeting of the American Political Science Association, Seattle, WA, September.

Washington Post. 2010. "Tea party" protesters accused of spitting on lawmaker, using slurs. Paul Kane, March 20.

Weber, R., and Crocker, J. 1983. Cognitive processes in the revision of stereotypic beliefs. *Journal of Personality and Social Psychology 45*: 961–977.

White, I. K. 2007. When race matters and when it doesn't: Racial group differences in response to racial cues. *American Political Science Review 101*: 339–354.

Winter, N. J. G. 2008. *Dangerous frames: How ideas about race and gender shape public opinion.* Chicago: University of Chicago Press.

CHAPTER 33

CIVIC NORMS AND COMMUNICATION COMPETENCE

Pathways to Socialization and Citizenship

DHAVAN V. SHAH, KJERSTIN THORSON, CHRIS WELLS, NAM-JIN LEE, AND JACK MCLEOD

THE question of political socialization and the role of communication in this process have been considered from a range of perspectives, across a number of fields, often with competing conclusions. Whether understood in terms of the institutions and structures through which social systems teach civic norms, values, and practices to citizens, especially to young people, or in terms of the dispositions, competencies, and opportunities that encourage individuals and groups to engage in processes of political development and learning, research on socialization has remained centrally concerned with the mechanisms that foster and support participatory citizenship (McLeod and Shah, 2009; Sapiro, 2004). There are few questions of greater importance for the health of civil society and democratic functioning, writ large. As such, the potential influence of communication, both mass media and interpersonal discussion, on modes of engagement with civic and political life has received considerable attention. The rapidly changing digital media environment of social and mobile platforms has sharpened this consideration, particularly on collective action formation and alternative modes of engagement (Bennett, Breunig, and Givens, 2008; Delli Carpini, 2000; Shah, McLeod, and Lee, 2009).

Before any discussion of the content and controversies of this research, we must begin with definitions of core concepts that serve as the basis for agreement and dispute. Among those most central to our review and synthesis are the notions of *civic norms* and the various sources from which they are acquired, *communication competence* and the challenges of navigating an increasingly complex media environment, *socialization* and attention to this ongoing process into adulthood, and *citizenship* and its changing styles and expanding boundaries. There are, of course, other relevant concepts; given space limitations we must gloss over these. Nonetheless, these core concepts provide the basis for reviewing the major points of development and dispute within the growing literature on political and civic socialization.

CORE CONCEPTS

Civic norms, one of the pillars of socialization, center on the constraints and incentives for engaging in civic and political life based on what is typical, expected, or accepta- ble behavior within households, among peers, in schools. Political communication research in this vein has examined family communication patterns, peer pressures and practices, and civic education and service learning in relation to different citi- zenship norms (Chaffee, McLeod, and Wackman, 1973; Fitzpatrick and Ritchie, 1994; Niemi and Junn, 2000; Walker, 2002). Recent work on norms has begun to explore how young people are moving beyond "dutiful" definitions of citizenship focused on government-centered activities such as formal memberships and electoral partici- pation toward "actualizing" styles of engagement tailored to personal meaning, such as political consumption and volunteerism (Bennett, 2008; Romer, Jamieson, and Pasek, 2009).

Complementing civic norms are communication skills and capabilities needed to "participate meaningfully and effectively in public life, . . . encompassing *media use*, particularly public affairs news consumption via broadcast, print, and online sources, and *interpersonal communication*, in terms of discussion of public affairs and politics at home, in school, and among peers" (Shah et al., 2009, 102). These discrete elements of communication competence are seen as interdependent and interconnected, consist- ent with the communication mediation model, with practices and skills developed in the home and the classroom shaping sophistication of media use, which in turn work through political exchanges to influence civic and political outcomes (Lee, Shah, and McLeod, 2013; McLeod, Shah, Hess, and Lee, 2010). This conception links competency with success in navigating the complexities of the digital media environment, a point we return to below.[1]

Socialization, then, is the long-term process of learning civic norms and developing communication competence in order to build civic and political capabilities. In contrast with early socialization research, which focused on the period prior to maturity as criti- cal (e.g., Hyman, 1959), this process is now thought to extend into adulthood. Attention to childhood and adolescence focused attention on life stages when parental and edu- cational influence are foregrounded, leading to overemphasis on these factors relative to the potential influence of media and peers (Galston, 2001; McDevitt and Chaffee, 2002). The most recent "third wave" of socialization research has expanded this to con- sider the possibilities of lifelong learning models, as attested by increasing attention to generational differences (Dennis, 1968; Jennings and Niemi, 1981; Niemi and Hepburn, 1995; Sears and Levy, 2003).

These socialization processes are thought to culminate in participatory *citizenship*, the result of increased knowledge, stronger opinion, and deeper reflection about the issues at hand. For the vast majority of political socialization research, participation focused on formal modes of political engagement, such as contacting a public official or participating in campaign activities. This has been linked to civics curricula that emphasized rights over obligations and formal knowledge over deliberative discussion (Gonzales, Riedel, Avery, and Sullivan, 2001; Hess, 2002). A growing list of scholars have asserted that younger Americans understand citizenship in more expansive ways, drawing upon different civic "repertoires" or "vocabularies" in enacting personalized styles of citizenship (Bennett, 2008; Dalton, 2008; Thorson, 2010). This perspective contends that modes of citizenship defined around civic norms of informed participation (i.e., linking political knowledge and voting behaviors) are giving way to a new kind of citizenship, comprising "highly personalized forms of identity politics anchored in lifestyles and consumer choices" (Bennett, 2003, 138). These include volunteering, club membership, social justice advocacy, political consumption, environmentalism, down-shifting, and boycotting (Stolle, Hooghe and Micheletti; 2005; Zukin, Keeter, Andolina, Jenkins, and Delli Carpini, 2006).

CONTROVERSIES AND CONCLUSIONS

Coming of age in the politically turbulent era of the 1960s, early research on political socialization emphasized stability and the handing down of political attitudes from one generation to another (e.g., Litt, 1963; for a critique, see Cook, 1985). These studies were dominated by a transmission metaphor that entailed a search for the mechanisms by which various agents of socialization "indoctrinated" younger generations of citizens. However, this assumption of transmission has been called into serious question by empirical evidence suggesting that socialization processes are much more reciprocal and contextual and involve much more activity on the part of young people. Current approaches emphasize the active role of young people in their own socialization and understand schools, peers, family, and media less as "agents" and more as sites for possible influence (McDevitt, 2005; McDevitt and Kiousis, 2007).

More recent work on socialization puts communication processes at the center and emphasizes the interdependence of various spheres of influence on the development of political identity among children and adolescents. Accompanying this new focus on agency and interdependence is something of a discursive turn, a move toward exploring how young people develop a sense of citizenship through the act of engaging in political discussion. Recognition of "trickle-up" phenomena, where children initiate political discussion in the home, has opened paths to demonstrate that parents' patterns of communication can shift in response to the actions of their children (McDevitt and Ostrowski, 2009). Recent studies examining the role of schools in civic education emphasize these institutions as sites for deliberative political discussion and focus on opportunities to practice civic skills as part of civics curricula and during engagement in associations such as student government and media (Hess, 2009).

There is much more controversy concerning the effects of mass media, particularly electronic media, on young people's involvement in social and political life. Scholars such as Putnam (2000), Nie (2001), and Ansolabehere and Iyengar (1995) have argued that television viewing, Internet use, and political ad exposure, respectively, erode trust and engagement. Youth, as heavy consumers of electronic media, purportedly experienced the negative influence of these mass communications to a disproportionate degree. Media reduce youth engagement, it has been argued, by promoting antisocial perceptions (i.e., cultivating beliefs in a "mean world"), displacing time from opportunities for social interaction, and generating cynicism toward politics and public affairs (Cappella and Jamieson, 1997; Putnam, 2000).

Although newspaper reading is viewed as the one exception to the deleterious effects of media on civic participation and democratic legitimacy, traditional print media have seen their readership, especially among youth audiences, displaced by the rise of television during the later half of the twentieth century and the ascendance of digital media during the first decade of this century (Kraut et al., 1998; Putnam, 2000; Shah, 1998; Uslaner, 1998; Wellman et al., 2001). Thus, shifts in media use are often named as the culprit in the loss of youth engagement. And these critics say that much has been lost. Not only are young people less knowledgeable about politics and less likely to consume the news than their parents were at their age but they are also less trusting of their fellow citizens and social institutions and less inclined to join social organizations, contact a public official, or vote (Rahn and Transue, 1998; Sirianni and Friedland, 2001).

Organizational disengagement is particularly consequential, for without it young people lack a context within which to develop the skills needed for effective political expression and other civic competencies (McLeod, Eveland, and Horowitz, 1998). Multigenerational analyses suggest that understanding low levels of conventional engagement among members of Gens X and Y is critical to reversing the decline (McLeod, 2000; Shah, McLeod, and Yoon, 2001b; Shah, Kwak, and Holbert, 2001a). For some, the answer to this puzzle lies in changing patterns of youth engagement and shifts away from these well-established indicators of political participation. For others, the solution can be found in the rise of digital and social media platforms that allow for information acquisition and exchange, potentially spurring political learning and deliberation.

The Emerging Information Paradigm

As this suggests, one important area for growth in the study of political socialization is coming to terms with the changing characteristics of the communication environment.

Young people in the early twenty-first century are confronting a markedly different media milieu than their counterparts faced in the late twentieth century (Jennings and Zeitner, 2003). Their media consumption patterns, particularly when it comes to learning about politics and public affairs, differ in important ways both from older generations today and from young generations in previous eras. Growth in information exchanges and socializing in online contexts have countered declines of youth consumption of news in conventional forms, especially via newspapers and television (Patterson, 2007). There is growing evidence that social networks deliver information of civic value (Bode, Vraga, Borah, and Shah, 2014; Hampton, Goulet, Rainie, and Purcell, 2011), yet the overall picture of young people's relationship to "news" is that the online world is not picking up the slack left by youth desertion of conventional news media (McLeod and Lee, 2012).

Nonetheless, for young people, consumption of news online has surpassed the impact of other forms of media in explaining levels of civic engagement (Lee et al., 2013). This is true for both exposure to conventional online news—such as mainstream news organizations websites such as cnn.com and nytimes.com—and nonconventional online news sources—such as blogs, candidate websites, and other emergent sources. Indeed, the latter sources appear to have their own independent impact on participation, an effect mediated by political messaging via the Internet. These trends bear directly on the study of communication competence, which posits that news use and political discussion are crucial steps in the pathway to engagement.

Making the need to develop communication competencies with new media all the more pressing, some scholars maintain that these changes are indicative of more fundamental shifts than the transformation of communication media. They argue that young citizens' media behaviors reflect the unique way in which they relate to the world of civic information, which has shifted from "dutiful" style of citizenship rooted in the twentieth-century's "modern" society to more "actualizing" civic style rooted in the norms of late modern society (Bennett, Freelon, Hussein, and Wells, 2012; Jenkins, Clinton, Purushotma, Robison, and Weigel, 2008).

From this perspective, youth enthusiasm for online interactive and expressive media and their ambivalence toward conventional news are embodiments of this trend: digital technologies and practices are seen as particularly well suited to the civic orientations of young people. The possibilities of personal expression through online video and social networking and the opportunities for forming personalized networks of interest and concern seem to help explain young people's preferences for receiving information, and expressing themselves, over social media rather than traditionally defined news media (e.g., Bennett et al., 2012).

Information Overload and Misinformation

Closely tied to larger social trends of declining faith in institutional authorities, one widely recognized characteristic of the emerging information environment is the dissolving importance of traditional notions of authority in information sources. Citizens decreasingly rely on a particular source of information, such as a local newspaper or a trusted broadcaster, solely because it is the voice of professional journalism. In the digital environment, news consumers increasingly choose to receive information from multiple sources and from sources that do not look like the professionalized journalism of even a few decades ago (Howard and Chadwick, 2009).

The declining role of authoritative voices importantly changes the information environment experienced by young citizens and creates challenges to being well informed. One such challenge is the difficulty of selecting helpful sources of information from the almost paralyzing multitude now available, known as information overload. The other is the problem of misinformation: while authoritative sources of information had their errors, the availability of rumors and false information in an information environment without established gatekeepers is greater (Vraga, Edgerly, Wang, and Shah, 2011). Citizens lacking the competency to deal with misinformation will find themselves increasingly confused and unable to navigate the voluminous communication environment they experience, encountering conflicting claims without the tools needed to distinguish between them and establish a coherent view.

Another possible solution to the problems of authentication and information overload may be the curation of individuals' information networks via social networks. Online social networking spaces are not only social spaces but also offer a flow of information of all sorts filtered through social contacts. As such, they enable an exchange of information between individuals that is more immediate and more voluminous than ever would be possible in person (boyd, 2007; Livingstone, 2008). Research is beginning to examine the degree to which the information flowing over online social networks constitutes civic information useful to being an engaged citizen (Bode et al., 2014).

Voice and Participation

The characteristic of the digital media society that perhaps best complements the "actualizing" style of citizenship is its multitude of opportunities for expressive participation (Jenkins et al., 2008). This convergence is evidenced by young citizens' high rates of participation in a variety of online activities requiring them to communicate their perspectives. As Rheingold (2008) puts it, "Whatever else might be said of teenage bloggers, dorm-room video producers, or the millions who maintain pages on social network services like MySpace and Facebook, it cannot be said that they are passive media consumers. They seek, adopt, appropriate, and invent ways to participate in cultural production" (97). Such creative production of media content may be particularly meaningful for participatory engagement.

Related to this is work exploring the role of participatory culture in promoting civic engagement (Jenkins, 2006). Here, the emphasis is on participation in practices related to media content creation, distributed collaboration, and making sense of networked information (Ekström and Östman, 2011). As Jenkins (2008, 3) states, "Access to this participatory culture functions as a new form of the hidden curriculum, shaping which youth will succeed and which will be left behind as they enter school and the workplace." Attention has broadened from concerns about whether young citizens have *access* to digital content to include concerns about unequal distribution of skills and practices surrounding new media technologies, as we discuss below.

Some are finding it hard to distinguish communication acts and participatory behaviors. In previous eras, communication could be conceptually distinguished from participation. The digital information environment disrupts this neat separation. Citizens are using communication online not only for consumption of information or even for deliberation or expression of views. They also are using digital media to directly influence others' ideas—as direct participants in the competition of ideas and public opinion (Castells, 2007). These perspectives fit nicely with recent work on *citizen communication mediation*, which emphasizes the role of expression, both face to face and online, as a conduit for dispositional and information factors on a range of participatory behaviors (Lee at al., 2013; Shah, Cho, Eveland, and Kwak, 2005).

Interdependence and Communication Mediation

Recent work has documented the interdependent roles that socializing sites play in cultivating civic norms and competencies among young people (Zukin et al., 2006). Norms and competencies learned in one context diffuse to different contexts; for example, deliberative norms students learn in a classroom diffuse to families and peer groups (McDevitt and Kiousis, 2006). Through the interplay of influences from schools, peers, and family, communication norms and skills are reinforced, reproduced, and normalized. In this way, the development of communication competence promotes continued political learning and sustained patterns of civic activism. Indeed, past research demonstrates the crucial role of civic norms and orientations in converting adolescent experiences into civic activism in the adulthood (Beck and Jennings, 1982). Some work draws attention to specific pathways to civic development and mobilization among youth. In particular, a growing body of research highlights online pathways through use of the Internet for information and expression to civic activism among youth. Mossberger, Tolbert, and McNeal (2007), for instance, found that online news gathering leads to higher rates of political knowledge, political interest, and increased political discussion with others.

Drawing on communication mediation models (Shah et al., 2005, 2007)—a series of theories emphasizing the critical role of information gathering and expressive activities in channeling effects of social structural factors toward various democratic outcomes—political socialization research has further theorized how the influence of families, schools, and peers is translated into communication competence. Lee, Shah, and McLeod (2013) have found that participation in deliberative classroom activities and democratic peer norms contribute to civic activism among youth but that these peer and school influences are largely indirect, working through informational use of conventional and online news and discussion of political ideas outside of classroom and family boundaries. This finding suggests that the communication processes that drive youth socialization are activated and cultivated through norms and competencies gained in the family, peer groups, and classroom.

Democracy Divide and Participatory Gaps

These pathways for civic activism, however, remain limited and are not open to everyone. As Kahne and Middaugh (2008) have demonstrated, opportunities for civic learning—such as engaging in civic simulations, participating in service learning, and discussing current events in the classroom—are inequitably distributed. In general, these researchers found that students from families of low socioeconomic status and those of color receive far fewer opportunities of this kind. McLeod and colleagues (2010) have also showed that adolescents less likely to attend college are unlikely to be exposed to active school experiences even though these experiences do benefit all who receive them. Such young people also have lower levels of news use, political discussion, and civic participation.

Moreover, these disparities in educational attainment produce similar gaps in communication and participation that widen from early to later adulthood. Gaps associated with news media use go beyond simple questions of *access* to the Internet—the *digital divide*—among the less educated; rather, they reflect more basic concerns about proficiency with how new media are used. McLeod, Shah, and colleagues (2010) propose expanding our concerns to a "democracy divide" that extends to participatory outcomes, one that is related to communication competencies across a range of contexts. Research has identified a participation gap between those who have attended college and those who have not, a gap that sets these groups onto distinct trajectories, one toward civic action and the other away from public life.

Along these same lines, Hargittai advocates recognition of a second-level digital divide to discriminate between more info-competent young citizens and their less skilled counterparts (Hargittai, 2002; Hargittai and Hinnant, 2008). Youth show wide variations in the ability to search for and evaluate the credibility of online information across a variety of domains (Hargittai, Fullerton, Menchen-Trevino, Thomas, 2010). New strategies are needed to teach adolescents communication competence skills that will help them use online media more effectively. Given the concerns associated with the quality of information on the Web, consumption of opinion-reinforcing information, and recruitment into homogeneous, polarized networks, media literacy would cultivate communication norms that value fact checking, the expression of minority views, tolerance for oppositional ideas, and validation of personal opinion through opinion exchange.

Challenges of Social Media

Another way to address these gaps in knowledge and participation is to rekindle civic norms in young people that might carry them into more active adult citizenship.

Although long understood as a key factor in promoting participation (Verba, Schlozman, and Brady, 1995), the origins of civic motivations have received little attention within the literature on youth engagement and socialization outside of an interest in partisanship. An environment increasingly focused on social media may contain perils and promise for fostering civic norms. At the most basic level, something as basic as preference for news over entertainment is thought to be increasingly important as digital tools diversify both content available to young citizens and their likelihood of exposure to political information given the plethora of choices (Prior, 2007). This is also true of the expended repertoires of action available within the realms of civic engagement (Bimber, Flanagin, and Stohl, 2005; Stolle et al., 2005; Thorson, 2010; Zukin et al., 2006).

On the one hand, our current era provides exciting new tools to transform the values of young citizens who, by dint of their school experiences and conversations with parents or peers, develop a sense of citizenship that is vast in its horizons and expansive in its action tendencies. They can deploy the power of social media and content creation to broadcast themselves. On the other, when citizenship is but one of many lifestyle choices, many will not choose civic engagement. One outcome of this may be accelerated gaps between the knowledge-rich and knowledge-poor as politically interested young citizens make the most of the new information environment to become self-made experts while those without such interest receive less incidental exposure to civic information (Bimber, 2001; Prior, 2007).

Yet the rise of online social network spaces brings with it a new source of incidental exposure as young citizens populate Twitter and Facebook news feeds with public affairs content curated from around the Web (Bode et al., 2014). Paradoxically, the new media environment creates even more opportunities for the most motivated of young citizens while excluding the less interested and less competent by removing many of the traditional, institutional pathways into public life. Optimistic views have tended to focus on practices related to digital media technologies as providing opportunities for young citizens to engage in public life (Jenkins, 2006; Bennett, Freelon, and Wells, 2010). Pessimistic views highlight the presence of "filter bubbles," where technology companies customize the information we encounter, creating tailored content to "serve up a kind of invisible autopropaganda, indoctrinating us with our own ideas, amplifying our desire for things that are familiar and leaving us oblivious to the dangers lurking in the dark territory of the unknown" (Pariser, 2011, 11). These technologies make it less likely that those who avoid political content will encounter it via social media.

FUTURE DIRECTIONS

As this tracing of the relationship of communication and socialization makes clear, much work remains to be done to understand the interplay of these factors in an increasingly complex media environment. Work must continue to examine the evolving development of the new information paradigm, the issues of information overload

and misinformation, the discursive turn in socialization research, and the interdependent pathways to active citizenship as well as the gaps in norms, knowledge, and actions
that limit engagement. This is especially true in the emerging social media environment,
which may be less under users; control than most realize, as the algorithms that curate
our content select sources that reinforce our perceptions.

To tackle these questions, scholars will need to employ a range of methodologies,
some established and others novel. At the most basic level, researchers need to deploy
research designs that track conventional, digital media use, face-to-face and online discussions, and civic learning and behavior from adolescence into adulthood. Efforts such
as the Future Voters Study (Lee et al., 2013; Bode et al., 2014) provide a model for the
types of research that might be done, though on a much shorter time frame, as well as
the recent Youth and Society study (Amnå and Östman, 2011; Ekström and Östman,
2011), which is structured as a multiyear study designed to follow adolescent and young
adult cohorts as they transition from one life stage into another. Additional investments
of this sort are needed.

Of course tracking the full range of communication and participation behaviors
over time will be sufficient only if the measurement of core concepts is both precise
and expansive. Too much of the work on political socialization attempts to draw conclusions about communication influence based on "days per week" metrics of media
use. Measurement needs to differentiate phenomena such as skimming, inadvertent
and incidental exposure, and purposeful information seeking. These measures need to
look across conventional print and broadcast media sources as well as established and
emerging digital, social, and mobile media technologies. Many of these media modalities allow for much finer tracking of media usage, in many cases down to the individual
click and keystroke (see Namkoong et al., 2010). Research that has examined actual patterns of digital and mobile media use based on analysis of server log files or coding of
harvested media content have permitted unique insights (Han et al, 2011; Sayre, Bode,
Shah, Wilcox, and Shah, 2010), although little work has specifically examined youth (see
Bennett et al., 2010). Such measures would provide new and important insights about
the nature of communication influence in socializing adolescents and adults into participatory engagement.

The four key sites of civic and political socialization—the family, school, peer groups,
and media—must also be considered in relation to one another. Much of the work to
date has focused on these factors in isolation or in pairs. The next phase of political
socialization research must consider how each of these essential socialization components work together in a complementary or contradictory fashion. Although there has
been some attention to the question of interdependence, research must also consider
how these factors work against one another at critical junctures. Are family communication and peer communication ever at odds? Do deliberative activities learned in the
classroom come into conflict with the tendency toward agreement cultivated in social
media settings? The complex interplay of these various sites of civic socialization must
be untangled in order to advance our understanding of the broader processes underlying the development of civic norms and competencies.

NOTE

1. This shares much in common with Dell Hymes's (1966, 1971) original formulation of the concept in the context of sociolinguistics, specifically as a means to assess the grammatical fluency, syntactical complexity, and related features of language use. Both conceptions attempt to link competency to fluency, see education as a means to improve competence, focus on the various contexts in which exchanges occur, and attempt to link connective thinking to action.

REFERENCES

Amnå, E., and J. Östman. 2011. Citizen styles and communication habits. Presented at Changing Styles of Citizenship: Communication, Media and Youth Engagement, Stockholm, September 29–30.

Ansolabehere, S., and S. Iyengar. 1995. *Going negative: How political advertisements shrink and polarize the electorate.* New York: Free Press.

Beck, P. A., and M. K. Jennings. 1982. Pathways to participation. *American Political Science Review,* 76: 94–108.

Bennett, W. L. 2003. Lifestyle politics and citizen-consumers: Identity, communication and political action in late modern society. In J. Corner, and D. Pels (Eds.), *Media and the restyling of politics* (pp. 137–150). London: Sage.

Bennett, W. L. 2008. Changing citizenship in the digital age. In W. L. Bennett (Ed.), *Civic life online: Learning how digital media can engage youth* (pp. 1–24). The John D. and Catherine T. MacArthur Foundation series on digital media and learning. Cambridge, MA: MIT Press.

Bennett, W. L., C. Breunig, and T. Givens. 2008. Communication and political mobilization: Digital media and the organization of anti-Iraq War demonstrations in the U.S. *Political Communication,* 25: 269–289.

Bennett, W. L., D. G. Freelon, M. Hussain, and C. Wells. 2012. Digital media and youth engagement. In H. A. Semetko and M. Scammell (Eds.), *Sage handbook of political communication* (pp. 127–141). New York: Sage.

Bennett, W. L., D. Freelon, and C. Wells. 2010. Changing citizen identity and the rise of a participatory media culture. In Lonnie R. Sherrod, Constance A. Flanagan, and Judith Torney-Purta (Eds.), *Handbook of research on civic engagement in youth* (pp. 393–423). New York: Routledge.

Bimber, B. A. 2001. Information and political engagement in America: The search for effects of information technology at the individual level. *Political Research Quarterly,* 54(1): 53–67.

Bimber, B. A., A. J. Flanagin, and C. Stohl. 2005. Reconceptualizing collective action in the contemporary media environment. *Communication Theory,* 15: 365–388.

Bode, L., E. K. Vraga, P. Borah, and D. V. Shah. 2014. A new space for political behavior: Political social networking and its democratic consequences. *Journal of Computer-Mediated Communication,* 19, 414–429.

Boyd, D. 2007 Why youth (heart) social network sites: The role of networked publics in teenage social life. In D. Buckingham (Ed.), *MacArthur Foundation series on digital learning—Youth, identity, and digital media.* Cambridge, MA: MIT Press.

Cappella, J. N., and K. H. Jamieson. 1997. *Spiral of cynicism: The press and public good.* New York: Oxford University Press.

Castells, M. 2007. Communication, power and counter-power in the network society. *International Journal of Communication*, 1: 238–266.

Chaffee, S. H., J. M. McLeod, and D. B. Wackman. 1973. Family communication patterns and adolescent political participation. In J. Dennis (Ed.), *Socialization to politics: A Reader* (pp. 349–364). New York: Holt, Rinehart and Winston.

Cook, T. E. 1985. The bear market in political socialization and the costs of misunderstood psychological theories. *American Political Science Review*, 79(4): 1079–1093.

Dalton, R. J. 2008. Citizenship norms and the expansion of participation. *Political Studies*, 56: 76–98.

Delli Carpini, M. X. 2000. Gen.com: Youth, civic engagement and the new information environment. *Political Communication*, 17: 341–349.

Dennis, J. 1968. Major problems of political socialization research. *American Journal of Political Science*, 12: 85–114.

Ekström, M. and J. Östman. 2011. Media engagement and political engagement: How specified forms of media use are related to young peoples participation in politics. Presented at Changing Styles of Citizenship: Communication, Media and Youth Engagement, Stockholm, September 29–30.

Fitzpatrick, M. A. and L. D. Ritchie. 1994. Communication schemata within the family: Multiple perspectives on family interaction. *Human Communication Research*, 20: 275–301.

Galston, W. A. 2001. Political knowledge, political engagement, and civic education. *Annual Review of Political Science*, 4: 217–234.

Gonzales, M. H., E. Riedel, P. G. Avery, and J. L. Sullivan. 2001. Rights and obligations in civic education: A content analysis of the national standards for civics and government. *Theory and Research in Social Education*, 29: 109–128.

Hampton, K., L. S. Goulet, L. Rainie, and K. Purcell. 2011. *Social networking sites and our lives.* Washington, DC: Pew Internet and American Life Project. Available at: http://www.pewinternet.org/Reports/2011/Technology-and-social-networks/Summary.aspx

Han, J. Y., D. V. Shah, E. Kim, K. Namkoong, S. Y. Lee, T. J. Moon, et al. 2011. Empathic exchanges in online cancer support groups: Distinguishing message expression and reception effects. *Health Communication*, 26: 185–197.

Hargittai, E. 2002. Second-level digital divide: Differences in people's online skills. *First Monday*, 7(4).

Hargittai, E., and A. Hinnant. 2008. Digital inequality: Differences in young adults' use of the Internet. *Communication Research*, 25: 602–621.

Hargittai, E., L. Fullerton, E. Menchen-Trevino, and K. Y. Thomas. 2010. Trust online: Young adults' evaluation of Web content. *International Journal of Communication*, 4: 468–494.

Hess, D. E. 2002. The pedagogical issues of teaching controversial public issues discussions in secondary social studies classrooms. *School Field*, 13: 113–132.

Hess, D. E. 2009. *Controversy in the classroom: The democratic power of discussion.* New York: Routledge.

Howard, P. N., and A. Chadwick. 2009. Political omnivores and wired states. In A. Chadwick and P. N. Howard (Eds.), *Routledge handbook of Internet politics* (pp. 424–434). New York: Routledge.

Hyman, H. 1959. *Political socialization.* Glencoe, IL: Free Press.

Hymes, D. H. 1966. Two types of linguistic relativity. In W. Bright (Ed.), *Socioliguistics* (pp. 114–158). The Hague: Mouton.

Hymes, D. H. 1971. *On communicative competence*. Philadelphia: University of Pennsylvania Press.

Jenkins, H. 2006. *Convergence culture*. New York: New York University Press.

Jenkins, H., K. Clinton, R. Purushotma, A. J. Robison, and M. Weigel. 2008. *Confronting the challenges of digital culture: Media education for the 21st century* (White paper) (p. 68). John D. and Catherine T. MacArthur Foundation. Cambridge, MA: MIT Press.

Jennings, M. K., and R. G. Niemi. 1981. *Generations and politics: A panel study of young adults and their parents*. Princeton, NJ: Princeton University Press.

Jennings, M. K., and V. Zeitner. 2003. Internet use and civic engagement: A longitudinal analysis. *Public Opinion Quarterly*, 67: 311–334.

Kahne, J., and E. Middaugh. 2008. Democracy for some: The civic opportunity gap in high school. (Working paper.) Available at: http://www.civicsurvey.org/democracy_some_circle.pdf

Kraut, R., M. Patterson, V. Lundmark, S. Kiesler, T. Mukopadhyay, and W. Scherlis. 1998. Internet paradox: A social technology that reduces social involvement and psychological well-being? *American Psychologist*, 53: 1017–1031.

Lee, N., D. V. Shah, and J. M. McLeod. 2013. Processes of political socialization: A communication mediation approach to youth civic engagement. *Communication Research*, 40 (5): 669–697.

Litt, E. 1963. Civic education, community norms, and political indoctrination. *American Sociological Review*, 28(1): 69–75.

Livingstone, S. 2008. Taking risky opportunities in youthful content creation: Teenagers' use of social networking sites for intimacy, privacy and self-expression. *New Media and Society*, 10 (3): 393–411.

McDevitt, M. 2005. The partisan child: Developmental provocation as a model of political socialization. *International Journal of Public Opinion*, 18: 67–88.

McDevitt, M., and S. H. Chaffee. 2002. From top-down to trickle-up influence: Revisiting assumptions about the family in political socialization. *Political Communication*, 19: 281–301.

McDevitt, M., and S. Kiousis. 2006. Deliberative learning: An evaluative approach to interactive civic education communication education. *Communication Research*, 55: 247–264.

McDevitt, M., and S. Kiousis. 2007. The red and blue of adolescence: Origins of the compliant voter and the defiant activist. *American Behavioral Scientist*, 50: 1214–1230.

McDevitt, M., and A. Ostrowski. 2009. The adolescent unbound: Unintentional influence of curricula on ideological conflict seeking. *Political Communication*, 26: 1–19.

McLeod, J. M. 2000. Media and civic socialization of youth. *Journal of Adolescent Health*, 27S: 45–51.

McLeod, J. M., W. P. Eveland, and E. M. Horowitz. 1998. Going beyond adults and voter turnout: Evaluation a socialization program involving schools, family and the media. In T. Johnson, C. Hays, and S. Hays (Eds.) *Engaging the public: How government and the media can reinvigorate American democracy*, (pp. 195–205). Lanham, MD: Rowman & Littlefield.

McLeod, J. M., and N.-J. Lee. 2012. Social networks, public discussion, and civic engagement: A socialization perspective. In H. A. Semetko and M. Scammell (Eds.), *Sage handbook of political communication* (pp. 197–208). New York: Sage.

McLeod, J. M., and D. V. Shah. 2009. Communication and political socialization: Challenges and opportunities for research. *Political Communication*, 26: 1–10.

McLeod, J. M., D. V. Shah, D. Hess, and N. Lee. 2010. Communication and education: Creating competence for socialization into public life. In L. R. Sherrod, C. A. Flanagan, and

J. Torney-Purta (Eds.), *Handbook of research on civic engagement in youth* (pp. 363–391). New York: Routledge.

Mossberger, K., C. J. Tolbert, and R. S. McNeal. 2007. *Digital citizenship: The Internet, society, and participation.* Cambridge, MA: MIT Press.

Namkoong, K., D. V. Shah, J. Y. Han, S. C. Kim, W. Yoo, D. Fan, et al. 2010. Expression and reception of treatment information in breast cancer support groups: How health self-efficacy moderates effects on emotional well-being. *Patient Education and Counseling,* 81S: S41–S47.

Nie, N. 2001. Sociability, interpersonal relations, and the Internet: Reconciling conflicting findings. *American Behavioral Scientist,* 45(3): 420–435.

Niemi, R. G., and Hepburn, M. A. 1995. The rebirth of political socialization. *Perspectives on Political Science,* 24: 7–17.

Niemi, R. G., and J. Junn. 2000 *Civic education: What makes students learn.* New Haven, CT: Yale University Press.

Pariser, E. 2011. *The filter bubble: What the Internet is hiding from you.* New York: Penguin Group.

Patterson, T. E. 2007. *Young people and news* (p. 33). Cambridge, MA: Shorenstein Center for Press and Politics.

Prior, M. 2007. *Post-broadcast democracy: How media choice increases inequality in political involvement and polarizes elections.* New York: Cambridge University Press.

Putnam, R. D. 2000. *Bowling alone: The collapse and revival of American community.* New York: Simon and Schuster.

Rahn, W. M., and J. E. Transue. 1998. Social trust and value change: The decline of social capital in American youth, 1976-1995. *Political Psychology,* 19: 545–565.

Rheingold, H. 2008. Using participatory media and public voice to encourage civic engagement. In W. L. Bennett (Ed.), *Civic life online: Learning how digital media can engage youth* (pp. 97–118). John D. and Catherine T MacArthur Series on Digital Media and Learning. Cambridge, MA: MIT Press.

Romer, D., K. H. Jamieson, and J. Pasek. 2009. Building social capital in young people: The role of mass media and life outlook. *Political Communication,* 26(1): 65–83.

Sapiro, V. 2004. Not your parents' political socialization: Introduction for a new generation. *Annual Review of Political Science,* 7: 1–23.

Sayre, B., L. Bode, D. V. Shah, D. Wilcox, and C. Shah. 2010 Agenda setting in a digital age: Tracking attention to California Proposition 8 in social media, online news and conventional news, *Policy and Internet,* 2.2: Article 2.

Sears, D. O., and S. Levy. 2003. Childhood and adult development. In D. O. Sears, L. Huddy, and R. L. Jervis (Eds.), *Handbook of political psychology* (pp. 60–109). New York: Oxford University Press.

Shah, D. V. 1998. Civic engagement, interpersonal trust, and television use: An individual level assessment of social capital. *Political Psychology,* 19: 469–496.

Shah, D. V., J. Cho, W. P. Eveland Jr., and K. Kwak. 2005. Information and expression in a digital age: Modeling Internet effects on civic participation. *Communication Research,* 32: 531–565.

Shah, D. V., J. Cho, S. Nah, M. R. Gotlieb, H. Hwang, N. Lee, R. M. Scholl, and D. M. McLeod. 2007. Campaign ads, online messaging, and participation: Extending the communication mediation model. *Journal of Communication,* 57: 676–703.

Shah, D. V., N. Kwak, and R. L. Holbert. 2001a. "Connecting" and "disconnecting" with civic life: Patterns of Internet use and the production of social capital. *Political Communication,* 18: 141–162.

Shah, D. V., McLeod, J. M., and Lee, N. 2009. Communication competence as a foundation for civic competence: Processes of socialization into citizenship. *Political Communication*, 26: 102–117.

Shah, D. V., J. M. McLeod, and S. H. Yoon. 2001b. Communication, context and community: An exploration of print, broadcast and Internet influences. *Communication Research*, 28: 464–506.

Sirianni, C., and L. A. Friedland. 2001. *Civic innovation in America: Community, empowerment, public policy, and the movement for civic renewal.* Berkeley: University of California Press.

Stole, D., M. Hooghe, and M. Micheletti. 2005. Politics in the supermarket: Political consumerism as a form of political participation. *International Political Science Review*, 26: 245–269.

Thorson, K. 2010. Finding gaps and building bridges: Mapping youth citizenship. Unpublished dissertation. Madison: University of Wisconsin.

Uslaner, E. M. 1998. Social capital, television, and the mean world: Trust, optimism and civic participation. *Political Psychology*, 19: 441–467.

Verba, S., K. L. Schlozman, and H. E. Brady. 1995. *Voice and equality: Civic voluntarism in American politics.* Cambridge, MA: Harvard University Press.

Vraga, E. K., S. Edgerly, B. M. Wang, and D. V. Shah. 2011. Who taught me that? Repurposed news, blog structure, and source identification. *Journal of Communication*, 61: 795–815.

Walker, T. 2002. Service as a pathway to political participation: What research tells us. *Applied Developmental Science*, 6: 183–188.

Wellman, B., A. Haase, J. Witte, and K. Hampton. 2001. Does the Internet increase, decrease, or supplement social capital? *American Behavioral Scientist*, 45: 436–455.

Zukin, C., S. Keeter, M. Andolina, K. Jenkins, and M. Delli Carpini. 2006. *A new engagement? Political participation, civic life, and the changing American citizen.* New York: Oxford University Press.

CHAPTER 34

....

FRAMING INEQUALITY IN PUBLIC POLICY DISCOURSE

The Nature of Constraint

....

OSCAR H. GANDY JR.

INTRODUCTION
....

MEDIA attention to the problem of economic, political, and social inequality rises and falls in response to a number of competing influences that include the release of government or research center reports and popular books that strike a chord with the public. Recent books by Hacker and Pierson (2010a) and Wilkinson and Pickett (2010) have helped to place the problem of income inequality back on the public agenda. Hopefully, with so much attention being paid to inequality, we might eventually see congressional hearings and legislative proposals focused on finding ways to address this problem. We might also expect to see an increase in scholarly assessments of the success or failure of these efforts. Some of this work will undoubtedly focus on how the options have been framed.

Although political scientists and others concerned with the nexus between political communication, public opinion, and public policy have revealed a growing interest in the role of framing in the policy process (D'Angelo and Kuypers, 2010; Johnston and Noakes, 2005; Reese, Gandy, and Grant, 2001; Schaffner and Sellers, 2010), studies that explore the framing of inequality are actually quite rare. This may be explained in part by the status of inequality as a social problem in the past. Page and Shapiro's (1992) assessment of fifty years of "American policy preferences" does not include inequality in its index. The term also fails to appear in the list of social problems that Baumgartner and Jones (1993) selected for their exploration of the relationship between the "dynamics of media attention" and the agendas of congressional hearings throughout the 1900s.

This marginal status may also reflect a determination that if there is sufficient attention being paid to poverty and the hardships faced by the poor (Grande, 2011; Guetzkow, 2010; Steensland, 2008), then there is no need to be concerned about more abstract targets of concern. In addition, not everyone agrees that inequality is actually a problem (Crenshaw, 2007). Indeed, mainstream economists suggest that at least under theoretically ideal conditions, inequality provides important benefits, such as enhancing national economic growth, as well as providing incentives for individuals to work hard and take risks (Birdsall, 2001). It may also be, as some suggest, that while Americans may actually believe that inequality is a problem, they tend to misunderstand the role that public policies play in maintaining or widening gaps in society (Bartels, 2005).

What the general public knows and feels about inequality depend to a great extent on the quality and extent of attention paid to it by the mass media. The public's orientation toward inequality also reflects the way that its character, causes, consequences, and constituents have been framed in the press. Social problems do not become policy issues unless they have been cast "in a way that they can be perceived as bad situations and moral wrongs that government can and should fix" (Gamble and Stone, 2006, 95).

After examining what we know about policy related framing in general, this essay will explore what we have learned so far about the framing of inequality.

THE ANALYSIS OF FRAMES

Framing is generally understood to refer to both a communicative process and the outcomes it may affect (Chong and Druckman, 2007; Entman, 1993). As a strategic resource and a political process, "framing" refers to efforts by a frame's sponsor to influence its distribution through a variety of communication channels (Gandy, 1982; Hallahan, 1999; Harris, 2010; Pan and Kosicki, 2001; Sellers, 2000). Social movement organizations (SMOs) rely on the mass media for assistance in attracting public attention and mobilizing their followers to take political action through the use of collective action frames (Benford and Snow, 2000; Nelson, 2004; Taylor, 2000) that often reflect an ideological position (Bartels, 2008). Scholars also recognize that journalists and their editors will affect the content, structure, and flow of policy relevant frames by virtue of the mix of personal, ideological, professional, and institutional constraints operating at a given point in time (Pollock, 2007).

Framing also refers to the ways that particular issues are understood and have their meanings altered when audiences are exposed to competing or novel constructions (McCombs and Ghanem, 2001; Scheufele and Tewksbury, 2007). The literature on the nature of media framing and its cognitive effects continues to expand to include taxonomies of frame types and framing strategies, as well as explorations into the complex interactions among frame types, topics, and a host of individual differences that constrain an affective or cognitive response (Schaffner and Sellers, 2010).

Gaps Are Identified by Type

When the media do focus on the problem of inequality, the coverage tends to be framed in terms of disparities, differences, or gaps between groups defined by class, race, gender, and age. In most of these cases, discussions focus on disparities in the quality of life that people enjoy (Phelan, Link, and Tehranifar, 2010).

Inequality is frequently explored at the national or international level where the contrasts are between states, regions, or nations framed as exemplars. Those comparisons are almost entirely focused on inequalities in income or wealth (Stiglitz, Sen, and Fitoussi, 2009) expressed in terms of convenient social binaries such as the "haves" versus the "have-nots." Frequently, these "characterizations are normative and evaluative, portraying groups in positive or negative terms through symbolic language, metaphors, and stories" (Schneider and Ingram, 1993, 334).

Public discourse regarding strategies for reducing economic disparities, especially those that involve redistribution, is frequently marked by harsh assessments of the moral status of the poor (Pasma, 2010). It is important to note how this status has been transformed by the criminalization of poverty, exemplified by reports about police in major US cities taking action against what has come to be called "quality of life crimes" such as public drunkenness or aggressive panhandling (Grande, 2011, 30–39).

Groups Are Labeled Strategically

Strategic contestation often takes place with regard to the selection and use of group labels. Even the familiar social and demographic categories of race, gender, and social class have been challenged with regard to the nature of the boundaries between groups and the determination of group membership. Similar definitional problems emerge with the identification, naming, and selection of causal influences, contributing factors, and responsible agents (Lucas and Beresford, 2010).

The linkage of negatively valenced targets to punitive policies has become a common practice during national election cycles in the United States (Schneider and Ingram, 1993, 337–338). The metaphoric construction of "welfare queens" became so closely linked to a stereotypically constructed and racialized image, that mere reference of welfare became capable of activating racial resentment years after its introduction into mainstream discourse (Winter, 2008).

Strategists attempt to characterize their opponents or their favored policies on the basis of associations with a particular category or class of individuals. Democratic strategists routinely characterize tax policies in terms of "the rich" versus everybody else (Harris, 2010, 49–50). Republican strategists, on the other hand, have managed to avoid this common polarization by relabeling "estate taxes," that presumably affected only upper income earners, into "death taxes," a risk that many came to believe they shared (Schaffner and Atkinson, 2010, 133).

Frames Vary Over Time and Across Contexts

An important body of research explores the way particular issues are framed at different points of time, perhaps reflecting the lifecycles of issue types (Baumgartner and Jones, 1993). In some cases, these analyses map the adjustments in frames that accompany changes in the identity of key actors or frame sponsors who promote the use of particular frames (Steensland, 2008).

Policy scholars have attempted to identify the shifting frames of emphasis that are placed on the causes, consequences, and policy options available to reduce particular gaps. It is difficult to determine if changes in the prominence of particular frames in the news media, public discourse, or public understanding can be attributed to the efforts of particular policy entrepreneurs or political strategists (Gandy, 1982; Pan and Kosicki, 2001), or whether these changes are the result of a complex process of policy learning that evolves in response to changing circumstances (Steensland, 2008).

Among the more important frames that are used to talk about economic inequality are those that assign blame or responsibility for the economic status of individuals or segments of the population. Frames that place primary responsibility on the shoulders of individuals (Hanson and Hanson, 2006; Limbert and Bullock, 2009) directly compete with frames that place that responsibility within the social structure (Bullock, Williams, and Limbert, 2003; Iyengar, 1996). Frames that "blame the victim" occasionally attach the responsibility for failure or loss to the values and cultural norms that the disadvantaged are presumed to learn from birth (Wilson, 2010).

Structurally oriented researchers have explored the way media in different cities use strategically altered frames to present the same facts to their audiences (Pollock, 2007). In some markets, the emphasis is on the winners; in others, it is the losers that dominate the frame. The racial composition of a newspaper's market has been shown to influence the framing of stories about race, especially with regard to identifying discrimination as the cause of some disparity (Gandy et al., 1997). The racial composition of a newspaper's staff has also been shown to affect the framing of editorials about affirmative action (Richardson and Lancendorfer, 2004).

Studies of Framing Impacts

The impact of media frames tends to be examined at the level of individuals, groups, and institutions, with the latter focused primarily on legislative decisions regarding controversial public policies. Audience-focused studies explore the relations between what publics feel about inequality and the policies they are willing to support. Many of these studies emphasize cultural constraints, such as an American reluctance to support the kinds of redistributive policies that are commonplace among most other high-income nations (McCall and Kenworthy, 2009).

The differences between people who place a high value on individualism compared with those who are more humanitarian in their orientation is reflected in their responses to policy proposals that would establish work requirements for welfare recipients (Shen and Edwards, 2005). Of course, public attitudes and policy preferences regarding inequality may also be based on false impressions of its nature and scope. Americans tend to underestimate the extent of wealth inequality at the same time that they express a preference for much greater equality than actually exists (Norton and Ariely, 2011).

Most audience studies rely on experimental and quasi-experimental designs to assess the effectiveness of particular frames. An increasing number of investigations make use of experiments embedded within large sample surveys (Brewer and Gross, 2010). While most of the studies of framing effects tend to focus on linguistic or textual presentations of alternative frames, an increasing number of them have examined the impact of visual cues (Ben-Porath and Shaker, 2010; Messaris and Abraham, 2003).

Scholars have also assessed the impacts of media frames at the institutional, system, or societal level. Their emphasis is primarily on changes in the logic and assumptions that govern a particular policy domain. Actual policy change is relatively rare; indeed, Baumgartner and colleagues suggest that such changes are unlikely to occur as a result of lobbying and other strategic communications (2009). Yet, there are several examples of shifts in policy over relatively short periods of time that are attributed to success in framing issues, target populations, or unexpected consequences in novel but compelling ways. Among the most striking is the dramatic shift in public opinion regarding the death penalty associated with a dramatic rise in the use of an "innocence frame" that emphasized flaws within the criminal justice system (Baumgartner, Linn, and Boydstun, 2010, 168).

While there are occasional shifts in policy that occur in response to critical events, including environmental disasters of one form or another (Nohrstedt and Weible, 2010), important alterations usually occur over longer periods of time during which the inertial forces protecting a particular "policy regime" are eventually overcome (McGuinn, 2006). As Hacker and Pierson suggest, it is important to understand how organized interests work to limit changes in policy that might otherwise arise in response to the altered circumstances and routines that they refer to as "policy drift" (2010b, 171, 191). It is in the analysis of these struggles over time, rather than in the short term battles to determine which candidate will be elected, that we are most likely to discover how those shifts are initiated, cultivated, and occasionally brought into being (Hacker and Pierson, 2010b, 168–169).

FRAMING INEQUALITY

Communicators seeking to influence the public's response to inequality nearly always comment on the nature and extent of the gaps within some system. In order to establish the importance of some gap as a social problem, the size of any disparity has to be compared with those found in other places, or at other times, or against some established standard.

There are several conventional measures of inequality, such as the Lorenz curve or the Gini coefficient that are used primarily with regard to income (Stiglitz, Sen, and Fitoussi, 2009). However, because their function within policy discourse is one of persuasion rather than enlightenment (Best, 2001), comparisons tend to be made between extremes, such as "the wealthiest one percent" versus "the middle class" (Noah, 2010).

As in other policy domains, the assignment of blame or responsibility for inequality is central to the mobilization of public opinion and popular support for a preferred policy option (Benford and Snow, 2000; Hanson and Hanson, 2006). Framing distributional considerations is also central to a determination of whether existing or predicted disparities are likely to raise moral and ethical concerns (Pelletier, 2010).

Communicators also understand that the persuasive impact of messages about in-group advantage will differ from that of messages about out-group disadvantage (Lowery and Wout, 2010). This impact also varies as a function of the strength of the audience's identification with or orientation toward either comparison group. While the identity of the beneficiaries and responsible parties is always important, it varies across particular domains, reflecting their social and normative constructions.

Health Disparities

Heckler's report on black and minority health (1985) was arguably the first and most influential attempt to put health disparities on the public policy agenda in the United States (Gamble and Stone, 2006). Part of the report's powerful influence has been attributed to its use of "excess deaths" as a metaphoric construction of a statistical reality that helped to emphasize the magnitude of the disparities as well as their moral weight (104).

Researchers seeking to understand the nature and causes of health disparities have identified individual, cultural, economic, and even genetic factors that determine how differences in exposure to a variety of pathogenic insults result in marked differences in quality of life (Krieger, 1999; Lynch et al., 2004; Mechanic, 2002; Phelan, Link, and Tehranifar, 2010). Characterizing the form, circumstance, and variety of discriminations people face is part of the challenge of demonstrating how social location determines the "pathways" to health disparities (Graham, 2004, 113).

Although mainstream news reports on this problem tend not to emphasize either causes or solutions to it, differences in emphasis among those few causal explanations are easily detected. It appears that in the United States, at least, newspaper coverage of racial disparities tends to emphasize behavioral causes, although references to problems in the healthcare delivery system are also occasionally found (Kim et al., 2010). Not surprisingly, behavioral changes dominate the solutions that are proposed for particular health problems.

This pattern of emphasis is consistent with an observed tendency to blame the victims for whatever hardships they suffer (Grande, 2011, 26; Hanson and Hanson, 2006, 426). To the extent that policies designed to reduce health disparities are framed in terms of the less sympathetic groups, such as those with drug dependencies, public support for them tends to be lower. Whereas when the policies are framed in terms of groups like military veterans, the elderly, or children, who are seen as more deserving, support tends to be higher (Rodriguez, Laugesen, and Watts, 2010).

Ironically, there is also evidence that emphasizing such disparities in the media leads toward mistrust and reluctance to make use of existing medical services and procedures on the part of African Americans (Nicholson et al., 2008).

Risk Frames

Differential exposure to a broad array of risks has been associated with group memberships defined by race, gender, and social class (Cooper, 2008; Gandy, 2009). The discourse of risk has become especially salient within public policy debates, and the communication of risk has become both a responsibility and a concern for a broad range of policy actors (Ericson and Haggerty, 1997; Garland, 2003; Hamilton, Adolphs, and Nerlich, 2007; Vaughan, 1995).

Some scholars have attempted to interpret media coverage of inequality in terms of "comparative risk" (Gandy, 1996; Gandy et al., 1997; Gandy and Li, 2005; Goshorn and Gandy, 1995). Comparative studies tend to focus on the negative side of risk where the emphasis in the media is on harm or loss rather than potential gain (Pettit and Western, 2004). Risk frames are also used as a resource for identifying competing sets of causal factors. Bad luck or unfortunate circumstances are readily distinguished from frames that place the blame for disparities on individual behavior, structural conditions, or institutional processes (Gandy, 2009, 145–182).

Although the Cultural Indicators research program of Gerbner and Gross (1976) did not explicitly identify the portrayals of the "winners and losers" and "violents and victims" as strategic frames introduced by policy oriented sponsors, these scholars did consistently link the social perceptions "cultivated" by exposure to prime-time television with a broad range of public policies (Gerbner et al., 1982). They also took pains to note that the risk ratios, or comparisons of relative risk faced by men, women, and people of color in the world of television were at substantial variance from those derived from an analysis of government statistics (Gerbner et al., 1994). Unfortunately, members of groups identified as being at greater comparative risk in the media have apparently incorporated those false constructions into their own conceptions of the world as a dangerous place (Flynn, Slovic, and Mertz 1994; Gandy, 2001).

Racial Inequality

Researchers who have investigated the way the story of racial inequality has been presented in the news typically emphasized the negative effects that were likely to flow from exposure to particular ways of framing the problem and its causes. After examining news reports over a six-year period focused on racial inequality, Iyengar (1991,

48) observed that this coverage tended to emphasize economic inequality as the problem, racial discrimination as the cause, and affirmative action as a proposed solution. He also suggested that because these stories were more likely to be dominated by episodic, rather than thematic frames, audiences would tend to place the blame on the victims, rather than institutional or structural factors.

After exploring the role of elite framing of issues at the heart of racial politics, Kinder and Sanders (1996) expressed a concern that strategic manipulation of public opinion might work through distorted impressions of the nature of the problems at hand and thereby result in an increase in what they termed "racial resentment" (283–285). Such resentment would likely be reflected in the public's response to government proposals to address a particular problem. Indeed, Gilens (1999) concluded that Americans were unwilling to support welfare programs in part because they assumed that the policy would primarily benefit African Americans, people thought to be underserving of such support (74–76).

The power of these frames is based in part on their use or activation of racial stereotypes. These stereotypes are easily recalled and activated by subtle cues in media-distributed policy frames (Loury, 2002, 55–107; Winter, 2008). Even the comparative statistics used in media stories about racial disparity help to activate racial stereotypes (Gandy and Baron, 1998), and in that way, they help to shape the audience's negative response to the policies being proposed.

News stories focused on racial inequality also tend to emphasize African American loss or victimization rather than white privilege or advantage (Gandy and Li, 2005). By framing inequality in this way, the media help socially dominant groups maintain a positive self-image (Powell, Branscombe, and Schmitt, 2005). At the same time, the absence of guilt makes it easier for them to justify withholding support for redistributive social policies (Lowery, Knowles, and Unzueta, 2007).

Strategic framing of affirmative action as "racial preferences" has been identified as a major strategic victory for those opposed to this redistributive social policy (Entman and Rojecki, 2000). The fact that supporters of affirmative action did not actively oppose this powerful frame but instead attempted to substitute "diversity" as a policy goal confirms the success of the strategy (Crenshaw, 2007; Davey, 2009; Rabinowitz et al., 2009).

Although most studies of racial policy frames emphasizes their success in opposing policies aimed at overcoming racial disparity, some success has also been observed for competing strategies that have focused on the structural and institutional practices held responsible for reproducing and extending inequality. These include the successful attempt to characterize race-based policing as illegal "racial profiling," while popularizing its consequences to include the "criminalization" of race itself, as in the so-called crime of "Driving While Black" (Gandy and Baruh, 2006; Meeks, 2000).

Knowledge, Achievement, and Performance Gaps

The *No Child Left Behind Act* of 2002 (NCLB) has been called "the most significant overhaul and expansion of the federal role in education since ESEA [The Elementary and

Secondary Education Act] was created in 1965" (McGuinn, 2006, 219). Given the stability of educational policy in the United States, the ability of a Republican president to accomplish such a major policy shift with broad bipartisan support helps to qualify this as a prime example of policy "regime change."

Although the Act was clearly focused on educational outcomes, it was framed and justified in terms of an explicit goal of reducing the disparity between groups disadvantaged by race, disability, or economic status (Jordan, 2010; Liu, 2009; McGuinn, 2006). Closing the "achievement gap" was not simply the pursuit of equality of opportunity, but it was an explicit commitment to equality of measured performance (William, 2010).

The fact that the legislation was supposed to correct racial disparities without requiring evidence of intentional discrimination also represented a departure from emergent trends in civil rights jurisprudence (Farmer, 2005). The majority of the public questioned the assumption that the "racial achievement gap" was due entirely, or even primarily, to schooling (Hess, 2006, 594). It is doubtful that most supporters of the legislation understood that accountability implied punitive sanctions on teachers and schools.

Goldstein and Beutel (2009) suggest, however, that the Bush administration felt that it would be easier to change teachers, and individual students or schools, rather than address "larger social, institutional, and structural barriers" to academic performance (279–280). Sources frequently cited in the press identified teachers' unions as "the primary obstacle to reforming education" (Goldstein, 2010, 15). At the same time, NCLB's policies tended to be framed as "achieving justice . . . particularly for those who have been least served in the past" (Goldstein, 2010, 22).

The Digital Divide

Inequality with regard to access to technology and the capacity to use it has been framed in terms of individual, community, and societal consequences. The metaphor of a "digital divide" emerged in common parlance across the globe in large part as the result of a series of reports from the US Department of Commerce's National Telecommunications Information Administration (NTIA).

Compaine (2001) questioned whether the so-called digital divide was a crisis in the making or was merely a mythic tale that should be ignored. Other critics suggested that the metaphor of a digital divide was part of a neoliberal project to shift responsibility from the government to the individual, while foreclosing a class analysis of the problem (Stevenson, 2009).

Selwyn (2004) argued against reliance on such an overly simplistic framing of the problem as one of the haves or the have-nots, or the "information rich" versus the "information poor" (345–346). Still others emphasized the myriad ways that limits on access to communications networks amplified other disparities, including those related to participation in the public sphere (Cooper, 2002).

The focus of the debate about the digital divide changed over time as the size of the gap declined. A "capabilities gap" and its relationship to productive uses of technology eventually moved to the forefront of the debate (Ferro, Helbig, and Gil-Garcia, 2007). By 2007, arguments about the impossibility of maximizing both equity and efficiency goals were dominating discussions of broadband telecommunications policy (Atkinson, 2007). In a manner similar to the shift in strategy by supporters of affirmative action, a coalition of minority organizations actually warned the Federal Communications Commission that its support of "net neutrality" as a standard for the Internet would forestall the introduction of new technologies and thereby "perpetuate the divide between the digital haves and have-nots" (Honig, 2010).

Environmental Inequalities and the Social Justice Frame

Environmental risks tend to be framed as problems of distributive justice or fairness, rather than of scientific confidence about the nature, extent, and likelihood that harms may result from the use of some product or device. Because of this emphasis, threats to public confidence and institutional trust become salient (Vaughan, 1995). Downey (2005) cites several studies emerging from environmental inequality research that draw critical distinctions between inequities associated with different causal models, as well as from the social and historical contexts that vary between nations.

To that point, environmental inequality had been discussed as a "fact of life," without a readily identifiable culprit. However, in the same way that Carson's *Silent Spring* (1962) helped to spark the environmental movement in the United States, Bullard's *Dumping in Dixie* (1990) helped to extend its scope under the banner of environmental justice (EJ).

For the environmental justice movement (EJM), injustice was elevated to the status of a master frame that examined environmental impacts "through the lens of race, class, and gender" (Taylor, 2000, 523). The fact that the EJM shared a taste for protest derived from its civil rights heritage may also explain some of its early success (Bullard and Johnson, 2000; Popescu and Gandy, 2004).

The EJ frame also tended to focus on corporate malfeasance and the failure of government agencies to be responsive to the concerns of the poor (Walker, 2009). As a result of its relatively unique emphasis on causal responsibility, the policy framework developed by the EJM was successful in helping to shift legal responsibility toward public agencies as well as moving public policy toward prevention (Bullard and Johnson, 2000). Somewhat ironically, the success of the EJM in the United States has meant that many toxic waste products generated in the West have been shipped to the Third World, thereby raising concerns about international equity (Walker, 2009, 372).

CONSTRAINTS ON THE INEQUALITY FRAME

The literature on framing helps to identify the disadvantages that burden SMOs as they attempt to move public policy agendas through an inequality framework (Nisbet, 2010).

This literature suggests (Johnston and Noakes, 2005) that frames that identify the broad mass of the population as being at risk are more likely to be successful than those that focus on unsympathetic victims. This strategy also reflects the fact that debates about policies designed to reduce disparities or even to mitigate the hardships that burden particular groups will nearly always find that the assessment of those policies will be shaped by public attitudes toward the groups identified as, or assumed to be, the beneficiaries.

In some cases, the true beneficiaries of a redistributive policy are rarely mentioned. For example, in one case strategists had apparently determined that it would be more effective to frame tax reductions that would benefit the wealthy as being motivated by a desire to support a more sympathetic group, such as senior citizens (Limbert and Bullock, 2009, 69–72). Along similar lines, the literature suggests that more success would be expected from frames that emphasize poverty rather than inequality (Gilens, 1999; Nisbet, 2010) because it is easier to introduce or elicit emotional responses to the real suffering and harms we associate with poverty (Guetzkow, 2010).

Nevertheless, it is important to note that some policy domains that are not explicitly discussed in terms of race still tend to be characterized in racial terms because of a process of "group implication" that develops over time (Dyck and Hussey, 2008; Goren, 2008). Indeed, it seems that "all social welfare discourse invokes race implicitly to some extent" (Winter, 2006, 416).

CRITICAL QUESTIONS THAT REMAIN

There is still considerable work to be done in identifying the factors that influence the rise and fall of equity frames in public discourse and on media agendas. These factors have to be examined in the context of lobbying and other forms of strategic communication. But we also have to find ways to incorporate longer, perhaps cyclical trends reflecting shifts in public sentiment and ideology as well as those in underlying sociotechnical systems (Webster, 2002). Because there are historically distinct periods within which differential patterns of enablement and constraint develop within social systems (Giddens, 1984), our understanding of the rise and fall of social problems, and the policies that are proposed to deal with them will require an expanded scope of inquiry.

Taking into account the many constraints on policy change that have been identified by Baumgartner et al. (2009) will require consideration of the myriad factors that alter the character and distribution of risk (Pellow, 2000). Giving due consideration to these complex structural relations will require a redistribution of energy and other resources away from what I believe has been a misplaced emphasis among scholars of political communication on individuals and their cognitive processes (Jacobs and Soss, 2010). Although I do believe that there is still much to be learned about how our identification with groups, and our orientations toward others shape our responses to the strategically framed messages that invoke them, we have much more to learn about how those messages come to be produced and distributed in the first place.

REFERENCES

Atkinson, R. 2007. Framing a national broadband policy. *Commonlaw Conspectus*, 16: 145–177.

Bartels, L. M. 2005. Homer gets a tax cut: Inequality and public policy in the American mind. *Perspectives on Politics*, 3: 15–31.

Bartels, L. M. 2008. *Unequal democracy: The political economy of the new Gilded Age*. Princeton, NJ: Princeton University Press.

Baumgartner, F. R., J. M. Berry, M. Hojnacki, D. C. Kimball, and B. L. Leech. 2009. *Lobbying and policy change: Who wins, who loses, and why*. Chicago: University of Chicago Press.

Baumgartner, F. R., and B. D. Jones. 1993. *Agendas and instability in American politics*. Chicago: University of Chicago Press.

Baumgartner, F. R., S. Linn, and A. E. Boydstun. 2010. The decline of the death penalty: How media framing changed capital punishment in America. In B. F. Shaffner and P. J. Sellers (Eds.), *Winning with words: The origins & impact of political framing* (pp. 159–184). New York: Routledge.

Ben-Porath, E. N., and L. K. Shaker. 2010. News images, race, and attribution in the wake of Hurricane Katrina. *Journal of Communication* 60: 466–490.

Benford, R. D., and D. A. Snow. 2000. Framing processes and social movements: An overview and assessment. *Annual Review of Sociology* 26: 611–639.

Best, J. 2001. *Damned lies and statistics: Untangling numbers from the media, politicians, and activists*. Berkeley: University of California Press.

Birdsall, N. 2001. Why inequality matters: Some economic issues. *Ethics & International Affairs* 15(2), 3–28.

Brewer, P. R., and K. Gross. 2010. Studying the effects of issue framing on public opinion about policy issues: Does what we see depend on how we look? In P. D'Angelo and J. A. Kuypers (Eds.), *Doing news framing analysis: Empirical and theoretical perspectives* (pp. 159–186). New York: Routledge.

Bullard, R. D. 1990. *Dumping in Dixie: Race, class, and environmental quality*. Boulder, CO: Westview Press.

Bullard, R., and G. S. Johnson. 2000. Environmental justice: Grassroots activism and its impact on public policy decision making. *Journal of Social Issues* 56(3), 557–578.

Bullock, H. E., W. R. Williams, and W. M. Limbert. 2003. Predicting support for welfare policies: The impact of attributions and beliefs about inequality. *Journal of Poverty* 7(3), 35–56.

Carson, R. 1962. *Silent spring*. Boston, MA: Houghton Mifflin.

Chong, D., and J. N. Druckman. 2007. Framing theory. *Annual Review of Political Science* 10: 103–126.

Compaine, B. M. 2001. Information gaps: Myth or reality? In B. Compaine (Ed.), *The digital divide: Facing a crisis or creating a myth?* (pp. 105–119). Cambridge, MA: MIT Press.

Cooper, M. 2008. The inequality of security: Winners and losers in the risk society. *Human Relations* 61 (9): 1229–1258.

Cooper, M. N. 2002. Inequality in the digital society: Why the digital divide deserves all the attention it gets. *Cardozo Arts & Entertainment Law Journal* 20: 73–134.

Crenshaw, K. W. 2007. Framing affirmative action. *Michigan Law Review First Impressions* 105: 123–133.

D'Angelo, P., and J. A. Kuypers (Eds). 2010. *Doing news framing analysis: Empirical and theoretical perspectives*. New York: Routledge.

Davey, L. 2009. Strategies for framing racial disparities: A FrameWorks messaging brief. Washington, DC: FrameWorks Institute.

Downey, L. 2005. Assessing environmental inequality: How the conclusions we draw vary according to the definitions we employ. *Sociological Spectrum* 25: 349–369.

Dyck, J. J., and L. S. Hussey. 2008. The end of welfare as we know it? Durable attitudes in a changing information environment. *Public Opinion Quarterly* 72(4): 589–618.

Entman, R. M. 1993. Framing: Toward clarification of a fractured paradigm. *Journal of Communication* 43(4): 51–58.

Entman, R. M, and A. Rojecki. 2000. *The black image in the white mind: Media and race in America.* Chicago: University of Chicago Press.

Ericson, R. V., and K. D. Haggerty. 1997. *Policing the risk society.* Toronto: University of Toronto Press.

Farmer, C. J. 2005. The No Child Left Behind Act: Will it produce a new breed of school financing litigation? *Columbia Journal of Law and Social Problems* 38: 443–481.

Ferro, E., N. C. Helbig, and J. R. Gil-Garcia. 2007. The digital divide metaphor: Understanding paths to IT literacy. NCDG Working Paper No. 07–001. Washington, DC: National Center for Digital Government.

Flynn, J., P. Slovic, and C. K. Mertz. 1994. Gender, race, and perception of environmental health risks. *Risk Analysis* 14 (6): 1101–1108.

Gamble, V. N., and D. Stone. 2006. U.S. policy on health inequities: The interplay of politics and research. *Journal of Health Politics, Policy and Law* 31(1): 93–126.

Gandy, O. H. 1982. *Beyond agenda setting: Information subsidies and public policy.* Norwood, NJ: Ablex.

Gandy, O. H. 1996. If it weren't for bad luck: Framing stories of racially comparative risk. In V. T. Berry and C. L. Manning-Miller (Eds.), *Mediated messages and African-American culture: Contemporary issues* (pp. 55–75). Thousand Oaks, CA: Sage.

Gandy, O. H. 2001. Racial identity, media use, and the social construction of risk among African Americans. *Journal of Black Studies* 31 (5): 600–618.

Gandy, O. H. 2009. *Coming to terms with chance: Engaging rational discrimination and cumulative disadvantage.* Burlington, VT: Ashgate.

Gandy, O. H., and J. Baron. 1998. Inequality: It's all in the way you look at it. *Communication Research* 25 (5): 505–527.

Gandy, O. H., and L. Baruh. 2006. Racial profiling: They said it was against the law! *University of Ottawa Law & Technology Journal* 3(1): 297–327.

Gandy, O. H., and Z. Li. 2005. Framing comparative risk: A preliminary analysis. *The Howard Journal of Communications* 16: 71–86.

Gandy, O. H., K. Kopp, T. Hands, K. Frazer, and D. Phillips. 1997. Race and risk: Factors affecting the framing of stories about inequality, discrimination, and just plain bad luck. *Public Opinion Quarterly* 61(1): 158–182.

Garland, D. 2003. The rise of risk. In *Risk and morality,* R. Ericson and A. Doyle (Eds.), (pp. 48–86). Toronto: University of Toronto Press.

Gerbner, G., and L. Gross. 1976. Living with television: The violence profile. *Journal of Communication* 26(2): 173–199.

Gerbner, G., L. Gross, M. Morgan, and N. Signorielli. 1982. Charting the mainstream: Television's contributions to political orientations. *Journal of Communication* 32(2): 100–127.

Gerbner, G., L. Gross, M. Morgan, and N. Signorielli. 1994. Growing up with television: The cultivation perspective. In J. Bryant and D. Zillman (Eds.), *Media effects: Advances in theory and research* (pp. 17–41). Hillsdale, NJ: Lawrence Earlbaum.

Giddens, A. 1984. *The constitution of society: Outline of the theory of structuration.* Cambridge, UK: Polity Press.

Gilens, M. 1999. *Why Americans hate welfare: Race, media, and the politics of antipoverty policy.* Chicago: University of Chicago Press.

Goldstein, R. A. 2010. Imaging the frame: Media representations of teachers, their unions, NCLB, and education reform. *Educational Policy* 25(4): 543–576.

Goldstein, R. A., and A. R. Beutel. 2009. "Soldier of democracy" or "enemy of the state"? The rhetorical construction of teacher through No Child Left Behind. *The Journal for Critical Education Policy Studies* 7(1): 276–300.

Goren, P. 2008. The two faces of government spending. *Political Research Quarterly* 61(1): 147–157.

Goshorn, K., and O. H. Gandy. 1995. Race, risk and responsibility: Editorial constraint in the framing of inequality. *Journal of Communication* 45(2): 133–151.

Graham, H. 2004. Social determinants and their unequal distribution: Clarifying policy understandings. *The Milbank Quarterly* 82(1): 101–124.

Grande, E. 2011. Against the poor: Homelessness in U.S. law. *Global Jurist* 11(1), (Advances), Article 2.

Guetzkow, J. 2010. Beyond deservingness: Congressional discourse on poverty, 1964–1996. *The ANNALS of the American Academy of Political and Social Science* 629(1): 173–197.

Hacker, J. S., and P. Pierson. 2010a. *Winner-take-all politics: How Washington made the rich richer—and turned its back on the middle class.* New York: Simon and Schuster.

Hacker, J. S., and P. Pierson. 2010b. Winner-take-all politics: Public policy, political organization, and the precipitous rise of top incomes in the United States. *Politics & Society* 38(2): 152–204.

Hallahan, K. 1999. Seven models of framing: Implications for public relations. *Journal of Public Relations Research* 11(3): 205–242.

Hamilton, C., S. Adolphs, and B. Nerlich. 2007. The meanings of "risk": A view from corpus linguistics. *Discourse & Society* 18(2): 163–181.

Hanson, J., and K. Hanson. 2006. The blame frame: Justifying (racial) injustice in America. *Harvard Civil Rights-Civil Liberties Law Review* 41: 413–480.

Harris, D. B. 2010. Partisan framing in legislative debates. In B. F. Schaffner and P. J. Sellers (Eds.), *Winning with words: The origins and impact of political framing* (pp. 41–59). New York: Routledge.

Heckler, M. 1985. *Report of the secretary's task force on black and minority health.* Washington, DC: U.S. Department of Health and Human Services.

Hess, F. M. 2006. Accountability without angst? Public opinion and No Child Left Behind. *Harvard Educational Review* 76(4): 587–610.

Honig, D., J. James, and J. Clary. 2010. *Comments of the National Organizations before the Federal Communications Commission in the matter of: preserving the open internet broadband industry practices.* Washington, DC.

Iyengar, S. 1991. *Is anyone responsible? How television frames political issues.* Chicago: University of Chicago Press.

Iyengar, S. 1996. Framing responsibility for political issues. *Annals of the American Academy of Political and Social Science* 546(1): 59–70.

Jacobs, L., and J. Soss. 2010. The politics of inequality in America: A political economy frame-work. *Annual Review of Political Science* 13: 341–364.

Johnston, H., and J. A. Noakes, (Eds.). 2005. *Frames of protest: Social movements and the fram-ing perspective.* Lanham, MD: Rowman & Littlefield.

Jordan, W. J. 2010. Defining equity: Multiple perspectives to analyzing the performance of diverse learners. *Review of Research in Education* 34(1): 142–178.

Kim. A., S. Kumanyika, D. Shive, U. Igweatu, and S. Kim. 2010. Coverage and framing of racial and ethnic health disparities in US newspapers, 1996–2005. *American Journal of Public Health*, Supplement 1 100 (S1): S224–S231.

Kinder, D. R., and L. M. Sanders. 1996. *Divided by color: Racial politics and Democratic ideals.* Chicago: University of Chicago Press.

Krieger, N. 1999. Embodying inequality: A review of concepts, measures, and methods for studying health consequences of discrimination. *International Journal of Health Services* 29(2): 295–352.

Limbert, W. M., and H. E. Bullock. 2009. Framing U.S. redistributive policies: Tough love for poor women and tax cuts for seniors. *Analyses of Social Issues and Public Policy* 9(1): 57–83.

Liu, G. 2009. The Bush administration and civil rights: Lessons learned. *Duke Journal of Constitutional Law & Public Policy* 4: 77–105.

Loury, G. C. 2002. *The anatomy of racial inequality.* Cambridge, MA: Harvard University Press.

Lowery, B. S., E. D. Knowles, and M. M. Unzueta. 2007. Framing inequity safely: Whites' motivated perceptions of racial privilege. *Personality and Social Psychology Bulletin* 33(9): 1237–1250.

Lowery, B. S., and D. A. Wout. 2010. When inequality matters: The effect of inequality frames on academic engagement. *Journal of Personality and Social Psychology* 98 (6): 956–966.

Lucas, S. R., and L. Beresford. 2010. Naming and classifying: Theory, evidence and equity in education. *Review of Research in Education* 34(1): 25–84.

Lynch, J., G. D. Smith, S. Harper, M. Hillemeier, N. Ross, G. A. Kaplan, and M. Wolfson. 2004. Is income inequality a determinant of population health? Part 1. A systematic review. *The Milbank Quarterly* 82(1): 5–99.

McCall, L., and L. Kenworthy. 2009. Americans' social policy preferences in the era of rising inequality. *Perspectives on Politics* 7(3): 459–484.

McCombs, M., and S. I. Ghanem. 2001. The convergence of agenda setting and framing. In S. D. Reese, O. H. Gandy and A. E. Grant (Eds.), *Framing public life: Perspectives on media and our understanding of the social world* (pp. 67–82). Mahwah, NJ: Lawrence Erlbaum.

McGuinn, P. 2006. Swing issues and policy regimes: Federal education policy and the politics of policy change. *The Journal of Policy History* 18(2): 205–240.

Mechanic, D. 2002. Disadvantage, inequality and social policy. *Health Affairs* 21(2): 48–59.

Meeks, K. 2000. *Driving while black: Highways, shopping malls, taxicabs, sidewalks: How to fight back if you are a victim of racial profiling.* New York: Broadway Books.

Messaris, P., and L. Abraham. 2003. The role of images in framing news stories. In S. D. Reese, O. H. Gandy and A. E. Grant (Eds.), *Framing public life: Perspectives on media and our under-standing of the social world* (pp. 215–226). Mahwah, NJ: Lawrence Erlbaum.

Nelson, T. E. 2004. Policy goals, public rhetoric, and political attitudes. *The Journal of Politics* 66(2): 581–605.

Nicholson, R. A., M.W. Kreuter, C. Lapka, R. Wellborn, E. M. Clark, V. Sanders-Thompson, H. M. Jacobson, and C. Casey. 2008. Unintended effects of emphasizing disparities in cancer communication to African-Americans. *Cancer Epidemiology, Biomarkers & Prevention* 17 (11): 2946–2953.

Nisbet, M. C. 2010. Knowledge into action: Framing the debates over climate change and poverty. In P. D'Angelo and J. Kuypers (Eds.), *Doing news framing analysis: Empirical and theoretical perspectives* (pp. 43–83). New York: Routledge.

Noah, T. 2010. The great divergence. *Slate*, Retrieved from http://img.slate.com/media/3/100914_NoahT_GreatDivergence.pdf.

Nohrstedt, D., and C. M. Weible. 2010. The logic of policy change after crisis: Proximity and subsystem interaction. *Risk, Hazards & Crisis in Public Policy* 1 (2), Article 1: 1–32.

Norton, M., and D. Ariely. 2011. Building a better America—one wealth quintile at a time. *Perspectives on Psychological Science* 6(1): 9–12.

Page, B. I., and R. Y. Shapiro. 1992. *The rational public: Fifty years of trends in Americans' policy preferences.* Chicago: University of Chicago Press.

Pan, Z., and G. M. Kosicki. 2001. Framing as a strategic action in public deliberation. In S. D. Reese, O. H. Gandy and A. E. Grant (Eds.), *Framing public life: Perspectives on media and our understanding of the social world* (pp. 35–66). Mahwah, NJ: Lawrence Earlbaum.

Pasma, C. 2010. Working through the work disincentive. *Basic Income Studies* 5(2), Article 4: 1–20.

Pelletier, N. 2010. Environmental sustainability as the first principle of distributive justice: Towards an ecological communitarian normative foundation for ecological economics. *Ecological Economics* 69: 1887–1894.

Pellow, D. N. 2000. Environmental inequality formation: Toward a theory of environmental injustice. *The American Behavioral Scientist* 43(4): 581–601.

Pettit, B., and B. Western. 2004. Mass imprisonment and the life course: Race and class inequality in U.S. incarceration. *American Sociological Review* 69(2): 151–169.

Phelan, J. C., B. G. Link, and P. Tehranifar. 2010. Social conditions as fundamental causes of health inequalities: Theory, evidence, and policy implications. *Journal of Health and Social Behavior* 51 (Supplement): S28–S40.

Pollock, J. C. 2007. *Tilted mirrors: Media alignment with political and social change—A community structure approach.* Cresskill, NJ: Hampton Press.

Popescu, M., and O. H. Gandy. 2004. Whose environmental justice? Social identity and institutional rationality. *Journal of Environmental Law and Litigation* 19(1): 141–192.

Powell, A. A., N. R. Branscombe, and M. T. Schmitt. 2005. Inequality as ingroup privilege or outgroup disadvantage: The impact of group focus on collective guilt and interracial attitudes. *Personality and Social Psychology Bulletin* 31(4): 508–521.

Rabinowitz, J. L., D. O. Sears, J. Sidanius, and J. A. Krosnick. 2009. Why do white Americans oppose race-targeted policies? Clarifying the impact of symbolic racism. *Political Psychology* 30 (5): 805–828.

Reese, S. D., O. H. Gandy, and A. E. Grant, (Eds.). 2001. *Framing public life: Perspectives on media and our understanding of the social world.* Mahwah, NJ: Lawrence Erlbaum.

Richardson, J. D., and K. M. Lancendorfer. 2004. Framing affirmative action: The influence of race on newspaper editorial responses to the University of Michigan cases. *The Harvard International Journal of Press/Politics* 9(4): 74–94.

Rodriguez, H. P., M. J. Laugesen, and C. A. Watts. 2010. A randomized experiment of issue framing and voter support of tax increases for health insurance expansion. *Health Policy* 98: 245–255.

Schaffner, B. F., and M. L. Atkinson. 2010. Taxing death or estates? When frames influence cit-
    izens' issue beliefs. In B. F. Schaffner and P. J. Sellers (Eds.), *Winning with words: The origins
    and impact of political framing* (pp. 121–135). New York: Routledge.

Schaffner, B. F., and P. J. Sellers, (Eds.). 2010. *Winning with words: The origins and impact of
    political framing.* New York: Routledge.

Scheufele, D. A., and D. Tewksbury. 2007. Framing, agenda setting, and priming: The evolution
    of three media effects models. *Journal of Communication* 57: 9–20.

Schneider, A., and H. Ingram. 1993. Social construction of target populations: Implications for
    politics and policy. *The American Political Science Review* 87(2): 334–347.

Sellers, P. J. 2000. Manipulating the message in the U.S. Congress. *The Harvard International
    Journal of Press/Politics* 5(1): 22–31.

Selwyn, N. 2004. Reconsidering political and popular understandings of the digital divide.
    New Media & Society 6(3): 341–362.

Shen, F., and H. Edwards. 2005. Economic individualism, humanitarianism, and welfare
    reform: A value-based account of framing effects. *Journal of Communication* 55(4): 795–809.

Steensland, B. 2008. Why do policy frames change? Actor-idea coevolution in debates over
    welfare reform. *Social Forces* 86(3): 1027–1054.

Stevenson, S. 2009. Digital divide: A discursive move away from the real inequities. *The
    Information Society* 25: 1–22.

Stiglitz, J. E., A. Sen, and J. P. Fitoussi. 2009. *Report by the Commission on the Measurement
    of Economic Performance and Social Progress.* Paris: Commission on the Measurement of
    Economic Performance and Social Progress.

Taylor, D. E. 2000. The rise of the environmental justice paradigm. *American Behavioral
    Scientist* 43(4): 508–580.

Vaughan, E. 1995. The significance of socioeconomic and ethnic diversity for the risk commu-
    nication process. *Risk Analysis* 15(2): 169–180.

Walker, G. 2009. Globalizing environmental justice: The geography and politics of frame con-
    textualization and evolution. *Global Science Policy* 9(3): 355–382.

Webster, F. 2002. *Theories of the information society.* 2nd ed. New York: Routledge.

Wilkinson, R. G., and K. G. Pickett. 2010. *The spirit level: Why equality is better for everyone.*
    London: Penguin.

William, D. 2010. What counts as evidence of educational achievement? The role of constructs
    in the pursuit of equity in assessment. *Review of Research in Education* 34(1): 254–284.

Wilson, W. J. 2010. Why both social structure and culture matter in a holistic analysis of inner-
    city poverty. *The Annals of the American Academy of Political and Social Science* 629(1):
    200–219.

Winter, N. J. G. 2006. Beyond welfare: Framing and the racialization of white opinion on Social
    Security. *American Journal of Political Science* 50(2): 400–420.

Winter, N. J. G. 2008. Dangerous frames: How ideas about race and gender shape public opin-
    ion. Chicago: University of Chicago Press.

....

CHAPTER 35

POLITICAL COMMUNICATION

Insights from Field Experiments

....

DONALD P. GREEN, ALLISON CARNEGIE, AND JOEL MIDDLETON

INTRODUCTION

....

EMPIRICAL investigation of cause and effect in the field of political communication has long been dominated by nonexperimental research. From the 1940s through the 1990s, political campaigns' effects on voter opinion and behavior were studied using survey data that compared people with different levels of exposure to campaigns and sometimes tracked these differences over time (Berelson, Lazarsfeld, and McPhee, 1986; Campbell, 1980; Freedman, Franz, and Goldstein, 2004; Johnston, Hagen, and Jamieson, 2004; Patterson and McClure, 1976). The methodological sophistication of these studies has improved over time as scholars have deployed much larger surveys (Romer, Kenski, Winneg, Adasiewicz, and Jamieson, 2006; Whiteley, 1988) and made use of improved technologies for measuring exposure to political messaging (Freedman and Goldstein, 1999; Goldstein and Freedman, 2002).

Nevertheless, an inherent limitation of nonexperimental research has been a growing source of concern. Because the analyst of observational data does not have control over the process by which people encounter political communication, any observed correlation between outcomes and exposure to political messages is subject to two interpretations: (a) exposure causes outcomes or (b) exposure is systematically related to unobserved factors that cause outcomes. For example, exposure to political advertising by presidential candidates may predict vote choice either because ads change opinions or because ads happen to coincide with viewers' pre-existing political preferences. The latter interpretation is hard to rule out when political campaigns strategically target their messages or when voters decide which messages to attend to.

One answer to this conundrum is to conduct experiments, a research method in which subjects are randomly assigned to treatment and control groups with known probabilities. The attractiveness of the experimental method derives largely from the fact that when political messages are assigned at random, there is no systematic relationship between the experimental intervention and subjects' political proclivities. Experiments in the field of political communication may be classified into two broad categories depending on whether they are conducted in the lab or field. Lab experiments expose subjects to messages in artificial settings. Although researchers often go to great lengths to recruit subjects from the general population, to make them feel at home in the lab setting, and to measure outcomes unobtrusively, applying the findings from laboratory studies to the world of politics requires supplementary assumptions. For example, in order to study the electoral effects of negative campaign tactics, Ansolabehere and Iyengar (1995) conducted a series of lab studies demonstrating that negative advertising depresses voter turnout, as measured by expressed intention to vote in postintervention surveys. Applying the lessons of the lab to the world of electoral politics, however, requires one to assume that subjects in the lab respond to advertising in the same way that ordinary television viewers do and that subjects stated vote intentions correspond to the way in which they would behave in a nonlab setting.

By focusing on political communication in real-world settings, field experiments are designed to shorten the distance between the experimental setting and the political setting to which the researchers intends to generalize. The push for realism and unobtrusiveness stems from the concern that unless one conducts experiments in a naturalistic manner, some aspect of the experimental design may generate results that defy generalization. The realism of a field experiment may be judged along four dimensions: whether the treatment used in the study resembles the intervention of interest in the world, whether the participants resemble the actors who ordinarily encounter these interventions, whether the context within which subjects receive the treatment resembles the context of interest, and whether the outcome measures resemble the actual outcomes of theoretical or practical interest. Field experiments vary in their degrees of realism but all share the randomized deployment of treatments in naturalistic settings.

The aim of this essay is to provide a brief overview of the field experimental literature in the domain of political communication. Recognizing that many readers may be unfamiliar with this style of research, we begin by describing some important features of experimental designs. This section discusses some of the challenges of conducting experiments in the field and explains how designs strike a balance between scholarly objectives and practical considerations. Next, we summarize the contributions of some illustrative field experiments in three substantive domains. First, we consider public information campaigns designed to encourage voters to hold public officials accountable for performance in office. Second, we discuss individually targeted information designed to encourage voters and taxpayers to comply with social norms. Finally, we review recent attempts to study the electoral effects of television and radio advertisements. The examples illustrate how field experiments may contribute to a broad range of important theoretical and policy debates.

Overview of Field Experimental Designs

In terms of research design, field experiments related to political communication may be classified along three different dimensions. The first dimension describes the unit of randomization. At the "micro" end of the spectrum are experiments in which individuals are each assigned to treatment or control conditions. On the other end of the spectrum are "place based" experiments (Boruch, 2005; Boruch et al., 2004) in which clusters of individuals, such as media markets or legislative districts, are assigned to treatment or control. A second dimension is whether subjects are presented with different treatments over time. A design that is strictly between-subjects focuses on a single point in time, comparing subjects who were randomly assigned to treatment or control. An alternative design traces subjects (which may be aggregate units, such as regions) over time as they respond to different treatments. A third dimension is the degree of correspondence between the assigned and actual treatment. In some settings, those implementing the intervention treat everyone in the treatment group and no one in the control group. In other settings, the experiment encounters some degree of noncompliance; some members of the assigned treatment group do not receive the treatment, or some members of the control group receive the treatment.

Before considering examples that illustrate these design dimensions, first consider some of the practical constraints and statistical considerations that lead researchers to implement different designs. Ordinarily, researchers aim to include as many units as possible in their experiments, since precision increases as the number of units in treatment and control increases. If an electoral constituency contains 100,000 voters, one would ideally like to assign them individually to treatment and control. Sometimes individual assignment is impossible. For example, given current technology, broadcast media send messages to geographically defined groups of voters; one cannot target randomly selected voters inside a media market. Sometimes the researcher aims to answer a question that lends itself to place-based randomization: instead of seeking to assess the effect of viewing a campaign message when one's neighbors do not, the researcher may wish to assess the effects of viewing a message when neighbors view it as well.

Second, the use of between-subjects designs makes sense when researchers have many experimental units, limited capacity to vary treatments over time, or limited capacity to measure outcomes over time. When only a small number of observations are available for experimental assignment and the experiment may be conducted repeatedly over time, researchers may compare observations both cross-sectionally and cross-temporally. The latter design is sometimes a matter of necessity when field-based research partners (e.g., political campaigns) refuse to conduct an experiment unless all units receive the treatment at some point. The so-called stepped wedge design rolls out the treatment in stages to selected subjects, until eventually every subject receives the treatment.

A final design dimension concerns the relationship between the assigned treatment and the treatment that subjects actually receive. Sometimes the aim of a study is to evaluate the effect of an attempt to expose subjects to a form of communication. For example, studies that evaluate the effects of direct mail (Gerber, Green, and Green 2003; Gerber, Green, and Larimer, 2008) assess the effect of sending mail, not the effect of actually reading what is sent. On the other hand, sometimes researchers have a different objective: they wish to study the effects of actually receiving a message. For example, studies that examine the effects of receiving a phone call from a political campaign must contend with the fact that only a portion of those who are randomly assigned to receive a call are in fact reached by canvassers. An experiment that encounters noncompliance cannot estimate the average effect of receiving the treatment for all subjects; instead, it can only estimate the effect of the treatment among "compliers," those who receive the treatment if and only if they are assigned to the treatment group. (For an extended discussion that defines compliers and reviews the assumptions necessary for estimation of the average treatment effect among compliers, see Gerber and Green, 2012.) Whether the average effect among compliers is of theoretical interest depends on one's research aims. If the aim is to estimate the average treatment effect of a policy that will expose everyone to the treatment, the answer is no; if the aim is to estimate the effect on compliers of an intervention that encourages exposure, the answer is yes.

Let's now consider three examples of research designs that vary along these dimensions and the reasons that scholars might choose one design over another. Shaw et al. (2012) report the results of a study that tests the persuasive effects of prerecorded messages on voting. The message in this experiment was an endorsement by the Republican governor of Texas, Rick Perry, of a conservative member of the State Supreme Court, who was facing reelection in a low-salience primary election. In order to assess the effects of the pre-recorded phone call on voter turnout, the calls were randomly assigned to more than 200,000 households with a history of voting in Republican primaries. To ascertain the effects on vote choice, the researchers conducted a parallel experiment in which the unit of assignment was the voting precinct. In the turnout experiment, outcomes were measured using official records indicating whether each individual voted; in the vote choice experiment, they were measured based on the number of votes that treatment and control precincts cast for the endorsed candidate. This study illustrates how the availability of outcome measures guides research design.

Another Texas experiment illustrates the advantages of tracing outcomes over time. Gerber et al. (2011) report the results of a multi–million dollar experiment in which eighteen Texas media markets were randomly assigned to varying levels of television and radio advertising. Because the number of media markets is fairly small, cross-sectional comparisons of treated and untreated markets were subject to considerable sampling variability. In this case, the treatments were rolled out gradually week by week, and outcomes were measured daily using tracking polls. The statistical power of this study derives in large part from the ability to track opinion in each media market over time. A final pair of examples illustrates the use of an encouragement design and the way in which noncompliance affects the interpretation of the results. Albertson and Lawrence (2009) report the results of an experiment that randomly encouraged subjects to watch a Fox News debate on affirmative action and gauged its effects on support for a ballot proposition on this issue, and Washington, Mullainathan, and Azari (2010) conducted an experiment that randomly encouraged New York voters to view a debate between mayoral candidates. Postdebate surveys gauged whether respondents in the treatment and control groups watched the debate. In both experiments, some subjects in the control group watched the treatment shows without being encouraged to do so, and some members of the treatment group failed to do so despite encouragement. These experiments therefore assess the effects of the experimental shows for compliers, those who view the shows if and only if encouraged to do so.

ILLUSTRATION OF SUBSTANTIVE CONTRIBUTIONS

This section reviews research from an assortment of different domains in order to illustrate the breadth of field experimental applications.

Public Information Campaigns Designed to Promote Electoral Accountability

In developing countries, the quality of governance tends to be poor even in countries where elections are conducted in an open and fair manner. Why does corruption and incompetence persist when voters regularly have the opportunity to punish candidates and political parties that misbehave in office? One hypothesis is that voters fail to punish official misconduct because they lack information about elected officials' levels of integrity and competence. This hypothesis lends itself to a field experiment in which voters are presented with "report cards" that grade officials' performances.

Two recent studies, one conducted in Mexico and another conducted in India, assess the effects of providing this type of information. A study by Banerjee et al. (2011) evaluates a multifaceted information campaign designed to inform slum dwellers in Delhi about the performance of incumbent state legislators. Legislators were graded based on their attendance at legislative sessions and local meetings, how they spent discretionary budgets, and their personal characteristics (such as whether they faced serious criminal charges). The researchers distributed report cards summarizing this information via door-to-door canvassing, group meetings, and newspapers in randomly selected polling precincts. Polling station outcomes were used to measure the treatment's effects on voter turnout and vote share for incumbents. A similar experiment by Chong et al. (2011) gauges the effect of providing Mexican voters with information about malfeasance in local governments. Information about integrity and performance was culled from reports from Mexico's federal government, which regularly audits municipal finances. Some municipalities received high marks (they spend authorized funds appropriately and without accounting irregularities symptomatic of corruption), and others did not. The researchers randomly assigned precincts within audited municipalities to one of four experimental conditions. Control precincts received a flyer shortly before the election with information about when and where to vote; treatment precincts received a flyer with this information plus a brief summary of the federal audit's findings. Specifically, the treatments reported one of three things: the auditor's assessment of the corruption in the municipality, how much of federally authorized funds the municipality spent (an indicator of bureaucratic competence), and how much of federally authorized money aimed at the poor the municipality spent. The outcome was the share of the vote that each precinct cast for the incumbent's party.

Banerjee et al. found that in areas where incumbent quality was poor, report cards significantly reduced votes for the incumbent. This finding is echoed by Chong et al., who find that in areas where auditors discovered corruption, leaflets that publicized corruption had substantial electoral effects, significantly reducing the vote share won by each incumbent's party in the subsequent election. Revelations about a government's failure to spend earmarked funds had no apparent effect. The implication seems to be that credible information causes voters to punish corrupt behavior, but voters are uncertain about or unmoved by allegations of bureaucratic incompetence, regardless of whether it means that the poor failed to receive authorized federal funds. The results of both studies seem to suggest that information with clear evaluative implications, such as charges of corruption, can lead voters to punish incumbents. This conclusion is bolstered by the findings of Ferraz and Finan (2008) showing that random audits of Brazilian municipalities that came to a critical verdict about municipal governance led to electoral reprisal against the incumbents, especially in areas where mass media publicized this information.

Individually Targeted Shaming Campaigns to Encourage Compliance with Norms

One of the longstanding puzzles in social science is the paradox of collective action: despite the fact that one person's contribution is extraordinarily unlikely to affect whether the collective goal is realized, individuals nevertheless vote, volunteer, and make other personal sacrifices for collective causes. One way to resolve this theoretical puzzle is to posit that people receive psychic benefits from doing the right thing, such as performing a civic duty. This hypothesis holds that the personal sacrifice of time or money is offset by two kinds of "selective incentives" (Olson, 1965): the intrinsic satisfaction that comes from upholding a social norm and the extrinsic utility of winning social approval (or avoiding social disapproval) from others. This theoretical argument has important practical implications: rather than offer material inducements, those seeking to encourage collective action could use tactics that increase the motivation to comply with social norms.

A series of recent field experiments has tested the effectiveness of encouragements that make social norms salient. Fellner, Sausgruber, and Traxler (2009) collaborated with an Austrian tax collection agency to examine the conditions under which people who own televisions without paying the mandatory annual fee will do so when confronted by an official letter from the tax collection agency. The researchers randomly varied the content of the mailings, emphasizing either (a) a threat of prosecution for tax evasion, (b) a fairness appeal to pay one's fair share rather than forcing others to bear one's tax burden, or (c) information stating the descriptive norm that 94 percent of households comply with this tax. These interventions were designed to accentuate three theoretically relevant factors: fear of punishment, concern for fairness, and conformity with perceived norms. The outcome was whether those who were apparently in arrears on their TV tax paid the tax in the wake of the letter. Their findings suggest that the letter's effectiveness was enhanced by threats of prosecution but not by appeals to fairness or descriptive norms. (For other large-scale experiments on the effects of warning letters from tax collection agencies, see Kleven et al., 2010, and Slemrod, Blumenthal, and Christian, 2001.)

A rather different pattern of results emerges when letters encourage voter turnout. A series of experiments beginning with that of Gross, Schmidt, Keating, and Saks (1974) has tested the effects of messages that manipulate the psychic benefits of voting by either encouraging people to do their civic duty or by reminding them that voting in elections is a matter of public record and that failure to vote will be a source of embarrassment. Gerber, Green, and Larimer (2008, 2010), for example, conducted a series of experiments in which tens of thousands of registered voters in Michigan were sent a letter that either (a) encouraged them to do their civic duty and vote in an upcoming election, (b) presented voters with records indicating whether they had voted in past elections and threatened to monitor whether they voted in an upcoming election, or (c) presented voters with records indicating whether they and their neighbors had voted in prior elections and threatened to update everyone about who voted in an upcoming election. Appeals to civic duty alone boosted turnout, but this effect was dwarfed by the powerful effects of disclosing voting records. These results have been replicated in other settings, again using very large samples (Mann, 2010; Panagopoulos, 2010; Sinclair, McConnell, and Green, 2012). Other field experiments have shown that turnout increases when messages encourage voters to join an honor roll of neighbors who vote (Panagopoulos, 2010) or thank voters for their past participation or interest in politics (Panagopoulos, 2011), suggesting that voters participate in elections in part to win the gratitude of others and to maintain positive self-images. Although direct mail that reminds people to vote in upcoming elections tends to have negligible effects (Bedolla and Michelson, 2012; Green and Gerber, 2008), mail that makes social norms salient tends to produce substantial increases in turnout.

Persuasive Effects of TV and Radio

Since the 1940s, scholars have attempted to measure the effects of TV and radio communication on political attitudes but have rarely employed experimental designs in naturalistic settings to do so (for exceptions, see Ball-Rokeach, Rokeach, and Grube, 1984). Recently, several experiments have demonstrated that field-based tests are possible and shed light on longstanding theories of opinion change.

Inspired by the large amount of nonexperimental literature on campaign spending and name recognition, Panagopoulos and Green (2008) conducted a study of mayoral elections in which the experimental intervention was a series of nonpartisan radio advertisements that mentioned the names and party affiliations of both mayoral candidates. The underlying hypothesis was that low levels of name recognition prevent challengers from running competitively against incumbents; by mentioning both candidates in an even-handed way, the intervention was expected to narrow incumbents' margins of victory. This prediction was borne out by electoral results from more than three dozen mayoral elections over a two year period, although their statistical results fall short of conventional levels of statistical significance.

One limitation of the Panagopoulos and Green (2008) study and related experiments that assess the effects of nonpartisan TV advertisements on voter turnout (Green and Vavreck, 2008; Panagopoulos and Green, 2011) is that they do not test the effects of partisan campaign advertisements aired by candidates. Gerber et al. (2011) attempt to fill this gap. Their experiment assesses the impact of millions of dollars of TV and radio advertising deployed by the campaign to re-elect Governor Rick Perry of Texas in 2006. As noted above, the study randomly assigned different amounts of TV and radio ads on a weekly basis in eighteen media markets over a three-week period in January 2006 at the start of campaign. Using daily tracking polls with approximately 1,000 respondents each day, the evaluation was able to gauge over time movement in voters' preferences as advertising was switched on or off in each market. The results showed a powerful but short-lived effect of TV ads. The statistical results suggest that 1,000 gross ratings points of TV advertising raised Perry's vote support by approximately 5 percentage points during the week in which the ads were aired; a week later, the ads had no apparent effect. Perhaps surprisingly, the TV ads' effects were unaffected by whether TV ads were aired by Perry's principal opponent, suggesting that one-sided and two-sided communication had roughly the same effect.

The fact that advertising had a momentary effect presents an interesting anomaly from the standpoint of rational learning theories, which characterize the public as Bayesian information processors (Gerber and Green, 1998). A Bayesian learning model would imply that an ad would move opinion markedly only if it conveyed a large amount of new information, in which case its effects should decline slowly unless the overall information environment was continually bombarding voters with important pieces of new information. But the Perry ad in this case was a feel-good one that conveyed little substantive content, and the informational environment during this period was fairly placid. Evidently, candidate ads can produce large momentary effects that are not easily reconciled with models of rational information processing.

DIRECTIONS FOR FUTURE RESEARCH

In the domain of political communication, field experimentation remains relatively rare, but recent research suggests that this type of inquiry is both feasible and informative (see Green, Calfano, and Aronow, 2014). In this section, we suggest some fruitful directions for future investigation, building on the brief literature review presented above.

Experiments have much to contribute to longstanding debates about the capacities of voters and the quality of public opinion. Social scientists have long been critical of the public's limited awareness of political facts (Delli Carpini and Keeter, 1997), its incoherent configuration of policy attitudes (Converse, 1964), and its lack of understanding of constitutional principles (McClosky and Brill, 1983). On the other hand, scholars have often praised the public's ability to adjust its policy views in light of current conditions (Page and Shapiro, 1983), to punish candidates based on retrospective performance evaluations (Fiorina, 1981), and to use decision shortcuts in order to sort out policy choices (Brady and Sniderman, 1985; Lupia, 1994). These claims all rest on observational data, and their characterization of the public is situated in a party system that narrows the range of "treatments" (candidate choices, messages, and messengers) to which citizens are exposed. In such cases, experiments are informative for two reasons: they overcome problems of unobserved heterogeneity, and they deploy treatments that would not ordinarily occur. For example, when left to its own devices, the political system rarely if ever generates radio ads that publicize the names of both parties' congressional candidates. If researchers want to test theories about the effects of these out-of-equilibrium forms of communication, they have no choice but to orchestrate these interventions themselves.

The recent line of field experiments that provide voters with information relevant to electoral choice could be expanded to address a variety of longstanding propositions about voter decision-making. We earlier reviewed interventions that provided information designed to assist voters in forming a retrospective performance evaluation (Fiorina, 1981), but the same experimental paradigm could be extended to other messages: issue positions, partisan cues, social identities, or endorsements by reference groups. Some initial attempts to conduct these sorts of theory-guided messaging tests may be found in the experimental literature on voter mobilization (Bedolla and Michelson, 2012; Trivedi, 2005); the next step is to extend this line of research to voter persuasion. This research agenda could also explore the possible interaction between information and other features of the political environment. For example, in India, caste tends to play a dominant role in shaping party preferences, and an interesting research question is whether interventions that lower the salience of caste have the effect of increasing the influence of issue—or performance-based evaluations (Banerjee et al., 2011). Similarly, one might conduct experiments in an array of different electoral settings to see whether the influence of information about incumbent performance depends on the availability of a viable alternative candidate.

Recent studies of attempts to increase compliance with social norms also point the way toward more systematic theoretically guided inquiry. The existing literature has focused primarily on *prescriptive* norms (what one ought to do) and *descriptive* norms (what others tend to do), and only recently have messaging experiments focused on other psychological propositions, such as idea that people are more likely to take action in the wake of an encouragement when they form a mental image of the steps they would take in order to perform the behavior (Rogers and Nickerson, 2010) or express a verbal commitment to perform the behavior that they are later reminded of (Michelson, Bedolla, and McConnell, 2009). Again, such messages could be studied in conjunction with other factors by concurrently varying source credibility or reference group cues.

Experimental investigations of mass media effects need to diversify along several dimensions. Field experiments have scarcely tested the relative effects of positive versus negative tone in candidate messaging. (For experiments that speak obliquely to this comparison with regard to voter turnout, see Gerber, Green, and Green, 2003, and Niven, 2006.) Researchers have only begun to test the rate at which messaging effects decay, and no experimental studies have tested whether the random introduction of ads on a specific topic changes the salience of that topic either in the minds of voters or in the media's campaign coverage. And beyond the traditional mass media, experimental researchers have paid relatively little attention to Internet-based advertising or messages deployed through social media, such as Facebook. (For experimental attempts to gauge the effects of email messaging on voter registration see Bennion and Nickerson, 2011; see Bond, Jones, and Fowler, 2011, and Broockman and Green 2014, on the effect of Facebook messaging on voter turnout and vote choice.) Despite the fact that Internet ads and applications are increasingly able to target specific individuals or small geographic regions, experimental researchers are only beginning to study the effects of political messaging. Given the immense reach of the Internet and the growing range of political actions that can be expressed through online behavior (e.g., petitions, donations, volunteering), experimental opportunities abound.

Can these opportunities be turned into actual field experiments? Prior to the 1990s, one might have supposed the answer to be no, but researchers in recent decades have steadily expanded the domain of what is thought possible. An increasing number of governments and nongovernmental organizations have been persuaded to use field experiments in order to evaluate their public outreach efforts. In the world of campaign politics, scholarly collaborations have occurred when candidates, interest groups, and political parties have sought to harness the power of randomized experiments in order to evaluate persuasive messages, fundraising appeals, and voter mobilization efforts. The field of political communication is gradually being transformed by this research method and the rigor that it brings to causal inference.

REFERENCES

Albertson, B., and A. Lawrence. 2009. After the credits roll: The long term effects of educational television on public knowledge and attitudes. *American Politics Research*, 37(2), 275–300.

Ansolabehere, S., and S. Iyengar. 1995. *Going negative: How attack ads shrink and polarize the electorate*. New York: Free Press.

Ball-Rokeach, S., M. Rokeach, and J. W. Grube. 1984. *The great American values test: Influencing behavior and belief through television*. New York: Free Press.

Banerjee, A. V., S. Kumar, R. Pande, and F. Su. 2011. Do informed voters make better choices? Experimental evidence from urban India. Unpublished manuscript. MIT and Harvard.

Bedolla, L. G., and M. R. Michelson. (2012). *Mobilizing inclusion: Redefining citizenship through get-out-the-vote campaigns*: New Haven, CT: Yale University Press.

Bennion, E. A., and D. W. Nickerson. 2011. The cost of convenience: An experiment showing e-mail outreach decreases voter registration. *Political Research Quarterly*, 64(4), 858–869.

Berelson, B., P. F. Lazarsfeld, and W. N. McPhee. 1986. *Voting: A study of opinion formation in a presidential campaign*. Chicago: University of Chicago Press.

Blumenthal, M., C. Christian, and J. Slemrod. 2001. Do normative appeals affect tax compliance? Evidence from a controlled experiment in Minnesota. *National Tax Journal*, 54(1), 125–138.

Boruch, R. F. (Ed.). 2005. *Place randomized trials: Experimental tests of public policy*. Thousand Oaks, CA: Sage.

Boruch, R., H. May, H. Turner, J. Lavenberg, A. Petrosino, D. De Moya, J. Grimshaw, and E. Foley. 2004. Estimating the effects of interventions that are deployed in many places: Place-randomized trials. *American Behavioral Scientist*, 47(5), 608–633.

Brady, H. E., and P. M. Sniderman. 1985. Attitude attribution: A group basis for political reasoning. *The American Political Science Review*, 79(4), 1061–1078.

Broockman, D. E., and D. P. Green. 2014. Do online advertisements increase political candidates' name recognition or favorability? Evidence from randomized field experiments. *Political Behavior*, 36(2): 263–289.

Campbell, A. 1980. *The American voter*. Chicago: University of Chicago Press.

Chong, A., A. L. De La O, D. Karlan, and L. Wantchekon. 2011. Information dissemination and local governments' electoral returns: Evidence from a field experiment in Mexico. Unpublished manuscript, Yale University.

Converse, P. E. 1964. The nature of belief systems in mass politics. In D. Apter (Ed.), *Ideology and discontent* (pp. 206–261). New York: Free Press.

Delli Carpini, M. X., and S. Keeter. 1997. *What Americans know about politics and why it matters*. New Haven, CT: Yale University Press.

Fellner, G., R. Sausgruber, and C. Traxler. 2009. Testing enforcement strategies in the field: Legal threat, moral appeal and social information. Working Paper, Max Planck Institute for Research on Collective Goods.

Ferraz, C., and F. Finan. 2008. Exposing corrupt politicians: The effects of Brazil's publicly released audits on electoral outcomes. *Quarterly Journal of Economics*, 123(2), 703–745.

Fiorina, M. P. 1981. *Retrospective voting in American national elections*. New Haven, CT: Yale University Press.

Fowler, J. H., J. Settle, J. Jones, R. Bond, and C. J. Fariss. 2011. Social networks, the diffusion of political information, and political engagement. Western Political Science Association 2011 Annual Meeting Paper.

Freedman, P., M. Franz, and K. Goldstein. 2004. Campaign advertising and democratic citizenship. *American Journal of Political Science*, 48(4), 723–741.

Freedman, P., and K. Goldstein. 1999. Measuring media exposure and the effects of negative campaign ads. *American Journal of Political Science*, 43(4), 1189–1208.

Gerber, A., J. G. Gimpel, D. P. Green, and D. R. Shaw. 2011. How large and long-lasting are the persuasive effects of televised campaign ads? Results from a randomized field experiment. *American Political Science Review*, 105(1), 135–150.

Gerber, A. S., and D. P. Green. 1998. Rational learning and partisan attitudes. *American Journal of Political Science*, 42, 794–818.

Gerber, A. S., and D. P. Green. 2012. *Field experiments: Design, analysis and interpretation.* New York: W.W. Norton.

Gerber, A. S., D. P. Green, and M. Green. 2003. Partisan direct mail and voter turnout: Results from randomized field experiments. *Electoral Studies*, 22, 563–579.

Gerber, A. S., D. P. Green, and C. W. Larimer. 2008. Social pressure and voter turnout: Evidence from a large-scale field experiment. *American Political Science Review*, 102(1), 33–48.

Gerber, A. S., D. P. Green, and C. W. Larimer. 2010. An experiment testing the relative effectiveness of encouraging voter participation by inducing feelings of pride or shame. *Political Behavior,* 32(3), 409–422.

Goldstein, K., and P. Freedman. 2002. Campaign advertising and voter turnout: New evidence for a stimulation effect. *Journal of Politics,* 64(3), 721–740.

Green, D. P., B. R. Calfano, and P. M. Aronow. 2014. Field experimental designs for the study of media effects. *Political Communication* 31(1): 168–180.

Green, D. P., and A. S. Gerber. 2008. *Get out the vote! How to increase voter turnout* (2nd ed.). Washington, D.C.: Brookings Institution Press.

Green, D. P., and L. Vavreck. 2008. Analysis of cluster-randomized experiments: A comparison of alternative estimation approaches. *Political Analysis,* 16(2), 138–152.

Gross, A. E., M. J. Schmidt, J. P. Keating, and M. J. Saks. 1974. Persuasion, surveillance, and voting behavior. *Journal of Experimental Social Psychology,* 10(5), 451–460.

Johnston, R., M. G. Hagen, and K. H. Jamieson. 2004. *The 2000 presidential election and the foundations of party politics.* New York: Cambridge University Press.

Kleven, H., M. B. Knudsen, C. Kreiner, S. Pedersen, and E. Saez. 2010. *Unwilling or unable to cheat? Evidence from a randomized tax audit experiment in Denmark.* Cambridge, MA: National Bureau of Economic Research.

Lupia, A. 1994. Shortcuts versus encyclopedias: Information and voting behavior in California insurance reform elections. *American Political Science Review,* 88(1), 63–76.

Mann, C. B. 2010. Is there backlash to social pressure? A large-scale field experiment on voter mobilization. *Political Behavior,* 32(3), 387–407.

McClosky, H., and A. Brill. 1983. *Dimensions of tolerance: What Americans believe about civil liberties.* New York: Russell Sage Foundation.

Michelson, M. R., L. G. Bedolla, and M. A. McConnell. 2009. Heeding the call: The effect of targeted two-round phone banks on voter turnout. *Journal of Politics,* 71(4), 1549–1563.

Mullainathan, S., E. Washington, and J. R. Azari. 2010. The impact of electoral debate on public opinions: An experimental investigation of the 2005 New York City mayoral election. In I. Shapiro, S. C. Stokes, E. Wood, and A. S. Kirshner (Eds.), *Political representation* (pp. 329–341). New York: Cambridge University Press.

Nickerson, D. W., and T. Rogers. 2010. Do you have a voting plan? Implementation intentions, voter turnout, and organic plan making. *Psychological Science,* 21(2), 194–199.

Niven, D. 2006. A field experiment on the effects of negative campaign mail on voter turnout in a municipal election. *Political Research Quarterly,* 59(2), 203–210.

Olson, M. 1965. *The logic of collective action: Public goods and the theory of groups.* Cambridge, MA: Harvard University Press.

Page, B. I., and R. Y. Shapiro. 1983. Effects of public opinion on policy. *The American Political Science Review*, 77(1), 175–190.

Panagopoulos, C. 2010. Affect, social pressure and prosocial motivation: Field experimental evidence of the mobilizing effects of pride, shame and publicizing voting behavior. *Political Behavior*, 32, 369–386.

Panagopoulos, C. 2011. Thank you for voting: Gratitude expression and voter mobilization. *Journal of Politics*, 73, 707–717.

Panagopoulos, C., and D. P. Green. 2008. Field experiments testing the impact of radio advertisements on electoral competition. *American Journal of Political Science*, 52(1), 156–168.

Panagopoulos, C., and D. P. Green. 2011. Spanish-language radio advertisements and Latino voter turnout in the 2006 congressional elections: Field experimental evidence. *Political Research Quarterly*, 64(3), 588–599.

Patterson, T. E., and R. D. McClure. 1976. *The unseeing eye: The myth of television power in national politics*. New York: Putnam.

Romer, D., Kenski, K., Winneg, K., Adasiewicz, C., and Jamieson, K. H. 2006. *Capturing campaign dynamics, 2000 and 2004: The National Annenberg Election Survey*. Philadelphia: University of Pennsylvania Press.

Shaw, D. R., D. P. Green, J. G. Gimpel, and A. S. Gerber. 2012. Do robotic calls from credible sources influence voter turnout or vote choice? Evidence from a randomized field experiment. *Journal of Political Marketing*, 11, 231–245.

Sinclair, B., M. McConnell, and D. P. Green. 2012. Detecting spillover effects: Design and analysis of multilevel experiments. *American Journal of Political Science*, 56(4), 1055–1069.

Trivedi, N. 2005. The effect of identity-based GOTV direct mail appeals on the turnout of Indian Americans. *The Annals of the American Academy of Political and Social Science*, 601(1), 115–122.

Whiteley, P. F. 1988. The causal relationships between issues, candidate evaluations, party identification, and vote choice—the view from rolling thunder. *Journal of Politics*, 50(4), 961–984.

Political Communication and Cognition

CHAPTER 36

COMMUNICATION MODALITIES AND POLITICAL KNOWLEDGE

WILLIAM P. EVELAND JR. AND R. KELLY GARRETT

IMPORTANCE OF THE AREA

THEORIES of democracy commonly assume that citizens must be at least minimally informed on matters related to the functioning of government and candidates for office (see Delli Carpini and Keeter, 1996). To make government responsive to their interests, citizens must be aware of government actions and candidate characteristics. Thus, a lack of information—or the presence of misinformation—among citizens about political matters can threaten democracy. In fact, considerable empirical research suggests both that, by comparison to those who are less well-informed, well-informed individuals are better able to translate their self-interest into political influence through public opinion (Althaus, 1996; Delli Carpini and Keeter, 1996; Gilens, 2001) and that often election outcomes would differ if the public were fully informed (Bartels, 1996). Citizens who are more knowledgeable are also more likely to participate in politics (Verba, Schlozman, and Brady, 1995), although it is not clear whether knowledge causes participation or if the intention to participate motivates individuals to become informed. And, considerable evidence indicates having political knowledge may moderate many different types of media effects, generally reducing susceptibility to influence and increasing future learning (e.g., Zaller, 1992).

Despite the apparent benefits of political knowledge, there is considerable evidence that the American public is, on the whole, relatively uninformed (e.g., Delli Carpini and Keeter, 1996). Given the democratic role the media are presumed to play in providing information, some scholars have placed at least part of the blame for low levels of citizen knowledge on the news media and have suggested possible changes to the content or structure of news to increase public knowledge (e.g., Entman, 2010; Gans, 2003; Graber, 1994; Jamieson and Waldman, 2003).

On the other hand, it has also been noted that even if perfect and complete information were available, rational citizens do not have a strong incentive to devote the considerable time and effort required to become fully informed. Rather, they most commonly use simple information shortcuts to make political decisions (Popkin, 1991). And, some argue, much of the time these shortcuts are sufficient to lead to "correct" decisions—or that individual errors in decisions are random and thus cancel out at the collective level (Page and Shapiro, 1992; but see Althaus, 2003; Lau, Andersen, and Redlawsk, 2008).

Major Findings to Date

Historically, research on the role of political media use in producing political knowledge has generally followed a relatively simple direct effects empirical model (see Eveland, 2001). Scholars have typically posited that a given modality[1]—newspapers, for instance, or television news—carries some valuable political information. Individuals who were exposed to this information would, through some cognitive process that would often go undescribed or unmeasured, gain this information and be able to demonstrate it by responding accurately to factual knowledge questions. By pitting use of various modalities of news against one another in statistical models, much of the research on the role of news media in producing political knowledge follows this direct effects approach (e.g., Drew and Weaver, 2006; Robinson and Levy, 1996). When the use of a given modality has a statistically significant coefficient in such models, authors infer a "media effect"; when the coefficient is nonsignificant, they assume the absence of effect.

The bulk of this literature suggests that in the United States, the use of print newspapers is more strongly associated with political knowledge—even after various demographic and other controls—than is the use of television news. More recent research in this vein indicates that those who use news online (e.g., Kenski and Stroud, 2006), listen to political talk radio (e.g., Jamieson and Cappella, 2008), and watch late night political comedy programs such as "The Daily Show" (e.g., Baek and Wojcieszak, 2009) also tend to be more informed than those who do not. However, considerable debate remains regarding the relative effectiveness of each modality and the consistency of positive effects from any one. There is also some evidence that such simple cross-modality comparisons are inappropriate (e.g., Holbert, 2005). On the whole, however, there is strong and consistent evidence that use of news and other political content is at least moderately associated with holding higher levels of political knowledge. In short, use of news modalities matters for political knowledge.

Another important stream of scholarship has focused closely on how news messages are processed. For instance, experimental studies have considered the implications of specific news content components such as verbal-visual redundancy, negativity (e.g., Reese, 1984; Reeves, Newhagen, Maibach, Basil, and Kurz, 1991), or structural features (e.g., Eveland, 2003; Lang, Potter, and Grabe, 2003) on learning and information processing. Taking just one of these examples, research has demonstrated both that there is a considerable lack of redundancy in the verbal and visual components of television news, and that the lack of redundancy hinders learning (Brosius, Donsbach, and Birk, 1996; Reese, 1984). Studies such as these have made it possible for journalistic practitioners to understand the implications of very specific aspects of their news products for political learning, including the use of narrative, visual-verbal redundancy, and emotion (see Lang et al., 2003), and may lead to better designed news in the future. Moreover, many of these studies are driven by models of information processing that link specific content or structural characteristics to their information processing demands and the allocation of limited processing resources of the individual (see Lang, 2000).

Building on these and other information processing theories of learning from news, empirical extensions of the basic direct effects model have incorporated explicit measures of cognitive effort or attention paid to the content in attempts to acknowledge the role of information processing in learning (Chaffee and Schleuder, 1986; McLeod and McDonald, 1985). These efforts ultimately produced mediation models that explicitly incorporated causal links among variables such as motivations, media use, information processing, and political knowledge (Beaudoin and Thorson, 2004; Cho, Shah, McLeod, McLeod, Scholl, and Gotlieb, 2009; David, 2009; Eveland, 2001). For instance, the cognitive mediation model (Eveland, 2001) argues that individual motivations for news use (e.g., to make decisions or to share information in discussions) drive attention, elaboration, and other media-related information processing activities and holds that these activities directly predict knowledge acquisition. The communication mediation model (see Cho et al., 2009) suggests that background characteristics (e.g., social status) affect political knowledge by influencing use of news and political discussion—and sometimes cognitive processing as well—which then produces knowledge.

Originally devised as a structural theory of media effects, the knowledge gap hypothesis (Tichenor, Donohue, and Olien, 1970) proposed that as media information enters a social system, individuals in a structurally advantaged position—those of higher social status, typically measured by education level—are able to gain this information more quickly, and thus social inequities are renewed or even increased. This structural theory has produced research on the moderating role of variables such as education or motivation on the impact of media use on knowledge (Eveland and Scheufele, 2000; Kwak, 1999; Grabe, Kamhawi, and Yegiyan, 2009). Work has also considered the implications of variations in content availability on education-based knowledge gaps (e.g., Jerit, 2009; Jerit, Barabas, and Bolsen, 2006). These studies are important because they demonstrate that the learning effects of a given unit of exposure to news are not necessarily equal across individuals with different levels of formal education (and thus presumably cognitive skills) or who bring different motivations to the exposure setting. However, the evidence for the moderating effects of education and motivation is complex and often inconsistent across studies (see Liu and Eveland, 2005), possibly due to variations in the study context (e.g., timing of study, level of community conflict, and community structure), the news modality under study, and the measure of knowledge used or the political issue or context under study.

More recent theorizing and research have advanced our understanding of the role of news media in producing political knowledge. Holbert (2005), for instance, has argued for explicit modeling of "intramedia mediation," which is the complex indirect effect of the use of one news modality on political knowledge through its prompting of use of other news modalities. He persuasively argues that use of a given political modality (e.g., candidate debates) will tend to prompt the use of other political modalities (e.g., subsequent newspaper coverage). Therefore, traditional models that pit different political modalities against one another as predictors of knowledge likely underestimate media effects because they ignore the stimulative effect of one modality on others. Eveland, Hayes, Shah, and Kwak (2005a) extend Holbert's idea to what they term "intracommunication mediation" by noting the longstanding argument that news media use and discussion of politics may drive one another, with news use prompting discussion of politics and anticipation of political discussions stimulating news use.

In addition to news use begetting further news use and political discussion, and thus producing a series of multiple mediation paths between various political communication modalities and political knowledge, it is also likely that the implications of the use of any given news modality is in some way contingent on the use of other news modalities or political discussion. Scheufele (2002) argues that the effects of news use depend on—or, in statistical terms, are moderated by—discussion of politics, such that news effects are greater in the presence than in the absence of discussion. The notion is that through discussion complex news information is made more comprehendible, and its relevance to one's prior political knowledge is made more apparent, thus increasing learning and retention. The evidence for this proposition is mixed, and scholars are continuing to determine when discussion may amplify or mitigate news use effects depending on the modality, nature of knowledge measure, or characteristics of the discussion itself (e.g., Feldman and Price, 2008; Hardy and Scheufele, 2009; Lenart, 1994). However, the notion of differential gains has spawned further consideration of the possibly synergistic—or alternatively diminishing returns—effects of the use of various combinations of news or other political modalities use under the term "intramedia interaction" (Shen and Eveland, 2010). Shen and Eveland argue that various combinations of news use may complement one another—producing amplification effects (or what Scheufele would call "differential gains")—but redundant information across modalities could lead to diminishing returns of each additional modality used. In still other cases, in which information from multiple modalities are effectively independent, simple additive effects may occur.

Unanswered Questions

There are a number of important, but as of yet unanswered, questions in the literature on media and political knowledge. Possibly first and most fundamental, questions remain about the appropriate conceptualization and operationalization of political knowledge. This is important because effect magnitudes of various forms of media use have been shown to vary according to type of knowledge measure (e.g., Chaffee, Zhao, and Leshner, 1994; Eveland, Seo, and Marton, 2002). This critique has several components. First, it is not clear whether, how, or when political knowledge should be treated as general and unidimensional or as grouped into a series of specialized topics based on issue domains (see Krosnick, 1990). Second, it is not clear whether, how, or when political knowledge should be divided into factual (differentiation) and structural (integration) components (Eveland, Marton, and Seo, 2004; Neuman, 1981). Third, it is not clear how to select indicators of knowledge that are relevant to the current political context and media environment without being ad hoc and thus incomparable over time and across studies. Finally, it is not clear how to come to agreement on what amount or type of political knowledge is necessary or sufficient for citizens to be considered "competent" (Weissberg, 2001).

A second unanswered question relates to the conceptualization and measurement of news media use. News use is among the most influential means of acquiring political information and is a central concern among political communication scholars. Although decades ago the case was made that exposure measures may be incomparable across media forms and so attention measures should be included in media effects studies (Chaffee and Schleuder, 1986), the operationalization of news use across studies remains highly inconsistent, and these inconsistencies have demonstrable consequences for the interpretation of study results (see Eveland, Hutchens, and Shen, 2009). Given the foundational nature of the concept of news use, scholars need to continue measurement work to validate current measures of news use or to develop alternatives (e.g., Eveland et al., 2009; Prior, 2009).

Finally, only limited empirical research addresses matters of causality in this literature. To what extent is news use producing political knowledge versus knowledgeable individuals seeking out news? Despite recent research on causal influence (e.g., Eveland, Hayes, Shah, and Kwak, 2005b; Strömbäck and Shehata, 2010), the causal connections among news use, political knowledge, and other variables such as political interest and political participation still remain at least somewhat ambiguous.

FUTURE DIRECTIONS

What has received insufficient attention until recently is an explicit model of how the sequential or contemporaneous use of media modalities (and interpersonal communication) may affect learning of political information. Attention to this process is particularly important in the changing political and media environment of the past two decades. During this time we have seen the rise of political talk radio and political comedy programs, the broad diffusion of the Internet—including online news and fact-checking websites as well as blogs and other forms of interactive online communication regarding politics—and a growing degree of partisan specialization, especially among cable news sources and blogs. We are also witnessing media convergence. People are increasingly reliant on computers and mobile phones for the delivery of political news, and these conduits tend to blur the lines among media produced for traditional delivery channels such as newspaper, radio, or television. Digital delivery also allows the inter-linking of content, facilitating seamless shifts across content types. Meanwhile, survey evidence indicates that rather than selecting a single modality for news, most individuals are exposed to multiple sources across multiple media forms (e.g., Kohut, Doherty, Dimock, and Keeter, 2010). Moreover, the political environment is changing, with greater partisanship and more clear alignment of parties and the public (e.g., Abramowitz, 2010). These trends have made simple, direct effect models of media effects on political knowledge inadequate, if they ever were so.

The changing political and information environment requires a reconsideration of fundamental assumptions about the relationship between news media use and political knowledge. The normative ideal for democracy resides in an uncontested (and consistent with the best available evidence) media environment producing accurate political knowledge in the public via learning from exposure to the news. Most prior research on learning from the news has assumed that the news conveys a relatively consistent, uncontested, and factually accurate portrait of political reality which audience members merely needed to recall, or possibly place in larger context, in order for political knowledge to be reproduced. This assumption may have been correct for the bulk of political information under consideration in the latter half of the twentieth century. For instance, the national broadcast news media were dominated by a few networks, all generally adhering to norms of balance and objectivity and covering the same topics in largely the same ways (e.g., Stempel, 1988). And, during the latter half of the twentieth century the vast majority of American cities were served by only a single daily newspaper rather than competing partisan papers as had been more common in the past (Busterna, 1988). Moreover, competing local television news stations did not differ considerably in the content of their coverage (Atwater, 1986). Today, however, the news media are more frequently characterized by divergent and contested political claims, at least at the national level (e.g., Holtzman, Schott, Jones, Balota, and Yarkoni, 2011).

What are the implications of the changing media environment for models of learning from the news and our conception of our "political knowledge" outcome variable? We begin by deriving insights into what may have been considered anomalies according to the old assumptions of political learning from the news. What happens when a particular news source "gets it wrong" and provides inaccurate information or information that could be misleading? Research on learning from conservative political talk radio (Hofstetter, Barker, Smith, Zari, and Ingrassia, 1999), news effects on racial beliefs (Dixon, 2008), and news effects on beliefs about the solvency of the Social Security system (Jerit and Barabas, 2006) all demonstrate that a simple factual learning model applied to inaccurate or misleading content can produce learning of inaccurate information among those more often exposed to the source. This should not be surprising; citizens can just as easily learn "wrong" information as they can learn "right" information from the media. But, given longstanding assumptions about the broad accuracy and consistency of news information among political learning scholars, this possibility has most often been ignored.

Exposure to news will produce consistent increases in factual political knowledge across a population only if the content of the news is undisputed and is viewed as unambiguously accurate. As information accuracy becomes more contested across sources, as it has in the current media environment, the citizenry's trust in the "facts" is replaced by individual judgment, and factual uncertainty (due to equivocal information) and inaccuracy are likely to rise. Judgment processes (versus simple recall) have not traditionally been part of models of media influence on political knowledge because they begin to blur the lines between learning of factual information and models of belief and attitude formation. They are, however, increasingly important. Faced with competing claims about political reality, individuals must integrate evaluation into the political learning process. This helps explain how citizens' understanding of political facts can diverge even as their exposure to political information increases. Thus, differences in beliefs between liberals and conservatives about weapons of mass destruction in Iraq (see World Public Opinion, 2006) presumably reflect differences in judgments concerning which information is most relevant and which sources are most trustworthy.

The nature of these judgments is controversial. Many scholars argue that polarization of beliefs across party lines is due to partisan biases in news exposure and interpretation (e.g., Bartels, 2002). This is consistent with evidence that individuals not only seek out information that confirms their prior beliefs but also counterargue information that challenges them (e.g., Taber and Lodge, 2006). Partisan biases are not, however, required to produce short-term divergence in political beliefs (Bullock, 2009). Instead, political learning can be understood as a series of Bayesian updates based on the perceived likelihood that new information is accurate (Gerber and Green, 1999). From this view, use of multiple sources of news (e.g., Fox News and the New York Times) can lead to exposure to competing factual claims, which reduces confidence in the veracity of incoming information, thereby increasing the relative influence of prior beliefs. Whether judgments are biased or not, in the presence of competing factual claims the learning process can no longer be modeled as the recall of uncontested facts. Rather, it must be understood as a process of judging and weighing competing evidence and claims.

Different credibility perceptions can also induce de facto partisan exposure biases, which could exacerbate the tendency of partisans to understand the political world differently. For instance, a preference for sources deemed more credible could lead people to adopt more ideologically homogeneous media diets. This is because credibility perceptions favor ideologically aligned sources (Turner, 2007), due in part to individuals' tendency to be more trusting of pro-attitudinal than counter-attitudinal information (Lord, Ross, and Lepper, 1979). As a consequence, we might expect that conservatives rely most heavily on Fox News and its ilk, whereas liberals turn to MSNBC and its ilk. But partisan selective exposure is likely to be imperfect and incomplete in such a diverse media environment (Garrett, 2009). In a media environment that is contested, and when partisan selective exposure does not entirely eliminate exposure to competing facts and interpretation, individuals must engage in probabilistic judgments of information accuracy in conjunction with simple recall in order to come to objective "accurate" knowledge. And, in many cases this process may produce inaccurate "knowledge" that is "learned" from the media, thus raising questions about the implied isomorphism between the notions of "learning from the news" and "gaining accurate political knowledge from the news." Rather, learning from the news may produce a set of probabilistic political beliefs that may or may not be accurate, depending on the quality of the media content to which an individual chooses to be exposed.

One important implication of partisan divergence in beliefs about factual information is that some individuals' views will become less accurate over time. Although political misperceptions can arise for a variety of reasons, those that arise from uncertainty generated by contested information environments may be the hardest to unseat. People have a variety of defenses against purposeful deception (see Harrington, 2009), and fact-checking by the news media can have corrective effects when these defenses fall short. But, the less individuals trust the news media, the less influence the information delivered by news organizations will have. When confidence in the accuracy of political information stored in memory is high, or when confidence in novel input is low, individuals are much less likely to update the stored information—in this case, to learn the correction—than when the reverse is true.

The literature today offers threads of theorizing that can be woven into a model of learning from the news that accounts for the altered political and media environment and changes in the way individuals must process mediated information. Hindman (2009) argues that the knowledge gap could be suitably reframed as the "belief gap," such that with increasing media information partisans diverge in their beliefs on polarized topics such as global warming, independent of objective reality. Although the mechanism remains unclear, this logic could be extended to much of the research on political knowledge. Understanding of how individuals arrive at probabilistic accuracy judgments can be informed by work on partisanship-motivated bias (e.g., Taber and Lodge, 2006) and by less politically colored factors. For example, the ease with which thoughts about a novel claim come to mind significantly influences the claim's perceived accuracy (Schwarz et al., 2007).

Holbert (2005) makes explicit the need to consider how use of one news modality may prompt use of another, and fact-checking may be one reason for this prompt. In today's environment, this could mean following a link on a partisan blog to the original article on the *New York Times* website (see Eveland and Dylko, 2007), picking up the morning paper after hearing a story on talk radio during the drive to work, or doing a Google search for further information on a topic mentioned in the evening network news (e.g., Weeks and Southwell, 2010). Much of this searching could be viewed as a form of fact-checking in which improbable or ambiguous information from one source could increase its perceived probability of accuracy through replication across sources, including more trusted or partisanship-consistent sources. And although not framed in the context of partisan differences, the intramedia interaction hypothesis (Shen and Eveland, 2010) and the differential gains hypothesis (Scheufele, 2002) both suggest that use of combinations of sources that are non-redundant—whether they are multiple media sources or a mix of media and interpersonal sources—can increase, decrease, or not affect the amount of accurate information gain from a single one of those sources. It would seem that from the partisan perspective, inconsistent information across sources could increase uncertainty about a given fact, whereas consistent information across sources would make learning much more likely.

NOTE

1. We define modality here as the intersection of medium of communication (i.e., television, print, radio) and genre or form (e.g., talk radio vs. radio news, magazine vs. newspaper, blog vs. online news article). We note that both content and form can vary across modalities, and so that any modality is composed of a "mix of attributes" that define it (Eveland, 2003).

REFERENCES

Abramowitz, A. I. 2010. *The disappearing center: Engaged citizens, polarization, and American democracy.* New Haven, CT: Yale University Press.

Althaus, S. 1996. Opinion polls, information effects, and political equality: Exploring ideological biases in collective opinion. *Political Communication, 13,* 3–21.

Althaus, S. L. 2003. *Collective preferences in democratic politics: Opinion surveys and the will of the people.* New York: Cambridge University Press.

Atwater, T. 1986. Consonance in local television news. *Journal of Broadcasting & Electronic Media, 30,* 467–472.

Baek, Y. M., and Wojcieszak, M. E. 2009. Don't expect too much! Learning from late night comedy and knowledge item difficulty. *Communication Research, 36,* 783–809.

Bartels, L. M. 1996. Uninformed votes: Information effects in presidential elections. *American Journal of Political Science, 40,* 194–230.

Bartels, L. M. 2002. Beyond the running tally: Partisan bias in political perceptions. *Political Behavior, 24,* 117–150.

Beaudoin, C. E., and Thorson, E. 2004. Testing the cognitive mediation model: The role of news reliance and three gratifications sought. *Communication Research, 31,* 446–471.

Brosius, H-B., Donsbach, W., and Birk, M. 1996. How do text-picture relations affect the informational effectiveness of television newscasts? *Journal of Broadcasting & Electronic Media, 40,* 180–195.

Bullock, J. G. 2009. Partisan bias and the Bayesian ideal in the study of public opinion. *Journal of Politics, 71,* 1109–1124.

Busterna, J. C. 1988. Trends in daily newspaper ownership. *Journalism Quarterly, 65,* 831–838.

Chaffee, S. H., and Schleuder, J. 1986. Measurement and effects of attention to media news. *Human Communication Research, 13,* 76–107.

Chaffee, S. H., Zhao, X., and Leshner, G. 1994. Political knowledge and the campaign media of 1992. *Communication Research, 21,* 305–324.

Cho, J., Shah, D. V., McLeod, J. M., McLeod, D. M., Scholl, R. M., and Gotlieb, M. R. 2009. Campaigns, reflection, and deliberation: Advancing an O-S-R-O-R model of communication effects. *Communication Theory, 19,* 66–88.

David, C. C. 2009. Learning political information from the news: A closer look at the role of motivation. *Journal of Communication,* 59, 243–261.

Delli Carpini, M. X., and Keeter, S. 1996. *What Americans know about politics and why it matters.* New Haven, CT: Yale University Press.

Dixon, T. L. 2008. Network news and racial beliefs: Exploring the connection between national television news exposure and stereotypical perceptions of African Americans. *Journal of Communication,* 58, 321–337.

Drew, D., and Weaver, D. 2006. Voter learning in the 2004 presidential election: Did the media matter? *Journalism & Mass Communication Quarterly,* 83, 25–42.

Entman, R. M. 2010. Improving newspapers' economic prospects by augmenting their contributions to democracy. *International Journal of Press/Politics,* 15, 104–125.

Eveland, W. P., Jr. 2001. The cognitive mediation model of learning from the news: Evidence from nonelection, off-year election, and presidential election contexts. *Communication Research,* 28, 571–601.

Eveland, W. P., Jr. 2003. A "mix of attributes" approach to the study of media effects and new communication technologies. *Journal of Communication,* 53, 395–410.

Eveland, W. P., Jr., and Dylko, I. 2007. Reading political blogs during the 2004 election campaign: Correlates and consequences. In M. Tremayne (Ed.), *Blogging, citizenship and the future of media* (pp. 105–126). New York: Routledge.

Eveland, W. P., Jr., Hayes, A. F., Shah, D. V., and Kwak, N. 2005a. Observations on estimation of communication effects on political knowledge and a test of intracommunication mediation. *Political Communication,* 22, 505–509.

Eveland, W. P., Jr., Hayes, A. F., Shah, D. V., and Kwak, N. 2005b. Understanding the relationship between communication and political knowledge: A model-comparison approach using panel data. *Political Communication,* 22, 423–446.

Eveland, W. P., Jr., Hutchens, M. J., and Shen, F. 2009. Exposure, attention, or "use" of news? Assessing aspects of the reliability and validity of a central concept in political communication research. *Communication Methods and Measures,* 3, 223–244.

Eveland, W. P., Jr., Marton, K., and Seo, M. 2004. Moving beyond "just the facts": The influence of online news on the content and structure of public affairs knowledge. *Communication Research,* 31, 82–108.

Eveland, W. P., Jr., and Scheufele, D. A. 2000. Connecting news media use with gaps in knowledge and participation. *Political Communication,* 17, 215–237.

Eveland, W. P., Jr., Seo, M., and Marton, K. 2002. Learning from the news in campaign 2000: An experimental comparison of TV news, newspapers and online news. *Media Psychology,* 4, 352–378.

Feldman, L., and Price, V. 2008. Confusion or enlightenment? How exposure to disagreement moderates the effects of political discussion and media use on candidate knowledge. *Communication Research,* 35, 61–87.

Gans, H. J. 2003. *Democracy and the news.* New York: Oxford University Press.

Garrett, R. K. 2009. Politically motivated reinforcement seeking: Reframing the selective exposure debate. *Journal of Communication,* 59, 676–699.

Gerber, A., and Green, D. 1999. Misperceptions about perceptual bias. *Annual Review of Political Science,* 2, 189–210.

Gilens, M. 2001. Political ignorance and collective policy preferences. *American Political Science Review,* 95, 379–396.

Grabe, M. E., Kamhawi, R., and Yegiyan, N. 2009. Informing citizens: How people with differ-ent levels of education process television, newspaper, and Web news. *Journal of Broadcasting & Electronic Media*, 53, 90–111.

Graber, D. A. 1994. Why voters fail information tests: Can the hurdles be overcome? *Political Communication*, 11, 331–346.

Hardy, B. W., and Scheufele, D. A. 2009. Presidential campaign dynamics and the ebb and flow of talk as a moderator: Media exposure, knowledge, and political discussion. *Communication Theory*, 19, 89–101.

Harrington, B. 2009. *Deception: From ancient empires to Internet dating*. Stanford, CA: Stanford University Press.

Hindman, D. B. 2009. Mass media flow and differential distribution of politically disputed beliefs: The belief gap hypothesis. *Journalism & Mass Communication Quarterly*, 86, 790–808.

Hofstetter, C. R., Barker, D., Smith, J., Zari, G. M., and Ingrassia, T. A. 1999. Information, mis-information, and political talk radio. *Political Research Quarterly*, 52, 353–369.

Holbert, R. L. 2005. Intramedia mediation: The cumulative and complementary effects of news media use. *Political Communication*, 22, 447–461.

Holtzman, N. S., Schott, J. P., Jones, M. N., Balota, D. A., and Yarkoni, T. 2011. Exploring media bias with semantic analysis tools: Validation of the Contrast Analysis of Semantic Similarity (CASS). *Behavior Research Methods*, 43, 193–200.

Jamieson, K. H., and Cappella, J. N. 2008. *Echo chamber: Rush Limbaugh and the conservative media establishment*. New York: Oxford University Press.

Jamieson, K. H., and Waldman, P. 2003. *The press effect: Politicians, journalists, and the stories that shape the political world*. New York: Oxford University Press.

Jerit, J. 2009. Understanding the knowledge gap: The role of experts and journalists. *Journal of Politics*, 71, 442–456.

Jerit, J., and Barabas, J. 2006. Bankrupt rhetoric: How misleading information affects knowl-edge about social security. *Public Opinion Quarterly*, 70, 278–303.

Jerit, J., Barabas, J., and Bolsen, T. 2006. Citizens, knowledge, and the information environ-ment. *American Journal of Political Science*, 50, 266–282.

Kenski, K., and Stroud, N. J. 2006. Connections between Internet use and political efficacy, knowledge, and participation. *Journal of Broadcasting & Electronic Media*, 50, 173–192.

Kohut, A., Doherty, C., Dimock, M., and Keeter, S. 2010. *Americans spending more time follow-ing the news—Ideological news sources: Who watches and why*. Washington, DC: The Pew Research Center for the People & the Press. Retrieved from http://people-press.org/files/legacy-pdf/652.pdf

Krosnick, J. A. 1990. Lessons learned: A review and integration of our findings. *Social Cognition*, 8, 154–158.

Kwak, N. 1999. Revisiting the knowledge gap hypothesis: Education, motivation, and media use. *Communication Research*, 26, 385–413.

Lang, A. 2000. The limited capacity model of mediated message processing. *Journal of Communication*, 50(1), 46–70.

Lang, A., Potter, D., and Grabe, M. E. 2003. Making news memorable: Applying theory to the production of local television news. *Journal of Broadcasting & Electronic Media*, 47, 113–123.

Lau, R. R., Andersen, D. J., and Redlawsk, D. P. 2008. An exploration of correct voting in recent U.S. presidential elections. *American Journal of Political Science*, 52, 395–411.

Lenart, S. 1994. *Shaping political attitudes: The impact of interpersonal communication and mass media*. Thousand Oaks, CA: Sage.

Liu, Y., and Eveland, W. P., Jr. 2005. Education, need for cognition, and campaign interest as moderators of news effects on political knowledge: An analysis of the knowledge gap. *Journalism & Mass Communication Quarterly*, 82, 910–929.

Lord, C. G., Ross, L., and Lepper, M. R. 1979. Biased assimilation and attitude polarization: The effects of prior theories on subsequently considered evidence. *Journal of Personality and Social Psychology*, 37, 2098–2109.

McLeod, J. M., and McDonald, D. G. 1985. Beyond simple exposure: Media orientations and their impact on political processes. *Communication Research*, 12, 3–33.

Neuman, W. R. 1981. Differentiation and integration: Two dimensions of political thinking. *American Journal of Sociology*, 86, 1236–1268.

Page, B. I., and Shapiro, R. Y. 1992. *The rational public: Fifty years of trends in Americans' policy preferences*. Chicago: University of Chicago Press.

Popkin, S. L. 1991. *The reasoning voter: Communication and persuasion in presidential campaigns*. Chicago: University of Chicago Press.

Prior, M. 2009. Improving media effects research through better measurement of news exposure. *Journal of Politics*, 71, 893–908.

Reese, S. D. 1984. Visual-verbal redundancy effects on television news learning. *Journal of Broadcasting*, 28, 79–87.

Reeves, B. R., Newhagen, J., Maibach, E., Basil, M., and Kurz, K. 1991. Negative and positive television messages: Effects of message type and context on attention and memory. *American Behavioral Scientist*, 34, 679–694.

Robinson, J. P., and Levy, M. R. 1996. News media use and the informed public: A 1990s update. *Journal of Communication*, 46(2), 129–135.

Scheufele, D. A. 2002. Examining differential gains from mass media and their implications for participatory behavior. *Communication Research*, 29, 46–65.

Schwarz, N., Sanna, L. J., Skurnik, I., and Yoon, C. 2007. Metacognitive experiences and the intricacies of setting people straight: Implications for debiasing and public information campaigns. In M. P. Zanna (Ed.), *Advances in experimental social psychology* (Vol. 39, pp. 127–161). New York: Academic Press.

Shen, F., and Eveland, W. P., Jr. 2010. Testing the intramedia interaction hypothesis: The contingent effects of news. *Journal of Communication*, 60, 364–387.

Stempel, G. H., III. 1988. Topic and story choice of five network newscasts. *Journalism Quarterly*, 65, 750–752.

Strömbäck, J., and Shehata, A. 2010. Media malaise or a virtuous circle? Exploring the causal relationship between news media exposure, political news attention and political interest. *European Journal of Political Research*, 49, 575–597.

Taber, C. S., and Lodge, M. 2006. Motivated skepticism in the evaluation of political beliefs. *American Journal of Political Science*, 50, 755–769.

Tichenor, P. J., Donohue, G. A., and Olien, C. N. 1970. Mass media flow and differential growth in knowledge. *Public Opinion Quarterly*, 34, 159–170.

Turner, J. 2007. The messenger overwhelming the message: Ideological cues and perceptions of bias in television news. *Political Behavior*, 29, 441–464.

Verba, S., Schlozman, K. L., and Brady, H. E. 1995. *Voice and equality: Civic voluntarism in American politics*. Cambridge, MA: Harvard University Press.

Weeks, B., and Southwell, B. 2010. The symbiosis of news coverage and aggregate online search behavior: Obama, rumors, and presidential politics. *Mass Communication & Society,* 13, 341–360.

Weissberg, R. 2001. Democratic political competence: Clearing the underbrush and a controversial proposal. *Political Behavior,* 23, 257–284.

World Public Opinion. 2006. *Percentage of Americans believing Iraq had WMD rises.* Washington, DC: World Public Opinion: Program on International Policy Attitudes.

Zaller, J. R. 1992. *The nature and origins of mass opinion.* New York: Cambridge University Press.

CHAPTER 37

....

SELECTIVE EXPOSURE THEORIES

....

NATALIE JOMINI STROUD

CITIZENS do not have the time, energy, desire, or ability to look at everything. Why do we gravitate toward some messages, some individuals, and some media and not to others? Investigations of selective exposure aim to provide some insight. Selective exposure is the motivated selection of messages matching one's beliefs. The availability of so many choices makes selectivity likely in the modern communication environment. This chapter is dedicated to summarizing what we know—and what we don't know—about what messages we select, why we select them, and what the consequences are.

IMPORTANCE OF SELECTIVE EXPOSURE
....

The concept of selective exposure can be traced to the 1940 presidential campaign, when Lazarsfeld, Berelson, and Gaudet (1948) noticed that partisans encountered congenial more often than uncongenial information. This observation in many ways previewed what has become the most frequently cited rationale for selective exposure, Festinger's (1957) cognitive dissonance theory. Festinger theorized that the selection of like-minded information could help people to reduce cognitive dissonance, an undesirable feeling that can arise when one has contradictory cognitions. Those experiencing dissonance are not expected to seek consonant information in all instances. When they are inundated with information contradicting their views, for example, people may forgo their original view instead of trying to bolster it with congenial information selection. When faced with moderate dissonance, however, Festinger believed selective exposure would result.

Early research on selective exposure built on Festinger's theory to explore the conditions under which it occurred (e.g., Abelson et al., 1968; Festinger, 1964). Research explored whether views held with a high degree of certainty, for example, would inspire less selective exposure than those less confidently held (Festinger, 1964). In the field of communication, selective exposure became a common explanation for why scholars had not uncovered more evidence of powerful media effects. According to this explanation, because people typically encountered like-minded perspectives, the media mainly reinforced attitudes rather than changed them (Klapper, 1960). In the mid-1960s, after nearly a decade of research on dissonance and selective exposure, reviews of the literature revealed mixed evidence, at best, of a preference for like-minded information (Freedman and Sears, 1965; Sears and Freedman, 1967). At least in part because of these critical reviews, research on selective exposure waned.

Selective exposure research was uncommon during the 1970s and 1980s. In the mid-1980s, however, several scholars advocated for a return to the intriguing hypothesis. Cotton (1985) and Frey (1986), for example, proposed that a number of methodological flaws may have been responsible for an inconsistent pattern of findings in earlier research. They called for more attention to moderators of selective exposure.

With a particular uptick over the past decade, selective exposure has received renewed research attention. The explosion of media choices (cable, Internet) has led to provocative theses about the possibility that the contemporary media environment may provide ideal conditions for selective exposure (Sunstein, 2001). Recent meta-analyses also document the existence of a selective exposure effect (D'Alessio and Allen, 2002; Hart et al., 2009). Although selective exposure is a phenomenon that extends beyond political communication research, stronger selective exposure effects have been found for political topics (Hart et al., 2009), making this subject especially relevant for this handbook.

MAJOR RESEARCH FINDINGS

Major findings about selective exposure can be divided into three categories: explanations of why selective exposure occurs, types of selective exposure, and moderators of selective exposure. I review each in turn.

Why Selective Exposure Occurs

Numerous explanations have been provided for why citizens may be motivated to select congenial messages. Below, I provide an overview of five different possibilities. The first and earliest explanation for selective exposure has been mentioned already: cognitive dissonance. Festinger (1957) proposed that when cognitions conflict, an individual can experience the highly undesirable state of cognitive dissonance. Selective exposure is one of several tools at an individual's disposal to reduce the dissonant state.

The second explanation is that motivations beyond cognitive dissonance prompt the seeking of supportive information. Kunda's (1990) theory of motivated reasoning suggests that people can be moved to select messages by accuracy goals and by directional goals. Those driven by directional goals should be more likely to seek like-minded information. Research by Kim (2007) provides support for the idea that accuracy and directional goals inspire different patterns of information search. Kruglanski's (1989) theory of lay epistemics also proposes that certain motivations will inspire a preference for congenial information. According to this theory, those wanting to reach a specific conclusion, such as that a certain candidate is the best choice, should engage in selective exposure.

A third explanation is that selective exposure occurs because processing like-minded information requires less cognitive effort than processing uncongenial information. According to this idea, citizens may engage in selective exposure because it is cognitively easier (Ziemke, 1980).

A fourth explanation is that moods and emotions can affect information search. In particular, moods can influence the selection of information such that negative moods enhance selective exposure (Jonas, Graupmann, and Frey, 2006). Emotions such as anger and fear also affect selective exposure—with respect to information about the economy, anger and fear may prompt different patterns of selective exposure (Kim, 2010). Valentino et al. (2009) also document that emotions affect information search. They refine this idea, however, by showing that anxiety sparks more balanced search when individuals expect that they will be asked to defend their views as opposed to when individuals do not have this expectation.

A fifth explanation for the occurrence of selective exposure is that people may make information selections based on their judgments about informational quality. High-quality information will be preferred over that which is of low quality. Quality judgments may be influenced, however, by one's beliefs (Fischer, Schulz-Hardt, and Frey, 2008). Selective exposure may occur, therefore, because people believe that like-minded information is high-quality information.

Although research suggests that all of these explanations can help us to understand why selective exposure occurs, we do not presently know which one best accounts for its occurrence. Several of these mechanisms may operate in concert or different explanations may account for selective exposure in different circumstances. Some have begun designing critical tests that pit one explanation against another. Fischer, Schulz-Hardt, and Frey (2008), for example, evaluate whether the dissonance, conservation of cognitive resources, or information quality explanation best accounts for why having many options yields higher levels of selective exposure than having fewer of them. Their results suggest that information quality is the best explanation in this case, but because they tested only a subset of possible explanations and looked only at these explanations in relation to the number of options provided to a subject, more research is needed.

Types of Selective Exposure

Selective exposure occurs in many different forms. One way to organize this literature is to examine the types of beliefs that motivate exposure. Below, I review four types of selective exposure that have been emphasized in recent literature: the selection of (1) news or entertainment, (2) messages about different issues, (3) a certain medium (e.g., the Internet), and (4) like-minded messages. The last type is most classically connected with selective exposure. The other types, however, also may be prompted by the cognitive and motivational mechanisms outlined earlier. For example, watching the news if it is not of interest may arouse dissonance. To avoid dissonance, these individuals may avoid the news. Further, sources covering issues seen as *un*important may be perceived as lower quality sources. This may lead people to spend more time with outlets covering issues perceived as important.

The first type of selective exposure examines whether people will opt for news or for entertainment when given the choice. When cable television diffused, the additional television channel options gave unengaged citizens more opportunities to avoid watching presidential speeches and debates (Baum and Kernell, 1999). The increased choice provided by cable enabled citizens to switch to entertainment if they so desired during these political moments. Prior's (2007) extensive research confirms that as media choice has increased owing to cable television and the Internet, citizens have been empowered to avoid the news. Prior's measure of "relative entertainment preference" shows that those preferring entertainment can and do opt out of news exposure when they have access to more media options.

The second type of selective exposure looks at which issues motivate people to gather more information. Some citizens are members of issue publics or groups finding certain issues to be particularly important (Converse, 1964). These citizens select information relevant to their issue-public membership more frequently than information about other issues. Healthcare workers, for example, are more likely than others to read healthcare information (Iyengar et al., 2008). Those finding an issue personally important tend to select more information on the issue versus those who do not find the issue as important (Kim, 2009).

The third type of selective exposure places less emphasis on the *content* selected and more emphasis on the chosen *medium*. In particular, some hypothesize that because the Internet allows more choice, people prefer to go online for information when they disagree with or do not trust the reportage in more mainstream outlets (Best, Chmielewski, and Krueger, 2005; Hwang et al., 2006; Tsfati and Cappella, 2003).

The fourth type of selective exposure that has received attention is the degree to which citizens choose like-minded political information. In interpersonal contexts, people tend to discuss politics with those with whom they already agree (Mutz, 2006), although there has been some debate regarding how frequently people encounter disagreement (Huckfeldt and Mendez, 2008; Mutz, 2006). In the contemporary media environment, some outlets are recognized as left- and right-leaning. Partisans are more likely to select like-minded media outlets (Hollander, 2008; Iyengar and Hahn, 2009; Morris, 2005; Stroud, 2008, 2011). People also favor information consistent with their views on political issues, such as abortion, affirmative action, and gun ownership (Knobloch-Westerwick and Meng, 2009; Taber and Lodge, 2006).

To this point, I have categorized selective exposure based on the sorts of beliefs motivating exposure. Similar approaches have been taken by others, such as Bennett and Iyengar (2008). Yet there are other ways of parsing the literature that prove useful in highlighting different aspects of the phenomenon. First, we could distinguish between mediated and interpersonal selective exposure. Mutz and Martin (2001) embarked on just such an endeavor with interesting results: People encountered more diverse political views through their media use than in their interpersonal interactions. The authors anticipated that as media choices increased, however, people might encounter less diversity in the media. Indeed, in the years since their data were collected in the 1990s, there have been considerable changes in the media environment. Second, selective exposure could be divided depending on the nature of the choice—whether people are making a one-time selection from different articles or are habitually turning to a source for news and information. These selections require different levels of commitment—a variable that featured prominently in early work on cognitive dissonance (Abelson et al., 1968; Brehm and Cohen, 1962; Festinger, 1964). Reading an article or browsing a website requires little dedication. A habit of relying on a particular source demonstrates a greater commitment. Organizing the literature in this way may reveal different patterns of selective exposure.

Moderators of Selective Exposure

Through the years, many moderators of selective exposure have been examined. Rather than attempting to review all the possibilities, I provide several examples of prominent and recently analyzed moderators. These can be organized in various ways; I propose two categories below: individual characteristics and environmental characteristics.

Individual characteristics can affect the extent to which people seek congenial information. Some characteristics enhance selective exposure. As previewed earlier, the certainty with which an individual holds a position moderates selective exposure. Although there has been some debate as to whether certainty will increase or decrease selective exposure (Festinger, 1964), several recent studies have found that certainty enhances it (Knobloch-Westerwick and Meng, 2009; Ziemke, 1980). Strongly held attitudes also motivate greater selective exposure than weaker ones (Brannon, Tagler, and Eagly, 2007; Stroud, 2010). Another characteristic affecting selective exposure is political knowledge. The politically knowledgeable are more likely to select politically like-minded media sources (Stroud, 2011; Taber and Lodge, 2006). Mortality salience, making people think about their deaths, enhances selective exposure in some cases (Jonas, Greenberg, and Frey, 2003; Lavine, Lodge, and Freitas, 2005). Other variables have been shown to reduce selective exposure, such as defensive confidence (Albarracín and Mitchell, 2004) and need for cognition (Tsfati and Cappella, 2005).

In addition to individual characteristics, environmental ones also affect selective exposure. Message content, for example, can affect it. Information utility has been proposed as one reason that some studies have not shown evidence of selective exposure—information perceived as useful may be selected more frequently whether it is congenial or not (Frey, 1986). Indeed, research does show that informational utility does prompt more exposure to online news (Knobloch, Carpentier, and Zillmann, 2003) and can override a bias for confirmatory information (Knobloch-Westerwick and Kleinman, 2012). The nature of one's choice also matters. When given more options from which to choose, people have greater opportunity to cater to their preferences. For example, those with a preference for entertainment are more likely to select entertainment as opposed to news when they have more options (Prior, 2007). People also are more likely to select like-minded information when given more choices (Fischer, Schulz-Hardt, and Frey, 2008). Constraints on how people select information also can affect selective exposure. When information is presented sequentially, as opposed to simultaneously, selective exposure is enhanced (Jonas et al., 2001). It also is heightened when people are limited in how much information they can select (Fischer, Jonas, Frey, and Schulz-Hardt, 2005). Beyond the messages and the nature of the choice, the presence of a group can influence selective exposure. More homogeneous groups are more prone to select like-minded information (Schulz-Hardt et al., 2000).

EMPIRICAL APPROACHES

A number of different empirical approaches have been utilized in the study of selective exposure. The increasing use of technology and improvements in experimental design promise new insights. Below, I describe four different approaches. The first two have been used since selective exposure was formally introduced in the 1950s. The latter two have been used more extensively recently.

Self-Report Studies

Self-report studies typically analyze the relationship between message content and the beliefs of the audience. This method is not ideally suited to show that people have a pref-erence for information matching their beliefs because of the presence of rival explana-tions (Freedman and Sears, 1965; Sears and Freedman, 1967). For example, people may encounter more like-minded information not because they prefer it but because they happen to encounter it in their environment. This is known as *de facto selective exposure*. Temporal order also is a question—do attitudes predict media exposure or vice versa? Studies that incorporate an over-time component allow for an examination of this issue (Slater, 2007; Sweeney and Gruber, 1984).

Measurement in self-report studies can be done in more or less direct ways. Some examine the correlation between participants' stated beliefs and their self-reported media exposure (Sweeney and Gruber, 1984). Others directly ask respondents the extent to which they prefer like-minded information (Johnson, Bichard, and Zhang, 2009). More work is needed to validate these approaches.

Laboratory Studies

Quasiexperiments whereby all participants are given access to the same political choices and asked to make a selection have shown a preference for like-minded sources (Chaffee and McLeod, 1973; Knobloch-Westerwick and Meng, 2009) and messages about issues of interest (Kim 2009). Experiments have varied the source of information and found that sources attract ideologically similar readers (Iyengar and Hahn, 2009).

Unobtrusive Measurement

Great advances have been made in understanding the selection of information by unobtrusively tracking people's online behavior and CD use (Iyengar et al., 2008; Kim, 2009; Knobloch-Westerwick and Meng, 2009), by observing their behavior in waiting rooms (Stroud, 2011), and by examining Nielsen television ratings (Webster, 2005) and Nielsen NetRatings (Tewksbury, 2005). These studies make it less likely that subjects will be able to guess the purpose of a study, and they provide a way of observing behavior in more natural settings.

Forced Versus Selective Exposure

In typical laboratory experiments, subjects are exposed to media content and their reactions monitored. Several current projects have proposed ways to incorporate selective exposure into these designs. Gaines and Kuklinski (2011) and Arceneaux, Johnson, and Murphy (2012) demonstrate various ways in which researchers can randomly assign participants either to a choice condition whereby they can select their media exposure or to a forced exposure condition whereby they are required to use media without choice. This innovative research design holds promise for providing more information on media effects, which may vary based on (1) differences between the self-selected audience and the experimental participants and (2) differences between the effects of messages on a self-selected audience versus experimental participants forced to engage with media.

UNANSWERED QUESTIONS AND THOUGHTS ON SELECTIVE EXPOSURE

The joy of doing research on selective exposure is that there are so many areas in need of additional research. In the paragraphs below, I pose questions and offer my thoughts on selective exposure. The first two questions probe the definition and boundaries of what we consider selective exposure. The next two ask about how message valence and the

Internet affect selective exposure. I then turn to an examination of what types of beliefs affect selective exposure. The final three questions aim to complicate and expand our understanding of selective exposure by putting selective exposure in conversation with other approaches, including incidental exposure, the role of political elites, and effects research.

How Do We Know Selective Exposure When We See It?

The definitional debate in selective exposure research comes in (at least) two forms. The first asks whether selective exposure is an all-or-nothing phenomenon. As an all-or-nothing phenomenon, people either (1) solely use like-minded information and engage in selective exposure or (2) are not engaging in selective exposure. This dichotomous view makes sense in laboratory settings where research subjects have only two options: selecting the like-minded option or selecting another option. In reality, however, it is unlikely that anyone would always encounter like-minded views. If we accept this definition, selective exposure does not occur in reality. As a result, I find a second view far more compelling: that selective exposure means exhibiting a preference for like-minded information. How to best measure this, however, is not altogether clear. If a person spends one minute with a congenial source, does this count as selective exposure? Five minutes? Two hours? These questions may be best answered by looking at the outcomes of selective exposure—a topic covered shortly. There also are important questions about whether we should focus on time with congenial sources *and* time with uncongenial sources or just the former, a topic to which I now turn.

What Is the Difference Between Selective Exposure and Selective Avoidance?

Selective exposure is sometimes coupled with selective avoidance—the motivated avoidance of messages discrepant with one's beliefs. Several scholars over the years have urged the separate consideration of selective exposure and selective avoidance (Chaffee et al., 2001; Frey, 1986; McGuire, 1968). In some contexts, selective exposure and avoidance are identical. When asked to choose between only two pieces of information—one congenial and one uncongenial—selective exposure *and* avoidance occur when a person selects the congenial information. The situation is more complicated, however, when people have the option to select multiple pieces of information and when information can contain both congenial and uncongenial perspectives. Garrett's (2009a, 2009b) work examines these sorts of instances. He finds that those gathering news via the Internet encounter arguments in favor of their preferred candidate more frequently. Yet their online news use does not reduce the frequency with which they encounter arguments *opposing* their preferred candidate (Garrett, 2009b). Garrett (2009a) also analyzes which websites people select on political topics of interest. Although sites believed to contain opinion challenging the viewer's information are selected less frequently, the avoidance of dissimilar views is weaker than the attraction to similar views. Garrett's work suggests that selective exposure and avoidance should not be combined. Although we may be prone to seek like-minded information, we may not be equally motivated to avoid information with which we disagree.

Additional work is required here, however, to understand how selective exposure and avoidance work in practice. People may encounter dissimilar views in contexts that primarily reinforce their views. After all, partisan sources do describe other views, even if only to inoculate their viewers and equip them with counterarguments (Jamieson and Cappella, 2008). Further, people's motivations for looking at other views—to laugh versus to counterargue versus to gain an appreciation for another viewpoint—should be taken into account. As Garrett (2009a) notes, we need more information about how people process uncongenial information. As a host of studies remind us, views can be strengthened in their original direction even when challenged by contradictory information (Lord, Ross, and Lepper, 1979; Meffert et al., 2006; Taber and Lodge, 2006). Further, other psychological reactions such as selective perception and retention occur in response to oppositional views (Jacobson, 2010). In sum, even if we do not avoid contradictory views with the same intensity with which we seek confirmatory views, the effects of exposure to contradictory information may only reinforce selective exposure effects.

Why Are There Differences Between Selective Exposure to Negative and Positive Information?

Certain forms of information may inspire selective exposure and avoidance. On this topic, several studies have revealed an interesting pattern. People seem to conform to the predictions of selective exposure when asked to select from positive information about their own view *and* positive information about an oppositional view. When given negative information about one's own view and the view of the opposition, however, selective exposure effects wane (Mills, Aronson, and Robinson, 1959). When people had access to both positive and negative information, Donsbach (1991) found clear selective exposure effects for the selection of positive information about a political figure but little evidence of selective exposure with respect to negative information. Meffert et al. (2006) uncovered a strong preference for negative information about one's preferred candidate. The consistency of this finding seems to suggest that exposure decisions are affected by valence and perhaps, as Meffert et al. (2006) suggest, the negativity bias is simply a stronger and more automatic drive than a preference for like-minded information.

How Does the Internet Encourage and Discourage Selective Exposure?

Although some find that people use the Internet to find like-minded views (Bimber and Davis, 2003; Sunstein, 2001) and to pursue their own narrow issue interests (Althaus and Tewksbury, 2002; Nie et al., 2010), others note that the Internet allows exposure to diverse perspectives (Brundidge, 2010; Gentzkow and Shapiro, 2011; Stromer-Galley, 2006; Wojcieszak and Mutz, 2009). Although both of these effects are occurring, at least to some extent, the real trick may lie in discovering structural characteristics that facilitate or discourage selective exposure. Holbert, Garrett, and Gleason (2010), for example, note that certain design features may inhibit selective exposure. In this vein, some work has focused on selective exposure on particular sites. Gaines and Mondak (2009), for example, find some evidence of ideological clustering among Facebook friends. Tewksbury (2005) finds that distinct news websites attract demographically distinguishable audiences. The research could go further, however, by examining characteristics that enhance or minimize selective exposure tendencies.

Which Beliefs Motivate Selective Exposure?

As previously reviewed, scholars have identified a host of beliefs that affect where people turn for information. These beliefs, however, do not capture everything that attracts audiences to political messages. Why do some beliefs affect message selection and not others? Or, as Holbert, Garrett, and Gleason (2010) ask, "When multiple attitudes have bearing on an issue, which one guides selectivity" (21)? Work on this topic has begun. Iyengar et al. (2008) looked at the extent to which issue-public membership and political predispositions predicted political information selection. Their results suggest that issue-public membership affects exposure decisions and provide some evidence that political predispositions matter. These patterns may be different today, however, as partisanship has taken a more central role in determining media selection (Bennett and Iyengar, 2008). In their meta-analysis, Hart et al. (2009) examine whether there are differences in patterns of selectivity across topics. Their results are suggestive: Politics and religion seem to inspire more selective exposure than other topics. Building on this, selective exposure may be particularly likely when the information content is about deeply held, chronically accessible, and emotionally charged topics. However, more formal testing of which beliefs matter most, when, and why, is needed.

How Do Selective Exposure and Incidental Exposure Operate?

Although people may prefer information consistent with their beliefs, it is unlikely that they always can screen out other views. There is a component of serendipity in message exposure. Known as incidental, or accidental, exposure, citizens sometimes encounter information that they were not seeking but happened across while doing other things. With respect to politics, citizens seem to learn about politics even when they are not looking for political information (Tewksbury, Weaver, and Maddex, 2001; Zukin and Snyder, 1984). Yet this sort of incidental exposure arguably is becoming rarer as more media choices enable better screening of information in which one has no interest (Prior, 2007). Indeed, incidental exposure to news is more common among those who already tend to seek news (Tewksbury, Weaver, and Maddex, 2001). We need to know more about the frequency and effects of incidental exposure in light of selective exposure.

How Do Elites, and Theories about the Role of Elites, Factor In?

In the study of political communication, research on selective exposure has focused predominately on the relationship between media and citizens. Yet the study of political communication often involves another important facet of the political landscape: elites. I discuss three ways in which elites can be and have been incorporated into the study of selective exposure. First, political elites can exacerbate selective exposure. Their cues direct citizens about which media outlets to use and which to avoid. When political elites criticize media coverage, educated and like-minded citizens base their opinions of the media on these comments (Ladd, 2010; Smith, 2010). Assuming that elites mainly criticize the media for expressing oppositional views (Watts et al., 1999), these critiques could reify avoidance of uncongenial outlets and the selection of like-minded media.

Second, just as some citizens respond to partisan news sources by relying upon like-minded sources, political elites also may be responding to a fragmented news environment. Instead of selective exposure, perhaps a form of *selective production* is occurring, whereby elites are more likely to give interviews to congenial outlets and divulge different information depending on an outlet's partisan leanings.

Building on these two research trajectories, selective exposure can be added profitably to Zaller's (1992) theory of elite leadership of public opinion. Zaller suggests that elite views transmitted via the media affect public views. Rather than measuring media exposure, he measures habitual news reception using political knowledge questions to account for whether people receive elite messages. Although selective exposure was not featured in the original version of his study and arguably was not as common when Zaller devised his conceptualization (Hollander, 2008; Prior, 2007), selective exposure could be incorporated into the model. In many ways, selective exposure findings underscore the utility of Zaller's model. Elites still affect public attitudes and behaviors. Research on selective exposure adds that elites affect attitudes about the media and that this may, in turn, affect information selection. Habitual news reception and partisanship continue to predict attitudes and behaviors. Selective exposure research adds that those with higher levels of education are more likely to respond to like-minded elite cues about bias (Ladd, 2010) and to select like-minded media (Stroud, 2011).

A potential modification could come from the addition of a measure of which media outlets people use. Instead of figuring out which views in a balanced news report correspond with their own—a task that would be rather challenging for someone without the requisite political knowledge—congenial information sources can provide unambiguous information about like-minded elite beliefs. Media exposure patterns, therefore, might be profitably added into Zaller's model. The seeds of this argument can be found in work by Lee and Cappella (2001), where they find that exposure has important effects in predicting political attitudes.

Should Selective Exposure Be Judged as Troubling or Not?

Although selective exposure research has been dominated by demonstrations of its occurrence and investigations of moderators, its consequences have attracted more attention recently. There are reasons to judge selective exposure as democratically troubling. After all, attending only or primarily to like-minded political content is related to polarization, different conceptions of the world in which we live, and heightened partisan reactions (Stroud, 2011; Taber and Lodge, 2006). The exodus from political life of those more interested in entertainment than the news also could be judged as troubling (Ksiazek, Malthouse, and Webster, 2010; Prior, 2007). On the other hand, selective exposure may not be terribly bad if it energizes the public and encourages participation (Dilliplane, 2011; Mutz, 2006; Stroud, 2011).

Although this is a normative question, more research into the consequences of selective exposure, particularly in today's fragmented media environment, is warranted. If we find that selective exposure is troubling, what is the solution? One popular idea is to encourage more exposure to diverse points of view. Yet exposure to the other side could ultimately lead to boomerang effects (Taber and Lodge, 2006) or to public inactivity (Mutz, 2006). How to (1) motivate engagement with the news and (2) encourage respectful consideration of other perspectives without deterring political involvement remain two pivotal challenges facing those who worry about political engagement.

Conclusion

Although it has garnered uneven research attention over time, selective exposure is a cornerstone of political communication research. If we do not understand when and why people select news and information, we will have an incomplete understanding of communication effects. Understanding selective exposure seems particularly vital in considering the role of communication in a democracy, because it has implications for citizen engagement, for the appreciation of diverse views, and for the creation of communities where citizens can agree on basic facts, to name but a few.

REFERENCES

Abelson, R. P., E. Aronson, W. J. McGuire, T. M. Newcomb, M. J. Rosenberg, and P. H. Tannenbaum (Eds.). 1968. *Theories of cognitive consistency*. Chicago: Rand McNally.

Albarracín, D., and A. L. Mitchell. 2004. The role of defensive confidence in preference for proattitudinal information: How believing that one is strong can sometimes be a defensive weakness. *Personality and Social Psychology Bulletin*, 30: 1565–1584.

Althaus, S. L., and D. Tewksbury. 2002. Agenda setting and the "new" news: Patterns of issue importance among readers of the paper and online versions of the *New York Times*. *Communication Research*, 29: 180–207.

Arceneaux, K., M. Johnson, and C. Murphy 2012. Polarized political communication, oppositional media hostility, and selective exposure. *Journal of Politics*, 74(1): 174–186.

Baum, M. A., and S. Kernell. 1999. Has cable ended the golden age of presidential television? *American Political Science Review*, 93: 99–114.

Bennett, W. L., and S. Iyengar. 2008. A new era of minimal effects? The changing foundations of political communication. *Journal of Communication*, 58: 707–731.

Best, S. J., B. Chmielewski, and B. S. Krueger. 2005. Selective exposure to online foreign news during the conflict with Iraq. *The International Journal of Press/Politics*, 10: 52–70.

Bimber, B., and R. Davis. 2003. *Campaigning online: The Internet in U.S. elections*. New York: Oxford University Press.

Brannon, L. A., M. J. Tagler, and A. H. Eagly. 2007. The moderating role of attitude strength in selective exposure to information. *Journal of Experimental Social Psychology*, 43: 611–617.

Brehm, J. W., and A. R. Cohen. 1962. *Explorations in cognitive dissonance*. New York: John Wiley & Sons.

Brundidge, J. 2010. Encountering "difference" in the contemporary public sphere: The contribution of the Internet to the heterogeneity of political discussion networks. *Journal of Communication*, 60: 680–700.

Chaffee, S. H., and J. M. McLeod. 1973. Individuals vs. social predictors of information seeking. *Journalism Quarterly*, 50: 237–245.

Chaffee, S. H., M. N. Saphir, J. Graf, C. Sandvig, and K. S. Hahn. 2001. Attention to counter-attitudinal messages in a state election campaign. *Political Communication*, 18: 247–272.

Converse, P. E. 1964. The nature of belief systems in mass publics. In D. E. Apter (Ed.) *Ideology and discontent* (pp. 206–261). New York: Free Press.

Cotton, J. L. 1985. Cognitive dissonance in selective exposure. In D. Zillmann and J. Bryant (Eds.), *Selective exposure to communication* (pp. 11–33). Hillsdale, NJ: Lawrence Erlbaum.

D'Alessio, D., and M. Allen. 2002. Selective exposure and dissonance after decisions. *Psychological Reports*, 91: 527–532.

Dilliplane, S. 2011. All the news you want to hear: The impact of partisan news exposure on political participation. *Public Opinion Quarterly*, 75 287–316.

Donsbach, W. 1991. Exposure to political content in newspapers: The impact of cognitive dissonance on readers' selectivity. *European Journal of Communication*, 6: 155–186.

Festinger, L. 1957. *A theory of cognitive dissonance*. Evanston, IL: Row, Peterson.

Festinger, L. 1964. *Conflict, decision, and dissonance*. Stanford, CA: Stanford University Press.

Fischer, P., E. Jonas, D. Frey, and S. Schulz-Hardt. 2005. Selective exposure to information: The impact of information limits. *European Journal of Social Psychology*, 35: 469–492.

Fischer, P., S. Schulz-Hardt, and D. Frey. 2008. Selective exposure and information quantity: How different information quantities moderate decision maker's preference for consistent and inconsistent information. *Journal of Personality and Social Psychology*, 94: 231–244.

Freedman, J. L., and D. O. Sears. 1965. Selective exposure. In L. Berkowitz (Ed.), *Advances in experimental social psychology*, vol. 2 (pp. 57–97). New York: Academic Press.

Frey, D. 1986. Recent research on selective exposure to information. In L. Berkowitz (Ed.), *Advances in experimental social psychology*, vol. 19 (pp. 41–80). New York: Academic Press.

Gaines, B. J., and J. H. Kuklinski. 2011. Experimental estimation of heterogeneous treatment effects related to self-selection. *American Journal of Political Science*, 55: 724–736.

Gaines, B. J., and J. J. Mondak. 2009. Typing together? Clustering of ideological types in online social networks. *Journal of Information Technology & Politics*, 6: 216–231.

Garrett, R. K. 2009a. Echo chambers online? Politically motivated selective exposure among Internet users. *Journal of Computer-Mediated Communication*, 14: 265–285.

Garrett, R. K. 2009b. Politically motivated reinforcement seeking: Reframing the selective exposure debate. *Journal of Communication*, 59: 676–699.

Gentzkow, M., and Shapiro, J. M. 2011. Ideological segregation online and offline. *The Quarterly Journal of Economics*, 126(4): 1799–1839.

Hart, W., D. Albarracín, A. H. Eagly, I. Brechan, M. J. Lindberg, and L. Merrill. 2009. Feeling validated versus being correct: A meta-analysis of selective exposure to information. *Psychological Bulletin*, 135: 555–588.

Holbert, R. L., R. K. Garrett, and L. S. Gleason. 2010. A new era of minimal effects? A response to Bennett and Iyengar. *Journal of Communication*, 60: 15–34.

Hollander, B. A. 2008. Tuning out or tuning elsewhere? Partisanship, polarization, and media migration from 1998 to 2006. *Journalism & Mass Communication Quarterly*, 85: 23–40.

Huckfeldt, R., and J. M. Mendez. 2008. Moths, flames, and political engagement: Managing disagreement within communication networks. *The Journal of Politics*, 70: 83–96.

Hwang, H., M. Schmierbach, H. Paek, H. Gil de Zuniga, and D. Shah. 2006. Media dissociation, Internet use, and antiwar political participation: A case study of political dissent and action against the war in Iraq. *Mass Communication & Society*, 9: 461–483.

Iyengar, S., and K. S. Hahn. 2009. Red media, blue media: Evidence of ideological selectivity in media use. *Journal of Communication*, 59: 19–39.

Iyengar, S., K. S. Hahn, J. A. Krosnick, and J. Walker. 2008. Selective exposure to campaign communication: The role of anticipated agreement and issue public membership. *Journal of Politics*, 70: 186–200.

Jacobson, G. C. 2010. Perception, memory, and partisan polarization on the Iraq War. *Political Science Quarterly*, 125: 31–56.

Jamieson, K. H., and J. N. Cappella. 2008. *Echo chamber: Rush Limbaugh and the conservative media establishment*. New York: Oxford University Press.

Johnson, T. J., S. L. Bichard, and W. Zhang. 2009. Communication communities or "cyber-ghettos?" A path analysis model examining factors that explain selective exposure to blogs. *Journal of Computer-Mediated Communication*, 15: 60–82.

Jonas, E., V. Graupmann, and D. Frey. 2006. The influence of mood on the search for supporting versus conflicting information: Dissonance reduction as a means of mood regulation? *Personality and Social Psychology Bulletin*, 32: 3–15.

Jonas, E., J. Greenberg, and D. Frey. 2003. Connecting terror management and dissonance theory: Evidence that mortality salience increases the preference for supporting information after decisions. *Personality and Social Psychology Bulletin*, 29: 1181–1189.

Jonas, E., S. Schulz-Hardt, D. Frey, and N. Thelen. 2001. Confirmation bias in sequential information search after preliminary decisions: An expansion of dissonance theoretical research on selective exposure to information. *Journal of Personality and Social Psychology*, 80: 557–571.

Kim, S. 2010. The role of emotion in selective exposure, information processing, and attitudinal polarization. Unpublished master's thesis. University of Texas at Austin.

Kim, Y. M. 2007. How intrinsic and extrinsic motivations interact in selectivity: Investigating the moderating effects of situational information processing goals in issue publics' Web behavior. *Communication Research*, 34: 185–211.

Kim, Y. M. 2009. Issue publics in the new information environment: Selectivity, domain specificity, and extremity. *Communication Research*, 36: 254–284.

Klapper, J. T. 1960. *The effects of mass communication*. Glencoe, IL: Free Press.

Knobloch, S., F. D. Carpentier, and D. Zillmann. 2003. Effects of salience dimensions of informational utility on selective exposure to online news. *Journalism & Mass Communication Quarterly*, 80: 91–108.

Knobloch-Westerwick, S. and J. Meng. 2009. Looking the other way: Selective exposure to attitude-consistent and counterattitudinal political information. *Communication Research*, 36: 426–448.

Knobloch-Westerwick, S., and S. Kleinman. 2012. Preelection selective exposure: Confirmation bias versus informational utility. *Communication Research*, 39(2): 170–193.

Kruglanski, A. W. (1989). *Lay epistemics and human knowledge: Cognitive and motivational bases*. New York: Plenum Press.

Ksiazek, T. B., E. C. Malthouse, and J. G. Webster. 2010. News-seekers and avoiders: Exploring patterns of total news consumption across media and the relationship to civic participation. *Journal of Broadcasting & Electronic Media*, 54: 551–568.

Kunda, Z. 1990. The case for motivated reasoning. *Psychological Bulletin*, 108: 480–498.

Ladd, J. M. 2010. The neglected power of elite opinion leadership to produce antipathy toward the news media: Evidence from a survey experiment. *Political Behavior*, 32: 29–50.

Lavine, H., M. Lodge, and K. Freitas. 2005. Threat, authoritarianism, and selective exposure to information. *Political Psychology*, 26: 219–244.

Lazarsfeld, P. F., B. Berelson, and H. Gaudet. 1948. *The people's choice: How the voter makes up his mind in a presidential election*. New York: Columbia University Press.

Lee, G., and J. N. Cappella. 2001. The effects of political talk radio on political attitude formation: Exposure versus knowledge. *Political Communication*, 18: 369–394.

Lord, C. G., L. Ross, and M. R. Lepper. 1979. Biased assimilation and attitude polarization: The effects of prior theories on subsequently considered evidence. *Journal of Personality and Social Psychology*, 37: 2098–2109.

McGuire, W. J. 1968. Selective exposure: A summing up. In R. P. Abelson, E. Aronson, W. J. McGuire, T. M. Newcomb, M. J. Rosenberg, and P. H. Tannenbaum (Eds.), *Theories of cognitive consistency* (pp. 97–800). Chicago: Rand McNally.

Meffert, M. F., S. Chung, A. J. Joiner, L. Waks, and J. Garst. 2006. The effects of negativity and motivated information processing during a political campaign. *Journal of Communication*, 56: 27–51.

Mills, J., E. Aronson, and H. Robinson. 1959. Selectivity in exposure to information. *Journal of Abnormal and Social Psychology*, 59: 250–253.

Morris, J. S. 2005. The Fox News factor. *International Journal of Press/Politics*, 10: 56–79.

Mutz, D. C. 2006. *Hearing the other side: Deliberative versus participatory democracy.* New York: Cambridge University Press.

Mutz, D. C., and P. S. Martin. 2001. Facilitating communication across lines of political difference: The role of mass media. *American Political Science Review,* 95: 97–114.

Nie, N. H., D. W. Miller, S. Golde, D. M. Butler, and K. Winneg. 2010. The World Wide Web and the U.S. political news market. *American Journal of Political Science,* 54: 428–439.

Prior, M. 2007. *Post-broadcast democracy: How media choice increases inequality in political involvement and polarizes elections.* New York: Cambridge University Press.

Schulz-Hardt, S., Frey, D., Lüthgens, C., and Moscovici, S. 2000. Biased information search in group decision making. *Journal of Personality and Social Psychology,* 78: 655–669.

Sears, D. O. and J. L. Freedman. 1967. Selective exposure to information: A critical review. *Public Opinion Quarterly,* 31: 194–213.

Slater, M. D. 2007. Reinforcing spirals: The mutual influence of media selectivity and media effects and their impact on individual behavior and social identity. *Communication Theory,* 17: 281–303.

Smith, G. R. 2010. Politicians and the news media: How elite attacks influence perceptions of media bias. *The International Journal of Press/Politics,* 15: 319–343.

Stromer-Galley, J. 2006. Diversity of political conversation on the Internet: Users' perspectives. *Journal of Computer-Mediated Communication,* 8: Article 6.

Stroud, N. J. 2008. Media use and political predispositions: Revisiting the concept of selective exposure. *Political Behavior,* 30: 341–366.

Stroud, N. J. 2010. Polarization and partisan selective exposure. *Journal of Communication,* 60: 556–576.

Stroud, N. J. 2011. *Niche news: The politics of news choice.* New York: Oxford University Press.

Sunstein, C. 2001. *Republic.com.* Princeton, NJ: Princeton University Press.

Sweeney, P. D., and Gruber, K. L. 1984. Selective exposure: Voter information preferences and the Watergate affair. *Journal of Personality and Social Psychology,* 46: 1208–1221.

Taber, C. S., and Lodge, M. 2006. Motivated skepticism in the evaluation of political beliefs. *American Journal of Political Science,* 50: 755–769.

Tewksbury, D. 2005. The seeds of audience fragmentation: Specialization in the use of online news sites. *Journal of Broadcasting & Electronic Media,* 49: 332–348.

Tewksbury, D., A. J. Weaver, and B. D. Maddex. 2001. Accidentally informed: Incidental news exposure on the World Wide Web. *Journalism & Mass Communication Quarterly,* 78: 533–554.

Tsfati, Y., and J. N. Cappella. 2003. Do people watch what they do not trust? Exploring the association between news media skepticism and exposure. *Communication Research,* 30: 504–529.

Tsfati, Y., and J. N. Cappella. 2005. Why do people watch news they do not trust? The need for cognition as a moderator in the association between news media skepticism and exposure. *Media Psychology,* 7: 251–271.

Valentino, N. A., A. J. Banks, V. L. Hutchings, and A. K. Davis. 2009. Selective exposure in the Internet age: The interaction between anxiety and information utility. *Political Psychology,* 30: 591–613.

Watts, M. D., D. Domke, D. V. Shah, and D. P. Fan. 1999. Elite cues and media bias in presidential campaigns: Explaining public perceptions of a liberal press. *Communication Research,* 26: 144–175.

Webster, J. G. 2005. Beneath the veneer of fragmentation: Television audience polarization in a multichannel world. *Journal of Communication* 55: 366–382.

Wojcieszak, M. E., and D. C. Mutz. 2009. Online groups and political discourse: Do online discussion spaces facilitate exposure to political disagreement? *Journal of Communication*, 59: 40–56.

Zaller, J. 1992. *The nature and origins of mass opinion*. New York: Cambridge University Press.

Ziemke, D. A. 1980. Selective exposure in a presidential campaign contingent on certainty and salience. In D. Nimmo (Ed.), *Communication yearbook*, vol. 4 (pp. 497–511). New Brunswick, NJ: Transaction Books.

Zukin, C., and R. Snyder. 1984. Passive learning: When the media environment is the message. *Public Opinion Quarterly*, 48: 629–638.

CHAPTER 38

THE HOSTILE MEDIA EFFECT

LAUREN FELDMAN

INTRODUCTION

THROUGHOUT the history of communication research, scholars have alternated between conceptualizations of the media audience as passively subject to media influence or active in its use and interpretation of mediated messages—although the latter view has come to predominate. Abundant evidence suggests that audiences, particularly those with strong prior beliefs and attitudes, are instrumental in determining when then will pay attention to a message and what meaning they will take away from it. A prominent example of this is the "hostile media effect," where opposing partisans perceive identical news coverage of a controversial issue as biased against their own side. To be sure, the hostile media *effect* is not an effect of the media per se but rather a response to media content, although this response has the potential to influence attitudinal and behavioral outcomes. For this reason, the hostile media effect is probably better referred to as a hostile media *perception* or hostile media *phenomenon*, but the terms are typically used interchangeably in the literature.

The hostile media effect was first demonstrated reliably by Vallone, Ross, and Lepper (1985) in the context of news about the ongoing Middle East conflict between the Israelis and Palestinians. In the study, Stanford University undergraduates—who self-identified as either pro-Arab, pro-Israeli, or neutral—were shown a selection of US network news coverage that detailed a 1982 massacre of Palestinians by a Lebanese militia group and raised questions about Israeli responsibility in its aftermath. Results demonstrated that students who characterized themselves as pro-Israeli saw the news as biased *against* Israel, whereas pro-Arab students saw it as biased in Israel's *favor*. Thus, both groups saw the same news coverage as hostile to their own position, whereas neutral viewers perceived the coverage as relatively balanced.

Using both experimental and survey methods, the hostile media phenomenon has been replicated in both its original (Giner-Sorolla and Chaiken, 1994; Perloff, 1989) and other issue contexts, including those surrounding primate research (Gunther, Christen,

Liebhart, and Chia, 2001), genetic modification of food (Gunther and Schmitt, 2004), election campaigns (Dalton, Beck, and Huckfeldt, 1998; Huge and Glynn, 2010), a UPS strike (Christen, Kannaovakun, and Gunther, 2002), and global warming (Kim, 2010). The hostile media effect even persists in a restricted press system, such as that of Singapore, where news coverage is highly regulated and people are aware of the government's control of the media (Chia, Yong, Wong, and Koh, 2007).

This chapter reviews the literature on the hostile media effect with an eye toward the theoretical explanations for this effect, its relationship to other psychological processes, and its broader implications for journalism and political behavior. The hostile media effect is more than just a perceptual phenomenon; it has important consequences for democratic society. Notably, recent national surveys paint a picture of a highly skeptical news audience, with wide disparities in Democrats and Republicans' perceptions of the credibility of various news organizations (Morales, 2010; Pew Research Center, 2010). Accordingly, a key objective of this chapter is to better understand the extent to which the hostile media phenomenon can help explain the public's eroding trust in the news media and the polarization among news audiences as well as to identify how future research can inform this discussion.

Explanatory Factors

Partisan Involvement

Stronger, more involved partisans are more likely to see news content as hostile (e.g., Choi, Yang, and Chang, 2009; Christen et al., 2002; Eveland and Shah, 2003; Vallone et al., 1985), suggesting that the hostile media effect is a situational response emerging from individuals' identification with a partisan group or issue (Gunther, 1992). Many studies of the hostile media effect have recruited partisan participants from interest groups, although some have relied on general population samples, categorizing partisans based on their attitude extremity. The latter method tends to locate weaker hostile media perceptions (Giner-Sorolla and Chaiken, 1994); however, there is some evidence that hostile media perceptions manifest even among the general population (Dalton et al., 1998; Gunther and Christen, 2002) and moderate partisans (Huge and Glynn 2010). A recent meta-analysis (Hansen and Kim, 2011) concluded that the hostile media effect persists regardless of whether participants are highly involved or not, although the effect is stronger with greater involvement.

To address concerns that "involvement" has been inconsistently conceptualizd and operationalized in earlier work (Choi et al., 2009), recent studies have tried to determine precisely what type of involvement contributes to hostile media perceptions. For example, Choi et al. (2009) found that value-relevant involvement, which occurs when concern about an issue is closely connected to one's personal and social values, was predictive of hostile media perceptions among South Korean students, whereas outcome-relevant involvement, which arises when an issue has future consequences for an individual, was not. And Gunther, Miller, and Liebhart (2009) found that group identification was associated with relatively unfavorable media perceptions, whereas attitudinal extremes were associated with relatively favorable media perceptions. Although there are conceptual parallels between value-relevant involvement and group membership on the one hand and outcome-relevant involvement and attitude extremity on the other, a fuller understanding of which aspects of involvement underlie the hostile media effect and whether this varies by issue, media source, or other factors requires additional research.

Message-Processing Mechanisms

Efforts to explain partisans' hostile media perceptions have generally coalesced around three psychological mechanisms (Giner-Sorolla and Chaiken, 1994; Schmitt, Gunther, and Liebhart, 2004). The first, *selective recall*, assumes that unfavorable content is more salient to partisans and therefore disproportionately remembered. With *selective categorization*, opposing partisans attend to, process, and recall the same content but interpret the valence of this content differently, classifying it as hostile to their own position. As suggested by Giner-Sorolla and Chaiken (1994), this second explanation is drawn from social judgment theory (Sherif and Hovland, 1961), which holds that highly involved partisans have wider "latitudes" of message rejection and will thus find more of the views expressed by the media to be disagreeable or biased than will weaker partisans, for whom the news is likely to fall into a latitude of acceptance or of noncommitment. Whereas selective recall and categorization assume a perceptual bias on the part of news consumers, scholars have also considered whether partisans might be vulnerable to an evaluative bias. This third explanation, dubbed the *different standards* mechanism, proposes that opposing partisans agree on the content and valence of a news story but have competing criteria for what constitutes a fair representation (Vallone et al., 1985). Specifically, only news stories that exclude information relevant to their opponents' claims would be deemed appropriate; an even-handed treatment would constitute bias. While early studies found evidence for different standards (Giner-Sorolla and Chaiken, 1994; Vallone et al., 1985), in recent research, using a more stringent test, selective categorization emerged as the most viable explanation (Gunther and Liebhart, 2006; Schmitt et al., 2004).

Source Heuristics

Scholars have also advanced a heuristic processing mechanism to explain the hostile media effect (Giner-Sorolla and Chaiken, 1994). Several studies suggest that existing beliefs about general media bias can contribute to hostile media perceptions (Giner-Sorolla and Chaiken, 1994; Chia et al., 2007, 2009). Indeed, given the persistent claims leveled by conservative elites about liberal media bias (Watts, Domke, Shah, and Fan, 1999), this could explain why Republicans are more likely to perceive a hostile media bias than are Democrats (Eveland and Shah, 2003). Moreover, as Eveland and Shah (2003) have demonstrated, Republicans' perceptions of bias follow directly not only from conservative elites' assertions that the media are biased against them but also from their discussions with like-minded others, who likely spread and reinforce these claims. Thus, elite cues, social networks, and individual partisanship appear to interact in complex ways to produce hostile media perceptions.

Also consistent with a heuristic processing mechanism, several studies indicate that hostile media perceptions are reduced when a media source is presumed to agree with one's own group and are heightened when the source is presumed to be disagreeable. For example, Arpan and Raney (2003) found that sports fans perceived a balanced news story about their town's sports team to be less hostile when it came from their hometown newspaper than when it came from either a neutral-town or rival-town paper. Likewise, Baum and Gussin (2007) demonstrated that the cable news channels Fox and CNN triggered perceptions of bias based on their assumed partisan leanings. For example, election news attributed to Fox was perceived as more hostile by liberals than conservatives, with the reverse true for an identical story from CNN. Ariyanto, Hornsey, and Gallois (2007) further demonstrated that the perceived alignment of a media source factors into people's judgments of bias. Specifically, Indonesian students believed that an article was biased against Christians when it appeared in a Muslim newspaper, but when the same article was credited to a Christian newspaper, it was seen as biased against Muslims.

Thus, a news source's real or imagined partisan loyalties may undermine its ability to convince opposing partisans that it reports current affairs fairly. Still, it is not entirely clear whether this is, in fact, a function of heuristic processing, whereby individuals forgo careful message processing and instead base their judgments of bias solely on assumptions about the source or if expectations of bias trigger the selective interpretation of message content. In the language of social judgment theory, it is quite possible that anticipated source bias creates wider latitudes of message rejection, thereby leading partisans to classify news content as hostile.

Perceived Reach

Not all information sources stimulate perceptions of a hostile bias. In fact, robust evidence exists in the social psychology literature for the opposite phenomenon, *biased assimilation*, whereby partisans interpret mixed evidence on an issue as supportive of their own point of view (Lord, Ross, and Lepper, 1979). To address this apparent contradiction, recent research has localized the hostile media effect to information sources that are perceived to be able to reach a wide audience and thereby exert a broad influence on public opinion. In this case, the perceived reach of the media content—and concern about its sway over a vulnerable public—are assumed to trigger defensive processing that makes otherwise benign information seem disagreeable (Gunther and Liebhart, 2006). Consistent with this explanation, studies have found that a newspaper article but not a student essay produces hostile media perceptions (Gunther and Liebhart, 2006; Gunther et al., 2009; Gunther and Schmitt, 2004) and that a national newspaper generates less favorable perceptions than does a regional one (Gunther et al., 2009). What's more, in these studies, the student essay generated assimilation effects, such that readers perceived it as supportive of their beliefs. Findings such as these prompt Gunther et al. (2009) to argue that hostile media perceptions and biased assimilation are "two ends of the same continuum" (760). This is perhaps best understood as a matter of dueling motivations. Assimilation effects are produced by information sources perceived to have limited reach, ostensibly because here, audiences interpret the information only relative to their own opinion, and their motivation is to protect their opinion by privileging supportive evidence. With greater perceived reach, the audience's outlook shifts to the influence on others, whom they are now motivated to guard from potentially harmful information. Theoretically, then, as perceived reach increases, partisans' latitudes of message rejection widen, triggering perceptions of bias in neutral news.

Questions remain, however, as to how finely audiences distinguish between the reach of sources: Will a front-page story generate more hostile perceptions than a story on page ten? What about a network television news story versus the same story on cable? It is also possible that issue dynamics alter the influence of perceived reach. For example, Huge and Glynn (2010) found that hostile media perceptions during an election campaign weakened as the race became less competitive. In other words, when people were confident that their candidate would win, they were less worried about the media's influence on others.

Democratic Consequences of Hostile Media Perceptions

While the tendency for individuals to perceive news coverage differently depending on their partisan orientation is of intrinsic theoretical interest, an emerging body of research suggests that the hostile media phenomenon also has important democratic consequences. As social psychologists and communication scholars have long recognized, "perceptions of reality, rather than actual observations of it, guide human beliefs, attitudes, and behaviors" (Hoffman and Glynn, 2008, 2945). Thus, although the hostile biases that partisans project on media coverage are, in many cases, not objectively real, these perceptions—justified or not—have been found to influence how people perceive the public opinion climate, the way they consume news, and their participation in political life.

Implications for Perceived Public Opinion

Several studies have found that hostile media perceptions lead partisans to also perceive public opinion as weighted against their own or less similar to theirs (Choi et al., 2009; Gunther and Chia, 2001; Gunther and Christen, 2002; Gunther et al., 2001). This is explained by the persuasive press inference model (Gunther, 1998), which posits that individuals infer public opinion from their perceptions of news coverage because of their assumption that it has substantial reach and influence on others. Thus, if people see news coverage as biased against their own point of view, they will likewise perceive others' opinions to be at odds with their own. Moreover, to the extent that individuals infer bias on the basis of *balanced* news coverage, their inferences about public opinion could be incorrect (Gunther and Chia, 2001). These perceptions then have the potential to influence *actual* public opinion, as theories such as the spiral of silence predict (Noelle-Neumann, 1984). Moreover, as Gunther et al. (2001) have observed, the connection between perceived media bias and perceived public opinion expands the role presumably played by the media in the spiral of silence. Specifically, it suggests that the media can cue audience impressions of the opinion climate even if they do not report on public opinion directly.

However, the persuasive press inference is at odds with the projection bias, also known as the looking-glass perception (Fields and Schuman, 1976), whereby people project others' opinions from their own. Some studies have found that the effects of projection on perceived public opinion overwhelm the effects of hostile media perceptions (e.g., Christen et al., 2002; Huge and Glynn, 2010). As Christen et al. (2002) have explained, because we are social animals, our motivation to validate our opinions by projecting them onto others is stronger than our motivation to see hostile media coverage as a persuasive force. In contrast, other scholars have found evidence for *both* projection and the persuasive press inference (e.g., Gunther and Chia, 2001; Gunther and Christen, 2002). According to Gunther and Christen (2002), the persuasive press inference helps mitigate projection effects, and the countervailing influences of the two phenomena end up producing more accurate perceptions of public opinion. Understanding the conditions that make projection and the persuasive press inference more or less influential on perceived public opinion is an important area for future study, as is the effect of hostile media perceptions on actual public opinion.

Implications for Journalism

Perhaps the most obvious consequence of the hostile media perception is its impact on the news media as an institution. The hostile media effect gives news organizations and professional journalists an impossible job—as even fair, balanced coverage of controversial issues is perceived as biased and antagonistic by members of the groups being covered. Indeed, content analyses have failed to find evidence for a systematic media bias (e.g., D'Alessio and Allen, 2000), yet claims of its existence—albeit divergent ones—abound.

Moreover, the perceived credibility of US news organizations on the whole is staggeringly low. In 2010, no more than a third of Americans said they believe all or most of the reporting by any one of fourteen major news organizations (Pew Research Center, 2010). While there are many reasons for this, it is plausible to assume that hostile media perceptions play some role, likely in interaction with other factors (see Ladd, 2010). For one, audiences tend to extrapolate from their perceptions of a hostile bias in a small sample of issue-relevant news coverage to the media's coverage of that issue in general (Kim, 2010) as well as to the media as a whole (Gunther et al., 2001; Tsfatiand Cohen, 2005). Perceptions of bias in news coverage at one point in time also predict perceived bias at a later point (Huge and Glynn, 2010). Moreover, if the recent explosion of available media content has prompted involved partisans to consume more news (Prior, 2007) *and* they are apt to see that news as hostile, this too could explain rising negativity toward the press.

One potential result is that partisans reject useful news content that exposes them to diverse viewpoints and instead find biased or like-minded content more appealing. This helps create a market for partisan news, which, in turn, may fuel the polarization of attitudes. Indeed, on cable television, by strategically catering to partisan audiences, both Fox News on the right and MSNBC on the left have met with considerable success—particularly relative to the more neutral CNN (Project for Excellence in Journalism, 2011). Several studies confirm that perceptions of a hostile media drive news consumers to alternative, ostensibly more friendly or ideologically similar media. Morris (2007) has demonstrated that individuals who perceived hostile bias in the mainstream media were more likely to use Fox News as their primary news source. Kim (2010) concluded that, among climate change believers and deniers, hostile media perceptions predicted selective exposure to like-minded news about global warming. Choi, Watt, and Lynch (2006) found that opponents of the Iraq War perceived the Internet as less aligned with the government's prowar position and as more credible than magazines, radio, newspapers, and television. Moreover, war opponents saw the Internet as significantly less prowar and therefore less hostile than did war supporters and nonpartisans; all other sources were seen as more antagonistic by war opponents. The Internet thus provided war opponents with an alternative, "nonhostile" channel. Although there is no research directly linking hostile media perceptions to the polarization of attitudes, the fact remains that to the extent that partisan selective exposure contributes to polarization (Stroud, 2010), the existing evidence is certainly suggestive. If hostile media perceptions lead people to reject independent, balanced coverage as biased and, in so doing, drive them to news sources that reinforce their views, this could indeed exacerbate gaps in public opinion and knowledge between opposing partisans.

Implications for Political Behavior

A third consequence of the hostile media effect is its influence on political behavior. The hostile media effect has been linked to feelings of indignation toward the media (Hwang, Pan, and Sun, 2008), generalized distrust of media and government institutions (Tsfati and Cohen, 2005), social and political alienation (Tsfati, 2007), and greater willingness to engage in "corrective actions" (Rojas, 2010), ranging from discursive participation (Hwang et al., 2008; Rojas, 2010) to violent protest (Tsfati and Cohen, 2005). In the best-case scenario, these findings offer encouraging evidence for deliberative democracy, seeing that hostile media perceptions motivate people to engage in political discussion. On the other hand, these results may be worrisome for democracy, in that hostile media perceptions appear to foster widespread contempt for democratic institutions and contribute to emotionally charged, polarizing discourse. Indeed, people are more likely to participate in the public sphere when they perceive the media as hostile and themselves as marginalized. In extreme cases (Tsfati and Cohen, 2005), hostile media perceptions undermine faith in the democratic process and engender opposition—even violent opposition—to democratic decisionmaking.

Strategies to Reduce Hostile Media Perceptions

The implications of hostile media perceptions raise an important normative question regarding whether efforts should be made to reduce them. Although the literature points to certain conditions that minimize the hostile media effect, such as low reach and agreeable sources, these are not modifications that can realistically be made to naturally occurring news content. To date there has been limited research examining practical ways to minimize hostile media perceptions, although a recent study (Vraga, Tully, Atkin, and Rojas, 2010) suggests that media literacy training can do so by signaling the importance of balanced news in a democratic society and deepening the audience's understanding of the journalistic process. A focus on shifting the perceptual processes that underlie hostile media perceptions (e.g., Gunther and Liebhart, 2006) and, in so doing, narrowing partisans' latitudes of message rejection is a productive area for future research.

UNDERSTANDING HOSTILE MEDIA PERCEPTIONS IN A CHANGING NEWS ENVIRONMENT

Hostile Media Perceptions in Biased News

When Vallone et al. (1985) first documented hostile media perceptions, their assumption of neutral news content was a logical one, given the journalistic paradigm of objectivity. In today's media environment, however, news outlets—particularly on cable—have begun to appeal to particular audience segments with targeted political messages. As journalistic norms of balanced reporting give way to overtly partisan and opinionated news, the question of how news that *is* biased is perceived by partisan audiences arises. However, the original hostile media phenomenon, with its inherent assumption of balanced coverage, lacks applicability to opinionated journalism. The *relative* hostile media effect (Gunther, Christen, Liebhart, and Chia, 2001) relaxes this assumption, extending the hostile media perception to content that is slanted in favor of or against a particular issue. In the presence of a relative hostile media effect, supporters and opponents of an issue perceive bias in a consistent direction (i.e., leaning toward one side), but each group perceives coverage as significantly more unfavorable to its own position relative to the other group. Put slightly differently, partisans perceive *less* bias in news coverage slanted to support their view than do their opponents on the other side of the issue.

Interestingly, then, whereas the implication of the original hostile media effect is a partisan public perceiving media bias where none exists and thus potentially discounting valuable information, the implications of the relative hostile media effect are somewhat different. Instead, in instances when a bias is congruent with their preexisting views, partisans may fail to fully recognize it in news that actually *is* in fact biased. Partisans for whom the news is attitudinally incongruent will overestimate bias. This phenomenon is concerning. Americans' trust in news sources has become deeply divided in recent years—with Republicans, for example, attributing more credibility to Fox News and less to most other news organizations than Democrats (Pew Research Center, 2010).

Several studies have documented a relative hostile media effect in response to opinionated cable news (Arceneaux, Johnson, and Murphy, 2012; Coe et al., 2008; Feldman, 2011), whereby opposing partisans identified a consistent directional bias but differed significantly in their perceptions of its extent. That is, those exposed to counterattitudinal news perceived more bias than those exposed to pro-attitudinal coverage. Arceneaux et al. (2012) call this "oppositional media hostility"—which occurs when people become suspicious of news content from outlets other than their ideologically preferred sources and make relative hostile judgments about them. When news—particularly on cable TV and online—is infused with ideologically driven commentary, partisans may find it easier to validate their personal political beliefs by embracing information that reinforces their views and rejecting counterattitudinal advocacy. Thus the relative hostile media effect may reflect not only partisan divides in news perceptions but may also contribute to the polarization of political attitudes and knowledge.

While the mechanism that produces the relative hostile media effect is not entirely clear, it probably results from a combination of selective processing of message content and heuristic processing of source cues (e.g., Baum and Gussin, 2007). Feldman's (2011) finding that relative hostile perceptions of opinionated news *stories* were less pronounced than hostile perceptions of the opinionated news *anchor* raises the possibility that obvious news bias washes out partisan differences in story perceptions, whereas relative hostile perceptions of the anchor, or host, persist. This explanation is consistent with the notion that the latter involves making a personal inference about the host— an ostensibly more subjective judgment than assessing favoritism in a blatantly opinionated news story. Alternatively, perceived host bias may not be a hostile media effect per se—whereby partisans categorize ambiguous news content as contrary to their own position—but rather a form of motivated reasoning, in which audiences attempt to protect their preexisting beliefs by discrediting the source of a counterattitudinal news story.

Selective Versus Forced Exposure

The strongest evidence for the hostile media effect comes from experimental studies that randomly assign subjects to view or read particular news content. This conclusion raises the possibility that hostile media perceptions will not persist in a high-choice media environment where audiences have agency over their media consumption. After all, with the proliferation of information outlets on cable and the Internet, citizens uninterested in politics can avoid news altogether (Prior, 2007), while partisans can confine their exposure to like-minded sources (Stroud, 2008). Thus, although maximizing internal validity, traditional experimental designs undermine external validity by failing to account for the fact that, in the real world, audiences self-select the media content to which they are exposed (Bennett and Iyengar, 2008). Indeed, recent evidence suggests that the "forced choice" approach used in traditional experimental studies can artificially inflate hostile media perceptions. Arceneaux et al. (2012) found that the opportunity for selective exposure—specifically the ability to opt out of counterattitudinal programming or of news programming altogether—blunted but did not eliminate hostile media perceptions in response to opinionated cable news. Under conditions of forced exposure, hostile perceptions were especially strong among those who indicated a preference for entertainment over cable news programming, suggesting that this group is driving the reduction in hostile media perceptions under conditions of choice. Mende (2008) likewise demonstrated that opposing partisan groups each saw a hostile bias in a balanced news article they were forced to read; but when they selected the article themselves, the groups did not differ significantly in their perceptions of bias.

Although these studies suggest that the hostile media effect could be a methodological artifact, it is important to recognize that selectivity did not completely erase hostile media perceptions. Moreover, if, as Arceneaux et al. (2012) attest, selectivity reduces hostile media perceptions primarily by permitting those who are disinterested in politics to opt for entertainment instead of news, this says nothing of the highly involved partisans who will continue to select news even in a high-choice environment, nor does it account for evidence of the hostile media effect identified by survey methods. Still, future studies should continue to probe the consequences of selectivity for hostile media perceptions. It will also be important to better clarify the mechanism by which selective exposure reduces hostile media perceptions. Explanations exist beyond those proposed by Arceneaux et al. The theory of cognitive dissonance (Festinger, 1957), for example, suggests that once people choose to consume—or pay to subscribe to—a particular media outlet, perceiving that outlet as biased would undermine that choice, thereby creating dissonance. Under those circumstances, selectivity may narrow one's latitude of rejection or, conversely, widen one's latitude of acceptance, thereby decreasing hostile media perceptions.

Conclusions and Unanswered Questions

By proving to be robust, the hostile media effect offers compelling evidence for the active audience paradigm. Audiences do not passively receive media content but rather actively interpret it in light of their own values and predispositions. Despite journalists' best intentions to report news in a fair and objective way, partisans are motivated to see balanced content as harboring a hostile bias. These hostile media perceptions emerge from a complex constellation of factors—including partisan involvement and the related impulse to protect a vulnerable public from undue media influence, a source's perceived like-mindedness, elite cues, discussion networks, and individuals' agency over their media consumption—all of which interact with the news message itself. Of course the hostile media phenomenon is of concern primarily because of its effects on political attitudes and behaviors. More than just an instantiation of selective perception, the hostile media effect has implications for perceived public opinion, news consumption patterns, attitudes toward democratic institutions, and political discourse and participation. Its very existence raises questions about whether media bias is something that can ever be objectively assessed. Still, it was only a few decades ago that the hostile media effect was first documented, and it generated sustained research attention only in the last several years. Thus, as highlighted throughout this chapter, a number of questions have yet to be answered, offering a productive agenda for future research.

First, deeper attention should be given to individual differences in hostile media perceptions. In addition to better clarifying the role of involvement, it would be beneficial to study other individual-level moderators of the hostile media effect. For example, political sophistication has generated mixed findings as a moderator of hostile media perceptions (e.g., Dalton et al., 1998; Vallone et al., 1985).

Whereas recent empirical research supports selective categorization as the psychological mechanism accounting for the hostile media effect, it is unclear whether this notion can account for the influence of prior beliefs about the media in general or about a particular media source on hostile media perceptions, or whether heuristic processing—or some other, unidentified mechanism—is at play (see Giner-Sorolla and Chaiken, 1994; Gunther and Liebhart, 2006). Similarly, the mechanisms at work in relative hostile judgments about biased news are as yet poorly understood. In seeking to clarify the processes by which people develop hostile media perceptions, the possibility of moderated mediation effects (Preacher, Rucker, and Hayes, 2007)—whereby the mechanism depends on the level of partisan involvement, the news source, or other contextual factors—should be explored. A fuller understanding of the mechanisms underlying the hostile media effect would, in turn, inform ways to encourage more accurate perceptions of media bias among news audiences—an area of research that has thus far been relatively ignored.

Ultimately the hostile media effect is only one of several perceptual phenomena that influence how citizens relate to and participate in a democratic society. Efforts to integrate the hostile media perception with associated processes—including projection, the persuasive press inference, biased assimilation, and the spiral of silence—will undoubtedly continue, with an eye toward better specifying the conditions under which these sometimes competing processes occur.

Importantly, the hostile media phenomenon seems to offer a critical tool for understanding the changes in and consequences of the contemporary media environment. For example, hostile media perceptions encourage selective exposure to like-minded news. Partisans, in turn, respond to opinionated and biased news by making relatively hostile judgments. In some cases, hostile media perceptions activate retaliatory communication and action. However, the conclusions that we can ultimately draw about the polarizing effects of hostile media perceptions are at this point quite tentative. Thus an important objective for future research is to probe the attitudinal and behavioral outcomes of hostile media perceptions in order to better understand the extent to which partisans' perceptual biases are serving to polarize news consumption, political attitudes, and discourse.

It is also important to consider how changes in our media landscape implicate hostile media perceptions. Research has only begun to explore whether the increased opportunity for media choice reduces hostile media perceptions; while the results are suggestive, replication of these studies in different contexts, using different messages and research designs, would be helpful, as would a broader exploration of the mechanisms by which selectivity weakens hostile media perceptions. Moreover, in today's media environment, audiences are not merely active but *interactive*—responding to, sharing, and producing new content from the media they consume. Thus audiences' interpretations of media content are shaped not only by their partisan motivations or elite cues but also by how their online social networks and the broader news audience reacts to the news in real time. Understanding the implications of these social influences for hostile media perceptions is an important area of future research. Finally, although scholars have begun to study the hostile media effect in nonwestern countries (e.g., Chia et al., 2007; Ariyanto et al., 2007), more research is needed to determine the generalizability of and variations in this phenomenon across cultures and media systems, particularly in news media traditions where the expectation is for bias instead of objectivity.

With trust in the US news media at its lowest point in more than two decades (Pew Research Center, 2009) and the media audience deeply fragmented across partisan and ideological lines (Pew Research Center, 2010), understanding how audiences perceive news content, as well as the reasons for and consequences of these perceptions, has never been more critical. Fortunately, empirical and theoretical efforts to elaborate the hostile media effect are well underway. With continued attention, this area of scholarship should yield fruitful insights into the implications of the active news audience for democratic life.

References

Arceneaux, K., M. Johnson, and C. Murphy. 2012. Polarized political communication, oppositional media hostility, and selective exposure. *Journal of Politics*, 74(1): 174–186.

Ariyanto, A., M., J. Hornsey, and C. Gallois. 2007. Group allegiances and perceptions of media bias: Taking into account both the perceiver and the source. *Group Processes & Intergroup Relations*, 10(2): 266–279.

Arpan, L. M., and A. A. Raney. 2003. An experimental investigation of news source and the hostile media effect. *Journalism and Mass Communication Quarterly*, 80(2): 265–281.

Baum, M. A., and P. Gussin. 2007. In the eye of the beholder: How information shortcuts shape individual perceptions of bias in the media. *Quarterly Journal of Political Science*, 3(1): 1–31.

Bennett, W. L., and S. Iyengar. 2008. A new era of minimal effects? The changing foundations of political communication. *Journal of Communication*, 58(4): 707–731.

Chia, S. C., S.Y.J. Yong, Z.W.D. Wong, and W. L. Koh. 2007. Personal bias or government bias? Testing the hostile media effect in a regulated press system. *International Journal of Public Opinion Research*, 19(3): 313–330.

Choi, J., M. Yang, and J. Chang. 2009. Elaboration of the hostile media phenomenon: The roles of involvement, media skepticism, congruency of perceived media influence, and perceived opinion climate. *Communication Research*, 36(1): 54–75.

Choi, J. H., J. H. Watt, and M. Lynch. 2006. Perceptions of news credibility about the war in Iraq: Why war opponents perceived the Internet as the most credible medium. *Journal of Computer-Mediated Communication*, 12(1): 209–229.

Christen, C. T., P. Kannaovakun, and A. C. Gunther. 2002. Hostile media perceptions: Partisan assessments of press and public during the 1997 United Parcel Service strike. *Political Communication*, 19(4): 423–436.

Coe, K., D. Tewksbury, B. J. Bond, K. L. Drogos, R. W. Porter, A. Yahn, and Y. Zhang. 2008. Hostile news: Partisan use and perceptions of cable news programming. *Journal of Communication*, 58(2): 201–219.

D'Alessio, D., and M. Allen. 2000. Media bias in presidential elections: A meta-analysis. *Journal of Communication*, 50(4): 133–156.

Dalton, R. J., P. A. Beck, and R. Huckfeldt. 1998. Partisan cues and the media: Information flows in the 1992 presidential election. *The American Political Science Review*, 92(1): 111–126.

Eveland, W. P., and D. V. Shah. 2003. The impact of individual and interpersonal factors on perceived news media bias. *Political Psychology*, 24(1): 101–117.

Feldman, L. 2011. Partisan differences in opinionated news perceptions: A test of the hostile media effect. *Political Behavior*, 33(3): 407–432.

Festinger, L. 1957. *A theory of cognitive dissonance*. Stanford, CA: Stanford University Press.

Fields, J. M., and H. Schuman. 1976. Public beliefs about the beliefs of the public. *Public Opinion Quarterly*, 40(4): 427–448.

Giner-Sorolla, R., and S. Chaiken. 1994. The causes of hostile media judgments. *Journal of Experimental Social Psychology*, 30(2): 165–180.

Gunther, A. C. 1992. Biased press or biased public? Attitudes toward media coverage of social groups. *Public Opinion Quarterly*, 56(2): 147–167.

Gunther, Albert C. 1998. The persuasive press inference. *Communication Research*, 25(5): 486–504.

Gunther, A. C., and S. C. Chia. 2001. Predicting pluralistic ignorance: The hostile media perception and its consequences. *Journalism & Mass Communication Quarterly*, 78(4): 688–701.

Gunther, A. C., and C. T. Christen. 2002. Projection or persuasive press? Contrary effects of personal opinion and perceived news coverage on estimates of public opinion. *Journal of Communication*, 52(1): 177–195.

Gunther, A. C., C. T. Christen, J. L. Liebhart, and S.C. Chia. 2001. Congenial public, contrary press, and biased estimates of the climate of opinion. *Public Opinion Quarterly*, 65(3): 295–320.

Gunther, A. C., and J. L. Liebhart. 2006. Broad reach or biased source? Decomposing the hostile media effect. *Journal of Communication*, 56(3): 449–466.

Gunther, A. C., N. Miller, and J. L. Liebhart. 2009. Assimilation and contrast in a test of the hostile media effect. *Communication Research*, 36(6): 747–764.

Gunther, A.C., and K. Schmitt. 2004. Mapping boundaries of the hostile media effect. *Journal of Communication*, 54(1): 55–70.

Hansen, G. J., and H. Kim. 2011. Is the media biased against me? A meta-analysis of the hostile media effect research. *Communication Research Reports*, 28(2): 169–179.

Hoffman, L. H., and C. J. Glynn. 2008. Media and perceptions of reality. In W. Donsbach (Ed.), *The international encyclopedia of communication*, Vol. VII (pp. 2945–2959). Malden, MA: Blackwell.

Huge, M., and C. J. Glynn. 2010. Hostile media and the campaign trail: Perceived media bias in the race for governor. *Journal of Communication*, 60(1): 165–181.

Hwang, H., Z. Pan, and Y. Sun. 2008. Influence of hostile media perception on willingness to engage in discursive activities: An examination of mediating role of media indignation. *Media Psychology*, 11(1): 76–97.

Kim, K. S. 2010. Public understanding of the politics of global warming in the news media: The hostile media approach. *Public Understanding of Science* (Online First July 27). doi: 10.1177/0963662510372313. Available at: http://pus.sagepub.com/content/early/2010/07/26/0963662510372313

Ladd, J. M. 2010. The neglected power of elite opinion leadership to produce antipathy toward the news media: Evidence from a survey experiment. *Political Behavior*, 32(1): 29–50.

Lord, C. G., L. Ross, and M. R. Lepper. 1979. Biased assimilation and attitude polarization: The effects of prior theories on subsequently considered evidence. *Journal of Personality and Social Psychology*, 37(11): 2098–2109.

Mende, A. 2008. Testing the hostile media effect under selective exposure. Paper Presented at the 58th Annual Conference of the International Communication Association, Montreal, Quebec, Canada, May 22-26.

Morales, L. September 29, 2010. Distrust in U.S. media edges up to record high. Gallup. Available at: http://www.gallup.com/poll/143267/Distrust-Media-Edges-Record-High.aspx

Morris, J. S. 2007. Slanted objectivity? Perceived media bias, cable news exposure, and political attitudes. *Social Science Quarterly*, 88(3): 707–728.

Noelle-Neumann, E. 1984. *The spiral of silence: Public opinion—our social skin*. Chicago: University of Chicago Press.

Perloff, R. M. 1989. Ego-involvement and the third person effect of televised news coverage. *Communication Research*, 16(2): 236–262.

Pew Research Center. September 12, 2010. Americans spending more time following the news. Available at: http://people-press.org/2010/09/12/americans-spending-more-time-following-the-news/

Pew Research Center. September 13, 2009. Press accuracy rating hits two decade low. Available at: http://people-press.org/2009/09/13/press-accuracy-rating-hits-two-decade-low/

Pew Research Center's Project for Excellence in Journalism. 2011. *The state of the news media 2011: An annual report on American journalism.* Available at: http://www.stateofthemedia. org/2011/

Preacher, K. J., D. D. Rucker, and A. F. Hayes. 2007. Assessing moderated mediation hypotheses: Theory, methods, and prescriptions. *Multivariate Behavioral Research*, 42: 185–227.

Prior, M. 2007. *Post-broadcast democracy: How media choice increases inequality in political involvement and polarizes elections.* New York: Cambridge University Press.

Rojas, H. 2010. "Corrective" actions in the public sphere: How perceptions of media and media effects shape political behaviors. *International Journal of Public Opinion Research*, 22(3): 343–363.

Schmitt, K. M., A. C. Gunther, and J. L. Liebhart. 2004. Why partisans see mass media as biased. *Communication Research*, 31(6): 623–641.

Sherif, M., and C. I. Hovland. 1961. *Social judgment: Assimilation and contrast effects in communication and attitude change.* New Haven, CT: Yale University Press.

Stroud, N. J. 2008. Media use and political predispositions: Revisiting the concept of selective exposure. *Political Behavior*, 30(3): 341–366.

Stroud, N. J. 2010. Polarization and partisan selective exposure. *Journal of Communication*, 60(3): 556–576.

Tsfati, Y. 2007. Hostile media perceptions, presumed media influence, and minority alienation: The case of Arabs in Israel. *Journal of Communication*, 57(4): 632–651.

Tsfati, Y., and J. Cohen. 2005. Democratic consequences of hostile media perceptions. *The Harvard International Journal of Press/Politics*, 10(4): 28–51.

Vallone, R.P., L. Ross, and M. R. Lepper. 1985. The hostile media phenomenon: Biased perception and perceptions of media bias in coverage of the Beirut massacre. *Journal of Personality and Social Psychology*, 49(3): 577–585.

Vraga, E. K., M. Tully, H.E. Atkin, and H. Rojas. 2010. Reducing hostile media perceptions for an environmental controversy through media literacy. Paper Presented at the Annual Meeting of the International Communication Association, Singapore, June 22.

Watts, M. D., D. Domke, D. V. Shah, and D. P. Fan. 1999. Elite cues and media bias in presidential campaigns. *Communication Research*, 26(2): 144–175.

CHAPTER 39

PUBLIC AND ELITE PERCEPTIONS OF NEWS MEDIA IN POLITICS

YARIV TSFATI

IMPORTANCE OF AREA

THIS chapter deals with individuals' perceptions about and attitudes toward the news media. People's views of media, particularly their conceptions of media influence, shape politics in many important ways. For example, many of the Egyptian protestors in Al-Tahrir Square carried signs in English, not because they anticipated that such signs would directly force President Hosni Mubarak to resign, but because they expected the international media to influence world elites to pressure Mubarak to do so. In the first six months of his presidency, President Barack Obama held four prime-time press conferences (the same number held by George W. Bush in his entire presidency) and made a record number of presidential appearances on talk shows, comedy shows, and online video messages. According to some analysts, this strategy was designed to influence the public to support his relatively unpopular policy initiatives (Senior, 2009). Some politicians participate in reality shows because they think doing so may positively affect voters. Some voters, in turn, change their votes because they think other voters are affected by media messages (Cohen and Tsfati, 2009; Golan, Banning, and Lundy, 2008).

Research investigating people's perceptions of media has focused on three main areas: trust in media, hostile media perceptions (HMPs), and perceptions of media impact ("third person perceptions"). In addition to reviewing the literature on *lay citizens'* views of media, this chapter argues that the perceptions about the news media among the *elite*, which by and large have been ignored by scholars working in this domain, are consequential in shaping the political world.

DEFINITIONS

The notion of trust in media applies the definition of the general concept of trust to the specific context of the relationship between the audience and media (Kohring and Matthes, 2007). General trust is defined as a "risky undertaking with the expectation of a future reward" (Luhmann, 1979, 42). The truster expects some benefit or at least reduced damage to result from the interaction with the trustee but has no empirical way to verify that this expectation is justified. In the context of the audience's trust in media, the potential gains for trusters include obtaining valid, accurate, comprehensive, and unbiased information about the world. The potential risks involve, for example, wasting one's time on news consumption only to discover later that the information obtained from the news was wrong. As a consequence, the potential "losses" resulting from violations of trust in media may include voting for the "wrong" candidate or party or buying the "wrong" stock, based on inaccurate media information. Research demonstrates that trust in media is composed of several elements, including the audience's trust in the news's selection of topics, journalists' selection of facts, the accuracy of depictions, and journalistic assessments and interpretation of the facts (Kohring and Matthes, 2007). Thus, trust in media may be defined as the expectation that journalists will report the news professionally (Tsfati, 2003a).

While trust in media is an expectation directed at news institutions in general, hostile media perceptions are targeted at particular messages. The hostile media phenomenon occurs when members of two opposing political groups evaluate the same, relatively even-handed, news clip (e.g., in the initial study, about the 1982 Beirut massacre) as biased against their point of view (Vallone, Ross, and Lepper, 1985). Later studies replicated these findings about hostile media in other contexts, using both experimental and survey designs. While the initial design in this paradigm used relatively balanced news clips as the stimulus material, the findings have since been extended to cases in which media coverage is clearly *imbalanced* (Gunther et al., 2001). Scholars have also documented a *relative* hostile media phenomenon "in which each group perceives news coverage to be either more hostile to, or at least less agreeable with, their own point of view than the opposing group sees it" (Gunther and Chia, 2001, 690).

Third person perceptions (TPP) relate not to perceptions of bias but rather to those of media influence. Such perceptions may focus on the news media in general or on the impact of a specific news message. Research on the third person effect stems from W. Phillip Davison's (1983) observation that people tend to perceive media messages as having a greater effect on others than on them. More recent work on the influence of presumed media influence (Gunther and Storey, 2003) has concentrated on general perceptions of media influence on others, particularly on the attitudinal and behavioral consequences of such perceptions.

Major Findings

Factors predicting and explaining trust in media, hostile media perceptions (HMPs), and TPPs have been reviewed elsewhere (e.g., Choi, Yang, and Chung, 2009; Lee, 2010; Perloff, 2009; Tal-Or, Tsfati, and Gunther, 2009). For the sake of brevity, the main explanations are summarized in Table 39.1. There is a relative consensus among scholars investigating the TPP that self-preservation processes play a role in shaping this phenomenon. On the other hand, most research on the predictors of the HMP has focused on cognitive processes. Relatively little is known about why people trust or mistrust the news media. While each of these perceptions is explained by similar but distinct psychological processes, all three produce important political consequences.

People's mistrust of media moderates the influence of media on the audience and shapes audience news media selections (e.g., Tsfati, 2002). At least when it comes to agenda setting (Tsfati, 2003b), framing (Druckman, 2001), priming (Miller and Krosnick, 2000), and public opinion perceptions (Tsfati, 2003a), trusting audiences are more influenced by the news media than audiences who are mistrustful of mainstream news coverage. Trusting audiences also tend to have more mainstream media exposure in their news diets, especially if they score low on cognitive needs (Tsfati and Cappella, 2005).

Trust in media may have macro-level political ramifications as well. According to some accounts, the increase in audience distrust of the news media over the past forty years has been an important contributor to the growing polarization of the American political system (Ladd, 2005).

While most research on the HMP has focused on the causes of this perceptual bias, several explorations have documented its consequences. Results indicated that HMPs can have an effect on opinion climate estimations, political and social alienation, and other outcomes (Tsfati, 2007). While an association between HMP and general trust in media has been documented, the causal mechanism underlying this association is still unclear. Some scholars argue that general attitudes toward media shape HMPs (Giner-Sorolla and Chaiken, 1994), while others contend that HMPs shape trust in media (Tsfati and Cohen, 2005a). Research also demonstrates that HMPs affect audience estimations of public opinion. According to this line of research, dubbed "the persuasive press inference," people perceive that slants in present media coverage will have an impact on future public opinion. Thus, HMPs contribute to perceptions of a hostile climate of opinion (Gunther, 1998; Gunther and Christen, 2002).

Most research on the outcomes of public perceptions of media has focused on the effects of perceptions about the impact of media. This line of research, also dubbed "the behavioral component of the TPP" or "the influence of presumed media influence," demonstrated that people's perceptions regarding media impact matter, albeit indirectly, because individuals react to these perceptions as if they were real (e.g., Tal-Or, Tsfati,

Table 39.1 Summary of the Main Explanations of Trust in Media, Hostile Media Perception, and Third Person Perception

	Trust in media	HMP	TPP
Cognitive explanations: Perceptions about media reflect respondents' use of social cues and information.	– Trust in media is influenced by the accuracy of media predictions (Major and Atwood, 1997). – Elite cues containing criticism of media shape media trust, over and above any real evidence of bias in news (Watts et al., 1999). This may explain why, in the US, conservatives (Lee, 2010) esp. frequent talk radio listeners, tend to mistrust media (Jones, 2004). – Journalistic practices (like quoting) shape audience trust in the message (e.g., Sundar, 1998). – Social information (e.g., stereotypes) about reporters and anchors is considered when people assess credibility (Weibel, Wissmath, and Groner, 2008).	– Different standards: Supportive information in news articles is treated as valid, but opposing arguments are perceived as invalid and are interpreted as bias (Giner-Sorolla and Chaiken, 1994; Gunther and Liebhart, 2007). – Selective categorization: The information is perceived differentially (e.g. to partisans, neutral arguments may seem hostile) in a way that makes the news segment on the whole seem more negative (Giner-Sorolla and Chaiken, 1994). – The source of the message and its perceived reach are factored in when people assess its hostility (Gunther and Liebhart, 2006; Gunther, Miller and Liebhart, 2009).	When assessing the impact of media on others, people use their knowledge of – The exposure of others (Eveland et al., 1999); – The perceived relevance of the message to the target audience (Elder, Douglas, and Sutton, 2006; Jensen and Hurley, 2005; Tsfati and Cohen, 2004); – In-group and out-group norms (self-categorization theory; Reid et al., 2007); and – The susceptibility of the audience to influence and the severity of the effect (Shah, Faber, and Youn, 1999). Other cognitive processes such as stereotypes (Scharrer, 2002) and attribution errors (Rucinski and Salmon, 1990) operate when estimating media impact on others.
Self-enhancement (motivational) explanations: Perceptions about media stem from internal motivation to preserve one's self-value.	People mistrust media when media messages conflict with their important beliefs and attitudes. This is why extreme partisans mistrust media (Gunther, 1988).	– The HMP is a strategy to enhance a positive in-group identity (social identity theory; Matheson and Dursun, 2001). – Ego-involvement, not outcome-involvement, explains HMPs (Choi, Yang, and Chang, 2009), probably because very ego-involved individuals are motivated to reject messages that threaten deeply held values.	– The TPP tends to decrease in response to high-quality or pro-social messages (White, 1997; Zhong, 2009) and may even reverse when it comes to positive messages (FPP; Gunther and Hwa, 1996). – The TPP tends to increase as the social distance between oneself and a comparison group increases (Chia, 2009; Ivory and Kalyanaraman, 2009). – The TPP is substitutable with other self-preserving biases (Tal-Or and Tfstai, 2007).
Personality and political factors	General trust and political trust (Lee, 2010), political conservatism, and attitude extremity (Gunther, 1988) shape trust in media.	Previous attitudes toward media predict HMPs (Giner-Sorolla and Chaiken, 1994).	Self-monitoring (Tal-Or and Drukman, 2010); Paternalism (McLeod et al., 2001).
Social factors	Cues from the interpersonal environment are factored into credibility judgments (Eveland and Shah, 2003).		Social relationships affect perceptions of media impact (Henriksen and Flora, 1999, Table 2).

and Gunther, 2009). Most work in this domain has focused on audience support of message restrictions in reaction to perceptions of influence of harmful political messages (Salwen, 1998; see Xu and Gonzebach, 2008, for a meta-analysis). However, TPPs are not as likely to predict support for censoring the news (e.g., Salwen and Driscoll, 1997) as they are to forecast the embrace of censorship of violent or sexual content, perhaps because public concern about freedom of speech is stronger in the political domain.

In addition to these "restrictive" reactions, scholars have proposed that some of the reactions to perceptions of media impact are "corrective." Rojas (2010), for example, demonstrated that those who attributed high levels of influence to biased media are more disposed to take political actions such as trying to persuade a friend to vote for a specific candidate or expressing their views offline (by attending rallies or protests or signing petitions) or online (by posting their views in online forums) in order to blunt the presumed effects and counteract the biased messages "that would otherwise sway public opinion" (343).

While Rojas focused on expressive "corrective" responses to perceptions about the effects of media—reactions in which "people use the communication tools at their disposal to make sure their views are heard" in what they perceive as a biased public sphere—other research has focused on more active behavioral outcomes. Golan, Banning, and Lundy (2008) suggested that when people conclude that less sophisticated others are influenced by political advertising, they may be more likely to vote in order to compensate for the possible electoral participation of those duped by such content. Similarly, Cohen and Tsfati (2009) demonstrated that in a multiparty system, perceived media influence on others may under some circumstances be related to strategic voting. Specifically, when people believed that media may have affected the voting decisions of others, they were more likely to vote for a party other than the one they most prefer. For example, people who had originally intended to vote for a small party may switch their support to a larger one, because they conclude that negative news coverage of their preferred party will cost it the votes needed to gain representation.

An extreme form of "corrective" political action may involve violent political protest. Right-wing Jewish settlers in the Gaza Strip who believed that Israeli public opinion about the settlements was heavily influenced by unfavorably biased media coverage were more likely to report that they would forcefully resist government efforts to uproot them (Tsfati and Cohen, 2005b). This reaction could also be perceived as corrective, because the settlers believed that without the role played by media, the public would never have supported what they saw as an irrational, unilateral withdrawal initiative. While behavioral intentions rather than actual behaviors were documented in this study, and while the study was conducted in a unique and extreme context, the results confirm that perceptions about the power of media may prompt various types of reactions that may include political violence.

According to some scholars, TPPs may not lead just to various restrictive and corrective political responses. Perceptions about the impact of media and the third person effect may also be involved in other theories about media effects and processes. Huck, Quiring, and Brosius (2009) propose that TPPs underlie the agenda-setting effect: Issues that receive media attention are not directly perceived as the most important collective problems. First, individual audience members perceive that the focus on these issues in news media makes the general public think that they are important. Consequently, individual audience members assume that if such issues matter to so many people (presumably, because of media coverage), then they must be important public issues. The TPP may also account for the spiral of silence effect. Noelle-Neumann's (1974) model implies that people may not express their personal opinions because they feel that the news media cause *other* people to hold *contrary* opinions (for a discussion of and evidence about the spiral of silence in the TPP context, see Mutz, 1989). Thus, the TPP may indirectly influence spiral of silence processes through its effect on perceptions about the climate of public opinion (Willnat, 1996).

When considering the consequences of the audience's perceptions about media, we must keep three important facts in mind. First, the effects of perceptions of media influence are amplified when they are coupled with perceptions of media hostility (Rojas, 2010), especially among audiences who are personally and emotionally involved in the issues on which the news media are reporting (Tsfati, 2007). Second, while many of these results are based on correlational designs that raise questions about causality, experimental research has established that perceptions of media impact are the *cause* of behavioral intentions (Dillard, Shen, and Vail, 2007; Tal-Or et al., 2010). However, the possibility of a reverse effect potentially operating simultaneously has never been examined experimentally. Finally, evidence demonstrates that the three distinct perceptions—trust in media, hostile media perceptions, and third person perceptions—are empirically related. While the statistically significant relationship between HMPs and TPPs has long been established (Vallone, Ross, and Lepper, 1985; Perloff, 1989), work documenting the association between both of them and trust in media is relatively recent (Choi, Yang, and Chang. 2009; Tsfati and Cohen, 2005a; Wei, Lo, and Lu, 2011).

ELITE PERCEPTIONS

In contrast to the huge volume of studies dedicated to public perceptions about media, relatively little study has addressed the possibly more consequential perceptions of the elite. Commenting on politicians' perceptions about media, several scholars used anecdotes to demonstrate that what politicians think about media power shapes political life (Cohen, Tsfati, and Sheafer, 2008). The most well-known example is Democratic candidate Gary Hart's decision to withdraw from the 1988 presidential primary race in the United States. Hart, a front runner at the time, withdrew from the race because of an embarrassing article that had not yet been printed but that was expected to undercut his prospects (Becker and Kosicki, 1995, 54; Mutz, 1989, 4). As Mutz put it, "Whether public sentiment in response to that article would have truly eliminated Hart from the race became a moot point; Hart's assumptions about media impact, right or wrong, changed the course of the election."

Very few scholars have investigated politicians' perceptions about the power of the media, probably because of the difficulty of obtaining the cooperation of elected legislators and officials. The few empirical investigations that are available—examining members of parliament in Sweden (Stromback, 2010), Israel (Cohen, Tsfati, and Sheafer, 2008), and Belgium and the Netherlands (Van Aelst et al., 2008); American congresspersons (Bennett and Yanovitzky, 2000); and local officials in Sweden (Johansson, 2004)—all demonstrated that politicians believe that the news media are enormously influential. In one of the studies, for example, 91 percent of Belgian politicians "completely agreed" that "the media make and break politicians," and 87.8 percent completely agreed that "the mass media have too much political power" (Van Aelst et al., 2008, 501; the equivalent rates in the Netherlands were 70.9 and 68.8 percent, respectively). Results also demonstrated that politicians' TPPs are significantly and substantially larger than those of average citizens (Johansson, 2004), and that the former's perceptions about the influence of the media are much stronger than those of journalists (Stromback, 2010; Van Aelst et al., 2008).

Research has documented that politicians' perceptions about the power of the media are not only sizeable, but they also shape their interactions with the news media. Cohen, Tsfati, and Sheafer (2008) interviewed members of the Israeli Knesset and obtained data from Knesset reporters about the motivation and efforts these members of Knesset (MKs) invest in pursuing news coverage. A very strong statistical association was found between MKs' perceptions about the impact of the media on the audience, their motivation to be covered by media, and the efforts they expended in obtaining such coverage. Given the important role of motivation as an almost-necessary condition for obtaining media coverage, the desire to gain such coverage and the amount of effort invested in achieving this goal were the best predictors of the actual amount of news media coverage received by the MKs, as measured by content analysis. The findings demonstrate that perceptions about the power of the media have a substantial, indirect effect on politicians' appearances in the media. This effect was fully mediated by the motivation to gain media coverage and the MKs' efforts in achieving this goal. For the most part, journalists' "routine" coverage of politics is initiated by the politicians themselves, and journalists do not often actively seek information that they are not "fed." Thus, politicians who invest in appearing in the news, issue press releases, maintain close ties with journalists, and cooperate with journalists' requests are very likely to receive such coverage. In other words, because of the degree to which most beat journalists tend to rely on or react to information they receive rather than initiating inquiries, the more politicians believe that the media have a strong influence on voters, the more they are covered frequently by the news media.

These findings, confirming both widespread belief among politicians in the impact of news media in politics and the effects of these beliefs on media motivation and efforts, may explain research findings demonstrating that politicians themselves report that much of the behavior of political actors is motivated by the urge to get journalists' attention and coverage, an urge that scholars call "media salacity" (Brants et al., 2010).

However, perceptions about news media power not only shape politicians' public relations efforts but also affect other aspects of their work. When a certain issue (such as drunk driving, the environment, or terrorism) is expected to receive substantial media attention, politicians react by initiating legislation (Baumgartner, Jones, and Leech, 1997; Yanovitky and Stryker, 2001). Presumably this institutional response takes place because legislators expect to receive news coverage as a result of their activity on the newsworthy topic, and because they expect that this coverage will bring them favorable public support. As Walgrave and Van Aelst note: "Political actors . . . do not primarily react on media coverage itself but on (presumed) public opinion. . . . [P]olitical actors anticipate the expected media impact on the public and build their political strategy on that premise" (2006, 100).

Scholars have also pointed out that much of the media activity of politicians is aimed at influencing their counterparts in the policymaking process. In other words, a politician may covet news coverage because she perceives that this coverage will affect fellow politicians, making her seem more prominent and attracting the attention of these fellow politicians to the issues and initiatives close to her heart (Cook, 1989; Kedrowski, 1996). It is well known that political actors use the media to communicate with each other (e.g., Walgrave and Van Aelst, 2006, 100), but at least part of the motivation for this mass-mediated communication within the political system seems to relate to the presumed reaction of other politicians to the communicated message.

Thus, politicians' belief that news media influence both voters and other political actors explains at least in part their pursuit of news coverage. These perceptions may be at the heart of a decades-long process scholars call "the mediatization of politics" (Altheide and Snow, 1979; Ericson, Baranek, and Chan, 1989). Defined by some as an "increasing intrusion of the media in the political process" (Mazzoleni and Schulz, 1999, 248) and by others as "the unconditional surrender of politics . . . to the logic of the media system" (Meyer, 2002, 71–72), mediatization processes seem to be driven to a large extent by politicians' perceptions that media have a powerful influence on politics. Drawing on their conviction that media make and break elections and political careers, politicians conclude that they need to comply with media demands and logic in order to succeed in the political realm (Stromback, 2010).

If elite perceptions about the impact of media on voters and politicians are the cause of the growing takeover of political life by the media, then perceptions about the impact of media may help us understand why the introduction of C-SPAN has had an influence on filibustering in the US Senate (Mixon, Gibson, and Upadhyaya, 2003), why during the 1970s and 1980s politicians were increasingly trying to speak in short sound bites in order to accommodate the production values of television news (Hallin, 1992, 13–14), and why politicians even admit time and again that attracting media attention is an indispensable part of their work. Thus, it would not be an exaggeration to say that politicians' perceptions about the power of the media have had a tremendous influence on their work and on their interactions with the news media.

Unanswered Questions and Future Research Directions

This chapter has focused on three empirically related perceptions: trust in media, hostile media perceptions, and perceptions of media impact. While ample research has been dedicated to the factors underlying these perceptions and their consequences for democratic *citizens*, not much empirical research has been devoted to the sources and consequences of *politicians'* perceptions of media. We do know that politicians believe that media have a stronger influence on others and on society than laypeople believe they do. In addition, there is some indication that the size of the effects of these perceptions of influence on politicians' behavior is larger than in the case of ordinary citizens. However, we do not know why politicians and laypeople differ in their perceptions about the influence of media or why the reaction of the former to perceived media impact seems to be much stronger than that of the latter. Is it merely because of politicians' greater involvement with media and politics? Or is it because politicians are possibly more paternalistic or score higher on self-monitoring than ordinary citizens? These questions should be addressed in future research.

Another set of issues for scholars relates to the accuracy of politicians' perceptions. Interestingly, while research on *lay citizens'* perceptions about media demonstrates that these views are rather sensible cognitive errors or self-serving misperceptions or exaggerations, research on *politicians* seems to argue that their perceptions of media impact are the result of careful deliberations and consultations with experts and that their reactions to these perceptions are strategically planned rather than spontaneous. Is it possible that politicians are wrong in perceiving that the mass media have a sizeable impact on their careers and on political life? It is difficult to answer this question conclusively, given the current state of research on the effects of communication on voters. Some empirical research shows that media coverage of candidates does indeed affect their electoral success (Bartels, 1988; Zaller, 1992). However, even in these studies the evidence points to statistically moderate effects, in a way that suggests the possibility that the image of the news media's make-or-break role in politics is at least somewhat exaggerated. Again, more research is needed to assess the accuracy of both lay citizens' and politicians' perceptions of media.

The chapter reviewed evidence that trust in media is empirically associated with HMPs and that both are correlated with perceptions of media power. Another set of unanswered questions relates to the mechanisms underlying these associations. Do trust and other deeply held attitudes toward news media undergird HMPs and TPPs, or is it possible that it is specific interactions with presumably hostile and influential texts that shape the more general trustful or mistrustful attitudes? The evidence reviewed in this chapter suggests that the perceptions about the news media held by the public and the elite are related. We know that elite cues regarding news media, especially elite allegations that they are untrustworthy, have a stronger impact on public trust in media than do the actual fairness and balance of the news media (Domke et al., 1999). However, could it be that the reason for politicians' attacks on the news media has to do with the negative public sentiments toward the news media expressed in public opinion polls? Could it be that blaming the news media, their so-called hostility and their power, is a strategy utilized by politicians to increase their own popularity and public support? The relationship between public and politicians' perceptions about media should also be further examined in future research.

Virtually all of the hundreds of studies about perceptions of media and their consequences occur in the context of traditional media channels. Another challenging question is how this model will play on the contemporary stage of online political communication. On the one hand, online media are often perceived as potent. Pundits and the general public have already pointed to this power to account for a variety of political consequences, from the "Facebook Revolution" in Egypt to the Obama "YouTube" and "MySpace" election. On the other hand, online media offer audiences a great deal of information about how others think and react to mediated messages. Audience reactions to online news stories may contain information that would positively or negatively affect our trust in the message and our perception of its hostility. Merely seeing how many readers visited a news story or watched or liked a political speech or an election ad may shape our perception of the power of these texts. Trust in media, HMPs, and TPPs are still inferences and will most probably remain inferences in the future. However, they are inferences potentially shaped by a technology that gives us all a new and far more interactive connection to the public sphere. That interactive connection increases our ability to learn what others are reading and watching, what they like, and how they are reacting—information that is pivotal to trust in media, HMPs, and presumed media influence.

The normative implications of these findings raise a final set of questions as well. Scholars investigating citizens' perceptions about media celebrate the fact that audiences emerge as more competent and powerful in research on the HMPs and TPPs and media trust (e.g., Tsfati, 2002) than in many other studies in the "effects" tradition, which portray audiences as less conscious and relatively more passive. *Citizens* appear from studies on media perceptions as critical and active, holding the ability to resist media portrayals in a reception-theory manner. When they react to media portrayals, they incorporate what they think they know about media and their influence in their reactions. However, when considering the ramifications of research on *politicians'* reactions and perceptions, it is not as clear that there is a reason for celebration. Are politicians' perceptions about the enormous effects of media and their actions in response to such perceptions detrimental for democratic life? Or, perhaps on the contrary, are such perceptions and reactions beneficial because they keep public officials attuned to the criticisms and concerns of the Fourth Estate?

The main implication of this chapter is that we should pay more attention to perceptions about the news media in political communication theory building. Audience perceptions about media shape politics in a variety of ways. They may also be a key mechanism underlying important political communication theories (such as agenda setting and the spiral of silence) and the explanation for important political processes such as the mediatization of politics. In addition to trying to explain audience mistrust of the media, HMPs, and TPPs, we should also try to understand how these perceptions affect the interactions among politicians, news media, and citizens. The consequences of HMPs, TPPs, and trust in media should be tested in additional contexts. Furthermore, we should demonstrate the temporal sequence advanced by current theories more rigorously. A more detailed explanation of the conditions under which politicians react to their perceptions about the power of media seems warranted. Thus, as always, much is left for further research.

References

Altheide, D. L., and Snow, R. P. 1979. *Media logic.* Beverly Hills, CA: Sage.

Bartels, L. M. 1988. *Presidential primaries and the dynamics of public choice.* Princeton, NJ: Princeton University Press.

Baumgartner, F. R., Jones, B. D., and Leech, B. L. 1997. Media attention and congressional agendas. In Shanto Iyengar and Richard Reeves (Eds.), *Do the media govern? Politicians, voters and reporters in America* (pp. 349–363). Thousand Oaks, CA: Sage.

Becker, L. B., and Kosicki, G. M. 1995. Understanding the message-producer/message-receiver transaction. In Philo Wasburn (Ed.), *Research in political sociology* (vol. 7, pp. 33–62). Greenwich, CT: JAI Press.

Bennett, C., and Yanovitzky, I. 2000. Patterns of congressional news media use: The questions of selection bias and third person effect. Paper presented to the Political Communication Division, 50th International Communication Association Annual Conference, Acapulco, Mexico.

Brants, K., de Vreese, C., Moller, J., and Van Praag, P. 2010. The real spiral of cynicism? Symbiosis and mistrust between politicians and journalists. *International Journal of Press/Politics* 15: 25–40.

Chia, S. C. 2009. When the east meets west: An examination of third-person perception about idealized body-images in Singapore. *Mass Communication & Society* 12: 423–445.

Choi, J., Yang, M., and Chang, J. J. C. 2009. Elaboration of the hostile media phenomenon: The roles of involvement, media skepticism, congruency of perceived media influence, and perceived opinion climate. *Communication Research* 36: 54–75.

Cohen, J., and Tsfati, Y. 2009. The influence of presumed media influence on strategic voting: Evidence from the Israeli 2003 and 2006 elections. *Communication Research* 36: 359–378.

Cohen, J., Tsfati, Y., and Sheafer, T. 2008. The influence of presumed media influence in politics: Do politicians' perceptions of media power matter. *Public Opinion Quarterly* 72: 331–344.

Cook, T. E. 1989. *Making laws and making news: Media strategies in the U.S. House of Representatives.* Washington, DC: The Brookings Institution.

Davison, W. P. 1983. The third-person effect in communication. *Public Opinion Quarterly* 47: 1–15.

Dillard, J. P., Shen, L., and Vail, R. G. 2007. Does perceived message effectiveness cause persuasion or vice versa? *Human Communication Research* 33: 467–488.

Domke, D., Watts, M. D., Shah, D. V., and Fan, D. P. 1999. The politics of conservative elites and the "liberal media" argument. *Journal of Communication* 49: 35–58.

Druckman, J. N. 2001. On the limits of framing: Who can frame? *Journal of Politics* 63: 1041–1066.

Elder, T. J., Douglas, K. M., and Sutton, R. M. 2006. Perceptions of social influence when messages favour "us" versus "them": A closer look at the social distance effect. *European Journal of Social Psychology* 36: 353–365.

Ericson, R. V., Baranek, P., and Chan, J. B. 1989. *Negotiating control: A study of news sources*. Toronto: University of Toronto Press.

Eveland, W. P., Jr., Nathanson, A. I., Detenber, B. H., and McLeod, D. M. 1999. Rethinking the social distance corollary: Perceived likelihood of exposure and the third-person effect. *Communication Research* 26: 275–302.

Eveland, W. P., Jr., and Shah, D. V. 2003. The impact of individual and interpersonal factors on perceived news media bias. *Political Psychology* 24: 101–117.

Giner-Sorolla, R., and Chaiken, S. 1994. The causes of hostile media judgments. *Journal of Experimental Social Psychology* 30: 165–180.

Golan, G. J., Banning, S. A., and Lundy, L. 2008. Likelihood to vote, candidate choice and the third-person effect: Behavioral implications of political advertising in the 2004 presidential elections. *American Behavioral Scientist* 52: 278–290.

Gunther, A. C. 1988. Attitude extremity and trust in media. *Journalism Quarterly* 65: 279–287.

Gunther, A. C. 1998. The persuasive press inference: Effects of mass media on perceived public opinion. *Communication Research* 25: 486–504.

Gunther, A. C., and Chia, S. C. 2001. Predicting pluralistic ignorance: The hostile media effect and its consequences. *Journalism and Mass Communication Quarterly* 78: 689–701.

Gunther, A. C, and Christen, Cindy T. 2002. Projection or persuasive press? Contrary effects of personal opinion and perceived news coverage on estimates of public opinion. *Journal of Communication* 52: 177–195.

Gunther, A. C., Christen, C. T., Liebhart, J., and Chia, S. C. 2001. Congenial public, contrary press, and biased estimates of the climate of opinion. *Public Opinion Quarterly* 65: 295–320.

Gunther, A. C, and Hwa, A. P. 1996. Public perceptions of television influence and opinions about censorship in Singapore. *International Journal of Public Opinion Research* 8: 248–265.

Gunther, A. C., and Liebhart, J. L. 2006. Broad reach or biased source? Decomposing the hostile media effect. *Journal of Communication* 56: 449–466.

Gunther, A. C, and Liebhart, J. L. 2007. The hostile media effect and opinions about agricultural biotechnology. In D. Brossard, J. Shanahan, and T. C. Nesbitt (Eds.), *The public, the media and agricultural biotechnology* (pp. 245–263). Cambridge, MA: CABI.

Gunther, A. C., Miller, N., and Liebhart, J. L. 2009. Assimilation and contrast in a test of the hostile media effect. *Communication Research* 36: 747–764.

Gunther, A. C., and Storey, D. J. 2003. The influence of presumed influence. *Journal of Communication* 53: 199–215.

Hallin, D. C. 1992. Sound bite news: Television coverage of elections 1968–1988. *Journal of Communication* 42: 5–24.

Henriksen, L., and Flora, J. A. 1999. Third-person perception and children: Perceived impact of pro- and anti-smoking ads. *Communication Research* 26: 643–665.

Huck, I., Quiring, O., and Brosius, H. B. 2009. Perceptual phenomena in the agenda setting process. *International Journal for Public Opinion Research* 21: 139–164.

Ivory, J., and Kalyanaraman, S. 2009. Video games make people violent—well, maybe not that game: Effects of content and person abstraction on perceptions of violent video games' effects and support of censorship. *Communication Reports* 22: 1–12.

Johansson, B. 2004. Mass media, interpersonal communication or personal experience? Perceptions of media effects among Swedish politicians. *Nordicom Review* 25: 259–276.

Jones, D. A. 2004. Why Americans don't trust the media: A preliminary analysis. *The International Journal of Press/Politics* 9: 60-77.

Kedrowski, K. M. 1996. *Media entrepreneurs and the media enterprise in the U.S. Congress.* Cresskill, NJ: Hampton Press.

Kohring, M., and Matthes, J. 2007. Trust in news media: Development and validation of a multidimensional scale. *Communication Research* 34: 231–252.

Ladd, J. M. 2005. Attitudes toward the news media and voting behavior. Paper presented at the annual meeting of the Midwest Political Science Association, Chicago, IL.

Lee, T. T. 2010. Why they don't trust the media? An examination of factors predicting trust. *American Behavioral Scientist* 54: 8–21.

Luhmann, N. 1979. *Trust and power.* Chichester, UK: Wiley.

Major, A. M., and Atwood, L. E. 1997. Changes in media credibility when a predicted disaster doesn't happen. *Journalism & Mass Communication Quarterly* 74: 797–813.

Matheson, K., and Dursun, S. 2001. Social identity precursors to the hostile media phenomenon: Partisan perceptions of coverage of the Bosnian conflict. *Group Processes & Intergroup Relations* 4: 116–125.

Mazzoleni, G., and Schulz, W. 1999. "Mediatization" of politics: A challenge for democracy? *Political Communication* 16: 247–261.

McLeod, D., Detenber, B. H., and Eveland, W. P. 2001. Behind the third-person effect: Differentiating perceptual processes for self and other. *Journal of Communication* 51: 678–695.

Meyer, T. 2002. *Media democracy: How the media colonize politics.* Cambridge: Polity Press.

Miller, J. M., and Krosnick, J. A. 2000. News media impact on the ingredients of presidential evaluations: Political knowledgeable citizens are guided by a trusted source. *American Journal of Political Science* 44: 301–315.

Mixon, F. G., Gibson, M. T., and Upadhyaya, K. P. 2003. Has legislative television changed legislator behavior? C-SPAN2 and the frequency of Senate filibustering. *Public Choice* 115: 139–162.

Mutz, D. 1989. The influence of perceptions of media influence. *International Journal of Public Opinion Research* 1: 3–23.

Noelle-Neumann, E. 1974. Spiral of silence: A theory of public opinion. *Journal of Communication* 24: 43–51.

Perloff, R. M. 1989. Ego-involvement and the third person effect of televised news coverage. *Communication Research* 16: 236–262.

Perloff, R. M. 2009. Mass media, social perception and the third person effect. In J. Bryant, and M. B. Oliver (Eds.), *Media effects: Advances in theory and research* (pp. 252–268). New York: Routledge.

Reid, S. A., Byrne, S., Brundidge, J. S., Shoham, M. D., and Marlow, M. L. 2007. A critical test of self-enhancement, exposure, and self-categorization explanations for first and third-person perceptions. *Human Communication Research* 33: 143–162.

Rojas, H. 2010. "Corrective" actions in the public sphere: How perceptions of media and media effects shape political behaviors. *International Journal of Public Opinion Research* 22: 343–363.

Rucinski, D., and Salmon, C. T. 1990. The "other" as the vulnerable voter: A study of the third-person effect in the 1988 presidential campaign. *International Journal of Public Opinion Research* 2: 345–368.

Salwen, M. B. 1998. Perceptions of media influence and support for message censorship: The third person effect in the 1996 presidential election campaign. *Communication Research* 25: 259–285.

Salwen, M. B., and Driscoll, P. D. 1997. Consequences of third-person perception in support of press restrictions in the O. J. Simpson trial. *Journal of Communication* 47: 60–75.

Scharrer, E. 2002. Third-person perception and television violence: The role of out-group stereotyping in perceptions of susceptibility to effects. *Communication Research* 29: 681–704.

Senior, J. 2009. The message is the message. *New York Magazine Online*. Retrieved April 4, 2011, from http://nymag.com/news/politics/58199/.

Shah, D. V., Faber, R. J., and Youn, S. 1999. Susceptibility and severity: Perceptual dimensions underlying the third-person effect. *Communication Research* 26: 240–267.

Stromback, J. 2010. Mediatization and perceptions of the media's political influence. *Journalism Studies* 12: 423–439.

Sundar, S. S. 1998. Effects of source attribution on perception of online news stories. *Journalism & Mass Communication Quarterly* 75: 55–68.

Tal-Or, N., Cohen, J., Tsfati, Y., and Gunther, A. C. 2010. Testing causal direction in the influence of presumed media influence. *Communication Research* 37: 801–824.

Tal-Or, N., and Drukman, D. 2010. Third-person perception as an impression management tactic. *Media Psychology* 13: 301–322.

Tal-Or, N., and Tsfati, Y. 2007. On the substitutability of third-person perceptions. *Media Psychology* 10: 231–249.

Tal-Or, N., Tsfati, Y., and Gunther, A. C. 2009. The influence of presumed media influence: Origins and implications of the third-person perception. In R. L. Nabi and M. B. Oliver (Eds.), *The SAGE handbook of media processes and effects* (pp. 99–112). Thousand Oaks, CA: Sage.

Tsfati, Y. 2002. The consequences of mistrust in the news media: Media skepticism as a moderator in media effects and as a factor influencing news media exposure. PhD diss., Annenberg School for Communication, University of Pennsylvania.

Tsfati, Y. 2003a. Media skepticism and climate of opinion perception. *International Journal of Public Opinion Research*, 15: 65-82.

Tsfati, Y. 2003b. Does audience skepticism of the media matter in agenda setting? *Journal of Broadcasting & Electronic Media* 47: 157–176.

Tsfati, Y. 2007. Hostile media perceptions, presumed media influence and minority alienation: The case of Arabs in Israel. *Journal of Communication* 57: 632–651.

Tsfati, Y., and Cappella, J. N. 2005. Why do people watch news they do not trust? The need for cognition as a moderator in the association between news media skepticism and exposure. *Media Psychology* 7: 251–272.

Tsfati, Y., and Cohen, J. 2004. Object-subject distance and the third-person perception. *Media Psychology* 6: 335–362.

Tsfati, Y., and Cohen, J. 2005a. Democratic consequences of hostile media perceptions: The case of Gaza settlers. *Harvard International Journal of Press/Politics* 10: 28–51.

Tsfati, Y., and Cohen, J. 2005b. The influence of presumed media influence on democratic legitimacy: The case of Gaza settlers. *Communication Research* 32: 794–821.

Vallone, R. P., Ross, L., and Lepper, M. R. 1985. The hostile media phenomenon: Biased perception and perceptions of media bias in coverage of the Beirut massacre. *Journal of Personality and Social Psychology 49*: 577–585.

Van Aelst, P., Brants, K., Van Praag, P., De Vreese, C., Nuytemans, M., and Van Dalen, A. 2008. The fourth estate as a superpower? An empirical study of perceptions of media power in Belgium and the Netherlands. *Journalism Studies 9*: 494–511.

Walgrave, S., and Van Aelst, P. 2006. The contingency of the mass media's political agenda setting power: Toward a preliminary theory. *Journal of Communication 56*: 88–109.

Watts, M. D., Domke, D., Shah, D. V., and Fan, D. 1999. Elite cues and media bias in presidential campaigns. *Communication Research 26*: 144–175.

Wei, R., Lo, Ven-Hwei, and Lu, Hung-Yi. 2011. Examining the perceptual gap and behavioral intention in the perceived effects of polling news in the 2008 Taiwan presidential elections. *Communication Research 38*: 206–227.

Weibel, D., Wissmath, B., and Groner, R. 2008. How gender and age affect newscasters' credibility. *Journal of Broadcasting and Electronic Media 52*: 466–484.

White, A. H. 1997. Considering interacting factors in the third-person effect: Argument strength and social distance. *Journalism & Mass Communication Quarterly 74*: 557–564.

Willnat, L. 1996. Mass media and political outspokenness in Hong Kong: Lining the third-person effect and the spiral of silence. *International Journal of Public Opinion Research 2*: 187–208.

Xu, J., and Gonzenbach, W. J. 2008. Does a perceptual discrepancy lead to action? A meta analysis of the behavioral component of the third person effect. *International Journal of Public Opinion Research 20*: 375–385.

Yanovitzky, I., and Stryker, J. 2001. Mass media, social norms and health promotion efforts: A longitudinal study of media effects on binge driving. *Communication Research 28*: 208–239.

Zaller, J. R. 1992. *The nature and origins of mass opinion*. New York: Cambridge University Press.

Zhong, Z-J. 2009. Third person perceptions and online games: A comparison of perceived anti-social and pro-social game effects. *Journal of Computer Mediated Communication 14*: 286–306.

CHAPTER 40

THE MEDIA AND THE FOSTERING OF POLITICAL (DIS)TRUST

MICHAEL BARTHEL AND PATRICIA MOY

INTRODUCTION

TRUST is central to the relationship between citizens and their government (Erber and Lau, 1990; Nye, Zelikow, and King, 1997). Citizens who distrust their government or hold cynical political views lack confidence that officials are working in their interest, that elections are being conducted fairly, or that information they receive—whether directly from the government or indirectly through the media—is accurate. Yet democratic structures are also designed to make productive use of citizens' skepticism about government officials. The system of checks and balances is designed with distrust in mind: given that branches of government are assumed to misbehave, other branches are given not only the power but the responsibility to intervene on the public's behalf. Officials are required to submit to timely elections so that, if they violate the trust placed in them, they may be removed from office (Miller, 1974). And because it is assumed that the current system safeguards actors from scrutiny, freedom of the press allows journalists to serve as independent assessors of political information. In democratic thought, this tendency toward misbehavior is assumed to be endemic to not only government, but also human nature, and so cynicism is a necessary component of any collective activity. "If men were angels," wrote Madison in Federalist No. 51, "no government would be necessary."

Though cynicism can be a valuable orientation from which to regard the government, it needs to be carefully balanced with enough trust to allow a legitimate government to function. Many scholars and politicians are concerned about the possible consequences of the public's high levels of cynicism for the government and even for society itself. President Barack Obama, in his first State of the Union address, cited "a deficit of trust" as one of the key issues faced by political leaders; these low levels of trust have been shown to problematically constrain the options of policymakers (Hetherington, 2006). More recently, when governments in the Arab world lost the confidence of their citizens because expectations for good governance were not being met, the result was a regional wave of systemic change.

The literature clearly indicates that cynical attitudes toward one's fellow citizens lower a society's overall level of social capital, depressing civic and political engagement (Putnam, 2000), while a trusting relationship between government and citizens can create a "virtuous spiral" that encourages better decisions and more public support (Mishler and Rose, 1997; see also Gamson, 1968). A society arranged around the consent of the governed cannot function well unless the governed and their leaders have some level of trust in one another. However, the point at which levels of cynicism work against society functioning healthily remains unclear. As Hamilton wrote in Federalist No. 29, "Where in the name of common-sense, are our fears to end if we may not trust our sons, our brothers, our neighbors, our fellow-citizens?"

In studying political trust, political communication scholars are concerned with the effects that the media have on influencing levels of it, or more often, political cynicism. After all, coverage of politics is consistently negative (Miller, Goldenberg, and Erbring, 1979; Patterson, 1993), and such negative coverage has been experimentally linked to increased cynicism (Cappella and Jamieson, 1997). This does not necessarily mean, however, that the relationship is a direct or uncomplicated one (Norris, 2000). Numerous aspects of the communication environment can shape the effects of a message on political trust. Moreover, as new venues for political information emerge, from infotainment to citizen-produced media content, these findings are constantly being revisited and revised.

In this chapter we map the terrain of research on political cynicism, ultimately identifying the most promising directions for future research. To do so, we first consider how political trust has been conceptualized and operationalized.

Conceptualization

One fundamental problem with trying to clearly explicate political trust is that it has been studied under so many different labels (Levi and Stoker, 2000). The concept has been used interchangeably with "confidence" (Lipset and Schneider, 1987; Dogan, 1994; Brehm and Rahn, 1997; Norris, 1999; Tarrow, 2000) and linked with "credibility" (Elster, 1989; Majone, 1997), "compliance" (Braithwaite and Makkai, 1994; Pettit, 1995), and "acceptance" (Tyler, 1990; Levi, 1997). Much research, however, has focused on the absence of trust or confidence, typically subsumed under the guises of distrust (Hardin, 2004), discontent or dissatisfaction (Shingles, 1981; Craig, 1996; Inglehart, 1997), and disaffection (Torcal and Montero, 2006). A significant body of research has focused on political cynicism and skepticism (Cappella and Jamieson, 1997; Mishler and Rose, 1997), with the latter reflecting dubiousness rather than an immutable predisposition to find fault (Cappella and Jamieson, 1997). Political trust (or its absence) has also been linked to apathy: the withdrawal from participation in conventional political activity (Citrin, 1974) or the unwillingness to become involved in the political process (Austin and Pinkleton, 1995). Yet political cynicism has been likened to perceived political normlessness, which Finifter (1970) identified as a component of political alienation. Both cynicism (or lack of trust) and perceived political normlessness derive from citizens believing that deviations from the accepted norms appear in the political process; that is, that the political process is not working as it should be (Hetherington, 2006).

Despite the conceptual murkiness, a general definition of political trust can be offered. Specifically, political trust is *the belief that the government, left to its own devices, will act in accordance with one's expectations* (see Miller and Listhaug, 1990). And while the profusion of terms and concepts may not be resolved here, there are certain dimensions along which a particular conception of trust can be oriented. For instance, trust may be *specific* or *diffuse* (Easton, 1965); that is, an individual's political trust may focus on either a particular government institution or actor (e.g., parliament or a member of parliament) or on government or politics as a whole (e.g., "the system").

In the United States the primary operationalization of political trust has comprised four questions in the American National Electoral Study (ANES), developed by Stokes (1962):[1]

(1) How much of the time do you think you can trust the government in Washington to do what is right: just about always, most of the time, or only some of the time?

(2) Do you think that people in government waste a lot of the money we pay in taxes, waste some of it, or don't waste very much of it?

(3) Would you say the government is pretty much run by a few big interests looking out for themselves, or that it is run for the benefit of all the people?

(4) Do you think that quite a few of the people running the government are crooked, not very many are, or do you think hardly any of them are crooked?

Stokes did not conceive of these as trust questions, intending them to "tap the basic evaluative orientations toward the national government" as well as "the ability and efficacy of government officials and the correctness of their decisions" (1962, 64). Only later did these items come to be conceived of as a trust scale. Despite its widespread adoption, this common operationalization of political trust does little to resolve the conceptual dilemmas just detailed. For instance, is the target of the attitude the political system as a whole (Miller, 1974) or individual incumbent leaders (Citrin, 1974)? From the term "the government in Washington" one might think the former, but "the people running the government" seems to indicate the latter.

Though Miller and Listhaug (1990) argue that the questions hold together as an assessment of the extent to which government's performance satisfies the public's expectations, other approaches have been proposed. Craig, Niemi, and Silver (1990) pilot-tested a new group of ANES trust items, and Erber and Lau (1990) proposed dividing up trust questions into "issue chronicity" and "people chronicity," differentiating between items that focus primarily on evaluations of the government's policies and those that focus on the officials currently in office. Meanwhile, professional polling organizations in the United States often use a single question such as "How much of the time do you trust the government in Washington?," which fails to specify either policies or officials as the primary target for the attitude.

KEY FINDINGS

Assessments of media impact on political trust assume that the media work in concert with individual, social, cultural, and economic forces (see Moy and Hussain, 2011, for a review). For instance, if education facilitates awareness of political processes and government deficiencies, then greater educational attainment may ultimately suppress levels of trust (Converse, 1972). Similarly, as the fabric of parts of society begins to disintegrate, citizens' expectations of government action become more salient, and the government's ability to address them becomes a basis of political distrust (Mansbridge, 1997). In the end, declining confidence in government stems from substantive failings or perceptions of substantive failings (Citrin and Green, 1986; Pfau, Moy, and Szabo, 2001)—perceptions fostered by mass-mediated content.

Early studies of political trust scrutinized media content to ascertain whether the valence of political coverage may be shaping political sentiment. Miller, Goldenberg, and Erbring's (1979) seminal study examined the articles on newspapers' front pages that referred to trust in government and found that over half had a negative tone. Moreover, citizens who read newspapers that tended to be more negative in their political coverage expressed higher levels of political distrust. Following Miller, Goldenberg, and Erbring's (1979) study of "type-set politics," content-analytic studies have examined the tone of news coverage about elected officials, and negativity about presidents and Congress has been found across a wide spectrum of media (Tidmarch and Pitney, 1985; Dowling, 1989; Robinson and Appel, 1979; Hart, Smith-Howell, and Llewellyn, 1990; Hallin, 1992; Moy, Pfau and Kahlor, 1999). Other early research in this area comes from Patterson (1993), who found that negative coverage of presidential candidates (in news magazines) had increased over time, an increase mirrored by the increase in not only distrust, but also the likelihood that journalists' own negative comments about candidates will replace the candidates' own negative statements.

The striking consistency of negative coverage and its connection to distrust and cynicism has been so firmly established that the tendency of the media to portray government in a negative light and to depress public confidence has been given its own name, "videomalaise," coined by Robinson (1976) with his particular focus on television news but later revised by Bennett and colleagues (1999) to "media malaise." Indeed, experimental research by Cappella and Jamieson (1997) found a link between press use of Patterson's "game frame" (which he found coincided with increased negative coverage) and increased cynicism.

Early research that attempted to explain the link between content and attitudes tended to focus on cultivation theory as a mechanism of influence. Adapting from the cultivation paradigm (Gerbner et al. 1994), it argued that the prevalence and relatively homogenous portrayals of groups on television shaped perceptions of reality. Moreover, the cultivation effects of television (and presumably the negative political coverage seen in the news media) would be magnified when individuals had no direct experience against which to evaluate the political goings-on outside of their immediate environment. And if individuals' own experiences with the government, an institution, or a politician resonated with media portrayals of that same entity, the cultivation effects of that media coverage would increase.

Despite this general set of robust findings, the relationship between media content and political cynicism is a nuanced one. After all, the mass media are not a unitary phenomenon, and the variance in coverage of politics is evident across media outlets. Early research has identified similar patterns of news coverage across certain media, with consistent findings for coverage of presidents in network television news (Hallin, 1992), newspapers (Dowling, 1989), news magazines (Hart, Smith-Howell, and Llewellyn, 1990), and political talk radio (Moy, Pfau, and Kahlor, 1999). However, coverage of Congress has been consistently negative in newspaper editorials (Tidmarch and Pitney, 1985) and network television news (Robinson and Appel, 1979).

Do these differences in coverage lead to differences in levels of political trust? The answer is a categorical affirmative. Research consistently has found that newspaper and magazine reading is positively associated with trust, while viewing television is negatively associated with trust—whether the target of political coverage is local government (Becker and Whitney, 1980), national government (McLeod et al., 1977), or democratic institutions in general (Moy and Pfau, 2000).

The distinction between print- and broadcast-media effects, however, needs to be reconsidered in light of today's media landscape. Today's tableau is the product of newspaper organizations and television networks having migrated online for a 24/7 news cycle, an exponential increase in the number of television outlets (Prior, 2007), and the blurring of news and entertainment (Williams and Delli Carpini, 2012). This means that media analyses, which traditionally have focused on "hard-news" outlets like newspapers, now need to consider an even broader array of modalities. After all, there are more genres of televised content now than when foundational research was conducted in the pre-cable era, and indeed, research has revealed differences in depictions and the effects of these portrayals.

Among the established formats, late-night talk shows and political talk radio have been found to be consistently hostile toward political institutions (Moy and Pfau, 2000), while television news magazines (*60 Minutes, 20/20, Dateline,* etc.) showed the most positive coverage of them (Fallows, 1996), though this may simply be due to their relatively nonpolitical focus. With specific regard to the courts, "sensational" media such as cable news and radio talk have been shown to produce less trusting attitudes than "sober" media like newspapers and broadcast news (Johnston and Bartels, 2010).

The effects on trust from newer sources of political information, however, are still somewhat inconclusive. When it comes to "infotainment" venues such as candidate appearances on entertainment talk shows and late-night comedy programs such as *The Daily Show*, research has shown divergent results. Some studies have identified a negative relationship between consumption of these media and trust: one study examined the effects of jokes on candidate evaluations (Baumgartner and Morris, 2006), and another investigated how exposure to satire affected attitudes toward government (Peterson, 2008). That humor depresses trust differs markedly from findings that exposure to specific instances of infotainment—e.g., late-night comedy shows (Cao and Brewer, 2008) and *The Daily Show* (Bennett, 2007)—can depress levels of *cynicism*. This empirical evidence showing that there are certain circumstances in which humor can lessen cynicism suggests that operational considerations of "media use" may shape the key relationships of interest.

Other than differing levels of negativity, what else can account for differences in media effects on political trust? According to some scholars, effects result from the inherent format of each medium. For instance, with their ability to accommodate significantly more information, print media may generate greater political awareness than does television news (Robinson and Levy, 1986). After all, newspapers and news magazines can convey abstract ideas (Graber, 1996) and include contextualizing information (Neuman, Just, and Crigler, 1992; see Guo and Moy, 1998, for a review). Coupled with the fact that greater effort is required to process print information, it is no surprise that individuals who rely on print news tend to have greater confidence in government.

Television news, on the other hand, is much less conducive to learning. Given the relatively superficial coverage of short and fragmented television news stories, viewers may have difficulty processing information, perceive that they are not learning anything from these stories, and as a result feel politically inefficacious. Consequently, they might believe that politicians are not responding to their concerns (Robinson, 1976). In addition, the fact that television producers are able to present content in novel ways has provided new ground for the study of political trust. For instance, the growing use of split screens in televised interviews and presidential debates has led researchers to study televised incivility, which can contribute to changes in political attitudes toward the individuals involved (Scheufele, Kim, and Brossard, 2007) and decreased trust in politicians, Congress, and the government (Mutz and Reeves, 2005). Incivility among individual politicians then appears to depress trust in much the same way incivility in media outlets depresses trust in the media (Thorson, Vraga, and Ekdale, 2010).

Given the different formats through which political information is delivered today, it is doubtful that the same mechanisms of influence are always at work. When the focus is not on abstract institutions but on political figures themselves, as is frequently the case in newer modalities such as infotainment, soft news, and online news, citizens may interact with these depictions differently than they do with the more straightforward framing of political information conveyed through traditional news sources. Although policymakers have become increasingly humanized through the blurring of public and private (Meyrowitz, 1985), they also have learned to use newer media outlets as a way to reach audiences without worrying about journalists filtering their messages. Consequently, politicians have begun to appear more and more often on talk shows and entertainment-oriented content. Person perceptions are an important part of political decision-making (Popkin, 1994), and by allowing citizens to see the private side of public figures, the media help to make these political actors appear more relatable. Indeed, citizens' evaluations of candidates or issues that appear on or are referenced in infotainment-based shows (such as those seen in late-night programming in the United States) change as a result of exposure to such content (Baumgartner and Morris, 2006; Moy, Xenos, and Hess, 2005). Televised political content—whether in traditional news sources or "nontraditional" outlets—has the ability to shape political attitudes through a variety of mechanisms.

CONTEMPORARY ISSUES AND OUTLOOK FOR RESEARCH

Methodological outlook. Current concerns about understanding political trust vis-à-vis the mass media are substantive in nature, but these discussions cannot be divorced from methodological discussions. It is common for political communication scholars to consider political trust an outcome of exposure or attention to media. As such, it is understandable that the early scholarship in this domain commonly involved media content analysis and survey methodology. These methods, used either singularly or in tandem, assumed an interest in media content and/or the effects of that content on political attitudes. Data collection efforts such as the American National Election Studies and the World Values Survey fortunately allow for trend analyses. However, as is the case with much cross-sectional research, issues of endogeneity arise. Although the ANES data afford scholars the opportunity to analyze panel data, the collection of survey- or experiment-based data from panels of respondents will allow for better understanding of the relationship between media use and political trust.

Experiments also have provided a useful way to link media content and beliefs (Cappella and Jamieson, 1997; de Vreese, 2004; Towner and Dulio, 2011). And focus groups, though not frequently employed, can be an excellent way of gaining deeper insights into citizens' political cynicism (Hibbing and Theiss-Morse, 2002). Studies in this area also can take advantage of integrating experimental treatments into focus groups to better understand the effects of specific media messages on dynamic, qualitative outcomes (such as citizen frames and discourse related to politics; see Neuman, Just, and Crigler, 1992).

A concept in need of continued theorizing. Methodological issues notwithstanding, fundamental issues related to clarifying trust as a concept remain. Decades of research on political trust and cynicism (and related concepts) have resulted in not fully consistent explications or operationalizations. Scholars therefore would benefit from more carefully understanding various aspects of political trust.

First, just as attitudes are directed at an attitude object, so too does trust have a *target*. Political trust can be directed at individuals (e.g., elected local officials, national-level politicians), agencies and institutions, political processes such as elections, as well as "the government." Given how both political knowledge and political trust can shape democratic outcomes, and given how the former can be disaggregated into information about "the rules of the game, the substance of politics, and people and parties" (Delli Carpini and Keeter, 1996, 65), examining how specific domains of knowledge and trust interrelate could shed light on exactly where citizens' expectations are not being met.

Second, the *antecedents and outcomes* of political trust remain in need of continued theorizing. Although this chapter has focused primarily on media effects on political trust, the media do not exert an impact on individuals entering the media environment as if they are *tabulae rasae* (McLeod, Kosicki, and McLeod, 1994). The orientations that one holds—whether it be a strongly instinctual assessment of a candidate's trustworthiness or a long-term frustration born of years of unresolved community tensions—will interact with mediated information to shape trust toward a particular target. That political communication scholars have begun to focus increasingly on the affective roots of political attitudes (Neuman, Just, and Crigler, 2007; see Crigler and Hevron, this volume) suggests that operationalizations of political trust might benefit from affect-based items as well as items that tap rational-actor considerations such as perceptions of government waste. At the same time, citizens' levels of political trust can exert an influence on other significant democratic outcomes. The keen interest in political trust as a criterion variable is grounded in strong normative concerns that relate to other outcomes such as voting behavior, political participation in its various iterations, and knowledge gain.

Trust and the shifting media landscape. Conceptual issues aside, the current terrain of scholarship in political trust would benefit from focused research in a few key areas, all derived from the changing media environment. Namely, as citizens encounter greater choice in their consumption of content, and as they increasingly produce content that can be disseminated to a mass audience, fundamental and novel questions about media effects arise.

Calling for a revisiting of media effects, Bennett and Iyengar (2008) argue that the fragmentation of national audiences and the proliferation of content-specific (and often partisan) outlets make it only more likely that media messages will reinforce audience members' predispositions. If citizens engage in selective exposure and as a result select information that is consonant with their beliefs and attitudes (Klapper, 1960), this use of "niche news" (Stroud, 2011) can profoundly shape what they know about their social world and how they feel about issues, and potentially mobilize them to action. Extrapolated to the domain of political trust, the new media environment therefore raises a key issue about causality: in determining the extent to which the media influence political trust, scholars also will need to consider how political trust influences one's exposure to mediated content.

The relationship between political trust and trust in the news media is nuanced, and one that deserves greater attention. As Tsfati (2003) noted, the degree to which individuals trust the media will influence not only the extent to which, but also how, messages are processed. If trust in the news media comprises various dimensions (Kohring and Matthes, 2007), then attempts to understand the relationship between trust in media and trust in government will need to consider the specific dimensions of the former. In other words, does the citizen trust the media's selectivity of topics, their selectivity of facts, the accuracy of their depictions, and/or their journalistic assessments? For the news consumer who has little faith in the media's production processes (and perhaps low levels of political trust to begin with), news content may have a very different effect on trust in government than for a news consumer who has a higher level of trust in the press.

The notion of trust in the media is confounded by its being in a state of flux brought on by citizens' newfound ability to produce media content themselves. If political information is coming not from a distant media source but from a fellow member of the public, it is seen as equally or more trustworthy than mainstream news sources (Johnson and Kaye, 2004). However, since online political content has been shown to be strongly related to content from the mainstream media (Johnson and Kaye, 2004), we would expect to see a similar tone taken toward government, which previous research has shown to be largely negative. This impact of being exposed to cynical content in the context of a trustworthy medium can produce both greater cynicism and greater efficacy among younger citizens (Towner and Dulio, 2011), although the audience for political content online tends to have greater cynicism and less efficacy than those who look at other kinds of blogs (Sweetser and Kaid, 2008).

Current social media platforms, however, do not require users to actively seek out political content. Political information may be contained in a Twitter feed alongside jokes and video links, while Facebook friends can argue about political topics while posting pictures of their children or relating the events of their day. This manner of communication, which Castells (2009) calls "mass self-communication," may have no effect on trust attitudes, since citizens' attitudes are largely shaped by their political beliefs and the mass media (Zaller, 1992). At the same time, the intertwining of political content with jokes and commentary (akin to what is seen on infotainment-oriented shows) has the ability to pique citizens' interest and motivate them to follow up on the issue. In this sense, the dearth of exposure to traditionally framed news about an issue in social media may allow these outlets to serve as an entree to more serious, detailed information found in the legacy media—a phenomenon dubbed the "gateway hypothesis" by Baum (2003).

Studies of political trust assume its normative significance in a democratic system. However, given large-scale recent political events around the globe, it is worthwhile to examine the process by which trust—or cynicism—emerges. After all, it is possible that the long-term force of *political culture* might normalize particular attitudes concerning trust in government and lead those within that culture toward similar attitudes. For instance, in comparing the influence of political culture and governmental behavior on political trust after the Soviet republics had become democratic states, Mishler and Rose (1997) found that trust attitudes changed, indicating that performance was more important than culture, which presumably remained constant. But elsewhere (Newton and Norris, 2000), performance has not been a factor in determining political trust. However, given the fairly major differences between political situations in a country transitioning from authoritarianism to democracy and a long-standing democratic society, their findings may not necessarily be applicable to the American or European context. Thus, more research is necessary to determine whether the near-exclusive focus on media effects is justified or if it might also be necessary to look at issues of culture in attempting to explain the sources of political trust.

It is important to consider the way trust attitudes themselves may feed back into political culture and have an effect on other attitudes, as well as behaviors (Gastil and Xenos, 2010). We know already that trust in government can affect the public's views on policy (Hetherington, 2006; Rudolph and Evans, 2005) as well as political participation (Mishler and Rose, 1997; Gamson, 1968). If political trust is inextricably linked with democracy, a clearer understanding of how political trust plays out in political life becomes increasingly important in the contexts of both emerging democracies and shifting notions of (digital) citizenship.

NOTE

1. Outside the United States, commonly employed measures of political trust are those included in the World Values Survey. These are single-item questions asking about "confidence" in different institutions such as the government, the legislature or parliament, and political parties.

REFERENCES

Austin, E. W., and Pinkleton, B. E. 1995. Positive and negative effects of political disaffection on less experienced voters. *Journal of Broadcasting and Electronic Media* 39: 215–235.

Baum, M. A. 2003. *Soft news goes to war: Public opinion and American foreign policy in the new media age.* Princeton, NJ: Princeton University Press.

Baumgartner, J., and Morris, J. S. 2006. The *Daily Show* effect: Candidate evaluations, efficacy, and American youth. *American Politics Research* 34(3): 341–367.

Becker, L. B., and Whitney, C. D. 1980. Effects of media dependencies: Audience assessment of government. *Communication Research* 7(1): 95–120.

Bennett, W. L. 2007. Relief in hard times: A defense of Jon Stewart's comedy in an age of cynicism. *Critical Studies in Media Communication* 24(3): 278–283.

Bennett, W. L., and Iyengar, S. 2008. A new era of minimal effects? The changing foundations of political communication. *Journal of Communication* 58(4): 707–731.

Bennett, S. E., Rhine, S. L., Flickinger, R. S., and Bennett, L. L. M. 1999. "Video malaise" revisited: Public trust in the media and government. *Harvard International Journal of Press/Politics* 4(4): 8–23.

Braithwaite, J., and Makkai, T. 1994. Trust and compliance. *Policing Society* 4: 1–12.

Brehm, J., and Rahn, W. M. 1997. Individual-level evidence for the causes and consequences of social capital. *American Journal of Political Science* 41(3): 999–1023.

Cao, X., and Brewer, P. R. 2008. Political comedy shows and public participation in politics. *International Journal of Public Opinion Research* 20(1): 90–99.

Cappella, J. N., and Jamieson, K. H. 1997. *Spiral of cynicism: The press and the public good*. New York: Oxford University Press.

Castells, M. 2009. *Communication power*. New York: Oxford University Press.

Citrin, J. 1974. Comment: The political relevance of trust in government. *American Political Science Review* 68(3): 973–988.

Citrin, J., and Green, D. P. 1986. Presidential leadership and the resurgence of trust in government. *British Journal of Political Science* 16: 431–453.

Converse, P. E. 1972. Changes in the American electorate. In A. Campbell and P. E. Converse (Eds.), *The human meaning of social change* (pp. 261–333). New York: Russell Sage Foundation.

Craig, S. C. 1996. The angry voter? Politics and popular discontent in the 1990s. In S. C. Craig (Ed.), *Broken contract: Changing relationships between Americans and their government* (pp. 46–66). Boulder, CO: Westview.

Craig, S. C., Niemi, R. G., and Silver, G. E. 1990. Political efficacy and trust: A report on the NES Pilot Study items. *Political Behavior* 12: 289–314.

De Vreese, C. 2004. The effects of strategic news on political cynicism, issue evaluation, and policy support: A two-wave experiment. *Mass Communication and Society* 7: 191–215.

Delli Carpini, M. X., and Keeter, S. 1996. *What Americans know about politics and why it matters*. New Haven, CT: Yale University Press.

Dogan, M. 1994. The pendulum between theory and substance: Testing the concepts of legitimacy and trust. In M. Dogan and A. Kazancigil (Eds.), *Comparing Nations* (pp. 296–313). Oxford: Blackwell.

Dowling, R. E. 1989. Print journalism as political communication: The Iran hostage crisis. *Political Communication and Persuasion* 6(2): 129–150.

Easton, D. 1965. *A systems analysis of political life*. New York: Wiley.

Elster, J. 1989. *The cement of society*. Cambridge, UK: Cambridge University Press.

Erber, R., and Lau, R. R. 1990. Political cynicism revisited: An information processing reconciliation of policy-based and incumbency-based interpretations of changes in trust in government. *American Journal of Political Science Review* 34: 236–253.

Fallows, J. 1996. *Breaking the news: How the media undermine American democracy*. New York: Pantheon Books.

Finifter, A. W. 1970. Dimensions of political alienation. *American Political Science Review* 64: 389–410.

Gamson, W. A. 1968. *Power and discontent*. Homewood, IL: Dorsey.

Gastil, J., and Xenos, M. A. 2010. Of attitudes and engagement: Clarifying the reciprocal relationship between civic attitudes and political participation. *Journal of Communication* 60: 318–343.

Gerbner, G., Gross, L., Morgan, M., and Signorielli, N. 1994. Growing up with television: The cultivation perspective. In J. Bryant and D. Zillmann (Eds.), *Media effects: Advances in theory and research* (pp. 43–68). Hillsdale, NJ: Lawrence Erlbaum.

Graber, D. A. 1996. Say it with pictures. *Annals of the American Academy of Political and Social Science* 546: 85–96.

Guo, Z., and Moy, P. 1998. Medium or message? Predicting dimensions of political sophistication. *International Journal of Public Opinion Research* 10(1): 25–50.

Hallin, D. C. 1992. The passing of the "high modernism" of American journalism. *Journal of Communication* 42(3): 14–25.

Hardin, R. 2004. Distrust: Manifestations and management. In R. Harding (Ed.), *Distrust* (pp. 3–33). New York: Russell Sage Foundation.

Hart, R. P., Smith-Howell, D., and Llewellyn, J. 1990. Evolution of presidential news coverage. *Political Communication and Persuasion* 7: 213–230.

Hetherington, M. J. 2006. *Why trust matters: Declining political trust and the demise of American liberalism*. Princeton, NJ: Princeton University Press.

Hibbing, J., and Theiss-Morse, E. 2002. *Stealth democracy: Americans' beliefs about how government should work*. Cambridge, UK: Cambridge University Press.

Inglehart, R. 1997. *Modernization and post-modernization: Cultural, political and economic change in 43 societies*. Princeton, NJ: Princeton University Press.

Johnson, T. J., and Kaye, B. K. 2004. Wag the blog: How reliance on traditional media and the Internet influence credibility perceptions of Weblogs among blog users. *Journalism and Mass Communication Quarterly* 81: 622–642.

Johnston, C. D., and Bartels, B. L. 2010. Sensationalism and sobriety: Differential media exposure and attitudes toward American courts. *Public Opinion Quarterly* 74(2): 260–285.

Klapper, J. T. 1960. *The effects of mass communication*. New York: Free Press.

Kohring, M., and Matthes, J. 2007. Trust in news media: Development and validation of a multidimensional scale. *Communication Research* 34(2): 231–252.

Levi, M. 1997. *Consent, dissent and patriotism*. New York: Cambridge University Press.

Levi, M., and Stoker, L. 2000. Political trust and trustworthiness. *Annual Review of Political Science* 3: 475–507.

Lipset, S. M., and Schneider, W. 1987. *The confidence gap: Business, labor, and government in the public mind*. Baltimore, MD: Johns Hopkins University Press.

Majone, G. 1997. Mutual trust, credible commitments and the evolution of rules for a single European market. In D. G. Mayes (Ed.), *The evolution of the single European market* (pp. 253–274). Cheltenham, UK: Elgar.

Mansbridge, J. 1997. Social and cultural causes of dissatisfaction with U.S. government. In J. S. Nye Jr., P. D. Zelikow, and D. C. King (Eds.), *Why people don't trust government* (pp. 133–153). Cambridge, MA: Harvard University Press.

McLeod, J. M., Brown, J. D., Becker, L. B., and Ziemke, D. A. 1977. Decline and gall at the White House: A longitudinal analysis of communication effects. *Communication Research* 4(1): 3–22.

McLeod, J. M., Kosicki, G. M., and McLeod, D. M. 1994. The expanding boundaries of political communication effects. In J. Bryant and D. Zillmann (Eds.), *Media Effects: Advances in Theory and Research* (pp. 123–162). Hillsdale, NJ: Lawrence Eribaum.

Meyrowitz, J. 1985. *No sense of place: The impact of electronic media on social behavior.* New York: Oxford University Press.

Miller, A. H. 1974. Political issues and trust in government: 1964–1970. *American Political Science Review* 68(3): 951–972.

Miller, A. H., Goldenberg, E. N., and Erbring, L. 1979. Type-set politics: Impact of newspapers on public confidence. *American Political Science Review* 73(1): 67–84.

Miller, A. H., and Listhaug, O. 1990. Political parties and confidence in government: A comparison of Norway, Sweden and the United States. *British Journal of Political Science* 20: 357–386.

Mishler, W., and Rose, R. 1997. Trust, distrust and skepticism: Popular evaluations of civil and political institutions in post-communist societies. *Journal of Politics* 59(2): 418–451.

Moy, P., and Hussain, M. M. 2011. Media influences on political trust and engagement. In L. Jacobs and Ro. Y. Shapiro (Eds.), *Oxford handbook of American public opinion and the media* (pp. 220–235). New York: Oxford University Press.

Moy, P., and Pfau, M. 2000. *With malice toward all? The media and public confidence in democratic institutions.* Westport, CT: Praeger.

Moy, P., Pfau, M., and Kahlor, L. 1999. Media use and public confidence in democratic institutions. *Journal of Broadcasting and Electronic Media* 43(2): 137–158.

Moy, P., Xenos, M. A., and Hess, V. K. 2005. Communication and citizenship: Mapping the political effects of infotainment. *Mass Communication and Society* 8(2): 111–131.

Mutz, D. C., and Reeves, B. 2005. The new videomalaise: Effects of televised incivility on political trust. *American Political Science Review* 99(1): 1–15.

Neuman, W. R., Just, M. R., and Crigler, A. N. 1992. *Common knowledge: News and the construction of political meaning.* Chicago: University of Chicago Press.

Neuman, W. R., Marcus, G. E., Crigler, A. N., and MacKuen, M. (Eds.) 2007. *The affect effect: Dynamics of emotion in political thinking and behavior.* Chicago: University of Chicago Press.

Newton, K., and Norris, P. 2000. Confidence in public institutions: Faith, culture or performance? In S. Pharr and R. Putnam (Eds.), *Disaffected democracies: What's troubling thetrilateral countries?* (pp. 52–74). Princeton, NJ: Princeton University Press.

Norris, P. 1999. Institutional explanations for political support. In P. Norris (Eds.), *Critical citizens: Global confidence in democratic government* (pp. 217–235). Oxford: Oxford University Press.

Norris, P. 2000. *A virtuous circle: Political communication in postindustrial societies.* Cambridge, UK: Cambridge University Press.

Nye, J. S., Jr., Zelikow, P. D., and King, D. C. (Eds.) 1997. *Why people don't trust government.* Cambridge, MA: Harvard University Press

Patterson, T. E. 1993. *Out of order.* New York: Alfred A. Knopf.

Peterson, R. L. 2008. *Strange bedfellows: How late-night comedy turns democracy into a joke.* New Brunswick, NJ: Rutgers University Press.

Pettit, P. 1995. The cunning of trust. *Philosophy of Public Affairs* 24: 202–225.

Pfau, M., Moy, P., and Szabo, E. A. 2001. Influence of prime-time television programming on perceptions of the federal government. *Mass Communication and Society* 4(4): 437–443.

Popkin, S. L. 1994. *The reasoning voter: Communication and persuasion in presidential campaigns.* Chicago: University of Chicago Press.

Prior, M. 2007. *Post-broadcast democracy. How media choice increases inequality in political involvement and polarizes elections.* Cambridge, UK: Cambridge University Press.

Putnam, R. 2000. *Bowling alone: The collapse and revival of American community.* New York: Simon and Schuster.

Robinson, M. J. 1976. Public affairs television and the growth of political malaise: The case of "The Selling of the Pentagon." *American Political Science Review* 70(2): 409–432.

Robinson, M. J., and Appel, K. R. 1979. Network news coverage of Congress. *Political Science Quarterly* 94: 407–448.

Robinson, J. P., and Levy, M. R. 1986. *The main source: Learning from television news.* Beverly Hills, CA: Sage.

Rudolph, T. J., and Evans, J. 2005. Political trust, ideology, and public support for government spending. *American Journal of Political Science* 49(3): 660–671.

Scheufele, D. A., Kim, E., and Brossard, D. 2007. My friend's enemy: How split-screen debate coverage influences evaluation of presidential debates. *Communication Research* 34(1): 3–24.

Shingles, R. D. 1981. Black consciousness and political participation: The missing link. *American Political Science Review* 75: 76–91.

Stokes, D. E. 1962. Popular evaluations of government: An empirical assessment. In H. Cleveland and H. D. Lasswell (Eds.), *Ethics and bigness: Scientific, academic, religious, political, and military* (pp. 61–72). New York: Harper.

Stroud, N. J. 2011. *Niche news: The politics of news choice.* New York: Oxford University Press.

Sweetser, K. D., and Kaid, L. L. 2008. Stealth soapboxes: Political information efficacy, cynicism and uses of celebrity Weblogs among readers. *New Media & Society* 10(1): 67–91.

Tarrow, S. G. 2000. Mad cows and activists: Contentious politics in the trilateral democracies. In S. Pharr and R. Putnam (Eds.), *Disaffected democracies: What's troubling the trilateral democracies* (pp. 270–289). Princeton, NJ: Princeton University Press.

Thorson, K., Vraga, E., and Ekdale, B. 2010. Credibility in context: How uncivil online commentary affects news credibility. *Mass Communication and Society* 13(3): 289–313.

Tidmarch, C. M., and Pitney, J. J., Jr. 1985. Covering Congress. *Polity* 17(3): 463–484.

Torcal, M., and Montero, J. R. 2006. *Political disaffection in contemporary democracies: Social capital, institutions and politics.* London: Routledge.

Towner, T. L., and Dulio, D. 2011. An experiment of campaign effects during the YouTube election. *New Media and Society* 13(4): 626–644.

Tsfati, Y. 2003. Media skepticism and climate of opinion perception. *International Journal of Public Opinion Research* 15(1): 65–82.

Tyler, T. R. 1990. *Why people obey the law.* New Haven, CT: Yale University Press.

Williams, B. A., and Delli Carpini, M. X. 2012. *After broadcast news: Media regimes, democracy, and the new information environment.* New York: Cambridge University Press.

Zaller, J. 1992. *The nature and origins of mass opinion.* Cambridge, UK: Cambridge University Press.

....

CHAPTER 41

CULTIVATION THEORY AND THE CONSTRUCTION OF POLITICAL REALITY

....

PATRICK E. JAMIESON AND DANIEL ROMER

AFTER defining the concept of cultivation and noting a number of ways in which it evolved over time, in this chapter we identify six broad political effects attributable to heavy use of either television in general or some genres of television in particular: increased fear of crime and increased identification of crime as a significant problem, activation of racialized perceptions, support for punitive policies and embrace of protective behaviors, identification as a political moderate, reduction in social trust and capital in adolescents, and activation of cynicism and depressed learning in political campaigns. We then specify a number of unanswered questions and indicate some directions for future research.

THE CONCEPT OF CULTIVATION

....

Conceptualized by George Gerbner in the 1950s, developed with his colleague Larry Gross in the 1960s and 1970s, and refined by Michael Morgan and Nancy Signorelli in recent decades, cultivation posits that, over time, heavy television viewers will see the world through the lens it provides (Gerbner and Gross, 1976). From 1969 to 1995 in the Cultural Indicators Project (CIP), Gerbner and his colleagues content analyzed the recurrent images in more than 3,000 programs and 35,000 characters of prime-time and weekend daytime TV and correlated the resulting findings with national survey data to compare ongoing over-time exposure to television content and the worldviews of viewers (Signorielli and Gerbner, 1995). Cultivation theory is heavily cited (Potter and Riddle, 2007), and a meta-analysis found effects that supported it (Morgan and Shanahan, 1997).

In this research tradition, the primary function of mass media is to reinforce and reproduce the existing social order. For Gerbner, "The mass production and rapid distribution of messages create new symbolic environments that reflect the structure and functions of the institutions that transmit them. These institutional processes of the mass-production of messages short-circuit other networks of social communication and superimpose their own forms of collective consciousness—their own publics— upon other social relationships" (Gerbner, 1970, 69). Whereas most media theories suggest that exposure changes attitudes and behaviors, cultivation presupposes that "cultural mass production" instead tends toward "the standardized and the safe rather than the diversified or critical" and "creates new problems in the theory and practice of self-government" (Gerbner, 1959, 276–277). "[T]he fundamental assumptions underlying cultivation analysis," notes Gross, "presume the existence of an ideologically coherent and consistent world view that is cultivated by the various arms of an industrialized, commercial media system" (Gross, 2012, xvii).

Because prime-time television programming features crime and violence, for example, gradually over long periods of time heavy viewers of television will come to view the world as a more violent, scary, and mean place than it actually is, resulting in a "mean world syndrome." The political implications were clear to Gerbner. "Fearful people are more dependent, more easily manipulated and controlled, more susceptible to deceptively simple, strong, tough measures and hardline postures—both political and religious," he told a congressional committee in 1981. "They may accept and even welcome repression if it promises to relieve their insecurities. That is the deeper problem of violence-laden television" (Gerbner, 1981).

In "Living with Television," Gerbner and Gross (1976) introduced their "cultivation differential," a measure of the difference between the views of issues of heavy and light viewers of television. Over time, heavy viewers' sense of the world would be more similar to that of other heavy viewers and dissimilar from that of light or nonviewers. They concluded, for example, that heavy viewers overestimated the amount of crime and the number of individuals employed in the criminal justice system. They found as well that heavy and light viewers differed in their perceptions of whether people can be trusted and whether most are "just looking out for themselves" (Gerbner, Gross, Morgan, and Signorielli, 1980b).

To their focus on differences in the worldviews of light and heavy viewers of television, cultivation scholars added the notions of mainstreaming, resonance, and first- and second-order effects. The television-created convergence of viewpoints among heavy viewers was for Gerbner and his team a form of socialization they called "mainstreaming" (Gerbner, Gross, Morgan, and Signorielli, 1980a). Through a process called "resonance," they argued that cultivation effects are minimized when they run counter to individual experience and magnified when experience and televised reality coincide (Gerbner et al., 1980a), a conclusion consistent with Weitzer and Kubrin's (2004) finding that watching local news and being fearful about crime were more clearly associated among those in high crime areas. Cultivation scholars also came to distinguish between first- and second-order cultivation effects (Hawkins and Pingree, 1982). First-order effects pertain to estimates about the prevalence of events such as the incidence of serious crime, probably arrived at through heuristic processing resulting from read-ier accessibility among frequent TV viewers (Shrum and O'Guinn, 1993). By contrast, second-order effects are reflected in value judgments and attitudes such as whether the world is a mean and scary place filled with untrustworthy people.

Critics of cultivation (Doob and Macdonald, 1979; Hughes, 1980, Hirsch, 1980, 1981; Heath and Petraitis, 1987) argued that the cultivation effects on fear of crime in particu-lar largely disappeared in the presence of controls. That is, after controlling for various demographic differences, such as education, age, black-white racial categories, and gen-der, heavy TV watching was no longer associated with cultivation effects. This suggested that rather than exposure to TV, more basic background factors were responsible for beliefs and attitudes related to a mean world syndrome.

In response scholars studying cultivation began controlling demographics and refin-ing their focus from television exposure in general to exposure to specific genres of tel-evision (Lee and Niederdeppe, 2011) and, within these genres, to specific characteristics of the messages themselves. In the process the perceived realism of prime-time crime dramas was isolated as a factor more powerful than exposure to TV itself in predicting fear of crime (Potter, 1986, 1988), and in studies we discuss below, a number of scholars stepped beyond Gerbner and his colleagues' focus on fictive television to hypothesize that exposure to local and national news would produce cultivation effects.

A recent study employing content analysis of TV dramas from 1972 to 2010 and asso-ciated Gallup Polls regarding fear of neighborhood crime showed that changes in vio-lent content in those dramas were associated with changes in the US population's fear of crime (Jamieson and Romer, 2014). This study suggests that some genres of TV fictional violence do affect public perceptions of crime and do so apart from changes in popula-tion demographics.

Inclusion of realism as a factor prompted important theorizing. We now know, for example, that whether content is considered realistic may be program or genre specific (Nabi et al., 2003). When carefully specified, some argue that "perceived realism of tel-evision content" may play a role in the heuristic process linking television exposure and social judgments (Busselle, 2001). Because the concepts of realism (Busselle and Greenberg, 2000) and fear (Morgan and Shanahan, 2010, 343) have been inconsistently defined, it is sometimes difficult to compare studies.

LOCAL AND NATIONAL TELEVISED NEWS AND FEAR OF CRIME

Coined by Coleridge, the notion of willing suspension of disbelief carries the idea that an involving narrative can transport the reader into a world of fiction and prompt her to ignore implausibilities in the plot. Whereas the prime-time fictional programming on which Gerbner focused requires suspension of disbelief, news does not. One might reasonably surmise that news programming, especially close to home at the local level, is as a result more likely than fiction to cultivate beliefs about the level of crime in one's community.

Several studies have correlated exposure to TV news coverage with fear of crime (Romer, Jamieson, and Aday, 2003; Lowry, Nio, and Leitner, 2003; Weitzer and Kubrin, 2004; Holbert, Shah, and Kwak, 2004). Working from the assumption that a significant proportion of local news programming in the United States was devoted to crime and that this coverage does not necessarily reflect actual local crime rates, Romer, Jamieson, and Aday (2003) found that independent of local crime rates, residents who were dependent on local TV news were more likely to be concerned about crime in their neighborhood. The beliefs about crime that were engendered by local news influenced the political agenda of viewers, with heavy viewers being more inclined to support stronger measures to reduce crime.

Using Federal Bureau of Investigation Uniform Crime Reports, Gallup data, national crime rates, and an analysis of media coverage of crime, Lowry, Nio, and Leitner (2003) isolated the same kind of effect resulting from national news exposure. Like Pritchard (1986) and Gebotys, Roberts, and DasGupta (1988), they identified an agenda-setting effect of crime reporting in national TV news, with crime news coverage correlating with perception of crime as a serious problem.

RACIALIZED PERCEPTIONS

Consistent with the finding that African Americans are overrepresented as perpetrators and underrepresented as crime victims in news (Dixon and Linz, 2000; Romer, Jamieson, and DeCoteau, 1998), higher levels of exposure to local news are also associated with increasing racialized belief in the guilt of black but not white suspects (Dixon, 2008). In a similar vein, Oliver and Armstrong (1998) found that viewing a "reality based" police TV show correlated with heightened reports among white viewers of African American involvement in crime.

CULTIVATION AND PROTECTION ACTION AND PUNITIVE POLICIES

Researchers have found political effects from exposure to specific genres of prime-time fiction and from both national and local television news. Nabi and Sullivan (2001, 814) concluded:

> [The] amount of television viewing was positively related to beliefs about prevalence of crime and violence in society . . . beliefs about prevalence of crime and violence

in society was positively related to the attitude that the world is a mean place ... the mean world attitude was positively related to intentions to take protective action ... and protection intentions were positively related to engagement in protective behaviors.

Similarly, Holbert, Shah, and Kwak (2004) found that viewing "police reality shows is both directly and indirectly related to the endorsement of capital punishment and handgun ownership, while also directly predicting a greater likelihood of actual handgun ownership" (343). And Goidel, Freeman, and Procopio (2006) associated TV news viewing with the false belief that rehabilitation is less effective than imprisonment and that sentencing of juveniles is not race-biased. These news findings are consistent with the mainstreaming hypothesis, which held that TV viewing "blurs traditional differences, blends them into a more homogenous mainstream, and bends the mainstream toward a 'hard line' position on issues dealing with minorities and personal rights" (Gerbner, Gross, Morgan, and Signorielli, 1982).

IDENTIFICATION AS MODERATES

Heavy viewers are more likely than light viewers to self-identify as political moderates (Gerbner, Gross, Morgan, and Signorielli, 1984), a socialization effect. According to Gerbner and his associates, "the mainstream does not mean the 'middle of the road'.... [A]lthough mainstreaming bends toward the right on political issues, it leans towards a populist stance on economic issues (e.g., demanding more social services but lower taxes), reflecting the influence of a marketing orientation and setting up potential conflicts of demands and expectations" (Gerbner, Gross, Morgan, and Signorielli, 1994, 32). After sociodemographic controls, party identification, and close following were taken into account, Hardy isolated this mainstreaming finding in the 2008 National Annenberg Election Survey data. His focus, however, was not on heavy television viewing but rather on higher levels of viewing campaign information on television (Hardy, 2012, 104–105).

CULTIVATION EFFECTS ON THE DEVELOPMENT OF ADOLESCENT SOCIAL CAPITAL

Concerns about disproportionately low voter participation among the young has raised questions about whether heavy adolescent TV viewing depressed later balloting (McLeod, 2000). In Putnam's (1995, 679) view, heavy TV viewing "may well increase pessimism about human nature," which subverts the trust needed to develop social capital and engagement in politics. It also may simply divert time away from social activity that enables the development of social capital. Here too evidence for the cultivation hypothesis is genre-dependent. Adolescents who follow news and watch a moderate amount of entertainment TV do not exhibit deficits in civic engagement or interpersonal trust (Pasek, Kenski, Romer, and Jamieson, 2006; Romer, Jamieson, and Pasek, 2009). However, heavy overall viewing of television regardless of genre is inversely related to trust in others (Romer, Jamieson, and Pasek, 2009). The mechanism behind this finding does not seem to hinge on the type of programming and may reflect other forms of content, such as advertising, which cultivates a materialistic worldview that interferes with trust formation (Rahn and Transue, 1998; Romer, 2008; Romer, Jamieson, and Pasek, 2009). Like Gerbner, Putnam (2000, 245) notes that TV advertising could cultivate "materialist values" that encourage "more of our time spent on goods and services consumed individually, rather than those consumed collectively."

Horse-race Schema Exposure Activates Cynicism and Depresses Learning

The focus on the "horse race" and tactics rather than issue substance in news is also likely to influence beliefs about electoral politics and to imbue a sense of cynicism about the democratic process, a finding whose significance is heightened by increased amounts of coverage focused on the horse race (Patterson, 1993). Jamieson (1992), Patterson (1993), and Cappella and Jamieson (1997) are among those noting that news coverage of politics in the United States relies on a news frame that emphasizes the strategic nature of politics (i.e., horse-race coverage) at the expense of coverage of policy differences. In a strategic news frame, the purpose of policy for politicians is to gain votes, increase poll numbers, and promote their candidacy, not advance serious solutions to the nation's problems.

By contrast, issue framing focuses on differences in policy positions that are important to voters rather than on how politicians are positioned to win or lose an election (Cappella and Jamieson, 1997, 34). In a field experiment in which they exposed participants to repeated examples of one of the two types of coverage over a week-long period, Cappella and Jamieson (1997, 228) found that unlike issue framing, horse-race coverage depressed learning and activated cynicism. Hardy (2012, 108) located similar results in 2004 Annenberg data, in which the belief that candidates never tell the truth about their opponents' records was predicted by exposure to 24-hour-a-day cable news and the Internet.

UNANSWERED QUESTIONS AND DIRECTIONS
FOR FUTURE RESEARCH

In the new media landscape, there are two significant unanswered research questions for those studying cultivation: Is there still a reason to hypothesize cultivation effects? If so, how would one expect them to differ from those found in the mass media age? After all, today's media climate is dramatically different from the one which in the 1950s prompted Gerbner to speculate about the effects of institutionalized mass-produced messages, which were at the time being transmitted through a single dominant medium controlled by a limited number of corporate owners. Unlike in the 1960s and 1970s, no single voice is now able to credibly say to a mass audience in the United States, as CBS news anchor Walter Cronkite once did, "That's the way it is." Gone too is the world captured by Bruce Springsteen's 1992 song, "57 Channels and Nothing On." Instead, at any time of the day or night, on portable and stationary screens and in various configurations, viewers can access 500 or more channels and watch and interact with what they want, when they want, rather than waiting for an episode or movie to air. At the same time, mass audiences have given way to niche ones, and the massed audiences for network news have declined. The notion of a dominant media voice has given way to media as menu and consumer as creator.

Some of the media and message structures central to cultivation persevere. Violence still dominates movies (Nalkur, Jamieson, and Romer, 2010; Jamieson et al., 2008; Bushman, Jamieson, Weitz, and Romer, 2013), female movie violence has increased (Bleakley, Jamieson, and Romer, 2012), and the movie suicide portrayal rate tripled from 1950 to 2006 (Jamieson and Romer, 2011). Violence is also common in video games (Huesmann and Taylor, 2006) and on television, with TV drama violence on the upswing (Jamieson and Romer, 2014) and local news trafficking crime on handheld devices. Moreover, it is possible that 24/7 connectivity is magnifying our exposure to fear-inducing messages rather than providing us with a means of avoiding them all together. At the same time, large-scale corporate ownership of the channels continues to characterize media industries, with Jeff Bezos owning the *Washington Post*, Rupert Murdoch the *Wall Street Journal* and Fox News, and NBC now being Comcast-NBC.

Indeed, one might hypothesize that micro-targeted communication based on detailed profiles of our consumer purchasing habits, voting dispositions, media preferences, and social media likes and dislikes may enhance cultivation effects. Determining whether it will, and if so how, as well as isolating the implications for our collective views of our political world, will drive research on cultivation in the coming decades.

REFERENCES

Bleakley, A., Jamieson, P. E., and Romer, D. 2012. Trends of sexual and violent content by gender in top-grossing US films, 1950–2006. *Journal of Adolescent Health* 51(1): 73–79.

Busselle, R. W. 2001. Television exposure, perceived realism, and exemplar accessibility in the social judgment process. *Media Psychology* 3(1): 43–67.

Busselle, R. W., and Greenberg, B. S. 2000. The nature of television realism judgments: A re-evaluation of their conceptualization and measurement. *Mass Communication & Society* 3(2–3): 249–268.

Cappella, J. N., and Jamieson, K. H. 1997. *Spiral of cynicism: The press and the public good.* New York: Oxford University Press.

Dixon, T. L. 2008. Crime news and racialized beliefs: Understanding the relationship between local news viewing and perceptions of African Americans and crime. *Journal of Communication* 58: 106–129.

Dixon, T. L., and Linz, D. 2000. Overrepresentation and underrepresentation of African Americans and Latinos as lawbreakers on television news. *Journal of Communication* 50: 131–154.

Doob, A. N., and Macdonald, G. E. 1979. Television viewing and fear of victimization: Is the relationship causal? *Journal of Personality and Social Psychology* 37(2): 170–179.

Gebotys, R. J., Roberts, J. V., and DasGupta, B. 1988. News media use and public perceptions of crime seriousness. *Canadian J. Criminology* 30: 3.

Gerbner, G. 1959. Education and the challenge of mass culture. *AV Communication Review* 7: 264–278.

Gerbner, G. 1969. Toward "cultural indicators": The analysis of mass mediated public message systems. *AV Communication Review* 17: 137–148.

Gerbner, G. 1970. Cultural indicators: The case of violence in television drama. *Annals of the American Academy of Political and Social Science* 388: 69–81.

Gerbner, G. 1981. Testimony of George Gerbner before the Subcommittee on Telecommunications, Consumer Protection, and Finance of the Committee on Energy and Commerce, U.S. House of Representatives, Washington, DC, October 21, 1981. Retrieved from http://www.asc.upenn.edu/gerbner/archive.aspx?sectionID=158&packageID=212

Gerbner, G., and Gross, L. 1976. Living with television: The violence profile. *Journal of Communication* 26(2): 173–199.

Gerbner, G., Gross, L., Morgan, M., and Signorielli, N. 1980a. The "mainstreaming" of America: Violence profile no. 11. *Journal of Communication* 30(3): 10–29.

Gerbner, G., Gross, L., Morgan, M., and Signorielli, N. 1980b. Some additional comments on cultivation analysis. *Public Opinion Quarterly* 44(3): 408–410.

Gerbner, G., Gross, L., Morgan, M., and Signorielli, N. 1982. Charting the mainstream: Television's contributions to political orientations. *Journal of Communication* 32: 100–127.

Gerbner, G., Gross, L., Morgan, M., and Signorielli, N. 1984. Political correlates of television viewing. *Public Opinion Quarterly* 48: 283–300.

Gerbner, G., Gross, L., Morgan, M., and Signorielli, N. 1994. Growing up with television: The cultivation perspective. In J. Bryant and D. Zillman (Eds.), *Media effects: Advances in theory and research* (pp. 17–41). Hillsdale, NJ: Lawrence Erlbaum.

Goidel, R. K., Freeman, C. M., and Procopio, S. T. 2006. The impact of television viewing on perceptions of juvenile crime. *Journal of Broadcasting & Electronic Media* 50(1): 119–139.

Gross, L. 2012. Foreword. In M. Morgan, J. Shanahan, and N. Signorelli (Eds.), *Living with television now: Advances in cultivation theory and research* (pp. xi–xix). New York: Peter Lang.

Hardy, B. 2012. Cultivation of political attitudes in the new media environment. In M. Morgan, J. Shanahan, and N. Signorielli (Eds.), *Living with television now: Advances in cultivation theory and research* (pp. 101–119). New York: Peter Lang.

Hawkins, R. P., and Pingree, S. 1982. Television's influence on social reality. In D. Pearl, L. Bouthilet, and J. Lazar (Eds.), *Television and behavior: Ten years of scientific progress and implications for the eighties* (pp. 224–247). Rockville, MD: National Institute of Mental Health.

Heath, L., and Petraitis, J. 1987. Television viewing and fear of crime: Where is the mean world? *Basic and Applied Social Psychology* 8(1–2): 97–123.

Hirsch, P. M. 1980. The "scary world" of the nonviewer and other anomalies: A reanalysis of Gerbner et al.'s findings on cultivation analysis, part 1. *Communication Research* 7(4): 403–456.

Hirsch, P. 1981. On not learning from one's own mistakes: A reanalysis of Gerbner et al.'s findings on cultivation analysis, part 2. *Communication Research* 8: 3–37.

Holbert, R. L., Shah, D. V., and Kwak, N. 2004. Fear, authority, and justice: Crime-related TV viewing and endorsements of capital punishment and gun ownership. *Journalism and Mass Communication Quarterly* 81: 343–363.

Huesmann, L. R., and Taylor, L. D. 2006. The role of media violence in violent behavior. *Annual Review of Public Health* 27(1): 393–415.

Hughes, M. 1980. The fruits of cultivation analysis: A re-examination of some effects of television watching. *Public Opinion Quarterly* 44(3): 287–302.

Jamieson, K. H. 1992. *Dirty politics: Deception, distraction and democracy.* New York: Oxford University Press.

Jamieson, P. E., More, E., Lee, S. S., Busse, P., and Romer, D. 2008. It matters what young people watch: Health risk behaviors portrayed in top-grossing movies since 1950. In P. E. Jamieson and D. Romer (Eds.), *The changing portrayal of adolescents in the media since 1950* (pp. 105–131). New York: Oxford University Press.

Jamieson, P. E., and Romer, D. 2011. Trends in explicit portrayal of suicidal behavior in popular U.S. movies, 1950–2006. *Archives of Suicide Research* 15(3): 277–289.

Jamieson, P. E., and Romer, D. 2014. Violence in popular US prime time TV dramas and the cultivation of fear: A time series analysis. *Media and Communication* 2(2): 31–41.

Lee, C. J., and Niederdeppe, J. 2011. Genre-specific cultivation effects. *Communication Research* 38(6): 731–753.

Lowry, D. T., Nio, T. C., and Leitner, D. W. 2003. Setting the public fear agenda: A longitudinal analysis of network TV crime reporting, public perceptions of crime, and FBI crime statistics. *Journal of Communication* 53: 61–73.

McLeod, J. M. 2000. Media and the civic socialization of youth. *Journal of Adolescent Health* 27: 45–51.

Morgan, M., and Shanahan, J. 1997. Two decades of cultivation research: An appraisal and meta-analysis. In B. R. Burleson (Ed.), *Communication yearbook 20* (pp. 1–45). Newbury Park, CA: Sage.

Morgan, M., and Shanahan, J. 2010. The state of cultivation. *Journal of Broadcasting & Electronic Media* 54(2): 337–355.

Nabi, R. L., and Sullivan, J. L. 2001. Does television viewing relate to engagement in protective action against crime? A cultivation analysis from a theory of reasoned action perspective. *Communication Research* 28(6): 802–825.

Nabi, R. L., Biely, E. N., Morgan, S. J., and Stitt, C. R. 2003. Reality-based television programming and the psychology of its appeal. *Media Psychology* 5(4): 303–330.

Nalkur P. G., Jamieson, P. E., and Romer, D. 2010. The effectiveness of the Motion Picture Association of America's rating system in screening explicit violence and sex in top-ranked movies from 1950–2006. *Journal of Adolescent Health* 47: 440–447.

Oliver, M. B., and Armstrong G. B. 1998. The color of crime: Perceptions of Caucasians' and African Americans' involvement in crime. In M. Fishman and G. Cavendar (Eds), *Entertaining crime: Television reality programs* (pp. 19–35). New York: Aldine de Gruyter.

Patterson, T. 1993. *Out of order: An incisive and boldly original critique of the news media's domination of America's political process.* New York: Alfred A. Knopf.

Pasek, J., Kenski, K., Romer, D., and Jamieson, K. H. 2006. America's youth and community engagement: How use of mass media is related to political knowledge and civic activity among 14 to 22 year olds. *Communication Research* 33: 115–135.

Potter, W. J. 1986. Perceived reality and the cultivation hypothesis. *Journal of Broadcasting and Electronic Media* 30: 159–174.

Potter, W. J. 1988. Perceived reality in television effects research. *Journal of Broadcasting & Electronic Media* 32(1): 23–41.

Potter, W. J., and Riddle, K. 2007. A content analysis of the media effects literature. *Journalism & Mass Communication Quarterly* 84(1): 90–104.

Pritchard, David. 1986. Homicide and bargained justice: The agenda-setting effect of crime news on prosecutors. *Public Opinion Quarterly* 50(2): 143-159.

Putnam, R. D. 1995. Tuning in, tuning out: The strange disappearance of social capital in America. *Political Science and Politics* 28: 664–683.

Putnam, R. D. 2000. *Bowling alone: The collapse and revival of American community.* New York: Touchstone.

Rahn, W. M., and Transue, J. 1998. Social trust and value change: The decline of social capital in American youth, 1976–1995. *Political Psychology* 19: 545–565.

Romer, D. 2008. Mass media and the socialization of adolescents since World War II. In P. E. Jamieson and D. Romer (Eds.), *The changing portrayal of Adolescents in the media since 1950* (pp. 3–26). New York: Oxford University Press.

Romer, D., Jamieson, K. H., and Aday, S. 2003. Television news and the cultivation of fear of crime. *Journal of Communication* 53(1): 88–104.

Romer, D., Jamieson, K. H., and DeCoteau, N. 1998. The treatment of persons of color in local television news: Ethnic blame discourse or realistic group conflict. *Communication Research* 25: 286–305.

Romer, D., Jamieson, K. H., and Pasek, J. 2009. Building social capital in young people: The role of mass media and life outlook. *Political Communication* 26: 65–83.

Shrum, L. J., and O'Guinn, T. C. 1993. Processes and effects in the construction of social reality. *Communication Research* 20(3): 436–471.

Signorielli, N., and Gerbner, G. 1995. Violence on television: The Cultural Indicators Project. *Journal of Broadcasting & Electronic Media* 39(2): 278–283.

Weitzer, R., and Kubrin, C. E. 2004. Breaking news: How local TV news and real-world conditions affect fear of crime. *Justice Quarterly* 21: 497–520.

CHAPTER 42

··

USES AND GRATIFICATIONS

··

R. LANCE HOLBERT

POLITICAL communication scholars interested in the study of media have long been concerned with the question: What is leading people to consume political media? This query is grounded in a broader "audience as agent" approach to the study of media consumers (Webster, 1998), with the central question associated with this metaphor being: What do people do with media? Political media scholars are also interested in what media people consume (i.e., audience as mass research), and there has been much attention paid of late to how best to measure patterns of political media use (e.g., Eveland, Hutchens, and Shen, 2009; Prior, 2009a, 2009b). The field is also interested in a broad range of democratic outcomes derived from the consumption of a variety of political media outlets (i.e., audience as outcome research), and the outcomes (e.g., issue salience, political knowledge, candidate thermometer ratings, voting) span the hierarchy of effects (e.g., Benoit, Hansen, and Verser, 2003; McCombs, 2004; Valentino, Hutchings, and White, 2002). While audience-as-mass and audience-as-outcome research may deal, either directly or indirectly, with elements of what is leading people to political media, audience-as-agent research in the uses and gratifications tradition treats as its primary and central focus the assessment of the internal mechanisms that drive individuals to consume media outlets that contain political content.

The question of what guides people to consume political media remains of central importance to the study of political communication. Prior (2007) argues that a far smaller percentage of the general population is turning to news media as a result of an expansion of media outlets, a vast majority of which focus on entertainment. A small percentage of the audience, 10–15 percent of the total population, consumes a great deal of political media (defined by Prior as "news junkies"), but most people who wish to eschew politics altogether can do so in today's media environment. What is driving some people to want to absorb enormous volumes of political media content, while others seek out media messages that have nothing to do with public affairs, civics, or basic democratic processes? Uses and gratifications research can provide some answers to this question.

In addition, some of the central debates among political communication scholars over the future of media influence center on what leads people to want to consume a broad range of political information outlets, from debates to news to blogs (see Bennett and Iyengar, 2008, 2010; Holbert, Garrett, and Gleason, 2010). Various political media experiences compete with an endless number of mass media alternatives (along with all of our nonmedia activities) for people's attention, but it is important from the standpoint of moving further toward our democratic ideals to gain a sense of who is consuming what political media material. In addition, we need a sense of when they are taking on political media and, most important, why they are choosing to engage this material. Inherent in these discussions are different perspectives on the all-important issue of endogeneity (see Iyengar, 2011). Bennett and Iyengar (2008, 2010) argue that any type of political media use should now be seen as a behavioral manifestation of an individual's political ideology and/or political party identification. Thus, ideology and party ID are contained within the act of media use itself. As a result, it is difficult to parse out the influence of media from that of ideology or party ID when the two are so deeply wedded. Holbert and colleagues (2010) argue that any single act of political media engagement is more than a mere reflection of one's political ideology, and a uses and gratifications perspective can shed some light on just how the consumption of a broad range of political media outlets can be driven by more than preexisting political orientations (Rubin, 2009). In short, the study of political media uses and gratifications remains relevant to the central issues and concerns driving the field.

Uses and gratifications research about political media has declined from its glory days of the late 1960s through the 1980s (see Blumler and Katz, 1974). Today's audience-as-agent research within the field of political communication is driven much more by the concept of selective exposure (e.g., Stroud, 2011) than by the broader framework that is uses and gratifications (see Rosengren, 1974). In addition, it is important to recognize that uses and gratifications is best defined as a framework or perspective for approaching the study of social and psychological processes leading to the formation of patterns of media use. Uses and gratifications is not a formal communication theory (see Berger, Roloff, and Ewoldsen, 2010; Pavitt, 2000, 2010). In addition, uses and gratifications retains some well-defined boundary conditions, the most important being a sole focus on the individual level of analysis. While other approaches to the establishment of patterns of media use embrace a broader, multilevel perspective (e.g., media systems dependency theory; see Ball-Rokeach and DeFleur, 1976), the main thrust of uses and gratifications research focuses on the individual. This is true of even the field's most recent uses and gratifications research efforts (e.g., Hanson and Haridakis, 2008; Holbert et al., 2007; Kaye, 2010; Krcmar and Strizhakova, 2009).

With these limitations in mind, uses and gratifications can and should remain a vital component of the study of political media consumption and effects (Ruggerio, 2000). As our media system continues to shift toward a model in which audience members increasingly control the ability to consume a seemingly infinite number of media outlets (Chaffee and Metzger, 2001), the types of questions both posed and addressed by uses and gratifications scholarship should provide much utility for the field.

With an eye toward uses and gratifications' continued relevance, this chapter focuses on seven topic areas that political communication scholars should wrestle with if they are to advance this framework for the study of media. First, given that uses and gratifications is more of a framework than a theory, several different theories have been linked to it to try to address the matter of (un)conscious selection of media. However, none has taken hold as a single best fit for what the broader uses and gratifications framework encapsulates. Second, if uses and gratifications is to move toward more formal theory development, then an honest and critical assessment is needed of what the core explanatory principles driving individual-level political media use are. Third, there needs to be a revisiting of what the field wishes to define as "political media." The heyday of political media uses and gratifications research retained a focus that was almost solely on news (i.e., the daily newspaper, broadcast television news), and any work done on alternative outlets (e.g., public television, talk radio, debates) was deemed novel (e.g., Armstrong and Rubin, 1989; Chaffee, 1978; Palmgreen and Rayburn, 1979). Fourth, moving beyond some core theory development concerns, there is the continuing issue of how best to operationalize political media gratifications sought and received at the individual level of analysis. Rubin (2009) notes that measurement has always been a lingering challenge for this area of study. If these measurement issues are not resolved in a systematic way, then there will remain a ceiling effect on the utility provided to the field by uses and gratifications research. These four points represent matters in the existing literature that require some degree of resolution.

In addition, although this is not an exhaustive list, there are three areas of potential development within the uses and gratifications framework that may be fruitful for political communication scholars. First is a shift within the broader study of mass communication to focus on dynamic processes, rather than simple, linear causal effects models (Lang and Ewoldsen, 2010), and much of the underlying discussion of uses and gratifications would point toward the emergence of dynamic processes (see Slater, 2007). Second, media scholars have assessed the gratifications sought and obtained for various political media outlets in relative isolation, but there is a growing body of work within political communication that looks at how various types of political media use are complementary (Holbert and Benoit, 2009). The study of uses and gratifications of political media may benefit from adopting a more complementary lens, and this notion is explored in some detail in this chapter. Finally, the study of anything involving media should encompass a broad assessment of McGuire's (1989) five communication input variables: message, source, recipient, channel, and context. The study of uses and gratifications is squarely focused on the recipient, but our emerging media environment and how various political media products are presented within it require paying attention to the other four inputs as well (especially a movement beyond gratifications sought and obtained in relation to specific message features). There is still much to be debated about the study of political media uses and gratifications, and addressing some of the issues raised in this chapter will serve to return this important framework to its proper place at the center of our field of study.

(Un)Conscious Selection

The study of seeking gratifications through media concerns itself with why or how individuals make conscious decisions to consume specific types of political media outlets or messages. Several theoretical approaches to conscious decision-making have been utilized in extant uses and gratifications research (LaRose, 2010): the theory of planned behavior (e.g., Oulette and Wood, 1998), expectancy value theory (Rayburn and Palmgreen, 1984), social cognitive theory (e.g., LaRose and Eastin, 2004), and selective exposure (e.g., Stroud, 2010). Each of these theories serves a very different purpose in uses and gratifications research. For example, the social cognitive approach offered by LaRose and Eastin (2004) links the concept of gratifications sought with Bandura's discussion of expected outcomes, and a connection is also made between the all-important concept of needs in uses and gratifications research (see more below) and Bandura's behavioral incentives. Social cognitive theory (Bandura, 1986) is a theoretical foundation that is more parsimonious than uses and gratifications, is internally consistent, and retains a high level of predictive power. These criteria are all elements for which uses and gratifications is lacking in terms of theory development. Likewise, the use of expectancy value theory (EVT) by Rayburn and Palmgreen (1984) allows for the formation of a more formulaic approach to the study of gratifications sought and obtained. Some of the initial models of uses and gratifications were unwieldy (see Rosengren 1974), but the use of EVT allows for the generation of more precise predictions concerning gratifications sought through political media use. However, no one theory has been able to take hold within the field that can serve as a foundation for the study of uses and gratifications. This is due in large part to the fact that the theories outlined above have been unable to retain a sufficient level of power to encompass all that uses and gratifications as a framework attempts to explain. However, the field should debate and attempt to reach some consensus on a proper bounding of uses and gratifications. If a proper set of boundaries can be established, then some of these theories may prove to be better fits than once thought.

There has also been work on media addictions (e.g., Young, 1996), dependencies (Wenner, 1982), and media habits (LaRose, Lin, and Eastin, 2003), and, as stated previously, the term "news junkie" has become part of our field's lexicon in the age of audience disaggregation (e.g., Prior, 2007). The use of terms like addiction, dependency, and habit tends to bring forward connotations of unconscious behavioral engagement, but LaRose (2010) has recently argued for a revisiting of the concept of habit to include a role for conscious selection. In particular, he outlines processes of habit acquisition and habit activation. Human beings seek to develop habits and then continually activate well-established habitual cognitive and behavioral systems in order to maximize efficiency and minimize cognitive activity. Humans are conscious of their efforts to establish habits, and the study of the habit formation and enactment may provide a foundation to allow uses and gratifications research to move toward becoming a formal theory.

REVISITING OF UNDERLYING CONCEPTS
AND EXPLANATORY PRINCIPLES

The classic definition of uses and gratifications places the concept of "needs" at the center of any processes that lead to media gratifications sought, patterns of media use, or media gratifications obtained (Katz, Blumler, and Gurevitch, 1974). These needs can be psychological or social in origin. However, there has been some revisiting of the concept of "needs" in the context of whether media consumption reflects "compensation" (i.e., making up for what can't be achieved through other means) or "enrichment" (i.e., building off of and expanding on meaningful nonmediated activities) (see Perse and Butler, 2005). This is a very interesting debate in relation to political media gratifications in particular. Let us take the surveillance function of media, which has long been the gratification most often associated with news media use (Becker, 1979). The desire to survey the world around us is associated with our need for safety; a feeling of safety derives from our gaining more information about the world around us and our role within it. So, does our seeking out news media to feel more secure in our environment represent our making up for what information could not be obtained through face-to-face communication with family members, coworkers, or members of our community? Or should we be viewing an activity like television news use as a communicative act that can serve to enrich other types of political communication activities (i.e., face-to-face political communication)? In addition, there is no reason to treat these queries as either-or scenarios. Perhaps there are specific individual-difference variables or other contextual factors that may serve as third-variable moderators and add predictive value for determining when a specific individual turns to a specific political media outlet to compensate for whatever need can't be gratified through a nonmediated activity or when the mediated communicative act serves to enrich those nonmediated communication acts we perform on a daily basis. Addressing these types of questions will lead to a better understanding of the role of media in our political lives.

The concept of needs should be revisited in parallel with a focus on some of the basic explanatory principles that have driven communication theory building in the past (e.g., the hedonic principle, understanding, consistency; see Pavitt, 2010). A fresh approach to uses and gratifications through a diversified set of core explanatory principles may place the concept of "needs" in better focus and allow it to become more useful for future research. In order for uses and gratifications to remain a relevant framework within the field, this type of fundamental theory building is necessary. The field of political communication is witnessing a shift in dominant explanatory principles, from understanding to consistency. Katz (1987) identified agenda setting as the quintessential example of the institutional paradigm, one of the three major critiques of Lazarsfeld's marketing-oriented approach to the study of media influence. The now seminal work of McCombs and Shaw (1972) represented a call for a focus on journalism as an "information profession" (Katz, 1987, S29), not as an activity designed to persuade. Agenda setting and other understanding-driven theories are now being called into question by many in the field (see Bennett and Iyengar, 2008), and more consistency-driven accounts of political media engagement appear to be replacing understanding in our research (e.g., partisan selective exposure; see, e.g., Knobloch-Westerwick and Meng, 2011). This shifting of explanatory principles will determine where the field moves theoretically over the next decade, and uses and gratifications, along with any other political communication-based theory, meta-concept, or framework, will need to wrestle with how best to situate itself within the debate if it is to remain relevant.

BOUNDARIES OF POLITICAL MEDIA

Much of the classic work on political media uses and gratifications focuses on news (e.g., Palmgreen, Wenner, and Rayburn, 1980), but other traditional political media outlets like debates (e.g., McLeod, Bybee, and Durall, 1982) have also been a focus of this approach to media. Uses and gratifications work has continued to expand over the years to bring within the fold such outlets as web news (Diddi and LaRose, 2006), radio (Albarran et al., 2007), and even *The Daily Show* (Holbert et al., 2007). A key issue that needs to be addressed by the field is where/how we establish the boundaries for what does and does not count as "political media." The establishment of these boundaries is open to much debate (compare Bennett and Iyengar, 2010 and Holbert et al., 2010), but this basic question needs to be resolved if this area of research is to move forward.

Take, for example, the case of political entertainment media, broadly defined (Holbert, 2005a). Tamborini and colleagues (2010) offer an argument using self-determination theory that media use satisfies the basic human needs of autonomy, competence, and relatedness, but these researchers nest all of these needs within a broader model of enjoyment. The concept of enjoyment has been woefully lacking in the study of political media use. Furthermore, to place this point of discussion within the broader context of revisiting uses and gratifications' core explanatory principles, Pavitt (2010) emphasizes the basic hedonic principle as a natural human drive that generates all types of communicative activities. The possible inclusion of even only a small subset of entertainment media that encompass various political themes makes all the more evident the necessity of including enjoyment in any discussion of political media uses and gratifications.

MEASUREMENT

Measurement is a messy business in uses and gratifications research. This research agenda's most immediate measurement issues focus on three core concepts: gratifications sought, gratifications obtained, and media use. It has long been established that gratifications sought and gratifications obtained are distinct concepts, but the measurement of each has remained problematic. It is especially troublesome/interesting conceptually (depending on one's point of view) that the relationship between the two gratification concepts is relatively low according to existing research. Some of the primary gratification dimensions explored to date are surveillance, escapism, to pass time, and entertainment (e.g., Diddi and LaRose, 2006). However, these dimensions should be revisited, especially in concert with the points outlined above concerning the boundaries of "political media" and the framework's core explanatory principles.

The study of media gratifications functions in concert with empirical assessments of media use, and there has been much debate recently over how best to measure political media use (see Eveland, Hutchens, and Shen, 2009; Prior 2009a, 2009b). A broad range of measurement options has been explored in other areas of communication as well (e.g., health communication; see Romantan et al., 2008), and these possibilities should be further explored by political communication researchers. It is essential to address the issue of media use measurement when thinking about how best to move forward in improving our operationalizations of political media gratifications (sought and obtained). The ultimate goal of uses and gratifications research is to better understand how and why people use media in various ways. However, if we can't even measure media use, much less its subdimensions of exposure and attention, in a valid and reliable manner, then it is easy to see how this set of circumstances places some fairly tight constraints on what uses and gratifications research can achieve over the long term.

Dynamic Processes

Conceptual models attempting to map out media gratification processes have been short on parsimony (see Rosengren, 1974). However, the core argument put forward by Palmgreen (1984) is that there is a reciprocal, mutually reinforcing relationship between gratifications sought and obtained, and that it is through their mutual reinforcement that patterns of media use solidify within individuals. Slater (2007) references uses and gratifications in the context of his proposal to study reinforcing spirals that form over time between media use and individual-level beliefs/attitudes (e.g., identity), and Rubin (2009) has argued that more work needs to be done on the study of the dynamic processes that exist among gratifications sought, gratifications obtained, and media use. There has been a general call to study a broad range of dynamic processes associated with media (e.g., Lang and Ewoldsen, 2010), and it is important for the field to address how best to approach the study of political media uses and gratifications from a dynamic perspective.

This important conceptual point manifests itself in an even broader set of methodological concerns. A vast majority of work on media uses and gratifications employs the use of cross-sectional surveys, but the limits of this type of design are well documented (see Eveland and Morey, 2011). There is a need for uses and gratifications research to be conducted using more complex survey designs (e.g., panel) and experimentation (especially the use of multistage designs; see Hansen and Pfau, 2011). Conceptually, uses and gratifications has always been seen as representing dynamic processes, and the field is now well situated to develop research designs to assess properly these complex processes of influence. Nonetheless, it is important that the field step away from the use of the cross-sectional surveys for the advancement of this area of research. The study of political media uses and gratifications is rich enough to require the use of multiple methods to gain true understanding of why people are choosing to consume a variety of political media outlets.

Assessing Networks of Political Media Gratifications

A vast majority of existing political media uses and gratifications research focuses either on a single outlet (e.g., television news, the web, debates, newspapers) or a series of outlets in relative isolation. A general call has been made to study how various types of political media use are related to one another, and how a broad range of processes of media influence form as a result of the establishment of these media-use-to-media-use relationships (Holbert, 2005; Holbert and Benoit, 2009). It can be argued that the gratifications sought and obtained in association with one political media outlet depend in part on the gratifications individuals associate with other political media outlets. As a result, studying the gratifications sought and obtained for a single political media outlet or multiple political media outlets in relative isolation will only provide limited insights. What needs to be assessed is how a web of gratification associations is formed in accordance with the use of multiple political media outlets. For example, let's focus on the concepts of reach and specificity (Schooler et al., 1998). My use of a reach-based political media outlet (e.g., *washingtonpost.com*) functions alongside my use of a specificity-based political media outlet (e.g., *The Huffington Post*). The gratifications I seek out through the use of the *Washington Post*'s website are determined in part by the gratifications I seek and receive from the *Huffington Post*. The two acts of political media engagement are linked. It is important for the study of political media uses and gratifications to explore how the gratifications sought and received in association with one outlet are determined by the gratifications associated with another outlet. From the standpoint of audience members, these outlets are not in competition with one another—they function in coordination with one another to enrich our understanding of politics, basic democratic processes, and what is happening in our communities.

Additional Recipient, Source, Channel, and Contextual Variables

Any discussion of the future of political media uses and gratifications research should include reference to other key audience variables: opinion leadership, personality strength, internal political self-efficacy, and cynicism (see Adriaansen, VanPragg, and DeVreese, 2010; Morrell, 2003; Scheufele and Shah, 2000; Shah and Scheufele, 2006). All of these characteristics have been shown to help shape political media use, and any measures of gratifications sought and obtained need to be constantly placed in their proper context relative to these other important audience variables. In addition, a variety of source characteristics, such as credibility (McCroskey and Teven, 1999), should be included in any assessment of political media use. People are not just drawn to political media for the messages being provided, but also for the personalities who are delivering these pieces of information. Rubin (2009) also mentions the need for continued study of not just message, but also form (channel). Eveland (2003) has posited a range of attributes that could influence political media gratifications sought and obtained: interactivity, locus of control, and channel (i.e., pure visual, pure audio, audiovisual; see also Walther, Gay, and Hancock, 2005). There is also a need to explore key contextual variables. For example, political media gratifications sought and obtained could vary widely based on whether there is a political campaign ongoing versus engaging political media outside the time frame of a specific election cycle.

Conclusion

Each area of study within the field of political communication experiences ups and downs in its centrality to current research efforts. It is safe to say that uses and gratifications research has hit a relatively low point, having occupied a high status position within the field for several decades leading up to the coming of the new century. However, with more of the onus being placed on citizens for determining political media use, one would be hard pressed to argue against the relevance of uses and gratifications in providing a foundation for explaining what this newfound power will mean for the functioning of basic democratic processes. The area of uses and gratifications will continue to work hard to resolve some central theoretical and methodological concerns, as well as to push the envelope over what types of communicative phenomena should be counted within its purview. It is argued in this chapter that continued exploration of a specific theory that can serve as an anchor for the uses and gratifications framework is needed, and that the search for an underlying theory should include a revisiting of the core explanatory principles driving future research agendas. The boundaries of the concept of "political media" need to be revisited, and an argument has been made for including entertainment-oriented outlets as political media. Regardless of where one takes a stand in this debate, almost everyone can agree on the need for improved measurement of uses and gratifications' central concepts (e.g., surveillance, escapism, entertainment). Uses and gratifications as a process needs to be studied dynamically to best reflect what has been argued theoretically for decades. In addition, gratifications sought and obtained relative to one outlet can't be looked at in isolation from other outlets. The political media gratifications obtained from one outlet will determine the political media gratifications sought through another. Finally, gratifications sought and obtained need to be understood as one small piece of a larger puzzle of recipient, message, source, channel, and contextual factors that help shape individual-level patterns of political media use. Addressing one or more of these points will propel the study of political media uses and gratifications forward and allow for new knowledge to be generated concerning how individual citizens use media to take part in various democratic processes.

REFERENCES

Adriaansen, M. L., VanPragg, P., and DeVreese, C. 2010. Substance matters: How news content can reduce political cynicism. *International Journal of Public Opinion Research 22*: 433–457.

Albarran, A. B., Anderson, T., Bejar, L. G., Bussart, A. L., Daggett, E., Gibson, S., Gorman, M., Greer, D., Guo, M., Horst, J. L., Khalaf, T., Lay, J. P., McCracken, M., Mott, B., and Way, H. 2007. What happened to our audience? Radio and new technology uses and gratifications among young adult users. *Journal of Radio & Audio Media 14*: 92–101.

Armstrong, C. B., and Rubin, A. M. 1989. Talk radio as interpersonal communication. *Journal of Communication 39*: 84–94.

Ball-Rokeach, S. J., and DeFleur, M. L. 1976. A dependency model of media effects. *Communication Research 3*: 3–21.

Bandura, A. 1986. *Social foundations of thought and action: A social cognitive theory.* Upper Saddle River, NJ: Prentice Hall.

Becker, L. B. 1979. Measurement of gratifications. *Communication Research 6*: 54–73.

Bennett, W. L., and Iyengar, S. 2008. A new era of minimal effects? The changing foundations of political communication. *Journal of Communication 58*: 707–731.

Bennett, W. L., and Iyengar, S. 2010. The shifting foundations of political communication: Responding to a defense of the media effects paradigm. *Journal of Communication 60*: 35–39.

Benoit, W. L., Hansen, G. J., and Verser, R. M. 2003. A meta-analysis of the effects of viewing presidential debates. *Communication Monographs 70*: 335–350.

Berger, C. R., Roloff, M. E., and Roskos-Ewoldsen, D. R. 2010. What is communication science? In C. R. Berger, M. E., Roloff, and D. R. Roskos-Ewoldsen (Eds.), *The handbook of communication science*, 2nd ed. (pp. 3–20). Thousand Oaks, CA: Sage.

Blumler, J. G., and Katz, E. 1974. *The uses of mass communications: Current perspectives on gratifications research.* Beverly Hills, CA: Sage.

Chaffee, S. H. 1978. Presidential debates—are they helpful to voters? *Communication Monographs 45*: 330–346.

Chaffee, S. H., and Metzger, M. J. 2001. The end of mass communication? *Mass Communication & Society* 4: 365–379.

Diddi, A., and LaRose, R. 2006. Getting hooked on news: Uses and gratifications and the formation of news habits among college students in an internet environment. *Journal of Broadcasting & Electronic Media* 50: 193–210.

Eveland, W. P., Jr. 2003. A "mix of attributes" approach to the study of media effects and new communication technologies. *Journal of Communication* 53: 395–410.

Eveland, W. P., Jr., Hutchens, M. J., and Shen, F. 2009. Exposure, attention, or "use" of news? Assessing aspects of the reliability and validity of a central concept in political communication research. *Communication Methods & Measures* 3: 223–244.

Eveland, W. P., Jr., and Morey, A. C. 2011. Challenges and opportunities of panel designs. In E. P. Bucy and R. L. Holbert (Eds.), *The sourcebook of political communication research: Methods, measures, and analytical techniques* (pp. 19–33). New York: Routledge.

Hansen, G. J., and Pfau, M. 2011. Multi-stage experimental designs in political communication research. In E. P. Bucy and R. L. Holbert (Eds.), *The sourcebook of political communication research: Methods, measures, and analytical techniques* (pp. 194–208). New York: Routledge.

Hanson, G., and Haridakis, P. 2008. YouTube users watching and sharing the news: A uses and gratifications approach. *Journal of Electronic Publishing* 11. Retrieved from http://hdl.handle.net/2027/spo.3336451.0011.305.

Holbert, R. L. 2005a. A typology for study of entertainment television and politics. *American Behavioral Scientist* 49: 436–453.

Holbert, R. L. 2005b. Debate viewing as mediator and partisan reinforcement in the relationship between news use and vote choice. *Journal of Communication* 55: 85–102.

Holbert, R. L., and Benoit, W. L. 2009. A theory of political campaign media connectedness. *Communication Monographs* 76: 303–332.

Holbert, R. L., Garrett, R. K., and Gleason, L. S. 2010. A new era of minimal effects? A response to Bennett and Iyengar. *Journal of Communication* 60: 15–34.

Holbert, R. L., Lambe, J. L., Dudo, A. D., and Carlton, K. A. 2007. Primacy effects of *The Daily Show* and national TV news viewing: Young viewers, political gratifications, and internal political self-efficacy. *Journal of Broadcasting & Electronic Media* 51: 20–38.

Iyengar, S. 2011. Experimental designs for political communication research: Using new technology and online participation pools to overcome the problem of generalizability. In E. P. Bucy and R. L. Holbert (Eds.), *The sourcebook for political communication research: Methods, measures, and analytical techniques* (pp. 129–148). New York: Routledge.

Katz, E. 1987. Communications research since Lazarsfeld. *Public Opinion Quarterly* 51: S25–S45.

Katz, E., Blumler, J. G., and Gurevitch, M. 1974. Utilization of mass communication by the individual. In J. G. Blumler and E. Katz (Eds.), *The uses of mass communications: Current perspectives on gratifications research* (pp. 19–32). Beverly Hills, CA: Sage.

Kaye, B. F. 2010. Uses and gratifications of the World Wide Web: From couch potato to web potato. *Atlantic Journal of Communication* 6: 21–40.

Knobloch-Westerwick, S., and Meng, J. 2011. Reinforcement of the political self through selective exposure to political messages. *Journal of Communication* 61: 349–368.

Krcmar, M., and Strizhakova, Y. 2009. Uses and gratifications as media choice. In T. Hartmann (Ed.), *Media choice: A theoretical and empirical overview* (pp. 53–69). New York: Taylor & Francis.

Lang, A., & Ewoldsen, D. (2010). Beyond effects: Conceptualizing communication as dynamic, complex, nonlinear, and fundamental. In S. Allen (Ed.), *Rethinking communication: Keywords in communication research* (pp. 111–122). New York: Hampton Press.

LaRose, R., and Eastin, M. S. 2004. A social cognitive theory of internet uses and gratifications: Toward a new model of media attendance. *Journal of Broadcasting & Electronic Media* 48: 358–377.

LaRose, R. 2010. The problem of media habits. *Communication Theory* 20: 194–222.

LaRose, R., Lin, C. A., and Eastin, M. S. 2003. Unregulated internet usage: Addiction, habit, or deficient self-regulation. *Media Psychology* 5: 225–253.

McCombs, M. E. 2004. *Setting the agenda: The mass media and public opinion.* Cambridge, UK: Polity.

McCombs, M. E., and Shaw, D. L. 1972. The agenda-setting function of mass media. *Public Opinion Quarterly* 36: 176–187.

McCroskey, J. C., and Teven, J. J. 1999. Goodwill: A reexamination of the construct and its measurement. *Communication Monographs* 66: 90–103.

McGuire, W. J. 1989. Theoretical foundations of campaigns. In R. E. Rice and C. K. Atkin (Eds.), *Public communication campaigns,* 2nd ed. (pp. 43–65). Newbury Park, CA; Sage.

McLeod, J., Bybee, C., and Durall, J. (1982). Evaluating media performance by gratifications sought and received. *Journalism Quarterly* 59, 3–12.

Morrell, M. E. 2003. Survey and experimental evidence for a reliable and valid measure of internal political efficacy. *Public Opinion Quarterly* 67: 589–602.

Oulette, J. A., and Wood, W. 1998. Habit and intention in everyday life: The multiple processes by which past behavior predicts future behavior. *Psychological Bulletin* 124: 54–74.

Palmgreen, P. 1984. Uses and gratifications: A theoretical perspective. *Communication Yearbook* 8: 20–55.

Palmgreen, P., and Rayburn, J. D. 1979. Uses and gratifications and exposure to public television: A discrepency approach. *Communication Research* 6: 155–179.

Palmgreen, P., Wenner, L. A., and Rayburn, J. D. 1980. Relations between gratifications sought and obtained: A study of television news. *Communication Research* 7: 161–192.

Pavitt, C. 2000. Answering questions requesting scientific explanations for communication. *Communication Theory* 10: 379–404.

Pavitt, C. 2010. Alternative approaches to theorizing in communication science. In C. R. Berger, M. E. Roloff, and D. R. Roskow-Ewoldsen (Eds.), *The handbook of communication science,* 2nd ed. (pp. 37–54). Thousand Oaks, CA: Sage.

Perse, E. M., and Butler, J. S. 2005. Call-in talk radio: Compensation or enrichment. *Journal of Radio & Audio Media* 12: 204–222.

Prior, M. 2007. *Post-broadcast democracy: How media choice increases inequality in political involvement and polarizes elections.* New York: Cambridge University Press.

Prior, M. 2009a. Improving media effects research through better measurement of news exposure. *Journal of Politics* 71: 893–908.

Prior, M. 2009b. The immensely inflated news audience: assessing bias in self-reported news exposure. *Public Opinion Quarterly* 73: 130–143.

Rayburn, J. D., and Palmgreen, P. 1984. Merging uses and gratifications and expectancy-value theory. *Communication Research* 11: 537–562.

Romantan, A., Hornik, R., Price, V., Cappella, J. N., and Viswanath, K. 2008. A comparative analysis of the performance of alternative measures of exposure. *Communication Methods & Measures* 2: 80–99.

Rosengren, K. 1974. Uses and gratifications: A paradigm outlined. In J. Blumler and E. Katz (Eds.), *The uses of mass communications: Current perspectives on gratifications research* (pp. 269–286). Beverly Hills, CA: Sage.

Rubin, A. M. 2009. Uses-and-gratifications perspective on media effects. In J. Bryant and M. B. Oliver (Eds.), *Media effects: Advances in theory and research* (pp. 165–184). New York: Routledge.

Ruggerio, T. E. 2000. Uses and gratification theory in the 21st century. *Mass Communication & Society 3*: 3–37.

Scheufele, D. A., and Shah, D. V. 2000. Personality strength and social capital: The role of dispositional and informational variables in the production of civic participation. *Communication Research 27*: 107–131.

Schooler, C., Chaffee, S. H., Flora, J. A., and Roser, C. 1998. Health campaign channels: Tradeoffs among reach, specificity, and impact. *Human Communication Research 24*: 410–432.

Shah, D. V., and Scheufele, D. A. 2006. Explication opinion leadership: Nonpolitical dispositions, information consumption, and civic participation. *Political Communication 23*: 1–22.

Slater, M. D. 2007. Reinforcing spirals: The mutual influence of media selectivity and media effects and their impact of individual behavior and social identity. *Communication Theory 17*: 281–303.

Stroud, N. J. 2010. Polarization and partisan selective exposure. *Journal of Communication 60*: 556–576.

Stroud, N. J. 2011. *Niche news: The politics of news choice.* Oxford: Oxford University Press.

Tamborini, R., Bowman, N., Eden, A., Grizzard, M., and Organ, A. 2010. Defining media enjoyment as the satisfaction of intrinsic needs. *Journal of Communication 60*: 758–777.

Valentino, N. A., Hutchings, V. L., and White, I. K. 2002. Cues that matter: How political ads prime racial attitudes during campaigns. *American Political Science Review 96*: 75–90.

Walther, J. B., Gay, G., and Hancock, J. T. 2005. How do communication and technology researchers study the internet? *Journal of Communication 55*: 632–657.

Webster, J. G. 1998. The audience. *Journal of Broadcasting & Electronic Media 42*: 190–207.

Wenner, L. A. 1982. Gratifications sought and obtained in program dependency: A study of networks news programs and *60 Minutes. Communication Research 9*: 539–560.

Young, K. S. 1996. Psychology of computer use: Addictive use of the Internet: A case that breaks the stereotype. *Psychological Reports 79*: 899–902.

....

CHAPTER 43

THE STATE OF FRAMING RESEARCH

A Call for New Directions

....

DIETRAM A. SCHEUFELE AND SHANTO IYENGAR

THE concept of framing embodies a context-sensitive explanation for shifts in political beliefs and attitudes. Framing defines a dynamic, circumstantially bound process of opinion formation in which the prevailing modes of presentation in elite rhetoric and news media coverage shape mass opinion (Iyengar, 1991; Scheufele, 1999). This definition stands in stark contrast to other models of opinion formation that explain attitudes on specific issues or events as a function of longstanding and stable political predispositions (Campell et al., 1960; Lazarsfeld, Berelson, and Gaudet, 1948), of persuasive messaging (O'Keefe, 2002), or of learning, information processing, and other cognitive processes (Brossard, Lewenstein, and Bonney, 2005; Delli Carpini and Keeter, 1996). As a result, framing effects refer to behavioral or attitudinal outcomes that are not due to differences in *what* is being communicated, but rather to variations in *how* a given piece of information is being presented (or framed) in public discourse.

In spite of its rather narrow conceptual definition, communication researchers have become infatuated with the framing concept. Today, virtually every volume of the major journals features at least one paper on media frames and framing effects. If we sample from the pages of *Political Communication* and *Journal of Communication*, the increased prominence of the concept is clear: According to Thomson Reuters' Web of Science, these two journals published a total of thirty-three papers on framing between 1991 and 2000, but eighty-six between 2001 and 2010. What accounts for the popularity of the framing paradigm, and does the recent surge in scholarly interest signal an advance in our understanding of political communication?

The purpose of this chapter is to sound a cautionary note. Current communications research on framing has largely abandoned the more rigorous (and narrow) definition of frames derived from psychology—frames as informationally equivalent labels—in favor of a much looser definition—stemming from work in sociology—that blurs the distinction between frames and other informational or persuasive features of messages. The upshot is a state of conceptual confusion whereby any attribute of information is treated as a frame and any response from the audience is deemed a framing effect. From this perspective, framing cannot be distinguished from other forms of media or social influence such as agenda setting, learning, or persuasion (Scheufele, 2000; Scheufele and Tewksbury, 2007).

We divide this chapter into three parts. After an introductory overview of the concept, we explore two of the most common conceptual misunderstandings related to framing and their implications for political communication research. This includes a conceptual overview of the different approaches to framing in political communication research and of the relationship between framing and related effects models, such as priming and agenda setting. Finally, we conclude with a recommendation that framing research be redirected away from confounded "emphasis frames" toward "equivalence frames" in the original tradition by expanding the sample of potential frames to include nonverbal visual cues. Specifically, current technology makes it possible to implement precise manipulations of designated attributes of images. In this sense, the use of nonverbal frames makes it possible to return to the original tradition of framing research.

FRAMING FALLACIES: WHAT FRAMING IS AND WHAT IT IS NOT

As we discussed earlier, framing effects refer to communication effects that are not due to differences in *what* is being communicated, but rather to variations in *how* a given piece of information is being presented (or framed) in public discourse. Given its interdisciplinary roots in sociology (Gamson and Modigliani, 1987, 1989; Goffman, 1974), psychology (Kahneman, 2003a; Kahneman and Tversky, 1979, 1984), and linguistics (Lakoff and Johnson, 1981), framing research has been characterized by significant levels of conceptual obliqueness and sometimes even fallacious reasoning (Scheufele, 1999). In order to help develop a clearer conceptual understanding of what framing is (and is not), it is necessary to first discuss two misconceptions underlying a significant portion of the work that is currently being done under the "framing" label in our field.

Equivalence versus Emphasis Frames

Framing research is often traced back to two largely unrelated traditions of thinking. The first emanates from research conducted by the psychologists Amos Tversky and Daniel Kahneman (Kahneman and Tversky, 1979, 1984) in which the term "framing" was used to describe subtle differences in the definition of choice alternatives. Subjects in these experiments were provided choices that were identical in their expected value, but which differed in the terms used to describe the choice options (e.g., a fixed probability of "winning" or "losing" some amount of money).

Tversky and Kahneman demonstrated that human choice was contingent on the description of choice problems. When presented with outcomes defined as potential gains, people showed risk aversion and chose the more certain payoff. But when the identical outcome was defined in terms that suggested potential losses instead of gains, people became risk seekers and preferred the outcome with the less certain payoff (for an overview, see Kahneman, 2003a).

This perspective on framing is dependent on the assumption that all "[p]erception is reference dependent" (Kahneman, 2003a, 459). In other words, how we interpret information differs depending on how that information is contextualized or framed. The effect is particularly pronounced for ambiguous stimuli, that is, pieces of information that are open to multiple interpretations. A good example is the "broken-B" stimulus used by psychologists Jerome Bruner and Leigh Minturn in the 1950s (Bruner and Minturn, 1955). It refers to a symbol that an observer could interpret as the number "13" or as a "B" with a slightly detached upright line. Bruner and Minturn showed the symbol to subjects after they had been exposed to a sequence of letters for the first experimental condition and a sequence of numbers for the second one, and found clear differences between the two groups in how they interpreted the ambiguous broken-B stimulus.

These psychological approaches to framing are based on two assumptions. The first assumption states that framing refers to differential modes of presentation for the exact same piece of information. The information that is being presented, as a result, is informationally equivalent across different frames. This tradition of framing research can therefore also be labeled "equivalence framing."

The second assumption is that framing—at least if tested in experimental designs—often leads to what Kahneman calls "complete suppression of ambiguity in conscious perception" (Kahneman, 2003b, 1454). In other words, participants interpret the stimulus in line with the context in which it is framed in the particular experimental condition, but have no reason to assume that it could also be seen differently if framed in an alternative way. This assumption, of course, is somewhat artificial, and does not take into account the complexity of everyday communication environments, where attitude formation is likely driven by an interplay of complementary or competing frames. Some scholars have therefore begun to investigate the simultaneous effects of competing or complementary frames by giving participants more than one perspective on the target phenomenon. These studies typically utilize longitudinal designs in which study participants are either exposed synchronously (at a single point in time) or repeatedly (e.g., Chong and Druckman, 2007, 2010). The evidence from this emerging literature suggests that the magnitude of framing effects depends not only on the number of frames encountered, but also on the information-processing strategies of the receivers (Druckman and Bolsen, 2011).

The concern about the lack of ecological validity of single-equivalence-frame studies is also addressed by a large body of framing research rooted in the social movements and general sociology literature (Ferree et al., 2002; Gamson, 1992; Gamson and Modigliani,

1987, 1989). Many of these researchers approach framing as a macro-level or meso-level phenomenon, rather than an individual-level phenomenon, and offer fairly broad and all-encompassing definitions of framing.

Gamson (1992), for example, conceptualizes framing very broadly as the relationship between ideas and symbols used in public discourse and the meaning that people construct around political issues. Frames emerge in public discourse in part as an outcome of journalistic routines that allow them to quickly identify and classify information and "to package it for efficient relay to their audiences" (Gitlin, 1980, 7). Probably the most widely cited and also all-encompassing definition of framing was provided by Gamson and Modigliani (1987), who see frames as "a central organizing idea or story line that provides meaning to an unfolding strip of events . . . The frame suggests what the controversy is about, the essence of the issue" (143).

Unfortunately, the great majority of framing studies rely heavily on this sociologically oriented tradition and converge on a relatively loose definition of framing as information that conveys differing perspectives on some event or issue. This tradition can also be labeled "emphasis" framing, since the observed framing effects represent differences in opinion that cannot be attributed exclusively to differences in presentation. Emphasis-based frames not only vary the perspective or underlying dimension for considering an event (e.g., freedom of speech in the case of some particular dissenting group), but they also differ in several other respects. Thus, the widespread adoption of the emphasis over the equivalence mode of framing makes it much more difficult to observe framing effects per se. Frames have morphed into messages, and the prevalence of emphasis framing in our field threatens to make the broader framing concept redundant as a theory of media effects. And the problem is not trivial, as it indicates an unintentional regression toward old media effects paradigms under the guise of conceptual refinement.

Framing, Priming, and Agenda Setting: Distinguishing Framing from Related Concepts

The confounding of equivalence frames with content elements has also been promoted by a second key fallacy underlying a substantial number of studies in this area: the difference between salience-based effects, such as priming and agenda setting, and applicability effects, such as framing, which assume that the effect of a message depends on the degree to which some aspects of that message resonate with (or are applicable to) a recipient's existing underlying cognitive schemas (Price and Tewksbury, 1997; Scheufele, 2004; Scheufele, 2000; Scheufele and Tewksbury, 2007; Tewksbury and Scheufele, 2009).

The term agenda setting usually refers to the transfer of salience from mass media to audiences. The original model posits that if a particular issue is covered more frequently or prominently in news outlets, audiences are also more likely to attribute importance to the issue. In their seminal study, McCombs and Shaw (1972) operationalized issue salience among audience members as judgments about the perceived importance of issues. Later studies replaced perceptions of importance with terms such as salience, awareness, attention, or concern (Edelstein, 1993).

Priming can in many ways be seen as a logical extension of agenda-setting processes. The concept is usually traced back to work on spreading activation theory in psychology. Psychologists Allan M. Collins and Elizabeth F. Loftus, for example, explain priming as the process that occurs after a construct is presented as highly salient to audiences: "When a concept is primed, activation tags are spread by tracing an expanding set of links in the network" (Collins and Loftus, 1975, 409). Or to put it differently, if media coverage makes an issue more salient in people's minds, this issue is also more likely to be used as one of "the standards by which governments, policies and candidates for public office are judged" (Iyengar and Kinder, 1987, 63).

Agenda setting and priming, as salience-based effects, are often grouped with framing. And historically, there are good reasons for discussing the three effects models together. They all mark a transition away from media effects theories, such as the Spiral of Silence (Noelle-Neumann, 1973, 1974) or Cultivation (Gerbner and Gross, 1974), which hypothesize unidirectional and unmediated media effects on various perceptual and behavioral outcomes. Agenda setting, priming, and framing do not necessarily predict less powerful effects overall, but they focus much more explicitly on the cognitive processes linking media stimuli to audience responses (Scheufele, 2000).

In spite of often being grouped together, however, agenda setting, priming, and framing outline effects models that are also based on clearly distinguishable theoretical premises. We will discuss these distinctions in greater detail below. In spite of these differences, however, some scholars have proposed to merge the three into a single conceptual framework. McCombs (1992, 8–9), for example, argues for conceptualization of framing as an agenda-setting effect:

> Agenda-setting is about more than issue or object salience. The news not only tells us what to think about; it also tells us how to think about it. Both the selection of topics for the news agenda and the selection of frames for stories about those topics are powerful agenda-setting roles and awesome ethical responsibilities.

Many of these efforts to subsume agenda setting, priming, and framing under a single conceptual model were motivated by one of the earlier definitions of framing developed in political communication that explicitly referred to news selection and salience as the theoretical underpinnings of framing:

> Framing essentially involves selection and salience. To frame is to select some aspects of a perceived reality and make them more salient in a communicating text, in such a way as to promote a particular problem definition, causal interpretation, moral evaluation, and/or treatment recommendation for the item described. (Entman, 1993, 52)

Entman's early work on framing (Entman, 1991, 1993) had a powerful catalytic effect on our field by setting the stage for numerous studies on framing over the course of the next thirty years. But its all-encompassing definition of framing also helped set the stage for a conceptual vagueness surrounding the concept of framing that is still lingering in many studies on the topic today. Some of Entman's early empirical work on the framing of two airline disasters is a good example. Under the label "framing," Entman examined how many pages *Time* and *Newsweek* devoted to each of the two disasters. Operationally, these measures of "framing," as Entman defines it, overlap significantly with the measures used by early agenda-setting researchers to tap issue hierarchies in the media agenda (Funkhouser, 1973a, 1973b; McCombs and Shaw, 1972). In other words, many of these first attempts to operationalize frames were interchangeable with measures of the media agenda.

The field of political communication has taken a long time to recover from some of these early imprecisions in definition. In fact, since the early 1990s the literature on framing, priming, and agenda setting has split off into two main schools of thought. A first group of researchers—trained mostly in the McCombs/UT Austin tradition (McCombs, 2004; McCombs and Shaw, 1972, 1993)—sees all three theoretical models as fundamentally related to the central concept of agenda setting and the salience-based explanations underlying it. Mass media, they argue, influence audience perceptions by highlighting the importance of issues (first-level agenda setting) or issue attributes (second-level agenda setting, which they see as equivalent to framing). This school of thought echoes Iyengar and Kinder's (1987) conceptualization of priming as an outcome of agenda setting, but also subsumes framing as an equivalent to second-level agenda setting.

This approach has been criticized on both conceptual and empirical grounds and a number of researchers have argued for a return to a more specific equivalency-based definition of framing (Scheufele, 2000; Scheufele and Tewksbury, 2007; Tewksbury and Scheufele, 2009). Expanding on Iyengar's (1991) seminal work on the framing of political messages, this second school of thought typically defines framing as only encompassing media effects that are due to variations in the mode of presentation for a given piece of information. Media effects that are an outcome of messages that present different facts, aspects of an issue, or even arguments do not fall under the framing label.

Scholars in this second school of thought also argue that the theoretical premises underlying framing, on the one hand, and agenda setting and priming, on the other hand, are distinctly different (Price and Tewksbury, 1997). And the different premises underlying each model are critically important for steering future research in each respective area (Scheufele, 2000).

Theoretical Underpinnings—And Why They Matter

Part of the confusion about (a) equivalence- and emphasis-based frames and (b) conceptual overlaps between framing and other cognitive effects models stems from the fact that researchers have paid limited attention to the historical and theoretical foundations of each concept, that is, the assumptions that help explain the mechanisms behind each of the three effects models.

As outlined earlier, agenda setting and priming are accessibility-based effects (Iyengar, 1990). Media coverage can influence perceptions of salience among lay audiences, either for particular issues (Funkhouser, 1973a, 1973b) or attributes of issues (Kim, Scheufele, and Shanahan, 2002). Increased salience means that relevant nodes in the minds of audience members get activated and that this activation spreads to related concepts (Collins and Loftus, 1975). As a result, these sets of nodes are more accessible and therefore retrievable from memory when we have to make decisions about candidates or policy choices (Zaller, 1992; Zaller and Feldman, 1992) and are more likely to influence our attitudes and evaluations (Iyengar, 1991).

Framing, on the other hand, is what Price and Tewksbury (1997) have called an applicability effect. Its earliest foundations can be seen in work on Gestalt psychology (Wertheimer, 1925) in the first half of the last century and subsequent thinking in attribution theory (Heider, 1978). Both areas of research dealt with human tendencies to make sense of seemingly unrelated pieces of information by detecting underlying patterns that were consistent with preexisting schemas in their minds.

The idea of applicability implicitly draws on this intellectual tradition and assumes that the effects of particular frames are strengthened or weakened, depending on how applicable they are to a particular cognitive schema. In other words, the mode of presentation of a given piece of information (i.e., frame) makes it more or less likely for that information to be processed using a particular schema. The applicability model is directly consistent with Bruner and Minturn's (1955) broken-B experiment, as outlined earlier. If presented (or framed) in a sequence of numbers, the stimulus is more likely to be processed as a number, but if presented in the context of other letters, it is more likely to be processed as a letter.

And these differential theoretical underpinnings of accessibility and applicability effects have important implications for our understanding of the mechanisms behind agenda setting, priming, and framing. In particular, they suggest that accessibility effects operate fairly universally across audiences. This is not to say that political sophistication or levels of preexisting knowledge on the issue may not moderate agenda setting or priming effects. In fact, some of the seminal work on the topic already suggested that they do (Iyengar and Kinder, 1987). But based on the underlying theoretical assumptions, an issue can be primed or made salient among mass audiences, even if they have never heard about it before.

Applicability models, in contrast, assume that effects, such as framing, are contingent or at least variant in strength, depending on an audience member's preexisting schema(s). As a result, the mode of presentation of a message or piece of information will be significantly more likely to have an impact if it resonates (or is applicable) to an audience member's mental schemas. If the relevant schema does not exist at all among audience members, framing effects are unlikely to occur.

Unfortunately, most work on framing, agenda setting, and priming to date has provided few empirical insights into this distinction between schema-independent effects, such as agenda setting and priming, and schema-dependent effects, such as equivalence framing. This has produced three collateral outcomes that all pose major challenges for our field in the future.

First, the theoretical underpinnings of each model help us clearly delineate the mechanism that each effects theory is concerned with. While magic bullet or hypodermic needle approaches before World War II were focused mostly on persuasive communication, that is, telling people what to think and believe, agenda setting explicitly rejected this idea of direct persuasion and instead focused on media's more subtle role in telling people what information to think about (Cohen, 1963). Framing—in contrast—is not concerned with either persuasion or agenda setting, but instead addresses how people make sense of information that they have received, that is, which mental "shelf" they put the new information on.

Second, schemas are culturally shared. As a result, tests of framing effects within a given culture are unlikely to produce applicability effects that are as strong as effects that could be observed in cross-cultural comparisons. For instance, the broken-B stimulus discussed earlier will only produce framing effects for audiences that are familiar with the Roman alphabet and Arabic numerals. In politics, habitual offender legislation in the United States is a good real-world example. Almost half of all US states have legislation that requires courts to hand down mandatory prison sentences to people who have been convicted of serious offenses on at least three occasions. These laws are often framed as "three strikes laws." This frame resonates with audiences that are familiar with the rules of baseball. It makes very little sense, however, in cultures, such as Germany, where a vast majority of citizens has virtually no knowledge of baseball and are therefore lacking the cognitive schema necessary to be susceptible to the "three strikes" frame. As a result, future research will have to examine much more carefully how variations in schemas across cultures can shape the outcomes of communication. A recent comparison among monocultural and multicultural individuals in Asia and the United States, for instance, suggests that there are in fact systematic variations that may provide fruitful insights for future framing research (Fung, 2010).

Third, and most importantly, the growing focus on emphasis rather than equivalence frames in the recent literature has likely masked any schema-dependent effects. As we discussed earlier, frames are increasingly tested as simple persuasive effects, by blurring the distinction between frames and other informational or persuasive features of messages. Similar to agenda setting and priming, these informational or persuasive effects are likely universal across audiences. As a result, they have little to do with the more rigorous definition of equivalence framing as a schema-dependent media effect.

NONVERBAL FRAMES: AN ARGUMENT FOR EQUIVALENCE DESIGNS

In this closing section, we recommend that framing research be redirected away from emphasis frames toward equivalence frames by expanding the sample of potential frames to include nonverbal, visual cues. One of the reasons scholars have come to rely on the emphasis approach to framing is the ease with which framing manipulations can be constructed. It is relatively costless to string together three or four paragraphs of text that provide different considerations concerning some underlying attitude target. But, as we have noted above, different words may convey more than differences in perspective and different individuals may "read" the same words quite differently.

One solution to the problem of semantic ambiguity is to utilize nonverbal cues as the vehicle for assessing framing effects. A picture may be worth a thousand words, but for framing research, pictorial manipulations have the added value of precision. It is possible to create alternative versions of a picture that differ along a specific dimension, but that remain identical on all other observable dimensions so that any variation in the audience response can be attributable only to the manipulated dimension. The visual *presentation* differs only in some relevant physical attribute, such as skin complexion. In a recent series of experiments, for instance, Bailenson and his collaborators (Bailenson et al., 2008) used face morphing techniques to alter a candidate's facial resemblance to individual voters. (Their methodology requires access to a photographic database of voters' faces and the ability to match individual faces to survey responses.) The researchers morphed a target candidate's face with either a particular respondent's face or with the face of some other respondent. For any given respondent, therefore, the candidate appeared either similar or dissimilar (see Table 43.1 for an example of the similarity manipulation).

Given the wealth of evidence suggesting that similarity is a compelling basis for attraction, Bailenson and his collaborators were able to compare the effects of facial similarity with similarity based on partisanship or policy preferences, or similarity according to group affiliation (i.e., gender or race). As expected, the effects of facial similarity were much weaker than the effects of partisan or ideological proximity, but they were significant nonetheless.

The morphing of photographs can be generalized to incorporate dimensions other than an individual's facial structure. It is also possible, for instance, to manipulate the prominence of group-based attributes associated with race or ethnicity. Social psychologists have shown that relatively prototypic Afrocentric facial features elicit more stereotypic evaluations of African Americans than relatively ambiguous or racially neutral features (see Blair et al., 2004; Eberhardt et al., 2006). In the case of skin complexion, there is ample evidence that the darker the target non-white individual, the more hostile the evaluations expressed by whites (for a review of the evidence, see Hochschild and Weaver, 2010).

Applying these findings concerning nonverbal racial cues to the political arena, we might expect that darkening a non-white candidate's complexion would have the effect of weakening that candidate's standing among white voters. To test this proposition, researchers presented a national sample of registered voters with relatively lighter and darker images of Senator Obama at two different stages of the 2008 campaign— early February and late October. The metrics of the complexion manipulation were

Table 43.1   Manipulating Facial Similarity between Candidates and Voters

Subject	"George Bush"	60:40 blend
Subject	"John Kerry"	60:40 blend

precise—the lighter and darker versions differed from the actual photograph by the exact same margin.[1] The results showed that whites' evaluations of Obama were significantly affected by skin complexion in February—the darker the complexion, the less positive the evaluation—but that as the campaign progressed and voters learned more about Obama, their evaluations came to be dominated by traditional cues (e.g., party affiliation and issue opinions) and were thus unaffected by the complexion manipulation (Iyengar et al., 2010).

As the facial similarity and complexion studies suggest, visual rather than semantic frames provide researchers with tight control over particular attributes of candidates. A candidate might be framed as an in-group member on the basis of race, gender, age, or other physical attributes. Not only does the visual medium provide greater precision and a return to the tradition of equivalence framing, but also visual stimuli are essential ingredients of the daily stream of political information. Ever since the advent of broadcasting, nonverbal cues have become critical ingredients of political and cultural discourse. In terms of sheer size, the broadcast news audience dominates the audience for print media; nonverbal cues thus represent an ecologically valid test of framing effects on mass opinion. And a further advantage for researchers is that the nonverbal channel is especially relevant for the communication of affect. Most attitude objects in the political domain are affectively laden; nonverbal frames therefore represent a potentially more powerful means of influencing political attitudes and actions.

In conclusion, this chapter makes an argument for new "traditional" directions in framing research. Over the course of the last two decades, the researchers in political communication have approached framing with a diverse and often incompatible set of conceptual definitions. And the resulting operational confusion surrounding the construct has made drawing broader inferences across different studies all but impossible.

We are therefore making another push for more fine-grained and precise conceptual thinking in political communication about framing and related cognitive effects models. Even within the concept of framing, we urge researchers to structure future empirical work around the original characteristics of the concept, that is, variations in the mode of presentation of a given stimulus, rather than manipulations of the informational or persuasive nature of messages.

The potential confounds between the information itself and the way it is being presented can be illustrated using an analogy from the art world. Framing is equivalent to the choices that an art dealer or gallery owner may make about how to display a painting. Reactions among potential buyers to a painting displayed in a large, gold-plated frame, for instance, will be distinctively different than they would be if the same painting were displayed in a simple aluminum frame. In other words, the art dealer can shape public reactions to the exact same painting based on fairly subtle variations in how she decides to present—or quite literally "frame"—that painting. Unfortunately, many political communication researchers have been studying paintings rather than frames over the last two decades. And not surprisingly, they found that audiences would indeed react differently to a Gauguin than they would to a Matisse. But that is an outcome of seeing two different paintings from two different artists, not two different frames.

NOTE

1. The complexion manipulations are calibrated along the brightness (V) component of the HSV color space, which ranges from zero to one. Lower values of V for facial pixels indicate a darker complexion (for details, see Messing et al., 2016).

REFERENCES

Bailenson, J. N., Iyengar, S., and Yee, N. 2008. Facial similarity between voters and candidates causes influence. *Public Opinion Quarterly* 72(4): 935–961.

Blair, I., Judd, C. and Chapleau, K. 2004. The influence of Afrocentric facial features in criminal sentencing. *Psychological Science* 15(10): 674–679.

Brossard, D., Lewenstein, B., and Bonney, R. 2005. Scientific knowledge and attitude change: The impact of a citizen science project. *International Journal of Science Education* 27(9): 1099–1121.

Bruner, J. S., and Minturn, A. L. 1955. Perceptual identification and perceptual organization. *Journal of General Psychology* 53: 21–28.

Campell, A., Converse, P. E., Miller, W. E., and Stokes, D. E. 1960. *The American voter*. Chicago: University of Chicago Press.

Chong, D., and Druckman, J. N. 2007. A theory of framing and opinion formation in competitive elite environments. *Journal of Communication* 57(1): 99–118.

Chong, D., and Druckman, J. N. 2010. Dynamic public opinion: Communication effects over time. *American Political Science Review* 104(4): 663–680.

Cohen, B. C. 1963. *The press and foreign policy*. Princeton, NJ: Princeton University Press.

Collins, A. M., and Loftus, E. F. 1975. A spreading-activation theory of semantic processing. *Psychological Review* 82: 407–428.

Delli Carpini, M. X., and Keeter, S. 1996. *What Americans know about politics and why it matters*. New Haven, CT: Yale University Press.

Druckman, J. N., and Bolsen, T. 2011. Framing, motivated reasoning, and opinions about emergent technologies. *Journal of Communication*, 61(4): 659–688.

Edelstein, A. S. 1993. Thinking about the criterion variable in agenda-setting research. *Journal of Communication* 43: 85–99.

Entman, R. M. 1991. Framing United States coverage of international news: Contrasts in narratives of the KAL and Iran Air incidents. *Journal of Communication* 41(4): 6–27.

Entman, R. M. 1993. Framing: Towards clarification of a fractured paradigm. *Journal of Communication* 43: 51–58.

Ferree, M. M., Gamson, W. A., Gerhards, J., and Rucht, D. 2002. *Shaping abortion discourse: Democracy and the public sphere in Germany and the United States*. New York: Cambridge University Press.

Fung, K. F. 2010. *Value framing, cultural cognitive systems and cultural cognition: Exploring how media framing effects vary across and within cultures*. Madison: University of Wisconsin-Madison.

Funkhouser, G. R. 1973a. The issues of the sixties: An exploratory study in the dynamics of public opinion. *Public Opinion Quarterly* 37(1): 62–75.

Funkhouser, G. R. 1973b. Trends in media coverage of the issues of the sixties. *Journalism Quarterly* 50: 533–538.

Gamson, W. A. 1992. *Talking politics*. New York: Cambridge University Press.

Gamson, W. A., and Modigliani, A. 1987. The changing culture of affirmative action. In R. G. Braungart and M. M. Braungart (Eds.), *Research in political sociology* (pp. 137–177). Greenwich, CT: JAI Press.

Gamson, W. A., and Modigliani, A. 1989. Media discourse and public opinion on nuclear power: A constructionist approach. *American Journal of Sociology* 95(1): 1–37.

Gerbner, G., and Gross, L. 1974. System of cultural indicators. *Public Opinion Quarterly* 38: 460–461.

Gitlin, T. 1980. *The whole world is watching: Mass media in the making & unmaking of the new left*. Berkeley: University of California Press.

Goffman, E. 1974. *Frame analysis: An essay on the organization of experience*. New York: Harper & Row.

Heider, F. 1978. Über Balance und Attribution [About balance and attribution]. In D. Görlitz, W.-U. Meyer and B. Weiner (Eds.), *Bielefelder symposium über attribution* (pp. 19–28). Stuttgart, Germany: Klett Verlag.

Hochschild, J., and Weaver, V. 2010. 'There's No One as Irish as Barack O'Bama': The policy and politics of American multiracialism. *Perspectives on Politics* 8(3): 737-759.

Iyengar, S. 1990. The accessibility bias in politics: Television news and public opinion. *International Journal of Public Opinion Research* 2(1): 1–15.

Iyengar, S. 1991. *Is anyone responsible? How television frames political issues.* Chicago: University of Chicago Press.

Iyengar, S., and Kinder, D. R. 1987. *News that matters: Television and American opinion.* Chicago: University of Chicago Press.

Iyengar, S., Messing, S., Hahn, K. and Banaji, M. 2010. Do explicit racial cues influence candidate preference? The case of skin complexion in the 2008 campaign. Presented at the Annual Meeting of the American Political Science Association.

Kahneman, D. 2003a. Maps of bounded rationality: A perspective on intuitive judgment and choice. In T. Frängsmyr. Stockholm (Ed.), *Les Prix Nobel: The Nobel Prizes 2002* (pp. 449–489). Sweden: Nobel Foundation.

Kahneman, D. 2003b. Maps of bounded rationality: Psychology for behavioral economics. *American Economic Review* 93(5): 1449–1475.

Kahneman, D., and Tversky, A. 1979. Prospect theory: Analysis of decision under risk. *Econometrica* 47(2): 263–291.

Kahneman, D., and Tversky, A. 1984. Choices, values, and frames. *American Psychologist* 39(4): 341–350.

Kim, S. H., Scheufele, D. A., and Shanahan, J. 2002. Think about it this way: Attribute agenda-setting function of the press and the public's evaluation of a local issue. *Journalism & Mass Communication Quarterly* 79(1): 7–25.

Lakoff, G., and Johnson, M. 1981. *Metaphors we live by.* Chicago: University of Chicago Press.

Lazarsfeld, P. M., Berelson, B. R., and Gaudet, H. 1948. *The people's choice: How the voter makes up his mind in a presidential campaign.* 2nd ed. New York: Duell, Sloan & Pearce.

McCombs, M. E. 1992. Explorers and surveyors: Expanding strategies for agenda-setting research. *Journalism Quarterly* 69(4): 813–824.

McCombs, M. E., and Shaw, D. L. 1972. The agenda-setting function of mass media. *Public Opinion Quarterly* 36(2): 176–187.

Messing, S., Jabon, M., and Plaut, E. 2016. Bias in the flesh: Skin complexion and stereotype consistency in political campaigns. *Public Opinion Quarterly*, 80(1): 44–65.

Noelle-Neumann, E. 1973. Return to the concept of powerful mass media. *Studies in Broadcasting* 9: 67–112.

Noelle-Neumann, E. 1974. The spiral of silence: A theory of public opinion. *Journal of Communication* 24(2): 43–51.

O'Keefe, D. J. 2002. *Persuasion: Theory and research.* 2nd ed. Thousand Oaks, CA: Sage.

Price, V., and Tewksbury, D. 1997. News values and public opinion: A theoretical account of media priming and framing. In G. A. Barett and F. J. Boster (Eds.), *Progress in communication sciences: Advances in persuasion (Vol. 13)* (pp. 173-212). Greenwich, CT: Ablex.

Scheufele, B. T. 2004. Framing-effects approach: A theoretical and methodological critique. *Communications* 29: 401–428.

Scheufele, D. A. 1999. Framing as a theory of media effects. *Journal of Communication* 49(1): 103–122.

Scheufele, D. A. 2000. Agenda-setting, priming, and framing revisited: Another look at cognitive effects of political communication. *Mass Communication & Society* 3(2&3): 297–316.

Scheufele, D. A., and Tewksbury, D. 2007. Framing, agenda setting, and priming: The evolution of three media effects models. *Journal of Communication* 57(1): 9–20.

Tewksbury, D., and Scheufele, D. A. 2009. News framing theory and research. In J. Bryant and M. B. Oliver (Eds.), *Media effects: Advances in theory and research* (pp. 17–33). Hillsdale, NJ: Erlbaum.

Wertheimer, M. 1925. *Drei Abhandlungen zur Gestalttheorie [Three essays about Gestalt theory].* Berlin: Philosophische Akademie.

Zaller, J. 1992. *The nature and origin of mass opinion.* New York: Cambridge University Press.

Zaller, J., and Feldman, S. 1992. A simple theory of survey response: Answering questions versus revealing preferences. *American Journal of Political Science* 36(3): 579–616.

....

CHAPTER 44

AGENDA-SETTING THEORY

The Frontier Research Questions

....

MAXWELL MCCOMBS
AND SEBASTIÁN VALENZUELA

FROM the welter of daily events the news media shine a tightly focused spotlight on a select few, a role that is central to the formation of public opinion. In *Public Opinion*, Walter Lippmann (1922) described this gatekeeping role as the primary bridge between "the world outside and the pictures in our head." Four decades later in Chapel Hill, North Carolina, during the 1968 US presidential election, McCombs and Shaw (1972) initiated a detailed explication of this idea grounded in a metaphor of public and media agendas. The media agenda is the pattern of news coverage over a period of days, weeks, months, and sometimes even years for a set of issues or other topics. In other words, the media agenda is a systematic compilation of the issues or topics presented to the public that identifies the degree of emphasis on these topics. Often this is presented in terms of their rank-order on the media agenda. The public agenda is the priority of these topics among the public, again frequently presented in terms of their rank-order. One of the most widely used measures of the public agenda is the venerable Gallup Poll question, "What do you think is the most important issue facing our country today?"

The seminal Chapel Hill study found a high correlation between the rank-order of the issues in the news coverage of the 1968 presidential campaign and the rank-order of these same issues among the public. That initial finding has stimulated hundreds of subsequent studies using panel studies and experiments in addition to cross-sectional designs to document the causal assertion of agenda setting that the media agenda influences the public agenda. This research has examined a wide variety of issues and other topics in both election and nonelection settings in every part of the world. Wanta and Ghanem's (2006) meta-analysis of this found a mean correlation of +.53 between the media and public agendas, with a very small variance.

Beyond these comparisons of media attention and public attention to the major topics of the day, agenda-setting theory has expanded to encompass five distinct areas of research, ranging from the origins of the media agenda to the consequences of agenda-setting effects on attitudes and opinions and on behavior (McCombs, 2014). This continuing evolution illustrates the productivity of agenda setting. In their overview of political communication as it entered the twenty-first century, Doris Graber and James Smith (2005, 489) stated, "Agenda setting remains the predominant theoretical approach to analyzing the impact of media messages on audiences."

Expanding on the basic agenda-setting effects found in Chapel Hill, the 1972 presidential election study in Charlotte, North Carolina (Shaw and McCombs, 1977) introduced a second theoretical area, the psychology of agenda setting, grounded in the concept of need for orientation (Weaver, 1977). Individual differences in the level of need for orientation explain both differences in attention to the media agenda and differences in the degree to which individuals reflect the media agenda. For recent discussions, see Chernov, Valenzuela, and McCombs (2011) and Matthes (2006).

The Charlotte study also introduced another theoretical area, the concept of a second level of effects, attribute agenda setting. In theoretical terms, the Chapel Hill study examined basic agenda-setting effects, the transfer of object salience from the media to the public. *Object* is used here with the same meaning used in social psychology for the term *attitude object*. For each object on the media agenda or the public agenda, an agenda of attributes also can be identified. This agenda is the hierarchy of attributes describing the object. Just as the rank-order of objects on the media and public agendas can be compared to measure basic agenda-setting effects, the rank-order of attributes on the media and public agendas can be compared to measure attribute agenda setting (Weaver et al., 1981; McCombs et al., 2000).

Attributes of an object have both a substantive and an affective dimension. Substantive attributes are the cognitive elements of messages that describe the denotative characteristics of an object. Examples of the substantive attributes of a political candidate are qualifications and issue positions. For issues, substantive attributes include subareas—for example, unemployment and budget deficits as attributes of the economic problem. The affective dimension is the positive, neutral, or negative tone in the descriptions of an object's substantive attributes.

In recent years a fourth theoretical area has emerged, investigations into the consequences of both first- and second-level agenda-setting effects for attitudes and opinions and behavior. This chapter focuses on the major contemporary research questions in all four of these areas. A fifth area of agenda-setting theory, which is discussed by David Weaver in this volume, concerns the origins of the media agenda. This area links agenda setting to another field of mass communication research, the sociology of news.

This continuing evolution of agenda setting across these five theoretical areas is characterized by two trends:

- A centrifugal trend of research in the expanding media landscape and in domains beyond the original focus on public affairs.
- A centripetal trend of research further explicating agenda setting's core concepts.

BASIC AGENDA SETTING

The expanding media landscape has prompted considerable research on online newspapers, interactive Internet sites, and the ever-growing panoply of social media. In many instances, the key questions of this new research replicate those of earlier decades when daily newspapers and television were the dominant news channels: "Do these media influence the public agenda?" and "Which of these channels is the more powerful agenda setter?" Although studies pursuing these questions have accumulated for more than a decade, a more comprehensive answer about basic agenda-setting effects in the new media landscape arguably can be provided by asking the first question in broader terms and downplaying the latter question about the relative strength of various channels. Decades of previous research on the comparative influence of newspapers and television provide useful guidance here. Despite dozens of studies, the relative impact of newspapers and television remains "on the one hand, on the other." About half of the time, there is no difference. For the remainder, the split is roughly two-thirds showing stronger newspaper effects and one-third demonstrating stronger TV effects.

Rather than attempting to tease out the relative impact of discrete media channels, a gestalt approach in recent empirical work demonstrates that agenda-setting effects among members of the public frequently are the cumulative result of the numerous channels that define most people's news environment. Stromback and Kiousis's (2010) study of the 2006 Swedish national election illustrates this perspective. Using a three-wave panel survey, they explicitly compared the impact of overall political news consumption versus media-specific news consumption on issue salience across nine different media channels (newspapers vs. television vs. radio) and media types (commercial media vs. public service media and elite newspapers vs. tabloid newspapers). Their results show that attention to political news exerts a strong influence on issue salience, and attention to political news matters more than attention to different newspapers or to specific news shows on television and radio.

These findings fit a wide range of previous research. There is compelling evidence dating from Chapel Hill about the high degree of convergence between the agendas of different news media. Across the world, the norms of journalism exert a powerful pressure toward similarity in telling the news of the day (King, 1997; McCombs, Lopez-Escobar, and Llamas, 2000; Jonsson and Stromback, 2007).

Boczkowski (2010) not only found a high level of homogeneity in the news agendas of the major print and online newspapers in Buenos Aires, but also noted the increasing similarity of these news agendas from 1995 to 2005. He attributes this to the facilitation of journalists' long-standing habit of monitoring the competition by the plethora of news now available on the Internet and television.

An overarching theme in these findings is that we swim in a vast sea of news and information, a gestalt of mass media channels in which the whole is much greater than the sum of its parts. Evidence regarding the interrelated nature of our mass communication experience dates from the earliest days of our field. In their bench-mark 1940 Erie County study, Lazarsfeld, Berelson, and Gaudet (1944) found substantial overlap in people's use of various mass media. Decades later, during the 1996 Spanish national election, McCombs, Lopez-Escobar, and Llamas (2000) found a high degree of similarity between the strength of people's agreement with their primary news source's agenda and their agreement with the agenda of that source's principal competitor. For example, among voters who identified *Diario de Navarra* as their primary news source, the agenda-setting correlation was +.62. Their level of agreement with the competing local newspaper was +.57. Across eighteen comparisons, the median difference in the correlations is .09.

Moving to the present, media use patterns among different generations do diverge somewhat because of the Internet. As a consequence, some have predicted the end of the agenda-setting role of the media (Chaffee and Metzger, 2001). However, drawing upon statewide surveys in North Carolina and Louisiana, Coleman and McCombs (2007) compared agenda-setting effects among the generations and found little difference. Particularly compelling is the comparison in Louisiana of the issue agendas of high and low Internet users to the issue agenda of the state's major newspapers. There is a differ-ence, but hardly a substantial one. For low Internet users the correlation with newspaper agendas is +.90. For high Internet users, the correlation is +.70.

There are powerful and influential newspapers, broadcast stations, and websites. However, the gestalt of media voices is integral to our social fabric. The collective influ-ence of the mass media also has the potential for expanding Shaw and Martin's (1992) seminal exploration of the role that news exposure has in citizens' consensus regarding the most important issues of the day. Their statewide study in North Carolina docu-mented that both increased use of newspapers and increased use of TV news resulted in greater agreement in the issue agendas of various demographic subgroups. Most com-monly, demographics are used to identify differences among subgroups. However, Shaw and Martin demonstrated that the issue agendas of various demographic subgroups— for example, younger persons vs. older persons—became more similar with increas-ing use of newspapers and television. This consensus-building role of the mass media regarding the most important issues of the day has been replicated in settings as cultur-ally and politically diverse as Spain and Taiwan (Lopez-Escobar, Llamas, and McCombs, 1998; Chiang, 1995).

Higgins (2009) further explicated this role of the news media in terms of second-level agenda setting. Focusing on the European Union's reaction to the attacks of September 11, 2001, in the United States, she examined how exposure to both national and transnational media in these fifteen countries increased the cohesion among var-ious demographic subgroups' attribute agendas for the issue of terrorism and their attribute agendas for the Muslim community in Europe. Use of national television was very strongly related to increased consensus regarding the attributes of terrorism and Muslims. Use of national newspapers also was linked with increased consensus for both of these agendas, but not as strongly as use of TV. The strength of transnational television was very similar to the national press. Other media showed far less impact.

Although borders still matter, especially for newspapers, the increasing availability of electronic transnational media may translate into increased influence as well. And what will be the collective impact of this expanding gestalt of news media?

PSYCHOLOGICAL DETERMINANTS OF ISSUE SALIENCE

Within the centripetal trend in agenda-setting research, a central question refers to the processes by which the media influence the public. Need for orientation remains the most studied individual-level factor for attributing differences in the strength of agenda-setting effects, and its central concept of relevance is at the forefront of research on the psychology of agenda setting. Evatt and Ghanem (2001) identified two substantive aspects of this concept, social relevance and personal relevance, and an affective aspect, emotional relevance. People can recognize that an issue may be important for society even if it is not important for them. Emotions, in turn, can increase the relevance of an issue even if it is not personally or socially relevant. These findings are consistent with statewide Texas polls in 1992 and 1996 exploring why respondents named a particular issue when answering the MIP question (McCombs, 1999). In this case, a stable set of five motivations emerged: self-interest and avocation—similar to Evatt and Ghanem's personal salience; civic duty and peer influence—resembling the social aspect of relevance; and emotional arousal—the same affective dimension identified by Evatt and Ghanem.

While the distinction between personal and national importance makes intuitive sense and is consistent with research on the dimensions of attitude strength (Miller and Peterson, 2004), emotional salience deserves further consideration. There is a long tradition in Western thought that downplays affect and emotion while highlighting the benefits of reason and cognition. However, neuroscientists have long contended that affective and cognitive processes are closely intertwined (Gray, 1990). In agenda setting, Miller's (2007) experiments found that some emotional responses to the news mediated agenda-setting effects, specifically when news stories about the issue of crime resulted in participants feeling sad or afraid. Other emotional responses, such as anger, pride, hope, and happiness, did not result in a greater salience of crime. Her finding that fear is a key mediator of agenda-setting effects is in line with affective intelligence theory (Marcus, Neuman, and MacKuen, 2000), which posits that anxiety activates greater attention to incoming information. However, the role of emotions is not circumscribed to triggering relevance. Coleman and Wu (2010) identified a significant, positive relationship between the televised images of the 2004 US presidential candidates and the public's negative emotional responses to George W. Bush and John Kerry. Emotions can be both a regulator and an outcome of agenda setting. This complex set of findings is suggestive of the fruitful venue for research that emotions bring to agenda-setting research.

Another source of the public's salience judgments is values, people's core beliefs about what are desirable and undesirable end-states of human life (Schwartz, 1992). Using a content analysis of newspapers, a panel survey, and a laboratory experiment, Valenzuela (2011) found that agenda-setting effects were stronger when the topics in the news agenda matched individuals' values. Based on Inglehart's (1977) theory of values, he found that individuals with materialist values exhibited larger agenda-setting effects for materialist issues such as the economy and crime than for postmaterialist issues such as the environment and political reform, whereas postmaterialist individuals exhibited larger agenda-setting effects for postmaterialist issues than for materialist issues. These results replicated across both aggregate- and individual-level analysis, providing strong support for the values-issues consistency hypothesis.

These different sources of relevance make it readily apparent that agenda-setting effects are not adequately explained by accessibility—the notion that issues become salient purely as a consequence of the frequency and recentness with which they are portrayed in the news—as argued by some scholars (Scheufele and Tewksbury, 2007). If this were the case, the effects of need for orientation, emotions, and values would be insignificant. Furthermore, empirical studies specifically addressing the role of accessibility in media effects, including agenda setting, priming, and framing, consistently have shown that the public reflects much more than just the most frequent or recent issues in the media agenda (Miller and Krosnick, 2000; Nelson, Clawson, and Oxley, 1997). Mutz (1998) also noted that responses to the MIP question tap more than just cognitive availability of issues; they reveal an affective judgment as well. Arguing that accessibility is the basis of agenda setting amounts to arguing that all easily accessible media information is considered important, something that is not supported by the available evidence.

LEARNING THE MEDIA AGENDA

A necessary condition for news' agenda-setting effects is exposure, either directly through media use or indirectly through communication about topics in the news within individuals' social networks. In either case, the traditional assumption is that people are actively exposed to public affairs. However, incidental exposure is an alternative route to acquiring the media agenda: learning passively without any significant involvement and intent to learn. This is a long-standing notion within educational psychology (e.g., McLaughlin, 1965), but only recently explored in political communication (Baum, 2002; Prior, 2007).

According to Frensch (1998), one of the routes for incidental learning is ubiquity. Individuals learn something about a particular object, person, or situation because it is omnipresent. As previously noted, the high degree of redundancy across media agendas increases the likelihood that the public will learn the media agenda even at low levels of news exposure. An empirical demonstration of incidental learning within the agenda-setting tradition is presented by Lee (2009), who found that participants instructed to pay only minimal attention to news stories (ten seconds or less) about the environment had significantly higher scores on the perceived importance of that issue than other participants who paid no attention whatsoever to these stories.

Another indirect way to learn the media agenda is provided by interpersonal and computer-mediated communication about news. Initial studies in the 1970s generally found that interpersonal discussion mediated the media's influence on issue salience (McLeod, Becker, and Byrnes, 1974; Shaw, 1976). Subsequent research, however, found that personal communications offset the media agenda setting (Atwater, Salwen, and Anderson, 1985; Lasorsa and Wanta, 1990). Most likely, the effects of citizen-to-citizen communication on agenda setting are contingent upon the content of the communication. When citizens' discussions deal with issues covered by the media, they should enhance the media's agenda-setting influence. When they deal with issues that receive little coverage, they should dampen the media's agenda-setting influence by providing alternative issue considerations (Wanta and Wu, 1992).

Taking a more nuanced approach, recent studies have been successful at integrating agenda-setting processes with communication processes within individuals' social networks (Weimann and Brosius, 1994; Yang and Stone, 2003). From this perspective, the issue agenda diffuses first from the news media to media users, and then from these to non-media users via personal communication, a process akin to the classic two-step flow of communication (Katz and Lazarsfeld, 1955). For instance, in a field experiment in Germany, Vu and Gehrau (2010) published an article about a new issue in a community magazine and two days later observed the agenda-setting processes and interpersonal communication triggered by it. They found a cascading effect: the article sparked conversations about the issue, and these conversations in turn increased the salience of the issue, even among those who had not read the article. Most notably, talking about the issue fully mediated the effects of reading the article on judgments of issue salience.

Although the transfer of salience from the media agenda to the public agenda can occur through a variety of means in addition to direct, motivated exposure to media messages, some observers—as noted earlier—have posited that agenda setting and other media effects are diluted in today's expanded media environment (e.g., Williams and Delli Carpini, 2004). On the one hand, some predict that with interactivity and the Web 2.0, "the key problem for agenda-setting theory will change from what issues the media tell people to think about to what issues people tell the media they want to think about" (Chaffee and Metzger, 2001, 375). On the other hand, there is the possibility that with higher media choice, selective exposure will become more prevalent: "People uninterested in politics can avoid news programming altogether by tuning into ESPN or the Food Network. And for political junkies, the sheer multiplicity of news sources demands they exercise discretionary or selective exposure to political information" (Bennett and Iyengar, 2008, 716). However, the evidence to date does not support these arguments. At least at the first level of agenda setting, blogs and other social media applications still echo the agenda of the traditional media (Asur et al., 2011; Meraz, 2009; Wallsten, 2007). Although more partisan television networks (think FOX News and MSNBC) cater to audiences that share their ideological stance, their agenda of issues is not that different from that of more centrists networks (Stroud, 2006). Certainly these are not definitive answers, and researchers will need to constantly reassess the merits of media influence in a changing media landscape.

ATTRIBUTE AGENDA SETTING

The first and second levels of agenda setting—object salience and attribute salience—are linked by the concept of compelling arguments that identifies situations in which one or two specific characteristics of an object on the media agenda resonate so strongly with the public that these attributes alone, rather than the full array of attributes on the media agenda, increase the salience of the object. Ghanem (1996) found that not only did crime coverage in the news generate high levels of public concern about crime as the most important problem facing the country, but an attribute of these crime stories—their psychological distance, operationally defined by drive-by shootings and local crime—influenced the salience of crime on the public agenda just as strongly as the overall level of crime coverage. In other words, the attribute of psychological distance was a compelling argument for the salience of crime as a major public issue.

Other studies of compelling arguments have documented the impact of negative tone in the news on the salience of the economy in Israel (Sheafer, 2007); the impact of positive and negative attributes of issues in 2004 Kerry political ads (but not Bush ads) on the salience of these issues on the public agenda (Golan et al., 2007); and across five US presidential elections, the impact of a specific candidate attribute in the news, moral quality, on the public salience of the candidates (Kiousis, 2005).

Although these studies illustrate that specific attributes on the media agenda can influence object salience on the public agenda, we do not have any systematic theoretical knowledge of which attributes function as compelling arguments. This focus on specific elements of media messages suggests renewed theoretical attention to message elements in the spirit of Hovland, Janis, and Kelly (1953) and renewed efforts to build what Maccoby (1963) termed a scientific rhetoric.

The larger point illustrated by the concept of compelling arguments is the ability of the news media to transfer the relationships presented within the media agenda to the public agenda. The concept of compelling arguments holds that news media can bundle an object with an attribute and make them salient in the public's mind simultaneously. However, in most research to date, the elements investigated are disaggregated objects or attributes ordered according to their frequency of occurrence. In terms of Lippmann's "pictures in our heads," a further question is: Are the news media able to transfer the salience of an integrated picture?

Some psychologists and philosophers hold that people's mental representations operate pictorially, diagrammatically or cartographically (Armstrong, 1973; Barsalou, 1998; Braddon-Mitchell and Jackson, 2007; Cummins, 1996). In other words, audiences map out objects and attributes in their heads as network-like pictures according to their interrelationships. This expands the traditional view that the public's perception of media agendas works logically according to their importance. From this "pictorialist" perspective, *the news media transfer the salience of relationships between a set of attributes to the public.*

In a pilot study to test this hypothesis, Guo and McCombs (2011) conducted network analyses on data sets initially collected by Kim and McCombs (2007). Studying candidates for Texas governor and US senator, Kim and McCombs found strong attribute-agenda-setting effects in analyses of each candidate separately, for both positive and negative attributes separately and combined, and for all four candidates, both positive and negative attributes separately and combined.

Reanalyzing these data, Guo and McCombs (2011) found significant network-agenda-setting effects consistent with the attribute-agenda-setting ones in the original study. For example, the overall correlation between the media and public attribute agendas in Kim and McCombs (+.65) corresponds with the correlation (+.67) between the media and public network agendas in Guo and McCombs. However, the details of the interrelationships in the network analysis provide a much richer picture of attribute agenda setting and suggest a wide range of new research regarding the impact of media agendas on the pictures in our heads.

Research on the concept of compelling arguments and on integrated attribute agendas reflects the trend of further explicating the core concepts of agenda-setting theory. This avenue is further illustrated by Son and Weaver's (2006) expansion of the media agenda, which takes into account the context in which the news media present the candidates and their affective attributes to the public. Focusing on the 2000 US presidential election, these authors investigated which news sources of candidate salience and which news sources of candidate affective attribute salience predicted changes in public opinion about each of the candidates, either immediately or cumulatively. The effects of both the first and second levels of agenda setting on the standings of the candidates in national public opinion polls were primarily cumulative rather than immediate, and different news sources had very different effects on them. For candidate salience, the reporters' analysis and polls had strong cumulative effects on the poll standings. For candidate attribute salience, statements by both the candidate himself and by members of the competing party had strong cumulative effects on the poll standings. Other news sources had little or no impact.

Son and Weaver's expanded perspective on attribute agenda setting suggests integrating object and issue salience with journalistic elements, such as sources, that characterize news stories. Their perspective also suggests the potential value of applying network analysis to these richer views of the media agenda.

Consequences of Agenda Setting

The transfer of salience of objects and their attributes from the media agenda to the public agenda is consequential for individuals' attitudes, including both their direction and strength, and for behavior. The most widely investigated attitudinal effect of agenda set-ting is media priming, the influence of the news media on the criteria used by citizens to evaluate political figures, governments, and political parties (Iyengar and Kinder, 1987). Asked their opinions about political topics such as performance of the president, most citizens do not engage in comprehensive analysis of their total store of informa-tion. Rather, individuals use information emphasized by the news media. The more the media cover a particular issue—prime that issue—the more people will rely on what they know about it to make political judgments. Ultimately, media priming may lead people to vote differently, providing a strong connection between agenda setting and behavioral effects.

Since Dietram Scheufele and Shanto Iyengar's chapter discusses media priming, here we concentrate on two other areas. First, researchers have identified attribute priming effects where the increased salience among the public of specific attributes emphasized in news coverage influences the weights people assign to those attributes in their evalua-tions of attitude objects. This process is usually a consequence of the valence of particu-larly salient attributes—that is, positive or negative attributes as perceived by the public. Sheafer (2007) referred to this influence as affective attribute priming and found signif-icant evidence for this effect across five Israeli elections. Specifically, the more negative the news coverage of the Israeli economy, the lower were the evaluations of the general performance of the incumbent political party. Not only did news prime the economy as a standard for judging incumbent party performance, but the affective tone of that cov-erage also influenced the direction of the evaluations.

A second aspect of the priming literature that is important for agenda setting asks which members of the public are more susceptible to media influence. At question is how competent citizens are at making political decisions. If priming effects occur because people are politically naïve, then the news media have a worrying power over citizens, as it would indicate that individuals' preferences are fully malleable by the media and political elites. If, on the other hand, priming occurs among more politi-cally sophisticated citizens, then media influence could be the result of a rather delib-erative process by which people actively filter news content. To date, the research results have been inconsistent. Some studies have found that higher knowledge facilitates priming, but higher interest and higher exposure reduce it (Krosnick and Brannon, 1993), while other studies have found that neither attentiveness nor gen-eral political knowledge is related to priming (Vanderbrug, Semetko, and Valkenburg, 2007). To reconcile these conflicting results, Valenzuela (2009) proposed that media priming varies across levels of political involvement. Priming should be strongest for citizens with moderate levels of involvement, who are interested enough in pub-lic affairs to follow the news, but lack the ideological strength to reject media cues. Using a content analysis of press coverage and a panel survey from the 2006 Canadian election, he found that, as predicted, priming was highest for citizens with medium levels of knowledge and discussion frequency and lowest for citizens at either extreme of these involvement measures. Compared to pessimistic and optimistic accounts of citizen competence, these findings present a more nuanced perspective on individuals' ability to filter and process news.

In addition to agenda-setting effects on the direction of opinions, there is mounting evidence about the role of the media agenda in shaping the strength of people's attitudes toward political figures and other objects in the news. According to McGuire's (1989) hierarchy of effects model, cognitive effects—the public's awareness of objects on the agenda—precede having opinions about those objects. Nevertheless, Kiousis and McCombs (2004) identified a different causal chain of effects. Using survey data from the 1996 US presidential election, they found that media salience of a political figure first influenced having an opinion about that person, which subsequently affected the salience of that person in people's minds. This study suggests that agenda setting relates not only to opinion formation, but also to opinion strength.

CONCLUSION

When connecting to the world outside our family, neighborhood, and workplace, we deal with a secondhand reality created by journalists and media organizations. However, due to time and space constraints, the mass media focus their attention on a few topics that are deemed newsworthy. Over time, those aspects of public affairs that are prominent in the media usually become prominent in public opinion. This ability to influence which issues, persons, and topics are perceived as the most important of the day was the first conceptualization of the agenda-setting role of the media, one that dates back to the 1968 Chapel Hill study. Over the last four decades, agenda setting has expanded into five different facets, from the origins of the media agenda to the consequences of agenda setting on attitudes and behavior.

In our review we have identified several engaging research questions across various aspects of agenda-setting theory, including the expanding media landscape, the psychological origins of issue relevance, and the transfer of a network of attributes of media objects from the media to the public. Looking to the future, creative scholars will refine the core ideas of agenda setting, expand the theory in new arenas, and produce new knowledge regarding the media's role in society.

REFERENCES

Armstrong, D. M. 1973. *Belief, truth, and knowledge*. London: Cambridge University Press.

Asur, S., Huberman, B. A., Szabo, G., and Wang, C. 2011. Trends in social media: Persistence and decay. *Social Science Research Network*, February 5. http://ssrn.com/abstract=1755748.

Atwater, T., Salwen, M. B., and Anderson, R. B. 1985. Interpersonal discussion as a potential barrier to agenda-setting. *Newspaper Research Journal 6*: 37–43.

Barsalou, L. 1998. Perceptual symbol systems. *Behavioral and Brain Sciences 22*: 557–660.

Baum, M. A. 2002. Sex, lies, and war: How soft news brings foreign policy to the inattentive public. *American Political Science Review* 96: 91–109.

Bennett, W. L., and Iyengar, S. 2008. A new era of minimal effects? The changing foundations of political communication. *Journal of Communication* 58: 707–731.

Boczkowski, P. J. 2010. *News at work: Imitation in an age of information abundance.* Chicago: University of Chicago Press.

Braddon-Mitchell, D., and Jackson, F. 2007. *Philosophy of mind and cognition.* 2nd ed. Cambridge, MA: Blackwell.

Chaffee, S., and Metzger, M. 2001. The end of mass communication? *Mass Communication and Society* 4: 365–379.

Chernov, G., Valenzuela, S., and McCombs, M. 2011. An experimental comparison of two perspectives on the concept of need for orientation in agenda-setting theory. *Journalism & Mass Communication Quarterly* 88: 142–55.

Chiang, C-Y. 1995. Bridging and closing the gap of our society: Social function of media agenda setting. Master's thesis, University of Texas, Austin.

Coleman, R., and McCombs, M. 2007. The young and agenda-less? Exploring age-related differences in agenda setting on the youngest generation, baby boomers, and the civic generation. *Journalism & Mass Communication Quarterly* 84: 495–508.

Coleman, R., and Wu, H. D. 2010. Proposing emotion as a dimension of affective agenda-setting: Separating affect into two components and comparing their second-level effects. *Journalism & Mass Communication Quarterly* 87: 315–327.

Cummins, R. 1996. *Representations, targets, and attitudes.* Cambridge, MA: MIT Press.

Evatt, D., and Ghanem, S. I. 2001. Building a scale to measure salience. Paper presented at the annual conference of the World Association of Public Opinion Research, Rome, Italy.

Frensch, P. A. 1998. One concept, multiple meanings. In M. A. Stadler and P. A. Frensch (Eds.), *Handbook of implicit learning* (pp. 47–104). Thousand Oaks, CA: Sage.

Ghanem, S. I. 1996. Media coverage of crime and public opinion: An exploration of the second level of agenda setting. PhD diss., University of Texas, Austin.

Golan, G. J., Kiousis, S. K., and McDaniel, M. L. 2007. Second-level agenda setting and political advertising: Investigating the transfer of issue and attribute saliency during the 2004 U.S. presidential election. *Journalism Studies* 8: 432–443.

Graber, D., and Smith, J. M. 2005. Political communication faces the 21st century. *Journal of Communication* 55: 479–507.

Gray, J. A. 1990. Brain systems that mediate both emotion and cognition. *Cognition and Emotion* 4: 269–288.

Guo, L., and McCombs, M. 2011. Network agenda setting: A third level of media effects. Paper presented at the International Communication Association annual conference, Boston, MA.

Higgins, V. M. 2009. News media roles in bridging communities: Consensus function of agenda-setting. PhD diss., University of Texas, Austin.

Hovland, C., Janis, I., and Kelley, H. 1953. *Communication and persuasion.* New Haven, CT: Yale University Press.

Inglehart, R. 1977. *The silent revolution: Changing values and political styles in advanced industrial society.* Princeton, NJ: Princeton University Press.

Iyengar, S., and Kinder, D. R. 1987. *News that matters: Television and American opinion.* Chicago: University of Chicago Press.

Jonsson, A. M., and Stromback, J. 2007. *TV-Journalistik i Konkurrensens tid: Nyhets-och Samh¨allsprogram i Svensk TV 1990-2004*. Stockholm, Sweden: Ekerlids forlag.

Katz, E., and Lazarsfeld, P. 1955. *Personal influence*. New York: Free Press.

Kim, K., and McCombs, M. 2007. News story descriptions and the public's opinions of political candidates. *Journalism & Mass Communication Quarterly 84*: 299–314.

King, P. 1997. The press, candidate images, and voter perceptions. In, M. McCombs, D. L. Shaw, and D. Weaver (Eds.), *Communication and democracy: Exploring the intellectual frontiers in agenda-setting theory* (pp. 29–40). Mahwah, NJ: Lawrence Erlbaum.

Kiousis, S. 2005. Compelling arguments and attitude strength: Exploring the impact of second-level agenda setting on public opinion of presidential candidate images. *Harvard International Journal of Press/Politics 10*: 3–27.

Krosnick, J. A., and Brannon, L. A. 1993. The impact of the Gulf War on the ingredients of presidential evaluations: Multidimensional effects of political involvement. *American Political Science Review 87*: 963–975.

Lasorsa, D. L., and Wanta, W. 1990. Effects of personal, interpersonal and media experiences on issue salience. *Journalism Quarterly 67*: 804–813.

Lazarsfeld, P., Berelson, B., and Gaudet, H. 1944. *The people's choice*. 2nd ed. New York: Columbia University Press.

Lee, J. K. 2009. Incidental exposure to news: Limiting fragmentation in the new media environment. PhD diss., University of Texas, Austin.

Lopez-Escobar, E., Llamas, J. P., and McCombs, M. 1998. Agenda setting and community consensus: First and second level effects. *International Journal of Public Opinion Research 10*: 335–348.

Maccoby, N. 1963. The new scientific rhetoric. In W. Schramm (Ed.), *The science of communication: New directions and new findings in communication research* (pp. 41–53). New York: Basic Books.

Marcus, G. E., Neuman, W. R., and MacKuen, M. B. 2000. *Affective intelligence and political judgment*. Chicago: University of Chicago Press.

Matthes, J. 2006. The need for orientation towards news media: Revising and validating a classic concept. *International Journal of Public Opinion Research 18*: 422–444.

McCombs, M. 1999. Personal involvement with issues on the public agenda. *International Journal of Public Opinion Research 11*: 152–168.

McCombs, M. 2014. *Setting the agenda: The mass media and public opinion*. 2nd ed. Cambridge, UK: Polity.

McCombs, M., and Shaw, D. L. 1972. The agenda-setting function of mass media. *Public Opinion Quarterly 36*: 176–187.

McCombs, M., Lopez-Escobar, E., and Llamas, J. P. 2000. Setting the agenda of attributes in the 1996 Spanish general election. *Journal of Communication 50*: 77–92.

McGuire, W. J. 1989. Theoretical foundations of campaigns. In R. E. Rice and C. K. Atkin (Eds.), *Public communication campaigns*, 2nd ed. (pp. 43–65). Newbury Park, CA: Sage.

McLaughlin, B. 1965. "Intentional" and "incidental" learning in human subjects: The role of instructions to learn and motivation. *Psychological Bulletin 63*: 359–376.

McLeod, J., Becker, L., and Byrnes, J. E. 1974. Another look at the agenda-setting function of the press. *Communication Research 1*: 131–166.

Meraz, S. 2009. Is there an elite hold? Traditional media to social media agenda setting influence in blog networks. *Journal of Computer-Mediated Communication 14*: 682–707.

Miller, J. M. 2007. Examining the mediators of agenda setting: A new experimental paradigm reveals the role of emotions. *Political Psychology 28*: 689–717.

Miller, J. M., and Krosnick, J. A. 2000. News media impact on the ingredients of presidential evaluations: Politically knowledgeable citizens are guided by a trusted source. *American Journal of Political Science 44*: 301–315.

Miller, J. M., and Peterson, D. A. M. 2004. Theoretical and empirical implications of attitude strength. *Journal of Politics 66*: 847–867.

Mutz, D. C. 1998. *Impersonal influence: How perceptions of mass collectives affect political attitudes.* Cambridge, UK: Cambridge University Press.

Nelson, T. E., Clawson, R. A., and Oxley, Z. 1997. Media framing of a civil liberties controversy and its effect on tolerance. *American Political Science Review 91*: 567–584.

Prior, M. 2007. *Post-broadcast democracy: How media choice increases inequality in political involvement and polarizes elections.* New York: Cambridge University Press.

Scheufele, D. A., and Tewksbury, D. 2007. Framing, agenda setting, and priming: The evolution of three media effects models. *Journal of Communication 57*: 9–20.

Schwartz, S. 1992. Universals in the content and structure of values: Theoretical advances and empirical tests in 20 countries. In M. P. Zanna (Ed.), *Advances in experimental social psychology*, vol. 24 (pp. 1–65). Orlando, FL: Academic Press.

Shaw, D. L., and Martin, S. E. 1992. The function of mass media agenda setting. *Journalism Quarterly 69*: 902–920.

Shaw, D. L., and McCombs, M. 1977. *The emergence of American political issues.* St. Paul, MN: West.

Shaw, E. F. 1976. The agenda-setting hypothesis reconsidered: Interpersonal factors. *Gazette 23*: 230–240.

Sheafer, T. 2007. How to evaluate it: The role of story-evaluative tone in agenda setting and priming. *Journal of Communication 57*: 21–39.

Son, Y. J., and Weaver, D. H. 2006. Another look at what moves public opinion: Media agenda setting and polls in the 2000 U.S. election. *International Journal of Public Opinion Research 18*: 174–197.

Stromback, J., and Kiousis, S. 2010. A new look at agenda-setting effects: Comparing the predictive power of overall political news consumption and specific news media consumption across different media channels and media types. *Journal of Communication 60*: 271–292.

Stroud, N. J. 2006. Selective exposure to partisan information. PhD diss., University of Pennsylvania, Philadelphia.

Valenzuela, S. 2009. Variations in media priming: The moderating role of knowledge, interest, news attention, and discussion. *Journalism and Mass Communication Quarterly 86*: 756–774.

Valenzuela, S. 2011. Materialism, postmaterialism and agenda-setting effects: The values-issues consistency hypothesis. *International Journal of Public Opinion Research 23*(4): 437–463.

Van der Brug, W., Semetko, H., and Valkenburg, P. 2007. Media priming in a multi-party context: A controlled naturalistic study in political communication. *Political Behavior 29*: 115–141.

Vu, H. N. N., and Gehrau, V. 2010. Agenda diffusion: An integrated model of agenda setting and interpersonal communication. *Journalism & Mass Communication Quarterly 87*: 100–116.

Wallsten, K. 2007. Agenda setting and the blogosphere: An analysis of the relationship between mainstream media and political blogs. *Review of Policy Research 24*: 567–587.

Wanta, W., and Ghanem, S. I. 2006. Effects of agenda setting. In R. W. Preiss, B. M. Gayle, N. Burrell, M. Allen, and J. Bryant (Eds.), *Mass media effects research: Advances through meta-analysis* (pp. 37–51). Mahwah, NJ: Lawrence Erlbaum.

Wanta, W., and Wu, Y. 1992. Interpersonal communication and the agenda-setting process. *Journalism Quarterly 69*: 847–855.

Weaver, D. H. 1977. Political issues and voters' need for orientation. In D. L. Shaw and M. E. McCombs (Eds.), *The emergence of American political issues: The agenda-setting function of the press* (pp. 107–120). St. Paul, MN: West.

Weaver, D. H., Graber, D., McCombs, M., and Eyal, C. 1981. *Media agenda setting in a presidential election: Issues, images and interest.* Westport, CT: Greenwood.

Weimann, G. and Brosius, H-B. 1994. Is there a two-step-flow of agenda-setting? *International Journal of Public Opinion Research 6*: 323–341.

Williams, B. A., and Delli Carpini, M. X. 2004. Monica and Bill all the time and everywhere: The collapse of gatekeeping and agenda setting in the new media environment. *American Behavioral Scientist 47*: 1208–1230.

Yang, J., and Stone, G. 2003. The powerful role of interpersonal communication in agenda-setting, *Mass Communication & Society 6*: 57–74.

CHAPTER 45

IMPLICIT POLITICAL ATTITUDES

When, How, Why, With What Effects?

DAN CASSINO, MILTON LODGE,
AND CHARLES TABER

WE are witnessing a revolution in how social and behavioral scientists think about how people think and reason. Three decades of research in the cognitive sciences (Davidson, Scherer, and Hill Goldsmith, 2003), backed by hundreds of well-crafted behavioral studies in social psychology (Bargh, 1999; Fazio, 1995), political psychology (Nosek, Graham, and Hawkins, 2010), and evidence from the neurosciences (Damasio, 1999; Gazzaniga, 2005), support *affect-driven dual-process models* of thinking and reasoning that directly challenge the way we social scientists think about, measure, and model the relationships among and between political beliefs, attitudes, and behavior.

Central to this social-psychological perspective is the distinction between unconscious ("automatic," "implicit," "System 1") and conscious ("controlled," "explicit," "System 2") processing. Implicit processes are spontaneous, fast, relatively effortless, and typically operate below conscious awareness, whereas explicit processes are slow, deliberative, and effortful, with hundreds of experiments documenting pervasive effects of consciously *un*noticed stimulus events on virtually every aspect of our social and mental life (Gawronski and Payne, 2010; Petty, Fazio, and Brinol, 2009).

This chapter reviews recent work on implicit political attitudes, detailing how, when, and why unconscious processes impact the explicit expression of political beliefs, attitudes, and preferences. What especially attracts our interest as social scientists to this dual-process model is strong theoretical and empirical evidence showing how and why preconscious processes operate throughout the judgment process from the earliest sensory experience to the explicit expression of a belief, attitude, or goal-directed behavior, as well as demonstrations that unconscious processes are extraordinarily receptive to all sensory aspects of the environment, both internal and external, that escape conscious awareness. What is more, outcomes of implicit processing routinely diverge from conscious responses, and implicit effects appear to be most influential when a stimulus event—say upbeat music at a campaign event—is noticed but its influence on decisions is unappreciated (Dijksterhuis, 2004; Wilson, 2002).

THRESHOLDS OF AWARENESS

Because much of our everyday experience is experienced unconsciously, outside of awareness, it is difficult to assess directly by traditional survey methods. Current estimates (Norretranders, 1998) show the human capacity for processing sensory experience to be about 11 million bits per second, of which we are consciously aware of no more than 1/200,000 bps. More limited still is our capacity to consciously think and reason, where we are able to keep in mind about 7±2 chunks of information (Miller, 1957). This being so, much of what we experience, our very connections to the outside world, come and go unnoticed.

An objective threshold, as can be measured by brain wave patterns, must be passed for an external stimulus event to enter one of the sensory systems. A subjective threshold is passed if the stimulus event enters conscious awareness. When this occurs, there are three possible outcomes (Lodge and Taber, 2011, 5–6):

- If the objective threshold is not passed, perception does not occur and there is no registration of the event on the senses. Essentially, a non-event with no impact on information processing.
- If the objective threshold is passed but the subjective is not, we have unconscious perception—a sensory experience passes objective thresholds without ever entering conscious awareness. Such *Consciously Unnoticed Events* (Type 1 CUEs or interchangeably called Type 1 primes) escape notice; seen, registered, but consciously unnoticed. An objectively perceived stimulus may not reach conscious awareness for many reasons: because it occurred too rapidly or too peripherally to be noticed, or one is momentarily distracted.
- If the subjective threshold is passed, we have explicit conscious perception, the stuff of everyday experience. But we may "see" the stimulus without realizing its influence on our thoughts, feelings, preferences, and choices. For such *Consciously Unappreciated Events* (Type 2 CUES or interchangeably Type 2 primes), the individual is consciously aware of the stimulus, say the American flag in the background of a candidate's speech, but its impact on thought, reasoning, and choice is not seen as being influential.

Although unconscious processes are present from start to finish and will inevitably impact all thoughts and feelings that come consciously to mind, this sequence—unregistered-unconscious-conscious processing—implies a continuum. As we shall see, unconscious stimulus events are ubiquitous in the real world (Bargh, 1997), and this dual-process model holds great promise as well as many headaches for the study of political communication.

This dual-process model takes its roots in memory. Metaphorically, the mind has two main memory structures: long-term memory (LTM) and working memory (WM). LTM has an enormous capacity to store information, so much so that the mind requires highly complex structures and efficient processes to recover relevant information in a timely manner. Since pioneering research in the 1960s (Collins and Quillian, 1969), these structures have been visualized as a web in which related concepts are connected according to the strength of their association. So, for instance, while it is the case that President Obama is a Harvard Law School graduate and a Democrat, and both these statements are equally true, the concept Democrat is more strongly linked with him than is the concept Harvard. In semantic association networks, concepts become linked through a version of Hebb's law (Hebb, 1949): concepts that fire together become wire together. When citizens encounter "Obama" and "Democrat" paired together time and time again, the two become closely linked, while the relatively smaller number of times Obama and Harvard are brought up together in the environment leads to a weaker connection between the two concepts.

In addition to these semantic relationships between concepts, LTM also organizes concepts in a parallel affective system (Bower, 1981; Forgas, 2001). Just as facts about George W. Bush, or any other concept in memory, are linked together based on their association to that object, they are also linked with other concepts of similar good-bad affective valence. So, for people who like Bush, the concept of "Bush" in LTM is linked with other things the individual likes about him, perhaps such directly related affectively charged traits as confidence and decisiveness. The strongest evidence for the existence of this parallel affective organization in LTM comes from priming studies where participants are exposed to a visual stimulus that is flashed so briefly that the individual is not consciously aware of having seen it, even though the brain is processing the stimulus. Researchers have normed a large number of words that have clear, population-wide positive or negative connections (Bradley and Lang, 1999): trait words such as ignorant and inarticulate, as well as such nouns as cancer, cockroach, and poison on the negative side, with handsome, honest, hugs, and joy on the positive side. When such affectively charged words are flashed on the computer screen—whether semantically related or not—concepts that are affectively related to the word become more accessible in memory. So, for an individual who liked President Bush, flashing the word "joy" on the computer screen will dispose them to more quickly recall more positive information him and evaluate him more favorably. Similarly, flashing "cancer" will inhibit their recall of positive information and evaluation of Bush, despite the fact that there is no semantic relationship between Bush and the target words. This process—*an affect-congruence effect*—is reliable enough that, among other things, researchers in political psychology can used this priming effect to provide an implicit, unconscious measure of how much a participant likes or dislikes political figures, groups, and issues (Burdein et al., 2006; Cassino and Lodge, 2007;

Lodge and Taber, 2013; Lodge, Taber, and Verhulst, 2011; Morris, Squires, Taber, and Lodge, 2003).

When an individual is exposed to a communication, the concepts in the message—whether consciously attended to or not—begin to activate the attendant concepts in long-term memory. Once a concept is activated, that activation spreads to all of the related concepts (Collins and Loftus, 1975), whether that connection is semantic or affective. This spreading activation moves through long-term memory: concepts that are part of the communication are activated, with that activation spreading almost instantaneously to all its related concepts. As political communications generally involve a large number of concepts coming into perception in rapid succession (think of television ads combining still images, words, or video with a voice over narration, all of which would simultaneously activate nodes in long-term memory), individual concepts become activated and reactivated in real time as they, and concepts related to them, are perceived. Over time, in a matter of moments, the activation level of the concept and its associated concepts decreases to make ready for what information comes next.

At this point in the process, the second type of memory becomes relevant. In contrast with long-term memory, working memory has a severely limited capacity: only about seven concepts can coexist in working memory simultaneously (Barsalou, 1992; Rumelhart and Ortony, 1977; Simon, 1967). These concepts in WM, in a very real sense, are what the individual is consciously thinking about at that time, and researchers have envisioned the process of moving concepts from long-term memory to working memory (as well as pattern recognition) through a pandemonium model (Neisser, 1967; Ratcliff, 1978; Larsen and Bundesen, 1996). In such models, activation is seen as a competition between all of the activated concepts, with those that are most activated, for whatever reason, being selected for further processing in working memory.

It is at this point that the parallel nature of the affective and semantic connections becomes critical. Those concepts that are most semantically implicated by the communication are of course likely to win the competition and to move into working memory. So, if an individual is reading a message about tax policy, the concept of taxes is going to be constantly activated and reactivated, as many of the concepts in the communication will either be about taxes directly, or about concepts closely related to taxes that will cause its further activation. However, the concepts related to taxes that are most likely to be brought into working memory—and therefore, potentially enter the conscious awareness of the individual as a relevant consideration—are those that are *both* semantically and affectively related to the concept. Suppose that taxes are viewed negatively, but there are an equal number of positively and negatively evaluated concepts that are semantically related to taxes (public works projects and tax refunds might be seen positively, while IRS audits and tax preparation might have a negative affective connection). Since the activation of the concept of taxes spreads both affectively and semantically, those concepts that are both semantically and affectively connected with the concept of taxes will most likely pop into working memory. So, when a message mentions taxes, a negatively viewed concept, the other associations that come into working memory are going to be biased in favor of other negatively viewed concepts: IRS audits rather than positively perceived public works projects are likely to win out.

Individuals may well be able to make reasoned decisions about the accuracy or implications of communications, but they can only do so with the information at their disposal. The mismatch in capacity between working and long-term memory means that there is a significant difference between *all* of the information that an individual might have about a communication, and the information about it that enters into working memory and then into the decision stream. An individual may attempt to make a cold, rational, effortful evaluation of a communication based on the information in working memory, but the considerations are biased from the outset because the sampling of information in working memory is already biased by the affective congruence effect spurred by one's prior attitude toward the object. Simply put, an individual can decide if a candidate is proposing good or bad ideas, but that evaluation is going to be largely based on concepts in working memory that are affectively congruent with one's prior attitude of the candidate. A liked candidate is going to bring to working memory more positively viewed attributes and concepts, while a disliked candidate will promote the opposite. Affect precedes and contextualizes cognition. Moreover, this is not a bias that an individual can easily overcome by trying hard to be even-handed, for it is a consequence of hard-wired processes that govern the retrieval of considerations (Bechara, Damasio, Tranel, and Damasio, 2005; Damasio, 1994, 1999).

IMPLICIT ATTITUDE DEFINED

Two somewhat diverging definitions of implicit attitude dominate the field: Greenwald and Banaji (1995) define implicit attitudes as "introspectively unidentified (or inaccurately identified) traces of past experiences that mediate favorable or unfavorable feeling, thought, or action toward social objects" (8). Accordingly, an implicit attitude is an unconscious effect sparked by some immediate environmental event—perhaps the attractiveness of a candidate—on feeling, thought, or behavior. The key here is that the individual is not consciously aware of the stimulus events' impact. Wilson et al. (2000) see implicit attitudes as "evaluations that (a) have an unknown origin (i.e., people are unaware of the basis of their evaluation); (b) are activated automatically; and (c) influence implicit responses, namely uncontrollable responses and ones that people do not view as an expression of their attitude and thus do not attempt to control" (104). Note that from this *dual-attitude perspective* implicit and explicit attitudes can coexist: an individual can—as is commonly found in studies of stereotyping—simultaneously hold an explicit positive attitude and an implicit negative attitude toward the same object. Which one gets triggered is driven by context.

THE UBIQUITY OF UNCONSCIOUS EFFECTS
IN EVERYDAY LIFE

Unconscious priming effects have been demonstrated experimentally on virtually all higher mental processes (see the overviews in Gawronski and Payne, 2010; Greenwald and Banaji, 1995; and Petty, Fazio, and Brinol, 2009). Of special interest to communication scholars are studies of attitude formation (Betsch, Plesser, Schwieren, and Gulig, 2001); the evaluation of political candidates and groups (Lodge and Taber, 2005); liberal-conservative ideology (Jost, Nosek, and Gosling, 2008); religious appeals (Albertson, 2011); the making of moral judgments (Haidt, 2001); group identifications (Perdue, Davidio, Gurtman, and Tyler, 1990); national symbols (Ferguson and Hassin, 2007); and a range of overt, goal-driven behaviors (Gollwitzer and Bargh, 1996), chief among them consumer preferences and behavior (Perkins and Forehand, 2010).

While much of this research involves experimentation inside a laboratory setting, more real-world demonstrations are coming to the fore. For example, Berger, Meredith, and Wheeler (2008) showed that budgetary support for education varied as a function of where people voted—whether in schools, churches, or firehouses—with voters more likely to favor raising state taxes to support education if voting in schools, even controlling for their political views. Clearly, the voters knew what building they were in, but they were not consciously aware of its influence on their vote choice. An extensive meta-analysis of ballot order effects (Schneider et al., 2008) found evidence of a primacy effect on ballot position, where being listed first increased the vote count for 80 percent of candidates. And for a final example of a Type 2 CUE, Achen and Bartels (2006) find that a string of shark attacks in the summer months before the 1916 presidential election cost Woodrow Wilson about ten percentage points in New Jersey beach communities, but produced no effect inland.

A major area of research on implicit attitudes focuses on facial attractiveness, with meta analyses reviewing over one thousand studies pointing to robust effects of facial attractiveness on multiple evaluations, attitudes, and behaviors (Eagly et al., 1991; Feingold, 1992; Langlois et al., 2000). Here, as in the stereotypic inferencing of traits from gender, age, and race, the visage is rapidly registered and spontaneously triggers stereotypic assumptions about the individual's character, attitudes, and behavior. Averaging over a hundred studies, a mere glance at an attractive face promotes a one-half standard deviation enhancement on positive personality traits, the attractive seen as being more socially competent (70 percent vs. 30 percent), more worthy of attention (74 percent vs. 26 percent), and more successful (68 percent vs. 32 percent). What is important here is that physical appearance is registered but its inferential impact on character perceptions, evaluations, and behavior is typically unappreciated by those making the judgments.

In an important series of experiments, Alex Todorov and his colleagues (2005) demonstrated that competence ratings based on a one-second exposure to two paired photos of competing congressional candidates predicted the 2004 House and Senate election outcomes at significantly better than chance levels (67.7 percent and 68.8 percent, respectively). Note here that competence ratings were made of *unfamiliar* candidates by *naive* experimental participants *before* the 2004 congressional elections, and the predictions were to the *actual* electoral outcomes, not vote intention. In other analyses, in addition to making competence judgments, participants evaluated the paired candidates on attractiveness, likability, trustworthiness, and other dispositional judgments, all well known to be important in the evaluation of political candidates (Kinder et al., 1980; Funk, 1999). The implication of this research is that people can make substantively important attributions on a mere one-second exposure to the facial photos of unfamiliar political candidates, and, what is more, these snap judgments (typically taking little more than one second) discriminate congressional winners from losers without any information or contextual cues. All this predictive power is accomplished without party identification, ideological proximity, or any of the traditional predictors of vote choice.

Numerous studies have replicated the general finding that both Type 1 and Type 2 CUES, when used in appearance-based judgments, predict election outcomes, while ruling out the alternative hypothesis that competence judgments simply reflect media-induced familiarity with the politicians (Lenz and Lawson, 2011). Antonakis and Dalgas (2009) pushed the research question deeper by asking 681 children aged 5 to 13 to play a computer game simulating a voyage on a difficult seagoing mission in which they chose which person (from the paired photos of French parliamentarians) they would want to captain the boat from Troy to Athens. The scenario for this study dates to Plato's *Republic* (1894/2008: 153), in which he argues that the crew (voters) cannot select a competent captain (ruler) because the crew is beguiled by appearances. The children in Antonakis and Dalgas's experiment predicted the French election outcome from their choice of ship captain with a correlation 0.71, which was indistinguishable from the adults' predictive success. These findings tell us that appearance-based trait inferences develop quite early and are surprisingly stable across age cohorts. Both children and adults can use facial cues to inform their preferences without any conscious in-depth processing.

Going one level deeper, there are many experiments in developmental psychology that show the effects of attractiveness on infants and toddlers (Pascalis and Slater, 2003). In one of many such experiments, Langlois and colleagues (1987) showed 6-month-old infants images of female faces previously rated as more to less attractive. For each pairing of faces (none were "drop-dead gorgeous" or "grotesque"), they found that the infants fixed their gaze longer on the more attractive face. Pushing the paradigm to its limits, the Langlois team (1991) next examined the preferences of 3-month-old infants to four types of faces—black men and women, white men and women—all previously rated on attractiveness. Results confirm earlier, less well-controlled studies, in showing that preference for attractive faces holds across genders and race.

Judgments of competence are clearly related to vote choice, as is shown repeatedly in the National Election Surveys, but the spontaneous process of making competence judgments appears to be preceded by an even earlier automatic assessment of attractiveness. Given the emerging consensus that judgments of attractiveness have a biological basis, with specific brain structures engaged in the recognition of faces and facial expressions (Ekman, 2007), it is not surprising that these thin-sliced, one-second evaluations of political candidates presented pairwise are influenced by an even more primary evaluation of attractiveness. In addition to predicting higher levels of competence, physical attractiveness of politicians significantly predicts higher levels of likability, integrity, and trust, all of which have also been repeatedly linked to the evaluation of political candidates and vote choice (Kinder et al., 1980). Specific to the automaticity of snap judgments, there are compelling demonstrations that people respond spontaneously to the affective components of a broad array of attitudinal objects (people, groups, and issues), even when—as we will see—the priming events are presented below the threshold of conscious awareness.

RESEARCH PARADIGMS MEASURING IMPLICIT ATTITUDES

This distinction between conscious ("explicit") and unconscious ("implicit") beliefs and attitudes has led to the development of *indirect* measures and experimental procedures designed to tap predispositions that escape conscious awareness (see the review by Wittenbrink, 2007). As a consequence, implicit attitudes must be measured *indirectly*, that is, one cannot directly ask a respondent if he or she was influenced by X. In addition to the problem of strategic responding, direct and indirect measures do not necessarily cohere or predict the same behaviors, with the correlation between measures of implicit and explicit attitudes often varying in the 0.3 to 0.6 range, dependent on one's strength of attitude, time constraints, context, and of course the individual's history of reinforcement (Nosek, Greenwald, and Banaji, 2005). Following De Houwer and Moors's (2005) analyses, a measurement strategy is implicit if responses are "uncontrolled, unintentional, goal independent, purely stimulus driven, autonomous, unconscious, efficient or fast" (188–189). While few measures satisfy all the criteria, indirect measures are proving to be extraordinarily sensitive and responsive to subtle environmental cues occurring outside conscious awareness. The key here is that indirect measures can assess a respondent's unconscious, spontaneous response to a stimulus that is not mediated by conscious thought, thereby tapping into automatically triggered beliefs, attitudes, and habitual behaviors, and circumventing strategic responding. Two research paradigms dominate the laboratory study of implicit beliefs and attitudes.

Implicit Association Test (IAT). The most popular method used to assess implicit attitudes is the Implicit Association Task (developed by Greenwald McGhee and Schwartz, 1998, and Greenwald and Banaji, 1995) and is widely used to measure the automaticity of social-psychological attitudes. Based on the basic premise of the associationist structure of long-term memory, which posits that cognitively accessible information is easier to respond to, thereby facilitating faster responses, the IAT employs an explicit categorization task to assess implicit associations. In a typical application to stereotyping, participants are presented with a set of words or pictures that vary along two separate dimensions; one dimension, perhaps, is of male and female faces, which can then be paired with an evaluative dimension comprised of a pleasant or unpleasant trait word, such as sensitive, hard-working, or emotional. The participant's job is to simply categorize the stimuli as quickly as possible along the gender dimension. The closer the association of face to trait the faster the response to categorize the word or picture, with recent work extending the categorical concepts to ideology, party identification, and a variety of other politically relevant stimuli (Nosek, 2004; Nosek, Graham, and Hawkins, 2010). A detailed description of the IAT setup, method, and measures is available at https://implicit.harvard.edu/implicit.

The Sequential Priming Paradigm. Sequential priming is a simple application of the classic memory-based associationist model. A prime word or picture activates a concept in LTM, with activation spreading along associative pathways to other related concepts. The length of time that it takes to respond to the target concept is the measure of the strength of the association between the prime and the target. Sequential priming can be used to effectively test the strength of association between semantic or affective categories. Researchers can test the automaticity or implicitness of the responses by precisely controlling the exposure time of the primes.

There are two types of sequential priming designed to measure the associative meaning(s) of concepts (Collins and Loftus, 1975; Collins and Quillian, 1969; Neely, 1976), one paradigm for measuring semantic associations, the other for measuring attitudinal responses. Lodge, Taber, and Vehhulst (2011) describe the two paradigms in detail with multiple examples. The semantic priming paradigm is based on a lexical decision task where, say, the prime "Obama" could be followed by a genuine English word, "Democrat," or a nonword such as "paslow." The participant's task is to, as quickly as possible without making too many errors, press the *Yes* response key if the target word is a genuine English word, or the *No* key if not. Here too, the basic idea is that the closer the semantic association between the prime and target concepts in long-term memory, the faster the reaction time to say whether the target is or is not a word. Note, this is an *in*direct measure, as subjects are not being asked if Obama is a Democrat, but simply whether "Democrat" is or is not a word. For strongly associated concepts we expect a facilitation effect, that is, relatively fast reaction times to verify that "Democrat" is a real word because of the close, well-learned semantic association between the two concepts in LTM. If the participant responds significantly faster to one prime-target pairing than the other, we can infer that the concept is more strongly (perhaps automatically) associated in long-term memory.

In the 1980s Fazio et al. (1986) adapted the semantic priming paradigm to study preconscious evaluations and test Zajonc's (1984, 2000) primacy of affect hypothesis. Here, a prime, say "Hitler" or any familiar leader, group, or issue is presented, followed by an unambiguously positive or negative target word. The participant's task is to indicate if the target word is a positive or negative concept. Assuming here we are not dealing with a psychopath, such affectively positive primes as "cockroach" will have a facilitatory effect, that is, promote a faster reaction time to indicate the target word "cockroach" is a negative word, while such affectively incongruent primes as "beautiful" or "healthy" promote an inhibition effect, a slower reaction time to identify a pleasant word as positive for disliked leaders, groups, and issues. Here, again, this is an indirect measure; we are not asking if Hitler is bad, but rather is the word cockroach a bad word. Affective primes make it easier (faster) for a participant to respond to affectively congruent targets and harder (slower) to respond to affectively incongruent targets. Given that the primes need not be substantively related to the target of evaluation, this affective-congruence effect is especially problematic, as the biasing effect easily escapes notice and is consequently less likely to be questioned.

In a major modification of the sequential priming paradigm, researchers have begun to gravitate toward the use of subliminal primes (Bargh, 2007; Lodge and Taber, 2005; Wittenbrink, 2007). By definition, subliminal primes are concepts (words or pictures) presented below the threshold for conscious perception, yet above the threshold for sensory perception. At prime exposure times from 14 to 100 milliseconds the prime appears as no more than a flicker on the computer screen. Thus, people are consciously unaware that they actually saw anything at all. When participants are subliminally primed, there is no opportunity for them to intentionally or consciously modify their response. A major finding of the affective priming paradigm is that a prime-valence by target-valence interaction holds here, even when there is no discernable semantic link between prime and target, say, terrorist and "toothache." These subliminal priming results offer strong support for the prevalence of hot cognition in political information processing which cannot be explained by purely cognitive models. Moreover, these effects are clearly outside conscious awareness, and so provide the first step in the cascade of automatic affective processes that drive motivated reasoning.

Conclusion

Political science in general and political psychology in particular have largely come to reject the view of individuals as rational actors, with a tsunami wave of evidence demonstrating that individuals are more like lawyers than scientists, often striving harder to defend their attitudes than correct them in the face of contrary facts and figures. The theoretical and empirical grounding for motivated reasoning models posits the primacy of emotional or affective responses on preference and choice. Still, many in political science have adopted a cognitively based dual-process model positing that individuals can jump from hot and cool reasoning, depending on their motivation and circumstances. The implication of this view is that although affect may dominate the evaluation process when individuals either don't care much about the outcome or aren't paying attention, the individuals can, with effort, override these tendencies and act rationally (Petty and Cacioppo, 1981), or at least use heuristic and similar strategies to approximate rational acting (Lau and Redlawsk, 2006).

Contrary to the way we routinely model how people form, update, and express their attitudes, individuals do not typically analyze their attitudes in a deliberative, conscious manner (Dijksterhuis, 2004; Wilson, 2002). Rather, their thoughts, feelings, and expressions of attitude are guided by a spontaneously activated semantic and instantly available affective appraisals. Whereas traditional questionnaires typically measure consciously constructed attitudes, implicit measures can index the automatic evaluation of social-psychological objects and so are particularly suited to the prediction of behaviors that are difficult to control, or behavior in situations where subjects are not strongly motivated to deliberate, or—this we think most common—in situations where the individual is aware of the stimulus event but unappreciative of its influence on thoughts and feelings.

Unnoticed and unappreciated "priming" events are ubiquitous in political communications and have been shown to significantly impact stated beliefs and attitudes. The affective organization of long-term memory running parallel to its semantic organization means that countervailing messages will have less impact on judgments when affectively incongruent with one's prior attitude. What is new here is that spontaneously activated semantic and affective inputs appear to enter the decision stream first, anchor the evaluation, and bias what considerations subsequently enter the decision stream. If people are made aware of this affective-congruence bias, it is possible, albeit difficult, to override its influence on perceptions and evaluations (Devine, 1989; Mendelberg, 2001). But when priming events go unnoticed or happen outside conscious awareness, there may be no registration of the event and hence no dissonance to motivate a correction. We see no easy way to fully overcome this bias, other than by repeated exposure to messages that activate countervailing considerations. One problem of course is that many of us live in an echo chamber that reverberates with attitudinally congruent beliefs and attitudinally reinforcing messages, with each congruent message strengthening one's prior semantic and affective associations.

REFERENCES

Achen, C., and Bartels, L. 2006. It feels like we're thinking: The rationalizing voter and electoral democracy. Paper presented at Annual Meeting of the American Political Science Association, Philadelphia, PA.

Albertson, B. 2011. Religious appeals and implicit attitudes. *Political Psychology*, 32(1): 109–130.

Antonakis, J., and Dalgas, O. 2009. Predicting elections: Child's play! *Science* 323(5918): 1183.

Bargh, J. 1997. The automaticity of everyday life. In R. Wyer (Ed.), *Advances in social cognition* (pp. 1–61). Mahwah, NJ: Erlbaum.

Bargh, J. 1999. The cognitive monster: The case against controllability of automatic stereotype effects. In S. Chaiken and Y. Trope (Eds.), *Dual process theories in social psychology* (pp 361–382). New York: Guilford.

Bargh, J. 2007. *Social psychology and the unconscious: The automaticity of higher mental processes*. Philadelphia, PA: Psychology Press.

Barsalou, L. 1992. *Cognitive psychology: An overview for cognitive psychology*. Hillsdale, NJ: Erlbaum.

Bechara, A., Damasio, H., Tranel, D., and Damasio, A. 2005. The Iowa gambling task and the somatic marker hypothesis: Some questions and answers. *Trends in Cognitive Science* 9(4): 159–162.

Berger, J., Meredith, M., and Wheeler, C. 2008. Contextual priming: Where people vote affects how they vote. *Proceedings of the National Academy of Sciences of the United States* 105(26): 8846–8848.

Betsch, T., Plessner, H., Schwiern, C., and Gutig, R. 2001. I like it but I don't know why: A value account approach to implied attitude formation. *Personality and Social Psychology Bulletin* 27: 242–253.

Bower, G. 1981. Mood and memory. *American Psychologist 36*: 129–148.

Bradley, M., and Lang, P. 1999. Affective norms for English words (ANEW). Instruction Manual and Affective Ratings. Technical Report C-1. The Center for Research in Psychophysiology, University of Florida.

Burdein, I., Lodge, M., and Taber, C. 2006. Automaticity of affect for political candidates, parties, and issues: An experimental test of the hot cognition hypothesis. *Political Psychology* 27(3): 359–371.

Cassino, D., Taber, C., and Lodge, M. 2007. Information processing and public opinion. *Politische Vierteljahresschrift 48*(2): 205–220.

Collins, A., and Loftus, E. 1975. A spreading-activation theory of semantic processing. *Psychological Review 82*(6): 407–428.

Collins, A., and Quillian, M. R. 1969. Retrieval time from semantic memory. *Journal of Verbal Learning and Verbal Behavior 8*(2): 240–247.

Damasio, A. 1994. *Descartes' error.* New York: Putnam.

Damasio, A. 1999. *The feeling of what happens: Body and emotion in the making of consciousness.* New York: Harcourt Brace.

Davidson, R., Scherer, K., and Goldsmith, H. 2003. *Handbook of the affective sciences.* New York: Oxford University Press.

De Houwer, J., and Moors, A. 2010. Implicit measures: similarities and differences. In B. Gawronski and K. Payne (Eds.), *Handbook of implicit social cognition: Measurement, theory, and applications* (pp. 176–193). New York: Guilford.

Devine, P. 1989. Stereotypes and prejudice: Their automatic and controlled components. *Journal of Personality and Social Psychology 56*(1): 680–690.

Dijksterhuis, A. 2004. Think different: The merit of unconscious thought in preference development and decision making. *Journal of Personality and Social Psychology 87*(5): 586–598.

Eagly, A., Ashmore, R., Makhijini, M., and Longo, L. 1991. What is beautiful is good, but . . . : A meta-analytic review of the research on the physical attractiveness stereotype. *Psychological Bulletin 110* (1): 109–128.

Ekman, P. 2007. *Emotions revealed: Recognizing faces and feelings to improve communication and emotional life.* New York: Henry Holt.

Fazio, R. 1995. Attitudes as object-evaluation associations: Determinants, consequences, and correlates of attitude accessibility. In R. Petty and J. Krosnick (Eds.), *Attitude strength: Antecedents and consequences* (pp. 247–282). Hillsdale: Erlbaum.

Feingold A. 1992. Gender differences in mate selection preferences: A test of the parental investment model. *Psychological Bulletin, 112*(1): 125–139.

Ferguson, M., and Hassin, R. 2007. On the automatic association between America and aggression for news watchers. *Personality and Social Psychology Bulletin 33*(12): 1632–1647.

Forgas, J. 2001. *Feeling and thinking: The role of affect in social cognition.* New York: Cambridge University Press.

Funk, C. 1999. Bringing the candidate into models of candidate evaluation. *Journal of Politics* 61(3): 700–720.

Gawronski, B., and Payne, K. (Eds.). 2010. *Handbook of implicit social cognition: Measurement, theory, and applications.* New York: Guilford.

Gazzaniga, M. 2005. Forty-five years of split-brain research and still going strong. *Nature Reviews: Neuroscience* 6(8): 653–659.

Gollwitzer, P., and Bargh, J. 1996. *The psychology of action: Linking cognition and motivation to behavior.* New York: Guilford Press.

Greenwald, A., and Banaji, M. 1995. Implicit social cognition: attitudes, self-esteem, and stereotypes. *Psychological Review* 102 (1): 4–27.

Haidt, J. 2001. The emotional dog and its rational tail: A social intuitionist approach to moral judgment. *Psychological Review* 108: 814–834.

Hebb, D. O. (1949). *The organization of behavior.* New York: Wiley & Sons.

Jost, J., Nosek, B., and Gosling, S. 2008. Ideology: Its resurgence in social, personality, and political psychology. *Perspectives in Psychological Science* 3(2): 126–136.

Kinder, D., Peters, M., Abelson, R., and Fiske, S. 1980. Presidential prototypes. *Political Behavior* 2(4): 315–337.

Langlois, J, Roggman, L., Casey, R., Ritter, J., Rieser-Danner, L., and Jenkins, V. 1987. Infant preferences for attractive faces: Rudiments of a stereotype? *Developmental Psychology* 23(3), 363.

Langlois, J., Kalakanis, L., Rubenstein, A., Larson, A., Hallam, M., and Smoot, M. 2000. Maxims or myths of beauty? A meta-analytic and theoretical review. *Psychological Bulletin* 126(3): 390–423.

Larsen, A., and Bundesen, C. 1996. A template-matching pandemonium recognizes unconstrained handwritten characters with high accuracy. *Memory and Cognition* 24(2): 136–143.

Lau, R., and Redlawsk, David. 2006. *How voters decide.* New York: Cambridge University Press.

Lenz, G., and Lawson, C. 2011. Looking the part: Television leads less informed citizens to vote based on candidates' appearance. *American Journal of Political Science* 55(3), 574-589.

Lodge, M., and Taber, C. 2005. The primacy of affect for political candidates, groups, and issues: An experimental test of the hot cognition hypothesis. *Political Psychology* 26(3): 333–487.

Lodge, M., and Taber, C. 2013. *The rationalizing voter.* New York: Cambridge University Press.

Lodge, M., Taber, C., and Verhulst, B. 2011. The indirect measurement of implicit political attitudes. In J. Druckman, D. Green, J. Kuklinski, and A. Lupia (Eds.), *Handbook of experimental political science.* New York: Cambridge University Press.

Mendelberg, T. 2001. *The race card: Campaign strategy, implicit messages, and the norm of equality.* Princeton, NJ: Princeton University Press.

Morris, J., Squires, N., Taber, C., and Lodge, M. 2003. The automatic activation of political attitudes: A psychophysiological examination of the hot cognition hypothesis. *Political Psychology* 24(4): 727–745.

Neely, J. 1976. Semantic priming and retrieval from lexical memory: Evidence for facilitatory and inhibitory processes. *Memory & Cognition* 4: 648–654.

Neisser, U. 1967. *Cognitive psychology.* East Norwalk, CT: Appleton-Century-Crofts.

Norretranders, T. 1998. *The user illusion: Cutting consciousness down to size.* New York: Penguin Books.

Nosek, B., Graham, J., and Hawkins, C. 2010. Implicit political cognition. In B. Gawronski and B. K. Payne (Eds.), *Handbook of implicit social cognition: Measurement, theory, and applications* (pp. 548–564). New York: Guilford Press.

Nosek, B., Greenwald, A., and Banaji, M. 2005. Understanding and using the implicit association test: II. Method variables and construct validity. *Personality and Social Psychology Bulletin* 31(2): 166–180.

Pascalis, O., and Slater, A. (Eds.). 2003. *The development of face processing in infancy and early childhood: Current perspectives.* New York: Nova Science.

Perdue, C., Dovidio, J., Gurtman, M., and Tyler, R. 1990. Us and them: Social categorization and the process of intergroup bias. *Journal of Personality and Social Psychology* 59(3): 475–486.

Petty, R. and Cacioppo, J. 1981. *Attitudes and persuasion: Classic and contemporary approaches.* Dubuque, IA: Brown.

Petty, R., Fazio, R., and Brinol, P. (Eds.). 2009. *Attitudes: Insights from the new implicit measures.* New York: Psychology Press.

Ratcliff, R. 1978. A theory of memory retrieval. *Psychological Review* 85(2): 59–108.

Rumelhart, D., and Ortony, A. 1977. The representation of knowledge in memory. In R. Anderson, R. J. Spiro, and W. E. Montague (Eds.), *Schooling and the acquisition of knowledge.* Hillsdale, NJ: Erlbaum.

Schneider, D., Krosnick, J. A., Ofir, E., Milligan, C., and Tahk, A. 2008. The psychology of voting: How and why the order of candidate names on the ballot and election laws influence election outcomes. In Annual meeting of the Society for Personality and Social Psychology, Albuquerque, NM.

Simon, H. 1967. Motivational and emotional controls of cognition. *Psychological Review* 74(1): 29–39.

Wilson, T. 2002. *Strangers to ourselves: Discovering the adaptive unconscious.* Cambridge, MA: Harvard University Press.

Wilson, T., Lindsey, S., and Schooler, T. Y. 2000. A model of dual attitudes. *Psychological Review* 107(1): 101–126.

Wittenbrink, B. 2007. Measuring attitudes through priming. In B. Wittenbrink and N. Schwarz (Eds.), *Implicit measures of attitudes* (pp. 17–58). New York: Guilford Press.

Zajonc, R. 1984. On the primacy of affect. *American Psychologist* 39(2): 117–123.

Zajonc, R. 2000. Feeling and thinking: Closing the debate over the independence of affect. In Joseph Forgas (Ed.), *Feeling and thinking: The role of affect in social cognition* (pp. 31–58). Cambridge, MA: Cambridge University Press.

CHAPTER 46

AFFECT AND POLITICAL CHOICE

ANN N. CRIGLER AND PARKER R. HEVRON

INTRODUCTION

AFTER watching an Al-Jazeera interview with a leader of the recent revolution in Egypt, an observer was quoted as saying that his emotions "exploded." The man turned off his television and immediately traveled to Tahrir Square in Cairo to take part in the protests that eventually toppled the decades-long regime of Hosni Mubarak (Faheem and El-Naggar, 2011). Now imagine a political world without emotions.[1] Every human being resembles Dr. Spock, the famously rational character from the television series *Star Trek*. Facial expressions reveal little affect, and decisions regarding how to govern are not made with concern for feelings or out of fear or compassion. Because emotions are integral to the political process, such a world is difficult to comprehend. Emotions are present at all stages of politics, influencing the decision-making processes of political leaders, media, and the public.

From ancient political philosophy to current political events and cutting-edge research in the neurosciences, affect, emotion, and mood are seen as an essential part of politics and political choices. In *Rhetoric*, Aristotle states that "the Emotions are all those feelings that so change men as to affect their judgments . . . " (91). His observations are borne out in a plethora of examples—from Barack Obama building a campaign theme around the discrete emotion of hope to his political opponents in the Tea Party movement unifying around anger; from the hate-filled burning of a copy of the Koran by a Florida minister to the outrage of those in Afghanistan who killed American soldiers in revenge. Whether political observers and participants applaud or decry the presence of emotions in political decision-making, scholars have begun to view the relationship between affect and reason as a key component of decision-making. In this chapter, we argue that emotions undergird acts of political choice, not simply as additional variables to explain preferences or actions but also as integral to the processing of information and decision-making.

THE SOCIAL CONSTRUCTION OF EMOTION

This chapter takes a constructionist view of the role of emotions in political choice. Even staunch social choice theorists emphasize the importance of the social construction of rationality to theories of behavior and decision-making (Arrow, 1986). Governing officials, political activists, journalists, and members of the public participate in a dynamic process of constructing political messages and meanings. With increasingly active social media, the construction of messages is not limited to political elites, but is open to anyone who might blog, use Facebook to share media stories, post YouTube videos, or tweet. Political meanings are also interpreted by all who are involved in making political choices. Participants decide what to pay attention to, judge the value of messages, weigh options, form preferences, reach decisions, and decide whether to act. Political choices are made by participants at each of these decision points in the process. Affect, emotion, and mood are important throughout—shaping expression, drawing attention, guiding judgments, and motivating actions.

Many political scientists think that political choices can be explained by individual preferences (e.g., Arrow, 1951; Downs, 1957), political partisanship (e.g., Campbell et al., 1960), or institutional arrangements (e.g., Schickler, 2001; Hacker, 2004). Why include measures of emotion in otherwise parsimonious models of political choice? Emotion is central to how people think, reason, and act (Damasio, 1994; Marcus et al., 2000; Lupia et al., 2000; Redlawsk, 2006; Neuman et al., 2007a). As research reviewed in this chapter illustrates, affect, emotion, and mood are vital to explaining four basic aspects of political choice, including: expressive, perceptual/attentional, appraisal, and behavioral ways of coping with the political world.[2] Emotions function as critical factors of political choice by explaining how people communicate about politics, how they seek information and learn, how they make judgments and form preferences, and how they participate.

To review the state of the field regarding emotion and political choice, the chapter begins with a brief definition of the terms and their measurement—both individually and collectively and preconsciously and consciously. The majority of the chapter analyzes the four basic emotion functions of political choice: expressive, perceptual/attentional, appraisal, and behavioral. Political communication questions and theories of emotion and political choice draw on multiple emotion functions. For example, George Marcus and his colleagues' affective intelligence theory (AIT) seeks to explain perceptual/attentional, appraisal, and behavioral functions of emotion (Marcus et al., 2000; Neuman et al., 2007a). The chapter concludes with recommendations and avenues for future research on affect and political choice.

Defining Affect, Emotion, and Mood

Intellectual histories of affect, emotion, and mood illustrate the difficulty scholars have had in establishing consensus definitions of the terms.[3] While there have been heated exchanges about whether emotion or cognition comes first in the processing of information, many current scholars argue that affect occurs both automatically or pre-consciously—as well as consciously (Lazarus, 1982; Zajonc, 1984; Murphy and Zajonc, 1993; Lerner and Keltner, 2000; Lodge and Taber, 2005; Lau and Redlawsk, 2006; Just et al., 2007; Redlawsk et al., 2007).[4] Affect is the experience of feeling emotions, which is often measured in directional or evaluative valence terms. Emotions are the relatively short-term states or longer-term traits of individuals or groups, which typically contain multiple components—perceptual, cognitive or evaluative, expressive, physiological/neurological, or behavioral (Planalp, 1999; Myers, 2004; Crigler and Just, 2012).[5] Emotions are measured in three different ways: categorical (discrete emotions such as happiness or sadness), valence (directional, as in positive or negative), or circumplex (Heilman, 1997; Plutchik and Conte, 1997; Marcus et al., 2000; Marcus, 2003). Circumplex models of emotion provide a multidimensional analytic structure to capture emotional response. One variant of the two-dimensional scheme has positivity-negativity along one axis dimension and levels of arousal along another. Another has positivity and negativity as orthogonal dimensions (Neuman et al., 2007b). Although closely related, emotion and mood differ in that emotions are usually stimulated by an identifiable target. Mood refers to a diffuse affective state experienced by individuals or groups. Although moods come and go, they are longer-lasting than emotions and can manifest themselves at the individual or group levels (Rahn and Hirshorn, 1999; Rahn, 2000).[6]

Measurement and Empirical Approaches

Understanding the interplay between emotion and political choice is difficult. Affect, emotion, and mood enter into the decision stream spontaneously at every stage of the process. A social constructionist approach to emotion and political choice acknowledges that emotions occur at multiple levels—from the firing of nerve synapses in the brain to the moods of large populations. This poses significant challenges for measurement, requiring clear specification and the use of multiple methods (Crigler and Just, 2012). Table 46.1 outlines some of the methodologies most commonly used to measure each of the four emotion functions that are central to political choice.

Expressive functions are examined through the verbal and nonverbal messages conveyed in politics. Studies of affective framing and political leaders' communications that

Table 46.1 Measurements of Emotional Functions in Political Choice.

Emotion Functions	Methods
Expressive	Content analysis Verbal Nonverbal Discourse analysis
Perceptual/Attentional	Physiological/neurological measures Survey Experiment Implicit Association Tests (IAT)
Appraisal	Interview Survey Experiment Focus Group
Behavioral	Ethnography/Observations Survey Experiment

employ content analysis and discourse analysis are included in this part of the chapter. The content analyses may be quantitative or qualitative, historical or contemporary. They require the examination of words and images, and also of tone, facial expressions, sounds, music, color, and symbols.

Perceptual/attentional functions center on the individual and his/her conscious and pre-conscious processing of emotions. These functions are evident in studies of subliminal messaging, newsworthiness, and agenda setting. Physiological and neurological measures (e.g., eye-tracking, galvanic skin response, heart rates, functional magnetic resonance imaging [fMRI], PET scans, or studies of patients with particular brain lesions) yield direct observations of bodily functions that are often associated with particular emotional responses (see Coronel, 2010). On one hand, these methods are useful in that they do not require individuals to put words to their embodied feelings. On the other hand, different emotions may elicit similar bodily responses (e.g., tears of joy or sadness) so that the interpretation of these tests depends on the researcher's ability to evaluate the results in the proper context. Perceptual/attentional functions are also measured through surveys and experiments. The survey and experimental questions are of two basic types. The first includes self reports in response to open- or closed-ended questions about emotional responses, and the second, Implicit Association Tests (IAT), measures the amount of time required to pair emotions and objects (Greenwald et al., 1998). An advantage of the IAT is that it obviates social desirability responses, replacing conscious choices with more subtle, and arguably accurate, measures of emotional appraisals.

Appraisal functions center on the forming of political judgments and preferences. This section reviews debates about theories of emotion and appraisal of candidates and policies. Emotional appraisals are made by individuals or groups based on evaluating political situations in relation to one's values, identities, and goals (Lazarus, 1991; Mackie et al., 2004; Smith et al., 2007). Appraisals can be both preconscious and conscious. Individual and group emotional appraisals are most often measured by survey or experimental methods, although focus groups and individual interviews are also used to elaborate on groups' emotional interactions and individuals' more nuanced emotional responses.

Behavioral functions of emotion are often outcomes of political choices that focus on the actions or proclivities to act politically. Information seeking and voter turnout are two examples of political behaviors that benefit from considering the emotional components of choice. Ethnographic and observational methods are used to measure actual emotions and behaviors as they occur. Surveys reveal respondents' self-reports of actions or tendencies to act. These methods are limited in establishing clear causal links between emotions and behaviors. Experiments address this deficiency by testing specific causal relations between elicited emotions and actions. Recent research has embedded experiments in surveys to improve the causality of surveys and generalizability of experiments.

To capture these four emotion functions of political choice, both preconsciously and consciously and at the individual and group levels, multiple methods are appropriate and necessary. This is especially true as researchers seek to analyze how emotional expressions and perceptions translate into judgments and actions.

Four Functions of Emotion in Political Choice

Expressive Functions

The capacity to express feelings is fundamental to the human experience and is an essential part of politics (Lane, 2001). Representative democracy depends on the ability of citizens and leaders to convey priorities and inspire and understand one another. This is evident in political campaigns where messages are often fraught with emotions (Kern, 1989). For example, Kaid and Johnston's content analysis of fifty years of presidential political advertising finds that 84 percent of ads made verbal or nonverbal emotional appeals (2001, 55). Brader's analysis of 1,425 presidential, gubernatorial, and congressional ads for the 2000 campaign finds that nearly 75 percent contained a strong emotional appeal (Brader, 2006, 171). Emotionally expressive content in political communications fundamentally affects how people pay attention to politics, how they appraise people and issues, and how they behave.

Affective Framing

Many scholars have focused on elites' messages to the public, analyzing the emotive and persuasive powers of leaders' appeals and framing of political coverage. Literature has begun to identify the role emotion plays in the processes underlying framing effects.[7] An example of the impact of affective framing lies in the emotional assessments of different types of frames (e.g., episodic versus thematic).[8] Experiments by Gross (2008) and Aarøe (2011) find that frames elicit particular emotional responses in viewers and lead to different feelings about policies. Gross finds that episodically framed stories about minimum sentencing stimulate emotions such as sympathy and pity and lead to different policy recommendations than thematic frames because of the emotional impact of episodic frames. Similarly, Aarøe conducts experiments concerning a controversial Danish immigration law and finds that people are more likely to be persuaded by episodic frames than thematic frames, due to the fact they elicit emotional reactions from study participants (208).

Political Leaders and Expression

In addition to verbal content, expressive functions of emotion are often conveyed visually through images, sound, and faces.[9] Ekman's foundational work on human faces shows that similar facial expressions are used to convey similar emotions even across different cultures.[10] How expressed emotions are perceived and "read" is vital to how leaders are judged, whether they are trusted, and ultimately to whether they are supported (Zebrowitz and Montepare, 2005). Extending Ekman's work, scholars argue that emotive expressions shape judgments of candidates across political contexts. In a series of articles, Masters and Sullivan find that American and French voters respond similarly to facial images of leaders, but Americans rely on personal characteristics and respond to emotive displays of happiness, while the French rely more on ideology and respond to displays of anger and threat (1989, 1991, and 1996). Lawson and colleagues' experiments extend the work of Ekman and Masters and Sullivan in two important ways (2010). First, they find that American and Indian subjects were able to predict election outcomes in Mexico and Brazil based on competence judgments of candidate faces, which suggests that expressive content translates across cultures. Second, like Masters and Sullivan, they find that political institutions play a role in how voters respond to expressive content of candidates. For example, Mexican gubernatorial and presidential elections are governed by plurality-winner rules. As a result, the authors find that candidate appearance matters more in those elections than in Mexican senate races, where candidates are primarily evaluated as party members (562). By using pictures of candidates who were unfamiliar to subjects, these findings dispel concerns that emotional appraisals are merely rationalizations of underlying preferences.

Perceptual/Attentional Functions

Emotion plays a key role in helping people determine the amount of attention to pay to the political process. When people pay attention to politics, they are more likely to participate politically. Research reveals that when people feel anxious, new sources of information are more likely to draw their attention, which diminishes reliance on preexisting habits (such as partisanship) (Marcus et al., 2000; Neuman et al., 2007a, b).

Subliminal Advertising and Precognitive Stimuli

The expression of emotion in political messages need not be recognized consciously to be effective. For example, subliminal messages in political advertising can preconsciously affect people as "precognitive" stimuli, meaning that voters have processed information and have been unaware of it.[11] In the 2000 US presidential campaign, the Republican National Committee ran an ad for George W. Bush against Al Gore that focused on Gore's prescription drug plan for seniors. The word "RATS" appeared for a fraction of a second as the narrator claimed that "bureaucrats decide." In separate experiments, researchers found that people who viewed the subliminal "RATS" ad were less likely to trust Democrats to protect Medicare and less likely to support Gore than those who saw the ad without the "RATS" prime (Steward and Schubert, 2006). To isolate the impact of the "RATS" prime, Westen and Weinberger ran an Internet experiment flashing "RATS" or its anagram, "STAR," before a photograph of an unknown candidate. The "RATS" prime led to significantly more negative ratings (Westen, 2007). These findings demonstrate the power of preconscious appraisals to shaping political choices.

Newsworthiness and Attention

Emotion also explains both why journalists perceive the importance of news stories (Fuller, 2010) and why people are more prone to pay attention to particular news (Graber, 2007). For journalists, newsworthiness is driven not only by market forces, but affective components, suggesting continued support for Gans's (1979) "if it bleeds, it leads" account of news programming (Fuller, 2010). Fuller argues that faced with an explosive increase in the availability of information, news media find themselves ratcheting up the emotional content of stories (2010, 72). Although journalists take for granted the fact that emotional content causes people to pay attention to stories, scholars have only recently begun to examine the mechanisms by which stories capture the public's attention. One way is that journalists indicate the importance of stories through repetition and placement within news coverage. Another is arousal. Graber's experiments using emotionally arousing news stories demonstrate that people are more likely to pay attention to fear-arousing stories, supporting AIT's finding that attention can be aroused through fear (2007).

Agenda Setting

The perceptual/attentional function of emotion helps to explain the processes underlying agenda-setting research. Agenda-setting theory argues that mass media influence the political process by affecting the salience of issues in the mind of the public (see for examples McCombs and Shaw, 1972; Kosicki, 1993; Dearing and Rogers, 1996; Young, 2003; McCombs and Reynolds, 2009). Including affect and emotion in agenda-setting studies explains the mechanisms by which agenda-setting effects occur and why the magnitude of the effects varies. Valence measures of emotions have been used to explain the causal mechanism of agenda-setting effects. In an experiment involving news stories about crime statistics, Miller finds that when media exposure leads a person to have more negative than positive emotions about an issue, the person is more likely to rate the issue as nationally important (2007, 702). Similarly, Sheafer's experiment in the context of Israeli national elections finds that as negative news coverage of the Israeli economy increases, subjects grow more likely to name the economy as Israel's most pressing public problem (2007).

Appraisal Functions

Appraisal functions comprise the bulk of research on affect and political choice. Here the literature is interdisciplinary, with publications in neuroscience, psychology, communication, economics, and political science showing how emotions are central to citizens' evaluations of political candidates, groups, and issues.[12] In this section we highlight two key aspects of the role of emotion in candidate and policy evaluations to illustrate that scholarship in the field of emotion and political appraisal remains far from settled.

Affective Intelligence Theory, Emotions, and Appraisal

AIT argues that people have dual emotion systems of disposition and surveillance that govern both thought and behavior (Marcus et al., 2000, 9). The disposition system is associated with enthusiasm and habitual behaviors. Anxiety and fear arouse the surveillance system, alerting people to possible threats. Marcus and colleagues' analyses of survey and quasi-experimental data from US presidential elections demonstrate that when respondents feel threatened or anxious, they make appraisals by relying more on current information and assessments and less on habitual preferences or ideology. This finding has evoked much debate (see Brader, 2005, 2006, 2011; cf. Ladd and Lenz, 2011).

Fundamental theoretical and methodological issues of AIT are at the heart of recent controversies. Ladd and Lenz argue that AIT's theory of dual emotion systems unnecessarily complicates the role of emotion in vote choice (2008, 2011). Instead, they contend that discrete conceptions of emotion are sufficient to explaining vote choice, because the discrete emotions directly affect comparative evaluations of political candidates.[13] Importantly, they examine the direct effects of emotion on preferences without considering how emotion shapes expression, perception, or behavior. The dual-processing system of AIT argues that emotion has important indirect effects (for example, suppositions that enthusiasm leads to participation, aversion pushes avoidance, and anxiety triggers learning) (Marcus et al., 2011, 331).

Candidate Appraisals

Whether emotions' roles directly persuade or indirectly affect surveillance, voters appraise political candidates in microseconds and also over the course of long campaigns. Affective appraisal works preconsciously, as evidenced by research that shows close correlations between rapid affective judgments of candidate competence and actual election outcomes (Todorov et al., 2005; Ballew and Todorov, 2007; Mattes et al., 2010; Lodge and Taber 2013).[14] Balmas and Sheafer conduct experiments and content analyses in the 2006 Israeli elections to argue that the affective tone of news coverage of candidate attributes primes the electorate through second-level agenda setting (2010). They argue that the most salient attributes of candidates stay with voters as they enter the voting booth, influencing their final judgments and vote choices.

Appraisals of People, Issues, and Groups

Emotional appeals are particularly influential on individuals' appraisals made on the basis of group identity. Although we have discussed the role of anxiety and threat in leading to positive actions, other research argues that they can also lead to negative behaviors. Studying the Israeli/Palestinian conflict, Halperin and co-authors conduct surveys of Israeli individuals' appraisals of out-groups and find that the discrete emotion of hatred leads to political intolerance, particularly during periods of heightened threat (2009).[15] In another example, Brader et al.'s experiments concerning group cues, emotional responses, and immigration policy find that affective reactions can lead to erroneous issue judgments (2008). Group cues regarding immigration policy elicit anxiety among white Americans when they highlight low-skilled Latino migrants and emphasize the negative consequences of immigration. Changes in anxiety, rather than perceived threat, mediate the impact of these cues on public opinion and political behavior (Brader et al., 2008, 975). In the same vein, Kinder and Sanders conduct experiments that mimic elite public discourse to examine the appraisal effects of news coverage of affirmative action policy (1990). They find that frames that trigger the salience of out-groups (e.g., affirmative action unfairly advantages minorities) lead to responses of anger, disgust, and fury. On the other hand, frames that trigger the salience of the in-group (e.g., affirmative action is reverse discrimination against whites) lead to appraisals rooted more in the perceived interests of the respondent and less in emotions (Kinder and Sanders, 1990; Visser et al., 2000).

Group appraisals can also manifest themselves as evaluations of candidates in political campaigns (Huddy and Mason, 2008; Baum et al., 2010). Intergroup emotions theory explains how news stories framed in terms of one candidate's position vis-à-vis other candidates can evoke fear or anger in the candidate's supporters, much like the twists and turns of a sporting event can lead to different reactions from fans for each side. For example, because of partisans' strong group attachment, they react differently to the horse race frames that are common to election coverage (Mackie and Smith, 2003; Baum et al., 2010). Future work should continue to clarify how group cues trigger emotions.

Behavioral Functions

The behavioral functions of emotion play out in many arenas, including information-seeking, voting and intention to vote, group formation and mobilization, and leaders' policy actions.[16] We will focus on only two in this chapter: acquiring information and voter turnout.

Information-seeking

As we have seen, Marcus and colleagues' analyses of survey and quasi-experimental data from US elections find that when respondents feel threatened or anxious, they seek new information (2000). Brader's experimental analyses argue that fear ads motivate people to pay more attention to related news stories and to seek information from political and non-political sources (Brader, 2006, 144). Extending these results, Valentino and his colleagues' experimental findings show that anxious subjects not only seek more information, but also retain it better than subjects who are angry (2008). Moreover, when study participants feel anxious about a politician or issue position of their own party, they are more likely to seek a balanced mix of information. In contrast, when people do not feel anxious, they seek information that reinforces their views.

Voter Turnout

The affective components of political advertising have long been the subject of scholarly debate (Ansolabehere et al., 1994; Ansolabehere and Iyengar, 1995; Freedman and Goldstein, 1999; Wattenberg and Brians, 1999; Lau et al., 1999; Goldstein and Ridout, 2004; Geer, 2006). Using experiments, Ansolabehere and colleagues find that negatively valenced "attack" advertising depresses intentions to vote (1994). Drawing on surveys, other scholars find that negative ads are associated with higher turnout. These conflicting findings may be reconciled by using more precise conceptions of negativity (Crigler et al., 2006) or emotion (Marcus and MacKuen, 1993; Brader, 2006). Findings based on AIT indicate that enthusiasm appeals in political advertising stimulate citizens' interest, involvement, and intentions to vote. These examples of the behavioral functions of emotion suggest some of the ways in which emotional judgments of individuals have consequences for political choices and actions. These findings have significant implications, not only for academic audiences but also for political practitioners seeking to move public opinion and citizens seeking to decode political appeals.

FUTURE AVENUES FOR RESEARCH

In the process of focusing on the four key functions of emotion in decision-making (i.e., expressive, perceptual/attentional, appraisal, and behavioral), this chapter has considered primarily the roles emotions play in individuals' political choices. We have shown emotion's central role in political choice through applications to basic concerns of political communication. These include questions of newsworthiness, framing, agenda setting, priming, attention, preference formation, and electoral participation. Although we have provided key examples of scholarship to illustrate the robustness of the field, we have omitted many others that deserve attention now and in future research. Avenues for further investigation are wide open.

Many of the basic concepts and theories in the field are still contested, including how best to measure affect, emotion, and mood; parse the differences between preconscious and conscious affective processing; analyze levels of emotional functions from the sub-cellular to the large group; and assess automatic, immediate, short-term, and longer-term effects of emotion on choice. Theories of emotion's roles in political choice abound. In *The Affect Effect*, the authors named twenty-three theories, models, and central concepts used by the contributors to analyze the dynamic process of emotion in political thinking and behavior (Neuman, Marcus, Crigler, and MacKuen, 2007b, 6). The abundance may be daunting, but it also provides enormous opportunities for further research.

Do valence, circumplex (or multidimensional), or discrete measures of emotion better explain different emotion functions in the process of making political choices? Political advertising research has often relied on valence measures to evaluate ads' persuasive and motivational impacts. Growing research suggests, however, that positive-negative valences fail to capture the different behavioral effects that would be expected from utilizing theories based on discrete or circumplex conceptions of emotion. More work must analyze the short-term and longer-term impacts of emotions such as anxiety and enthusiasm (Brader, 2005), anger (Lerner and Tiedens, 2006), regret (Connolly and Butler, 2006) or hope (Just et al., 2007). This research also must expand across content, political contexts, and cultures to see how robust the persuasive effects of political campaign content are.

Disagreements exist about whether emotions lead people (directly or indirectly) to certain political preferences and action or whether people simply rationalize their emotional choices post hoc. These problems of endogeneity are ripe for creative, interdisciplinary, and multi-method research to analyze emotions' functions throughout the process of making choices—from the framing of expressions, to perception, appraisal, and behavioral responses. More experimental work needs to be done to isolate the independent emotional effects on political choice. Experimental research, however, is limited in that it is often heavily reliant on self-report data that require conscious and verbal expression. For example, immediate (preconscious) judgments might lead to one action, but after thinking about reactions (consciously), subjects might report differently. As a result, the research designs for measuring emotion effects must employ measures to get at both conscious and preconscious processing. Research should use physiological and neurological, as well as implicit and explicit, measures of emotions. Finally, the impact of more illusory nonverbal expressions of emotion and public mood are areas ripe for experimental research both in the lab and in the field. Political communication, with its interests in the expression, communication, and assessment of political messages, should take the lead in exploring the connections among affect, emotion, mood, and political choice.

Notes

1. See Patricia Paperman (1995).
2. For an example, see Peters et al. (2006), who theorize that affect serves four roles in judgments and decision-making, or Planalp (1999), and Crigler and Just (2012), who describe a componential model of emotions and its role in the political communication process.
3. For philosophical debates, see Solomon (2003). For debates in psychology, see Frijda (2010).
4. The term cognition is often used as a synonym for information processing; others commonly use it as a synonym for thinking (Marcus et al., 2000). Michael Spezio and Ralph Adolphs (2007) argue that the term cognition is used within most treatments of decision-making to denote "conscious, intentional processes" (76).
5. Affect and emotion are often used interchangeably in the political communication literature.
6. Mood has been extensively studied in the laboratory using experiments (Schwarz and Clore, 1983; Bless et al., 1992; Peters et al., 2006; Caruso and Shafir, 2006), and we must continue to examine its effects in "real world" political decision-making.
7. For examples, see Gross (2008), Aarøe (2011), Druckman (2001, 2005), Druckman and McDermott (2008), Druckman and Parkin (2005), Kinder and Sanders (1990), and Kahneman and Tversky (1979).
8. Episodic frames "present an issue by offering a specific example, case study or event oriented report," whereas thematic frames place issues in a broader context (Gross, 2008, 171).
9. For examples, see Keating et al. (1981) (1999), Barry (1997), Ekman and Friesen (1978), McHugo et al. (1985), Ekman and Rosenberg (1997), Russell and Fernandez-Dols (1997), Bucy (2000), Scherer (2004), Brader (2006), and Bailenson et al. (2009).
10. Although some expressions are universal, scholarship demonstrates cross-cultural differences in perception of smiling and non-smiling faces and raised and lowered eyebrows. Keating and co-authors found that among Western experimental subjects, lowered brows are associated with social dominance, whereas among non-Westernized subjects the association between lowered brows and social dominance disappears (1981, 624).
11. Neuroscience suggests that people process information along a "high road" and a "low road," in which the "high road" controls much of people's conscious behavior and the "low road" processes information quickly and automatically (LeDoux and Phelps, 2010; Stewart and Schubert, 2006, 105).
12. E.g, see for political candidates, Glaser and Salovey (1998), Brader (2005, 2006), Just et al. (2007), Mattes et al. (2010), Balmas and Sheafer (2010). For groups, see Halperin et al. (2009), Lerner and Keltner (2000), Valentino et al. (2002), Brader et al. (2008). For issues, see Miller (2007) and Brader et al. (2008).
13. Ladd and Lenz change the dependent variable from Marcus et al.'s (2000) vote intention to a candidate-feeling thermometer (2008, 2011). The resultant effects of AIT are subsumed by affect transfer.
14. Additionally, by using pictures of actual politicians that have run against each other for office, Mattes and colleagues overcome the problem of external validity that often plagues laboratory experiments (201).
15. They argue that these effects are moderated by political sophistication. Similarly, Wendy Rahn (2000) argues that the influence of "public mood" on political reasoning is greater among less politically sophisticated individuals than the well informed.

16. For group formation and mobilization, see Tiedens and Leach (2004), Mackie et al. (2004), and Goodwin et al. (2001). For leaders' policy actions, see Blight (1990), Greenstein (2000), and McDermott (2008).

REFERENCES

Aarøe, L. 2011. Investigating frame strength: The case of episodic and thematic frames. *Political Communication* 28(2): 207–226.

Ansolabehere, S., and Iyengar, S. 1995. *Going negative: How political advertisements shrink and polarize the electorate.* New York: Free Press.

Ansolabehere, S., Iyengar, S., Simon, A., and Valentino, N. 1994. Does attack advertising demobilize the electorate? *American Political Science Review* 88: 829–838.

Aristotle. 1954. *Aristotle's rhetoric.* Translated by W. Rhys Roberts with an Introduction by Friedrich Solmsen. New York: Random House.

Arrow, K. J. 1951. Alternative approaches to the theory of choice in risk-taking situations. *Econometrica* 19: 404–437.

Arrow, K. J. 1986. Rationality of self and others in an economic system. *The Journal of Business* 59(4) (2): S385–S399.

Bailenson, J. N., Iyengar, S., Yee, N., and Collins, N. A. 2009. Facial similarity between voters and candidates causes influence. *Public Opinion Quarterly* 72(5): 935–961.

Ballew, C. C., and Todorov, A. 2007. Predicting political elections from rapid and unreflective face decisions. *Proceedings of the National Academy of Science* 104: 17948–17953.

Balmas, M., and Sheafer, T. 2010. Candidate image in election campaigns: Attribute agenda setting, affective priming, and voting intentions. *International Journal of Public Opinion Research* 22 (5): 1–26.

Barry, A. M. 1997. *Visual intelligence: Perception, image, and manipulation in visual communication.* Albany, NY: SUNY Press.

Baum, M., Crigler, A., Just, M., and Mills, J. 2010. Emotions, the horserace metaphor, and the 2008 presidential campaign. Paper presented at the annual meeting of the American Political Science Association, Washington, DC.

Bless, H., Mackie, D. M., and Schwarz, N. 1992. Mood effects on attitude judgments: Independent effects of mood before and after message elaboration. *Journal of Personality and Social Psychology* 63(4): 585–595.

Blight, J. G. 1990. *The shattered crystal ball: Fear and learning in the Cuban Missile Crisis.* Savage, MD: Rowan and Littlefield.

Brader, T. 2005. Striking a responsive chord: How campaign ads motivate and persuade voters by appealing to emotions. *American Journal of Political Science* 49(2): 388–405.

Brader, T. 2006. *Campaigning for hearts and minds: How emotional appeals in political ads work.* Chicago: University of Chicago Press.

Brader, T. 2011. The political relevance of emotions: "Reassessing" revisited. *Political Psychology* 32(2): 337–345.

Brader, T., Valentino, N. A., and Suhay, E. 2008. What triggers public opposition to immigration? Anxiety, group cues, and immigration threat. *American Journal of Political Science* 52(4): 959–978.

Bucy, E. 2000. Emotion and evaluative consequences of inappropriate leader displays. *Communication Research* 27(2): 194–226.

Campbell, A., Converse, P. E., Miller, W. E., and Stokes, D. E. 1960. *The American voter.* Chicago: University of Chicago Press.

Caruso, E. M., and Shafir, E. 2006. Now that I think about it, I'm in the mood for laughs: Decisions focused on mood. *Journal of Behavioral Decision Making* 19(2): 155–169.

Connolly, T., and Butler, D. 2006. Regret in economic and psychological theories of choice. *Journal of Behavioral Decision Making* 19(2): 139–154.

Coronel, J. 2010. If citizens with severe brain lesions can make reasonable voting decisions, then so can everyone else. Paper presented at the California Institute of Technology Neuroscience Workshop, Pasadena, CA.

Crigler, A. N., and Just, M. R. 2012. Measuring affect, emotion and mood in political communication. In H. Semetko and M. Scammell (Eds.), *Handbook of political communication* (pp. 211–225). Thousand Oaks, CA: Sage.

Crigler, A. N., Just, M., and Belt, T. 2006. The three faces of negative campaigning: The democratic implications of attack ads, cynical news and fear arousing messages. In D. P. Redlawsk (Ed.), *Feeling politics: Affect and emotion in political information processing* (pp. 135–63). New York: Palgrave/Macmillan.

Damasio, A. R. 1994. *Descartes' error.* New York: Harper.

Dearing, J. W., and Rogers, E. M. 1996. *Agenda-setting: Communication concepts.* Los Angeles: Sage.

Downs, A. 1957. *An economic theory of democracy.* New York: Addison Wesley.

Druckman, J. N. 2001. Does political information matter? *Political Communication* 20: 515–519.

Druckman, J. N. 2005. Media matter: How newspapers and television news cover campaigns and influence voters. *Political Communication* 22: 463–481.

Druckman, J. N., and McDermott, R. 2008. Emotion and the framing of risky choice. *Political Behavior* 30: 297–321.

Druckman, J. N., and Parkin, M. 2005. The impact of media bias: How editorial slant affects voters. *Journal of Politics* 67: 1030–1049.

Ekman, P., and Friesen, W. V. 1978. *The facial action coding system: A technique for the measurement of facial movement.* Palo Alto, CA: Consulting Psychologists Press.

Ekman, P., and Rosenberg, E. (Eds.). 1997. *What the face reveals: Basic and applied studies of spontaneous expression using the facial action coding system (FACS).* New York: Oxford University Press.

Faheem, K., and El-Naggar, M. 2011. Violent clashes mark protests against Mubarak's rule. *New York Times.* Retrieved April 24, 2011, from http://www.nytimes.com/2011/01/26/world/middleeast/26egypt.html?_r=2&src=twrhp.

Freedman, P., and Goldstein K. 1999. Measuring media exposure and the effects of negative campaign ads. *American Journal of Political Science* 43(4): 1189–1208.

Frijda, N. 2010. The psychologist's point of view. In M. Lewis, J. Haviland-Jones, and L. F. Barrett (Eds.), *Handbook of emotions,* 3rd ed. (pp. 68–87). New York: Guilford Press.

Fuller, J. 2010. *What is happening to news? The information explosion and the crisis in journalism.* Chicago: University of Chicago Press.

Gans, H. J. 1979. *Deciding what's news: A study of CBS Evening News, NBC Nightly News, Newsweek and Time.* New York: Vintage Press.

Geer, J. G. 2006. *In defense of negativity: Attack advertising in presidential campaigns.* Chicago: University of Chicago Press.

Glaser, J., and Salovey, P. 1998. Affect in electoral politics. *Personality and Social Psychology Review* 2(3): 156–172.

Goldstein, K., and Ridout, T. N. 2004. Measuring the effects of televised political advertising in the United States. *American Political Science Review* 7: 205–226.

Goodwin, J., Jasper, J. M., and Polletta, F. (Eds.). 2001. *Passionate politics: Emotion and social movements.* Chicago: University of Chicago Press.

Graber, D. 2007. The road to public surveillance: Breeching attention thresholds. In W. R. Neuman, G. Marcus, A. Crigler, and M. MacKuen (Eds.), *The affect effect: Dynamics of emotion in political thinking and behavior* (pp. 265–290). Chicago: University of Chicago Press.

Greenstein, F. 2000. *The presidential difference: Leadership style from FDR to Clinton.* New York: Free Press.

Greenwald, A. G., McGhee, D. E., and Schwartz, J. L. K. 1998. Measuring individual differences in implicit cognition: The implicit association test. *Journal of Personality and Social Psychology* 74(6): 1464–1480.

Gross, K. 2008. Framing persuasive appeals: Episodic and thematic framing, emotional response, and policy change. *Political Psychology* 29(2): 169–192.

Hacker, J. 2004. Privatizing risk without privatizing the welfare state: The hidden politics of social policy entrenchment in the United States. *American Political Science Review* 98(2): 243–260.

Halperin, E., Canetti-Nisim, D., and Hirsch-Hoefler, S. 2009. Emotional antecedents of political intolerance: The central role of group-based hatred. *Political Psychology* 30: 93–123.

Heilman, K. M. 1997. The neurobiology of emotional experience. *Journal of Neuropsychiatry and Clinical Neuroscience* 9(3): 439–448.

Huddy, L., and Mason, L. 2008. Heated campaign politics: An intergroup conflict model of partisan emotions. Paper presented at the annual meeting of the American Political Science Association, Boston, Massachusetts.

Just, M. R., Crigler, A. N., and Belt, T. 2007. Don't give up hope: Emotions, candidate appraisals and votes. In W. R. Neuman, G. E. Marcus, A. N. Crigler, and M. B. MacKuen (Eds.), *The affect effect: Dynamics of emotion in political thinking and behavior* (pp. 231–260). Chicago: University of Chicago Press.

Kahneman, D., and Tversky, A. 1979. Prospect theory: An analysis of decisions under risk. *Econometrica* 47(2): 263–291.

Kaid, L. L., and Johnston, A. 2001. *Videostyle in presidential campaigns: Style and content of televised political advertising.* Westport, CT: Praeger/Greenwood.

Keating, C. F., Mazur, A., Segall, M. H., Cysneiros, P. G., Divale, W. T., Kilbride, J. E., Komin, S., Leahy, P., Thurman, B., and Wirsing, R. 1981. Culture and the perception of social dominance from facial expressions. *Journal of Personality and Social Psychology* 40(4): 615–626.

Keating, C. F., Randall, D., and Kendrick, T. 1999. Presidential physiognomies: Altered images, altered perceptions. *Political Psychology* 20(3): 593–610.

Kern, M. 1989. *30-second Politics: Political advertising in the eighties.* New York: Praeger.

Kinder, D. R., and Sanders, L. M. 1990. Mimicking political debate with survey questions: The case of white opinion on affirmative action for blacks. *Social Cognition* 8: 73–103.

Kosicki, G. M. 1993. Problems and opportunities in agenda-setting research. *Journal of Communication* 43: 100–127.

Ladd, J. M., and Lenz, G. S. 2008. Reassessing the role of anxiety in vote choice. *Political Psychology* 29: 275–296.

Ladd, J. M., and Lenz, G. S. 2011. Does anxiety improve voters' decision making? *Political Psychology* 32(2): 347–361.

Lane, R. 2001. *The loss of happiness in market democracies.* New Haven: Yale University Press.

Lau, R. R., and Redlawsk, D. R. 2006. *How voters decide: Information processing during election campaigns.* Cambridge: Cambridge University Press.

Lau, R. R., Sigelman, L., Heldman, C., and Babbit, P. 1999. The effect of negative political advertisements: A meta-analytic assessment. *American Political Science Review 93*(4): 851–875.

Lawson, C., Lenz, G. S., Baker, A., and Myers, M. 2010. Looking like a winner: Candidate appearance and success in new democracies. *World Politics 62*(4): 561–593.

Lazarus, R. S. 1982. Thoughts on the relations between emotions and cognition. *American Physiologist 37*(10): 1019–1024.

Lazarus, R. S. 1991. *Emotion and adaptation.* New York: Oxford University Press.

LeDoux, J. E., and Phelps, E. A. 2010. Emotional networks in the brain. In M. Lewis, J. M. Haviland-Jones, and L. F. Barrett (Eds.), *Handbook of emotions,* 3rd ed. (pp. 159–179). New York: Guilford.

Lerner, J. S., and Keltner, D. 2000. Beyond valence: Toward a model of emotion-specific influences on judgment and choice. *Cognition and Emotion 14*(4): 473–493.

Lerner, J. S., and Tiedens, L. Z. 2006. Portrait of the angry decision maker: How appraisal tendencies shape anger's influence on cognition. *Journal of Behavioral Decision Making 19*: 115–137.

Lodge, M., and Taber, C. S. 2005. The automaticity of affect for political leaders, groups, and issues: An experimental test of the hot cognition hypothesis. *Political Psychology 26* (3): 455–482.

Lodge, M., and Taber, C. S. 2013. *The rationalizing voter.* New York: Cambridge University Press.

Lupia, A., McCubbins, M. D., and Popkin, S. L. (Eds.). 2000. *Elements of reason: Cognition, choice, and the bounds of rationality.* Cambridge: Cambridge University Press.

Mackie, D. M., Silver, L., and Smith, E. R. 2004. Emotion as an intergroup phenomenon. In C. W. Leach and L. A. Tiedens (Eds.), *The social life of emotions,* (227–245). Cambridge: Cambridge University Press.

Mackie, D. M., and Smith, E. (Eds.). 2003. *From prejudice to intergroup emotions.* New York: Psychology Press.

Marcus, G. E. 2003. The psychology of emotion and politics. In L. Huddy, D. Sears, and R. Jervis (Eds.), *The oxford handbook of political psychology,* (pp. 182–221). New York: Oxford University Press.

Marcus, G. E., and MacKuen, M. B. 1993. Anxiety, enthusiasm, and the vote: The emotional underpinnings of learning and involvement during political campaigns. *American Political Science Review 87*(3): 672–685.

Marcus, G. E., MacKuen, M. B., and Neuman, W. R. 2011. Parsimony and complexity: Developing and testing theories of affective intelligence. *Political Psychology 32*(2): 323–335.

Marcus, G. E., Neuman, W. R., and MacKuen, M. B. 2000. *Affective intelligence and political judgment.* Chicago: University of Chicago Press.

Masters, R. D. 1991. Individual and cultural differences in response to leaders' nonverbal displays. *Journal of Social Issues 47*: 151–165.

Masters, R. D., and Sullivan, D. G. 1989. Nonverbal displays and political leadership in France and the United States. *Political Behavior 11*(2): 123–156.

Mattes, K., Spezio, M., Kim, H., Todorov, A., Adolphs, R., and Alvarez, R. M. 2010. Predicting election outcomes from positive and negative trait assessments of candidate images. *Political Psychology 31*(1): 41–58.

McCombs, M. E., and Reynolds, A. 2009. How the news shapes our civic agenda. In J. Bryant and M. B. Oliver (Eds.), *Media effects: Advances in theory and research* (pp. 1–16). New York: Taylor & Francis.

McCombs, M. E., and Shaw, D. L. 1972. The agenda-setting function of mass media. *Public Opinion Quarterly* 36: 176–187.

McDermott, R. 2008. *Presidential leadership, illness and decision making*. Cambridge: Cambridge University Press.

McHugo, G. J., Lanzetta, J. T., Sullivan, D. G., Masters, R. D., and Englis, B. G. 1985. Emotional reactions to a political leader's expressive displays. *Journal of Personality and Social Psychology* 49(6): 1513–1529.

Miller, J. M. 2007. Examining the mediators of agenda setting: A new experimental paradigm reveals the role of emotions. *Political Psychology* 28(6): 689–717.

Murphy, S. T., and Zajonc, R. 1993. Affect, cognition and awareness: Priming with optimal and suboptimal stimulus exposures. *Journal of Personality and Social Psychology* 64: 723–739.

Myers, D. G. 2004. *Theories of emotion in psychology*. 7th ed. New York: Worth.

Neuman, W. R., Marcus, G. E., Crigler, A. N., and MacKuen, M B. 2007a. *The affect effect: Dynamics of emotion in political thinking and behavior*. Chicago: University of Chicago Press.

Neuman, W. R., Marcus, G. E., Crigler, A., and MacKuen, M. 2007b. Theorizing affect's effects. In W. R. Neuman, G. Marcus, A. Crigler, and M. MacKuen (Eds.), *The affect effect: Dynamics of emotion in political thinking and behavior* (pp. 1–20). Chicago: University of Chicago Press.

Paperman, P. 1995. L'absence d'émotion comme offense. In P. Paperman and R. Olgen (Eds.), *La Couleur Despensées* (pp. 175–196). Paris: éditions de l'école des Hautes études en Sciences Sociales.

Peters, E., Vastfjall, D., Garling, T., and Slovic, P. 2006. Affect and decision making: A "hot" topic. *Journal of Behavioral Decision Making* 19: 79–85.

Planalp, S. 1999. *Communicating emotion: Social, moral, and cultural processes*. Paris: Cambridge University Press and Editions de la Maison des Sciences de l'Homme.

Plutchik, R., and Conte, H. R. 1997. *Circumplex models of personality and emotions*. Washington, DC: American Psychological Association.

Rahn, W. M. 2000. Affect as information: The role of public mood in political reasoning. In A. Lupia, M. D. McCubbins, and S. Popkin (Eds.), *Elements of reason: Cognition, choice, and the bounds of rationality* (pp. 130–152). Cambridge: Cambridge University Press.

Rahn, W. M., and Hirshorn, R. M. 1999. Political advertising and public mood: A study of children's political orientations. *Political Communication* 16(1): 387–407.

Redlawsk, D. (Ed.). 2006. *Feeling politics: Emotion in political information processing*. New York: Palgrave Macmillan.

Redlawsk, D., Civettini, A. J., and R. Lau. 2007. Affective intelligence and voting: information processing and learning in a campaign. In W. R. Neuman, G. Marcus, A. Crigler and M. MacKuen (Eds.), *The affect effect: Dynamics of emotion in political thinking and behavior* (pp. 152–179). Chicago: University of Chicago Press.

Russell, J., and Fernandez-Dols, J. (Eds.). 1997. *The psychology of facial expression*. Cambridge: Cambridge University Press.

Scherer, K. 2004. Which emotions can be induced by music? What are the underlying mechanisms? And, how can we measure them? *Journal of New Music Research* 33(3): 239–251.

Schickler, E. 2001. *Disjointed pluralism: Institutional innovation and the development of the U.S. Congress*. Princeton, NJ: Princeton University Press.

Schwarz, N., and Clore, G. 1983. Mood, misattribution, and judgments of well-being: Informative and directive functions of affective states. *Journal of Personality and Social Psychology* 45(3): 513–523.

Sheafer, T. 2007. How to evaluate it: The role of story-evaluative tone in agenda setting and priming. *Journal of Communication* 57: 21–39.

Smith, E. R., Seger, C., and Mackie, D. M. 2007. Can emotions be truly group-level? Evidence regarding four conceptual criteria. *Journal of Personality and Social Psychology* 93: 431–446.

Solomon, R. (Ed.). 2003. *What is an emotion?* 2nd ed. New York: Oxford University Press.

Spezio, M. L., and Adolphs, R. 2007. Politics and the evolving neuroscience literature. In W. R. Neuman, G. Marcus, A. Crigler, and M. MacKuen (Eds.), *The affect effect: Dynamics of emotion in political thinking and behavior* (pp. 71–95). Chicago: University of Chicago Press.

Stewart, P. A., and Schubert, J. N. 2006. Taking the "low road" with subliminal advertisements: A study testing the effect of precognitive prime "RATS" in a 2000 presidential advertisement. *The Harvard Journal of International Press/Politics* 11: 103–114.

Tiedens, L., and Leach, C. W. (Eds.). 2004. *The social life of emotions*. Cambridge: Cambridge University Press.

Todorov, A., Mandisodza, A. N., Goren, A., and Hall, C. C. 2005. Inferences of competence from faces predict election outcomes. *Science* 308(5728): 1623–1626.

Valentino, N. A., Hutchings, V. L., Banks, A. J., and Davis, A. K. 2008. Is a worried citizen a good citizen? Emotions, political information seeking, and learning via the Internet. *Political Psychology* 29(2): 247–273.

Valentino, N. A., Hutchings, V. L., and White, I. K. 2002. Cues that matter: How political ads prime racial attitudes during campaigns. *American Political Science Review* 96(1): 75–90.

Visser, P. S., Krosnick, J. A., and Lavrakas, P. J. 2000. Survey research. In C. M. Judd and H. Reis (Eds.), *Research methods in social psychology* (pp. 223–252). Cambridge: Cambridge University Press.

Wattenberg, M. P., and Brians, C. L. 1999. Negative campaign advertising: Demobilizer or mobilizer? *American Political Science Review* 93(4): 891–899.

Westen, D. 2007. *The political brain: The role of emotion in deciding the fate of the nation*. New York: Public Affairs.

Young, J. R. 2003. The role of fear in agenda setting by television news. *American Behavioral Scientist* 46(12): 1673–1695.

Zajonc, R. 1984. On the primacy of affect. *American Psychologist* 39(2): 117–123.

Zebrowitz, L. A., and Montepare, J. M. 2005. Appearance DOES matter. *Women's Health* 308(5728): 1565–1566.

INTERPERSONAL AND SMALL GROUP POLITICAL COMMUNICATION

CHAPTER 47

....

TWO-STEP FLOW, DIFFUSION, AND THE ROLE OF SOCIAL NETWORKS IN POLITICAL COMMUNICATION

....

BRIAN G. SOUTHWELL

INTRODUCTION

MORE than five and a half decades ago, Katz and Lazarsfeld's (1955) *Personal Influence* highlighted what might seem a mundane notion—the idea that people talk to one another and serve as important sources of information—while also expanding our thinking about mass media effects beyond the moment of initial broadcast and forecasting a path for future mass communication research. During the present era of social media, in which many people log onto *Facebook* instead of reading a morning newspaper, the relevance of social networks in explaining political information spread, influence, and decision-making may seem to need little explanation. As Kenski, Hardy, and Jamieson (2010) note, for example, the full story of the 2008 presidential campaign cannot be told without mention of both "interpersonal microtargeting" to encourage people to recruit others in their social network to work for the Obama-Biden campaign and "viral slurs" spread by email and word-of-mouth among opponents of the Obama-Biden effort (307). More recently, we have seen social networking tools used for political organizing in Egypt and elsewhere in northern Africa and the Middle East. News coverage of the 2011 protests in the region often explicitly mentioned the role of social media in mobilizing people. Despite the omnipresence of social networking technologies, however, we still have much to learn about the roles of interpersonal connections in shaping and affecting mass political communication and behavior.

An increasing array of political communication scholars and political scientists now include interpersonal communication as part of their models, such as Druckman and Nelson (2003), Mutz and Martin (2001), McClurg (2004), or Roch (2005). The central theoretical foundation for much of that work nonetheless owes much to two long-running literatures directly intersecting in, and stemming from, *Personal Influence*: research on the two-step flow and investigation of information diffusion. Consequently, a broad overview of political communication theories calls for a discussion of the theoretical underpinnings of the two-step flow (and its linkage to diffusion), major findings to date, and future directions for research.

THE IMPORTANCE OF SOCIAL NETWORKS IN EXPLAINING POLITICAL INFORMATION FLOW

Drawing on earlier speculation by Lazarsfeld, Berelson, and Gaudet (1944), Katz and Lazarfeld (1955) asserted that interpersonal conversation serves as a mediating bridge between the general broadcast of information and individual engagement of, and action on, that information. In explaining their decision-making in various domains, women in the Decatur, Illinois, study cited other people as an important source of information. Katz and Lazarsfeld also observed the pivotal role played by so-called opinion leaders, individuals who both engage news and other media sources and, in turn, dispense information from those sources to networks of followers. Scholars subsequently extended the original notion of a two-step flow to the possibility of a multistep flow (Brosius and Weimann, 1996; Katz, 1987).

While popular discussion of the book often invokes the "two-step flow" phrase, it would be a misstep to label the simple empirical observation of a two-step flow, from broadcast media outlets to opinion leaders to other individuals, as the defining contribution of *Personal Influence* to political communication research. As we will discuss, scholars have noted important methodological limitations in the original studies of the two-step flow notion. The broader contribution instead is likely one of theoretical orientation toward an understanding of audiences as networked and socially situated. As Kadushin (2006) has pointed out, *Personal Influence* offers a foundation for nothing less than a theory of action, an account of "basic human character" at the same level of generalizability as theorizing by Hobbes or Parsons (272). From this perspective, the two-step flow model posits a fundamental assumption about human decision-making, namely that because it often is social in nature it might be vulnerable to community-level influence. As such, we now have theoretical license to probe the impact of immediate and distal social networks on an individual's political choices and behavior, certainly a crucial source of variance over and above an individual's direct exposure to mass propaganda.

One actually can trace intellectual interest in information diffusion back much further than *Personal Influence* (1955) or *The People's Choice* (1944). For example, early observations of imitation in groups by Tarde (1903) suggested the social nature of humans as an explanation for the spread of ideas; the human tendency to converse offers a key route for information diffusion. In the early twentieth century, numerous examples emerged of information quickly spreading via interpersonal channels. For example, Scanlon (1998) noted how quickly news of the 1917 Halifax explosion spread across Canada as telephone switchboards lit up. Yet not all information appeared to diffuse in the same way. As DeFleur (1987) has noted, contrasting political news studies in the 1940s and 1950s provided a complicated array of evidence. Whereas Miller (1945) claimed that more than 90 percent of a college student population heard about the death of US President Franklin D. Roosevelt within half an hour of official news reports by talking with someone about it, Larsen and Hill's (1954) study of how people found out about the death of Ohio Senator Robert Taft pointed to radio, rather than word-of-mouth, as the primary source of information. Recognition of such complexity, in turn, inspired a generation of diffusion studies (e.g., DeFleur and Larsen, 1958; Rogers, 1962; Rosengren, 1973) that sought to go beyond simple documentation of information spread to investigation of who adopts innovative beliefs in what order and other questions.

What the two-step flow approach did, beyond resonating with other evidence of interpersonal diffusion, was to relate the decision-making of individuals to groups and social networks rather than simply tying it to the impact of broadcast propaganda. As Katz (2006) succinctly notes, a key conclusion of *Personal Influence* is that "choices are made in the informal deliberations of small groups of family and friends, not by a tyrannical majority or by hegemonic duplicity" (312). Crucially, the perspective suggested by *Personal Influence* grants agency to members of audiences to engage both media content and one another. Livingstone (2006) has observed that this perspective both assumes that mass media are not monolithic in content or influence and also acknowledges that audiences are far from defenseless objects of broadcast persuasion attempts.

The particular importance of conceptualizing an electorate as comprised of interconnected networks rather than a mass of atomized individuals becomes clear as we note the technology changes that have arrived in the 21st century. No longer are we in a world of relatively limited mass media outlets, for example, and patterns of social interaction undoubtedly have been affected by technology trends. As Simonson (2006) adeptly suggests, the "two-step flows of Decatur women in 1945 are not the two-step flows of today" (21). Moreover, as Bennett and Manheim (2006) have observed, it has increasingly become possible for campaigns to directly target individuals with tailored messages, which might allow campaign staff to circumvent conventional opinion leaders and reach potential voters directly. Bennett and Manheim go so far as to claim that this situation has led to the rise of a "one-step flow" of communication (213). From this perspective, opinion leaders are often not leading in the sense of providing completely new information as much as they are guiding response to information widely available to everyone in a network.

MAJOR FINDINGS TO DATE

In the more than half a century since *Personal Influence* first appeared, the empirical evidence for the two-step flow hypothesis has been contested in a variety of ways. Katz (1957) offered an early critique, noting in a *Public Opinion Quarterly* piece that the Decatur study highlighted in *Personal Influence* was limited in key ways. Specifically, what Katz and Lazarsfeld (1955) report regarding opinion leader attributes is largely a function of self-designated opinion leadership; while researchers attempted to interview those supposedly influenced by opinion leaders in Decatur (as a way of validating the opinion leader designation), the task proved overwhelming (Katz, 1957). Moreover, the Decatur study documents the attribution of decision-making influence to interaction with interpersonal sources, but does not actually trace the flow of specific items of information, meaning *Personal Influence* is not a specific item diffusion study, per se.

Katz and colleagues later began to address the question of specific information diffusion with a study of physicians (Coleman, Katz, and Menzel, 1957). We see a similar focus on explicit tracking of information flow through social networks in diffusion of innovations research in the 1970s and beyond, as described by Rogers (1995, 2003). Weimann (1991), among others, highlights the methodological requirements for such inquiry with his study of interpersonal influence in Israel, which used sociometric mapping to identify social networks and then traced the flow of released information through ties that had been mutually identified by pairs of participants. Such work has confirmed that, in fact, some people are diffusion hubs relative to others. In the Weimann study, for example, those identified as influential activated more (mutually identified) ties in distributing information to which they were exposed than did others.

The Weimann (1991) study also highlights a major theme of the empirical evidence on the two-step flow to date, namely the idea that the *sequential* two-step flow notion might not be universally accurate. In other words, the assumption that influence primarily flows from general mass media outlets through opinion leaders to their followers appears to require important caveats. In an early example, Troldahl (1966) observed some direct influence from mass media on those who were ostensibly followers (rather than opinion leaders); this led him to call for a modified two-step flow model that allowed for direct exposure to mass media among virtually all individuals in a system. (This finding resonates with Bennett and Manheim's aforementioned 2006 proposal of a one-step flow possibility.) Weimann also found no significant difference between the mass media exposure of those designated as an influential and those not designated as such. Similarly, in Roch's (2005) more recent study, those designated as opinion leaders actually were no more likely than nonleaders to watch television (or use other mass media) in general, a finding consistent with other prominent studies such as Kingdon (1970) and Robinson (1976). Moreover, as Robinson (1976) demonstrated, at least some peer influence on decision-making in elections appears to operate solely at the interpersonal level without any direct reference to specific mass media content at all, making the role of mass media at best distal or even ambiguous or nonexistent at times.

Interpersonal social networks sometimes also can rival mass media outlets as a source of information and influence. Rawan (2001) highlights the example of Iran in the 1970s, where information crucial to the Iranian Revolution of 1979 spread largely through social networks connected to mosques rather than through electronic media channels (which were essentially controlled by the Shah regime). Indeed, Rawan suggests that the Shah government may not have fully grasped the importance of such traditional and oral means of communication. (One might even suggest those earlier patterns forecast the more recent role of social networks in political upheaval in the spring of 2011 in the Middle East.) More recently, de Vreese and Boomgaarden (2006) contended that interpersonal channels might even matter more than media exposure for questions of opinion change among "politically sophisticated" individuals because the interpersonal networks of such people will tend to deliver more relevant and ostensibly credible information than mass audience programming (19).

Despite these findings, both the two-step flow concept and the notion of diffusion have guided later political communication scholarship in a variety of ways. For decades, studies of political knowledge have explicitly included interpersonal interaction as a variable. Moreover, the literature on campaign strategy has often referred to the predominant two-stage nature of campaigning in which political campaign staff workers directly reach out to voters and, in turn, that campaign effort prompts voters to engage their personal social networks, thereby verifying indirect mobilization possibilities (McClurg, 2004; Rosenstone and Hansen, 1993).

In the decades following *Personal Influence*, however, political communication research nonetheless has left some of the two-step flow and diffusion terrain surprisingly uncultivated empirically, though that oversight has begun to be remedied in recent years. (See Southwell and Yzer, 2007, for a discussion.) The 1990s, for example, saw rediscovery of some of the critical elements of the two-step flow process in various political contexts. Mondak (1995) demonstrated a relationship between media exposure and political discussion, for example, and Huckfeldt (2001) found that during the 1996 US presidential election people tended to talk more with expert peers who were relatively knowledgeable about politics as opposed to people perceived to be less knowledgeable. (See also Huckfeldt and Sprague, 1995.) In the early twenty-first century, attention has turned to several key questions involving opinion leadership and the existence of additional dynamics involving talk, media exposure, and political behavior beyond those described in Katz and Lazarsfeld's work.

As Roch (2005) has noted, much of the political science research that has formally invoked the two-step flow has focused on the basic task of predicting opinion leadership. In attempting to account for opinion leadership researchers have assessed individual difference models employing variables such as socioeconomic status, media use, level of political knowledge, and preexisting political involvement, such as Black (1982),

Kingdon (1970), Levy (1978), Pan et al. (2006), or Robinson (1976). Roch's (2005) own work continues in this vein, though, importantly, she improves upon some past opinion leadership work by identifying opinion leaders through peer nomination (rather than self-identification) and also by assessing the nature of leaders' social networks. Roch's investigation of the issue of school choice finds that reading *specialized* information sources, such as topical newsletters, and having relatively *unique* personal contacts helps to set people apart as opinion leaders in that policy arena, as people with such resources were more likely to be identified as a leader than their peers.

Other research has focused on reexamining explanations for the basic bivariate relationship between political talk and political knowledge (Lenart, 1994). Some of this recent inquiry has questioned whether the relationship between conversation (with opinion leaders or others) and gains in political knowledge is always direct and causal. In other words, might talking with others about politics sometimes not just be a simple mechanism for indirect exposure to information but instead bear a more complicated relationship to one's own intentional information seeking and past and future media use? Using data from US election surveys, for example, Eveland (2004) found that the talk-knowledge relationship was actually better understood as a function of people's anticipation of conversations and consequent elaboration as a result of them than as a function of simple learning through exposure to political conversation. While Eveland discovered a positive relationship between political discussion and political knowledge, he did not identify any specific boost in knowledge from speaking with a relatively knowledgeable partner, per se. By contrast, in a study of mass media priming effects on voting decisions, Druckman (2004) found that exposure to interpersonal conversation played a *reinforcing* role, rather than simply producing main effects. That study concluded that the impact of media campaign exposure was most apparent in those voters who also reported regular interpersonal discussion about politics. In other words, conversations sometimes can reinforce campaign effects, which is a crucial but nonetheless different effect than the sort of persuasive impact of talk with an opinion leader often associated with the two-step flow.

Such studies should not be taken as evidence that the original two-step flow account of the relationship of mass communication and interpersonal communication is not plausible under some circumstances. Instead, what such work suggests is that we need a multifaceted account of the *various* roles conversation can play in understanding political campaign effects and political news impacts. (See Southwell and Yzer, 2007, for a discussion.) We also likely need to take what is being said into account before estimating the potential for interpersonal talk to act as a conduit for information and knowledge gain, suggesting that certain types of talk might matter more than others. That point is nicely illustrated by work on conversational disagreement and deliberation (Price, Cappella, and Nir, 2002). Interpersonal communication is not always particularly informative, per se. As such, a basic knowledge diffusion account alone does not sufficiently acknowledge the full array of possibilities suggested by the networked audience perspective introduced by *Personal Influence*.

What's Next? Unanswered Questions and Continuing Dilemmas

Despite advances, there remain a number of critical unanswered questions about the roles of interpersonal conversation and interaction in shaping mass media effects on political perceptions and behavior in the early twenty-first century. (See also Southwell and Yzer, 2009, for a discussion.) In general, these questions involve how conversational networks arise, whether conversational modality matters, and whether contextual factors moderate the influence of interpersonal influence.

How Do Conversational Networks Arise?

On a basic level, we need to continue to ask not only *who* serves as an opinion leader, influential, or network hub, but also *under what circumstances* such opinion leadership might occur. This general question has lingered since Katz and Lazarsfeld's original analysis. Katz (1957) concluded that opinion leadership is not simply a matter of personality (forecasting the inadequacy of a host of later studies that would focus only on individual difference variables); he noted that serving as such a hub is a function of who one is and what one knows but also whom one happens to know. How latent or potential networks get activated by circumstances is, as a result, a critical question. As Kadushin (2006) later observed, *Personal Influence* did not explicitly categorize the latent and active sources of influence in participants' social networks, which means we do not know who might have been influential under different circumstances, for example. That, in turn, suggests we need to know more about how conversational networks develop.

At least since Simmel's (1922/1955) observation that individuals stand at the intersection of multiple social circles beyond their immediate family unit, researchers have asked questions about how social networks develop and evolve and what the consequences of one's affiliations are for information exposure. Much political communication research has focused on ideological stance and network homogeneity or heterogeneity (and its consequences for debate and deliberation). Mutz and Martin (2001) summarize this literature, claiming that interpersonal networks tend to be ideologically homogeneous, at least in terms of information sharing, and even suggest that interpersonal networks expose people to more homogeneous information than do mass media outlets. Constraints on the availability of conversation partners and our tendency to selectively affiliate with like-minded people limit the potential for interpersonal networks to expose people in any particular network to vivid accounts of differing viewpoints. One answer to the question of whom opinion leaders tend to be, then, is that they tend to be similar to those whose perceptions they inform, influence, and reinforce.

Whether these patterns reflect active selection and construction of ideologically similar networks, though, is a matter of some debate. Huckfeldt and Mendez (2008) recently argued that there is actually considerable political viewpoint heterogeneity in people's conversation networks, partly as a function of environmental factors. What instead appears to explain observed patterns of homogeneity in viewpoint exposure in this study is people's tendency to avoid conversations with those in their network with whom they have experienced prior disagreement. What this suggests again is that we might usefully distinguish between active and potential networks and also that we likely need to view conversational networks as evolving over time as a result of both structural opportunity and individual experience. Work in political science, network sociology, and organizational dynamics to pinpoint the ways in which individuals activate and engage political conversational networks from among their general sets of associations will be vital to moving our understanding ahead. We need to know not just how networks form in general but also how parts of networks get activated for information sharing or conversation.

Does Conversational Modality Matter?

People can now talk using a number of different modalities, including not only face-to-face interaction and telephone conversations but also exchanges online. Consequently, we need to ask whether modality matters specifically for the types of effects we have discussed. Can new communication technologies sufficiently change conversational contexts in ways that render our current theoretical ideas moot? Available evidence suggests that there is reason to extend much of our thinking about offline discussion to online exchange. Many now rate offline and online discussion as roughly equivalent in quality; Baym and colleagues (2004) reported, for example, that college students perceived Internet-based conversation as only slightly lower in quality than face-to-face interaction. We also know, for example, that both online and face-to-face exchanges can affect political perceptions and outcomes. Price, Cappella, and Nir (2002) discovered that online dialogue between those with differing viewpoints (conducted through a WebTV project) appeared to facilitate opinion change, just as face-to-face discussion sometimes can. Hardy and Scheufele (2005) directly compared the effects of reported face-to-face discussion about politics and relevant computer-mediated interactions such as chat and found similar effects in both cases.

At the same time, there is more to exchanges in a social network than dyadic perceptions of interaction quality. We also can ask questions about the structure and extent of networks, for example, especially in light of the tangible associations now made possible by social media applications such as *Facebook*. Vilpponen and colleagues (2006) have suggested that the very structure of what they call electronic communication networks is likely different than conventional interpersonal networks. A major question in this vein involves scale and scope: To what extent do new technologies make it possible for some influential persons or opinion leaders to influence much larger networks of followers than ever before? While certainly social media provide a platform for unconventional voices (e.g., bloggers) to broadcast their views and many citizens are ostensibly connected to sizable networks online, a person is not necessarily functionally engaged in political talk with everyone to whom they are nominally connected online. The number of one's Facebook friends may not be as meaningful as the size of one's active political conversation network online, an observation that resonates nicely with Kadushin's (2006) distinction between latent and active connections between people. Efforts to assess opinion leadership as a function of Facebook friend quantity, for example, seem especially problematic in this regard. Specifically, we need to develop more sophisticated online social network measures of political conversation.

Does Context Dictate the Influence of Interpersonal Influence?

A major theme of a special issue of *Communication Theory* on conversations and campaigns was the conditional nature of conversation's place in explaining media campaign effects (Southwell and Yzer, 2009). One critical source of conditioning factors undoubtedly is situational context. Because historical, geographical, and cultural circumstances likely dictate the nature and content of interpersonal conversations that can and do occur, the two-step flow and the related impact of conversational networks on political communication should vary across time and place.

Jamieson and Kenski (2006), for example, demonstrated that the amount of political discussion in the US electorate varies over time and seems to be affected by campaign events. Later, Hardy and Scheufele's (2009) longitudinal study of a US presidential election campaign also highlighted the impact of timing on what it is that people actually discuss, which in turn seems to suggest a rise and fall in the importance of talk in campaign effects over time. A discussion that happens on the day following a major presidential debate, for example, is more likely to focus on conflict between candidate stances or rhetorical prowess than might be the case at other times during the year. When a conversation occurs in an election cycle—its situational context—likely impacts the topical priming potential and knowledge sharing potential of any given exchange between two people, which in turn should affect the extent to which that conversation is a two-step flow exemplar, a reinforcing force, or a relatively ineffectual exchange. A promising future agenda for work rooted in the two-step flow tradition could focus on better understanding this moderating impact of timing and context.

CONCLUDING THOUGHTS

The social nature of humanity guarantees the enduring relevance of the two-step flow for political communication theories. While evidence has suggested a somewhat more complicated picture of the sequence of information and influence flow than described in the earliest formulations of the two-step flow hypothesis, the general theoretical orientation suggested by that tradition continues to be relevant to political communication in the twenty-first century. As we search for ways that the connections between people complement and complicate the impact of mass media content on political behavior, future work in this vein should address questions of social network genesis, the impact of conversational modality, and the role of environmental context.

References

Baym, N. K., Zhang, Y. B., and Lin, M.-C. 2004. Social interactions across media: Interpersonal communication on the Internet, telephone, and face-to-face. *New Media & Society,* 6, 299–318.

Bennett, W. L., and Manheim, J. B. 2006. The one-step flow of communication. *The Annals of the American Academy of Political and Social Science,* 608, 213–232.

Black, J. S. 1982. Opinion leaders: Is anyone following? *Public Opinion Quarterly,* 46, 169–176.

Brosius, H. B., and Weimann, G. 1996. Who sets the agenda? Agenda-setting as two-step flow. *Communication Research,* 23, 561–580.

Coleman, J. S., Katz, E., and Menzel, H. 1957. The diffusion of an innovation among physicians. *Sociometry,* 20, 253–270.

DeFleur, M. L. 1987. The growth and decline of research on the diffusion of news, 1945–1985. *Communication Research,* 14, 109–130.

DeFleur, M. L., and Larsen, O. N. 1958. *The flow of information.* New York: Harper & Brothers.

De Vreese, C. H., and Boomgaarden, H. G. 2006. Media message flows and interpersonal communication: The conditional nature of effects on public opinion. *Communication Research,* 33, 19–37.

Druckman, J. N. 2004. Priming the vote: Campaign effects in a U.S. Senate election. *Political Psychology,* 25, 577–594.

Druckman, J. N., and Nelson, K. R. 2003. Framing and deliberation: How citizens' conversations limit elite influence. *American Journal of Political Science,* 47, 729–745.

Eveland, W. P. 2004. The effect of political discussion in producing informed citizens: The roles of information, motivation, and elaboration. *Political Communication,* 21, 177–193.

Hardy, B. W., and Scheufele, D. A. 2005. Examining differential gains from Internet use: Comparing the moderating role of talk and online interactions. *Journal of Communication,* 55, 71–84.

Hardy, B. W., and Scheufele, D. A. 2009. Presidential campaign dynamics and the ebb and flow of talk as a moderator: Media exposure, knowledge, and political discussion. *Communication Theory,* 19, 89–101.

Huckfeldt, R. 2001. The social communication of political expertise. *American Journal of Political Science,* 45, 425–438.

Huckfeldt, R., and Mendez, J. M. 2008. Moths, flames, and political engagement: Managing disagreement within communication networks. *Journal of Politics,* 70, 83–96.

Huckfeldt, R., and Sprague, J. 1995. *Citizens, politics, and social communication: Information and influence in an election campaign.* New York: Cambridge University Press.

Jamieson, K. H., and Kenski, K. 2006. Why the National Annenberg Election Survey? In D. Romer, K. Kenski, K. Winneg, C. Adasiewicz, and K. H. Jamieson (Eds.), *Capturing campaign dynamics, 2000 and 2004: The National Annenberg Election Survey* (pp. 1–13). Philadelphia: University of Pennsylvania Press.

Kadushin, C. 2006. *Personal Influence*: A radical theory of action. *The Annals of the American Academy of Political and Social Science, 608*, 270–281.

Katz, E. 1957. The two-step flow of communication: An up-to-date report on an hypothesis. *Public Opinion Quarterly, 21*, 61–78.

Katz, E. 1987. Communications research since Lazarsfeld. *Public Opinion Quarterly, 51*, s25–s45.

Katz, E. 2006. Afterword: True stories. *The Annals of the American Academy of Political and Social Science, 608*, 301–314.

Katz, E., and Lazarsfeld, P. F. 1955. *Personal influence*. Glencoe, IL: Free Press.

Kenski, K., Hardy, B. W., and Jamieson, K. H. 2010. *The Obama victory: How media, money, and message shaped the 2008 election*. New York: Oxford University Press.

Kingdon, J. W. 1970. Opinion leaders in the electorate. *Public Opinion Quarterly, 34*, 256–261.

Larsen, O. N., and Hill, R. J. 1954. Mass media and interpersonal communication in the diffusion of a news event. *American Sociological Review, 19*, 426–433.

Lazarsfeld, P. F., Berelson, B., and Gaudet, H. 1944. *The people's choice: How the voter makes up his mind in a presidential campaign*. New York: Columbia University Press.

Lenart, S. 1994. Shaping political attitudes: The impact of interpersonal communication and mass media. Thousand Oaks, CA: Sage.

Levy, M. R. 1978. Opinion leadership and television news use. *Public Opinion Quarterly, 42*, 402–406.

Livingstone, S. 2006. The influence of *Personal Influence* on the study of audiences. *The Annals of the American Academy of Political and Social Science, 608*, 233–250.

McClurg, S. D. 2004. Indirect mobilization: The social consequences of party contacts in an election campaign. *American Politics Research, 32*, 406–443.

Miller, D. C. 1945. A research note on mass communication. *American Sociological Review, 10*, 691–694.

Mondak, J. 1995. Media exposure and political discussion in U.S. elections. *Journal of Politics, 57*, 62–85.

Mutz, D. C., and Martin, P. S. 2001. Facilitating communication across lines of political difference: The role of mass media. *American Political Science Review, 95*, 97–114.

Pan, Z., Shen, L., Paek, H.-J., and Sun, Y. 2006. Mobilizing political talk in a presidential campaign: An examination of campaign effects in a deliberative framework. *Communication Research, 33*, 315–345.

Price, V. J., Cappella, J. N., and Nir, L. 2002. Does disagreement contribute to more deliberative opinion? *Political Communication, 19*, 95–112.

Rawan, S. M. 2001. Interaction between traditional communication and modern media: Implications for social change in Iran and Pakistan. In K. Hafez (Ed.), *Mass media, politics, and society in the Middle East* (pp. 175–196). Cresskill, NJ: Hampton Press.

Robinson, J. P. 1976. Interpersonal influence in election campaigns: Two-step flow hypothesis. *Public Opinion Quarterly, 40*, 304–319.

Roch, C. H. 2005. The dual roots of opinion leadership. *Journal of Politics, 67*, 110–131.

Rogers, E. M. 1962. *Diffusion of innovations* (1st ed.). New York: Free Press.

Rogers, E. M. 1995. *Diffusion of innovations* (4th ed.). New York: Free Press.

Rogers, E. M. 2003. *Diffusion of innovations* (5th ed.). New York: Free Press.

Rosengren, K. E. 1973. News diffusion: An overview. *Journalism Quarterly, 50*, 83–91.

Rosenstone, S. J., and Hansen, J. M. 1993. *Mobilization, participation, and democracy in America*. New York: MacMillan.

Scanlon, J. 1998. The search for non-existent facts in the reporting of disasters. *Journalism & Mass Communication Educator*, 53, 45–53.

Simmel, G. 1922/1955. *Conflict and the web of group affiliations*. Translated by K. H. Wolff and R. Bendix. New York: Free Press.

Simonson, P. 2006. Introduction. *The Annals of the American Academy of Political and Social Science*, 608, 6–24.

Southwell, B. G., and Yzer, M. C. 2007. The roles of interpersonal communication in mass media campaigns. In C. Beck (Ed.), *Communication Yearbook 31* (pp. 420–462). New York: Lawrence Erlbaum Associates.

Southwell, B. G., and Yzer, M. C. 2009. When (and why) interpersonal talk matters for campaigns. *Communication Theory*, 19, 1–8.

Tarde, G. 1903. *The laws of imitation*. Translated by E. W. C. Parsons. New York: H. Holt.

Troldahl, V. C. 1966. A field test of a modified "two-step flow of communication" model. *Public Opinion Quarterly*, 30, 609–623.

Vilpponen, A., Winter, S., and Sundqvist, S. 2006. Electronic word-of-mouth in online environments: Exploring referral network structure and adoption behavior. *Journal of Interactive Advertising*, 6, 71–86.

Weimann, G. 1991. The influentials: Back to the concept of opinion leaders? *Public Opinion Quarterly*, 55, 267–279.

....

CHAPTER 48

TAKING INTERDEPENDENCE SERIOUSLY

Platforms for Understanding Political Communication

....

ROBERT HUCKFELDT

STUDIES of social networks and social contexts have integrated the study of political communication directly into the study of elections, voting, and public opinion, not as a set of factors external or exogenous to individuals but rather as a process that creates interdependence among individuals. Hence the study of political communication conceives an electoral whole that is different than the sum of its citizen parts. Political communication is not self-contained and isolated from the rest of democratic politics but rather imbedded within it. Equally important, the primary focus on individuals that arises in public opinion, voting, and participation research is understood within patterns of communication linking these individuals together.

An important point in the evolution of this view dates to the efforts of scholars at the Bureau of Applied Social Research of Columbia University. Paul Lazarsfeld and colleagues revolutionized our understanding of politics and political communication with their studies of the 1940 and 1948 presidential elections as they unfolded in Elmira, New York (Lazarsfeld et al., 1948) and Erie County, Ohio (Berelson et al., 1954). Their contributions were at once substantively revealing, theoretically significant, and methodologically innovative. They revealed the lack of involvement and sophistication on the part of voters—a state of affairs commonly alleged (Ortega, 1932; Schumpeter, 1950) but seldom documented at the level of individual citizens. In their recognition of politics as a "social experience," they articulated a theoretical vision of politics built on the interdependence of citizens within the electorate, pointing toward electorates that are organized in systematic yet complex ways, with important and sometimes difficult-to-predict consequences both for individual and aggregate outcomes.

Their methodological contribution was equally profound. The Columbia studies produced the first large-scale academic effort to study public opinion, elections, and campaigns based on survey research. In doing so, these investigators introduced methodological individualism into the empirical study of electoral politics. At the same time, they were attentive to particular forms of social organization and their consequences for political communication. This was especially true for the second study, *Voting* (Berelson et al., 1954), which constitutes a classic point in the evolution of our collective understanding regarding the social dynamics underlying electoral politics (see Huckfeldt, 1983a; McPhee, 1963).

The implications of individual interdependence within electorates carry far-reaching consequences, and the aftershocks of the Lazarsfeld moment that identified politics as a "social experience" continue to reverberate not only for the way we think about politics but also for the methods and ways in which we observe the political process—in time, in space, and subject to locally specific social contingencies. Hence this chapter locates the contribution of Lazarsfeld and colleagues in a historical, intellectual context; it reviews the progress that has been made since their studies; and it points in promising directions of continued future progress.

GETTING AN OBSERVATIONAL HANDLE ON DEMOCRATIC POLITICS

The birth of modern social sciences dates at least to the 1776 publication of Adam Smith's *The Wealth of Nations*, but progress in recognizing the implications of interdependence among actors has been slow in coming.[1] The tempo increased during the second half of the nineteenth century with the development of modern sociology and fundamentally important turn-of-the-century contributions by Emile Durkheim, Max Weber, and others. For our purposes, Durkheim's contributions lie both in seeing societies as macro realities and in his ingenious analyses of the societal implications arising due to associated individuals (Durkheim, 1952). And Weber's contributions (1968, 2001) lie in the development of individualistic models for understanding these macro realities. One might say that Weber introduced Smith to Durkheim (Boudon, 1986), thereby drawing attention to the micro-macro manifold in the creation of social dynamics (Eulau, 1996).

The development of modern statistics in the late nineteenth and early twentieth centuries by Francis Galton, Karl Pearson, Ronald Fisher, and others gave rise to the growth of empirical analyses within the social sciences; but for sociologists, economists, and political scientists, the available data were nearly all based on aggregate units. This meant, in practical terms, that many analyses were based on (Pearsonian) correlations among the aggregate characteristics of spatial units. Even during this early period, as Achen and Shively (1995) demonstrate, progress was being made by a number scholars in recognizing the difficulties inherent in making cross=level inferences regarding the behavior of individuals based on the aggregate units within which those individuals were located.

An example of this awareness with respect to politics comes in the work of Tingsten (1963, 1937), who demonstrated a keen sensitivity to the issues involved in cross-level inference. In particular, his aggregate analysis of social democratic voting in Stockholm precincts pays particular attention to the likelihood of socially contingent voting on the part of working-class residents. In complementary fashion, Key's (1949) analysis of southern politics also recognizes the role of the social contingencies underlying racial hostility.

Robinson's (1950) exposé of ecological fallacies revolutionized observation in the social sciences. In short order, the sensitivities of social scientists to misleading inferences based on aggregate correlations were on high alert. Not only ecological fallacies but aggregate data in general were called into question. The message that many took away from the debate was that individual-level data are uniformly better and to be preferred. This came at an important moment in the development of the social sciences, with high-quality, large-scale surveys becoming increasingly available. Hence, for many, the obvious lesson seemed to be that problems of cross-level inference can be resolved by relying on individual-level data.

In this context, Goodman's early contributions (1953, 1959) continue to provide an important corrective. As he shows, the potential for ecological fallacies arises when the individual probabilities (p_{ij}) that a particular class of individuals (i) will engage in particular behaviors vary across aggregation units (j). If these individual-level probabilities are constant across aggregation units, the danger of ecological fallacies is eliminated. In contrast, if southern whites were more likely to be hostile toward blacks in counties with higher proportions of African Americans in the population, a simple county-level correlation between levels of support for candidates such as George Wallace or David Duke and the black proportion of the population might well be positive, but it would be a grotesque ecological fallacy to assume that African Americans were more likely to support racist candidates.

Moreover, individual-level data do not resolve the problem. That is, surveys of white citizens in the South would certainly have produced individual-level estimates of support for David Duke and George Wallace. The problem is that, without correctly specifying the interdependence between black population densities and white behavior, the individual-level model would also be misspecified, underestimating white racial hostility in some contexts and overestimating it in others. Hence the shift in the level of analysis would simply replace an ecological fallacy with an individualistic fallacy (Giles and Buckner, 1993; Voss, 1996; Wright 1976, 1977).

If individuals are interdependent, significant dangers arise in an analysis that infers either individual or group behavior simply on the basis of individual-level correlations. By combining individual-level observation with the observation of the social groups and environments where individuals were located, the Columbia research program laid the foundation for a revolution in the study of political communication that was not only substantive and theoretical but methodological as well. This revolution has not, however, fully run its course. New platforms for studying political communication are only beginning to be employed, and they carry the potential for further transformations in the ways that we understand the consequences of political communication for individual voters as well as for electorates.

CONTEXTUAL ANALYSES, INTERDEPENDENCE, AND THE IMPORTANCE OF COMMUNICATION

Admirers of the Columbia contributions have sometimes criticized the subsequent series of election studies conducted by scholars at the University of Michigan for failing to pursue the focus on individual interdependence and the social contingencies arising from political communication. Such a view ignores the important contributions of the Michigan studies and the revolution in the study of political behavior that they inspired. An accounting of the contributions made by Morningside Heights and Ann Arbor does not reduce to a zero-sum game, as several examples make vividly clear.

Miller's (1956) study of one-party politics and the voter locates survey respondents within the political contexts of their counties, demonstrating the disabling consequences for political minorities. Converse (1969) addresses the development of democratic values and political learning in his analysis "Of Time and Partisan Stability," anchoring survey data in both time and space. Butler and Stokes (1974) studied the class composition of British parliamentary constituencies and the implications for party support.[2] Jennings and Niemi (1968) and Jennings and Stoker (2008) transformed the study of political socialization by studying politics and political behavior in the context of the family, both in the cross section and over time.

Multilevel contextual analyses of politics and political behavior such as these have played a fundamental role in the growing awareness of interdependence and social contingencies in the analysis of individual political behavior. Indeed, by the early 1970s, contextual analysis had gained currency and was often seen as a way of reincorporating aggregate reality and individual interdependence into analyses of politics absent ecological fallacies.[3] At the same time, Hauser (1974) and others were articulating the dangers of "contextual fallacies." The most enduring criticisms included a failure to account fully for individual-level sources of variability before relying on contextual explanations for individual behavior, endogeneity problems, and the mechanisms responsible for producing the contextual effects. The first of these is perhaps most easily addressed, but the two latter problems are enduring issues in the study of social contingencies and interdependence.

COMMUNICATION, INTERDEPENDENCE, AND SOCIALLY CONTINGENT BEHAVIOR

A central challenge in studying contextual effects is the identification of mechanisms responsible for creating socially contingent behavior. Analysts have been well aware of the problem from the beginning of the literature (Huckfeldt, 1983a, 1983b; Langton and Rapoport, 1975; Putnam, 1966; Tingsten, 1963). Two mechanisms stand out: (1) the stochastic, probabilistic effects of social contexts on social interaction within and among social groups and (2) party mobilization efforts.

Party Mobilization Efforts

A long and distinguished literature in political science has examined the efforts on the part of party and candidate organizations to mobilize support by personally contacting individuals and encouraging them to vote, support a party or cause, or support a candidate. The earliest empirical effort was undertaken by Harold Gosnell (1927), who implemented a controlled field experiment in Chicago aimed at assessing the consequences of such contacting. By demonstrating appreciable effects, Gosnell's effort set the stage for several generations of studies that addressed party mobilization efforts (e.g., Katz and Eldersveld, 1961) based on survey self-reports.

This survey-based literature suffered from several problems related to the lack of an experimentally controlled treatment. Perhaps most important, party canvassers are opportunistic. They focus their efforts where they are likely to find supporters; hence contacting is endogenous to support in several ways. First, voter registration offices provide parties and candidates with lists of registered voters that typically include measures of party support—registration with a party or participation in a particular party's primary election. Second, even if individual-level identification is impractical, political organizations can use precinct voting returns to target particular neighborhoods. Hence party mobilization efforts key off that information, making it difficult to tell whether those who report being contacted are more likely to vote or support a party regardless of whether they are contacted (Huckfeldt and Sprague, 1992).

The study of get-out-the-vote efforts has been reinvigorated by Green and Gerber (2008; Gerber and Green, 2000) and their reintroduction of controlled field experiments. In addition to demonstrating the exogenous effects of contacting, they have helped us to reconsider its importance as a catalyst in the political communication process. Indeed, Nickerson (2008) shows that contacting is responsible for second-order effects—the contact stimulates a social communication process, magnifying the effect of the initial contact.

Social Interaction Effects

Most analyses of contextual effects have centered on a generalized social interaction mechanism as the primary vehicle for individual influence. These efforts were most immediately inspired by a series of contributions regarding cross-level inference, based on aggregate analyses, and aimed at addressing a central question regarding ecological fallacies (Achen and Shively 1995; Przeworski, 1974; Sprague 1976). If, as Goodman (1953, 1959) suggests, the problem of ecological inferences regarding individual behavior is that the behavior varies across aggregation units, why not model these effects directly?

The Sprague contribution is particularly noteworthy in this regard. Based on a social interaction argument, he employs an extension of the Goodman model to address the group-specific support for a party within spatially defined contexts. Absent individual-level data, the analysis assumes aggregate data regarding party support and group composition within each context. For ease of exposition, I am defining terms within the Tingsten framework: the political behavior of interest as the proportion voting for a social democratic candidate (D), and the social groups of interest as the working-class (S) and the nonworking-class (1-S) population proportions.

Sprague's effort is based on a traditionally employed random mixing assumption with respect to social interaction: the probabilities of interaction with working-class and non–working-class individuals are set to the proportions of these groups within the context. The level of social democratic voting is thus expressed as a function of six factors: the individual propensities that workers and nonworkers would vote for the social democratic candidates; in-group interaction effects—workers on workers and nonworkers on nonworkers; and out-group interaction effects—workers on nonworkers and nonworkers on workers.

The Sprague formulation demonstrates the problem that lies at the heart of the ecological fallacy—a lack of sufficient information for identifying behavioral parameters. The model yields six unknown behavioral parameters that are in principle estimable but only three observables—D, S, and S^2. There are two immediate solutions to this problem: arbitrarily assume that some of the behavioral parameters are zero or employ data on individuals. The primary advantage of individual-level data is that they make it possible to move beyond the logjam of indeterminacy. Hence many subsequent analyses turned to individually based contextual models, where information on individuals is combined with aggregate measures on their contexts (Books and Prysby, 1991; Dogan and Rokkan, 1974; Huckfeldt, 1986; Huckfeldt and Sprague, 1995).

While many of the problems presented by ecological regressions are resolved in contextual models, an unambiguous specification of the particular social interaction mechanism often lies beyond reach. Consider the efforts of Langton and Rapoport (1975) in Santiago and Huckfeldt (1984) in Detroit. Both efforts consider partisan behavior and working-class densities defined at the neighborhood level. Both show substantial contextual effects—members of the working class are more likely to support Allende (in

Santiago) and the Democratic Party (in Detroit). The Santiago results suggest that the effect is mediated by social interaction effects on working class loyalties. The Detroit results suggest that the political effect is mediated directly by social interaction—in particular, by the class membership of a respondent's friendship group. And a self-selection counterargument is that working-class loyalties and working-class friends encourage individuals to support corresponding parties and candidates as well as to locate themselves in working-class neighborhoods. In short, these problems lead directly to a concentrated focus on the mechanisms of interaction and communication.

INTERACTION, COMMUNICATION, AND NETWORKS

One common criticism of contextual effects such as those coming from the Detroit and Santiago studies is that neighborhoods are irrelevant to social interaction. One argument is that people choose their residential locations to reflect their social and political preferences (Bishop, 2009). Another argument is that modern societies are not organized around residential neighborhoods but rather around workplaces, places of recreation, and so on. A third argument is that people reside in a variety of locales—household, work, school, recreation—and each produces opportunities and constraints on social interaction.[4]

These issues encourage an effort to incorporate communication networks into an understanding of the micro-macro divide between voters and electorates. By incorporating network information, the *assumption* of a social interaction mechanism can instead become a focus of analysis. Social interaction and the creation of networks within contexts is not conceived as a purely random process but rather as a process in which associational preferences play a role. In a perfect world, most people would prefer enlightened associates who share their political preferences (Downs, 1957); but in the world as it is, people have multiple preferences that are realized relative to the readily available set of choices. Your perfect associate may be a Democrat who is a Dodgers fan with a great sense of humor, but such an alternative may not be available within the set of choices defined by the contexts within which you reside.

Building on an insight from Coleman (1964, chapter 16), that view is implemented in a mathematical argument and evaluated empirically in several different contexts (Huckfeldt, 1983a; Huckfeldt and Sprague, 1988). The results suggest that associational preferences can be swamped by supply—the stochastic odds of interaction are set by the mix of associational alternatives available relative to the particular contexts within which an individual resides. Members of social and political minorities may resolutely inflict their associational preferences on the construction of a communication network, but the mathematically compounding logic of the odds in a dynamic process of network formation does not favor their success.[5]

While it is often assumed that these spatial effects on the stochastic odds of interaction are primarily localized (workplaces, churches, etc.), Huckfeldt, Pappi, and Ikeda (2005) also demonstrate higher-level macro constraints on network formation and social communication. In a cross-national comparison of elections in Germany, Japan, and the United States, supporters of minor parties and their candidates are much more likely to be imbedded in communication networks that are politically heterogeneous. That is, supporters of minor German parties, minor Japanese parties, and Ross Perot's 1992 American presidential candidacy are more likely to encounter disagreement within their communication networks. In short, while it is appropriate to recognize the constraints of locally defined contexts on network formation, the effects are not *only* local, and they can be understood at much higher levels of aggregation.

These efforts sustain the argument that communication networks reflect the social contexts within which an actor is imbedded, thereby bridging the micro-macro divide in our understanding of electoral politics. Belonging to a group and developing appropriate political loyalties is not simply a matter of individual characteristics. Rather, it is a matter of being connected to the group through networks of communication and association. Finally, these efforts also suggest that communication networks, as well as the patterns of communication and interdependence they produce, cannot be wholly understood apart from the aggregate realities that lie behind their formation.

Networks as Laboratories to Study Political Communication

Until recently, most of the progress in studying network effects on political communication has come in the context of egocentric networks and snowball surveys. Individual respondents to a first-stage survey identify the individuals with whom they discuss political affairs. They respond to batteries of questions regarding their own opinions and preferences, the discussants' opinions and preferences, the nature of their relationships with each of the discussants, the frequency of communication and disagreement with the discussants, and more. A sample of these discussants is then interviewed in a subsequent survey, which poses many of the questions previously asked of main respondents.[6] These procedures, in turn, result in virtual laboratories, generating a wide range of results with respect to political communication networks among citizens. A sampling of these is summarized below.

Judgments of Others' Opinions

While main respondents are generally quite accurate in their assessments of a discussant's preferences and opinions, their perceptions are biased by their own preferences as well as by the preferences of other discussants. For example, if they support the Republican candidate and if they believe their other discussants support the Republican candidate as well, they are likely to miss the fact that one of their discussants actually supports the Democratic candidate (Huckfeldt, 2007; Huckfeldt and Sprague, 1987).

Social Contingencies on Persuasion

The persuasiveness of a socially communicated opinion is contingent on the distribution of opinions within the entire network. Hence the persuasiveness of a discussant who communicates an opinion increases when the opinion is widely shared in the remainder of the recipient's network. In this way we can say that the influence of any single informant depends on the messages sent by other informants in the network (Huckfeldt, 2007; Huckfeldt, Johnson, and Sprague, 2004).

The Importance of the Messenger's Preference Strength

The persuasiveness of a message also depends on the messenger. Informants with deeply held, unambiguous opinions are more likely to be correctly perceived and hence to be more persuasive. In contrast, there is no evidence to suggest that individuals with strongly held preferences are less likely to recognize the preferences of others (Huckfeldt, Johnson, and Sprague, 2004).

The Role of Informant Expertise

Citizens are fully capable of recognizing the political experts in their midst. Respondents' judgments regarding informant expertise are driven primarily by the informant's self-reported interest in politics and how well the informant performs on a political knowledge battery (Huckfeldt, 2001). In comparison, shared opinions between the respondent and the informant produce a very modest effect on the respondent's judgment of informant expertise (but also see Mendez and Osborn, 2010; Ryan, 2011a).

The Role of Experts

Respondents report more frequent communication with informants whom they judge to be expert, and there are likely to be two separate factors driving this effect. First, in keeping with the insights of Downs (1957), small group experiments suggest that individuals are motivated primarily by expertise rather than shared preferences in the search for informants (Ahn, Huckfeldt, and Ryan, 2010). Second, network surveys show that interested, knowledgeable individuals are more likely to discuss politics frequently

(Huckfeldt, 2001). Hence the social airwaves of democratic discussion tend to be dominated by interested citizens who have invested in the acquisition of information.

Limitations on Expert Influence

At the same time that experts are overrepresented as participants in the democratic discussion, there is no evidence to suggest that their influence is determinate or, all else equal, even that they are more influential (Huckfeldt and Sprague, 1995). Moreover, while experts may raise the level of the political conversation in aggregate terms, they also introduce their own biases. Indeed, experts can provide misleading as well as illuminating information (Ahn, Huckfeldt, and Ryan, 2010; Ahn, Huckfeldt, Mayer, and Ryan, 2013; Ahn, Isaac, and Salmon, 2008; Ryan 2010, 2011b). In short, the influence of experts is realized through their disproportionate share of air time within political discussion networks, not by any simple model of opinion leadership in which the poorly informed submit passively to expert, beneficent guidance.

Opinion Leaders and Disagreement

Opinion leaders are politically expert and interested and hence more likely to engage in political discussion (Huckfeldt, 2001). Their commitment to politics attracts them to discussion even if disagreement is the consequence, much as moths are attracted to a flame (Huckfeldt and Mendez, 2008). At the same time, the potential influence of opinion leaders depends on their location within communication networks—their influence is realized only if they come into contact with people who hold preferences that diverge from their own (Huckfeldt, Johnson, and Sprague, 2002).

The Persistence of Disagreement

Very few individuals are located in communication networks where their opinions and preferences constitute a minority viewpoint. At the same time, most individuals are located in networks where their political preferences are less than unanimously held (Huckfeldt, Johnson, and Sprague, 2004). The previous two sentences must be understood in tandem—the fact that individuals can resist persuasion by minority viewpoints makes it possible to sustain disagreement within social networks. Beth and Tom may regularly talk about politics even though they persistently disagree, but neither is likely to persuade the other so long as the remaining individuals in their respective communication networks sustain their own individually held viewpoints.

Disagreement and Ambivalence

Ambivalence is usefully seen as the consequence of multiple attitudes that point in different directions. For example, a conservative Democrat is likely to be ambivalent with respect to a wide range of contemporary political choices. Thompson, Zanna, and Griffin (1995) suggest that ambivalence is more pronounced to the extent that an individual is more intense (has more related attitudes) but less polarized (has more related attitudes that point in different directions). In this context, research efforts have shown that people located in politically heterogeneous networks are not less likely to hold politically intense attitudes regarding political candidates, but they are less likely to hold polarized attitudes. In short, higher levels of political disagreement within communication networks are likely to generate higher levels of ambivalence (Huckfeldt, Mendez, and Osborn, 2004).

Ambivalence and Political Engagement

The consequences of socially induced ambivalence for political engagement produce mixed results (Huckfeldt, Mendez, and Osborn, 2004; McClurg, 2006a, 2006b; Mutz, 2002, 2006; Nir, 2005; Nir and Druckman, 2008), and there are reasons not to be surprised. First, no one disputes that higher levels of polarization and intensity stimulate higher levels of engagement. The interesting case arises for ambivalent individuals who are high on intensity but low on polarization—a common circumstance among citizens located in large, diverse communication networks. The conclusive case has yet to be made that polarization consistently trumps intensity in lowering levels of engagement. Second, the emotional response to ambivalence is likely to be anxiety, and the response to anxiety in this context is not entirely clear. One might imagine individuals who withdraw from politics because they dislike being anxious, but one might also imagine individuals who reduce their anxiety by more in-depth processing of political stimuli. More work remains to be done (Lavine et al., 2012; Rudolph and Popp, 2007).

MOVING FORWARD: NEW PLATFORMS
FOR TAKING INTERDEPENDENCE SERIOUSLY

People do not make political choices in a social vacuum, and relatively few individuals hold views that can be reconciled with the majority viewpoint that exists among their direct social contacts. At the same time, the implications of interdependence are complex, and a great deal of progress remains to be made. The political psychology of communication and influence among and between individuals produces a wide range of questions and unresolved puzzles, and further progress depends on innovation in locating decision making relative to concrete patterns of relations among individuals (Granovetter, 1985).

One way to take interdependence seriously is to reinvigorate the study of small self-contained populations by social and political psychologists, political economists, and political scientists. The good news is that all three groups are indeed responding with novel studies of network formation in small groups. Visser and Mirabile (2004) and Levitan and Visser (2009) have produced innovative field experiments that address the development of social networks among college freshmen. These studies provide convincing evidence that self-selection does not generate politically homogeneous networks of political communication (also see Huckfeldt, 2007; Huckfeldt and Mendez, 2008; Klofstad et al., 2009) and that network composition has important consequences for attitude formation and attitude strength.

In a similar study, Lazer and colleagues (2010) follow the development of communication networks among first-year graduate students at the Kennedy School of Government. While homophily is produced along various criteria, political preference is a generally unimportant factor, even among advanced policy students. In short, self-selection along political lines is not a central factor in network construction in any of these experimental studies; hence political heterogeneity persists within the networks.

Increasingly large numbers of economists, political economists, and others (Ahn, Isaac, and Salmon, 2008; Fehr and Gächter, 2001; Ostrom, Walker, and Gardiner, 1992) are also engaged in studies of small group networks based on incentivized experiments. A great deal of this work is organized around the resolution of collective action problems through social communication, but other work addresses communication in relationship to expertise and political decision making (Ahn, Huckfeldt, and Ryan, 2010).

This new wave of small-group studies includes several crucial ingredients. First, the studies are experimental; hence the work is positioned to consider many of the difficult causal issues that are seen when attempts are made to address the network effects arising in a context where the networks are endogenous. Second, these small-group studies include an explicitly network component; hence they are designed and equipped to address concrete patterns of communication and their higher-order consequences. For example, if Betty talks to Claude, and Claude talks to Dan, and Dan talks to Ellen, the possibility of communication between Betty and Ellen can be addressed as well. More generally, we are able to move beyond the study of dyads to address the dynamic complexity of networks as well as the consequences for both individual and aggregate outcomes (Christakis and Fowler, 2009; Fowler, 2005).

Finally, a range of opportunities are currently under development for addressing complete networks of relations as opposed to samples of independent dyads. One form of this work is accomplished by intensive sampling within self-contained, naturally occurring populations. These designs have been in use by sociologists for more than fifty years (see White et al., 1976), but it is only recently that they have been entertained as useful tools for political analysis and for understanding political communication networks (Cranmer and Desmarais, 2011). Moreover, the rise of electronic social networking creates still more opportunities for studying higher-order communication networks (Goel, Mason, and Watts, 2010).

Progress in measurement and observation creates opportunities to carry forward the revolution that was begun by Lazarsfeld and colleagues. Populations of interdependent individuals tied together in recurrent patterns of communication produce electorates and electoral outcomes that are far different from those arising from a population of individuals who obtain information individually, analyze it alone, and act on it in isolation. The result will be an analytic framework that moves smoothly between individuals and aggregates tied together via networks of political communication. These networks, in turn, produce complex patterns of behavior and path-dependent outcomes, with important implications for polarization, opinion thresholds, and seemingly random yet perfectly explained events (Boudon, 1986; Huckfeldt, Johnson, and Sprague, 2004). We are, in short, at another Lazarsfeld moment in scholarly development, where future theoretical progress is being stimulated by innovation in our methods of observation.

Taking advantage of this moment requires more than a solely micro focus or a solely macro focus. The Lazarsfeld contribution addressed individuals within structured patterns of interaction relative to the connective tissue between individuals and aggregates. A renewed commitment to this strategy promises to provide insights regarding not only networks, contexts, and structures but also the psychology, economics, and politics of individual decision making within a constrained set of choices. In the language of communication networks, both the nodes (individuals) and the edges (relationships), can be addressed simultaneously, thereby revealing the complexity of the whole.

NOTES

1. Smith certainly recognized the dangers of interdependent actors for creating social contingencies on the play of free markets: "People of the same trade seldom meet together, even for merriment and diversion, but the conversation ends in a conspiracy against the public, or in some contrivance to raise prices" (2008/1776: book I, chapter 10, paragraph 82).
2. For a more recent update, see Anderson and Heath (2002).
3. For substantive and contextual discussions regarding contextual analyses, see Dogan and Rokkan (1974), Huckfeldt (1986), Boyd and Iversen (1979), Bryk and Raudenbush (2002), Huckfeldt and Sprague (1995, chapter 5), Steenburgen and Jones (2002).
4. This discussion is focused primarily on forms of association that are ongoing and personal, omitting less personal contacts encountered in everyday undertakings. These less personals encounters may be politically significant as well, but they pose challenges not addressed here.
5. The survey employed came from Edward Lauman's 1966 Detroit Area Study of white men, merged together with contextual data at the census tract level (see Laumann, 1973).
6. See Huckfeldt and Sprague (1995) and Huckfeldt, Johnson, and Sprague (2004) for methodological details.

REFERENCES

Achen, C. H., and W. P. Shively. 1995. *Cross level inference.* Chicago: University of Chicago Press.

Ahn, T. K., R. M. Isaac, and T. C. Salmon. 2008. Endogneous group formation. *Journal of Public Economic Theory* 10(2): 171–194.

Ahn, T. K., R. Huckfeldt, A. K. Mayer, and J. B. Ryan. 2013. Expertise and bias in political communication networks. *American Journal of Political Science,* 57: 357–373.

Ahn, T. K., R. Huckfeldt, and J. B. Ryan. 2010. Communication, influence, and informational asymmetries among voters. *Political Psychology,* 31(5): 763–787.

Andersen, R., and A. Heath. 2002. Class matters: The persisting effects of contextual social class on individual voting in Britain, 1964–1997. *European Sociological Review,* 18: 125–138.

Berelson, B. R., Paul F. L., and W. N. McPhee. 1954. *Voting: A study of opinion formation in a presidential election.* Chicago: University of Chicago Press.

Bishop, B., and R. G. Cushing. 2009. *The big sort: Why the clustering of like-minded America is tearing us apart.* New York: Houghton Mifflin.

Books, J. W., and C. L. Prysby. 1991. *Political behavior and the local context.* New York: Praeger.

Boudon, R. 1986. *Theories of social change.* Berkeley: University of California Press.

Boyd, L. H., Jr., and G. R. Iversen. 1979. *Contextual analysis: Concepts and statistical techniques.* Belmont, CA: Wadsworth.

Butler, D., and D. Stokes. 1974. *Political change in Britain.* 2nd ed. London: MacMillan.

Christakis, N. A., and J. H. Fowler. 2009. *Connected.* New York: Little, Brown.

Coleman, J. S. 1964. *Introduction to mathematical sociology.* New York: Free Press.

Converse, P. E. 1969. Of time and partisan stability. *Comparative Political Studies,* 2: 139–171.

Cranmer, S. J., and B. A. Desmarais. 2011. Inferential network analysis with exponential random graph models. *Political Analysis,* 19: 66–86.

Dogan, M., and S. Rokkan. 1974. *Social ecology.* Cambridge, MA: MIT Press.

Downs, A. 1957. An economic theory of democracy. New York: Harper & Row.

Druckman, J. N., and K. R. Nelson. 2003. Framing and deliberation: How citizens' conversations limit elite influence. *American Journal of Political Science,* 47: 728–744.

Durkheim, E. 1952. *Suicide.* J. A. Spaulding and G. Simpson, Transl. London: Routledge. Originally published in 1897.

Eulau, H. 1996. *Micro-macro dilemmas in political science.* Norman: University of Oklahoma Press.

Fehr, E., and S. Gächter. 2001. Altruistic punishment in humans. *Nature,* 415: 137–140

Fowler, J. H. 2005. Turnout in a small world. In A. Zuckerman (Ed.), *Social logic of politics.* New York: Temple University Press.

Fowler, J. H., and O. Smirnov. 2005. Dynamic parties and social turnout: An agent based model. *American Journal of Sociology,* 110: 10710–1094.

Gerber, A. S., and D. P. Green. 2000. The effects of canvassing, telephone calls, and direct mail on voter turnout: A field experiment. *The American Political Science Review,* 94(3): 653–663.

Giles, M. W., and M. A. Buckner. 1993. David Duke and black threat: An old hypothesis revisited. *Journal of Politics,* 55: 702–713.

Goel, S., W. Mason, and D. J. Watts. 2010. Real and perceived attitude agreement in social networks. *Journal of Personality and Social Psychology,* 99(4): 611–621.

Goodman, L. A. 1953. Ecological regressions and the behavior of individuals. *American Sociological Review,* 18: 663–666.

Goodman, L. A. 1959. Some alternatives to ecological correlation. *American Journal of Sociology*, 64: 610–625.

Green, D. P., and A. S. Gerber. 2008. *Get out the vote*. 2nd ed. Washington, DC: Brookings.

Gosnell, H. F. 1927. *Getting out the vote: An experiment in the stimulation of voting*. Chicago: University of Chicago Press.

Granovetter, M. 1985. Economic action and social structure: The problem of embeddedness. *American Journal of Sociology*, 91(3): 481–510.

Hauser, R. M. 2000. Context and consex: A cautionary tale. *American Journal of Sociology*, 75: 645–664.

Hauser, R. M. 1974. Contextual analysis revisited. *Sociological Methods and Research* 2: 365–375.

Huckfeldt, R. 1983a. Social contexts, social networks, and urban neighborhoods: Environmental constraints on friendship choice. *American Journal of Sociology*, 89: 651–669.

Huckfeldt, R. 1983b. The social context of political change: Durability, volatility, and social influence. *American Political Science Review*, 77: 929–944.

Huckfeldt, R. 1984. Political loyalties and social class ties: The mechanisms of contextual influence. *American Journal of Political Science*, 28: 399–417.

Huckfeldt, R. 1986. *Politics in context*. New York: Agathon.

Huckfeldt, R. 2001. The social communication of political expertise. *American Journal of Political Science*, 45: 425–438.

Huckfeldt, R. 2007. Unanimity, discord, and the communication of public opinion. *American Journal of Political Science*, 51: 978–995.

Huckfeldt, R., K. Ikeda, and F. U. Pappi. 2005. Patterns of disagreement in democratic politics: Comparing Germany, Japan, and the United States. *American Journal of Political Science*, 49: 497–514

Huckfeldt, R., P. E. Johnson, and J. Sprague. 2002. Political environments, political dynamics, and the survival of disagreement. *Journal of Politics*, 64(01): 1–21.

Huckfeldt, R., P. E. Johnson, and J. Sprague. 2004. *Political disagreement: The survival of diverse opinions within communication networks*. New York: Cambridge University Press.

Huckfeldt, R., and J. M. Mendez. 2008. Moths, flames, and political engagement: Managing disagreement within communication networks. *Journal of Politics*, 70: 83–96.

Huckfeldt, R., J. M. Mendez, and T. Osborn. 2004. Disagreement, ambivalence and engagement: The political consequences of heterogeneous networks. *Political Psychology*, 26: 65–96.

Huckfeldt, R., and J. Sprague. 1987. Networks in context: The social flow of political information. *American Political Science Review*, 81: 1197–1216.

Huckfeldt, R., and J. Sprague. 1988. Choice, social structure, and political information: The information coercion of minorities. *American Journal of Political Science*, 32: 467–482.

Huckfeldt, R., and J. Sprague. 1992. Political parties and electoral mobilization: Political structure, social structure, and the party canvass. *American Political Science Review*, 86: 70–86.

Huckfeldt, R., and J. Sprague. 1995. *Citizens, politics, and social communication*. New York: Cambridge University Press.

Huckfeldt, R., J. Sprague, and J. Levine. 2000. The dynamics of collective deliberation in the 1996 election: Campaign effects on accessibility, certainty, and accuracy. *American Political Science Review*, 94: 641–651.

Jennings, M. K., and R. G. Niemi. 1968. The transmission of political values from parent to child. *American Political Science Review*, 62: 169–184.

Jennings, M. K., and L. Stoker. 2008. Of time and the development of partisan polarization in the United States. *American Journal of Political Science,* 52: 619–635.

Katz, D., and S. J. Eldersveld. 1961. The impact of local party activities upon the electorate. *Public Opinion Quarterly,* 25: 1–24.

Katz, E. 1957. The two step flow of communication: An up-to-date report on an hypothesis. *Public Opinion Quarterly,* 21: 67–81.

Katz, E., and P. F. Lazarsfeld. 1955. *Personal influence: The part played by people in the flow of mass communications.* New York: Free Press.

Key, V. O., Jr. 1949. *Southern politics in state and nation.* New York: Knopf.

Klofstad, C. A., S. D. McClurg, and M. Rolfe. 2009. Measurement of political discussion networks: A comparison of two name generator procedures. *Public Opinion Quarterly,* 73: 462–483.

Langton, K. P., and R. Rapoport. 1975. Social structure, social context and partisan mobilization: Urban workers in Chile. *Comparative Political Studies,* 8: 318–344.

Laumann, E. O. 1973. *Bonds of pluralism: The form and substance of urban social networks.* New York: Wiley.

Lavine, H. G., C. D. Johnston, and M. R. Steenbergen. 2012. *The ambivalent partisan: How critical loyalty promotes democracy.* New York: Oxford University Press.

Lazarsfeld, P. F., B. Berelson, and H. Gaudet. 1948. *The people's choice: How a voter makes up his mind in a presidential campaign.* New York: Columbia University Press.

Lazer, D., B. Rubineau, N. Katz, C. Chetkovich, and M. Neblo. 2010. The coevolution of networks and political attitudes. *Political Communication,* 27: 248–274.

Levitan, L. C., and Visser, P. S. 2008. The impact of the social context on resistance to persuasion: Effortful versus effortless responses to counter-attitudinal information. *Journal of Experimental Social Psychology,* 44(3): 640–649.

Levitan, L. C., and Visser, P. S. 2009. Social network composition and attitude strength: Exploring the dynamics within newly formed social networks. *Journal of Experimental Social Psychology,* 45(5): 1057–1067.

McClurg, S. D. 2003. Social networks and political participation: The role of social interaction in explaining political participation. *Political Research Quarterly,* 56(4): 449–464.

McClurg, S. D. 2004. Indirect mobilization: The social consequences of party contacts in an election campaign. *American Politics Research,* 32(4): 406–443.

McClurg, S. D. 2006a. The electoral relevance of political talk: Examining the effect of disagreement and expertise in social networks on political participation. *American Journal of Political Science,* 50(3): 737–754.

McClurg, S. D. 2006b. Political disagreement in context: The conditional effect of neighborhood context, discussion, and disagreement on electoral participation. *Political Behavior,* 28(4): 349–366.

McPhee, W. N. 1963. *Formal theories of mass behavior.* New York: Free Press.

Mendez, J. M., and T. Osborn. 2010. Gender and the perception of knowledge in political discussion. *Political Research Quarterly,* 63: 269–279.

Miller, W. E. 1956. One party politics and the voter. *American Political Science Review,* 50: 707–725.

Mutz, D. C. 2002. The consequences of cross-cutting networks for political participation. *American Journal of Political Science,* 46(4): 838–855.

Mutz, D. C. 2006. *Hearing the other side: Deliberative versus participatory democracy.* New York: Cambridge University Press.

Mutz, D. C., and J. J. Mondak. 2006. The workplace as a context for cross-cutting political discourse. *Journal of Politics*, 1: 140–155.

Nickerson, D. 2008. Is voting contagious? Evidence from two field experiments. *American Political Science Review*, 102: 49–57.

Nir, L. 2005. Ambivalent social networks and their consequences for participation. *International Journal of Public Opinion Research*, 17(4): 422–442.

Nir, L., and J. N. Druckman. 2008. Campaign mixed-message flows and timing of vote decision. *International Journal of Public Opinion Research*, 20(3): 326–346.

Ortega y Gasset, J. 1932. *The revolt of the masses*. New York: Norton.

Ostrom, E., J. Walker, and R. Gardner. 1992. Covenants with and without a sword: Self-governance is possible. *American Political Science Review*, 86(2): 404–417.

Przeworski, A. 1974. Contextual models of political behavior. *Political Methodology*, 1: 27–61.

Putnam, Robert D. 1966. Political attitudes and the local community. *American Political Science Review*, 60(3): 640–654.

Raudenbush, R. W., and A. S. Bryk. 2002. *Hierarchical linear models*. 2nd ed. Thousand Oaks, CA: Sage.

Robinson, W. S. 1950. Ecological correlations and the behavior of individuals. *American Sociological Review* 15: 351–357.

Rudolph, T. J., and E. Popp. 2007. An information processing theory of ambivalence. *Political Psychology*, 28(5): 563–585.

Ryan, J. B. 2010. The effects of network expertise and biases on vote choice. *Political Communication*, 27(1): 44–58.

Ryan, J. B. 2011a. Accuracy and bias in perceptions of political knowledge. *Political Behavior*, 33(2): 335–356.

Ryan, J. B. 2011b. Social networks as a shortcut to correct voting. *American Journal of Political Science*, 55(4): 753–766.

Schumpeter, J. A. 1950. *Capitalism, socialism and democracy*. 3rd ed. New York: Harper & Row.

Smith, A. 2008. *An inquiry into the nature and causes of the wealth of nations: A selected edition.* K. Sutherland (Ed.). Oxford, United Kingdom: Oxford University Press. The first edition was published in 1776.

Sprague, J. 1976. Estimating a Boudon type contextual model: Some practical and theoretical problems of measurement. *Political Methodology*, 3: 333–353.

Steenbergen, M. R., and B. S. Jones. 2002. Modeling multilevel data structures. *American Journal of Political Science*, 46: 218–237.

Thompson, M. M., M. P. Zanna, and D. W. Griffin. 1995. Let's not be indifferent about (attitudinal) ambivalence. In R. E. Petty and J. A. Krosnick (Eds.), *Attitude strength: Antecedents and consequences* (pp. 361–386). Mahwah, NJ: Erlbaum.

Tingsten, H. 1963. *Political behavior: Studies in election statistics*. V. Hammarling (Transl.). Totowa, NJ: Bedminster Press. Originally published in 1937.

Visser, P. S., and Mirabile, R. R. 2004. Attitudes in the social context: The impact of social network composition on individual-level attitude strength. *Journal of Personality and Social Psychology*, 87(6): 779–795.

Voss, D. 1996. Beyond racial threat: Failure of an old hypothesis in the New South. *The Journal of Politics*, 58: 1156–1170

Weber, M. 1968. *Economy and society*. G. Roth and C. Wittich (Eds.). E. Fischoff, H. Gerth, A. M. Henerson, F. Kolegar, C. W. Mills, T. Parsons, M. Reinstein, G. Roth, E. Shils, and

C. Wittich (Transl.). New York: Bedminster Press. Originally published posthumously in 1921–1922.

Weber, M. 2001. *The Protestant ethic and the spirit of capitalism*. Talcott Parsons (Transl.). New York: Routledge. Originally published in 1905.

White, H. C., S. A. Boorman, and R. L. Breiger. 1976. Social structure from multiple networks. I. Blockmodels of roles and positions. *American Journal of Sociology*, 81: 730–780.

Wright, G. C. 1977. Contextual models of electoral behavior: The Southern Wallace vote. *American Political Science Review*, 71(June): 497–508.

Wright, G. C. 1976. Community structure and voter decision making in the South. *Public Opinion Quarterly*, 40(Summer): 201–215.

CHAPTER 49

....

DISAGREEMENT IN
POLITICAL DISCUSSION

....

LILACH NIR

INTRODUCTION

....

OBSERVERS of public discourse in contemporary American politics frequently lament the deterioration of what used to be polite exchanges between citizens into heated partisan rancor and invective-driven disagreement. What is less often noted is that exposure to disagreement—polite or otherwise—is virtually inevitable in democracies that strive to accommodate the competing political goals of multiple social groups and actors. This is not to say that the experience of encountering a difference of opinion in conversation is always comfortable or convenient. Consider, however, whether the alternatives are any better: the elimination of expressed disagreement that characterizes state-controlled public space in authoritarian regimes or the consensus and unanimity between members of a millenarian cult.

Everyday political disagreement "refers to conversations where individuals are exposed to viewpoints that are different from their own" (Klofstad, Sokhey, and McClurg, 2013, 121). Exposure to disagreement is not only inevitable in modern democracies but also a desired feature that goes hand in hand with espousing democratic values such as political tolerance. This chapter considers whether the resulting democratic education in pluralism and difference carries a toll, as some argue, and whether perhaps eternal uneasiness and self-guessing are the price of liberty.

First we review the literature on exposure to disagreement in ordinary political conversation and suggest promising directions for future research. The first section outlines the importance of disagreement as a concept for research in political communication, distinguishes it from related notions, and details different operational definitions that researchers have employed in the past. The next section highlights some of the major findings on the consequences of disagreement in political discussion among citizens.

The concluding section points to unanswered questions and outlines goals for future research on exposure to disagreement.

The Importance of Disagreement

Normative theory extols the virtues of disagreement to democracy. Theorists from Aristotle to Mill, Dewey, and Arendt praise the benefits of careful and reflective political judgment that results from encountering views unlike one's own. Diversity encourages "enlarged mentality" (Arendt, 1968, 241) and "enlightened understanding" (Dahl, 1989, 105). By interacting with others of a different view, we are made aware of competing perspectives and values, enabling us to recognize and sometimes rebut counterarguments. Disagreement thus prompts reflection about and formation of better-reasoned, higher-quality opinions. In addition to opinion quality, an increased awareness of human experiences unlike our own fosters greater understanding of and increased political tolerance for the ideas and values of different groups. Moreover, publicly aired disagreements over policy alternatives such as healthcare or education reform reveal a decision-making process that is grounded on reason rather than arbitrary (Mutz, 2002a).

Broadly defined, political disagreement is the "interaction among citizens who hold divergent viewpoints and perspectives regarding politics" (Huckfeldt et al., 2004, 3–4). Key in this definition is an expressed *divergence* of viewpoints; not just any political conversation qualifies as airing disagreements or different perspectives. The benefits of *discussing* politics in general are reviewed in Chapter 48 of this volume (Huckfeldt), whereas the current chapter focuses on the correlates of *disagreement*. Another important component of the definition is its inclusion of the interaction among *citizens*, a definition that encompasses discussions of ordinary women and men and not elites in a parliament or legislative body, journalists, or jurors whose potential disagreements on a case will be resolved by arriving at a consensual decision. Finally, disagreement is a feature of an *interaction* among citizens—between talkers in a dyad—in contrast to the benefits of exposure to non–like-minded content through mass-mediated channels (Matthes and Valenzuela, 2012).

In their groundbreaking voting studies of the 1940s, Paul Lazarsfeld and colleagues proposed the "cross pressures" hypothesis as the explanation for a form of political paralysis rooted in the conflicts and inconsistencies in voters' environments, which pulled them in opposite directions, delayed decisions, and discouraged voting (Lazarsfeld, Berelson and Gaudet, 1948). However, little empirical evidence exists to show that cross pressures dampen interest. More recently Mutz's recasting of cross pressures as "cross-cutting networks" brought to the fore inherent tensions between two models of democracy, suggesting that "the kind of environment widely assumed to encourage an open and tolerant society is not necessarily the same kind of environment that produces an enthusiastically participative one" (2002, 851).

Various conceptualizations of exposure to political differences in conversation have given rise to interrelated terms, among them *exposure to disagreement, heterogeneity, crosscutting networks, network heterogeneity, network ambivalence, dangerous discussion*, and *diverse discussion* (for further reading on terminology, see Scheufele, Hardy, Brossard, Waismel-Manor, and Nisbet, 2006; Eveland and Hively, 2009). Table 49.1 summarizes these differences.

A summary of definitions in over twenty studies reveals four main conceptualizations and measurement strategies for capturing disagreement among citizens that have emerged since the Columbia School's pioneering work on cross pressures. One measures whether the respondent's self-report registered perception of disagreement with discussants in general (e.g., see, in Table 49.1, Spencer; ED2k Baseline; DDB-Chicago). A second focuses on vote preference of the main respondent and his or her discussants, and assesses disagreement by either taking into account the number of Republican candidate supporters and number of Democratic candidate supporters as separate measures or by computing the proportion within the network that does not share the main respondent's preference (e.g., American National Election Studies [ANES]; St. Louis). A third constructs a network heterogeneity index based on the frequency of discussing politics with individuals who differ from the main respondent with respect to age, gender, education, ethnicity, and political views (e.g., Cornell; Wisconsin; Michigan). A final measurement strategy codes the observed expression in discussion groups; researchers varied systematically the composition of these groups (of opposing or like-minded partisans) to ensure high or low exposure to disagreement (e.g., Electronic Dialogue 2000 [ED2k] groups; Virtual Agora).

With a better understanding of the different definitions of disagreement in the literature, the conceptual divergence between discussing politics and disagreement and the different measurement strategies used to capture disagreement, we turn next to survey the literature addressing its consequences for various politically relevant outcomes.

MAJOR FINDINGS TO DATE

The effects of disagreement in citizens' conversations has attracted considerable scholarly attention over the past decade, for two main reasons. First, empirical evidence confirms that benefits result from exposure to political difference. Moreover, the debate about whether disagreement is beneficial or detrimental to public engagement has generated evidence to support both positions and thus continues to inspire research and conceptual refinements. This section highlights several outcomes that are unequivocally (seem and unequivocally are incompatible) associated with exposure to disagreement including greater tolerance, reflection, news exposure, careful decision-making, and acknowledgments of opposite points of view. Next, we turn to some less conclusive findings on the relative benefits of disagreement and explore whether it increases or

Table 49.1 Definitions of Disagreement

	Name	Fielding (N)	Disagreement Measures	References
1	The People's Choice, Erie County, OH	05–11/1940 Multiwave panel (N = 600)	Cross-pressures 6-item index (pp. 56–61).	Lazarsfeld et al., 1944
2	Voting Elmira, NY	06–11/1948 (n = 538)	"Attitudinal x-pressures" (p. 27): Mismatch of issue position and candidate/party choice.	Berelson et al., 1954
3	South-Bend, IN, Network Study	1984 (N = 1,512)	Ego-discussant vote preference mismatch.	Huckfeldt and Sprague, 1995
4	Cross-National Election Project, US (CNEP)	09/1992–02/1993 (N = 1,318)	Ego-discussant vote preference mismatch.	Mutz and Mondak, 2006
5	Indianapolis-St. Louis Network Study	03/1996–11/1997 (N = 2174, main Rs; N = 1,475 discussants)	Network composition: ego-discussant vote preference (mis)match (i.e., Clinton voter, Dole discussant) index of dyadic (dis)agreement in the network. Each respondent reported perception of up to five discussants.	Huckfeldt et al., 2004 Klofstad et al., 2009 McClurg, 2006a
6	British Election Study (BES)	1992 (N = 2,676) 2005 (N = 2,340)	How often they disagree with political discussion partners. 2005: Count number of groups (spouse/partner; family; friends; neighbors; workmates) for which each respondent reported that either some or all of their discussion partners supported a different party. Percent of R's net size disagreeing.	Pattie and Johnston, 2008, 2009
7	Spencer Foundation Study	1996 National (N = 780)	Crosscutting network. Perceived disagreement (3-point) on five dimensions, with up to three discussants. Differences: political views; party preference; 1996 presidential candidate preference; opinion on most political issues; and reported frequency of disagreement.	Mutz 2002a,b; 2006; Mutz and Mondak, 2006
8	U Wisconsin–Madison's Understanding Deliberation	10-11/1997 (N = 416) RDD Madison, WI, and contiguous cities, townships, and villages	Heterogeneity: four characteristics of the respondents and their primary discussion networks: age, gender, social ideology, and political information. Respondents' perceptions of the characteristics of their main discussion partners were subtracted from their own reports of these characteristics. The four difference scores were standardized and combined into an additive index.	McLeod, Scheufele, Moy, et al., 1999

(*continued*)

Table 49.1 continued

	Name	Fielding (N)	Disagreement Measures	References
9	Electronic Dialogue 2000: Surveys (ED2k)	02–03/2000 Two waves (N = 1,684) National	Perceived disagreement, 1–5 "almost never" to "almost all the time" with up to four discussants; averaged. Perceived vote preference mismatch, trial heat.	Cappella, Price, and Nir, 2002; Feldman and Price, 2008; Price, Cappella, and Nir, 2002
10	Electronic Dialogue 2000: Discussion groups	04/2000–01/2001 Multiple waves National	Experimental condition (group ideology); perceptions of opinion diversity; observed disagreement (coded utterances).	Price, Nir, and Cappella, 2005, 2006
11	American National Election Study	09–12/2000 (N = 1,551)	Ego-discussants up to four vote preference mismatch (choice of candidate for president).	Huckfeldt et al., 2004; Mutz and Mondak, 2006; Nir, 2005, 2011; Richey, 2008; Ryan, 2010
12	*Talking Politics*	10–11/2002 (N = 392) Ann Arbor, MI, contiguous cities, townships, and villages	Heterogeneity of discussion network: 10-point scale, from not at all to very often, was used for each item: frequency of political discussion with those with different characteristics with respect to age, gender, education, ethnicity, and political views; additive index.	Kwak et al., 2005
13	Social Structure and Citizenship	11–12/2002 (N = 787) RDD National	Network heterogeneity: 10-point scale, how frequently Rs discussed politics with (a) men, (b) women, (c) people with extreme right views, (d) people with extreme left views, and (e) people of a different race or ethnicity.	Scheufele et al., 2004
14	Cornell Data	10–11/2003 (N = 781)	Discussion heterogeneity: 10-point scale, how frequently respondents discuss politics with (a) men, (b) women, (c) people with extreme right views, (d) people with extreme left views, (e) people who are Democrats, (f) people who are Republicans, and (g) people of a different race or ethnicity. Structural and racial heterogeneity: county-level voting tallies, 2000 presidential; and 2000 census data by zip code on race composition.	Scheufele et al., 2006; Brundidge, 2010

(*continued*)

Table 49.1 continued

	Name	Fielding (*N*)	Disagreement Measures	References
15	Virtual Agora on Pittsburg Schools	07/2004 (N = 568) Pittsburg city residents; 179 talked online	Coded transcripts of deliberations for thought that signals disagreement with what a prior speaker said, e.g.: "I'm not sure about that," "That's not right;" "I agree . . . but. . . . "	Stromer-Galley and Muhlberger, 2009
16	Ohio State	11/2004 postelection (N = 600) Ohioans	Dangerous discussion: frequency of discussion with alters who identified with a party opposite that of the ego; safe discussion: frequency of discussion with alters who identified with same party.	Eveland and Hively, 2009
17	DDB-Chicago Life Style	02/2002–07/2005 (N = 1,446) mail in, multiple waves	Heterogeneous political talk: how frequently respondents discussed politics during the previous 3 months with (a) coworkers and (b) people who disagreed with them.	Binder et al., 2009
18	Neo-Nazi and radical environmentalist groups, online chats	Summer 2005 nonprobability sample (N = 210) (n = 114) Neo-Nazis sample only, NMandS	Averaged items on perceptual dissimilarity, in core and weaker ties ("How many of them do you think generally have opinions on political issues that are different from yours?," 1= almost none to 5 = almost all), exposure to dissimilar opinions ("How often do they express views on political issues that are different from yours?"), and political disagreement ("How often do you disagree with them when you talk about politics?").	Wojcieszak, 2009, 2010
19	Polish Dialogue Project Warsaw	2007, Pro/anti-gay issues; activist groups, students; nonprobability sample (N = 182)	Estimated frequency with which R disagreed with the views expressed by other group members (from 1, never, to 10, always).	Wojcieszak, 2011
20	American National Election Studies 2008–2009 Panel Study	09–11/2008 Multiple waves	Rs name up to 3 people that they talked to about government or politics in the last 6 months. Rs then asked how different each discussant's opinions are from their own views; responses range from 1= not different at all, to 5 = extremely different. Responses summed across all discussants and divided by net size to create the average amount of political disagreement in a respondent's social network.	Parsons, 2010; Klofstad et al., 2013

decreases political knowledge, polarizes or depolarizes attitudes, inspires or dampens participation, or is unrelated to these.

Rather than debating whether disagreement is good or bad, this review posits the conceptual coherence of the theoretical *mechanisms* researchers offer to explain how disagreement brings about these outcomes. We shall also keep in mind the considerable *variation* across studies in sampling (probability, network, or volunteer sample of die-hard activists), measurement of disagreement (see Table 49.1), measures of the different engagement outcomes, and cultural and national context.

Consensual Findings on Disagreement

Several studies agree that exposure to disagreement in conversation affects awareness of reasons for different positions, political tolerance, ambivalence, and a longer, careful consideration of vote choice. First among the benefits is an understanding of the reasons that ground ideologically different points of view. Political discussion that expresses diversity encourages "enlarged mentality" (Arendt, 1968, 241) and "enlightened under-standing" (Dahl, 1989, 105). Interacting with others who hold a different view makes us aware of perspectives and values unlike our own and prepares us to recognize and rebut counterarguments to our position. Past research offers two slightly different ways to tap such considerations: *argument repertoire* (Cappella, Price, and Nir, 2002; Price, Cappella, and Nir, 2002) and *awareness of rationales* (Mutz, 2002b). Argument reper-toire captures being cognizant of the reasons why one favors party A and dislikes party B and why other voters hold *opposite* preferences as well as reasons in favor and oppo-sition to them. Awareness of rationales captures differences in issue positions as well (e.g., Regardless of your own views, what reasons can you think of for people favoring or opposing a position such as devolution to state governments? For favoring or opposing affirmative action programs?). Despite small differences in wording, findings point to a positive association between disagreement in discussion networks and understanding the reasoning of opposite views (Mutz, 2002b; Price et al., 2002). Related analyses con-firm that disagreement in the workplace heightened awareness of rationales for opposite views (Mutz and Mondak, 2006).

Disagreement not only increases awareness of the reasons for diverse positions but also expands the capacity to tolerate detested views. *Political tolerance* refers to indi-viduals' willingness to put up with the ideas of objectionable people and groups. A per-son might detest a group of people that believes in communism, intelligent design, or feminism, but the mark of a tolerant individual is a willingness to extend civil liber-ties and free expression to his or her least liked group (Sullivan, Piereson, and Marcus, 1982). Disagreement affects tolerance by a cognitive route (i.e., awareness of reasons that ground different views) and an affective route (e.g., having a close friend who holds a different view) (Mutz, 2002b, 114). As analyses of the Spencer survey show, both famil-iarity with non–like-minded social ties and awareness of opposing rationales were asso-ciated with greater tolerance (118). Experimental tests have confirmed that exposure to *dissonant* views, and not just views more generally, increases tolerance levels (Mutz, 2002b, 122) and does so in particular when these views are attributed to an in-group member (Robinson, 2010). Furthermore, in analyses focusing on the workplace as a locus of conversation across ideological difference, Mutz and Mondak (2006) found that people who disagreed with workmates were also more tolerant of a least liked group.

Finally, research shows that exposure to disagreement also prompts consideration of conflicting information at greater length, elicits greater ambivalence, and may delay vote decisions. *Ambivalence*, an individual's simultaneous endorsement of opposite considerations that are relevant to evaluating an attitude object, carries important electoral consequences: it leads to greater variability in candidate assessments, lengthens the time for vote preference to crystallize, and weakens the correlation between preference and vote choice (Lavine, 2001). Previous research suggests that two mechanisms trigger this effect: exposure to dissent either makes people uncertain of their own views (Mutz, 2002a) or increases the salience of considerations from different perspectives (e.g., Feldman and Zaller, 1992; Huckfeldt et al., 2004; Zaller, 1992). A number of studies indeed show that disagreement correlates with greater ambivalence (Huckfeldt et al., 2004; Mutz, 2002a; Nir, 2005) and that ambivalence mediates the relationship between disagreement and late decision (Mutz, 2002a, 2006).

Mixed Findings on Disagreement

Next, we review less widely accepted findings on the effects of disagreement: Does it mobilize or demobilize voters to political action? Does it polarize or depolarize political evaluations? And what is the effect of disagreement on political knowledge?

Participation

Scholars disagree about whether disagreement in social networks mobilizes or demobilizes participation and turnout. On the one hand, divergent viewpoints deter participation: disagreement induces "cross pressures," sources of conflict and inconsistency that drive voters in opposite directions, diminish interest, foster ambivalence, delay vote crystallization, and discourage turnout (Berelson, Lazarsfeld, and McPhee, 1954, chapter 7; Lazarsfeld et al., 1948, chapter 6). According to an influential rethinking of the Columbia School's "cross pressures" hypothesis, disagreement demobilizes voters (Mutz, 2006). Crosscutting networks, Mutz has proposed, denote an individual's self-reported exposure to non–like-minded views within discussion networks. If so, disagreement deters political activity because it introduces internal ambivalence and ramps up pressures to preserve social harmony and refrain from taking sides in order not to alienate a group of non–like-minded discussants.

Additional research, however, shows divergent viewpoints do not deter participation: Indicators of sociopolitical diversity in heterogeneous networks are actually associated with higher willingness to participate in a public forum (McLeod, Scheufele, Moy, et al., 1999) as well as higher participation (Pattie and Johnston, 2009; Scheufele et al.,

2006; Scheufele, Nisbet, Brossard, and Nisbet, 2004). Forms of participation—such as attending a political meeting, rally, or speech, or circulating a petition for a candidate or issue and contacting a local public official—are predicted by network heterogeneity, even after network size and discussion frequency are taken into account (Kwak, Williams, Wang, and Lee, 2005). Political heterogeneity neither deters engagement (Huckfeldt et al., 2004) nor discourages other campaign activities (Nir, 2005). Whereas being the heroic holdout in a network completely antagonistic to one's views discourages participation, a diverse network encourages it (Nir, 2011a; but see Eveland and Hively, 2009).

Still others both show disagreement in and of itself has only a marginal effect on interest in the campaign and find no adverse effect on opinion expression and turnout (Huckfeldt et al., 2004; Pattie and Johnston, 2009; Stromer-Galley and Muhlberger, 2009). Moreover, research suggests that any effects of disagreement on decision timing and participation are *conditional*. Moderators of the effects were neighborhood ideological composition (McClurg, 2006b), an individual's opinion strength (Nir, 2005), whether the network includes knowledgeable discussants (McClurg, 2006a), and whether respondents report a tendency for conflict avoidance (Mutz, 2006) or indifference and alienation (Jang, 2009).

Depolarization

The literature also paints a less conclusive picture on attitude polarization following exposure to disagreement. The argument that disagreement depolarizes attitudes and facilitates persuasion rests on the explanation that exposure makes people uncertain of their own views or creates intrapersonal conflict and ambivalence (Mutz, 2002b, 2006). Most past research concurs with the depolarization thesis—that is, exposure precipitates *less* extreme reactions (e.g., Huckfeldt et al., 2004; Mutz, 2006; Nir, 2005). An ideologically mixed social network dampens campaign interest and delays the crystallization of vote decision, especially among the most ambivalent voters, who, as these studies show, are deterred from turning out. In addition to depolarizing attitudes and behavioral intentions, exposure to disagreement depolarizes emotions as well. For example, when exposed to disagreement, partisan respondents in the 2008 US election felt more hopeful and proud and less angry and fearful of the *out*-party candidate, and experienced a reverse pattern of less positive and more negative emotions toward the *in*-party candidate; in other words, exposure to disagreement did *not* polarize affective reactions to the out-party candidate (Parsons, 2010). Moreover, less polarized affective reactions to the candidates were correlated with the reduction of political interest, issue placement accuracy, and political participation (Parsons, 2010).

A second nuanced look suggests that depolarization may not always occur as a result of exposure to disagreement. Rather than depolarizing them, exposure to disagreement may further polarize *subgroups* such as those made up of extreme individuals and committed partisans, while it *de*polarizes moderates and the noncommitted. These individual differences highlight theoretical processes of inoculation and resistance to persuasion (McGuire, 1962, cited in Nir, 2005, 426–427). Indeed, as analyses of a representative sample of American voters have shown, exposure to disagreement affected nonambivalent individuals in a very different way than ambivalent ones; non-ambivalent voters were more likely to participate and form early a vote preference following exposure to disagreement in their network (Nir, 2005).

As a different example, a study of Polish pro- and anti-gay groups showed a face-to-face disagreement with activists from the opposite side increased some individuals' rates of high-risk activism, including their contacting media and politicians, petitioning, distributing information, taking part in actions, and joining an organization (Wojcieszak, 2011). Disagreement drove participation for individuals who held extreme attitudes. However, Wojcieszak also found that extremism in these groups was due not only to disagreement but also to the effect of high *similarity* (i.e., *agreement*), in strong and weak social ties (2010, 646). In short, it is unclear from these studies what communicative processes matter to attitude polarization, since they seem to suggest that extreme activists become equally motivated by agreement and disagreement, opinion similarity and dissimilarity.

Knowledge

A third body of divergent findings addresses whether disagreement enhances political knowledge or detracts from it. For example, early work by Mutz (2002b) and by Price et al. (2002) showed that exposure to disagreement goes hand in hand with understanding the reasoning of those holding opposing positions and with commanding a higher level of factual political knowledge. Subsequent work by Feldman and Price, however, suggested that disagreement confuses voters: specifically it dampens the positive effects of discussing politics by decreasing issue knowledge among those who frequently discussed with disagreeing others (2008). The three-way interaction, discussion frequency x disagreement x media exposure, was negatively associated with lower issue knowledge, but—importantly—only when "media" were measured as debate viewing and not when measured as newspaper and television news exposure (77).

Additional evidence paints a more positive picture of the effects of disagreement on factual issue knowledge. Network heterogeneity (i.e., discussing politics with people of different ideology and demographics) was a *positive* and significant predictor of issue knowledge, in addition to network size and discussion frequency (Kwak et al., 2005, 98).

Still others proposed to measure not factual bits of issue information, but Knowledge Structure Density (KSD), which is defined as "the extent to which individuals see connections or relationships among various concepts within the political domain—issues, individuals, or organizations" (Eveland and Hively, 2009, 212). Contrasting KSD to issue stance knowledge revealed that *less* disagreement ("safe discussion") was marginally correlated with more issue stance knowledge but unrelated to KSD. However, KSD was predicted by exposure to *more* disagreement (217) (dangerous discussion frequency, and diverse discussion). Dangerous and diverse discussions were not related to issue knowledge but were significant predictors of integration of idea elements in politically sophisticated thinking.

Summary

Mixed findings on the effect of disagreement on participation, depolarization, and knowledge may be partly reconciled by parsing the substantial variations across studies. First, studies differ considerably in their measure of exposure to "disagreement," "heterogeneity," "crosscutting networks," "deliberative," or "dangerous" discussion (see Table 49.1 in this chapter; see also Eveland and Hively's 2009 introduction for further distinctions between heterogeneity and dangerous or diverse networks and Nir [2011a] for distinguishing between competition and opposition in social networks).

Second, studies also vary in conceptualizations of "engagement" outcomes: Whereas some research views turnout and campaign recruiting as participation, other work looks at interest, attitude extremity, intention to participate in a deliberative forum, or signing petitions as an outcome. Important differences in the conceptualization and measurement of political knowledge also lead to potential divergence.

Third, some mixed findings may be attributable to differences in the population whose exposure is studied. The evidence shows differences between studies of nationally representative samples, such as the ANES, and activist samples, online or in countries outside the United States. Differences across issues are also important; it is reasonable to surmise that disagreement over the devolution of federal power to state governments (the Spencer study) or choice of candidate or party (see, in Table 49.1, ANES, ED2k, Indianapolis-St. Louis) has a slightly different dynamic than, for example, disagreement among activists in mostly Catholic Poland about gay marriage.

Fourth, a cursory inspection of the literature suggests that we, as researchers, would benefit from a wider discourse that collapses the traditional disciplinary divides between communication and political science. As reviewed, much work in the field of communication confirms scholarship developed in political science; however, the synergy between these two bodies of work is frustrated when work published in specialized journals in one discipline is not read by those in the other discipline. It is time to build cumulative knowledge through a cross-disciplinary conversation that takes into account theoretical implications of past disagreements about the effects of disagreement.

Unanswered Questions and Future Directions

Although recent scholarship has advanced our collective knowledge on disagreement, a number of questions remain worthy of further investigation. The first two involve micro-level processes. First, what underlying causal mechanisms explain different reactions to disagreement? Second, do the content and structure of disagreement alter its effects? Other unanswered questions focus on macro-level settings. What contextual and structural features, such as federalism or multiple parties, accommodate and perhaps facilitate civil exchange that acknowledges differences of opinion as an inherent part of democratic politics?

What Explains the Divergence Between Polarization and Depolarization as Reactions to Disagreement?

Research has tested both the expectation that disagreement fosters internal ambivalence (producing *less* extreme attitudes; e.g., Mutz, 2002a; Huckfeldt et al., 2004) and that it polarizes attitudes (producing *more* extreme attitudes; e.g., Wojcieszak, 2010). Understanding the mechanisms that lead from exposure to disagreement to either more ambivalence and openness to persuasion, or, in contrast, to more polarization and resistance is a first step toward resolving the debate on the effects of disagreement on political participation as well.

Three advances in research may shed light on potential explanations: personality, motivated cognitions, and situational cues. First, "Big Five" personality factors (openness to experience, conscientiousness, extraversion, agreeableness, and neuroticism) correlate predictably with individuals' reported social network size and structure; people who score high on extraversion appear to report more disagreement, whereas people high in agreeableness tend to surround themselves with like-minded others (Mondak, Hibbing, Canache, Seligson, and Anderson, 2010). Individual differences in personality may explain the correlation between respondents' reports of homogeneous networks and higher rates of participation (Nir, 2011a).

Second, in order to understand why some individuals perceive disagreement more than others do, perhaps we ought to study differences in motivation to detect and perceive disagreement. Some individuals process information as motivated partisans in search of preferred conclusions, whereas others are motivated by accuracy goals. When motivated by accuracy, people search for both confirming and disconfirming information, attend to issue-relevant information more carefully, invest cognitive effort in reasoning, and process the information more deeply, using more complex rules (Kunda, 1990). These differential motivations could explain low receptivity to counterattitudinal information (Taber and Lodge, 2006) and subsequent (mis)perceptions of public opinion and opinion climate in groups (Nir, 2011b), resulting in behaviors and actions that are based on misperceptions of agreement.

Third, recent work suggests why, in certain situations, exposure to disagreement (higher network heterogeneity) correlates with depolarization and greater openness to persuasion, whereas in other situations exposure to disagreement results in *more* resistance and polarization—cueing moral considerations such as right and wrong, fair and unfair (Ben-Nun Bloom and Levitan, 2011). In a carefully designed experiment involving two different political issues, the researchers tested whether moral cues and network composition interacted to predict persuasion. Results demonstrate that when participants were *not* cued to consider morality, increased network heterogeneity predicted greater persuasion in the counterattitudinal direction. However, when identical messages were presented in a way that invoked morality, the impact of network heterogeneity disappeared and even reversed marginally (the "boomerang" effect).

What Is the Content of Exchanges and How Is That Content Linked to Outcomes?

In addition to individual differences and situational cues, we ought to consider actual content of exchanges across lines of political difference. What is discussed in mixed partisan company and how, if at all, does the content of conversation differ from a conversations with like-minded others? We still know very little about the content of political conversations because most research relies on survey responses of reported disagreement with others rather than analyses of the content of interactions (Sokhey and Djupe, 2011). Some scholars have pioneered efforts to systematize coding of exchanges and link them to polarization in expression, opinion crystallization, satisfaction with outcomes, and so forth (Price, Nir and Cappella, 2005; Stromer-Galley, 2007; Stromer-Galley and Muhlberger, 2009). Building on the richness of this evidence from structured group deliberation, we might also consider whether exchanges in natural settings among people who disagree are necessarily bitter and hostile and deteriorate to conflict that detracts from participation.

As a second point, we ought to consider plausible mechanisms that tie exposure to disagreement with lower turnout: Perhaps in amicable crosscutting exchanges individuals focus on finding a common denominator across ideological differences; such a common denominator is often dissatisfaction with politics (Rosenberg, 1954). A commonly shared cynicism and apathy across partisan stripes, and cross-partisan *consensus* on the futility of political activity, may deter participation more than hearing *opposing* ideological arguments from others.

What Contextual, Structural, and Cultural Factors Explain Disagreement?

Additional fruitful directions point to contextual features that help to accommodate political disagreements. Past research explains why neighborhoods, workplaces, and the Internet are important contexts for the survival of disagreement by noting that since citizens (1) cannot control the composition of such structurally diverse spaces, exposure to difference is inevitable, and (2) may appreciate other amicable and praiseworthy qualities in their "wrongheaded" colleagues or neighbors. Moreover, (3) effects of such interactions may not be due to opinion differences, but rather to learning from discussing politics with knowledgeable others (see, e.g., Brundidge, 2010; Garrett, 2009; Huckfeldt et al., 2004; Huckfeldt and Sprague, 1995; McClurg, 2006; Mutz and Mondak, 2006; Scheufele et al., 2004, 2006).

These different context-level explanations can be conceptualized at larger units of analysis, such as entire countries in a cross-national comparative research. Party systems, for example, are institutional mechanisms that help contain political disagreements. How does the context of multiple parties (versus the two parties in the United States) affect citizen's discussion and disagreement? Does it help legitimate oppositional points of view? Does this form of disagreement mobilize voters? That is, does it go hand in hand with higher participation rates? Recent studies show that cross-country variations in institutional features such as multiple parties predictably correlate with discussion frequency and exposure to disagreement (Nir, 2012; Smith, 2012).

Additional cross-national variations worth exploring are the degree to which politics and media systems mirror other overlapping social cleavages (Hallin and Mancini, 2004). Disagreement in interpersonal discussions may fare very differently in a political context that is covered by a decades-old tradition of partisan press, such as that found in several European countries (e.g., Hopmann, 2012; Shehata and Strömbäck, 2011; van Kempen, 2007). Perhaps "agreeing to disagree" is relatively easier for citizens who are socialized in a civic context where political and media institutions offer a larger repertoire of political choices and outlooks.

Finally, we would do well to study the cross-national variations in valuing disagreement. In other words, we should consider conflict avoidance, argumentativeness, or outspokenness, not only as individual differences but also as culturally variable. Open opposition is negatively sanctioned in cultures that emphasize harmony and uniformity; Japanese respondents report fewer discussants and less disagreement than do their American or German counterparts (Huckfeldt, Ikeda, and Pappi, 2005; Ikeda and Huckfeldt, 2001). Others, such as Greeks or Israelis, have long held high the tradition of opposition and disputation, as inherent both to discussions of public matters and to the dialogic search for truth (Blum-Kulka, Blondheim, and HaCohen, 2002; Kakava, 2002). In a sociolinguistic study of the *dugri* form of direct speech among native Hebrew speakers, Katriel (1986) showed that this cultural way of speaking is preferred to indirectness by most Israelis. Whereas "straight talk" affirms the identity of the speakers and the trust and familiarity between them, profuse politeness is culturally interpreted as evasive, masking ulterior motives, insincere, and artificial. There is reason to expect, therefore, that avoiding open disagreements in the United States may be a cultural exception rather than the rule, and that exposure to disagreement *and* high mobilization—more often than not—go hand in hand elsewhere in the world. These related questions are well suited to a cross-national comparative investigation.

Concluding Thoughts

Exposure to disagreement in political discussion networks continues to be relevant for political communication as it highlights a normative tension between two opposing democratic ideals, the deliberative and the participatory (Mutz, 2006). Considerable research fuels this debate. An inclusive review of research over the past decade, however, suggests that neither is disagreement unequivocally and positively associated with deliberative outcomes such as knowledge gains, nor does disagreement always lead to depolarization, moderation, or decreases participation. To advance research in this area, we need to understand better the role that depolarization and polarization processes play in mediating and moderating the effects of ideologically diverse social networks on political attitudes and behavior. Future work on disagreement should consider new directions—individual differences in reporting disagreement, the content of crosscutting exchanges, and cross-national differences in political institutions, press-party parallelism, and cultural preference for outspokenness—as potentially productive avenues for further theorizing and research.

REFERENCES

Arendt, H. 1968. Truth and politics. In *Between past and future: Eight exercises in political thought* (pp. 227–264). New York: Viking Press.

Ben-Nun Bloom, P., and L. C. Levitan. 2011. We're closer than I thought: Social network heterogeneity, morality, and political persuasion. *Political Psychology*, 32(4): 643–665.

Berelson, B., P. F. Lazarsfeld, and W. N. McPhee. 1954. *Voting: A study of opinion formation in a presidential campaign*. Chicago: University of Chicago Press.

Binder, A. R., K. E. Dalrymple, D. Brossard, and D. A. Scheufele. 2009. The soul of a polarized democracy: Testing theoretical linkages between talk and attitude extremity during the 2004 presidential election. *Communication Research*, 36(3): 315–340.

Blum-Kulka, S., M. Blondheim, and G. HaCohen. 2002. Traditions of dispute: From negotiations of Talmud texts to the arena of political discourse in the media. *Journal of Pragmatics*, 34(10–11): 1569–1594.

Brundidge, J. 2010. Encountering "difference" in the contemporary public sphere: The contribution of the Internet to the heterogeneity of political discussion networks. *Journal of Communication*, 60(4): 680–700.

Cappella, J. N., V. Price, and L. Nir. 2002. Argument repertoire as a reliable and valid measure of opinion quality: Electronic dialogue during campaign 2000. *Political Communication*, 19(1):73–93.

Dahl, R. A. 1989. *Democracy and its critics*. New Haven, CT: Yale University Press.

Eveland, W. P., and M. H. Hively. 2009. Political discussion frequency, network size, and "heterogeneity" of discussion as predictors of political knowledge and participation. *Journal of Communication*, 59(2): 205–224.

Feldman, L., and V. Price. 2008. Confusion or enlightenment? How exposure to disagreement moderates the effects of political discussion and media use on candidate knowledge. *Communication Research*, 35(1): 61–87.

Feldman, S., and J. Zaller. 1992. The political culture of ambivalence: Ideological responses to the welfare state. *American Journal of Political Science*, 36(1): 268–307.

Garrett, R. K. 2009. Politically motivated reinforcement seeking: Reframing the selective exposure debate. *Journal of Communication*, 59(4): 676–699.

Hallin, D. C., and P. Mancini. 2004. *Comparing media systems: Three models of media and politics*. New York: Cambridge University Press.

Hopmann, D. N. 2012. The consequences of political disagreement in interpersonal communication: New insights from a comparative perspective. *European Journal of Political Research*, 51(2): 265–287.

Huckfeldt, R., K. Ikeda, and F. U. Pappi. 2005. Patterns of disagreement in democratic politics: Comparing Germany, Japan, and the United States. *American Journal of Political Science*, 49(3): 497–514.

Huckfeldt, R., P. E. Johnson, and J. Sprague. 2004. *Political disagreement: The survival of diverse opinions within communication networks*. New York: Cambridge University Press.

Huckfeldt, R., J. M. Mendez, and T. Osborn. 2004. Disagreement, ambivalence, and engagement: The political consequences of heterogeneous networks. *Political Psychology*, 25(1): 65–95.

Huckfeldt, R., and J. Sprague. 1995. *Citizens, politics and social communication: Information and influence in an election campaign.* New York: Cambridge University Press.

Ikeda, K., and R. Huckfeldt. 2001. Political communication and disagreement among citizens in Japan and the United States. *Political Behavior*, 23(1): 23–51.

Jang, S. J. 2009. Are diverse political networks always bad for participatory democracy? Indifference, alienation, and political disagreements. *American Politics Research*, 37(5): 879–898.

Kakava, C. 2002. Opposition in modern Greek discourse: Cultural and contextual constraints. *Journal of Pragmatics*, 34 (10–11: Negation and Disagreement): 1537–1568.

Katriel, T. 1986. *Talking straight: Dugri speech in Israeli Sabra culture.* New York: Cambridge University Press.

Klofstad, C. A., A. E. Sokhey, and S. D. McClurg. 2013. Disagreeing about disagreement: How conflict in social networks affects political behavior. *American Journal of Political Science*, 57(1): 120–134.

Kunda, Z. 1990. The case for motivated reasoning. *Psychological Bulletin*, 108: 480–498.

Kwak, N., A. Williams, X. Wang, and H. Lee. 2005. Talking politics and engaging politics: An examination of the interactive relationships between structural features of political talk and discussion engagement. *Communication Research*, 32: 87–111.

Lavine, H. 2001. The electoral consequences of ambivalence toward presidential candidates. *American Journal of Political Science*, 45: 915–929.

Lazarsfeld, P. F., B. Berelson, and H. Gaudet. 1948. *The people's choice: How the voter makes up his mind in a presidential campaign*, 2nd ed. New York: Columbia University Press. Originally published in 1944.

Matthes, J., and S. Valenzuela. 2012. Who learns from cross-cutting exposure? Motivated reasoning, counterattitudinal news coverage, and awareness of oppositional views. Presented at the annual conference of the International Communication Association, Phoenix, Arizona, May 24–28.

McClurg, S. D. 2006a. The electoral relevance of political talk: Examining disagreement and expertise effects in social networks on political participation. *American Journal of Political Science*, 50(3): 737–754.

McClurg, S. D. 2006b. Political disagreement in context: The conditional effect of neighborhood context, disagreement and political talk on electoral participation. *Political Behavior*, 28(4): 349–366.

McLeod, J. M., D. A. Scheufele, P. Moy, E. M. Horowitz, R. L. Holbert, W. W. Zhang, S. Zubric, and J. Zubric. 1999. Understanding deliberation—The effects of discussion networks on participation in a public forum. *Communication Research*, 26(6): 743–774.

Mondak, J. J., M. V. Hibbing, D. Canache, M. A. Seligson., and M. R. Anderson. 2010. Personality and civic engagement: An integrative framework for the study of trait effects on political behavior. *American Political Science Review*, 104: 85–110.

Mutz, D. C. 2002a. The consequences of cross-cutting networks for political participation. *American Journal of Political Science*, 46(4): 838–855.

Mutz, D. C. 2002b. Cross-cutting social networks: Testing democratic theory in practice. *American Political Science Review*, 96(1): 111–126.

Mutz, D. C. 2006. *Hearing the other side.* New York: Cambridge University Press.

Mutz, D. C., and J. J. Mondak. 2006. The workplace as a context for cross-cutting political discourse. *Journal of Politics*, 68(1): 140–155.

Nir, L. 2005. Ambivalent social networks and their consequences for participation. *International Journal of Public Opinion Research*, 17(4): 422–442.

Nir, L. 2011a. Disagreement and opposition in social networks: Does disagreement discourage turnout? *Political Studies*, 59(3): 674–692.

Nir, L. 2011b. Motivated reasoning and public opinion perception. *Public Opinion Quarterly*, 75(3): 504–532.

Nir, L. 2012. Cross-national differences in political discussion: Can political systems narrow deliberation gaps? *Journal of Communication* 62(3): 553–570.

Parsons, B. M. 2010. Social networks and the affective impact of political disagreement. *Political Behavior*, 32(2):181–204.

Pattie, C. J., and R. J. Johnston. 2008. It's good to talk: Talk, disagreement and tolerance. *British Journal of Political Science*, 38: 677–698.

Pattie, C. J., and R. J. Johnston. 2009. Conversation, disagreement and political participation. *Political Behavior*, 31(2): 261–285.

Price, V., J. N. Cappella, and L. Nir. 2002. Does disagreement contribute to more deliberative opinion? *Political Communication*, 19(1): 95–112.

Price, V., L. Nir, and J. N. Cappella. 2005. Framing public discussion of gay civil unions. *Public Opinion Quarterly*, 69(2): 179–212.

Price, V., L. Nir, and J. N. Cappella. 2006. Normative and informational influences in online political discussions. *Communication Theory*, 16(1): 47–74.

Richey, S. 2008. The autoregressive influence of social network political knowledge on voting behaviour. *British Journal of Political Science*, 38: 527–542.

Robinson, C. 2010. Cross-cutting messages and political tolerance: An experiment using evangelical Protestants. *Political Behavior*, 32(4): 495–515.

Rosenberg, M. 1954. Some determinants of political apathy. *Public Opinion Quarterly*, 18(4): 349–366.

Ryan, J. B. 2010. The effect of network expertise and biases on vote choice. *Political Communication*, 27(1): 44–58.

Scheufele, D. A., B. W. Hardy, D. Brossard, I. S. Waismel-Manor, and E. Nisbet. 2006. Democracy based on difference: Examining the links between structural heterogeneity, heterogeneity of discussion networks, and democratic citizenship. *Journal of Communication*, 56(4): 728–753.

Scheufele, D. A., M. C. Nisbet, D. Brossard, and E. C. Nisbet. 2004. Social structure and citizenship: Examining the impacts of social setting, network heterogeneity, and informational variables on political participation. *Political Communication*, 21(3): 315–338.

Shehata, A., and J. Strömbäck. 2011. A matter of context: A comparative study of media environments and news consumption gaps in Europe. *Political Communication*, 28(1): 110–134.

Smith, A. E. 2012. Conflict and diversity: Electoral systems, social network disagreement, and turnout in cross-national perspective. Paper presented at the Annual Meeting of the Southern Political Science Association, New Orleans.

Sokhey, A. E., and P. A. Djupe. 2011. Interpersonal networks and democratic politics. *PS-Political Science and Politics*, 44(1): 55–59.

Stromer-Galley, J. 2007. Measuring deliberation's content: A coding scheme. *Journal of Public Deliberation* 3(1), article 12. Available at: http://services.bepress.com/jpd/vol3/iss1/art12

Stromer-Galley, J., and P. Muhlberger. 2009. Agreement and disagreement in group deliberation: Effects on deliberation satisfaction, future engagement, and decision legitimacy. *Political Communication*, 26(2): 173–192.

Sullivan, J. L., J. Piereson, and G. E. Marcus. 1982. *Political tolerance and American democracy*. Chicago: University of Chicago Press.

Taber, C. S., and M. Lodge. 2006. Motivated skepticism in the evaluation of political beliefs. *American Journal of Political Science*, 50: 755–769.

van Kempen, H. 2007. Media-party parallelism and its effects: A cross-national comparative study. *Political Communication*, 24(3): 303–320.

Wojcieszak, M. 2009. "Carrying online participation offline": Mobilization by radical online groups and politically dissimilar offline ties. *Journal of Communication*, 59(3): 564–586.

Wojcieszak, M. 2010. "Don't talk to me": Effects of ideologically homogeneous online groups and politically dissimilar offline ties on extremism. *New Media and Society*, 12(4): 637–655.

Wojcieszak, M. 2011. Pulling toward or pulling away: Deliberation, disagreement, and opinion extremity in political participation. *Social Science Quarterly*, 92(1): 207–225.

Zaller, J. R. 1992. *The nature and origins of mass opinion*. New York: Cambridge University Press.

CHAPTER 50

THE INTERNAL DYNAMICS AND POLITICAL POWER OF SMALL GROUP POLITICAL DELIBERATION

JOHN GASTIL, KATHERINE R. KNOBLOCH, AND JASON GILMORE

INTRODUCTION

AGGREGATIVE models of democracy, which presuppose that institutions combine the private opinions and votes of individual citizens, dominate both American politics and political communication scholarship. This view fits both a public opinion research tradition that privileges the individual over the individual's groups and associations, and it squares with the actual counting of individual ballots. The guts of both democracy and politics, however, consist of group decision-making, public judgment, and collective action.

Deliberative democratic theory arose as a counterpoint to this and related models of democracy (Barber, 1984; Cohen, 1989; Fishkin, 1991; Mansbridge, 1983). Roughly speaking, a public or governing body engages in democratic deliberation when it undertakes a rigorous analysis of relevant values, information, and arguments to make a collective decision through an egalitarian and respectful process (Burkhalter, Gastil, and Kelshaw, 2002; Gastil, 1993). Deliberative democratic theory argues that political preferences emerge in the course of experience and through discourse. The quality of our public talk can vary from propagandistic and simple-minded name calling at one extreme to substantive but narrow and strategic debate, but there also exists the potential for more reflective and engaged deliberation. Where a representative system of government lands on the deliberative spectrum says much about the quality of its institutions, its political associations, and, ultimately, its collective decisions. More public deliberation, theorists claim, yields more skilled, responsible, and respectful citizens, more conscientious political elites, and better public policy (Chambers, 2003; Gutmann and Thompson, 2004).

This essay summarizes the implications of this body of work for the study of political communication as it occurs in small social bodies, from dyadic conversations and small groups to structured deliberative bodies, such as citizens' assemblies. We begin by illustrating the growth, impact, and importance of this relatively new area of study in political communication. The heart of the essay then reviews the findings of key studies relevant to, influenced by, or designed to advance deliberative theories of group behavior. The third section emphasizes one particular subarea of importance in this body of work—the potential power of connecting small group deliberation with large-scale public judgment. In the final section, we identify some of the key unanswered questions about group deliberation.

IMPORTANCE OF THE AREA

Writings on deliberative democracy initially had a theoretical impact by shifting attention toward forms of politics and public engagement previously neglected in the literature (e.g., Barber, 1984; Fishkin, 1991). By focusing on the quality of public talk, the deliberative theoretical framework highlighted neglected topics such as political conversation, online political discussion groups, public and town meetings, the internal dynamics of activist groups, deliberation on criminal and civil juries, and the group decision making of public officials in committees, boards, and councils (Gastil, 2008).

Initially, theoretical critique reinterpretations of the relevant works of German social theorist Jürgen Habermas (1979, 1989) yielded numerous conceptual advances (Bohman and Rehg, 1997; Dahlberg, 2005; Dryzek, 2010; Elster, 1998; Gutmann and Thompson, 1996). These debates clarified the strategic obstacles to creating new deliberative groups and institutions, the need for pluralism in both the participants and designs of deliberative forums, and the importance of deliberation complementing rather than suppressing complementary forms of politics and public discourse (Elstub, 2010; Mansbridge et al., 2010; Pearce and Littlejohn, 1997; Sanders, 1997).

While political theorists refined the deliberative model of democracy, communication scholars and others in fields as diverse as environmental studies, public affairs, social work, and geography began accumulating empirical studies of actual deliberative practices, from field case studies to surveys and laboratory experiments (Delli Carpini, Cook, and Jacobs 2004; Delli Carpini, Huddy, and Shapiro, 2002; Gastil, 2008; Karpowitz and Mendelberg, 2007; Mendelberg, 2002; Rosenberg, 2007; Ryfe, 2005; Xenos, 2011). Another body of work bridged theory, research, and practice in what some would call action research, public scholarship, or engaged scholarship. The latter studies yielded detailed accounts of experiments involving deliberative events, programs, or even institutions (Fishkin, 2009; Fung and Wright, 2003; Gastil and Levine, 2005; McCombs and Reynolds, 1999; Nabatchi et al., 2012; Renn, Webler, and Widemann, 1995; Warren and Pearse, 2008).

Taken together, these theoretical, empirical, and practical writings contributed to a rapid growth in academic work on public deliberation. Figure 50.1. shows the growth in peer-reviewed articles explicitly addressing (in their titles/abstracts) "deliberation" in the context of civic life, citizen behavior, and/or public or political issues.[1] Beginning in 1990, there were fewer than ten articles on the subject. By the end of the decade, there were more than fifty per year, and each year thereafter, there were at least 100 new articles and essays. Now, over 300 new works arrive each year, with some appearing in the *Journal of Public Deliberation*, which began publication in 2005.

The net result has been to reorient political communication research and democratic theory to look more closely at micro-level political talk and the deliberative quality of both micro and macro political processes. In the following section, we review the main findings regarding public deliberation as it occurs in groups—from its design and quality to its impact. Afterward, we look specifically at how micro-level deliberation can influence larger-scale political communication and decision-making.

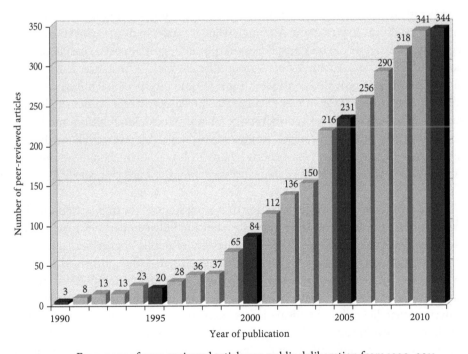

FIGURE 50.1. Frequency of peer-reviewed articles on public deliberation from 1990–2011

Note. Results shown are the total number of peer-reviewed articles per year found in a search of *Expanded Academic Index* titles and abstracts with the terms = "Deliberation" AND (Civic OR Citizen OR Political OR Public). A full-text search yields roughly ten times as many results, though that cruder method yields many false positives.

Major Research Findings

With the number of articles on deliberative democracy now numbering in the thousands, it is no longer necessary to bemoan the absence of empirical work investigating deliberative theory. Though many important propositions remain untested and there exists no consensus operationalization of deliberation itself, one can still glean important insights from the past two decades of scholarship on the subject.

Our review of that work proceeds in three parts. We begin by looking at informal public talk, followed by public forums designed specifically to promote deliberation. After doing so, we consider the factors that encourage the creation of deliberative spaces and the general public's participation in deliberation and related activities. We then address the fundamental measurement question—how one decides whether, or to what degree, a group has deliberated. Finally, we look at the question that has drawn the most interest from political communication researchers—the net impact of deliberation on participants and the wider public.

Informal Discussions

Democratic deliberation has relevance to a wide spectrum of activities, the most informal being political conversation. Although when it occurs in dyads, conversation is not a group process, it would be a mistake to sharply distinguish between casual conversations and equally unstructured small-group discussions. For instance, Huckfeldt and his colleagues have provided considerable insight into interpersonal influence through social networks, which sometimes entail dyadic linkages and other times small groups, such as gatherings of relatives, coworkers, or friends (Huckfeldt, Johnson, and Sprague, 2004; Huckfeldt and Sprague, 1995). Among other things, this research shows that when the balance of one's social connections begins to lean heavily toward an alternative political viewpoint, that creates a social pressure to move one's own views in a similar direction.

Mutz's (2006) research on conversation draws out some of the implications of diverse conversation networks. Her work suggests a tension between participatory models of democracy, which stress the volume and intensity of public engagement and a deliberative orientation that wants higher *quality* engagement—more informed and reflective and less impulsive and expressive. She finds that crosscutting political networks can promote ambivalence and a reluctance to take action. The debilitating effects of a conversational diet rich in political disagreement are worst for those averse to conflict; for them, an action such as choosing a candidate and voting requires an exceedingly painful process of confronting conflicting internal and social judgments. In the end, however, Mutz concludes that if she had to choose "between promoting like-minded networks and political activism, or heterogeneous networks and tolerance," she would "come down on the side of promoting greater heterogeneity" (148). People will always find fellow travelers, she reasons, but we must be vigilant in ensuring sufficient diversity in our political contacts.

Other works have looked more specifically at informal discussion in groups, per se. One of the earliest such studies was by Gamson (1992), who found that the media have a profound impact on the character of focus group conversations about politics. Gamson noted that people tended to draw on what they had recently heard in the media to provide content to their conversations. Years later, Walsh (2004) found the same thing in an intensive ethnographic study of a group of older friends who regularly met to talk about both personal and political topics. With online access and social media bringing media content even closer, this pattern likely characterizes informal discussion more than ever. In sum, informal political exchanges in conversational networks and discussion groups can exert considerable influence on political preferences, and political content accessed at the macro level carries through to those exchanges, if not necessarily in a formal "two-step flow."

Deliberative Designs

Though some theorists count such informal exchanges as the most commonplace manifestations of quasi-deliberation (Mutz, 2006) or "discursive participation" (Jacobs, Cook, and Delli Carpini, 2009), settings more relevant to the deliberative ideal involve more consciously designed public spaces. The least demanding of these are civic educational spaces, such as the National Issues Forums created by the Kettering Foundation, which aim to inform participants' public judgments, if not reach a collective decision (Gastil and Dillard, 1999a; Melville, Willingham, and Dedrick, 2005). These processes involve considerable disagreement, leading to an ideological sharpening of political viewpoints (Gastil and Dillard, 1999b). At the same time, participants engage in rich narrative exchanges (Ryfe, 2006) that may combine with the robust debate to increase their general appetite for future deliberation (Gastil, 2004).

Though National Issues Forums may be among the most widely practiced forms of public deliberation, the deliberative polls[2] have garnered the most international attention (Fishkin, 2009) and have even been tagged as the "gold standard" for deliberation (Mansbridge, 2010). As Fishkin and his colleagues have demonstrated more than once, the deliberative poll can produce a significant increase in political knowledge, even after taking into account gains one might have expected from simply reading the briefing booklets that accompany these events (Fishkin 2009; Luskin, Fishkin, and Jowell, 2002). The deliberative poll goes a step beyond an issues forum by extending the discussion from two hours to two or three days and by bracketing the discussion with pre- and post-deliberation questionnaires to glean the "reflective judgment" of the public, as measured by the aggregated private opinions of the poll's participants. The polls take a step back, however, in orienting most of the discussion toward querying experts and advocates, thereby spending relatively little time on directly discussing policy alternatives in small groups. Similar processes, such as twenty-first-century town

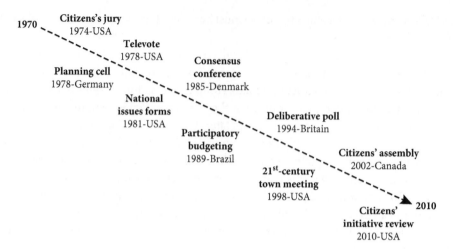

FIGURE 50.2. A timeline of selected modern deliberative designs

meetings (Lukensmeyer, Goldman, and Brigham, 2005), have used alternative designs to promote more intensive face-to-face deliberation while still aggregating the collective sentiments of those in attendance.

Issues forums and polls often operate as educational exercises, only informally advisory to a government body (though there have been exceptions, as illustrated by Fishkin, He, Luskin, and Siu, 2010). By contrast, there exists an array of deliberative designs meant to give concrete advice to policymakers or even set policy, often on administrative questions. These intensive citizen processes typically last a week or are held over a series of weeks or months and go by names such as citizens' juries (Crosby and Nethercutt, 2005; Smith and Wales, 2000) or consensus conferences and planning cells (Hendriks, 2005). With a history of practice dating to the 1970s, the citizens' juries and many other public engagement methods have created a track record of deliberative performance that predates both issues forums and deliberative polls, as shown in Figure 50.2.

Finally, the past few years have brought into being processes that combine the intensive policy deliberation of citizens' juries with the institutional power previously reserved for such exceptional processes as Brazil's Participatory Budgeting (Wampler, 2007). Innovations such as the British Columbia Citizens' Assembly (Warren and Pearse, 2008) and the Oregon Citizens' Initiative Review (Knobloch et al., 2013) that provide smaller deliberative bodies of citizens with the power to set the agenda or influence voters in initiative and referenda elections will receive special consideration in the next main section of this essay.

Promoting and Participating in Deliberation

Many of the deliberative processes shown in Figure 50.2. use clear and powerful incentives to ensure public participation in their events. These include money (direct

payments for participants' time, honoraria, and/or reimbursement for travel and lodg-
ing expenses), public recognition, or even a clear role in shaping public policy. Short
of these, however, one line of research has found little public interest in deliberation,
arguing that the average citizen actually prefers to stay on the sidelines and let elected
officials govern for them (Hibbing and Theiss-Morse, 2002). Subsequent research has
suggested that this view aptly describes only the least politically engaged strata of the
public (Lipsitz, Trost, and Grossman, 2005) or grossly underestimates the general public's appetite for more meaningful participation in public discussion, at least when it
involves low-stress direct encounters with public officials (Neblo et al., 2010).

More fundamentally, researchers have considered the underlying cultural forces that
make a society more or less inclined to deliberate (Keith, 2007). Dryzek (1990, 2010) has
tracked the way changing norms of government and public discourse have facilitated
the emergence of deliberative ideals, but there appears to exist an even broader cultural
sense of how public discussion is *supposed* to occur (Bormann, 1996). Researchers have
traced norms for democratic group deliberation back to social movements, which have
proved particularly important in readying disenfranchised group "enclaves" for wider
public deliberation (Evans and Boyte, 1992; Karpowitz, Raphael, and Hammond, 2009;
Polletta, 2002). Deliberative habits and expectations can also be elicited by institutions,
for example, from serving on juries (Gastil et al., 2010), participating in public forums
(Walsh, 2003), or engaging in structured community programs designed to reinforce
deliberative norms (Potapchuk, Carlson, and Kennedy, 2005).

Measuring Deliberation

*The diversity of deliberative settings makes measuring their deliberative quality increas-
ingly important.* Evaluations generally begin by conceptualizing ideal deliberation, and
although the theoretical and empirical understandings of it have not always evolved in
tandem (Thompson, 2008), a growing consensus has begun to articulate deliberation
as an egalitarian exchange of information oriented toward forming better judgments
(Benhabib, 1996; Cohen, 1989; Gutmann and Thompson, 1996). This definition, which
takes into account lived-inequalities while maintaining deliberation's commitment
to rationality, has three broad criteria: (1) analytic rigor based on the careful weighing of information, values and consequences, (2) democratic discussion requiring
equal participation and mutual respect and consideration, and (3) a noncoercive and
information-based decision-making process (Gastil, Knobloch, and Kelly, 2012).

To assess whether deliberative events satisfy these critera, deliberation scholars
rely on three primary methods: transcript analysis, participant assessments, and/or
case studies. Transcript analysis may be undertaken using several distinct methods,
including close textual analysis (Mendelberg and Oleske, 2000), narrative analysis
(Black, 2008; Ryfe, 2005, 2006), or content analysis (Hart and Jarvis, 1999; Haug and
Teune, 2008, Polletta and Lee, 2006; Steenbergen et al., 2003; Steiner, 2012; Stromer-
Galley, 2007), the former two allowing scholars to closely analyze the transcripts, and

the latter facilitating the analysis of large amounts of text—an increasing necessity as large-scale, intensive deliberation often produces thousands of pages of transcripts. Alternatively, scholars using participant assessments have relied on surveys, questionnaires, and interviews of participants to examine whether participation meets normative conceptions of deliberation (Button and Mattson, 1999; Gastil and Sawyer, 2004; Jacobs, Cook, and Delli Carpini, 2009; Polletta, 2008; Ryfe, 2007), providing indications of deliberative processes, such as the presence of respect and comprehension, not easily operationalized through other methods (Gastil and Sawyer, 2004; Hartz-Karp, 2005). Finally, case studies allow scholars to integrate content analysis, close textual analysis, and participant assessments as well as participant observations, interviews with organizers, and analyses of media coverage to provide a more in-depth assessment of a group's deliberation (Button and Mattson, 1999; Edwards, Hindmarsh, Mercer, and Rownland, 2008; Hartz-Karp, 2005; Mendleberg and Olseke, 2000).

The Quality of Deliberation in Groups

Using these methods, scholars have begun to parcel out which processes can promote deliberation and which obstruct it, though specific understandings of the relation between structure and deliberative quality remain underdeveloped (Black, 2012; Ryfe, 2006). Perhaps most importantly, homogeneity can prevent deliberation from occurring. Without diversity in demographic make-up, cultural orientation, and political leanings, deliberation can devolve into enclave communication as participants fail to confront one another with opposing information or viewpoints, a situation that often results in movement toward more extremist positions (Mendelberg and Oleske, 2000; Mutz, 2006; Sunstein, 2000). Even with diversity, however, pressure toward consensus can hamper deliberation when people feel pressure to conform to majority opinion (Karpowitz and Mansbridge, 2005).

Quality deliberation also often depends on the structure of the deliberative event. The incorporation of expert testimony, question-and-answer sessions, and the integration of small- and large-group discussions can facilitate deliberation, but the exclusion of other processes, such as values discussions, may hinder the participants' ability to fully engage in it (Edwards et al., 2008; Knobloch et al., 2013). Similarly, though facilitation can encourage turn-taking, equitable and informative conversation, and progress toward the end goal, overly directive facilitation or an inability for participants' to make changes to the agenda can disrupt the flow of conversation and prevent participants from engaging in passionate conversations or seeking outside solutions (Mansbridge et al., 2006; Polletta, 2008; Ryfe, 2006).

Furthermore, discussion, emotion, humor (Mansbridge et al., 2006), and storytelling (Black, 2008; Ryfe, 2006) foster deliberation by creating alternative means for providing information and promoting a positive social atmosphere, even though the presence of intensely negative emotions may actually hinder deliberative discussion (Mansbridge et al.). Overly technical language, or jargon, can also prevent equitable deliberation, either because participants find the discussion hard to follow or are intimidated by the expertise implied by the use of such vocabulary (Edwards et al., 2008; Mansbridge et al.).

Finally, deliberative events may be evaluated based on the outcomes they produce (Barrett, Wyman, and Coelho, 2012; Kinney, 2012; Pincock, 2012). For example, Goodin and Dryzek (2006) have charted eight ways that deliberative forums may affect the larger community, such as incorporation in the policy process and legitimating public decisions. Without connections to governing institutions and decision-making organizations or significant publicity campaigns, however, deliberative events risk having little impact on the larger public.

The Impact of Group Deliberation

Gauging the success of deliberative groups, however, requires not only measuring deliberative quality but also examining the *impact* of these events on participants and the wider public. The early theoretical literature on deliberation included many protohypotheses, the most basic of which argued that deliberation can have an educative effect on citizens (Nabatchi, 2010) and promote attitudes and actions consistent with a more deliberative democracy (Burkhalter et al., 2002; Carcasson and Christopher, 2008; Cohen, 1989; Fung and Wright, 2003; Gutmann and Thompson, 2004; Pincock, 2012).

Perhaps deliberation's most consistently validated impact is increased participant knowledge. Presenting discussants with expert testimony and an opportunity to ask questions and converse on the topic with fellow citizens, face-to-face (Barabas, 2004; Fishkin, 1991, 1995, 2009; Gastil and Dillard, 1999a) and in online deliberative forums (Esterling, Neblo, and Lazer, 2011; Luskin, Fishkin, and Iyengar, 2006; Min, 2007) can increase participants' knowledge of the issue on which the process has focused. At times, participants will also update their opinions to match their knowledge gains (Barabas; Luskin, Fishkin, and Jowell, 2002).

Deliberation has also been shown to produce changes in participants' attitudes toward political processes, other citizens, and themselves. Several forms of deliberative participation, ranging from informal discursive participation to jury service and large deliberative events, have been shown to boost external efficacy or trust in governing officials and institutions (Fishkin, 2009, 141; Gastil et al., 2010; Goidel et al., 2008; Jacobs et al., 2009; Nabatchi, 2010). Further, as individuals engage in the practice of deliberation, they often begin to understand their capacities for engaging in governance and political involvement, which increases their internal and external efficacy (Gastil and Dillard, 1999b; Fishkin, 2009). Moreover, as a result of the process of working with other members of their community to solve a common problem, participants often begin to feel a sense of collective identity (Hartz-Karp et al., 2010).

In addition to these cognitive changes, participants often experience behavioral changes, increasing both their civic skills and their political and deliberative engagement. Deliberation likely allows participants to build communicative skills necessary for engagement in political life, including the ability both to engage in civil conversation with those who hold opposing views and to evaluate arguments and claims (Burkhalter et al., 2002; Fung and Wright, 2003). Likely stemming from the development of such skills, deliberative participation is particularly effective at increasing communicative or deliberative engagement, such as attention to political media, engagement in political conversations, and attendance at public forums, and has been shown to increase the diversity of participants' conversation networks (Gastil, 2004; McLeod et al., 1999). Similar effects have been found in more traditional or institutionalized forms of engagement with both face-to-face and online deliberation shown to increase participation in voting, electoral engagement, and volunteering (Gastil, 2000; Gastil et al., 2010; Jacobs et al., 2009; Price and Cappella, 2002).

Such cognitive and behavioral effects may not be limited to those who directly participate in the deliberative process. As discussed in the following section, several deliberative forums attempt to connect small bodies of deliberative citizens with the larger public. When this occurs, deliberation may have cascading effects, increasing the public's perception of the legitimacy of the decision-making process and possibly its political engagement and the wider public's knowledge, efficacy, and identity (Dryzek, 2010; Fung, 2003; Goodin and Dryzek, 2006), though these claims have not yet received significant empirical scrutiny.

CONNECTING MICRO- AND MACRO-LEVEL DELIBERATION

Among the many promising directions in the theory and practice of small group deliberation, what stands out are efforts to link these small bodies to larger political units. Dryzek (2010) has referred to this as the "macro consequences" of "mini-publics," and he outlines a range of potential impacts, from direct policymaking to a strong policy-advisory role to guiding the course of public debates and public opinion. Here, we highlight two examples to show how smaller deliberative groups can affect the decision-making processes of larger publics.

The 2004 British Columbia Citizens' Assembly (Warren and Pearse, 2008) gathered 160 randomly selected citizens to engage in a series of face-to-face meetings on how to reform the province's electoral process. After small- and large-group meetings, public hearings, and diverse expert testimony, the Assembly voted 146-7 in favor of replacing the status quo with a Single Transferable Vote model, which lets voters rank candidates within multimember districts. From the outset, it was understood that the Assembly's recommendation would go before the people of British Columbia for ratification, and in 2005, a majority of voters in 77 of British Columbia's 79 ridings (districts) approved the Assembly's proposal, with 57 percent of all votes cast in favor of the proposal. Unfortunately, the British Columbian legislature had set the bar for passage at 60 percent of the popular vote. More importantly, however, voter surveys showed that considerable support for the proposal came from the public's perception that the deliberative process had been legitimate (Cutler and Johnson, 2008). Many of those who reported being confused by the proposed system nonetheless voted in favor of it because they had confidence in the deliberative quality of the citizens' assembly itself. As Dryzek (2010) sees it, this case demonstrated how small-scale public deliberation can play a representative role with potentially more public legitimacy than an elected body—something particularly important for setting policies, such as electoral reforms, which directly affect the fortunes of elected officials.

The 2010 Oregon Citizens' Initiative Review (CIR) provides a case where micro deliberation may have improved the quality of macro public deliberation when the larger public has already been tasked with making policy decisions through the initiative process. The CIR convened two small deliberative groups of randomly selected Oregon citizens to study upcoming ballot measures. The first panel deliberated on a proposal to increase minimum sentences for repeated cases of felony sex crimes or driving while inebriated. The second reviewed a proposal to establish a more robust medical marijuana supply system in Oregon. The CIR had a direct connection to voters through a pair of one-page citizens' statements it place in the official Voters' Pamphlet, which Oregon's secretary of state mailed to every registered voter's household. A combination of panel and rolling cross-sectional surveys showed that reading the CIR's statements had a strong negative effect on voters' likelihood of supporting both measures, and at the same time increased policy knowledge about each (Gastil and Knobloch, 2010). The success of the CIR led the Oregon state legislature to make it a permanent part of that state's electoral process.

These and other examples from across the globe (Dryzek, 2010) show the potential for small-group deliberation to influence public opinion and public policy. Though it remains important to study small political groups in their own right, these examples of institutional innovation suggest that the size of the deliberative body does not necessarily determine the extent of its impact.

Unanswered Questions

The sheer volume of scholarship on deliberative democracy and political deliberation in small groups can obscure the limited knowledge that has accumulated on these subjects in the past two decades. The preceding sections show some of the insight gained to this point, but the subject domain remains so vast that the specific questions have only been answered partially. Moreover, the answers gained often have untested cultural and temporal boundaries, with the bulk of the research and experimentation on the subject happening in a handful of countries, particularly the United States, Canada, Australia, Brazil, England, and the European Union. Much can be learned from newer studies that use deliberative democratic theory to frame cross-national research questions (Steiner,

2012) or studies based in novel settings, such as rural town meetings in India (e.g., Ban, Jha, and Rao, 2012).

Among the most pressing questions are those concerning the deliberative process itself. The most robust public deliberation processes, for instance, use professional facilitators, but little has been done to categorize the different facilitation strategies and their net impact on different deliberative groups. The role of experts and professional briefing materials has also been taken for granted, but we need to know more how to incorporate these elements in a way that breaks through preexisting citizen biases without giving undue credence to the expert sources, which are usually chosen by the organizers of the deliberative process. We also know that storytelling and emotion play a sizeable role in deliberation, but we lack a clear sense of how to integrate these with the argument and reason-giving norms fundamental to deliberative success. Finally, all of these questions require a contextual sensitivity to the widely varying purposes of different deliberative fora, from civic education to community building to policymaking.

The other pressing set of questions concerns long-term cultural and institutional effects. The case of the jury system shows how taken-for-granted deliberation can become cultural and political practice (Dwyer, 2002), but it provides only limited insight into what will happen should newer forms of group deliberation become "embedded" in society (Fagotto and Fung, 2006). Over time, how might deliberative processes like the Oregon CIR affect the interplay of values and knowledge in public opinion formation? Can events like the British Columbia Citizens' Assembly set new norms for public debate within bodies of elected officials? Can regularized citizen deliberative bodies, like the Danish Board of Technology (Kluver, 2000), change the relationship between public officials and the lay public, restoring each group's confidence in the other's judgment, when formed in more deliberative environments?

Questions such as these will continue to interest scholars for years to come. Already, this area of research has drawn the attention of preeminent political communication researchers while also inspiring new generations of researchers to identify this topic as their primary area of study. The combined forces of these different generations, spread across a wide range of academic fields, should provide considerable insight into why, how, and to what effect citizens deliberate together in small groups.

NOTES

1. To identify only articles that were directly related to deliberation scholarship we searched for the word "deliberation" coupled with "civic, citizen, political, or public" within the title and abstract in Academic Search Complete (ASC). The ASC database offers a uniquely robust and reliable overview of peer-reviewed journal articles available in the social sciences. The same search terms used in more inclusive databases yield larger returns; Google Scholar, for instance, finds 11,000 articles on deliberation in the social sciences in 2010 alone.

2. Note that this and many other of the proper-noun processes listed herein have registered service marks or trademarks. Their names can be used to describe public processes only with the explicit permission of their affiliated organizations.

References

Ban, R., S. Jha, and V. Rao. 2012. Who has voice in a deliberative democracy? Evidence from transcripts of village parliaments in south India. *Journal of Development Economics*, 99, 428–438.

Barabas, J. 2004. How deliberation affects policy opinions. *American Political Science Review*, 98(4), 687–701.

Barber, B. R. 1984. *Strong democracy: Participatory politics for a new age*. Berkeley: University of California Press.

Barrett, G., M. Wyman, and V. Coelho. 2012. Assessing policy impacts of deliberative civic engagement: Comparing engagement in the health policy processes of Brazil and Canada. Pp. 181–204 in *Democracy in motion: Evaluating the practice and impact of deliberative civic engagement*, ed. T. Nabatchi, J. Gastil, M. Weiksner, and M. Leighninger. New York: Oxford University Press.

Benhabib, S. 1996. Toward a deliberative model of democratic legitimacy. In S. Benhabib (Ed.), *Democracy and difference: Contesting the boundaries of the political* (pp. 67–94). Princeton, NJ: Princeton University Press.

Black, L. 2012. How people communicate during deliberative events. In T. Nabatchi, J. Gastil, M. Weiksner, and M. Leighninger (Eds.), *Democracy in motion: Evaluating the practice and impact of deliberative civic engagement* (pp. 59–82). New York: Oxford University Press.

Black, L. W. 2008. Deliberation, storytelling, and dialogic moments. *Communication Theory*, 18(1), 93–116.

Bohman, J. F., and W. Rehg, eds. 1997. *Deliberative democracy: Essays on reason and politics*. Cambridge: MIT Press.

Bormann, E. G. 1996. Symbolic convergence theory and communication in group decision making. In R. Y. Hirokawa and M. S. Poole (Eds.), *Communication and group decision making*, 2nd ed. (pp. 81–113). Beverly Hills: Sage.

Burkhalter, S., J. Gastil, and T. Kelshaw. 2002. A conceptual definition and theoretical model of public deliberation in small face-to-face groups. *Communication Theory*, 12, 398–422.

Button, M., and K. Mattson. 1999. Deliberative democracy in practice: Challenges and prospects for civic deliberation. *Polity*, 31(4), 609–637.

Carcasson, M., and E. Christopher. 2008. *The goals & consequences of deliberation: Key findings and challenges for deliberative practitioners*. Kettering Foundation Research Report No. 52706.

Chambers, S. 2003. Deliberative democratic theory. *Annual Review of Political Science*, 6, 307–326.

Cohen, J. 1989. Deliberation and democratic legitimacy. In P. Pettit and A. Hamlin (Eds.), *The good polity* (pp. 17–34). New York: Basil Blackwell.

Crosby, N., and D. Nethercut. 2005. Citizen juries: Creating a trustworthy voice of the people. Pp. 111–119 in *The deliberative democracy handbook: Strategies for effective civic engagement in the 21st century*, ed. J. Gastil and P. Levine. San Francisco: Jossey-Bass.

Cutler, F., and R. Johnston. 2008. Deliberation, information and trust: The BC Citizens' Assembly as agenda setter. In M. Warren and H. Pearse (Eds.), *Designing deliberative democracy: The British Columbia Citizens' Assembly and democratic renewal* (pp. 166–191). New York: Cambridge University Press.

Dahlberg, L. 2005. The Habermasian public sphere: Taking difference seriously. *Theory and Society*, 34, 111–136.

Delli Carpini, M. X., F. L. Cook, and L. R. Jacobs. 2004. Public deliberation, discursive participation, and citizen engagement: A review of the empirical literature. *Annual Review of Political Science*, 7, 315–344.

Delli Carpini, M. X., L. Huddy, and R. Y. Shapiro, (Eds.). 2002. *Research in micropolitics*. Vol. 6, *Political decision-making, deliberation and participation*. New York: Elsevier.

Dryzek, J. S. 1990. *Discursive democracy: Politics, policy, and political science*. Cambridge: Cambridge University Press.

Dryzek, J. S. 2010. *Foundation and frontiers of deliberative governance*. New York: Oxford.

Dwyer, W. L. 2002. *In the hands of the people*. New York: St. Martin's.

Edwards, P. B., R. Hindmarsh, M. B. Mercer, and A. Rowland. 2008. A three-stage evaluation of a deliberative event on climate change and transforming energy. *Journal of Public Deliberation*, 4(1), Article 6. Retrieved from http://services.bepress.com/jpd/vol4/iss1/art6

Elster, J., ed. 1998. *Deliberative democracy*. Cambridge: Cambridge University Press.

Elstub, S. 2010. The third generation of deliberative democracy. *Political Studies*, 8, 291–307.

Esterling, K. M., M. A. Neblo, and D. M. Lazer. 2011. Means, motive, and opportunity in becoming informed about politics: A deliberative field experiment with members of congress and their constituents. *Public Opinion Quarterly*, Advance Accesses, 1–21.

Evans, S. M., and H. C. Boyte. 1992. *Free spaces: The sources of democratic change in America*. Chicago: University of Chicago Press.

Fagotto, E., and A. Fung. 2006. Embedded deliberation: Entrepreneurs, organizations, and public action. *William and Flora Hewlett Foundation*, 1–151.

Fishkin, J. S. 1991. *Democracy and deliberation: New directions for democratic reform*. New Haven, CT: Yale University Press.

Fishkin, J. S. 1995. *The voice of the people: Public opinion and democracy*. New Haven, CT: Yale University Press.

Fishkin, J. S. 2009. *When the people speak: Deliberative democracy and public consultation*. New York: Oxford University Press.

Fishkin, J. S., B. He, R. C. Luskin, and A. Siu. 2010. Deliberative democracy in an unlikely place: Deliberative polling in China. *British Journal of Political Science*, 40, 435–448.

Fung, A. 2003. Survey article: Recipes for public spheres: Eight institutional design choices and their consequences. *Journal of Political Philosophy*, 11(3), 338–367.

Fung, A., and E. O. Wright, (Eds.). 2003. *Deepening democracy: Institutional innovations in empowered participatory governance*. London: Verso.

Gamson, W. A. 1992. *Talking politics*. Cambridge: Cambridge University Press.

Gastil, J. 1993. *Democracy in small groups: Participation, decision making, and communication*. Philadelphia, PA: New Society Publishers.

Gastil, J. 2000. Is face-to-face citizen deliberation a luxury or a necessity? *Political Communication*, 17(4), 357–361.

Gastil, J. 2004. Adult civic education through the National Issues Forums: Developing democratic habits and dispositions through public deliberation. *Adult Education Quarterly*, 54, 308–328.

Gastil, J. 2008. *Political communication and deliberation*. Thousand Oaks, CA: Sage.

Gastil, J., and J. P. Dillard. 1999a. The aims, methods, and effects of deliberative civic education through the National Issues Forums. *Communication Education*, 48, 1–14.

Gastil, J., and J. P. Dillard. 1999b. Increasing political sophistication through public deliberation. *Political Communication*, 16, 3–23.

Gastil, J., and K. Knobloch. 2010. *Evaluation report to the Oregon State Legislature on the 2010 Oregon Citizens' Initiative Review*. Retrieved from http://healthydemocracyoregon.org/sites/default/files/Oregon%20Legislative%20Report%20on%20CIR%20v.3-1.pdf

Gastil, J., K. Knobloch, and M. Kelly. 2012. Evaluating deliberative public events and projects. Pp. 205–260 in *Democracy in motion: Evaluating the practice and impact of deliberative civic engagement*, ed. T. Nabatchi, J. Gastil, M. Weiksner, and M. Leighninger. New York: Oxford University Press.

Gastil, J., and P. Levine, eds. 2005. *The deliberative democracy handbook: Strategies for effective civic engagement in the twenty-first century*. San Francisco, CA: Jossey Bass.

Gastil, J., and K. Sawyer. 2004. When process matters: An exploration of different approaches to operationalizing public deliberation. Paper presented at the annual meeting of the Western States Communication Association.

Goidel, R. K., Freeman, C. M., Procopio, S., and Zewe, C. F. 2008. Who participates in the "public square" and does it matter? *Public Opinion Quarterly*, 72(4), 792–803.

Goodin, R. E., and J. S. Dryzeck. 2006. Deliberative impacts: The macro-political uptake of mini-publics. *Politics & Society*, 34(2), 219–244.

Gutmann, A., and D. F. Thompson. 1996. *Democracy and disagreement*. Cambridge, MA: Harvard University Press.

Gutmann, A., and D. F. Thompson. 2004. *Why deliberative democracy?* Princeton, NJ: Princeton University Press.

Habermas, J. 1979. *Communication and the evolution of society*. Boston: Beacon Press.

Habermas, J. 1989. *The structural transformation of the public sphere*. Cambridge, MA: MIT Press.

Hart, R., and S. Jarvis. 1999. We the people: The contours of lay political discourse. Pp. 59–84 in *The poll with a human face: The National Issues Convention experiment in political communication*, ed. M. McCombs and A. Reynolds. Mahwah, NJ: Lawrence Erlbaum.

Hartz-Karp, J. 2005. A case study in deliberative democracy: Dialogue with the city. *Journal of Public Deliberation*, 1(1), Article 6.

Hartz-Karp, J., P. Anderson, J. Gastil, and A. Felicetti. 2010. The Australian Citizens' Parliament: Forging shared identity through public deliberation. *Journal of Public Affairs*, 10(4), 353–371.

Haug, C., and S. Teune. 2008. Identifying deliberation in social movement assemblies: Challenges of comparative participant observation, *Journal of Public Deliberation*, 4 (1), Article 8. Retrieved from http://servies.bepress.com/jpd/vol4/iss1/art8

Hendriks, C. M. 2005. Consensus conferences and planning cells: Lay citizen deliberations. Pp. 80–110 in *The deliberative democracy handbook: Strategies for effective civic engagement in the 21st century*, ed. J. Gastil and P. Levine. San Francisco: Jossey-Bass.

Hibbing, J. R., and E. Theiss-Morse. 2002. *Stealth democracy: Americans' beliefs about how government should work*. Cambridge: Cambridge University Press.

Huckfeldt, R., P. E. Johnson, and J. Sprague. 2004. *Political disagreement: The survival of diverse opinions within communication networks*. New York: Cambridge University Press.

Huckfeldt, R., and J. Sprague. 1995. *Citizens, politics, and social communication: Information and influence in an election campaign*. Cambridge: Cambridge University Press.

Jacobs, L. R., F. L. Cook, and M. X. Delli Carpini. 2009. *Talking together: Public deliberation and political participation in America*. Chicago: University of Chicago Press.

Karpowitz, C. F., and J. Mansbridge. 2005. Disagreement and consensus: The importance of dynamic updating in public deliberation. In J. Gastil and P. Levine (Eds.), *The deliberative democracy handbook: Strategies for effective civic engagement in the 21st century* (pp. 237–253). San Francisco: Jossey-Bass.

Karpowitz, C. F., C. Raphael, and A. S. Hammond IV. 2009. Deliberative democracy and inequality: Two cheers for enclave deliberation among the disempowered. *Politics & Society*, 37, 576–615.

Karpowitz, C. F., and Mendelberg, T. 2007. Groups and deliberation. *Swiss Political Science Review*, 13, 645–662.

Keith, W. 2007. Democracy as discussion: *The American Forum Movement and civic education*. Lanham, MD: Rowman and Littlefield.

Kinney. B. 2012. Deliberation's contribution to community capacity building. In T. Nabatchi, J. Gastil, M. Weiksner, and M. Leighninger (Eds.), *Democracy in motion: Evaluating the practice and impact of deliberative civic engagement* (pp. 163–180). New York: Oxford University Press.

Kluver, L. 2000. The Danish Board of Technology. In N. Vig and H. Paschen (Eds.), *Parliaments and technology: The development of technology assessment in Europe* (pp. 173–197). Albany, NY: SUNY Press.

Knobloch, K., J. Gastil, J. Reedy, and K. C. Walsh. 2013. Did they deliberate? Applying an evaluative model of democratic deliberation to the Oregon Citizens' Initiative Review. *Journal of Applied Communication Research*. Retrieved from http://www.tandfonline.com/doi/abs/10.1080/00909882.2012.760746

Lipsitz, K., C. Trost, and M. Grossmann. 2005. What voters want from political campaign communication. *Political Communication*, 22, 337–354.

Lukensmeyer, C. J., J. Goldman, and S. Brigham. 2005. A town meeting for the twenty-first century. Pp. 154–163 in *The deliberative democracy handbook: Strategies for effective civic engagement in the 21st century*, ed. J. Gastil and P. Levine. San Francisco: Jossey-Bass.

Luskin, R. C., J. S. Fishkin, and R. Jowell. 2002. Considered opinions: Deliberative polling in Britain. *British Journal of Political Science*, 32, 455–487.

Luskin, R. C., J. S. Fishkin, and S. Iyengar. 2006. *Considered opinions on U.S. foreign policy: Face-to-face versus online deliberative polling*. Center for Deliberative Democracy, Stanford University. Retrieved from http://cdd.stanford.edu/research/papers/2006/foreign-policy.pdf

Mansbridge, J. J. 1983. *Beyond adversary democracy*. Chicago: University of Chicago Press.

Mansbridge, J. J. 2010. Deliberative polling as the gold standard. *The Good Society*, 19, 56–63.

Mansbridge, J., J. Bohman, S. Chambers, D. Estlund, A. Follesdal, A. Fung, C. Lafont, B. Manin, and J. L. Marti. 2010. The place of self-interest and the role of power in deliberative democracy. *The Journal of Political Philosophy*, 18, 64–100.

Mansbridge, J., J. Hartz-Karp, M. Amengual, and J. Gastil. 2006. Norms of deliberation: An inductive study. *Journal of Public Deliberation*, 2(1), Article 7. Retrieved from http://services.bepress.com/jpd/vol2/iss1/art7

McCombs, M., and A. Reynolds, (Eds.). 1999. *The poll with a human face: The National Issues Convention experiment in political communication*. Mahwah, NJ: Lawrence Erlbaum.

McLeod, J. M., D. A. Scheufele, P. Moy, E. M. Horowitz, R. L. Holbert, W. Zhang, S. Subric, and J. Subric. 1999. Understanding deliberation: The effects of discussion networks on participation in a public forum. *Communication Research*, 26(6), 743–774.

Melville, K., T. L. Willingham, and J. R. Dedrick. 2005. National Issues Forums: A network of communities promoting public deliberation. In J. Gastil and P. Levine (Eds.), *The deliberative democracy handbook: Strategies for effective civic engagement in the 21st century* (pp. 37–58). San Francisco: Jossey-Bass.

Mendelberg, T. 2002. The deliberative citizen: Theory and evidence. *Political Decision Making, Deliberation and Participation*, 6, 151–193.

Mendelberg, T., and J. Oleske. 2000. Race and public deliberation. *Political Communication*, 17(2), 169–191.

Min, S. J. 2007. Online vs. face-to-face deliberation: Effects on civic engagement. *Journal of Computer-Mediated Communication*, 12(4), 1369–1387.

Mutz, D. C. 2006. *Hearing the other side: Deliberative versus participatory democracy*. New York: Cambridge University Press.

Nabatchi, T. 2010. Deliberative democracy and citizenship: In search of the efficacy effect. *Journal of Public Deliberation*, 6(2), Article 8. Retrieved from http://services.bepress.com./cgi/viewcontent.cgi?article=1135&context=jpd

Nabatchi, T., J. Gastil, M. Weiksner, and M. Leighninger, eds. 2012. *Democracy in motion: Evaluating the practice and impact of deliberative civic engagement*. New York: Oxford University Press.

Neblo, M. A., K. M. Kennedy, R. P. Lazer, D. M. J. Sokhey, and A. E. Esterling. 2010. Who wants to deliberate—and why? *American Political Science Review*, 104, 566–583.

Pearce, W. B., and S. W. Littlejohn. 1997. *Moral conflict: When social worlds collide*. Thousand Oaks, CA: Sage.

Pincock, H. 2012. Does deliberation make better citizens? In T. Nabatchi, J. Gastil, M. Weiksner, and M. Leighninger (Eds.), *Democracy in motion: Evaluating the practice and impact of deliberative civic engagement* (pp. 135–162). New York: Oxford University Press.

Polletta, F. 2002. *Freedom is an endless meeting: Democracy in American social movements*. Chicago: University of Chicago Press.

Polletta, F. 2008. Just talk: Political deliberation after 9/11. *Journal of Public Deliberation*, 4(1), Article 2. Retrieved from http://services.bepress.jpd/vol4/iss1/art2/

Polletta, F., and J. Lee. 2006. Is telling stories good for democracy? Rhetoric in public deliberation after 9/11. *American Sociological Review*, 71(5), 699–723.

Potapchuk, W. R., C. Carlson, and J. Kennedy. 2005. Growing governance deliberatively: Lessons and inspiration from Hampton, Virginia. In . Gastil and P. Levine (Eds.), *The deliberative democracy handbook: Strategies for effective civic engagement in the 21st century* (pp. 254–270). San Francisco: Jossey-Bass.

Price, V and J. N. Capella. 2002. Online deliberation and its influence: The Electronic Dialogue Project in campaign 2000. *IT and Society*, 1(1), 303–328. Retrieved from http://www.stanford.edu/group/siqss/itandsociety/v01i01/v01i01a20.pdf

Renn, O., T. Webler, and P. Wiedemann, eds. 1995. *Fairness and competence in citizen participation: Evaluating models for environmental discourse*. Boston: Kluwer Academic.

Rosenberg, S. W., ed. 2007. *Democracy, deliberation and participation: Can the people decide?* London: Palgrave Macmillan.

Ryfe, D. M. 2005. Does deliberative democracy work? *Annual Review of Political Science*, 8, 49–71.

Ryfe, D. M. 2006. Narrative and deliberation in small group forums. *Journal of Applied Communication Research*, 34, 72–93.

Ryfe, D. M. 2007. Toward a sociology of deliberation. *Journal of Public Deliberation*, 3(1), Article 3. Retrieved from http://services.bepress.com/cgi/viewcontent.cgi?article=1048& context=jpd

Sanders, L. M. 1997. Against deliberation. *Political Theory*, 25, 347–76.

Smith, G., and C. Wales. 2000. Citizens' juries and deliberative democracy. *Political Studies*, 48, 51–65.

Steenbergen, M. R., A. Bachtiger, M. Spordnli, and J. Steinger. 2003. Measuring political delib-
    eration: A discourse quality index. *Comparative European Politics*, 1(1), 21–48.

Steiner, J. 2012. *The foundations of deliberative democracy: Empirical research and normative
    implications.* New York: Cambridge University Press.

Stromer-Galley, J. 2007. Measuring deliberation's content: A coding scheme. *Journal of Public
    Deliberation*, 3(1), Article 12. Retrieved from http://services.bepress.com/jpd/vol3/iss1/art12.

Sunstein, C. R. 2000. Deliberative trouble: Why groups go to extremes. *The Yale Law Journal*,
    110(1), 71–119.

Thompson, D. 2008. Deliberative democratic theory and empirical political science. *Annual
    Review of Political Science*, 11, 497–520.

Walsh, K. C. 2003. *Communities, race, and talk: An analysis of the occurrence of civic inter-
    group dialogue programs.* Presented at the annual meeting of the American Political Science
    Association, Pennsylvania.

Walsh, K. C. 2004. *Talking about politics: Informal groups and social identity in American life.*
    Chicago: University of Chicago Press.

Wampler, B. 2007. *Participatory budgeting in Brazil: Contestation, cooperation, and accountabil-
    ity.* University Park: Penn State University Press.

Warren, M., and H. Pearse. (Eds.). 2008. *Designing deliberative democracy: The British
    Columbia Citizens' Assembly.* Cambridge University Press: Cambridge.

Xenos, Michael A. 2011. Deliberation. *Oxford bibliographies online.* New York: Oxford
    University Press. Retrieved from http://www.oxfordbibliographiesonline.com/view/docu-
    ment/obo-9780199756841/obo-9780199756841-0043.xml

CHAPTER 51

....

ETHNOGRAPHY OF POLITICS AND POLITICAL COMMUNICATION

Studies in Sociology and Political Science

....

EEVA LUHTAKALLIO AND NINA ELIASOPH

WHY ETHNOGRAPHY AND POLITICS ARE A NECESSARY MATCH

....

AN essay on ethnography of political communication must begin with two questions: What do we mean by "political," and what do we mean by "ethnography"? Depending on these definitions, there are either very few ethnographies of political communication or a substantial number, spanning the disciplines of communication, sociology, political science, history, business, and policy. As for the definition of "political ethnography" and its salience, recent debates, especially in the field of political science, have argued about different definitions of the concept and its position in the academic field with such zeal that we consider it unnecessary to enter this fray (see Tilly, 2006; Auyero 2006; Auyero and Joseph, 2007; Yanow, 2009; Kubik, 2009; Pachirat, 2009; Warren, 2009; Schatz, 2009a, 2009b; Wedeen, 2010). Instead, we focus on discussing the findings and consequences of the ethnographic approach to political phenomena, by means of a few particularly illustrative examples.

In the widest possible sense, the ancestors of today's political ethnographers wrote travel descriptions first, and anthropological accounts a little later, about distant cultures in which societies were organized and the polis was constituted and acted on in ways unfamiliar to Western traditions. These historical accounts continue to remind us that understanding politics requires multiple strategies of analysis.

A similar challenge to our taken-for-granted definitions of "politics" confronts Western-educated investigators who conduct cross-cultural ethnography. These temporal and spatial leaps force the researcher to confront something that other researchers can more easily avoid: the puzzle of defining some interactions and activities as "politics" and others as "not politics" a priori, without deeply understanding the context and situation. As Clifford Geertz (1973, 311–312) noted, politics is one of the principal arenas in which the structures of meaning we habitually call "culture" unfold and become observable. What unfolds, then, is not limited to political institutions or decision-making practices, but both reflects and constitutes a vast array of activities and meanings with widely different scopes of political consequences, ranging from the obstacles of politicization experienced in a poor French suburb to the motivations of keeping up with exhausting political work in US Senate-level campaigning (cf. Hamidi, 2009; Mahler, 2006).

In this chapter we argue that the ethnographic approach has particular potential for studying political communication through enlarging common understandings of political institutions and expanding common definitions of "politics." First, widening *institutional understanding* takes advantage of ethnography's capacity to open windows that traditional analysis of political institutions leaves shut. By prying these windows open, ethnography, when done well, forces us to see what meanings-in-context constitute these institutions. Peering inside the "big," institutional structures of politics shows how they are intricately and precisely composed of elements that typical research does not theorize as part of "politics"; by the same token, ethnography also forces us to notice atypical political processes and arenas, outside of the institutionalized forums. Thus, second, ethnography is uniquely able to examine *new forms of engagement* that people have not *yet* defined as "politics." Third, studying political communication ethnographically also means expanding the *modes of communication* and activity examined to include, for example, nonverbal and virtual communication. In addition to their impact on empirical outcomes, such as patterns of voting and activism, varied media that include nonverbal and virtual communication can have implications that challenge standard definitions of politics.

Current political ethnographies are undeniably indebted to streams of writing and research going back to the early modern Europeans' travelogues describing exotic cultures, and from there on to the tradition of linguistic anthropology. Nonetheless, in this text we concentrate principally on the work of ethnographers from the past couple of decades to stress the crucial role of ethnography in understanding what is most proper to current political communication: mediated flows in globalized, complex, and transnational settings. The need to understand these transformations brings us to the particular and increasing importance of political ethnography today. In the current plurality of contexts for political communication, multiple levels, styles, and means of communication are simultaneously influential, and the lack of tools to grasp this multiplicity hampers political analysis. In a world of global and "glocal" (Brenner 2004) crisscrossing meanings, weak signs grow in importance. Political ethnography is at best a form of inquiry that specializes in weak, barely visible signs, habits and practices hidden from news headlines, and the counter trends that may be bubbling underneath them, sometimes taking the headlines as well as macro-level political analysis by surprise.

How Different Organizations Close Down, Open Up, and Shape Political Communication

So how surprising have the news headlines from the political ethnography channel been, in recent years? What have we learned, really, and what is specifically ethnographic about these findings? In this section we explore political ethnography from three overlapping perspectives: the ethnographic accounts of studying "established" political institutions or action; the grasp of political processes and capacity to recognize politics in fragile, new, and/or unexpected contexts of an ethnographic approach; and the ethnographers' tools to analyze and understand obstacles, hindrances, and the lack of politics that largely escape other research approaches. We look at these perspectives by sketching bodies of studies that share certain features and through illustrative examples highlighting those features.

Ethnographic research on politics sensitizes analysis of the ways that different organizations invoke different kinds of political engagement. It does so by taking into account the "nitty-gritty details and effects of different forms of political action, networks and tactics," as Auyero and Joseph (2007, 3) describe the benefits of political ethnography in introducing their edited volume on the theme. In other words, ethnographic studies show how political practices reflect, construct, and occasionally transform organizations, expanding, contracting, or reshaping the possible places for political expression.

This feature makes ethnography a useful approach for studying various kinds of political organizations and processes, with the promise of results that reach beyond not just surveys and policy analysis, but also interview-based studies. Be it "business as usual" or change and crisis moments of more or less institutional politics, NGOs, collective action, and social movements, ethnographic studies show that political communication takes shape and has various consequences as it unfolds in different types of organizations, contexts, and situations, and that general talk about political cultures should always be evaluated with precaution, with a careful inspection of the everyday practices through which the "cultures" materialize (e.g., Abèles, 1991; Lichterman, 1996; Sampson, 1996; Eliasoph, 1998; Mische, 2009; Moore, 2001; Elyachar, 2002; Baiocchi, 2005; Mahler, 2006; Steinhoff, 2006; Yon, 2009; Eliasoph, 2011; Luhtakallio, 2012).

Learning Participation, Displacing Politics?

One example is the worldwide "participation industry," which has been given the task of renewing and saving democracy from a crisis (e.g., Moore, 2001; Baiocchi, 2005; Talpin, 2006; Polletta and Lee, 2006; Lee, 2010). But what does participation actually produce, and can it save democracy by simply being implemented? In a comparative ethnography of organs of participatory democracy in France and Italy, Talpin (2006) describes the "effects" of deliberation among the participating citizens. He notes that over time, something indeed changes in the participants' actions; they learn how to participate—appropriately. This means that they, in his words, learn to "play good citizens," which includes asking the right kind of questions and avoiding saying anything that might seem too controversial or "out of place." Talpin concludes that it seems arbitrary to try to separate deliberation as a practice from its supposed effects, as deliberation is the process itself. Separating deliberation from its effects would be like separating the dancer from the dance. What the citizens learned first and foremost was to deliberate according to the guidelines set and kept by the local political leaders. As Lee's startling studies also show in the US context, playing good citizen in these situations that the participation industry tends to create can often require entering a rather apolitical or even depoliticizing game (Lee, 2010).

This example is not chosen to show that participatory democracy is a sham, but to stress that the internationally promoted image of participatory democracy does not actually capture these processes. Rather, these forums teach people a kind of organizational style (Eliasoph and Lichterman, 2003). They learn to follow the "rules of the game." One cannot become a decent member of the neighborhood council, the bureaucracy, or the activist group, for that matter, until one knows what the unspoken "organizational style" is. The importance of mastering the organizational style to learn appropriate modes of participation is not new; Mansbridge (1983) describes how and why, in the classic site of civic engagement, Vermont town meetings, working-class people routinely could not bear to be outspoken participants.

In a more current site of civic life, Eliasoph (2011) portrays programs that aim at fighting social exclusion and promoting empowerment among underprivileged youth. These "empowerment projects" end up doing something quite different from what they are designed to do. In the whirlpool of project-based government funding, evaluations, and unspoken missions, the young people learn to represent "underprivileged youth" and talk and act in a fashion that satisfies the expectations of the program planners. Instead of being empowered in ways that the doctrine of these programs promises, they become capable of playing in the world of projects where money is scarce, goals unrealistic, and the results sought are very far from their own realities. They learn how to navigate these quasi-governmental, quasi-civic, quasi-political organizations that receive funding from state and nonprofit sources—a skill that may come in handy if they themselves end up getting jobs in this increasingly prevalent "hybrid" nonprofit sector. In this way, participants are in fact learning how to navigate our current *political* world, in which it is increasingly difficult to find the boundary between "government" and "nongovernmental organization" all over the world—where some NGO's budgets and political power exceed those of many governments. Along with this political structure comes a political culture—for example, in the form of an increasingly international language that an anthropologist studying NGO's efforts at building civic life in Albania calls "projectspeak" (Sampson, 1996).

This is not to say that the "structure" of an organization determines its styles of communication. In the Brazilian, university-based activist groups that Mische studied, three very different styles predominated. In one, members tried hard to always agree and bond and express their feelings; in another type of group, members sharpened their swords with loud debate verging on fights; and in still a third type of activist group, members explored ideas without feeling the need to conclude anything (2001).

Studies such as Mische's show that we should be uneasy when we talk about political culture "in general" and wary of making broad international comparisons. Instead, the spectrum of comparative analysis widens and gains in color, detail, and pertinence when carried out with ethnographic tools. In comparing French and Finnish styles of politicization, Luhtakallio (2012) showed that broad international comparisons are nonetheless possible. There are features that characterize large cultural entities, and analyzing how they come to be—that is, through and in what kind of processes they actually exist—is the key to understanding what is it that makes them "general features." At the same time, important fissures and weak signs of change that mainly escape the eyes of policy analysis–based model builders become apparent, and seeing these seemingly insignificant features of political engagement makes it possible to get beyond two-dimensional comparisons. Luhtakallio, for example, concluded that on the one hand, when examined close up, the French contentiousness in interactions between activists and decision-makers included activists' implicit knowledge that they were contending with stagnant, out-of-reach hierarchies that kept the power configurations intact. On the other hand, the Finnish culture of consensus and inclusive decision-making included putting a lot of effort into quelling conflicts and depoliticizing issues of controversy, instead of dealing with them through a political process.

Finally, all these examples show that be it the "participation industry" or another type of political institution or group, careful ethnography can tell us an additional, a different, and sometimes even the opposite tale from the official story, and the stakes can be high.

"Politics" in the Making . . . and Not

The second perspective elaborates on the ways ethnography provides for tools to recognize politics in the making and the crucial but hard-to-catch processes of politicization and depoliticization, politics happening and failing to happen (Carrel, 2006; Eliasoph, 1998, 2011; Hamidi, 2006, 2010; Luhtakallio, 2012; Lichterman, 2005). Both are features that statistical, macro, interview-based, and even multimethod analysis mainly ignore: to render something visible that is all but not there yet, or does not happen, requires ethnographic crafting. Yet these processes are crucial in grasping the essence of politics. Here the question is how new issues emerge, and what hinders them from emerging, on the agenda.

Ethnographers often become interested in new, nascent forms of politics before other students of politics notice them. Political ethnographies bring to the fore the blurring of borders of habitual fields of action in showing things that are emerging and have not yet solidified into "politics" but are social work, or theater, or voluntary aid work. This is due not only to their sensitivity in recognizing political processes but also to the logic of ethnographic research: no institution, structure, or research context is a "given" when the meanings and meaningfulness of action are under scrutiny. Furthermore, the ethnographic approach is probably the most prominent tool for analyzing the whys and hows of the *absence* of politics: the variety of hindrances and obstacles to politicization and fragilities and failures of political processes. (Huspek and Kendall, 1991; Eliasoph, 1998; Carrel, 2006; Wolford, 2006; Auyero and Swistun, 2007; Näre, 2011). We next consider these two sides of how ethnographic research captures situations that constitute politics.

Hamidi (2006, 2010) envisions a conception that can include political action (*le politique*) that takes place outside the sphere of institutional politics (*la politique*), such as established social movements, but also activities that are not easily recognized as political to begin with and in which the actors do not necessarily "actually think" they are engaged in political activism. Hamidi talks about graffiti writing, asking whether tagging is a form of "political communication." She says that the question is a bit wrong: whether tagging is a form of politics depends on how the taggers imagine it and talk about it in relation to what Hamidi calls "organized conflict." This approach steers a middle ground between searching too "low" and saying that tagging is, of course, a form of vague "resistance," versus searching too "high," only examining official, public discourse aimed at changing policy. Hamidi's definition combines the necessary "conflictualization" (Duchesne, 2003) that denaturalizes a problem—the essential first step in politicization—with an approach that organizes varied objects into a category that is large enough to act upon. The latter can mean naming the forty-seven humiliations experienced by immigrant youth as "examples of racial discrimination." This is the process of "raising the problem to a level of generality" as the authors of *On Justification*, the influence of which in European political research is nearly inescapable, put it (Boltanski and Thévenot, [1991] 2006). It is also the key to the process that leads from the "I want" to the "we have the right to" that Hanna Pitkin described as the metaphor for a process leading to public-spirited thinking and principles of justice.

Hamidi's study (2006) also puts her "enlarged concept of politicization" to work when figuring out why there seemed to be so little "politics" going on in the associational activities of immigrant-dominated suburbs. Despite the often conflictual setting of the activities, conversations in the associations were rarely "political" in any obvious sense. It turned out that there were features that were particularly efficient in taming political expressions, such as defining a problem as being of a psychological nature or stressing the urgency of the case of, for instance, a victim of domestic violence, instead of including political reflection in the process of helping out.

In a similar manner, Eliasoph (1998) concludes that particular organizational styles turned situations and activities that could have a political dimension into something else: people combating a proposed toxic dump in their neighborhood could analyze the corporate policies that make so much toxic production possible, and they could discuss the government's role in allowing so much toxic production, its lax regulation, and its own share of toxic waste production, when they mention that the US military is the largest toxic producer in the nation. They could say to one another quite clearly that the waste should not go in someone else's backyard. They could say this kind of thing over breakfast with one another or in casual conversations outside of meetings with one another. But the moment the radio and TV mikes go on in a press conference, these same people say, "I care because I'm a mom," and express concerns about their own local neighborhood. There was a pattern: what they can easily say in one context—in casual contexts—was hard for them to say in another—the press conference—and the result was an evaporation of political speech from public situations.

Carrel (2006) notes in her study—concerning politicization processes in consciousness groups for residents of a disadvantaged neighborhood—that as important as recognizing politicization is recognizing the fragility of these processes. Carrel tells the story of "Lila," who has been on the list of applicants for government housing for several years. Lila is a participant in a social worker–led group in what is called a "difficult neighborhood" in Paris. She is an unemployed young mother, a French citizen of Algerian origin. In the kick-off meeting of the group, she is angry and aggressive, reluctant to participate at all. A social worker had put in a great deal of effort persuading her to attend. The principal reason for her attitude was that she had waited for a long time to get an answer to her housing application and had become convinced that her application had been deliberately "blocked" by a Mrs. Martin, manager of the housing services, whom she openly accused of racism. She rocked between resignation and rage, having received no detailed explanation for the failure of her application. Over a period of six months, Lila and Mrs. Martin engaged in an exchange and an inquiry into the procedures that determine who gets public housing. Lila learned that while the local council collects applications and decides on a preselection, the final decision is made elsewhere. Thus, Mrs. Martin was but one link in a long chain of decision-making. Lila debated and confronted, along with the group, the inadequate provision of public housing and the opacity of the granting procedures. During this experimental program of participatory democracy, she shifted from "I am a victim of racism, they don't want to give me housing" to "As applicants for public housing, we demand explanations from elected representatives and administrative authorities." Lila's shift provides Carrel with a textbook case of a Pitkin-inspired instance of "I want" becoming "we have the right to." At the end of this project, Lila gave a public speech before the housing management committee criticizing the opacity of the process and the inadequate provision of affordable housing in the area. This was the peak of her engagement, however. After finally acquiring an apartment, she withdrew from political activities (Carrel, 2006).

Lila's is a story of a successful political learning process, and at the same time a story of the fragility of these processes. Even once it happens, politicization is not something a person possesses or an achieved group characteristic. It may be tempting to think of it as an achieved state of affairs, which comes with a big solid box of "civic skills" (Verba, Brady, and Schlozman, 1995), but following the process over time, with the patience and eyes of an ethnographer, reveals the situational nature of politics and politicization. Political emancipation of "the poor and marginalized," as this case would seem to be, may not be a lasting, linear progress story even once it has started, but exactly the kind of "come-and-go" of "raising justifications to a level of generality" that Hamidi (2006) describes. Undeniably, Lila went through a process of emancipation of some kind, and yet a year later, when the ethnographer returned to the field, Lila was not an activist, nor did she express any political interest—on the contrary, she had withdrawn from all participation, going nearly all the way back to her original position, except that now she was no longer homeless. Should the people who ran this experiment in participatory democracy call this a success? In some ways, it certainly was—she was no longer homeless. But in another way, it was not: Lila's passion for democratic participation was evanescent and vanished when she got the apartment she needed.

In a study of environmental suffering in the "Flammable" shantytown in Buenos Aires, Auyero and Swistun (2007) show how an ethnographic approach can reveal reasons for collective passivity. Inhabitants of a polluted poor neighborhood in the vicinity of an oil refinery kept *waiting* for a change in their dangerous living conditions, instead of acting. They were hesitant and confused, living in a generalized cloud of not knowing what to do and when, not knowing if a change was about to take place or not. The authors show how this general atmosphere came into being, defining everyday life in the neighborhood. The antipoliticizing effects of small enhancements and vague but constant (and mainly unkept) promises by the authorities and corporate representatives positioned the local inhabitants' sense of time, as Bourdieu has put it. Rather than living on their own calendars, it was as if they were living on a calendar that was oriented to others.

By slowing down the camera like this, ethnography can reveal obstacles to political engagement and the personal and social consequences of political engagement and its absence. In sum, it can uncover the fragility of political processes.

THEORIZING POLITICS
THROUGH ETHNOGRAPHIC EVIDENCE

It may seem obvious that if one wants to study political communication, one should study a political organization—an activist group, political party, or public hearings, for example—and theories from Tocqueville onward point to civic associations as the places to go if a person is looking for the cultivation of civic skills. When the ethnographer selects a site according to what seems, in the light of theory or "common sense," to be the dependent variable, she usually finds something other than the expected. An ethnographer can discover the qualities of relationships and material conditions in workplaces, or churches, or political activist organizations that shape political communication one way or another, showing how and why political communication arises where it does, and when, and between whom. Ethnography, in other words, takes the concepts of Burke's "pentad" (1945) and shows how they reflect and create everyday *situations*.

These situations, repeated often enough in a widespread enough way, create organizational forms that shape the kinds of political communication that can unfold therein. Milburn's remarkable book (2009) on communication patterns in nonprofit organizations in the United States shows this "sedimentation (Ricoeur 1991" clearly. "Often enough" and "widespread enough" are, of course, admittedly vague terms; further research could clarify how and when people come to recognize what is acceptable in a new kind of organization. Eliasoph's (2011) exploration of these processes in nonprofit- and government-sponsored youth volunteer programs offers an initial way of thinking about the processes of sedimentation. In an era of state "devolution" of crucial government functions—for example, social services, education, policing—to nonprofits and "community-based organizations," studying these cases, which are more and more prevalent, is a way of examining the state's new configuration. This is the new face of the state—which is still the first thing people mean when they say "politics." The problem is that it is no longer as easy as it once was to say, with certainty, "this is 'government,' and this is 'not government.'" Now the state's boundaries are not so clear. "Widespread enough" and "often enough" may be good enough for now, since our seemingly solid structures are more obviously *processes*, sedimenting and eroding and re-sedimenting into things that look solid, till they dissolve again. Ethnography helps remind us that history does not "freeze," but is a series of path-dependent events that never just stop (Warren, 2009).

Another way that ethnography makes us retheorize political engagement is by showing how people "embody" it. For example, Mahler (2006) examines extremely dedicated "politicos," who work day and night with seemingly boundless energy. Mahler's case consists of politicians and campaign workers on the Senate level and the questions of what has made them take politics as a vocation and what keeps them at it. Mahler shows—with a rather rare approach (in ethnography) based on biographical and historical accounts—that the observable political actions are not what makes the political experiences special, but instead the "feel": the way people enact them together, fueling and refueling each other's passion in a mutual conflagration of spiraling energy, that allows these super-activists to survive with almost no sleep for weeks and even months at a time when they are working hard on a campaign.

Detailing the levels of engagement in political processes can be the principal objective of a study, as it was in Olga Koveneva's comparative study of the alternative grounds for the protection of environment and defense of the area in a French and a Russian nature park, which portrayed the differences in how actors in the two contexts related themselves to the material world they were defending and the ways in which these differences affected political action (Koveneva, 2011). The park was a shared political space in both contexts, but the process of politicization grew differently and had different impacts according to the level of "communicating the common" the people practiced. The French nature-defenders spoke and acted on a public level of justifying their arguments, proving the representative nature of their groups, and grounding their claims on expert knowledge. The Russians, in contrast, refrained from public justifications and communicated mainly on the level of familiar, local loyalties and engagements, diminishing the possibility of a public political process considerably. Thévenot's (2006, 2007) theoretical work provides the idea of the three regimes of engagement: publicly justifiable engagement, engagement in a plan, and familiar engagement. The first is the level of "politics," with its anchorage in public justifications. Nevertheless, as Mahler's and Koveneva's works both show in different ways, political action and processes of politicization do not reside exclusively in the realm of "public," but are instead complex combinations of routines, habits, plans, and choices. The key question in understanding these processes and their different grounds in different contexts is the question of moving from one "level" to another and transforming people's personal and particularistic attachments into issues of higher levels of generality. In all these studies, it becomes clear how the "how" and "why" are related; to learn how a quality of engagement arises opens a route to finding out why it does. This theoretical apparatus is almost exclusively based on ethnographic research that provides tools sensitive enough to capture these momentary processes (see Thévenot, Moody, and Lafaye, 2000; Doidy, 2005; Thévenot, 2006, 2007; Koveneva, 2011; Breviglieri et al., 2009 Charles, 2012).

UNANSWERED QUESTIONS AND CURRENT CHALLENGES

Many ethnographers have recently begun to explore virtual communities and the multilevel and multimedia mobilizations taking place online, creating new understanding of belonging and corporeality in political processes (Fay, 2007; Laine, 2011). Corporality and its absence present a new, underexplored avenue for thinking about political ethnography. Feeling its absence in online communication heightens our awareness of just how much political communication is nonverbal.

The following example from before the Internet era highlights both the nonverbal and the materialized features of politics: When East and West Germany merged after the fall of the Berlin Wall, and police officers from the former communist East and capitalist West had to get along and forge a new government body in their new republic, their everyday habits were different, in major and minor details. For the East German officers, for example, it was normal to take off the uniform at home, while for the former West Germans, it was proper to take it off before leaving the precinct office. This difference in habits makes sense when one considers that in East Germany, housing was allocated mainly through a person's job, whereas in the former West Germany, private, home life was as separate from work life as it is for us in the United States; home and work were more separate. The taking off of the uniform solidifies this in a convenient "device," as Latour (2005) or Thévenot (2006) would put it. Participants implicitly know that the uniform, or its absence on the way home, summarizes a whole way of life and a whole political system. In the spirit of this anecdote, we need more research, not necessarily on Web activism in a vacuum, but on the relations between embodied and disembodied political communication (e.g., Polletta and Lee, 2006; Laine, 2011;

Luhtakallio, 2013). The problem in this regard is how to track these kinds of underlying features of politics deliberately: Where do we look if we don't know where it is? How do people, and organizations, connect and disconnect their embodied selves to/from their online selves?

Another set of challenges for ethnography of political communication is the puzzle of doing comparative research. In the pressing task of increasing transnational understanding on political engagement, ethnography is an important research strategy. But it is difficult to know what can stand as equivalents from one society to the next. Already in this chapter, American readers reading about Carrel's case of public housing would have a very different set of assumptions about it than the French people in her case. Our US welfare state is (still) so much weaker and smaller than theirs that it might even seem strange that anyone, much less an immigrant, would take housing as a right that the state must guarantee. If we were to conduct ethnography in the United States, could a public housing project stand as equivalent enough to function as a comparison? We doubt it. In Hamidi's studies of French immigrants from North Africa, could we use them as equivalents to immigrants to the United States? Or would they be equal to African Americans, since immigrants from France's former colonies in North Africa are, de jure anyway, full citizens, as blacks are here? If we wanted to study a nonprofit here, would it be the same as studying one in a nation that had a strong welfare state? One way around this puzzle is to study the same organization across various nations—for example, Amnesty International (Gray, 2007). Another is to do what Luhtakallio (2012) has begun, by showing how activities that look similar in different nations face similar tensions in meshing their different missions, but solve them very differently.

Finally, as the discussion of Web-based citizenship and activism shows, it is a great challenge, and an even greater opportunity, for ethnographers to find out how to delocalize our inquiries. Since early ethnographers such as Gluckman wrote about seemingly local events, it has been clear that the "here and now" is never just here and now. In Gluckman's famous colonial-era case (1958, 1967), a bridge in Zululand was inaugurated, and the local ceremony reflected and embodied and reproduced not only local power relations but also a whole set of relations between colonizers and colonized. His task was to show that a participant simply could not understand the ceremony without this implicit background knowledge. When, to take a more current example, Mexican immigrants in Los Angeles become union activists in their new place of residence, they have one imaginary foot in LA and the other in Mexico; the activism is both here and there, and the money, the people, and the imaginations flow back and forth (Fitzgerald, 2004). The local is never just local, but is always haunted by these invisible ghosts. Ethnography's challenge is to reveal these invisible ghosts as they proliferate and move faster and faster.

References

Abèles, M. 1991. *Quiet days in Burgundy: A study of local politics.* Paris: Editions de la Maison de science de l'homme.

Auyero, J. 2006. Introductory note to politics under the microscope. In special issue on political ethnography. *Qualitative Sociology* 29(3): 257–259.

Auyero, J., and Joseph, L. 2007. Introduction: Politics under the ethnographic microscope. In L. Joseph, M. Mahler, and J. Auyero (Eds.), *New perspectives in political ethnography* (pp. 1–13). New York: Springer.

Auyero, J., and Swistun, D. 2007. Confused because exposed: Towards an ethnography of environmental suffering. *Ethnography* 8(2): 123–144.

Baiocchi, G. 2005. *Militants and citizens: The politics of participatory democracy in Porto Alegre.* Stanford, CA: Stanford University Press.

Boltanski, L., and Thévenot, L. (1991) 2006. *On justification: Economies of worth.* Princeton, NJ: Princeton University Press. [De la justification. Des economies de grandeur. Paris: Gallimard].

Brenner, N. 2004. *New state spaces: Urban governance and the rescaling of statehood.* New York: Oxford University Press.

Breviglieri, M., Lafaye, C., and Trom, D. 2009. *Compétences critiques et sens de la justice.* Colloque de Cerisy. Paris: Economica.

Burke, K. 1945. *A grammar of motives.* Berkeley: University of California Press.

Carrel, M. 2006. Politisation et publicisation: Les effets fragiles de la délibération en milieu populaire. *Politix* 19(75): 33–51.

Charles, J. 2012. Les charges de la participation. *Sociologies,* 15 Novembre 2012, http://sociologies.revues.org/4151.

Doidy, E. 2005. (Ne pas) juger scandaleux: Les électeurs de Levallois-Perret face au comportement de leur maire. *Politix* 71: 165–189.

Duchesne, S. 2003. Dons et recherche de soi, l'altruisme en question aux Restaurants du Coeur et à Amnesty International. *Les Cahiers du Cévipof* 33(Janvier). http://www.cevipof.com/fr/les-publications/les-cahiers-du-cevipof/bdd/publication/437

Eliasoph, N. 1998. *Avoiding politics: How Americans produce apathy in everyday life.* Cambridge, UK: Cambridge University Press.

Eliasoph, N. 2011. *Making volunteers: Civic life after welfare's end.* Princeton, NJ: Princeton University Press.

Eliasoph, N., and Lichterman, P. 2003. Culture in interaction. *American Journal of Sociology* 108(4, January): 735–794.

Elyachar, J. 2002. Empowerment money: The World Bank, non-governmental organizations, and the value of culture in Egypt. *Public Culture* 14(3): 493–513.

Fay, M. 2007. Mobile subjects, mobile methods: Doing virtual ethnography in a feminist online network. *Forum: Qualitative Social Research* 8(3): Art. 13.

Fitzgerald, D. 2004. Beyond "transnationalism": Mexican hometown politics at an American labor union. *Ethnic and Racial Studies* 27(2): 228–247.

Geertz, C. 1973. *The interpretation of cultures.* New York: Basic Books.

Gluckman, M. 1958. *Analysis of a social situation in modern Zululand.* Manchester: Manchester University Press for The Rhodes-Livingston Institute.

Gluckman, M. 1967. Introduction to *The Craft of Social Anthropology,* by A. L. Epstein (pp. xi–xx). London: Tavistock.

Gray, C. M. 2007. "The gulag of our times": Diplomatic postures and dactivist dramatics in human rights NGO strategies. Paper presented at the International Studies Association 48th Annual Convention, Chicago, IL, February 28. http://www.allacademic.com/meta/p179521_index.html.

Hamidi, C. 2006. Eléments pour une approche interactionniste de la politisation: Engagement associatif et rapport au politique dans des associations locales issues de l'immigration. *Revue Française de Science Politique* 56(1): 5–25.

Hamidi, C. 2010. *La société civile dans les cités: Engagement associatif et politisation dans des associations de quartier*. Paris: Economica.

Huspek, M., and Kendall, K. E. 1991. On withholding political voice: An analysis of the political vocabulary of a "nonpolitical" speech community. *Quarterly Journal of Speech* 77: 1–19.

Koveneva, O. 2011. Les communautés politiques en France et en Russie. *Annales. Histoire, Sciences Sociales* 3/2011, 787–817.

Kubik, J. 2009. Ethnographic innovations in the study of post-communism: Two examples. *Qualitative & Multi-Method Research* 7(2): 37–41.

Laine, S. 2011. Grounded globalizations of transnational social movement: Ethnographic analysis on free hugs campaign at the World Social Forum Belém 2009. *Ephemera* 11(3): 243–257.

Latour, B. 2005. *Reassembling the social: An introduction to actor-network-theory*. Oxford: Oxford University Press.

Lichterman, P. 1996. *The search for political community. American activists reinventing commitment*. Cambridge, UK: Cambridge University Press.

Lichterman, P. 2005. *Elusive togetherness: Church groups trying to bridge America's divisions*. Princeton, NJ: Princeton University Press.

Luhtakallio, E. 2012. *Practicing democracy: Local activism and politics in France and Finland*. Basingstoke, UK: Palgrave Macmillan.

Luhtakallio, E. 2013. Bodies keying politics. Visual frame analysis of gendered local activism in France and Finland. *Research in Social Movements, Conflict and Change* 35, 27–54.

Mahler, M. 2006. Politics as a vocation: Notes toward a sensualist understanding of political engagement. *Qualitative Sociology* 29: 281–300.

Mansbridge, J. 1983. *Beyond adversary democracy*. Chicago: Chicago University Press.

Milburn, T. 2009. *Nonprofit organizations: Creating membership through communication*. Cresskill, NJ: Hampton Press.

Mische, A. 2009. *Partisan publics: Communication and contention across Brazilian youth activist networks*. Princeton, NJ: Princeton University Press.

Moore, S. F. 2001. The international production of authoritative knowledge. *Ethnography* 2(2): 161–189.

Näre, L. 2011. The informal economy of paid domestic work: The case of ukrainian and polish migrants in naples. In M. Bommes, and G. Sciortino, (Eds.) *Foggy social structures: Irregular migration and informal economy in Western Europe* (pp. 67–87). Amsterdam: Amsterdam University Press.

Pachirat, T. 2009. Shouts and murmurs: The ethnographer's potion. *Qualitative & Multi-Method Research* 7(2): 41–44.

Polletta, F., and Lee, J. 2006. Is telling stories good for democracy? Rhetoric in public deliberation after 9/11. *American Sociological Review* 71(October): 699–723.

Ricoeur, P. 1991. Life: A story in search of a narrator. In M. Valdés (Ed.), *Reflection and imagination: A Paul Ricoeur reader* (pp. 482–490). Toronto: University of Toronto Press.

Sampson, S. 1996. The social life of projects. Importing civil society to Albania. In C. Mann and E. Dunn (Eds.), *Civil society: Challenging western models* (pp. 121–142). London and New York: Routledge.

Schatz, E. 2009a. Ethnography and American political science: Two tribes, briefly character-ized. *Qualitative & Multi-Method Research* 7(2): 48–50.

Schatz, E. (Ed.). 2009b. *Political ethnography: What immersion contributes to the study of power.* Chicago: University of Chicago Press.

Steinhoff, P. G. 2006. Radical outcasts versus three kinds of police: Constructing limits in Japanese anti-emperor protests. *Qualitative Sociology* 29: 387–408.

Talpin, J. 2006. Jouer les bons citoyens. Les effets contrastés de l'engagement au sein de disposi-tifs participatifs. *Politix* 19(75): 13–31.

Thévenot, L. 2006. *L'action au pluriel: Sociologie des régimes d'engagement.* Paris: La Découverte.

Thévenot, L. 2007. The plurality of cognitive formats and engagements moving between the familiar and the public. *European Journal of Social Theory* 10(3): 409–423.

Thévenot, L., Moody, M., and Lafaye, C. 2000. Forms of valuing nature: Arguments and modes of justification in French and American environmental disputes. In M. Lamont and L. Thévenot (Eds.), *Rethinking comparative cultural sociology: Repertoires of evalua-tion in France and the United States* (pp. 229–272). Cambridge, New York, and Melbourne: Cambridge University Press.

Tilly, C. 2006. Afterword: Political ethnography as art and science. *Qualitative Sociology* 29(3): 409–412.

Verba, S., Brady, H., and Schlozman, K. 1995. *Voice and equality: Civic voluntarism in American politics.* Cambridge, MA: Harvard University Press.

Warren, D. 2009. Studying politics with an ethnographic and historical sensibility. *Qualitative & Multi-Method Research* 7(2): 44–48.

Wedeen, L. 2010. Reflections on ethnographic work in political science. *Annual Review of Political Science* 13: 255–272.

Wolford, W. 2006. The difference ethnography can make: Understanding social mobilization and development in the Brazilian Northeast. *Qualitative Sociology* 29: 335–352.

Yanow, D. 2009. What's political about political ethnography? Abducting our way toward rea-son and meaning. *Qualitative & Multi-Method Research* 7(2): 33–37.

Yon, K. 2009. Quand le syndicalism s'éprouve hors du lieu de travail: La production du sens confédéral à Force ouvrière. *Politix* 22(85): 57–79.

CHAPTER 52

....

SELF-CENSORSHIP, THE SPIRAL OF SILENCE, AND CONTEMPORARY POLITICAL COMMUNICATION

....

ANDREW F. HAYES AND JÖRG MATTHES

INTRODUCTION

....

IN December 2010, a fruit and vegetable cart in Tunisia was closed by government officials, who accused its operator, Mohamed Bouazizi, of not having a proper license. During the altercation, Mr. Bouazazi was reportedly laughed at, spit upon, and allegedly beaten by officials of the Tunisian government (Watson and Karadsheh, 2011). After a failed attempt to remedy his predicament by a visit to a local government office, he doused himself with gasoline in the middle of the street outside that office and set himself ablaze. This act of political expression set off a wave of angry protests in Tunisia, with the people demanding reforms to a corrupt government that was failing its people, limiting their opportunities for economic success, and controlling their destiny, and that suppressed political dissent. After a few weeks and some bloodshed, Tunisian president Zine el-Abidine Ben Ali gave up his hold on power and resigned his office, fleeing to Saudi Arabia.

The events in Tunisia encouraged similar protests elsewhere in the Middle East, where activists ignored threats and overt acts of government retribution and took to the streets to protest governmental repression. Structured and person-on-the-street media interviews of participants in these demonstrations revealed a common sentiment. People were tired of living in fear, and they were willing to die at the hands of the government as a consequence of their actions rather than remain silent and continue to live as victims of oppression and censorship.

To those living in a democracy, the plight of those living under totalitarian rule is hard to fathom. Within broad limits, citizens of democratic nations are afforded the right to speak their minds and to contribute to the political process through elections, serve in government office, protest, and engage in open dialogue with leaders about the governance of a community or nation. Indeed, one could construe these as *human* rights rather than simply *political* ones; for a government to rule its people with a heavy fist and through the suppression of speech is akin to slavery and an affront to humankind. Perhaps as a result, such citizens take free expression for granted, as this right is a liberty seemingly so "inalienable" that it hardly requires much thought in day to day life.

But this does not mean that political expression in democracies is entirely open or that fear of some kind plays no role in democratic political discourse. Although democratic governments have little to no authority to censor public expression of political speech, people still experience censorship of a different variety. Acts of *self-censorship*, in which a person chooses to refrain from engaging in a form of expression given the opportunity, sometimes are motivated by fear, but of a kind different from that felt by the Tunisians. Even in democracies, to varying degrees people may choose silence over expression as a result of "social fears," occasioned by concern about the regard of peers or of the community at large (see e.g., Hayes, 2007; Hayes, Scheufele, and Huge, 2006; Hyde and Ruth, 2002; Ulbig and Funk, 1999; Wyatt et al., 1996). Indeed, such concerns about disrupting one's social life through candid political expression can be a powerful force that serves as the "motivational trigger" (Lin and Pfau, 2007) for a process Noelle-Neumann called the *spiral of silence* (1974, 2003).

In this chapter we review the theoretical propositions of spiral of silence theory as it relates to the interplay among the media, interpersonal talk, and political processes. We briefly summarize the findings to date as they relate to public discourse about the political process and comment on where we see the theory's relevance to modern-day political communication. Finally, we offer some new directions for research and theorizing in the tradition of spiral of silence theory.

The Spiral of Silence, Public Opinion, and Politics

Spiral of silence (SoS) theory attempts to explain the ebb and flow of public opinion around a particular social or political controversy. It is relevant to political communication and the political process insofar as the affect, cognition, and behavior of the citizens of a community (e.g., their attitudes and evaluation of their leaders and their participation in the political process) and/or of its leaders or those involved in governing are determined at least in part by an understanding (mistaken or correct) of public sentiment on the issues that politicians and the people confront during the governance process. The theory consists of a series of propositions anchored by the notion that fundamentally, people are social beings motivated to avoid ostracism, ridicule, and isolation from members of the surrounding community. To successfully navigate the social world and avoid appearing to be on the "wrong side" of public debate, people are constantly monitoring what other people think about controversial issues of the day. Through such observation, people develop a sense of the climate of opinion, primarily based on what the media convey about public sentiment and, to a lesser extent, what they perceive during day-to-day political discussion. According to SoS theory, people whose "quasi-statistical sense" leads them to believe that their own opinion about a given social controversy is in the minority (currently or in the future) will be more reticent to express their views in public situations (e.g., interpersonal discussion, giving interviews to reporters, and so forth) than will individuals who perceive themselves to be in a majority. When those whose beliefs are in a minority choose to self-censor, and when the media fail to represent the minority perspective, ignore it, or construe it as on the fringe, this further alters the perceptions others have of the prevailing climate of opinion, leading to a downward spiraling of the apparent popularity of the minority position that continues until only a small group of "hard cores" choose to express their views.

The theory's major contribution to political communication scholarship has been to increase awareness of the role of social reality perceptions in determining public behavior and collective thinking. Furthermore, Noelle-Neumann's work marks a conceptual turn in the history of media effects as it renewed belief (and interest) in the concept of powerful mass media, one of the classic debates in the field (Peter, 2004). By combining theorizing about mass opinion formation with the substantive body of experimental small-group research on social conformity, the theory also established a vital link between micro-psychological and macro-sociological approaches. The increasingly divisive nature of politics throughout the world makes the theory as relevant today as it was when first conceived in the 1960s. However, as we discuss, we believe that relative to a few decades ago, today it has greater applicability as a theory of group dynamics in the context of small-scale political processes than it does as a theory of media effects or an as explanation for large-scale political outcomes.

The Current State of the Empirical Literature

Noelle-Neumann repeatedly stressed that SoS theory explains a complex and dynamic process and should not be empirically reduced to a test of one single core hypothesis. Yet most studies premised on SoS theory have done just that by focusing on one and sometimes two key assumptions of the theory. The most frequently investigated hypotheses concern (1) the role of perceived (or actual) congruence between one's own opinion and public sentiment on the decision to self-censor and (2) fear of social isolation as a motivation for self-censorship.

Perception of the Opinion Climate and Public Opinion Expression. In almost every published empirical paper testing SoS theory, the effect of perceived congruence between one's opinion and the prevailing climate of opinion on willingness to express that opinion publicly is assessed. Typically, this proposition is tested in an interpersonal context by asking a person to contemplate whether he or she would choose to express his or her opinion or remain silent when engaged in a conversation about a controversial topic with an individual or group. Noelle-Neumann originally used a conversation with passengers on a train as the hypothetical scenario, and thus this paradigm has come to be known as the "train test." Variations on this approach have described the social context as a bus ride (Shamir, 1997), an airplane flight (Salmon and Neuwirth, 1990; Lasorsa, 1991), a party or social gathering (Hayes, 2007; Moy, Domke, and Stamm, 2001; Mutz, 1989; Scheufele, Shanahan, and Lee, 2001), an interview with a reporter or journalist (Kim et al., 2004; Salmon and Neuwirth, 1990; Shamir, 1997; Tokinoya, 1989, 1996), a doctor's waiting room (Petric and Pinter, 2002), a wedding (Willnat, Lee and Detenber, 2002), or a public meeting (Gonzenbach and Stephenson, 1994), among others. Along with this measurement of "willingness to speak out," participants' beliefs and what they believe some reference group of others believes about the issue at hand are assessed. Based on these responses, a measure of self-other opinion congruence is constructed. Studies have used "the public" broadly construed (Lasorsa, 1991; Shamir, 1997) as the reference group, people in the study participant's country (Petric and Pinter, 2002; Willnat, Lee, and Detenber, 2002), the local community (Gonzenbach and Stephenson, 1994; Mutz, 1989; Salmen and Neuwirth, 1990), the media (Kim et al., 2004), recent conversational partners (Scheufele, Shanahan, and Lee, 2001), or friends or family (Moy, Domke, and Stamm, 2001). Frequently, investigators measure self-other congruence with respect to several reference groups simultaneously (e.g., Moy, Domke, and Stamm, 2001; Salwen, Lin, and Matera, 1994; Salmen and Neuwirth, 1990).

Twenty years after SoS theory was first published, the hypothesis that opinion expression is less likely (i.e., self-censorship is more likely) when perceived self-other opinion congruence is low had been examined with such frequency that a meta-analysis of findings was warranted and eventually published in 1997 (Glynn, Hayes, and Shanahan, 1997). This meta-analysis revealed a weak relationship between perceived self-other opinion congruence and willingness to publicly express one's opinion. To explain what seems like a nonintuitive result, a number of boundary conditions and methodological explanations have been offered (Shanahan, Glynn, and Hayes 2007). The inability of past work to find strong effects has been attributed to scholars' failure to account for individual differences between people that relate to public opinion expression, the lack of opinion consonance in media coverage in today's media environment, greater choice in where one obtains news and commentary about political events and issues, the hypothetical nature of the situations participants are asked to contemplate in research to date, or the multidimensional nature of public opinion expression in general.

There is also some debate about how to test this central part of the theory. Such debates include, for example, which "other" should self-other congruence measure, whether the use of hypothetical scenarios such as Noelle-Neumann's original train test or comparable spin-offs can capture how people actually behave, and whether a true test of SoS theory requires acknowledgment of the evolution of public opinion over time. Furthermore, it remains unresolved whether, how, and under what boundary conditions perceptions of public opinion can influence other forms of political expression (such as the display of yard signs, signing petitions) or more private acts, such as voting or donating to a political campaign or party.

Fear of Social Isolation. Noelle-Neumann theorizes that "[a]s social beings, most people are afraid of becoming isolated from their environment" (1977). She adds: "*As a result of* this fear of social isolation, individuals are constantly trying to assess the climate of opinion" [italics ours] (1993, 202; see also 1977, 144; 1991, 260). Fear of social isolation is acknowledged in almost every single SoS study, yet in the vast majority, fear is treated as a given and a social constant of human nature that does not necessitate an empirical test. Some researchers have broken from this tradition by acknowledging that there are individual differences in such fear that should be related to willingness to express opinions publicly. The studies that have directly assessed this relationship generally yield the expected, albeit weak negative association (e.g., Moy, Domke, and Stamm, 2001; Petric and Pinter 2002; Scheufele 1999; Scheufele, Shanahan, and Lee, 2001), but some that find fear of social isolation and opinion expression are unrelated do not, at least after various statistical controls (Kim et al., 2004; Shoemaker, Breen, and Stamper, 2000).

Although there is some consistency in findings, there is little to none in operationalization of fear of social isolation across studies. In most studies, measures of fear of social isolation were constructed ad hoc, providing no evidence of discriminant validity of their measurement from competing constructs (such as shyness). In some cases, reliability is much lower than is generally accepted in the social sciences. Furthermore, the measures sometimes confound their measure of fear of social isolation with the criterion it is being used to predict (see Hayes, Matthes, and Eveland, 2013, for a discussion).

Fear of social isolation may motivate self-censorship, but at least as important is its role as a motivator for people to seek information about the distribution of opinion in the public opinion landscape. Surprisingly, since the search for information about the opinion climate is clearly conceptualized by SoS theory as the *outcome* of our fear of isolation (see the quote above), it took close to forty years for this proposition to be tested. Hayes, Matthes, and Eveland (2013) found that in six of eight countries they examined (United States, England, France, Germany, South Korea, China, Mexico, and Chile), those who measured relatively high in fear of social isolation also reported greater attention to one source of information about the opinion climate: mass media reports of public opinion polls. Only in the two Spanish-speaking countries (Mexico and Chile) was this association absent. This finding suggests that fear of social isolation indeed motivates our quest for knowledge of what others are thinking. Unfortunately, it is one of only a handful of studies (e.g., Huang, 2005) that have taken seriously Noelle-Neumann's (1993, 205) argument that "any theory of public opinion must be internationally applicable" by testing for cross-cultural consistency or variation in results across countries.

Observations about Spiral of Silence Theory as Conceived and Tested

Whether one loves or hates it, whether one construes the evidence as primarily dis-confirming or supporting its basic propositions, SoS theory long ago passed one of the basic tests of a theory by demonstrating its heuristic value. It influenced the way com-munication scholars and political scientists construe public opinion—as a process that interlinks a powerful mass media and interpersonal discourse about matters of pub-lic relevance. Along the way, it has generated myriad empirical studies that pepper the social science literature and conference programs, as well as many journal articles and book chapters both praising and critiquing it. In this section we add our own observa-tions about SoS theory to this literature.

Spiral of Silence Is a Theory of Media Effects. The SoS theory was conceived to help explain changes in public opinion aggregated over individuals within a society and how the mass media influence the ebb and flow of mass opinion. In its original and purest form, SoS is a theory of media effects, not, as it is often described and tested, a theory of interpersonal communication. As Noelle-Neumann first stated in the 1974 *Journal of Communication* article that introduced the theory, "Mass media are part of the system which the individual uses to gain information about the environment. *For all questions outside his immediate personal sphere* he is almost entirely dependent on mass media for the facts and for his evaluation of the climate of opinion" (Noelle-Neumann 1993, 50–51; emphasis added). Her focus is also reflected in her stand on whether the media determine or are a reflection of the public agenda: "[T]he mass media have to be seen as creating public opinion: they provide the environmental pressure to which people respond with alacrity, or with acquiescence, or with silence" (Noelle-Neumann, 1993, 51). In other words, the media influence what people think or should think. If the mass media do not provide a consistent or *consonant* message about where the mass public resides on matters of public relevance, they can do little other than confuse the public about which stand is widely shared or gaining approval and which is a minority per-spective. For this reason, a consonant mass media is an important condition for a spiral of silence to develop at a mass scale. So as originally conceived in SoS theory, the mass media are the primary source of information about the climate of opinion, and from this information people make decisions about how comfortable they are voicing an opinion publicly that runs counter to what the consonant and ubiquitous mass media report. Thus, although the media affect the way we interact with each other, spiral of silence ultimately is a theory about how we are affected by the media.

Of course, by talking about politics and public policy, people can learn what others within their local community, neighborhood, or sphere of friends and family think. But what people are willing to say publicly during such discussions plays a relatively minor role in the public opinion dynamics on a mass scale that SoS theory attempts to explain. A person's "willingness to speak out" is more an operationalization used for testing the fear of social isolation explanation, since it is an inherently meaningful input into peoples' "quasi-statistical organ": the mental calculus that leads a person to understand what the public thinks vis-à-vis his or her own opinion. Thus, studies that attempt to confirm or disprove SoS theory by asking people to articulate what they believe others in their proximate surroundings think are arguably irrelevant, unless such a question is being construed as a proxy for what the mass public thinks. Furthermore, studies that pit various measures of opinion congruence vis-à-vis different reference groups (the mass public, one's community, one's friends and family, and so forth) are beside the point, again according to SoS theory's original set of propositions. Indeed, most every example, empirical or otherwise, that Noelle-Neumann used in her writings focused specifically on people's beliefs about what the general public thinks, not about what a person's friends, family, or members of the person's local community think.

If it is true that the mass media are the main conduit through which information about the climate of opinion is transmitted to the public, then we believe that biases that people assume exist in the media and relatively recent changes in the media industry greatly reduce the modern relevance of SoS theory as it was originally conceived when it comes to understanding the evolution of public opinion on a mass scale. A pervasive finding in communication research is that the mass media are perceived as biased, primarily in a direction against the perceiver's own ideological orientation and especially on topics that people believe are important to them (Hansen and Kim, 2011). So there is some question about the credibility that a significant fraction of the public will ascribe to traditional media when assessing the climate of opinion on a particular public affairs controversy. Furthermore, cable television and especially the Internet have changed the way people acquire information about public affairs. These days, people can choose their news, who delivers it, and the spin they prefer (e.g., news that leans conservative or liberal). This means that people who are so inclined can and often do find voices supporting their position. In this environment, those who are not motivated to selectively expose and who instead sample from the news content in a fairly nonbiased way, may find a lack of media consonance.

Morality, Goodness, and Spiral of Silence Processes. Noelle-Neumann insisted (e.g. 1991, 275; 1993, 200) that a spiral of silence can only develop when the issue at stake is controversial and involves questions of morality or ethics. If one's position reveals little about one's goodness as a person, one's morality, spiritual pureness, or personal ethics, espousing it is unlikely to carry fears of social isolation driven by the disapproval of one's community or peers. Taking a minority stand on a controversial topic that revolves around morality and ethics is an interpersonally risky proposition because of the implications that expression has for perceptions of the morality or goodness of the expressive individual. It is only when interpersonal risks are high that fear of social isolation should operate to suppress the voicing of minority viewpoints.

We don't doubt that the stakes of open dialogue are much higher when the topic of debate focuses on policies or decisions that divide the public along religious, moral, or ethical lines. Yet we question the extent to which this is a necessary condition for a spiral of silence to develop. After all, much of the early empirical research upon which SoS theory is based—for example, Asch's work on conformity—shows that various social pressures can hinder open communication about one's beliefs even when the topic of controversy is as mundane as the lengths of lines on a card. Furthermore, research on social identity using the minimal group paradigm (Brewer, 2007; Tajfel, 1970) has shown that people divided into entirely arbitrary and even random groups make distinctions between those in their group and those outside of it, and such otherwise meaningless "us versus them" distinctions can influence evaluations of the out-group and how the out-group is treated. So there is no reason to assume that social pressures to self-censor are restricted to topics that are highly controversial and morally loaded. Conceivably, any topic on which there is variation in beliefs that allows people to make us-versus-them distinctions could evoke the kind of social pressures to self-censor Noelle-Neumann described.

But more important, there is empirical evidence that when people feel strongly (e.g., Baldassare and Katz, 1996) or care highly about the issue or topic of debate (e.g., Mutz, 1989; Willnat, Lee, and Detenber, 2002), or are more certain that their beliefs are "correct" (e.g., Lasorsa, 1991), or when principles of morality serve as the foundation for those beliefs (Hornsey et al., 2003), self-expression is more likely than when they are less certain or feel less strongly, or their attitudes aren't rooted in deep moral principles. Social issues and public debates that are tinged with questions of morality and ethics are likely to elicit strong beliefs and certain attitudes, perhaps because they are guided by religious doctrine or political ideology. Work by Hornsey and colleagues (2003) supports the notion that such factors can influence the extent to which cues about the opinion climate influence the choice to self-express or self-censor. They experimentally manipulated information about the climate of opinion prior to assessing participants' willingness to express their opinions publicly. They found that among those who said their attitudes were based on moral principle, either the opinion climate was irrelevant to the choice to self-censor (study 1), or self-censorship was *less* likely when the climate was perceived to be *hostile* (study 2). In a similar vein, Matthes, Morrison, and Schemer (2010) provide evidence that attitude certainty moderates the effect of cues about the climate of opinion on public opinion expression. Specifically, when the perceived climate was friendly, self-censorship in a hostile climate was more likely among those less certain of their attitudes. Among those highly certain of their attitudes, perceived opinion climate was either less related or unrelated to willingness to speak out.

Thus, there is some empirical evidence telling us that there is reason to be skeptical that SoS processes operate to suppress less widely shared views primarily when the topic is one that is morally loaded. As Hornsey and colleagues (2003) and Lasorsa (1991) describe, when people's beliefs are guided by moral principles or deep convictions, they may feel the need to act according to those principles. As a result, standing up to an immoral majority may outweigh their need to belong and fit in (also see Moscovici, 1991). These may be the "hard core" that Noelle-Neumann talked about, but on such morally loaded topics—topics that characterize some of the more visible public debates about policy and governing—these hard-core people are likely large in number and their voices sufficiently loud in the public discourse that they most certainly would inhibit a spiral of silence from evolving on a large scale.

Suggestions for Future Research

As originally conceptualized, SoS theory assumed the existence of an omnipresent mass media conveying a consonant message to a mass public, who modify their public communication about controversial, morally loaded topics to avoid the social isolation that can result from expressing unpopular viewpoints. According to this view, empirical research that attempts to test SoS theory absent a morally loaded controversy and an omnipresent, consonant media disseminating information about the opinions of a mass public is misleading.

We believe that SoS theory is best conceptualized in future research not as literally applicable word-for-word, tenet-for-tenet to modern political communication, but instead as a handy heuristic tool for thinking about the interplay among public discussion, perceptions of what others think, and informed decision-making about matters of small-scale or local relevance that are less likely to garner media attention. Absent sufficient media coverage or consonant cues from the media about what the public think, we have no choice but to rely on what we hear other people say, and what they do, to guide our thinking about the opinion climate and where our beliefs reside in that distribution. We have argued that SoS theory probably has little contribution to make these days when it comes to understanding mass political movements or the ebb and flow of opinion on a national scale. Nonetheless, it offers a way to make sense of local political movements that garner little media attention, and it can explicate the dynamics of local political decision-making, whether the actions of a school board, parent-teacher association, or city council. It can also be applied to the political decision-making of small government committees, whether national, state/provincial, or local. Thus, researchers should offer no apologies for using the ideas expressed in SoS theory to guide their own theorizing about local political dynamics, even if the research context does not meet the criteria described in SoS theory for a spiral to develop.

No doubt most of us prefer not to be seen as outcasts, outsiders, strange, deviant, and unusual, for those who are perceived as such rarely have much influence in group interaction and decision-making. But there is reason to believe that individuals vary widely in the amount of fear they bring to social interaction and in the extent to which concern about social isolation inhibits their self-expression. A new measurement tool shows promise in measuring these individual differences reliably and validly (Hayes, Matthes, and Eveland, 2013). Using this instrument, it is worth understanding more about those who let fear govern their day to day discourse and how it influences the direction of political discussion and the quality of group decisions. As noted above, research suggests that such people are more attentive than their low-fear counterparts to what others think about issues of the day. If so, we would expect them to be more accurate in their knowledge of the opinion climate. Yet new evidence suggests that at least on issues that are highly important, those high in fear of social isolation are more likely to falsely assume congruence between their own opinions and the opinions of others (Morrison and Matthes, 2011). But they are also more likely to engage in chronic self-censorship than those relatively low in such fear (Matthes et al., 2010). These conflicting findings tell us that we have much to learn about how fear of social isolation influences people's perceptions of those around them and how those perceptions regulate their public communication.

The citizens of a community can participate in its governance in many different ways, including voting, donating money to a campaign, canvassing a neighborhood, advocating a particular policy or decision, displaying yard signs or bumper stickers, participating in protests, writing letters to elected officials or a local newspaper, joining a school board, running for local political office, talking to one's neighbors about political matters, and so forth. Hayes and colleagues (2006) argue that with the exception of voting, virtually all forms of participation can be construed as public forms of opinion expression. But as acts of opinion expression, different forms of political participation are not equally public.

Researchers (e.g., Scheufele and Eveland, 2001) have described the public versus private distinction vis-à-vis its relevance SoS theory and how different forms of participation may be differentially affected by the process the theory describes (although Noelle-Neumann, 2001, discounted the value of this exercise). If this line of inquiry is to bear theoretical or empirical fruit, the "publicness" of an act of opinion expression needs better explication and operationalization. No doubt publicness of opinion expression can be conceptualized and quantified in multidimensional terms. The dimensions future investigators might consider include how much information the behavior conveys with respect to the opinion of the person engaging in the act, how individuated or personally identifiable the person is when engaging in the behavior, the size of the audience witnessing the action, and the ability of the audience to administer sanction or disapproval.

Finally, we close by taking our own public stand and offer a perspective that may not be widely shared. We suggest that researchers abandon their quest to formally test SoS theory by using the same research paradigm that dominates the existing literature, asking people from population A what they believe about topic B; gauging the congruence between their position and "public opinion" as measured in reference group C, D, and E; and seeing how willing they are to express their opinion in context F. We've been there and done that ad nauseum, and we have learned that public opinion expression is a complex phenomenon guided by many forces, and that no single theory can account for the variation in results that have been observed. The SoS theory is most certain wrong to some extent, like most theories. Instead, we can applaud what Noelle-Neumann has offered to the field of political communication and public opinion and use its tenets to guide us in how we think about how political decision-making contexts can be structured so as to maximize the quality of community decisions and actions.

References

Baldasarre, M., and Katz, C. 1996. Measures of attitude strength as predictors of willingness to speak to the media. *Journalism and Mass Communication Quarterly* 73: 147–158.

Brewer, M. B. 2007. The importance of being We: Human nature and intergroup relations. *American Psychologist* 62: 728–738.

Glynn, C. J., Hayes, A. F., and Shanahan, J. E. 1997. Perceived support for one's opinions and willingness to speak out: A meta-analysis of survey studies on the "spiral of silence." *Public Opinion Quarterly* 61: 452–461.

Gonzenbach, W. J., and Stevenson, R. L. 1994. Children with AIDS attending public school: An analysis of the spiral of silence. *Political Communication* 11: 3–18.

Hansen, G. J., and Kim, H. 2011. Is the media biased against me? A meta-analysis of the hostile media effect research. *Communication Research Reports* 28: 169–179.

Hayes, A. F. 2007. Exploring the forms of self-censorship: On the spiral of silence and the use of opinion expression avoidance strategies. *Journal of Communication* 57: 785–802.

Hayes, A. F., Matthes, J., and Eveland, W. P., Jr. 2013. Stimulating the quasi-statistical organ: Fear of social isolation motivates the quest for knowledge of the opinion climate. *Communication Research* 40: 439–462.

Hayes, A. F., Scheufele, D. A., and Huge, M. E. 2006. Nonparticipation as self-censorship: Publicly-observable political activity in a polarized opinion climate. *Political Behavior* 28: 259–283.

Hornsey, M. J., Makjut, L., Terry, D. J., and McKimmie, B. M. 2003. On being loud and proud: Non-conformity and counter-conformity to group norms. *British Journal of Social Psychology* 42: 319–335.

Huang, H. 2005. A cross-cultural test of the spiral of silence. *International Journal of Public Opinion Research* 17: 324–345.

Hyde, C. A., and Ruth, B. J. 2002. Multicultural content and class participation: Do students self-censor? *Journal of Social Work Education* 38: 241–256.

Kim, S-H., Han, M., Shanahan, J., and Berdayes, V. 2004. Talking on "sunshine in North Korea": A test of the spiral of silence theory as a theory of powerful mass media. *International Journal of Public Opinion Research* 16: 39–62.

Lasorsa, D. L. 1991. Political outspokenness: Factors working against the spiral of silence. *Journalism Quarterly* 68: 131–140.

Lin, W-K., and Pfau, M. 2007. Can inoculation work against the spiral of silence? A study of public opinion on the future of Taiwan. *International Journal of Public Opinion Research* 19: 155–172.

Matthes, J., Hayes, A. F., Rojas, H., Shen, F., Min, S. J., and Dylko, I. 2010. Testing the spiral of silence theory in nine countries: An individual difference perspective. Paper presented at the annual meeting of the International Communication Association, Singapore.

Matthes, J., Morrison, K. R., and Schemer, C. 2010. A spiral of silence for some: Attitude certainty and the expression of minority political opinions. *Communication Research* 37: 774–800.

Morrison, K. R., and Matthes, J. 2011. Socially motivated projection: Need to belong increases perceived consensus on important issues. *European Journal of Social Psychology* 41: 707–719.

Moscovici, S. 1991. Silent majorities and loud minorities. *Communication Yearbook* 14: 256–287.

Moy, P., Domke, D., and Stamm, K. 2001. The spiral of silence and public opinion on affirmative action. *Journalism and Mass Communication Quarterly* 78: 7–25.

Mutz, D. C. 1989. The influence of perceptions of media influence: Third person effects and the public expression of opinions. *International Journal of Public Opinion Research* 2: 3–23.

Noelle-Neumann, E. 1974. The spiral of silence: A theory of public opinion. *Journal of Communication* 24: 43-51.

Noelle-Neumann, E. 1977. Turbulences in the climate of opinion: Methodological applications of the spiral of silence theory. *Public Opinion Quarterly* 41: 143–158.

Noelle-Neumann, E. 1991. The theory of public opinion: The concept of the spiral of silence. *Communication Yearbook* 14: 256–287.

Noelle-Neumann, E. 1993. *The spiral of silence: Public opinion—Our social skin.* 2nd ed. Chicago: University of Chicago Press.

Noelle-Neumann, E. 2001. Commentary. *International Journal of Public Opinion Research* 13: 59–60.

Peter, J. 2004. Our long "return to the concept of a powerful mass media"—A cross-national comparative investigation of the effects of consonant media coverage. *International Journal of Public Opinion Research* 16: 144–168.

Petric, G., and Pinter, A. 2002. From social perception to public expression of opinion: A structural equation modeling approach to the spiral of silence. *International Journal of Public Opinion Research* 14: 37–54.

Salmon, C. T., and Neuwirth, K. 1990. Perception of opinion "climates" and willingness to discuss the issue of abortion. *Journalism Quarterly*, 67: 567–575.

Salwen, M. B., Lin, C., and Matera, F. R. 1994. Willingness to discuss "official English": A test of three communities. *Journalism Quarterly* 71: 282–290.

Scheufele, D. A. 1999. Deliberation of dispute: An exploratory study examining dimensions of public opinion expression. *International Journal of Public Opinion Research* 11: 25–58.

Scheufele, D. A., and Eveland, W. P., Jr. 2001. Perceptions of "public opinion" and "public" opinion expression. *International Journal of Public Opinion Research* 13: 24–44.

Scheufele, D. A., Shanahan, J., and Lee, E. 2001. Real talk: Manipulating the dependent variable in spiral of silence research. *Communication Research* 28: 304–324.

Shamir, J. 1997. Speaking up and silencing out in the face of changing climate of opinion. *Journalism and Mass Communication Quarterly* 74: 602–614.

Shanahan, J., Glynn, C. J., and Hayes, A. F. 2007. The spiral of silence: A meta-analysis and its impact. In R. Preiss, M. Allen, B. Gayle, N. Burrell, and J. Bryant (Eds.), *Mass media effects: Advances through meta-analysis* (pp. 415–427). Mahwah, NJ: Erlbaum.

Shoemaker, P. J., Breen, M., and Stamper, M. 2000. Fear of social isolation: Testing an assumption from the spiral of silence. *Irish Communication Review* 8: 65–78.

Tajfel, H. 1970. Experiments in intergroup discrimination. *Scientific American* 223: 96–102.

Tokinoya, H. 1989. Testing the spiral of silence theory in East Asia. *KEIO Communication Review* 10: 35–49.

Tokinoya, H. 1996. A study on the spiral of silence theory in Japan. *KEIO Communication Review* 18: 1–13.

Ulbig, S. G., and Funk, C. L. 1999. Conflict avoidance and political participation. *Political Behavior* 3: 265–282.

Watson, I., and Karadsheh, J. 2011. The Tunisian fruit seller who kickstarted Arab uprising. Retrieved October 30, 2011, from http://articles.cnn.com/2011-03-22/world/tunisia.bouazizi.arab.unrest_1_fruit-vendor-sidi-bouzid-abedine-ben-ali?_s=PM:WORLD.

Willnat, L., Lee, W., and Detenber, B. H. 2002. Individual-level predictors of public outspokenness: A test of the spiral of silence theory in Singapore. *International Journal of Public Opinion Research* 13: 391–412.

Wyatt, R. O., Katz, E., Levinsohn, H., and Al-Haj, M. 1996. The dimensions of expression inhibition: Perception of obstacles to free speech in three cultures. *International Journal of Public Opinion Research* 8: 229–247.

CHAPTER 53

....

COLLECTIVE
INTELLIGENCE

The Wisdom and Foolishness
of Deliberating Groups

....

JOSEPH N. CAPPELLA, JINGWEN ZHANG,
AND VINCENT PRICE

THE Internet has created substantial interest in and use of various forms of online collectives to generate knowledge and information and even to solve scientific problems. The best-known example is *Wikipedia* and its variants, which allow a wide variety of contributors and contributions that distill content through a combination of bottom-up and top-down processes. News outlets have allowed and even encouraged readers to offer substantive commentary on articles while communicating back to the readership which topics are being widely read, forwarded, and liked. Other more complex processes provide recommendations for movies, books, and products tailored to the interests of each user based on content and preference similarities, also known as recommendation systems (Adomavicius and Tuzhilin, 2005).

Some scholars identify all these examples as types of collective intelligence, casting a wide net to include the blogosphere and the many forms of social media as falling under the umbrella of collective intelligence (Alag, 2009). Any process by which information is collected and aggregated is treated by some as a case of collective intelligence (Bettencourt, 2009). This approach is too broad, in our opinion, both as a way to understand the strengths and weaknesses of collective information generation and certainly for the demands of this chapter.

Instead, we restrict our focus to collectives of individual who identify themselves as a group or not (voters in a congressional district as well as a company's board of directors), who must make a decision on some issue (voting for a congressional candidate; granting health insurance to domestic partners in the company) and who are in direct deliberation (board) or essentially independent decision-makers. Collective intelligence (or foolishness), in our view, requires an assessment of the quality of the decision reached by the collective through deliberation or through simple aggregation of judgments.[1] The focus here is on the role of deliberation in enhancing or undermining collective intelligence with collective decisions of a large group of independent (that is, nondeliberating) persons serving as the baseline of comparison.

The core issue surrounding the value and utility of these collective deliberations is captured in two articles appearing in the *New York Times* in the span of just a few days in early 2012. One extols the effectiveness of collaborative scientific inquiries made possible in large part by the ease with which collective groups of scientists can come together to work on common problems with differential but relevant expertise (Lin, 2012). The other makes clear (Cain, 2012) that intelligent, creative outcomes are as likely and sometimes more likely when people are allowed the solitude and concentration of individual deliberation. At heart, these articles contrast the power of group versus individual deliberation—the core question raised in this chapter. Are collectives capable of being more intelligent than the individuals making them up? If so, under what conditions will the deliberation of collectives yield greater wisdom than foolishness?

Although the upsurge in interest in various forms of collective intelligence—as well as its benefits and pitfalls—appears to be the result of increased attention to emerging media, the idea of collective intelligence is, in fact, an old one, having its roots in the work of John Dewey (1927, 1993), the group social psychologies of the 1950s, and studies in political communication extolling the value of deliberation for successful democracy. The core questions that emerged early in these arenas include whether groups could make better decisions than individuals and under what conditions, whether discussion assisted in the decision-making process or whether the simple aggregation of individual opinion was sufficient to enhance the quality of a decisional outcome, and under what conditions groups produced poorer—foolish—decisions rather than wiser ones.

In this chapter, we take up the question of collective intelligence through a broad review of pertinent literature crafting the following framework for collective intelligence: (1) Simple aggregation of individual opinion (or judgment) is a poor substitute for reasoned opinion by collectives (i.e., deliberation) except in limited circumstances. However, the simple aggregation of opinions serves as the baseline for any improvement in intelligence by a collective. (2) There is no "gold standard" for intelligent decisions by groups except in the case of uninteresting problems such as how many colored balls there are in a large jar. What constitutes an intelligent decision on consequential matters of ethics, public policy, or governance requires approximations to the ideal of what is intelligent. (3) The research on deliberation in various types of collectivities has suffered from many problems—weak or nonexistent theoretical explanations, causal direction, nonindependence of observations, insufficient control, missing data, failure to show that discussion content is linked to outcomes, outcomes that are inconsequential to participants, the absence of any stake in the decision by deliberants, and so on. The most significant problem, however, has been the failure to identify outcomes that are somehow better or worse—that is more and less intelligent—as the crucial consequence of deliberative activity. Instead, outcomes have included opinion change, equality of contributions, satisfaction or dissatisfaction, feelings of isolation or connection, reports of greater or lesser tolerance, and so forth (Delli Carpini et al., 2004). If collective deliberation is to be useful, then its outcomes must be improved decisions, more accurate conclusions, solutions to problems that work—in short, intelligent outcomes by some standard. (4) Collective deliberations will sometimes yield greater foolishness than wisdom, poorer rather than better decisions, less effective or efficient solutions. Understanding the conditions which can enhance and retard collective intelligence is a challenge for the research community. We will examine some established factors, specifically diversity of opinion and information and its impact on collective intelligence. (5) We conclude that deliberation in collective units within society can lead to more intelligent outcomes when opinion, knowledge, and judgment within a collective is diverse at the outset and when this diversity is expressed and thus made available to others in deliberation. (6) This suggests that the trends within emerging media toward increasingly narrow, partisan sources of information, toward selective exposure and avoidance, and toward balkanization of collectives will depress the possibilities of collective intelligence that emerging media would on their surface seem to enhance.

A Baseline for Intelligent Collective Judgments: The Condorcet Jury Theorem

Cass Sunstein (2006) begins *Infotopia* with a discussion of the Condorcet jury theorem (CJT), which sets an important baseline against which to compare any collective decision made by a group in interaction to that aggregate decision of a group of people not in interaction. The CJT asks "under what conditions does the aggregate, independent judgment of a set of individuals yield a better outcome than the most competent person alone or any random person alone?"

Let us suppose that you have a decision to make with two choices, A and B (Stanford or Yale; Romney or Gingrich; policy X will work versus backfire; more white or colored balls in a large jar). You can make the decision on your own or you can consult a number of other people and just get their votes (not their knowledge or their commentary). Which of the following would give the best decision and under what conditions? Your decision ignoring everyone else; the average decision of the group (e.g., 55 percent say Yale); the average decision of the most competent members of the group?

The answer in general is the average of the group's judgments. This is true in general but a variety of conditions need to exist. They include the following: a single, simple, distinct decision (i.e., A or B), no obvious bias affecting everyone in the group (e.g., color blindness, or all rich, or all alumni, or all pessimists); rational deliberators seeking the correct decision, not necessarily a decision that will undermine the process (e.g., voting for a write-in because democracy is a perversion!). The idea here is that averages of judgments are reasonable indicators and better indicators of decisions than is the case for any individual choice, given a clear decision in the face of uncertainty. For example, one would never use this approach in bridge design using a general population because the likelihood of being wrong (the probability of correct decisions not being greater than .50) for a large number of people in the sample is quite high. The CJT sets out a criterion against which decisions by deliberating groups should be set: Does deliberation enhance the quality of the outcome over what it would be for N people who did not deliberate?

The CJT also suggests that simple aggregation of individual judgments can often be successful, so that in this simple sense collectives have a very real chance of being intelligent under a variety of circumstances, although certainly not in general. The CJT has often been tested with relatively simple rather than complex or nuanced tasks (such as policy preferences or ethical decisions). So one issue that must be addressed is whether it is even possible to consider tasks with no clear correct or incorrect outcome. If not, then our ability to study collective intelligence may be so stymied and thus remain merely theoretical.

Is There a Gold Standard for Intelligent Decisions?

With simple technical problems such as the "desert survival problem" or group solutions to a sodoku puzzle, the quality or speed of the solution can be assessed. However, such technical problems are not very interesting and say little about real-world solutions to real-world problems, such as national debt reduction. Mercier and Landemore (2012) argue that even in the case of moral and complex policy decisions, some criteria for better outcomes are possible. Although the actual success of a selected policy may have to await future outcomes, Mercier and Landemore argue that the "epistemic bases" for such decisions are themselves indirect measures of the possible success of the policy selected. They hold that the epistemologic bases for successful decisions are important and necessary, although not sufficient, conditions for intelligent decisions.

In previous research, we have taken a similar approach, arguing that a particular measure of opinion quality—called *argument repertoire* (Cappella, Price and Nir, 2002)—is an indicator of enhanced epistemic grounding for opinion and, therefore, a necessary indicator of increased intelligence in group deliberations. Argument repertoire (AR) is derived from the conceptual and empirical work by Kuhn (1991) on reasoning in daily life. She focuses less on what people think than on *why* they think it. Kuhn's real innovation is directly eliciting and assessing *counter*arguments.

The generation of counter-arguments requires people to envision conditions that would falsify their explanations. This level of reasoning, especially if accompanied by genuine counterevidence, suggests a sophisticated knowledge of the topic well beyond that represented by reasons and evidence for one's own position. In several applications, coders were able to make reliable assessments of the relevant reasons people have for their opinions and reasons that others might have for holding opposed opinions.

AR is also a valid measure of anchored opinion. Those with higher AR are better educated, have greater political knowledge, more interest in politics, more exposure and attention to news, higher interpersonal communication about politics, more commitment to their political parties, and are older (Cappella, Price, and Nir, 2002). Respondents with higher AR scores are more likely to participate in online discussion groups and, once there, to talk more on topic and offer more arguments. Most important, AR is sensitive to the effects of deliberation. Those exposed to substantive conversation on specific issues have elevated AR scores after discussion (Cappella, Price, and Nir, 2002).

AR sidesteps the question of accuracy of reasons and evidence in favor of a simpler but effective measure of anchored opinion. When AR is coupled with standard measures of domain-specific factual knowledge, the two begin to triangulate the epistemic bases for intelligent decisions, as Mercier and Landemore would argue.

However, AR and domain-specific factual knowledge cannot be considered anything but indicators of intelligence regarding an issue. How can preferred solutions be assessed as wise or foolish other than waiting for future outcomes that may never be realized? One solution to this problem is to use aggregate expert opinion as a criterion for judging the success of open-ended problems. While there is no guarantee that expert opinion will yield solutions that work objectively in the real world, opinion from such a group—not from individual experts, mind you, but a group—has a higher probability of working and being fully informed than does the opinion of nonexperts or the opinion of an individual randomly selected expert, at least that is what the CJT would suggest. Such experts offer a greater chance of meeting the criteria set forward for success in the CJT, namely that their individual judgments have a probability above chance of being correct so that—in the absence of other serious biases—their aggregate opinion would be more likely to constitute a wise outcome than would be the case for a random set of individuals or a randomly selected expert.

Although no unassailable standard for assessing intelligent decisions is able to be stated, a combination of criteria establishes the epistemic bases for intelligent decisions and aggregate opinion of domain-specific experts as standards against which individual and group judgment can be assessed.[2]

INTELLIGENT (AND FOOLISH) OUTCOMES FROM DELIBERATING GROUPS

Intelligent Outcomes

Substantial evidence supports the finding that groups in deliberation can in some cases produce enhanced decisions in contrast to individuals or even in comparison to the most competent member. This has been true with mathematical and logical problems (Laughlin and Ellis, 1986; Moshman and Geil, 1998), induction problems (Laughlin, Bonner, and Miner, 2002), causes of death (Sniezek and Henry, 1989), project teams with a group history working outside the laboratory (Michaelsen, Watson, and Black, 1989, see also Bainbridge, 2002; Watson, Michaelsen, and Sharp, 1991; West and Anderson, 1996). In the research on deliberation in political science and political communication, there is a sense that more intelligent outcomes result (Barabas, 2000; Cook and Jacobs, 1998; Fishkin and Luskin, 2005; Gastil and Dillard, 1999), reviewers of this literature acknowledge (Mackie, 2006; Mercier and Landemore, 2012) the tenuous relationship between the outcome measured in most of these studies and real intelligence. For example, opinion change resulting from discussion is not a clear indicator of wisdom or foolishness, as opinions can polarize in undesirable directions.

Research from our own projects on deliberation and intelligence are worth highlighting as well. One project (gPOD[3] for "genetics, public opinion, and deliberation") focused on deliberation by groups sampled from the general public (8 to 12 per group) who met online synchronously on three separate occasions to discuss ethical issues about genetics testing and research. Participants provided information on the epistemic bases for decision quality at various points including factual knowledge about genetics, AR regarding participation in genetics research, and structures of semantic and social networks derived from open-ended responses.

The key comparisons are between those deliberating and others in various nondeliberating control conditions. Young Min Baek (2010) explored changes in factual knowledge by investigating the effects of deliberation participation on a citizen's basic genetic knowledge change. Active deliberation reduced "uncertainty," in that participants became better informed by replacing uncertain knowledge with accurate knowledge. Discussion of bioethical issues mainly influences the "certainty" of their knowledge, which helps the public form more accurate understanding of an issue and thus contribute to stable and solidified opinion. Deliberation, however, does not seem to correct misinformation.

AR was also affected by deliberative activity in contrast to nondeliberating controls (Kim and Cappella, 2010). The quality of opinion—measured as the reasons for one's own and for other's opposed views—is higher for those deliberating than for those not deliberating and especially for those deliberating twice or more in contrast to those not deliberating. The findings are consistent across multiple topics about ethical issues in genetics (e.g., from "duty to warn" to "volunteering"). Deliberation affected the basis of opinion. In support of the importance of opinion anchors, Kim and Cappella (2010) also showed those with more anchored opinions having greater opinion stability over time than those with opinions formed without deliberation.

In his dissertation, Young Min Baek (2011)—also using gPOD data—examined the effect of deliberation on both social and semantic networks while taking into account the positivity and negativity of concepts. A small set of themes was identified as capturing a large percentage of ethical issues regarding genetics. Four outcome measures were examined from the network of social and semantic connections: (1) *size*—for example, how many ties a node has in a given social network; (2) *range*—for example, how many mediations a node enables between nodes in a given social or semantic graph; (3) *integration*—for example, the degree of interconnection within a set of nodes with the same valence in a given network; and (4) *differentiation*—for example, the degree of disconnection between two sets of nodes with opposite valence in a given network.

The most pertinent conclusions are as follows: (1) Deliberation about bioethical issues in genetics made people and concepts more highly interconnected than controls. (2) The dominant valence of the group's discussion (pro or con messages) increased (network) solidarity between people of the same valence. (3) Postdiscussion semantic networks were the result of both prediscussion networks and, more importantly, group-level semantic networks emerging from deliberation (51 of 60 groups).

Results from the gPOD project so far are encouraging regarding the epistemic bases for intelligent decisions by deliberating groups. However, gPOD has not yet employed the opinions of bioethicists as a comparison standard for deliberating versus nondeliberating participants. However, in an earlier deliberation study on healthcare reform, experts were a part of the sample whose positions offered a specific comparison to non expert members of the public.

Studies using protocols similar to gPOD have investigated health policy problems and solutions. One particularly important set of findings yielded the following pattern: that (1) groups' views on health policy change through deliberation in contrast to those not deliberating; (2) the change is in the direction of elite opinion on healthcare policy as revealed in baseline surveys; and (3) change is not dependent on having elites in the deliberating group (Price, Feldman, Freres, Cappella, and Zhang, 2005). For example, elite opinion does not favor tax solutions to health insurance problems initially, whereas citizen opinion does; but citizen opinion changes toward that of elites on this issue even when elites are not in the deliberating group. These results are encouraging.

Other evidence from the healthcare dialogue study indicates that discussion increases the complexity of opinion structures (Price, Arnold, Baek, and Cappella, 2009). Confirmatory factor analysis (CFA) and structural equation modeling (SEM) were used to examine the latent dimensions underlying multiple opinions on healthcare policies and then to test the impact of participation in the online discussions on that latent structure. Results indicate that deliberation produced a significantly more complex and differentiated structure of opinions. Comparisons between "elite" and nonelite respondents further indicate that this deliberation-induced change can be confidently interpreted as reflecting an increase in cognitive sophistication.

Baek and Cappella (2010) have studied the complexity of expressed opinion (not self-reported opinion) in discussing issues in healthcare reform over two time periods. Ordinary citizens and experts' are compared after having discussions with other experts at time one; the expressions at time two show that ordinary citizens' become more complex while those of experts become less complex. These findings indicate that citizens learn the complexities of healthcare options over time from a low base, while experts refine the complex views with which they begin to become more focused on the positions they believe are most effective.

Both existing and new research indicate that deliberation can affect both the epistemic bases for and quality of policy recommendations with deliberation. This conclusion certainly does not and cannot mean that deliberating groups will necessarily produce intelligent outcomes.

Foolish Decisions

Groups do not always make better decisions. Summaries of the literature make clear that certain processes common in group deliberation can distort the information available to discussants through suppression of minority opinion, polarization, and the development of risky shifts (Laughlin, 2011; Turner, 1991). Sunstein (2002, 2008) popularized some of the problems in group deliberation using language that makes clear their consequences for collective intelligence. (1) The predeliberation errors of group members can be amplified, not merely propagated, as a result of deliberation. (2) Groups may fall victim to cascade effects, as the judgments of initial speakers or actors are followed up in successive commentary, while contrary information is withheld (Bikhchandani et al., 1992; Banerjee, 1992; Chamley, 2004). Nondisclosure may be a product of either informational or reputational cascades. (3) Group polarization can lead to more extreme judgments in line with the group's predeliberation dispositions (Nocetti, 2008). Although polarization can lead in desirable directions, there is no assurance of this consequence. (4) In deliberating groups, shared information often dominates or crowds out unshared information, reducing diversity of information and ensuring that groups do not acquire the full range of information available.

FACTORS AFFECTING INTELLIGENT DECISION-MAKING THROUGH DELIBERATION

Researchers have long held that high-quality group decisions depend on the diversity of opinion expressed in group deliberations. Taylor and Faust (1952) claimed that group decisions were superior to individual decisions because groups presented more views of the problem and greater information pertinent to solutions. Since Janis (1982) proposed that successful handling of the Cuban Missile Crisis in 1962 resulted in part from Robert Kennedy playing the role of "devil's advocate," this has been considered one of the prototypical intervention strategies to improve group decision-making performance. The mechanism for improved decisions in "devil's advocate" (DA) procedures may very well be that it increases opinion diversity. SunWolf and Seibold (1999) conclude from their review that the DA procedure improves group decisions; but the groups included only students and focused on well-defined decision tasks. Salazar (1997) found that opinion similarity in groups decreased task-relevant communication, while diverse prior opinions worked to enhance both communication and decision quality. Maznevski (1994) showed that ethnic and cultural diversity improved decision-making performance, again presumably because the information about and frames for viewing alternative outcomes were more diverse. The evidence from controlled group experiments supports Stasser's (1992) conclusion that the quality of group decisions depends significantly on the diversity of information discussed. When status diversity reflects variance in knowledge, expertise, and values, then status diversity can increase the likelihood of high-quality decisions (Berger et al., 1977; Kirchler and Davis, 1986).

Research in political deliberation and political talk has shown that "disagreement" can provide exposure to multiple perspectives and is thus thought to foster the kind of careful reflection needed to arrive at a reasoned opinion. For example, Arendt (1968, 241) stresses the importance of exposure to oppositional views for encouraging an "enlarged mentality," or the ability to form a more representative, informed opinion by considering a particular issue from alternative standpoints. In the view of deliberative theorists, then, political disagreement (or expressed diversity) should enhance learning. Social networks research also suggests that weaker, more heterogeneous ties carry a higher likelihood of transmitting novel information (Granovetter, 1973; Weimann, 1982). Kwak, Williams, Wang, and Lee (2005) and Scheufele et al. (2004) found that talking with people from diverse sociopolitical backgrounds is related to political knowledge.

Exposure to political disagreement has shown that network diversity fosters a better understanding of multiple perspectives on issues (Mutz, 2002a; Price et al., 2002). The ability to rationalize other people's viewpoints might be considered an indirect measure of fact-based issue knowledge. Although one's repertoire of arguments may very well be expanded via political disagreement, this is not to say that these arguments and the issues that support them are necessarily conveyed or interpreted accurately.

Feldman and Price (2008), analyzing data from online group deliberations about the 2000 presidential election, report an interaction effect between amount of political discussion and the perceived disagreement present in discussion networks. Those with the lowest levels of factual knowledge about political issues are embedded in low-disagreement networks with little political talk. Those in high-disagreement networks or low-disagreement, high-talk networks have elevated issue knowledge. Although these data are about people talking politics with others, disagreement plays a consequential role in advancing issue knowledge measured as accurate responses on political issue questions.

Political deliberation is not the only source of support for claims about the importance of information heterogeneity. For example, Giles's (2005) study compares the quality of *Wikipedia* articles to those of the *Encyclopedia Britannica* in terms of the number of acknowledged errors finding them comparable. Surowiecki (2005) suggests that the aggregate knowledge of a large group can be superior to that of a single or small set of experts when diversity of opinion, independence, decentralization, and aggregation characterize the collective. Arazy, Morgan, and Patterson (2006) tested forty-two *Wikipedia* articles to determine the effect of crowd size and diversity on article quality. Quality was defined as the number of errors; crowd size was the number of authors plus number of edits. Diversity was measured as the number of words in the discussion page and the number of edit wars. The results showed that size and diversity had positive effects on quality (see also Arazy, Nov, Patterson, and Yeo, 2011).

Woolley et al. (2010) had small groups of people working on a wide variety of tasks. The groups were shown to have a general "group intelligence," in that performing well on one kind of task was also associated with performance on other quite unrelated tasks. This group intelligence is only weakly related to the average intelligence of individuals in the group or to the intelligence of the most intelligent person. However, it is strongly related to social sensitivity of the group members and to more symmetric distribution of discussion in the group. This equality of discussion is important to information sharing and to effective performance on the assigned tasks. Group intelligence results in large part from social skills inviting the sharing of whatever diverse information and skill is present in the group.

Summary, Implications, and Next Steps

The purpose of this essay has been to invite researchers to reactivate interest in an old problem in the context of the interest created by emerging media in the promise of collective deliberation yielding intelligent outcomes. The old problem is obviously the situation in which groups produce higher-quality decisions than individuals in the context of interaction about those decisions. Our review suggests that deliberating groups can be effective in advancing the epistemic bases for good decisions and for enhancing the quality of decisions for certain types of tasks and for certain criteria for quality. In addition, some consensus in the research literature has emerged over the importance of expressed diversity of opinion, judgment, and knowledge as one important causal factor in assuring the effect of deliberations on decision quality.

However, many challenges remain. The criteria for defining a decision as intelligent rather than foolish are open to considerable debate, especially with open-ended tasks regarding policy, ethics, and governance. We have tried a variety of approaches in our work, including using factual knowledge and argument repertoire as indicators of the epistemic bases for intelligent decisions and comparisons to aggregate elite opinion as an indicator of the quality of a group's decision. Approaches that move beyond simple opinions and judgments (even of experts) to more complex semantic network representations of complex issues hold real promise, we believe (Baek, 2011; Morgan, Fischhoff, Bostrom, and Atman, 2002), especially when aggregate semantic representations of elites are the comparison base for that of the deliberating group. In the end, there is no gold standard, but certainly the issue is worth attention.

Although deliberating collectives are capable of intelligent decisions, they are also capable of foolish ones. No comprehensive theoretical account has emerged for distinguishing the conditions for one or other type of decision even though specific factors such as diversity of expressed information is certainly implicated in intelligent outcomes. Other factors that will need to be considered in any account distinguishing quality of decisions will be a theory of types of tasks and vested interest in the decision's outcome. Both have received attention in the research literature (Hackman, 1969; McGrath, 1984), with the latter factor widely considered in the work on prediction markets.

As has been the case in much of the research on the consequences of political deliberation, few convincing explanations have arisen for why deliberative processes should produce changes in tolerance, engagement, and social capital. The same is true of deliberation and collective intelligence. Certainly arguments about bounded rationality, the analogy to genetic diversity and survival, and other biological analogies have appeal. However, no strong causal account has arisen even to explain why collective deliberation can be intelligent.

If expressed diversity of opinion, judgment, and knowledge is as important to intelligent decisions as some research already suggests, then social, political, psychological, and media systems factors that increase the likelihood of the balkanization of knowledge and opinion will undermine the chances of intelligent deliberation. Jamieson and Cappella (2008) and many others have addressed this issue (Sunstein, 2001, 2009), but in the context of a burgeoning interest in collective deliberation and intelligence, the effects of balkanized knowledge on deliberation—whether by elites or nonelites—take on renewed urgency.

Notes

1. Public opinion is not concerned with the quality of the outcome rendered by the expressed opinions, just their outcome.
2. Another approach to defining tasks whose outcomes can be compared to real-world decisions is the use of prediction markets to predict future events (Servan-Schreiber et al., 2004; Wolfers and Zitzewitz, 2004), such as the success of upcoming movies (Foutz and Jank, 2010), political stock markets (Forsythe et al., 1999) and sports betting markets (Spann and Skiera, 2009), as well as election outcomes (e.g., in contrast to political polling results) (Erikson and Wlezien, 2008; Pagon, 2005; Wolfers and Zitzewitz, 2009). However, these forums for collective intelligence replace deliberation with online monetary decisions; therefore, while relevant to collective decision making, they are irrelevant to deliberative processes except under the most generous interpretation of the equivalence of betting with the exchange of symbolic information.
3. Research from gPOD is mostly unpublished or currently under review. For a copy of the final report from this project, providing some of the detailed results and analyses, or for copies of individual papers cited, contact the first author.

References

Adomavicius, G., and Tuzhilin, A. 2005. Toward the next generation of recommender systems: A Survey of the state-of-the-art and possible extensions. *IEEE Transactions on Knowledge and Data Engineering* 17(6): 734–749.

Alag, S. 2009. *Collective intelligence in action.* Greenwich, CT: Manning.

Arazy, O., Morgan, W., and Patterson, R. 2006. Wisdom of the crowds: Decentralized knowledge construction in Wikipedia. Proceeding of the 16th Workshop on Information Technologies & Systems (WITS'06). Unpublished paper. Available at: http://papers.ssrn.com/sol3/papers.cfm?abstract_id=1025624

Arazy, O., Nov, O., Patterson, R., and Yeo, L. 2011. Information quality in Wikipedia: The effects of group composition and task conflict. *Journal of Management Information Systems,* 27(4): 73–100.

Arendt, H. 1968. Truth and politics. In H. Arendt (Ed.), *Between past and future: Eight exercises in political thought* (pp. 227–264). New York: Viking Press.

Baek, Y. M. 2010. From uncertain to accurate: How citizens are informed in deliberation. Unpublished manuscript.

Baek, Y. M. 2011. The impact of deliberation on social and semantic networks: Citizens mental models of bioethical issues in genetics using automated textual analysis. University of Pennsylvania. ProQuest Dissertations and Theses. Available at: http://search.proquest.com/docview/893843412?accountid=6167

Baek, Y. M., and Cappella, J. N. 2010. When citizens meet experts: Effects of issue experts' mental models on citizens' opinion as textual network. Unpublished manuscript. Philadelphia: Annenberg School for Communication.

Bainbridge, S. M. 2002. Why a board? Group decision making in corporate governance. *Vanderbilt Law Review* 55(1): 1–55.

Banerjee, A.V. 1992. A simple model of herd behaviour. *Quarterly Journal of Economics* 107(3): 797–817.

Barabas, J. 2000. Americans discuss social security: How deliberation affects public opinion. Northwestern University. ProQuest Dissertations and Theses. Available at: http://search.proquest.com/docview/304632708?accountid=6167

Berger, J., Fisek, M. H., Norman, R. Z., and Zelditch, M., Jr. 1977. *Status characteristics and social interaction.* New York: Elsevier.

Bettencourt, L.M.A. 2009. The rules of information aggregation and emergence of collective intelligent behavior. *Topics in Cognitive Science* 1: 598–620.

Bikhchandani, S., Hirshleifer, D., and Welch, I. 1992. A theory of fads, fashion, custom, and cultural change as informational cascades. *Journal of Political Economy* 1005: 992–1026.

Cain, S. January 13, 2012. The rise of the new groupthink. *New York Times.* Available at: http://www.nytimes.com/2012/01/15/opinion/sunday/the-rise-of-the-new-groupthink.html

Cappella, J. N., Price, V., and Nir, L. 2002. Argument repertoire as a reliable and valid measure of opinion quality: Electronic dialogue in campaign 2000. *Political Communication* 19(1): 73–93.

Chamley, C. P. 2004. *Rational herds: Economic models of social learning.* Cambridge, UK: Cambridge University Press.

Cook, F. L., and Jacobs, L. R. 1998. *Deliberative democracy in action: Evaluation of Americans discuss social security.* Washington DC: Report to the Pew Charitable Trusts.

Delli Carpini, M. X., Cook, F. L., and Jacobs, L. R. 2004. Public deliberation, discursive participation, and citizen engagement: A review of the empirical literature. *Annual Review of
Political Science* 7: 315–344.

Dewey, J. 1927. *The public and its problems.* New York: Holt.

Dewey, J. 1993. Philosophy and democracy. In D. Morris and I. Shapiro (Eds.), *John Dewey: The
political writings* (pp. 38–47). Indianapolis, IN: Hackett. Original work published in 1919.

Erikson, R. S., and Wlezien, C. 2008. Are political markets really superior to polls as election
predictors? *Public Opinion Quarterly* 722: 190–215.

Feldman, L., and Price, V. 2008. Confusion or enlightenment? How exposure to disagreement moderates the effects of political discussion and media use on candidate knowledge.
Communication Research 35(1): 61–87.

Fishkin, J. S. and Luskin, R. C. 2005. Experimenting with a democratic ideal: Deliberative polling and public opinion. *Acta Politica* 40: 284–298.

Forsythe, R., Rietz, T. A., and Ross, T. W. 1999. Wishes, expectations, and actions: A survey on
price formation in election stock markets. *Journal of Economic Behavior and Organization*
39: 83–110.

Foutz, N. Z., and Jank, W. 2010. Research note—Prerelease demand forecasting for motion
pictures using functional shape analysis of virtual stock markets. *Marketing Science* 29(3):
568–579.

Gastil, J., and Dillard, J. P. 1999. Increasing political sophistication through public deliberation.
Political Communication 16: 3–23.

Giles, J. 2005. Internet encyclopedias go head to head. *Nature* 438(15): 900–901.

Granovetter, M. 1973. The strength of weak ties. *American Journal of Sociology* 78: 1360–1380.

Hackman, J. R. 1969. Toward understanding the role of tasks in behavioral research. *Acta
Psychologica* 31: 97–128.

Jamieson, K. H., and Cappella, J. N. 2008. *Echo chamber: Rush Limbaugh and the conservative
media establishment.* New York: Oxford University Press.

Janis, I. L. 1982. *Groupthink,* 2nd ed. Boston: Houghton Mifflin.

Kim, J. W., and Cappella, J. N. 2010. Effects of deliberation on reasoned and stable opinions
about genetics research. Unpublished manuscript. Philadelphia: Annenberg School for
Communication.

Kirchler, E., and Davis, J. H. 1986. The influence of member status differences and task type on
group consensus and member position change. *Journal of Personality and Social Psychology*
51(1): 83–91.

Kuhn, D. 1991. *The skills of argument.* Cambridge, UK: Cambridge University Press.

Kwak, N., Williams, A. E., Wang, X., and Lee, H. 2005. Talking politics and engaging politics: An examination of the interactive relationships between structural features of political
talk and discussion engagement. *Communication Research* 32: 87–111.

Laughlin, P. R. 2011. *Group problem solving.* Princeton, NJ: Princeton University Press.

Laughlin, P. R., Bonner, B. L., and Miner, A. G. 2002. Groups perform better than the best
individuals on letters-to-numbers problems. *Organizational Behavior and Human Decision
Processes* 88: 605–620.

Laughlin, P. R., and Ellis, A. L. 1986. Demonstrability and social combination processes on
mathematical intellective tasks. *Journal of Experimental Social Psychology* 22: 177–189.

Lin, T. January 16, 2012. Cracking open the scientific process. *New York Times.* Available at:
http://www.nytimes.com/2012/01/17/science/open-science-challenges-journal-tradition-
with-web-collaboration.html

Mackie, G. 2006. Does democratic deliberation change minds? *Philosophy, Politics and Economics* 10(5): 279–303.

Maznevski, M. L. 1994. Understanding our differences: Performance in decision-making groups with diverse members. *Human Relations* 47(5): 531–552.

McGrath, J. E. 1984. *Group interaction and performance.* Englewood Cliffs, NJ: Prentice Hall.

Mercier, H., and Landemore, H. 2012. Reasoning is for arguing: Understanding the successes and failures of deliberation. *Political Psychology* 33(2): 243–258.

Michaelsen, L. K., Watson, W E., and Black, R. H. 1989. A realistic test of individual versus group consensus decision making. *Journal of Applied Psychology* 74: 834–839.

Morgan, M. G., Fischhoff, B., Bostrom, A., and Atman, C. J. 2002. *Risk communication: A mental Models approach.* New York: Cambridge University Press.

Moshman, D., and Geil, M. 1998. Collaborative reasoning: Evidence for collective rationality. *Thinking and Reasoning* 4(3): 231–248.

Mutz, D. C. 2002. Cross-cutting social networks: Testing democratic theory in practice. *American Political Science Review* 96: 111–126.

Nocetti, D. 2008. The biasing effects of memory distortions on the process of legal decision-making. *Review of Law and Economics* 4(1): 314–334.

Pagon, A. 2005. Polls and markets in the 2004 presidential election: A risk premium to explain deviations between polling predictions and market prices. Department of Economics working paper, Stanford University. Available at: http://economics.stanford.edu/files/Theses/Theses_2005/Pagon.pdf

Price, V., Arnold, A. K., Baek, Y. M., and Cappella, J. N. 2009, Deliberation, constraint and complexity. Unpublished manuscript. Philadelphia: Annenberg School for Communication.

Price, V., Feldman, L., Freres, D., Cappella, J. N., and Zhang, W. 2005. Informing public opinion about health care reform through online deliberation. Unpublished manuscript. Philadelphia: Annenberg School for Communication.

Price, V., Nir, L., and Cappella, J. 2002. Does disagreement contribute to more deliberative opinion? *Political Communication* 19: 95–112.

Salazar, A. J. 1997. Communication effects on small group decision-making: Homogeneity and task as moderators of the communication-performance relationship. *Western Journal of Communication* 61(1): 35–65.

Scheufele, D. A., Nisbet, M. C., Brossard, D., and Nisbet, E. C. 2004. Social structure and citizenship: Examining the impacts of social setting, network heterogeneity, and informational variables on political participation. *Political Communication* 21: 315–338.

Servan-Schreiber, E., Wolfers, J., Pennock, D. M., and Galebach, B. 2004. Prediction markets: Does money matter? *Electronic Markets* 14(3): 243–251.

Sniezek, J. A., and Henry, R. A. 1989. Accuracy and confidence in group judgment. *Organizational Behavior and Human Decision Processes* 43: 1–28.

Spann, M., and Skiera, B. 2009. Sports forecasting: A comparison of the forecast accuracy of prediction markets, betting odds and tipsters. *Journal of Forecasting* 28: 55–72.

Stasser, G. 1992. Information salience and the discovery of hidden profiles by decision-making groups: A "thought experiment." *Organizational Behavior and Human Decision Processes* 52: 156–181.

Sunstein, C. R. 2002. The law of group polarization. *Journal of Political Philosophy* 10 (2): 175–195.

Sunstein, C. R. 2001. *Republic.com.* Princeton, NJ: Princeton University Press.

Sunstein, C. R. 2006. *Infotopia: How many minds produce knowledge.* New York: Oxford University Press.

Sunstein, C. R. 2009. *Republic.com 2.0.* Princeton, NJ: Princeton University Press.

Sunstein, C. R., and Hastie, R. 2008. Four failures of deliberating groups. John M. Olin Law and Economics working paper no. 401, University of Chicago. Available at: http://www.law.uchicago.edu/files/files/401.pdf

SunWolf and Seibold, D. R. 1999. The impact of formal problem solving procedures on group processes, members, and task outcomes. In L. R. Frey (Ed.), D. S. Gouran, and M. S. Poole (Assoc. Eds.), *The handbook of group communication theory and research* (pp. 395–431). Thousand Oaks, CA: Sage.

Surowiecki, J. 2005. *The wisdom of crowds.* New York: Random House.

Taylor, D. W., and Faust, W. L. 1952. Twenty questions: Efficiency in problem solving as a function of size of group. *Journal of Experimental Psychology* 44: 360–368.

Turner, J. C. 1991. *Social influence.* Pacific Grove, CA: Brooks/Cole.

Watson, W. E., Michaelsen, L. K., and Sharp, W. 1991. Member competence, group interaction, and group decision making: A longitudinal study. *Journal of Applied Psychology* 76: 803–809.

Weimann, G. 1982. On the importance of marginality: One more step in the two-step flow of communication. *American Sociological Review* 47: 764–773.

West, M. A., and Anderson, N. R. 1996. Innovation in top management teams. *Journal of Applied Psychology* 81: 680–693.

Wolfers, J., and Zitzewitz, E. 2009. Using markets to inform policy: The case of the Iraq War. *Economica* 76: 225–250.

Wolfers, J. and Zitzewitz, E. 2004. Prediction markets. *Journal of Economic Perspectives* 18(2): 107–126.

Woolley, A. W., Chabris, C. F., Pentland, A., Hashmi, N., and Malone, T. W. 2010. Evidence for a collective intelligence factor in the performance of human groups. *Science* 330: 686–688.

THE ALTERED POLITICAL COMMUNICATION LANDSCAPE

CHAPTER 54

BROADCASTING VERSUS NARROWCASTING

Do Mass Media Exist in the Twenty-First Century?

MIRIAM J. METZGER

THE DEMASSIFICATION OF MASS COMMUNICATION

WITHER mass communication? In a 2001 article titled "The End of Mass Communication?" Chaffee and Metzger observed that a profound change was occurring such that the defining features of mass communication that had been in place since the early twentieth century were being undermined by significant changes in the communication technologies used to produce, disseminate, and exhibit media content in the twenty-first century. Specifically, whereas "mass communication" of the past could be characterized in terms of the production of broad-appeal content by a handful of large and powerful media institutions, and by little content choice at the audience level due to a limited number of available channels and formats, contemporary media present a vastly different environment to media consumers. The "new" media environment not only offers a massive amount of information from a multitude of sources that can transmit their content over many channels but also places more control over both content creation and selection in the hands of audience members themselves. These changes precipitated a shift from mostly broad-appeal programming to a sizable portion of content produced to appeal to more narrow audiences. As a result, Chaffee and Metzger (2001) argued that contemporary media are "demassifying" mass communication.

Demassification is particularly evident in recent media production and consumption patterns. The one-to-many model of media content production that has traditionally defined "mass" communication and set it apart from other forms of communication now finds itself having to accommodate newer models of many-to-many communication.

Opportunities afforded to users of digital media for producing and distributing their own media content to large audiences (i.e., "user-generated content") undermine the long-held assumption that large organizations are required to produce and distribute media content at a mass scale. In other words, whereas mass media producers of the past were "big and few," today they are also "small and many" (Chaffee and Metzger, 2001).

Moreover, the enormous popularity of Web-based platforms such as YouTube, blogs, and other forms of digital and social media may divert audience attention from media content delivered via traditional media channels. Indeed, there is evidence to show that this is happening in the realm of news and political information. Data from a recent *State of the News Media* annual report, for example, show that while digital platforms for news are gaining in audience share, all other mass media sectors—including cable news for the first time—are experiencing declines in their audience numbers (Rosensteil and Mitchell, 2011). And, as the plethora of choices expands, audiences will continue to be stretched thinner across all the options of media sources and channels. In sum, then, the two key defining characteristics of mass communication historically, namely the size of mass media producers and the size of the audience for any particular media content, appear to be "demassifying" in large part as a result of changes in the communication technologies used to produce and deliver media content.

This chapter examines these changes in the media landscape to address the question of the continuing relevance of mass media at the dawn of the new millennium. It begins by tracing the history of media content production, distribution, and consumption first from broadcasting to narrowcasting, and then to more recent trends toward "hyper-personalization" in the digital media environment. The chapter then focuses on what these changes mean for politics and for political communication theory. It concludes by attempting to answer the question "Do mass media exist in the twenty-first century?" and by posing some questions about the future of mass media that are intended to serve as a call for research into the changing nature, circumstances, and effects of mass communication in the contemporary media environment.

Media Content: From Broadcasting to Narrowcasting

The original "broadcast model" of media content production to mass audiences was a rational response to early mass media systems' economic and physical resource scarcity. Under such constraints the best way to attract the largest portion of the audience share was to produce the programming with the broadest appeal. But a significant effect of the explosion of channels made available by digital networked communication technologies in the waning decades of the twentieth century has been to diffuse the audience for any particular media product, as discussed earlier. The result, which again was a rational response to changing market conditions, has been toward increasingly niche-oriented media content delivered over increasingly specialized channels (Owen and Wildman, 1992). This trend away from "broadcasting" and toward "narrowcasting" (see Massey, 2004) and its sociopolitical impacts has been discussed by several scholars (e.g., Bennett and Iyengar, 2008; Mendelsohn and Nadeau, 1996; Prior, 2007; Ranney, 1990; Sunstein, 2001, 2007, 2009; Turow, 1997).

Although the shift from broadcasting to narrowcasting is evident across several genres of media content, news provides a particularly interesting case study. In the heyday of traditional mass communication in the twentieth century, major media outlets, including the leading urban newspapers and television network news broadcasts, dominated the news audience share in most US media markets. For example, the audience for the three major network newscasts (ABC, CBS, and NBC) in the mid-twentieth century typically reached over seventy million Americans (Prior, 2007). That has changed dramatically, with only about a fifth of Americans now tuning in on an average weeknight (Rosensteil and Mitchell, 2011). Although data show steady declines in audiences for network news over the last thirty years, during which time the networks lost 55.5 percent of the share of viewership they once had, this does not mean that most people have abandoned news altogether. Instead, they appear to be gravitating to other news platforms (Rosensteil and Mitchell, 2011).

The appearance of cable and satellite technologies in the 1980s and 1990s offered the first serious alternatives to broadcast network news, and both these and more recent digital networked communication technologies accelerated the decline in both television news viewership and print newspaper readership. Perhaps more importantly, however, the fracturing of audiences for traditional news outlets prompted product differentiation and experimentation with new forms of news,[1] including more partisan news outlets (Bae, 1999, 2000; Iyengar and Hahn, 2009). Fox News is the most obvious example, and Iyengar and Hahn (2009) argue that Fox News emerged in part by audience fragmentation resulting from channel proliferation in the 1990s. Mullainathan and Shleifer (2005) further show that there is economic incentive for ideological specialization in news products, as audiences tend to prefer information that confirms their beliefs, and media organizations that respond to audience demand stand to reap greater profits. In other words, niche news is an effective competitive strategy in an increasingly crowded news marketplace.

The rise of media channel proliferation and narrowcasting increased audience choice in media content and, consequently, audience members' opportunities for selective exposure (Chaffee and Metzger, 2001; Iyengar and Hahn, 2009). Although niche media (e.g., radio, magazines) predate cable, satellite, and Internet media technologies, and while audience selectivity has been observed with traditional mass media content as well (see Sears and Freedman, 1967 for a review), the appearance of partisan news affords greater opportunity for a particular type of audience selectivity—selective exposure to ideologically congenial news and public affairs information.

Several scholars argue that this type of selectivity may significantly reduce citizens' exposure to political difference (see, for example, Bennett and Iyengar, 2008; Sunstein, 2001). Also, while narrowcasting and increased consumer control over media exposure reduced the size of the available audience share for all types of programming, demand for mainstream news information, which used to provide an "information commons" or shared context for receiving public affairs information, has shrunk over the years, particularly among younger audiences (Bennett and Iyengar, 2008).[2] Even among politically interested citizens, niche media provide attractive alternatives to traditional news outlets, while facilitating politically uninterested audiences to tune out completely. Bennett and Iyengar (2008, 707) consequently question whether the concept of mass media has been "made obsolete by audience fragmentation and isolation from the public sphere." For many of the same reasons, Chaffee and Metzger (2001) similarly wondered whether history will show that "mass media" was a purely a twentieth-century phenomenon.

Media Content: From Narrowcasting to Hyperpersonalization

The latest development in the move from broadcasting to narrowcasting, coupled with niche news and the expansion of opportunities for selective exposure afforded by modern media technology, is what Bennett and Iyengar (2008, 723) call "the personally mediated society." Similar to Negroponte's (1995) concept of the "Daily Me," which refers to news content that is customized according to individuals' personal tastes, Bennett and Iyengar argue that the diversified information environment allows individual news consumers to limit their news information to, for example, include only those sources and perspectives that share their ideological views. Indeed, Turow's historical analysis of media marketing strategies shows a progression toward what he calls the "hypersegmentation" of audiences by media firms and advertisers in order to take better advantage of the narrowcasting opportunities made possible by channel proliferation in the contemporary media environment (Turow, 1997). Thus, whether it is by their own hand via selective exposure, or by the hand of media firms and their advertisers via target marketing, media audiences are increasingly likely to receive information that is customized to their personal tastes, interests, and political viewpoints to the possible exclusion of other information.

The personally mediated society may be exacerbated by Web 2.0 applications, such as social media including social networking platforms (e.g., Facebook), social bookmarking sites (e.g., Digg or Reddit), and political blogs. These platforms and applications allow for a new level of customization that is based on personal interests that we both consciously and inadvertently express via our activity on the Web, including the sites we visit, the search terms we use, the interests and actions we disclose in online social networks, and even those of our peers with whom we are connected via our various online communities. Writing about this development, Sunstein (2007, 4) comments:

> Negroponte's prophecy was not nearly ambitious enough. As it turns out, you don't
> need to create a Daily Me. Others can create it for you. If people know a little bit
> about you, they can discover, and tell you, what "people like you" tend to like—and
> they can create a Daily Me, just for you, in a matter of seconds.

Pariser (2011) similarly argues that as algorithmic gatekeepers and recommendation systems replace human ones, each communication we receive will be chosen in advance based on algorithmic filters, which themselves are based on the traces that we leave of ourselves via our online actions. This creates a form of "hyperpersonalization" of news and other media content, as well as a new form of preselected selective exposure that is outside the direct control of audience members. A case in point is that the exact same Google search performed by two people now returns quite different results. Moreover, Facebook envisions a future in which all of the information we receive online is filtered through our personally tailored social networks such that, rather than querying a search engine like Google as we seek advice on what camera to buy or dentist to see, we will instead query our "social graph," which consists of our network of friends, colleagues, peers, and family with whom we are connected online (Vogelstein, 2009). Given that humans tend to associate with others who share similar attributes and attitudes (e.g., Byrne, 1971), this may further limit the diversity of information that people are exposed to and create an echo chamber effect as they engage with information and others online.

Major Research Findings

An important question stemming from these trends asks what these shifts in the media landscape mean for politics and for political communication theory? As it turns out, there is considerable research to help answer this question, but it is not without controversy. Two major areas of scholarship pertaining to the first part of this question are whether narrowcasting leads to greater audience selective exposure, and whether selective exposure will foster political polarization that serves to undermine democracy. Another area of scholarship addresses the second part of the question by examining whether new forms of media content (e.g., niche news) and patterns of their consumption necessitate entirely new theorizing and expectations about media effects on political outcomes. These issues are discussed next.

Implications of Narrowcasting and Hyperpersonalization for Democracy

Several scholars have written about the impact of selective exposure due to the rise of narrowcasting and hyperpersonalization of media content on democracy, arguing that exclusive attention to like-minded others exacerbates rifts in society between ideologically divergent groups, and thus impedes the cooperation that is needed to address the complex problems facing modern society (e.g., Mendelsohn and Nadeau, 1996; Stroud, 2010; Sunstein, 2001, 2007, 2009). Stroud (2010), for instance, looked at news consumption behavior over time, and found strong evidence that repeated selective exposure to attitude-consistent information resulted in increased political polarization. Sunstein (2007) argues that selective exposure to ideologically congenial information undermines the preconditions for a well-functioning democracy, which include exposure to political difference and a shared information commons. Without these, he says, common understandings between groups will be more difficult to achieve and society will have a much harder time in addressing its social problems. Others have similarly discussed the implications of channel proliferation on creating political attitude extremity and partisan echo chambers (e.g., Jamieson and Cappella, 2009).

Of course, whether the most drastic political implications are ever realized is contingent on the extent to which narrowcasting encourages audience members' selective exposure to exclusively attitudinally congruent news information in the first place. This topic has received a good deal of attention over the years. While early research on selective exposure in general found weak or mixed evidence for the phenomenon (see, for example, Kinder, 2003; Sears and Freedman, 1967), more recent empirical work provides strong evidence for its prevalence today (Iyengar and Hahn, 2009; Stroud, 2007, 2008, 2010, 2011; Tewksbury, 2005). Although this research has largely settled the debate over people's tendency to selectively attend to attitude-consistent political information, disagreement concerning whether they actively avoid attitude-discrepant information—which is an important component of normative views of the effects of selective exposure—continues. Research by Stroud (2010) and by Iyengar and Hahn (2009) showing evidence of selective avoidance is countered by studies showing no evidence for the phenomenon (e.g., Garrett, 2009a, 2009b; Kobayashi and Ikeda, 2009; Webster, 2007). Holbert, Garrett, and Gleason's (2010, 22) overview of this literature concludes that despite having a preference for congenial information, people do engage with discrepant viewpoints under certain circumstances. Thus, these scholars conclude that "selective exposure and encounters with attitude-discrepant information can co-exist."

There are also questions about the prevalence of selective exposure and avoidance across the political spectrum. One of the circumstances under which selective exposure appears to occur is with news consumers who possess strong political attitudes (Brannon, Tagler, and Eagly, 2007). Indeed, Knobloch-Westerwick and Meng (2009) found that partisanship interacts with selectivity. In their study, although people chose attitude-consistent sources of news information, and spent more time reading news from these sources than news from counter-attitudinal sources, this effect was more pronounced for people who felt strongly about their beliefs. Evidence for selective avoidance by stronger partisans is also seen in the blogosphere, where studies have found a tendency for blog readers to avoid those that challenge their ideological views (Johnson, Bichard, and Zhang, 2009), and for bloggers to avoid linking to political videos that challenge their ideological positions (Wallsten, 2011). The question of whether selective avoidance operates only or primarily among strong partisans, while the majority of citizens receive a fairly balanced diet of attitudinally consistent and inconsistent information, is important because this would weaken claims that narrowcasting will necessarily have drastic negative repercussions for democratic society.

Finally, there is debate about the effects of selective exposure on political participation. Stroud (2011) concludes from her research that selective exposure influences how average people engage with politics. She argues that on the one hand, citizens may become increasingly polarized as a result of using media that coheres with their political beliefs, causing them to experience political frustration and apathy, and perhaps culminating in decreased voter turnout. On the other hand, however, she also finds that partisan selective exposure may encourage participation at the individual level by encouraging political engagement. Sunstein (2009) similarly argues that political extremism can be good in that it can bring like-minded individuals together, spurring heightened political involvement and collective action. As the title of his book suggests, like minds can both unite and divide.[3]

Implications of Narrowcasting for Political Communication Theory

In addition to debates on the extent to which selective exposure exists and leads to political polarization, there is contention over whether the shifting foundations of modern mass communication media are creating fissures in our central and long-held theories of political communication effects (Bennett and Iyengar, 2008; Chaffee and Metzger, 2001; Holbert et al., 2010; Metzger 2009; Neuman and Guggenheim, 2011). This first took the form of Chaffee and Metzger's (2001) proposition that several of our core media effects theories are challenged by demassification brought on by digital networked media. Metzger (2009) further suggested media effects theories that assume mass exposure to relatively uniform content (e.g., exposure to a limited set of news information and perspectives emanating from three dominant broadcast networks), such as agenda setting, cultivation theory, and the spiral of silence, are either untenable in the contemporary media environment or that their basic premises should be seriously reexamined.

The debate over media effects in the new media landscape has centered more recently on whether the effects of political communications in this environment are likely to be minimal or substantial. Bennett and Iyengar (2008) argue that the trend toward narrowcasting is likely to produce only minimal effects of political communication on audiences, at least in the realm of persuasive media effects. This is true for several reasons, they say. First, channel proliferation encourages selective exposure to attitudinally congruent media content (and selective avoidance of dissonant information), which serves to reinforce rather than change news consumers' preexisting attitudes. In addition, given most people's preference for entertainment media content, all but the most politically interested citizens will be exposed to less news information overall and so collectively, the electorate will know less about and thus participate less in politics. Third, it will be difficult for survey researchers to prove that audiences have been persuaded by a media message when those audiences self-select messages that confirm their views, and media audiences will be more likely to resist messages that challenge their preexisting attitudes. This means that reinforcement effects will be found even among those who are exposed to counter-attitudinal information. As an example of the last point, they discuss survey data showing that many Republicans continued to believe that Iraqi President Saddam Hussein possessed weapons of mass destruction even after receiving overwhelming information to the contrary.

While Holbert et al. (2010) agree with much of Bennett and Iyengar's analysis, they disagree with their conclusion. They instead argue that recent changes in the media environment facilitate "pull" rather than "push" media, which means that those who do choose to expose themselves to political information in high-choice media environments may be more motivated to process that information, and thus will be affected by it. They rely on theories of persuasion such as the Elaboration Likelihood Model, which show that, under conditions of high motivation to process information (i.e., central route processing), people are more receptive to influence, and that central route processing produces attitude change that is more permanent and resistant to counter-persuasion attempts. Thus, they argue that the effects of political communication in the new media environment may not be so minimal after all.

Perhaps most important, these discussions have called for new theorizing, as well as for refinement of existing theory, to accommodate serious changes in the contemporary media landscape. This stands as the field's greatest challenge at the moment. The way forward will include devising new methods and measures of media exposure, as well as considering carefully what has and has not changed about both media content and audience experience when theorizing about effects in the altered media landscape. While some effects may be diminished by the expansion of media choice, others will be enhanced, and most will likely change in interesting ways. For example, although mainstream media's ability to set the public agenda may wane as people turn to individually customized news diets, the power of the public to set the media and policy agendas via blogs and user-generated news may increase. In addition, peer-to-peer agenda setting via online social networking and other forms of social media becomes an interesting and important area to study.

Similarly, as technology increasingly enables media audiences to connect with those who share similar views, mechanisms driving the spiral of silence may disappear. At the same time, however, "reinforcement spirals" may take their place and result in stronger in-group allegiances and out-group suspicion (Slater, 2007). Alternatively, new venues for spirals of silence to emerge may appear, particularly within social media environments such as Facebook, whose usage is often motivated by a desire for popularity and where pressure to conform to peer opinion may be quite powerful (see Metzger, 2009 for a fuller discussion of these and other theoretical extensions to traditional media effects theories due to technological changes).

BROADCASTING VERSUS
NARROWCASTING: A FALSE DICHOTOMY

The discussions of the future media landscape and its effects on audiences imply that a dichotomy exists between broadcast and narrowcast content by suggesting that narrowcasting is replacing general-appeal content. Some even imply that narrowcasting and hyperpersonalization threaten the very survival of the "mass" media. These concerns are overblown. The reality is that the contemporary media environment can and does include both specialized and mass appeal content. Also, as mentioned earlier, while partisans may gravitate more readily toward one-sided news, the majority of the audience so far does not avail itself of niche news, and typically prefers more "objective" journalism found in traditional and online versions of mainstream newspapers and nonpartisan cable or television news stations (Takeshita, 2006). Also, only about 9 percent of Americans obtain news via blogs regularly, and they tend to supplement these sources with other news sources as well (Pew Research Center, 2010). Indeed, many people consider blog credibility to be suspect. Consequently, demand still exists for mass-appeal news and political information, and economic incentives for media firms to produce broad-appeal programming are still in place, even in multiple channel markets (Waterman, 1992).

In fact, setting newspapers aside, most mass media organizations (e.g., traditional broadcast and cable television firms such as CBS or CNN) are in many ways bigger and more powerful than ever before, and they now venture far outside the national borders that once contained them. They have also managed to escape the delivery channels that used to bound and distinguish them, now often offering the same content delivered over a variety of print, broadcast, cable, *and* digital channels. When readership of their online versions is factored in, the major newspapers, television, and cable news outlets still have a stranglehold over content production and command a large percentage of the audience share for news (Pew Research Center, 2010). At the same time, mainstream media are incorporating narrowcasting into their products in several ways, including developing their own blogs, affording opportunities for user commentary and user-generated news on their websites (e.g., CNN's iReport), and maintaining a presence in social networking sites. In other words, broadcast and narrowcast content can and do coexist. An interesting question is whether this new hybrid form of news offers the best scenario for democracy by offering greater and more enticing chances for political engagement while providing enough of an information commons to avoid polarization?

So, one thing that is clear is that mass media do still exist in the twenty-first century and are likely to survive for quite some time. They are, however, changing as a response to emerging information technologies, and mass media news firms of the future may ultimately bear little resemblance to what they looked like at the beginning of the twenty-first century. For example, as news consumers have become agnostic about the channel through which they receive news information, consuming broadcast, cable, or print news content all via the same digital medium, news organizations have been forced to abandon their channel-specific formats by offering a mix of text (print) and video (broadcast, cable) journalism, as well as interactive formats of news information and commentary through their websites. This has created considerable duplication in the industry that now threatens the survival of even the leading news brands. To achieve efficiencies, one possibility is that search engines such as Google, Microsoft's Bing, and Yahoo! could replace the former channel-specific news monoliths such as CBS News, CNN, and the *New York Times* to become the mainstream news brands of the future.

Another thing that is clear is that communication scholars must change their definitions of mass communication to better describe what is happening in today's media landscape. As Napoli (2008, 2) contends, mass communication still has relevance today only if it is redefined with a new interpretive approach that is not exclusive to institutional communicators and "that allows the term 'mass' to extend to both the senders and receivers of messages." In other words, whereas mass communication was traditionally defined by the number receivers of a message, digital forms of distribution allow for masses to communicate with masses. So, while Napoli's suggestion retains the one-to-many aspect of mass communication at its core, it enables the term "mass" to describe *both* the number of receivers *and* the number of sources in the definition of mass communication. Digital networked media necessitate this more expansive definition of mass communication.

UNANSWERED QUESTIONS

As the previous sections demonstrate, the rapid and dramatic shifts in the media environment that have taken place since the 1990s beckon reconceptualizations of mass communication and mass media effects. Many challenges loom for political communication scholars seeking to understand the scope, nature, and impacts of the new forms of mass communication and media content available to audiences. The following questions represent some starting points in this line of inquiry:

- To what extent are theories of mass media effects still useful? What is the best way to evaluate existing theories of political communication processes and effects in light of the new media configurations, and how should communication scholars go about developing new theories and methods to better fit the changing sociotechnical circumstances? Some suggest that media attribute or variable-centered approaches to theorizing about media in the future will prove the most fruitful (Eveland, 2003; Lang, 2011; Sundar, 2009). These approaches privilege studying media messages at the feature level, rather than at the channel level, which is useful as audiences are less tied to single-channel news outlets. Others suggest that the key to media effects may now lie in the interpersonal interactions surrounding mass media content reception, such that complex multi-step flows of communication via a combination of mass and social media shape public opinion in new ways. As such, understanding mass media effects may require a new type of scholar trained broadly in theories of both interpersonal and media influence.

- Assuming that exposure to political communication is a precursor to effects, what methodological innovations are needed to measure exposure to media messages in the future, as message delivery and audience consumption practices expand and change rapidly? What was once a relatively simple task of measuring news exposure is now quite difficult as audiences are exposed to mass media content through so many channels and alternate venues (e.g., a news story posted on a friend's Facebook profile). Some scholars argue that researchers must now incorporate options for audience selective exposure into their research designs, rather than assuming or forcing exposure to the same messages and issues in order to properly understand the magnitude of media effects on society (Bennett and Iyengar, 2008). Related to this, scholars must learn more about the ratio of partisan to objective news that different types or groups of people are exposed to. Which do people find more credible? How do patterns of and motives for both selective exposure and avoidance affect political knowledge, attitudes, and propensity for political engagement?

- While channel proliferation has made it more difficult to measure what information news consumers receive, with hyperpersonalization even the same channel can now produce different information for different individuals (Pariser, 2011). How can communication scholars track these forms of "pre-filtered selective exposure" and how might our theories of media effects take this into account? On the one hand, tracking exactly what information people are exposed to is complicated by networked digital media, yet these technologies also allow for precise monitoring of online behavior. In fact, tracking when people are exposed to what content online, as well as directly observing the multi-step flow of communication, may be easier via technology and may provide more accurate data than self-reports. An important question is how communication scholars can build partnerships with technology organizations and computer scientists to help them harness these data.

- How will younger generations who are not as steeped in traditional media perceive the relevance of mass communication in the future? Also, as younger people become accustomed to increased opportunities to create content, to what extent will audience members participate in news production themselves, and how might doing so impact political participation in the future? Scholarly work on this question is only just beginning.

Conclusion

This chapter posed the question of whether mass media will continue to endure in an environment of vast choice and increased audience control over both media content production and its reception. Implications of the shift from broadcasting to narrowcasting, and to hyperpersonalization of content, invite political communication scholars to reexamine long-held theoretical assumptions about whether, where, and how media effects are likely to occur and to devise new methods to study them. While the chapter made clear that mass media will likely endure, it also raised new questions that will have to be addressed as scholars strive to understand the nature and effects of mass communication in the future.

Notes

1. Or, perhaps more correctly, the fracturing of media audiences for traditional news has recathected old forms of news, in that what we are witnessing today is the return of the partisan press (Abrahamson, 2006).
2. Recent research by the Pew Research Center's Project for Excellence in Journalism (Rosensteil and Mitchell, 2011) found a rebound in time spent with news in 2010 compared to previous years, but this trend was not evident among younger adults.
3. Sunstein's title is *Going to Extremes: How Like Minds Unite and Divide*. There is also some debate surrounding whether political polarization is primarily a result of narrowcasting and selective exposure to attitudinally consistent news information, or whether it is due to other factors, such as people's preference for entertainment over news media content, which leads to inequalities in political knowledge and participation among those who are more versus less politically interested (see Prior, 2007).

References

Abrahamson, D. 2006. The rise of the new partisan press: Forward into the past. *Journal of Magazine and New Media Research* 8(1): 1–4.

Bae, H.-S. 1999. Product differentiation in cable programming: The case in the cable national all-news networks. *Journal of Media Economics* 12(4): 265–277.

Bae, H.-S. 2000. Product differentiation in national TV newscasts: A comparison of the cable all-news networks and the broadcast networks. *Journal of Broadcasting & Electronic Media* 44(1): 62–77.

Bennett, W. L., and Iyengar, S. 2008. A new era of minimal effects? The changing foundations of political communication. *Journal of Communication* 58(4): 707–731.

Brannon, L. A., Tagler, M. J., and Eagly, A. H. 2007. The moderating role of attitude strength in selective exposure to information. *Journal of Experimental Social Psychology* 43(4): 611–617.

Byrne, D. 1971. *The attraction paradigm.* New York: Academic Press.

Chaffee, S. H., and Metzger, M. J. 2001. The end of mass communication? *Mass Communication and Society* 4(4): 365–379.

Eveland, W. P. 2003. A "mix of attributes" approach to the study of media effects and new communication technologies. *Journal of Communication* 53(3): 395–410.

Garrett, R. K. 2009a. Echo chambers online? Politically motivated selective exposure among Internet news users. *Journal of Computer-Mediated Communication,* 14(2): 265–285.

Garrett, R. K. 2009b. Politically motivated reinforcement seeking: Reframing the selective exposure debate. *Journal of Communication* 59: 676–699.

Holbert, R. L., Garrett, R. K., and Gleason, L. S. 2010. A new era of minimal effects? A response to Bennett and Iyengar. *Journal of Communication* 60(1): 15–34.

Iyengar, S., and Hahn, K. S. 2009. Red media, blue media: Evidence of ideological selectivity in media use. *Journal of Communication* 59(1): 19–39.

Jamieson, K. H., and Cappella, J. 2009. *Echo chamber: Rush Limbaugh and the conservative media establishment.* New York: Oxford University Press.

Johnson, T. J., Bichard, S. L., and Zhang, W. 2009. Communication communities or "cyber-ghettos?": A path analysis model examining factors that explain selective exposure to blogs. *Journal of Computer-Mediated Communication* 15(1): 60–82.

Kinder, D. R. 2003. Communication and politics in the age of information. In D. O. Sears, L. Huddy, and R. Jervis (Eds.), *Oxford handbook of political psychology* (pp. 357–393). Oxford: Oxford University Press.

Knobloch-Westerwick, S., and Meng, J. 2009. Looking the other way: Selective exposure to attitude-consistent and counterattitudinal political information. *Communication Research* 36(3): 426–448.

Kobayashi, T., and Ikeda, K. 2009. Selective exposure in political web browsing: Empirical verification of "cyber-balkanization" in Japan and the USA. *Information, Communication, & Society* 12(6): 929–953.

Lang, A. 2011. *The shifting paradigm of mass communication research.* Paper presented to the Mass Communication Division of the International Communication Association annual conference. Boston, MA.

Massey, K. 2004. Narrowcasting. The Museum of Broadcast Communications. Retrieved March 23, 2008, from http://www.museum.tv/archives/etv/N/htmlN/narrowcasting/narrowcasting.htm.

Mendelsohn, M., and Nadeau, R. 1996. The magnification and minimization of social cleavages by the broadcast and narrowcast news media. *International Journal of Public Opinion Research* 8(4): 374–389.

Metzger, M. J. 2009. The study of media effects in the era of Internet communication. In R. L. Nabi and M. B. Oliver (Eds.), *The Sage handbook of media processes and effects* (pp. 561–576). Thousand Oaks, CA: Sage.

Mullainathan, S., and Shleifer, A. 2005. The market for news. *American Economic Review* 95: 1031–1053.

Napoli, P. M. 2008. Revisiting "mass communication" and the "work" of the audience in the new media environment. *McGannon Center Working Paper Series.* Paper 24. http://fordham.bepress.com/mcgannon_working_papers/24.

Negroponte, N. 1995. *Being digital.* New York: Knopf.

Neuman, W. R., and Guggenheim, L. 2011. The evolution of media effects theory: A six-stage model of cumulative research. *Communication Theory* 21(2): 169–196.

Owen, B. M., and S. S. Wildman. 1992. *Video economics.* Cambridge, MA: Harvard University Press.

Pariser, E. 2011. *The filter bubble: What the Internet is hiding from you.* New York: Penguin.

Pew Research Center. 2010. Americans spending more time following the news: Ideological news sources: Who watches and why. http://people-press.org/2010/09/12/americans-spending-more-time-following-the-news/.

Prior, M. 2007. *Post-broadcast democracy: How media choice increases inequality in political involvement and polarizes elections*. New York: Cambridge University Press.

Ranney, A. 1990. Broadcasting, narrowcasting, and politics. In A. S. King (Ed.), *The new American political system*, 2nd ed. (pp. 175–202). Washington, DC: The AEI Press.

Rosensteil, T., and Mitchell, A. 2011. The state of the news media 2011: An annual report on American journalism. Project for Excellence in Journalism. http://stateofthemedia.org/2011/overview-2/.

Sears, D. O., and Freedman, J. L. 1967. Selective exposure to information: A critical review. *Public Opinion Quarterly* 31(2): 194.

Stroud, N. J. 2007. Media effects, selective exposure, and Fahrenheit 9/11. *Political Communication* 24(4): 415–432.

Stroud, N. J. 2008. Media use and political predispositions: Revisiting the concept of selective exposure. *Political Behavior* 30: 341–366.

Stroud, N. J. 2010. Polarization and partisan selective exposure. *Journal of Communication*, 60: 556-576.

Stroud, N. J. 2011. *Niche news: The politics of news choice*. New York: Oxford University Press.

Sunstein, C. 2001. *Republic.com*. Princeton, NJ: Princeton University Press.

Sunstein, C. 2007. *Republic.com 2.0*. Princeton, NJ: Princeton University Press.

Sunstein, C. 2009. *Going to extremes: How like minds unite and divide*. New York: Oxford University Press.

Takeshita, T. 2006. Current critical problems in agenda-setting research. *International Journal of Public Opinion Research* 18(3), 275–296.

Tewksbury, D. 2005. The seeds of audience fragmentation: Specialization in the use of online news sites. *Journal of Broadcasting and Electronic Media* 49(3): 332–348.

Turow, J. 1997. *Breaking up America: Advertisers and the new media world*. Chicago: University of Chicago Press.

Vogelstein, F. 2009. Great wall of Facebook: The social network's plan to dominate the Internet—and keep Google out. *Wired Magazine*, 17.07. http://www.wired.com/techbiz/it/magazine/17-07/ff_facebookwall.

Wallsten, K. 2011. Many sources, one message: Political blog links to online videos during the 2008 campaign. *Journal of Political Marketing* 10(1) (January): 88–114.

Waterman, D. 1992. "Narrowcasting" and "broadcasting" on nonbroadcast media: A program choice model. *Communication Research* 19(1): 3–28.

Webster, J. G. 2007. Diversity of exposure. In P. M. Napoli (Ed.), *Media diversity and localism: Meaning and metrics* (pp. 309–326). Mahwah, NJ: Erlbaum.

CHAPTER 55

....

ONLINE NEWS CONSUMPTION IN THE UNITED STATES AND IDEOLOGICAL EXTREMISM

....

KENNETH M. WINNEG, DANIEL M. BUTLER,
SAAR GOLDE, DARWIN W. MILLER III,
AND NORMAN H. NIE

INTRODUCTION

....

THE news media landscape is evolving, expanding, and becoming increasingly fragmented. Over the past two decades cable news has replaced broadcast network news as the source for national and international news. Also during this time, the ideologically conservative Fox News Channel has become the leading news cable channel (Morris, 2007; Pew, 2008). This shift coincided with an unprecedented expansion in Internet access. It is increasingly common for consumers to use the Internet as their primary source of news and information (Bimber and Davis, 2003; Davis and Owen, 1998; Pew, 2011; Tewksbury, 2006).

In this essay, we combine insights from theories of selective media exposure from social psychology and political communication with economic theories of differentiated products markets to develop a theoretical framework for understanding how the Internet continues to affect the US political news market. The driving force behind this framework is the dramatically lower cost of production for Internet news sources relative to traditional television news. Lower cost of production allows Internet news providers to profitably provide content to consumers with more diverse and less centrist political views. Combining this insight with the concept of selective media exposure—the idea that consumers tend to seek out media that conform to their own political tastes—leads to the testable predictions that consumers of Internet news sources should, on average, hold political views that are farther away from the center, and be interested in more diverse political issues than those who solely consume mainstream television news.

In an earlier study, we found evidence that supported these predictions using data covering the period April 2000 to June 2007 (Nie et al., 2010). Here we test whether the same patterns hold using data from the 2008 National Annenberg Election Survey online panel (NAES) conducted during the 2008 presidential election cycle. It is important to determine whether the same pattern continues to hold as the Internet grows as a regular source of news for more and more citizens.

We believe this research is important for several reasons. First, our framework generates new predictions about the relationship between individuals' news viewership and their political views. Because the Internet allows consumers to fit their news exposure to their own political preferences, these predictions tie our study to the large and emerging literature on political polarization. Second, these results highlight the importance of considering interaction effects when studying the impact of the Internet (Bimber, 2005). Third, and perhaps most important, our framework can give theoretical grounding for future work on the consequences of changes in the political news market.

Previous Empirical Research

Much of the previous empirical work on the relationship between consumers' political attitudes and views and their news source(s) comes out of the literature on the political fragmentation of news consumers. Sunstein (2001) has argued that the Internet will lead to fragmentation and what he calls "balkanization." Rather than operating in an open society of diverse ideas and discussion, citizens interact in an echo chamber, limiting their discussion and interaction to those whose opinions are similar to theirs, where there is little opportunity for their ideas to be challenged. In Sunstein's view, the diversity of communication options and increased choice will lessen the opportunities for common public experiences, shared realities and effective public deliberation.

The growth of "new" media has greatly expanded the number of available channels of communication, leading to increased audience fragmentation. Davis and Owen (1998), for example, compare the attitudes of talk radio listeners, television news magazine viewers, and those who acquire news and political information on the Internet using data from the 1996 American National Election Study (ANES) and found significant differences among these groups. More recently, in a national survey of 1,506 adults, Mardenfeld et al. (2006) found that self-identifying liberals and moderates were less likely to choose the Fox News Channel than they were to choose ABC, CBS, NBC, and CNN for their news. Those who self-identify as conservatives were more likely to choose Fox News. Similarly, Morris (2007) found, using surveys from Pew conducted in 2004 and 2005, that Fox News Channel viewers had distinct attitudes toward both President Bush and his opposition. Stroud (2008), using data from the 2004 NAES, showed that people's political beliefs are related to their media exposure, a pattern that persists across media types (newspapers, political talk radio, cable news, and Internet).

While there is a literature on political fragmentation and the media news market, the majority of previous studies have focused on network, cable, and talk radio, not the Internet (see also, e.g., Dimmick et al., 2004; Jones, 2001; Mardenfeld et al., 2006; Morris, 2005). While Davis and Owen (1998) did include the Internet in their study, their research used data collected well before the Internet explosion and the rise of such cable news channels as Fox News (CNN has been around since the 1980s) so it is unclear whether their results still describe the situation today.

Our prior work on which this essay is based (Nie et al., 2010) was among the first to study the relationship between a consumer's source of news and his or her political attitudes while looking simultaneously at network, cable, and Internet information sources. Here, we follow the theoretical framework of the political news market we developed for that study and test predictions derived from that framework using more recent data.

Theoretical Framework

Premise I: The Demand Side—Selective Exposure

The first premise underlying our model is that consumers tend to expose themselves to news content that covers issues they care about and is in line with their own political views. This premise is supported by a long line of literature from social psychology and public opinion and communications research.

Several political studies, going back to the seminal work by Lazarsfeld et al. (1944) and Berelson et al. (1954), point to evidence of selective exposure when it comes to seeking political information. Selective exposure is "any systematic bias in audience composition" (Sears and Freedman, 1967, 195). The psychological theory of cognitive dissonance, developed by Festinger (1957) is the foundation for selective exposure. Festinger posits that people seek out reinforcing messages to reduce and avoid dissonance.

In the field of communication, the concept of selective exposure was incorporated into the "limited effects" model of media exposure developed by Klapper (1960). In this model, which dominated the field for many years, selective exposure was used as a means for asserting that the media have little to no effect on social and political behavior. "Attitude predispositions largely determine the communications to which the individual is exposed" (Klapper, 1963, 67). Individuals seek information that supports rather than disputes their point of view (Sears and Freedman, 1967). Voters sought information that conformed to one's existing values and predispositions (Berelson and Steiner, 1964). For example, Schramm and Carter (1959) found that Republicans were more likely than Democrats to watch a Republican-sponsored telecast.

Over time, the evidence proved to be more equivocal about whether people selectively seek out only information reinforcing their own view. Critics of selective exposure include

Sears and Freedman (1967), who, in a review of prior research, argued that no empirical case had been made for its existence. Much of the research following their review has reached similar conclusions, citing other factors explaining media exposure patterns (e.g., Cotton, 1985; McCombs and Becker, 1979; O'Keefe and Atwood, 1981; Severin and Tankard, 1979). Chaffee and Miyo (1983) found that while selective exposure did occur, the underlying assumptions of this theory were questionable. Selective exposure was found mainly among those with the lowest political involvement and electoral experience.

Years later, D'Alessio and Allen (2002, 2007) conducted a meta-analysis of experimental studies testing selective exposure and provided evidence to support the notion that cognitive dissonance is weakly associated with it. Criticizing prior reviews, they argue, for example, that flaws in Freedman and Sears' (1967) meta-analysis explain their inconsistent results. Despite criticisms of the studies, researchers who found other explanations never fully discounted the idea of selective exposure as a means of ideological reinforcement. (O'Keefe and Atwood, 1981; Severin and Tankard, 1979).

More recent studies point to evidence that selective exposure does contribute to media effects. Chaffee et al. (2001) found that people were somewhat more likely to pay attention to information about their preferred candidate. Taber and Lodge (2006) concluded that when faced with pro and con arguments, people uncritically accept the arguments they support, and counter argue the ones which they oppose. When they are given the option to self-select a source of information, they pick the ones which are most likely to confirm their arguments. In a political advertising study of the 1996 campaign, Kaid (1997) shows that Democrats became more positive toward Bill Clinton after seeing a Clinton advertisement and Republicans became more positive toward Dole after seeing one of his political spots. Stroud (2007) suggests that selective exposure may play a role in increasing polarization, finding that those who viewed Michael Moore's film "Fahrenheit 9/11" had significantly higher negative feelings toward President Bush than those who intended to see it but had not.

Studies show that those who rely on the Internet for information have not abandoned mainstream sources altogether. Still, the Internet is distinctly different from network television and cable news because it is an interactive medium that promotes more than a one-way communication. "The Internet does not represent a singular mode of communication, but a flexible and adaptable set of opportunities for communication that can be exploited by individuals and groups in many ways" (Bimber, 2005, 16). As a result, Bimber argues, it is difficult for researchers to determine a single main effect.

In an early study of online use, Johnson and Kaye (1998) found that those online tended to be less trustful of government and less likely to vote. While the Internet had a positive and significant impact on political interest, there was a negative impact between reliance on the Internet and trust in government, efficacy, and voting behavior (1996 elections).

To be clear, we do not argue that selective exposure is all that drives media selection. There are other factors such as interest in news and current affairs that are also likely to affect the sources of news one seeks. Our claim is that, *ceteris paribus*, people will seek out news presented by sources with an ideological slant similar to their own (Iyengar, 2007).

Premise 2: The Supply Side—Internet News Saturates the Taste Space

The second premise is that the news content available on the Internet covers a wider range of political opinions and issues than that available from more traditional news sources. This assertion is theoretically grounded in the large difference in cost of production for Internet news sources relative to television news sources (Baum, 2003; Hamilton, 2004; Prior, 2007) and the need for news producers to recover their production costs.[1] When production costs are high, a large number of consumers are needed before profits can be made and so the market can only support a few producers. When only a few producers enter the market, they place themselves in a position designed to reach a lot of consumers, typically toward the center of the distribution. When costs are low, producers need fewer consumers to be viable, so more producers will enter the market and, among them, cover a greater range of locations in the market space. We argue that it is reasonable to view the Internet as a medium that effectively saturates the entire taste space for political news because of its low production costs.

The models of differentiated products markets from the field of economics provide theoretical support for why lower costs increase competition and cause programming to become more diverse. Originally developed by Hotelling (1929), these models describe behavior in markets where consumers have tastes that are distributed according to some distribution function and prefer products close to their ideal point in the distribution; producers in these markets select product positions so as to maximize profits. One of the key results in the product differentiation literature is that when people consume the product nearest to their ideal point (i.e., when selective exposure occurs), lower production costs leads to saturation (see Eaton and Lipsey, 1989, for a comprehensive, if somewhat outdated, survey of the literature).

Figure 55.1 provides a graphical illustration of our argument. The mainstream television news sources are all located relatively close to the center where they can attract a large enough audience to cover their high production costs. The Internet, however, has saturated the taste space by providing news from all different ideological perspectives.

Together these premises predict that individuals whose ideological preferences are not completely served by mainstream television news sources (because their views are farther from the center) will tend to search the Internet to get news that is more complementary to their views. We test this prediction by looking at the news consumption of those getting news from television sources that appeal most to the viewers on the left (CNN and MSNBC in our data set) and right (Fox News in our data set).

For the purposes of our model, it is useful to divide those who are using noncentrist cable television news sources into three groups. Let us use Fox News viewers as an example. There are viewers who are more conservative than Fox News, viewers who have roughly the same ideological position as Fox News, and viewers who are more liberal than Fox News. Viewers who are more liberal than Fox and those with roughly the same

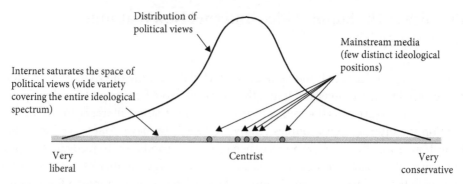

FIGURE 55.1. Graphic representation of the model. Here, the distribution of political views within the population represents the local demand for political bias, and high cost mainstream media locate at discrete points close to the center of this distribution. Due to the very low cost of production and distribution of Internet news, there are minimal barriers to entry that lead us to model the Internet as filling in the entire continuum and saturating the taste space for political bias. Thus, when viewing online content, consumers can choose news that fits their political opinion exactly.

ideological position should be able to satisfy their ideological preferences with the coverage they can find on television (either on Fox or more liberal sources). However those Fox News viewers who are more conservative than Fox News cannot supplement their news consumption by using an additional television news source that is more conservative than Fox. Because the most widely available option open to these consumers is the Internet, we should find that the most conservative Fox viewers supplement their Fox News viewership with Internet news content.

> H1: Of those who watch the Fox News Channel, individuals who also get news from the Internet will be more conservative than other Fox News Channel viewers.

Similarly for those using CNN and MSNBC (the most liberal television sources in our study):

> H2: Of those who watch CNN/MSNBC news, individuals who also get news from the Internet will be more liberal than other CNN/MSNBC news viewers.

As H1 and H2 suggest, one motive for seeking Internet news can be a search for greater ideological purity in issue coverage. Interest in issues not covered by mainstream broadcast news may provide another motive. Mainstream broadcast news is time-constrained and thus chooses to cover a subset of issues most viewers find important. In contrast, Internet news can focus on niche issues. Therefore, people who are interested in more diverse political issues are more likely to seek out news on the Internet. People interested in a broad range of political issues are more likely to identify a low salience issue as the single most important current issue than people with a narrow range of political interest. Combining these two observations about people with a broad range of political interests yields our final hypothesis:

> H3: Individuals who use the Internet for news should be more likely to identify low-salience political issues as important than those who rely solely upon mainstream television content.

RESEARCH DESIGN AND RESULTS

To address these hypotheses, we analyze data from the 2008 NAES online panel. For our analyses looking at citizens' ideology/partisanship we use a sample that includes about 4,000 regular Fox News viewers, 2,000 regular CNN viewers, and 1,000 regular MSNBC viewers. Because the sampling scheme employed in administering surveys can potentially cause certain groups to be overrepresented or underrepresented in the sample, we use rim weights to adjust our sample composition to match that of the national population. We also present the results of these analyses when using unweighted sample means and running OLS regressions with all available demographic variables as controls.

Recall that our theoretical framework suggests that consumers whose ideological perspectives are not adequately covered by the mainstream media should be more likely to use the Internet for news. Using this insight, we predict that among those who watch news from the rightmost television news source, the Fox News Channel, those who also get news from the Internet will be more conservative than Fox News viewers who do not cite the Internet as a news source (see H1). To test this hypothesis, we limited the sample to those who responded that they watched a regularly scheduled Fox News program ("Fox News Sunday" and/or "The O'Reilly Factor") frequently[2] and compared the ideological position of consumers who searched the Internet for news on at least a weekly basis[3] to those who searched the Internet for news less frequently.

We measured the ideological/partisan position of respondents in two different ways. First, we used their self-identified liberal-conservative position on a 7-point scale[4] (with increasing values indicating increasing levels of conservatism). Second, we used respondents' self-identified five-point party identification, where increasing values indicate increasing levels of attachment to the Republican Party.[5] For both measures, we calculated the difference between Fox viewers who consume Internet news and those who do not. The results are presented in Table 55.1 and show that Fox News viewers who also search for news online are more conservative and have a stronger attachment to the Republican Party than do Fox News viewers who do not use online news sources. The estimated differences are substantively significant. For example, the difference in

Table 55.1 The Ideological/Partisan Difference between Internet News Users and Non-Internet News Users Among Fox News Viewers

	Weighted Means	Unweighted Means	OLS
DV = Party Identification			
Difference	0.84***	0.86***	0.55***
Std. Error	0.11	0.05	0.06
N	2,233	3,875	3,546
DV = Liberal-Conservative Position			
Difference	0.99***	0.98***	0.77***
Std. Error	0.13	0.06	0.06
N	2,222	3,850	3,523

Notes: (*) significant at 10% level, (**) significant at 5% level, (***) significant at 1% level. Control variables included in the OLS regression include controls for age and dummies for gender, marital status, race / ethnic groups, levels of education, levels of religious participation, and income levels.

conservatism between Fox News viewers who search the Internet for news and those who do not is nearly a full point on a 6-point scale. Given that the sample is limited to those who watch Fox News, and so are located right of center, this large of a difference is striking.

We found similar results when we tested our hypothesis that frequent[6] CNN viewers (i.e., those who watched "The Situation Room with Wolf Blitzer" and/or "Late Edition with Wolf Blitzer") and MSNBC viewers (i.e., those who watched "Hardball with Chris Matthews") who also get news from the Internet are more liberal than CNN/MSNBC news viewers who do not. As with the analysis of Fox News viewers, we measured respondents' positions by using both their self-identified liberal-conservative position and their party identification. The results are presented in Table 55.2 and show that CNN and MSNBC viewers who also search for news online are more liberal and more attached to the Democratic Party than their counterparts who do not. The results are substantively significant but because of the smaller sample sizes, the differences do not always achieve statistical significance. Still, the difference is always in the predicted direction, is substantively significant, and in 75 percent of the cases, statistically significant. On balance the results provide evidence that the CNN/MSNBC news viewers who also use the Internet for news are more ideologically extreme than those who do not use the Internet to get news.

Our final hypothesis, H3, is that those who use the Internet for new, whether or not they also use television sources, will be more likely to identify low-salience issues as

Table 55.2 The Ideological/Partisan Difference between Internet News Users and Non-Internet News Users Among CNN and MSNBC News Viewers

	Weighted Means	Unweighted Means	OLS
CNN Viewers			
DV = Party Identification			
Difference	−0.34	−0.36***	−0.45***
Std. Error	0.24	0.12	0.15
N	1,095	1,977	1,729
DV = Liberal-Conservative Position			
Difference	−0.94***	−0.75***	−0.49***
Std. Error	0.36	0.15	0.17
N	1,092	1,963	1,716
MSNBC Viewers			
DV = Party Identification			
Difference	−0.51*	−0.41*	−0.44
Std. Error	0.29	0.21	0.29
N	582	1,098	959
DV = Liberal-Conservative Position			
Difference	−0.95**	−0.82***	−0.45
Std. Error	0.24	0.21	0.28
N	580	1,093	955

Notes: (*) significant at 10% level, (**) significant at 5% level, (***) significant at 1% level. Control variables included in the OLS regression include controls for age and dummies for gender, marital status, race / ethnic groups, levels of education, levels of religious participation, and income levels.

being important than those who rely solely on television sources for news content.[7] For the dependent variable in the analysis we use whether the respondent choose the "Other" category when responding to the question "In your opinion, what is the most important issue facing the U.S. today?" Respondents could choose one of seven specified answers (Taxes, Education, War on terrorism, Situation in Iraq, Economy/Jobs, Moral issues, Healthcare) or choose "Other (please specify:____)." Because the available answers to the question represent the issues that are dealt with most frequently in the mainstream media, the likelihood of choosing "Other" represents interest in a wider variety of issues than those available in mainstream media. Table 55.3 reports the

Table 55.3 Difference between Internet News Users and Non–Internet News Users in Terms of the Diversity of Issues Considered Important Likelihood of Identifying "Other" as Most Important Issue

	Weighted Means	Unweighted Means	OLS
Difference	0.3	0.6	0.4
Std. Error	1.6	0.7	0.8
N	2,544	5,544	4,909

Notes: (*) significant at 10% level, (**) significant at 5% level, (***) significant at 1% level. Control variables included in the OLS regression include controls for age and dummies for gender, marital status, race / ethnic groups, levels of education, levels of religious participation, and income levels.

difference, in percentage points, of the weighted means between the two groups. In this case, there is no evidence for H3. The estimated differences are all small (sometimes as low as 0.3 percentage points) and statistically insignificant.

Discussion

In this essay, we have followed up on an earlier study looking at how the Internet has changed the political news market (Nie et al., 2010). The key theoretical contribution from that earlier study, which we have reiterated here, is that the reduced costs of producing and distributing news, combined with the consumers' tendency to selectively expose themselves to media with which they agree, has changed the US political news market by giving consumers more control over their information environment. From this model we derived three observable implications about the difference between those who use the Internet for news and those who do not. In our initial report, we found evidence for all three hypotheses when using data collected between April 2000 and June 2007.

Since the Internet has grown and become a more regular source of news for more and more citizens, we wanted to see whether these patterns continued to hold using data from the 2008 presidential election. We found further support for the ideological extremity hypotheses (i.e., H1 and H2). Those who use the Internet to supplement their consumption of news from the most noncentrist television sources (CNN, MSNBC, and Fox) are farther from the ideological center than their counterparts who do not. However, we no longer find evidence that those who use the Internet for news are interested in a broader array of issues than those who do not (i.e., H3). We suspect that this reflects that fact that as the Internet becomes the primary source of news for more and more individuals, the topics covered by Internet and non-Internet sources are similar.

Instead, the difference is the slant, with the Internet providing content that is more ideologically extreme.

Notes

1. Hamilton's analysis, which is the closest to ours, focuses on the effects of lowered costs on the provision of "soft" vs. "hard" news (assuming that "hard" news has the positive externality related to encouraging voters to vote and assisting them in making more-informed voting decisions). In contrast, we focus on differentiation along the dimension of political bias or slant, which has a more symmetric structure of both costs and preferences.
2. In the case of "Fox News Sunday," this is defined as watching this show either "every week or almost every week" or "one to three times a month." For the "O'Reilly Factor," a frequent watcher is someone who indicated watching the show either "every night or almost every night" or "a few times a week."
3. This included respondents who indicated that they searched wither "three times a week or more" or "every week or almost every week." Respondents were not asked what type of news they were seeking online, which websites they went to or to what extent and in which direction were these online news sources biased.
4. The liberal-conservative scale in the Knowledge Networks data has the following values: 1 = extremely liberal, 2 = liberal, 3 = slightly liberal, 4 = moderate, middle of the road, 5 = slightly conservative, 6 = conservative, and 7 = extremely conservative.
5. The respondent's party id were determined as part of a two-stage question—the first about which party they identify with, and the second question (asked only if the response to the first one was "Democrat" or "Republican") about the strength of party association. The scale takes the following values: 1 = strong Democrat 2 = weak Democrat, 3 = Independent, 4 = weak Republican, 5 = strong Republican
6. For the show "Late Edition," a frequent viewer is defined as someone who watches this show either "every week or almost every week" or "one to three times a month." For the shows "Hardball" and the "Situation Room," a frequent watcher is someone who indicated watching the show either "every night or almost every night" or "a few times a week."
7. Specifically, the comparison group is those who did not search the Internet for news frequently, but did report frequently watching television news programs from at least one of the following sources: national network news, CNN, MSNBC, or Fox News.

References

Baum, M. A. 2003. *Soft news goes to war: Public opinion and American foreign policy in the new media age.* Princeton, NJ: Princeton University Press.

Berelson, B., Lazarsfeld, P. F., and McPhee, W. F. 1954. *Voting: A study of opinion formation in a presidential campaign.* Chicago: University of Chicago Press.

Berelson, B., and Steiner, G. A. 1964. *Human behavior: An inventory of scientific findings.* Oxford, England: Harcourt, Brace & World.

Bimber, B. 2005. The Internet and political fragmentation. Paper prepared for presentation at the Democracy in the 21st Century Conference, University of Illinois Urbana-Champaign.

Bimber, B., and Davis, R. 2003. *Campaigning online: The Internet in U.S. elections.* New York: Oxford University Press.

Chaffee, S. H., Saphir, M. N., Graf, J. Sandvig, C., and Hahn, K. S. 2001. Attention to counter-attitudinal messages in a state election campaign. *Political Communication, 18*(3), 247–272.

Chaffee, S., and Miyo, Y. 1983. Selective exposure and the reinforcement hypothesis: An inter-generational panel study of the 1980 presidential campaign. *Communication Research, 10*, 3–36.

Cotton, J. 1985. Cognitive dissonance in selective exposure. In D. Zillmann and J. Bryant (Eds.), *Selective exposure to communication.* Hillsdale, NJ: Lawrence Erlbaum.

D'Alessio, D., and Allen, M. 2002. Selective exposure and dissonance after decisions. *Psychological Reports, 91*(2), 527–532.

D'Alessio, D., and Allen, M. 2007. The selective exposure hypothesis and media choice processes. In R. W. Preiss, B. M. Gayle, N. Burrell, M. Allen, and J. Bryant (Eds.), *Mass media effects research: Advances through meta analysis* (pp. 103–118). Hillsdale, NJ: Erlbaum.

Davis, R., and Owen, D. 1998. *New media and American politics.* New York: Oxford University Press.

Dimmick, J., Chen, Y., and Zhan, L. 2004. Competition between the Internet and traditional news media: The gratification-opportunities niche dimension. *Journal of Media Economics, 17*(1), 19–33.

Eaton, B., and Lipsey, R. G. 1989. Product differentiation. In R. Schmalensee and R. Willig (Eds.), *Handbook of industrial organizations.* Amsterdam: North-Holland.

Festinger, L. 1957. *A theory of cognitive dissonance.* Stanford, CA: Stanford University Press.

Hamilton, J. T. 2004. *All the news that's fit to sell: How the market transforms information into news.* Princeton, NJ: Princeton University Press.

Hotelling, H. 1929. Stability in competition. *Economic Journal, 39*(1), 41–57.

Iyengar, S., and Hahn, K. S. 2009. Red media, blue media: Evidence of ideological selectivity in media use. *Journal of Communication, 59*(1), 19–39.

Johnson, T., and Kaye, B. 1998. A vehicle for engagement or a haven for the disaffected? Internet use, political alienation, and voter participation. In T. J. Johnson, C.E. Hays, and S. P. Hays (Eds.), *Engaging the public: How the government and media can reinvigorate democracy* (pp. 123–135). Lanham, MD: Roman and Littlefield.

Jones, D. A. 2001. The polarizing effect of new media messages. *International Journal of Public Opinion Research, 14*(2), 158–174.

Kaid. L. L. 1997. Effects of the television spots on images of Dole and Clinton. *American Behavioral Scientist, 40*, 1085–1094.

Klapper, J. T. 1960. *The effects of mass communication.* New York: Free Press.

Klapper, J. T. 1963. The social effects of mass communication. In W. Schramm (Ed.), *The science of human communication.* New York: Free Press.

Lazarsfeld, P., Berelson, B., and Gaudet, H. 1944. *The people's choice: How the voter makes up his mind in a presidential campaign.* New York: Columbia University Press.

Mardenfeld, S., Taylor, C. E., Kirkyla, A., and Anderson, A. 2006. Choosing media based on political stance. Presentation at the 2006 Annual Conference of the New Jersey Communication Association.

McCombs, M. E., and Becker, L. 1979. *Using mass communication theory.* Englewood Cliffs, NJ: Prentice-Hall.

Morris, J. S. 2005. The Fox News factor. *The Harvard International Journal of Press/Politics 10*(3), 56–79.

Morris, J. S. 2007. Slanted objectivity? Perceived media bias, cable news exposure and political attitudes. *Social Science Quarterly, 88*(3), 707–728.

Nie, N. H., et al. 2010. The world wide web and the U.S. political news market. *American Journal of Political Science, 54*(2), 428–439.

O'Keefe, G. J., and Atwood, L. E. 1981. Communication and election campaigns. In D. D. Nimmo and K. R. Sanders (Eds.), *Handbook of political communication.* Beverly Hills, CA: Sage.

Pew Research Center. 2008. Internet's broader role in campaign 2008. *Research Report.* Retrieved from www.pewInternet.org

Pew Research Center. 2011. Understanding the participatory news consumer: How Internet and cell phone users have turned news into a social experience. *Research Report.* Retrieved from http://www.pewInternet.org/~/media//Files/Reports/2010/PIP_Understanding_the_Participatory_News_Consumer.pdf

Prior, M. 2007. *Post-broadcast democracy: How media choice increases inequality in political involvement and polarizes elections.* New York: Cambridge University Press.

Schramm, W., and Carter, R. F. 1959. Effectiveness of a political telethon. *Public Opinion Quarterly, 31,* 194–213.

Sears, D. O., and Freedman, J. L. 1967. Selective exposure to information: A critical review. *Public Opinion Quarterly, 31*(2), 194–213.

Severin, W. J., and Tankard, J. 1979. *Communication theories.* New York: Hastings House.

Stroud, N. J. 2007. Media effects, selective exposure, and Fahrenheit 9/11. *Political Communication, 24*(4), 415–432.

Stroud, N. J. 2008. Media use and political predispositions: Revisiting the concept of selective exposure. *Political Behavior, 30*(3), 341–366.

Sunstein, C. R. 2001. Republic.com. Princeton, NJ: Princeton University Press.

Taber, C. S., and Lodge, M. 2006. Motivated skepticism in the evaluation of political beliefs. *American Journal of Political Science, 50*(3), 755–769.

Tewksbury, D. 2006. Exposure to newer media in a presidential primary. *Political Communication, 23*(3), 313–332.

CHAPTER 56

....

NEW MEDIA AND POLITICAL CAMPAIGNS

....

DIANA OWEN

THE 1992 presidential election ushered in a new era of campaign media. Candidates turned to entertainment venues to circumvent the mainstream press's stranglehold on the campaign agenda. This development was marked by the signature moments of businessman Ross Perot launching his third party presidential bid on *Larry King Live* and Democratic nominee Bill Clinton donning dark shades and playing the saxophone on the *Arsenio Hall Show*. At the same time, voters became more visibly engaged with campaign media, especially through call-in radio and television programs. Communication researchers speculated about the dawn of a new era of campaign media, alternately praising its populist tendencies and lamenting its degradation of political discourse. These forms of new media primarily made use of traditional print, radio, and television media platforms.

In the years since, new technologies have transformed the campaign media system and in the process altered the ways in which campaigns are waged by candidates, reported on by journalists, and experienced by voters. New campaign media have proliferated and become increasingly prominent with each passing election. Candidates employ complex media strategies incorporating an ever-changing menu of innovations in conjunction with traditional media management techniques. Campaign reporting is no longer the exclusive province of professional journalists, as bloggers and average citizens cover events and provide commentary that is widely available. Voters look to new media as primary sources of information and participate actively in campaigns through digital platforms.

THE NEW MEDIA CAMPAIGN ENVIRONMENT

....

A multilayered communication environment exists for election campaigns. The media system is transitioning from a broadcast model associated with traditional media where general-interest news items are disseminated to the mass public through a narrowcasting model where carefully crafted messages target discrete audience segments. On the one hand, the mainstream press maintains an identifiable presence. Much original and investigative campaign reporting is conducted by professional journalists, even as financial pressures have forced the industry to reduce their numbers drastically. Mainstream media still validate information disseminated via new media platforms, such as blogs and Twitter feeds. At the same time, the proliferation of new media has increased the diversification and fragmentation of the communication environment. Media are more politically polarized, as niche sources associated with extreme ideological positions appeal to growing sections of the audience. The abundance of new sources makes it possible for voters to tailor their media consumption to conform to their personal tastes (Sunstein, 2000; Jamieson and Cappella, 2008; Stroud, 2011).

The evolution of campaign communication in the new media era can be construed as three distinct yet overlapping phases, as depicted in Figure 56.1.

Old Media, New Politics

During the "old media, new politics" phase, candidates used established nonpolitical and entertainment media to bypass mainstream press gatekeepers, who reduced their messages to eight-second sound bites sandwiched between extensive commentary. Candidates sought to reach voters who were less attentive to print and television news through personal appeals in the media venues they frequented. "Old media, new politics" thrives in the current era, as candidates seek the favorable and widespread coverage they can garner from a cover story in *People Weekly* and appearances on the talk and comedy show circuit (Baum, 2005). This type of election media laid the foundation for the personalized soft news coverage that permeates twenty-first-century new media campaigns. While rudimentary websites, or "brochureware,"—defined as web versions of traditional print campaign flyers—that served as digital repositories of campaign documents first appeared in 1992 (Davis, 1999), old media technologies remained dominant during this phase.

New Media, New Politics 1.0

The second phase—"new media, new politics 1.0"—witnessed the introduction of novel election communication platforms made possible by technological innovations. By the year 2000 election, all major and many minor candidates had basic websites that were heavily text-based (Bimber and Davis, 2003). Campaign websites incorporating interactive elements—including features that allowed users to engage in discussions, donate to candidates, and volunteer—became standard in the 2004 election. Election-related blogs also proliferated, offering voters an alternative to corporate news products

	Characteristics	Examples
Old Media, New Politics 1992-1994	Established nonpolitical and entertainment media formats accommodate election communication; web campaigning is primitive	Call-in Radio and Television Late Night Television Shows News Magazine Programs Music Television (MTV) Print and Television Tabloids "Brochureware" Websites
New Media, New Politics 1.0 1996-2006	Internet technology facilitates the development of new forms of campaign communication with interactive capabilities	Websites with Interactive Features Email Discussion Boards Blogs Meetups
New Media, New Politics 2.0 2008-2010	Expanded and sophisticated use of digital technology for campaign applications characterized by higher levels of interactive information sharing, networking, collaboration, community-building, and engagement	Full-Service Websites Social Media Video Sharing Sites Twitter Microblogging Sites Mobile Device Applications iMedia Applications

Figure 56.1 Phases of new media in election campaigns.

(Cornfield, 2004; Foot and Schneider, 2006). Internet use in midterm elections lagged somewhat behind presidential campaign applications. Many congressional candidates had basic websites in 2006, but few included blogs, fundraising tools, or volunteer-building applications (The Bivings Group, 2006).

New Media, New Politics 2.0

The 2008 presidential election marked the beginning of the third phase in the evolution of election media—"new media, new politics 2.0." This period is distinguished by innovations in digital election communication that facilitate networking, collaboration and community building as well as active engagement. Campaign websites became full-service multimedia platforms where voters could find extensive information about the candidates as well as election logistics, access and share videos and ads, blog, and provide commentary, donate, and take part in volunteer activities. The most notable development in 2008 was the use of social media, such as Facebook, and video sharing sites, like YouTube, for peer-to-peer exchange of election information, campaign organizing, and election participation. Mainstream media organizations kept pace with these developments by incorporating social media and video sharing features into their digital platforms. These new media innovations were amplified in the 2010 midterm elections, with Twitter and microblogging sites featured more prominently in the election media mix.

The Importance of New Media
in Elections

The new media's influence on elections has been substantial. Campaigns provide a laboratory for the development of political applications that carry over to postelection politics and establish new norms for media politics in subsequent contests. The social media innovations that rose to prominence in the 2008 presidential contest became standard practice in the 2010 midterm elections and set the stage for the more prolific development of political applications for handheld devices than was the case in 2004, when the Bush campaign used handheld devices to show campaign ads door to door.

Campaign Organizations, Parties, and Grassroots Movements

Candidates have incorporated new media into their organizational strategies for informing, contacting, and mobilizing voters. Candidate websites have come a long way from the days of brochureware and provide users with the opportunity for an individualized experience that can range from simply access biographical information to networking with supporters from across the country. Campaigns have also developed advanced microtargeting methods, including the use of focused text messages to reach specific constituencies, such as ethnic group members and issue constituencies (Hillygus and Shields, 2008).

The Democratic and Republican parties have developed digital media strategies for enhancing personal outreach to voters. Their websites have become social media hubs that can engage voters during and after elections. The dominant function of the two major parties' new media strategy is fundraising, and the "donate" button features prominently on all of their platforms. The parties' outreach to voters continues between elections, especially through the use of regular email and text messages to supporters.

Grassroots political movements have employed new media as a means of getting their message out and mobilizing supporters. In the 2010 midterm elections, the Tea Party movement used websites, blogs, social media, and email to bring national attention to state and local candidates and to promote its antigovernment taxing and spending message (Lepore, 2010). Mainstream and new media coverage of the Tea Party was substantial and resulted in increased public awareness of and momentum behind little-known candidates (Project for Excellence in Journalism, 2010). At the same time, new media strategies can backfire when the mainstream press publicizes unflattering or embarrassing information about candidates. Christine O'Donnell, an unsuccessful Tea Party-backed candidate for the Senate in Delaware in 2010, received extensive national press coverage for statements about witchcraft she had once made that helped to derail her campaign.

At the same time, campaigns have had to adapt to a more negative and volatile electoral environment. Candidates are subject to constant scrutiny, as their words and actions are closely recorded. Reporters and average citizens can compile information and disseminate it using inexpensive technologies that link easily to networks, where rumors can be spread instantaneously. New media can sustain rumors well after an election. Rumors promulgated by the "birther movement"—that Barack Obama was not qualified to be president because he was not born in the United States—continued to circulate long after he took office.

Media Organizations

The relationship between traditional and new media has gone from adversarial to symbiotic, as new media have become sources of campaign information for professional journalists. Average citizens have become prolific providers of election-related content ranging from short reactions to campaign stories to lengthy firsthand accounts of campaigns events. Mainstream media have tacked new media features onto their digital platforms, which have become delivery systems for content that originates from websites, Twitter feeds, blogs, and citizen-produced videos. As a result, messages originating in new media increasingly set the campaign agenda.

New media constitute an abundant source of election information for an increasing number of voters. While television remains the main source of election news for a majority of people, online sources are gaining popularity (Smith, 2011). The Internet has gone from a supplementary resource for election information to a main source of news for more than a third of voters during presidential campaigns and a quarter of voters during midterm elections. The use of the Internet as a main source in presidential elections has climbed from 3 percent in 1996 to 36 percent in 2008. Mainstream television news exposure and hardcopy print newspaper use has dropped markedly over time. Radio's popularity as a resource for information on presidential elections has increased slightly since the 1980s and early 1990s, largely due to talk radio's popularity (Table 56.1).

The Electorate

The role of the new media in fostering a more active electorate is perhaps their most consequential contribution to campaigns. Voters use new media to participate in campaigns in traditional and novel ways, such as producing and distributing campaign content, including news stories, short observations, opinion pieces, audio and video accounts, and independent ads. Citizens can not only access and share information through peer-to-peer networks using email and an ever-increasing array of digital platforms but also engage in structured activities organized digitally by campaign organizations, parties, and interest groups; or they can organize campaign events on their own using social media.

Table 56.1 Main Sources of Election News

	Television	Newspaper	Radio	Magazine	Internet
Presidential Elections					
1992	82%	57%	12%	9%	–
1996	72%	60%	19%	11%	3%
2000	70%	39%	15%	4%	11%
2004	76%	46%	22%	1%	21%
2008	68%	33%	16%	3%	36%
Midterm Elections					
2002	66%	33%	13%	1%	7%
2006	69%	34%	17%	2%	15%
2010	67%	27%	14%	2%	24%

Note: Respondents could volunteer more than one main source.

Source: Pew Research Center, November 13, 2008; Pew Internet and American Life Project, March 17, 2011.

MAJOR RESEARCH QUESTIONS AND FINDINGS

A research tradition begun in the 1992 presidential campaign has addressed both macro-level issues about the importance of new media for democratic participation and also more specific questions about the form, content, role, audiences, and effects of new media in particular campaigns. Since the new media's influence in elections has been dynamic, research findings should be considered within the context of the phases of new media development. As new media have matured, they have become more integral to the electoral process, and their effects are more pronounced.

Form, Function, and Content of New Election Media

In order to address issues dealing with the form, function, and content of new election media, researchers have asked: What distinguishes new media from traditional media in campaigns? Studies examining the characteristics of new media in elections have provided snapshots of new media developments in specific elections and tracked their evolution over time. Dominant traits that set new media apart from traditional ones are interactivity and the ability to dynamically engage audience members in elections. New media are also flexible and adaptable, as they can accommodate a wide range of campaign applications. Some, such as fundraising, have offline counterparts, while others, like voter-produced election ads, are unique to the digital realm.

Research on candidate websites provides an illustration of research on the form, function, and content of new election media. Studies have traced the rising sophistication of websites across election cycles and analyzed their changing strategic value in campaigns (Bimber and Davis, 2003; Cornfield, 2004; Davis, 1999; Druckman, Hennessy, Kifer, and Parkin, 2010; Druckman, Kifer, and Parkin, 2007, 2010; Foot and Schneider, 2006; Stromer-Galley, 2000).

Despite the apparent boundary lines of the phases noted earlier, it has become increasingly difficult to draw clear-cut distinctions between traditional and new media. Technology enables the convergence of communication platforms and the formation of hybrid digital media. *Convergence* refers to the trend of different communication technologies performing similar functions (Jenkins, 2006). Video sharing platforms, like YouTube, have converged with television in elections as they host campaign ads (Burgess and Green, 2009; Pauwels and Hallriegel, 2009). As standard formats take on new media elements, hybrid media have evolved. For example, online versions of print newspapers that originally looked similar to their offline counterparts have come to resemble high-level blogs in style and function. Online newspapers have not only become less formal and more entertainment-focused but now also include mechanisms for interactive engagement and accommodate significant multimedia and user-generated content. Research examining the influence of convergence and hybridity on campaign communication has not kept pace with developments that have important consequences for elections.

Campaign Strategy

Scholars have addressed the ways in which candidates, campaign organizations, and political parties incorporate new media into their strategies. Successful political organizations employ multitiered strategies that integrate traditional and new media tactics. As they take into account the audiences for particular media forms, the strategies of candidates and political parties have become more specialized. A strong majority of senior voters rely primarily on traditional print and electronic sources for campaign data, while younger voters are inclined to consume such information on their smart phones. Digital media have made it possible for campaigns to gather data on voters ranging from their voting history and political leanings to their consumer product preferences. They can also take stock of the electorate's pulse through a wide range of digital polling tools (Howard, 2005).

The question of how much control candidates have over their campaign messaging in the new media environment has also been raised. Some candidacies are better suited to new media strategies than others (Davis and Owen, 1999). Presidential candidates

Bill Clinton and Barack Obama were able to negotiate old and new media comfortably. Others such as George H. W. Bush in 1992 and John McCain in 2008, had greater difficulty adapting to the less formal, more relational style of new media.

The growth in the number of actors who can actively participate in the media campaign in the new media era has created challenges for candidates seeking to control their message. Political organizations such as 527 groups, which are not subject to campaign contribution and spending limits, can run campaign ads and mobilize voters online as long as they do not coordinate with a candidate's campaign committee. The ads they disseminate can complicate messaging strategies even for candidates they are meant to help.

New Media Audiences

Another body of research focuses on the audiences for new media in elections. Here the most basic question is: Who makes up the audiences for new election media? The answer has changed as Internet penetration has become more widespread and people adopt new forms of digital technology. Early political Internet users were younger, male, and educated. However, as the audiences for new election media have expanded exponentially, they increasingly resemble the general population (Zickuhr, 2010).

Fifty-five percent of voters in the 2010 midterm contests used Internet media for some election-relevant purpose (Smith, 2011). Still, younger and more educated people are the most inclined to use the most pioneering platforms. Enthusiasm over new media developments in campaigns can at times overshadow the reality that the audiences for all but a few political media sites are generally small (Hindman, 2009) and use of the most innovative campaign applications can be slight (Owen 2011a, 2011b).

Related research examines the extent to which new outlets supplement or supplant mainstream media for voters. The dynamics underlying audience media use differ for presidential and midterm elections. Voters are gravitating from traditional television and print sources and moving to the Internet for presidential campaign news (Owen and Davis, 2008). Rather than abandoning traditional sources entirely, many people are adding Internet media as a new source of information during midterm elections (Smith, 2011). Local television news, in particular, remains important for midterm election voters (Owen, 2011b). Young people, however, are inclined to use online sources to the exclusion of television and print newspapers in both types of campaigns.

Audience use of campaign media is a research focus that raises a key question: What motivates voters to use new election media? Attempts to address this issue have employed uses and gratifications frameworks to examine the motivations underpinning voters' media use. Many of these studies rely heavily on lists of media motivations and uses that were developed in the pre–new media era (see Blumler, 1979; Owen, 1991). Studies adopting these frameworks reveal that voters use new campaign media for guidance, surveillance/information seeking, entertainment, and social utility (Kaye and Johnson, 2002) as well as to reinforce their voting decisions (Mutz and Martin, 2001).

These standard uses and gratifications have been supplemented by campaign media motivations and uses that take into account digital media's interactivity, networkability, collaborative possibilities, ability to foster engagement (Ruggiero, 2000), and convenience. New media use involves experiences that are more active and goal-directed than those associated with traditional media. These include problem solving, persuading others, relationship maintenance, status seeking, personal insight, and time consumption. Scholars have also identified uses and gratifications that are linked to specific aspects of new election media use (Johnson and Kaye, 2008). Gratifications are derived from participating in virtual communities, as by establishing a peer identity (LaRose and Eastin, 2004). The use of social media fulfills needs including enhancing social connectedness, self-expression, sharing problems, sociability, relationship maintenance, and self-actualization (Quan-Haase, 2010; Shao, 2009).

New Media Effects in Elections

Researchers have also investigated the relationship between voters' use of new media and their levels of political attentiveness, knowledge, attitudes, orientations, and engagement. Early studies of the effects of new media on voters' acquisition of campaign knowledge produced mixed results, while newer research reveals more consistent evidence of information gain (Bimber, 2001; Drew and Weaver, 2006; Norris, 2000; Prior, 2005; Weaver and Drew, 2001; Wei and Lo, 2008). Scholars have also examined the influence of the use of new election media on the development of political attitudes and orientations, such as efficacy and trust (Johnson, Braima, and Sothirajah, 1999; Kenski and Stroud, 2006, Wang, 2007; Zhang, Johnson, Seltzer, and Bichard, 2010).

Some studies have found a connection between exposure to online media and higher levels of electoral engagement and turnout (Gueorguieva, 2008; Gulati and Williams, 2010; Johnson and Kaye, 2003; Tolbert and Mcneal, 2003; Wang, 2007). However, the effects may not be overwhelming (Boulianne, 2009). The online environment may be most relevant for people who are already predisposed toward political engagement (Park and Perry, 2008, 2009). The use of social media does not necessarily increase electoral participation, although it has a positive influence on civic engagement, such as community volunteerism (Baumgartner and Morris, 2010; Zhang, Johnson, Seltzer, and Bichard, 2010).

Young Voters

Young voters, those under age 30, came of political age during the Internet era. Unlike older citizens, who established their campaign media habits in the print and television age, this generation has embraced the election online from the outset. A growing body of literature focuses on the ways in which young voters are using new election media and their effects. Studies indicate that this demographic group is out front in terms of using new media for accessing information (Lupia and Philpot, 2005; Shah, McLeod, and Yoon, 2001); indeed, many ignore traditional print and broadcast media and rely exclusively on digital sources (Owen, 2011b). Young people are also at the forefront of new election media innovation and participation (Owen, 2008–2009; Baumgartner and Morris, 2010).

UNANSWERED QUESTIONS AND NEW DIRECTIONS

Research to date has established useful baselines for understanding new media and elections. However, many of the questions that guided early work remain contested or only partially addressed. Much of the existing scholarship has employed well-worn theoretical frameworks that are not entirely appropriate for the new media age and have relied on orthodox methodological approaches, such as survey research and content analysis. In order to track new developments and voters' use of campaign media innovations, theories explaining the new media's role in elections should be refined or recast. Creative research methodologies such as the use of time gliders to catalogue the emergence and development of new campaign media should be employed.

Going forward, scholars should critically and creatively address the basic question: How can new media's influence in elections be identified, measured, assessed, and explained in the current environment? Since the new media environment is changeable, and tracking developments is difficult, this is a challenging proposition. New media applications are introduced and modified, and they sometimes disappear quickly. Audiences' new media tastes shift, and their engagement with particular platforms can be mercurial. Candidates, parties, media organizations, and average citizens experiment with new media and introduce new scenarios in virtually every campaign.

Theoretical frameworks should be tested for their capacity to accommodate the unique characteristics of new media, with their inherent multipath interactivity, flexibility, unpredictability, and opportunities for more active engagement. Theories should elucidate the challenges new media present to entrenched media and political hierarchies. They also should address the manner in which new media are influencing campaign logistics and strategies. To address the effects of complex audience dynamics, scholars need to develop analytical categories beyond demographics and basic political orientations. Much excitement has been generated by the prospect of using new media for electoral engagement, but the substance and significance of these forms of activation are barely understood. Studies might more deeply assess whether or not this engagement constitutes meaningful and effective political activation.

Standard methodological approaches should be updated for the new media age or used in conjunction with cutting edge methods. Some of the very same tools that are employed by users of digital media can be used by scholars to collect and analyze data. Electronic sources—such as blogs, discussion forums, and email—can function as archives of material that can be automatically searched, retrieved, extracted, and examined using digital tools. Audience analysis also can benefit from fresh methodological approaches. People do not consume news online in the same linear fashion that they read the morning newspaper. Instead, they explore news offerings by following a series of links to particular content. Web crawler techniques can be used to examine online election communities. Digital utilities, such as online timeline creators, visually chart the development of new election media and serve as research tools (Owen, 2011a). Journals that can handle digital scholarship using multimedia graphics, and interactive exhibits should be developed.

References

Baum, M. A. 2005. Talking the vote: Why presidential candidates hit the talk show circuit. *American Journal of Political Science* 49(2), 213–234.

Baumgartner, J. C., and J. Morris. 2010. MyFaceTube politics: Social networking websites and political engagement of young people. *Social Science Computer Review* 28(1), 24–44.

Bimber, B., and R. Davis. 2003. *Campaigning online: The Internet in U.S. elections.* New York: Oxford University Press.

The Bivings Group. 2006. *The Internet's role in political campaigns.* Research report. Washington, DC: The Bivings Group.

Blumler, J. G. 1979. The role of theory in uses and gratifications studies. *Communication Research* 8(1), 9–36.

Boulianne, S. 2009. Does Internet use affect engagement? A meta-analysis of research. *Political Communication* 26(2), 193–211.

Burgess, J., and J. Green. 2009. *YouTube: Online video and participatory culture.* Malden, MA: Polity Press.

Cornfield, M. 2004. *Politics moves online: Campaigning and the Internet.* New York: The Century Foundation.

Davis, R. 1999. *The web of politics.* New York: Oxford University Press.

Davis, R., and D. Owen. 1999. *New media and American politics.* New York: Oxford University Press.

Drew, D., and D. Weaver. 2006. Voter learning in the 2004 presidential election: Did the media matter? *Journalism and Mass Communication Quarterly* 68(1), 27–37.

Druckman, J. N., C. L. Hennessy, M. J. Kifer, and M. Parkin. 2010. Issue engagement on congressional candidate web sites, 2002–2006. *Social Science Computer Review* 28(1), 3–23.

Druckman, J. N., M. J. Kifer, and M. Parkin. 2007. The technological development of congressional candidate web sites. *Social Science Computer Review* 25(4), 425–442.

Druckman, J. N., M. J. Kifer, and M. Parkin. 2010. Timeless strategy meets new medium: Going negative on congressional campaign web sites, 2002–2006. *Political Communication* 27(1), 88–103.

Foot, K. A., and S. M. Schneider. 2006. *Web campaigning.* Cambridge, MA: MIT Press.

Gueorguieva, V. 2008. Voters, MySpace, and YouTube: The impact of alternative communication channels on the 2006 election cycle and beyond. *Social Science Computer Review* 26(3), 288–300.

Gulati, G. J. "Jeff," and C. B. Williams. 2010. Congressional candidates' use of YouTube in 2008: Its frequency and rationale. *Journal of Information Technology and Politics* 7(2), 93–109.

Hillygus, D. S., and T. G. Shields. 2008. *The persuadable voter.* Princeton, NJ: Princeton University Press.

Hindman, M. 2009. *The myth of digital democracy.* Princeton, NJ: Princeton University Press.

Howard, P. N. 2005. Deep democracy, Thin citizenship: The impact of digital media in political campaign strategy. *The Annals of the American Academy of Political and Social Science 597,* 153–170.

Jamieson, K. H., and J. N. Cappella. 2008. *Echo chamber.* New York: Oxford University Press.

Jenkins, H. 2006. *Convergence culture: Where old and new media collide.* New York: New York University Press.

Johnson, T. J., M. A. M. Braima, and J. Sothirajah. 1999. Doing the traditional media sidestep: Comparing the effects of the Internet and other nontraditional media with traditional media in the 1996 presidential campaign. *Journalism & Mass Communication Quarterly 76*(1), 99–123.

Johnson, T. J., and B. K. Kaye. 2003. A boost or bust for democracy? How the Web influenced political behaviors in the 1996 and 2000 presidential elections. *The International Journal of Press/Politics 8*(3), 9–34.

Johnson, T. J., and B. K. Kaye. 2008. In blog we trust? Deciphering credibility of components of the Internet among politically interested Internet users. *Computers in Human Behavior 25*(1), 175–182.

Kaye, B. K., and T. J. Johnson. 2002. Online and in the know: Uses and gratifications of the Web for political information. *Journal of Broadcasting & Electronic Media, 46*(2), 54–71.

Kenski, K., and N. J. Stroud. 2006. Connections between Internet use and political efficacy, knowledge, and participation. *Journal of Broadcasting & Electronic Media 50*(2), 173–192.

LaRose, R., and M. S. Eastin. 2004. A social cognitive theory of Internet uses and gratifications: Toward a new model of media attendance. *Journal of Broadcasting & Electronic Media 48*(3), 358–377.

Lepore, J. 2010. *The whites of their eyes.* Princeton, NJ: Princeton University Press.

Lupia, A., and T. S. Philpot. 2005. Views from inside the net: How websites affect young adults' political interest. *Journal of Politics 67*(4), 1122–1142.

Mutz, D. C., and P. S. Martin. 2001. Facilitating communication across lines of political difference: The role of mass media. *American Political Science Review 95*(1), 97–114.

Norris, P. 2000. *A virtuous circle? Political communications in post-industrial democracies.* Cambridge: Cambridge University Press.

Owen, D. 1991. *Media messages in American presidential elections.* Westport, CT: Greenwood Press.

Owen, D. 2008–09. Election media and youth political engagement. *Journal of Social Science Education 38*(2), 14–25.

Owen, D. 2011a. Media: The complex interplay of old and new forms. In S. K. Medvic (Ed.), *New directions in campaigns and elections* (pp. 145–162). New York: Routledge.

Owen, D. 2011b. The Internet and voter decision-making. Paper presented at the conference on Internet, Voting, and Democracy, Center for the Study of Democracy, University of California, Irvine, and the European University Institute, Florence, Laguna Beach, CA, May 14–15.

Owen, D., and R. Davis. 2008. United States: Internet and elections. In S. Ward, D. Owen, R. Davis, and D. Taras (Eds.), *Making a difference: A comparative view of the role of the Internet in election politics* (pp. 93–112). Lanham, MD: Lexington Books.

Park, H. M., and J. L. Perry. 2008. Do campaign web sites really matter in electoral civic engagement? *Social Science Computer Review* 26(2), 190–212.

Park, H. M., and J. L. Perry. 2009. Do campaign websites really matter in electoral civic engagement? Empirical evidence from the 2004 and 2006 Internet tracking survey. In C. Panagopoulos (Ed.), *Politicking online* (pp. 101–124). New Brunswick, NJ: Rutgers University Press.

Pauwels, L., and P. Hellriegel. 2009. Strategic and tactical uses of Internet design and infrastructure: The case of YouTube. *Journal of Visual Literacy* 28(1), 51–69.

Prior, M. 2005. News vs. entertainment: How increasing media choice widens gaps in political knowledge and turnout. *American Journal of Political Science* 49(3), 577–592.

Project for Excellence in Journalism. 2010. Parsing election day media—How the midterm message varied by platform. Research report. Washington, DC, November 5. Available at: http://www.journalism.org/analysis_report/blogs_%E2%80%93_commentary_and_conspiracies (Accessed May 11, 2011.)

Quan-Haase, A., and A. L. Young. 2010. Uses and gratifications of social media: A comparison of Facebook and instant messaging. *Bulletin of Science and Technology* 30(5), 350–361.

Ruggiero, T. E. 2000. Uses and gratifications theory in the 21st century. *Mass Communication and Society* 3(1), 3–37.

Shah, D., D. M. McLeod, and So-Hyang Yoon. 2001. Communication, context, and community: An exploration of print, broadcast, and Internet influences. *Communication Research* 28(4), 464–506.

Shao, G. 2009. Understanding the appeal of user-generated media: A uses and gratification perspective. *Internet Research* 19(1), 7–25.

Smith, A. 2011. *The Internet in campaign 2010*. Research report. Washington, DC: Pew Internet and American Life Project.

Stromer-Galley, J. 2000. On-line interaction and why candidates avoid it. *Journal of Communication* 50(4), 111–132.

Stroud, N. J. 2011. *Niche news*. New York: Oxford University Press.

Sunstein, C. R. 2000. *Republic.com*. Princeton, NJ: Princeton University Press.

Tolbert, C. J., and R. S. Mcneal. 2003. Unraveling the effects of the Internet on political participation. *Political Research Quarterly* 56(2), 175–185.

Wang, Song-In. 2007. Political use of the Internet, political attitudes, and political participation. *Asian Journal of Communication* 17(4), 381–395.

Weaver, D., and D. Drew. 2001. Voter learning and interest in the 2000 presidential election: Did the media matter? *Journalism & Mass Communication Quarterly* 78(4), 41–65.

Wei, R., and Ven-hwei Lo. 2008. News media use and knowledge about the 2006 U.S. midterm elections: Why exposure matters in voter learning. *International Journal of Public Opinion Research* 20(3), 347–362.

Zhang, W., T. J. Johnson, T. Seltzer, and S. L. Bichard. 2010. The revolution will be networked: The influence of social network sites on political attitudes and behavior. *Social Science Computer Review* 28(1), 75–92.

Zickuhr, K. *Generations 2010*. Research report. Washington, DC: Pew Internet and American Life Project.

CHAPTER 57

POLITICAL DISCUSSION AND DELIBERATION ONLINE

JENNIFER STROMER-GALLEY

As a variety of information and communication technologies (ICTs)—including email listservs, Usenet/Google groups, blogs, microblogs, wikis, and social sites—diffuse globally, much research has focused on their democratizing potential. Since the early 1990s, scholars have examined how Internet-channeled communication might facilitate a variety of political behaviors, including talk about politics and social issues with friends and family or acquaintances and strangers. Some of that talk is formal, structured deliberations, but most is informal political conversation. This chapter examines the research on both of these forms of political discussion online, identifies the importance of this research area, signals its major findings, and examines key unanswered questions. First, it explains the importance of scholarship focused on informal political conversation and of more formal political deliberation over the Internet as well.

IMPORTANCE

Several theorists have argued that ICTs and political conversation, discussion, and deliberation have important functions in democracies. John Dewey (1946), Harold Lasswell (1941), and Jürgen Habermas (1962/1989; 1984) among others, advanced the idea that informal conversation that critically engages political and social topics is a necessary component of a functioning democracy. Through political conversation, citizens' opinions and perspectives are represented in their government, and in turn their government is more responsive to its citizens. Moreover, Benjamin Barber (1984) argued that interactive technologies can be harnessed to create a "strong democracy," bringing citizens together for discussion and deliberation on community and policy matters, thus enabling them to better engage in the surveillance of their governments and to provide feedback to them.

For these reasons Internet–based political deliberation and discussion are important foci of research within political communication. Although much prior scholarship in political communication has been preoccupied with understanding the relationship between mass-media use and political knowledge, opinions, and participation, there have been moments that focused on face-to-face political talk. Empirical research from the 1950s on "two-step flow" (Katz and Lazersfeld, 1960), for example, posited the importance of opinion elites within interpersonal communities as elite opinion leaders pass mass media information onto others who are not exposed to media information directly. In the first decade of this century, others have theorized the role of *informal conversation* as an important moderating factor in political participation (Nisbet and Scheufele, 2004) and recognized the value of informal political conversation in shaping and informing public opinion to mobilize and sometimes demobilize political action (see, for example, Mutz, 2002). In a similar vein, political theorists have focused attention on *political deliberation*, which brings an interested public together to talk through a common problem and come to consensus on a solution, giving the practice of deliberation a more direct role in informing on public policy (Coleman and Blumler, 2009; Fishkin, 2009; Gutmann and Thompson, 2004).

As ICTs have proliferated, intellectual interest in the role of social and deliberative political talk online has grown. These communication channels, most notably occurring through the Internet but also on mobile phone devices and interactive television, have been examined for their potential to increase the opportunities for political conversation and direct participation in policymaking (Coleman, 1999; Froomkin, 2004). Channel characteristics such as decreased perceived distance between people, increased speed of communication, nearly limitless volume and storage, and enhanced interactivity between people and between people and ICTs have been identified as opportunities for increased political talk and deliberation.

Not everyone has heralded ICTs as a panacea for democratization, however. Scholars have pointed to the increased opportunities for surveillance by governments that use the information to monitor and sanction their citizens and by campaigns to narrowcast to relatively small subsets of the public (Howard, 2006). In response to the optimism expressed in the early days of the World Wide Web, some have argued that in the United States in particular and the Western world in general, a "normalization" ensures that the same hierarchies, power dynamics, and disparities seen in political life offline inevitably will be reproduced online (Margolis and Resnick, 2000).

Also of concern is the prospect that ICTs will contribute to fragmentation and polarization. Fragmentation has been of particular interest in the digital age, given the greater choices the public has for its media diet. If people act on their disposition to enclave themselves in a world filled with like-minded friends, associates, and media, there can be no common public (Sunstein, 2001). This, in turn, risks severely harming democratic society, which requires some shared basis of common information and experience upon which to associate and to solve its problems (Davis and Owen, 1998; Selnow, 1998; Sunstein, 2001). The related concern, polarization, may be the by-product of a high choice media environment. If so, those interested in politics will become more knowledgeable as well as ideologically extreme and rigid in their perspectives, while the less interested "middle" becomes less knowledgeable and involved (Prior, 2007). This potentially creates more extreme ideological positions with less room for compromise on policy or political matters.

With these concerns as a backdrop, researchers have asked who engages in online discussion and who does not, why they do so, what is the quality of such discussions, and what role the technological infrastructure and context plays in shaping those discussions. In the sections that follow, I synthesize their answers and note areas requiring additional work.

THE STATE OF KNOWLEDGE

One of the most basic questions for scholars of ICTs is who participates in online political discussions, whether informal or deliberative. This can be a challenging question to answer, in part because observing online forums does not reveal much about user identity, given the fairly anonymous nature of much online interaction. The surveys that have been the best sources of information on who participates are often limited because those who talk politics are a relatively small percentage of the online population. As a result, our basic understanding of who participates in informal political conversations or more formal deliberations is still surprisingly thin. What the research suggests is that relatively few people in the United States use the Internet to seek political information (Hindman, 2009; Tewksbury, 2003) and that those who actually talk politics online are an even smaller minority, especially in nonelection years. A recent study of the 2008 presidential election suggests that 38 percent of surveyed Internet users reported talking about the election online (Nam and Stromer-Galley, 2012), and in 2012 nearly 35 percent reported encouraging others to vote and posting their thoughts about the election through social media (Rainie, Smith, Schlozman, Brady, and Verba, 2012). Sometimes up to three times as many people read or "lurk" than post, however (Albrecht, 2006; Davis, 1999; Tsaliki, 2002). For most ordinary Internet users, exposure to cross-cutting political views and disagreements tends to happen on sites or channels that are not necessarily devoted to political topics (Graham, 2010; Wojcieszak and Mutz, 2009).

Those who do participate in online political discussions are historically advantaged and enfranchised groups. Specifically, those who are more affluent and have more education are more likely to participate; this was as true in the late 1990s as it is today for both informal conversation and formal deliberation (Baek, Wojcieszak, and Delli Carpini, 2012; Davis, 2005; Johnson et al., 2007; Nam and Stromer-Galley, 2012; Trénel, 2004). An example of this can be found in blog writing, where authors are likely to be well-educated professional white men (Hindman, 2009). Although blog readership is relatively small, weblogs influence the larger political discussion within the public sphere because their audience is populated with political elites and journalists (Farrell and Drezner, 2008; Perlmutter, 2008).

Although young people tend to be less engaged in and knowledgeable about politics, research on informal political discussions finds that they are relatively overrepresented in online discussions in the United States (Baek, Wojcieszak, and Delli Carpini, 2012; Davis, 2005) and in European countries (Albrecht, 2006; Calenda and Mosca, 2007). This can be partly explained because young people are more likely to use ICTs over the Internet than are older people; however, young people are not necessarily overrepresented in all online communication channels. Research suggests that younger individuals are drawn to newer Internet-channeled communications—for example, social media sites like Facebook (Nam and Stromer-Galley, 2012), while those who are older tend to use blogs and older ICTs, such as listservs and Usenet/Google groups (Stromer-Galley, 2002b).

A noteworthy gender gap exists in online political conversation, with men more likely to participate in online political discussions in the United States (Davis, 1999; Garramone, Harris, and Pizante, 1986; Harp and Tremayne, 2006; Hill and Hughes, 1998; Savicki, Lingenfelter, and Kelley, 1996; Stromer-Galley, 2002a; Trammell and Keshelashvili, 2005) and in European countries (Albrecht, 2006; Hagemann, 2002; Jankowski and van Selm, 2000; Jensen, 2003), which raises questions about how representative such discussions can be. So, for example, Harp and Tremayne's (2006) analysis of top political blogs in the United States finds a "boys' club." Male bloggers are less likely to link to blogs authored by women, and when women are part of the conversation, they are attacked, marginalized, and sexualized, making it harder for them to be part of the conversation. As well, the issues that tend to be the focus of political discussions online are typically not "female" ones, such as child care and education (Davis, 2005). This lack of focus on issues of particular concern to women may further exclude them.

The relationship between race and political conversation online has been and continues to be an understudied area. Few studies specifically examine differentials in participation or the reasons why. This absence may be attributable in part to the rhetoric in the early days of the World Wide Web's diffusion, which stressed the idea that when online we were identity-free; one's bodily identity could be left behind and a new one constructed (Turkle, 1995). Yet there is good reason to think that race cannot be left behind (Burkhalter, 1999). One potentially empowering aspect of ICTs is enabling marginalized and minority groups to find each other online. In her interviews with Latino/Latina and African American bloggers, Pole (2010) found influential activism among groups of African American and Latino bloggers on issues related to race and immigration. Yet, Byrne's (2007) examination of social media sites notes that few are dedicated to African Americans and issues of particular concern to them. Additionally, race and age cannot be readily disentangled online. Garcia-Castañon, Rank, and Barreto (2011) find that in the 2008 US election, when an African American ran for president and won, young racial minorities were as proportionally engaged in ICTs such as campaign-related blogs during the election as were young whites; but among older voters, whites were more likely to use ICTs related to the 2008 election, suggesting that the digital and access divide may disproportionately affect older minorities.

One of the potential benefits of informal political discussion and especially more formal political deliberation is the opportunity for discussants to be exposed to other opinions and values. Online exposure to different, cross-current points of view and to discussions where disagreements are expressed have been shown to increase "argument repertoire," defined as the ability of people to articulate both reasons for their own perspectives and for those held by others holding opposing positions (Price, Cappella, and Nir, 2002). Online discussion also has the potential to shift people's opinions. Research that examined a political discussion on sexual minorities and same-sex marriage found that those who had strong opinions on the topic did not change their positions, but those who were strong supporters shifted to a more moderate position on the issue (Wojcieszak and Price, 2010).

Even though there is evidence of increased opinion sophistication and opinion shift because of online deliberation, scholars have raised concerns about the quality of online discussions, especially informal discussions that one might find on blogs, in open chat rooms, and on message board forums. In theory, a high-quality discussion would include not only opinion expression but also reason-giving for those opinions, sustained interaction with others in the discussion, focus on the topic at hand and not to other unrelated topics, a limit on ad hominem attacks but the presence of a mixture of agreement and respectful disagreement, and a range of evidence in support of arguments, including linking to Web sources and providing personal experience (Stromer-Galley, 2007). If those are one's expectations, much research suggests that online political discussion is severely lacking (Benson, 1996; Noveck, 2000; Streck, 1998). Several scholars have characterized online discussions as not delving deeply into important political issues (Wilhelm, 1998), exhibiting fairly low rationality (Hagemann, 2002) and underdeveloped arguments (Ellis and Maoz, 2007; Weger and Aakhus, 2003), and a lack of understanding or even an attempt at understanding ideologically opposed perspectives (Jankowski and van Selm, 2000; Schneider, 1996). Some research suggests that online discussions tend to be dominated by a few outspoken people rather than exhibiting equality of participation (Davis, 1999; Koop and Jansen, 2009; Robinson, 2005).

However, the character of online discussion is not uniformly bleak. Other work suggests that synchronous chat is more coherent and engaged than that on other topics (Stromer-Galley and Martinson, 2009), and political topics tend to draw in a broader network of people (Gonzalez-Bailon, Kaltenbrunner, and Banchs, 2010). Some scholars even provide evidence for a fairly high degree of rationality (Graham, 2010). For instance, collaborative editing on the *Wikipedia* exhibits a genuine quest for high-quality information and of inclusion in the discussion of anyone who shares that goal (Klemp and Forcehimes, 2010). Online discussants make use of URL-link posting in their discussions, which generates greater interaction among participants but also seems to foster even greater opinionated rather than informed discourse (Polletta, Chen, and Anderson, 2009).

Why people participate in online discussions given this mixed picture of its quality is another topic of interest. Understanding the motives that drive particular people to engage in political conversations might prove useful in considering ways to encourage more people to participate in online discussions, given the possibility for increased opinion sophistication for those who participate. Some research suggests that people participate to be sociable, to become more informed on political topics, to hear diverse perspectives including those from the "other side," to learn more about their own opinions, and to vent their anger at current events or policies (Stromer-Galley, 2003). People also report that they feel less inhibited about expressing their opinions online than face to face (Ho and McLeod, 2008) and that, when online, they experience fewer negative emotions and more consensus but also are exposed to more extreme ideological positions (Baek, Wojcieszak, and Delli Carpini, 2012). Little similar research exists that measures motives for online formal political deliberations.

Research is mixed with regard to fragmentation and polarization, two concerns raised earlier. Some research supports the fragmentation hypothesis, concluding that linking practices in the blogosphere reveal that liberal and conservative bloggers are more likely to connect their own work to other blogs that share their political worldview (Hargittai, Gallo, and Kane, 2008). Yet other scholarship suggests that some seek online discussions that engage a diverse range of perspectives (Kelly, Fisher, and Smith, 2005; Stromer-Galley, 2003). Related research suggests that fears of online echo chambers of like-minded people only talking with each other may be unfounded, because people, even those with strong ideological leanings, tend to link to neutral third-party sites, giving the two polarized sides a common information stream and frames of reference (Reese et al., 2007).

Scholars agree that the structure of the online environment affects the quality of the discussions that happen within it (Beierle, 2004; Noveck, 2004; Wright, 2006). Researchers have found that recruiting people who are interested in and knowledgeable about the topic increases discussion quality (Wright and Street, 2007), and that having political elites and politicians coparticipate in the discussion also elevates quality (Coleman, 2004; Jensen, 2003). A moderator who oversees and manages the discussion also helps (Albrecht, 2006; Trénel, 2004). The open, nonthreaded, unmoderated discussions that take place on social media sites such as Facebook are not conducive to quality discussion. The jokes, flames, and parodies on YouTube, for example, may hamper engaged and sustained political critique and discussion (Hess, 2009).

Researchers have investigated ways in which to harness ICTs for discussion. New digital mapping technologies, such as Google maps, that allow people to tag locations and comment, can be employed to facilitate online deliberations that deal with spatial/geographic issues (Rinner, Kessler, and Andrulis, 2008). Argument mapping has been viewed as a way to structure formal political deliberations by having discussants tag their messages with a predefined tag set, such as *question* or *disagree*, which then invites visual mapping of threads of discussion and the polarities within those discussion threads. Some research suggests, however, that although they view such systems favorably, participants resist the predefined tag set, and moderation and guidance is needed to help users with the system (Gürkan et al., 2010).

CONTEMPLATIONS ON THE STATE
OF THIS AREA OF INQUIRY

One of the central challenges in studying political communication behavior and ICTs is the fact that the channels for communication are ever-evolving. Although some have existed since the 1970s and 1980s, such as email and bulletin board systems respectively, others, such as microblogging and social network sites, have emerged only in the past decade. These evolving technologies mean that on the horizon there seems always to be yet another new technology whose effects we need to investigate. Yet that focus on individual technologies overlooks the larger social, media, and political ecology in which we now live and often fails to see the forest for the trees. Put another way, by focusing on the diffusion of each new ICT, scholars fail to examine the broader social and media context and the larger media system into which each is set. As well, this emergent digital communication environment often leads researchers to focus on the "newest" or "hottest" online discussion forums, often at the expense of a richer understanding of some of the long-standing online discussion environments and discourse practices and their effects, such as email listservs and message board forums, which still serve as outlets for political talk.

The scholarship also tends to concentrate on research questions that are relatively easy to pursue, without investigating similarly pressing questions in environments that are more challenging to access. For example, as described earlier, a few studies now have looked at the link practices across blog sites to determine whether blogs or message boards of one political ideology connect to those of opposed ideologies (see, for example, Kelly, Fisher, and Smith, 2005). This is a relatively easy pattern to study, since these forums are publicly available, relatively easily "scraped," and their links categorized. We have not seen similar investigations on newer social media forums or on older channels such as email lists. Part of the reason for this omission is the difficulty in gaining access to often private discussion spaces in order to study actual conversations occurring in those online domains.

Despite the challenges in so doing, a small number of scholars are studying actual talk. Since systematic content analysis, thematic analysis, and other qualitative examinations of the interactions are slow, time-consuming, and labor-intensive, increasingly communication scholars are partnering with computer scientists who have developed lexicons (large lists of words, their meanings, and their relationships to other words), machine learning algorithms, and Natural Language Processing capabilities to process large volumes of text. These systems are being used to visualize online discussions (Kelly, Fisher, and Smith, 2005) and to analyze their characteristics (e.g., leadership within forums [Huffaker, 2010; Broadwell et al., 2013]). Such partnerships will be fruitful in years to come.

Not only the media environment but also the population using ICTs is changing. Research conducted about political discussion online in the 1980s and 1990s depicted a stereotypic actor: highly educated, likely employed in the high-tech sector or in higher education, overwhelmingly male, and fairly antiestablishment (Garramone, Harris, and Pizante, 1986; Hill and Hughes, 1998), a conclusion that reflected the relatively small percentage of Americans who were using the Internet at that time. As it has diffused and digital and mobile technologies become more ubiquitous especially in Western countries, speculation has centered on "digital natives," the political actors born and raised in the digital era who may learn, socialize, and engage with politics in ways that differ from those of earlier generations. Thus, as the generational cohorts change, what we think we now know about political discussion online may not hold.

Finally, two conceptual problems plague research in this area. The first relates specifically to the terminology used to characterize discussion online. The second, which stems from the first, is the adequacy of the metric or yardstick used to assess online deliberation. In writing about online discussion, many researchers use the term *deliberation*, which as described earlier connotes a formal process of discussion with a clearly identified problem and a common task of identifying consensually agreed-upon solutions. The trouble, however, is that much political discussion that occurs online is framed as deliberation and so little of it satisfies that definition. For example, Graham's (2010) research on the fan site for *Big Brother*, UK, finds political discussions infused with nonpolitical ones. Yet, it is important to note that the fans who congregate on that website are not there to solve any particular problem or find consensus on a solution. Theirs, then, is a very different type of conversation from that studied by Trénel (2004) and Black (2009), who examined online deliberations that brought New Yorkers together to discuss the redesign and development of Ground Zero, the former World Trade Center site in lower Manhattan, a shared problem for a community that had a collective need to identify agreed-upon solutions. Framing the latter as *deliberation* makes conceptual sense, but applying that term to political chat that emerges as part of a conversation about a TV show does not and leads to the related problem discussed next, that of assessing the character and quality of the discussion.

Scholars' study of the quality of online discussions often has been informed by deliberative theory, especially that of Jürgen Habermas. Unsurprisingly, much of this work finds that online discussions fail to live up to Habermasian ideals of rational-critical discussion (Dahlberg, 2001). It is worth mentioning that the rational-critical deliberative ideal that Habermas envisioned was never meant as a measuring stick against which to assess discussions on or off line. Having said that, most informal political conversations cannot and should not be expected to do the heavy work assigned to more formal deliberations. Put another way, neither a conversation about homosexuality that emerges on the fan site for *Big Brother* nor any other informal online political discussion should be expected to embody rational-critical, deductive argumentation, with high reciprocity and equality of participation. That is not the function of such a discussion and likely does not fit with the motives of those who are there to share their thoughts. Put simply, being clear about the function or purpose of the interaction for the participants and within the broader social context would go a long way to clarifying the scholarship on online political talk.

KEY UNANSWERED QUESTIONS

As suggested earlier, in this area of work, several significant questions remain unanswered. We need to know more about who participates, who does not, and why. For example, the reasons for the gender disparity in online discussion and deliberation remain something of a mystery. In-depth interviews and surveys with women who do and who do not participate in online informal political discussions or deliberations and participant observation of their online discussions to identify and better understand the discourse practices in these environments would be a helpful addition to this body of scholarship. Relatedly, scholars need to understand in more detail the racial divide online, determine where it does and does not exist, and identify the motives and the social, political, and technological enticements and obstacles that bring certain racial groups but not others to informal talk or formal deliberation online.

We need to better understand which variables affect the quality of informal discussion and formal deliberations. What exactly causes opinion to shift and does the type of digital channel matter (e.g., email, Twitter, chat forums)? Are there particular methods of moderation that produce better discussions and that create better decision outcomes for formal deliberations? Are there particular digital affordances, such as synchrony (time) or visual presence (e.g., pictures of participants), that facilitate higher-quality discussions? What mechanisms—such as gamification techniques (e.g., badges, points, stars)—might promote greater sustained engagement and broader involvement of participants? Are there more effective mechanisms for participants to self-moderate and self-govern in order to produce higher-quality discussions and better outcomes? These and related questions would be best addressed by researchers conducting controlled experiments. Most research about online discussion, however, analyzes individual case studies or surveys of people who report discussing politics online. Careful experimentation would help researchers to identify explanatory variables as well as isolate the digital and structural characteristics that promote high-quality discussion and better decision outcomes.

Fragmentation and polarization have been identified as key social processes that have been exacerbated by our increasingly diverse media environment, with potentially devastating consequences to democratic societies. The scholarship is mixed with regard to whether people seek homophilous or heterogeneous others with whom to talk politics. My own suspicion is that it is not an either/or situation; that is, in some instances people seek out like-minded others, but at other times they want diverse opinions. We need to better understand the underlying motives and the exigencies that give rise to such media choices. More research is needed to chart and characterize fragmentation and polarization in the context of political talk online and to examine its consequences, both desirable and dire.

Finally, little research has examined how national, political, and cultural climates shape online political discussion and more formal deliberation. One study that analyzed newspaper comments online in three countries—Brazil, the United States, and France—before and after the terrorist attacks in the United States on September 11, 2001, found noteworthy differences in the length of comments, the use of humor and ad hominem attack, and methods of argument across the three countries (Robinson, 2005). More scholarship is needed to reveal whether channel characteristics or the national, social, and political culture explain some of the communication practices exhibited in and effects of online discussion. We need to better understand, for example, the ways and functions of political talk online in authoritarian regimes, such as on *Sina Weibo* in China, or the use of social media in highlighting political issues in authoritarian and transitioning governments as in Egypt.

Conclusion

Online political discussion and deliberation will remain important areas of scholarship in the years ahead, especially as ICTs continue to diffuse and are used not only in democratically organized governments but also in authoritarian and oligarchic regimes. Although we now know a fair amount about who uses particular channels for political talk, have identified some of their motives for doing so, and have gathered insight into the positive and negative effects of these behaviors, more work is needed. First, we have yet to unpack the factors that lead women and minorities to engage or avoid online discussions and formal deliberations. Second, more experimental work is needed to understand what produces higher-quality discussions and decision outcomes. Third, scholars must work toward conceptual clarity about the phenomenon of interest. Because informal political conversation and formal deliberation are distinctly different in purpose and in character, analysis of online discourse must attend carefully to its purpose. Fourth, more research is needed that extends across ICTs, cross-culturally and beyond democratically governed societies. As globalization continues, we need to shift our focus beyond the United States and the democratic West to understand nonwestern social and political environments and the nature and function of online political discussion within them.

References

Albrecht, S. 2006. Whose voice is heard in online deliberation? A study of participation and representation in political debates on the Internet. *Information, Communication & Society* 9: 62–82.

Baek, Y. M., M. Wojcieszak, and M. X. Delli Carpini. 2012. Online versus face-to-face deliberation: Who? Why? What? With what effects? *New Media & Society* 14: 363–383.

Barber, B. 1984. *Strong democracy: Participatory politics for a new age.* Berkeley: University of California Press.

Beierle, T. C. 2004. Digital deliberation: Engaging the public through online policy dialogues. In P. M. Shane (Ed.), *Democracy online: The prospects for political renewal through the Internet* (pp. 155–166). New York: Routledge.

Benson, T. W. 1996. Rhetoric, civility, and community: Political debate on computer bulletin boards. *Communication Quarterly* 44: 359–378.

Black, L. 2009. Listening to the city: Difference, identity, and storytelling in online deliberative groups. *Journal of Public Deliberation* 5 (1). Available at: http://services.bepress.com/jpd/vol5/iss1/art4

Broadwell, G. A., J. Stromer-Galley, T. Strzalkowski, S. Shaikh, S. Taylor, U. Boz, A. Elia, L. Jiao, T. Liu, and N. J. Webb. 2013. Modeling socio-cultural phenomena in discourse. *Journal of Natural Language Engineering* 19: 213–257. Available at: http://dx.doi.org/10.1017/S1351324911000386

Burkhalter, B. 1999. Reading race online: Discovering racial identity in Usenet discussions. In M. A. Smith and P. Kollock (Eds.), *Communities in cyberspace* (pp. 60–75). New York: Routledge.

Byrne, D. N. 2007. Public discourse, community concerns, and civic engagement: Exploring black social networking traditions on BlackPlanet.com. *Journal of Computer-Mediated Communication* 13 (1). Available at: http://jcmc.indiana.edu/vol13/issue1/byrne.html

Calenda, D., and L. Mosca. 2007. The political use of the Internet: Some insights from two surveys of Italian students. *Information, Communication & Society* 10: 29–47.

Coleman, S. 1999. Cutting out the middle man: From virtual representation to direct deliberation. In B. N. Hague and B. D. Loader (Eds.), *Digital democracy: Discourse and decision making in the information age* (pp. 195–210). New York: Routledge.

Coleman, S. 2004. Connecting Parliament to the public via the Internet. *Information, Communication & Society* 7: 1–22.

Coleman, S., and J. Blumberg. 2009. *The Internet and democratic citizenship: Theory, Practice, and Policy*. New York: Cambridge University Press.

Dahlberg, L. 2001. The Internet and democratic discourse: Exploring the prospects of online deliberative forums extending the public sphere. *Information, Communication & Society* 4: 615–633.

Davis, R. 1999. *The web of politics: The Internet's impact on the American political system*. New York: Oxford University Press.

Davis, R. 2005. *Politics online: Blogs, chatrooms, and discussion groups in American democracy*. New York: Routledge.

Davis, R., and D. Owen. 1998. *New media and American politics*. New York: Oxford University Press.

Dewey, J. 1946. *The Public and its problems: An essay in political inquiry*. Chicago: Gateway Books.

Ellis, D. G., and I. Maoz. 2007. Online argument between Israeli Jews and Palestinians. *Human Communication Research* 33: 291–309.

Farrell, H., and D. W. Drezner. 2008. The power and politics of blogs. *Public Choice* 134: 15–30.

Fishkin, J. S. 2009. *When the people speak: Deliberative democracy & public consultation*. New York: Oxford University Press.

Froomkin, A. M. 2004. Technologies for democracy. In P. M. Shane (Ed.), *Democracy online: The prospects for political renewal through the Internet* (pp. 3–20). New York: Routledge.

Garcia-Castañon, M., A. D. Rank, and M. A. Barreto. 2011. Plugged in or tuned out? Youth, race, and Internet usage in the 2008 election. *Journal of Political Marketing* 10: 115–138.

Garramone, G. M., A. C. Harris, and G. Pizante. 1986. Predictors of motivation to use computer-mediated political communication systems. *Journal of Broadcasting & Electronic Media* 30: 445–457.

Gonzalez-Bailon, S., A. Kaltenbrunner, and R. E. Banchs. 2010. The structure of political discussion networks: A model for the analysis of online deliberation. *Journal of Information Technology* 25: 230–243.

Graham, T. 2010. Talking politics online within spaces of popular culture: The case of the Big Brother Forum. *Javnost-The Public* 17(4): 25–42.

Gürkan, A., L. Iandoli, M. Klein, and G. Zollo. 2010. Mediating debate through on-line large-scale argumentation: Evidence from the field. *Information Sciences* 180: 3686–3702.

Gutmann, A., and D. Thompson. 2004. *Why deliberative democracy?* Princeton, NJ: Princeton University Press.

Habermas, J. 1984. *The theory of communicative action: Reason and the rationalization of society*, Vol. 1. T. McCarthy (Transl.). Boston, MA: Beacon Press.

Habermas, J. 1962/1989. *The structural transformation of the public sphere: An inquiry into a category of bourgeois society*. T. Burger (Transl.). Cambridge, MA: MIT Press.

Hagemann, C. 2002. Participation in and contents of two Dutch political party discussion lists on the Internet. *Javnost-The Public* 9(2): 61–76.

Hargittai, E., J. Gallo, and M. Kane. 2008. Cross-ideological discussions among conservative and liberal bloggers. *Public Choice* 134: 67–86.

Harp, D., and M. Tremayne. 2006. The gendered blogosphere: Examining inequality using network and feminist theory. *Journalism & Mass Communication Quarterly* 83: 247–264.

Hess, A. 2009. Resistance up in smoke: Analyzing the limitations of deliberation on YouTube. *Critical Studies in Media Communication* 26: 411–434.

Hill, K. A., and J. E. Hughes. 1998. *Cyberpolitics: Citizen activism in the age of the Internet*. Lanham, MD: Rowman & Littlefield.

Hindman, M. 2009. *The myth of digital democracy*. Princeton, NJ: Princeton University Press.

Ho, S. S., and D. M. McLeod. 2008. Social-psychological influences on opinion expression in face-to-face and computer-mediated communication. *Communication Research* 35: 190–207.

Howard, P. N. 2006. *New Media campaigns and the managed citizen*. Cambridge, MA: Cambridge University Press.

Huffaker, D. 2010. Dimensions of leadership and social influence in online communities. *Human Communication Research* 36: 593–617.

Jankowski, N., and M. van Selm. 2000. The promise and practice of public debate in cyberspace. In Kenneth T. Hacker and Jan van Dijk (Eds.), *Digital democracy: Issues of theory and practice* (pp. 149–165). Thousand Oaks, CA: Sage.

Jensen, J. L. 2003. Public spheres on the Internet: Anarchic or government-sponsored—A comparison. *Scandinavian Political Studies* 26: 349–374.

Johnson, T. J., B. K. Kaye, S. L. Bichard, and W. J. Wong. 2007. Every blog has its day: Politically interested Internet users' perceptions of blog credibility. *Journal of Computer-Mediated Communication* 13(1). Available at: http://jcmc.indiana.edu/vol13/issue1/johnson.html

Katz, E., and P. F. Lazersfeld. 1960. *Personal influence: The part played by people in the flow of mass communications*. New York: Free Press.

Kelly, J., D. Fisher, and M. A. Smith. 2005. Debate, division, and diversity: Political discourse networks in Usenet newsgroups. Paper Presented at the Online Deliberation Conference. Palo Alto, CA.

Klemp, N. J., and A. T. Forcehimes. 2010. From town-halls to Wikis: Exploring Wikipedia's implications for deliberative democracy. *Journal of Public Deliberation* 6(2). Available at: http://services.bepress.com/jpd/vol6/iss2/art4

Koop, R., and H. J. Jansen. 2009. Political blogs and blogrolls in Canada: Forums for democratic deliberation? *Social Science Computer Review* 27:155–173.

Lasswell, H. D. 1941. *Democracy through public opinion.* New York: Bantam.

Margolis, M., and D. Resnick. 2000. *Politics as usual: The cyberspace "revolution."* Thousand Oaks, CA: Sage.

Mutz, D. C. 2002. The consequences of cross-cutting networks for political participation. *American Journal of Political Science* 46: 838–855.

Nam, T., and J. Stromer-Galley. 2012. The democratic divide in the 2008 U.S. presidential election. *Journal of Information Technology and Politics,* 9: 133–149.

Nisbet, M. C., and D. A. Scheufele. 2004. Political talk as a catalyst for online citizenship. *Journalism & Mass Communication Quarterly* 81: 877–896.

Noveck, B. S. 2000. Paradoxical partners: Electronic communication and electronic democracy. In P. Ferdinand (Ed.), *The Internet, democracy, and democratization* (pp. 18–35). London: Frank Cass.

Noveck, B. S. 2004. Unchat: Democratic solutions for a wired world. In P. M. Shane (Ed.), *Democracy online: The prospects for political renewal through the Internet* (pp. 21–34). New York: Routledge.

Perlmutter, D. D. 2008. *Blogwars.* New York: Oxford University Press.

Pole, A. 2010. *Blogging the political: Politics and participation in a networked society.* New York: Routledge.

Polletta, F., P. Ching, B. Chen, and C. Anderson. 2009. Is information good for deliberation? Link-posting in an online forum. *Journal of Public Deliberation* 5(1). Available at: http://services.bepress.com/jpd/vol5/iss1/art2

Price, V., J. N. Cappella, and L. Nir. 2002. Does disagreement contribute to more deliberative opinion? *Political Communication* 19: 95–112.

Prior, M. 2007. *Post-broadcast democracy: How media choice increases inequality in political involvement and polarizes elections.* Cambridge, UK: Cambridge University Press.

Rainie, L., A. Smith, K. L. Schlozman, H. Brady, and S. Verba. 2012. Social media and political engagement. Pew Internet and American Life Project. Available at: http://www.pewinternet.org/Reports/2012/Political-engagement.aspx

Reese, S. D., L. Rutigliano, K. Hyun, and J. Jeong. 2007. Mapping the blogosphere: Professional and citizen-based media in the global news arena. *Journalism* 8: 235–261.

Rinner, C., C. Kessler, and S. Andrulis. 2008. The use of Web 2.0 concepts to support deliberation in spatial decision making. *Computers, Environment and Urban Systems* 32: 386–395.

Robinson, L. 2005. Debating the events of September 11th: Discursive and interactional dynamics in three online fora. *Journal of Computer-Mediated Communication* 10(4). Available at: http://jcmc.indiana.edu/vol10/issue4/robinson.html

Savicki, V., D. Lingenfelter, and M. Kelley. 1996. Gender language style and group composition in Internet discussion groups. *Journal of Computer-Mediated Communication* 2(3). Available at: http://jcmc.huji.ac.il/vol2/issue3/savicki.html

Schneider, S. M. 1996. Creating a democratic public sphere through political discussion: A case study of abortion conversation on the Internet. *Social Science Computer Review* 14: 373–393.

Selnow, G. W. 1998. *Electronic whistle-stops: The impact of the Internet on American politics.* Westport, CT: Praeger.

Streck, J. M. 1998. Pulling the plug on electronic town meetings: Participatory democracy and the reality of Usenet. In C. Toulouse and T. W. Luke (Eds.), *The politics of cyberspace* (pp. 18–47). New York: Routledge.

Stromer-Galley, J. 2002a. New voices in the public sphere: A comparative analysis of interpersonal and online political talk. *Javnost-The Public* 9(2): 23–42.

Stromer-Galley, J. 2002b. New voices in the public sphere: Political conversation in the Internet age. Philadelphia: Annenberg School for Communication.

Stromer-Galley, J. 2003. Diversity and political conversations on the Internet: Users' perspectives. *Journal of Computer-Mediated Communication* 8 (3). Available at: http://jcmc.indiana.edu/vol8/issue3/stromergalley.html

Stromer-Galley, J. 2007. Measuring deliberation's content: A coding scheme. *Journal of Public Deliberation* 3(1). Available at: http://services.bepress.com/jpd/vol3/iss1/art12

Stromer-Galley, J., and A. Martinson. 2009. Coherence in political computer-mediated communication: Analyzing topic relevance and drift in chat. *Discourse & Communication* 3: 195–216.

Sunstein, C. R. 2001. *Republic.com*. Princeton, NJ: Princeton University Press.

Tewksbury, D. 2003. What do Americans really want to know? Tracking the behavior of news readers on the Internet. *Journal of Communication* 53: 694–710.

Trammell, K. D., and A. Keshelashvili. 2005. Examining the new influencers: A self-presentation study of A-list blogs. *Journalism & Mass Communication Quarterly* 82: 968–982.

Trénel, M. May 2004. Facilitating deliberation online: What difference does it make? Paper presented at the Second Online Deliberation Conference. Palo Alto, CA.

Tsaliki, L. 2002. Online forums and the enlargement of public space: Research findings from a European project. *Javnost-The Public* 9(2): 95–112.

Turkle, S. 1995. *Life on the screen: Identity in the age of the Internet*. New York: Simon & Schuster.

Weger, H., Jr., and M. Aakhus. 2003. Arguing in Internet chat rooms: Argumentative adaptations to chat room design and some consequences for public deliberation at a distance. *Argumentation and Advocacy* 40(2): 23–38.

Wilhelm, A. G. 1998. Virtual sounding boards: How deliberative is on-line political discussion? *Information, Communication & Society* 1: 313–338.

Wojcieszak, M. E., and D. C. Mutz. 2009. Online groups and political discourse: Do online discussion spaces facilitate exposure to political disagreement? *Journal of Communication* 59: 40–56.

Wojcieszak, M., and V. Price. 2010. Bridging the divide or intensifying the conflict? How disagreement affects strong predilections about sexual minorities. *Political Psychology* 31: 315–339.

Wright, S. 2006. Design matters: The political efficacy of government-run discussion boards. In S. Oates, D. Owen and R. K. Gibson (Eds.), *The Internet and politics: Citizens, voters and activists* (pp. 80–99). London: Routledge.

CHAPTER 58

THE POLITICAL EFFECTS OF ENTERTAINMENT MEDIA

MICHAEL X. DELLI CARPINI

INTRODUCTION

FOR understandable reasons, most research about the media's effects on citizens' political attitudes, opinions, knowledge, and behaviors has focused on the news. After all, it is this portion of our mediated environment that is explicitly devoted to informing the public about public affairs, a "social responsibility" ceded to professional journalists and explicitly codified, in the United States, in such places as the Hutchins Commission's report (1947) and Siebert, Peterson, and Schramm's *Four Theories of the Press* (1956). Under this arrangement the remaining media are freed from public interest obligations; as Gary Marshall, executive producer of several television sitcoms, remarked, "If television is the education of the American public, then I am recess!"

In recent years political communication scholars have begun to question this assumption, building a small but important body of quantitative research suggesting that the consumption of entertainment media can affect how citizens learn about, think about, and act in the political world. However, while this work is an important starting point, the way we have approached it limits our ability to more fully understand the media's political impact. This is so because we have treated research on entertainment media as a distinct and somewhat ghettoized area of study, while at the same time relying largely on theories originating in the study of public affairs media. My argument in this chapter is that our notions—as citizens and scholars—of what constitutes such fundamental concepts as "politics," "political engagement," "political effects," and "politically relevant media" are not based on inherent qualities of a particular genre, medium, or topic, but are rather socially constructed (and hence amenable to influence by entertainment genres?). This has always been true, but is arguably more so in the information environment of the twenty-first century, which for a variety of reasons challenges the presumed distinction between "news" and "entertainment." In short, if one of our goals as political communication scholars is to understand the ways in which the mediated environment influences citizens' participation in the democratic process, we must both broaden and refine our objects of study.

To make this case, this chapter is organized into four sections. First, I review the small but growing research on the effects of entertainment media on political attitudes, opinions, knowledge, and behavior, highlighting both major findings and areas of scholarly disagreement.[1] I then discuss how traditional definitions of "politics," "political engagement," "political effects," and "politically relevant media" help explain why the political impact of entertainment media has been either ignored or studied in relatively limited ways. I conclude with several suggestions for how we might approach the study of media and politics in ways that are more appropriate to the new information environment.

THE STATE OF RESEARCH ON THE POLITICAL EFFECTS OF ENTERTAINMENT MEDIA

Mainstream studies of the effects of media on citizens' political engagement generally ignore entertainment. For example, the *Handbook of Political Communication Research* (Kaid, 2004) devoted no more than a few lines to this topic. The research that does exist can be loosely parsed into two camps: the first sees entertainment media as at best a distraction from politics and at worst a cause of active disengagement; the second casts such media as an alternative venue for many of the same processes of learning, persuasion, or mobilization that occur through traditional public affairs genres.

Entertainment Media as a Distraction or a Source of Disengagement

The somewhat parallel trends in the United States of the declining size of news audiences and drops in several key indicators of citizens' political involvement over the last three decades has led some to suggest that the former is causally linked to the latter. One of the strongest proponents of this view is Robert Putnam (1995a, 1995b, 2000), whose argument consists of three components. First, social capital—defined as a connectedness of citizens to others in their community—produces a wide range of individual and collective benefits, including a more participatory democracy (2000, 287–363). Second, social capital has severely eroded in the United States over the past half century. And third, television viewing, especially among recent generations, has dampened the development of social capital and with it democratic engagement by usurping time that could be (and in the past was) used for more social and civic-minded activities, fostering psychological effects that inhibit social participation, and trafficking in content that undermines civic motivations (2000, 237).[2]

An important connector in the hypothesized link between entertainment media use and social capital is the dispositional orientation toward others in one's community, known as "social (or interpersonal) trust." High social trust indicates feelings of connectedness to and faith in fellow citizens, or more simply, "a 'standing decision' to give most people—even those whom one does not know from direct experience—the benefit of the doubt" (Rahn and Transue, 1998, 545). Those scoring high on social trust are more likely to interact with fellow citizens informally as well as through membership in community groups and to engage in a range of civic and political activities (Borgida et al., 1997; Brehm and Rahn, 1997; Rahn and Transue, 1998; Uslaner, 1995). In short, social trust is a psychological measure of the more behavioral and collective concept of social capital.

The level of social trust in the United States has fallen significantly over the past thirty years (General Social Survey, 1972–2010), especially among younger adults, paralleling other indicators of declining social capital (Brehm and Rahn, 1997; Putnam, 2000). As with social capital, entertainment television has been singled out as a major cause of the decline in social trust. Shah, Kwak, and Holbert (2001) summarize the reasoning underlying this view:

> Time spent with television is thought to privatize leisure time at the expense of civic activities and to foster beliefs that the world is as threatening as the social reality of the "airwaves" (Brehm and Rahn, 1997; Gerbner, Gross, Morgan, and Signorielli, 1980; Morgan and Shanahan, 1997). Likewise, epidemiological research has connected amount of television viewing with lower levels of physical and mental health (Sidney et al., 1998). These studies, albeit crude in their operationalization of media variables, lend support to the view that media use is related to changes in life contentment, social trust, and civic participation. (143)

This argument has been extended to the Internet. Nie and Erbring (2000) found that time spent online comes at the direct expense of more social activities, leading heavy Internet users to become physically and psychologically disconnected from their social environment. And Kraut and colleagues conclude that "[l]ike watching television, using a home computer and the Internet generally implies physical inactivity and limited face-to-face social interaction" (1998, 1019).

Additional research both supports and complicates the argument that entertainment media use decreases social trust. In one of the more comprehensive efforts to explore this relationship, Shah, Kwak, and Holbert (2001) distinguish among overall television use; the use of television for "hard news"; overall newspaper use; the use of newspapers for "hard news"; overall Internet use; and the use of the Internet for "social recreation," "product consumption," "financial management," and "information exchange." They find that when controlling for demographic characteristics, using newspapers for hard news and using the Internet for information exchange (measured as "exploring an interest or hobby," "searching for school or educational purposes," or "sending an e-mail") had a small but significant positive overall effect on social trust, though they also found differences by age. For the "Civic Generation" (pre–baby boomers), reading newspapers for hard news was the only type of media consumption that was significantly (positively) correlated with social trust. For baby boomers, however, only using the Internet for information exchange was correlated (again positively) with social trust. And for Generation Xers, use of the Internet for social recreation produced a significant negative effect, while using it for information exchange produced a significant positive one. In more recent research Williams (2006) found a decline in social capital among online game players, with some evidence for increases in a diffuse sense of community among players themselves.

Research on the negative civic and political consequences of entertainment media has extended to other aspects of democratic citizenship, such as political attitudes, opinions, efficacy, knowledge, and participation (e.g., Baumgartner and Morris, 2006; Besley, 2006; Bonfadelli, 2002; Couldry and Markham, 2007; Hess, 2006; Hooghe, 2002; Johnson and Kaye, 2003; Kaye and Johnson, 2002; Keum et al., 2004; Kim and Han, 2005; Kim and Vishak, 2008; Morgan and Shanahan, 1997; Scheufele and Nisbet, 2002; Sweetser and Kaid, 2008). Particularly relevant is work by Markus Prior (2005, 2007) suggesting that the proliferation of choice in the new media environment allows citizens who express a preference for entertainment to essentially opt out of news consumption, with the effect of widening the gap between those who are politically involved and those who are not.

Though the results of some studies have been equivocal (Baumgartner, 2007; Moy and Scheufele, 2000; Nabi, Moyer-Guse, and Byrne, 2007; Pasek et al., 2006), the tentative conclusion emerging from this line of research is that "informational and communicative uses of the media may prove beneficial to the health of society, whereas recreational and entertainment uses may erode public involvement" (Shah, Kwak, and Holbert, 2001, 144). The same studies suggest that while this erosion is produced in part from simple time displacement, it also results from factors that include the availability of greater non-news choices, the physiological effects of passive media experiences, the particular ways in which humor and other forms of entertainment are attended to and processed, and the actual content of the consumed entertainment media.

These conclusions remain tentative, in part because of the still rapidly changing nature of the information environment. For example the growth in online social networking sites is challenging the notion that Internet use necessarily takes away from other forms of social connectedness. Indeed, Hampton and colleagues (2011) found that users of social network sites reported *higher* levels of social trust than nonusers, as well as of other indicators of social capital such as "instrumental aid" (i.e., having someone they can call on to help them when they are in need of assistance), emotional support, and companionship (see also Hampton et al., 2009; Pew Research Center, 2011). And they remain tentative because a new strand of research is challenging the assumption that entertainment media need always and only serve as a form of distraction from and disengagement with politics.

Entertainment Media as an Alternative Source of Political Engagement

A growing body of research argues—and finds—that just as traditional news media vary in their form, content, and audiences and thus their effects on political attitudes and actions, so too do entertainment media. For example, Baum (2002, 2003a, 2003b) concludes that "soft news" sources such as talk shows and infotainment news can increase awareness about major public issues among those who are unmotivated to learn about these issues through traditional news venues. Baum (2005) and Baum and Jamison (2006) find that watching candidate appearances on talk shows such as *Oprah* increases the likelihood that such viewers (if they are not very politically motivated to begin with) will vote for a candidate whose stances most closely reflect their own preferences.

The logic of this research is straightforward: a large and growing number of citizens eschew traditional news, but do attend to soft news outlets, often for their entertainment value. However, as Baum demonstrates, such shows increasingly include politically relevant and easily digestible information, coincidently exposing viewers to this information. In short, these studies suggest that entertainment media can serve as an alternative source of political information, especially for those who do not attend to more traditional news sources. This conclusion is partially disputed by Prior (2003), however, who finds no evidence of increased political knowledge among viewers of infotainment. And while generally supporting Baum's research, Brewer and Cao (2006) reported that watching presidential candidates on late-night talk shows correlated with greater political knowledge, but watching them on morning talk did not (watching them on news magazine talk shows produced mixed results).

Attending to entertainment can also affect viewers' political opinions. For example, Glynn and colleagues (2007), drawing partly on agenda-setting theory and partly on cultivation analysis (discussed below), locate support for the notion that exposure to daytime talk shows such as *Oprah* increases support for government intervention in the social issues being discussed, even moderating the effects of political ideology. Jackson and Darrow (2005) and Jackson (2007) find that young adults are more likely to support issue positions that are endorsed by well-known celebrities. Jamieson and Cappella (2008) find that conservative talk radio shows act as an "echo chamber," reinforcing and increasing the conservative views of listeners and the negative images they hold of political opponents. Talk radio can also increase listeners' likelihood of holding and expressing a political opinion even if the opinion is unpopular, and increase the likelihood that listeners will participate in politics (Lee, 2007). Similar effects on opinion expression and participation have been found for both late-night television comedy and daytime television talk shows, though the effects of the former are especially pronounced for politically sophisticated viewers (Moy, Xenos, and Hess, 2005a).

A particularly well-developed body of research focuses on the political influence of humor. To date, the results are mixed on whether this genre enhances, detracts from, or is unrelated to democratic engagement, and under what conditions it does so. Analysis by Baumgartner and Morris (2006) suggests that levels of self-efficacy mediate the potential positive effects of watching programs such as *The Daily Show*. Hollander (2005) finds that watching late-night political satire and comedy can increase recognition of political figures and topics, but not recall of them. Young (2004) finds some evidence that citizens' ratings of candidate traits (e.g., honesty or intelligence), when mediated by partisan dispositions and prior levels of political knowledge, can be influenced by the way these traits are caricatured on late-night talk shows. Cao (2008) observes that watching political comedy is associated with greater political knowledge for younger and more educated viewers, but less political knowledge for older or less educated ones. Moy, Xenos, and Hess (2005b) find that voters' evaluations of presidential candidates are shaped by candidates' appearance on late-night comedy shows. And more recent research (Nabi, Moyer-Guse, and Byrne, 2007; Young, 2008; Polk, Young, and Holbert, 2009; Holbert et al., 2011; Hoffman and Young, 2011) has begun to parse the distinctive effects of different types of humor. For example, Hoffman and Young find that viewing satire or parody (such as *The Daily Show*) has positive, significant effects on political participation, while viewing traditional late-night comedy (e.g., *The Tonight Show*) does not. Holbert and colleagues (2011) provide an even more fine-grained analysis of the effects of different forms of satire, and Polk, Young, and Holbert (2009) offer evidence that irony reduces viewers' argument scrutiny relative to the effects of sarcasm.

Additional research on humor and satire focuses on their interactions with traditional news use. Diddi and LaRose (2006) find that college students are "news grazers" whose specific mix of traditional news, cable news, satire, and the Internet depends on a combination of learned habits and sought after gratifications. Young and Tisinger (2006) find that watching *The Daily Show* complements and reinforces rather than substitutes for traditional news consumption. And Xenos and Becker (2009) confirm that watching political comedy can serve as a gateway to seeking political information from more hard news sources. However, Holbert and colleagues (2007), using an experimental design, caution that the order in which one watches entertainment news (*The Daily Show*) and traditional news (CNN) affects the impact of the second genre watched (e.g., the political gratification obtained from traditional news is lower among viewers with low political efficacy who first watched satirical news).

Two entertainment genres with longer (if still limited) histories of being studied by researchers interested in the political effects of media are dramas and docudramas. This small body of research generally concludes that exposure to these genres can influence political attitudes. For example, Adams and colleagues (1985), using a quasi-experimental field experiment, concluded that watching the Hollywood movie *The Right Stuff* (about the original US astronauts) produced increased positive feelings about the presidential candidacy of former astronaut John Glenn. Carlson (1985) reported that viewing prime-time law enforcement dramas eroded support for civil and criminal rights. Using a panel survey, Lenart and McGraw (1989) found that watching the docudrama *Amerika* (in which the United States is taken over by the

Soviet Union) increased support for conservative policies toward the Soviet Union (see also Lasorsa, 1989). Holbert and colleagues (2003), using a pre-test, post-test experimental design, found that watching *The West Wing* led both to an increased belief in the importance of a president being "engaging" and to improved ratings for both George W. Bush and Bill Clinton, suggesting that the positive feelings toward the fictional president on *The West Wing* carried over to the current and former president through priming. Exposure to prime-time dramas that presented more progressive views of women increased support for greater gender equality, while tuning to shows with more traditional gender roles did the opposite (Holbert, Shah, and Kwak, 2003). Holbrook and Hill (2005), using both surveys and experimental designs, found that watching crime dramas increased concerns about crime in the real world, and through priming subsequently affected ratings of the president. Similarly, watching Michael Moore's *Fahrenheit 9-11* primed opinions about George W. Bush, but only when mediated through citizens' levels of partisanship, affective ambivalence, and need for closure (Holbert and Hansen, 2006). And Stroud (2007) found that, controlling for other factors, those who viewed *Fahrenheit 9/11* had significantly more negative attitudes toward President Bush and were more likely to engage in political discussion.

Taken as a whole, this body of research takes us several steps beyond the "distraction and disengagement" hypotheses. It does so first by focusing on specific genres (and even specific films or shows) that have political content, rather than treating "entertainment media" as an undifferentiated category. Second, it is more sophisticated than earlier work in theoretical orientation and in the kinds of effects hypothesized. In particular, this body of scholarship not only draws on extant theories used in the study of news (e.g., agenda setting, framing, priming, uses and gratifications, persuasion, information processing, selective exposure), but occasionally adapts them in ways that acknowledge the potentially unique contributions of specific non-news genres (e.g., the utility of narrative in political learning or the ability of humor to bypass more central information processing). Third, it more subtly parses the negative and positive political consequences of entertainment media, acknowledging the possibility of either or both. Fourth, it uses more nuanced measures of media exposure. Fifth, it employs more varied and sophisticated methods, including panel designs, field experiments, and laboratory experiments. And finally, it takes into account the conditional aspects of influence, allowing for differential effects across different genres and contexts and among different types of audiences/citizens.

Nonetheless, even this work by and large accepts the assumptions underlying the larger study of political communication: that there is a clear distinction between "news" and "entertainment" genres, that "politics" (and political engagement) is centrally about elections and governance, and that "effects" are manifest only in change. The result is research designed to determine whether or not attending to entertainment media either works at cross purposes to the effects of news consumption or has effects (in direction and magnitude) similar to those found for news.

Rethinking "Politics," "Political Engagement," "Political Effects," and "Politically Relevant Media"

To date scholarship focused on the political effects of entertainment programming has been hampered by constrictive definitions. For example, those interested in the effects of communication on political attitudes and actions tend to cast "politics" in ways consistent with the Merriam-Webster dictionary's view that this phenomenon is a) "the art or science of *government*; b) the art or science concerned with guiding or influencing *governmental* policy; or c) the art or science concerned with winning and holding control over *government*" (emphases added). In addition, media "effects," and similar terms such as "influence" or "impact," are generally defined as *change* attributable to the media (e.g., the formation of new or modified opinions, the learning of new facts, or the engagement in more or new behaviors). Finally, "news" and "entertainment" media are treated as conceptually distinct.[3]

Problems inhere in traditional meanings attached to news as well, which is typically defined in one of two ways. The first, based on content, is some variation of "the report of an event that happened or that was disclosed within the previous twenty-four hours and treats an issue of ongoing concern" (Jamieson and Campbell, 2000, 40).[4] The second focuses on the source; news is what is produced and disseminated by professional journalists working within news organizations or divisions (Gans, 1980; Romano, 1986; Jamieson and Campbell, 2000). Similarly, "entertainment media" are typically defined as having content that is either amusing or diversionary (Postman, 1986), or as being produced and disseminated by non-news divisions or types of media organizations.

When combined, these definitions delimit research on the political effects of the media to understanding how the consumption of news affects what citizens believe and think about government and those who vie for control of it, and how citizens act on these beliefs, attitudes, and opinions to influence who governs (e.g., through voting) and what government does. In the process these definitions have shaped—and circumscribed—the study of the political effects of entertainment media. To make sense of such effects requires a more expansive definition of "politics," "political engagement," "political effects," and "politically relevant media."

Expanding What We Mean by Politics, Political Engagement, and Political Effects

Certainly candidates and officeholders, political parties, campaigns and elections, government policymaking and implementation, and so forth, are central to any meaningful definition of politics. But limiting ourselves to these people, processes, and institutions (and citizens' knowledge and opinions about and behaviors toward them) is nonetheless problematic. Missing in this conception are the numerous public figures (actors, musicians, bloggers, radio and television personalities, business leaders, parents, peers, etc.), processes (informal talk and formal deliberation, consumption choices, work and leisure habits, etc.), and institutions (unions, corporations, churches, neighborhood associations, online communities, Internet providers, etc.) that are politically relevant. Also missed are more "foundational" aspects of politics such as attitudes and beliefs about race, gender, justice, equality, individualism, community, freedom, fairness, etc. Too often these people, processes, institutions, or beliefs, when considered at all, are relegated to the sidelines as "control variables" or to subfields such as democratic theory or political socialization. What I am suggesting is that we reclaim definitions of politics such as Lasswell's (1936) "who gets what, when, how," or Easton's (1965) "the authoritative allocation of goods, services and values."

In addition, the definition of "political engagement" (i.e., politics applied to the role of citizens) should be equally expansive: understanding, deliberating, and acting on the conditions of one's everyday life, the life of fellow community members, and the norms and structures of power that shape these relationships (Williams and Delli Carpini, 2011). And our definition of "effects" should be expanded to encompass not only *change*, but also *formation* and *reinforcement* (Holbert, Garrett, and Gleason, 2010). Again, these approaches are not new; mainstream scholars of political participation do consider opinions and behaviors that go beyond the usual fare, and the notion that effects should include more than change was noted as early as 1948 by Paul Lazarsfeld. But in practice we tend to treat these alternative forms of engagement as peripheral to the "real stuff" of politics and to be unimaginative in our thinking about what kind of knowledge, opinions, and behaviors might be relevant, or how one might study effects other than change.

Expanding What We Mean by Politically Relevant Media

Finally, we need to move beyond the increasingly outmoded distinction between "news" and "entertainment" and toward a more useful and integrated notion of "politically relevant media." I suggest this for three reasons.[5] First, despite the seeming naturalness of the distinction, it is remarkably difficult to identify the structural or substantive characteristics upon which it is based. The opposite of "news" is not "entertainment," as the news is often diversionary or amusing (the definition of entertainment), and what is called "entertainment" is often neither of these things. One would be hard pressed to find any substantive topic found in the news that has not also been the subject of ostensibly non-news media. And what is ordinarily called the news regularly addresses issues of culture, celebrity, and personality.

Second is the context-dependent nature of the news versus entertainment distinction. A historical perspective reveals that in the United States we have lived through a number of relatively distinct "media regimes" (Williams and Delli Carpini, 2011), each with its own economically, politically, culturally, and technologically driven assumptions about the role of media, citizens, and elites in democratic life. Each of these earlier regimes—the explicitly "partisan press" of the early US republic, the salacious "penny press" of the mid-nineteenth century, the "age of realism" in the latter nineteenth century, and the "progressive era" of the early twentieth century—had unique strengths and weaknesses. Each eventually came to be seen as "natural." Each eventually gave way to a new regime. But none reified the news versus entertainment distinction to the extent seen in the era dominated by broadcast news.

This leads to a third reason for questioning the news versus entertainment distinction: we have, for the last two decades, been living in a world anathema to it. The underlying political, economic, cultural, and technological conditions that produced and maintained this distinction have changed beyond recognition. In short, the media regime in place during the latter half of the twentieth century has been dismantled, and with it the utility of the news versus entertainment distinction. At a minimum this requires political communication scholars to examine our theories, methods, and findings, most of which developed in tandem with the age of broadcast news.

Taken together, these expanded notions of politics, political engagement, political effects, and politically relevant media suggest an equally expansive goal for research on the political effects of the media: *to conceptualize and empirically document how the mediated information environment influences the individual and collective ways citizens understand, deliberate about, and act on the conditions of one's everyday life, the life of fellow community members, and the norms and structures of power that shape these relationships.*

FUTURE DIRECTIONS

Where does this leave scholars interested in the political effects of mediated information generally, and entertainment media more specifically?

Building on Existing Research

At a minimum, my brief review suggests the need for more of the same; although extant research has demonstrated that entertainment media can affect citizens' political attitudes, opinions, knowledge and behaviors, we are nowhere near understanding their full relevance to existing theories such as agenda setting, framing and priming, persuasion, information processing, and so forth. Nor are we close to understanding the varied effects of different kinds of entertainment genres (e.g., comedy, satire, drama, docudramas, advertisements, reality shows, films, music, comic books, flash videos, etc.), and in the process determining for whom these effects are most likely (e.g., by various demographic, emotional, cognitive, or political characteristics), or under what circumstances they are likely to occur (e.g., in interaction with other types of media consumption, during periods when certain issues are foregrounded in the "real world," when imbedded viewpoints are consistent across a range of media, etc.). Were we to "simply" focus on addressing these questions, we could make strides in understanding the political effects of entertainment media in a way more akin to the much larger and more developed body of research that exists for news and public affairs media. We would also know more about the circumstances under which these effects are similar to or different from those found for public affairs media. And we would know more about which existing theories developed for studying public affairs media apply to entertainment media, and where we are in need of revised or new theories.

Expanding What We Mean by Political Engagement

More ambitiously, my review suggests the need to expand what we mean by our central dependent variable, political engagement. Our research should include a wider range of norms, values, attitudes, beliefs, knowledge, opinions, behaviors, and skills than we typically study, drawing on public opinion and behavior research from other areas such as children and media, political socialization, entertainment-education, and so forth, as well as other disciplines such as psychology, sociology, education, and marketing. We should also take seriously notions of citizenship (emerging largely from cultural and critical studies) that are less instrumental and more identity-based, performative, discursive, and aesthetic (Miller, 1998; Jenkins, 2006; Dahlgren, 2007; Bennett, 2008; Jacobs, 2012). It seems likely that these more expanded notions of engagement and citizenship are particularly influenced by entertainment media of various kinds and thus potentially fruitful areas of inquiry.

Moving Beyond Change

Also more ambitious—and particularly difficult for quantitative researchers—is the need to expand what we mean by effects to include formation and reinforcement, especially of foundational attitudes and beliefs. Here theories and research more commonly thought of as fitting within the subfield of political socialization may be particularly helpful. Also relevant is the work of Zaller (1996), which while focusing largely on persuasion, provides a theoretical framework that can apply to both the formation and reinforcement of political attitudes, beliefs, and behaviors.

Perhaps most useful in this regard is "cultivation analysis," originating in the seminal work of George Gerbner and his various colleagues (1978, 1980, 1982, 1984, 1986, 2002; see also Morgan, Shanahan, and Signorielli, 2009). One of the earliest theories regarding the political influence of entertainment media, cultivation analysis posited and provided empirical evidence that the content of mainstream media was largely homogeneous, that it presented a view of the world that was often at odds with reality, and that the social and political perspectives of heavy users of the media were influenced by this content. As such, it cultivated worldviews that in turn could influence more proximate opinions about political issues and public figures of the day. Implicit in this approach was the notion that the biases contained in mainstream entertainment media were not random, but rather reflected the dominant social, economic, and political agendas of those in positions of power.

Despite its continued reference and occasional use (e.g., Saito, 2007; Morgan, Shanahan, and Signorielli, 2009), cultivation analysis was and remains something of an outlier in quantitative communication research, due in part to its polyglot nature. On the one hand, its acceptance of the sociopolitical power of entertainment and of the subtle, long-term, collective, and hegemonic implications of consuming such media connect it to a variety of more developed traditions within critical media studies that raise concerns over "mass culture" (e.g., Horkheimer and Adorno, 1947/2002; Adorno, 1941, 1963/1975), "cultural imperialism" (e.g., Tunstall, 1977; Schiller, 1976), "media concentration" (e.g., Bagdikian, 1983), and "mass propaganda" (e.g., Lasswell, 1927). On the other hand, its focus on how citizens' attitudes and opinions are shaped by mediated messages, and its use of survey research and quantitative analyses, connect it with more mainstream media effects research.

While demonstrating suggestive relationships between heavy television use and a variety of political and social attitudes (see also, Besley, 2006, 2008), cultivation analysis was and remains largely cut off from its mainstream and critical genealogy. Regarding the former, the effort to use quantitative methods arguably better suited to uncovering specific, short-term effects to test theories that were based on more collective, long-term processes proved problematic, suffering from several familiar methodological shortcomings: less than optimal measures of media exposure, limited data, and simplistic statistical methods. As a result, scholars have found it difficult to draw convincing conclusions regarding causality (see Hirsch, 1980). Regarding the latter, while the notion of a largely hegemonic worldview might have been an accurate description of the media environment of the 1970s and 1980s, this is less clearly the case in the more complex and diverse mediated world of the twenty-first century. In addition, the growing popularity of audience response analysis and the realization that citizens are not simply empty vessels, but rather can take an active role in constructing meaning from the media they consume, has further challenged the theory underlying cultivation research. Despite these shortcomings, cultivation analysis seems a valuable starting point for theorizing and testing entertainment media's formative and reinforcing effects.

Toward an Integrated Theory of Media Effects

Ultimately, and most ambitiously, we should move away from a focus on specific genres and toward theories and research based on the underlying attributes found in individual media texts, media, and ultimately systems: for example, the amount and type of politically relevant information they contain; the presence or absence of textual, visual, and/or aural information; the degree of interactivity allowed; argument presence and strength; the presence of emotional appeals; the use of devices such as narrative, humor, and sensation arousal; and so forth.[6] After all, it is these kinds of attributes that are likely to influence the public's attitudes and actions, yet genres are increasingly poor substitutes for them, since such attributes do not map neatly onto artificial and rapidly changing distinctions such as news, comedy, drama, and so forth.

Such an integrated approach to media effects, using attributes rather than genres as its starting point, would bring the study of entertainment media more directly into the mainstream, melding it in useful ways with studies of news and public affairs. It would allow us to empirically determine if and how particular genres, media, and information environments vary along dimensions based on relevant attributes. And it would help us better hypothesize and test how specific qualities of the media affect citizens' individual and collective attitudes and actions, and thus their agency to act as democratic citizens and a democratic citizenry.

NOTES

1. Given my focus on individual-level political effects, I am giving short shrift to a much larger body of media scholarship that has long studied entertainment media, either in its own right (e.g., film or literary studies) or as a social force (e.g., "entertainment-education" research on children and media or health-related behaviors; or content, rhetorical, and discourse analyses of the political and social messages embedded in entertainment genres). I also focus mainly on research conducted within the United States. I believe, however, that the research discussed below is collectively both of relevance to and could benefit from these other research traditions.
2. Putnam's argument has been disputed by scholars such as Norris (1996, 2000), though tellingly for the purposes of this chapter, Norris focuses largely on the positive benefits of the news content of television and the Internet.
3. Other terms sometimes substitute for either: for example, "public affairs media" in the former case and "popular culture" in the latter. For the purposes of this chapter I treat these alternatives as equivalent to "news" and "entertainment media," respectively, as do most political communication scholars.
4. Jamieson and Campbell's definition refers to "hard news," but this is typically the core component of journalists' public function and the type of news typically of interest to political communication scholars.
5. For a fuller explication, see Williams and Delli Carpini (2011).
6. Such an approach can build on work already being done by political communication scholars (e.g., Holbert, 2005; Holbert, Garrett, and Gleason, 2010; Holbert and Young, forthcoming), as well as in other areas such as health communication (e.g., Strasser et al., 2009; Lee et al., 2011).

REFERENCES

Adams, W. C., Salzman, A., Vantine, W. Suelter, L., Baker, A., Bonvouloir, L., Brenner, B., Ely, M., Feldman, J., and Ziegel, R. 1985. The power of *The Right Stuff*: A quasi-experimental field test of the docudrama hypothesis. *Public Opinion Quarterly* 49(3): 300–339.

Adorno, T. 1941. On popular music. *Studies in Philosophy and Social Sciences IX*: 17–48.

Adorno, T. 1963/1975. Culture industry reconsidered. *New German Critique* 6(1): 12–19.

Bagdikian, B. 1983. *The media monopoly*. Boston: Beacon Press.

Baum, M. 2002 Sex, lies and war: How soft news brings foreign policy to the inattentive public. *American Political Science Review* 96(1): 91–109.

Baum, M. 2003a. Soft news and political knowledge: Evidence of absence or absence of evidence? *Political Communication* 20(2): 173–190.

Baum, M. 2003b. *Soft news goes to war: Public opinion and American foreign policy in the new media age*. Princeton, NJ: Princeton University Press.

Baum, M. 2005. Talking the vote: Why presidential candidates hit the talk show circuit. *American Journal of Political Science* 49(2): 213–234.

Baum, M., and Jamison, A. S. 2006. The *Oprah* effect: How soft news helps inattentive citizens vote consistently. *Journal of Politics* 68(4): 946–959.

Baumgartner, J. C. 2007. Humor on the next frontier: Youth, online political humor, and the jibjab effect. *Social Science Computer Review* 25: 319–338.

Baumgartner, J., and Morris, J. S. 2006. The *Daily Show* effect: Candidate evaluations, efficacy, and American youth. *American Politics Research* 34: 341–367.

Bennett, W. L. (Ed.). 2008. *Civic life online: Learning how digital media can engage youth*. Cambridge, MA: MIT Press.

Besley, J. C. 2006. The role of entertainment television and its interactions with individual values in explaining political participation. *Harvard International Journal of Press-Politics* 11(2): 41–63.

Besley, J. C. 2008. Media use and human values. *Journalism & Mass Communication Quarterly* 85(2): 311–330.

Bonfadelli, H. 2002. The Internet and knowledge gaps: A theoretical and empirical investigation. *European Journal of Communication* 17(1): 65–84.

Borgida, E., Sullivan, J., Haney, B., Burgess, D., Rahn, W., Snyder, M., and Transue, J. 1997. A selected review of trends and influences of civic participation. Research paper for the Center for the Study of Political Psychology, Minneapolis.

Brehm, J., and Rahn, W. 1997. Individual-level evidence for the causes and consequences of social capital. *American Journal of Political Science* 41: 999–1023.

Brewer, P. R., and Cao, X. 2006. Candidate appearances on soft news shows and public knowledge about primary campaigns. *Journal of Broadcasting & Electronic Media* 50: 18–35.

Cao, X. 2008. Political comedy shows and knowledge about primary campaigns: The moderating effects of age and education. *Mass Communication & Society* 11: 43–61.

Carlson, J. M. 1985. *Prime-time law enforcement*. New York: Praeger.

Couldry, N., and Markham, T. 2007. Celebrity culture and public connection: Bridge or chasm? *International Journal of Cultural Studies* 10: 403–421.

Dahlgren, P. (Ed.). 2007. *Young citizens and new media: Learning for democratic participation*. New York: Routledge.

Diddi, A., and LaRose, R. 2006. Getting hooked on news: Uses and gratifications and the formation of news habits among college students in an Internet environment. *Journal of Broadcasting & Electronic Media* 50: 193–210.

Easton, D. 1965. *A systems analyses of political life*. New York: John Wiley and Sons.

Gans, H. 1980. *Deciding what's news: A study of CBS Evening News, NBC Nightly New, Newsweek and Time*. New York: Vintage Books.

General Social Survey. 1972–2010. National Opinion Research Center. http://www3.norc.org/GSS+Website/.

Gerbner, G., Gross, L., Jackson-Beeck, M., Jeffries-Fox, S., and Signorielli, N. 1978. Cultural indicators: Violence profile no. 9. *Journal of Communication* 28: 178, 193.

Gerbner, G., Gross, L., Morgan, M., and Signorielli, N. 1980. The "mainstreaming" of America: Violence profile no. 11. *Journal of Communication* 30: 10–29.

Gerbner, G., Gross, L., Morgan, M., and Signorielli, N. 1982. Charting the mainstream: Television's contribution to political orientations. *Journal of Communication* 32: 100–127.

Gerbner, G., Gross, L., Morgan, M., and Signorielli, N. 1984. Political correlates of television viewing. *Public Opinion Quarterly* 48: 283–300.

Gerbner, G., Gross, L., Morgan, M., and Signorielli, N. 1986. Living with television: The dynamics of the cultivation process. In J. Bryant and D. Zillmann (Eds.), *Perspectives on media effects* (pp. 17–40). Hillsdale, NJ: Lawrence Erlbaum.

Gerbner, G., Gross, L., Morgan, M., Signorielli, N., and Shanahan, J. 2002. Growing up with television: Cultivation processes. In J. Bryant and D. Zillmann (Eds.), *Media effects: Advances in theory and research* (pp. 43–67). Mahwah, NJ: Lawrence Erlbaum.

Glynn, C. J., Huge, M., Reineke, J. B., Hardy, B. W., and Shanahan, J. 2007. When Oprah intervenes: Political correlates of daytime talk show viewing. *Journal of Broadcasting & Electronic Media* 51: 228–244.

Hampton, K., Goulet, L. S., Rainie, L., and Purcell, K. 2011. Social networking sites and our lives: How people's trust, personal relationships, and civic and political involvement are connected to their use of social networking sites and other technologies. Washington, DC: Pew Research Center's Internet and American Life Project.

Hampton, K., Goulet, L. S., Her, E. J., and Rainie, L. 2009. Social isolation and new technology: How the Internet and mobile phones impact Americans' social networks. Washington, DC: Pew Research Center's Internet and American Life Project.

Hess, V. K. 2006. Political apathy among young adults: The influence of late-night comedy in the 2000 election. PhD diss., University of Washington.

Hirsch, Paul. 1980. The "scary world" of the nonviewer and other anomalies: A reanalysis of Gerbner et al.'s findings on cultivation analysis, part I. *Communication Research* 7(4): 403–456.

Hoffman, L. H., and Young, D. G. 2011. Satire, punchlines, and the nightly news: Untangling media effects on political participation. *Communication Research Reports* 28(2): 1–10.

Holbert, R. L. 2005. A typology for the study of entertainment television and politics. *American Behavioral Scientist* 49: 436–453.

Holbert, R. L., Garrett, R. K., and Gleason, L. S. 2010. A new era of minimal effects? A response to Bennett and Iyengar. *Journal of Communication* 60: 15–34.

Holbert, R. L., and Hansen, G. J. 2006. *Farenheit 9-11*, need for closure and the priming of affective ambivalence: An assessment of intra-affective structures by party identification. *Human Communication Research* 32: 109–129.

Holbert, R. L., Lambe, J. L., Dudo, A. D., and Carlton, K. A. 2007. Primacy effects of *The Daily Show* and national TV news viewing: Young viewers, political gratifications, and internal political self-efficacy. *Journal of Broadcasting & Electronic Media* 51(1): 20–38.

Holbert, R. L., Pillion, O., Tschida, D., Armfield, G., Kinder, K., Cherry, K., and Daulton, A. 2003. *The West Wing* as endorsement of the U.S. presidency: Expanding the bounds of priming in political communication. *Journal of Communication* 53: 427–443.

Holbert, R. L., Shah, D. V., and Kwak, N. 2003. Political implications of prime-time drama and sitcom use: Genres of representation and opinions concerning women's rights. *Journal of Communication* 53: 45–60.

Holbert, R. L., and Young, D. G. (2013). Exploring relations between political entertainment media and traditional political communication information outlets: A research agenda. In E. Scharrer (Ed.), *The international encyclopedia of media studies, volume V: Media effects/media psychology* (pp. 484–504). West Sussex, UK: Blackwell-Wiley.

Holbert, R. L., Hmielowski, J., Jain, P., Lather, J., and Morey, A. 2011. Adding nuance to the study of political humor effects: Experimental research on Juvenalian satire versus Horatian satire. *American Behavioral Scientist* 55(3): 187–211.

Holbrook, R. A., and Hill, T. G. 2005. Agenda setting and priming in prime time television: Crime dramas as political cues. *Political Communication* 22(3): 277–295.

Hollander, B. A. 2005. Late night learning: Do entertainment programs increase political campaign knowledge for young viewers? *Journal of Broadcasting and Electronic Media* 49(4): 402–415.

Hooghe, M. 2002. Watching television and civic engagement: Disentangling the effects of time, programs, and stations. *Harvard International Journal of Press Politics* 7(2): 84–104.

Horkheimer, M., and Adorno, T. W. 1947/2002. *Dialectic of enlightenment: Philosophical fragments*. Edited by G. S. Noerr, translated by E. Jephcott, Stanford, CA: Stanford University Press.

Hutchins Commission [Commission on Freedom of the Press]. 1947. *A free and responsible press*. Chicago: University of Chicago Press.

Jackson, D. J. 2007. Selling politics: The impact of celebrities' political beliefs on young Americans. *Journal of Political Marketing* 6: 67–83.

Jackson, D. J., and Darrow, T. I. A. 2005. The influence of celebrity endorsements on young adults' political opinions. *Harvard International Journal of Press Politics* 10(2): 80–98.

Jacobs, R. (2012). Entertainment media and the aesthetic public sphere. In J. Alexander, R. Jacobs, and P. Smith (Eds.), *Oxford handbook of cultural sociology* (pp. 318–341). New York: Oxford University Press.

Jamieson, K. H., and Campbell, K. K. 2000. *The interplay of influence: News, advertising, politics and the mass media*. Belmont, CA: Wadsworth.

Jamieson, K. H., and Cappella, J. N. 2008. *Echo chamber: Rush Limbaugh and the conservative media establishment*. New York: Oxford University Press.

Jenkins, H.. 2006. *Fans, bloggers, and games: Exploring participatory culture*. New York: New York University Press.

Johnson, T. J., and Kaye, B. K. 2003. Around the World Wide Web in 80 ways: How motives for going online are linked to Internet activities among politically interested Internet users. *Social Science Computer Review* 21(3): 304–325.

Kaid, L. L. (Ed.). 2004. *Handbook of political communication research*. Mahwah, NJ: Lawrence Erlbaum.

Kaye, B. K., and Johnson, T. J. 2002. Online and in the know: Uses and gratifications of the Web for political information. *Journal of Broadcasting and Electronic Media* 46(1): 54–71.

Keum, H., Devanathan, S., Deshpande, S., Nelson, M. R., and Shah, D. V. 2004. The citizen-consumer: Media effects at the intersection of consumer and civic culture. *Political Communication* 21(3): pp. 369–391.

Kim, S., and Han, M. 2005. Media use and participatory democracy in South Korea. *Mass Communication & Society* 8(2): 133–153.

Kim, Y. M., and Vishak, J. 2008. Just laugh! you don't need to remember: The effects of entertainment media on political information acquisition and information processing in political judgement. *Journal of Communication* 58: 338–360.

Kraut, R. E., Scherlis, W., Patterson, M., Kiesler, S, and Mukhopadhyay, T. 1998. Social impact of the Internet: What does it mean? *Communications of the ACM* 41(12): 21–22.

Lasorsa, D. L. 1989. Real and perceived effects of *Amerika*. *Journalism Quarterly* 66(2): 373–378.

Lasswell, H. D. 1927. *Propaganda technique in the World War*. London: Kegan Paul, Trench, Trubner.

Lasswell, H. D. 1936. *Politics: Who gets what, when, how*. New York: McGraw Hill.

Lazarsfeld, P. 1948. Communication research and the social psychologist. In W. Dennis (Ed.), *Current trends in social psychology* (pp. 218–273). Pittsburgh: University of Pittsburgh Press.

Lee, F. L. 2007. Talk radio listening, opinion expression and political discussion in a democratizing society. *Asian Journal of Communication* 17: 78–96.

Lee, S., Cappella, J. N., Lerman, C., and Strasser, A. A. 2011. Smoking cues, argument strength, and perceived effectiveness of antismoking PSAs. *Nicotine and Tobacco Research* 13(4): 282–290.

Lenart, S., and McGraw, K. M. 1989. America watches *Amerika*: Television docudramas and political attitudes. *Journal of Politics* 51(3): 697–713.

Miller, Toby. 1998. *Technologies of truth: Cultural citizenship and popular media*. Minneapolis: University of Minnesota Press.

Morgan, M., and Shanahan, J. 1997. Two decades of cultivation research: An appraisal and meta-analysis. *Communication Yearbook* 20: 1–45.

Morgan, M., Shanahan, J., and Signorielli, N. 2009. Growing up with television: Cultivation processes. In J. Brant and M. B. Oliver (Eds.), *Media Effects: Advances in Theory and Research* (pp. 34–49). New York: Routledge.

Moy, P., and Scheufele, D. A. 2000. Media effects on political and social trust. *Journalism and Mass Communication Quarterly* 77(4): 744–759.

Moy, P., Xenos, M. A., and Hess, V. K. 2005a. Communication and citizenship: Mapping the political effects of infotainment. *Mass Communication & Society* 8: 111–131.

Moy, P., Xenos, M. A., and Hess, V. K. 2005b. Priming effects of late-night comedy. *International Journal of Public Opinion Research* 18: 198–210.

Nabi, R., Moyer-Guse, E., and Byrne, S. 2007. All joking aside: A serious investigation into the persuasive effect of funny social issue messages. *Communication Monographs* 74: 29–54.

Nie, N., and Erbring, L. 2000. Internet and society: A preliminary report. Stanford Institute for the Quantitative Study of Society, Stanford University.

Norris, P. 1996. Does television erode social capital? A reply to Putnam. *PS: Political Science and Politics* 29: 474–479.

Norris, P. 2000. *A virtuous circle: Political communications in postindustrial societies*. New York: Cambridge University Press.

Pasek, J., Kenski, K., Romer, D., and Jamieson, K. H. 2006. America's youth and community engagement: How use of the mass media is related to civic activity and political awareness in 14 to 22 year olds. *Communication Research* 33(3): 115–135.

Pew Research Center. 2011. Internet and American Life Project. January 18. http://www.pewinternet.org/~/media//Files/Reports/2011/PIP_Social_Side_of_the_Internet.pdf.

Polk, J., Young, D. G., and Holbert, R. L. 2009. Humor complexity and political influence: An elaboration likelihood approach examining *The Daily Show with Jon Stewart*. *Atlantic Journal of Communication* 17: 202–219.

Postman, N. 1986. *Amusing ourselves to death: Public discourse in the age of show business*. New York: Penguin Books.

Prior, M. 2003. Any good news in soft news? The impact of soft news preference on political knowledge. *Political Communication* 20(2): 149–171.

Prior, M. 2005. News versus entertainment: How increasing media choice widens the gap in political knowledge and turnout. *American Journal of Political Science* 49(3): 577–592.

Prior, M. 2007. *Post-broadcast democracy: How media choice increases inequality in political involvement and polarizes elections.* New York: Cambridge University Press.

Putnam, R. 1995a. Bowling alone: America's declining social capital. *Journal of Democracy* 6: 65–78.

Putnam, R. 1995b. Tuning in, tuning out: The strange disappearance of social capital in America. *PS: Political Science and Politics* 27: 664–683.

Putnam, R. 2000. *Bowling alone.* New York: Simon and Schuster.

Rahn, W., and Transue, J. 1998. Social trust and value change: The decline of social capital in American youth, 1976–1995. *Political Psychology* 19: 545–565.

Romano, C. 1986. What? The grisly truth about bare facts. In R. K. Manoff and M. Schudson (Eds.), *Reading the news.* New York: Pantheon Books.

Saito, S. 2007. Television and the cultivation of gender-role attitudes in Japan: Does television contribute to the maintenance of the status quo? *Journal of Communication* 57: 511–531.

Scheufele, D. A., and Nisbet, M. C. 2002. Being a citizen online: New opportunities and dead ends. *Harvard International Journal of Press-Politics* 7(3): 55–75.

Schiller, H. 1976. *Communication and cultural eomination.* White Plains, NY: International Arts and Sciences Press.

Seibert, F., Peterson, T., and Schramm, W. 1956. *Four theories of the press: The authoritarian, libertarian, social responsibility and Soviet Communist concepts of what the press should be and do.* Champaign-Urbana: University of Illinois Press.

Shah, D. V., Kwak, N., and Holbert, R. L. 2001. "Connecting" and "disconnecting" with civic life: Patterns of Internet use and the production of social capital. *Political Communication* 18: 141–162.

Sidney, S., Sternfeld, B., Haskell, W. L., Jacobs, D. R., Chesney, M. A., and Hulley, S. B. 1998. Television viewing and cardiovascular risk factors in young adults: The CARDIA study. *Annals of Epidemiology* 6: 154–159.

Strasser, A. A., Cappella, J. N., Jepson, C., Fishbein, M., Tang, K. Z., Han, E., and Lerman, C. 2009. Experimental evaluation of anti-tobacco PSAs: Effects of message content and format on physiological and behavioral outcomes. *Nicotine and Tobacco Research* 11(3): 293–302.

Stroud, N. J. 2007. Media effects, selective exposure, and Fahrenheit 9/11. *Political Communication* 24: 415–432.

Sweetser, K. D., and Kaid, L. L. 2008, Stealth soapboxes: Political information efficacy, cynicism and uses of celebrity weblogs among readers. *New Media & Society* 10: 67–91.

Tunstall, J. 1977. *The media are American.* New York: Columbia University Press.

Uslaner, E. 1995. Faith, hope and charity: Social capital, trust and collective action. Paper presented at the Annual Meeting of the American Political Science Association. Chicago.

Williams, D. 2006. Groups and goblins: The social and civic impact of online gaming. *Journal of Broadcasting and Electronic Media:* 651–670.

Williams, B., and Delli Carpini, M. X. 2011. *After broadcast news: Media regimes, democracy and the new information environment.* New York: Cambridge University Press.

Young, D. G. 2004. Late night comedy in election 2000: Its influence on candidate trait ratings and the moderating effects of political knowledge and partisanship. *Journal of Broadcasting and Electronic Media* 48(1): 1–22.

Young, D. G. 2008. The privileged role of the late-night joke: Exploring humor's role in disrupting argument scrutiny. *Media Psychology* 11: 119–142.

Young, D. G., and Tisinger, R. M. 2006. Dispelling late-night myths: News consumption among late-night comedy viewers and the predictors of exposure to various late-night shows. *Harvard International Journal of Press/Politics* 11: 113–133.

Xenos, M. A., and Becker, A. B. 2009. Moments of zen: Effects of *The Daily Show* on information seeking and political learning. *Political Communication* 26: 317–332.

Zaller, J. (1996). The myth of massive media impact revived: New support for a discredited idea. In D. Mutz, P. Sniderman, and R. Brody (Eds.), *Political persuasion and attitude change* (pp. 17–78). Ann Arbor: University of Michigan Press.

CHAPTER 59

THEORIES AND EFFECTS OF POLITICAL HUMOR

Discounting Cues, Gateways, and the Impact of Incongruities

DANNAGAL G. YOUNG

BACKGROUND

As both an art form and a mode of persuasive discourse, political humor dates back to ancient Greece and Rome. For centuries politicians, citizens, and elites have marveled at and feared its powerful—and magical—influence on public opinion (Caufield, 2007; Test, 1991). Writing almost four hundred years BC, the Athenian playwright Aristophanes, "the comic genius of political criticism" (Schutz, 1977, 10), explored themes of status, power, and war, all within the frame of a play that rendered his satire both humorous and incendiary. Socrates, the great ironic "sage satyr" (Schutz, 1977, 79), offered subtle critiques of Athenian society through the voice of a playful clown. In spite of this rich history, scholars have only just begun to quantify the impact of political humor on attitudes, cognitions, and behaviors.

Scholars from linguistics, psychology, and sociology have developed theories to account for humor's role in society and impact on the audience. The core empirical work on the impact of *political* humor has emerged over the last decade from the disciplines of communication, political science, and psychology. In the late 1990s, as political candidates appeared on entertainment programs and talk shows, media effects scholars began studying the impact of nontraditional forms of political information on the audience. While first included under such umbrella terms as "soft news" (Baum, 2003) or "talk shows" (Davis and Owen, 1998), political humor soon became a dedicated area of media effects research.

The rise in scholarly attention to political humor can be attributed to the increasing prevalence of hybrid forms of political information over the past twenty years. This includes the frequency of political themes in the monologues of late-night comedians like David Letterman and Jay Leno throughout the 1990s; the emergence of dedicated political satire programs on the cable network Comedy Central (*The Daily Show* with Jon Stewart, which launched in 1999, and the *Colbert Report* with Stephen Colbert, which debuted in 2005); and alternative entertainment political formats like *Politically Incorrect* with Bill Maher (first introduced on Comedy Central in 1993), as well as the rise of online political humor sites such as *Funny or Die* (launched 2006) or the *Onion News Network* (launched 2007). As chronicled by Geoff Baym (2009a), these hybrid forms of political content have their roots in the deregulation of the media industry in the 1980s and the simultaneous rise in digital technologies in the 1990s. Together, these changes fostered a media environment in which the once-formal distinction between news and entertainment disappeared (see also Williams and Delli Carpini, 2002). As news programs had to compete with entertainment shows for ratings, news executives increasingly adopted entertainment production norms. Meanwhile, the rise in digital technologies meant that media conglomerates could efficiently repurpose content across their many outlets and platforms (see Jenkins, 2006). Hence, entertainment creators increasingly experimented with political themes—leading to the late 1990s influx of hybrid political entertainment genres.

The Content of Political Humor

When scholars discuss the content of contemporary political humor, they are usually referring to a set of texts ranging from the political jokes of late-night comedians like Jay Leno or David Letterman, to online political parodies, to the playful cultural critiques on the animated series *The Simpsons,* to longer ironic or satirical segments from Jon Stewart or Stephen Colbert. Early studies of the content of late-night comedy monologues suggested that late-night political jokes tended to focus on the executive branch and were almost "devoid" of policy content, focusing instead on personalities and weaknesses of individual politicians (Niven, Lichter, and Amundson, 2003). Recent research on the content of televised political humor complicates these initial observations. The *themes* included in the content of *The Daily Show*, for example, are often more issue-oriented than those of Leno or Letterman (National Annenberg Election Survey, 2004). In fact, scholars have found comparable treatment of substantive issues across the content of *The Daily Show* and network news broadcasts during the same time period (Fox, Koloen, and Sahin, 2007).

These competing findings reflect an evolving political media landscape, but also an imperative need to understand what we're talking about when we say "political humor."

"Political humor" is an umbrella term that encompasses any humorous text dealing with political issues, people, events, processes, or institutions. Within that broad category, political *satire* occupies a specific role. According to humor scholar George Test (1991), political satire is playful and is designed to elicit laughter, while simultaneously casting judgment. It is this function of "casting judgment" that separates satire from broader notions of political humor. Jokes and texts that treat political topics in a lighthearted manner but offer no criticism of institutions, policies, or societal norms do not constitute satire. Rather, satire questions the existing political or social order, usually by juxtaposing the existing imperfect reality with visions of what *could* or *should* be. So, while satire can be biting and even aggressive in tenor, the underlying premise of a satirical text is often optimistic, as it suggests we (collectively) deserve better. In the words of Bloom and Bloom (1979), "The satirist who goes about his task skillfully gives the reader a double reward: the pleasure of an aesthetic experience coupled with the reasonable hope that a stable political order may be attainable" (1979, 38).

Parody, a subcategory of humor that often overlaps with satire, relies on the audience's prior knowledge of an original text or concept by exaggerating its most familiar aspects (Gray, 2005; Gray, Jones, and Thompson, 2009). Caricatures, or visual exaggerations of a known person's most identifiable characteristics, are an example of parody. Other examples include impersonations of political figures as well as programs and texts that exaggeratedly (or ironically) mimic a political concept, event, or genre. *The Colbert Report* with Stephen Colbert, for instance, constitutes parody, as the structure of his mock cable-news program and his very persona are based on Bill O'Reilly's *No Spin Zone* on Fox News (see Baym, 2009a). While parodies are not always satirical, they can be. Friendly political impersonations, such as those of Rich Little in the 1970s and 1980s, offer physical and verbal exaggerations without casting judgment. Other parodies, such as *Saturday Night Live* comedian Tina Fey's impersonation of vice-presidential candidate Sarah Palin, constitute political satire. Fey's Palin impersonation not only exaggerated the Alaskan governor's folksy accent and winking appearance, but also criticized her conservative issue positions with statements such as, "I think that Global warming is . . . just God huggin' us closer" (Tina Fey and Amy Poehler, 2008).

In addition to satire and parody, it is important to consider the role played by irony in a political context. Irony is present when a text exposes a gap between what is stated and what is meant. Bergson notes: "Sometimes we state what ought to be done, and pretend to believe that this is just what is actually being done; then we have irony" (1921, 127). Irony is a common rhetorical tool of the satirist. Just as satirical texts present critiques of society's ills through a humorous lens, irony offers a useful mechanism to playfully expose the gap between the way things are and the way things should be. Jonathan Swift's (1729) *A Modest Proposal*, for example, proposes a detailed plan to remedy the economic and social problems of Ireland by feeding poor malnourished children to Ireland's upper class. The text is both *ironic*, as Swift certainly does not mean what he says, and *satirical*, as the act of comprehending the text requires the reader to question the dispassionate rational perspective underlying his economic argument. Similarly, *The Colbert Report* is a complex example of satirical irony (see Lamarre, Landreville, and Beam, 2009). Colbert's character rails against liberal policies under the guise of an ill-informed right-wing pundit, who doesn't let facts get in the way of "truth." This playful inversion of reality (the real Colbert believes the opposite of what he states on the show) forces the audience to see the conservative arguments made by his character as short-sighted and ill-informed at best or hypocritical and malevolent at worst.

Several additional approaches to the categorization of political humor have helped make sense of this rich body of content. The Roman satirists Horatio and Juvenal codified two broad subgenres of political satire: Horatian satire was lighthearted and playful, and Juvenalian satire articulated outrage and pessimism about the evils of society through sarcasm and irony. These categories continue to inform how political communication researchers think about political humor's content and impact (Holbert et al., 2011). Integrating a more generalizable vocabulary into the study of political humor, Paletz's (1990) typology considers it as a function of four elements: target, focus, acceptability, and presentation. Together these dimensions determine how a humorous political text ranks on a spectrum, from "supportive" of the existing political order to "subversive."

The Audience of Contemporary Political Humor

Much of the interest in political humor as a source of political influence stems from its perceived accessibility to broad audiences. During the past decade several reports from the Pew Center for the People and the Press concluded that young people, more so than older people, were increasingly reporting learning about politics from comedy shows (Pew, 2004). At the same time, young people were reporting lower rates of learning from traditional news programming. Yet the contention that young people are abandoning traditional news in favor of comedy programming is *not* supported by existing research (Young and Tisinger, 2006). Youthful late-night comedy viewers are *more* likely to be consuming news on cable networks, on the radio, and online than their non-comedy-viewing counterparts. Cross-sectional studies also contradict the assumption of the "politically disengaged" audience, as late-night comedy viewers, particularly those of the *Daily Show*, are more politically knowledgeable, more participatory, and more attentive to politics than non-late-night viewers (Brewer and Cao, 2006; Cao, 2010; Cao and Brewer, 2008; Young and Tisinger, 2006).

Humor Theory

For centuries, philosophers, psychologists, and sociologists have attempted to untangle the mystery that is "humor." Why do people enjoy humor? How does humor work? In addressing these questions, scholars have pursued several broad theoretical perspectives. Superiority theory, the roots of which are in the writings of Hobbes (1650), proposes that humor capitalizes on the "sudden glory" of realizing that we may be superior to someone else. Release or tension theories in humor research are an extension of concepts from Freudian psychology. Here humor is conceptualized as a "safety valve" that expels excess energy or passions that might otherwise transform into sexual or aggressive energy (see Raskin, 1985, for a review). Finally, the class of humor theories most often integrated into cognitive models of media effects is "incongruity theory." While incongruity theory has been elaborated upon by Koestler (1964) and Suls (1972), among others, the approach is often attributed to Kant's observation that "laughter is an affection arising from the sudden transformation of a strained expectation into nothing" (2007, 133). This notion of unmet expectations has been adapted by cognitive scholars who see humor as the intersection of two incompatible schemas in memory.

Perhaps because of its compatibility with concepts such as mental models, schemas, and associative networks in memory, much of the recent empirical work on the cognitive impact of political humor has been theoretically grounded in incongruity theory (Nabi, Moyer-Guse, and Byrne, 2007; Young, 2008). Incongruity theory assumes that a humorous text begins with one apparent or conventional script: an initial story or set of predictable constructs (Raskin, 1985). Side by side with the conventional script is one that is hidden until it intersects with the first (Koestler, 1964). Humor is experienced when the listener becomes aware of the two coexisting incompatible scripts or frames (Attardo, 1997) and has to reinterpret the old information in light of the new (Giora, 1991). This is ultimately the unique element of humor as a form of discourse: the participatory role of the audience in "reconciling" the incongruity and interpreting the original schema in light of this new frame of reference (Koestler, 1964). Because the audience of a humorous text must participate in its construction and appreciation, the audience is complicit in the creation of its meaning.

THE QUESTION OF IMPACT

Persuasion, Priming, and Cognitive Elaboration

While Athenian society viewed satirists as possessing a magical persuasive power (Caufield, 2007), historians do not agree on the amount of influence these humorous texts actually had on Athenian citizens. Lord argues that Aristophanes's audience could not "distinguish between the caricature [of Socrates] and the reality" (1925, 40), hence leading to Socrates's conviction and execution. Stow (1942), on the other hand, argues that Aristophanes's impact on the citizens of Athens was negligible—his power was in revealing the sentiments of Athenians, not in shaping them.

Contemporary empirical research remains focused on this same question: Is political humor an agent of influence or merely a barometer of public opinion? If the audience is complicit in the creation of meaning through humor, could that enhance its persuasive capacity? Intuitively we know that topics treated in a humorous way are often perceived as less offensive than when presented seriously. If humor can playfully present information or argument without eliciting a negative audience reaction, then employing it could be a promising way to incite attitude change. Indeed, research consistently indicates that humor reduces counterargumentation, or argument scrutiny, in response to the premise of that humorous text (Nabi, Moyer-Guse, and Byrne, 2007; Young, 2008). However, the mechanism responsible for this phenomenon remains elusive. On the one hand, some scholars suggest that the complex task of reconciling incongruity reduces cognitive resources available to scrutinize message arguments (Young, 2008). On the other, some studies suggest that the reduction in argument scrutiny is a result of the listener discounting the message as "just a joke," a mechanism referred to as a discounting cue (Nabi, Moyer-Guse, and Byrne, 2007). While this debate may seem tedious, the implications are profound. If humor's ability to suspend argument scrutiny of the listener stems from the listener's decision to treat the text as "just a joke," then the potential power of humor depends on the audience's willingness to play along. If, however, the reduction in counterargumentation is a result of humor's drain on cognitive resources, then the listener is at the mercy of the humorous text.

In spite of political humor's documented ability to suspend argument scrutiny, researchers have yet to find strong and consistent evidence of humor's *persuasive* capacity. Young (2004) found more negative appraisals of candidates' most caricatured personality traits as an outcome of viewing late-night comedy programming, particularly among those low in political knowledge. Similarly, Morris (2009) documented more negative ratings of Republican candidates among viewers of *The Daily Show* during the 2008 Republican conventions, consistent with the tenor of the show's content during that time. Research has also demonstrated that exposure to political humor can increase the salience of certain issues or constructs in the minds of the audience (Moy, Xenos, and Hess, 2006; Young, 2006). Here, the focus is not on attitude change per se, but rather on the priming of certain issues, events, or traits that could affect subsequent decision-making processes (see Iyengar and Kinder, 1987).

Learning, Recall, and Information Seeking from Political Humor

In addition to examinations of humor's role in persuasion, scholars have studied how political humor affects information acquisition—both directly and indirectly. To date, studies suggest that exposure to political humor may be associated with information recognition and a viewer's *sense* of being informed (Hollander, 2005). However, experimental research indicates that exposure to late-night comedy may result in lower acquisition of detailed factual and issue knowledge than traditional news viewing (Kim and Vishak, 2008). Complicating these findings is the observation that viewers of late-night comedy programs consistently score higher on political knowledge tests than nonviewers, even in the face of controls (Cao, 2008; National Annenberg Election Survey, 2004). Overall, it seems that political humor audiences likely come to the viewing experience with above average political knowledge, but the direct impact of that exposure on information acquisition remains an open question.

Additional research has moved beyond direct learning models to assess political humor's possible "gateway" effect (Baum, 2003). According to Baum, "soft news" (including political humor) serves as a gateway to politics for viewers who are otherwise politically inattentive. By covering politics in an entertaining way, these programs may motivate politically inattentive viewers to seek out additional political information. Cross-sectional research supports Baum's general model, with evidence that viewers of late-night comedy are more attentive to politics (Cao, 2010; Young and Tisinger, 2006) and that exposure to political humor among politically inattentive audiences is associated with increased attention to high-profile political stories (Cao, 2010) as well as issue-specific news items (Feldman, Leiserwitz, and Maibach, 2011). Time series analyses reveal that viewers of late-night comedy programming experience a steeper increase in news attention than noncomedy viewers during primary campaigns (Feldman and Young, 2008). Also consistent with the gateway hypothesis, experimental work by Xenos and Becker (2009) illustrates enhanced attentiveness to news after exposure to political humor programming among less politically interested viewers. In this same study, politically inattentive viewers experienced higher rates of learning from subsequent news exposure. Together, these findings speak to the potential of political humor to increase viewers' attention to politics, hence indirectly fostering certain kinds of political learning, particularly among those with the least political interest from the start.

Political Participation, Discussion, Engagement, and Trust in Government

At the heart of this effects research is a question of how political humor might affect democracy. The US Supreme Court has consistently upheld parody and satire as protected forms of expression, a fact that speaks to humor's privileged role in a democratic society. As conceptualized by literary scholars Bloom and Bloom, satire is intended to "plead with man for a return to his moral senses" (1979, 38). When successful, they state, satire can "effect a gradual moral reawakening, a reaffirmation of positive social and individual values" (17). If these contentions were true, exposure to political satire, such as *The Daily Show*, should result in higher rates of political participation and discussion and other characteristics of an engaged citizenry, such as attention to politics or political efficacy (see Jones, 2009).

Cross-sectional studies consistently find that the audience of *The Daily Show* with Jon Stewart participates in politics more (Cao and Brewer, 2008; Hoffman and Young, 2011) and is more likely to discuss politics with friends, family, and coworkers than are nonviewers (Young and Esralew, 2011). Using panel data, Landreville, Holbert, and

Lamarre (2010) demonstrated that *Daily Show* viewers experienced increases in political discussion, a process mediated by increased debate viewing. Such findings suggest that Baum's (2003) gateway mechanism might extend beyond attention and learning, to include other beneficial democratic behaviors like political discussion. Moy, Xenos, and Hess (2005) found that late-night comedy viewing in general (which includes exposure to Leno and Letterman) was associated with increased vote intention and political discussion, though these effects were limited to political sophisticates. Although not all of this research establishes causality between exposure and participation/discussion, experimental and time-series studies of political attention and information seeking have pointed to a causal relationship, with exposure to political humor fostering these democratically healthy outcomes (Feldman, Leiserwitz, and Maibach, 2011; Feldman and Young, 2008; Xenos and Becker, 2009).

Because of contemporary political humor's frequent criticism of politicians and governing institutions, some fear that routine exposure to such critical examinations of government may erode citizens' trust in institutions and faith in the democratic process (Baumgartner and Morris, 2006; Hart and Hartelius, 2007). While isolated studies have found that viewers of *The Daily Show* are less trusting of government (Baumgartner and Morris, 2006), questions remain regarding whether a *lack of government trust* is necessarily a bad thing for democracy, as government trust is often lowest among our most politically active and engaged citizens (Cappella and Jamieson, 1997; de Vreese and Semetko, 2002; de Vreese, 2005). If the fundamental proposition of political satire is that we deserve—and can attain—something better, then it is logical that audiences would see this message as both an indictment of the existing political order and a call to strive for its improvement.

The reason for scholars' fundamentally different conclusions about satire's role in a democratic society may stem from the polysemy inherent in humor. The meaning of humor is not in the text itself. Instead, it is in the reconciliation of the incongruity which, in turn, is at the mercy of whatever the listener brings to the text. Perhaps this is why we find such differences in the effects of political humor as a function of various individual-level characteristics: political knowledge (Young, 2004), interest in politics (Xenos and Becker, 2009), age (Cao, 2008), and political ideology (Lamarre, Landreville, and Beam, 2009). With different experiences and understandings of politics, these distinct groups will likely construct different meanings from political humor, thereby fostering different processes and different outcomes.

Illustrative of the importance of a listener's cognitive contribution to meaning construction in humor are Lamarre, Landreville, and Beam's (2009) findings regarding the perceived meaning of *The Colbert Report* among conservatives and liberals. The authors found that liberals interpreted Colbert's ironic performance accurately—as a criticism of conservative policies and values. Meanwhile, conservatives found humor in Colbert's show, but interpreted it literally, as an exaggerated indictment of liberal politics. Hence, selective perception altered the audience's construction of Colbert's meaning. Such findings demonstrate the importance of exploring individual differences as moderating variables in studies of humor's impact.

WHERE WE ARE AND WHERE WE'RE GOING

At present, political humor's impact on knowledge, attitudes, and behaviors is far from clear. Reports of humor disrupting argument scrutiny, but not necessarily leading to attitude change, suggest that whatever counterargument-disruption mechanism is operative in humor might suspend other forms of processing as well. Humor's limited ability to foster detailed information recall, in spite of its positive impact on construct recognition (Hollander, 2005) and overall impressions of political constructs (Kim and Vishak, 2008), illustrates a similar phenomenon. Perhaps political humor activates online, rather than memory-based, processing (see Kim and Vishak, 2008), rendering it suitable for impression formation and heuristic evaluation, but not for central message processing or detailed information acquisition (see Baum, 2003). These micro-level processes need to be better explicated, perhaps through the integration of physiological measurements or with novel imaging techniques emerging from neuroscience (Coulson, 2001; Coulson and Williams, 2005).

Because the comprehension of and meaning derived from political humor depend on the cognitive contribution of the audience, future work on political humor's impact ought to link detailed analyses of humorous texts to audience characteristics, psychology, and viewing motivations. In particular, future work ought to develop effects mechanisms that emphasize the importance of the structure elements of the humorous texts and the individual-level characteristics of the audience:

1) Structural elements of the humorous text: Since humorous texts are incomplete until reconciled by the audience, the nature of the incongruity helps determine what kind of contribution a listener will make and hence what that text will ultimately come to mean. In the case of a punchline-oriented late-night joke, the incongruity might simply be a pun or play on words that unexpectedly highlights a candidate's physical or personality flaws. In the case of satirical irony, the incongruity is presented by the gap between what is said and what is meant—or between what reality is and what it ought to be. To better understand the potential power of humor to shape audiences, scholars must dissect these underlying incongruities and link them with cognitive contributions made to reconcile them.

2) Individual-level characteristics: Once an incongruity is presented, the audience takes over in constructing the text's meaning. The cognitive contribution made by the listener depends on what he or she brings to the table: political knowledge, political beliefs or ideology (selective perception), as well as psychological characteristics and viewing motivations. Hmielowski, Holbert, and Lee's (2011) "Affinity for Political Humor Scale" is a first step toward understanding what brings people to the viewing experience. Future studies need to further integrate uses and gratifications approaches (Katz, Blumler, and Gurevitch, 1974) into studies of

political humor effects. By understanding why people consume political humor, we can better capture the various cognitive processes underlying different viewing experiences.

To pursue some of the core questions regarding political humor's role in a democratic society, researchers may need to look across discipline and method. Whether political satire is good or bad for democracy has proven exceptionally difficult to address with empirical effects studies. For example, operationalizing political cynicism with three items designed to measure trust in government might not adequately capture the meaning of contemporary political satire. If viewers come away from Stewart or Colbert critically challenging the current system, but striving for something better, perhaps qualitative methods (focus groups, long-form interviews, ethnographies, or textual analysis) would help us better understand these complex processes.

Indeed, humanistic studies of political humor have contributed rich theoretical and historical understanding to the approach being taken by scholars across epistemological boundaries (Holbert and Young, 2013). Qualitative and cultural research has chronicled how and why the once-strict divide between entertainment and news no longer exists (Baym, 2009a; Williams and Delli Carpini, 2002), and that scholars should explore political humor *not* as an alternative *to* political information, but as an alternative form *of* political information (Baym, 2009b). Work by Baym (2005, 2009a) highlights how political humor challenges the notion that journalistic practices such as objectivity and sensationalism are necessary or beneficial to society. Work by Jones (2009) and Van Zoonen (2005) suggests that by addressing political themes outside the traditional elite model of political discourse, political humor might invite more people into the political conversation.

As political comedians capitalize on advances in digital technologies to translate their message across platform and genre (Jenkins, 2006), scholars will benefit from the integration of qualitative and quantitative approaches to the study of these phenomena. Baym and Shah (2011), for example, tracked the flow and context of digital segments of *The Colbert Report* across the Internet landscape. Their work illustrates how activists and organizations repurpose relevant clips to help attain informational, community-building, and deliberative goals. Such innovative approaches will advance our understanding of newly emerging political humor phenomena. For example, in October 2010 Stewart and Colbert mobilized people from around the country to travel to Washington, DC, to playfully restore civility to political discourse. Through social networking sites and broad media appearances, the shows' hosts gathered a crowd of more than 200,000 people (Tavernise and Stelter, 2010). The rally—a mix of music festival, variety show, and political commentary—stumped journalists and politicos, who struggled to make sense of the event. And just as the rally did not fit neatly within the news/entertainment dichotomy, neither did it fit neatly into linear models of media effects.

In just the past year, numerous examples of political humor operating across platforms highlight the need for scholars to work across methodological and epistemological traditions to understand what this all means. In September 2010 Stephen Colbert appeared in character to ironically testify before Congress on the issue of immigration reform. Throughout 2010 and 2011 Jon Stewart engaged in satirical critiques of Fox News on his own show, while appearing as a guest on Bill O'Reilly's *No Spin Zone* (on Fox) to debate and mock the host. In March 2011 Colbert launched the ironically self-aggrandizing Colbert SuperPAC, a political action committee designed to raise unlimited funds to help "make a better a better tomorrow, tomorrow" (colbertpac.com).

FINAL WORD

To anchor this body of research in generalizable concepts, we must formally recognize that humor arises not only from audience perception but also from structural elements within the text that *invite* or *signal* that audience participation. The act of returning to the basic concept of incongruity and audience reconciliation will encourage scholars to build upon existing theory to advance our understanding of micro-level processes involved in humor comprehension. Finally, the complexity of the multiplatform digital environment means that linear sender-receiver models of effects will not be adequate to capture the full scope of political humor's impact. Instead, scholars of political humor will increasingly be called upon to embrace diverse methods and innovative approaches. Only through collaborative and discursive research models will the political meaning and significance of this diverse set of humorous texts and performances be adequately understood.

REFERENCES

Attardo, S. 1997. The semantic foundations of cognitive theories of humor. *Humor: International Journal of Humor Research* 10(4): 395–420.

Baum, M. A. 2003. Soft news and political knowledge: Evidence of absence or absence of evidence? *Political Communication* 20: 173–190.

Baumgartner, J., and Morris, J. S. 2006. The Daily Show effect. *American Politics Research 34*: 341–367.

Baym, G. 2005. *The Daily Show*: Discursive integration and the reinvention of political journalism. *Political Communication* 22: 259–276.

Baym, G. 2009a. *From Cronkite to Colbert: The evolution of broadcast news.* Boulder, CO: Paradigm.

Baym, G. 2009b. Real news/fake news: Beyond the news/entertainment divide. In S. Allen (Ed.), *The Routledge companion to news and journalism studies* (pp. 374–383). New York: Routledge.

Baym, G., and Shah, C. 2011. Circulating struggle: The on-line flow of environmental advocacy clips from *The Daily Show* and *The Colbert Report*. *Information, Communication & Society 14*(7), 1017–1038.

Bergson, H. 1921. *Laughter.* New York: Macmillan.

Bloom, E., and Bloom, L. 1979. *Satire's persuasive voice.* Ithaca, NY: Cornell University Press.

Brewer, P. R., and Cao, X. 2006. Candidate appearances on soft news shows and public knowledge about primary campaigns. *Journal of Broadcasting & Electronic Media* 50: 18–35.

Cao, X. 2008. Political comedy shows and knowledge about primary campaigns: The moderating effects of age and education. *Mass Communication & Society* 11: 43–61.

Cao, X. 2010. Hearing it from Jon Stewart: The impact of *The Daily Show* on public attentiveness to politics. *International Journal of Public Opinion Research* 22: 26–46.

Cao, X. and Brewer, P. 2008. Political comedy shows and public participation in politics. *International Journal of Public Opinion Research* 20(1): 90-99.

Cappella, J. N., and Jamieson, K. H. 1997. *Spiral of cynicism: The press and the public good.* New York: Oxford University Press.

Caufield, R. P. 2007. The influence of "infoenterpropagainment." In J. S. Morris and J. C. Baumgartner (Eds.), *Laughing matters: Humor and American politics in the media age* (pp. 3–20). New York: Routledge.

Coulson, S. 2001. *Semantic leaps: Frame-shifting and conceptual blending in meaning construction.* New York and Cambridge: Cambridge University Press.

Coulson, S., and Williams, R. F. 2005. Hemispheric asymmetries and joke comprehension. *Neuropsychologia* 43: 128–141.

De Vreese, C. H. 2005. The spiral of cynicism reconsidered: The mobilizing function of news. *European Journal of Communication* 20: 283–301.

De Vreese, C. H., and Semetko, H. A. 2002. Cynical and engaged: Strategic campaign coverage, public opinion and mobilization in a referendum. *Communication Research* 29: 615–641.

Davis, R., and Owen, D. 1998. *New media and American politics.* New York: Oxford University Press.

Feldman, L., Leiserowitz, A., and Maibach, E. 2011. The science of satire: *The Daily Show* and *The Colbert Report* as sources of public attention to science and the environment. In A. Amarasingam (Ed.), *The Stewart/Colbert effect: Essays on the real impact of fake news* (pp. 25–46). Jefferson, NC: McFarland.

Feldman, L., and Young, D. G. 2008. Late-night comedy as a gateway to traditional news: An analysis of time trends in news attention among late-night comedy viewers during the 2004 presidential primaries. *Political Communication* 25(4): 401–422.

Fox, J. R., Koloen, G., and Sahin, V. 2007. No joke: A comparison of substance in *The Daily Show with Jon Stewart* and broadcast network television coverage of the 2004 presidential election campaign. *Journal of Broadcasting & Electronic Media* 51: 213–227.

Giora, R. 1991. On the cognitive aspects of the joke. *Journal of Pragmatics* 16(5): 465–486.

Gray, J. 2005. Television teaching: Parody, *The Simpsons*, and media literacy education. *Critical Studies in Media Communication* 22(3): 223–238.

Gray, J., Jones, J. P., and Thompson, E. 2009. *Satire TV: Politics and comedy in the post-network era.* New York: New York University Press.

Hart, R. P., and Hartelius, J. 2007. The political sins of Jon Stewart. *Critical Studies in Media Communication* 24: 263–272.

Hmielowski, J. D., Holbert, R. L., and Lee, J. 2011. Predicting the consumption of political TV satire: Affinity for political humor, *The Daily Show*, and *The Colbert Report*. *Communication Monographs* 78: 96–114.

Hobbes, T. [1650] 2008. *Human nature.* New York: Oxford.

Hoffman, L. H., and Young, D. G. 2011. Satire, punch lines, and the nightly news: Untangling media effects on political participation. *Communication Research Reports* 28(2): 1–10.

Holbert, R. L., Hmielowski, J., Jain, P., Lather, J., and Morey, A. 2011. Adding nuance to the study of political humor effects: A study of juvenalian satire versus horatian satire. *American Behavioral Scientist* 55: 187–211.

Holbert, R. L., and Young, D. G. 2013. Exploring relations between political entertainment media and traditional political communication information outlets: A research agenda. In E. Scharrer (Ed.), *Media effects/media psychology* (pp. 484–504). West Sussex, UK: Wiley-Blackwell.

Hollander, B. 2005. Late-night learning: Do entertainment programs increase political campaign knowledge for young viewers? *Journal of Broadcasting & Electronic Media* 49(December): 402–415.

Iyengar, S., and Kinder, D. R. 1987. *News that matters*. Chicago: University of Chicago Press.

Jenkins, H. 2006. *Convergence culture: Where old and new media collide*. New York: New York University Press.

Jones, J. P. 2009. *Entertaining politics: Satire television and political engagement*. Lanham, MD: Rowman & Littlefield.

Kant, I. 2007. *Critique of judgement*. New York: Cosimo.

Katz, E., Blumler, J. G., and Gurevitch, M. 1974. Uses and gratifications research. *Public Opinion Quarterly* 37: 509–523.

Kim, Y. M., and Vishak, J. 2008. Just laugh! You don't need to remember: The effects of the entertainment media on political information acquisition and processing. *Journal of Communication*, 58: 338–360.

Koestler, A. 1964. *The act of creation*. London: Hutchinson.

LaMarre, H. L., Landreville, K. D., and Beam, M. A. 2009. The irony of satire. *International of Journal of Press/Politics* 14: 212–231.

Landreville, K., Holbert, R. L., and LaMarre, H. L. 2010. The influence of late-night TV comedy viewing on political talk: A moderated-mediation model. *International Journal of Press/Politics* 15: 482–498.

Lord, L. E. 1925. *Aristophanes: His plays and his influence*. New York: Cooper Square.

Moy, P., Xenos, M. A., and Hess, V. K. 2006. Priming effects of late-night comedy. *International Journal of Public Opinion Research* 18: 198–210.

Moy, P., Xenos, M. A., and Hess, V. K. 2005. Communication and citizenship: Mapping the political effects of infotainment. *Mass Communication & Society* 8: 111–131.

Nabi, R. L., Moyer-Guse, E., and Byrne, S. 2007. All joking aside: A serious investigation into the persuasive effect of funny social issue messages. *Communication Monographs* 74: 29–54.

National Annenberg Election Survey. 2004. *Daily Show* viewers knowledgeable about presidential campaign, National Annenberg Election Survey. Sept 21. Retrieved 2.1.14 from http://www.naes04.org

Niven, D., Lichter, S. R., and Amundson, D. 2003. The political content of late night comedy. *Harvard International Journal of Press/Politics* 8: 118–133.

Paletz, D. L. 1990. Political humor and authority. *International Political Science Review* 11: 483–493.

Pew Center for the People and the Press 2004. Cable and Internet loom large in fragmented political news universe. Pew, January 11. Retrieved 2.1.14 from http://www.people-press.org/2004/01/11/cable-and-internet-loom-large-in-fragmented-political-news-universe/

Raskin, V. 1985. *Semantic mechanisms of humor*. Dordrecht, Netherlands: D. Reidel.

Schutz, C. E. 1977. *Political humor: From Aristophanes to Sam Ervin*. Rutherford, NJ: Fairleigh Dickinson University Press.

Stow, H. L. 1942. Aristophanes' influence upon public opinion. *Classical Journal 38*: 83–92.

Suls, J. M. 1972. A two-stage model for the appreciation of jokes and cartoons. In J. H. Goldstein and P. E. McGhee (Eds.), *The psychology of humor* (pp. 81–100). New York: Academic Press.

Swift. J. [1729] 1986. A modest proposal. In M. H. Abrams (Ed.), *The Norton anthology of english literature*, 5th ed. (Vol. 1, pp. 2174–2181). New York: W. W. Norton.

Tavernise, S., and Stelter B. 2010., At rally, thousands—billions?—respond. *New York Times*, October 30.

Test. G. 1991. *Satire: Spirit and art*. Tampa: University of South Florida Press.

Tina Fey and Amy Poehler address the SNL nation. 2008. *ComedyCritic.com*, September 14. http://www.comedycentric.com/2008/09/14/tina-fey-and-amy-poehler-address-the-snl-nation-transcript/

Van Zoonen, L. 2005. *Entertaining the citizen: When politics and popular culture converge*. Boulder, CO: Rowman and Littlefield.

Williams, B. A., and Delli Carpini. M. X. 2002. Heeeeeeeeeeeere's democracy! *The Chronicle of Higher Education*, April 19, B14–B15.

Xenos, M. A., and Becker, A. B. 2009. Moments of zen: Effects of *The Daily Show* on information seeking and political learning. *Political Communication 26*: 317–332.

Young, D. G. 2004. Late-night comedy in election 2000: Its influence on candidate trait ratings and the moderating effects of political knowledge and partisanship. *Journal of Broadcasting & Electronic Media 48*: 1–22.

Young, D. G. 2006. Late-night comedy and the salience of the candidates' caricatured traits in the 2000 election. *Mass Communication and Society 9*: 339–366.

Young, D. G. 2008. The privileged role of the late-night joke: Exploring humor's role in disrupting argument scrutiny. *Media Psychology 11*: 119–142.

Young, D. G., and Esralew, S. 2011. Jon Stewart a heretic? Surely you jest: Political participation and discussion among viewers of late-night comedy programming, In A. Amarasinga (Ed.), *The Stewart/Colbert effect: Essays on the real impact of fake news* (pp. 99–116). Jefferson, NC: McFarland.

Young, D. G., and Tisinger, R. 2006. Dispelling late-night myths: News consumption among late-night comedy viewers and the predictors of exposure to various late-night shows. *International Journal of Press/Politics 11*: 113–134.

....

CHAPTER 60

MUSIC AS POLITICAL COMMUNICATION

....

JOHN STREET

THE politician and social theorist Jacques Attali (1985, 3) makes this bold assertion: "For twenty-five centuries, Western knowledge has tried to look upon the world. It has failed to understand that the world is not for beholding. It is for hearing. It is not legible, but audible." This radical claim suggests that our understanding of human communication comes not through the eyes and the business of reading and watching, but through our ears and the business of hearing and listening. Hart (1987, 120) makes the same point more modestly when he observes of media coverage of US politics: "Generally the networks depict a silent president." We know, of course, that presidents, and especially presidential campaigns, have a soundtrack, and one that communicates much about the occupant of the White House and those who aspire to occupy it. To take but one example, during the 2008 US presidential campaign millions of Americans listened to Barack Obama's "Yes We Can" speech, remixed with will.i.am's beats and lilting choruses (http://www.youtube.com/watch?v=SsV2O4fCgjk).

Attali's bold assertion resonates with those who claim that Adolph Hitler's rise to power owed much to the invention of the loudspeaker (Schafer, 1994, 91). Or with those who note how, on assuming power in Afghanistan, the Taliban began by making the performance of music a criminal offense (Baily, 2004). Or with those who argue that the fall of the Berlin Wall owed much to the intervention of rock musicians (Wicke, 1992). Such instances give credence to, if not proof of, the importance of sound in general, and music in particular, to the conduct of politics. But to register these examples is one thing; it is quite another to identify what precisely music contributes to the communication of politics and how its contribution might be analyzed and evaluated.

Despite Attali's sweeping generalization, we are not, in fact, entering uncharted territory. The founding figures of political science were, after all, acutely aware of the importance of music. Both Plato and Aristotle, albeit in different ways, discussed the place of music in the moral and political order of ancient Greece. Much later, in the eighteenth century, Jean-Jacques Rousseau gave his "Essay on the Origin of Languages" the subtitle

"In Which Melody and Musical Imitation Are Treated." In this essay Rousseau (1998) dwelt at length on the place of music in the formation and maintenance of human society. This emphasis on the political importance of music finds further sustenance in subsequent centuries in the writings of Friedrich Nietzsche, particularly *The Birth of Tragedy* (1999); John Dewey (1919); and Theodor Adorno (2002), whose ideas about the relationship of sound and social order continue to occupy scholars today. But these scholars—and this is where Attali's point may strike home—are not typically located in the field of political communication.

The study of political communication has tended to overlook sound in its concern with the written word and the visual image. It sometimes seems, as Hart observed, that politics is conducted in silence. The neglect of sound is not peculiar to political communication. In film studies, the soundtrack receives less attention than the visuals and the dialogue. More generally, semioticians, and those other researchers concerned with "reading" media texts, tend to pay less heed to what is heard than what is seen, although there are notable exceptions (Franklin, 2005; van Leeuwen, 1999). By way of correcting this imbalance in the analysis of political communication, this chapter does three things. It begins, in the next section, with an account of the more obvious ways in which music has become associated with political communication: as protest, propaganda, and resistance. The subsequent section raises a more profound set of questions about how music, as "organized sound," can be understood to communicate politics. What is it about music that enables it to convey political ideas and inspire political acts? The final section points to how scholars of political communication might contribute further to our appreciation of music's role by focusing on the relationship of music to the public sphere and civic engagement. This concluding discussion is framed by the question, to put it at its most stark, of why it might matter to the communication of politics if the world was rendered musically silent.

THE POLITICAL USES OF MUSIC

Music as Protest

The most familiar form of music as political communication is the protest song, a broad, perhaps ill-defined category, that contains such examples as "This Land Is Your Land," "We Shall Overcome," "Blowin' in the Wind" and "Give Peace a Chance." These songs serve to articulate, in musical form, an explicit political sentiment. They constitute, if not a genre, a type of music the purpose of which is established by its explicit desire to communicate political sentiments.

A recent history of the protest song (Lynskey, 2011) refers to some thirteen hundred examples in the period 1939 to 2004, ranging from Billie Holiday's "Strange Fruit" to Green Day's "American Idiot." This, though, is only a small sample. Protest songs of various kinds appear throughout much of recorded history (Palmer, 1988).

They are to be found too in many countries and contexts (Fischlin and Heble, 2003; Peddie, 2006).

The ubiquity of the protest song owes much to music's particular characteristics. Lyrics, like poetry, allow for meaning to be hinted at, rather than stated explicitly. Messages, in this sense, are more difficult to censor. And unlike film or television, music demands far less in terms of capital costs and bureaucratic compliance. It is a more democratic art form. It is also more mobile: songs can be performed almost anywhere. Music too, in its uses of melody and rhythm, has the capacity to move people directly, even spontaneously. These features of the protest song have been highlighted in the work of scholars of social movements (most notably the civil rights movement), who have pointed to the use of song to articulate and animate the cause (Saul, 2003; Smith, 1999; Ward, 1998). The protest song therefore has been seen as a means of conveying political ideas, and its singers as "bearing witness" to the righteousness of their cause (Eyerman and Jamison, 1998). Important though the protest song has been in conveying political ideas and inspiring political actions, there is a danger in focusing only on this particular musical form and this particular kind of politics.

Music as Propaganda

Political protest is not the only type of political communication expressed in sound. The business of securing support for a party, a nation, or a government can also draw on music's communicative powers. The same capacity that is used to express a critical sentiment can also be deployed to endorse the established order or to win support for a party.

Those who study election campaigns are aware that they are noisy affairs. On the stump, there is the sound of the bands that accompany the candidate; on television and radio, and increasingly online, there is the music that acts as the soundtrack to the political advertisements. Tony Blair's New Labour choreographed their 1997 election campaign to the pop sound of D:Ream's "Things Can Only Get Better," while in the previous decade US presidential contenders Ronald Reagan and Walter Mondale squabbled over which of them was the rightful heir to Bruce Springsteen's "Born in the USA." Such apparently trivial matters may be more significant than they seem. The music selected by the campaign team serves to "brand" its candidate's message.

In keeping with the Downsian (1957) view that parties have an incentive to provide cheap information, music serves to lower the cost of political communication and to help identify key messages. This is how music is used in commercial advertising, and there is no reason to suppose that it is any different in political advertising. Parties and politicians at least devote care and attention to the music that accompanies their campaigns and select music that in some sense "speaks" to their manifesto (Beck, 2000). Indeed, Hart sees the connection as being even closer, with political communication emulating the pop form. He (1987, 66) writes of how Reagan's speeches "resemble the controlled artistry of rock videos," and of how the president made use of his previous experience in vaudeville in presenting himself to the voters.

Music does not just contribute to electoral communications. It also forms part of the repertoire of devices that governments use to communicate with their citizens. Where music as message takes a relatively benign form in the choreographing of state occasions—whether a presidential inauguration or the commemoration of a presidential death, or marking a national victory or a national disaster—it assumes more malign aspects when that state is a totalitarian one. In *Nineteen-Eighty-Four*, George Orwell describes the Party's "Hate Song," a key part of Hate Week: "It had a savage, barking rhythm which could not exactly be called music, but resembled the beating of a drum. Roared out by hundreds of voices to the tramp of marching feet, it was terrifying" (Orwell 1989, 155). Orwell's dystopian vision echoes through accounts of the deliberate marshaling of music and musicians by Stalin and Hitler (Blanning, 2008; Caute, 2005; Kater, 1997; Meyer, 1991; Ross, 2007). Such regimes took particular care to ensure that music reinforced messages that were not simply to be encoded in the libretto and lyrics, but also in the style of the music. The regimes created bureaucracies designed to promote music that encapsulated the virtues and visions of the dominant order and to repress music and musicians who failed to communicate the "correct" message. The authorities in apartheid South Africa, for example, insisted that those radio stations that served black workers should play rural music only. Urban music, the state reasoned, would encourage such workers to believe that they belonged in the cities, whereas rural music would reinforce official policy: that the black workers belonged in their "homelands" (Andersson, 1981).

Music as Resistance

Protest and propaganda are perhaps the most obvious ways in which music communicates politics. They are marked by two features. The first is the explicit and literal identification of the politics that they seek to communicate: "this land is my land, "my country 'tis of thee." The second is the intentionality that they embody. They are commissioned, composed, and performed to meet identifiable political goals. They are designed to accompany national celebrations or rituals of nationhood, or they are used to identify a cause or rally a movement. But sometimes songs can communicate political sentiments and ideas that owe nothing to the formal intentions of their author or those who commission them. This can be the case with what Dave Laing (2003) labels "songs of resistance" that come to have political significance by virtue of the context in which they are performed and the meaning they hold for those who sing or hear them. For example, the magazine *Index on Censorship* (1998) released an illicit recording of Tibetan nuns, imprisoned for their opposition to China's role in their country, singing traditional songs. The songs themselves were not "political" in their content, but the manner and context of their singing made them so.

Another instance of the resistance song is provided by the schoolchildren of Soweto who adopted Pink Floyd's line "We don't need no education" (from "Another Brick in the Wall") in their protest of the attempt by the apartheid regime to impose the Afrikaans language on them. Many of the songs adopted by the protesters during the so-called Arab Spring of early 2011 were not overtly political, but they too served to articulate the politics of those who gathered to protest and in the process embodied a sense of group identity, rather than supplying information or laying claim to a cause (as is the case with a protest song).

Songs of resistance were important to oppositional political communication in the Soviet Union, when directly expressed political protest was impossible, but resistance could be encoded in (often Western) music (Cushman, 1995; Starr, 1983; Szemere, 2001; Urban, 2004). As the musician Daniel Barenboim (Barenboim and Said, 2004, 44) once noted: "If you look at the role that music, and much more than music—theater and opera—played in societies and the totalitarian regimes, it was the only place that political ideas and social totalitarianism could be criticized. In other words, a performance of Beethoven ... under any kind of totalitarian regime ... suddenly assumes the call for freedom." The key point is that in giving form to resistance, it is the use of sound (rather than the literal content of lyrics) that constitutes the form of the political communication.

How Music Communicates Politics

The examples of music as protest, propaganda, and resistance help to illustrate how music can serve as political communication. The connection is usually drawn by way of either the content (protest and propaganda) or the context (resistance). Music is "read" in each case as communicating a set of political ideas, by virtue of either what it appears to be "saying" or how it functions in a particular setting. However, these interpretations of music's capacity to communicate politics tend to skate over questions of how exactly music—as "organized sound"—communicates with those who hear it. In order to consider what music does to its audience, and how it does this, this discussion begins with music's capacity to convey a sense of unity.

The Sound of Unity

Nationhood is often evoked in sound, typically in the form of a national anthem (Revill, 2000). While we can read national anthems as variants on music-as-propaganda, this is to miss a singular feature of the form. National anthems are sung, and sung by large ensembles. At sporting events there may be a professionally trained singer leading the crowd, but it is the massed human voices that define the sound. For Anderson (1983), the business of imagining the national community is directly implicated in the *act of singing*. It is the singing itself that generates the experience of collectivity that allows the imagination to work. National anthems, he writes (1983, 132), are "occasions for unisonality, for the echoed physical realization of the imagined community."

National anthems are not the only examples of music communicating and creating a sense of communality. Thomas Turino (2008), in studying the role of music in political participation, draws a distinction between two musical forms: the "presentational" and the "participatory." The latter actively engages the audience, while the former is performed to a largely passive gathering. Of course no listener is entirely passive, but Turino's intention is to highlight how musical *form* matters to what is communicated and experienced.

A more radical version of this same idea is offered by the sociologist Kevin McDonald (2006), who argues that musical rhythms communicate the *experience* of political engagement. According to McDonald, social movements are best understood as "experience movements," as entities that function by generating specific sensations that serve to animate their participants. McDonald (2006, 225) suggests that "we can think of movements as closer to music [than to texts or messages]." This provocative claim is sustained more by speculation than by evidence. Nonetheless, it serves to indicate how sound (in the form of music) can be understood as communicating ideas and values out of which are formed collectivities. And there are instances to which McDonald's argument seems to apply, most notably the case of the Infernal Noise Brigade, a marching band that accompanied the anticapitalist and antiglobalization demonstrations of the late twentieth and early twenty-first centuries. The band choreographed the protestors through the rhythms that they played (Whitney, 2003).

Ideological Sound

In the earlier discussion of music as protest and propaganda, the "politics" of the music was assumed to be explicitly and literally contained in the lyrics. And clearly, in asking what music communicates, the words may be key to understanding what is being "said." But as with any media text, music is polysemic. In the case of songs, the lyrics tell only part of the story. To be interpreted, they need to be heard and in the process marked by sincerity or irony, commitment or criticism. This, in part, was the source of the argument between the presidential rivals over "Born in the USA." Where the Reagan team heard it as a patriotic anthem, to those in Mondale's camp it was a barbed complaint. When Randy Newman sang "Short People" ("they got no reason to live"), was this a simple expression of prejudice, or a satirical comment on discrimination? Sometimes a close reading of the lyrics may reveal an answer to such questions, but more often than not, other elements will be brought into play: the sound of the voice, the genre, or the context.

Voice and words are not the only bearers of meaning. Melodies and rhythms may do so as well, although how and with what consequences is complex (Frith, 1996). This is perhaps most evident in the debates about the composer Richard Wagner, whose own anti-Semitism is well-documented, as is the adoption of his music by the Nazi elite. But the question "Is his music also racist or fascist?" has occupied writers from Friedrich Nietzsche onward. Theodor Adorno (2002), Edward Said (Barenboim and Said, 2004), and Alain Badiou (2010), among many others, have contributed to the argument. What is at issue is, on the one hand, whether a style of music, a way of organizing sound, can also be read as conveying a set of political ideas. And on the other, if it can, what does any given melody "say?" In the debate about Wagner, for example, it is contended that his "endless melodies" have a repressive effect on his listeners (Badiou, 2010).

Similar debates have emerged in discussion of the sexual politics of such diverse genres as heavy metal and disco (Negus, 1996). Here the arguments have been about how particular combinations of sounds construct or express—a crucial difference— gender and sexual identities. The point is that the argument is not simply about what the words say, but about how they sound, and indeed about what the combinations of rhythms and melodies convey or create.

The Power of Music

Underlying the question of what sounds mean or how they generate a sense of community is a further set of claims about how sound affects its audience. From Plato onward, writers have argued that different forms of music generate, or are directly associated with, different forms of conduct, and there is much work in social psychology to support this idea (Hallam, 2001, 2010). This presumption also underlies the regulation of sound by those in authority. It also informs the censorship of music (and extreme examples of this, such as the Taliban's outlawing of music in Afghanistan). Johnson and Cloonan (2009, 37), for instance, argue that the noise pollution policy in sixteenth-century England was motivated by the desire to stamp out the subversive sounds of the minstrels who populated London streets.

A modern variant of this is the zoning of the urban environment and the regulation and sequestering of music venues into particular areas at the behest of dominant interests. Such policies have yielded challenges, most notably in New York, where the lawyer Paul Chevigny (1991), acting on behalf of the Musicians' Union, established that local city laws restricting the performance of music violated the rights of musicians under the First Amendment. The New York County Supreme Court found that the Constitution's protection of free speech extended to the right to perform music in particular ways. In other words, the issue was not the right to perform the written notes in a given order, but to create a particular *sound* in doing so. In this decision (*Chiasson v. NYC Department of Consumer Affairs*, 1988), music (as a set of sounds) was deemed a form of communication, and as such worthy of protection as conventional speech.

Hearing Others

In his discussion of political oratory, Hart (1987) describes how the sound of speech serves to convey the "humanness" of the speaker. Sound, Hart suggests, conveys meanings and insights that mere words cannot. The political philosopher Martha Nussbaum

(2001) develops this suggestion further, arguing that music communicates the emotional experiences of others and elicits compassion in its audience. Her argument recalls that of Rousseau, who also saw music as communicating and sharing emotional experiences: "The passions have their gestures, but they also have their accents, and these accents, which make us tremble, these accents, from which we cannot shield our organ, penetrate by it to the bottom of the heart, and in spite of us carry to it the movements that wrest them, and make us feel what we hear. Let us conclude that visible signs convey a more precise imitation, but what interest is aroused more effectively by sound" (Rousseau, 1998, 292). Both Nussbaum and Rousseau suggest that music contributes to our capacity to understand each other, and in particular our feelings and emotions, a capacity central to individual deliberation about who "we" are and what constitutes the good life.

Music, the Public Sphere, and Civic Engagement

The second part of the chapter has taken us from the obvious forms of music as political communication (as protest, propaganda, and resistance) to consider the question of how music more generally might work as a form of communication, and how it might register protest and resistance in the sounds it makes, rather than in the words it uses or the contexts in which it is performed and heard. It has documented music's communicative capacity to generate a sense of community, articulate ideas, and communicate emotional insights. What these capacities represent is an argument for considering music as a particular type of political communication, requiring different approaches and questions than those applied to other media forms. But although the meanings and effects that may be attributed to music have been considered, this chapter has said nothing about the conditions that enable it to act in these ways.

At one level, this is to touch upon issues familiar to scholars of political communication. Questions of ownership and diversity apply to the production of music in much the same way they do to other media (Wikstrom, 2009). What is perhaps less often noted in this context is how music might be incorporated within the notions of the public sphere and of civic engagement, although Jürgen Habermas (1992), in the definitive text on the public sphere, devotes several pages to music.

In his comparative study of democracy in different regions of Italy, *Making Democracy Work*, Robert Putnam (1993) attributes the propensity to participate politically to the presence of, among other things, local choirs. He insists that this association is more than a correlation, and that the choirs are not themselves a side effect of political engagement. Choral societies generate social capital, in part by teaching "self-discipline" and the value of "successful collaboration" (Putnam 1993, 90). Later, in *Bowling Alone*, Putnam (2000, 411) returns to the value of singing together, arguing that it is important to the regeneration of a civic culture. In other words, he offers arguments and evidence for the association of choirs and singing with the communication of a sense of community and the generation of social capital.

Putnam's focus on music's potential is vividly illustrated by the West-Eastern Divan Workshop and Orchestra, set up by Edward Said and Daniel Barenboim (2004), in which young musicians from across the Middle East played together. The performers' musical collaboration symbolized an ideal of peaceful coexistence, but it did more than this. It produced—albeit in limited form—the conditions for, and experience of, such coexistence. Something similar is to be found in the El Sistema scheme, which originated in Venezuela, but which has been adopted by other governments, including New Labour in the United Kingdom. El Sistema enables young children from socially deprived areas to learn a musical instrument and perform in orchestras. The result, it is claimed by Andrea Creech and her colleague (2013), is a new self-respect and sense of social worth, born of their musical experience. What these examples represent, in summary, are cases of music embodying a vision of the "good society," one that transcends the harsh realities of daily life. These claims have direct equivalents in the arguments made for the value of traditional media in serving democracy. They find their most explicit expression in A Music Manifesto for Scotland, published by the Royal Society of Scotland to coincide with the country's elections: "We hold these truths to be self-evident: Humans make music and music makes us human. There are no societies without music and music is the dynamic spirit of a society. Music is what we do together. It is through music that peoples best express and understand themselves" (Frith and Cloonan, 2011, 1).

If we share such sentiments, their implications are important. They raise questions of how, if music is an important form of political communication capable of generating social capital or conveying powerful ideas, it should be organized. Just as students of other forms of political communication become exercised about the regulation of news media corporations, so those concerned with music as a form of political communication need to address the power of the global media industry and the (de-)regulation of broadcasting. The issues at stake are not just those of plurality and diversity, but of civic engagement as well.

Conclusion

This chapter began with Attali's stark assertion that for too long we have watched the world, when we should instead have been listening to it. While the claim may be exaggerated, it does serve to raise an important issue for students of political communication. Sound, and in this case the sound of music, communicates political ideas and inspires political actions. There are the obvious examples of music's use as a form of protest, propaganda, and resistance, but underlying them is the matter of *how* music as sound performs the communicative roles assigned to it. Without pretending to comprehensiveness, this survey illustrated how music might unify and move people, how it can be read as expressing an ideology, how it can be employed to cause people to act in particular ways, and how it provides insights into the inner lives of citizens. In all these respects, music is a form of political communication. The last section of this chapter raised, albeit briefly, the ways in which regulation can expand or enervate music's capacity to perform its communicative role.

This chapter has indicated what is entailed in thinking of music as a form of political communication. For a number of reasons, music—and sound more generally—should feature more prominently in analysis of political communication, particularly in a multichannel, multimedia environment: music is a site both of the exercise of power and of resistance to it; it provides a voice for the powerful and for the powerless. How it is organized and used has consequences for the communication of politics.

References

Adorno, T. W. 2002. *Essays on music.* Edited by R. Leppert. Berkeley: University of California Press.

Anderson, B. 1983. *Imagined communities: Reflections on the origins and spread of nationalism.* London: Verso.

Andersson, M. 1981. *Music in the mix: The story of South African popular music.* Johannesburg: Ravan Press.

Attali, J. 1985. *Noise: The political economy of music.* Minneapolis: University of Minnesota Press.

Badiou, A. 2010. *Five lessons on Wagner.* London: Verso.

Baily, J. 2004. Music censorship in Afghanistan before and after the Taliban. In M. Korpe (Ed.), *Shoot the singer: Music censorship today* (pp. 19–28). London: Zed Books.

Barenboim, D., and Said, E. W. 2004. *Parallels and paradoxes: Explorations in music and society* Edited by A. Guzelimian. London: Bloomsbury.

Beck, A. 2000. Music in the party election TV broadcasts of 1997. Retrieved from hhtp://www.tagg.org/students/Liverpool/partyelect97.html.

Blanning, T. 2008. *The triumph of music: Composers, musicians and their audiences, 1700 to the present.* London: Allen Lane.

Caute, D. 2005. *The dancer defects: The struggle for cultural supremacy during the Cold War.* Oxford: Oxford University Press.

Chevigny, P. 1991. *Gigs: Jazz and the cabaret laws in New York City.* New York: Routledge.

Creech, A., Gonzalez-Moreno, P., Lorenzino, L and Waitman, G. 2013. *El Sistema and Sistema-inspired programmes: A literature review of research, evaluation, and critical debates.* San Diego, CA: Sistema Global.

Cushman, T. 1995. *Notes from underground: Rock music counterculture in Russia.* Albany: State University of New York Press.

Dewey, J. 1919. *Democracy and education: An introduction to the philosophy of education.* New York: Macmillan.

Downs, A. 1957. *An economic theory of democracy.* New York: Harper & Row.

Eyerman, R., and Jamison, A. 1998. *Music and social movements: Mobilizing traditions in the twentieth century.* Cambridge, UK: Cambridge University Press.

Fischlin, D., and Heble, A. (Eds.). 2003. *Rebel musics: Human rights, resistant sounds, and the politics of music making.* Montreal: Black Rose Books.

Franklin, M. (Ed.). 2005. *Resounding international relations: On music, culture and politics.* Houndmills, Basingstoke, UK: Palgrave Macmillan.

Frith, S. 1996. *Performing rites: On the value of popular music.* Oxford: Oxford University Press.

Frith, S., and Cloonan, M. 2011. *A music manifesto for Scotland.* Edinburgh: Royal Society of Edinburgh.

Habermas, J. 1992. *The structural Transformation of the public sphere: An inquiry into a category of bourgeois society.* Cambridge, UK: Polity.

Hallam, S. 2001. *The power of music.* London: PMRS.

Hallam, S. 2010. The power of music: Its impact on the intellectual, social and personal development of children and young people. *International Journal of Music Education* 38(3): 269–289.

Hart, R. 1987. *The sound of leadership: Presidential communication in the modern age.* Chicago: University of Chicago Press.

Index on Censorship. 1998. Smashed hits: The book of banned music. No. 6.

Johnson, B., and Cloonan, M. 2009. *Dark side of the tune: Popular music and violence.* Aldershot, UK: Ashgate.

Kater, M. 1997. *The twisted muse: Musicians and the music in the Third Reich.* Oxford: Oxford University Press.

Laing, D. 2003. Resistance and rotest. In J. Shepherd, D. Horn, D. Laing, P. Oliver, and P. Wicke (Eds.), *Continuum Encyclopedia of Popular Music of the World* (pp. 345–346). London: Continuum.

Lynskey, D. 2011. *33 Revolutions per minute: A history of protest music.* London: Faber and Faber.

McDonald, K. 2006. *Global movements: Action and culture.* Oxford: Blackwell.

Meyer, M. 1991. *The politics of music in the Third Reich.* New York: Peter Lang.

Negus, K. 1996. *Popular music in theory.* Cambridge: Polity.

Nietzsche, F. 1999. *The birth of tragedy and other writings.* Edited by R. Geuss and R. Speirs. Cambridge, UK: Cambridge University Press.

Nussbaum, M. 2001. *Upheavals of thought: The intelligence of emotions.* Cambridge, UK: Cambridge University Press.

Orwell, G. 1989. *Nineteen eighty-four.* Harmondsworth, UK: Penguin.

Palmer, R. 1988. *The sound of history: Songs and social comment.* Oxford: Oxford University Press.

Peddie, I. (Ed.). 2006. *The resisting music: Popular music and social protest.* Aldershot, UK: Ashgate.

Putnam, R. 1993. *Making democracy work: Civic traditions in modern Italy.* Princeton, NJ: Princeton University Press.

Putnam, R. 2000. *Bowling alone: The collapse and revival of American community.* New York: Simon & Schuster.

Revill, G. 2000. Music and the politics of sound: nationalism, citizenship, and auditory space. *Environment and Planning D: Society and Space* 18(5): 597–613.

Ross, A. 2007. *The rest is noise: Listening to the twentieth century.* New York: Farrar, Straus and Giroux.

Rousseau, J-J. 1998. *Essay on the origin of languages and writings related to music.* Translated and edited by J. T. Scott. Hanover and London: University Press of New England.

Saul, S. 2003. *Freedom is, freedom ain't: Jazz and the making of the sixties.* Cambridge, MA: Harvard University Press.

Schafer, R. M. 1994. *The soundscape: Our sonic environment and the tuning of the world.* Rochester, VT: Destiny Books.

Smith, S. 1999. *Dancing in the street: Motown and the cultural politics of Detroit.* Cambridge, MA: Harvard University Press.

Starr, F. 1983. *Red and hot: The fate of jazz in the Soviet Union.* Oxford: Oxford University Press.

Szemere, A. 2001. *Up from the underground: The culture of rock music in postsocialist Hungary.* University Park: Pennsylvania State University Press.

Turino, T. 2008. *Music as social life: The politics of participation.* Chicago: University of Chicago Press.

Urban, M. 2004. *Russia gets the blues: Music, culture, and community in unsettled times.* London: Cornell University Press.

Van Leeuwen, T. 1999. *Speech, music, sound.* Houndmills, Basingstoke, UK: Palgrave Macmillan.

Ward, B. 1998. *Just my soul responding: Rhythm and blues, black consciousness and race relations.* London: UCL Press.

Whitney, J. 2003. Infernal noise: The soundtrack to insurrection. In Notes from Nowhere (Eds.), *We are everywhere: The irresistible rise of global anticapitalism* (pp. 216–227). London: Verso.

Wicke, P. 1992. "The times they are a-changin": Rock music and political change in Eastern Germany. In R. Garofalo (Ed.), *Rockin' the boat: Mass music and mass movements* (pp. 81–93). Boston: South End Press.

Wikstrom, P. 2009. *The music industry.* Cambridge, UK: Polity.

CHAPTER 61

CONDITIONS FOR POLITICAL ACCOUNTABILITY IN A HIGH-CHOICE MEDIA ENVIRONMENT

MARKUS PRIOR

COMMUNICATION technology has changed dramatically in recent decades, and with it the way people consume news. This chapter asks how changes in the media environment affect political accountability in a democratic system. The chapter's purpose is to sketch several conditions for accountability in a high-choice media environment and discuss their empirical plausibility.

The level of political knowledge among ordinary citizens is an important factor in determining how, and how well, elected officials are held accountable. Representatives typically have more information about conditions and policies than the people who choose them, so "the main difficulty both in instructing governments what to do and in judging what they have done is that we, citizens, just do not know enough" (Manin et al., 1999, 23). But even though governments and representatives have an inherent informational advantage, a more-informed electorate may produce greater political accountability than a less-informed one.

For a citizenry to be informed, information about government and elected officials must be available. Two critical sources of such information are news media and election campaigns. Studies suggest that politicians covered more heavily by the news media are more accountable to their constituents (e.g., Cohen et al., 2004; Snyder and Strömberg, 2010). Elections are more likely to vote out of office those who ignore the preferences of the people they represent (e.g., Canes-Wrone et al., 2002). How much information is being produced by media and campaigns—and whether new technologies have systematically altered production—are very difficult to quantify. On one hand, cable channels, Web-based news providers, online databases (Schudson, 2010), and amateur journalists (Bentley, 2008) have added new sources of information about public affairs. On the other hand, these additions may not compensate for the loss of traditional media coverage due to intensified competition and declining advertising revenue. Hard news is under attack from entertainment-heavy soft news, especially on television, and news organizations are closing foreign bureaus. Some areas of journalism, including local public affairs coverage (Starr, 2009), have suffered stark losses in resources and personnel.

Undeniably, however, more public affairs information is available to individual media users than before the rise of digital media. Many traditional media outlets that used to be available only in some parts of the country or the world now have websites, and news aggregators organize this content conveniently. Information collected by governments or interest groups that used to be difficult to access—including public opinion data, roll call votes, and government expenditures—is now a mouse click away for anyone with an Internet connection.

Greater availability of information has not translated into greater use of information across the board, however. Starting in the 1970s, cable television slowly offered television viewers more programming choices. Some viewers—people who prefer entertainment to news programming—began to abandon the nightly newscasts in favor of more entertaining programs. In the low-choice environment before cable TV, they encountered politics at least occasionally, because they liked watching television—even television news—more than most other leisure activities. With access to numerous entertainment-oriented cable channels and Internet websites, entertainment fans learn less about politics than they used to and vote less often. The transition from the low-option environment to the high-choice world of cable and Internet had the opposite effect on people who prefer news to entertainment. These news junkies take advantage of more information to become more knowledgeable and more likely to vote than in the past. Hence, the growth of new media has increased inequality in the distribution of political knowledge and concentrates knowledge among those who like the news (Prior, 2005, 2007).

New Media and Political Accountability

The combination of greater availability of information and mounting inequality of its use might seem like a quintessential case of good news/bad news. If political accountability is roughly proportional to total consumption of political information by all members of an electorate, then an accounting of changing news audiences can determine if the bad news outweighs the good news. I illustrate such an accounting below.

But it is critical to realize that not all citizens have to follow the news in order for detailed media coverage to strengthen accountability, because an evenly well-informed electorate is not a necessary condition for political accountability. Accountability requires only that wrongdoing, incompetence, and shirking by representatives will be revealed and sanctioned at least some of the time (e.g., Ferejohn, 1986; Key, 1961). It does not require that every such instance is known to all citizens. Instead, elected officials, aware that their behavior is being monitored or may be subject to an "audit" (Arnold, 1990), anticipate sanctions for abusing their power, acting incompetently, or ignoring constituents' preferences. When evidence for any of these behaviors is revealed, the representative risks losing her job. Ferejohn (1999) shows that competition between agents (candidates for office) can lead to more effective monitoring because principals (voters) tend to prefer agents who commit to making their actions transparent. And as long as the representative believes that she may be monitored, she will not take (full) advantage of the information asymmetries in her favor.

A representative seeking reelection thus has an incentive to act according to her constituents' preferences, even if constituents do not have full information about her actions. When selecting an action, reelection-seeking representatives must gauge "latent opinion" (Key, 1961), that is, the state of public opinion that might develop if their actions or the consequences of their actions are revealed by election time. Actions and consequences may remain private, so latent opinion may never become actual opinion, in which case representatives will not be judged against latent opinion at all. Yet, the mere possibility that actual opinion might catch up with representatives' behavior can be a powerful incentive for them to keep their constituents' best interests in mind— even when constituents have uninformed, vague, or no opinions on the subject (Arnold, 1990; Canes-Wrone et al., 2001; Zaller, 2003a).

For this incentive structure to work, it is not necessary that all or even a majority of citizens monitor representatives' behavior. Writing about accountability of congressional representatives, Arnold (2004, 13) emphasizes that

> [n]ot every citizen needs to be a front-line sentry to keep representatives on their toes. As long as a cadre of individuals and organizations monitor what representatives are doing in office and stand ready to inform other citizens when they see something out of line, representatives know that they are being watched. Much more important is that information regularly flows to those who act as watchdogs, that these watchdogs reflect the diversity of interests in a constituency, and that they have easy ways to communicate with other citizens when they discover representatives doing disagreeable things.

This mechanism does not require that all citizens are well informed and does not provide a hard lower bound for the number of well informed. If the presence of well-informed "watchdogs" is a crucial requirement for accountability, then higher levels of news exposure and political knowledge in a relatively small subset of the population might improve overall accountability of a democratic system, even when the population as a whole does not consume more news and some citizens consume noticeably less than they used to. If the level of information among the politically most involved citizens is a critical condition for political accountability, then new media may in fact strengthen accountability because news junkies are more informed than in the past. And increasing the share of ill-informed citizens will not necessarily reduce the effectiveness of the accountability mechanism. To be sure, Arnold's prescription for accountability involves more than well-informed watchdogs. For a relatively small number of news junkies to serve as watchdogs and strengthen accountability, they must hold similar political attitudes as other citizens and be able to alert them.

With a basic understanding of the principal (citizen)–agent (representative) relationship in place, the conditions under which recent changes in the media environment strengthen or weaken accountability become more nuanced. The remainder of this chapter offers some crude empirical assessments of these conditions.

Total News Consumption and Political Accountability

One way to assess changes in accountability is to consider if a given news story or piece of information is as likely to be seen, read, or heard as it was in the past. The question here is *not* if as many people as in the past follow the news. Rather, the critical condition is that information about abuse of power or incompetence by elected officials finds its way to some members of the public, who can then help spread it to inattentive publics through interpersonal channels or by organizing amplifying protest activities. The extent to which Americans collectively attend to information produced by the news media becomes a rough gauge of accountability. This would make overall consumption of news and political information the relevant indicator to trace.

Conceptually, Total News Consumption is simple to define. It is the total amount of news consumed in a given interval by a group of people, in this case the American public. Practically, measuring Total News Consumption poses considerable challenges, made more daunting by the diversification of news options. Signs of audience fragmentation are taken prematurely as indication of declining news consumption. Traditional indicators of news media use—network news ratings and daily newspaper circulation—have indeed declined. But news options that were not available in the past or have expanded in scope have gained audiences. Cable television, all-news radio, news Websites, and the online editions of newspapers all add to the overall news audience. Individually, these new audiences may seem rather small, but together they make up a large share of news media use.

Unfortunately, measuring Total News Consumption across all these platforms by simply asking a representative group of survey respondents is bound to yield misleading results because people are not adept at estimating the amount of time they spend doing things, including watching, reading, or listening to news (Price and Zaller, 1993; Prior, 2009, 2013a, 2013b). As a result, audience research firms monitor television viewing to provide consumption estimates that do not depend on self-assessment. A similar measurement approach has become common for online news consumption, but it is not obvious how either can be compared to consumption of offline print media, which is most validly assessed by the number of copies in circulation.

In *Post-Broadcast Democracy* (Prior, 2007), I offered a very rough accounting of trends in Total News Consumption. Even though many people consume less news than they used to, the total amount of news consumed has probably not declined. New media generate so much more news media use that the American public likely consumes more news than in the past.

Today, by far the greatest contributor to overall television news exposure is cable news. Even though each half-hour nightly broadcast network news program still draws about twice the audience as the highest-rated cable news shows, the accumulation of small cable news audiences over a 24-hour day exceeds the combined network news audience. In 1980, the nightly network news enjoyed its highest-ever combined yearly average with a rating of 38. That is, 38 percent of all US households watched one of the three evening network newscasts—30 minutes of news (including commercial breaks). For the average household, this amounted to 11.4 minutes (30 minutes × .38) of news per weekday. By 2004, the combined rating had dropped to 18.5. In that year, the three major cable networks (CNN, Fox News Channel, and MSNBC) had a combined average rating of 1.4. But since this is a rating over a 24-hour period, it adds up to more news consumption than network news at its peak. A 1.4 rating for the three cable networks means that 1.4 percent of all US households watched one of the three cable networks *during the average minute of the day*. For the average household, this amounts to 20.2 minutes (60 minutes × 24 hours × .014) of news per day.

Other significant contributions to news consumption on broadcast networks come from prime-time news magazines, Sunday morning talk shows, and morning news. In the early 1980s, the most popular news magazine, *60 Minutes*, contributed about the same amount to Total News Consumption in its one weekly hour as CNN, then the only cable news network, did with its 24/7 schedule. Although other broadcast programs tried to copy the success of *60 Minutes*, their ratings were lower at the outset, and all news magazines have suffered large audience losses since. The networks' Sunday morning interview shows draw small audiences and add relatively little to overall news consumption. Yet the extension of *Meet the Press* to one hour in 1992 and the addition of *Fox News Sunday* in 1996 increased average news consumption of the Sunday morning shows temporarily. Audiences for weekday morning news on ABC, CBS, and NBC have been fairly stable over the last two decades. Local newscasts tend to draw somewhat larger audiences than national broadcast news. Over recent decades, their ratings have declined at similar rates as nightly network news (see Prior, 2007, ch. 3; Project for Excellence in Journalism, 2011b).

Adding up the time the American public spends watching cable and broadcast news reveals remarkably stable television news consumption between the early 1980s, when CNN appeared on the scene, and the end of the 1990s, when broadcast news had lost a considerable share of its audience and cable access had reached two-thirds of all American households. Driven by increased cable news viewing, Total Television News Consumption increased by about 50 percent in 2001 in the aftermath of 9/11. Sustained, at least in part, by the war in Iraq and perhaps by the addition of the successful Fox News Channel, it stayed at this level and reached an even higher mark during the 2008 presidential campaign.

Between 2005 and 2010, nightly network news programs lost another 19 percent of their audience, while cable news grew by about 15 percent, even though ratings dropped considerably after the first months of the Obama administration (Project for Excellence in Journalism, 2011b). Since cable news provided three to four times the news consumption as network news midway through the decade, this implies that Total Television News Consumption continues to exceed the levels of the 1980s and 90s.

Nor is there clear evidence that the overall amount of newspaper reading has declined. Although it is difficult to compare circulation data with metrics for use of newspaper websites, declining print circulation may well be offset by increased online reading. Between 1995 and 2010, daily newspaper circulation dropped by about 15 million, declining from 58.2 million to 43.4 million, according to *Editor & Publisher*. In a given month, US newspaper websites currently draw about 100 million unique visitors (from within the United States), according to comScore data published by the Newspaper Association of America. Although this number has doubled since 2005, it inflates the online newspaper audiences. By tracking cookies comScore counts the same users multiple times if they use different browsers or delete cookies (Project for Excellence in Journalism, 2011b).

The great majority of "unique visitors" spend very little time on newspaper websites each month. The average monthly time spent per visitor is just over 30 minutes (down about 10 percent from 2005.) An analysis of online news consumption by the Project for Excellence in Journalism (2011a) found that about two-thirds of visitors to the top twenty-five news websites do not return to the site in the same month and fewer than 10 percent spend more than an hour per month on the site. But these estimates are website-specific and do not reveal how many people follow news on any combination of websites for more than an hour per month (or week). Clearly, only a small fraction of the 100 million unique monthly visitors estimated by comScore actually read articles on a more or less daily basis. Yet, even though it is difficult to determine the share of serious online readers, 30 minutes of news consumption per month by 100 million visitors—plus traffic to other news sites—probably go a long way toward compensating for the decline in print circulation.

Radio news consumption, too, appears to be relatively stable, with National Public Radio increasing its audience over the last decade and political talk radio fairly stable (Project for Excellence in Journalism, 2011b).

If political accountability is indeed proportional to overall consumption of political information, there is little reason to conclude that it has been weakened by new technologies and greater media choice.

News Junkies as Monitors

The argument that political accountability is proportional to overall news consumption ignores some of the insights generated by principal-agent models. The effectiveness of accountability mechanisms depends in part on who monitors representatives. An arrangement where all or most citizens do the monitoring is not necessarily more effective than monitoring by a smaller set of people and organizations, especially when these people and organizations are attentive and knowledgeable. Instead of using overall news consumption as an indicator of accountability, it may be more relevant to focus on how a changing media environment affects the distribution of news consumption and thereby modifies the monitoring capacity of the attentive public.

Writing about the capacity of Congress to hold the executive branch accountable, McCubbins and Schwartz (1984) famously contrasted two approaches to oversight. Members of Congress could collect and review detailed information on all aspects of executive behavior. Or they could devise mechanisms that flag problematic behavior. McCubbins and Schwartz referred to the former as "police patrols" and the latter as "fire alarms." Fire alarms are more efficient than police patrols. When the system produces so much information that police-patrol oversight cannot process all of it, they are also more effective because police-patrol oversight will miss evidence of shirking or incompetence in the ocean of irrelevant or benign information.

Fire-alarm oversight draws its effectiveness from the threat that shirking may be caught by monitors. This threat is only credible if there is in fact a good chance that someone will notice shirking and sound an alarm. In McCubbins and Schwartz's (1984) fire-alarm model, various watchdogs, including interest groups and ordinary citizens, monitor executive branch behavior and alert Congress or the courts when legislative goals are violated.

Both Zaller (2003b) and Arnold (2004) subsequently drew on fire-alarm oversight to specify what role news media should play in fostering political accountability. Arnold (2004, 13–16) describes different types of watchdogs using different information to monitor the actions of elected officials. "Professional watchdogs," such as opposition politicians and interest groups, have the resources to engage in their own police-patrol oversight. "Amateur watchdogs" are interested ordinary citizens—roughly what I call news junkies—who do not have such resources and must therefore rely on news coverage for their monitoring. News media are needed to perform police-patrol oversight as well because none of the other watchdogs are prone to unearth the information that journalists produce.

According to Zaller, most media should be evaluated based on how well they alert citizens to danger, not based on how well they inform them on mundane political matters. Noting that many citizens lack interest in providing police-patrol oversight, Zaller's (2003b) "burglar alarm" news standard charges news media with more of the monitoring. Zaller believes that "it is the job of reporters . . . to decide what requires attention and bring it to the public." Citizens "should be alerted to problems requiring attention and otherwise left to private concerns" (121).

Even though Zaller (2003b) draws heavily on Schudson's (1998) idea of ordinary people as "monitorial citizens," he does not entrust citizens with the same responsibility to hold officials accountable as Schudson does. In Schudson's view, the ideal of an informed citizen who carefully studies policy issues and candidate platforms before casting a vote was always an ideal against which most citizens looked ill informed and ineffective. Although Schudson does not deny the benefits of an informed citizenry, it is neither realistic nor necessary, in his view, to expect citizens to be well informed about every aspect of their increasingly complex role in society. Rather than being widely knowledgeable about politics, citizens merely need to "be informed enough and alert enough to identify danger to their personal good and danger to the public good" (Schudson, 2000, 22). In order to fulfill this "monitoring obligation," citizens "engage in environmental surveillance rather than information-gathering"—they "scan (rather than read) the informational environment in a way so that they may be alerted on a very wide variety of issues for a very wide variety of ends" (1998, 310–311). Media provide much of the input for monitoring, but citizens do more than respond to journalists' alarms.

An average citizen may well be closer to Zaller's pessimistic diagnosis than to Schudson's ideal. But from an agency perspective on accountability, that is not the relevant question. The more attentive and knowledgeable citizens, not the average Joe, contribute to accountability. Today's news junkies certainly look like excellent monitors. The current high-choice media environment provides them with unprecedented resources to perform as monitorial citizens, so the expansion of media choice may make it easier to spot the dangers. They consume a lot of information—and a lot more than before the days of cable and online news (Prior, 2007). They also take advantage of new media technologies to share and debate the results of their monitoring (e.g., Adamic and Glance, 2005; Lawrence et al., 2010). Most importantly, news junkies do not mind the monitoring obligation. They enjoy following the news. Hence, new media may strengthen accountability because some citizens, news junkies, and "amateur watchdogs," become more knowledgeable and can more effectively monitor elected officials.

Representative News Junkies or Biased Fire Alarms?

For "monitorial news junkies" to maintain or even improve accountability in a high-choice media environment, their increased monitoring capacity must compensate for those who lack the interest to monitor their representatives. Entertainment fans, who actively try to avoid exposure to news, can hardly be effective monitors. Their news exposure and political knowledge dropped as they obtained access to cable television and the Internet. For new media to strengthen accountability, it is not sufficient that one segment of the population, news junkies, becomes more knowledgeable as a result of new and easily accessible sources of information. The news junkies also need to be representative of the population as a whole. If monitoring by a subset of citizens were to foster overall accountability in a political system, it must be clear that citizens who monitor and citizens who do not monitor *would* sound the alarm under the same circumstances (or amplify an alarm sounded by the media or interest groups).

This added requirement may be of little importance for the punishing abuse of power and major incompetence. The representativeness condition is met to the extent that there is wide agreement regarding the standards to which elected officials ought to be held and the criteria by which these standards can be assessed. Impeachable offenses, ethics violations, and perhaps even dramatically incompetent or ineffective performance in office could be detected and sanctioned by monitorial news junkies as stand-ins for those who would rather enjoy entertainment fare.

But the definition of political accountability offered by Manin et al. (1999, 10) goes far beyond alarms that everybody can agree on. Instead, "governments are 'accountable' if citizens can discern representative from unrepresentative governments and can sanction them appropriately." Government is "representative" if it acts in the collective interest of the citizens or, when interests collide, "pursues the best interest of a majority" (7). Unless one wants to rely on altruism and magnanimity of news junkies, this leads to Arnold's requirement that "these watchdogs reflect the diversity of interests in a constituency." The demographic background and political attitudes of the monitors are critical, if political accountability includes electoral sanctions for failing to serve one's constituents on inherently contestable issues.

It may still not be necessary for all citizens to engage in monitoring, because some citizens can in fact fill in as monitors for others. But those who sound or amplify alarms must effectively represent the interests of those who are tuning out. Political accountability could be strengthened if more effective monitoring by news junkies can help detect unrepresentative government and trigger sanctions. But if news junkies have different interests than the rest of the population, their monitoring may actually lead to less representative government and thus lower accountability by Manin et al.'s definition. It becomes a matter of empirical analysis to determine if monitorial news junkies sound, or react to, the same alarms as non-monitoring entertainment fans.

One way this could happen is if monitoring news junkies resembled the population except for their greater preference for news consumption and interest in politics. I measured people's preference for news over entertainment—their Relative Entertainment Preference (REP)—in two different ways. The first REP measure asked respondents to rank how much they liked news compared to other programming genres. Out of ten genres, news ranked first for 5 percent of the respondents and was among the three most-liked genres for 30 percent. In the second survey item measuring REP, respondents were asked which of four cable premium channels they would order, assuming that they would not have to pay a monthly charge. The four alternatives were a music channel, a news channel, a "movie and entertainment channel," and a sports channel. Instead of making respondents pick one channel, the question allowed them to assign a "percent chance" to each of the four channels (following a design developed by Charles Manski). Respondents could thus express their preference structure more precisely. The movie channel was most popular with an average percent chance of 50, and the news channel was next with an average percent chance of 23. (For more details on these measures, see Prior, 2007, ch. 4.) Separately or as a combined two-item measure, REP is a powerful determinant of news exposure, political knowledge, and turnout among people with access to cable television or the Internet. Among people without new media access, REP is unrelated to those indicators of political involvement.

Who are the news junkies that take advantage of new media to become more knowledgeable about politics? Demographically, it turns out, they are very similar to the rest of the population. On a variety of variables, including race, marital status, education, income, employment status, and media access, few differences emerge. Although college-educated people, men, the wealthy, and the unemployed are significantly fonder of news, these differences are substantively small (less than a fifth of one standard deviation of REP). The only sizable predictor of REP is age. Young people enjoy entertainment more than news and political information, while people over 64 prefer news quite strongly. Without age in the model, demographic variables explain only 7 percent of the variance in REP. Even with age included as a set of four categories, the R^2 is only .13.

Descriptive representation (Pitkin, 1967) does not appear to suffer much as entertainment fans tune out, leaving news junkies in charge of monitoring elected officials and sounding alarms. As far as demographics are concerned, news junkies look like potential stand-ins for the political dropouts of the high-choice media environment. Importantly, a preference for entertainment is not a proxy for education or socioeconomic status. The chances that a wealthy, well-educated American and a poor American without a high-school diploma prefer entertainment to news are essentially the same. As a result, the chances are essentially the same that either one of them will abandon the news in the high-choice media environment.

Yet, demographic similarity between news and entertainment fans is not a sufficient condition for effective representation. It does not imply shared political values or issue preferences. Demographic similarity cannot assure us that news junkies are ready to sanction elected officials who hurt the interests of inattentive entertainment fans. But the similarities between these groups go beyond demographics. Collectively, news junkies do not have a fundamentally different view of politics than entertainment fans. Party identification and ideology are not related to REP. News junkies are not systematically more liberal, more conservative, more Republican, or more Democratic than entertainment fans.

In one respect, however, news fans differ substantially from entertainment fans: They are far more partisan. At one extreme, almost 40 percent of the people who decidedly prefer news (bottom eighth of REP) identify strongly with a party, and an additional 26 percent identify weakly. Respondents at the other extreme—those who most clearly prefer entertainment—are the least partisan of all. Only 25 percent of them identify strongly with a party. Forty percent are either independent or completely apolitical, not reporting any party preference. As we move from low to high REP, the share of strong partisans drops by about a third, while the share of apoliticals and independents doubles (Prior, 2007, ch. 7).

Since news junkies are about evenly split into Democrats and Republicans, they might still effectively alert others when government threatens to pass laws that do not represent the interests of a majority. Even though they do not include many monitors with centrist views, they will sound the alarm about non-centrist policy proposals—the ones that are inconsistent with their own partisan leanings.

But news junkies may also raise their voices and drum up opposition to centrist policies or candidates. In fact, liberal and conservative news junkies might both sound alarms about centrist proposals. The disproportionate and growing political involvement of relatively partisan Americans may further encourage candidates to take more extreme political positions, especially in primaries (Aldrich, 1995; Fiorina, 1999). So the only manifest difference between news junkies and the rest of the population—the intensity of partisan feelings—reduces the likelihood that monitors would advocate, or at least not punish, the moderate policy positions that entertainment fans seem to favor.

CONCLUSION

As a result of more media choice, the task of holding elected officials accountable rests increasingly on a relatively narrow segment of the population—the news junkies. Many others have simply withdrawn into the inattentive public that is roused only if enough news junkies make noise. But the changing media environment has equipped news junkies with newly abundant political information that may well make them more effective "monitorial citizens." News junkies consume so much news that Total News Consumption has probably remained fairly constant, even though many entertainment fans abandoned the news audience once cable television and the entertainment offered them more attractive programming at all times of the day.

These developments give power to news junkies—and raise the question of how likely these news monitors are to use their power responsibly. As news junkies resemble the rest of the population in many demographic and even political characteristics, they may often just have to follow their own interests and preferences to effectively represent entertainment fans. In cases of politically unambiguous abuse of power or dramatic incompetence, news junkies will probably be good proxies for others and alert the wider public. But since they are on the whole considerably more partisan, news junkies will not always guard or facilitate the centrist policies that the rest of the population would prefer. In those instances, news junkies could strengthen political accountability only if they consider the collective interest of the citizenry, rather than their own self-interest, while performing their monitoring tasks.

If rising inequality in political involvement does reduce responsiveness of elected officials to the interests of citizens who prefer entertainment to news, these entertainment fans will have mostly themselves to blame. Unlike most other forms of inequality, this one is a second-order consequence of *voluntary* consumption decisions, not differences in abilities or resources. Entertainment fans abandon politics not because it has become harder for them to be involved—many people would argue the contrary—but because they decide to devote their time to media that promise greater gratification than the news. Whether the harm from lack of representation outweighs the added consumption value of more entertainment is a difficult question to answer for researchers and entertainment fans alike.

In this chapter, I have argued that a clearer understanding of accountability mechanisms can bring political communication research one step closer to an answer. This chapter raises many questions that require further theoretical development and focused empirical examination. Two areas of research seem particularly critical. The first concerns journalism. To judge the effectiveness of monitoring by news junkies, it is important to understand what news junkies can learn. How much relevant public affairs information do news media, governments, and interest groups produce? Arnold's (2004) detailed study of newspaper coverage of Congress is an excellent model, but the current media environment requires content analysis across platforms and types of information providers. The ongoing data collection by the Pew Research Center's Project for Excellence in Journalism (http://www.journalism.org) provides content data for an unprecedented number of different media outlets. But it is not deliberately designed to evaluate accountability journalism. Better data would allow us to adjudicate between Zaller (2003b), Bennett (2003), and Arnold (2004), who offer widely different assessments of the capacity of news organizations to sound appropriate alarms.

With more detailed content data, it would become easier to assess viable business models for accountability journalism. Millions of former newspaper readers who used to pay for their paper and serve as targets for mass advertisements have either abandoned news or turned into online users who access news free of charge and do not respond to ads as frequently as advertisers have hoped. It is too early for obituaries of market-provided accountability journalism. But in some areas, market mechanisms have failed in the past (Hamilton, 2004) and will only become less effective as bundling declines. Ironically, the corollary of more efficient fire-alarm oversight by a small group of news junkies is a reduced customer base for commercial news providers. And we should think twice before charging avid news consumers more steeply—they are, after all, doing the important monitoring for everyone else.

A second critical research area involves the diffusion of alarms. How and how effectively do various watchdogs, including news junkies, spread fire alarms to inattentive citizens? If elected officials do not expect that the problems uncovered by fire-alarm oversight will ultimately trickle down to large segments of the voting public, they will be able to ignore the alarms. The growing sophistication of online communication and the popularity of social media offer some prospect that news junkies may manage to alert the rest of the citizenry. But the abundance of distractions and obfuscations creates a formidable wall of noise that news junkies' voices must penetrate. Assessments of their success will likely benefit from a growing academic interest in network analysis and closer attention to existing theories of democratic accountability but will also need to understand "new" and "old" kinds of news production.

References

Adamic, L. A., and Glance, N. 2005. *The political blogosphere and the 2004 U.S. election: Divided they blog.* Proceedings of the 3rd International workshop on Link Discovery, pp. 36–43.
Aldrich, J. 1995. *Why parties?* Chicago: University of Chicago Press.
Arnold, R. D. 1990. *The logic of congressional action.* New Haven, CT: Yale University Press.
Arnold, R. D. 2004. *Congress, the press and political accountability.* Princeton, NJ: Princeton University Press.

Bennett, W. L. 2003. The burglar alarm that just keeps ringing: A response to Zaller. *Political Communication* 20(2): 131–138.

Bentley, C. H. June 2008. Citizen journalism: Back to the future? Paper presented at the Carnegie-Knight Conference on the Future of Journalism, Cambridge, MA.

Canes-Wrone, B., Brady, D. W., and Cogan, J. F. 2002. Out of step, out of office: Electoral accountability and House members' voting. *American Political Science Review* 96(1): 127–140.

Canes-Wrone, B., Herron, M. C., and Shotts, K. W. 2001. Leadership and pandering: A theory of executive policymaking. *American Journal of Political Science* 45(3): 532–550.

Cohen, M., Noel, H., and Zaller, J. 2004. Local news and political accountability in U.S. legislative elections. Paper presented at the Annual meeting of the American Political Science Association, Chicago.

Ferejohn, J. 1986. Incumbent performance and electoral control. *Public Choice* 50(1/3): 5–25.

Ferejohn, J. 1999. Accountability and authority: Toward a theory of political accountability. In Adam Przeworski, Susan C. Stokes, and Bernard Manin (Eds.), *Democracy, accountability, and representation* (pp. 131–153). Cambridge: Cambridge University Press.

Fiorina, M. P. October 1999. Whatever happened to the median voter? Paper presented at the MIT Conference on Parties and Congress, Cambridge, MA.

Hamilton, J. T. 2004. *All the news that's fit to sell: How the market transforms information into news.* Princeton, NJ: Princeton University Press.

Key, V. O. Jr. 1961. *Public opinion and American democracy.* New York: Alfred A. Knopf.

Lawrence, E., Sides, J., and Farrell, H. 2010. Self-segregation or deliberation? Blog readership, participation, and polarization in American politics. *Perspectives on Politics* 8(1): 141–57.

Manin, B., Przeworski, A., and Stokes, S. C. 1999. Introduction. In A. Przeworski, S. C. Stokes, and B. Manin (Eds.), *Democracy, accountability, and representation* (pp. 1–26). Cambridge: Cambridge University Press.

McCubbins, M. D., and Schwartz, T. 1984. Congressional oversight overlooked: Police patrols versus fire alarms. *American Journal of Political Science* 28(1): 165–179.

Pitkin, H. F. 1967. *The concept of representation.* Berkeley: University of California Press.

Price, V., and Zaller, J. 1993. Who gets the news? Alternative measures of news reception and their implications for research. *Public Opinion Quarterly* 57(2): 133–164.

Prior, M. 2005. News v. entertainment: How increasing media choice widens gaps in political knowledge and turnout. *American Journal of Political Science* 49(3): 577–592.

Prior, M. 2007. *Post-broadcast democracy: How media choice increases inequality in political involvement and polarizes elections.* New York: Cambridge University Press.

Prior, M. 2009. The immensely inflated news audience: Assessing bias in self-reported news exposure. *Public Opinion Quarterly* 73(1): 130–143.

Prior, M. 2013a. The challenge of measuring media exposure: Reply to Dilliplane, Goldman, and Mutz. *Political Communication* 30(4): 620–634.

Prior, M. 2013b. Media and political polarization. *Annual Review of Political Science* 16: 101–27.

Project for Excellence in Journalism. 2011a. *Navigating news online: Where people go, how they get there and what lures them away.* Washington, DC.

Project for Excellence in Journalism. 2011b. *The state of the news media 2011.* Washington, DC.

Schudson, M. 1998. *The good citizen: A history of American civic life.* New York: Martin Kessler Books.

Schudson, M. 2000. Good citizens and bad history: Today's political ideas in historical perspective. *Communication Review* 4(1): 1–20.

Schudson, M. 2010. Political observatories, databases and news in the emerging ecology of public information. *Daedalus* 139(2): 100–109.

Snyder, J. M., and Strömberg, D. 2010. Press coverage and political accountability. *Journal of Political Economy* 118(2): 355–408.

Starr, P. 2009. Goodbye to the age of newspapers (hello to a new era of corruption). *The New Republic*, 240(3): 28–35.

Zaller, J. 2003a. Coming to grips with V. O. Key's concept of latent opinion. In M. MacKuen and G. Rabinowitz (Eds.), *Electoral democracy* (pp. 311–336). Ann Arbor: University of Michigan Press.

Zaller, J. 2003b. A new standard of news quality: Burglar alarms for the monitorial citizen. *Political Communication* 20(2): 109–130.

CONCLUSION

CHAPTER 62

....

POLITICAL COMMUNICATION

Looking Ahead

....

KATE KENSKI AND KATHLEEN HALL JAMIESON

PROCLAIMING that the action was a response to US-led airstrikes in Iraq, in late August 2014 a group identifying itself as Islamic State of Iraq and the Levant (ISIL), also known as ISIS (Islamic State in Iraq and Syria) or IS (Islamic State), posted a video showing the beheading of freelance journalist James Foley, who had at an earlier point worked for the Defense Department's *Stars and Stripes* newspaper. In short order, YouTube and Twitter also relayed into the international media agenda videos of the execution of US journalist Steven Sotloff and British aid worker David Haines. "If you threaten America, you will find no safe haven," responded President Barack Obama. "Our objective is clear and that is to degrade and destroy (ISIL) so that it's no longer a threat" (Remarks by President Obama, 2014). Vice President Joe Biden put it more bluntly when he declared that the United States would pursue the killers to the "gates of hell" (Topaz, 2014). That rhetoric signaled the US action that followed in the form of airstrikes against ISIS in Syria.

Propelled by media manipulation by ISIS, two phenomena legitimized presidential military action. According to an NBC/WSJ poll, by the end of the first week in September, more than nine out of ten Americans (94 percent) had heard about the beheadings—a higher percentage than for any news event measured by that poll in the past five years. At the same time the poll found that 61 percent approved military action against ISIS (Murray, 2014).

We open with this ISIS-US-media account because it illustrates two important ways in which the political landscape, and with it political communication, have changed. A group without national standing commandeered media outlets that did not exist at the turn of this century to set a US media agenda and in the process parlayed the killing of single individuals into national disapproval that in effect licensed both rhetorical and military response by the president of the United States.

At the beginning of this handbook we offered two definitions of political communication: "making sense of symbolic exchanges about the shared exercise of power" and alternatively "the presentation and interpretation of information, messages or signals with potential consequences for the exercise of shared power." Neither of these initial conceptions specifies the subjects sharing power. In decades past, political communication theorists focused on the ways in which heads of state or elected representatives obtained and deployed power and on the ways in which others challenged those uses or maneuvered to increase their access to or share of it. The field arose, after all, from concerns about authoritarian leadership (e.g., Hitler, Mussolini) and abuses of the capacity to persuade. During the past several decades, media systems and the loci of power both were national. By contrast, in the current environment media structures are increasingly transnational, and the nation-state model is challenged by nonstate actors, such as ISIS, and cross-national collectivities, such as the Eurozone. Those who exercise power are no longer identifiable solely through status conferred by nominations and elections. The preoccupation with concerns over authoritarianism is not manifest in the same ways today as groups, such as ISIS, magnify their power and influence through digital messages transmitted globally over the Internet rather than through traditional media structures.

Such changes in the relationships among leaders, media, and publics invite the question: Do the theories and models developed in earlier decades retain relevance today? The synthetic reviews of the political communication literature provided by the contributors to this handbook suggest that the formative theories retain utility, but at the same time require rethinking in light of the changing ways in which power can and cannot be symbolically constructed and shared. As a number of the chapters in this volume attest, such changes require that scholars rethink how political communication shapes and is shaped by individual attitudes and behaviors; group dynamics; media structures and content; public policy; and other political, social, and technological processes.

In our introduction and opening chapters, we outlined the ancestry of the political communication field through five decades (1940s–1990s). Just as the models developed in the 1940s were questioned by the scholarship of mass-media era scholars, so too have the digital media of the twenty-first century created complexities not envisioned by the workhorse theories of the broadcast age. Because the books' chapters are structured to feature recommendations for future work, there is no need in this essay to perform that function. Instead, we thread together some of the signals the previous chapters send about challenges facing political communication theorists in an age in which nonstate actors wield influence through social media channels.

The old paradigms of communication require reconceptualization in a media age in which agents can reach large audiences virally without the complicity of the gatekeepers employed by corporate media structures and without purchasing ad time or owning a media outlet. This change has empowered not only insurgent groups such as ISIS, but also artists such as the Black Eyed Peas' Will.i.am, who in 2008 elicited more than twenty million views for a viral homage to Democratic aspirant Barack Obama.[1] That musical collage, which for practical purposes functions as a mobilizing ad, punctuated clips of celebrities echoing the words of Barack Obama's concession speech in the New Hampshire primary with their and his invocation of the Obama slogan, "Yes we can."

The absence of gatekeepers has also opened large-scale access to claims such as one that Michelle Obama is actually a man, a video that has received almost three million views,[2] and messages implying that comedian Joan Rivers was murdered because she revealed that Barack Obama is gay and his wife a transsexual.[3] The capacity to relay such viral content from like-minded person to ideological kin not only makes it difficult for journalists to identify and debunk deceptive content trafficked in this form, but also increases its reach and visibility. Importantly, those who reported receiving viral content from friends during the 2008 election were more likely to believe the deceptions found in those forms (Kenski, Hardy, and Jamieson, 2010).

Audience control over access to content has changed political dynamics as well by effectively minimizing common mass political experiences. So, for example, during the 2008 presidential campaign prospective voters had access to a sophisticated video on demand structure that permitted Obama supporters to view reinforcing content at times of their own choosing. This increased control has political consequences. Some who habitually scan multiple broadcast evening news programs for content of interest evince a higher level of knowledge about politics than non-channel switchers (Jamieson and Hardy, 2011). Others use channel control to search out entertainment, avoiding news content more systematically than was possible in past eras (Prior, 2007). Still others seek out content compatible with their preexisting political beliefs (Jamieson and Cappella, 2010).

Presidential debates remain one of the few remaining national political events able to attract a large audience, but here too the viewing experience is increasingly individualized. As Pew found in 2012, "11% of live debate watchers [of the first presidential debate of 2012] were 'dual screeners,' following coverage on a computer or mobile device at the same time as following television coverage. Another 3% say they followed the debate live exclusively online" (Pew Research Center for the People and the Press, 2012). Grappling with this personalized media experience, researchers are asking such questions as: Does tweeting or following Twitter while viewing a debate increase learning, as one study suggests (Houston, Hawthorne, Spialek, Greenwood, and McKinney, 2013), or depress it, as another finds (Gottfried, Hardy, Winneg, and Jamieson, 2013)? Does it affect what is learned, with Big Bird, "binders full of women," and bayonets primed in the 2012 Twitter-verse and less salient among those offline?

Making sense of the political implications of this altered media environment and of innovative methods for dealing with it requires abandoning static notions of communication for an integrative approach consistent with a more dynamic understanding of phenomena in context. At the same time, political communication theories need to account for the capacities and constraints that changing geopolitical and media structures place on the construction of meaning and the ways in which meaning can be created through collaborative creation or noncooperative co-optation. Aiding in this process of addressing this changed media-political landscape are sophisticated tools such as social network analysis, isolation of underlying rhetorical regularities through big data mining, and psychophysiological and neurological measures of affect and cognition that open alternative ways of seeing political communication and also challenge us to develop theoretical paradigms encompassing new types of evidence.

We also need to ask whether, and if so how, our conceptualizations of political communication should be recast in light of the research agendas that emerged in the handbook's chapters. In particular the concepts on which the second definition pivots—information, messages, signals—are legacies of the transmission model and as such less useful in a communication environment in which boundaries between sender signal and audience are frequently blurred.

Although the definition of communication varies from scholar to scholar, the thread across definitions usually comes down to messages. Yet in an environment in which ideas are turned into content that is quickly spread, adapted, and modified by users, messages are neither stable nor tightly bounded by readily discerned beginnings and obvious endings. Because the viral social media environment churns out permutations of messages, recognizing, capturing, and making sense of the variations become challenges for researchers. Consequently, one call to researchers is to adopt a new lexicon focused on *messaging*, rather than messages. Some messaging morphs in ways that the originator intends as a series of collaborative creative acts. Other messaging highjacks, subverts, or co-opts an original communicative act. For example, Republican nominee Mitt Romney's statement in a 2012 presidential general election debate that he would end the government subsidy of the Public Broadcasting System included the disclaimer, "I love Big Bird. I actually like you, [moderator Jim Lehrer] too. But I'm not going to keep on spending money on things to borrow money from China to pay for it." Within minutes, Web memes appeared showing Big Bird holding a "willing to work for food" sign on his back with an arrow through his chest, extending a finger to reinforce the message to Romney: "This message is brought to you by the letters FU." Each visually reframed the Romney message to one not susceptible to traditional forms of rebuttal. The rise of comedic news shows such as *The Daily Show with Jon Stewart*, the *Colbert Report*, and more recently *Last Week Tonight with John Oliver* also ensures a regular stream of meta-communication about political content past and present. So for example, in 2012 *The Daily Show* parodied the Will.i.am "Yes we can" video with a rendition rife with dashed hopes, titled "Yes we can, but . . ."

Much political communication research in earlier decades concerned itself with mass communication delivery systems in the broadcast age. Beginning in the 1980s the growth of cable resulted in research observing differences in messages between media outlets and concentrating on segmentation based on ideological affinity. In the process, the implications of narrowcasting elicited scholarly attention. The availability of technologies hospitable to tailoring of information based on user preference redirected these discussions to focus on personal casting, with messaging addressing individuals identified by attributes they share with a subset of others.

The explosion in the numbers of channels and opportunities for messaging has also revived interest in theories such as two-step flow, developed during earlier decades. Balances of power shift when ordinary people can select ideologically hospitable gatekeepers and act as gatekeepers in their own right for their networks of followers. Yet it is important to note that elements of the transmission model of communication do retain some utility in the vastly changed media environment, with many responding as in decades and centuries past by assimilating the offered message.

While the concept of two-step flow was useful in accounting for the flow of information in a pretelevision age in which elites consumed more and different types of media, the era of the mass media and massed audience made it less likely that ideas would flow from media to opinion leaders and from them to followers. The notion is again gaining currency in the digital world, in which reliance on curators makes sense. However, whereas in earlier decades opinion leaders were often elites, such as union figures, politicians, or anchormen, today they are less likely to carry institutionally certified authority.

To take into account the media environment and the constraints and changing forms of non-state-based leadership, we offer a few tentative modifications to the definitions offered in the opening chapter. First, political communication is the making sense of symbolic exchanges about the exercise of power, including but not necessarily requiring shared power. Second, political communication is the study of how, why, when, and with what effect humans make sense of symbolic exchanges about sharing and shared power. Third, political communication is the study of how humans claim, lose, or share power through symbolic exchanges, a process that includes creative collaboration and creative co-optation. All three definitions include the concept of power not predicated on top-down models of understanding. The third definition in particular emphasizes the process and focuses on the "how."

Although this handbook covers much ground, its scope has two limitations of which we are especially aware: its focus on US-based scholarship and the absence of a section on the methods most often used by political communication researchers. We recognize that significant work on political communication is being generated around the globe and hope that successive editions of this handbook will emphasize its importance. We anticipate that the field will increasingly incorporate and harmonize international rather than national perspectives. Another limitation of this handbook was the decision to not delve into methodological breakthroughs in the social sciences. The choice was driven by the fact that fine work of this sort already exists in Bucy and Holbert's *Sourcebook for Political Communication Research: Methods, Measures, and Analytical Techniques* (2011). When we parsed this volume's chapters into categories, we were aware of the many alternative placements that would have made equal sense. Because this handbook is being published online as well as in traditional print, we anticipate that users will create as many different rearrangements as there are readers.

The study of political communication has come a long way since Chaffee's edited volume *Political Communication: Issues and Strategies for Research* appeared in 1975. But as a dynamic field devoted to studying a complex and changing set of institutional and social structures, we anticipate that the study of political communication will continue to do as it has in decades past and borrow the best from cognate fields, even as it continues to develop its own insights about the ways in which individuals create intersections between power and symbols and use symbols to gain, hold, and contest power.

Notes

1. See https://www.youtube.com/watch?v=jjXyqcx-mYY.
2. See https://www.youtube.com/watch?v=gvuulZPbfBg&spfreload=1 (accessed December 17, 2014).
3. See https://www.youtube.com/watch?v=ERiipNGMSrI (accessed December 17, 2014).

References

Bucy, E. P., & Holbert, R. L. (Eds.) 2014. *Sourcebook for political communication research: Methods, measures, and analytical techniques.* New York: Routledge.

Chaffee, S. (Ed.). 1975. *Political communication: Issues and strategies for research.* Beverly Hills, CA: Sage.

Gottfried, J., Hardy, B., Winneg, K., and Jamieson, K. 2013. Social networking sites and knowledge of the 2012 presidential election. Paper presented at the annual convention of the National Communication Association, Washington DC, November 21–24, 2013.

Houston, J. B., Hawthorne, J., Spialek, M. L., Greenwood, M. S., and McKinney, M. S. 2013. Tweeting during presidential debates: Effect on candidate evaluations and debate attitudes. *Argumentation & Advocacy 49*: 301–311.

Jamieson, K. H., and Cappella, J. N. 2010. *Echo chamber: Rush Limbaugh and the conservative media establishment.* New York: Oxford University Press.

Jamieson, K. H., and Hardy, B. 2011. The effect of media on public knowledge. In G. Edwards III, L. Jacobs, and R. Shapiro (Eds.), *The Oxford handbook of American public opinion and the media* (pp. 236–250). New York: Oxford University Press.

Kenski, K., Hardy, B. W., and Jamieson, K. H. 2010. *The Obama victory: How media, money, and message shaped the 2008 election.* New York: Oxford University Press.

Murray, M. 2014. Poll: Americans feel unsafe, support action against ISIS. *MSNBC.com.* Retrieved from http://www.msnbc.com/msnbc/poll-americans-support-action-against-isis.

Pew Research Center for the People and the Press. 2012. One-in-ten "dual screened" the presidential debate. Retrieved from http://www.people-press.org/2012/10/11/one-in-ten-dual-screened-the-presidential-debate/.

Prior, M. 2007. *Post-broadcast democracy: How media choice increases inequality in political involvement and polarizes elections.* Cambridge, UK: Cambridge University Press.

Remarks by President Obama and President Ilves of Estonia in joint press conference. 2014. White House Briefing Room. Retrieved from http://www.whitehouse.gov/photos-and-video/video/2014/09/03/president-obama-holds-press-conference-president-ilves-estonia#transcript.

Topaz, J. 2014. Joe Biden: We'll follow ISIL to "gates of hell." *Politico.* Retrieved from http://www.politico.com/story/2014/09/joe-biden-isil-react-110558.html.

INDEX

Page references followed by a *t* indicate tables; *f* indicate figures.

on framing, 623–24
on media bias, 403, 412–13
on war, 304
environmental inequality, 492
environmental justice movement (EJM), 492
equivalence framing, 63, 620–22,
  626–29, 628f
Erasmus, 207
Erber, R., 583–84
Erbring, L., 31, 853
  on political trust, 584
Erjavec, K., 111
"Essay on the Origin of Languages" (Rousseau,
  J.-J.), 885–86
Esser, F., 49, 55
  on CPCR, 287, 291
The Ethics of Rhetoric (Weaver), 139
ethnography
  organized conflict and, 754
  political action and, 754
  of political communication, 749–59
  theorizing and, 756–58
Eulau, H., 6
Evatt, D., 637
Eveland, W. P., Jr., 520, 552
  on disagreement, 723
  on social networks, 688
  on SoS, 767
  on uses and gratifications, 613
Everitt, J., 168
EVT. *See* expectancy value theory
expectancy theory, 154
expectancy value theory (EVT), 608
Experiments on Mass Communication
  (Hovland), 21
experts, 703–4
expressive functions, of emotion, 665–68
external pluralism, 104
Eyal, C., 6
Eysenbach, G., 420

Facebook, 186–87, 472, 475, 574
  advertising on, 510
  diplomacy, 324
  hyperpersonalization on, 799
  political campaigns and, 825
  political trust and, 589

selective exposure and, 540
social networks on, 690–91
face-to-face canvassing
  as niche communication, 181–82
  for voter turnout, 71–72
FactCheck.org, 249
Fahrenheit 9/11 (Moore), 812, 857
Fairness Doctrine, 337
Farrell, H., 367
Faust, W. L., 784
Fazio, R., 657
FCC. *See* Federal Communications
  Commission
fear of social isolation, 767
Federal Communications Commission
  (FCC), 278–79
  net neutrality and, 492
  public-service model and, 337
Federal Elections Commission, 102
Feldman, L., 785
Feldman, O., 21
  on disagreement, 722
  on hostile media effect, 557
  on partisanship, 136, 138
Fellner, G., 507
Fenster, M., 306
Ferejohn, J., 899
Ferraro, Geraldine
  in debates, 168
  game schema and, 383
Ferree, M. M., 114
Festinger, L., 531–32
  on selective exposure, 811
Fey, Tina, 873
field experiments
  on advertising, 504–5
  on civic norms, 506–7
  design of, 503–5
  on electoral accountability, 505–6
  on persuasion, 508
  on political communication, 501–10
"57 Channels and Nothing On"
  (Springsteen), 601
Finifter, A. W., 583
Finkel, S. E., 15, 35
First Amendment, 96
Fischer, P., 533

confirmation bias and, 536
de facto, 536
elites and, 541–42
emotion and, 533
to entertainment, 534
Fox News and, 813–16, 818*t*
hostile media effect and, 558–59
incidental exposure and, 540–41
on Internet, 540, 809–19, 814*f*, 816*t*–818*t*
judgment of, 542
laboratory studies on, 537
moderators of, 535–36
motivating beliefs for, 540
MSNBC and, 814, 816, 817*t*
narrowcasting and, 797–98
negativity and, 539
partisanship and, 534, 811–12
polarization and, 428
political knowledge and, 535
positivity and, 539
recognition of, 538
selective avoidance and, 538–39
self-report studies on, 536
source credibility and, 426–27
types of, 533–35
unobtrusive measurement of, 537
why it occurs, 532–33
selective incentives, 506–7
selective production, 541
selective recall, 551
self-censorship
    in freedom of the press, 240–41
    opinion climate and, 770
    political communication and, 763–72
self-determination theory, 610
self-report studies, 536
self-selection bias, of audience, 257, 258–59
SEM. *See* structural equation modeling
Semetko, H. A., 288–89
    on journalism norms, 368
September 11. *See* 9/11
sequential priming, 657
Serazio, M., 226
sex offenders, 115
Shah, C., 880
Shah, D. V., 520, 552
    on crime, 599

on entertainment, 853
on socialization, 473, 474
Shamir, J., 89
Shamir, M., 89
Shanks, J. M., 441
Shapiro, J. M., 279
    on media bias, 410
Shapiro, R. Y., 483
Shaw, D., 6, 28, 73
    on agenda setting, 61, 623, 633, 636
    on minimal effects model, 31
Shaw, D. L., 609
Shaw, D. R., 504
Sheafer, T., 571
    on emotion, 671
    on priming, 642
Sheehan, M. A., 383
Sheets, P., 111
Shehata, A., 290, 293–94
Sherr, S., 147, 152
Shibutani, T., 23
Shields, T.
    on direct mail, 183
    on niche communication, 189
Shively, W. P., 696–97
Shleifer, A., 410
Shoemaker, P., 291
    on agenda setting, 359
    on gatekeeping, 353
    on journalism norms, 368
"Short People" (Newman), 890
Siebert, F. S., 239–40, 851
Sigal, L. V., 361
Sigelman, L., 154
Signorelli, N., 595
Silent Spring (Carson), 492
Silver, G. E., 583–84
Silverstone, R., 340
Simmel, G., 689
Simms, A., 342
Simon, A.
    on advertising, 154
    on voter turnout, 150
Simonson, P., 685
The Simpsons, 872
Sina Weibo, 845
Singer, J. B., 368–69

Lightning Source UK Ltd.
Milton Keynes UK
UKHW051528060821
388083UK00014B/637

9 780190 090456